THE BUILDINGS OF ENGLAND

FOUNDING EDITOR: NIKOLAUS PEVSNER
ADVISORY EDITOR: JOHN NEWMAN
EDITOR: BRIDGET CHERRY

NORTHUMBERLAND

JOHN GRUNDY, GRACE McCOMBIE, PETER RYDER,
HUMPHREY WELFARE AND NIKOLAUS PEVSNER

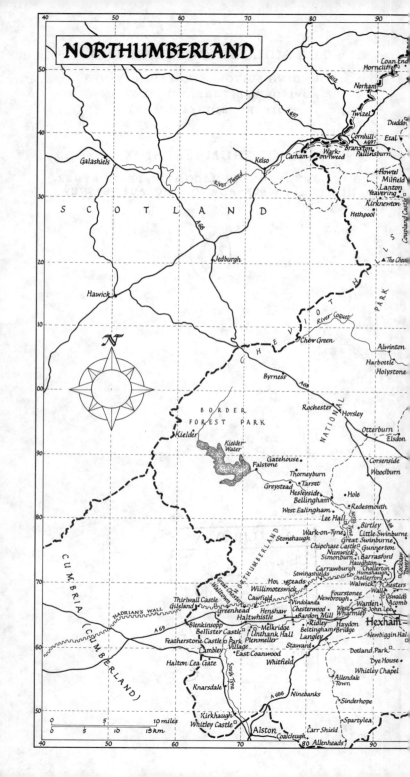

NORTHUMBERLAND

Loan End
Horncliffe
Norham
Twizel
Duddo
Cornhill
Etal
Wark-on-Tweed
Branxton
Pallinsburn
Carham
Flowtel
Milfield
Lanton
Yeavering
Kirknewton
Hethpool
Coupland Castle
The Cheviot
River Coquet
Chew Green
Alwinton
Harbottle
Holystone
Byrness
Rochester
Horsley
Otterburn
Elsdon
BORDER FOREST PARK
Kielder
Kielder Water
Gatehouse
Falstone
Corsenside
Woodburn
Thorneyburn
Tarset
Greystead
Hesleyside
Hole
Bellingham
Redesmouth
West Ealingham
Lee Hall
Birtley
Wark-on-Tyne
Little Swinburne
Stonehaugh
Great Swinburne
Chipchase Castle
Gunnerton
Nunwick
Barrasford
Simonburn
Haughton
Carrawburgh
Chollerton
Humshaugh
Sewingshields
Chollerford
Housesteads
Walwick
Chesters
Willimoteswick
Wall
Cawfield
Vindolanda
Fourstones
Warden
Acomb
Newbrough
West John Lee
Thirlwall Castle
Greenhead
Henshaw
Chesterwood
Wharmley
Gilsland
Haltwhistle
Bardon Mill
St Oswald's
Blenkinsopp
Ridley
Haydon
Hexham
Melkridge
Beltingham
Bridge
Featherstone Castle
Unthank Hall
Langley
Newbiggin Hall
Park Plenmeller
Village
Staward
Cambley
East Coanwood
Dotland Park
Halton Lea Gate
Whitfield
Dye House
Whitley Chapel
Knarsdale
Allendale Town
Ninebanks
Sinderhope
Kirkhaugh
Spartylea
Whitley Castle
Alston
Carr Shield
Coalcleugh
Allenheads

SCOTLAND
Galashiels
River Tweed
Kelso
Jedburgh
Hawick

CUMBRIA (CUMBERLAND)
HADRIAN'S WALL
NATIONAL PARK
NORTHUMBERLAND
Great Chesters
Whitlow

0 5 10 miles
0 5 10 15 km

The publishers and authors gratefully acknowledge
the support given by
the Napper Collerton Partnership

Northumberland

BY
JOHN GRUNDY, GRACE McCOMBIE,
PETER RYDER, HUMPHREY WELFARE
AND
NIKOLAUS PEVSNER

INDUSTRIAL BUILDINGS
BY STAFFORD LINSLEY

THE BUILDINGS OF ENGLAND

PENGUIN BOOKS

PENGUIN BOOKS
Published by the Penguin Group
27 Wrights Lane, London w8 5tz, England

Viking Penguin, a division of Penguin Books USA Inc.,
375 Hudson Street, New York, New York 10014, USA
Penguin Books Australia Ltd, Ringwood, Victoria, Australia
Penguin Books Canada Ltd, 10 Alcorn Avenue, Toronto, Ontario, Canada m4v 3b2
Penguin Books (NZ) Ltd, 182–190 Wairau Road, Auckland 10, New Zealand

Penguin Books Ltd, Registered Offices: Harmondsworth, Middlesex, England

First published 1992

ISBN 0 14 0710590

Copyright 1957 by Nikolaus Pevsner
Copyright © John Grundy, Stafford Linsley, Grace McCombie,
Douglas Robson, Peter Ryder, Humphrey Welfare
and the estate of Nikolaus Pevsner, 1992

Made and printed in Great Britain
by Butler & Tanner Ltd, Frome and London
Set in Monotype Plantin

To the memory of
DR ROSA SCHAPIRE
enthusiastic and indefatigable in her collaboration
on 'The Buildings of England' as in
everything else
1875–1954

CONTENTS

LIST OF TEXT FIGURES AND MAPS

MAP REFERENCES

The numbers printed in italic type in the margin against the place names in the gazetteer of the book indicate the position of the place in question on the index map (pp. 2–3), which is divided into sections by the 10-kilometre reference lines of the National Grid. The reference given here omits the two initial letters (formerly numbers) which in a full grid reference refer to the 100-kilometre squares into which the county is divided. The first two numbers indicate the *western* boundary, and the last two the *southern* boundary, of the 10-kilometre square in which the place in question is situated. For example, Bamburgh (reference 1030) will be found in the 10-kilometre square bounded by grid lines 10 and 20 on the *west* and 30 and 40 on the *south*; Bardon Mill (reference 7060) in the square bounded by grid lines 70 and 80 on the *west* and 60 and 70 on the *south*.

FOREWORD TO THE FIRST EDITION (1957)

This is the first joint volume of *The Buildings of England*. The Roman parts of Introduction and Gazetteer, which amount to a great deal, are the work of Professor Ian Richmond. I am most grateful to him for having agreed to undertake this work. The paragraphs on geology in the Introduction are written by Professor K. C. Dunham, the pages and passages on prehistory have been provided, as in the preceding six volumes, by Mr Jon Manchip White. All the rest of the preliminary extracting lay once more in the hands of Dr R. Schapire. Northumberland was to be the fourth volume of this series prepared by her. However, her full life ended before it could be published. Her corpus of extracts was supplemented by Miss M. Littlemore. All the travelling which was necessary for writing my text, I did myself (driven indefatigably by my wife). It was my intention to see everything that needed description. Where I have failed, brackets mark the item described.

Amongst those who have been of help, first place is due to the late H. L. Honeyman, who read the proofs of my text and made many valuable additions and corrections. I am as grateful to him as I am to the Ministry of Housing and Local Government (here abbreviated MHLG), who have a statutory duty of drawing up lists of buildings of architectural or historic interest and who, with their customary kindness, have again put at my disposal the lists collected by the Chief Investigator and his staff. I am equally grateful to Mr Cecil Farthing and Mrs Parry of the National Buildings Record for their kindness and helpfulness. The signs GR and TK will by now be familiar to users of this series. They stand for Mr H. S. Goodhart-Rendel's list of Victorian churches and Sir Thomas Kendrick's list of Victorian glass which I had once more the privilege of using. Amongst librarians in the county I specially want to thank Mr E. Austin Hinton of the Central Library, Newcastle for much help with difficult questions, and also Mr E. G. Hatton of Tynemouth Public Library and Mr F. Fordham of Berwick Public Library. The Head Vergers of Hexham Abbey and the Cathedral at Newcastle, Mr W. T. Taylor and Mr W. J. Liversedge, went to much trouble, too, to reply to queries of mine. So did Lady Ridley, Mr B. Beresford Peirse, and Major Charles Mitchell. In addition I have to thank the Rectors and Vicars of many churches who answered questions of mine put to them in writing, and the owners of many houses – open or closed to the public – who allowed me to visit them or tried to elucidate for me obscure historical or architectural points. We found all round quite an exceptional willingness to help and the friendliest hospitality. Yet with all the help received by me and all the work put into this book by others it is bound to contain plenty of errors and omissions. Would users be so good as to advise the publisher or myself of any they may notice?

The foreword had been written up to this point in the summer of 1955 and the volume was already in the hands of the printers. Circumstances then arose which theatened the whole future of *The Buildings of England*. Penguin Books had, from the outset, undertaken their publication at a loss in the desire to offer what they contain to as wide a public as possible at the lowest practicable price but the loss now proved greater than could be sustained...

After striving to find some way out of this impasse the immediate problem has been solved by a generous grant from The Leverhulme Trust which will provide for the cost of the research; Birkbeck College of the University of London at the same time accepted the responsibility for administering the grant.

In addition Messrs Arthur Guinness, Son & Company Ltd have placed at the publisher's and my disposal a substantial sum with which to cover part of the production costs and establishment expenses particular to the series.

I take this opportunity of expressing my gratitude to The Leverhulme Trustees, Messrs Guinness, and the Governors of Birkbeck College, and hope that readers of this and succeeding volumes will join their appreciation to mine.

NIKOLAUS PEVSNER

FOREWORD TO THE SECOND EDITION

Since 1957, when the first edition of *Northumberland* was published, much has changed on Tyneside and in the industrial south-east of the county. Coalmining has declined and the old heavy industries which were the backbone of the region's economy have all but disappeared. Newcastle itself was dramatically transformed in the 1960s and early 1970s, but its elegant C 19 heart and much of its ancient riverside have thankfully been preserved and revived. The political changes of the 1970s were equally radical: Tyneside was hived off from Northumberland in 1974 into the new metropolitan county of Tyne and Wear, making Morpeth the county town rather than Newcastle. Elsewhere in the county, changes have been much less dramatic, and little new has been built. However, new research has enriched and extended our understanding. Our view of pre-historic vernacular architecture and of the buildings of the Roman frontier has undergone a revolution. The C 16 bastle houses which are unique to the Border area have been properly recognized and described and the vernacular traditions of the county thoroughly evaluated for the first time. Familiar buildings have been re-examined and re-interpreted, and many building types brought within the scope of the revision in response to growing interest and new discoveries: for example, industrial and agricultural buildings are discussed within their historical context, country houses are set more firmly in their parks and gardens, and Victorian and Edwardian architecture is brought into closer focus.

The vast amount of material that has been added to the first edition explains why this revision has been such a long-drawn-out process. It was begun while three of us (John Grundy, Grace McCombie and Peter Ryder) were involved in the Resurvey of Listed Buildings for the counties of Northumberland, Durham and Tyne and Wear, and it would not have been possible without the help, advice and support of a large number of people. Some of them are the authors of the books and articles which have appeared since the first edition was issued, and they (or as many of them as possible) are referred to in Further Reading at the end of the Introduction. However, Northumberland is a relatively unresearched county in architectural matters, and in many cases our information has been provided directly by those involved in writing and research and by the owners or occupiers of properties.

Of those involved in research, a number must be singled out. Dr Stafford Linsley contributed the introductory essay on industrial archaeology and was an ever-present help when we were working both on the Resurvey and on this gazetteer. Dr Douglas Robson kindly agreed to use his unparalleled knowledge of the geology of the county to prepare a revised essay for the Introduction.

There are also many people who helped us in their official capacity, but whose assistance went far beyond the bounds required by their jobs. Dolly Potter, our guide, mentor and guard, Inspector for the region for English Heritage and passionate watchdog in the cause of Northumbrian architecture, must get first mention, but there are many more. Also at English Heritage, Jill Kerr, Richard Halsey and Peter Leach have all offered information or written reports on individual buildings and architects which have proved invaluable. J. M. McDonald, Director of Planning at Berwick-upon-Tweed, identified a number of buildings which might well have been missed. R. Gard, the (retired) County Archivist of Northumberland, and his extremely helpful staff; the equally helpful people at the Local Studies Department of the Central Library in Newcastle, and in particular F. Manders and D. Bond; all of these earned our gratitude. The Tyne and Wear Archives hold much of the information on Newcastle and Wallsend, and since 1990 on North Shields and Tynemouth. The expertise of the former archivist, W. A. L. Seaman, his successor, B. Jackson, and their assistants was particularly valuable. E. Hollerton of the former branch of that service in North Shields helped us with research into North Shields and Tynemouth. In the Northumberland National Park, Beryl Charlton and Albert Weir, among others, provided useful information about their areas. In Newcastle and North Tyneside, the members of the Joint Conservation Team of the former Tyne and Wear County Council Planning Department provided much information for the Listed Buildings Resurvey, which was carried out from that department. The newspaper research of A. G. Chamberlain was an invaluable source of information on buildings and building materials. Their successors in the Design Team of the Planning Department of the City of Newcastle upon Tyne must be thanked for patiently answering numerous enquiries, especially R. B. Harbottle (who kindly read part of the text on North Tyneside and Newcastle), P. Jubb and D. Lovie. Others in the Planning Department who provided information about post-World War II buildings were J. G. W. Stabler, D. Bolland and A. H. Smithson. For the co-operation of his department the City Planning Officer, R. M. Angell, is thanked. A. Austin and E. Heatherington of the City Engineer's Department kindly obtained information about prefabricated houses. Thanks are also due to the City of Newcastle for permission to copy a plan of the Civic Centre. The Newcastle Population Office provided statistics. The staff of North Tyneside Planning Department were equally helpful, especially P. Brown and P. Harle. P. Dillon in that department, and G. D. Halliday and A. Brack in the Department of Planning and Economic Development of Northumberland County Council, explained the genesis of Killingworth and Cramlington.

Many individuals made valuable contributions, some on behalf of their firms or societies: P. Cormack (information on C19 and C20 stained glass); W. J. Mitchinson, Director of Estates, RVI (tiled pictures); Neil Moat (stained glass of all periods); E. Nicklin (The Ryder Nicklin Partnership); A. Rylance (the University of Newcastle upon Tyne); J. Weatherley (Kempe and Kempe & Co.). Certain organizations also deserve our thanks. The Civic Trust and the Royal Institute of British Architects both have architectural awards which proved to be excellent signposts to the best of current work. The University of Newcastle upon Tyne supplied a plan of its campus; the Tyne and Wear Passenger Transport Executive and Newcastle United Football Club provided information. Humphrey Welfare is grateful to his colleagues in RCHME for much cheerful discussion.

For individual buildings, groups of buildings and estates, the number of people who offered information, advice or even just permission to poke around seems absolutely legion, and the following list is bound unintentionally to omit people to whom we feel gratitude. Overall, it needs to be said that the welcome and kindness (not to mention cups of tea) offered to us during our researches tended to confirm all of the stereotypical images of northern openness, and we wish we had them all to visit again. Here is the list, incomplete though it must be: G. Allinson (Eldon Square); Frank Atkinson (Ovingham); Adrian Bennet (Chillingham); British Gas; Major Brown (of Callaly, now sadly deceased); R. Connell (of Reavell & Cahill, Architects, Alnwick); F. M. Cowe (Berwick); P. Deakin (Alnwick and Belford Hall); R. Fern and M. Wills (University of Newcastle upon Tyne); R. Foster (Dockwray Square); R. Gilbert (Alfred Gilbert); J. Greenacombe of RCHME (T. R. Spence); A. Greg (Pendower); B. Jobling (Tyne and Wear Preservation Trust, Buttress); G. Long (St Bartholomew, Longbenton); J. McHarg (Fowberry); Lesley Milner; A. Moody, Douglas Wise & Partners (Vale House, Jesmond); L. G. Mouchel & Partners (the C.W.S. warehouse, Quayside, Newcastle); W. Naylor and F. McTavish (Procter & Gamble); the late Father Nicholson, for help with the history of many of the Roman Catholic churches in the county; D. Noble-Rollin (Natural History Society of Northumbria); C. Parish and M. Nowell (Literary and Philosophical Society); C. Rainford (St Mary's R. C. Cathedral); W. Render (Mary Magdalene and Holy Jesus Hospitals); G. M. Robson (Hole Farm, Bellingham); Lord Roddam (Roddam); A. Rudd of the Fortress Study Group (Northumberland Record Office); W. Stonor (Faulkner Browns); Canon Strange and R. Conliffe (St Nicholas's Cathedral); G. M. Taylor (Elsdon); R. Tillotson (Byker); A. N. Tweddle (Morpeth); Commodore Wilkinson and Mr Green (Trinity House of Newcastle upon Tyne); A. Wilson (John George Joicey Museum, Tyne and Wear Museums Service).

In short, we are indebted to all of those incumbents, owners and tenants of houses, principals of schools and colleges, and directors of business concerns who have taken the often considerable trouble to help us, to answer our letters and to show us around their demesnes.

We are also grateful to all who responded to the invitation in the first edition to send in corrections and additions. The bulging file on our desk has been a constant reminder of how gimlet-eyed and knowledgeable the readership is for this series, and we suffer from constant worry about what sort of file will be needed to store the responses to the second edition. This list of the observant includes Frank Rutherford (in the pages of the *Transactions of the Architectural and Archaeological Society of Durham and Northumberland*), M. U. Beasley, R. Bibby, N. Bosanquet, Dr G. K. Brandwood, H. D. Briggs, L. D. Butler, C. N. Dallison, J. A. Finch, R. Green, R.

Neville Hadcock, R. H. Kamen, E. Kerr, P. Reid, A. C. Sewter and
J. T. Smith.

Other organizations and individuals gave us financial and material
support which made it possible for us to work on this revision. Some
gave money. Berwick District Council, North Tyneside M.B.C., the
Hadrian Trust, the Joicey Trust, Northumberland County Council,
the Knott Trust, the Northern Rock Building Society, Tyne Tees
Television Holdings plc, Greggs plc, Fenwicks Ltd, and the Arup
Trust all helped to provide the funds which allowed us to travel and
see each of the buildings described in the present volume. Others
helped in different ways, especially the Newcastle Council for Voluntary Service, which was good enough to administer the grants
that had been made to us; and the Napper Collerton Partnership,
which housed us with great kindness and tolerance throughout the
Listed Buildings Resurvey of Northumberland and Durham and
supported us splendidly in the early days of this revision. We must
thank those who helped to turn our typescript into this book; Judith
Wardman, who meticulously edited the text; Eddie Ryle-Hodges,
who took so many superb photographs; Richard Andrews, who drew
the plans; and Reg Piggott, who painstakingly composed the maps.
Finally, we must offer our gratitude for the support and advice given
to us by the staff of *The Buildings of England* at Penguin Books, to
Bridget Cherry, Judy Nairn (who sadly died during the final stages
of preparation of this volume), Susan Rose-Smith for her long search
for the best possible illustrations, and to Elizabeth Williamson, our
patient and gentle editor whose savage pencil we have forgotten
about and forgiven . . . almost. Once again corrections and additions
will be welcome.

Finally an explanatory note. The Introduction to this edition incorporates many of Sir Nikolaus's stimulating insights, but also includes
new interpretations made in the light of new research and new
interests, for example in vernacular and industrial buildings. The
gazetteer is necessarily only a selection of the county's architecturally
significant buildings. Anglican churches built before *c.* 1830 are all
included, but not all churches that belong to other denominations
and not all of those built after that date. They are listed as follows:
Anglican churches, Roman Catholic churches, and then those of
other denominations in alphabetical order. Churches now in secular
use still appear under their ecclesiastical names, though often with
cross-references to descriptions elsewhere. Convents and cemeteries
are listed after churches. Public buildings are grouped together in
what, according to *Buildings of England* tradition, is rank order: that
is, municipal and public offices; museums, libraries and theatres;
colleges and schools; hospitals and parks; and, finally, public utilities
and transport buildings.

A word of warning: churches are nearly always locked (although
their custodians are almost invariably kind when approached for
access), and many of the secular buildings included are private and
not freely accessible, even when the interior has been mentioned.
As a rule, we have avoided describing in detail the interiors of minor
buildings to which there is no hope of admission. Church furnishings
are described where they are noteworthy (except plate and moveable
objects), but furniture and paintings in secular buildings are omitted,

unless they form part of a decorative scheme. Buildings demolished since the first edition was published are mentioned very exceptionally.

INTRODUCTION

Northumberland is a rough county: that is its great attraction. Rough are the winds, the moors, the castles, the dolerite cliffs by Hadrian's 2 Wall and on the coast; rough is the stone of the walls which take the place of hedges; and even the smoother and more precisely worked stone of Newcastle seems rough. It is a wild county too; wild and empty on the Cheviots and the Pennines, wild and windswept on 1 the coast, so that the gentler aspects of building in Northumberland – the spacious village greens of Elsdon, Stamfordham and Wall, the priories embedded fairy-fashion in greenery at Brinkburn and at Hulne – are as much a surprise as the deeply cut denes and valleys, almost invisible until you are upon them.

There is indeed much more variety of scenery in the county than superficial knowledge would reveal. And no wonder, for Northumberland is a large county; with its 2,000 square miles it is the fifth largest of the old English counties (after Yorkshire, Lincolnshire, Devon and Norfolk). The diversity and the contrasts include the dunes and sandy beaches between Bamburgh and Dunstanburgh or from Whitley Bay to Alnmouth, the splendid monotony of the tidal flats between Holy Island and the mainland, the sandstone cliffs of Tynemouth, the sheer angular fluting of the dolerite crags on which Hadrian's Wall stands or at Dunstanburgh and the Farne Islands, and the broad green valley of the lower Tyne, at Wylam, at Bywell, at Hexham. There is the infrequent but dramatic desecration of open-cast mining and the tawdry sub-countryside that makes up much of the south-east of the county; but there is also the grand sweep of the infertile Fell Sandstone ridges, rising to Simonside and Ros Castle, their dark moors clad with heather and bracken, the dense trees and the hump-backed bridges down along the winding Wansbeck, the Coquet, the Till and the Aln, the more dramatic Pennine hills and rivers in the south-west with their melancholy ruins of deserted leadmines. Beyond Hadrian's Wall, the scarplands of North Tynedale, like some choppy petrified seascape, merge into the vast conifer forests of Kielder, centred on still waters. Further to the north the bare green Cheviots above Otterburn on the Rede, above Bellingham on the North Tyne, and west of Alnham and Ingram and Wooler, climb to the high watershed of the Border. A rough country veined with softness.

GEOLOGY AND TOPOGRAPHY

BY DOUGLAS ROBSON

The focus of Northumberland's GEOLOGY is centred on the Cheviot Hills. The Cheviot rocks derive from a long history of intense igneous activity that occurred almost 400 million years ago, during the Lower Old Red Sandstone period. This activity was heralded by volcanic outbursts of explosive violence when ash (finely disseminated rock fragments) was hurled into the air from a number of individual vents, extending along the line from E of Carter Bar to Wooler. These vents can no longer be identified in the field, but Thirlmoor, at the head of the River Coquet, together with the flanks of Gaisty Law, is composed mainly of the products of the outbursts. There followed a long period during which the outpouring of lava flows occurred, interrupted by occasional explosions, which provided further ash beds. In all, the volcanic products (mainly lavas) accumulated to a thickness of several thousand metres.

After this long-lasting volcanic episode, tranquillity returned to the region, and erosive activity by streams and rivers began to reduce the volcanic pile. However, after an interval of some ten million years, a stock or great mass of molten rock, eight to nine kilometres in diameter, and having the composition of granite, was thrust up into the body of the volcanic succession, but without reaching what was then the surface. Gradually, the granite cooled and solidified, losing its heat to the immediately adjacent lavas, which themselves became heated and recrystallized to form a metamorphic ring or aureole, more resistant to erosion than the normal volcanics, around the margin of the granite.

Further activity followed, in the form of the injection of numerous dykes (vertical veins) of granite-like material. These dykes were intruded both into the volcanics and into the central granite mass. Associated with the dyke intrusions a body of similar material, in the form of a laccolith (an elongated haystack-like form, though with a much smaller volume than that of the granite), was pushed up into the lavas, towards their southern boundary, with a N–S trend. The laccolith outcrops at Biddlestone. Apart from a later injection of a number of siliceous veins, this ended the igneous history of the Cheviot Hills, and subsequent erosion has cut down the lavas, exposing both the granite stock, the dykes and the laccolith, at the present surface.

The mode of occurrence of igneous rocks controls their rate of cooling, and slow cooling promotes crystallization. Therefore a huge body like a stock will cool slowly and will be coarsely crystalline. A dyke or a laccolith will lose its heat more rapidly, producing finer crystal grains; whereas a lava flow, rapidly losing heat at the Earth's surface, will be composed of minute grains, or it may even form a solid like a glass, without any crystalline texture. All these features are well displayed in the various igneous rocks of the Cheviot Hills.

Though sandstones of Old Red Sandstone age were being laid down during the Cheviot igneous activity over what are now the lowlands of Scotland, none of these deposits extended into Northumberland. However, in the geological period which followed, that known as the Carboniferous, the geographical conditions were such that a great land-mass lay well to the N of the Border, from which rivers brought material – sand and mud – spreading it out across the shallow sea which is now Northumberland. The whole of this region constituted a slowly subsiding trough, and in all some 3,000 metres of sediments accumulated during Carboniferous times.

The Carboniferous deposits in Northumberland are sub-divided into groups or series. The earliest of these, the Cementstones, were laid down by slow-flowing rivers as mud (which subsequently became compacted into shale) and sand (which became sandstone). Occasional thin calcareous beds accumulated; these were derived from the shells of marine organisms which became compacted into limestones – but such marine conditions (and they were generally muddy) were rare during deposition in Cementstone times. It is from these beds that the group has been given its name. In the group which followed, that of the Fell Sandstones, the deposits were almost exclusively of sand – indicating a more rapidly flowing river, with an abundant supply of material at source.

The next part of the succession, the Scremerston Coal Group, contains an assemblage of sandstones and shales with some limestones and coal seams. The presence of limestones, thicker and less contaminated with mud than those of the Cementstone Group, indicates an interval during which deposition from the land had practically ceased, and marine shelled organisms were able to flourish in the clear-water conditions. Coal seams, on the other hand, point to the filling-up of the trough or basin to sea-level, with the growth of plants and trees in the consequent swampy conditions. Compaction of this vegetable matter, as it decayed, led to the eventual formation first of peat then, with further compaction, of lignite and finally of bituminous coal.

The three succeeding groups, those of the Lower, Middle and Upper Limestones, are made up of a succession similar to the underlying Scremerston Coal Group, though with limestones more dominant, but still with some coal seams. The overlying group, the Longhoughton Grits, are similar to the Fell Sandstones, though they are less thick and much less widespread. The Coal Measures Group, the youngest and last of the Carboniferous succession in Northumberland, is made up of sandstones, shales and coal seams; the latter are both thicker and more abundant than in any of the underlying groups. There is a total lack of limestones in this group, indicating an absence of marine incursions.

An important igneous rock, the Great Whin Sill, outcrops across Northumberland. This rock, a dolerite, was injected between, rather than through, the layers of the Carboniferous succession as a sill, fed from below by a number of broad dykes. The most notable of these dykes is exposed along the southern edge of Lindisfarne, on which the castle stands. The sill outcrops from Belford in the N to the SW boundary of Northumberland, near Greenhead. This intrusion occurred before the next system of rocks, the Permian, was laid down. The latter occurs only across the old SE boundary of Northumberland, now Tyne and Wear, namely at Cullercoats and Tynemouth. These Permian rocks consist, at the base, of consolidated dune sand, succeeded by the Magnesian Limestone. The latter is a form of limestone containing about equal proportions of

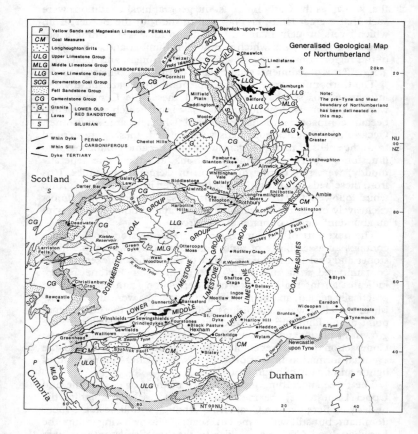

Generalised Geological Map
of Northumberland

calcium and magnesium; it is thicker and more widespread than any of the limestones in the underlying Carboniferous formations.

At a much later date, during Tertiary times, a number of dykes, in composition quite similar to the Great Whin Sill, were intruded across the county, linked to the much more extensive series of igneous dykes which radiate from the Isle of Mull. Of those in Northumberland, the most noteworthy is the Acklington dyke, which can be traced from the Scottish border, across the southern fringe of the Cheviot lavas, to the village of Acklington, and then on to the Northumberland shore.

The latest deposits, laid down during the Ice Age, are to be found covering most of the low ground of Northumberland. The ice advanced from the N in great sheets which scoured and blanketed the underlying rock. When this ice eventually melted, a great amount of debris, in the form of gravels, sands and clays, covered – and as yet still covers – the low ground, sometimes to a depth of 30 metres (100 ft). When the melt waters were blocked by stagnant ice still lying in the valleys, temporary lakes were formed; these overflowed and, in doing so, cut deep channels in the solid rock. The most outstanding of these channels in Northumberland is that immediately s of Powburn, through which the main road runs.

The TOPOGRAPHY of the county reflects very precisely the nature of the underlying rock. The present lava sequence of the Cheviot region has been eroded down by swiftly flowing rivers and burns, to form a deeply dissected plateau, approaching 500 metres (about 1,650 ft) above sea-level. The E central part of the region, occupied by the granite, is a rather higher, inner plateau, at about 600 metres (2,000 ft). Cheviot itself, a triangular-shaped plateau of peat hags, almost bereft of rock exposures, is over 800 metres (2,676 ft). The twelve hundred square kilometres (about 460 square miles) of the Cheviot region is a remote country, accessible for vehicles only along narrow, single-track roads. It is the domain of the hill shepherd, his dogs, his sheep and, alas, to an increasing extent the forest conifers. The lavas support grassland, while heather is confined to the central granite. The metamorphic aureole of the recrystallized lavas can be recognized by a broken ring of tors, especially on the eastern and western flanks of the granite mass.

The sedimentary rocks of the Northumberland trough were, of course, laid down in horizontal layers adjacent to, and to some extent across, the igneous rocks of the Cheviot region. Subsequently, earth movements uplifted the Cheviot mass, which then became subject to erosion. The surrounding sedimentary layers were therefore tilted to the E, SE and S, in the form of a huge, broken half-dome around the igneous core. Finally, erosion removed all but the Cementstones from the region immediately adjacent to the Cheviots, while the overlying rocks were planed off eastwards, so that the complete succession is now only preserved in the SE of the county (*see* the map).

Since all these layered rocks tilt down (or dip) away from the Cheviot massif, each of the thick, resistant formations, especially the sandstones, forms inward-facing scarp features. Of all these scarps, none is so prominent as those of the Fell Sandstones, which can be traced, in an almost unbroken series of ridges, from the Kyloe Hills, s to Chillingham and to Alnwick, then w to the Longframlington Moors, Simonside Hills, the Harbottle Hills and at last to the Larriston Fells and Christianbury Crag, on Cumbria's border. It would take the rambler several days to make the journey along those seldom frequented ridges from Berwick to Bewcastle, for he would find the heather tracks rough going.

The Fell Sandstone country is as remote as the Cheviots, but these two upland regions are as contrasting in topography and vegetation as they are in rock-type; the Cheviots are rounded, the Fell Sandstones angular, and while the former are largely grassland, the latter are mostly clothed in heather. To the local people, they are known respectively as 'the white country' and 'the black country'.

Beneath the Fell Sandstones, the soft shales of the Cementstone Group form the low cultivated areas of Milfield Plain, Whittingham Vale, Callaly and the low ground w of Thropton. There is nothing remote about the Cementstone country, whereon are many farms and villages, well provided with roads.

Many of the sandstones in the succession above those of the Fell Sandstones likewise form scarps facing towards the Cheviot massif. Chief among them are those of the Lower Limestone Group at

Ottercops, the sandstones of the Middle Limestone Group N of Hadrian's Wall (the motorist, travelling N from Corbridge to West Woodburn, cannot fail to notice the effect of these sandstone features as the road switchbacks up the dip-slope and down the scarp face of each ridge), and those of the Upper Limestone Group at Rothley, Shaftoe and Ingoe. Wherever these sandstones outcrop, they form rough, heather-clad, Fell Sandstone-type of country, though on a much more restricted scale.

In the Coal Measures region between the coast and a line joining Amble to Wylam, occasional ridges of sandstone occur, either within the Longhoughton Grits (especially at Harlow Hill), but more often in the Coal Measures. Examples of these Coal Measures ridges may be seen at Earsdon, Kenton and Heddon, but much of the solid rock in this low-lying region is covered by glacial deposits.

The Great Whin Sill forms many crags across Northumberland, outclassing all but the most prominent of the sandstone scarps. Many of these crags and, indeed, those of the sandstones also have been sharpened by the passage of ice across them. Noteworthy whin land-forms can be seen at Bamburgh, Dunstanburgh and Ratcheugh (near Alnwick), then at Thockrington and Bavington further S, and finally as the crags along Hadrian's Wall at Sewingshields, Winshields and the Nine Nicks of Thirlwall.

BUILDING STONES

BY JOHN GRUNDY

What the architectural traveller needs to know is how the county's geology and topography has affected its buildings and their materials. The Cheviot region by its nature has no villages and few farms. Its igneous rocks are hard and unyielding, and so their impact on the architecture of the county has been slight. However, in the deep valleys which cut into the hills, such as those of the Breamish, the Harthope Burn and the Coquet, the walls of the farms are built of igneous rock, while the door and window surrounds are built of softer, more manageable sandstone imported from outside the hills. Often the igneous rock used is in the form of boulders gathered from the beds of streams and therefore from a variety of geological sources. Some of the most attractive walls of this type are to be found on the northern edge of the region, around Kirknewton and Akeld, where the browns and soft pinks, greys, purples and reds of the igneous rocks contrast beautifully against the buff sandstone dressings. Coupland Castle, Akeld Bastle and the C 20 buildings at Hethpool are among the few major buildings built in this way, but there are many minor examples, and in addition the igneous rocks create splendid field walls, with broad bases and steeply battered sides.

Outside of the Cheviot area it is the rocks of the Carboniferous succession which have provided the stone for the vast majority of the county's buildings. From these deposits, the shale and limestone have provided no building materials (though the limestone has been extensively quarried and burned for agricultural purposes); the coal has of course been mined; the sandstone has become the dominant building material of the county. Northumberland is, perhaps to a greater extent than any other English county, a region of sandstone building.

All of the different Carboniferous groups described above, from the earliest Cementstones to the latest Coal Measures, have produced sandstone for building. They are, moreover, very often excellent building stones, relatively free from mica (which causes the rock to split into thin slabs) and massively bedded, with the grains well cemented together so that the rock can be cut easily into any shape. Which of the groups was chosen for a particular building was (until the advent of improved transportation) a decision controlled only by locality. So a village like Glanton in the Cementstones area is built of sandstone from that group; Rothbury and Cragside are from the Fell Sandstone quarry at Pondicherry just to the W of Rothbury; and houses like Capheaton and Belsay and most of the buildings in the Tyne Valley and on the coastal plain are built from sandstones in the various limestone groups.

Even a town as important as Newcastle is no exception; until the arrival of the railways made the import of alien materials a practical alternative, all the stone buildings in the town were of local sandstone. The castle, the medieval churches, the town walls and the Grainger redevelopment are all of local stone from quarries in the Coal Measures group, either immediately S of the river or at Kenton Bar, Heddon and Wideopen.

Experts can divide these sandstones into their various groups by examining the way they are bedded and by analysis of their mineral content, but the amateur would find it difficult to differentiate between them. That is not to say that there are no visible differences. The range is remarkable, even though the bulk of them contain iron oxide (limonite) which imparts to them a light buff colour. Some of the stone (e.g. that at Blagdon, Nunwick or Hesleyside) is an exquisite pale biscuit colour; Wallington, on the other hand, is a soft grey, while Belsay (and nearby Milbourne Hall) are built of a beautiful golden stone flecked with little nodules of iron which rust when exposed and stain the surface with runnels of brown. Some of the sandstones are notable for the way in which they cut and weather especially well. The village of Harbottle (even though it rests on the Cementstones) is largely built of big soft-edged blocks of honey-coloured Fell Sandstone from an outcrop just outside the village on the N bank of the Coquet. Even stones from closely related groups can vary greatly. Within the Limestone Groups, Dunstanburgh Castle is built of an extremely coarse-grained sandstone, while that used at Nunnykirk Hall is just the opposite, extremely fine-grained.

Buff and grey are the commonest but not the only colours to be found. The presence of haematite in the stone means that parts of the NE of the county have a great deal of red and pink sandstone, most notably that still quarried at Doddington near Wooler, and formerly quarried at Cheswick opposite Holy Island and near Bamburgh. The red is rarely harsh, just a quiet blush through the

grey, but it is unmistakable at Bamburgh Castle and Church, at
Lindisfarne Priory (where the stone in many places has weathered
into extraordinary, almost vermiculate patterns), and further inland
at Fowberry Tower and around the village of Doddington itself.
The occasional red building further N still (e.g. Horncliffe House,
on the Tweed, and Sanson Seal, near Berwick) is usually built of
the much older Old Red Sandstone of southern Scotland.

The dramatic crags of the Great Whin Sill and its associated dykes
have not only had a marked influence on the topography of the
county but provide settings for some of its most spectacular buildings – for Lindisfarne, Bamburgh and Dunstanburgh castles, and of
course for Hadrian's Wall.

The Romans chose to follow the line of dolerite cliffs in the centre
section of their Wall because of the wonderful natural defences
provided by the site. On the other hand they did not find the stone
itself useful for building. The hard dolerite (or whinstone) proved
too irksome to dress into regular facing stones (though it was used
in its rough state for the core of the Wall), and the Romans turned
instead, like most Northumbrian builders since, to nearby sources
of sandstones. Few others have used the dolerite; just occasionally
in the C 18 and early C 19 it was used to provide picturesque contrast
with paler sandstone dressings. The Georgian additions to Craster
Tower are the major example, but there are also a Greek Doric
house in Bamburgh, some farms near Embleton and one or two
cottages on Holy Island.

Building materials other than stone are dealt with later in this
introduction (*see* the section on Small Domestic Buildings). The
same is true of roofing materials, but mention might be made here
of those roofs in which once again sandstone plays a part. Easily
split, mica-rich sandstones from the Allen Valley provided roofing
flags which are still very common in the extreme S of the county
and quite common in the Tyne Valley. Stone flags are, however,
extremely rare further N in the county.

THE EARLIEST VERNACULAR STYLES:
PREHISTORIC NORTHUMBERLAND

BY HUMPHREY WELFARE

The gradual climatic improvement after the end of the last glaciation
eventually tempted relatively small groups of MESOLITHIC people
into northern England and southern Scotland some time after about
8000 B.C. These bands, who were probably largely nomadic,
depended on hunting and the gathering of seasonal foodstuffs. Their
presence in Northumberland is identifiable only by the simple tools
of flint and chert that they discarded. These have been found in
Mid Tynedale and in Allendale, but the contemporary coastline (a
favoured area) has been largely destroyed by changes in sea level and
by erosion. There is some evidence for the occasional occupation of
rock-shelters in the crags of the Fell Sandstone hills, but little is

known of the less durable shelters that these Mesolithic people may have constructed elsewhere.

The dawn of the NEOLITHIC period in the fifth millennium B.C. was marked by a slow but irrevocable revolution: the introduction of agriculture, a change which must also have brought about a more sedentary settlement pattern. The characteristic polished stone axes have been found all over the county, except in the hills over 300 metres (c. 1,000 ft) and on some of the heavier clay soils. Finds have been particularly plentiful in Coquetdale, the lower Breamish and upper Till, and in the Ponteland–Heddon area. Very many of the axes were evidently imported from the Langdale–Scafell area of the central Lake District, but other tools found in the county were made of rock from unidentified sources along the Whin Sill and from the greywackes of southern Scotland. The contemporary settlements of the fourth and third millennia B.C. have been equally elusive, and they have only been pinpointed when later sites have been excavated (e.g. Yeavering in Glendale and Thirlings near Ewart Park); even then the scraps of evidence provide scant coherence, consisting of little more than pits and gullies in the subsoil, associated with Neolithic artefacts.

Slightly more is known of the structures built for the dead. There seems to have been a Neolithic tradition (perhaps reserved for selected individuals or dynasties) of successive and collective burial under cairns. Some of these were probably large and circular on plan, but these are difficult to tell apart from their Bronze Age counterparts, and it is the LONG CAIRNS that are the most distinctive. There are two good examples in Northumberland, each constructed of rubble and with almost parallel sides: the Devil's Lapful, which stretches for about sixty metres (190 ft) down a conifer-clad hillside near Kielder, and the enormous Bellshiel Law cairn (112 metres (370 ft) long) lying on its impressive skyline site within the Otterburn Ranges near Rochester. Although the Bellshiel cairn may contain some structural slabs, no burial chambers have yet been identified within any long cairn in the county, and the nature of the mortuary arrangements that these huge constructions cover is uncertain.

By the last few centuries of the third millennium B.C. a highly organized late Neolithic social structure seems to have evolved. In the Milfield plain, land-divisions were laid out and a cluster of seven labour-consuming ritual centres (henges) was constructed. Unfortunately none of these is visible above ground, being known only from cropmarks on aerial photographs and from excavations. Nevertheless, it is clear that ritual played an important role in everyday life, though the remnants of that ritual, as revealed by archaeology, are often difficult to understand. This period of transition from the late Neolithic to the early Bronze Age produced the most puzzling remains of all, the rock-carvings known as CUP-AND-RING MARKS. The simplest of these symbols is a small cup-shaped hollow pecked out of the rock, but more elaborate examples abound: a cup may be surrounded by single, multiple, annular or penannular rings; long grooves or gutters may lead away from them, often linking with others to create more complex designs. In some cases the overall effect is almost pictorial, as on Dod Law (*see* Doddington), where clusters of cups are surrounded by grooves enclosing a sub-rectangular area. The carvings at Morwick, on the Coquet, are wholly exceptional, for they include sophisticated arrangements of conjoined spirals executed on the vertical face of a cliff, rather than on a level outcrop. (These designs are closer in style to the Megalithic art of Ireland and the Western seaways.) Not surprisingly, the distribution of cup-and-ring marks is determined by the geology, and in Northumberland the majority are on the Fell Sandstone hills from Rothbury to Ford. The best and most accessible examples are on Garleigh Moor s of Rothbury (*see* Hesleyhurst) and at Roughting Linn between Milfield and Lowick (*see* Doddington). The meaning of the carvings, impossibly obscure to us, must have been self-evident at the time, in the same way that the symbolism of a holy child and mother, or (for most of the twentieth century) of a sickle and a hammer, are instantly recognizable to us.

In the s of the county, cup marks are found on STANDING STONES, including those at Ingoe and Matfen. Again, little is known of the social or ritual compulsion that was satisfied by the erection of these pillars, for which a general Neolithic or Bronze Age date is usually cited. Some are minor triumphs of early engineering, for those at Great Swinburne and Yeavering are 3 metres (10 ft) high. As for STONE CIRCLES, Northumberland has but a handful: good examples survive at Threestoneburn (*see* Ilderton) and Duddo. From both of these there is shadowy evidence of burning or of burial, although the oxymoronically named 'four-poster' stone circles seem to have had burial as their principal function. This type of 'circle' is more common further N, and the examples at Ravensheugh Crags near Wark in Tynedale and the Three Kings near Rochester in Redesdale (*see* Byrness) are isolated from their main distribution, in NE and SW Scotland.

A more conventional resting-place for the dead was under a CAIRN. These piles of rubble, conspicuously positioned on summits or skylines, varied greatly in size. The largest survivors, at Thirlmoor near Chew Green and Russell's Cairn on the border with Roxburgh (Alwinton), are 16 metres (52 ft) across and over 2 metres (6½ ft) high. Bulk counted for more than architectural sophistication; the best that can be hoped for is a kerb of large blocks. However, the simple ruinous exterior frequently conceals a complex structural history, as has been revealed at Chatton Sandyfords and at Blawearie near Old Bewick. In contrast to the collective burials of the Neolithic, the usual practice during the Bronze Age was for the central burial (either a cremation or inhumation) to be that of a single individual, accompanied by a pottery vessel containing food or drink for the long journey. Subsequently the cairn would commonly be used for other burials, perhaps over a period of several centuries. A stone CIST (a box of stone slabs) protected the body from the weight of the cairn. Examples are exposed at Blawearie, Hole Farm, on Garleigh Moor to the s of Rothbury (*see* Hesleyhurst) and below Hepburn Crag near Chillingham. Such cists are also frequently found in modern arable land, without any apparent cairn or marker.

Clusters of very much smaller cairns can be seen on the shoulders of the middle Breamish valley and when the heather is burnt off the Fell Sandstone ridges. Although some of these small cairns were used for burial, many seem to have been the result of clearing stones from extensive areas of new arable land *c.* 2000 B.C. Settlements of the second millennium B.C. have been identified, but since they consist of unenclosed and often isolated stone hut-circles, their remains are usually difficult to identify and are largely of specialist interest. Those that survive have been found at relatively high altitudes, such as the group of houses at about 400 metres (1,300 ft) near Tathey Crags in the Cheviots, overlooking Threestoneburn (*see* Ilderton). The houses of one settlement dating to the C 15–13 B.C., excavated near Linhope in the upper Breamish, had a ring of substantial timber uprights to support the roof; the walls seem to have been of wattle and were surrounded by a bank of stones (all that is usually visible) cleared from the fields.

Soon after the beginning of the first millennium B.C., necessity or fashion dictated that some settlements on the hilltops and spurs should surround themselves with substantial timber palisades. The incredible stability of the turf in the Cheviots has preserved a small number of these stockades as readily visible surface features. At High Knowes, Alnham, the shallow trenches cut in the subsoil to receive the uprights can still be seen. Elsewhere, as at the huge example on Old Fawdon Hill, S of Ingram, only the practised eye will spot the evidence. Some settlements, like that above Hosedon Linn on Clennell Street (*see* Alwinton), never developed further and still display the circular grooves that mark the closely packed timber houses. However, most of the palisaded sites offering natural defensive potential were redeveloped, in a variety of fortifications, throughout the Iron Age. Thus it is often (but by no means invariable) that a palisade is found to be the first phase in the structural sequence of a HILLFORT. Throughout the Borders, excavation at sites such as Fenton Hill (*see* Doddington) has demonstrated a broadly predictable sequence in which one or more palisaded phases are replaced by defences consisting of a single wall faced with timber or stone. There are good examples of these univallate forts at Hepburn Crag (*see* Chillingham), Witchy Neuk (*see* Hepple) and the first phase at Harehaugh (*see* Holystone). In the later first millennium B.C. many such sites were reconstructed with the deep defences afforded by several ramparts formed of material upcast from external ditches (a multivallate fort), often at the expense of some of the area enclosed. On the rounded summits so common in the Borders, especially in the rolling coastal plains, the ramparts of multivallate and bivallate forts follow the contours and are oval or circular (e.g. Fenton Hill, Colwell Hill, and Fawdon Hill near Otterburn); elsewhere, as at Roughting Linn (Doddington), Monday Cleugh (Akeld) and Brinkburn, the natural defences afforded by cliffs or promontories could be economically utilized. Occasionally, as at Harehaugh, some impression of the development of the fortification can be gauged from the surface, but more often than not the earthworks of a deceptively simple final phase conceal a complex structural history.

Although this general and over-simplified sequence (palisade – univallate wall – multivallate upcast ramparts) is reasonably clear, the stratigraphical combinations on individual hillforts are legion in their diversity. Even contemporary sites are anything but uniform: contrast the elaborate stone walls of Brough Law in the Breamish Valley (near Ingram) with the humbler farmstead nearby at Ingram

Hill, which is defended only by a shallow ditch and by an embanked
palisade. Both sites date to the C 4 or early C 3 B.C. As with the twin
3 forts at Old Bewick, the social history implied by these remains
cannot be uncovered by archaeological methods.

The hillforts of Northumberland are small in size; although Yeavering Bell enclosed 5.5 hectares ($13\frac{1}{2}$ acres) the overwhelming
majority of sites cover less than half a hectare. A conspicuous position, as at Ros Castle near Chillingham and Tosson Burgh in
Coquetdale (*see* Great Tosson), must have made up in prestige what
the fort lacked in area. Overall size is, however, a poor guide to
population, as the high-density housing at Wether Hill (Ingram),
High Knowes (Alnham) and Old Fawdon Hill (Ingram) amply
demonstrates.

By the mid-first millennium B.C., contemporary with the hillforts,
lightly defended rectangular settlements seem to have become
common on the undulating lowlands of the coastal plain. Although
they are principally known only from the cropmarks of their surrounding ditches, excavation has shown these homesteads to have
been occupied over many generations, at least as late as the C 2 A.D.
Their durability is in some way indicative of the success of the Pax
Celtica that preceded the disruptions that heralded the imposed Pax
Romana. Many still survive in the higher pastures of North Tynedale
and Redesdale, their overall uniformity of design confirmed by
excavation at Tower Knowe (*see* Kielder), Riding Wood (*see*
Bellingham) and Woolaw (*see* Rochester). Inside a rectangular perimeter wall, three or four circular stone-founded buildings looked
out onto well-worn cobbled stockyards. The successive replacement
of earlier, timber buildings confirms that these conservative farmers
doggedly retained the same plan for centuries during the late Iron
Age and Roman periods. Although the contemporary homesteads
6 in the Cheviots, such as those on Haystack Hill near Ingram, were
usually curvilinear rather than rectangular, no one, it seems,
departed too radically from the basic design. Nevertheless, these
homesteads often appear to have extra buildings within their interior
or tacked onto their perimeters, suggesting the natural growth of a
prosperous community.

Elsewhere it was probably pressure upon the intensively farmed
landscape that dictated the redevelopment for housing of the most
obvious areas that could neither be ploughed nor grazed: the redundant defences of the abandoned hillforts. Circular stone houses of
Romano-British type overlie the ruins and shelter in the lee of the
ramparts at Grieve's Ash (near Ingram) and on Garleigh Moor (*see*
Hesleyhurst). This is a common occurrence; most of the buildings
are quite unenclosed and undefended, speaking tacitly of quiet
times, although on West Hill above Kirknewton the outer rampart
of the fort is overlain, predictably, by an enclosed rectangular settlement.

The abiding attraction of those sites offering good natural
defences is underlined by the long continuity of settlement beneath
the coastal castles of Bamburgh, Dunstanburgh and Tynemouth;
each of them probably began as a hillfort and was occupied during
the Roman period.

The architecture of late prehistory and of the Roman countryside
in Northumberland appears to have been staggeringly conservative.

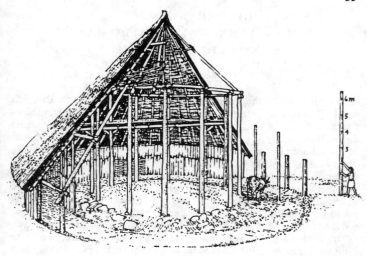

Iron Age architecture. Cut-away reconstruction of a round timber house with, perhaps, an upper floor

For at least 1,500 years there was no departure from a circular ground-plan. Although only the foundations of the buildings are known (a severe handicap in any attempt to reconstruct early vernacular style), fieldwork and excavation have sketched in some details.

The surface evidence for Iron Age buildings is often confined to a scatter of circular hollows and platforms within hillforts and settlements. The simplest form of superstructure, identifiable only in excavation, is still much as it had been in the second millennium B.C.: one or more rings of timber uprights protected by an outer skin of wattle and daub. The conical roof would have been thatched with heather, perhaps with a lining of turf. On some sites, such as Wether Hill near Ingram, the outer ring of posts was set in a continuous bedding-trench, which may still be traceable as a 'ring-groove' in the upland turf. As with most early houses, the entrance is usually in the SE quadrant.

Around the mid-first millennium B.C. a variation appeared: the 'ring-ditch' house, visible on the surface as a penannular depression (e.g. at High Knowes near Alnham). Substantial buildings (as much as twenty metres in diameter), each contained within its outer timber wall a shallow concentric ditch. This possibly resulted from the stalling of cattle, and could, in essence, have been similar in conception to the medieval long-house. Instead of having the two elements end to end, the Iron Age farmers would have had the byre wrapped round the central dwelling space, with all the benefits of winter insulation that this would bring. An upper floor, for living quarters or a hay-loft, is also a possibility.

BORDER COUNTRY:
HADRIAN'S WALL AND ROMAN
NORTHUMBERLAND

BY HUMPHREY WELFARE

Although it lacks the sophisticated urban buildings and the rich rural villas of the southern half of the province of Britannia, Northumberland can boast some of the finest Roman military remains in the Empire. By A.D. 79, thirty-six years after the initial invasion of the Channel coast, the governor, Agricola, had advanced to the Tay, and four years later he defeated the Caledonians at Mons Graupius, somewhere in NE Scotland. Although roads were built and forts were garrisoned at strategic points as far N as the S edge of the Highlands, the success was not pursued; by A.D. 90 all positions N of the Forth–Clyde isthmus had been evacuated. About a decade or so later the Romans fell back to the natural routeway of the Tyne Gap, where a road, known as the Stanegate, had been built by Agricola or his successors to link the forts at Corbridge and Carlisle (each of which stood on roads leading to the S). Within Northumberland, the fort at Vindolanda was also occupied, and the fortlet at Haltwhistle Burn (*see* Cawfields) was built soon after the turn of the century. Carvoran (*see* Greenhead) may have been garrisoned, and it is conceivable that a fortlet at Newbrough was also occupied at this time. Although at least one signal tower was built (later incorporated into Hadrian's Wall as Turret 45a: *see* Walltown), no regular signalling system has been identified. Indeed, despite the fact that the garrisons along the Stanegate were then on the N limit of the occupied zone, there is no evidence that the road formed any kind of formal frontier line as such. Certainly its course is not readily defensible, as modern travellers may appreciate as they follow its route from Fourstones almost to Vindolanda.

Early in the reign of Hadrian (117–138), there seems to have been some trouble. Whatever form it took, it concentrated the mind of the Emperor upon a serious problem: how could the Roman province be protected from any threat that might come from the unconquered lands to the N? It was probably during Hadrian's visit to Britain in 122 that the grand design was conceived for the security of this narrow N flank. With no continuous natural barrier to fix on, the radical alternative was to build an artificial one. This could make some use of the E–W communications already provided by the Stanegate and of the garrisons stationed along it, for the road itself had done little more than join the two routes running N and S on either side of the Pennines. To be effective the new barrier had to extend for seventy-six miles from a new bridge at the lowest crossing point of the Tyne at Newcastle to the shores of the Solway at Bowness in Cumberland. In planning the line, advantage was taken of the local topography wherever practicable; this was achieved most spectacularly in the wild central sector from Sewingshields to Greenhead, where the high crags of the Whin Sill could be made almost impregnable.

In order to make it more easily comprehensible, the original design of HADRIAN'S WALL will be described here, followed by an account of the modifications it underwent over the next three centuries (pp. 38–42). A final section (pp. 42–8) will outline the character of the Roman remains most readily visible within the county, and of the buildings in the contemporary countryside.

The original specification for Hadrian's Wall was a relatively simple regular scheme (no doubt the Emperor's own design) which sometimes took little account of the variations in local topography. At first it was rigidly adhered to, but extensive modifications were rapidly introduced. The Wall itself was to be ten Roman feet wide (about 9 ft 7 ins or 2.9 metres: the so-called Broad Wall) and was to be of stone from Newcastle to the River Irthing, just over the Cumbrian border; further W it was initially to be of turf. The stone Wall had a level berm, 6 metres (20 ft) wide, dividing it from a V-shaped Ditch to the N; this was usually about 8 metres (26 ft) broad and 3 metres (10 ft) deep. The Ditch was dug through solid rock if necessary (e.g. at Limestone Corner, W of Chesters), but on the Whin Sill crags it was not needed. In such a massive undertaking every economy was of importance, and the legionaries made the most of the building materials available locally. The faces of the Wall were usually made of roughly dressed coursed sandstone rubble won from small quarries (e.g. those on the crest S of Housesteads), although whinstone was occasionally used, especially in subsequent repairs and additions. The sandstone blocks were set in mortar and were of a manageable size; indeed, their general character is so uniform that they are readily recognizable wherever they have been reused (as so frequently) in later buildings. (By the early C 3, if not before, a final weather-proofing of thick lime-mortar wash or cement rendering seems to have been applied – deliberately or incidentally – to the face of the Wall in some places. As a dazzling white streak slashing across the landscape it must have struck awe into all who confronted it.) Between the wall-faces the rubble core might be bonded in mortar if limestone was available to hand, although in many places it seems that economics and the urgency of the initial phase of building dictated that the core was set in nothing better than earth. Puddled clay (from the Ditch) could also be used; indeed blocks of cut clay sometimes replaced the rubble itself as the core material. On the crags of the Whin Sill, chunks of the hard dolerite taken from the scree were often included in the core. Even then the assemblage of materials was incomplete: limestone outcrops had to be quarried and the rock burnt for mortar, and water had to be carried to the building gangs. The gangs themselves would each have consisted of a 'century' (about eighty legionaries), who usually signed their work with a terse inscription, the so-called 'centurial stones'.

We do not know either how high the Wall was or how the upper portion was designed. Estimates centre on a height of about 4.6 metres (15 ft), or perhaps 6 metres (20 ft) if there was a parapet. The latter would only be necessary if there was a patrol-walk on top of the Wall, for which there is no certain evidence either way. Unlike a castle wall, this was not intended to be a fighting-platform; rather it was a barrier to control movement and from which a watch might be kept. A patrol-walk may have been superfluous, for enough vantage points were provided by regularly spaced towers: the mile-castles and turrets.

4   At every Roman mile there was a MILECASTLE, essentially a cross
between a gateway and a fortlet. Every one had a N and S gate (each
probably with a tower above) to provide access through the Wall
itself; a small barrack-block was provided and often an ancillary
building too – sufficient accommodation for the men who controlled
the gates and kept watch over the Wall on either side. The role of
the milecastle was to be a base for patrols along the Wall and (at
least initially) a depot for repairs and maintenance. In the effort to
carry out the imperial scheme to the letter, regularity of design
sometimes seems to have taken precedence over function and topography. Hence, although the precipitous crags might make a N
gate superfluous and unusable, one was provided nevertheless: e.g.
Milecastle 42* at Cawfields, where, in addition, the interior slopes
so steeply as to make the construction of the internal buildings most
difficult.

Equally spaced between each pair of milecastles stood two
TURRETS. These small towers were simple observation posts, with
no sleeping-quarters, recessed into the rear of the Wall. The remains
visible at ground level usually consist of a door in the S side and,
next to it, a stone platform which probably supported a timber
ladder giving access to the first floor (e.g. Turret 7b at Denton,
Newcastle upon Tyne). As to its exterior appearance, several reconstructions are possible. The turret built conjecturally at Vindolanda
in 1973 has a flat roof and a castellated parapet. It is perhaps just as
likely that the watch stood on a timber gallery which projected from
all four walls at second-floor level. If so, the roof may have been
hipped or gabled and covered with tiles of stone or clay.

Changes in strategy, changes in design

These then were the key elements in the original scheme: Wall,
Ditch, milecastles and turrets. The forts along the Stanegate, in the
rear of the new frontier, were at first to be the bases for the garrison.
The response to any attack would therefore not have been immediate, but then this was a barrier designed to do no more than control
movement; no trouble was expected. Nevertheless in c. 124, before
work on the Wall was complete, a decision was taken which affected
the whole design of the military zone. New forts were to be built at
roughly regular intervals, six to nine miles apart, bringing the troops
and the command up onto the line of the Wall itself. In Northumberland, the first of the new forts were at Benwell, Rudchester,
Haltonchesters, Chesters and Housesteads. All of these (with the
exception of Housesteads, where the topography prevented it) were
designed to lie astride the Wall; in this way three gates could open
beyond the curtain (on the N side), thus providing the mobility that
was central to Roman field tactics. The character and constituent
parts of these forts are discussed below (pp. 44–6).

A wholly new element in this revamped scheme was the impressive
earthwork known as the VALLUM. This seems to have been a
demarcation line for the S side of the military zone, rather than an
insuperable barrier; it consists of a broad flat-bottomed ditch,
flanked to both N and S by a level berm and a continuous bank.

* The milecastles and turrets are numbered sequentially from E to W.

Carefully built, its earthen scarps were revetted with turf or stone where necessary. A causeway across the Vallum was provided opposite the S gate of each fort (a single example is still visible, at Benwell: *see* Newcastle upon Tyne), effectively controlling access into the strip under military control. Its course closely follows that of the Wall, except on the crags W of Sewingshields, where the Vallum takes to the lower ground. Little is known for certain, but it is likely that the line was originally laid out as a service track during the early stages of the construction of the Wall. If so, the track (now to be on the N berm) may have been provided with protective earthworks when the 'fort decision' was taken *c*. 124.

The construction of the Vallum must have weakened the need for the milecastles to serve one of their original functions, as gates through the Wall, since access to the military zone from the S could now only be achieved at forts. This was ironic, for the milecastles and turrets (both crucial as watch-towers) had almost all been completed by the time the frontier was redesigned. Each had been built with a stubby 'wing-wall' on either side: a short length of curtain that could be neatly bonded in when the legionary gangs arrived to complete the rest of the Wall above the foundations, already laid out. However, one facet of the new scheme was the decision that the Wall itself could be narrower, about eight Roman feet (2.3 metres) thick (thinner stretches survive, the results of later repairs and reconstruction). This must have speeded completion and certainly represents an enormous saving in building materials. A new E extension, from Newcastle to a new fort at Wallsend, was wholly built as this Narrow Wall. Elsewhere the superseded foundations of the original Broad Wall can frequently be seen extending S of the Narrow Wall; a detached section, which was never built upon, is exposed on the rocky knoll E of Milecastle 39. A point of reduction between the two gauges is preserved at Planetrees, just E of the North Tyne at Chollerford (*see* Wall). Several of the turrets, notably those at Brunton (26b: *see* Wall) and Black Carts (29a: *see* Chesters), illustrate how their Broad wing-walls were awkwardly bonded with the Narrow curtain; the reductions are always on the southern face. Only at Denton (7b), close to the Newcastle Western Bypass, can the Broad Wall be seen bonding into the turret as originally intended. In a few cases the new forts were set on the site of the recently built milecastles and turrets. This is only visible at Housesteads, where the foundations of Turret 36b have been exposed close to the N edge of the fort.

The forts themselves were garrisoned by auxiliary units raised throughout the western Empire, although the frontier works were originally built by legionaries. Inscriptions, and distinctive details in the design of milecastles and turrets and in the construction of the Wall itself, have enabled a complex picture to be sketched of the allocation of the work between the Second, Sixth and Twentieth Legions.

Modifications continued. It was quickly realized that the forts need not be set astride the Wall, and two of the last to be built illustrate this: Great Chesters, dated by an inscription to between A.D. 128 and 138, and Carrawburgh, which overlies an infilled stretch of the recently constructed Vallum. In the earlier forts that did project N, the three N gates were soon found to be an over-provision; lack of use eventually led to many of them being walled up. The fort at Carvoran, which may have preceded the Wall as a timber-built base on the Stanegate, was reconstructed in stone *c*. A.D. 136.

Two years later Hadrian died. Almost at once the new emperor, Antoninus Pius, decided to advance into Scotland, and by A.D. 139 the preparations were in hand, including the reoccupation of the forts on Dere Street: Corbridge (which had been abandoned as the Wall was built) and High Rochester. The next three years were occupied with campaigns in southern Scotland and culminated in the construction of a new frontier line across the narrow isthmus between the Forth and the Clyde: the Antonine Wall (*see* Buildings of Scotland: *Glasgow* and *Lothian*).

No longer in the forefront of military affairs, Hadrian's Wall was not wholly abandoned, although the garrisons were probably reduced to a skeletal level. The physical barrier now had no purpose: the milecastle gates were opened or removed entirely, and in some places regularly spaced gaps were driven through the N and S mounds of the Vallum, the material forming causeways across the ditch.

However, the advance into Scotland may not have long survived Antoninus Pius himself. Some time after his death in 161 the order was given for a strategic retreat to the southern Wall. By *c*. 169 the Antonine Wall was abandoned, but the forward forts on Dere Street, including a new one at Risingham, at the crossing of the Rede (*see* Woodburn), were retained for a time to act as centres for patrols throughout the eastern Borders. On Hadrian's Wall the milecastle gates were replaced and in each fort there was extensive refurbishment. The ditch of the Vallum was cleared out, producing a third mound on the S lip, which is best seen S of Milecastle 42 (Cawfields). A new road, the Military Way, was built between the Wall and the Vallum to improve communications (*see* below). Frontier life settled down again, but the troops were still spread thinly and the Wall could never have been held against a concerted attack from a large force; in any case Roman tactics would always have preferred a set-piece engagement in the field, well away from the Wall. In the early 180s, however, the intelligence reports must have broken down or the forward garrisons must have been out-manoeuvred. An invasion swept down from the N, the Wall was crossed, and there is evidence of destruction at Haltonchesters, Rudchester and Corbridge. Risingham may also have suffered. Peace was restored in 184 by the new governor, Ulpius Marcellus. The crossing of the Wall must almost inevitably have led to a review and shake-up of its defences, although some of the changes introduced at about this time are difficult to date with accuracy and may not have taken place until the early C 3.

In the forts many of the garrisons seem to have been changed. Most of the milecastles were apparently retained, but their gates (which had rarely been very effective) were blocked or narrowed to posterns, e.g. Milecastle 37 (Housesteads) or 39 (Castle Nick: *see* Housesteads). A good number of the turrets were declared obsolete and abandoned: doorways were walled up, and in some cases (clearly visible at 33b and 35a: *see* Sewingshields) the tower was demolished and the curtain wall carried flush across the face of the old recess.

The Roman frontier in the third and fourth centuries A.D.

The last decades of the C 2 were troubled times in Britain: a mutinous army and the civil war that followed the murder of the Emperor Commodus in 192 must have meant that the needs of the N frontier of Britain had a comparatively low priority. The garrisons of the Wall must to some extent have been drained for these campaigns, a time of weakness which enabled the Highland tribes to make trouble in southern Scotland. Whether the frontier itself was ever threatened is uncertain. Whatever the case, the early C 3 saw the beginning of a long building programme at many places along the Wall and in the outpost forts.

Renewed trouble, or the anticipation of it, brought the Emperor Severus to Britain in 208 with his sons Caracalla and Geta. Once again an advance was made up Dere Street into Scotland, penetrating into the NE. However, the death of the Emperor at York in February 211 brought, as so often before, a swift reversal of policy. Caracalla concluded a treaty with the northern tribes and returned to Rome. The Scottish forts were abandoned soon afterwards, but the outpost forts on Dere Street, at High Rochester and Risingham, were retained. They, together with their western counterparts at Bewcastle and Netherby in Cumbria, were the eyes and ears of the Wall. From them scouts were sent out to patrol and police the uplands of the later Border, providing a deep buffer zone.

Along the Wall itself some gradual changes took place during the long peace of the third century. Within the forts the garrisons had time to maintain and renew their premises. Repairs to the curtain Wall itself seem to have amounted, in many places, to a wholesale reconstruction at a gauge even thinner than the Hadrianic Narrow Wall. This often entailed the use of a particularly durable mortar which appears to have been applied so generously that the facing-stones must have been, in effect, rendered. The vertical offsets often encountered in the S face of the Wall seem to have been a feature of this rebuilding. The Vallum probably slipped out of use at about this time; beside the forts it was filled in by the inhabitants and entrepreneurs of the civil settlements that flourished outside their walls.

The evidence for the civilian lifestyle dependent upon the military is particularly good in the C 3 and C 4. In the prosperous garrison town at Corbridge the houses, shops and taverns made good use of the soldiers' pay. The best-known civil settlements, at Housesteads and Vindolanda, probably dwarfed the forts that had spawned them and eventually achieved a measure of self-government. In the later C 3, during this long period of stability, some bases, such as Rudchester and Haltonchesters, seem to have been run down. However, at Vindolanda the civil settlement itself may have dwindled after *c.* 270, although the reason for this is unclear.

At the very end of the C 3 or in the early C 4, rebuilding in the forts sometimes took a rather different form, especially in the barrack-blocks. This is known from a number of sites but is only clearly visible at Housesteads, where at least two barrack-blocks were completely remodelled into a series of separate units, nicknamed 'chalets'. The change may have coincided with a general decrease in the size of the garrison on the Wall. The outpost forts were not neglected (building projects included the grand W gateway at High Rochester), but these more isolated bases could hardly remain secure for ever; some destruction is attested at both High Rochester and Risingham at about this time.

In 314 the Emperor Constantine assumed the title Britannicus Maximus, probably as a result of successful but otherwise unrecorded wars in Britain. Further trouble in 342 also brought the Emperor Constans to the N, and in the 360s the disturbances became more frequent. In 367 a wild confederacy of 'barbarians' mounted a concerted attack upon Britain, the northern frontier of which had been rendered fatally vulnerable by the duplicity of the scouts. The Franks and Saxons ripped into the S and E, while the Scots (from Ireland) and the Picts and Attacotti (from Scotland) surged over the N and W. It took a substantial new army, under Count Theodosius, to restore order and to begin some reconstruction.

How much the Wall suffered, if at all, is unclear, for the raiders may have come by sea. Nevertheless the northern command must have been severely shaken. Haltonchesters and Rudchester were reconstructed (perhaps largely in timber) and reoccupied; elsewhere, however, it seems that military, social and architectural standards in the late C4 were not what they had been. At Housesteads, parts of the central administration block were turned into living quarters (as at Vindolanda) and into an armoury. It may have been about this time that the buildings of the civil settlements at Housesteads and Carrawburgh were apparently cleared away from the fort walls in order to insert double banks as extra defences. The camp-followers may have been living within the fort itself by then, but the evidence for this is shadowy at best. Even less is known for certain about the forward patrolling N of the Wall in the C4, or exactly when the outpost forts were abandoned. The dwindling number of late Roman artefacts found in the native settlements (*see* p. 48) may suggest that contacts with the tribes beyond the Wall were steadily decreasing. As the C5 dawned, troops were being drained away from Britain to defend the heartlands of the Empire. The forts of the Wall were still manned in some way up to 411, when the last British appeals were sent, in vain, to Rome for military and financial assistance. Continuing C5 occupation is suggested at Corbridge and at Vindolanda, although by now all the strongholds may have taken on the role of fortified villages, slowly declining, rather than the proud bastions of an imperial frontier that they once had been.

The surviving remnants of Rome

The most durable legacy of the Roman period in Northumberland is not buildings at all but the ROADS, probably laid out by Agricola or his immediate successors. The principal route was Dere Street, which led N from the centre of the military command at York to the fort at Corbridge, built to guard the crossing of the Tyne. Passing through Hadrian's Wall at Portgate, its course is followed by the A68 for most of the way to Rochester in Redesdale. Over this section the road is straight for several miles, a roller-coaster ride over the rapidly succeeding crests of E Tynedale. A more dignified and atmospheric stretch lies beyond High Rochester, in the Otterburn

Ranges used by the c 20 army. The narrow modern road on the Roman line leads up the valley of the Sills Burn and over Foulplay Head to the w shoulder of Thirlmoor, above the head of Coquetdale, the best viewpoint for the installations at Chew Green. At last free of tarmac, the road swings up to 480 metres (1,575 ft) on Brownhart Law to follow the Border line for a short distance, with half of the Scottish county of Roxburgh laid out below. Thereafter its course lay NNW, to the fort at Elginhaugh near Dalkeith and to the Antonine Wall.

Soon after leaving Corbridge, a road long nicknamed the Devil's Causeway branched away from Dere Street just N of Portgate. It was heading for an unlocated fort and harbour at Berwick or Tweedmouth. Apart from short lengths of bridleway and lane w of Longhorsley and Longframlington, the only viable length is the modern road from Horton, near Wooler, to Lowick. A single fort, levelled by the plough, is known on the Devil's Causeway at Low Learchild between Whittingham and Edlingham. From there, however, another road pushed w across Whittingham Vale and Coquetdale to meet Dere Street at High Rochester. Portions of it can be traced in the heather w of Holystone.

In the s of the county the Stanegate connected Corbridge with Carlisle; it is rarely an impressive survival, although its route can be followed for several miles on the back road leading w from New-brough towards Vindolanda, where a milestone (and the stump of another) can be seen. At Carvoran (*see* Greenhead) the Stanegate met the Maiden Way, which ran up South Tynedale to Whitley Castle and over the high fells to Kirkby Thore in the Eden Valley. However, perhaps the most readily appreciated Roman road in the county is also the least typical: the later c 2 Military Way serving the garrison of Hadrian's Wall. It flouts all the usual Roman rules (long straight stretches; changes of direction only on summits) by wriggling up hill and down dale to keep close to the Wall. A low green cambered mound, often bounded by kerbstones, it is clearly visible for most of the way from Sewingshields, past Housesteads to Cawfields and near Walltown. Its late survival as a road is empha-sized by the number of field-gates on its line; indeed it was only finally superseded by the much later Military Road built to link Newcastle and Carlisle after the Jacobite rebellion of 1745.

At the end of each journey lay either a temporary CAMP or a fort. Good examples of the former can be seen to the s of the quarry at Cawfields on Hadrian's Wall, and at Chew Green close to the s Scottish border. Their defences are unimpressive, no more than a single bank of earth and turf, derived from an outer ditch; normally laid out like a playing-card on plan, some enclose as much as 16 hectares (39 acres). They could, in theory, be thrown up for a single night to protect the leather tents of an army on the march or on manoeuvre. However, some of them were probably used for a sea-son's campaigning or were reused over a period of years.

More substantial permanent posts, known as FORTLETS, were built to house a small detachment. Northumberland has three par-ticularly good examples. One, occupied from *c.* 105 to 204, lies on the Stanegate beside the Haltwhistle Burn at Cawfields, protected by a simple outwork. Elsewhere, isolation called for deeper defences, as at Longshaws near Stanton, where the fortlet is on a cliff above

the River Font; well away from any known Roman road, this site
probably belongs to the early years of the conquest in the late C I.
At Chew Green on Dere Street, just below the modern Border, a
roadside post was also provided with multiple ramparts.

The usual base of each garrison was, however, the FORT. This
almost invariably followed a general plan standard throughout the
Empire, although they varied greatly in detail. No Roman fort in
Northumberland has been exposed and displayed in its entirety but
the best impression of the overall arrangements can be gauged at
Housesteads (see pp. 345–9). A playing-card shape was again the
norm, and in the C I the perimeter of a typical fort would have
been defined by a timber stockade backed by a substantial earthen rampart; beyond a level berm lay one or more external ditches. In the
C 2 the timber revetment was almost invariably replaced in stone. The
principal gate was set in the centre of one of the short sides. From
it a road ran a third of the way into the interior of the fort, down
its long axis, to meet a cross-street linking the two lateral gateways.

At this junction, facing back towards the main gate, was the
HEADQUARTERS BUILDING, the administrative centre of the fort
and the focus of regimental loyalty. Excellent examples of these key
buildings can be seen at Chesters, Housesteads and Vindolanda.
Passing through a central archway, visitors found themselves in a
colonnaded courtyard. Here information could be exchanged and
perhaps notices posted; at Chesters and Vindolanda a well was sunk
within the court. Across the rear of this courtyard, through some
double doors, was a lofty hall, a basilica, which was probably lit by
a clerestory. At the right-hand end a raised platform or dais was
provided, upon which the commanding officer sat during briefings
or tribunals. Opening onto the further long side of the hall would
be five small rooms. At Vindolanda the decorated slabs that formed
the low screens fronting these rooms can still be seen. The space
above them may have been filled with open ironwork. The central
room was the shrine to the gods of the army itself, the chapel of the
regimental standards where all the sacred military regalia was kept.
Later modifications in many forts recognized that this was also the
safest place in which to store the unit's pay-chest. At Chesters, Great
Chesters and Corbridge the modern visitor can descend worn steps
or peer into the vault of a sunken strongroom concealed below the
raised floor of the shrine. An unusual and very narrow variant
survives at Vindolanda. The rooms on either side of the shrine were
occupied by administrative staff. To the left were the offices of the
standard-bearers, who dispensed the soldiers' pay and ran a savings
bank. The rooms to the right were occupied by the adjutant and his
staff. The later changes in use so commonly found in these offices,
and throughout the headquarters building, reflect the eventual
decline in central discipline, in the dignity of the command and in
the coherence of the fighting unit.

Two other distinctive types of building usually flank the headquarters, completing the administrative range in the central third of
the fort. The GRANARIES are easily recognizable by their closely
spaced massive buttresses which counteracted the outward thrust
of a roof of stone slates, and also of the sacks or bins filled with grain
and other foodstuffs. Low openings through the outer walls provided
much-needed ventilation underneath a floor of stone slabs raised

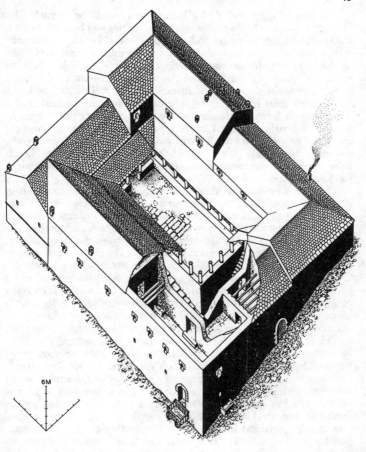

Housesteads. Reconstruction of the Commanding Officer's House

upon low sleeper walls or pillars (compare the fine survivals at Corbridge and Housesteads). On the other side of the headquarters stood the COMMANDING OFFICER'S HOUSE. This was a gentleman's residence, the rooms ranged around a courtyard, with ample space for his family and for official entertaining. A small private bath-suite was almost invariably provided. The remains at Chesters are complicated by later alterations, but the building at Housesteads is more readily appreciated, although the variation in ground level seems to have complicated the arrangements and provided an extra storey at the SE angle. Also at Housesteads, behind the headquarters, the HOSPITAL has been excavated; its individual rooms are again laid out around a courtyard, an arrangement more suited to the climate of the Mediterranean than to that of Northumberland.

The rest of the interior of a Roman fort would be occupied by even more austere buildings: workshops, stables and barrack-blocks. Each of the latter was long and narrow, divided behind a verandah into a number of compartments, ten in an infantry unit and eight in the cavalry (who presumably required extra space in which to store and maintain the harness). In marked contrast to the CO's quarters, one of these compartments housed eight men, and was itself subdivided into sleeping accommodation at the rear and a living area in front. At the end of the block, closest to the rampart, a projecting suite of rooms housed the centurion. Two incomplete examples of such barracks are exposed at Chesters. At Housesteads, by way of contrast, the C 4 type has been excavated and consolidated: here the compartments are separate units ('chalets') with only a back wall in common.

There was no central Mess in a Roman fort; food was eaten in the front rooms of the barracks but was cooked in an oven set into the rampart (e.g. beside the W gate at Chesters) in order to minimize the fire risk. LATRINES, however, were always communal rather than individual. They varied greatly in size, from the large suite at Housesteads, which made such good use of the fort's sparse water-supply, to the much smaller (but by no means cosy) block near the NE corner of the fort at Vindolanda. The Roman soldier had to be sociable in all his ablutions, and the BATH-HOUSE was an important component of his civilization. The baths were almost invariably placed well outside the fort and were constructed of stone, pre-cautions essential to guard against the constant danger presented by the sparks from the furnaces that heated the water. The well-preserved example at Chesters stands a short distance away from the fort, by the banks of the North Tyne, and, like its counterpart visible at Vindolanda, it was probably engulfed by the expansion of the civil settlement. Within each building a succession of rooms provided various gradations and combinations of conditions, hot or cool, moist or dry, with a continuous supply of water. Thus a choice was usually provided for the bather depending upon which route was taken: Turkish bath or sauna. The waste water was used to flush a latrine. The design and construction of the building as a whole, though often standardized, was dictated by its function. In the hotter rooms the floors were heated by hot air, which circulated first through hypocausts and then upwards through vertical flues to warm walls clad in waterproof plaster. The windows were glazed (with glass that was translucent rather than truly transparent), and the door-jambs were of stone to prevent warping and rot. The roofs were barrel-vaulted, with an insulated construction of stone voussoirs and tiles, and were probably rendered.

In their religious life the Romans worshipped a wide pantheon, as the variety of altars recovered so vividly illustrates. The TEMPLES to these gods, built outside the fort on the edge of the civil settlement, were small by later ecclesiastical standards but varied greatly in design. The shrine to Coventina at Carrawburgh had the square plan of a Romano-Celtic temple but was a simple construction and may have been open to the sky. The temple to Antenociticus, who seems to have been a local god, is a straightforward apsidal structure, now in suburban Benwell (see Newcastle upon Tyne). It was built to house the fine statue of the deity and could accommodate only a few worshippers. The aisled temple of the eastern god Mithras at Carrawburgh is larger but also has no architectural pretensions. Like all *mithraea* it was designed to resemble the cave in which the god slew the primordial bull (the scene depicted in the relief on the reredos), thus releasing all the powers of untamed creation for the benefit of man.

Of the secular buildings in the civil settlements the most typical was the 'strip-house', remains of which can be seen at Housesteads and Vindolanda. These had a long and narrow ground-plan, with only one gable-end fronting onto the street. Some seem to have been shops, a groove in their sills suggesting a shuttered front or a counter; a workshop or living quarters may have occupied the back rooms. More sophisticated and varied properties existed within the urban centre of Roman Corbridge, but little is known of their individual functions.

The reconstruction of any of these buildings from the archaeological evidence is fraught with problems. Only the granaries and the baths are likely to have been constructed entirely of stone. The other 'stone' buildings in the forts and civil settlements were probably timber-framed. All that survives are low walls that carried the sill-beams; above this, posts and studs were presumably infilled with wattle-and-daub. The provision of a second storey would therefore have presented no particular problem, although how often this may have occurred is unknown. More certainty attaches to the roofs, which seem usually to have been covered with tiles or stone slates.

Within the context of early Britain the buildings erected by the Romans were of exceptional quality. By classical standards, however, those put up by the army in the N were coarse: building rather than architecture. Plaster rendering must have covered a multitude of masonry sins. To the eyes of a stonemason, even the more respectable survivals (such as the N gate of Milecastle 37 or the W gate at Housesteads) only consisted of good block-in-course work improved by chiselled margins on the quoins. True ashlar is rare (e.g., surprisingly, in the gateway of the Vallum crossing at Benwell), and elsewhere standards varied widely. Part of the Chesters bridge-abutment has facing-blocks neatly punched in curving furrows, whereas on the outer face of the W range of the unfinished market at Corbridge only the margins of the blocks were dressed, leaving heavy rustication. Whatever Hadrian and his successors may have wished for, it seems (according to Hill) that the Wall was regarded by its masons 'not so much as a superb monument to the Emperor as a gigantic exercise in utility civil engineering'.

In the countryside of Roman Northumberland the farmhouses could hardly have been more different from the southern villas. Their architecture sprang directly from their Iron Age antecedents, the only major change coming in about the C1 or C2 A.D., when a low wall of uncoursed and unmortared rubble became fashionable as the outer skin. Some still had a ring of timber uprights round the inner face, but elsewhere the wall was lined with wattle. The provision of a timber porch seems to have been common, if not essential, as the rafters probably rested on the low wall-head. Paved floors, averaging about five to six metres in diameter, give no indication of the arrangement of the posts set up on them to support the roof. In a few cases wattle partitions have been recovered within the interior; an off-centre hearth, lined with slabs, was usually provided.

The dating evidence for the settlements of the Roman countryside is pitifully poor, dependent all too often upon a scrap of abraded pottery or the presence of a glass bead. In the C3 even these meagre clues gradually dry up; thereafter, for several centuries, archaeology is almost completely silent.

MEDIEVAL ARCHITECTURE AND SCULPTURE

BY PETER RYDER

Pre-Conquest

The known story of SAXON ARCHITECTURE in the county is, as usual, almost entirely that of CHURCH BUILDING, and church building in stone. Before turning to that, we should note that no secular or timber buildings remain, although our archaeological knowledge of the rural palaces of Yeavering and Milfield, with their buttressed barn-like halls, gives some indication of the architectural sophistication available in the C6 and C7. However, *grubenhäuser* (small, simple huts with sunken floors) may have been more typical as a vernacular style. These have been recorded as cropmarks in the lowlands around the Till, but elsewhere nothing whatever is known.

The key events in the history of the Christianization of Northumbria are well documented: King Edwin's baptism at York in 627, King Oswald's decisive defeat of the pagan British at Heavenfield in 634, Aidan's arrival at Lindisfarne in 635, the Synod of Whitby in 664, Cuthbert's death in his cell on Farne in 687 and the closing of the 'Golden Age' with the Danes sacking Lindisfarne in 793. The Lindisfarne Gospels are testimony to the monkish craftsmanship of the period, as are some of the surviving pieces of stone sculpture; but as regards its buildings and architecture we still know relatively little. Wilfrid, champion of the Roman cause at Whitby, started to build a monastery at Hexham *c.* 670, and his church was elevated to cathedral status eight years later; his biographer Eddius penned a glowing description of this building, which he considered without parallel 'on this side of the Alps'. But despite the attempts of generations of antiquaries and archaeologists to reconcile his description with extant and recorded remains we still 9 know very little about it, with the exception of its crypt (very like that of Wilfrid's earlier monastery at Ripon), which survives intact. Constructed of Roman stone, its passages and small chambers encircle a central relic chamber; the concept has been held to be inspired by Wilfrid's visit to the Catacombs. A monastery and episcopal seat such as Hexham would have possessed a whole cluster of churches; it is recorded that Wilfrid built at least two more, but one of these (St Peter) is now lost and for the other (St Mary) we only have fragments of its medieval successor. The Saxon St Mary would appear to have been a building of unusual interest, as Aelred of Rievaulx, writing in the C 12, describes it as being circular in plan, with four apses facing the cardinal points.

Three or perhaps four churches, all close to the Tyne and within a dozen miles downstream of Hexham, preserve fabric which the Taylors have classed as of period 'A', i.e. before 800 and the Danish invasions. These are all churches of the 'Northumbrian' type well known from Jarrow and Monkwearmouth in County Durham, typi- fied by long, tall and narrow naves and the use of megalithic angle quoins laid in side-alternate fashion, that is, large slabs, equivalent in height to two or three courses of ordinary walling, laid on their sides with their longer faces along alternate walls. Corbridge has remains of a typical nave, with a w porch later raised (as at Monkwearmouth and also Ledsham in Yorkshire) into a tower; Bywell St Andrew also has a late Saxon tower which may incorporate 7 an older porch, whilst Bywell St Peter preserves parts of a large nave (possibly even longer than that at Monkwearmouth) and chancel, with evidence of *porticus* overlapping their junction as at Escomb in County Durham. Heddon-on-the-Wall is dated to this early period on the basis of its nave having thin walling and massive side-alternate eastern quoins. All these churches, like the majority of pre-800 stone churches in Northumbria, were probably initially monastic. There was another early monastic church at Rothbury, where it appears that, as at Jarrow, a late Saxon tower (possibly built above a porch) linked two churches set on the same E–W axis. Sadly its last remains were cleared away in the cause of Victorian restoration.

Most of the other surviving pre-Conquest churches in the county probably date to the last century of the Saxon period, when some degree of peace and prosperity had returned after Viking raiding and settlement. This was a century of TOWER BUILDING right across Europe. Tynedale remained important, and has a fine series of late Saxon towers at Warden, Corbridge, Bywell St Andrew and 7 Ovingham. The last two are the best-preserved, with belfry openings 8 showing proto-tracery, where paired openings are set within an arch outlined by stripwork, with a circular piercing in the tympanum. At Bywell there is a further pair of small circular openings above and to either side of each main opening. Both churches have doorways on the S immediately below the belfry, now opening about 12 metres (40 ft) above ground level; their function remains a mystery. Most of these features are shared by the very similar tower at Billingham (*see* Buildings of England: *County Durham*). The tower at Bolam, 15 m. N of the Tyne, is quite different in style from Bywell and Ovingham, and has its belfry openings not in the top storey but in the one below; the openings are still paired, with a mid-wall shaft, but here there is no enclosing arch of stripwork. The overall effect is plainer and more massive than the Tynedale towers. The only other Saxon tower is at Whittingham, and this suffered from a savage gothicization in 1840; its oddity is that both tower and nave w end have long-and-short quoining, which is distinctively a South-of- England ('Mercian') type; the next most northerly outliers of the style are in Yorkshire at Bolton-on-Dearne and Laughton-en-le- Morthen near Sheffield, and Barton-on-Humber.

At other churches Saxon remains are more fragmentary, and difficult to date. Hartburn, Newburn and Stamfordham all show heavy side-alternate quoining. Woodhorn has remains of one quoin

and a pair of single-splayed windows cut into by the Norman
12 arcades; one has strange geometric doodlings incised on its lintel.
The parish church on Holy Island, where plaster-stripping has
revealed remains of an early chancel arch and an opening above,
poses a puzzle; is this the late Saxon mother church of Islandshire,
or the new church recorded as having been built by a monk called
Edward when the first Benedictines arrived in the 1080s?

Other churches preserve fabric which, although lacking distinctively Anglo-Saxon architectural features or quoining, by its
relationship with Norman parts of the building implies a Saxon or
Saxo-Norman date. Chillingham and Old Bewick have massive
rubble walling that contrasts with their well-squared C 12 ashlar;
Ingram and Seaton Delaval other fabric that seems to pre-date their
C 12 parts. At Longhoughton the massive simplicity of the slightly
horseshoe-shaped chancel arch contrasts with the clearly Norman
tower arch. The list could go on; overall, around a third of the
county's medieval churches have fabric or features showing Saxon
style or tradition, which must date them to before c. 1100.

Turning to SCULPTURE, the British Academy *Corpus** lists 154
pieces of pre-Conquest stone sculpture in the county, and another
forty of Saxo-Norman or 'Overlap' or uncertain date; together they
come from thirty-six different sites. Many of these are of course
minor fragments, but there are a number of important pieces, which
are a more tangible demonstration of the artistic achievements of
the period than the surviving buildings. The collection at Hexham
includes carved imposts and sections of friezes from Wilfrid's late
C 7 church, and the spectacular Acca Cross of c. 740. The surviving
10 pieces of the early C 9 Rothbury Cross are also of major importance.
The design of these two crosses is no longer quite so uncannily
sophisticated as the earlier Ruthwell and Bewcastle crosses, but with
their birds and beasts in vine-scrolls and figure sculpture they are
infinitely superior to Continental work before the Carolingian
Renaissance. Charlemagne was well advised to draw Alcuin to his
court from York and make him head of the school at Tours. The
other major collection of sculpture is at Lindisfarne, which includes
many small grave markers ranging in date from the C 7 to the late
C 9. One of the latest is a strangely moving piece; one side shows a
procession of warriors brandishing Viking-style swords and axes and
the other figures kneeling before a cross with both sun and moon
above, symbolic of the Doomsday and Last Judgement that the
monks must have thought had come upon them. At Hexham is
another impressive relic of Northumberland's pre-Conquest *flo-*
11 *raison*, a stone chair of c. 675–700, called the Frith Stool or Wilfrid's
Chair.

Northumberland was the butt of many Viking raids, but it was
never a county of major Scandinavian settlement as Yorkshire was.
Viking influence is seen in a scatter of C 10 and C 11 crosses and
monuments (there is one late C 10 hogback grave cover at Hexham)
but there is nothing of real importance. As with the church buildings,
it is difficult to distinguish between pre- and post-1066 in this minor
sculpture. The small headstones or grave markers at Chollerton and

* R. Cramp, *Corpus of Anglo-Saxon Sculpture in England* I: Part 1, *County Durham and
Northumberland* (1984).

Woodhorn, the churchyard crosses at Kirkhaugh and Warden and a number of simple cross-slab grave covers are all in the tradition of simple but functional monuments that continued at least until the C 13, a tradition on which the new Norman overlordship made little recognizable impact.

Medieval ecclesiastical architecture

The era of NORMAN dominance dawned troubled, with a succession of rebellions, put down by William with his customary ruthlessness. The Norman presence was soon realized both in the castles springing up throughout the county – or at least at its major river crossings and strategic points – and in the appearance of a growing number of MONASTIC HOUSES, although there was never anything here on the scale of the Cathedral Priory of Durham or the great Yorkshire abbeys. Two pre-Conquest foundations were re-established as priories of Benedictine monks, Lindisfarne in 1083 19 as a dependency of Durham, and Tynemouth at about the same time, first dependent on Durham and then on the remote St Albans. Extensive ruins of their churches survive, sufficient to be of considerable architectural importance, and we have at least the ground-plans of their principal monastic buildings. There are also interesting remains on a much smaller scale of the Benedictine cells on Coquet and Farne Islands; nothing survives above ground of a third cell at Warkworth. There were Benedictine nuns at Holystone and Lambley (each with minor structural remains and *ex-situ* fragments) and at Newcastle, where nothing but street names survives to indicate the site. Northumberland had only one Cistercian house, Newminster (founded 1138), a daughter house of Fountains which today presents fragmentary ruins (largely re-erected masonry) on a confused and partly excavated site.

The county's two best-preserved monastic churches belonged to Augustinian priories, at Hexham (founded 1113) and Brinkburn 28, 25–6 (founded before 1135). Both are monuments of major architectural importance, and have typical Augustinian naves with N aisles only (that at Hexham rebuilt in 1908 on the old foundations). The remains of their monastic buildings (more extensive at Hexham) have been complicated by incorporation in post-medieval houses. Of the other Augustinian houses, little survives at Bamburgh (founded 1121) and nothing above ground at Carham (founded *c.* 1131); Bamburgh was initially a cell of Nostell, Carham a cell of Kirkham, another Yorkshire house. Hexham had a cell at Ovingham, a late foundation (1378) of which some remains survive. The Premonstratensian canons had abbeys at Alnwick (founded 1147) and 36 Blanchland (founded 1165). Of the former a gatehouse survives and the ground-plan has been excavated; at the latter, parts of the church, cloister and outer court buildings are delightfully tangled up with an C 18 village. Guyzance had a small priory of the same order, initially a nunnery but later a cell of Alnwick; it is not clear whether the ruined church there was monastic or not.

In the C 13 all four main orders of friars (Franciscan, Dominican, Austin and Carmelite), along with the Trinitarians and the Friars of the Sack, established themselves in Newcastle. Quite extensive remains of Black Friars (Dominican) have now been rescued from 47

dereliction, excavated and conserved; there is also a fragment of
the Austin friars' church, strangely sandwiched between a post-
Dissolution tower and the C17 Holy Jesus Hospital. There are slight
remains of the Dominican house at Bamburgh. The Carmelites also
27 had a house at Hulne (founded 1242), in a quite different rural
situation, and here there are ruins that are both extensive and
picturesque, their appeal enhanced but their archaeology confused
by C18 'improvements'. Another unusual survival is the ruin of
the Knights Hospitallers' preceptory at Chibburn (founded before
1313), which like Newcastle Black Friars narrowly survived a C20
threat, this time from opencast coalmining. In addition to these
twenty-six religious houses, Knowles and Hadcock, in *Medieval
Religious Houses in England and Wales* (2nd ed., 1971), list forty-two
medieval hospitals, which as usual have suffered more severely;
above-ground relics are few. As for medieval colleges, Northumberland was too turbulent to favour their establishment. The
undercroft and footings of what was intended to be a collegiate
chapel survive within the bailey of Warkworth Castle, but the foundation was never established. There was a small college at Ponteland,
but no visible remains survive.

In 1296 hostilities were renewed across the Border, accompanied
by a general absence of law and order. These conditions had a
profound effect on both secular and ecclesiastical architecture;
neither the largest monastery nor the smallest parish church was
exempt from threat. It was Durham Cathedral that was once
described as 'half church of God, half castle 'gainst the Scot', but
this epithet would also have been true of almost every medieval
monastic house in Northumberland. The fire and slaughter of many
raids have been chronicled; each religious house needed to be a
'walled city' in order to survive. Nowhere is this better seen than at
Tynemouth, where castle and priory are one. Defensive features
even extended to the churches: at Lindisfarne the C14 added a
chamber above the nave vault with cruciform crossbow loops in its
W wall; at Tynemouth and Brinkburn upper chambers were built
above the choir. The Lindisfarne cloister and outer court are more
like the inner and outer bailey of a castle, with a gatehouse between
them that has a distinctly military barbican. Hulne is girdled by
what is virtually a curtain wall, over which peers a tower-house of
1486 which, as at Blanchland, served as the prior's lodging (like the
towers at Carlisle and Lanercost in Cumbria). The Benedictine cells
of Coquet and Farne also have towers, as also the Augustinian
Bamburgh and Carham.

For reasons already spelled out, Northumberland is not a great
county for PARISH CHURCHES. There are barely fifty relatively
intact medieval buildings, and about another twenty which incorporate some pre-Reformation fabric. As a general rule they are
relatively small and show little architectural elaboration. Here and
there a church sheltering under the castle of some rich patron
14-16 (e.g. the Norman Norham and Warkworth, and the Perpendicular
45 Alnwick) shows an outburst of carved detail and ornament, contrasting strangely with the simple and almost vernacular features of
scattered hill-country churches like Alnham, Bellingham and
Elsdon. In the more remote W and N of the county, towers are rare;
there is a group of picturesque and irregular bellcotes (Bothal,

Felton, Ford, Holy Island), but these may all be post-medieval.
Turning to the architectural styles of the churches, the poverty of
the war-torn centuries after 1300 is stressed by the almost complete
absence of new Decorated and Perpendicular buildings. Many
churches show some Norman (or earlier) work; then we have the
beginnings of the flowering of the Gothic in thirty or so buildings
extended or remodelled in the Early English style – and the curtain
came down.

NORMAN WORK occurs on a variety of scales. The largest
churches are monastic; that at Lindisfarne (c. 1093–c. 1140) can 19
be considered a smaller-scale version of the contemporary mother
church at Durham. It had a tri-apsidal E end, twin western towers
and a central tower; the alternating patterns of the nave piers, and
the early rib vaults, all echo the greater church. The first Priory
Church at Tynemouth, of much the same period, had a more
complex aisled eastern arm terminating in three radiating apsidal
chapels. In both cases, the apses (except for those of the transepts
at Lindisfarne) were done away with in favour of square E ends, at
Lindisfarne as early as c. 1140, at Tynemouth at the end of the C 12.
Another link with Durham (and Lindisfarne) is seen in the rib vault
over the chancel at Warkworth; this seems to have been square-
ended from the first, and may be of c. 1130. Heddon too has a rib
vault over its mid-C 12 chancel extension. Another rib vault, quite
richly ornamented, occurs in the chapel in the keep at Newcastle.
There are plain barrel vaults over the chancels at Seaton Delaval 20
and Thockrington, churches which originally had a three-cell plan
and preserve both chancel and sanctuary arches. This plan form
occurs again at Old Bewick, where the apsidal sanctuary survives.
The responds of another sanctuary arch can be seen at Bolam. The
surviving fragment of the chapel in Mitford Castle shows that
the chancel (or sanctuary?) had thicker walls, presumably to receive
the thrust of a vault.

Much of the Norman work in the county is of a very simple
character; a number of churches (e.g. Birtley and Corsenside) retain
chancel arches so plain and simple that they have sometimes been
given an Anglo-Saxon date. At the other end of the Romanesque
spectrum, the sumptuous late Norman of Bishop Le Puiset's Gallery
in Durham Castle, with its emphasis on zigzag ornament, is seen in
another church with strong Durham connections, at Norham. Here 16
the S wall of the chancel is the showpiece; the S arcade, by contrast,
has deeply moulded arches with zigzag confined to a small frieze
above. Ancroft, although much smaller, shows some remains of
good Norman detail in its corbel table and (blocked) S door. The N
arcade of c. 1150 at Chollerton has monolithic circular piers that
may be reused Roman material; Bolam has a good chancel arch of
three orders with jamb shafts and scalloped capitals, and a slightly
later S arcade where the piers take on a quatrefoil section. In Newcastle, St Andrew has a lofty chancel arch with two orders of zigzag 17
and plainer nave arcades that may be of the same date; in addition
there are Norman fragments at St Nicholas's Cathedral, and old
illustrations show a Norman door at the old All Saints. The most
sumptuous piece of Norman architecture in the city, however, is the
chapel in the Castle keep.

Only a few Norman churches have contemporary towers (all at

13 the w end) – Edlingham, Embleton, Longhoughton, Ponteland –
and none but Newburn preserves a contemporary belfry. One explanation might be that the original belfries were timber and needed
replacement within a century or two. Another might be that the
prime function of the tower was as a refuge (calling to mind the
original Middle English form 'berfrey', a combination of words
meaning 'to protect' and 'peace'); this was certainly true in some
c 13 and c 14 examples with barrel-vaulted basements, such as Hartburn and Ancroft. A vault with transverse ribs was inserted into the
Norman tower at Embleton. The towers at Bywell St Peter and
Edlingham also look as if they were built with an eye to defence.

The first signs of the transition from Romanesque to GOTHIC are
changes in the treatment of ornamental details. Waterleaf capitals
appear at Norham church and in Newcastle Castle chapel. The s
arcade at Bolam, perhaps dating to the 1180s, still has plain stepped
round arches, but the piers are of a slightly keeled quatrefoil plan.
Perhaps a decade later comes Longframlington, where the arches
(chancel and s door) are still round, with plain square orders, but
they rest on shafts with waterleaf capitals. The inspiration for these
may have been the cloister arcades (now re-erected) at Newminster.
The transition – or, really, more of an admixture – between the old
and new styles is most strikingly seen at Brinkburn. Here the n door
is an exuberant late Norman piece, but the contemporary blind
arcade of trefoiled-pointed arches above is pure Early English; the
arcade piers are octagonal, with pointed double-chamfered arches,
and the e and w ends, along with the aisle, have lancets, but the
triforium openings and clerestory windows use the round arch.
Building began c. 1190 and admittedly might have extended over
three or four decades, but it is difficult to sort out a chronology of
construction based on style alone.

The other two great MONASTIC CHURCHES are grander in scale
and show a more fully developed Early English style, with fine sheer
wall-faces and arcades framing typical North-of-England lancets.
28 At Hexham, construction seems to have begun, from the e end,
c. 1180. The compound piers of the choir and transepts are basically
of quatrefoil form, with smaller shafts in the diagonals, major and
minor shafts all being keeled. Capitals and arches are all richly
moulded. The only round arches are in the triforium gallery, where
31 they enclosed pairs of pointed openings. At Tynemouth, the eastern
arm of the Norman church was rebuilt c. 1190 with an aisled five-
bay choir (with compound piers very like Hexham) and an aisleless
four-bay presbytery; this has blind arcading below the windows (like
the n transept at Hexham) and an e end with three tiers of windows,
three tall stepped lancets at the bottom, two shorter lancets flanking
a vesica, and finally, in the gable, a single taller lancet flanked by
blind arcading. Thirty years later the Tynemouth nave was extended
two bays westwards; the new w front has blind arcading and a
central portal with dogtooth ornament.

The c 13 is the great period of PARISH CHURCH REBUILDING
and remodelling in Northumberland. The trend for eastward extension, seen in the mid-c 12 substitution of the square e end for
the apse, continued with the proliferation of new chancels, always
aisleless and with their lengths two to three times their breadth. This
Early English remodelling is especially well seen in the Tyne Valley,

where Haltwhistle, Simonburn, Warden, Corbridge, Ovingham and the Bywells are all predominantly of the period. Further N, Bothal, Felton, Hartburn, Ponteland and Rothbury have typical chancels of the period; Bamburgh, doubtless through its connection with the Augustinian priory there, has an especially fine example, with a continuous wall-arcade internally. Transepts became common as well, even when naves remained aisleless (Bywell St Andrew, Warden); one group shows the rather unusual plan feature of a W aisle to the transept (Bellingham, Corbridge, Elsdon, Ovingham, Rothbury). There are W towers at Eglingham, Ingram, and on a larger scale at Warkworth, with bell openings that are simply paired lancets; more characteristic of the county are sturdy W bellcotes, at Bothal, Felton, Ford and Thockrington carried on one W buttress as broad as a chimneybreast, at St Mary on Holy Island on a pair of buttresses linked high up by an arch. It is difficult to say whether any of the bell turrets themselves are genuinely medieval in their present picturesque diversity of forms. External elevations remained relatively plain; ranges of well-spaced lancet windows (with some-times a 'low-side window', a feature which intrigued an earlier generation of antiquaries and has never been satisfactorily explained) lit chancel side walls, whilst the E end almost invariably had a stepped triplet. In details such as east-end fenestration, an evolutionary sequence can be traced from Norman origins (Haydon Old Church) through three separate lancets (most of the Tyne Valley examples) to three lancets under one arch internally (Bolam), one arch externally (Meldon, restored) and finally the simple bar tracery of *c.* 1300 at Newbiggin. The influence of the monasteries upon the parish churches is shown less in their plans and elevations – which reflect their differing functions – than in their ornament and minor detail. Thus the dogtooth which is a hallmark of Tynemouth and all but the earliest work at Hexham is seized upon and used rather heavy-handedly in the S door at Hartburn and most oddly, between the shafts of a compound pier, at Whalton. The thin buttresses at Brinkburn and Hexham which turn semi-octagonal in their upper stages appear again at Hartburn and Ovingham. 32

The beginnings of WINDOW TRACERY come in the mid-C 13. The Bamburgh chancel has its lancets arranged in pairs; at Heddon-on-the-Wall the spandrels of close-set lancet pairs have sinkings with worn carved heads (cf. Aydon Castle). The sinking becomes a vesica-shaped piercing at Simonburn, and plate tracery proper on the S side of the choir at Hulne Priory, where two unfoiled lights have a plain circle above. It is worth following tracery patterns on from here. From the simplest of plate tracery of *c.* 1250 at Hulne it seems a long step to the elaborate Geometrical patterns in the head of the five-light S aisle E window at Felton, with an eight-petalled flower at its apex; both window heads, however, are each cut from a single slab of sandstone, part of a tradition of monolithic window-head construction in the area which is seen in both ecclesiastical and secular buildings. This tradition is a long one, extending at least into the C 17 from origins before the Norman Conquest. G. W. D. Briggs has shown that over a third of the surviving medieval traceried window heads in the county are of this type. One building (if it can be called such) that demands a mention at this point is the Warkworth Hermitage, where the entire chapel and sacristy, groined 'vaulting' and a variety of features, including a four-light window with flowing tracery, were cut into the natural sandstone of a river-cliff overhanging the Coquet in *c.* 1330–40. As already explained, post-1300 work is relatively rare (and more or less confined to the 'safer' area s of Alnwick and within twenty miles of the coast). Intersected and bar tracery of *c.* 1300 is seen at Newbiggin, Newburn and Morpeth 37, 20 and reticulated forms at Kirkharle, Morpeth, Seaton Delaval, Widdrington and (rather surprisingly, considering its proximity to the Border) at Elsdon. In the hills there are one or two hard-to-date architectural curiosities that presumably relate to the troubled later 30 medieval centuries, none stranger than the low tunnel vaults of chancel and s transept at Kirknewton. The quadrant vaults over the aisles at Elsdon may, like the ribbed vaults at Bellingham, be postmedieval. As a rule, however, after the Black Death added to Northumberland's miseries in the mid-C 14 there was very little church building, except at a handful of sites.

Newcastle's walls sheltered it at least from the Scots; some of the better LATE MEDIEVAL WORK in the county is preserved within their circuit. Extensive building works were being carried out at 39 St Nicholas's Church in the mid-C 14, and the PERPENDICULAR STYLE makes its appearance in the (restored) chancel windows. The nave arcades have octagonal piers from which double-chamfered arches spring without the intervention of any capital, a form also seen at nearby St John, a few miles outside the city at Ponteland, and across the Tyne at Gateshead St Mary (County Durham). The 44 dominant feature of St Nicholas is, however, the western tower with its 'crown'; this is all late-C 15 work, pre-dating similar features at Edinburgh St Giles and King's College, Aberdeen. The peculiarity of transepts with western aisles, already noted in the context of C 13 buildings, appears again in the C 14 and C 15 at all three of Newcastle's medieval churches, St Nicholas, St Andrew and St John. The best Perpendicular church in the county is undoubtedly 45 Alnwick. In plan it is a fully aisled parallelogram (the only example in the county, except, it is claimed, the C 13 St Mary's Church at Hexham); there are a variety of tracery forms, and the chancel arcades have compound piers with major and minor shafts of filleted ogee section and richly carved capitals. The contemporary chancel roof survives, with the oddity of a strainer beam linking the trusses beneath the ridge-piece (as at nearby Lesbury, which also sheltered 31 under the Percy umbrella). At Tynemouth the tiny Percy Chantry tacked incongruously onto the base of the towering C 13 E end in the mid-C 15 is another important Perpendicular piece, notable for its carved roof bosses. At Hexham, Prior Leschman's chantry chapel of the last decade of the C 15 displays a riot of intriguing carvings in a style somewhere between the eclectic and the vernacular, hardly great art. And that, beyond a scatter of windows with simple panel tracery (e.g. the w window at Hartburn), is all.

In terms of most types of CHURCH MONUMENTS Northumberland is not especially rich. There are about two dozen monumental effigies; a C 13 priest at Stamfordham is one of the earliest, a knight of *c.* 1330 at Warkworth one of the best-preserved. 38, 48 There is another early C 14 knight at Seaton Delaval. Chillingham has the mid-C 15 alabaster effigies of Sir Ralph Grey and his wife on a carved tomb-chest; of lesser quality, and about seventy years later in date, is a monument of the same type to Ralph Ogle at Bothal. The dramatic effigy of Prior Leschman († 1491) at Hexham, his 49 cowl pulled over his eyes, also deserves a mention; and there is a fine sandstone effigy of a knight in armour, found at the Augustinian Friary, Newcastle, in the John George Joicey Museum. The only brass of any note is the spectacular monument of Roger Thornton † 1429 (formerly in All Saints' Church, Newcastle; now removed to St Nicholas's Cathedral). But if Northumberland is relatively poor in monuments of the ruling classes, it is rich in cross-slab grave covers, humbler memorials to those a little further down the social scale. Most of the 700 or so surviving slabs are of C 12 and C 13 date (they continue in use until the Reformation, and very occasionally beyond, but later medieval examples are less common), and, as is usual in the North of England, they often bear emblems denoting the trade or rank of the deceased. There are several major collections in Tynedale (Bywell, Corbridge, Hexham); the hand of the rustic or vernacular stone-carver, well seen in so many post-medieval churchyard monuments, is clear in a delightful series of medieval 29 slabs at Ryal.

When it comes to CHURCH FURNISHINGS, Hexham Priory alone 46 retains an interesting collection of medieval woodwork. This is of the C 15 or early C 16, and includes a rood screen, reredos and lectern, all with contemporary paintings, stalls, sedilia, and the Leschman and Ogle chantries. None are great art by national standards, but some pieces (notably the carving on the stone parts of the Leschman Chantry) show vigorous vernacular touches; in this part of the country the whole assemblage is a precious survival. Relatively few churches retain medieval FONTS; those at Chollerton and Haydon Bridge, near Hadrian's Wall, are fashioned from Roman altars. The C 15 font at St Nicholas's Cathedral, Newcastle, 50 has a spectacular cover of c. 1500, and there is a similar font cover nearby at St Andrew's Church. At St Nicholas there is also a brass eagle LECTERN which no doubt comes from a workshop responsible for many identical lecterns in England (e.g. Southwell, Coventry, Lowestoft). Little medieval STAINED GLASS survives: the C 14 Jesse window at Morpeth is the most important piece, and there are more fragmentary remains at Bothal and Ponteland. Morpeth also preserves several doors with C 14 IRONWORK and contemporary ROOFS to nave and aisles; other later medieval roofs, all relatively plain, survive at Alnwick, Bothal and Lesbury. Other than these, there is a scatter of pieces of SCULPTURE which do not fall into any of the categories already discussed. Kirknewton has a charming 18 Adoration of the Magi that might be C 12, Alnwick a pair of C 15 statues and Stamfordham a very decayed stone reredos of the C 14.

FORTIFIED BUILDINGS

BY PETER RYDER

England's border with Scotland was so turbulent throughout the later Middle Ages that, except within the walls of Newcastle, there is no surviving secular building in Northumberland of the period 1301–1550 in whose construction defence was not a prime consideration. Many fortified or defensible buildings do survive, at least

21, 23 in part; great fortresses like Alnwick, Bamburgh, Dunstanburgh
52 and Warkworth reinforce Northumberland's claim to be 'England's castle county *par excellence*'. Yet only a small proportion of its fortified buildings are genuine castles (i.e., with the usual appurtenances of gatehouse, curtain wall etc.); the great majority are 'towers', a loose and rather confusing classification covering a variety of building types. Most of these lesser fortified or defensible structures are best seen as the Borderland equivalent of the small manor house.

Economy of effort was an important consideration in the building of EARTHWORK AND TIMBER CASTLES in the generations after the Norman Conquest. Prehistoric defences were almost certainly revamped at Tynemouth, Dunstanburgh and Bamburgh, and possibly also at Warkworth. On a smaller scale, good use was made throughout the county of natural promontories; these were cut off by a single ditch and an internal bank at Dally, Lowick, Tarset, Cornhill and the massive Green Castle near Wooler. At Warden and Ha' Hill (Morpeth) the scarps of a hilltop were trimmed to a motte-like appearance, and the same was probably true of the first phase at Prudhoe. Most of the true mottes in the county were reused in later fortifications, but there are good survivors at Styford (*see* Bywell) and Gunnerton. The motte-and-bailey at Harbottle, where the later stone phases are now reduced to scattered fragments, remains a dramatic monument. In the second phase at Prudhoe a large ringwork was constructed, but by far the most impos-

24 ing remains are at Elsdon, where the ringwork has a bailey of complementary bulk. Though often ignored, the remains of the earthwork bank of the early bailey at Warkworth are also very substantial.

Not long after their arrival, the Norman lords were ringing their baileys with stone curtain walls. It is here that the earliest masonry survives, at the great strongholds of Alnwick and Warkworth; such remains are largely mute as to the overall form and features of the contemporary castle. No C 11 hall such as those at Richmond (North Yorkshire) and Chepstow (Gwent) survives in the county. Although the great Norman introduction, the KEEP, had been in vogue on the Continent for half a century before William the Conqueror's invasion, it does not seem to have appeared in Northumberland until the middle of the C 12. When Hugh de Puiset, Bishop of Durham, in about 1160 fashioned a formidable stone castle on the earthworks of Bishop Flambard's motte-and-bailey at Norham, he reared a hall keep of 25.6 by 18.3 metres (84 by 60 ft) in the inner ward. Access was by an external stone stair to a hall with a magnificent arched recess at the dais end (cf. St Mary's Guild, Lincoln).

Hall keeps such as Norham can be seen as the successors to earlier
Norman stone halls such as those at Chepstow, Richmond and
Castle Acre (Norfolk). The near-contemporary keep at Bamburgh,
21.1 by 18.9 metres (69 by 61½ ft), can also be classed a hall keep
although much squarer in plan; it is exceptional in that the formidable natural defences of the site allowed the building of a keep
with a ground-floor entrance. Two other keeps, Newcastle and
Prudhoe, are both of the more common tower-keep form, in which
the accommodation was forced into a more vertical arrangement,
with the entrance placed in a forebuilding. The former was built by 35
Henry II in 1168–78, and it is a late but sophisticated example of a
Norman keep with a rib-vaulted chapel in the base of the forebuilding; Prudhoe is probably of the same date, but is much smaller,
12.6 by 13.5 metres (41 by 44 ft), and more ruinous. At the same
time, shell keeps, circular, oval or polygonal, with a central open
courtyard were being built; they brought less weight to bear on
foundations dependent on the made-up ground of a motte, and had
no acute corners to render them vulnerable to mining. The Alnwick
keep of the first half of the C 12 was presumably of this type; Wark-
on-Tweed (1153–6) was an irregular octagon in plan. Two castles
that have not been adequately investigated had shell keeps: Harbottle had a polygonal shell, whilst Mitford seems to have had a
large oval shell wall, which may be early C 12, with a tower or
'blockhouse' inside, replaced early in the C 13 by a strange little
pentagonal keep.

NORMAN GATEHOUSES survive at Prudhoe and, in a more 22
ruinous state, at Norham. At Alnwick the only recognizable remnant
of the early keep is its gateway arch with chevron ornament. Such
gatehouses were, by later standards, relatively simple and unsophisticated. It was the C 13 and early C 14 that saw the development of
CURTAIN WALL DEFENCES, after the Crusaders had appreciated
the strength of walls studded with semicircular or semi-polygonal
towers in the Near East. The new gatehouse of c. 1200 at Warkworth
was flanked by semi-octagonal towers with spectacular arrow loops,
and the Carrickfergus Tower at the SW corner took the same form.
At Newcastle the Black Gate of 1247 was built, barbican-like, in 35
front of the older gatehouse; in form it can be described as a large
oval tower, or two D-shaped towers set back-to-back flanking the
gate passage. Berwick Castle may have been largely C 13, with many
round and half-round towers; it seems to have had a circular keep
(cf. Barnard Castle in Durham), but its remains fell victim to C 19
railway development. It was the beginning of the C 14 before the
Norman curtain of Alnwick received an impressive set of towers; its
shell keep was transformed into a cluster of seven semicircular
towers, a more sprawling version of the C 13 clustered donjons at
Pontefract and Sandal in Yorkshire.

The FOURTEENTH CENTURY was a century of almost permanent
warfare with the Scots, and one that spawned much castle-building,
in a variety of forms; a dominant theme was the strengthening of
the GATEHOUSE. Those of already existing fortresses were strengthened by the addition of barbicans, a forework or extension providing an extra gateway, and within it an enclave in which attackers
would come under hostile fire from above as they tackled the main
gate. Alnwick has a splendid barbican to its outer gatehouse, and 40

another to its keep; there are good barbicans at Prudhoe and Tynemouth as well.

One new idea in castle design can be traced to the great series of
Welsh castles built by Edward I. They have no keeps, but at several,
including Harlech and Beaumaris, the gatehouse functions as one.
This change has been ascribed to the waning confidence of the lord
in his own garrison, in that he now controlled the main access
to the castle himself. Dunstanburgh, begun in 1314, is the great
Northumbrian example, with its hall set above the gate passage and
fronted by a pair of lofty D-shaped towers. Although this arrangement had some obvious drawbacks (indeed at Dunstanburgh John
of Gaunt walled up the gateway in the later C 14 and made a new
one, with an elaborate barbican, in the curtain a little to the N), it
was one that kept reappearing in humbler castles for the next two
centuries. Bothal (licence to crenellate 1343) is a good example;
Bywell, around a hundred years later in date, is of precisely the same
type and, as at Hylton in County Durham (c. 1400), the gatehouse
seems to have been the most substantial part of its castle. Other mid-
to late-C 14 gatehouses are at Morpeth Castle and the Archbishop of
53 York's Moot Hall at Hexham; the latter, however it related to other
buildings on the site, is very much a gatehouse with quite prestigious
apartments on the upper floors. The earlier hall house at Willimoteswick had by the late C 15 or early C 16 become part of a larger
castle or fortified manor house with a big rectangular gatehouse
tower in the same tradition.

Another distinctive castle type to appear in the C 14 is the QUAD-
RANGULAR CASTLE, a square or rectangular enclosure with a tower
at each corner. This is another type with its origins on the Continent;
it has been suggested that it began in castles created by the Emperor
Frederick II in the S of Italy and Sicily c. 1230 (Augusta, Syracuse,
Catania), was taken over by the Prussian knights in the mid-C 13
and later was widely accepted in Italy and France. In the North of
England two variants are visible; the earlier seems to be the castle
where the corner towers contain the principal accommodation, with
only subsidiary buildings, perhaps of timber, backing onto the cur-
67 tains between them. Chillingham (licence to crenellate 1344) is a
good example of this, and Ford (licence to crenellate 1338) was
originally of the same type. Etal (licensed 1341) is superficially
similar, although here the SE tower is in fact quite a sophisticated
gatehouse, whilst the large rectangular NW tower seems to have
originated as a C 13 or early C 14 upper-floor hall house (old drawings
show the destroyed NE tower at Ford to have been of similar elongate
plan, and it too may have been an earlier building incorporated in
the C 14 castle). Castles where the main apartments are housed in
substantial stone ranges linking the corner towers are a slightly later
type, such as Bolton in North Yorkshire (1379) and Lumley in
County Durham (1392); the smaller Cartington in Northumberland
seems to be derived from this form. Old accounts suggest that Ogle
was a strongly moated quadrangular castle of the type with circular
angle towers (cf. Bodiam in Sussex), but today only late medieval
internal domestic buildings, and part of the moat, survive.

The FIFTEENTH CENTURY in Northumberland was marked by
the provision of improved accommodation within castles rather than
by an increase in their military strength. Nowhere is this better seen

than in the construction of the Warkworth keep. This was not so 52
much a defensive last resort, as Norman keeps had been, but a
dramatic tower-house – or more a tower-palace. A successful
attempt at combining the needs of defence with the comforts of a
manor house, it also provided a splendid symbol of the might of the
Percys. The extraordinary shape of the keep – a square with a
projecting block near the centre of each side – may have been
conditioned by its being fashioned from the remains of its predecessor. Within this the unknown C 15 architect produced a central
light well and beside it a tall and slender turret. There was enough
space for plenty of sizeable rooms, and hall, kitchen, buttery, pantry,
solar, chapel were all placed, thanks to an ingenious layout, on the
same floor. The hall is 12.2 by 7.6 metres (40 by 25 ft) and reaches
through two storeys, with a minstrels' gallery. Alnwick and Bamburgh Castles also received late medieval suites of state rooms – of
which little has survived – but without such radical innovations as
at Warkworth.

The blanket term 'TOWERS' is generally applied to the largest
group of fortified medieval buildings in the county, structures generally consisting of a single defensible block of building without any
curtain wall. Often rather unhappily referred to as 'pele' or 'peel'
towers (a term derived from the same root as the modern word
'palisade', and correctly referring to a timber fortification), their size
and character distinguish them from the larger fortresses, although
many (e.g. Haughton and Langley) are generally referred to as
'castles'. Overall, towers form a group that is sufficiently coherent
to be treated separately from castles proper, although anything more
than the most cursory survey reveals that they include a variety of
quite different building types, spanning three centuries. Three basic
medieval types can be distinguished: the hall tower; the solar tower;
and the later medieval solitary tower or tower-house. Two further
variants, the stronghouse and the bastle house, are technically post-
medieval buildings, but are included here because they are so
strongly linked in function with what went before. No system of
nomenclature for these building types has been established; the
names used here, qualified by their accompanying descriptions,
should be regarded as terms of convenience.

Before looking at towers themselves, it is worth considering a
handful of HALL HOUSES in the S of the county which date from
before the onset of what H. L. Honeyman used to call 'The Three
Hundred Years' War'. Aydon, the best-known example, was orig- 33
inally a manor house, only lightly fortified, of the late C 13, quite
akin to Markenfield (North Yorkshire). The first-floor hall was
reached by an external stone stair, and has a solar with a good
fireplace on the first floor of the cross wing. Unusually for Northumberland there is some architectural elaboration in several two-
light windows and a pretty little chimneystack with lancet-shaped
vents for the smoke to escape. With the outbreak of hostilities with
the Scots, Aydon's owner received a licence to crenellate in 1305.
He added an embattled courtyard wall, and a little later an outer
curtain with two rather weak towers. It may have been the very
inadequacy of these defences – the house changed hands several
times without any serious siege – that ensured the survival of virtually
the whole 'castle' in a relatively unaltered state. Even less defensible,

and thus more heavily altered as the need for fortifications increased,
68 were ground-floor halls such as Featherstone, Halton and Low Hall
in Corbridge; in each case the C 14 or C 15 saw a tower solar built
at the high end of the hall. The so-called towers at the Blackbird
Inn (Ponteland) and Shield Hall may be the solar wings of similar
houses, built over barrel-vaulted basements.

Whilst no major new castle in the county was founded in the C 13,
it did see the emergence of a whole new group of fortified buildings,
the upper-floor hall houses or HALL TOWERS. These seem to have
had a dual ancestry; one parent may have been the first-floor hall
house of the Aydon type, the other, more elevated socially, the hall
keep of the castles of the previous century. Unlike the castle keeps,
hall towers often stood more or less alone, without a curtain wall or
stone outer defences; they may have had stockades and ditches, but
evidence of such enclosures rarely survives. Such structures are the
Northumberland equivalent of manor houses of the type represented
in less troubled areas by hall-and-cross-wing houses with their
accommodation at ground level. The hall towers have their halls set
on the first or even the second floor of a rectangular block that
typically had projecting square turrets at some or all of the angles,
a characteristic Northumberland form of the later C 13 and early
C 14. They range in sophistication from Sir William Felton's lordly
first-floor hall of c. 1300 at Edlingham, with its octagonal corner
turrets, to the bleak and virtually windowless Thirlwall, probably a
little later in date but notably devoid of architectural features or any
34 evidence of refinement. Haughton is another good example, and
42 Langley may also have been of the same form; both were remodelled
and heightened in the mid-C 14. Tarset, Dally (near Greystead) and
Bellister, more ruinous, all seem to have been hall towers with typical
corner turrets. At Willimoteswick, only one end of the hall, with a
pair of strangely slender turrets, survives. Blenkinsopp seems to have
lacked turrets, but instead was additionally strengthened by being
closely girdled by a concentric curtain wall. Further N, Preston
Tower seems to be one end of a hall tower very like Langley.

A large group, appearing from the mid-C 14 onwards, consists of
the SOLAR TOWERS. Unlike the hall towers they did not stand
alone, but only formed part of a larger establishment, usually being
sited at one end of a hall block, where they provided the owner's
private apartments with both prestige and additional security. It
has been suggested that some might also have provided in-house
lodgings for the autonomous household of an owner's parent or
sibling. Such towers often seem to have been added to pre-existing
hall blocks, as in the case of the early Tynedale halls already mentioned. Close examination of towers often quoted as having been
self-contained 'tower-houses' frequently shows evidence of a vanished hall, either demolished to make the building more readily
defensible or simply thought old-fashioned and replaced by a more
41, 65 gracious house in the late C 16 or C 17 (e.g. Belsay, Chipchase, West
Bitchfield). A typical solar tower had a vaulted basement beneath
principal domestic accommodation on the first and second floors.
Entry was either by a mural stair from a ground-floor lobby, or
occasionally (as at Cocklaw) through a first-floor door reached by
an external stair or a bridge from some other structure. Garderobes
or small chambers might be set in the thickness of the walls, as in a

Norman keep. At wall-top level the embattled parapet might be set forward on corbels, and there were often bartizans – corbelled-out turrets – at the corners, as at Belsay and Chipchase. These features 41, 43 are of course shared with other contemporary buildings, such as the Moot Hall and Prison at Hexham and the towers and gatehouses of many castles. The seminal site for our understanding of solar towers has been Edlingham Castle, where recent excavations have shown that the earlier hall tower received a curtain wall and gatehouse in the mid-C 14 and then, c. 1400, a swagger new solar tower. The position of this tower on the external periphery of the castle, and its large windows, suggest that prestige was more important than defensibility.

Whilst the majority of Northumberland's C 14 and early C 15 towers (and especially those in the S of the county) can now be shown to have been parts of larger houses, there is one group that does appear to have stood alone, the 'VICAR'S PELES'; the parish priest was often a man of some substance and needed the protection of a tower as much as did the lord of the manor. Here there can be no quarrel with the name 'tower-house'. Corbridge is by far the best example, retaining features such as a stone reading desk built into the wall beside one window; others survive, in whole or in part, at Alnham, Embleton, Ford, Ponteland, and Whitton. Tower building continued through the C 15 and C 16, and solitary towers or TOWER-HOUSES became commoner, especially towards the Border. These reflect some contemporary Scottish trends; the early C 16 Cockle Park has a projecting wing or 'jamb' containing the stair turret but also reflecting its internal first-floor division into hall and solar; the corbelled-out bartizans are still very much like those of the towers of a hundred years before. In the N of the county the towers at Coupland Castle, Duddo (now fallen) and Hetton Hall, and in the S that at Dilston, show another 'Scottish' feature in having a broad newel stair giving access to the first floor, above which a narrower stair rose in a corbelled-out 'pepperpot' turret. The provision of a corbelled-out machicolation covering a ground-level entrance is good evidence for a tower having stood alone; this is well seen at the tiny Burradon, which measures little over 7.7 by 6.8 metres (25 by 22 ft) externally and had only a single room on each of its three floors; it is thought to have been built c. 1550. The larger Elsdon, in the notorious wilds of Redesdale, is another late example.

By the LATE SIXTEENTH CENTURY, towers were at last becoming old-fashioned, although the prudent landowner was still concerned for his security. DEFENSIBLE HOUSES became the norm; several strands can be recognized in their development, although the evidence is sometimes harder to distinguish than in the case of medieval buildings proper; a C 16 house remodelled in the C 17 is less easy to recognize than a tower conversion. For the upper classes, at least two distinctive house types are clear. One is the conversion of a medieval tower into one wing of a larger house; often this involved the rebuilding of an older hall block rather than the addition of a new building. The result might be a tall H-plan structure with a service wing balancing the old tower; old prints show Belsay and Widdrington in this form, which survives in a humbler (and more altered) guise at East Shaftoe Hall (near Capheaton) and Whalton

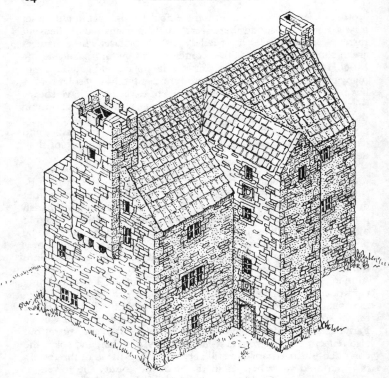

Stronghouse. Reconstruction loosely based on Witton Shields Tower

Rectory. Where a new house was built from scratch, a type of
building here termed a 'STRONGHOUSE' often resulted, in plan a
more elongate rectangle than most towers, three storeys high and
often with a small gabled stair wing either housing or flanking the
entrance door. A group of houses in the N of the county, including
Akeld and Pressen (near Carham), have vaulted basements in the
usual tower-house manner, but others such as Doddington
(formerly with a 1584 datestone) and Witton Shields (dated 1608)
seem to have had living accommodation on all floors. Doddington
had a parapet walk; in other cases, small turrets or roof-level lookouts, as at Harnham and formerly at Healey Hall and the demolished
Low Hirst 'Tower', remained a wise provision.

All the buildings so far described have been the homes of landowners, and of the ruling classes. However, they were not the only
people whose security was under threat. The persistence of local
unrest and cattle thieving forced the smaller farmers to build their
own defensible houses in the C16, and so Northumberland's
BASTLE HOUSES, straddling the divide between military and vernacular architecture, appear on the scene. As a class they appear to
have superseded earlier structures of a type exemplified by the 'peles

of Tynedale', mentioned in the 1541 survey as consisting 'of walls and roofs of squared oak trees bound together and morticed. The whole is covered with earth and turves so that they may not be set on fire and they are so strong that only with great force and numbers could they be cast down.' Sadly none of these peles – here there can be no argument with the term – survives today, nor have any been recognized in archaeological excavations. Bastle houses (illustrated on p. 66) are not unique to Northumberland – there is a scatter of them across the Border to the N, and in County Durham's Weardale to the S, and rather more in Cumberland to the W – but the great majority of the recorded examples lies within its boundaries. The Royal Commission on Historical Monuments' use of the term is followed here; 'bastles', 'bastle houses', 'stronghouses', 'stone houses', 'peels' and 'peel houses' are all used in contemporary documents without regard for specific building types.

Around 200 bastle houses survive today, whole or in part. They are concentrated in the upland W, and especially SW, of the county. The vast majority are rectangular buildings of about 10 by 5.5 metres (33 by 18 ft) externally,* with a ground-floor byre below first-floor living accommodation. Their walls are around one metre (3–4 ft) thick and their doorways have massive block surrounds, sometimes with arched or gabled monolithic heads that would not look out of place in pre-Conquest churches. The byre door is generally set centrally in one gable end, and in some cases (e.g. Bog Head, near Gatehouse) has had a chute or 'quenching hole' in the wall above, so that water could be poured down on a fire set against the door. The upper door is usually in the side wall, and was originally gained by a removable ladder, often replaced by a stone external stair. Windows were small and heavily barred; Black Cleugh (Unthank) and High Shaw (Redesdale: see Hepple) have basement gunloops. Although as a class bastle houses are remarkably uniform in size and plan, there are a few interesting variants. In North Tynedale and Redesdale the byre is sometimes barrel-vaulted; elsewhere, and notably S of the Tyne, heavy and close-set transverse beams carry the flagstones of the upper floor. A scatter of examples in the S of the county differ from the majority in that they are squarer in plan, and some (e.g. Sinderhope Shield in Allendale) seem to have had three floors; a poor man's tower? The square buildings seem to be a relatively early type, although dating evidence is hard to come by; where they are attached to other 'bastle-period' buildings they generally seem to be the earliest member of the group. There are also a number of rather superior bastle houses, distinguished either by their size or by architectural elaboration (a relative term!), which might go as far as moulded door surrounds and stone-mullioned windows. Brinkheugh (see Brinkburn Priory) and Thropton Peel in Coquetdale and Eltringham in Tynedale have both doorways set in one gable-end, whereas Westside near Whitfield in Allendale and Low Cleughs near Woodburn in Redesdale have both upper and 89 lower doorways in the long side wall. The extraordinary Snabdaugh (see Greystead) appears to be a bastle house with an attic-level vault. A few cases (e.g. Woodhouses at Holystone and Tower House at

* Bastles in the S of the county tend to be a little smaller, on average 9 metres (30 ft) long.

Bastle house. Reconstruction based on Nine Dargue, Allendale

Tow House, near Henshaw) have an internal stair and thus dispense
with the upper doorway. Further variations arise in the relationship
between bastles. Quite often one bastle is built onto the end of an
earlier one, the two thus sharing a single byre door; more rarely,
'terraced' examples (with their byre doors in the side walls) enclose
a yard or green, as at Chesterwood and on a larger scale at Wall, N
of Hexham. Haltwhistle in the wild W of Tynedale at one time
seems to have been largely composed of bastles.

The dating of bastles is still problematical; the Royal Commission
on Historical Monuments ascribes them to the later C 16 and early
C 17, with the few dated examples belonging to the latter period. It
was the middle of the C 17 before the Northumberland hill farmer
could rebuild his house on more conventional lines and come downstairs to live in relative peace.

It was of course not only individual households that required
security; Border towns required their own TOWN DEFENCES. The
54 town walls of Newcastle were built in the late C 13 and C 14, with
six gates and seventeen towers, mostly D-shaped. They were re-

paired and garrisoned as late as the Napoleonic Wars, but today only about a sixth of the circuit survives, with six towers but no gates. Alnwick had C 14 walls, of which only one gatehouse survives, and Corbridge had an enclosing ditch. Berwick had two-and-a-half miles of walls in the late C 13, but their remains are fragmentary and partly concealed by the C 16 defences which succeeded them. Enclosing 56 only about two-thirds of the medieval area, these are without parallel in the country as a complete set of walls and bastions, with associated earthworks. Constructed on Italian lines, they are very much a state-of-the-art expression of contemporary fortification; construction began in 1558, and two Italian engineers, *Portinari* and *Jacopo a Contio*, were later consulted. The cannon was all-important, firing from triangular bastions set forward from the line of the main rampart (these were filled with earth soon after their construction to provide raised platforms or 'cavaliers'), and from flankers, emplacements set on either side of the narrow neck or collar of the bastion's platform, to cover the wall-face on either side. Berwick's walls, although maintained and periodically 'improved' for almost three centuries, were never put to the test; it is arguable how effective a defence they might have provided.

The medieval curtain walls of Tynemouth Castle, the strategic guardian of the mouth of Northumberland's greatest river, were also partly rebuilt after the dissolution of the Priory provided a convenient supply of dressed stone. Similar sources of building material were utilized on Lindisfarne, where an artillery fort was built across the bay to the E of the Priory, and at Harbottle, where, after the castle had passed into Royal hands in 1545, the keep was largely rebuilt, using stone from the monasteries of Holystone and Brinkburn; evocative fragments survive, complete with oval cannon-loops. But it was the end of the age of the castle; Harbottle was soon in ruins again, and by 1588 the thieves of Teviotdale had broken in and 'carried awaie much goods without either showt or crie'.

ARCHITECTURE FROM 1550 TO 1800

BY JOHN GRUNDY AND GRACE MCCOMBIE

Of C 16 SECULAR BUILDINGS there is absurdly little to talk about which has not already been covered in the discussion of defensible buildings. The reasons are only too obvious. The nobility of Northumberland at the time of the Pilgrimage of Grace and after were not in a position to build fine mansions, and warfare was still endemic throughout the century. No big new houses were built, and only at Ford among the major buildings was any domestic improvement introduced. Here, before 1589, still within the protection of the curtain walls, a new S front was put onto the N range on the common Elizabethan E-plan with big regular mullioned-and-transomed windows. At Chillingham in the early C 17 changes took 67 place within the castle courtyard, and in addition the entrance to the castle from the outside world was given one of those fashionable three-storey frontispieces with columns which are so familiar at Oxford and had been introduced from France some seventy years earlier.

But that was after the Union and before the Civil War, and in those years of the FIRST HALF OF THE C 17 a little more was undertaken. Indeed, as the threat of warfare receded, owners of castles and towers were quick to take the opportunity to make improvements. Most of these were additions or alterations to existing buildings. The only independent new Jacobean mansions are Denton Hall of 1622, close to Newcastle, and Mitford, where a house in the Jacobean style, dated 1637, was erected quite away from the medieval castle.

Elsewhere the process of change is more problematical. As has already been stated, the old notion of a solitary tower gradually being added to as times improved has been superseded by the recognition that most, if not all, of the towers had other buildings around from the start; thus the new wings which began to appear in the C 17 were either replacements or modifications of existing
41 wings or additions to existing complexes. One example is Belsay Castle, where a new two-storey wing was added in 1614, the earliest of the C 17 wings; but here detailed evidence from the tower itself reveals that there must have been an accompanying building from the start, probably a hall block, so that the building of 1614 was a replacement of an earlier structure, not a new departure. Another example is Welton Hall (near Horsley-on-the-Hill), where the Jacobean work is also dated 1614 but where again a closer look shows that the Jacobean detail is no more than an alteration of a medieval fabric which actually pre-dates the tower beside it. The significance of the new wings that began to appear all over the county in the early C 17 is not so much that there was a dramatic increase in the size of houses as that Northumberland was at last finding the freedom to catch up with the taste of the rest of the country.
65   The best of the new wings is at Chipchase, where the work is dated 1621. It is an E-plan range with a three-storey porch-tower, quite richly decorated, with plenty of strapwork, elaborate openwork parapet and, flanking the doorway, small inaccurate Ionic columns bearing statues. The alterations at Chillingham are of much the same date as Chipchase, and here, as well as the three-stage frontispiece with columns, there is an arrangement in the courtyard which also relies on small Ionic columns bearing statues. Nothing else of this period in the county has the same degree of elaboration, though there are smaller examples of almost equal sophistication. At Belsay the doorway is flanked by paired Tuscan columns, and at Mitford the surviving porch-tower of the ruined manor house shows plenty of strapwork and other ornament; but elsewhere plainness is the order of the day. Simple mullioned windows, occasional mullioned-and-transomed windows, doorways with four-centred-arched lintels, doorways with roll-moulded surrounds, scattered fenestration with or without hoodmoulds (as at Horsley Tower in Longhorsley); these are the features that one looks for, and the only real sense of progression one finds is a gradual ordering of the façade. In the earliest or simplest examples this is done with no more than hoodmoulds and windows placed reasonably in relation with each other, as at Dilston Castle or the Blackbird Inn, Ponteland. At Shortflatt Tower and Denton Hall the hoodmoulds are joined

together by a stringcourse which rises above the windows. Other houses have stringcourses which are straight and properly moulded. East Shaftoe Hall (near Capheaton) is an example of this, as is Ovingham Vicarage; but here, while the façade is properly ordered, the doorway (round-headed with a pendant keystone – also characteristic features of the period) is off-centre, still in the medieval position. The same reluctance to arrive at new forms can be found throughout the county. Even Denton Hall, the largest of the new buildings, has its doorway off-centre.

The surviving FURNISHINGS of the early C17 are few. Most are rough and rustic. Fireplaces with four-centred arched lintels abound; a few are decorated with dates and initials (Coupland Castle, 1619), a few have simple geometric patterns (the Blackbird Inn, Ponteland), but furnishings of any pretension are rare indeed. Nos. 28–30 the Close, Newcastle upon Tyne, has remarkable plasterwork applied to heavy ceiling beams after the manner of the painted ceilings in Scotland. The style of all this is still essentially Jacobean or even Tudor. In the rural area, Chillingham has the only surviving plaster ceiling earlier than the mid-C17 outside Newcastle; it also has two big and ambitious stone fireplaces. There is a more interesting group of fanciful overmantels of c. 1630. One is at Chipchase. The second is now at Haughton Castle (where there is also an Elizabethan fireplace), but it came from a house in Sandhill in Newcastle. The third, dated 1636, is in the Merchant Venturers' 59 Hall at Newcastle's Guildhall. The fourth has now gone to Beamish Museum, but, like the Haughton Castle example, it came from elsewhere in Newcastle. This tight group, with its exuberant carving and lively figure reliefs, is probably the work of local carvers, a reminder that Newcastle at that time was a very different place from the rest of the county – a rich and major city.

At the Newcastle Guildhall (1655–8) we meet for the first time a Northumbrian architect whose name we know and whose style comes alive to us. ROBERT TROLLOPE († 1686) was born in York. Not a great deal is known about him, but one thing is certain: he did not hanker after the serene classicism of Palladio and Inigo Jones. The Guildhall exterior is not preserved, but we know it from engravings. It was in a bastard style, with round arches and pointed arches, rustication and crazy gothicizing tracery, very much the sort of mixture that can be seen at the almost contemporary Holy Trinity, Berwick. The interior, with its thin double-hammerbeam roof and 60 its rusticated round arches, confirms our impression of the exterior.

It might be argued that the Guildhall was a special job, so it is lucky that we know Trollope also as a house designer. Capheaton 66 dates from 1668, and in these ten years (which saw the beginnings of Wren's activity as an architect) Trollope had acquainted himself with such things as giant pilasters and pediments and garlands. But his pilasters are banded or rock-faced, his pediments broken, open and curly, and his garlands far too heavy to frame a door or window. For one doorway he uses columns with vines twining round them. Moreover he goes on using mullioned windows. In short, Mannerist trappings are to him no more than welcome additions to his repertoire of flourishes. The case is not unusual in England, which did not at once take to the discipline of Italy and France. Oxford and Cambridge in 1660 were perhaps grander, but not purer; other examples are Bolsover and Nottingham Castle. Trollope was inexhaustible in his oddities. The sundial at Capheaton has a frame of dogtooth, and other houses in Northumberland which can be attributed to him have frames of Norman zigzag and all sorts of other surprising ornamental gambols. The group includes Bockenfield, where the doorway has spiral-fluted columns, and the windows are mullioned and transomed and framed with a cable moulding. At Callaly Castle in 1676 the mixture is if anything even odder. The façade, with its bolection mouldings, pediments with pulvinated oak-leaf friezes, and, especially, the sash windows replacing the original cross ones, may at first glance look rather more purely classical than the others. It has, however, an almost absurd Baroque compression, the three centre bays absolutely crushed together; and the details further reveal the man: there are trophies in the pediments, strapwork above the door, and the mouldings around door and windows are all very much in c 16 or early c 17 style. The doorway even has a four-centred head with a pendant keystone. Eshott Hall of *c*. 1660 and Netherwitton Hall of *c*. 1685 are less certainly attributed to Trollope, but Netherwitton especially, with its complex pattern of pediments and zigzag ornament, is in his style.

There are no other houses which can be attributed to Trollope, but right up to 1700 and beyond (i.e. well after his death), motifs recur which are characteristic of him and might suggest the power of his influence. Woolsington Hall has thick bead-moulded surrounds to the windows and primitive depressed shells instead of pediments over the windows. The curly open pediment, a favourite motif, is found, for example, at Hexham Grammar School in 1684, at Bywell Vicarage and at Errington. One group of houses uses the curly open pediment but as part of façades which are beginning to be calmer, to open the way to the classicism of the early c 18. At Halton Tower a wing with an excellent façade, built onto the medieval tower in 1696, has lightly moulded window surrounds under plain cornices. West Bitchfield has architrave surrounds to the windows and proper cornices too.

TIMBER FRAMING in Northumberland is entirely restricted to Newcastle, and even there it is now, sadly, visible only in a small group of buildings in the Close and at Sandhill, though it was formerly much more widespread. Most of the timber-framed buildings, including those early examples already mentioned, are solid and functional rather than displaying any special sophistication in their use of timber; but the best-surviving example in Newcastle,
63 the mid-c 17 Bessie Surtees' House, is more elaborate, with four tiers of widely spaced vertical studs, decorated with reeded pilasters; the rest of the façade is filled with glass with a freedom rarely seen before the c 20. The WINDOW GLASS is itself important, for it was easier to achieve such glazing in Newcastle than in any other provincial town in the c 17. Newcastle had become a leading producer of window glass with the setting up of coal-fired glass furnaces at the mouth of the Ouse Burn. In the INTERIORS of the houses too a new richness is discernible, or at least the richness has survived. The Sandhill timber-framed houses are full of plasterwork, panelling
64 and carved fireplaces, though some of it is pastiche and some is *ex situ*.

Towards the end of the century, a group of houses appeared

which were classical in a much more metropolitan sense. They were mainly in Newcastle. The Mansion House of 1691 and the two wings which Sir William Blackett added at about the same time to his vast Newcastle mansion, Anderson Place, have not survived and we know them only from illustrations, but they were of brick, with sash windows. BRICK indeed was the new popular material in Newcastle, though it shows little sign of having spread outside the town at this early date. Higham Dykes is the only brick country house of C 17 date, and Morpeth, by the end of the century, the only other town to be building extensively in brick. But in Newcastle, where there was plenty of clay and ample coal, brick became common. The Holy Jesus Hospital of 1681 is of brick with an arcade 62 of thirty moulded-brick arches; and brick façades were added to some older buildings in the C 18.

Intermittent raiding and fighting in the Border counties had continued into the C 16 and early C 17, so it is not surprising that little energy seems to have gone into building or improving PARISH CHURCHES. The threat of attack from marauders affected the remodelling of churches as well as that of houses, and any work done to country churches tended to be to increase the protection they could offer their congregations. A stone vaulted roof might be constructed, as at Bellingham, where the nave and transepts were given ribbed barrel vaults c. 1609, or Elsdon, where quadrant vaults were built. The only new C 17 church was Holy Trinity, Berwick, 57 particularly unusual because it was built during the Commonwealth, in 1650–2. Its original design, with a mixture of classical and Gothic, resembled, before C 19 alterations, that of St Katherine Cree, London (1628–31); the Northumbrian building which most closely parallels its mixture of styles is *Trollope*'s Newcastle Guildhall of 1655–8. Inside, the woodwork shows an equally surprising jux- 60 taposition of Jacobean strapwork and intersecting arches like Norman arcading.

In the churches a minimum of FURNISHING was done, except that a number of FONTS were replaced or provided in the 1660s. The new fonts, like those provided throughout England, are very plain, either still Perp in character (Chillingham, Alnham) or decorated with the most elementary geometrical patterns (Eglingham, Ingram, Kirknewton, Rothbury). Few C 16 and C 17 furnishings equal the luxurious standard of the domestic overmantels of that period, and there is little to match the beautiful C 17 WOODWORK found in County Durham. Northumberland was part of the diocese of Durham until 1882, and there are some pieces of woodwork in Bishop Cosin's most sumptuous Baroque-Gothic style, which Archdeacon Charles Thorp, that great furniture remover and architectural salvage specialist, removed from Durham to the Farne Islands and to Norham in the C 19. Much more remarkable, because complete and unchanged, are the furnishings of Trinity House 58 Chapel, Newcastle, installed in the 1630s; the screens, pews, pulpit and lecterns, with finials, buttons and cherubs' heads, the latter carved by *Richard Newlove*. Notable late C 17 woodwork can be seen in St Nicholas's Cathedral and St John, Newcastle; in the former there is an organ case built for a *Renatus Harris* organ in 1676, and the latter has a font cover of Gothic inspiration and a pulpit which

combines classical acanthus and Corinthian columns with Jacobean faceted lozenges. As for MONUMENTS, two wall monuments of the
51 1630s have survived in St Nicholas, to the Hall and Maddison families, both with rows of children kneeling below their parents in prayer, and all in their best clothes. There is a rather rustic monument to Bertram Reveley († 1622) at Mitford, a vigorous if unsophisticated memorial, with much scrollwork, to John Swinburn († 1623) at Stamfordham, and part of one at Simonburn (1637). The Hopper Mausoleum in the graveyard of St Andrew, Greymare Hill, is unique in the county, but can be compared with a smaller, more mutilated mausoleum at St Mary, Gateshead (County Durham), which is said to be *Trollope*'s own.

Although much energy went into house building in the later C17, none went into churches; but the increasing peace and prosperity during the next century made church building possible. The C18 CHURCHES were built to replace ruinous structures or to meet new needs. They were usually little more than preaching boxes, with arched or 'churchwarden' windows, which were made definitely Gothic in the C19, for example Carham of 1790, Kyloe of 1792 and Lowick of 1794. The exceptions are significant and reflect the secular fashions of the period. At Chipchase Castle a chapel was built *c.* 1735 by the owner, John Reed, which, with its heavily moulded round-arched windows and bellcote, is reminiscent of Vanbrugh. It has a complete scheme of furnishings, with pulpit, choir stalls and reading desk, all enriched with Corinthian pilasters. A new church was built at Beadnell *c.* 1740, but on Tyneside rather more happened.

In Newcastle the only significant ecclesiastical work of the first half of the century was the S porch added to St Andrew. Then, in 1764–8, the medieval chapel of St Anne was rebuilt to serve the rapidly increasing populace of the Sandgate suburbs by the river. It is a preaching box but a fine one, designed by the Newcastle architect *William Newton* (*see* also p. 75) in his usual conventional but elegant classical style. It has no separate sanctuary or aisles, but it does have the distinction of a pedimented Tuscan portico below a pedimented W gable carrying a tower with urns and a steeple. A few years after St Anne was completed, All Saints, the mother church of St Anne, began to collapse, and it was eventually entirely rebuilt in 1786–96 after a competition won by *David Stephenson* (*see* also p. 77), the first Newcastle man to study architecture in London. This is an
69–70 extraordinarily satisfying building, sophisticated in its oval plan and classical elevations, and with a superb tower and spire, which were, surprisingly, an afterthought. The design was probably inspired by James Gibbs's proposal for a centrally planned St Martin-in-the-Fields, as Andrew Greg has pointed out. There is less ambitious classical work by *John Dodds*, who rebuilt the parish church of Tynemouth at North Shields and the chapel of St Nicholas at Gosforth. In Longbenton, one of the old villages close to Newcastle, the church was repaired and the tower rebuilt in 1790 by *William Newton*, who gave it windows in late GOTHIC STYLE, a style he had used only twice before and then for country houses. Also Gothic are the sadly decayed but charming chancel arch at Longhorsley of 1783, its imitator of 1811 at Thropton, and the 'churchwarden' windows of Kyloe, 1792. The earliest NON-

CONFORMIST buildings, very simply classical, belong to the Presbyterian Church. Morpeth, of 1722, is the oldest, then comes Great Bavington, 1725 (but much altered), and then Branton, 1781. In addition to these there is the Friends' Meeting House at East Coanwood, 1760, in its lovely rural setting.

Very few C18 FURNISHINGS are to be seen in parish churches in the rural areas of the county. There is a wrought-iron communion rail at Warkworth, altar rails at Branxton with heavy turned balusters, and a neat Georgian organ at Norham. In Newcastle much of the magnificent interior of All Saints survives, with pews in elegant mahogany and Corinthian columns supporting the gallery. At Christ Church, North Shields, there is a Georgian font. Newcastle churches have many of the best C18 MONUMENTS. St Nicholas had many memorials which were set up after the alterations of 1784 and were swept away a century later, but the most sophisticated monument in the cathedral, by *John Bacon* to Matthew Ridley, 1787, is still there. There are rewarding C18 headstones at Falstone and Hartburn. 72, 73

Now for C18 SECULAR BUILDINGS. In Newcastle, brick was still the building material but used in remarkably varied styles. Alderman Fenwick's House from the very end of the C17 and the new Trinity House Banqueting Hall of 1721 are entirely up to date, with sash windows (at least from 1723 at Alderman Fenwick's House), quoins, moulded stringcourses and cornices; but the Keelmen's Hospital of 1701 seems quite archaic with its two-light mullioned windows, oddly inaccurate brick pediments and shaped gables. In the county too, small buildings continued the traditions of the C17. Cross windows were still used as late as 1724 in a farmhouse at High Callerton. Swarland Old Hall has often been attributed to *Trollope*, so similar in feel is it to his designs, and yet it dates from the early 1700s, well after his death. But at a higher social level things were beginning to change. The landed gentry was at last settling down to a comfortable untroubled life. Old families rebuilt their houses. New wealth began to flow into building from the spectacular growth of coalmining and the coal trade.

The first architectural event of the C18 was, alas, to remain an episode. VANBRUGH, who by his nature understood the virile robust character of Northumberland better than anyone else from the south, came up and built the Morpeth Town Hall in 1714 and Seaton Delaval in 1718–29. The Town Hall at Morpeth was burnt out and restored in the C19 and is thus no longer pure Vanbrugh, but Seaton Delaval is his alone. Here was the staid, orderly, classical 74–5 style of London, of the 'tame sneaking south', as Vanbrugh wrote, turned into something cyclopean. Here was an architecture for the storm and the driving cloud, for sombre ships and battering sea. Seaton Delaval can never have been a comfortable home – the plan is singularly ruthless – but it is a monument of Baroque grandeur and a passionate power unmatched in England, even in Vanbrugh's own work. The sympathy of the building with the country that surrounds it is indeed uncanny. For instance, the outward bulging bands of rustication that form the base on which Seaton Delaval stands had already been used by Northumbrian builders before Vanbrugh ever set foot in the county – at Capheaton by *Trollope* in 1668, at Halton Tower in 1696, and at Bywell St Peter in 1706 (and perhaps by the Romans at Corbridge). It is clear that the Baroque style had not left Northumberland; but it is not clear on the other hand whether Vanbrugh was responding to continuing tradition or whether at some point the county began to respond to him. There are a large number of buildings which are frankly Vanbrughian in character. There is, for example, the curious structure which the Newcastle Ships' Carpenters' Company built on top of the Sallyport of the old Town Walls to create the Sallyport Tower c. 1716. The barracks at Berwick of 1717–21 have often been thought to be by Vanbrugh himself, but they are now known to be by his partner *Nicholas Hawksmoor*, with the designs probably modified during building by *Andrews Jelfe*. There are many other buildings that show echoes of Vanbrugh's style, especially those façades of the 1720s in which doorways and all windows are crushed by frames with the same heavy alternating rustication of the wings at Seaton Delaval. 80 Such are the Simonburn Rectory dated 1725, No. 19 Priestpopple in Hexham, and Newmoor Hall.

It should be remembered, though, that however potent and appropriate Vanbrugh's passionate Baroque might seem, it did not stand alone, even in the first quarter of the century. There was a whole group of COUNTRY HOUSES which were closer to the mainstream of English taste. Bavington Hall, completed by Vanbrugh's client Admiral Delaval, admittedly has heavy door surrounds with cyclopean lintels, but the rest of the house is notable for its simplicity and restraint. At Hesleyside in 1719 a wing was built with the heavily segment-headed windows typical of that date all over England. Eglingham Hall of 1728 is quite Baroque with its triple keystones and rusticated corners, but Eslington Park of *c.* 1720 is much quieter in mood, a simple classical house with no more decoration than moulded surrounds to the windows, and an Ionic porch. Callaly Castle demonstrates how interchangeable styles were in the early c 18. In 1707, right next to the Trollope front, a wing was built in the plainest Queen Anne style; a few years later, before 1727, a two-storey arcaded loggia was added on the W front which was frankly Vanbrughian in mood.

Seaton Delaval ought to have been enough to establish Vanbrugh's as the true style of the North, yet by the 1730s the chaste PALLADIANISM promulgated in London in the 1720s had spread N to Northumberland, and for the rest of the century, in spite of Vanbrugh, the county built in the style that became dominant throughout England. It naturally used stone where some other parts of the country may have used brick, and some of its stone is of a ravishing biscuit or honey colour (Blagdon, Nunwick). Pure Pal- 88 ladianism appears first of all in the Thomlinson Library which Sir Walter Blackett gave to St Nicholas, Newcastle, in 1736, then at 76, 78 Wallington, designed by *Daniel Garrett* in the 1730s and 40s, in the garden front at Blagdon of 1752 and at Nunwick in 1748–52, two other houses possibly designed by Garrett, and again in the houses *James Paine* designed for Northumbrian clients in the 1750s (the 79, 82 bridge at Wallington, Gosforth House, Belford Hall, Bywell Hall). The restraint of these designs was offset, however, in some cases by an interior decoration of the most exuberant Rococo, the work of a group of Italians whom Sir Walter Blackett had settled at Cambo. They worked at Wallington, in the even more splendid saloon at 77 Callaly, and possibly also at Littleharle Tower and Blagdon.

Blagdon was begun *c.* 1735, extended *c.* 1752, and remodelled in the 1780s by *James Wyatt*, who also provided a lodge and the stables. Other work of the late C 18 includes Close House, Heddon-on-the-Wall, of 1779, Shawdon Hall, also of 1779, and the almost identical Acton House, *c.* 1781. Spital, near Hexham, *c.* 1802, is a rather brittle elegant design, and Horncliffe House of about the same time remains a fine Palladian composition. No architects' names are recorded for these and many other late C 18 houses, but it has been suggested that two of them (Acton House and Shawdon Hall) might be by a local architect, WILLIAM NEWTON (1730–98). Newton's houses (and the list of his known works is still growing) make quite an impressive collection. He was not a great architect, but he was clearly very competent and at home in a range of idioms. Backworth Hall of 1778–80, possibly his most successful house, is quite Adamish in style, with the openings set in high blank arches. Howick Hall of 1782 has a distinct quality of Paine about it, while Dissington Hall of 1794 and the similar Whitfield Hall have an unadorned solid plainness, relying for their effect on the quality of their splendid stonework. Newton's other works include the Temple of 1783 from Heaton Hall (now at Blagdon) and a wing of 1796 at Hesleyside.

Newton is also known as a designer of churches and public buildings, of which more has been said elsewhere, but only once in the county did he design secular work in the GOTHIC STYLE: at Kielder Castle, the Duke of Northumberland's remote hunting lodge, which Newton designed in 1775. But if gothicism is rare in Newton's work, Northumberland as a whole committed itself to the style earlier and more wholeheartedly than many other counties. The spirit if not the appearance of the style can even be found right at the beginning of the century at Seaton Delaval, which had a decidedly medieval as well as a primeval quality, for instance in the polygonal bays which look like the towers of a gatehouse, and the mighty towers which flank the centre block. This connection with the Gothic may seem tenuous, but in the 1720s Dr Sharp at Whitton built a folly tower for his vicarage and made it circular and gave it battlements. The windows are, however, still round-arched. In 1762, with the help of his parishioners, he built another battlemented tower, at Hartburn.

Larger landowners were soon eagerly erecting Gothic buildings to embellish their LANDSCAPED PARKS. Sir Walter Blackett of Wallington built Rothley Castle to the design of *Daniel Garrett*, *c.* 1755, as part of a picturesque landscape a few miles N of his house. The landscape, Rothley Park, contains a second, later folly, Codger Fort by *Thomas Wright*, and two ornamental lakes by *Capability Brown*. The lakes at Rothley Park are only part of Brown's work for the Wallington estate. He was born nearby at Kirkharle in 1715 and went to school at Cambo. His first employer was Sir William Loraine of Kirkharle, and he returned twice during his career to work for the Loraine family. His work at Wallington was done in the 1760s, and in the 60s and 70s he was extensively employed at Alnwick. In both places he designed garden buildings in the Gothic style. His designs for Wallington were never executed (though the fine classical Garden House is reputed to be his), but at Alnwick he seems to have been partly responsible for the Gothic additions to Hulne Priory. The other architect involved there was *Robert Adam*, who, under the patronage of the first Duke of Northumberland, was probably responsible more than anyone else for the emergence of the Gothic Revival as a Northumbrian fashion. Adam very completely and very daintily gothicized Alnwick between *c.* 1760 and the mid-1770s. A hundred years later the fourth Duke ripped out all Adam's work and replaced it by his Italianate decoration, which, whatever else one may say about it, certainly looked more substantial than Robert Adam's fragilities. All that is left of Adam's work now is two fireplaces and some furniture. Concurrently with the changes to the castle the domain was punctuated with gothicisms – the 84 observatory on Ratcheugh Cliffs, and Brizlee Tower; a medievalizing bridge, a pretty summerhouse within the walls of Hulne Priory and sundry cottages; in Alnwick itself, a Gothic fountain built in 1765 and Pottergate Tower, a sham medieval gatetower built on the site of one of the original defences in 1768. Finally, high up in the North Tyne Valley the Duke built the shooting lodge, Kielder Castle, which began this survey of Gothic building.

Meanwhile other landowners had followed suit. Sir John Hussey Delaval in 1761 began the process of gothicizing Ford Castle – a process which was to continue into the 1790s, when he built the 83 beautiful forecourt walls and gateways. The builders, part of a rather confusing story, seem to have been two local men, *George Raffield* and *Alexander Gilkie*, under the supervision of a Kelso architect, *James Nesbit*, whose name appears regularly in the northern part of the county. He was the architect for Sir Francis Blake, who in 1770 decided to outdo the Duke of Northumberland and build for himself, on the cliffs above Twizel Bridge, a castle of prodigious bulk. It was never entirely completed and now stands as a ruin with ivy hanging down – more Gothic in the sense of the C 18 than it ever could be if it was occupied. Nesbit was also the architect when Fowberry Tower was enlarged and made most originally Gothic in 1776. It has charming interiors. Elsewhere Mr Craster at Craster Tower built embattled walls around his house *c.* 1769 and at the same time gothicized the hall on the upper floor of his medieval tower. In 1768 Sir Lancelot Allgood at Nunwick put up kennels in the Gothic taste; the Roddams at Roddam Hall put up stables and estate buildings, probably to the designs of the Duke of Northumberland's estate architect, *Vincent Shepherd* (*c.* 1750–1812). Ewart Park, designed for himself by *Count Horace St Paul*, has one quite convincing and effective round tower. This list is by no means complete and, as we shall see, the northern taste for the Gothic was to continue unabated into the C 19; but before we reach that period we must step back and consider the public buildings of the second half of the C 18.

Outside Newcastle, PUBLIC BUILDINGS are usually small (Town Hall, Alnwick, 1731; Shambles, Hexham, 1766) and only 85 the Town Hall at Berwick, 1754–61, with its giant portico on top of a flight of stairs and its tall tower, has greater ambitions. It gave an architectural climax to a town of increasing civility. No formal 86 terraces or squares, but a multiplicity of good Georgian houses turned Berwick into the county's Georgian country town *par excellence*. But Newcastle was beginning to establish a city character. A fine new infirmary was built in 1751–2 and a Theatre Royal in 1788 (though both have now been replaced). More formal streets and squares of terraced brick houses with simple classical details, such as *William Newton*'s Charlotte Square (1770), began to appear in Newcastle and in North Shields. Newton also designed the Assembly Rooms in a fine Adamish style in 1774–6, and in 1796, with *David Stephenson*, he remodelled the N front of the Guildhall in a similar style. DAVID STEPHENSON (1757–1819), like Newton, was a local man about whose career far too little is known. He became architect to Newcastle Corporation and played an important part in the expansion of the city by laying out Mosley Street and Dean Street *c*. 1787. He was the designer of the Cale Cross, formerly at the foot of the Side (now at Blagdon). This was built in 1783, and in 1786 Stephenson designed his finest building, All Saints' Church, which we have already discussed. His style, like Newton's style, indeed Newcastle's style, towards the end of the century, tended towards a delicate Neo-classicism, though the northern part of the county was, as we have seen, still to a large extent gripped by the taste for the Gothic. A more robust Neo-classicism was to arrive in the early years of the C19 (*see* p. 104). But before we turn to C19 architecture, we must take account of the other aspects of the county's built fabric: the traditional domestic buildings of the countryside, and the transformations wrought by agrarian and industrial change from the mid-C18 onwards.

SMALL DOMESTIC BUILDINGS OF THE COUNTRYSIDE

BY JOHN GRUNDY

Rural Northumberland is scattered with small domestic buildings, but it is not the county in which to see great variety of them. Most date from the C18 and later, for the general insecurity of the area, from the medieval period right through to the middle of the C17, gave rise to a situation where anyone who could afford it built himself a defensible house, and those who could not afford it lived in houses too mean to have survived. Throughout the C17 and C18 security and prosperity were of course increasing, but the process was slow and the county has always been thinly populated. So not until the new wealth created by the agrarian transformation began in turn to revolutionize the farmsteads of rural Northumberland in the late C18 and early C19 (as Stafford Linsley describes in the next section) do we begin to find surviving small houses in any number, and by that time the varieties in style and plan form had largely been ironed out. Many of these C18 and C19 houses, however, are buildings of great solidity and even beauty, so that what the county may lack in range and variety, it makes up for in quality.

Since no early small domestic houses survive in Northumberland, we have to return to excavation, in particular to the DESERTED MEDIEVAL VILLAGES, to find out what they were like. Low Buston and Belsay, each consisting of houses set along a single street, were destroyed by the creation of parkland at the beginning of the C19, but the more usual pattern was one of gradual decline and eventual abandonment in the post-medieval period, attributable to a variety of reasons. A common layout, identifiable in the earthworks at South Middleton, Ogle, Great Bavington, West Whelpington (near Kirkwhelpington) and Middleton Old Town (near Ilderton), consisted of two rows of houses facing each other across a broad village green. At Old Shipley (near Eglingham) a third side was built up. In the marginal land of the upper Breamish, Alnhamsheles (*see* Ingram) grew up on either side of the Rowhope Burn, much as the surviving village of Whittingham is divided by the Aln. At a simpler level, the village of Hartside (*see* Ingram), on the SE slopes of Dunmoor, was no more than a single straggling row.

One medieval village, West Whelpington, has been examined in some detail by excavation (prior to its destruction by the quarrying of the whinstone knoll on which it stood). In its later medieval form it consisted of a series of terraces of long-houses flanking a broad green. Each consisted of a single-storey two-cell building with opposed entrances into a paved through passage which separated a byre at one end from living accommodation at the other. West Whelpington, like many Northumberland villages, shrank during the C 15 and C 16; Scottish raids, local outlawry and outbreaks of disease combined to blight rural life. In the later C 16 the bastle house (*see* above) was developed. At West Whelpington, while the older houses continued in use, a single bastle appeared on the village green, perhaps housing a socially prominent villager or one with more possessions to protect. Elsewhere (notably in the wilder western uplands) rows of terraced bastles (as at Wall) echoed the earlier terraced long-houses. Evistones in Redesdale (*see* Horsley), one of the most evocative deserted village sites of all, in true wild Border style consisted of a tight protective corral of individual bastles. Long-houses continued into the Tudor period and beyond; and in the remote upland areas where transhumance was being practised, even more rudimentary low-walled huts or shielings continued in use well into the C 18. The walls of all these buildings were low and of rubble or boulders, roughly bonded with clay; the roofs were probably hipped and thatched in heather (none have survived).

BUILDING MATERIALS for smaller houses and farm buildings were restricted to those found locally. Of ROOFING MATERIALS, THATCH, now the rarest, was at one time extremely widespread. There are two types. More normal straw thatch was common throughout the coastal plain and along the River Tweed in the N. Photographs right into the early years of the C 20 show it in use in villages like Wark-on-Tweed. Now it is restricted to Etal, where its survival is due to the picturesque taste of Lord Joicey. The upland areas and the Tyne Valley used heather thatch, and once again photographs reveal how widespread its use was. Pictures by Gibson, the Hexham photographer, show it even on houses in Gilesgate right in the middle of the town as late as the second half of the C 19. Only a very few heather roofs still exist, all of them, as far as is known, in the Bardon Mill area. There are barns at High Meadow just E of the village and at Tow House near Henshaw; and there is Causeway House on the Stanegate near Vindolanda. None of these are early buildings (indeed Causeway House is dated 1770) and yet they all have roofs characterized by the roughest construction, roughly cut crucks or upper crucks, rafters of unfinished branches and heather still attached to its roots and earth. They are extremely steeply pitched, with raised coping at the gables, often of reversed triangular stones. Such steepness and such coping are to be found on hundreds of buildings roofed in different materials throughout the county, and in many cases it seems to be a reasonable assumption that these were also thatched originally.

Roofs of sandstone FLAGS are still common in parts of the county and were formerly more widespread. They were, and are, commonest in places where thinly bedded, easily split sandstone occurs and that is principally in the s of the county, in the South Tyne Valley and the valley of the River Allen, but they are found, though more rarely, further N as well, at least as far as Bellingham. On more substantial buildings they are found throughout the county.

Northumberland has no natural SLATE, but like the rest of the country it has been largely buried beneath the ubiquitous Welsh slate, which is first recorded as arriving on Tyneside in 1798. More attractive, because it is rougher-textured and more receptive to lichen, is the Scottish slate used on many late C 18 and early C 19 houses in the northern parts of the county. Finally there are PAN-TILES, which are found in a broad swathe down the coastal plain. Some of the most effective roofs, though, are quite well inland, between Wooler and the Border, where the weathered orange of the roofs is combined with beautiful pink and grey walls built of the igneous rocks which have been washed down from the Cheviot massif.

This brings us to BUILDING STONE. It has been made clear earlier in this introduction that the vast majority of the buildings of Northumberland are made of buff sandstone, and this is equally true of the smaller buildings. The only areas which differ are the Wooler district and the valleys which cut deep into the Cheviots, where the igneous rocks are to be found, and the Doddington/Bamburgh/Holy Island area, where a delicious pink sandstone predominates. It is a soft stone which weathers easily, often into the most extraordinary patterns, as can be seen in the walls of Lindisfarne Priory and among the gravestones of Bamburgh. Dolerite, the county's other volcanic rock, though it provides in the Whin Sill the most dramatic of all its landscapes, is rarely used for building. Craster Tower is one 'polite' building which uses it; there are one or two cottages on Holy Island and one or two houses at Bamburgh, and that is all.

Outside of Tyneside and before the Victorian period BRICK is uncommon. Its use in Newcastle in the late C 17 and in the C 18 has already been recorded, and mention was also made of Morpeth, where a late C 17 fire led to extensive rebuilding in brick from c. 1700 onwards. Most of the other towns have some C 18 brick but not much. At Alnwick, Dorothy Forster's House on Narrowgate is an example, and Berwick has, e.g., the Old Vicarage in Church Street. None of these is of high quality. There seems to have been little or no tradition of bricklaying in Northumberland, and virtually all the brickwork, right into the early C 19, is in the most basic of bonds, the English Garden Wall, varied in Morpeth by the occasional brick stringcourse and more frequently by gables of tumbled-in brickwork. In the countryside, brick is even rarer; the earliest houses are early

C 18 and are almost without exception of more substantial quality
than other small houses of the period. The Croft, Stamfordham, of
1711, is a typical brick house of the period, three bays with stone
dressings, quoins and plinth. Brick cottages are few and far between
before the middle of the C 19.

Whether the first bricks to be used were imported, as is popularly
claimed, as ballast from the Low Countries, or whether they were
home-made, as the Newcastle bricks possibly were, is not certain.
By the early C 19, however, brick kilns were relatively common. A
prominent example is the group beside the A 696 just S of Belsay.
Ewart, near Wooler (*see* Ewart Park), had the reputation of having
the finest clay and producing the finest bricks. Its kilns were in
production by 1814 and are still standing, and the cottages and
houses on the estate, where they are not painted, are indeed of a
deep rich pink brick. It was not until the growth of the coal industry
with its attendant need for miners' housing, and the huge expansion
of industry on Tyneside, that brick finally became common for
houses. From the mid-C 19, brick terraces swamped the SE part of
the county, so that places like Ashington, Blyth, Wallsend and the
industrial suburbs of Newcastle are visually dominated by red brick,
though almost always, at the historical or social core of each settlement, the county reverts to its more natural sandstone.

LONG-HOUSES continue into the C 16 and C 17, though surviving
examples are very rare; indeed none appears to have survived in pure
unaltered form. Wooley Farmhouse (*see* Allendale Town) seems to
have been a rather superior long-house with domestic accommodation above the byre; it may date from the early C 16. No. 6
Riverside, Felton, is probably early C 17 and has a stone-walled cross
passage between the house and a down-house or service room,
perhaps used for brewing.

More common are CROSS-PASSAGE HOUSES, which are more
likely to be developments of the true long-house plan. Here the
accommodation is divided between house and down-house with
both parts intended for human habitation. One example, probably
from the later C 17, is Alloa Lea near Greenhead.

It was not long before the SMALL HOUSES in the county began
to develop one comparatively standard form, with a central or near
central doorway between the two ground-floor rooms. Among minor
manor houses of vernacular quality the form was already being
established by the end of the C 16 and the very beginning of the C 17.
The C 16 date on Clennell Hall near Biddlestone does indeed seem
puzzlingly early for an unfortified wing so close to the Border, but
as early as 1613 Blackheddon is a standard two-roomed farmhouse.
Other examples from later in the century include Corsenside (1686),
The Hagg, Allendale (1691), Crooked Oak, Allensford (1684). All of
these are plain in the extreme. They have (or had) simple mullioned
windows and often doorways with flattened triangular-shaped
heads. They are one room deep only.

Alongside these there are a few buildings which, while still quali-
fying for a small-house classification, are a little more ambitious.
Stringcourses attempting to establish an order to the façade are
61 found occasionally (No. 2 Holy Island, Hexham, 1657), and others
have straight labels or pieces of entablature above the windows (East
Hartford near Cramlington, probably *c.* 1670; Knarsdale Hall).

Others, possibly under the influence of Robert Trollope's country houses, have decorated window surrounds of rounded section (Aydon White House, 1684; Redesmouth House). One characteristic of the very end of the C 17 and the early C 18 is a tall and very narrow window shape. Bankfoot in Anick, Mainbank near Stamfordham and the impressive West Ord are all examples of a type which may have been associated originally with mullioned-and-transomed cross windows (cf. New Deanham; Callerton House in High Callerton).

Before we leave the C 17 we must return to the BASTLE HOUSE FORM and record the existence of a group of intensely conservative houses which continue the notion of first-floor living long after the defensive need for it had disappeared. Low Row near Kirkhaugh and Rowantree Stob, Sinderhope, are just two examples, both prob- 90 ably of the late C 17, which retain strong bastle-like characteristics and first-floor living. Such houses continue, especially s of the Tyne, right into the C 18.

More normal C 18 HOUSES fall into a number of patterns. The vast majority are two storeys high and three bays wide, with a central doorway. The earliest are one room deep only, and one strand of development is the gradual deepening of the house-plan, with the addition first of all of single-storey, lean-to outshuts holding sculleries to the rear of the house. Then come more substantial kitchens to the rear of the main rooms, integrated into the main structure under one great sweeping pitch of roof, a 'catslide roof'. The Old Butchers Shop in Whittingham is an excellent example of this type. Finally, towards the end of the century, houses begin to appear which are two full rooms deep under a single roof. They are too numerous to specify.

The architectural details associated with these C 18 farmhouses deserve a mention. The humblest are entirely plain; the windows, until the last years of the century, are cut sharp through the wall without any internal splay. Roofs are steep and gabled, with flat coping, and kneelers cut in a gentle S-curve. Buildings of slightly higher status often have broad, flat raised stone surrounds to their doors and windows; these can be found almost throughout the century (High Town House, Melkridge, 1741; Monkridge Hall, Otterburn, c. 1774). Elaboration beyond this is rare indeed, and Northumberland largely lacks the classical farmhouses so common in other counties. There are exceptions, of course: Brandon Farmhouse has a pedimented doorway and rusticated quoins; Glenwhelt, Greenhead (1757), has a segmental pediment on Corinthian columns and friezes with vermiculated rustication over the windows. The pedimented Corneyside (c. 1730–40) at Matfen is the most 81 completely classical farmhouse in the county.

These C 18 farmhouses have certain recurrent INTERNAL FEATURES. As in other areas, two quite distinct lines of roof carpentry co-exist side by side from beginnings in the medieval period until vernacular forms were supplanted by country-wide copy-book designs in the late C 18 and early C 19 centuries. Principal rafter roofs, very much in the 'Highland' tradition – there seem to be no 'Lowland' or common-rafter forms in the county – are of the simplest form, a simple triangle of tie-beam and principals, with a collar-beam often added for strength. This type is seen at Wooley Farmhouse near Allendale Town in the C 16 and in a few bastles, and continues relatively unaltered; its strength and solidity make it ideal for stone-flag roofs. The second line is that of cruck construction, seen in the upper-cruck trusses (at both first- and second-floor levels) well into the C 17 and early C 18 houses in Hexham and elsewhere, notably in the S of the county. It is tempting to link the use of upper crucks with heather thatch, although the two techniques are by no means mutually exclusive. Staircases are few in pattern and highly conservative in style. Until c.1750 many houses have roughly turned balusters with a square projecting knop at about the mid-point. Later in the century, everywhere adopts the perfectly simple, square-section stick balusters which continue virtually unchallenged until the middle of the C 19.

And it was without any doubt the FIRST HALF OF THE C 19 which was the great period of rebuilding in rural Northumberland. The vast majority of farmhouses date from this period. Mackenzie, writing his *History of Northumberland* in the 1820s, wrote 'most of the farmhouses were formerly very shabby and ill-contrived ... Those that have been erected of late years are substantial neat buildings, excellently adapted to the various purposes wanted for extensive farms and improved cultivation. The farmsteads built by the Commissioners of Greenwich Hospital are remarkably convenient and handsome.'

The Greenwich Hospital farms are on the estates confiscated from the Earl of Derwentwater for his part in the 1715 Jacobite Rebellion. They are to be found, e.g., round Scremerston, where Town Farm and Inlandpasture are characteristic, intensely plain and dignified, and built of the finest ashlar. Other big estates were not left behind. The Duke of Northumberland's farms were rebuilt in huge numbers between 1800 and 1850. A typical house on the larger farms is Chattonpark, near Chatton, which is square, solid, four bays wide, in stone, with a square porch and a roof of broad overhanging eaves on big unmoulded stone brackets.

Similar rebuilding was going on throughout the county, and particularly impressive examples can be found on estates belonging to the Haggerston family (e.g. South Hazelrigg, near Hetton Hall), the Tankervilles (Chillingham Castle), the Ridleys (Blagdon Hall) and many others. All of them are built of stone, and all of them are exceptionally plain. Very occasionally a doorway will be set in a blank arch, but decoration is quite unusual. Windows especially are cut straight through the wall without any surrounds. Roofs are almost always gabled. Kneelers tend to become more complex in profile as the century progresses. These houses are so large and impressive, especially in the lowland parts of the county, because they were the focus of very extensive farms, farms which needed large numbers of workers to run them and which were, in effect, more like hamlets than normal farms. They are known as 'STEADINGS' in the county, and their buildings, which were being rebuilt at the same time as the farmhouses, are described in the next section; but the cottages for the workers deserve a mention here.

Farm labourers' COTTAGES older than this great period of rebuilding during the agrarian transformation are quite uncommon in many parts of the county, and indeed one receives mainly distressing notions from the early C 19 writers as to why the rebuilding was necessary. Mackenzie again: '... but in many parts of the county the landlords still appear shamefully ignorant of the advantages which result from increasing the comfort of the labourer. It is shocking that a man, his wife, and half a dozen children should be obliged to live huddled together in one miserable hovel ... Many of the old cottages [he says this about Holburn near Lowick] ... were built chiefly with oak trees which in many instances rested upon the ground and were joined at the top. These rude log-houses are now replaced with neat well-built cottages.'

'Neat well-built cottages' began to spring up in the later years of the C 18. A new village street at Capheaton, erected by Sir John Swinburne, was of single-storey, two-room cottages with concrete barrel-vaulted roofs, which were, alas, replaced by more conventional roofs shortly afterwards. At Calder on the Roddam Hall estate, cottages were built in 1788 which were also single-storey but had a granary above, forming a second floor. Single-storey cottages are more normal, however, especially in the N half of the county. Rows of them can be seen at hundreds of large farms, and they can form quite impressive groups (e.g. at East House Farm, Cheswick, or West Learmouth, near Carham, where they step down hillsides). At Akeld they form a complete square, formerly with the privies in a block in the middle. Squares of single-storey fishermen's cottages are also to be seen at Low Newton-by-the-Sea and at Low Hauxley 123 (see High Hauxley). These single-storey rows, often with large gardens, sometimes with pantile roofs, give the landscape in the N part of the county a distinctly Scottish feel. Further S, at Chollerton, for example, and elsewhere in the Tyne Valley, two-storey cottages are common, and not just for agricultural workers: at Allenheads, in the extreme S of the county, terraces of two-storey cottages were built from the 1790s for workers in the leadmines.

PLANNED SETTLEMENTS, or at least purpose-built ones, are quite a feature of Northumberland. The prettiest and best-known is Blanchland, developed rather than rebuilt out of the ruined outer courtyard of the Abbey at the behest of the Lord Crewe Trustees. Many medieval fragments remain incorporated into the mid-C 18 cottages. The new village at Belsay was probably begun c. 1816 by Sir Charles Monck, who gave it an Italianate arcade to go with his Grecian mansion. Capheaton has already been mentioned. Cambo, probably laid out by *Daniel Garrett*, is very pretty. Many villages are totally or effectively estate villages rebuilt all at one time; Chillingham in the 1830s and Denwick a little later, in the Tudor style for the Duke of Northumberland, are just two of many examples. Lady Waterford began to build a model village at Ford c. 1860. She started rather dully (apart from the beautiful school), and it was left to Lord Joicey to make it pretty after 1907, as he did also in nearby Etal. Finally one curious planned village is the Swarland Settlement laid out in 1934–9 by Commander Clare Vyner and the Fountains Abbey Settlers Society, with their architect *Miss M. P. Reavell*, to house homeless families from Tyneside.

Meanwhile cottage building continued on the estates right through the C 19 and into the C 20, and two later examples might be singled out for mention. *Norman Shaw*'s Addycombe Cottages 111 in Rothbury for the Cragside Estate were built in 1876. They are in fact two-storey flats, eminently picturesque from the front and composed with almost geometric care to the rear. Hethpool Cottages in the College Valley were built by *Robert Mauchlen* in 1926 in a pretty Arts-and-Crafts style. These were both built for industrialist owners; industrial housing, which dominates the SE of the county, is described in the following section.

EIGHTEENTH TO TWENTIETH CENTURY: AGRARIAN TRANSFORMATION AND INDUSTRIAL REVOLUTION

BY S. M. LINSLEY

Some ninety per cent of Northumberland has never been other than agricultural, and poor though much of the high ground is, there are considerable tracts of land along the coastal plain and the valleys of the lower Tyne, Till, Tweed etc. which are particularly fertile. It was in these areas and particularly in Glendale that Northumberland's AGRARIAN TRANSFORMATION became most obvious during the second half of the C 18.

In 1766 William Hutchinson contrasted Northumberland then with its supposed condition some 200 years earlier. His prose is undoubtedly purple but nonetheless interesting: 'The ferocity of the inhabitants is [now] subdued; traffic, arts, sciences, manufactories and navigations, have taken the place of the brutal warfare, which is extinguished; Cultivation, with all the comeliness of Plenty, laughs in the valleys; the streams are taught to labour in mechanic systems, to aid the manufacturer; every Creek and Bay is thronged with Ships ... Desert plains stained with Slaughter and track'd with the progress of Rapine and Violence, formerly spread forth an extensive scene of desolation, where now rising woods, inclosed farms, villages and hamlets are disposed under the smiles of Prosperity. The original naked inhabitants ... [have] furnished the land with a race, who, at the time they enjoy the comforts of life, reap the fruits of industry and the profits of genius, and thereby are progressively advancing their families towards opulence. Happy reverse!'

The changes which were evident then continued at a pace which might have astonished Hutchinson, for, although the spirit of improvement was not universal throughout the county, sufficient farmers and agents adopted and developed the changed systems of agriculture to make the 'Northumberland system of husbandry' a farmhouse-hold phrase. Many facets of the 'Age of Improvement' need not be discussed here; suffice it to say that the enclosing and dividing of large areas of ground, usually by quickset or other hedges, the adoption of 'alternate husbandry' making the land more productive, the establishment of plantations on poorer land and the building of new farmsteads were integral features of improvement. Such developments were not unique to Northumberland, but the dominance of its major landowners and the relative paucity of common-field agricultural systems enabled such developments to proceed with little contention. Consequently hundreds of square miles of rural Northumberland demonstrate landscapes of improvement. There are few Enclosure Acts for the arable parts of Northumberland, simply because owners with so much land under their control could enclose and divide as and when they saw fit. Before improvement, much land in the N of the county seems to have been husbanded on the infield-outfield system, whereby large outfield areas of potential arable land were only sporadically tilled. Consequently these near-virgin lands could be brought into permanent cultivation when the opportunity arose to profit from the increased demands for agricultural produce.

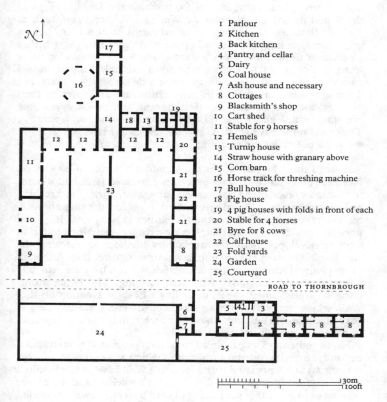

1 Parlour
2 Kitchen
3 Back kitchen
4 Pantry and cellar
5 Dairy
6 Coal house
7 Ash house and necessary
8 Cottages
9 Blacksmith's shop
10 Cart shed
11 Stable for 9 horses
12 Hemels
13 Turnip house
14 Straw house with granary above
15 Corn barn
16 Horse track for threshing machine
17 Bull house
18 Pig house
19 4 pig houses with folds in front of each
20 Stable for 4 horses
21 Byre for 8 cows
22 Calf house
23 Fold yards
24 Garden
25 Courtyard

ROAD TO THORNBROUGH

30m
100ft

Thornbrough High Barns (Aydon). Early C19 planned farm

As has been mentioned (*see* p. 80), there is evidence that Northumberland's early FARMSTEADS were characterized by a linear building comprising house, byre and barn, but with an enclosed cross passage separating the house from the other offices. Such arrangements were clearly inadequate for the industrialized farming which improving landlords, agents and tenants sought. New arrangements of steading, neatly arranged around a central foldyard, sometimes with proper accommodation for farm workers, emerged after 1750, occasionally with architect/builders involved. New farm plans were devised after the Scotsman Andrew Meikle invented and subsequently patented the first successful threshing machine in the 1780s. This machine, a fixture within the barn, needed a waterwheel, wind tower, horsewheel or steam engine to power it. Fixed barn threshers were rapidly introduced throughout the arable areas of Northumberland, until few if any mixed-arable farms of more than 200 acres did not employ one. Whilst the threshing machine could sometimes be incorporated into an existing barn with its prime mover on the opposite side of an outer wall, ergonomics resulted in new farmstead arrangements from which the familiar 'E-plan' developed during the Napoleonic War period. Architects such as *John & Benjamin Green* later designed farms on this plan, but its originator is unknown. Generally the county's farmsteads, whether 121 planned or unplanned, are excellent examples of vernacular architecture. Most FARMHOUSES are uniformly double-fronted on two storeys, with overall dimensions varying little across the county, but there is much more variety in the architecture and form of farm workers' cottages. Some have one and some have two storeys; some are single-entry and some double; most are plain but some are Tudorish; some have small Yorkshire sashes at first-floor level but some do not. Like the steadings themselves, farmhouses and cottages mainly date from the C 19.

A word must be said about the apparent absence of BARNS on Northumbrian farms. In fact every mixed-arable farm had a barn, not for the storage of the unthreshed harvest but rather for threshing and processing only. Northern farmers regarded the huge timber-built storage barns of the southern counties as 'very unsightly' and unnecessary, for even with their less clement weather Northumbrian farmers developed perfectly satisfactory methods of stacking the corn harvest in an open yard until it was time for threshing. Although many planned and unplanned farmsteads survive, they are generally unsuited to the demands of modern farming. The large, multi-purpose, steel-framed sheds, as at Bay's Leap at Heddon-on-the-Wall, which best serve farming needs in the late C 20 may be less attractive than the buildings they replace, but they too are responses to changing agricultural needs and ideas.

Northumberland's agriculture has always generated related activities and industries, the most obvious of which was CORN MILLING. WATER MILLS associated with Hadrian's Wall have been identified at Willowford Bridge (Cumbria) and Cawfields, and there are reasons to suppose that the milling of corn by waterpower continued up to and through the early medieval periods. Certainly there are sufficient C 12 and C 13 references to indicate their widespread presence. Some 300–400 were at work during the C 18, many being enlarged or rebuilt during the Age of Improvement and the Napoleonic War period. For example Waren Mill, on a C 12 site, shows extensive rebuilding in the 1780s, with further extensions and the installation of a steam engine in 1819 and yet more extensions in 1835 – developments encouraged by the fact that Waren was accessible to coasters via Budle Bay. Such enlargements are not, however, universal: Linnels Mill on the Devil's Water near Hexham still retains an early C 18 form. With the spread of improved transport systems, many water mills in the more marginal arable areas closed down during the C 19. Concomitantly corn imports were growing, and large port-orientated steam-powered mills were built. One such at Willington-on-Tyne, built c. 1799, was seven storeys high and was said to have cost above £4,000. Water-powered sites, however, remained highly prized, and often mills underwent changes of use. At Oliver's Mill in Morpeth, for example, a three-storey, stone-built, water-powered woollen mill of c. 1830 was subsequently converted to a corn mill. In 1899 a new, brick-built extension was added for steam milling, its fine brickwork details in sharp contrast with the plain vernacular of the older mill. WINDMILLING in Northumberland, as in the rest of the United Kingdom, came much later than water milling. The earliest windmill recorded for the U.K. dates from 1185, and Northumberland's earliest identified windmill stood for a short while on Coquet Island c. 1200. In a county well endowed with rivers suitable for water milling, windmills were mainly built within five miles of the coast and in the urban areas, notably at Newcastle, where only the tower survives of one of *Smeaton's* two Chimney Mills of c. 1782. Somewhat unusually, at Great Whittington and Acomb, wind and water mills stood almost side by side: the water mill at the latter site was provided with an auxiliary steam engine, presumably to cover for all eventualities. But nothing could slow the growing dominance of the port mills; eventually, often after turning to provender milling for a few years, all of the county's wind and water mills ceased operation, the last of them just surviving into the mid-C 20.

Another activity clearly supported by agriculture was the county's WOOLLEN INDUSTRY. Weavers, dyers, fullers and wool merchants are recorded in the 1296 Lay Subsidy Roll for Northumberland, with weavers being particularly concentrated at Corbridge. There is every reason to assume that the woollen industry continued throughout the medieval period, with some evidence of diversification into linens, sacking, sailcloth etc. It is clear that many fulling mills became small WOOLLEN MILLS with the advent of mechanization in the late C 18, but Northumberland did not become a significant textile county. A number of woollen mills continued to operate into the C 20, e.g. at Newminster, Otterburn, Great Tosson and possibly Haltwhistle; mill buildings remain at all these locations. Towards the end of the C 18 some COTTON MILLS were established, for instance at Stannington and Netherwitton, the latter being a short-lived venture which soon converted to woollens before becoming a saw mill; in 1988 this fine Georgian mill was converted into apartments.

ROPE MAKING perhaps just deserves to be classified as a textile industry, and rope was always in great demand in the mining and shipbuilding industries. Not surprisingly therefore many ropewalks and later 'patent' ropeworks were established on Tyneside, but there were also ropewalks in the rural areas to serve agricultural demands; the only surviving ropewalk building of note is at Hexham, dating from the second quarter of the C 19.

The LEATHER INDUSTRY was also supported in part by local agriculture, and in the C 13 Newcastle was regarded as the nation's premier hide-exporting port. In 1833 it was still being described as 'the leather metropolis of the north', and in 1863 it was said to be 'at the head of the trade in seal, calf and sheep skins'. Although Newcastle dominated the county's leather trade, there was activity elsewhere; Hexham had become, certainly by the C 17, noted for the manufacture of leather gloves, the so-called 'Hexham Tans'. In the 1820s one fifth of Hexham's population was employed in its leather industries; at least five tanneries were at work and more than 23,000 dozen gloves per year were produced, being cut and sewn mainly by women in outwork. Largely through a failure to mechanize, the county's leather industry became greatly diminished as the C 19 proceeded, succumbing in particular to Yorkshire enterprise as the Leeds tanneries all but cornered the market. The last Newcastle tannery closed down in the 1970s, and now only at Hexham can the once familiar wood-louvred drying lofts be seen.

A short digression seems appropriate here, for drying lofts were
117 also a feature of PAPER MILLS; at Haughton Castle is one of the finest such lofts in the country. The first ever provincial newspaper was produced in Newcastle in 1639, which pre-dates any local paper mills, the earliest in the North East being at Chopwell (Blackhall Mill), County Durham, in 1697. In fact the region's paper industry was mainly concentrated in County Durham, although the reasons for this are unclear. Initially the mills required waterpower and produced only hand-made paper. Thus Haughton Castle paper mill was established in 1788, and by 1825 it operated with four vats. Although the mill seems to have closed down before 1887, its shell survives and its magnificent drying loft stands nearby. At Fourstones the earliest of the three waterpowered vat mills in the county is still working, although little survives of its original buildings. Founded in 1763, Fourstones was one of only a few waterpowered vat mills in the region, and indeed in the country, to successfully make the transition to steam-powered, machine-made paper and to use imported esparto grass as the basic raw material instead of rags. Generally such changes favoured the establishment of new mills near ports, and again Durham gained more from this change than Northumberland. Few early fireproof mills have been identified within the county, but one such was a paper mill at Scotswood on Tyne, demolished in the late 1970s and believed to date from the 1820s.

The last of the larger industries to be directly supported by agriculture generated one of Northumberland's most famous and popular products – beer. MALTING AND BREWING were once as widespread in Northumberland as anywhere else; now they are equally concentrated. For centuries Newcastle has been famous for its beer and claims (as does Stone in Staffordshire) to be the first town in England to brew ale. There are numerous references to breweries in the C 18, and by the mid-C 19 Newcastle alone had thirty-two breweries. The ease with which barley could be grown in many parts of the county, and the thirst for beer in both rural and industrial districts, led to the development of dozens of maltings and breweries throughout the county, from Allendale in the S to Berwick in the N. There were no breweries with architecture to match the 'Capital Brewhouses' elsewhere, and the maltings were generally quite plain, but the late C 18 brewery and maltings at Tweedmouth (see under Berwick) present vernacular industrial architecture at its best.

The county's early INDUSTRIAL FORTUNES sprang from a complex geological matrix. Its extractive industries have included lead, silver, barytes, witherite, ironstone, whinstone, sandstone, limestone, clay and above all coal. The utilization and marketing of these resources were greatly assisted by the county's natural harbours and navigable rivers, of which the Tyne was easily the most important. With such intrinsic advantages, and a succession of gifted inventors, engineers, industrialists and agricultural improvers, supported by a growing and adaptable workforce, it is perhaps not surprising that Northumberland should play an important role during the nation's industrial revolution.

Although some of Northumberland's ROADS have ancient origins, it was in the C 18 and C 19 that a coherent road pattern was developed through the agency of turnpikes, an attempt to build new roads or improve existing routes on the novel principle that road users should pay for their upkeep. Between 1747 and 1826 some nineteen trusts were established with complete TURNPIKES or lengths of turnpike in the county. The early turnpikes were mainly trunk routes like the Great North Road, or routes radiating from Newcastle. The later turnpikes largely filled the gaps or, as in the case of the Alston Roads, provided a carefully planned network in a particular area to serve particular needs. The earliest turnpikes, like that from Hexham to Alnmouth or the section between Whittingham and Powburn (Acts passed in 1752), usually followed pre-existing routes, often through enclosed land, passing through several towns or villages. They were constructed with minimal engineering works, many sharp bends and steep hills, although they may be quite straight when constructed through unenclosed land. In contrast the 'New Line' from Belsay to near Otterburn (Act of 1830) and the Whittingham 'bypass' of 1842 have smoother gradients, embankments and cuttings and pay no particular heed to existing villages. The only buildings that Turnpike Trustees were obliged to erect were TOLLHOUSES. Of the eighty-five which once existed in the county only about a dozen remain. They are usually very simple, single-storey structures with small gable-end windows offset to the road side of the house (as at Allendale or Farnley, for example), although the one at Langley Castle has an unusual plan form. Turnpike Trustees were also required to set up mile posts at one-mile intervals, so that in theory some 500 ought to have been provided in the county. Certainly some interesting MILESTONES remain, as on the Alston, the Hexham to Alnmouth, and the Percys Cross to Milfield turnpikes. There were very few significant TURNPIKE BRIDGES (the 1820 Union Bridge [113] at Loan End being an exception), the Trustees generally using pre-existing bridges over the wider rivers, as at Rothbury, or relying on individuals or Bridge Trusts to risk their finances on large bridges, as at Hexham (1781) and Coldstream, near Cornhill (1766), respectively. Still, one or two unusual turnpike bridges do remain, as at Corbys Letch (1754, with later modifications; see Edlingham) between Alnwick and Rothbury. Turnpikes had fallen out of popular and government favour by the middle of the C 19, and not without good reason. Trusts were steadily discontinued as railway competition strengthened in the 1860s and 1870s, and, as trust income declined, their roads ultimately passed to highway authorities. Little used then for a few decades, it was pressure from the cycling and later the motoring lobbies which focused attention once more on road transport. The c 20 decline in the railway system and the rise of the dual carriageway and the motorway are well known – but this may not be the end of the story.

Historically the development of the coalfield has been governed by those inter-related technological, economic and social factors which influence industrialization generally. But no other part of the kingdom was better placed to meet increasing national demand for COAL than the North East, where shallow seams of high-quality coals outcropped on or near the banks of the navigable reaches of the Tyne. Cliff-face and surface outcrop workings can be found throughout the Coal Measure areas, often with bell pits just to the
119 dip of the outcrop, as at Stublick (Langley), where colliery buildings remain from the early c 19. Such readily accessible resources were finite, but pits more than about three miles distant from navigable water needed more economical transport systems than packhorses or carts, and deeper mines needed adequate winding and pumping machinery. When Huntingdon Beaumont constructed a horse-drawn waggonway near Bedlington *c.* 1606, it was the county's first 'railway' and the second in Great Britain. Waggonways increased the economic distance from pit to navigable water to about eight miles, and over the following two centuries they facilitated the enlargement of the active area of the coalfield. Before 1700 many mines had been drowned out, but when a lifebelt in the shape of the Newcomen pumping engine became available, it was grabbed with enthusiasm by coal owners in Northumberland. Although no Newcomen ENGINE HOUSES remain in the county, Scremerston and Ford (both 1840s) have houses from a later generation of pumping engine. Through these and other improvements the North East coal trade grew from about 250,000 tons per annum in 1600 to ten times that amount by 1800.

It is curious that PORT AND HARBOUR IMPROVEMENTS played little part in Northumberland's share in this growth, the notable exception being at Seaton Sluice (Hartley Harbour), where, in the 1760s, the c 17 harbour was improved by driving an artificial cut through surface rock to provide safer access to the old natural harbour as well as a small but effective wet dock. Closed since the 1870s the impressive cut still remains; this and the nearby 'Octagon' building (once a harbour office, now a private residence) are the only substantial c 18 features which survive at Seaton Sluice. Between 1750 and 1850 the village also boasted a large glass-works, salt pans, copperas works, iron works, limekiln, brewery, three public houses, chapel, windmill, market square, shops and offices. Other c 18 port and harbour works were much less significant, although Beadnell and Seahouses had enclosing piers before 1800, to aid fishing and the export of lime, and Blyth acquired a new breakwater and leading light; the small harbour of Cullercoats, constructed in 1677, closed down in 1730.

The c 19 was to see great CHANGES IN THE COAL INDUSTRY and in the railways, ports and harbours which principally served the coal trade. Firstly, to meet the growing demands of the industrial revolution, the coal industry further expanded its output and area of activity. Output from Northumberland and Durham grew from about 2.5 million tons per annum in 1800 to 45 million tons per annum by 1900, the increase being achieved by more efficient working systems both above and below ground, by the sinking of new and deeper pits, and by better transport facilities over land and water. This technological progress was not without its dangers. Deeper and more extensive underground workings were more difficult to ventilate and drain; safety lamps were a double-edged sword, for they could be used by unscrupulous coal owners as a substitute for better ventilation. Above ground the larger mines needed a complex of buildings, with winding and pumping engine houses, headstocks, screens, workshops, sheds and offices, and sometimes had associated brick works, gas works or coke works. Some idea of the scale of these complexes can be gained at the preserved site at Woodhorn (*see* Ashington). Many new MINING VILLAGES were created, e.g. in the Bedlington and Ashington areas, where new mines were sunk from the 1840s and 1860s respectively. At Bedlington the mining communities were grafted onto a village of medieval origins, whereas at Ashington a wholly new mining town was created: in 1841 the area that was to become Ashington had a population of 58. The 'Fell-em-Doon' shaft was sunk in 1846 and this was followed by the Bothal Pit (1867), the Carl Pit (1887), Linton Colliery (1896) and Woodhorn Colliery (1898). By the 1850s the settlement consisted of two rows of houses, increasing to eight rows (335 houses) by 1880 and eleven rows (665 houses) by 1890. A further 1,300 houses were built over the next quarter-century. All the houses had gardens and reasonable but communal water supplies; sewers were well drained and the streets lit by gas. Compared with certain parts of Newcastle at that time (and perhaps even in the 1990s), living conditions at Ashington were quite civilized, its gridiron layouts in no way detracting from its essential homeliness. The scale of colliery house provision on the Great Northern Coalfield was unique. By 1913 the coalfield employed nearly one quarter of all the colliery workmen in Great Britain but it contained almost one half of all colliery-owned houses.

The horse-drawn WAGGONWAYS which had carried coal from pit to navigable water continued to operate into the early C 19, but by then horses were being augmented by rope-worked systems. George Stephenson, born in 1781 in a small house which stands by the side of the Wylam waggonway, and first employed in keeping cattle off the Walbottle Moor Waggonway, was one of a number of Northumbrians who continued the work of Richard Trevithick in advancing the claims of the steam locomotive as a viable alternative to horse-worked and ultimately to rope-worked railways. Although first aimed at the carriage of coal, and hence only used on former waggonways and new mineral lines, the steam locomotive was soon to transform the country with the efficient carriage of people as well as goods on interconnected railway systems. Hence in Northumberland a new pattern of PUBLIC RAILWAYS was superimposed over the existing weave of horse-, rope-, and locomotive-worked mineral lines. Of particular importance amongst the new railways was the Newcastle and Carlisle Railway (N & C R). Opened in sections between 1834 and 1839, it was the first railway built across England, the first line to use what became standard gauge throughout, the longest railway in the world at that time and, most importantly for the student of architecture, the first railway line anywhere to provide proper passenger facilities at intermediate stations. *Francis Giles*, who had worked extensively with *John Rennie*, was appointed engineer to the company, much to the chagrin of the Stephensons, but in 1834 *John Blackmore* was appointed as 'operating engineer' with Giles nominally retained as consulting engineer. Another who came to work on the line as an engineer under Giles was *Wylam Walker*. He subsequently lived at Hexham, established a firebrick and earthenware pottery at Corbridge and acquired the famous Prudham sandstone quarry at Fourstones which supplied stone for many prestigious structures such as Barnes Bridge over the Thames and Newcastle Central Station. Whilst it is not yet known who designed or built the early lineside STATIONS on the N & CR, one or all of these men may have been involved. Biddle has suggested that *Benjamin Green* may have been their architect, recognizing similar stylistic effects in some later railway stations by him. However, at the various opening celebrations, reported quite fully in the Newcastle newspapers, neither Green nor any other architect is mentioned in the long lists of formal thanks. So the mystery remains, but fortunately so do many of the stations – Wylam, Hexham, Bardon Mill, Haltwhistle – all in neo-Tudor style but differing in their detailed arrangements. As Dr Granville observed in 1841 (*Spas of England*), the N & CR was: 'Unquestionably by far the prettiest railroad in England. It is exceedingly neat and well kept and its station-houses built of freestone, are perfect specimens of taste and style in architecture.'

'LINESIDE STYLE' was therefore first instituted on the N & CR and subsequently imitated throughout the world. *Benjamin Green*'s stations on the 1847 Newcastle to Berwick line, generally much grander than those of the N & CR, are again mainly neo-Tudor

115 (e.g. Chathill Station at Preston), but with no two stations alike, ranging from cottage-like structures to buildings of manorial proportions (*see* Morpeth and Belford, for example). The later stations (1877) on the Alnwick to Cornhill branch railway, probably by *William Bell*, again have a distinctive style, somewhat extravagant, with rugged stonework, half-hipped dormers, cross gables, elaborate bargeboards and attractive wrought-iron finials; Ilderton and Akeld are good examples. In contrast, but again probably by *Bell*, the extraordinary seaside stations of Tynemouth (1882) and Whitley Bay (1910) illustrate the structural and decorative potential of brick, cast iron, wrought iron and glass. Of course Northumberland's most impressive railway station is Newcastle Central (1850). As its architect, *John Dobson*, noted: 'Railway buildings ought to do much for architecture, being a new class of structures erected for purposes unknown until ... the present generation ... They are especially public works ... and might therefore do much towards improving the tastes of the public.'

116, 130 Newcastle Central Station, with its classical frontage and innovative train-shed roof, was the physical embodiment of Dobson's philosophy. Railway engineering offered many other challenges to architects and engineers, notably in the design of BRIDGES AND VIADUCTS. Their responses were frequently bold and imaginative, witness *Robert Stephenson*'s High Level Bridge (Newcastle upon Tyne, 1849) and Royal Border Bridge (Berwick, 1850), *John &*

Benjamin Green's Ouseburn and Willington viaducts of 1837–9 (*see* Wallsend and Newcastle upon Tyne respectively), and the Border Counties Railway skew viaducts at Chollerton (1858) and Kielder (1862), by *Robert Nicholson* and/or *John Furness Tone*.

Alongside the development of the railways, and frequently at the behest of railway companies, Northumberland's PORTS were slowly but surely transformed to meet the new demands of the C 19. As always, the Port of Tyne dominated trade, although it was not until after the River Tyne Commission was formed in 1851 that much improvement took place, the fine piers at the harbour mouth not being completed until the early C 20. To the N, Tweedmouth Dock, Seahouses Harbour, Warkworth Harbour (Amble) and the Port of Blyth, with its impressive coal staiths and long breakwaters, were all essentially developments of the C 19.

Another once great extractive industry, that of LEAD ORE MINING AND PROCESSING, has virtually disappeared from the county, although certainly not without trace. Evident at least from the C 15 in the Blanchland area of Northumberland, the industry was already well established and important throughout the Northern Pennines. Over the following four centuries the lead industry dominated that part of Northumberland which lies within the North Pennine orefield, and few aspects of its landscapes are not directly derived from that industry. The single most important mine in the orefield, and possibly in Europe, was at Allenheads, where mining had probably begun in the C 16 and lasted until the late C 19. It was here that the Beaumont family as land and mine owners encouraged Thomas Sopwith, their agent from 1845 to 1871, to develop what was almost a model village around the central mining and processing area. Thus at Allenheads and nearby 'Dirt Pot', offices, houses, a school, reading room, library, church and chapels were constructed, while extensive tree planting provided as sylvan a retreat as might reasonably be expected at an altitude of some 400 metres (1,300 ft). Nor was this the highest lead settlement in Northumberland, for nearby Coalcleugh is at 530 metres (1,740 ft). Around both Allenheads and Coalcleugh there is abundant evidence for the establishment of the smallholdings, often above the 500-metre contour, which enabled miners to simultaneously practise a limited degree of marginal farming; no polite architecture here, but a vast field archive for the student of the vernacular.

Mechanization played little part in the lead industry until the C 19, when increased capital investment was necessary to win deeper and declining resources, and to process the ore with minimum waste. Thus the evidence for huge pumping engines near Blanchland (the Shildon mine, *c.* 1808) and Newbrough (the Stonecroft mine, *c.* 1850), and thus also the need for a settled workforce in company villages. There was little scope for mechanization of lead smelting processes, but again the growing need to avoid waste, and the wish to capitalize on a period of particularly high lead prices, brought about the construction of 'horizontal chimneys' in the first decade of the C 19. In essence these were long, stone-built condensers which trapped the lead and silver vapours or particles that would escape from the normal short chimney of a lead-smelting furnace; periodically the flue deposits were scraped down and recovered. At the Allendale Smelt Mill three flues, with a combined length of about eight miles, wind their way up the fell to the SW, terminating in two crumbling vertical chimneys. At Langley, where the Greenwich Hospital Commissioners, then land and mineral royalty owners of Alston Moor, built a smelt mill *c.* 1770, many of the developments outlined above can be seen. The collapse of the industry in the late C 19 as reserves declined and imported lead undercut indigenous supplies, deprived Northumberland of a long-established industry but provided today's industrial and landscape archaeologists with an immense field resource and an intricate and frequently exhilarating road and footpath network for the traveller by foot or by wheel.

Although coal and lead ore represented the county's major EXTRACTIVE INDUSTRIES there were others of economic significance; few, however, had much impact on the built landscape. QUARRYING is one of the obvious exceptions, since high-quality freestone was a widely available building material. Some quarries produced building stone which was highly prized beyond the county's boundaries. Blaxter and Darney quarries, for example, found regular customers in Edinburgh and elsewhere. The nature and use of building stones in the county are dealt with above, and little further needs to be noted here. The CLAY PRODUCTS INDUSTRY of Northumberland may be of some antiquity, although the ease with which clay and clay products could be imported as ballast is a complicating factor. Newcastle had a Company of Bricklayers from 1454 and a Company of Slaters and Tylers from at least 1691. There were attempts to establish BRICK WORKS in and around the town during the C 17, perhaps with some success, but it cannot be said with certainty that Newcastle's brick buildings of the C 17 (Holy Jesus Hospital of 1681, for example) used locally produced bricks. However, during the C 18 many brick and tile works were established throughout the county, serving the growing urban areas, the market towns and rural Northumberland in general. Thus bricks and pantiles were made at Cottingwood (Morpeth) at least from 1739. The agrarian transformation during the second half of the C 18 brought additional demands for bricks and tiles even within the traditional sandstone areas. When Sir John Hussey Delaval's Ford estate was being improved during the second half of the C 18, the early establishment of a brick and pantile works was seen to be a desirable enterprise, and by 1771 it was producing some 100,000 bricks per year and the same number of pantiles. Although sandstone remained the dominant building material on the estate, the use of brick and tile is evident in brick party walls, pantiled roofs and the former works site, where a long-abandoned tile kiln remains. Similar evidence survives at many of the larger estates, such as Ewart, Dilston and Capheaton, and it should be of no surprise that near Berwick, with its splendid pantiled roofscape, one tile works was established *c.* 1762 and another in 1788; together they produced some 350,000 tiles a year by 1799. One of the manufacturers offered a no-quibble guarantee period of six years! The rural brick and tile works probably developed still further in the C 19, switching production to clay drainage tiles, but they were in sharp decline by the early C 20. This decline was no doubt related to the growth of larger brickmaking concerns in the S of the county and the relative ease with which their products could be carried by railways. The demand for bricks in the urban and industrial areas was much greater than in rural Northumberland, and some measure of the scale of this demand can be gauged by the fact that the glass cone at Lemington (now the only survivor of perhaps one hundred such structures in the North East) is said to have required one and three-quarter million bricks for its construction in 1797.

It was geologically fortuitous that suitable clays were often associated with coal, and this enabled several colliery concerns to establish their own brick works. Parallel clay product developments of the C 18 were the fireclay and earthenware pottery industries, mainly located along the Tyne Valley from Haltwhistle in the W to near the mouth of the Tyne. The POTTERY INDUSTRY was probably the earlier of the two, being first established by Warburton on Tyneside c. 1730; several other firms became established as the C 18 proceeded. Their tidewater locations allowed the easy importation of ballasted raw materials and the export of the finished products both coastwise and overseas. Warburton, however, soon abandoned his riverside site and moved two miles S of the river to Gateshead (County Durham). Once powdered flint came to be an essential ingredient of the clay body, after c. 1720, flints were brought in as ballast to be ground locally. During the C 19 most, if not all, of the clay was likewise brought in cheaply on returning colliers. Certainly one reason for the eventual decline of the Tyneside industry was the growing use of water-ballasted colliers from 1852 onwards. Only one Tyneside pottery was to survive the general decline. From its beginnings on Wearside in 1762 the Maling Pottery grew to be the most important on Tyneside, the Ford B Pottery at St Lawrence, Newcastle, being the largest integrated pottery in Britain at the time of its construction in 1878. It was finally closed in 1963, but the main buildings survive as a furniture repository.

The FIRECLAY INDUSTRY seems to have begun in the second half of the C 18, but its heyday was in the C 19. Much of it was devoted to the manufacture of firebricks for industrial purposes, but many houses were also built of this material – there are examples in the west end of Newcastle, in Normanton Terrace, for example, and at Clayton Park Square near the city centre, both from the 1870s. The Broomhill Collieries Ltd established a firebrick works at Amble c. 1870, and many houses in the town were built using their bricks. C 19 concerns for hygiene, however, brought a new use for fireclay in the manufacture of salt-glazed sanitary ware. Many works were active on both sides of the river along the Tyne Valley between North Shields and Haltwhistle, and at Corbridge the 'Old Pottery', established by Wylam Walker c. 1840 and closed down c. 1910, still retains two 'Newcastle' kilns and two 'bottle ovens'. At Bardon Mill the fireclay works occupied a former woollen mill building to produce a wide range of goods (salt-glazed decorative garden ware is still manufactured); nearby houses show how varied its products had once been. The development and widespread use of plastic pipes and fittings has been mainly responsible for the closure, from the 1960s, of all the sanitary ware works. Mention must be made of the once famous Adamsez works at Scotswood-on-Tyne (Newcastle upon Tyne). Taking over an ailing brick and tile works and neighbouring paper mill in 1903, Charles and Moses Adams transferred their Leeds sanitary ware business to Scotswood and began to

make products which can still be seen in public and private
conveniences around the world. After Adamsez closed in 1975,
some of its remaining buildings at Scotswood were used as a pie
factory.

The rhythms of geological time ensured that Northumberland
had widespread limestones as well as coals, ores, clays and sandstones. The Romans had used burnt lime both for cements and for
agricultural purposes, and the uncovering of eight LIMEKILNS
dated to the C 15 during an archaeological excavation on the Newcastle quayside in 1990 suggests a substantial enterprise for the late
medieval period, perhaps based on ballasted imports of limestone.
But the great age of lime burning in the county was from c. 1750 to
1900. Lime was used in agriculture to neutralize acid soils at least
from the C 17; its popularity undoubtedly grew during the early C 18,
and it came into near-universal use on mixed-arable lands during
the 'Age of Improvement'. Where burnt lime could be transported
only by horse and cart and the industry was confined to areas where
limestone and coal were easily come by, only small kilns were built;
there are many such just to the S of the Military Road beside
Milestone House, near Cawfields. Where more distant markets were
available, as in the N of the county, which supplied some of the
lime-free areas of southern Scotland, somewhat larger kilns were
built, as at Lowick. If sea transport was possible, even larger concerns
were established (see Holy Island, Seahouses and Beadnell). With
the building of railways some huge banks of kilns, with direct rail
access, were constructed to serve markets many miles distant (see
Littlemill, Wall (Brunton) and Fourstones). There is therefore considerable variety of form in the county's limekilns, but only the 1888
kiln at Great Tosson is known to have benefited from the attentions
of an architect – *George Reavell* of Alnwick. Hundreds more,
however, survive; but with the advent of chemical fertilizers and the
ability to crush limestone to powder, all have ceased operating
during the past century or so.

Northumberland's medieval IRON INDUSTRY does not seem to
have been of any great significance. Only one blast furnace is known
to have been worked for part of the C 16 (Wheelbirks, near
Stocksfield) and another for part of the C 17 (Allensford). Neither
of these appears to have been very long-lived, and for most of the
C 18 iron ore was smelted only at Bedlington (briefly), and possibly
also at Lee Hall. There were other iron-working enterprises in the
county, however, for it was well-placed to receive imported wrought
iron from Sweden, in particular, but also from Russia, as well as pig
iron from America. This was the basis of the considerable Crowley
enterprise in the Derwent Valley in County Durham, where the
imported irons were reworked or converted into steel by the cementation process for use in the manufacture of a variety of products.
There were similar but smaller undertakings in the town of Newcastle, especially that at Busy Cottage in Jesmond Dene, and also at
the small water-powered forge at Ford. At Guyzance by the River
Coquet a foundry for iron and tin was started by 'a firm of speculators' (actually members of the Kendall dynasty of ironmasters)
between 1775 and 1778. In spite of having the services of the great
John Smeaton, who designed the dam and waterwheel machinery,
the firm collapsed, and in 1791 the premises were bought by a

Newcastle draper who converted them into a woollen mill and dyehouse. Some of the buildings have now been adapted for domestic accommodation, but Smeaton's dam remains one of the finest C 18 examples in the country. Towards the end of the C 18, large-scale, integrated iron ore smelting and working was introduced to Northumberland with the establishment of the Tyne Iron Works at Lemington. Located by the tidal Tyne for ease of import and export, the works were freed from the need for waterpower by the installation of a Boulton & Watt blowing engine. Such engines increased the desirability of associated coal and ironstone measures for the location of ironworks, and in Northumberland works were set up at Wylam (1836), Ridsdale, near Woodburn (1836), Walker (1842), Brinkburn (c. 1845) and Haltwhistle (1856). These works were short-lived, wilting either through geographic isolation or in the face of competition from the rapidly expanding iron industry in Durham and on Teesside. However, there are interesting (and at Ridsdale dramatic) remains at some of the sites noted, testimony to a brief ironmaking flourish in the county. W. G. Armstrong developed an ironworks at Elswick (Newcastle upon Tyne) in 1860 primarily to supply his own engineering concern at the same location, but although this works continued into the C 20 Northumberland could no longer be described as a significant iron-making county. Small-scale steel production in Newcastle continued into the C 19, but the major development took place at Newburn in 1822. John Spencer had served an apprenticeship in Sheffield before working for Crowley and Millington at Winlaton. He began his own business in Newcastle as a file manufacturer in 1810, then moved to Newburn, soon to be known locally as 'New Sheffield'. Beginning with a small water-powered corn mill, which he converted to file grinding, Spencer went on to create a steel works which had few equals in the North East, employing up to 2,000 workers on a site of some eleven acres before its collapse in c. 1925–6.

It is perhaps appropriate to note at this point that coalmining, coal transport and iron-working led quite naturally to the development of an important ENGINEERING AND SHIPBUILDING industry, located mainly on Tyneside. Defoe had noted that at Newcastle 'they build ships to perfection', and the building of wooden sailing colliers on the Tyne had preceded his visit by centuries. Although the region's first iron vessel (a rowing boat) was launched on the Tyne in 1822 it was not until the second half of the C 19 that steam-powered iron ships were built in large numbers. Like the wooden sailing ships before them, the new breeds of vessel were generally constructed in the open air, although there was one covered ship-yard, at St Peter's, Newcastle, by 1860. There are therefore few significant buildings associated with shipbuilding other than some office blocks of the C 20. Ships were also built at Blyth, Amble and Berwick, while fishing boats were built at several ports and harbours along the coast and are still built at Seahouses in a manner that would be generally recognizable to a C 17 shipwright. Steam propulsion gave birth to marine engineering, and pioneering firms like R. & W. Hawthorn of Newcastle supplied marine and other steam engines from the 1820s. In the last decade of the C 19 Charles Parsons built the world's first turbine-powered ship, as throughout the century ship and engine builders had broken records and introduced innovations with seemingly effortless regularity – a situation regrettably unlikely to recur after the decline in shipbuilding which has accelerated through the C 20.

Of other forms of engineering the most significant were in loco-motive building, hydraulic engineering and armaments manu-facture. Robert Stephenson & Company established the world's first LOCOMOTIVE BUILDING factory on Forth Banks, just outside Newcastle's Town Wall, in 1823; their immediate neighbours, R. & W. Hawthorn, also built steam locomotives. The Stephenson works had early vicissitudes but survived to become one of the most important concerns of its kind in the country. The site was aban-doned by the company in 1902 and taken over in part by Hawthorns and in part by Doves, the builders' merchants; although some of the factory buildings were wilfully demolished in the early 1980s, a significant group survives in South Street and Orchard Street. The even more famous Armstrong Engineering Works in the west end of Newcastle at Elswick has been entirely swept away to allow the site to be redeveloped for retail, domestic and leisure purposes.

Armstrong's works were established in 1847, being initially set up to produce novel HYDRAULIC MACHINES which soon achieved international fame, and widespread use, on railways, in docks, ware-houses, swing bridges etc. The Tyne Swing Bridge of 1876, still hydraulically powered by its original engines, is a product of the Armstrong Works, as is the machinery for London's Tower Bridge. Armaments and shipbuilding came later as the concern became one of the foremost engineering works in the world. The official opening of the Tyne Swing Bridge gives a measure of the importance of the Elswick works. It was, at the time, the largest such bridge in the world, and the first vessel to pass it was heading for Elswick to take on board the largest gun that had ever been manufactured. At Elswick the gun was hoisted aboard by the world's largest hydrauli-cally powered sheer-legs, and after the sea voyage to Italy it was unloaded by a hydraulic crane, also the largest in the world. Bridge, gun, sheer-legs and crane had all been designed and built at Arm-strong's Elswick works. It is difficult now to appreciate the versatility offered by hydraulic engineering before the electrical age was ushered in.

Another legacy of concerns like Armstrong's and the shipyards to the E of Newcastle is the rows of terraced INDUSTRIAL HOUSING, 122 often of the characteristic 'Tyneside flat' form (*see* pp. 100–1). These dwellings, not built exclusively for the working classes, are two-storey terraces of flats, with one family occupying the ground floor and another the upper floor; each tenement has its own entrances and frequently its own back yard. Tyneside flats are a peculiarity of NE England; some 44.5 per cent of Newcastle's population lived in flats in 1911, compared with 3.7 per cent for all the urban areas of England and Wales. Vast acreages of land on Tyneside were taken over for the building of these flats, as at Elswick, for example, where, mainly under the impact of the Armstrong Works, population grew from 400 in 1811 to 3,540 in 1851 and 14,345 by 1861. Although many Tyneside flats have been replaced by high-rise developments and flat-roofed maisonettes, the survivors are often highly prized.

Of the once great Northumbrian industries, perhaps only the GLASS INDUSTRY still needs to be noted. It was first established on

Tyneside *c.* 1618 by Sir Robert Mansell under a crown monopoly; later the cheapness of coal and the relative ease of import and export drew others to establish glassworks in the North East. Mansell's works were just to the E of Newcastle at Mushroom, St Lawrence, and this location, together with the neighbouring St Peter's area and other sites along the Tyne, continued to attract glassmakers; by 1800 there were about a dozen works along the N bank of the river. Away from Tyneside the only other glassworks in Northumberland was at Seaton Sluice, where the Delavals' 'Royal Hartley Bottle Works' was opened in 1762; by 1788, with three bottle houses in production, it was the largest such works in the kingdom. It included a 'handsome building 220 feet in front, the side walls to the roof 36 feet', and a maze of underground tunnels for bringing raw materials in from the quay and taking finished products out. All that now survives of the Hartley works is the tunnels under the modern housing development s of the road bridge, and heaps of glass slag. Of all of the county's glassworks, only that at Lemington, established in 1787, is still in production. Its surviving glass cone (*see* p. 95 above) is one of the 118 country's most outstanding C 18 structures. In the later C 19 the glass industry, like several others in Northumberland, failed to match up to competition from elsewhere in the country, partly through a reluctance to innovate.

The great industrial developments of the C 19, the huge increases in population, the explosive growth of urban areas and new colliery villages generated service industries such as WATER, GAS AND ELECTRICITY supplies. Many were established by profit-making organizations, but eventually most came under public, local or national control, only to be returned to the private sector in the last decades of the C 20.

Until the C 19 there was little attempt at generalized PROVISION OF WATER in Northumberland outside of Newcastle. Indeed it was not until the 1830s that the Newcastle Subscription Water Company made serious attempts, not always successfully, to supply the town with reliable clean water. Rival companies emerged after parliamentary reports into living conditions strongly advocated the universal need for pure water; from the 1840s, reservoirs such as those at Whittle Dene near Horsley-on-the-Hill (1846), Hallington (1863 and 1880), Little Swinburne and Coltcrag (*c.* 1880) were built. Some of these reservoirs, however, fell well short of their design expectations, perhaps not surprisingly when the Swinburne reservoir, for example, was fed by three streams of which two were called 'Small Burn' and the other was named 'Dry Burn'! Throughout this period the companies involved also extracted water from the increasingly polluted River Tyne; river extraction pumping engine houses still remain at Newburn (1855) and Wylam (1874). The construction of the Catcleugh Reservoir, near Byrness (1891–1905), was the most ambitious water-supply scheme of the C 19 and without doubt the most successful in achieving an ample and reliable supply. During the building of this reservoir a hutted village provided living accommodation for workers and their families, and surprisingly one of these dwellings survives. Ironically the latest significant chapter in the county's water-supply history has provided, in Kielder Water (1975–81), 'the largest man-made lake in Europe'; but demand for its water has been almost non-existent. Elsewhere in Northumberland

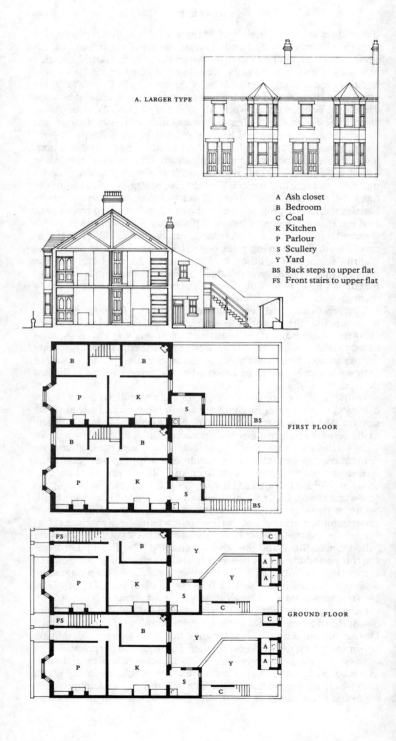

A. LARGER TYPE

A Ash closet
B Bedroom
C Coal
K Kitchen
P Parlour
S Scullery
Y Yard
BS Back steps to upper flat
FS Front stairs to upper flat

FIRST FLOOR

GROUND FLOOR

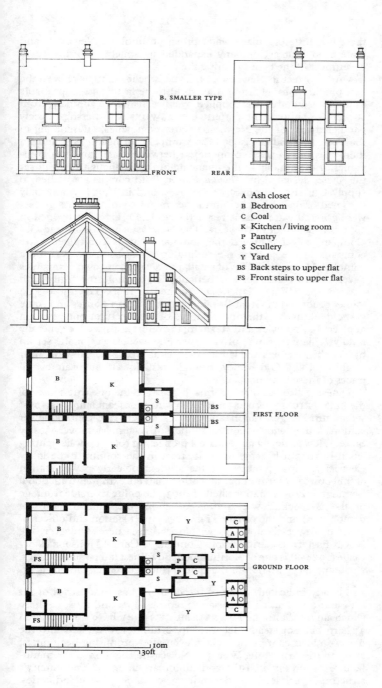

B. SMALLER TYPE

FRONT   REAR

A Ash closet
B Bedroom
C Coal
K Kitchen / living room
P Pantry
S Scullery
Y Yard
BS Back steps to upper flat
FS Front stairs to upper flat

FIRST FLOOR

GROUND FLOOR

10m
30ft

Tyneside flats

there was little organized water provision until the Newcastle and Gateshead Water Company expanded its sphere of influence to cover most of the county during the C 20.

Mosley Street in Newcastle on Tyne is believed to have been the first public thoroughfare in the world to be lit by gas. Improbable as it may seem, this was supplied by a fire insurance company from 1818. The subsequent pattern of GASWORKS ownership closely paralleled that of the Newcastle water companies, culminating in the Newcastle and Gateshead Gas Company formed in 1838. Indeed there was often close co-operation between water and gas companies, most notably in the financing of the Redheugh Bridge over the Tyne, designed by *Thomas Bouch*. Both companies wished to supply Gateshead from N of the river, and in Bouch's unusually designed bridge the upper and lower members of the truss girders were gas and water mains respectively. The bridge was opened in 1871 and lasted for thirty years. The Newcastle and Gateshead Gas Company never achieved the dominance of its equivalent water company in the county; the technology of distribution was more complex. Hence a number of small, mainly market-town companies developed in rural Northumberland, for example the 'Alnmouth Gas and Salt Water Baths Co.', formed in 1860. Town gas is no longer produced in Great Britain, but small retort houses and some gasholders, usually the only features of architectural note, remain at places like Alnwick and Hexham; the retort houses were generally mildly Italianate. Small private gasworks were occasionally set up by wealthier farmers and landowners, as at West Side, Newton, near Corbridge, and Old Ridley, near Stocksfield, although almost all traces of these have now gone.

Tyneside also has many claims to be called the one true source of the ELECTRICITY INDUSTRY: Swan's incandescent lamp, Parsons' steam turbine generation and Merz's designs for central power stations with integrated control support this claim. Moreover Mosley Street, Newcastle, again took on a pioneering role in public lighting when in 1880 it became the first street in the country to be lit by electricity. Little remains for the student of early power station architecture in Northumberland other than the extremely functional Lemington Power Station shell of 1903, the polite riverside frontage of the Berwick Power Station of about the same date (now demolished) and the ornate Tramways power station and offices of 1901 in Newcastle upon Tyne. No Battersea here! However, the North Eastern Electric Supply Company's Carliol House in Newcastle (1924–8) is one of Northumberland's finest inter-war buildings, a triumphal celebration of the central role of electricity in our lives.

As already indicated, some of the county's basic industries of the C 18 and C 19 had all but disappeared by 1900, and most of those which survived into the TWENTIETH CENTURY have since suffered a sharp but not steady decline. Opportunities to expand into the newer industries were not taken, even after promising beginnings, as when the Armstrong Works in Newcastle abandoned the manufacture of aircraft in 1919 and motorcars in 1920. The county's structural weakness, its dependency on a few basic industries, exacerbated by declining coal reserves, has beset its industrial areas since the 1920s, and the effects continue to be felt.

The C 20 has witnessed only retrenchment in Northumberland's once prosperous coal industry. There were about 120 coalmines in the county in 1913 but only 67 by Vesting Day in 1947. In that year the total manpower in mining exceeded 40,000 and output was nearly 11 million tons; by 1987–8 the only remaining deep mine, Ellington, employed under 2,000 men and produced 2.2 million tons for the Alcan aluminium smelter power station nearby at Lyne-mouth. Accompanying this collapse has been the abandonment or reduced significance of the former mineral railways. Nor-thumberland retains only two mainline railways, the N & C R and the Newcastle to Berwick, neither of which has working branches. The rural lines have all been closed, although the commuter lines on Tyneside received a new lease of life through electrification and integration into the Metro Rapid Transit System in the 1970s and 80s, reusing some existing stations, such as Whitley Bay and Monk-seaton, and building new ones, as at Haymarket in Newcastle. Shipbuilding has also seen massive contractions since the early 1960s, a decline which in the face of foreign and often heavily subsidized competition has not been halted by the rationalization, nationalization and privatization to which it has been subjected. Construction and repair of rigs for the North Sea oilfields has taken the place of several redundant shipyards. Not surprisingly the county's major ports have witnessed a concomitant decline – the former coal-exporting port at Amble ceased that trade in 1969 but now boasts the region's largest marina, thanks in large measure to the European Economic Development Fund. Although agriculture remains strong, mechanization since the 1950s has resulted in a greatly decreased workforce and has threatened the fragile viability of several small communities, although afforestation, with all its attendant environmental problems, has provided work opportunities in upland areas. Greater threats now face these areas with the changing emphases in upland farming.

There have been some positive developments since the mid-C 20. Alcan was directed to Northumberland by government persuasion in 1968 and the Lynemouth works was in production by 1972. The smelting shop advertises its product through the extensive use of aluminium in the cladding, curtain walls and window frames of its construction; the £65 million complex, constructed by *Gleeson Civil Engineering Ltd* with *Yorke, Rosenberg, Mardall* as architects, was described as 'An admirable example of a great industrial enterprise housed in a planned way' by the judges of the *Financial Times* Industrial Architecture competition. Some former coalminers found work there, belying their new occupation in the vast, airy smelting shops by squatting in their customary underground manner. It is the service industries which have provided new industrial structures of distinction. Carliol House in Newcastle (*see* above) of 1924–8 was the first; more recent examples are the British Gas Engineering Research Station at Killingworth (1967), the water tower at Morwick (1961) and the Newcastle Airport terminal at Woolsington (1964–7).

The ADAPTIVE REUSE of old and not so old buildings at last seems to be finding favour, as at the medieval Dove's and other later warehouses on Newcastle's quayside, at the former Wills cigarette factory in the city's suburbs, at the C 18 cotton mill at Netherwitton in rural Northumberland and in numerous farm building and railway station conversions for private accommodation, craft workshops and computer-based enterprises. But there has been little concerted effort to maintain the county's industrial and agricultural heritage. After years under the threat of demolition, Tynemouth Station has gained a new lease of life and is a popular place for specialist shopping and live music. Part of one coalmine, Woodhorn Colliery near Ashington, has become a museum, while other relics of that industry survive only through neglect in the rural areas. The Northumberland National Park has a programme to conserve the lime-kilns within its boundaries as well as the navvies' hut at Catcleugh. The National Trust also has in its care a number of industrial structures as well as several working farmsteads, and at Cragside it has refurbished some Armstrong engineering equipment to create a 'power trail'. Little is being done to save relics of the once important lead industry other than the restoration of the smelt mill chimney at Stublick, near Langley, and valiant community efforts at Allenheads. Not one of the many splendid planned farms of the C19 is being actively preserved, and only one watermill has been restored for the benefit of the public. Northumberland is not an economically rich county and unfortunately this will mean that much of its industrial and agricultural heritage will sooner or later be lost.

NINETEENTH- AND TWENTIETH-CENTURY ARCHITECTURE

BY JOHN GRUNDY AND GRACE MCCOMBIE

The first major new C19 SECULAR BUILDING erected in Northumberland was a COUNTRY HOUSE, Barmoor, begun in 1801 to the designs of *John Paterson* of Edinburgh. Paterson was a pupil and partner of the Adam brothers and an important exponent of their 'castle style', so that Barmoor acts as a summary of the C18 and a useful introduction to the new century. Here elegant classical oval rooms are fitted into a Gothic exterior; but a few years later, at Milbourne Hall, Paterson used the same oval Neo-classical rooms behind a classical exterior, so superficial was the preference for one set of forms over another.

Was it any different when the severe forms of the GREEK REVIVAL and especially the Greek Doric Order were first used? It
93 is doubtful. The case is Belsay Hall, built by *Sir Charles Monck*, who had been in Athens, become enamoured with Periclean Athens and wanted a Parthenon to live in. The result is a house, Palladian in its
94 bones, but with Doric trim and a fine, temple-like hall inside with galleries, in two orders. Sir Charles designed it himself. He also provided Grecian lodges, a remarkable garden and incidentally a nicely and not at all Grecianly planned village street of stone cottages with an arcade. The date of Belsay Hall is 1807, early in the Greek Revival; William Wilkins, it is true, did Doric then, but there were still very few who had the courage to try to domesticate the style.

Within a very few years the Greek Doric had become the accepted style in the county. As early as 1810, the Moot Hall at Newcastle, that is a public building, was given a Greek Doric portico. It was designed by *John Stokoe* (c. 1756–1836), the first of a pantheon of local architects who emerged in the early part of the C 19. The most prominent and most talented of the group was JOHN DOBSON (1787–1865), who produced a full-blown Greek Doric design in the same year, 1810: the Royal Jubilee School, Newcastle. Sadly it has not survived, but as designed it was a pure and perfect Greek temple. Over the next quarter of a century Dobson continued to use the style with an increasing freedom and sophistication which place him among the best architects of his generation in the whole of England. His earliest surviving Greek houses are small and restrained, notable for a perfection of masonry finish which Dobson himself claimed derived from the demands made on his masons by Sir Charles Monck at Belsay. Prestwick Lodge (1815) is the plainest and small-est, with no more decoration than Doric pilasters framing the doorway. Villa Real, Newcastle (1817), and Doxford Hall (1818) are given porticoes of Greek Doric columns. But it was the decades of the 1820s and 30s which brought a sequence of Dobson's finest Grecian designs. Mitford Hall of 1823 was almost a reprise of Doxford Hall, the most successful of the earlier houses, but Longhirst Hall, designed the following year, broke entirely new ground. For a start it abandoned the Doric order for the first time and used the Corinthian instead. It is not a large house, but the entrance front is a splendid design, exciting and theatrical. It has a tightly compressed full-height Corinthian portico with a pediment, the only time Dobson used a pediment on any of his houses. Inside the drama continues with a two-storey hall of unpainted, beautifully veined sandstone. The ceiling has a series of shallow coffered Soanian domes. Longhirst was followed by Nunnykirk Hall (1825), a remodelling and enlarging job this time, characterized again by the most exquisite stonework. Here a recessed three-storey centre is flanked by projecting two-storey wings with an Ionic loggia between them. The main block is rusticated in its entirety, a feature not otherwise found in Dobson's work but used more regularly by his friend Ignatius Bonomi in County Durham. Meldon Park (1832), the last of the great Greek houses, was marked in the design by a return on a larger scale and with a little more sophistication to the simple elegance of Mitford.

Dobson was equally happy to design in the GOTHIC STYLE, though the results are not so unreservedly successful. His earliest attempts, Cheeseburn Grange (c. 1813) in a restrained Tudor, and West Jesmond House (1817) in a spiky Gothic, are both pretty; and the surviving gatehouse and court house to his massive gaol at Morpeth (1821) are in an overpowering castellated Gothic style. His best Gothic buildings are substantial country houses. Lilburn Tower (1828–9), built in the middle of his finest Grecian period, is in reality a symmetrical classical design wrapped in a Tudor-Gothic veneer. It is a beautiful house, nevertheless, wonderfully sited (as almost all Dobson's houses were) and with a fine and complete set of his own decorations and furnishings. Beaufront Castle (1836–41) is Gothic in a far more picturesque sense, an irregular assembly of towers and battlements, at times massed romantically and at times with an almost Vanbrughian sense of drama.

The vast majority of the country house work in the county during the first half of the c 19 was done by Dobson, but he was not quite the only architect to be represented. Apart from the designs of Paterson already mentioned there is a house of 1819 by *William Burn* (Adderstone Hall), one by *George Wyatt* which has been demolished (Twizell House, Adderstone, of *c*. 1812), and several others whose architects have not been recorded (Budle Hall, Lorbottle Hall near Callaly, The Spital near Hexham). Matfen Hall (1828–30) was designed in a very large and lavish mixed Tudor and Gothic, partly by *Rickman* and partly by the owner, *Sir Edward Blackett*, who seems to have taken over control in the middle of the building process. *John Shaw* also built a house in the county, Cresswell Hall of 1821–5 (which has been demolished). It had many similarities with Dobson's designs, especially Longhirst; the surviving stables and fragments of colonnades reveal that the masonry was also of similar standard to contemporary houses elsewhere in the county.

In Newcastle and on Tyneside, from 1800 to 1850 the types of buildings were much more varied than in the countryside. Tyneside's c 19 PUBLIC BUILDINGS were all by local architects. The most important of the early c 19 was *John Stokoe*'s Moot Hall in Newcastle, which has already been mentioned. The Greek Revival remained dominant until the 1830s. *John Dobson*'s Scotch Church of 1811 in Howard Street, North Shields, was in that style, and so was the colonnaded Fish Market he created at the E end of Newcastle's Guildhall in 1823. *John Green*'s Literary and Philosophical Society in Westgate Street, Newcastle (1822–5), has handsome Doric columns *in antis*. Dobson's most impressive public building, Newcastle's Central Station (1850), has already been mentioned by Dr Linsley (*see* p. 92); that was in a majestic Roman Doric style. For CHARITABLE AND EDUCATIONAL BUILDINGS, Jacobean and Tudor were as popular on Tyneside as in the rest of the country. Jacobean was used by *John & Benjamin Green* in North Shields for the Poor Law Building in Howard Street and Saville Street to which *Dobson* attached his Tudor Town Hall in 1845, and for their mariners' almshouses at Tynemouth (1837). In Newcastle, *Dobson*'s Lying-in Hospital of 1826 is Tudor Gothic, though his much earlier House of Recovery (1804) is simply classical.

The most significant public buildings were those associated with the development of NEWCASTLE'S TOWN CENTRE. This began with *Richard Grainger*'s purchase in 1834 of the Anderson estate, which lay within the Town Walls. Grainger had established his reputation as a Newcastle builder-developer with the building of Blackett Street and Eldon Square in 1827, designed by *Thomas Oliver and John Dobson*, and of the suburban Leazes Terrace and
97 Crescent (1829–30), designed by Thomas Oliver (*see* pp. 413–15). Grainger's purchase of the Anderson estate proved a turning-point in the town's architectural history; his plan to develop this large central area, with the help of several architects and the approval of the Common Council, might be compared to the development of Edinburgh's New Town, except that Newcastle's 'new town' was within its medieval boundaries and limited by its medieval streets. Grainger's architects were *John Wardle* and *George Walker* from his own office, *John Dobson* and *John & Benjamin Green*. A prerequisite

for the new development was the demolition of a market which the Corporation had built as recently as 1808 and its replacement by the Grainger Market, probably designed by *John Dobson*, with a rationally planned interior. It opened in 1835. The new centre was virtually complete by 1837, with its main thoroughfare, the gently curving Grey Street, climbing uphill past *Green*'s noble classical portico of the Theatre Royal (1836–7) to what became the focal point of Grainger's scheme, the Column to Lord Grey, also designed by Green, of 1838. Grainger and his architects brought a new sophistication to the town, and a classical grandeur combined with Picturesque planning influenced by Nash's London developments. Where brick had reigned supreme, there were now smooth stone fronts; where details had been modest floor and sill bands and classical doorcases, there were now giant classical orders, with rusticated basements supporting giant pilasters and full entablatures. Suburban developments were of plainer, classical brick terraces, but on the fringes of the town (and now within the city boundary) there are houses by *Dobson*: the Gothic West Jesmond House (later Jesmond Towers) of 1817–27 and the Tudor Benwell Towers of 1831.

In other Tyneside towns, PLANNED DEVELOPMENT was less extensive, though what can now be seen is only a shadow of what was built. At North Shields a grid of new streets with simple classical terraces was built away from the riverside *c.* 1800. There is also the relic of the most ambitious planned development outside Newcastle, that is, one section of the handsome Neo-classical terraces designed by *David Stephenson* in 1806–17 to enclose the New Quay. The building of handsome seaward-facing terraces established Tynemouth's resort character in the 1830s. Tyneside's defences were much strengthened in the face of the threat from France in the first years of the C 19. New BARRACKS were built on the Castle Leazes at Newcastle in the first decade of the C 19, perhaps to the designs of *James Wyatt*, then Architect to the Board of Ordnance. Clifford's Fort at North Shields was strengthened, and there are early C 19 houses said to have been built for officers connected with the (demolished) late C 18 barracks.

The best churches to be built in the second half of the C 18, St Anne and All Saints in Newcastle, were buildings of real quality and raised hopes of a new era to come in ecclesiastic building. It never arrived. The C 19 CHURCHES in the county are almost all ordinary. Plenty of new churches were built to meet the needs of the rising population of the industrial centres, but very few were built with ambition. One group has at least the distinction of an interesting history; the group of parishes carved out of the huge parish of Simonburn in 1818 (Greystead, Humshaugh, Thorneyburn, Wark) were all provided with churches to the designs of *H. H. Seward*, pupil of Soane and house architect to Greenwich Hospital, which had owned Simonburn (and lots of the rest of Northumberland) since the execution of the ill-fated Earl of Derwentwater for his part in the 1715 Rising. The churches were built, it is said, to provide work for redundant chaplains after the end of the Napoleonic Wars. They are plain, lancet-style preaching boxes, typical of their period but well proportioned and provided with parsonages which form, with the churches, curious islands of urbanity in their wild moorland settings.

Everywhere the lancet style was the order of the day, but though many were built, few are memorable. *John* and *Benjamin Green* did several simple little churches with nave, chancel and bellcote, true in a sense to the commonest medieval type in the county, but uninspiring in imitation. Examples of these are Dalton (1836) and Holy Saviour, Sugley (1836–7; *see* Lemington). Their more ambitious churches are Earsdon (1836–7) and Cambo (1842); but the best of the E.E.-style churches are by *John Dobson*, and the best 99 of his work is the early St Thomas in Newcastle, done in 1827–30. This is a strong and personal design. There is a similar strength on a smaller scale in Dobson's work at St Mary, Belford, in 1828; it was less personal but more archaeologically accurate at St Cuthbert, Greenhead, done a year or two earlier in 1826. This, minus the tower, is almost a copy of the genuine E.E. nearby at Haltwhistle. Dobson was also willing to work in the Norman fashion, though his only neo-Norman church within Northumberland is the extremely early example of 1831 at St James, Benwell. The *Greens* also turned to the Norman style once, in a fairly minor way, at Horsley in Redesdale in 1844. Indeed most of the neo-Norman work is small and minor, e.g. Duddo, 1832 by *Ignatius Bonomi*, North Sunderland, 1834 by *Salvin*, Cresswell, *c.* 1836, and Branxton, 1849; but the county contains one quite spectacular neo-Norman church, St 103-4 James, Morpeth, of 1843–6 by *Benjamin Ferrey*.

The mention of Ferrey is a reminder, as we move into the Victorian age, of how few churches there are in Northumberland by 100 architects of national repute. *Pugin* built the Roman Catholic Cathedral for Newcastle in 1842–4 (with the soaring spire added by *Dunn & Hansom* in 1860); *Salvin* built several serious and not very inspired churches for the Duke of Northumberland; *Butterfield* did one not especially interesting chapel (at Etal in 1858), *Blomfield* a completely uninteresting church at Longhirst in 1876. There is not a single *Scott* church in the county (though he did extensive restoration at St Nicholas, Newcastle), and the only national figure to supply a church of outstanding merit is *Pearson*, whose St George, Cullercoats, 1882–4, is the only C19 church in the county which is stone-vaulted throughout. It would be interesting to speculate why so few of these great men were able to respond to the quality of the county in the way *Shaw* achieved at Cragside. A useful model, perhaps, would have been the local architect *Thomas Austin* († 1875), whose beautiful restoration of Brinkburn Priory in 1858–9 showed respect for the solidity and plainness of the best medieval Northumbrian architecture. Austin, and in particular his later partner *R. J. Johnson* (1832–92), did much of the creditable church work in the county later in the century. Johnson's best churches (St Mary, Stannington, 1871; St Matthew, Summerhill Street, Newcastle, 1877; St Oswin, Wylam, 1886; All Saints, Gosforth, 1887) all show originality, increasing eclecticism, and a strong sense of mass and spatial awareness. He had been a pupil of G. G. Scott in his youth, along with J. J. Stephenson and E. R. Robson, and on his death was described by *The Builder* as among the best architects in England to have worked exclusively in the provinces. He does not stand alone. We have already had occasion to comment on the powerful group of local talents working in Newcastle in the first half of the C19, and their successors later in the century also included some good

architects. *Dobson* spans two generations. His later churches sometimes have an intricacy and delicacy not found in his earlier work
(St John, Otterburn, 1858) and sometimes an originality of design
(Jesmond Parish Church, Newcastle, 1857–61). Others who did
work which is worthy of attention were *A. B. Higham* (Holy Trinity,
Whitfield, 1859–60), *F. W. Rich* (St Gabriel, Heaton, Newcastle,
1898–1905), and in particular *Hicks & Charlewood*, who were the
most successful firm in the last years of the C 19 and on into the
C 20. Their churches and restorations are to be found throughout
the county and are almost always sensitively done.

Before we reach the end of the C 19, two unusual churches deserve
a mention. One is the extremely odd St John, Healey, of 1860 by
Major C. E. Davis of Bath; the other is the more interesting and
highly eclectic St Christopher, Gunnerton, of 1899 by the *Rev. J. C.
Hawes*. The most interesting church of all in the later years of the
C 19 is also a special case – St George, Jesmond, built in 1888–9 at 101–2
the expense of Charles Mitchell, Lord Armstrong's partner, to the
designs of *T. R. Spence*. The exterior is very noble and restrained
with a tall Italian campanile, but the interior is richly decorated in
an Arts-and-Crafts style approaching *art nouveau*. The scheme is a
rich synthesis of glass and woodwork, mosaic and bronze, and
includes two monuments by *Frampton* (who is represented, incidentally, elsewhere in the county by a statue of the young Victoria
at the Royal Victoria Infirmary, Newcastle, and some pieces of
garden statuary formerly at Pallinsburn, a house belonging to Mitchell's son, and now at Whitfield Hall).

The interior of St George's brings us to DECORATION, which is
generally a rather patchy affair in the C 19 churches. Very little
survives from the early part of the century. There are galleries at St
Thomas, Newcastle, at Belford and at Cornhill; box pews still at
Carham and Chillingham; a set of neo-Norman furnishings by *Ferrey*
at Morpeth, with frescoes by *Clayton & Bell* (1871); but most of the 104
early C 19 and early Victorian churches are bare. MONUMENTS of
any quality are few. The best of them by far are to be found in St
Nicholas, Newcastle, where there is a group of figures of 1801 by 71
Webber, author of the Garrick monument in Westminster Abbey.
Flaxman did one in 1813, *Rossi* a rather sensational one for Admiral
Collingwood in 1810, and *Baily* a nobly sentimental one in 1815 and
another in 1823 (also two at Whalton, of 1831 and 1846). There are
tablets everywhere by *Green* and by *Davies* of Newcastle and *Jopling*
of Gateshead. To the 1830s belong the impressive portraits in monuments large and small by *Dunbar*, and the three works by *Chantrey*
in the county, one being a fireplace made for Buckingham Palace
(at Matfen Hall), the other two monuments (Hartburn, 1834, Bamburgh, 1839). And that brings us into the Victorian age and especially
the work of the Northumbrian *John Graham Lough* (1798–1876),
responsible for monuments at Norham (1857) and Allendale, as well
as the 7 metre (23 ft) high statue on the Collingwood Monument of 109
1847 at Tynemouth. Two other highly characteristic early Victorian
monuments are to be found at St Paul, Alnwick, c. 1847 by *J. E.
Carew*, and at Howick, 1850 by *John Francis*. The Collingwood
Monument, designed by *Dobson*, is, of course, a public monument.
Two other much later C 19 monuments need mentioning here: both
fine studies of the elderly Queen Victoria, one at Tynemouth by

110 *Alfred Turner* (1902), the other at Newcastle (1903) in *Gilbert*'s exuberant style.

By the middle of the century the situation with regard to CHURCH DECORATION has begun to change a little, and there is plenty of STAINED GLASS of reasonable quality. *William Wailes*, one of the most successful artists in stained glass, was a Newcastle man, and a great deal of his work survives, though in the absence of documentary evidence it is not always certainly identified. Indeed much of the most attractive glass is without attribution. Among many anonymous windows, mention might be made of those at St Bartholomew, Whittingham, and St Maurice, Ellingham. At Haltwhistle Church (and also at Cragside) there is *Morris* glass of an early date. At Jesmond Presbyterian Church (now United Reformed – a fine church, incidentally, by *W. L. Newcombe*) there is later glass by *Morris & Co.* as well as a whole series by *Kempe*, whose glass is to be found in other churches in the county, too many to mention individually. *William Dyce* did the cartoons for a window carried out in Munich for St Paul, Alnwick – in a pure, entirely Raphaelesque style. *Henry Holiday* did a window at Hexham. *John W. Brown* and *C. W. Mitchell* did the fine windows at St George, Jesmond, where we started this survey of C 19 church decoration. Finally there is a group of churches in the N part of the county which have older glass inserted in the mid-C 19 by Archdeacon Thorp. They are large figures, probably C 17 Flemish, badly preserved but beautifully drawn and they are to be found, for example, at Bamburgh and Ellingham. A similar case concerns the C 16 stained glass at Earsdon Church, which came supposedly from the Great Hall, Hampton Court. It was installed, restored and probably enlarged by *Willement* and was the gift of Lord Hastings in 1874. No survey of C 19 glass in Northumberland should ignore the often beautiful plain glass which was inserted into many churches during restorations in the 1860s and 70s. These elaborate patterned leaded lights can produce coruscating effects with the light and the landscape. Most of them, in churches such as Ponteland, Elsdon and Bolam, are the work of the local architect *F. R. Wilson*, whose restorations take a little getting used to but can grow on one, especially the coarse but vigorous hammerbeam roofs he evidently had a penchant for.

And finally the FURNISHINGS AND FITTINGS of the later C 19. *Lutyens* did a very early reredos for Berwick, but once again most of the best work is local. The Newcastle carver *Ralph Hedley* and the firm he founded were capable of work of the highest order. It is to be found among other places at All Saints, Gosforth, St George, Jesmond, and St Nicholas, Newcastle. *Hicks & Charlewood* also designed fittings of a high standard for their churches and restorations; especially fine is Hicks's St John Lee.

So far no mention has been made of the ROMAN CATHOLIC CHURCH in Northumberland except for a brief reference to the Cathedral in Newcastle. A few relatively early churches are to be found in the county. The earliest is an C 18 house at Morpeth, which is no longer in use as a church; the oldest proper church is All Saints at Thropton of the late C 18 or early C 19 (much altered in 1842), which has the charming motif of a tripartite division between the

nave and the chancel, the division being by means of pendants where
one might have expected columns. Berwick built its Catholic chapel
in 1829, and Hexham has a particularly pretty church of 1830 in a
castellated Gothick style. It was designed by the incumbent, *Fr
Singleton*. *Bonomi* was responsible for St Oswald at Bellingham
(1839), and *Goldie* did a competent job at Wooler (1856); but most
of the later churches are by the firm of *A. M. Dunn* and *E. J. Hansom*.

The earliest NONCONFORMIST CHAPEL of the C 19, and the
most impressive, is the Brunswick Methodist Chapel of 1820–1 at
Newcastle. Blyth has the large Central Methodist Church (1868) in
the Italianate style, with a lavish interior. Nothing else is as impressive as these, except the Jesmond Presbyterian Church by Newcombe
which has already been mentioned and the large former Congregational Church, St James, Northumberland Road, Newcastle,
designed in 1882 by *T. Lewis Banks* and highly original for its date.

The VICTORIAN AGE meant to Northumberland a prodigious
rise of Tyneside industry, of shipyard and ordnance factory, and
also of coal export ($3\frac{1}{4}$ million tons in 1846; 12 million in 1894; 20
million in 1911). Names like George Stephenson and Lord Armstrong are the real heroes of C 19 Northumbrian history, and the
great civil engineering works like the Royal Border Bridge at Berwick
(1847–50) and Newcastle Central Station (1845–50) are the chief
monuments of the age. In 1855, when, at Ruskin's suggestion, the
inner courtyard at Wallington was glazed and the arcades and walls
filled with wall paintings of Northumbrian history by the young Pre-
Raphaelite *William Bell Scott*, the last of the pictures was made to
deal with iron and coal. It shows the brand-new High Level Bridge
at Newcastle and working drawings for a railway locomotive. These
images of a new world are side by side with botanically accurate
portraits of plants – a Victorian ideal of ornamentation – of which
Ruskin himself did one. Ruskin incidentally was also interested in
the curious educative and artistic enterprise of *Louisa, Marchioness* 108
of Waterford, who in 1861 began to paint wall paintings of suitable
subjects for the village school of her planned estate village at Ford.
He was in the end disappointed with her work, which is indeed more
influenced by Michelangelo than the pre-Raphaelites.

Lady Waterford felt very much the châtelaine at her castle at
Ford, and as there was not very much there for a baronial life except
two towers from the medieval castle and a mansion made very
Gothic in the late C 18, she made up her mind to make Ford what
it might have been. *David Bryce* of Edinburgh was her chosen
architect and work on a big scale went on in the 1860s. But Lady
Waterford had been preceded by the Duke of Northumberland,
who in the 1850s secured *Salvin*'s services to convert Alnwick 21
from a flimsy Gothic fantasy into a serious and substantial castle.
Much was lost in the process, since Robert Adam's interiors were replaced. But the new work, designed and made for the Duke by a
team of Italians, is the essence of mid-Victorian opulence, rich,
glowing and intricate, far more comfortable, perhaps, than Adam's
elegance.

So much for events in the castles. Otherwise, except for those fine
engineering jobs which are dealt with above in a separate section of
this introduction, Northumberland has surprisingly little to con-
tribute to the picture of Victorian architecture. There is a reasonable

collection of COUNTRY MANSIONS. A brief list will suffice: Middleton Hall, near Belford (1871), possibly by *David Brandon*; Longridge
Tower, near Horncliffe (*c.* 1876), by *J. C. & C. A. Buckler*; Tillmouth
Park, near Twizel (1882), by *Charles Barry Jun.*; Ridley Hall (1891)
by *Horatio Adamson*; and work at Jesmond Dene House in the 1890s
by *F. W. Rich*. All of these are in the Tudor style, with the latest,
Jesmond Dene House, as one might expect, the most freely composed. There are also a few Gothic houses. One is Shotley Hall,
designed in 1863 by the owner, *Thomas Wilson*; another is by *F. R.
Wilson*, Salvin's assistant at Alnwick, who built Cheswick House in
a jolly High Victorian Gothic in 1859–62. But none of these is of
more than local interest. Only one architect produced work of wider
significance in the second half of the C 19, and that was *Norman
Shaw*. Shaw did a number of buildings in Northumberland. An
outstanding example of his later Baroque manner is Chesters of
1891, an enlargement of a house of 1771. It is a composition of
considerable sweeping grandeur, a quite splendid re-interpretation
of the early C 18, with perhaps an acknowledgement of Northumberland's Roman past in the curved colonnade that overlooks
the Roman fort of Chesters. Shaw used the same style on a gigantic
scale at Haggerston Castle, a house now surviving only in fragments,
but fragments which clearly reveal how monumental the house was.
106 Twenty years earlier he had found a quite different style for Cragside,
built in its highly Wagnerian position near Rothbury for Lord Armstrong – one expects all the time to hear Valkyries ride through
the skies over its manifold gables and chimneystacks. And this
romanticism remained unquenchable in the Northumbrian air. It
persuaded Lord Armstrong in 1894 to restore Bamburgh Castle into
his second grand residence, and it was bound to attract *Sir Edwin
Lutyens*.

In his CONVERSIONS of existing buildings without radically changing their character, Lutyens served the county well. At Whalton in
1908–9 he executed a very subtle conversion of four village houses
to form Whalton Manor, a charming composition of house and
garden. At Meldon Park, *c.* 1930, he altered the staircase, putting
new balusters in and adding stucco wall decoration; presumably he
also did the Venetian stair window, the whole a Baroque insertion
rather at odds with the Neo-classical house. At Blagdon Hall he
reordered the gardens in the 1930s. But his most admired Northumbrian work is the transformation, begun in 1903, of the old fort
107 on Holy Island into Lindisfarne Castle, an eyrie with nine bedrooms,
for his ideal client, Edward Hudson, owner of *Country Life*. It has a
handkerchief-sized *Jekyll* garden nearby.

From Lutyens to *Baker*, his friend and enemy. Sir Herbert is also
represented by a conversion – an ambitious one at Howick, after a
fire, in 1928. Somewhat earlier, in the 1880s and 90s two of *Dobson*'s
country houses on the fringes of Newcastle were extended and the
interiors lavishly refurbished in the Arts-and-Crafts style for local
manufacturers. At Jesmond Dene the architects were *F. W. Rich*
and *Norman Shaw*, at Jesmond Towers (now La Sagesse School)
T. R. Spence, the Armstrong-Mitchell firm's architect. Country
house design other than this was mostly the work of two local
firms. *Mauchlen & Weightman* in the years after 1918 were the
most popular. Their best new house, Whitton Grange (1921), is a

successful essay in late C 17 style. Elsewhere they made effective
additions to houses like Doxford Hall and Tughall Hall. *George
Reavell* of Alnwick was the principal of the other firm. His best house
is the solidly Arts-and-Crafts Hethpool House (1919).

TYNESIDE SECULAR ARCHITECTURE of 1850 to 1914 presents a
different story from the rest of the county. As in the first half of the
C 19, the architects were almost exclusively talented local men.
Richard Grainger, as we have seen, had given Newcastle a centre of
great spaciousness, dignity and unity. It was surrounded by medieval
streets of varying width, fronted by mostly C 17 and C 18 timber-
framed and brick houses. Many of these were demolished in the
second half of the C 19 and replaced by premises more suitable
for the commercial enterprises which met the needs of a rapidly
increasing population. The fashionable Gothic style was adopted
for many of the new buildings, especially those of the 1870s on the
W extension of Grainger Street, created to link the town centre with
the railway station, and for the richly ornamented Neville Hall of
the Institute of Mining and Mechanical Engineers of 1869–72 by
A. M. Dunn. Both medieval and Tudor styles were successfully
adapted by *Dunn, Hansom & Dunn*, who designed the new Medical
School for Durham University (1887; now used by Newcastle
Polytechnic), and *W. H. Knowles* for the College of Art and Design
(1911; now the Fine Art Department of Newcastle University). The
College of Science by *R. J. Johnson* (1887–8; now the Armstrong
Building of the University) shares the Tudor style, which was
popular until the mid-C 20 for academic buildings, as the University's Old Library Building of 1923–6 by *A. Dunbar Smith* shows.

For financial institutions, Italian Renaissance was the favoured
style. The change from early Renaissance to Baroque can be followed: the Trustee Savings Bank of 1862–3 by *J. E. Watson*, in
the later part of Grainger Street, has round-headed windows and
pedimented centres; the National Provincial Bank in Mosley Street,
1870–2 by *Gibson*, giant pilasters and pedimented windows; and
the bank built in Collingwood Street for Hodgkin, Barnet, Pease,
Spence & Co. by *R. J. Johnson* in 1891, a *piano nobile* with Gibbs
surrounds and a magnificent swagged frieze below a deep modillion
cornice and balustrade. Towards the end of the century, Tyneside
kept pace with the growing popularity of the Free Style. The great
lightening of spirit is seen in the work of *F. W. Rich* and of *B. F.
Simpson*, whose style is a cheerful mixture of flowing *art nouveau*,
noble Baroque and exotic Oriental. Simpson enlivened the city
centre with his exuberant Emerson Chambers (*c.* 1903) and possibly
with the *art nouveau* Reid shopfront, also in Blackett Street. Like
Emerson Chambers, *Simpson, Lawson & Rayne*'s Half Moon Chambers in Bigg Market (1902–5) is a large composition full of lively
detail. Their more sober office and power station building of 1901
in Melbourne Street for the Electric Tramways skilfully combines
utility and beauty.

The BAROQUE REVIVAL extends from the vigour of Sunlight
Chambers (1901–2 by Lever's architect, *W. & S. Owen*) in the Bigg
Market to the cool clarity of the Royal Grammar School of 1907 by
Sir Edwin Cooper, extremes of a movement which at its centre
produced such comforting and dignified civic buildings as the Town

Hall and the group beside it at Wallsend, by *E. F. W. Liddle & P. L. Brown* (1907–8). Free Baroque unifies the linked pavilions and administration block of Newcastle's Royal Victoria Infirmary by *Newcombe & Adams* (1900–6). W. L. Newcombe was a Newcastle architect; Percy Adams had begun his career with Stephen Salter, architect to the Royal College of Surgeons. The highly original work of *F. W. Rich*, displayed in 1893 at the Ouseburn Schools, carried on into the new century, with the long frontage of his Bolbec Hall (1907–9) in Westgate Road neither overwhelming its Greek Revival neighbour, the Literary and Philosophical Society, nor shrinking from its challenge. References to Italian origins were still popular with banks. Barclays Bank in Collingwood Street was especially elaborate, because the original intention was to build a hotel. It was completed in 1903 by *Cackett & Burns Dick*, but begun in 1899 by *Oliver & Leeson*, a firm which built many large offices in Edwardian Newcastle, always with well-executed detail and grand proportions. Cathedral Buildings and Milburn House in Dean Street, the former Co-operative Wholesale Society warehouse and offices in Blandford Square (now the Science Museum and Archives Department) and the Sun Insurance office in Collingwood Street are all good examples of their work. *Cackett & Burns Dick* were notable among local practices working in this mood, which tended towards the *art nouveau* in the Laing Art Gallery of 1903–4. Their Cross House (1911) in Westgate Road is a particularly imposing wedge-plan building, its steel frame clad in Portland stone. After the 1914–18 war, *R. Mackellar* joined the firm, which subsequently designed several important public buildings: a red-and-white Tudor Students' Union for King's College, Durham University (now the University of Newcastle); the architectural detailing of the Tyne Bridge; and the Central Police Station and Magistrates Court of 1931 in Pilgrim Street. *Cackett & Burns Dick*'s Spanish City at Whitley Bay, a domed pleasure palace of 1908–10 for Tyneside workers on holiday, was built of ferro-concrete, the most important new building material of the 1890s and 1900s. It was employed early on Tyneside because of the opening of a local branch of the civil engineers *L. G. Mouchel*, who were licensed to use the *Hennebique* method of construction. It made massive proportions and wide spans possible, and gave a stone-like appearance with a facility for creating moulded detail. The best surviving examples N of the Tyne show its versatility: the stark classicism of the warehouse built in 1899–1900 at the E end of Newcastle's Quayside for the Co-operative Wholesale Society contrasts with the Spanish City's frivolous Baroque.

Now for C 20 PUBLIC BUILDINGS in county and city. As local administration has developed, so new MUNICIPAL BUILDINGS have been provided. Northumberland County Hall, which was set in Newcastle's royal castle, was built in 1910 by *J. A. Bain*, hugely enlarged by *Cackett, Burns Dick & Mackellar* in 1929–34, and then replaced in 1982 with a spreading building of informal style in brick at Morpeth. Newcastle's Town Hall opposite St Nicholas's Cathedral survived the transition to City in 1882, but by the mid-C 20 could not contain all the City's offices. It was demolished and they were more efficiently housed on a site outside the medieval
126 town N of the present commercial area in the rather grand Civic

Centre of 1960–8 by the City Architect, *George Kenyon*, full of prestigious works of art and using traditional materials of the highest quality to clad a steel frame. Newcastle's UNIVERSITY BUILDINGS had demonstrated the academic world's fondness for the Tudor and Jacobean style, as we have seen. A very different spirit ruled post-1945, after the master plan had been drawn up by the Professor of Architecture, *W. B. Edwards*, and *Sir Howard Robertson*. The elegant Stephenson Building by *Edwards & Manby* (1952), *Easton & Robertson, Cusdin, Preston & Smith*'s rear extension of the library, with full-height glazed apse (1959), and the striking Herschel Building, completed as the Physics Building in 1962 by *Sir Basil Spence*, represent the best of their time. Also in the early 1960s, *William Whitfield* made monumental additions to the Students' Union. At the time of writing the most recent addition has been the highly successful Robinson Library of 1983 by *Faulkner Brown Hendy Watkinson Stonor*.

During the inter-war period the COMMERCIAL CENTRE OF NEWCASTLE took on a new shape and scale. The most advanced and cosmopolitan building of the 1920s is the North Eastern Electricity Supply Company's Carliol House in Pilgrim Street, designed by *Burnet, Tait & Lorne* with the local firm *L. J. Couves & Partners*. The change of scale is particularly noticeable in the large shops which were built throughout the 1920s and 1930s, especially in Northumberland Street, which became a main route after the opening of the Tyne Bridge in 1928 and the straightening of Pilgrim Street. The Newcastle Co-operative Society replaced most of its C19 buildings in Newgate Street, in two stages from 1931, with a superb Art Deco store designed by *L. G. Ekins* of the C.W.S. London office. In passing, it is worth noting two buildings elsewhere in the county which are also International in inspiration: West Monkseaton Railway Station (1936; *see* Whitley Bay), with its flat roof, curved white entrance walls and metal window frames, and the pithead baths erected for the Miners Welfare Committee by *F. G. Frizzell*, of which, sadly, the only good example to have survived N of the Tyne is at Lynemouth Colliery. (Over a dozen were noted in the First Edition of 1957.)

After the Second World War, Newcastle became established as the major shopping and entertainment centre of the region and the massive replanning of the city centre which was undertaken in the 1960s was followed by a transport scheme of similar scale. By the time the huge and introverted Eldon Square Shopping Centre was opened in 1978 and the Tyneside Rapid Transport System ('the Metro') began operating in 1980, some aspects of the plans of the 1960s had been dropped; but not before many of the buildings of the historic centre had been destroyed for new roads and new developments which were not always of the highest quality.

Tyneside beyond the centre of Newcastle changed rapidly after the First World War. Much of the Victorian and Edwardian HOUSING, described by Henry A. Mess in his social survey *Industrial Tyneside* (1928) as small, densely packed and overcrowded, was demolished and the inhabitants moved to large new LOCAL AUTHORITY HOUSING ESTATES on the edges of the towns, begun under the 1919 Housing Act and continued with varying forms of government help between the wars. Despite best efforts, only the estimate of 4,700 'working class houses' needed in Newcastle and 424 needed in Whitley Bay had been met by 1928, Mess noted.

Mess recognized the sound construction, fair accommodation and near-uniqueness of the Tyneside flat (described on p. 98 by Dr Linsley), but criticized the layout of the streets. In general they cut straight across the contours, which may have been efficient for drainage but made walking and transport difficult. Mess pointed to the better layout at Lemington, where Newburn Urban District Council had begun a different sort of housing after the 1919 Housing Act under the guidance of *W. A. Harvey*, whose best-known housing was designed for Cadbury at Bournville. These inter-war council estates showed the influence of the garden city movement. In Newcastle the first sign of the new philosophy had already been seen as early as 1908 at Walkerville, at the E boundary, where in Rosewood Crescent and its neighbours still surviving semi-detached 'model cottages' for sale were designed by a group of architects for the Walker Model Housing Exhibition. In Newcastle these principles were developed in the Walker Estate ('the garden suburb') begun in 1919 by *F. L. Thompson, R. Dann and S. P. Taylor*, High Heaton Estate of the 1930s, designed by *R. G. Roberts*, the Corporation Architect, and taking variety of form and materials from the vernacular revival movement, and the Pendower Estate, Benwell, which was also begun in 1919 but continued in the 1920s by *Cackett, Dick & Mackellar*. Along the main roads out of the Tyneside towns spread ribbons of 'semi-detached' private houses of modest pretension and little design consciousness, which only sometimes followed garden suburb examples in their layout.

It was not until the YEARS AFTER 1945 that new ideas appeared, again in the public sector, where the need for more houses was met by prefabricating as much of the buildings as possible in factories. Of the many designs which were adopted, two are particularly notable on Tyneside for their success; the most numerous is the single-storey Tarran, the most surprising the two-storey 'Howard' by *F. Gibberd*. Examples of both are to be found in Gosforth, e.g. St Aidan's Close and Rydal Road. Greatly increased demand led public authorities away from factory-built individual homes towards larger and taller buildings containing many units – the high-rise flats of the sixties. The best have survived, the worst have gone. Among the best are the multi-storey blocks in Jesmond Vale and Shieldfield, Newcastle, designed by *Douglas Wise & Partners*, 1967. The poor seven-storey blocks at Elswick have been demolished and replaced with low-rise housing, and at Killingworth, though the two-storey houses of the post-1945 development are still in use, the linked tower blocks have gone. Private housing seldom took the multi-storey form, but where it did it was built to high standards, e.g. the Beacon House flats (1962) near St Mary's Island at Whitley Bay, the only one built of three blocks designed for the site by *Ryder & Yates* in the early 1960s.

In the 1960s two large comprehensive development areas were created by local authorities in the form of TOWNSHIPS – Killingworth to take overspill from Tyneside, Cramlington to give new life to a decayed industrial area. In neither place, despite the provision of leisure and shopping facilities, were cohesive communities successfully established. The same is true of the contemporary

Kenton Bar Estate in Gosforth (1964–8 by *Ryder & Yates & Partners*), with its stark uncluttered design. In reaction to this type of mass rehousing, the community architecture movement began and found its supreme expression in the world-famous redevelopment of Byker by *Ralph Erskine* for the City of Newcastle, from 129 1968. Here, where Tyneside flats once filled the hillside between the shipyards below and the engineering works above, small houses cluster and the high flats of the 'Byker Wall', as it is affectionately known, undulate behind them. The steeply sloped old people's home rides high over all at the w end of the wall, with views of the whole river. Variety of scale and form, texture and colour are the visible signs of the architect's high regard for the human part of the equation which makes good housing. The whole undertaking was carried out in consultation with the people of the area.

A parallel development of shopping from the corner shop of the C19 through the high-street grocers of the earlier C20 to the supermarkets on the outskirts of the town built in the 1980s has given the suburbs of Newcastle, as of all large towns, a sort of tithe barn of our time. While providing large-scale shopping areas they adopt the style of the aisled barn, with high gabled doors for the trolleys.

The heavy engineering industries which had generated so much wealth and filled Tyneside with parallel ridges of Welsh slate on the long terraces of Tyneside flats had also engendered FACTORIES AND WORKSHOPS, memorable mostly for their enormous mass of hard red brick and for the black smoke from their tall chimneys. Most of them vanished in the years of reconstruction, between 1960 and 1980, replaced by sleek clean sheds. In w Newcastle, where once Armstrong's factories spread along the riverbank from Elswick to Scotswood, there is now at Scotswood *Ryder, Yates & Partners'* Vickers factory, a bold design of 1981–2 set alongside the river. More often the striking buildings of a shipbuilding yard or a colliery have been replaced by a cluster of modest little factories and workshops for small enterprises and light industries, seldom distinguished, seldom offensive, and, with their brick-clad walls and brightly painted doors, as like houses as they can be. More impressive are the big post-1945 buildings which met the needs of new industries on entirely new sites. The first of these is Northumberland's only outlier of the modern movement factories so numerous around London: the Wills Factory, designed by the company's own architect 125 and built just inside Newcastle's boundary in 1946–50, has an enormous brick-and-concrete-clad steel frame which belongs to the 1930s in style, and may have been designed before the war. The best example of such architecture from after the Second World War is the friendly offices designed in the 1950s for Messrs Hedley (now Procter & Gamble) by *Sidney Burn* with *Anthony Chitty*, which fit unobtrusively into suburban Gosforth. The offices and research station at Killingworth commissioned by the gas industry from 127–8 *Ryder, Yates & Partners* in the 1960s introduced a new language of design: clear bold statements on a site newly landscaped to obliterate the dereliction of dead collieries.

In 1974, the historic county of Northumberland was divided into two. In the larger part – rural Northumberland, with a population of 299,905 in 1981 – much of the uplands is a designated National

Park, with the care for the landscape and its buildings that results. In the country, though most houses are still in the hands of private owners, some have found new uses or, like Callaly Castle, have been skilfully converted into flats. The geographically smaller but more populous part (the Districts of Newcastle upon Tyne and North Tyneside) belongs to Tyne and Wear (population 1,143,245 in 1981) which straddles the Tyne, with commercial and population pressures centred on the City of Newcastle (population 192,454 in 1981). There has been much sweeping away of old industrial buildings along the banks of the Tyne, where the 'Regeneration of the Quayside', begun by Newcastle City Council in 1980, has been continued by Tyne and Wear Development Corporation, the planning authority for the banks of the Tyne from Newcastle to the harbour at the river's mouth. In Newcastle at least, old buildings in Sandhill and the Close have been expertly restored for new uses (for example, Nos. 28–30 the Close by *Simpson & Brown*), and new buildings, such as Blue Anchor Quay by the *Napper Collerton Partnership* (1987), designed sympathetically to fill the gaps. The impressive Law Courts of 1986–90 by the same architects, a major feature of this renewal, is set among the surviving evidence of many centuries of Tyneside's endeavour – from the medieval houses in the Close, to Trinity House on its C16 site in Broad Chare and the C19 warehouses of Pandon and Milk Market – and is dramatic evidence of the late C20 concern for integrating old and new.

FURTHER READING

Northumberland has a long tradition of archaeology, beginning with John Horsley's unsurpassed *Britannia Romana* of 1732, followed by Henry MacLauchlan's surveys for the Duke of Northumberland in the 1850s and Collingwood Bruce's monographs on Hadrian's Wall from 1863 onwards. In 1893, before the *Victoria County History* was conceived, the Northumberland County History Committee had started on an independent *History of Northumberland*; over the next half-century fifteen volumes were published, covering most of the county not included in John Hodgson's important and exhaustive but incomplete earlier *History* (1820–58). The coverage of individual buildings in the early C 20 set is rather variable; there are some good detailed accounts by writers such as W. H. Knowles and H. L. Honeyman, who also contributed many papers to periodicals such as those of the Society of Antiquaries of Newcastle upon Tyne (the excellent *Archaeologia Aeliana* and *Proceedings*) and the *Transactions of the Architectural and Archaeological Society of Durham and Northumberland*. Among general guide books, that of W. W. Tomlinson (1888) is useful, although J. E. Morris's volume in the *Little Guide* series (1916) is more reliable on matters architectural, although necessarily brief. Valuable recent accounts of a number of the county's more important sites and buildings, compiled when the Royal Archaeological Institute held its Summer Meeting at Newcastle, can be found in the pages of the *Archaeological Journal* for 1976.

Most of the archaeology of Northumberland has appeared in the pages of *Archaeologia Aeliana*, a county journal of exceptional quality. A notable achievement was that of George Jobey, who recorded the surviving prehistoric earthworks in more than a score of papers in '*AA*' between 1957 and 1988. A wide-ranging collection of essays on the archaeology of the county, with an extensive bibliography, was published in a volume presented to Jobey in 1984: *Between and Beyond the Walls* (ed. R. Miket and C. Burgess). The literature relating to the Roman period, and especially to Hadrian's Wall, is immense. Only three or four titles, however, are essential to the enquirer: J. C. Bruce's *Handbook to the Roman Wall* (13 editions, 1863 to 1978) which describes the remains; Eric Birley's *Research on Hadrian's Wall* (1961), which recounts the progress of antiquarian knowledge and provides some valuable summaries; and two readable and complementary overviews, both with the same title, *Hadrian's Wall*, one by David Breeze and Brian Dobson (3rd ed. 1987), the other by Stephen Johnson (1989). For later periods, a benchmark excavation of medieval buildings in the county was that at West Whelpington, to be found in *Archaeologia Aeliana* for 1962, 1970 and 1987.

H. M. Colvin, *The History of the King's Works* (1973–82), provides insight into a number of places, particularly Bamburgh and Berwick, as part of its national survey; but the most detailed account of the castles and medieval fortified buildings of Northumberland is still Cadwallader Bates's *Border Holds of Northumberland* (1891), first published as a volume of *Archaeologia Aeliana*; unfortunately its coverage is only partial. A fuller list, with pocket histories and an excellent bibliography, is provided by J. D. C. King, *Castellarium Anglicanum* (1983). The RCHM *Shielings and Bastles* (1970) provides a more in-depth study of two types of post-medieval building, although based on rather localized fieldwork. Several of the better-known buildings have their own guide books, which as usual are very variable in quality; the English Heritage guides (Aydon, Berwick, Norham and Prudhoe) set a high standard.

As regards ecclesiastical architecture, valuable accounts of pre-Conquest churches are to be found in the Taylors' *Anglo-Saxon Architecture* (1965), and the form of the early cathedral at Hexham has taxed many researchers from C. C. Hodges onwards; for a reconstruction, see the account by Edward Gilbert in *Saint Wilfred at Hexham* (1974).

The later medieval parish churches have received less attention. F. R. Wilson's *An Architectural Survey of the Churches in the Archdeaconry of Lindisfarne* (1870) is a valuable source for plans and drawings before and after Victorian restorations; and in the 1970s and 80s a number of parish churches received detailed attention from G. W. D. Briggs in the pages of *Archaeologia Aeliana*. There is no overall county-wide account of the monastic sites of Northumberland, but Brinkburn, Lindisfarne and Tynemouth are covered by English Heritage guides.

When it comes to post-medieval buildings, very little has been published especially on vernacular architecture; this lack is reflected in the pages of general architectural works covering the whole country, which regularly dismiss Northumberland in a few frustrating lines, although H. M. Colvin's *Biographical Dictionary of British Architects 1600–1840* (1978) is an essential tool. A selection of the larger country houses have appeared in the pages of *Country Life*, e.g. Gervase Jackson-Stop's accounts of Beaufront (5 February 1976) and Eglingham Hall (27 November 1975). Belsay has a very good English Heritage guide. Kerry Downes, *Vanbrugh* (1977), provides some useful insights on Seaton Delaval. A. Saint, *Richard Norman Shaw* (1976), is equally useful on the county. Peter Leach, *The Life and Work of James Paine* (1989), features several important Northumbrian houses. Peter Willis wrote an effective account of Capability Brown in Northumberland for the *Journal of the Garden History Society* (1983). T. Faulkner and A. Greg's *John Dobson: Newcastle Architect* (1987) covers the manifold works of one of the region's most prolific talents.

So much for the county as a whole. C. Rayne, *The History and Antiquities of North Durham* (1852), deals with those parts of Northumberland which until 1844 were detached parts of County Durham. Newcastle upon Tyne is fortunate in having one of the earliest of all English town histories – *Chorographia or a survey of Newcastle upon Tyne* by William Grey, published in 1649 and reprinted in 1970 by Frank Graham from Reid's 1884 edition. With Grey, as with so many writers, accounts of contemporary events and of the town as he knew it are more reliable than his interpretations of the preceding centuries. Two scholarly writers of the C18 give us descriptions of the town's public buildings and transcripts of historical documents as well as much that relates to the history and economy of the whole area. The first was Henry Bourne, whose *The History of Newcastle upon Tyne* was published in 1739, three years after his death. The second was John Brand, whose two-volume *The History and Antiquities of the Town and County of Newcastle upon Tyne, including an Account of the coal Trade* (1789) is an indispensable source. The next major book to describe the town was by Eneas Mackenzie: *A Descriptive and Historical Account of the Town and County of Newcastle upon Tyne, including the Borough of Gateshead* (1827). (His *An Historical, Topographical and Descriptive View of the County of Northumberland* (1825) is also extremely useful.) Thomas Oliver, *A New Picture of Newcastle* (1831, reprinted by Frank Graham in 1970), Collard and Ross, *Architectural and Picturesque Views in Newcastle upon Tyne* (1841), and W. H. Knowles and J. R. Boyle, *Vestiges of Old Newcastle and Gateshead*, are among the most useful of many C 19 publications. Further reading can usefully include maps: a superb source is Oliver's large-scale 1830 map of Newcastle and Gateshead, which with its accompanying Book of Reference identifies the owners of all the properties in the town. Engraved views of the town, especially taking a southern viewpoint, are plentiful. *The Prospect of Newcastle upon Tyne from the south* (1745), by the Buck brothers, is a wonderful aid to research as well as to the imagination (*see* pp. 408–9 below). In 1723 James Corbridge published a map with little pictures of buildings around the border, as was the fashion then.

In the C 20, archaeological research in the city (up to 1976) is summarized in R. B. Harbottle and P. A. G. Clack, 'Newcastle upon Tyne: Archaeology and Development', which forms Appendix A of *Archaeology in the North*, ed. Harding (1976). Much of the research appeared in the pages of *Archaeologia Aeliana*, and the volumes of the fifth series contain many reports and studies since then, especially concerning the Castle, the Town Wall and Black Friars (articles by R. B. Harbottle and her colleagues M. Ellison, R. Fraser and J. Nolan), the Quayside area (C. O'Brien), and Trinity House (G. McCombie). Further down the river, D. C. Kear's 'Clifford's Fort and the Defence of the Tyne', in *Archaeologia Aeliana* (1986), is an excavation report with a history of the fort.

The River Tyne has of course made Newcastle what it is and many of the buildings along its banks can be understood with the help of J. Guthrie, *The River Tyne, its History and Resources* (1880). S. Middlebrook, *Newcastle upon Tyne* (1950 and 1968), is a fine study pulling together all strands of history and not forgetting buildings. The riverside's buildings are helpfully drawn into their historical context in the Royal Commission on the Historical Monuments of England, *Tyne and Wear, vol 1, Tyneside, An Architectural Survey of Urban Development Corporation Areas* (1990). For the wider setting, N. McCord, *North East England: an Economic and Social History* (1979), and Fraser and Emsley, *Tyneside* (1973), are especially useful.

For the C 18 and early C 19 buildings of Newcastle there is no better introduction than the Tyne and Wear Museums 1980 exhibition catalogue *The Tyneside Classical Tradition*. A fuller account of the activities of Richard Grainger is L. Wilkes and G. Dodds, *Tyneside Classical: the Newcastle of Grainger, Dobson and Clayton* (1964), and the factors involved in the redevelopment of central Newcastle are examined by T. Faulkner in 'The early nineteenth century planning of Newcastle upon Tyne', in *Planning Perspectives 5* (1990). The Faulkner and Greg catalogue to accompany the John Dobson exhibition in 1987 has already been mentioned. For inter-war buildings on Tyneside there is a useful and well-illustrated survey in Buckley and Walker, *Between the Wars. Architecture and Design on Tyneside 1919–1939*, a Newcastle Polytechnic Gallery catalogue of 1982. The buildings of the University are described in A. R. Roberts's B.Arch dissertation, Newcastle (1988), *An Architectural History of the University of Newcastle upon Tyne, 1887–1958*. Humbler buildings have fared no better in Newcastle than in the county at large. The only published study to set the Tyneside flat in its national context is S. Muthesius, *The English Terraced House* (1982). There is much information on churches in *A Social History of the Diocese of Newcastle*, ed. W. S. F. Pickering (1982). Finally there are two more Tyne and Wear Museums Service exhibition catalogues, one on *Twelve Newcastle Churches* (1982), which is brief but good, and a catalogue/book of 1988 on the work of the sculptor Ralph Hedley.

NORTHUMBERLAND

ACKLINGTON

ST JOHN THE DIVINE. 1860 by *James Deason*. E.E. style; four-bay aisled nave and chancel, with tall steep-pitched roofs.

The village is no more than a single street, with some minor but attractive C19 buildings. W of the church is the OLD VICARAGE of 1861, quite a creditable essay in a Gothic-cum-Tudor style.

ACKLINGTON STATION, ½ m. SW. 1847 by *Benjamin Green* for the Newcastle and Berwick Railway Company. Now a private house. H-plan, in the Greens' usual Tudor style (cf. Warkworth). Well-preserved contemporary GOODS SHED with big segmental-pointed arches and smaller arched openings in the gables.

BRAINSHAUGH. *See* p. 199.

ACOMB

The old village, once a leadmining centre, is no more than a single street. There are quite a number of dated houses. On the N side from W to E are CHARE HEAD, 1691, with its doorway moulding stepped on the lintel; TOWN HEAD, 1796, still with a plain chamfered doorway; TYNEVALE HOUSE, 1754, with a band and tooled wedge-shaped lintels, and MIDDLE FARMHOUSE, 1826. On the S side is ACOMB HIGH HOUSE, with a doorway dated 1694 but much enlarged *c.* 1820, then the little square with a PANT, an C18 stone structure with a C19 cast-iron lion mask hydrant. Further E the MINERS ARMS of 1750 and NORTH VIEW with an upper-cruck roof where the carpenter's numbering is, unusually, in arabic numerals. THE BARRACKS, 1730, is interesting and seems to have been built as a semi-detached pair: it is said to derive its name from having been used as a leadminers' lodging. Finally, further down the hill, the 1871 METHODIST CHAPEL with the usual gabled front.

ACOMB HOUSE, to the S of the square. Five-bay three-storey house, dated 1737. Rusticated quoins, and doorway and windows in keyed segmental-arched surrounds. Panelling and other internal features suggest that C17 fabric is incorporated. NW wing of *c.* 1900 and E wing of 1925.

ACOMB MILL, ¼ m. S on the Birkey Burn. Late C18 three-storey mill, with integral miller's house dated 1728. The millstream was insufficient to turn the internal overshot wheel in dry summers, so the watermill was operated first probably in conjunction with the WINDMILL on the hill to the S and then in the C19 with a steam engine on the gable wall. The windmill, now part of

LANTHORN COTTAGE, retains a round, tapered three-storeyed tower with chamfered windows and a doorway dated 1720, with the initials RR (Richard Ridley).

HALFWAY HOUSE COTTAGES, $\frac{1}{2}$m. N. One cottage is a picturesque conversion of the ENGINE HOUSE of the former Fallowfield Lead Mine, built in 1779. The three-stage chimneystack still functions as the cottage chimney. The second cottage to the E was the miners' 'shop' or lodging house.

ST JOHN LEE. *See* p. 557.

1000

ACTON
1 m. N of Felton

ACTON HALL. The five-bay two-storey S front is almost identical with that dated 1732 at Elyhaugh. The central door has a big bolection-moulded surround with the mouldings carried up over a semicircular lintel panel containing a coat of arms. A cornice above the door has been removed but its console brackets remain. The windows are all in surrounds with a bold convex moulding. Door and ground-floor windows have detached segmental bands, hardly big enough to be called pediments, above. The W end shows earlier masonry and a big stepped stack; the rear span of the house probably goes with the early C 18 front, whilst the three-bay E extension must be early C 19. STABLE BLOCK dated 1724, altered early C 19, with centre tower-cum-dovecote. The GATE-SCREEN beside the road to the N has low piers with bulgy rustication and odd drum-like finials with rustic plant designs carved in relief. These may be late C 17 or perhaps rather rustic early C 18 work.

ACTON HOUSE. Quite a grand house of *c.* 1781, attributed to *William Newton*, for Robert Lisle. The design here is very close to that of Shawdon Hall (q.v.). Two-storey seven-bay ashlar front with a three-bay centrepiece, where panelled giant Ionic pilasters carry a fluted frieze and a pediment. The interior is largely contemporary, with many good features, including an imperial stair with a Roman Doric screen at the foot and an Ionic screen at the top. In the entrance hall is a fireplace with a cast-iron radial hearth, similar to two at Newton Hall (Newton-on-the-Moor). An earlier C 18 house was incorporated as a NE wing, but this was largely remodelled *c.* 1920.

NELSON MONUMENT, $\frac{1}{2}$m. NW beside the old A1. Obelisk erected in 1805 after Trafalgar by the obsequious Alexander Davison (*see* Swarland), 'to the Memory of Private Friendship' with Nelson.

RASHERCAP, on the E side of the old A1 $\frac{1}{4}$m. N of the monument. Possibly a TOLLHOUSE, a small C 18 cottage with a steep pyramidal roof.

ADDERSTONE HALL

2 m. SE of Belford

1819 by *William Burn*. Quite a large house. Classical style in fine ashlar. Five bays with large *porte cochère*, all very severe and unadorned. Lower service wing to the l. The full-height central hall has balconies r. and l. with scrolled iron balustrade; it is top-lit from a glazed drum.

TWIZELL HOUSE, 1 m. SW at Warenford on the A1, a large and quite splendid house by *George Wyatt*, *c.* 1812, was demolished in the 1950s. It was the home of Prideaux Selby, the naturalist, and his walled garden remains. The NORTH LODGE, on the A1, is late C 19, with a loggia of square piers on the ground floor.

AKELD

AKELD BASTLE. Stronghouse or bastle house of the early C 16 and of a type not at all common in the county. It is *c.* 19 metres (63 ft) long and therefore longer than most bastles, and the ground-floor vault is higher and more rounded. The ground-floor doorway is towards the end of one of the long sides. The first floor was probably rebuilt in the early C 19, although the quoins show no signs of alteration. The side walls on the first floor are very low, and the roof is steeply pitched. The proportions and size distinguish the building from the bastles further S in the county but link it, on the other hand, to a small group near the River Tweed (Pressen Bastle at Carham and Castle Heaton, near Twizel). The tunnel vault is pierced by a ladder hole only 37 by 27 cm (14 by 11 ins.).

AKELD MANOR. Plain but substantial six-bay farmhouse, late C 18 or early C 19, rendered with raised stone surrounds to doors and windows. Nice Scottish slate roof.

Adjacent to the house a large but compact group of PLANNED FARM BUILDINGS, and beside them single-storey WORKERS' COTTAGES built round a square, with the former privies in the middle. They bear a date 1892 but were in existence by 1860.

RAILWAY STATION, ¼ m. N. By *William Bell*, one of his series of line-style stations on the former Alnwick to Cornhill railway, which opened in 1887 and closed in 1965. Station offices, goods shed, weigh cabin house and cottages in a pleasant red sandstone; the main buildings, like others on this line, are somewhat extrava-gantly designed with half-hipped dormers, cross gables, decorated bargeboards and wrought-iron finials. Now in domestic use.

GLEADSCLEUGH, ¾ m. SW. Dramatically sited inland promontory fort defended by two short ramparts on the N and entered from the NE. Scoops within the interior mark sites of timber houses.

BATTLE STONE, ¾ m. E. A prehistoric standing stone nearly 2 metres (6½ ft) high, traditionally associated with the battle of Hom-ildon Hill (1402). A burial cist, plausibly contemporary, was found close to it.

HUMBLETON HILL, 1 m. SE, is crowned by a massive hillfort, its natural defences enhanced by the steep-sided valley to the SW. Approached from the SE, a broad outer band of rubble, spread to a width of 9 metres (30 ft), conceals two roughly parallel walls, each up to 3 metres (10 ft) thick. These followed the contours, the upper wall utilizing a line of crags on the W. The summit itself had an extra inner wall along its E side. From the slopes to the dry valley on the W round to the ENE is an outer wall enclosing an annexe much larger than the fort itself. The rubble core of this wall is retained by angular boulders set on edge. Shallow scoops and platforms for timber houses can be traced on the summit and in the annexe.

MONDAY CLEUGH, ¾ m. s. A multivallate hillfort N of Gains Law that makes good use of a steep cliff as a natural defence on its E side. Round stone houses of a secondary, Romano-British, settlement are visible in the interior.

8050

ALLENDALE TOWN

A most attractive little town set amongst trees at the head of a steep bank above the River Allen.

ST CUTHBERT, set back at the NE corner of the square. 1874 by *Austin and Johnson*, who kept the lower part of the tower of its 1807 predecessor. A sound, uneventful Gothic edifice, splendidly placed high above the river. An 1842 sundial on the S wall cites the latitude (54°50') in reference to Allendale Town being the geographical centre of Britain. Above the tower arch, MEMORIAL TABLET to the Stephenson family by *John Lough*, c. 1830.

The MARKET PLACE is large and square with the fortuitously picturesque motif of two islands of houses in it. Late C 18 and C 19 houses and hotels, with little of especial note except for the three-bay Georgian PATH HOUSE of 1813, at the head of the bank down to the bridge, and the former TRUSTEE SAVINGS BANK of 1873, a pleasant essay in C 17 style, which has kept its railings.

C 19 prosperity came initially from the valley's leadmines, and on the riverbank below the church is the portal of BLACKETT LEVEL, the driving of which was begun in 1854 in an ambitious attempt to drain the mines of the whole valley. It was worked until 1903 but never completed.

ALLENDALE TOWN BRIDGE. 1825. One segmental arch with a moulded arch ring. Beside the bridge the apparently contemporary former CORN MILL; the three-storey mill has an external hoist and is on an L-shaped plan with mill house attached. There are remains of a massive timber-piled masonry dam which fed the head-race; the tail-race was taken underground for half a mile, to serve as head-race for waterwheels at the ALLEN SMELT MILL, worked c. 1780–1896. One substantial late C 19 building survives, along with remains of the flues, which extend 2 miles to the SW to two ruined chimneys prominent on the moortop skyline. Nearby, ALLENMILL BRIDGE, 1813, with two segmental arches, and ¼ m. N on the W bank of the river, the earthworks and some masonry of an earlier lead-smelting mill, probably pre-1692.

There are two former TOLLHOUSES on the Allendale Roads Turnpike (1826), one at BRIDGE END and the other, the LEADGATE

TOLL HOUSE, at s end of the village. Small gabled cottages with a single offset window in each end wall.

Many of the scattered farms of Allendale incorporate remains of BASTLE HOUSES. Traces of about 40 have been identified within the parish (*see* also Sinderhope, Spartylea and Whitfield). MOOR HOUSES, 1 m. to the NE, is a typical example, with the original bastle extended in the later C 17, and a C 19 cottage built onto the end of the range.

At WOOLEY, 1 m. to the SW, an intriguing group of buildings is grouped round a triangular yard, forming a complex that was clearly intended to be defensible. The farmhouse on the E seems to have been a true long-house, with a central cross passage between a formerly open hall and a byre with a chamber above; it may be early C 16. On the N is a range of bastle-like later C 16 or C 17 buildings, and on the w is a square bastle (now ruinous) with a tall mid-C 18 house (with a contemporary stair and an upper-cruck roof) built onto its s end. The narrow entrance between the house and a bastle-like s extension of the farmhouse is closed by a gate, which could afford some measure of security to cattle shut in the yard; if real danger threatened they could be taken into the buildings.

Across the fields to the s are NINE DARGUE, another ruined bastle with a round-headed byre door typical of the area, and THE HAGG, dated 1691, a conventional farmhouse with two- and three-light mullioned windows, built when it was safe again to live at ground level.

ALLENHEADS   *8040*

At the head of the valley of the East Allen amongst the wild Pennine moors, and now (1991) being developed as a centre for tourism.

ST PETER. 1825 by *W. Crawhall*. Away from the village to the N, and now a house. Preaching box with Y-tracery windows and an embattled E gable; on the N of the W porch is a reset classical door surround dated 1701, from the previous chapel.

Most of the buildings in the village relate to Allenheads' C 19 heyday as an important leadmining centre (*see* Introduction, p. 93); time has healed most of the scars to the surrounding landscape. FAWSIDE GREEN (dated 1790) and DUDLEY PLACE are purpose-built terraces for mineworkers, with the former ALLENHEADS SCHOOL of 1849 perched on the hillside high above and NEW HOUSES (1788), another terrace, further NE. A small railed enclosure in front of the mid-C 19 ESTATE OFFICES was the entrance to the HORSE TRACK, a spiral incline descending into the deep mines beneath the village. Down the hill in the village centre several mining relics are displayed, and a former public house, long disused, has been converted into the ALLENHEADS HERITAGE CENTRE by *Jowett Buckley & Curry* for the Allenheads Village Trust (1987), a rare example of community architecture in a rural setting. Over the road is the ALLENHEADS INN, largely C 18 but retaining a C 17 fireplace; adjoining to the w is ICETON HOUSE, once the miners' pay office; ashlar, with rusticated quoins and door surround and weathervane dated 1790. The road running N passes the BEAU-MONT MINE, recently worked for fluorspar but preserving various relics of the leadmining past: a row of workshops, a BOUSE TEAM (stone-built range of ore bunkers) and the horseshoe-arched portal of FAWSIDE LEVEL of 1776. Further on is the early C 19 ALLENHEADS FARM, arranged round a paved yard with a central pond, now infilled, where the ponies stabled here could be washed on coming out of the workings.

ALLENHEADS HALL, amongst trees SE of the village, with its heavily corbelled porch and shouldered lintels was built in 1847 by *E. B. Lamb*, and occupied by Thomas Sopwith, the celebrated mine agent to the Beaumont family. Instead of rosebeds the garden had little mounds of purple fluorspar and white quartz crystals from the mines beneath.

At DIRT POT, 1 m. N, was a LEAD SMELTING MILL. The long peat house is the only building intact; all else is ruined. Round the moorland edges are many cottages and small farmhouses built in the C 19 by leadminer/smallholders. Most are derelict and ruinous. On the Coalcleugh road from Dirt Pot is the SLAG HILL LIMEKILN, a bank of two elliptical-plan kiln pots, each with a single E-facing segmental-headed draw arch.

0050   ALLENSFORD

ALLENSFORD MILL FARMHOUSE. The taller C 17 part is to the r. of a C 18 range with stone-surround windows. In the early C 19 it housed the unlikely combination of an inn (The Belsay Castle) and a Nonconformist chapel.

BLAST FURNACE, on the N bank of the Derwent, *c.* 250 metres NE of the bridge. Ruined square furnace. Further up the hillside, a calciner with a round-arched circular kiln. Established in the C 17; last used *c.* 1740.

CROOKED OAK, 1½ m. W. Two-bay farmhouse with mullioned windows and a centre doorway dated 1684, in a lugged bolection-moulded surround. Inside, a fireplace with a bold moulded sur-round dated 1717.

DURHAMFIELD, 1½ m. NW. Rather similar to Crooked Oak, but here the doorway has a simpler moulding stepped on the lintel, which is dated 1691. Another doorway of this type is at SUM-MERFIELD on the A68, dated 1721.

9010   ALNHAM

ST MICHAEL. Nave with bellcote, lower chancel, transepts and S porch. A N aisle was pulled down, but the three-bay arcade can still be seen embedded in the N wall. The church had been ruinous for a long time when it was restored in 1870 by *F. R. Wilson*. The original features that remain point to a date *c.* 1200. Chancel arch on demishafts with simple moulded capitals. Transept arches single-chamfered on the s, double-chamfered on the N side. Parts of the w window, i.e. the bases and one capital to the shafts, are original. s porch and doorway are probably of the C 16 or early C 17; single-chamfered, round-headed doorways and tunnel-vaulted porch. C 15 recess in the chancel s wall. However, the church is much older than it seems, for there are Saxon quoins at NE and SE corners of the nave. – FONT. Dated 1664, octagonal, small bowl with moulded profile, still meant to be in the Gothic tradition. – MONUMENTS. Several coffin lids.

TOWER HOUSE, beside the church. Called in 1541 the mansion of the vicarage, that is, a 'vicar's pele' like those at Corbridge, Whitton and Ford. The upper parts are all redone, but there was apparently no corbelled top. Ground floor tunnel-vaulted. Described as 'long uninhabited and uninhabitable' in 1821, but in use again by 1844.

LITTLE RYLE FARMHOUSE, 1½ m. E. A bastle house of the C 16 with some slightly later mullioned windows. The original ground-floor door is in the middle of the long s side, with the first-floor door blocked above it, an arrangement which is found in a number of other bastles (e.g. Low Cleughs, near Woodburn; Shittleheugh, near Otterburn). The ground floor is tunnel-vaulted, though the vault has been pierced by a C 19 staircase. At one end of the vault, an early C 18 panelled room; and on the first floor a stone C 17 fireplace with four-centred arch and moulded surround.

CASTLE. Prominent green mound, 200 metres SE of the church; mentioned in 1405, probably burnt by Scotts of Teviotdale in 1532. In 1586 'the faire stronge stone Tower' was 'strongly vaulted over … the Gates and Dores be all of great stronge Iron Barres … the House is now ruinous and in some decay, by reason the Farmer useth to carry his sheep up the stares and to lay them in the Chambers which rotteth the vaultes …'

CASTLE HILL, ¾ m. W. Multivallate hillfort with deep defences, the inner rampart robbed away. On the SE an extra rampart, ditch and entrance were added. Fragments of a Romano-British settlement overlie the NE quadrant; another lies immediately outside on the SE; a third, within a rectangular enclosure, is crossed by the field wall just to the N.

HIGH KNOWES. A circular homestead of the mid-first millennium B.C., with the parallel slots for its double timber palisades startlingly visible, on a summit 1 m. SE of Ewartly Shank and 300 metres NE from the road. The course of the perimeter is represented by a slightly raised band exhibiting an unmistakable vegetation change. This is bounded by the grooves that demonstrate the minimal silting of the continuous narrow trenches which, with packing-stones, held the close-set upright timbers. The entrance lay on the E. Within the NE arc of the interior stood a large ring-ditch house and a smaller ring-groove building (*see* p. 35); these are smoothed by excavation but another of each type can still be traced immediately SW.

On a lower knoll, 100 metres E, is a smaller, pear-shaped settlement, its double palisade less well preserved. At least sixteen buildings (marked by a ring-ditch, ring-grooves and hollows) are closely set in the interior and apparently spill outwards on the

s. A later stone building, perhaps Romano-British, overlay the palisades close to the E entrance.

ALNHAMSHELES *see* INGRAM

2010

ALNMOUTH

ST JOHN THE BAPTIST. 1876. Simple lancet Gothic, aisleless, with a W tower and spire and a polygonal apse. – STAINED GLASS. Several later C 20 windows by *Evetts*.

ST WALERIC. The C 12 church stood on Church Hill, cut off from the village by the new river mouth formed after the 1806 storm; the same storm toppled the last fragment of an unusual cruciform Romanesque church. Nothing but the odd C 18 headstone remains visible on the hill, but below the W slope is a roofless MORTUARY CHAPEL of 1870; its weathered S door now looks convincingly Norman.

FRANCISCAN FRIARY (formerly Lint Close). 1902–16 by *W. H. Knowles* for the Scholefield family. On a bold hillside site overlooking the village, a large and quite impressive house with an eclectic mixture of Gothic and Baroque motifs.

THE DUCHESS'S BRIDGE. 1864. Rock-faced, with four segmental arches.

Alnmouth has an aura of departed greatness. A planned medieval port, it retained its importance through the C 18 (a turnpike road from Hexham to Alnmouth was constructed in 1752–66) and until the fateful storm of Christmas 1806, when the Aln changed course. After this the harbour slowly silted up and became unusable, although timber and slate were still being imported and a substantial fishing industry flourished in the 1880s. The village retains its medieval plan, with burghal strips recognizable on both sides of NORTHUMBERLAND STREET, which runs down the spine of the spur on which it is built. On the E side of Northumberland Street, s of the church, is PROSPECT PLACE, with an C 18 granary, converted in the C 19 into a row of houses, leading to a flight of steps beside the MARINE HOUSE HOTEL, also built as a granary but converted in the C 19 into the vicarage. Then comes a row of varied C 18 and C 19 houses; THE GALLEON is early C 18, with a moulded doorway. NETHER LODGE, *c.* 1840, was built by the Pease family, a picturesque mixture of Italianate Gothic towers and half-absorbed C 18 cottages. Further on is the HINDMARSH HALL, another C 18 granary gothicized in the C 19; attached to it, Nos. 1–4 VICTORIA PLACE, a row of late C 17 or early C 18 cottages rewindowed in the mid-C 19.

Returning up the W side of Northumberland Street, No. 14 is a low C 17 building with its gable end to the street, with jointed upper crucks. It is worth turning l. down Garden Terrace to see the old harbour wall and THE GRANGE, a Victorian conversion of yet another granary. In its garden, the OLD WATCH TOWER, a brick gazebo-like structure which in the C 18 was the harbour master's office. ALN HOUSE is a five-bay house of *c.* 1740, built of brick with ashlar dressings. GROSVENOR TERRACE was fashioned in the early C19 out of former outbuildings to the sadly decayed early C18 GROSVENOR HOUSE at the far end; linked to this, but looking E across the river, is LOVAINE TERRACE, *c.* 1860, eight houses of experimental concrete blockwork construction. Rendered and variously colourwashed, they form a prominent element in distant views of Alnmouth from the W. Back in Northumberland Street there are other C18 houses further N and then, set back, THE HALL, early C18, brick and of five bays. The Victorians made various additions, including an odd tower at the back.

GUANO SHED, ½m. S. Now standing alone amongst the fields but built on the bank of the pre-1806 Aln, a long C18 barn-like structure designed to store imported guano (used as fertilizer). Guano was kept as far from the village as possible: it smelt dreadful.

HIGH BUSTON HOUSE, 1½m. SW. Late C18 five-bay villa with contemporary stableyard group and outbuildings.

ALNWICK

1010

Alnwick is the ducal town of Northumberland; one is never far from the lion or crescent, ever-present reminders of seven centuries of the Percy family. The town sprawls over gently rising ground on the side of the Aln valley, S of the castle and the two bridges; the castle, although on a vast scale, only dominates when one enters the town from the N across the Lion Bridge, or in distant views from the E. Alnwick and its environs satisfy the architectural traveller in no fewer than four fields: military architecture (of course), ecclesiastical architecture – parish church, abbey gatehouse and a remarkably preserved friary – urban architecture, where the C18 and C19 make their contribution, and, last but not least, architecture more decorative than functional in the buildings of the Duke's park, scattering up the Aln valley to where the spectacular Brizlee Tower claims the skyline.

CHURCHES

ST MICHAEL. The church lies at the W end of the town and does not really form part of its pattern. The churchyard overlooks the River Aln and the wooded banks of the park to the N. From outside, St Michael's is a completely Perp church, of a unity and a size uncommon in Northumberland. One is used to prosperous late medieval churches with completely homogeneous parallelogram plans in other parts of England; in Northumberland, where the C14 and C15 were not a period of peace and riches, they hardly exist. Moreover, Alnwick church can be dated with some accuracy. In 1464 Henry VI granted Alnwick a port and some tolls to 'make and repair their church'. In common with the castle, the church was gothicized in the late C18 (an old painting shows a spectacular plaster fan vault over the chancel), but all evidence of this was swept away by *Salvin* in 1863. Alnwick church

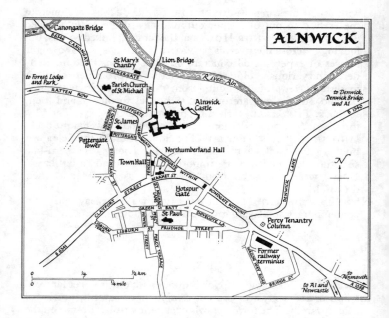

has a nave with wide aisles of five bays and a chancel with three-bay chapels, organ chamber (1890, by *F. R. Wilson*) and vestries on the N. The E end is straight, the W end modified a little by the fact that the tower is over the W bay of the S aisle; that is the only major irregularity of the plan. The tower is not high and has an excessive number of setbacks to the buttresses; with its battlements and small pinnacles it gives a feeling of strength and trustworthiness. The S porch, contemporary with the tower, is likewise simple and functional. The three-light W window of the nave is Salvin's, replacing a Dec original; the windows on the S, the show front of the church, are all of three lights, with renewed panel tracery; the wall is embattled, with pinnacled buttresses. The S aisle E window has five lights, the N aisle E window four, and both have more complex tracery (restored), exceptional in the county; they flank the E end of the chancel, which, with its five-light window and flanking buttresses, seems to be wholly of 1863. At the E angle of the S aisle is a polygonal turret with a corbelled-out top and adjacent chamber (originally rather larger) above the roof; whether this was simply a priest's room or had some military function is uncertain. All this is of after 1464. Evidence of earlier building activity is scarce externally and even internally does not change the late Perp character of the church. Externally all that can be seen is the small W window of the N aisle, a trefoiled lancet very close to the nave; this and the adjacent masonry prove a former narrower aisle of *c.* 1300, the foundations of which have been excavated. The aisle was widened in the later C14 and given its present windows, with segmental heads and cusped ogee heads to the three lights beneath (cf. Newcastle).

Inside the church there is more evidence of earlier phases. Above the chancel arch, not *in situ*, are stones with Norman diaper work. They belong to a church which excavations showed to consist of a narrow aisleless nave and apse. Then comes the addition of the aisles with double-chamfered arches. The S arcade has octagonal piers, interfered with at the W in the C 15, when the tower, with a big buttress reaching out into the nave, was built. The N arcade has odd hexagonal piers with fluted faces; unfortunately everything except the W respond looks C 19. The old arcade had been removed to permit the insertions of galleries. The chancel arch also looks C 19, but the arcades to the chapels are unusually ornate late C 15 work and of great interest. The piers consist of four large and four smaller shafts, of filleted ogee section, running up behind traceried panels at the top; the capitals are richly carved with stylized foliage of different types. The 'Hotspur' capital on the N carries the crescent and fetterlocks, a combination first used, it is said, by the fourth Earl of Northumberland (1470–89). The nave roof is of the same period, and has contemporary bosses. The arch-braced trusses vary in detail; two have cusping. There is a moulded strainer beam just below the ridge (cf. Lesbury). – SCULPTURE. Statues of Henry VI and a martyr saint pierced by arrows, under the tower. Late C 15 and not of good quality. – CHEST. Flemish, early C 14, one of the best of the type in any English church. The decoration is mostly foliage and dragons, but there is also a hunting scene. None of the tracery motifs usual in the later Middle Ages. – STAINED GLASS. In N aisle W window, C 15 fragments, including a small roundel with a pelican. The rest of the church offers an uncommonly complete and enlightening survey of Victorian glass, as follows: baptistery W, *Clayton & Bell*, 1871, S, *Baguley*, 1897. W window, *Clayton & Bell*, c. 1865–70 – N aisle from W, *Baguley*, 1872, *Lavers, Barraud & Westlake*, 1871, *Burlison & Grylls*, 1884, *Atkinson*, 1882, *Lavers, Barraud & Westlake*, 1871 (behind the organ and the next two windows E). – S aisle next to porch, *Atkinson*, c. 1890, centre, *Powell*, E end, *Powell*, 1868. – S chancel chapel, all *Clayton & Bell*, all c. 1865–70. Chancel, all *Ward & Hughes*, 1866. Some of the glass, especially that in the N aisle, is badly faded. – MONUMENTS. Under the tower and outside W of the porch about twenty C 12–14 CROSS SLABS, some with unusual emblems, e.g. a hammer and anvil, bows, a hunting horn and a mason's square. – In the S chapel, EFFIGIES of a knight and a lady, early to mid-C 14, under projecting crocketed canopies. (In the porch on the N of the chancel, later C 14 effigy of a clerk.) – In the S chapel, tablets to Alexander Bane † 1737, with etched portrait on bronze roundel, and Collingwood Foster † 1766 by *T. King* of Bath. – Under the tower, tablets to Frances Selby † 1790 and Henry Collingwood Selby † 1839, by *Dunn* of Alnwick. – Many C 17 and C 18 ledger stones, mostly of blue limestone, in chancel.

ST MARY (R.C.), Bailiffgate. 1836 by *John Green* in the lancet style. Narrow gable to the street, with trefoil loops flanking the door, lancets flanking a two-light window above. At the top, a window in the form of a four-pointed star, flanked by little blind lancets.

ST PAUL (formerly Anglican, now R.C.), Percy Street. 1846 by *Salvin*. A large, competent, serious-minded Dec church built at

the expense of the third Duke of Northumberland. Nave of five
bays with aisles, chancel with two-bay aisles and a big s vestry
like an outer aisle; big w tower. Wheel window in the nave E
gable. Plastered inside with dressings of very grey stone. The
impressive pitch-pine fan vault is an insertion of c. 1865. –
STAINED GLASS. E window (Paul and Barnabas preaching)
designed by *Dyce* and made by *Ainmüller* of Munich, 1856. The
design highly Raphaelesque, the architectural surrounds bristly
Gothic, the colouring somewhat garish. – MONUMENT. Third
Duke of Northumberland † 1847, by *J. E. Carew*. Asleep in his
garter robes with coronet on his head, a curiously incongruous
composition, and proof of the remarkably untroubled conscience
of the early Victorian nobleman.

ANGLICAN MISSION HALL (now disused), tucked away off the s
side of Pottergate. Dated 1886, and by *F. R. Wilson*. The poor
man's parish church, with soup kitchens etc. below a first-floor
hall. Plenty of fussy but cheaply done detail to the timber-framed
canted bays on each side, and two little turrets on the ridge;
canted apse at the s (liturgical E) end, with a gablet and fancy
bargeboards. An interesting piece of social history.

ST JAMES UNITED REFORMED CHURCH (formerly Presbyterian), Pottergate. Designed 1883–4 by *Hicks & Charlewood*
but dated 1894. Free Perp style, not one of their best. Big sw
porch tower with a corbelled-out stair turret and spirelet. The
church is set back behind the Church Hall by *Reavell*, 1904, in a
rather eclectic style with keyed round arches to the ground-floor
windows, under square-headed windows with little classical
columns as mullions.

UNITED PRESBYTERIAN CHURCH (now Sheraton House), Clayport Street. 1846, attributed to *Smith*. Somewhere between Tudor
and Gothick, with a gabled centrepiece between embattled octagonal towers.

METHODIST CHURCH, Chapel Lane (off Clayport Street). 1786;
remodelled and gothicized in 1886.

SION MEETING HOUSE (now a warehouse), Chapel Lane. Dated
1815; two storeys and four bays with arched windows, a moulded
cornice and a hipped roof.

RUINS OF ST LEONARD'S HOSPITAL CHAPEL, on the w side of
the A1068, about 500 metres N of the Lion Bridge. Founded
between 1193 and 1216 by Eustace de Vescy for the benefit of the
soul of Malcolm King of Scots, slain nearby. In ruins by 1535.
The hospital seems to have consisted of a hall with a narrower
chapel to the E and another range to the s. The remains were
rediscovered during ploughing in 1845: the standing fragments,
which comprise a round-arched s door with continuous chevron
moulding and an indented hood, and a fragment of the moulded
arch between hall and chapel, were reconstructed by *F. R. Wilson*
using excavated masonry.

ALNWICK ABBEY, in the Duke's Park w of the Eglingham road,
just across Canongate Bridge. Founded in 1147 by Eustace Fitz-
John for Premonstratensian canons. The plan was ascertained by
St John Hope in excavations of 1884 and was marked out on the
ground, but is now barely traceable; the chief peculiarity was the
horseshoe-shaped E end of the chapter house. The only above-

ground survival is the C 15 GATEHOUSE, close to the Eglingham 36 road just beyond Canongate Bridge. It is quite big, with four strongly projecting square turrets and battlements. The recessed N wall between has two niches for statues above the segmental arch, and a machicolated parapet. Oddly there is another blocked arch between far-projecting turrets, with high-level machicolations, on the E. The W face shows a corbelled-out garderobe at parapet level. The gate passage has a segmental tunnel vault, with a straight stair in the W wall and a newel in the SE turret. The upper floor has several longish straight-headed two-light windows with transoms and big hoodmoulds.

ALNWICK CASTLE

Alnwick Castle is approached from Bailiffgate, that is the W. The 21 castle covers an area of c. 2.8 hectares (7 acres). Much of that is now well-tended turf, and beyond the walls to the E, S and N stretches the green of deliciously landscaped grounds; they are the work of *Capability Brown*, probably done at about the same time as Syon House was landscaped for the Duke of Northumberland, i.e., c. 1765. These must be forgotten if one wishes to evoke the medieval appearance of the castle. Its natural position was excellent, protected on the N side by the River Aln and on the S and E by the ravine of the former Bow Burn.

The castle probably began its existence as a motte-and-bailey with wooden buildings, although it seems to have been fully walled in stone before the death of Eustace Fitz-John in 1157. In overall plan the castle is an elongate triangle fitted to its spur-end site, with the short W side fronting onto Bailiffgate. A large shell keep on a levelled-down motte stood between the two baileys; the plan is somewhat reminiscent of Windsor. On the N the keep itself formed part of the *enceinte* (cf. Warkworth), whilst on the S a cross wall between the baileys ran from the keep to the Middle Gate, set against the S curtain. There may have been minor changes at some points in the line of the curtain since the C 12, but the distinctive squared Norman masonry, sometimes laid in courses which seem to follow lost undulations in the ground surface, can be seen at the NW corner of the W bailey and possibly in its S wall near the Middle Gate, in both N and S walls of the E bailey, and in the gate passage to the keep.

In 1309 the castle came by purchase to Henry de Percy, and he added and strengthened much. Due to him are the semicircular towers closely besetting the shell keep; there were originally seven but only that nearest the gateway on the E now shows any old masonry externally. He also refaced the curtain wall and provided it with strong towers of a variety of forms – rectangular, circular and D-shaped – and smaller turrets or 'garrets' between. When Henry de Percy died in 1315, the work was continued by the second Henry, who built the present gatehouse with its barbican, the best in the country, and also the gateway into the keep; by the time of his death in 1352 the castle had assumed its present character. The fourth Lord de Percy was raised to an earldom, and eleven earls followed before the male Percy line became extinct; the heiress, Lady Elizabeth Seymour, married Sir Hugh Smithson, who took the family

name and became the first Duke of Northumberland (1750–86).
The Percys have continued in possession to the present day.

We know from such illustrations as Canaletto's painting of *c.* 1750
how ruinous the castle was in the early days of the first Duke. He
decided to make it once again habitable and presentable, and in the
latter was vigorously supported by the Duchess, who wanted to
enjoy her life and riches. 'Junketaceous' is the term Horace Walpole
applied to her. Walpole mentions building going on in 1752, and
this may have been directed by *Paine*. But it cannot have amounted
to much, or else would have been mentioned in the descriptions in
a book published in 1758. In the 1760s, however, more must have
been done. Paine continued to visit Alnwick, and in addition *Robert
Adam* was called in. He gave Alnwick the most complete and fanciful
Gothick decorations he ever designed. The masons in charge were
Matthew and *Thomas Mills*. Hardly anything of this work of Adam's
for the interior survives. A guidebook of 1822 calls it 'in the gayest
and most elegant style of Gothick architecture'. But the Gothick
style of Alnwick is reflected in such buildings as Hulne Priory,
Craster, Fowberry and Ford. It was the fourth Duke (1847–65) who
condemned Adam's work to death, because it must have seemed to
him both ignorant and flimsy. *Anthony Salvin* was his architect. He
began work in 1854, and he spent a quarter of a million pounds on
building and decorating. The Prudhoe Tower at the NW end of the
keep is entirely his, and the adjoining chapel with its polygonal W
apse. These and the inner courtyard of the keep corresponded to
the fourth Duke's vision of chivalry, the wholly Italian state rooms
inside to his requests for domestic display.

We can now look at the individual parts of the castle topographically.

40 GATEHOUSE AND BARBICAN (*c.* 1310–1320). The barbican has
square projecting towers l. and r. of a round-arched entrance.
The upper parts of the towers are corbelled out, and the battlements carry figures of soldiers. They look C 18, but no doubt
replace original apotropaic figures such as also exist on other
North Country castles (Raby and Hylton in County Durham, and
Bothal in Northumberland). Past the entrance the visitor goes
under a vault with transverse single-chamfered arches, and comes
out in the open again. He is however narrowly flanked by tall
walls l. and r. until he reaches the gatehouse itself. Originally there
was a ditch here as well and one could only walk on a drawbridge
which worked on a horizontal pivot in front of the gatehouse arch.
The pivoting was devised in such a way that, when opened, half
the drawbridge was in the ditch and half in front of the entrance.
The entrance was further protected by a portcullis and double
doors. The gateway is vaulted and again has transverse arches.
To the l. and r. are guardrooms. The flanking towers are polygonal
with spurs at their bases, and again have little figures.

CURTAIN WALL AND TOWERS. Inside the W bailey, to the N the
curtain, of a variety of medieval builds, runs past a well-preserved
garret to the rectangular ABBOT'S TOWER at the NW corner,
early C 14 with a good rib-vaulted basement; the wall then turns
E to *Salvin*'s FALCONER TOWER, with a large carving of the
fourth Duke's Victoria Cross on the E side; the medieval curtain
from here ran SE to join the keep, but has been replaced by the

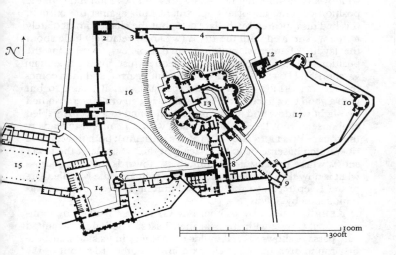

1 Gatehouse and barbican   7 Auditor's Tower   13 Keep
2 Abbot's Tower   8 Middle Gate   14 Stable Court (Salvin)
3 Falconer Tower   9 Garden Gate (Salvin)   15 Riding School (Salvin)
4 Gun Terrace   10 Record Tower   16 West Bailey
5 Avener's Tower   11 Constable Tower   17 East Bailey
6 Clock Tower   12 Postern Tower

Alnwick Castle. Plan

broad GUN TERRACE (mid-C 18, extended in the C 19), which
runs across to join the N curtain of the E bailey. Returning to the
gatehouse, the S section of the W curtain has been much restored
and refaced, with the small AVENER'S TOWER of the 1760s and
at the SW corner the round CLOCK TOWER (formerly the Water
Tower), of which only the plinth is visibly medieval. The E part
of the S curtain has been replaced by the estate office range, where
some Gothick interiors survive, notably in the Commissioner's
Dining Room; embedded in the range is the D-shaped AUDI-
TOR'S or BEEFSTAND TOWER, and then some old masonry
incorporated in a C 19 range brings us to the MIDDLE GATE,
c 14, with its upper parts remodelled c. 1440. The round-arched
gateway is flanked on the N by a semicircular tower. Beyond,
through a gate passage with a segmental vault on chamfered ribs,
is the E bailey. On the S is a C 19 range ending in *Salvin*'s GARDEN
GATE, theatrically aligned with the gatehouse of the keep, but
with a brewhouse and an icehouse practically tucked away beneath
the vaulted gate passage. The medieval curtain then reappears,
with a well-preserved garret and then a series of garderobe projections just before the RECORD TOWER at the extreme E end
of the castle; this was originally open-backed, but was rebuilt
above its lowest stage in 1880. The curtain then turns back NW;
in this part, between two big buttresses, two blocked two-light

windows (their internal recesses with window seats) indicate the position of some important apartment built against the curtain; this had disappeared by the late C 16, but the chapel, immediately to the W, survived until the 1750s (we know relatively little about the layout of internal buildings in the baileys, except for the positions of the stables and exchequer just inside the main gatehouse). HOTSPUR'S SEAT is a rebuilt garret, and then comes the CONSTABLE'S TOWER, its apsidal external face C 19 but with a good C 14 front to the bailey showing an original transomed two-light window and a stair projection rising to a steeply gabled caphouse at roof level. More curtain with C 12 masonry leads to the square POSTERN TOWER (now a museum); both towers have rib-vaulted basements. C 18 refacing at the SW angle of the tower shows where the curtain continued SW towards the keep, across what is now the Gun Terrace. The range linking the Middle Gate to the Keep replaced the medieval curtain in the C 18, and was remodelled by Salvin.

The KEEP is entered by another fine GATEWAY flanked by semi-octagonal turrets with spurs at their bases. The long rib-vaulted gate passage shows several builds of masonry in its side walls; the first round arch has reset chevron in the outer order, but at the far end of the passage is a genuine early C 12 arch; it has two orders of chevron and a hotchpotch of a hoodmould with lozenges and tegulae, which looks reset. The INNER COURT is mostly Salvin's 1854 etc.); it has a strong Wagnerian flavour (Tannhäuser 1845, Lohengrin 1848), especially in the vaulted approach to the main entrance leading to the state rooms. This is in the NW corner. To the r., as one enters through the Norman gate, the lower section of the wall is early C 14 and has a triple-arched well recess within a keel-moulded surround. Here was the hall, at first-floor level above an undercroft and entered by an external stair (cf. Aydon Castle), with the solar to its S above the gateway and the kitchen to its N; the C 19 works revealed some remains of the hall, including a buffet recess (cf. Hexham Moot Hall), but they were not preserved. More is known of Robert Adam's arrangements, in the size and functions of rooms largely taken over by Salvin. He replaced Adam's splendid staircase in its circular well (similar in type to that at Home House, Portman Square, London) by his Prudhoe Tower with the Library and Adam's State Dressing Room by his Chapel. Of all Adam's decorations and furnishings nothing is left but a few Gothick chairs and two semi-Gothick fireplaces, one with a combination of blank tracery and honey-suckle ornament (Housekeeper's Room, Steward's Room or present Art Rooms not open to the public).

Salvin's Chapel is rib-vaulted, with a polygonal apse and an upper family pew. To its N is the Library, the largest room in the castle. The bookcases were made by George Smith in London but designed by an Italian, Giovanni Montiroli. The fourth Duke believed in the superiority of baronial Gothic for exteriors but Italian Renaissance at its most sumptuous for interiors. So he obtained the services of a team of Italians who worked for him at Alnwick and in Italy. Montiroli was still extremely young. He appeared as an assistant to the distinguished Luigi Canina, who had been called to Alnwick to make plans for the interior remodelling but died on the way back after a short stay. The other main characters were the sculptor *Strazza*, professor at the Brera of Milan, and the painter *Mantovani*, who had worked for the popes in the Lateran, Vatican, and Quirinal palaces, and the woodcarver *Bulletti*. In the Library the chimneypieces are mostly by *Strazza*.

The Library is connected by an ante-room with the staircase. *Salvin* handled the transition from the Gothic exterior to the Italianate interior with some care; beyond its vaulted porch the Entrance Hall is stone-walled with a simple stucco ceiling, with marble decoration appearing in the Lower Staircase Hall and on the stair. At the foot of the staircase are two statues (Action and Repose) by *John Gibson*, the Romanized British sculptor, and friezes high up by the popular German decorator *J. Götzenberger*. On the other side of the ante-room follows the main suite of state rooms, the Music Room with a chimneypiece by *Nucci*, the Drawing Room with a chimneypiece by the same and a frieze by *Mantovani*, and the Dining Room, the large bay window of which looks towards the distant eyecatcher on Ratcheugh Crag. The bacchante of the fireplace is by *Strazza*, the faun by *Nucci*. The ceiling, like all the others, is heavy with dark and gilt wooden coffering. *Salvin*'s big well-vaulted kitchen and service apartments lay beyond the Middle Gate in the range s of the w bailey; food for the State Dining Room had to be wheeled through a white-tiled tunnel beneath the E bailey to a serving room and then taken up a lift.

Salvin also greatly extended the stable complex outside the SW corner of the W bailey; to the W beyond the big rectangular STABLE COURT is his RIDING SCHOOL, which has a covered ride behind a big timber arcade around an open oval green at the centre. It is the embattled screen wall enclosing this that one first sees on the Narrowgate approach to the castle.

Ornamental buildings in and around the Park

These are mostly due to the first Duke of Northumberland and his enthusiasm for the Picturesque.

MALCOLM'S CROSS. To commemorate the death of Malcolm, King of Scotland, at the siege of Alnwick in 1093. The present Gothick cross is dated 1774; fragments of a medieval predecessor to one side.

BRIZLEE TOWER, 2 m. NW of the Castle and a prominent object 84 on its hilltop. From close at hand it is quite stunning. It was built in 1781, probably to *Adam*'s design, although sometimes credited to the Duke himself. In plan a circle with four rectangular projections, it is 24 metres (78 ft) high, with an encircling verandah entered by four tripartite archways. Three upper storeys, divided by quatrefoil and fluted friezes, then a balcony on fan corbels with a pieced quatrefoil balustrade. The top has a crenellated parapet and a big cast-iron fire basket. Lots of fancy Gothick detail. Inside is a stone newel stair. At the NINE YEAR AUD HOLE, 210 metres (230 yds) SW, an C 18 statue of a bearded hermit, like those of friars at Hulne, stands in a cave entrance.

Also in the Park are the little Gothick MOOR LODGE of *c.* 1775, ¼ m. W of the Forest Lodge entrance, perhaps by *Bell* of Durham;

PARK FARM, 1 m. NW of Forest Lodge, with a farmhouse dated 1832 and impressive ashlar-faced planned farmbuildings – the s range symmetrical around a big pedimented gateway – dated 1827 and probably by *J. & B. Green*; more farm buildings with both classical and Gothick touches at EAST BRIZLEE, 2 m. NW; and the ornamental triple-arched CAST-IRON BRIDGE, $\frac{1}{4}$ m. s of Hulne Priory, dated 1812 and by *I. & T. Cookson* of Newcastle. In connection with these buildings the tower in Pottergate (*see* below) and the Summer House inside the ruins of Hulne Priory (q.v.) should be referred to.

Then the three bridges. The LION BRIDGE of 1773 is by *John Adam*. Gothick, with a segmental arch flanked by circular arches. Embattled parapet, semicircular lookouts and a cast lead Percy lion in the middle of the E parapet. DENWICK BRIDGE is dated 1766 and may be by *Robert Mylne*. It has a single round arch and polygonal lookouts with fan corbelling, and a balustrade of interlinked Percy crescents. The E face, facing away from the Park, is much plainer. CANONGATE BRIDGE on the Eglingham road is of 1821, and has three segmental arches; the only decoration here is moulded roundels in the arch spandrels.

Finally there are the two columns. The PERCY TENANTRY COLUMN at the E end of the old town was erected in 1816 to the design of *David Stephenson*. The Greek Doric column, 22.8 metres (75 ft) high, stands on a stepped plinth with a recumbent lion at each corner, and is capped by a balcony and a drum topped by the Percy lion. It was erected by the Duke's tenants in gratitude for a 25-per-cent rent reduction; the next Duke soon increased the rents again, and the column became locally known as the 'Farmers' Folly'. – The PEACE COLUMN in Swansfield Park was erected to commemorate the peace of 1814, and is a smaller Tuscan column with a bell on top, surrounded by trees. It stands within the abraded and damaged remains of an oval univallate HILLFORT. Only the outer scarp of the rampart survives.

PUBLIC BUILDINGS

TOWN HALL, Fenkle Street. 1731. A five-bay block with a big hipped roof and a square tower projecting from the centre of the front. Rusticated quoins, a passage through to the Market Place with a rusticated round arch at each end, and tall first-floor windows with moulded surrounds. The tower, said to have been built or rebuilt in 1767 by *John Bell* of Durham, has a parapet with a small open pediment on each side, corner pinnacles and a tall swept lead dome. The elevation to the Market Place has a datestone above the central first-floor window and an ornate 1790 rainwater head, both with the names of contemporary chamberlains of the Alnwick burgesses. External stair to the first-floor door now covered by a later porch.

NORTHUMBERLAND HALL, Market Street. 1826. The architect seems to be unrecorded. The Hall, much larger than the Town Hall, was built at the expense of the third Duke. It consists of a ten-by-three-bay rectangle with Doric giant pilasters and a range of blind windows below the top cornice, with at the E end a lower polygonal extension. Both parts have an open arcaded ground floor.

ALNWICK LIBRARY (originally the Duke's School), Green Batt. 1810 datestone. Plinth and rusticated quoins; the Tudor windows and Gothic bellcote must be later C 19.

DUKE'S SCHOOL (now Barndale House Special School), Windsor Gardens. 1852–3 by *Thomas Robertson* of Alnwick, altered in 1903 by *J. W. Douglas*. Tudor style, E-plan and single-storey except for a room above the centre porch (cf. Nedderton).

DUKE'S COUNTY MIDDLE SCHOOL (formerly the Duke's Grammar School), The Dunterns. Turn-of-the-century Tudor, quite elaborate, with much carved heraldry etc.

DUCHESS'S GIRLS SCHOOL, Bailiffgate. *See* Perambulation, below.

VICTORIA INFANTS' SCHOOL. *See* Perambulation.

POLICE STATION, Prudhoe Street. *c.* 1935. Brick with ashlar dressings and green slate roof; Neo-classical.

RAILWAY TERMINUS. *See* Perambulation.

PERAMBULATION

A good place to start is at the junction of the Alnmouth and Newcastle roads, at the SE end of the town. On the l. here is the early C 19 and rather Dobsonesque BELVEDERE TERRACE, six three-bay ashlar houses with a rusticated basement and pretty cast-iron balconies under the first-floor windows, alternately continuous and individual. Then comes the former RAILWAY TERMINUS of 1887, probably by *William Bell*, rock-faced stone with segmental-headed openings and a cast-iron canopy above the entrance. Passing the Percy Column (see above) and the WAR MEMORIAL of 1920–2 with three mourning figures (by *R. Hedley*), the pre-1800 town starts as BONDGATE WITHOUT. On the l. little early C 19 COLUMN COTTAGE (traditionally, 'Wager Cottage', built in a fortnight by the Duchess, who thus won a wager with the Duke). Humbly Tudor, with the ubiquitous Percy crescent over the door. Close by, Nos. 1–3, a well-preserved pair of a common Alnwick type, late C 18 (the eaves heightened in the C 19), stone, three storeys and quite plain. The door of No. 1 has a stone hood on cusped brackets, typical of the area. No. 8, opposite, is very similar. On the l. again, and set back from the road, is BONDGATE HALL (Inland Revenue offices), a three-bay villa of *c.* 1810 with a pedimented centre, its form echoed by a humble little stable block to the W. Close to the end of Bondgate Without, GREENWELL ROAD on the r. affords a glimpse of an embattled C 19 TOWER in the Castle gardens.

Bondgate Without ends where the road is spanned by the HOTSPUR GATE, part of the town walls; licence to fortify was given in 1434 but building seems to have spanned half a century after this. Segmental archway and ribbed vault, flanked by semi-octagonal projections with slit windows; over the arch a much-decayed lion rampant, and corbels once carrying a machicolation. The inner face has a mullioned and a cross window.

On the N side of BONDGATE WITHIN, some typical C 18 houses;

No. 8 is a good example, with sill bands. Then comes the WHITE SWAN. Its mid-C 19 front is not special, but at the back lies the remarkable Olympic Room, salvaged from the *Titanic*'s sister ship (1910–35) when she was broken up at Jarrow. A contemporary writer described it as 'a noble apartment in the Louis Quinze style, the details being taken from the Palace of Versailles'. It is 18 by 19 metres (59 by 63 ft) and over 3.6 metres (12 ft) high, with two three-bay screens, much carved wood, an ornate panelled plaster ceiling and a marble fireplace. Further along, a row of banks; early C 20 LLOYDS BANK, *c.* 1910, by the local architect *George Reavell,* is the best; BARCLAYS BANK incorporates an early C 18 house. The row ends in the mid-C 20 DISTRICT COUNCIL OFFICES, cheap and uninspiring.

Opposite, on the s side of the broad street (beyond the asphalt road, a wide slope of cobbles up to the pavement makes a very effective feature) is a row of unassuming late C 18 and early C 19 properties. At the top of a triple flight of nicely worn stone steps, the former CORN EXCHANGE of 1862, fronted by a two-storey block holding two round arches with big triple keystones, under a bellcote; a taller gable rises behind. The side walls are bleak and windowless. At this point Market Street branches off w.

Back in Bondgate Within, Nos. 69–75 is a three-storey eight-bay early C 18 block, brick with rusticated quoins and stone dressings. On the N, Nos. 58–60 may be late medieval, although disguised by render and with the ground floor ruthlessly removed by modern shops. On the front, the Percy arms and crossed croziers (for Alnwick Abbey) in a panel under a Tudor-style hoodmould.

Bondgate Within then becomes NARROWGATE, much narrower than Bondgate and curved so as to vary vistas. Fenkle Street joins at an acute angle from the l., and on the narrower corner site is the former SAVINGS BANK, No. 11, built in 1835 by *William Smith*. Playful Gothick, with a one-bay front on the street corner between polygonal buttresses ending in tall turrets. Almost opposite, the more sober No. 28, three storeys and three bays with a cornice, flat-topped parapet and two 1790 rainwater heads. Just beyond, YE OLDE CROSS is partly C 17, with some chamfered windows which have lost their mullions. The road then widens at the base of POTTERGATE, which rises up steeply to the l.; the junction is spoiled by an obtrusive modern garage facing the DUKE'S COTTAGES by *Robert Lutyens* (designed 1941, built 1948), a row of four in brick with a projecting wing at each end. Pedimented stone door cases with Gibbs jambs, and steep gables alternating with hip-roofed dormers; said to follow the style of some old houses formerly in Narrowgate. The final section of Narrowgate becomes BAILIFFGATE halfway along, here over-shadowed by the C 19 embattled wall of the Castle's equestrian exercise yard on the r. On the l. here are GENERAL LAMBERT'S HOUSE, early C 19 ashlar of three storeys and seven bays, and the humbler early C 18 DOROTHY FORSTER'S HOUSE, two storeys and four bays, brick with stone dressings; then Nos. 1–1c Bailiffgate, three-storey C 18 houses, ashlar and brick.

The road now suddenly expands into Bailiffgate proper, a broad and tree-lined avenue leading w from the drama of the Castle gatehouse towards the church. Once more there are good-quality

later c 18 and c 19 houses. At the E end on the N side, the
DUCHESS'S GIRLS SCHOOL originally built as the Estate Commissioners house, supposedly in 1797; a dignified tall five-bay
house with Venetian stair windows at the rear. At the back are
1976 extensions by *D. C. Jeffrey* (the County Architect) including
two ashlar-faced blocks with tall and narrow windows set in pairs
of recessed panels.

It is worth continuing beyond the parish church down CANON-
GATE. The road drops steeply, between an old buttressed wall
retaining the churchyard and a PANT of 1770, to a highly picturesque series of estate cottages and small houses; most have the
Percy crescent, and many are dated. The CHURCH HALL up on
the r. is free Perp of 1913. Further down the hill is a convincing
essay (dated 1983, by *Ray Connell* of *Reavell & Cahill*) in the local
vernacular which was current around 1800, sandwiched between
a genuine c 18 house and an early c 19 pair.

Coming back uphill, it is worth making a detour l. along WAL-
KERGATE to see the ruins of ST MARY'S CHANTRY, probably
of 1449, although much patched. It seems to have been a priest's
house (and later the first school in the town) and has a cross
passage with an arched doorway at each end, set E of centre; the
doorway to the street has Perp mouldings, and to its l. is a cross
window at first-floor level with trefoiled heads to its upper lights.
To the r., a later Tudor-arched doorway, perhaps a c 17 insertion.

From the churchyard gate, turn S along NORTHUMBERLAND
STREET. On the l., an early c 19 ashlar two-storeyed terrace, with
mid-c 20 continuations in the same style but using reconstituted
stone. On the r., set back, is the VICARAGE of *c.* 1840, designed
by *the Duchess* herself (with the help of *William Barnfather*, clerk
of works) in the typical Tudor style of the early c 19 estate buildings (cf. Denwick village and Westfield House in Longhoughton).
At the top of the hill on the l. stands POTTERGATE TOWER,
Gothick of 1768 by *Henry Bell* and replacing a medieval gateway
(a little older-looking squared stone seems to survive on the
external face). Round-arched gateway with ribbed vault; the inner
face of the tower is the more elaborate, with traceried panels. Until
1812 the tower had a 'crown' like that of Newcastle Cathedral.

Starting again in Bondgate Without, we go up MARKET STREET.
On the r. behind the Northumberland Hall (*see* above) is the
MARKET PLACE, effectively kept clear of all main streets. The
MARKET CROSS has a c 19 panelled and traceried head on the
older shaft and stepped base. Nearby, on the E side, two tall c 18
houses; No. 10 has sashes with thick architraves to the first and
second floors, and little Yorkshire sashes beneath the eaves; the
adjacent house, on the corner, has a 1738 sundial towards Market
Street, which now becomes CLAYPORT STREET. Here is the
pretty ST MICHAEL'S PANT (Gothick of 1765 by *Bell*); opposite,
FENKLE STREET leads off N and is worth a sidetrack. On the r.,
beyond the Town Hall, the CO-OP BUILDING of 1907, Arts-
and-Crafts classical, is marred by later changes on the ground
floor. Opposite, the TERRITORIAL DRILL HALL of *c.* 1834 looks
quite imposing, with a Greek Doric porch *in antis*, angle bays with
giant pilasters and a big balustrade.

Back on Clayport Street, on the S the OLD POST OFFICE, No.

1, a handsome early C 19 building with a Tuscan porch and pedimented centrepiece. Opposite, after the late C 20 bus station, another detour along DISPENSARY STREET to see the early C 19 BREWERY, a good massing of lofty but plain ranges. Opposite No. 25 Clayport Street stood (until 1804) the C 15 gateway that gave the street its name. Outside Westgate House is another PANT, this time dated 1755. A little further up the hill, LISBURN TERRACE joins from the l., with, on the corner, the striking TERRITORIAL ARMY CENTRE, 1983, by *Frank Harrison* of the *Mauchlen, Weightman & Elphick Partnership*; light fawn brick with pilasters of dark brown brick, a six-bay part with a taller three-bay part at the back. Big hipped roofs with overhanging eaves on triangular brackets; the entrance at the SE end is flanked by triangular oriels.

Lisburn Terrace becomes LISBURN STREET (on the r. the former VICTORIA INFANTS' SCHOOL; of the 1830s, Tuscan, single storey and three bays) and then PRUDHOE STREET, which, with the parallel GREEN BATT to the N and several linking N–S streets, is the focus of the HOWICK STREET development. This superior-quality residential suburb was created in the 1830s by *William Smith*, on land formerly belonging to General Lambert, with written-in specifications for ashlar fronts, chimneys and slate roofs. A variety of styles was used, from chaste Georgian to Gothick. The suburb is still virtually unspoiled though few of the buildings demand individual notice. The former MECHANICS INSTITUTE by *William Smith*, 1831–2, with giant Doric pilasters with honeysuckle capitals and a very Grecian doorway, forms part of a composition of two-storeyed houses facing St Paul's Church. GREEN BATT HOUSE is a hip-roofed villa; GLEBELANDS LODGE, across the road NE of Green Batt House, is a slightly earlier single-storey Gothick lodge. Return to the centre by ST MICHAEL'S LANE (due N from St Paul), past the former Sion Meeting House and under an archway into Market Street again.

There are a few worthwhile buildings outside the perambulation: ST THOMAS FARM, on the N where Clayport Street has steepened into Clayport Bank. Tudor style, dated 1829, with the rear wall of an adjacent outbuilding transformed into a pretty Gothick screen with arrow slits. There is a similar little eyecatcher about 200 yards S in the wall on the W side of Swansfield Park. Swansfield House (1823, by *Dobson*) has been demolished, but the Peace Column in its grounds survives (*see* above). The FOREST LODGE AND STOCKINGATE, at the end of Ratten Row, branching W off Canongate opposite the parish church, 1854, may be by *F. R. Wilson* (it resembles his reworking of the Shilbottle Vicarage tower). The segmental archway, beside an embattled tower with trefoil-headed lights and a taller turret, forms the main entrance to the Duke's Park.

HEIFERLAW TOWER. *See* p. 313.
HULNE PRIORY. *See* p. 353.

ALWINTON   9000

ST MICHAEL. S of the river on the slope of the bank. This position gives the church a dramatic W front and an even more dramatic rising of the chancel above the nave. There are ten steps up to the chancel. The crypt underneath has not been seen for over a hundred years. Apart from the chancel, which is medieval, only the N aisle E wall, part of the N aisle N wall, and parts of the W wall, with some blocked windows, pre-date 1851, when the church was largely rebuilt by *Pickering*. He used the E.E. style. The W front has two lancets and two smaller lancets at the W end of the aisles. Some lancet windows along the sides. In the outer S wall of the S transept there is a cross-shaped stone with coat of arms, initials and the date 1672. The chancel was built in the C 12, as can be seen from one small original S window, and it was altered in the C 14, as can be seen from the two low-side lancets with shouldered rere-arches, and a two-light Dec window. C 19 E window. Inside, the chancel arch, and nearly everything else, is Pickering's, though the nave arcades may be over-restored C 13. – STAINED GLASS. All by *Wailes*. – MONUMENTS. Wall tablets by *Jopling* of Gateshead (1796) to Percy Clennell, and by *Bulman* of Newcastle (1849) to Thomas Clennell. – In the N aisle two rustic but finely carved table tombs of 1701 and 1745.

CHEW GREEN. *See* p. 225.

CLENNELL STREET. One of the medieval roads over the Border, from Alwinton to Hownam. A prominent CROSS-RIDGE DYKE, 270 metres (880 ft) long and cunningly set in a gully, guards its passage 1 m. N. Early enclosed and unenclosed settlements beside the route include GALLOW LAW, 800 metres (870 yards) N, a large hillfort with a rocky interior and a good E entrance; its two slight stony ramparts have strong natural defences overlooking the village. Aspiring students of early vernacular architecture can test their powers of observation above the steep slopes of Hosedon Linn: on a ledge immediately W of the Street, where it crosses the summit 300 metres N of the cross dyke, stood an Iron Age settlement of nine timber houses; their sites are marked by circular grooves in the turf. At least two had double rings of posts supporting the roof.

RUSSELL'S CAIRN, on the Border at the summit of Windy Gyle (619 metres, 2,030 ft). A massive rubble cairn 16 metres (50 ft) in diameter and 2.5 metres (8 ft) high. Probably Bronze Age, but traditionally associated with the murder of Lord Francis Russell on a day of truce in 1585; however, the deed may have been done on Cock Law, a mile ENE.

AMBLE   2000

Amble was little more than a hamlet before the construction of its harbour (originally known as Warkworth Harbour) in 1838–49. *Rennie* was its designer; the contractors were *John and James Welch* (until 1842) and then *Sandersons*, who also commenced a planned urban development around Queen Street. (*See* Introduction,

p. 103.) Today Amble is a not unpleasant small town but has few buildings of distinction.

St CUTHBERT. 1870 by *Austin & Johnson* of Newcastle. Aisleless but quite large, in the Dec style. 1929 s vestry.

VICARAGE. Church Street, across the road from the parish church. Quite a handsome Jacobean-style house of 1876 by *Johnson & Hicks*.

In Queen Street and on the w side of the adjacent North Street, some of the original 1837 terraces survive, at least at first-floor level. Their stonework is of almost ashlar quality, with some odd arrangements of pilasters ending below the moulded eaves cornice. On the N side of High Street, immediately w of the mid-c 20 R.C. Church, is a fragment of wall with a c 15 window, square-headed and of two trefoiled lights with uncusped sunk panels above. Though it may seem unlikely, this is an *in-situ* fragment of the medieval MANOR HOUSE. It belonged to Tyne-mouth Priory and may have served as a monastic cell.

HIGH HAUXLEY. *See* p. 334.

NORTH TOGSTON. *See* p. 532.

0040

ANCROFT

St ANNE. The w half of the nave is Norman and contains a s doorway which is important, though blocked and badly decayed. It is set slightly forward from the wall-face under a gable and has three orders of colonnettes with heavy arches. The outer arch has worn beakhead. This s side of the church also has a genuine c 12 corbel table and a large buttress which formerly marked the SE corner of the nave. Above the corbel table, in the late c 13, a tower, like a vicar's pele, was built, blocking the doorway. It can of course be called a fortified church tower. It has a tunnel-vaulted ground floor, just like the other Northumbrian tower-houses, a spiral stair in the SE corner, and on the upper floor a room with three deeply splayed one-light lancet windows. At the w end the roof mark of the gable of the original c 12 towerless church can be seen, as can the band where the corbel table was cut away. On the N side one arch of the corbel table remains. The church was restored in 1836 and again in 1870 (by *F. R. Wilson*), when the nave was extended to the E, the chancel rebuilt and the door and windows replaced, all in imitation of the original. Inside, the chancel arch, 1870, has quite elaborate chevron mouldings. – GRAVESTONE, just w of the church. Inscribed:

> To the Memory of Mary Catherine Smith
> deceased the 20th of Jan 1799 · · · · ·
> · · · · · · · Superior
> of the Religious Community who by the
> Bounty of SIR CARNABY HAGGERSTON
> Bart. were received and lodg'd at his castle
> during 12 years after the French Revolution.

The stone then records the names of nine more nuns buried in the same place.

BERRINGTON HOUSE, 1½ m. s. Not a large house, just three by two bays. It looks a characteristically early c 19 house for this area, in fine ashlar with no more decoration than raised quoins, a moulded eaves cornice, a plain parapet and, above the centre bay, a higher parapet with some guilloche moulding. Inside, the staircase has the same balustrade as Barmoor Castle, with wrought-iron balusters in the form of stylized palm fronds. Raine, writing in 1852, says that the house was rebuilt for John Grey of Kimmerston 'some ten or twelve years since'. It looks older than that, and, indeed, Mackenzie suggested in 1825 that it had already been built for John Clavering.

The WALLED GARDEN is a splendid affair, with walls of many periods from the late medieval to the c 18. Incorporated into the s side are parts of the c 17 manor house of the Claverings. A gable and some windows are clearly visible.

EAST ALLERDEAN, 2 m. WNW. Large and impressive farm buildings of c. 1880 (cf. Murton, Ord; East House, Cheswick).

CHESWICK. See p. 225.

HAGGERSTON. See p. 295.

ANGERTON
½ m s of Hartburn

0080

ANGERTON HALL. 1842 by *John Dobson*; NE wing c. 1920. Reduced in size 1957. Tudor style. Irregular H-plan with symmetrical s front and mullioned-and-transomed windows. At the back a big gabled porch leads into an entrance hall with a coffered ceiling and ornamental bosses. – The GARDENS were laid out in 1904 by *Lutyens*. Rock-faced terrace walls and fancy wrought-iron gates s of the house, a little summerhouse to the E, and pergola and gateways in the Victorian walled garden to the NE.

LOW ANGERTON BRIDGE, over the infant Wansbeck. 1908 by the *British Concrete Steel Company*. Reinforced concrete with open-work wrought-iron parapet.

To the E, behind a c 19 house, is a ruined BASTLE HOUSE, unusual this far E in the county. All that survives is the lower part of its w end, with a central round-arched byre door.

ANICK
1 m. NE of Hexham

9060

ANICK FARMHOUSE. Good example of a bastle house remodelled as a conventional farmhouse (c. 1700). Of the earlier phase, the thick walls of roughly coursed rubble and remains of byre and upper doors in heavy block surrounds, both on the s; of the latter, the present moulded doorway and windows (which have the proportions of mullioned windows but are without mullions) with stepped surrounds, now holding Yorkshire sashes. Also of the second phase, two fireplaces, one with a bolection moulding.

HOMEWAY. Moulded doorway dated 1694 between windows of

the Anick Farmhouse type, except that here they have stone mullions (renewed): upper floor later C 19.

BANKFOOT, ¼ m. S. Five-bay late C 17 house with central moulded doorway and rather tall and narrow windows: at the rear, smaller blocked windows with steeply chamfered stone surrounds. Typical reverse-stepped gables to the steep roof, which must once have been thatched. Formerly an inn.

ASHINGTON

HOLY SEPULCHRE. 1887–96 by *W. S. Hicks*. Five-bay fully aisled plan in Hicks's usual Perp style, with a W narthex (cf. St Cuthbert at Blyth). The NE bell tower was never completed, because the Ashington Coal Company, which provided most of the money, was worried that the bells would wake its night-shift workers. To the S is the VICARAGE, *c.* 1897, of snecked stone in a free Tudor style with some Arts-and-Crafts touches.

ST ANDREW THE APOSTLE, Seaton Hirst. 1932. Big brick basilica.

ST JOHN THE EVANGELIST, Seaton Hirst. 1896, enlarged in 1905 and again in 1945. Snecked stone, in a plain lancet style.

ST AIDAN (R.C.), Station Road. 1905. Lancet style, in hard orange brick.

METHODIST CENTRAL HALL, Woodhorn Road. 1923 by *Brocklehurst & Co.* of Manchester. Art Deco style, in glazed brick with terracotta dressings. This was the era of the cinema's burgeoning popularity, and its influence is plain, with the organ framed by a proscenium arch and even a projector room.

POLICE STATION, Station Road. 1897. Red brick with red sandstone dressings. Behind is the MAGISTRATES' COURT of 1926, brown brick and ashlar, with its two doorways set in big rusticated arches with round windows above.

ASHINGTON DISTRICT HOSPITAL. By *Powell & Moya*, completed 1991. Distinguished. Low (to minimize the effect of icy blasts from the North Sea) and domestic in outline, with hipped roofs and clusters of slender white flues.

Before the opening of the coalpits in the mid-C 19, Ashington was a single farm (which survives, ¾ m. SW of the present centre). The town owes its growth to the Ashington Coal Company (*see* Introduction, p. 91), which built the first 300 houses between *c.* 1855 and 1878. These were in a series of E–W terraces at the W end of the town, just N of the parish church. The large area of N–S terraces E of the railway, called Hirst, is an early C 20 development. The original centre is marked by FIRST ROW, a relatively unaltered terrace of *c.* 1870. These are rather superior brick cottages, varying in size, with painted stone lintels and sills; they were built for the colliery manager and officials. The other rows, of humbler dwellings, have all been much altered. To the rear of each row there was originally a tramway system for removing rubbish and waste from the ash closets. The present centre of the town, further E at the far end of Station Road, is architecturally undistinguished. On Woodhorn Road is the Baroque CO-OPERATIVE SOCIETY BUILDING, designed in 1924 by *Harrison*,

Ash & Blyth of Newcastle, as a terracotta-fronted shopping arcade with offices and a ballroom above. The formerly open ground floor is now filled in by small units, but the grand imperial stair with contemporary bronze handrails survives.

WOODHORN COLLIERY, 1 m. E. Colliery buildings of *c.* 1895–1900, being converted to a museum (1991). All the buildings are of yellow Ashington brick made from clay brought out of the colliery: there are two shafts with headgear and winding houses, fan and engine houses, a long range of workshops and a stable. Most of the openings are round-headed, with gauged brick arches; the windows are iron-framed casements.

AYDON   *0060*

A small village with three quite substantial houses. On the N side of the road are NORTH FARMHOUSE, a symmetrical early C 18 five-bay house with bands and wedge lintels, and SOUTH FARM-HOUSE, which has a three-storey late C 18 part and a lower wing, dated 1722, with details still in the C 17 tradition. On the S of the road, AYDON HOUSE, a five-bay three-storey building dated 1727, with a moulded doorway and windows with wedge lintels tooled to imitate voussoirs. The parallel rear range and the E wing, which replaces a C 17 house, are of 1885 by *Septimus Oswald & Son*, and so is the pretty wooden verandah.

AYDON CASTLE, ½ m. NW, is beautifully and strongly placed above the Cor Burn, which winds round it on three sides. The slopes are steep and densely wooded. The castle consists of an outer bailey to the N, where the site is exposed to attack, and a square courtyard (which hardly merits the term inner bailey), with the hall range along its S side, backed by the steep valley side. Aydon has no keep, and that gives it its outstanding architectural importance. Here is a very early case of a fortified house rather than a castle; indeed until recently it was still sometimes referred to as 'Aydon Hall'. Licence to crenellate was granted to Robert de Reymes in 1305, but the architecture of the hall range looks a little earlier, perhaps by twenty or thirty years. It has been assumed that 1305 refers to the finishing, that is to the actual crenellating of the house and the addition of the NW range and courtyard walls. An additional range W of the hall block (now largely removed) and the outer bailey walls are later C 14 additions. Subsequent alterations have been remarkably few. The main buildings were for many years a farmhouse, but the internal evidences of this phase have now been stripped out, with the result that the C 13 and C 14 work is all exposed, but there is a slightly gutted feel to the interiors.

The hall range is worth close study. The hall itself is at first-floor level. At its E end is a cross wing containing the solar, and beyond that a projecting wing making a roughly cruciform plan. Solar and E wing are of *c.* 1280: there is some evidence that they were additions to an older hall block which was rebuilt a few years after their construction. An outer staircase leads up to the double-chamfered hall doorway, beneath the roof-line of a former porch.

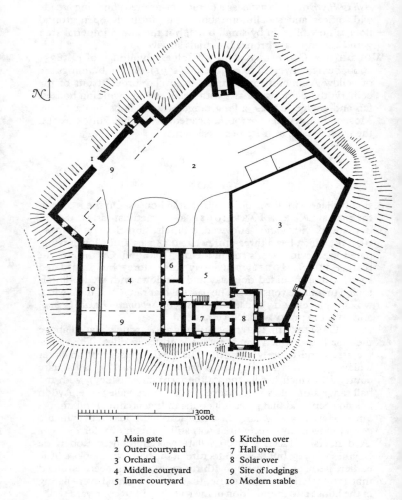

Aydon Castle. Plan

1 Main gate	6 Kitchen over
2 Outer courtyard	7 Hall over
3 Orchard	8 Solar over
4 Middle courtyard	9 Site of lodgings
5 Inner courtyard	10 Modern stable

This led into a screens passage with a gallery over, as can be seen
from the window arrangements in the s wall; this may be a c 14
rather than a c 13 feature, as the chamber w of the entry was
probably in its original form a kitchen. Alterations and the insertion of a floor probably took place in the early c 14, when the
kitchen was moved to the new NW range. The dais end of the hall
was lit by a two-light window in each wall. Below the hall was a
room with a fireplace (the hall presumably had to make do with
a brazier), and the outer projection of the fireplace in the s wall
is one of the most remarkable features of the building. It ends

below the eaves line of the range in a semicircular attached shaft with lancet openings for the smoke to escape. To the W of this room is a vaulted chamber beneath the original kitchen. The solar at the E end of the hall is clearly distinguished by an excellent fireplace, treated more sumptuously than the others. To the s is a window like those flanking the hall dais, of two pointed lights under an arched hoodmould. The windows to the E and N are more elaborate, with sunk quatrefoils in the spandrel, that on the N containing a bearded head. 33

There has been some speculation as to how the house actually functioned. The apparent duplication of apartments on ground- and first-floor levels has led to the suggestion that it was designed for dual occupation, but the obviously inferior status of the lower rooms makes it more likely that they simply housed the owner's personal attendants. The small E wing is another puzzle; by analogy with other houses it should have housed a private chapel. Possibly there was a chapel on a second floor removed in antiquity; its size suggests some function other than giving access to the well-preserved garderobes in a s projection which are now its main feature.

The C 14 NW wing has a barrel-vaulted basement and mutilated remains of a large kitchen fireplace. Windows with shouldered arches to the individual lights characterize the C 14 work: there are more in the curtain wall which formed the s side of the former W wing. The courtyard wall has a chamfered gateway arch, a wall-walk and battlements which may be an addition. The outer bailey is an irregular pentagon in plan: neither the segmental-arched gateway facing NW nor the single D-plan tower at the N corner (only its basement survives) is of especial defensive strength. From the C 16 and C 17 are the simple principal-rafter truss roofs, and two basement doorways with lintel dates in the 1660s; a few simple sash windows remain from the last phase of occupation as a farmhouse. But these are details. The aesthetic and historical significance is all comprised in the view up from the s to the broad and secure walls of the hall and its dependent apartments. This represents the amount of space and of comfort which could be afforded in the Border country c. 1300.

THORNBROUGH HIGH BARNS, $\frac{3}{4}$ m. SE. 1816. The earliest of the planned farms built for Greenwich Hospital for which a plan survives (see Introduction, p. 85). The farmhouse is much altered but the buildings survive. Single-storey ranges on three sides of a yard open to the s, with a two-storey barn running back from the centre of the N range and a loose-box in the centre of the yard.

WHITE HOUSE, 1 m. NE. Late C 17 T-plan house. The front has a moulded doorway dated 1684 and mullioned windows. The window mullions and surrounds are of rounded section (cf. Capheaton etc.). C 19 wing, altered in 1953 by *H. L. Honeyman*, linking the rear wing to a barn which may be contemporary with the house. The WALLED GARDEN to the SE, probably of the mid-C 18, includes a garden house or gazebo with Venetian windows which was obviously planned to be part of a larger building.

BACKWORTH

3m. w of Whitley Bay

In the Middle Ages there were two villages, East and West Backworth. The E end of Backworth Lane is the attractive main street
of the present village. It shows no sign of building before the C 18
but has a pleasing irregularity of plot size and building line, with
the expected mixture of farms, cottages, pubs and school. C 19
and C 20 houses lie to the E around Church Road, and, since the
1980s, have been built to the W, off the road to Killingworth.
The C 19 colliery has gone almost without trace; where once the
sandstone tower of the pit engine winding house stood to the SE
of the village, there is now a light industrial estate and just a few
remaining one-storey cottages.

BACKWORTH HALL (now Backworth Miners' Welfare Hall). The
grounds back onto the S side of the village street. 1778–80 by
William Newton for R.W. Grey, replacing a C 17 house. Generously spaced five-bay S front. Half-basement of rusticated sandstone, the other one-and-a-half storeys smooth ashlar; all the
masonry is of high quality. Stairs up to the central doorway, which
is of the Venetian type favoured by Robert Adam. The ground-
floor windows have fluted friezes below cornices, the intermediate
ones are pedimented, and those above have architrave surrounds.
Three-bay dentilled pediment on a dentilled cornice which wraps
round the sides as far as the rear corner pilasters. The rear elevation (N) also has a three-bay projection under a plain pediment.
Wings project from the NE and NW corners. These originally
consisted of one-bay, one-storey connecting links and three-bay,
one-and-a-half-storey pavilions with pediments, making a very
civilized and elegant design, but they have been reduced to one
storey; the W one is only a façade, the E one has a flat roof, and
the arched window panels are blocked. They cry out to be
restored. The fire which spoilt the interior *c.* 1960 was probably
to blame for their mutilation. The entrance hall still has a Venetian
screen in front of the renewed staircase; the stair well is lit from
above by a glass dome.

DUKE'S COTTAGES, Nos. 1–4 Front Street. An attractive row of
estate workers' cottages in a subdued C 17 style, built as six houses
c. 1840 for the Duke of Northumberland. Restored 1981–2 by
J. & D. Darbyshire for Buttress, the Tyne and Wear Building
Preservation Trust.

BAMBURGH

ST AIDAN. The church is large and forms part of a wonderful group
with the castle. From the outside, however, it is more varied than
impressive. It has a W tower, and nave, transepts and aisles with
roofs so flat as to be almost invisible, and a chancel with a
high and steeply pitched roof. The chancel is the finest piece of
architecture. It was built *c.* 1230, after the Pope had settled a
dispute over the ownership of the church in 1221, and is one of the
typical long, aisleless chancels of the North. Fine, high moulded
plinth. At the E end three lancets of the same height separated by

buttresses, and beneath them three small lancets to the crypt. On the s side, five bays. In four of them, paired lancets under a continuous dripstone. The second bay has a priest's door altered externally and given a high gable in 1830. Original corbel table. On the N side, windows in two bays only, and a low-side window with a cinquefoil cusped head. The rainwater heads are dated 1830 and bear the crest of Lord Crewe. The s transept and aisle have renewed Dec windows. The aisles embrace the tower, which has medieval stonework below, with C 18 or early C 19 lancets, and was rebuilt above, possibly in 1830. The N aisle has renewed windows also, but the beautiful large blocks of weathered stone show that the N wall must have been rebuilt in the C 15. The stonework of the N transept, on the other hand, is small and square, clearly earlier than anything else visible from the outside and characteristically C 12.

Inside, the E window of the N transept has a round rere-arch, and there are several other small pieces of evidence to suggest the C 12 predecessor to the present church, in particular another stretch of clearly C 12 masonry in the s transept above the arch into the crossing. The confusing evidence in this part of the church points to the existence of an earlier aisleless nave. The present nave is late C 12 or early C 13. The arcades to the N and s aisles differ from each other. The older ones are on the N side and have circular piers, except for the w respond, which is a corbel. The capitals are round. The first one is very plainly moulded, the second a little more elaborately, the third has a wreath of upright stiffleaves. The arches are double-chamfered and steeply pointed. The E arch rests on a semicircular respond which begins, rather oddly, on a corbel halfway up the pier. This arch is also very narrow, another of the puzzles of the church for which there is no satisfactory explanation. The corresponding arch of the s arcade is narrow also, but less so. Both abut against the angles of the transepts, which, as we have seen, were already in existence (and not parallel with each other); so perhaps the arcade was built from the w with the assumption that the existing transepts were to be demolished, and when this for some reason was not carried out, the arcades had to be finished in this squashed manner. The N arcade seems *c.* 1190–1200. The s arcade is similar but, with its more elaborately moulded capitals, a little later. The s aisle is very wide, a C 14 rather than a C 13 trait. It must have been rebuilt. It has a remarkably wide double-chamfered arch. The other arches to the crossing are again puzzling, for they look older than the arcades; towards the nave and the N aisle they have two very slight chamfers, towards the transept an unmoulded arch. Above the s arcade there are blocked square clerestory windows now within the roof. Can they be original or are they C 16? The C 16 seems the most likely date for the square newel stair in the tower. The three tower arches (i.e. towards the nave and aisles) are triple-chamfered. The tower ceiling has an old forked beam associated with the legend of the death of Aidan. The N aisle has old tie-beams.

Double-chamfered chancel arch. To the r. of it, a squint – a large square opening of Dec tracery. The chancel is the architectural high point, but it was once even more sumptuous. Above the windows one can still see a long arcade of pointed arches apparently on moulded corbels. In fact the corbels are the capitals of long slender shafts which divided up the whole of the chancel walls. There are two low-side windows, the S one blocked. In the S wall the C 14 group of SEDILIA and PISCINA with simple pointed trefoiled heads. Opposite, an AUMBREY with a top of the same shape; also another piscina whose original drain can still be seen outside – REREDOS. 1895 by *W. S. Hicks* as part of his restoration. Large and elaborate, with sculpture. – ALTAR RAILS. C 17. – STAINED GLASS. Large C 17 Flemish figures in the chancel S windows; inserted in the mid-C 19 during Archdeacon Thorp's incumbency. They are part of the same sequence as those at Ryton Church (*see* Buildings of England, *County Durham*). – S aisle, 1936 by *J. M. Ballantyne*. – MONUMENTS. Next to the sedilia a low large recess with the effigy of a slender knight with crossed legs. The most probable date is *c.* 1325. – Claudius Forster † 1623. A black marble cartouche in an aedicule on the chancel N wall. – Forster family † 1711, also on the chancel N wall. A well-carved white marble wall monument with an interesting inscription. – Sharp monument. W end of N aisle. 1839 by *Chantrey*. A seated girl looking down; beside her the bust of Dr John Sharp on a pedestal. – The recumbent effigy of Grace Darling in the N aisle is by *Raymond Smith*, 1844. Formerly in the churchyard, where a facsimile now lies in a Gothic shrine with metal colonnettes and a canopy (by *Hicks*, 1895). – W of the church, a broken column of 1843 with an excellent inscription to the Rev. John Mackenzie who died in the wreck of the steamship *Pegasus*.

Beneath the S side of the chancel is a CRYPT vaulted in an unusual way. Two bays separated by a transverse arch, and each bay with a cinquepartite rib vault, i.e. additional ridge ribs only rising from the middle of the W and E walls to the apexes of each bay. The ribs are single-chamfered and rest on corbels.

Beneath the N third of the chancel is a corridor with a pointed tunnel vault.

BAMBURGH CASTLE. The castle looks its grandest from the village, though for views from afar also there are not many castles in
23   England that can vie with it. It is placed on a precipitous outcrop of the Whin Sill rising up to 46 metres (150 ft). Views from the castle extend across the dunes to Holy Island. The site is long and narrow in a W–E direction. It comprises 3.2 hectares (8 acres) and is the very ideal of natural fortification. It has been used as such since very early times; indeed excavations in the W ward revealed a sequence of continuous occupation from the late pre-Roman Iron Age, when the rock probably held a hillfort. Throughout Saxon times it was a fort and royal palace. Of all this nothing remains visible except part of a cross shaft and some pieces of jewelry found during excavation and preserved in the castle museum. The castle now consists of a C 12 keep and three baileys – the East Ward, the West Ward and the Inner Ward.

The keep lies between the East Ward and the Inner Ward. It is the principal relic of the Norman castle. There are records of expenditure on it in 1164, but the amounts are so small as to suggest that it had been started a little earlier under Scottish rule

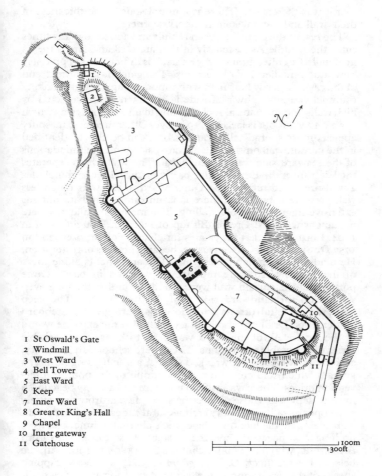

1 St Oswald's Gate
2 Windmill
3 West Ward
4 Bell Tower
5 East Ward
6 Keep
7 Inner Ward
8 Great or King's Hall
9 Chapel
10 Inner gateway
11 Gatehouse

Bamburgh Castle. Plan

and that this money was only to complete existing work. In plan
and appearance it resembles Carlisle, which was built in the 1150s.
It is 21.1 by 18.9 metres (69 by 61½ ft) and 23.7 metres (78 ft)
high – sturdy proportions. High moulded plinth, square turrets
at the corners and buttresses strengthening the walls. A remarkable and very rare feature, proving how secure one could feel on
the dolerite rock, is the position of the principal entrance on the
ground floor. It has two orders of renewed colonnettes and a plain
stepped round arch. Inside much was altered in the C18, but the
basement is vaulted with two parallel tunnel vaults rising from
huge square piers. On the first floor, the armoury is vaulted also.
The room is divided into bays by flat pilasters, and the bays are
groin-vaulted. The E end of the room is apsidal, which suggests

that it was the chapel. There is a mural stair in the thickness of the E wall and a spiral stair in the NW corner.

The rest of the castle has been rebuilt and added to many times since the Middle Ages, mainly in the late C 18 and late C 19. As no detailed architectural survey exists, it is difficult to say precisely how much medieval work remains. The gatehouse at the E end of the castle is partly Norman, with rounded angle towers flanking a tunnel-vaulted archway. Inside is a sunken road protected by high walls and the natural rock, leading to an inner gateway which has a C 12 vault but is largely C 19 above. Other medieval masonry appears more sporadically. Patches of it can be clearly identified in the curtain wall on the S (landward) side, and the foundations of the seaward side wall are medieval. The wall which separates the West from the East Ward is partly medieval too and includes a well-preserved turret. The Outer Ward to the W is much less well-preserved, but what there is is unrestored and it contains extensive fragments of old walling. The medieval buildings were in ruins when Lord Crewe, Bishop of Durham, bought them in 1704. Lord Crewe left his estates for charitable purposes, and in 1757 Dr Sharp, as a Crewe trustee, began a process of restoration. He made the keep habitable again. The apartments along the S of the Inner Ward were rebuilt and restored in parts. Large portions of the curtain wall were rebuilt including the long even section on the landward side E of the Bell Tower. The keep was given fanciful turrets and the walls were given pasteboard battlements. Dr Sharp also built a windmill at the extreme W end of the castle. All of this work was used to house a remarkable series of charitable institutions. There were schools, an infirmary, accommodation for shipwrecked sailors, a free lending library, a granary which sold corn from the windmill to the poor at intervention prices. There was a lifeboat system and a safety beacon – a mass of activities whose pioneering social adventurousness surely outshone the rather ordinary architectural endeavours which went with them. By the late C 19 the castle's charitable functions were no longer so necessary and the trustees chose to sell it to Lord Armstrong, who made major changes from 1894 to 1904 with the help of his architect, *C. J. Ferguson* of Carlisle. Avray Tipping speaks of the restoration as the 'acme of expenditure with a nadir of intelligent achievement'. This is not fair. Ferguson and Lord Armstrong remodelled work which had already been altered by Dr Sharp and his successors. Their principal contribution is a series of state rooms and apartments along the S side of the Inner Ward on the site of and including remnants of the great hall, the kitchens and the captain's lodgings. The style is Perp to early Tudor, relatively free and varied externally and equally varied inside. The porch has a sophisticated umbrella vault and there is a cantilevered stair with *art nouveau* balusters. The King's Hall is grand in scale, with a false hammerbeam roof, a fireplace with joggled lintel and full-height overmantel of Perp stone tracery, and beautifully detailed bay windows on the S side. These add greatly to the picture of the castle from the village. This hall is on the site of the great hall built in 1384–90 by Sir John Fenwick. The three original service doors at the lower end survive. The two outer doors lead to the original pantry and buttery, both of which have high pointed tunnel vaults. The middle door opens onto a corridor which leads to the great kitchen. It has three huge segmental-arched fireplaces. There are also two vaulted larders. Beneath all of these rooms and the captain's lodgings to the W are preserved medieval cellars, especially the vault underneath the so-called Captain's Hall, which has ten single-chamfered transverse arches.

In the middle of the Inner Ward are the ruins of a CHAPEL of the C12. Nave, square chancel and apse, all buttressed. The apse has shafts inside between the windows, which are themselves shafted – it must once have made quite a rich ensemble.

VILLAGE. Bamburgh village is dominated by the castle. The church lies at the far end of a triangular green. The S side has mainly C18 and C19 cottages, though one is dated 1699 on a window lintel. Nos. 17–22 are Gothick single-storey cottages dated 1809. Of more substantial houses there are, up lanes just to the S of Front Street, BAMBURGH HOUSE, Greek Doric of 1830–40, and ARMSTRONG HOUSE (Abbeyfield Homes), built as a rest home for Lord Armstrong's Tyneside workers and designed in Arts-and-Crafts style by *Ernest J. Hart*, Lord Armstrong's agent, in 1914. In a field just S of the house, a tall beehive-shaped medieval DOVECOTE similar to those at Embleton, at Buckton near Kyloe and at Gainford Hall in County Durham. Gothick PANT on the green, *c.* 1830.

Beside the church, and forming an attractive group with it, is BAMBURGH HALL, with a dignified early C19 ashlar four-bay façade; much older masonry behind, including a large external chimney-stack. The wall between the Hall and the church incorporates medieval masonry from the Augustinian cell founded from Nostell in 1121. The cell had its own master, and the surviving stretch of old walling is referred to as the MASTER OF BAMBURGH'S TOWER

Of the Dominican friary, licensed in 1265, little more can be seen than the site, now FRIARY FARM, to the S of the B1342 road to Belford, $\frac{1}{4}$m. from the church. The farm buildings are fine in themselves, incorporating some medieval masonry and a blocked C16 doorway. A fragment of high, ivy-covered stonework to the l. of the farm is the NE corner of the church.

BUDLE. *See* p. 203.
WAREN MILL. *See* p. 609.

BARDON MILL 7060

On the N bank of the South Tyne, and dominated by a POTTERY, converted from a stone-built, water-powered woollen mill of *c.* 1800 after a fire destroyed the woollen milling equipment in 1876. The mill building is of two adjoining bays of two and three storeys but was evidently once higher; it has an internal waterwheel behind the road-end gable and an external steam engine bed alongside. It made salt-glazed sanitary ware, bricks etc., and still uses circular downdraught kilns, although it is now a pottery for garden ware; there are horizontal-draught 'Newcastle' kilns in the same yard.

STATIONMASTER'S HOUSE. Early C 19 Tudor, but in a rather different style (cf. particularly the gable finials) to the other early buildings on the Newcastle–Carlisle line, which are assumed to be by the *Greens*.

MILLHOUSE GRANGE. An ashlar-fronted three-bay house of the early C 19; to the NW is a BASTLE HOUSE, now a garage, with a flattened Tudor arch to its blocked upper door; inside, heavy transverse beams carrying the first floor, and a central principal rafter roof truss. Across the road to the W, a terrace of cottages incorporating three more bastles built end-to-end.

Other BASTLE HOUSES in the area include BIRKSHAW, $\frac{3}{4}$ m. N, GRANDY'S KNOWE, 2 m. N (more ruinous; attached early C 18 house with upper crucks), and several around THORNGRAFTON, $\frac{1}{2}$ m. NE. At WHITSHIELDS, I m. E, is a larger bastle-type building with a cross wing at one end.

HIGH MEADOW, I$\frac{1}{2}$ m. E. To the N of an C 18 cottage is a six-bay CRUCK BARN, a precious vernacular survival, in a parlous condition at the time of writing. Roughly shaped full cruck trusses with purlins carried on the overlapped ends of the collars and the ridge between the overlapped ends of the blades. The rafters are simply uncut branches carrying heather thatch. Despite the antique appearance of the roof structure, the neatly squared stonework shows that the date is no earlier than the mid-C 18.

Beside a minor road at CRINDLEDIKES, I$\frac{1}{2}$ m. N, in the scarp country S of the Wall, a quarry in one of the tilted limestone bands has an impressive LIMEKILN, sub-circular, with three lofty corbelled drawing arches.

HOUSESTEADS. *See* p. 345.

VINDOLANDA. *See* p. 597.

WILLIMOTESWICK. *See* p. 631.

0039

BARMOOR

1m. w of Lowick

The house was designed in 1801 for Francis Sitwell by *John Paterson* of Edinburgh. Paterson had been a pupil and partner of the Adam brothers and after their death became one of the leading exponents of the 'castle style' they had developed. Barmoor is an excellent example of the type. The entrance side is five bays and three storeys high; castellated, with mullioned and transomed windows. The broad centre bay is a higher tower, boldly projecting from the rest of the façade. This has, in its turn, two diagonally set turrets. The doorway is in a shallow, single-storey, bow-like porch between these turrets. The effect is quite powerful and grand.

Each of the house's formal façades is different in mood from the others. The garden side was the banqueting suite. It is still castellated, with round corner towers, but with its large sash windows and three-bay, two-storey central bow it looks rather more classical. The rear elevation is similar to this, but the central bow is set into a three-storey projecting tower. So it is a house externally of mixed stylistic leanings, slipping comfortably between the Gothic and the classical. Inside, however, all is

classical. The entrance hall is oval with niches, and behind it is a
three-storey cantilevered staircase with wrought-iron balusters in
the form of palm fronds. Over the stairs is an oval glass dome,
and beyond the staircase is an oval saloon, its doorcases with
pediments and anthemion friezes. Two have more elaborate
Adamish *sopraporte*.

BARRASFORD
1 m. NW of Chollerton

9070

The village is chiefly notable for the romantic views of Haughton
Castle across the North Tyne.

ELWOOD HOUSE, ¼ m. NW. Late C 18 three-bay house. Rusticated
quoins and pedimented door surround, with fluted frieze and
paterae. Flanking two-storey shallow bay windows. The detail is
similar to the remains of the house at Swinburne Castle nearby
(*see* Great Swinburne).

OLD SCHOOL, ½ m. NW. 1831 by *Dobson*. Ordinary.

Romano-British SETTLEMENT, ¼ m. NW of Barrasford Park: three
stone houses, approached by stone causeways across sunken
yards.

BAVINGTON HALL
½ m. S of Great Bavington

9070

Sizeable stone house begun by the Shafto family in the late C 17 but
altered and extended by Admiral Delaval (*see* Introduction, p.
74), who bought the property *c.* 1720. Seven bays, two-and-a-half
storeys. The top floor with the shaped gables is an addition of the
early C 19. On the entrance side, a heavy arched doorway with
a Gibbs surround. Sash windows with thick glazing bars and
architrave surrounds. The garden side is, alas, roughcast. It has
a doorway with a Gibbs surround and a pediment. Lower C 20 E
wing and, behind it, the kitchen wing, with two big arched
windows. Inside, several features of the early C 18. One room has
a fireplace and overmantel flanked by two elegant Corinthian
pilasters right to the ceiling. In another room, original panelling,
an excellent fireplace with termini caryatids in profile l. and r.,
and a curly open pediment to crown the overmantel. Staircase
with fat turned balusters and a heavily moulded handrail.

In the garden a small early C 18 GAZEBO with a pedimented
Ionic front. The grounds were formerly landscaped on a grand
scale, with lakes and avenues of trees. Of this all that remains are
fragments of a GROTTO with cyclopean masonry; a brick pedestal
presumably for a giant statue; and, a little to the SW, an EYE-
CATCHER in the form of a miniature castle with a raised centre.
Its similarity to Garrett's Rothley Castle a few miles away is
striking.

BAYBRIDGE

9050

¾ m. w of Blanchland

A hamlet just across the Derwent from the village of Hunstanworth
in County Durham. The latter was rebuilt in 1862–3 by *S. S.
Teulon*, and a number of buildings on the Northumberland side
of the river look like his work as well. GROVE COTTAGE was a
gate lodge to Newbiggin Hall. Of snecked stone with white brick
quoins and dressings of both sandstone and brick; varied Gothic
fenestration and one polygonal stone chimney. The METHODIST
CHAPEL, dated 1867 and of rock-faced stone, is also quirky
Gothic, with gable-headed windows, a steep roof and some elaborate wrought-iron finials.

NEWBIGGIN HALL, ½ m. w. The seat of Teulon's patron, the Rev.
Daniel Capper, but the present house was rebuilt, in Neo-classical
style, in 1906 after a fire of 1904, as a Latin inscription on the w
wall tells us.

BEADNELL

2020

ST EBBA. Built *c.* 1740 and enlarged 1792 by *William Athey*. The
tower and spire are of this later date, and although the odd pierced
octagonal screen at the base of the spire, with its quatrefoils and
grotesque heads, looks C 18 also, it was in fact added in 1860, at
the same time as the windows on the N side of the nave were
thoroughly gothicized. The architect was *F. R. Wilson*. Plain Y-
tracery windows on the s side of the nave. – STAINED GLASS.
One s nave window is signed by *Wailes*, 1851. – The E window
and a chancel N window, of 1854 and 1853 respectively, are
unsigned but clearly by him also. – Attractive and unusual Second
World War Memorial window in the nave by *J. E. Nuttgens*. –
MONUMENTS. Thomas Taylor †1802, with a draped urn. –
Henry Howey †1816, with a nice garlanded urn; by *Dennis, Lee &
Welsh* of Leeds.

BEADNELL HALL. A late C 17 or early C 18 house embedded on
three sides in later C 18 Gothick. Castellated gables and the typical
quatrefoils and broad-pointed sash windows. The entrance front
is of the earlier period; windows in architrave surrounds and a
porch with heavily moulded pedimented door surround. Inside,
good late C 17 or early C 18 panelling in four rooms.

CRASTER ARMS. Pretty two-bay C 18 front with coat of arms and
over-large foliage trails carved in stone. To the rear, the first two
floors of a small medieval tower. The basement, which is divided
in two by a cross wall, has a rough four-centred vault and a mural
stair at the E end.

The medieval chapel of ST EBBA stood on the rocks to the NE of
Beadnell Harbour. There is nothing more of it visible than some
humps in the grass and some bits of masonry. The surviving
details point to an early C 13 date, but the isolated position on the
headland suggests that the church was of much earlier foundation.

Near the site of the chapel, and considerably more prominent, the
extremely impressive group of disused LIMEKILNS, 1798, by
Richard Pringle for John Wood of Beadnell Hall. Wood was also

responsible for extending the attractive little late C 18 HARBOUR, probably to a design of Robert Cramond; piers heightened 1886 on the advice of *J. Watt Sandeman*.

ANNSTEAD, 1 m. N. Early C 19. Three bays with pedimented centre and projecting one-bay service wings with blank Venetian windows in the gable ends.

WEST FLEETHAM, 3 m. W. The farmhouse is probably C 16 in origin. The l. half of it has thick walls, and inside is a doorway with a four-centred lintel. The house was extended to the r. in the C 18 and altered *c.* 1810.

TUGHALL. *See* p. 586.

BEAUFRONT CASTLE
½ m. w of Sandhoe

9060

A country house of 1836–41 by *Dobson* for William Cuthbert. There was a medieval tower here, but nothing of it is now visible. What survives of the late C 17 Errington mansion built onto the tower is now well disguised. An extremely ambitious enterprise in Dob- 105 son's 'domestic castellated' style, a free mixture of Perpendicular and Tudor Gothic. Asymmetrically planned. The w side has the main entrance in a tall tower, with another tall block to the s showing the tall transomed windows (with glass by *Wailes*) of the main staircase. The s front, looking out across the valley, has an oriel and large buttresses, and a setback wing ending in the East Tower with a big polygonal stair turret. On the N, an attached stable court entered between smaller towers and a screen with wrought-iron gates between piers carrying C 18 statues. Inside, the *pièce de résistance* is the billiard room, with a rib-vaulted cloister on three sides. A simple but noble C 18 fireplace survives in the dining room. Below are extensive cellars with cavity walling, a device thought to have been inspired by the remains of the Roman bath-house at Haltonchesters which Dobson is known to have planned in 1827.

The SOUTH LODGE, of *c.* 1870, is by *J. A. Hansom*, who made some minor additions to the main house. A small-scale but very effective composition, following Dobson's style. The WALLED GARDEN lies 100 metres SW of the castle. John Errington expended a great deal of money on the construction of extensive gardens and hothouses in the last decades of the C 18, and parts at least of the walls and associated buildings are his. Late C 18 also the ICEHOUSE, about 500 metres N of the castle, of all-stone construction (unlike the usual C 19 types).

BEAUFRONT RED HOUSE, ¾ m. SW. Beside the new A69 dual carriageway is a big tower-like Gothick DOVECOTE, converted into a house in the C 20.

BEAUFRONT WOODHEAD, ½ m. NW. Picturesque farmhouse of several C 18 dates, with lots of reverse-stepped gables. Its complicated nature probably results from the sequential rebuilding of an older house.

BEDLINGTON

St Cuthbert. The nave is basically c 12, with a porch-like c 14 s chapel. The blocked round-arched windows date from a mid-c 18 remodelling in which the nave was turned through 90° liturgically and given a big bowed projection on the N. The c 18 chancel was rebuilt in the mid-c 19 and the w tower (which had been genuine c 12) in 1868, both in a heavy Romanesque style. In 1911–12 the nave was restored to a more conventional form and a broad N aisle added. The chancel arch is an uncommonly interesting piece of late Norman building. It rests on semicircular responds with a carved impost band. The arch is four-centred (suggesting that it was reset in the c 15) and has an inner order moulded with a half-roll between sunk quadrants, an outer order with zigzag and a worn carved hood. To the r. of the arch, a c 14 ogee-headed niche, to the l. a trefoil-headed squint. The s chapel is barrel-vaulted and has a segmental-arched recess on the w. The c 19 chancel has what are in effect stone roof trusses, round-arched, with chevron ornament. – SCULPTURE. Romanesque panel, with two standing figures, in s chapel. – MONUMENTS. Seven c 12–14 CROSS SLABS at the w end. – STAINED GLASS. Burdon Memorial Window at w end of aisle, *c.* 1911, with a strange mixture of Christian and masonic imagery.

Bedlington's character is now that of a coalfield village (the first mine was sunk in the 1840s), but it has a long history. It was once the capital of Bedlingtonshire, which formed part of the County Palatine of Durham. There is a long and wide High Street called Front Street and a c 18 MARKET CROSS in the form of an obelisk. A few old houses survive. E of the church is the Old Vicarage of 1835, a three-bay villa preserving its c 18 predecessor as a service wing to the rear. On the N side of the road, some distance w, is the King's Arms, of five bays and two storeys; doorway with segmental pediment and windows with keyed architraves. The c 16 Old Hall opposite has been demolished.

Hartford Hall. *See* p. 306.
Nedderton. *See* p. 402.
West Sleekburn. *See* p. 622.

BELFORD

St Mary. Norman chancel arch. It is double-chamfered, with chevron moulding on the E side and traces of chevron moulding on the w side. The responds are c 19. Built into the wall above it are various Norman bits, so the whole is probably reset. The only other surviving details of the old church are the priests' door, dated 1615, and a two-light window above with cusped segmental heads to the lights. The chancel was restored by *Dobson* in 1828, and he followed this window's Tudor style throughout. In 1829 he rebuilt the nave and added a N aisle and w tower. On the s side he repeated the exceptionally elongated paired lancets he had designed for St Thomas, Newcastle; the effect is quite striking. The N side has tall single lancets. The tower has lancets and

pinnacles. The porch was added in 1844. In 1965 the N gallery
was blocked off to form a parish hall. – ROYAL ARMS of George I;
well carved and painted. – STAINED GLASS. E window of 1883
and chancel S window of 1902, both by *Kempe*. – MONUMENT.
William Clark † 1837, with good marble bust on a big pedestal
filled by a long inscription; the whole in a neo-Norman niche.

The VILLAGE is nice and neat; the chief vista up the High Street to
the N is closed by the long low C 18 front of the BLUE BELL INN,
built in brick, which is unusual in a village characterized by rows
and terraces of early C 19 ashlar houses. At the S end of the
High Street, THE VILLA and THE CROFT are the two most
substantial houses. Off the N end of the High Street, CLARK
PLACE is the best of the terraces. It must date from *c*. 1820.

BELFORD HALL. The main block of five by five bays and two-and- 82
a-half storeys was built in 1754–6 by *James Paine* for Abraham
Dixon. It is a typical Paine design, at once both restrained and yet
animated. The basement is rusticated and the principal doorway is
in the *piano nobile*, approached by a flight of balustraded steps.
The three-bay centre breaks forward slightly; it has a pediment
over and four giant engaged Ionic columns flanked by two giant
Ionic pilasters. The openings are simply treated. Only the outer
windows on the *piano nobile* are given special attention; they have
pediments, swept architrave surrounds and balustraded aprons,
a familiar Paine characteristic. This is one of his most satisfying
designs; according to Dr Leach, 'a wonderfully complete and
subtle essay in movement'. Paine's original design included wings
but these were never built. The present wings, lying back and
extending l. and r., were added *c*. 1817–18 by *Dobson* for a new
owner, William Clark. They are four bays long, with the end bay
on each side a slightly higher pavilion. The style is faithful to, and
cleverly suggestive of, Paine's original, but subtly changed. The
rusticated basement and the first-floor windows in the pavilions
copy Paine, but the overall effect is more severe and Grecian, with
broad, flat and very plain pilasters. At the same time Dobson
remodelled the rear of the main block and installed a new entrance
with an Ionic portico *in antis*. This façade is also severe in its
details, but clever and Romantic in its massing. The house
remained empty and derelict for many years after 1945, and
Paine's fine suite of state rooms was all but lost. It has been
rescued under the auspices of the Northern Heritage Trust, and
was converted into flats by *Reavell & Cahill* of Alnwick, 1983–7.
A few features were retained, e.g. the fireplace in the entrance
hall. The plasterwork was lost but it has in part been recreated in
a series of friezes with bucrania and metopes in imitation of
Paine's style. The staircase and some fine doorcases have been
reconstructed.

The SOUTH LODGE is probably by *Dobson*. Single-storey, with
a very plain little portico of square pillars. N of the house, an
ICEHOUSE, just a grassy hump from outside but ashlar inside
and connected to the kitchens of the house by a long vaulted
underground passage. About 200 metres E of the house, a ruined
Gothick SUMMERHOUSE by *Paine*.

BELFORD STATION, 1 m. SE. *c*. 1847 by *Benjamin Green* for the
York, Newcastle and Berwick Railway. In the Tudor style.

EASINGTON GRANGE, $1\frac{1}{2}$ m. NE. A substantial farmhouse of the early C 17, altered in the C 18. The doorway has a multi-moulded surround which has a canted Tudor-arched head and a pendant keystone.

MIDDLETON HALL, I m. N. 1871 for Colonel Leather, possibly by *David Brandon*. Quite large, irregular and Tudor, with a wing added in similar style in 1925. Set in a romantic Victorian landscape of lakes, waterfalls and rhododendrons.

TOLLGATE COTTAGE, I m. S. A single-storey early C 19 tollhouse formerly on the Great North Road but now bypassed. Two projecting bays flank a central door with the roof carried over and between the bays to form a shallow porch.

ADDERSTONE HALL. *See* p. 125.

NAVIGATION BEACONS, Ross Sands. *See* p. 341.

BELLASIS

1070

$1\frac{1}{2}$ m. SW of Stannington

BELLASIS FARMHOUSE. Dated 1694 on the lintel of a doorway with a simple chamfered surround. The end bays of the five-bay front have oddly narrow blocked windows (cf. Hepscott Hall).

BELLASIS BRIDGE. Attractive old hogback bridge over the River Blyth, with two segmental arches of 5.6 and 12.6 metre ($18\frac{1}{2}$ and $41\frac{1}{2}$ ft) span, the larger, N one double-chamfered, and a cutwater carried up as a refuge (triangular on the W, rectangular on the E) between.

BELLINGHAM

8080

ST CUTHBERT. A church of considerable interest, low and without a W tower, as they so often are in Northumberland. Chancel of the early C 13 with a single lancet on the S side, and at the E end three widely spaced lancets of even height, with monolithic heads and trefoiled rere-arches inside. The chancel arch is of the same date. The church at that time had a nave with aisles. Of the arcades no more is now visible than the four C 13 responds, now embedded in the side walls. The long S transept had a W aisle until the C 17 rebuilding, and the fine C 13 triple-shafted corbel respond of the aisle arcade remains. It has a little nail-head decoration in the abacus. Then, some time after 1609, the aisles were demolished and the church remodelled. The most remarkable feature of that renovation is the vaults of nave and transept, stone vaults, carried in the most orthodox fashion by narrowly set chamfered transverse arches, fifteen in the nave and seven in the transept. The arches are broached; so is the round-headed arch into the transept. The rere-arches of the windows are single-chamfered too. In short, the whole of the detail is essentially still medieval, survival emphatically and not revival. At the same time the nave was given a S door. It is Tudor in style, and above it a coarsely detailed niche with a roll-moulded surround. The C 17 roof is exceptional in Northumberland. It has alternate strips of single and double thickness of stone slabs running vertically down the roof pitch. The same design is to be found at Ladywell in Berwickshire, another stone-vaulted church, built by James IV after 1500. In both places, one assumes, the motive was protection. The nave windows pose a problem. They are lancets, but are they original, reused from the aisles in the rebuilding? Or are they c 17? In either case their use is remarkable at this date. The nave buttresses are attributed to the c 18. – FONT. Bowl on octagonal shaft with simple geometric c 17 decoration. – MONUMENTS. Against the outside of the chancel s wall, a tombstone of 1628 to a Charlton of Redesmouth, with wildly set-out relief lettering. – N of the chancel, the so-called 'Long Pack', a gravestone associated with a famous local legend. It is a c 13 coped grave slab. – Inside the chancel, a marble wall monument to Archibald Reed † 1729, with Ionic columns and a curly open pediment.

RECTORY. 1818 by *H. H. Seward* in exactly the same style as the rectories at Wark, Thorneyburn etc.

ST OSWALD (R.C.), on the B6320, ¼ m. w. 1839 by *Ignatius Bonomi*, in the lancet style, but with a bellcote and rather fanciful detail on the w front. – MONUMENT by *G. Green* of Newcastle, 1841.

BRIDGE. By *John Green*, 1834, with a small single-storey toll-house.

The little town has not much that is old, but it is attractive nevertheless, characterized by good c 19 shopfronts and a wealth of late c 19 railings. The main street is called FRONT STREET. Nos. 1–3, on the NW side, is a quite large early c 18 house, now subdivided. It is of three storeys, with moulded surrounds to door and windows. On the opposite side of the street, the TOWN HALL with a playful lead clock turret surmounted by a small lead spire and four spirelets. In the square behind the Town Hall, a BOER WAR MEMORIAL FOUNTAIN, *c.* 1903, with a statue of a soldier.

HARESHAW IRON WORKS. Only a few rows of cottages on the E bank of the Hareshaw Burn and the remains of spoil heaps higher up the hillside remain from these important workings, opened in 1838 and closed ten years later. Upriver are the remains of the iron works dam, some 9.5 metres (31 ft) wide and originally about 6 metres (20 ft) high.

CEMETERY, on the B6320, s of the bridge. First World War Memorial lychgate in the Arts-and-Crafts style by *Robert Mauchlen*.

THE RIDING, 1 m. NW. A bastle, extended and converted into a house in the c 18. Walls *c.* 1½ metres (5 ft) thick.

RIDING WOOD, 1½ m. NW. A subrectangular homestead, of late Iron Age and Romano-British date, within double banks. Excavations revealed at least four round stone-founded houses; these looked out onto two enclosed yards, each with its own entrance, which flanked a central gateway.

HESLEYSIDE. *See* p. 316.

HOLE. *See* p. 335.

REDESMOUTH. *See* p. 547.

THE REENES. *See* p. 582.

WEST EALINGHAM. *See* p. 622.

7060

BELLISTER CASTLE
1m. sw of Haltwhistle

On a natural motte-like mound, artificially scarped, the ruins of the N end of a C 13 fortified hall house of the Haughton type, with a later C 13 or C 14 NW tower. Few architectural features survive except for the square buttress-like projections at the corners, fragments of a newel stair and garderobe and one square-headed window at second-floor level on the N of the tower, which has a roll-moulded frame of C 16 type. The adjacent house was remodelled in 1827 by *Dobson* and altered *c.* 1890 and again, after a fire, 1902–5. It incorporates some thick walls, but the oldest visible features are a moulded doorway with a flattened ogee head (cf. Featherstone Castle) and a 1669 datestone. To the NE, a good group of late C 18 or early C 19 FARM BUILDINGS, including a square gingang.

BELLSHIEL LAW *see* ROCHESTER

0070

BELSAY

In terms of both its architecture and its landscape features, Belsay is one of the most important sites, not only in Northumberland, but in the whole country. It is in a sense an encapsulation of English history. The earliest surviving element is a hillfort on Bantam Hill to the w of the grounds. The castle at the foot of the hill was built by the de Middleton family in the C 14, extended in the early C 17 by the addition of a manor house, and emparked by Sir William Middleton in the mid-C 18. Sir William's son, Sir Charles Monck, abandoned the castle after his honeymoon in Germany and Greece and in 1807 began to build the magnificent Grecian mansion with all its richness of associated gardens and ancillary buildings. Sir Charles's grandson, Sir Arthur Middleton, completed the gardens in the second half of the C 19. Now, following a period of neglect after the Second World War, the property is maintained by English Heritage.

BELSAY CASTLE. The site has no natural defences, having a steep hill immediately above it to the w and a gentle slope away to the E and N. It is one of the most impressive castles in Northumberland, and one of the most rewarding to study. It is a tower-house which, although it appears at first square in plan, is really an oblong with short wings at the sw and NW corners flanking the recessed entrance. Yet the genealogy of the plan is the L-type, in itself an extension of the normal rectangular Norman keep. The L-plan, for instance, remains at Chipchase, a castle in its details very near to Belsay. At Belsay the main part of the tower has three big rooms above each other. The lowest has a pointed tunnel vault and was used as a kitchen. Above this is the hall, with a comparatively large two-light window to the s and another to the N. The hall has a large fireplace and the rather faded remains of some C 15 mural decoration. Above the hall is the great chamber, also with a fireplace. The SW wing has the staircase, especially well protected in the re-entrant angle, and there are small chambers on six different levels, including one at the same level as the hall which may have been an oratory. The two lowest and the two highest of the chambers are vaulted. The top one is well above the roof-line and has to be approached by an open stair from the roof. The NW wing has rooms on four different levels.

So much for the plan; in appearance the castle is even more exciting. The masonry is beautiful – even, squared, honey-col- 41 oured sandstone. On the S side there are three windows. The two-light hall window has a transom and the lights are cusped. Above the arch is a blank arch with blank tracery. A similar but smaller window without the transom lights the oratory to the l. The great chamber is lit by a small two-light window with cinquefoil heads to the lights. But the crowning glory is the roof-line, with four rounded bartizans boldly corbelled out and machicolated battlements between. Three of the bartizans are of the same height; the fourth, with the staircase and the vaulted room mentioned above, rises a good deal higher and forms the most striking ornament of Belsay.

The history of the castle is not entirely clear. The tower appears to have been built c. 1370, when the de Middletons regained possession of the estates from the de Strivelyns after a break of more than half a century. The manor was already in the possession of the de Middletons in 1270 and it was sufficiently well appointed to receive Edward I in 1278. Nothing is known of the appearance of the original manor or of its relationship to the present tower. It seems reasonable to assume that the tower did not stand alone. There is a doorway, for example, at second-floor level above the present doorway which must have connected with something; and the lower windows on the staircase are cut through the wall at a pronounced skew which suggests that it was necessary to avoid looking out onto an existing wall. There are, moreover, walls of clearly late medieval character in the building attached to the N of the tower. Whatever was there was replaced in 1614 by the two-storey manor house which now adjoins the tower on the W. This house, with its mullioned and transomed windows, was 41 extensively remodelled in 1862, but its porch, with coupled Tuscan columns and its inscription above to Thomas Middleton and Dorothy his wife, is largely original. It is now roofless. It formerly had a wing to the W which may have been built in 1711, the date on a sundial now at West Bitchfield Tower (q.v.). The remains of this wing are only fragmentary.

Massively detailed early C 18 STABLES just to the N of the castle. Also pretty mid-C 19 KENNELS and much castellated WALLING.

BELSAY HALL, 300 metres E of the castle. *Sir Charles Monck* (who in 1799 had changed his name from Middleton to satisfy the terms of his maternal grandfather's will) built Belsay Hall in 1807–17 to his own designs based on studies undertaken in 1804–6 on his honeymoon in Germany, where his diary records that he saw,

sketched and approved several of the recent Neo-classical buildings, including the Brandenburg Gate, and in Athens, where he
met Sir William Gell, a more experienced antiquary and a member
of the Cambridge Hellenists. Gell's *Troäd* had come out in 1804,
and he may well have influenced the design of the house, although
the existence of more than 200 drawings in Monck's own hand
is clear evidence that the design is his. Suggestions that the young
John Dobson contributed have never been proved. Monck's
design is Doric, which in 1807 was still a rarity in the English
country house, and few of the professional architects were convinced of it. William Wilkins was the leading Grecian. His Grange
Park (Hampshire) was designed in 1804. But Belsay is very different from Grange Park and very different in fact from all other
Greek Doric houses in Britain.

93   It is a block seven by six bays, exactly one hundred feet square,
raised like a Greek temple on a podium of three steps. It has no
portico: instead, at the entrance, there are two mighty Doric
columns *in antis*. Each façade is punctuated by four giant Doric
pilasters. The windows are cut in without any mouldings, and the
building is crowned by an enormous triglyph frieze and a far-
projecting cornice. It is a totally original synthesis of Greek
elements. Each feature has absolute classical authority, but the
details have been subordinated to the most severe design imaginable. The exterior of the house is characterized most of all by a
pure and noble simplicity. Only at the back, around the service
court, is this perfect symmetry lost. Here three storeys are pushed
in in place of two and the façade has an ungainly and unfinished
quality.

          The interior is as severe and unique as the exterior. The house
94   is planned round a clerestory-lit oblong central hall more like the
atrium of a Roman house than anything purely Greek. The hall
is surrounded by colonnades on two storeys, slim fluted Ionic
columns below, Roman Doric columns above, which is an odd
inversion of the normal rules. The columns are especially well
executed, perfectly carved volutes on the ground floor, pretty
anthemion necking on the first floor. There are fine brass railings
with acanthus scrolls between the Roman Doric columns. The
staircase, also with a brass balustrade, is at the side of the hall,
somewhat squashed in behind the colonnade. The main rooms
lie along the s front. They seem very plain after the elaboration
of the hall. The largest is the former library with a fireplace of
yellow scagliola and marble. The bookcases are said to echo,
on a reduced scale, measurements made by Monck on the
Erechtheion. The ceilings throughout the main rooms are coffered, with deep friezes of palmettes and Greek key. The dining
room has a white marble fireplace with attached Doric columns.
Under the house there are very extensive vaulted cellars.

          The material of the house is a lovely honey-coloured sandstone
flecked with little bits of iron ore. It is dressed with the most
remarkable precision; how the masons achieved this skill is not
known, but Dobson was to claim later that 'Monck introduced a
style of masonry previously unknown' and that, subsequent to
Belsay, Northumbrian masons were renowned throughout the
country.

STABLES with projecting wings; pedimented centre and pedimented fronts to the side wings. The octagonal lantern was influenced by the Tower of the Winds in Athens.

The GROUNDS provide a neat introduction to C 18 and C 19
garden design. To the N of the castle lies a mid-C 18 landscaped
PARK. Woods and specimen trees were planted to frame the view
from the castle to BANTAM FOLLY, a *ferme ornée* built for Sir
William Middleton (the third Baronet) before 1757. All around
the castle, ha-has opened up the parkland, and ornate bridges
spanned the Coal Burn. One in particular, immediately N of the
castle, is worthy of note. There were walled gardens S of the
castle, but these disappeared when the gardens were created
around the new hall. Monck's gardens are eminently picturesque,
a rare and splendid Romantic setting in wonderful contrast to the
severity of the house. Most notable is the garden made in the
quarry from which the house was built, but there are also terraces
and lakes, dells and ponds and cascades. The work was continued
throughout the C 19 and into the early years of the C 20 by Sir
Charles's grandson, Sir Arthur Middleton. There are a number
of built features in the park. The LODGES are in the Greek style,
especially the HALL FIELD LODGE, due E of the hall, which has
an attached temple front of two Greek Doric columns.

Of earlier elements in the park, two must be mentioned:

BANTAM HILL. A small bivallate hillfort, on the summit of
the spur ⅓ m. W of the castle, has an outer line of defence (one
end of which is overlain by Bantam Folly); there is an unusually
wide gap between the two.

VILLAGE CROSS, *c.* 250 metres E of the castle. Medieval, with
a large square base and a tapering square shaft, *c.* 2.7 metres (9 ft)
high. The shaft has chamfered edges. It is *ex situ*, of course; it was
placed here when the old village was removed by Sir Charles (*see*
below).

BELSAY VILLAGE. The old village lay SW of the castle in the area
cut by the western quarry. By the early C 19 there were about
eighteen houses. They were scrapped by Sir Charles Monck,
apparently *c.* 1816. The new village is said to have been built,
away from the hall on the main road, between 1830 and 1840, but
it seems probable that it was started during the building of the
Hall. It is just one long terrace of houses with arcaded ground
floor in the Italian taste. The former inn, WOOD HOUSE, is dated
1836. The OLD SCHOOL, round the corner in Whalton Road,
has a date of 1829 on a beam inside, though it is said to have
opened as a school in 1841. The present school, BELSAY
COUNTY FIRST SCHOOL, is an agreeable Gothic building of *c.*
1870.

SWANSTEAD, ¼ m. NNE of the hall, and visible across the fields from
the drive. Originally built for Sir William Middleton's brother,
Captain Thomas Middleton, *c.* 1759. Restored and altered *c.* 1950
for Sir Stephen Middleton by *Claud Phillimore*, who created a new
entrance hall and added a two-storey bow window on the N
side. The house is built of well-dressed stone and is solid and
unpretentious, with a plain five-bay front and a high hipped
roof. The original intention, following Sir Stephen's decision to
abandon the hall after the Second World War, had been to build

a new house onto the castle, but this was prevented by the local authority.

BRICK AND TILE KILNS, 1 m. s on the A696. A prominent group of low early c 19 kilns.

BOLAM. *See* p. 195.

BRADFORD. *See* p. 304.

HARNHAM. *See* p. 303.

WEST BITCHFIELD TOWER. *See* p. 621.

BELTINGHAM

7060

A sweet hamlet amongst trees, set back from the s bank of the South Tyne.

ST CUTHBERT. The church (formerly a chapel of ease of Haltwhistle) was over-zealously restored in 1884. In form it is a six-bay unaisled rectangle. The E part seems to date from *c.* 1500, with the three w bays thought to be a later c 17 addition. The chapel was called 'almost quite ruinate' in 1650. S windows of three trefoil-headed lights under elliptical arches, the sills of those in the second and fifth bays set higher to allow for doorways beneath. The western door has an elliptical arch and the eastern a blocked four-centred arch dated 1691. Thin stepped buttresses between the windows. The w window and the single N window are similar. E window of five cinquefoil-headed lights. Inside there is no structural division. The three easternmost windows on the s have interesting rustic carvings (a rabbit, flowers, fleur-de-lys and a grotesque mask) on their inner splays. The large corbels flanking the E window, with chevron and sunk-star ornament, may be genuine c 12 work. Set in the recess of the blocked SE doorway is an early CROSS SLAB, which may be pre-Conquest. Squint with old iron bars from a former sacristy or chapel on the site of the 1884 vestry, in the E wall of which is an odd reset window with a triangular head and a raised ball in the apex of the chamfered surround. Is it c 16? – STAINED GLASS. E window by *Kempe*, 1891. – w window on N of chancel by *Kempe & Co.*, 1926. – MONUMENT. A tablet of 1828 by *L. Blain* of Carlisle. – In the churchyard a plain CROSS, probably c 13, with most of its head broken away. Outside the w end of the nave, a ROMAN ALTAR; parts of another built into the wall beside the churchyard gate.

BELTINGHAM HOUSE, beside the churchyard, is a nice three-bay building of the mid-c 18 with rusticated quoins, a modillion cornice, and pediments to the centre-bay architraves. On the other side of the churchyard entrance is the older WHITE HEATHER COTTAGE, a bastle house remodelled in the c 18; boulder plinth and massive rubble in end and rear walls; it has a 'wrestler' roof, a vernacular form (now rare) in which the stone slates at the ridge are shaped and interlocked, projecting alternately above the ridge so as to give a serrated roof-line (cf. Abbey Cottage at Blanchland and Shankhead, below). The VICARAGE has an ashlar three-bay front with a centre curved bow, and is dated 1845 although in style thirty years earlier.

SHANKHEAD, 1½ m. SSW. A pair of houses, now farm buildings; the W one is late C17 and has upper crucks, the E one, dated 1764, still has heavy quoins and lintels and preserves another 'wrestler' roof (*see* above).

RIDLEY. *See* p. 549.

WILLIMOTESWICK. *See* p. 631.

BENWELL *see* NEWCASTLE UPON TYNE

BERWICK-UPON-TWEED

9050

Berwick is one of the most exciting towns in England, a real town, with the strongest sense of enclosure, a town of red roofs on grey houses with hardly any irritating buildings anywhere, and a town of the most intricate changes of levels. In the description of its streets these levels will have to be considered, though the transition from one to the other, as one goes through the town, cannot be adequately brought out. In addition there is the sombre fascination of its history between England and Scotland, the constant battle for ownership throughout the medieval period; and even after the Union of the Crowns, its prolonged existence as almost a free town, mentioned separately in Acts of Parliament until 1746. Finally there is its position along an estuary crossed by three bridges and along the open sea.

Tweedmouth and Spittal, now part of Berwick, are treated separately on pp. 185–6 below.

CHURCHES

HOLY TRINITY, Wallace Green. A building of quite exceptional 57 architectural interest. It was built afresh and to one consistent plan in 1650–2, on the initiative of Colonel George Fenwicke, Governor of Berwick, as a replacement to the apparently dilapidated and undistinguished medieval church which stood on the site. There are not many churches in England of *c.* 1650, or indeed of the C17, and every one deserves attention. Holy Trinity was built by a London mason, *John Young* of Blackfriars, to his 'own Moddell and Draught'. In character and certain details it is surprisingly like St Katherine Cree in the City of London, a church of 1628–31. Externally, St Katherine Cree is a curious mixture of Gothic and semi-classical motifs. It has a large Gothic E window, and elsewhere odd stepped tripartite windows with flat tops, like proto-Venetian windows. Windows of this type are now to be found at Holy Trinity only in the clerestory, where they alternate with round-headed windows, but an engraving of 1799 in Fuller's *History of Berwick* shows that the church at that time had them throughout. The engraving also shows that the church had a large Gothic W window with rather sparse Dec tracery.

There was a similar window at the E end, battlemented parapets to the aisles and N chapel, and small octagonal turrets with spirelets on the W angles of the nave; all of which suggests how closely Young's design resembled the London church. However, in 1855 Holy Trinity was restored in a way that made it more classical than before. The large Gothic windows at the W and E ends were replaced by equally large Venetian windows (at the same time the short chancel was added). The other windows in the church were made into proper Venetian windows and the W turrets were given a frill of classical arcading and ogee tops to replace the spirelets. The only Gothic feature to be retained was the battlemented parapet to the aisles.

What one sees from the outside now, therefore, is a classical church which is more of an amalgam of the C 17 and the C 19 than is generally acknowledged. It comprises nave and aisles, clerestory, chancel and no tower. It is said that one was intended but omitted at the request of Cromwell, who passed through Berwick on his way to the battle of Dunbar. In the middle of the W front is a small original doorway with pediment on Tuscan columns, and above it and to the l. and r. one each of the Venetian windows which we have seen are now typical of the whole church. The nave is five bays long. The centre bay on the S side has a shorter window above a low round-headed doorway. Above this centre bay, the battlements of the aisle are broken by a sundial with flanking scrolls – the new sense of symmetry of the coming classical style.

The interior has been less altered. It has an arcade of five bays on Tuscan columns and with round arches. The keystones of the arches are carved with small cartouches. The N chapel, though of two bays, is divided from the aisle by one broad depressed arch. – W GALLERY of wood in the Jacobean taste, and beneath it screens forming a lobby at the back of the church. The gallery and the screens have the remarkable motif of intersected arcading combined with strapwork – a case of Norman revival to be compared with certain details of Bishop Cosin's work in County Durham. There were N and S galleries as well, and also, a Presbyterian touch, one E gallery. They all gradually disappeared. – FONT. C 17. Small, hexagonal and plain. – REREDOS. 1893, a pleasant early design of *Lutyens* with Tuscan columns and balusters, standing against the E window. – PULPIT. Jacobean type, though of c. 1652. It has a tester. – CHOIR STALLS. C 19 but incorporating C 17 panels of intersected arcading and strapwork similar to the W gallery. – STAINED GLASS. In the W window, a large number of small roundels; Flemish or Dutch C 16 and C 17. – MONUMENTS. S aisle, a nice modest black marble cartouche to Colonel Fenwicke (*see* above) †1656. – N aisle, Patrick Boge, Laird of Byne, †1681. Relief lettering and coat of arms in a moulded frame. – Chancel. Mr James Graham †1816, a sarcophagus, signed by *Davies* of Newcastle. – George Johnston †1855, by *Young & Cole*. – The churchyard has tall rusticated GATEPIERS with pineapple finials. Dated 1750 and signed by the church wardens.

ST MARY, Castlegate. 1858 by *J. Howison*. E.E., with small SW tower ending in an octagonal turret.

ST MARY AND ST CUTHBERT (R.C.), Ravensdowne. The church
is attached to the back of No. 64, its presbytery. It lies back from
the street, under a castellated archway and up an alley. Built in
1829; the polygonal apse and Dec tracery are later.

METHODIST CHURCH, Walkergate. 1878. Behind it the original
chapel of 1797; five bays with arched windows and intersecting
glazing bars.

PRESBYTERIAN CHURCH OF SCOTLAND, Wallace Green. 1858–
9 by *J. D. & I. Hay* of Liverpool. In the Dec style, with a large spire
starting low and enriched by angle spirelets and large dormers. It
is a somewhat arrogant design, completely obscuring Holy Trinity
which lies behind it.

UNITED REFORMED CHURCH, Bankhill. Next to the Academy
(*see* Perambulation 1, below). Formerly the Presbyterian Church
of England. 1835–6. The usual type, with two large windows
flanked by doorways with smaller windows over.

PUBLIC BUILDINGS

FORTIFICATIONS. In the three hundred years up to 1482, when it
changed hands for the last time, the town of Berwick had been
captured or sacked no fewer than fourteen times. Since 1482 it has
remained part of England but for many years after that date it was
considered the most vulnerable town in the kingdom. Right through
the Anglo-Scottish wars of the C16 it was under threat, and not
until 1603 did the threat subside. Such a town in such a place needed
fortifications more than it needed anything else, and the walls and
castle at Berwick provide us with one of the most complete overviews
we have of the development of military architecture in Britain. The
medieval remains are, as we shall see, fragmentary but still of great
interest, while the Tudor works, beginning with a few piecemeal
modifications to the existing walls and culminating in the great
Italianate bastions of the Elizabethan age, are almost perfectly preserved and of immense historical significance.

CASTLE. The castle lay outside the NW angle of the medieval town,
separated from it by a ditch, and connected to it by a bridge across
the ditch and a gatehouse in the town wall. Of these no trace
survives, but of the castle itself there are considerable remains,
though they are scattered and rather difficult to find. That such
an important castle should be in such a fragmentary state is due
in part to the arrival of the railway and the building of the railway
station, which is placed in the very middle of the site; but the
process of decay had begun far earlier than that. There was a
proposal to demolish the castle in 1558, and from *c.* 1611 it was
entirely abandoned and became a convenient quarry for later
building in the town.

The castle is first mentioned in 1160, but the earliest surviving
sections date from the remodelling which took place after Edward
I captured the town in 1296. The castle as built then consisted of
a curtain wall strengthened by towers and turrets. The domestic
buildings were set against the curtain on the S and W sides. There
are two main chunks which survive. In Castle Vale Park and the
grounds of the Abbeyfield Home is the SE angle tower and a

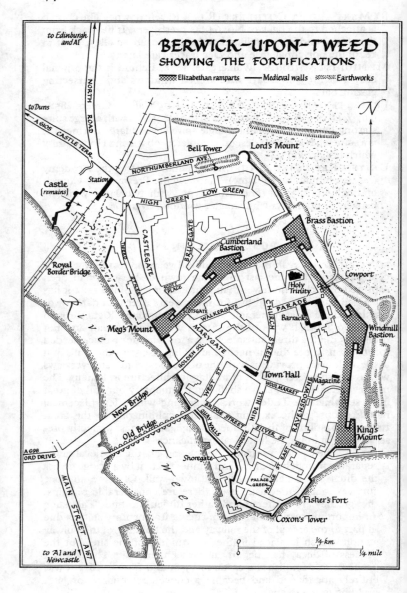

to Edinburgh
and A1

to Duns

NORTH ROAD

A 6105 CASTLE TERR.

Castle
(remains)

Station

BERWICK-UPON-TWEED
SHOWING THE FORTIFICATIONS
▨▨▨ Elizabethan ramparts —— Medieval walls ⠿⠿ Earthworks

N

Bell Tower   Lord's Mount

NORTHUMBERLAND AVE.

HIGH   GREEN   LOW   GREEN

Brass Bastion

Royal
Border Bridge

CASTLEGATE

TWEED STREET

BRIDGE STREET

SCOTS PLACE

Cumberland
Bastion

Cowport

Holy
Trinity

Meg's Mount

SCOTSGATE

WALKERGATE

MARYGATE

CHURCH STREET

PARADE

Barracks

Windmill
Bastion

GOLDEN SQ.

WEST ST

HIDE HILL

RAVENSDOWNE

Town Hall

WOOLMARKET

Magazine

New Bridge

BRIDGE STREET

QUAY WALLS

SILVER ST.

SANDGATE

EAST ST

NESS ST.

King's
Mount

A 698
ORD DRIVE

Old Bridge

Shoregate

PALACE
GREEN

Fisher's Fort

MAIN STREET A 167

Coxon's Tower

River

Tweed

to A1 and
Newcastle

0   ¼ km
0   ¼ mile

stretch of adjoining curtain wall. The tower, known as the Constable Tower, is especially fine. The lowest courses look to be
C 12, and above them rises a polygonal tower in exceptionally
well-cut ashlar. It is not known for sure whether it dates from
Edward I or from Edward III, but comparison of the fish-tail
arrow slits with, say, Dally Castle (*see* Greystead) would suggest

the earlier date. There is also a garderobe chute. The other
surviving portion is the NW wall of the castle which can be seen
from the outside in Coronation Park, and from the inside from
the station platform. At the N end is a tall tower. At the S end,
commanding the top of the hill overlooking the Tweed, is a
semicircular gun turret of *c.* 1540. Other towers of the same period
and style may have been added elsewhere.

Descending from the SW angle to the river bank is the spectacular WHITE WALL of 1297–8, built to prevent the castle being
bypassed. At its foot on the river bank is the WATER TOWER
which was rebuilt, like the SW angle tower, *c.* 1540. It has three
casemates for cannon.

The MEDIEVAL TOWN WALLS were begun by Edward I as soon as
he had captured the town in 1296. At first there was just a palisade,
but as early as 1297 work started to rebuild in stone. By 1318, when
Robert the Bruce captured the town, the walls were complete but
too low, and the Scots undertook to heighten them. When the
Elizabethan bastions were built (*see* below), the northern half of
the town was abandoned and the walls there allowed to decay. In
the southern half of the town the old walls were either replaced
by or incorporated in the new fortifications, and those portions
of them that survive will be described below during the perambulation of the Elizabethan ramparts. The best-preserved
stretch in the northern half of the town is high up along the
edge of the cliff between Meg's Mount and the Border Bridge.
NORTHUMBERLAND AVENUE, opposite the station, lies just
outside the line of the wall, and contains, at its E end, a stretch
of ditch and mound, substantial chunks of masonry and the tall
octagonal Elizabethan Bell Tower, built on Edwardian foundations, probably in the 1570s as a watch tower. Lord's Mount,
just beyond the Bell Tower, formed the NE angle of the medieval
town walls. It was built 1539–42 as the first of a series of piecemeal
attempts to strengthen the old walls in the years before they were
finally abandoned. It is a massive circular fortification with walls
almost 6 metres thick containing casemates for artillery. Henry
VIII himself is said to have been involved in the design. S of Lord's
Mount the line of the abandoned wall can be clearly seen.

The ELIZABETHAN RAMPARTS. As we have seen, attempts to
strengthen the existing walls to cope with artillery had begun at
least as early as the 1530s, and in 1550, during the reign of Edward
VI, work began on a major new citadel on the E side of the
town. It was never completed and in 1558 it was abandoned and
superseded by a much more ambitious plan. In that year Calais
had been lost and there was considerable nervousness about the
presence of French troops in Scotland and the possibility of a
further war against the Scots. It was therefore decided that the
defences of Berwick needed to be put on a proper footing. *Sir
Richard Lee*, who in 1545 had designed at Portsmouth the earliest
Italianate bastions in England, was appointed Chief Surveyor.
The system he chose is based on those that had been developed
earlier in the C16 in Italy, especially at Verona in the 1530s. They
consist of bastions or platforms facing the attacker with an obtuse
angle and connected to the main curtain wall by a collar piece or
gorge narrower than the bastion. The recesses between the wall,

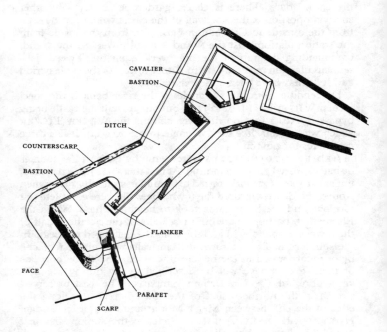

Berwick-upon-Tweed, fortifications

the gorge and the bastion are called flankers. They are provided with guns to fire parallel with the wall. The guns are placed behind screen walls with segment-headed, window-like openings. The flankers are accessible by means of tunnels. In front of the wall is a broad shallow ditch, originally water-filled and with an unexpected and much deeper ditch in its middle. Beyond the ditch is a bank called the counterscarp which was intended to be capped by a wall. Such was the system that Lee derived from Italy; in this form it was still quite recent and had hardly been tried in northern Europe, but Lee carried it a stage further. His walls are not very high (4 metres) and only moderately thick. From the outside they are quite smooth, with a slight batter and a bold roll moulding at the base of the parapet. They are heavily buttressed internally, with the buttresses linked together by arches; but what gives the system its real strength is not the walls but the huge thickness of earthwork behind them. The counterscarp was intended to prevent a direct artillery assault on the walls, so that the force of the attack would be borne and absorbed by the soft earthworks. There is no contemporary system quite like it and it may well have been Lee's own invention.

Work began in 1558 and continued until 1569, when it was more or less abandoned; it was never completed. The plan had been to cut off the lower s end of the town along the river bank and create a complete fortress on the high ground. In the event this was not done and only the ramparts along the N and E sides were built. The S and W sides of the town continued to use the old medieval wall. There were other problems too. After complaints about Lee, the Italian engineer *Portinari* was called in to assess the work in 1560. In general he approved but felt that the whole of the peninsula should have been included within the walls. Nothing was done about his suggestions, but in 1564 he was consulted again, along with *Jacopo a Contio*, and this time they criticized the design of the flankers, saying that they were too narrow and too difficult of access. Changes were made to the size but not to the access. The earth embankments which now tower above the bastions and the walls, and which were such an integral part of Lee's original design, were not added until 1639–53. The ditch was never completed and the wall on top of the counterscarp never even begun. This unfinished work, which in the view of most contemporaries left the town still seriously underdefended, cost Elizabeth's government £128,648 5s. 9½d. It was by far the costliest single work undertaken during the reign.

Whatever their immediate military effectiveness, however, the Berwick walls were the culmination of decades of fumbling towards an understanding of new forms of defence and they are of immense historical importance for the whole of northern Europe. They are, moreover, wonderful to look at and walk around, and the perfect place to commence this perambulation is Meg's Mount at the NW angle of the Elizabethan fortifications.

MEG'S MOUNT was begun in 1558. It is only half a bastion, since only the eastern part was built. It was intended to complete it, but SW from here the defences continue along the river by the reconstructed medieval wall. Just E of Meg's Mount, SCOTSGATE opens through the Elizabethan wall. It was one of the original gates, widened in 1815 and altered again in 1858. CUMBERLAND BASTION, in the centre of the N wall, is a complete bastion, with two flankers, and is well-preserved, so that a description of it will serve as a general guide to the others. The flankers are narrow at the rear and widen out by splayed walls towards the front. This was the result of the rebuilding after Portinari and Contio had criticized the size of the original flankers in 1564. The original cross walls were demolished and new ones built closer to the end of the bastion. In the S wall of the flankers, doorways with four-centred arched heads lead to narrow passageways through the ramparts. On top of the bastion there are earthworks of 1638–52 on two different levels: an earthwork parapet immediately behind the wall, and a high central platform called a cavalier, with its own earthwork parapet; guns were placed at both levels and embrasures can still be seen. BRASS BASTION stands at the NE 56 angle of the walls and is essentially similar to the others, the only difference being the high arches which were built in 1564 to carry the sentry path over the extended flankers. Behind the W flanker a short stretch of the original cobbled sentry path has been exposed; elsewhere on the ramparts it was covered up by the C 17 earthworks. The ditch in front of the wall and the counterscarp beyond it are well-preserved at this point. S of Brass Bastion, COWPORT is the only gate in the walls more or less in its original state. It was constructed in 1596, according to the Calendar of Border

Papers, and along with the adjacent bridge, cost £489 4s. 9d. It
is tunnel-vaulted, with a portcullis groove. Excavation has
revealed the portcullis superstructure, partly demolished and
buried by the C 17 heightening of the earthwork rampart. It also
uncovered the cobbled sentry walk immediately inside the
parapet, backed by a wall that seems to have retained an original
earth rampart. The gates themselves are mid-C 18, and there is a
little guard house of 1755. WINDMILL BASTION in the centre of
the E side is complete and well-preserved. Stone and concrete
gun emplacements on it date from the C 19 and from the First
World War. Outside the walls opposite Windmill are a series of
earthworks. The largest, called WINDMILL BULWARK, dates
from 1522–3 and was added to an angle of the medieval defences.
The others, immediately to the S, have two elements: the banks
forming the E edge of the public park and playground are part of
the medieval circuit; to the E, portions of the two E bastions of
the unfinished Edward VI Citadel project beyond the earlier line.
KING'S MOUNT is the last of the Elizabethan bastions, and as
with Meg's Mount only half of it was built. It was intended at this
point to turn the line of the wall at right angles back towards
Meg's Mount, thereby creating a complete fortress on the high
ground, but this was never done. Instead the line continues down
the hill using the medieval walls. One semicircular turret remains.
At the foot of the hill the NESS GATE of 1816 was cut through
the wall to provide access to the new pier (*see* below). From this
point on, the defences continue along the shore on the line of the
medieval walls. Much of the masonry is clearly medieval, but,
equally, a great deal of it was rebuilt in the C 18. Some of the
detail, such as the semicircular moulding at the foot of the parapet,
is the same as on the Elizabethan walls, so perhaps parts of this
section received minor alteration too. Below the Ness Gate is a
projecting gun battery called FISHER'S FORT, built in 1522–3
but partly reconstructed in the C 18. COXON'S TOWER forms
the SE angle of the town. Its upper parts have been rebuilt, but
the basement has a fine early C 14 rib vault with single-chamfered
ribs rising from corbels. The window embrasures have shouldered
rere-lintels. From this point on along the river front most of what
one sees is Georgian. There are two batteries of *c.* 1745 designed
to cover the mouth of the river. SHOREGATE at the foot of
Sandgate is a reconstruction of the 1760s. It has rusticated voussoirs and its original doors. At Bridge End, where the line of the
wall crosses the old bridge, was the site of the English Gate,
demolished finally in 1825. Beyond Bridge End the wall climbs
steeply back up the hill until it joins Meg's Mount and the perambulation is complete.

BARRACKS, The Parade. Begun in 1717, occupied in 1721. They
were just one of an important series of military buildings begun
by the newly formed Board of Ordnance. Woolwich Arsenal and
Chatham Naval Dock Yard are two even more major works of
this series, but Berwick has the distinction of being the earliest
barracks to be built in Britain. The motive which initiated the
work at Berwick must have been worry following the Jacobite
uprising of 1715. The identity of the designer has long been a
source of speculation, and *Vanbrugh* has frequently been cited.

He certainly was part of the circle of the Duke of Marlborough and Lord Cobham, who were the driving force at the Board of Ordnance. However, a drawing from the Wilton House papers and in the Wiltshire County Record Office proves that the designer was *Nicholas Hawksmoor* (information kindly provided by Richard Hewlings). The drawing is signed and dated April 1717, just one month after authorization was given for the job to be undertaken. In March 1719 *Andrews Jelfe* was appointed by the Board to be architect and clerk of works to all of its buildings in the North and in Scotland, and it seems likely that he modified Hawksmoor's design, since the gateway as built is simpler than shown in the original drawing, though still clearly identifiable. The executant on the spot was the Board's local representative, Captain Thomas Philips.

The Barracks comprise three independent buildings on three sides of a quadrangle. The fourth side is closed by a high wall with a gatehouse. The two side blocks were built first. They are three storeys high and twenty-two bays long, with segment-headed windows and heavily rusticated quoins. The buildings end in stepped gables, a remarkable archaism. The gateway is of great strength and solidity – a tall, plain, tower-like centre pierced by a round arch with massive triple keystone and flanked by heavy square buttresses. Above the arch are the Arms of George I in an elaborate cartouche. The building facing the gateway, known as the Clock Block, was built in 1739 and replaced an earlier gunpowder magazine. It is nine bays long. The centre bay has a full height blank arch with a pediment over. Round-headed openings on the ground floor, segment-headed above; and once again stepped gables, even more archaic by 1739.

MAGAZINE. *See* Perambulation 3, below.

TOWN HALL. 1754–61, designed by *S. & J. Worrall*, but signed surprisingly conspicuously right above the main entrance by *Joseph Dods*, Architect. What seems to have happened is that the Worralls were paid for designs which the Town Hall Committee or the Guild of Freemen rejected, handing over the work to Dods, who was one of their number. He probably did little more than tinker with the original plan. The front part of the building was completed in 1754 and then extended to the rear in 1761. An excellent focal point for Marygate. Tall, very severe, somewhat 85 Vanbrughian giant portico of Tuscan columns up a high flight of steps; and behind it a tall belfry, 46 metres (150 ft) high, formed on the pattern of Gibbs's St Martin's-in-the-Fields, but much sturdier in proportion. It has four stages: a square bell stage with louvred round-headed window and four pilasters on each side, a clock stage with the clocks framed in open-pedimented surrounds, an octagonal upper stage with attached Ionic columns at the angles and an open balustraded parapet, and finally a stone spire. The ground floor is arcaded at the sides and to the rear. At the back there is a large Venetian window. Inside, in the Council Chamber, there is a pretty stucco figure of Justice blindfold in a large Rococo cartouche. This was done in 1789 by *Joseph Alexander*. The top floor was the town gaol and is preserved in its original state.

BOROUGH COUNCIL OFFICES, Wallace Green. Built in 1848–9

as the gaol in a cheerful Tudor. Symmetrical with gables, castellated bay windows and many tall octagonal chimneys.

POLICE STATION AND MAGISTRATE COURT. *See* Perambulation
1 below.

SWIMMING BATHS. *See* Perambulation 2.

CUSTOMS HOUSE. *See* Perambulation 3.

SCHOOLS. *See* Perambulations 3 and 4.

INFIRMARY. *See* Perambulation 4.

OLD MILITARY HOSPITAL. *See* Perambulation 4.

RAILWAY STATION. *See* Perambulation 4.

PIER. 1810–21 by *Rennie*. The LIGHTHOUSE was added in 1826.

55 OLD BRIDGE (BERWICK BRIDGE). Begun in 1611 and completed
c. 1626, though the accounts were not closed until 1634. The
surveyor was *James Burrell*. A beautiful red sandstone bridge of
fifteen segmental arches with Doric columns on many of the
cutwaters. It is 355 metres (1,164 ft) long and 14 metres (45 ft)
high at its highest point near the N shore.

ROYAL BORDER BRIDGE. 1847–50 by *Robert Stephenson*. It has
twenty-eight arches, each of 18.75-metre (61½-ft) span, and they
tower high up like those of a Roman aqueduct. The piers are of
rock-faced stone, the round arches of brick, stone-faced. Height
38.5 metres (126½ ft).

NEW BRIDGE (ROYAL TWEED BRIDGE). Designed 1925–8 by
L. G. Mouchel & Partners, the concrete engineers. It spans 428
metres (1,405 ft) in four long leaps, with segmental arches, each
built up on four ribs. The uprights in the open spandrels are
rather heavy. The bridge has nothing of the elegance of Maillart's
concrete bridges in Switzerland and some in Germany and
America – a pity, as the opportunity in a town like Berwick and
within sight of the other two bridges was enormous. Even worse
than this lost opportunity was the damage done by the New Bridge
to the integrity of Marygate (*see* Perambulation 1 below).

PERAMBULATIONS

Berwick is a small but a complex town, so the perambulations have
been divided into four short walks, the first three encompassing the
area within the Elizabethan walls, and the fourth covering the area
outside the walls.

1. Town Hall, Marygate, Walkergate, the Parade and Church Street

A walk through Berwick ought to start by the Town Hall (*see* Public
Buildings, above). It faces up MARYGATE and here at once the
theme is set – a fine town, with closed streets, houses not all of
great architectural merit but blending well with each other and
the fortifications and the sea. Behind their fronts are back wings
and back alleys. But Marygate is also a good place to start because
it disposes straightaway of most of the few irritations which the
town has to offer. Its unity and compactness have been sadly
damaged by the street which cuts into it from the New Bridge,
and by the bus station facing it. It is the main shopping street and
here, as nowhere else in the town, the usual rash of cavernous
C 20 shopfronts has spoilt the scene. But there are still a few

buildings worth looking at. Nos. 47–51 on the s side, though much altered on the ground floor, must have been quite a grand house. Six bays with architrave surrounds to the windows, a bold eaves cornice and those fine scrolled kneelers, like half Ionic volutes, which are a feature of so many c 18 houses in Berwick. Parts of the street from the New Bridge are old. It is called GOLDEN SQUARE and before the bridge was built it was an alley off Marygate. At its sw end is the simple four-bay former CORPORATION ACADEMY of 1798. Beyond this, on BANK-HILL, overlooking the Tweed, is the LADY JERNINGHAM STATUE, designed by her husband, *Sir Hubert Jerningham*, with the assistance of *Walter Ingram*, and carved by *Penachini* in 1906. Marygate ends at Scotsgate (*see* Public Buildings, above). Off to the e is WALKERGATE. Nos. 1–3, built as a Baptist Chapel in 1810, has three tall arched windows. In COXON'S LANE there is a very good former Temperance Hall, dated 1874 but surely earlier, since it has a fine pedimented three-bay ashlar front with round-headed door and windows in blank arched recesses. It looks *c.* 1800. Walkergate ends at WALLACE GREEN. The odd, highly decorated MASONIC HALL of 1872 is on the corner; opposite is the United Reformed Church and next to it the Borough Council Offices (for both, *see* above). The large open space between the Parish Church and the Barracks (*see* above) is called THE PARADE. Along its s side is an irregular but harmonious row of brightly painted houses much earlier than their mainly c 19 detail. CHURCH STREET leads back down the hill towards the Town Hall. No. 61 is the stately OLD VICARAGE, a mid-c 18 five-bay brick house with stone angle pilasters and doorcase. No. 57 is a funny little house with a doorway with Tuscan columns and pediment, and to its r. just one Venetian window on the ground floor and one on the first; that is all. On the other side of the road are the POLICE STATION AND MAGISTRATE COURT, a nice free Baroque building of 1899–1901 with touches of Art Nouveau; Tudor windows, Gibbs surrounds, a tower not placed in the middle, and at its top stumpy columns and a bulgy dome. The architect was *R. Burns Dick*. The street starts on the w side with a long early c 19 ashlar group which is rusticated on the ground floor.

2. *From the Town Hall to the lower town and back, via West Street, Bridge Street, Sandgate and Hide Hill*

The second perambulation again starts from Marygate and turns down WEST STREET. Nos. 32–36 was one seven-bay c 18 house with quoins and quoins to the centre bay. No. 57 has a pedimented door surround. The steep descent of West Street marks the change from the high town level of the Town Hall and the New Bridge to the lower level of the Old Bridge. At the end of West Street, facing the Old Bridge and the river is BRIDGE TERRACE. No. 2 is brightly painted and has a handsome doorcase with Tuscan pilasters set in front of a rusticated surround. BRIDGE END, with a dignified ashlar block of 1804 on one side of the road and a Gothic house of 1864 on the other, leads into BRIDGE STREET. This is the lowest level of Berwick and was the main entry into the town until the New Bridge was built; now it is much quieter, rather neglected and consequently unspoilt. Nos. 64–66 (with No. 57 West Street, q.v.) has an attractive Victorian shopfront with slender fluted columns and pediments over the two doors. Nos. 54–60, the best house on the street, is of *c*. 1800, with eleven windows with rusticated quoins of even length and long tapering Tuscan giant pilasters flanking the centre bay. Nos. 45–53 opposite is an early C 18 house with two doorways, an original one with a bolection-moulded surround and a pedimented later door. On the first floor, eight windows in bolection-moulded surrounds. Nos. 48–52 has similar windows and is also early C 18, but its rear wing is timber-framed with a jettied upper storey and so probably C 17. It is the only timber framing in the county outside of Newcastle. No. 9 has a rusticated ground floor and a particularly boldly moulded eaves cornice. Late C 18. Bridge Street is crossed at the end by SANDGATE, which dips under the Quay Wall by the Shoregate. Nos. 11–15 (including the Hen and Chickens), a good mid-C 18 group, are typical of Berwick with their bright paintwork, moulded window surrounds, scrolled kneelers and steeply pitched roofs. Then the SWIMMING BATHS, mixed Renaissance style of 1858, formerly the Corn Exchange, and the BANK OF SCOTLAND, 1886 by *Kinnear & Peddie*. From the end of Sandgate, HIDE HILL rises again to the Town Hall level, and here, looking up, the KING'S ARMS HOTEL makes a fine picture. It is designed just like a typical Georgian country house. Two parts, the lower of six bays and two-and-a-half storeys and quoins, the upper of three bays and two-and-a-half storeys, with rather clumsily provincial Venetian windows on the upper floors. In the yard behind the hotel, much altered but still recognizable, is a large theatre or assembly rooms of 1845. On the W side of the street there is an equally attractive group of houses, all nicely painted and varied. They are mainly three storeys high and four bays wide. Nos. 18–28 are all late C 18, with raised or moulded window surrounds and scrolled kneelers. Nos. 6–12 are very plain, ashlar and early C 19. The top of Hide Hill brings us back to the Town Hall.

3. *From the Old Bridge along Quay Walls, Palace Green, Ravensdowne to the Parade*

This perambulation starts from the end of the Old Bridge and begins
86 along QUAY WALLS, which is a splendid street of well-restored and maintained Georgian houses built immediately behind the riverside town wall, indeed with the wall-head forming the pavement outside the houses. None of the houses is a disappointment, and some deserve to be singled out. No. 4, late C 18, is of five bays with a pedimented Tuscan door surround and an especially ornate Venetian inner doorway. No. 8, early C 19, has two adjoining doorways tied together by one big and awkward pediment. No. 18 is the CUSTOMS HOUSE, a neat later C 18 house of five bays and two storeys, with arched windows on the ground floor and a Venetian doorway. No. 21 is a two-bay house with all Venetian windows, the panes of which are rectangular and horizontal after a more Scottish pattern. Nos. 22 and 23 have nice

doorcases. Just beyond the end of Quay Walls, still on the circuit of the ramparts, is WELLINGTON TERRACE, a nice row of three red sandstone ashlar Grecian houses, each on a slightly different pattern. No. 1 has a Greek Doric porch and harpoons and other images of whaling carved on the friezes and the capitals of the pilasters. The row was built just before 1816, but No. 3 is said to have been built in 1852. If it was, it was an extremely conservative design for the date, because it looks just like the others.

From here one can continue the walk around the walls but that perambulation has already been described above (*see* Public Buildings) and it is at least as enjoyable to dive down behind Wellington Terrace into Palace Street and Palace Green, i.e. again right into the lowest level of the town. In PALACE STREET the re-erected mid-C18 MAIN GUARD, which stood originally in Marygate until it was moved here in 1815. It must have been altered when it was moved because the tripartite windows set in blank segmental arches are clearly of 1815 and not the mid-C18. As it stands now it is single-storey and of five bays, with the middle bays a low squat Tuscan portico and steep pediment. Some of this looks original (i.e. the columns); other parts are a renewal, and indeed the engraving of the building in Fuller's 1799 *History of Berwick* is significantly different from what one sees now. PALACE GREEN is a delicious oasis of old dark trees surrounded by dignified buildings. On the E side, the former GOVERNOR'S HOUSE, characteristically early C18. Five bays and three storeys, with two-storey wings. The centre has its angle bays flanked by giant pilasters. The wings have oddly archaic gabled centres and stepped end gables (cf. the Barracks). No. 4 on the N side has a pedimented door surround with a pretty frieze. No. 9 on the S side (Bower Villa) has a coloured bust of Wellington over the doorway. The rest of the S side is taken up with the long three-storey ST AIDANS, the former British School of 1859, in a vaguely Italianate style with round-headed windows and overhanging eaves. On into PALACE STREET EAST, which is continued in Ravensdowne and forms the elegant Georgian quarter of Berwick. It starts, on the corner, with No. 10, a mildly Art Nouveau design of 1913. No. 6 has a porch with Corinthian columns. AVENUE HOUSE (No. 4) is particularly pretty, brightly painted, four plus one bays, iron balconies with acanthus scrolls and a fine painted coat of arms of the Call family. The rear of the house (No. 11 WEDDELL'S LANE) has a mid-C18 pedimented doorway and in the garden a few medieval fragments built into a wall. They consist of two short pieces of C13 column, one keeled and the other triple-shafted. Above them is a crown. They are assembled like a fireplace. Opposite Avenue House is THE AVENUE, an C18 rope walk, again lined with pleasant Georgian houses. No. 4 has a mansard roof. THE RETREAT, at the far end, is C18 brick. Back on Palace Street East, the former GRAMMAR SCHOOL (No. 1) is of 1754, six bays, three storeys, lying back in its garden, which has a wall which ends in an unusual large spiral volute.

In RAVENSDOWNE nearly all the houses are worth a glance. The stepped skyline of the street rising gently to upper or Town Hall level is very pretty. Nos. 2–4 are quite handsome, early C19, with Adamish doorcases in blank arches. Nos. 6–8, also early C19, have a thin pierced parapet of intersected pointed arches with a large pineapple flanked by scrolls in the centre. Nos. 10–22 are plainer but still very satisfying, early C 19 and built of a delicate pink sandstone ashlar. No. 5 opposite was the BOYS' NATIONAL SCHOOL (1842). No.7 has a beautiful porch with detached Roman Doric columns. The next section of the street has, on the E side, a high wall with doorways. These were late C 18 ICEHOUSES associated with the salmon industry. Beyond them, steps and a narrow alleyway lead up on to the walls and more especially to THE LIONS HOUSE, a three-storey five-bay early C 19 house in a splendidly prominent position overlooking the walls. On its gatepiers, the eponymous lions are endearingly ill-carved and leer cheekily. Below the house (which is on the site of the unfinished Edward VI citadel) is THE MAGAZINE, or gunpowder store, of 1749. It belonged to the Barracks, of course, but was suitably detached from it. It is a fascinating place. High walls surround it, with a narrow pedimented doorway on the E side. The building itself has a similar doorway, no windows, stone roof and massive lean-to buttresses all along the sides. It looks very strong.

Back on Ravensdowne at this point it is necessary to glance to the l. into WOOLMARKET, to be rewarded with a house (No. 35) with some crazy mason's display of tooling, vertical fluting, diagonal tooling l. to r. and r. to l., and diverse kinds of knotwork of vaguely neo-Greek origin. The date will be 1830 or 1840. The top end of Ravensdowne has a different quality from the rest, quieter and more closed in. Nos. 34–36 are in effect semi-detached Georgian, i.e. seven bays with two pedimented doors side by side in the middle. Nos. 52–54 is a nice Adamish house with rusticated pilasters and paterae in the frieze. The house also has a castellated parapet. No. 72 is Grecian. No. 76 has attached Ionic columns to the doorcase. On the opposite side of the road, Nos. 51–53 are a pair of early C 19 Grecian semis with angle pilasters. Finally the OLD MILITARY HOSPITAL, set behind a high wall with a dignified pedimented doorway (cf. the Magazine). A simple two-storey three-bay house of the 1740s. The top of Ravensdowne brings us to the Parade and the Parish Church.

4. Beyond the ramparts to the N via Castlegate

Back to Marygate and N through Scotsgate and along CASTLE-GATE, which starts on the l. with Meg's Mount and the marble JUBILEE FOUNTAIN of 1897 and on the r. with a visually inappropriate but doubtless useful supermarket. No. 1 is a Grecian house with panelled pilasters and attached Ionic columns to the doorcase. It is built of ashlar and dates presumably from the 1820s. No. 19 is just the same but painted and rendered. The WAR MEMORIAL at the head of the street is a fine bronze eagle on a tall square rusticated plinth; it was designed by *Alexander Carrick*. The area to the r. of Castlegate is known as Low Greenses. It can be approached along SCOTT'S PLACE, a row of late C 18 or early C 19 ashlar houses with rusticated quoins and scrolled kneelers. Beyond, on WELLCLOSE SQUARE, the INFIRMARY is of 1874, except for the maternity wing to the N, which occupies the former poor-house and has small sixteen-pane sash windows.

NORTHUMBERLAND AVENUE, apart from the Bell Tower and the remains of the Edwardian wall (*see* above), has BERWICK MIDDLE SCHOOL, which is made up of a number of early C 20 elements. The earliest is the former Infants School of *c.* 1900, single-storeyed, rock-faced, with quite a hint of Art Nouveau in the curved lintels and parapets and the battered chimneys. In 1932 it became a senior school and was added to in brick, quite humanely with long fully-glazed corridors. The former Girls' Grammar School, on the opposite side of the road, was built in 1927 and as befitted its higher status was given a somewhat grander neo-Georgian quality. To the l. of Castlegate, RAILWAY STREET and TWEED STREET have, on the corner between them, a house which is crazy enough to be worth a detour. Towards Railway Street is an early C 19 three-bay house, conventional enough except for the busts of poets which adorn the parapet; but around the corner the house was extended in 1854 in the most bizarre manner imaginable. The walls are a positive riot of ornament. All the windows have carved and scrolled architrave surrounds; the lintels and keystones are all carved with masks; the entire wall surface is covered with carved patterns; there is an acanthus cornice and the parapet is littered with busts and a large stone eagle. The man responsible was a local sculptor, *William Wilson* (*see* also Wilson Terrace in Spittal). The STATION, which is further along Railway Street, was rebuilt in vague Classical style in 1924–7.

CASTLE HILLS, ½ m. W. Formerly the home of the Askew family. Early C 19. Castellated. Three-bay centre with higher projecting end wings. Gothick lodge.

SANSON SEAL, 2 m. NW. Red sandstone house of the late C 18; five bays wide with one-bay open pediment.

TWEEDMOUTH

Now part of Berwick-upon-Tweed, which it faces from the S bank of the Tweed, but with some distinct character of its own.

ST BARTHOLOMEW. 1783; chancel added and generally gothicized by *F. R. Wilson* 1866. Of 1783, the W tower with the quatrefoil motifs below the battlements; a quatrefoil window also at the W end of the nave, N of the tower. The church formerly had Y-tracery windows throughout and still has them on the N side. The N transept has a round arch towards the nave. – STAINED GLASS. One S window by *Kempe*, 1887. – Remarkably overcrowded GRAVEYARD. The OLD VICARAGE, opposite, is by *F. R. Wilson* also. Around the church is an area still with a real village atmosphere, nicely enclosed, though with no houses of special quality.

TWEED DOCK. By *Messrs David* and *Thomas Stevenson* of Edinburgh, with *Morrisons and Sons*, also of Edinburgh, as contractors. Opened officially in 1876, giving some 1.4 hectares (3½ acres) of enclosed wet dock and *c.* 500 metres (1,640 ft) of quayside – the only wet dock ever constructed on the Northumberland coast. Still in regular use. Facing the harbour and served by it is a grain mill and behind this a disused C 18 brewery and maltings.

The MAIN STREET of Tweedmouth runs close to the Tweed. The best house is No. 4, part of a good group of largely C18 houses opposite the end of the OLD BRIDGE (*see* above). It has seven narrow bays, the centre three projecting to form a loggia of four Tuscan columns with a Venetian window above and a pediment. Pedimented door and flanking niches behind the loggia. No. 46 is of three storeys and three bays with full-height bow windows flanking the doorway. WEST END is a successful blend of old and new houses at the w end of Main Street. The work was done by the Berwick-upon-Tweed *Borough Architects* in 1975. On the hill behind the houses, the KINGDOM HALL of the Jehovah's Witnesses, built in 1848 as a Scottish Presbyterian Church. The s front has large arched windows flanked by two round windows over doors with hoodmoulds. The N front is of two bays, flanked by taller octagonal castellated towers. Next to the church is the former manse, with a doorway set in a blank segmental arch.

SPITTAL

Now part of Berwick-upon-Tweed and almost a continuation of Tweedmouth, but with a distinct character. The name comes from the C13 Hospital of St Bartholomew, the site of which is no longer known.

ST JOHN, Main Street. Completed *c.* 1870–1. Four-bay nave, N aisle and short chancel. SW tower added later. Geometric style. Scissor-brace roof.

ST PAUL'S UNITED REFORMED CHURCH, Main Street. Formerly Presbyterian. 1878, with a NW broach spire that looks earlier.

Broad, tree-lined and quite attractive MAIN STREET, with no buildings of special distinction except the extraordinary Nos. 178–80 and the adjacent WILSON TERRACE built *c.* 1850 by *William Wilson*, a local sculptor. The fronts of these houses are a riot of bizarre decoration; every stone of the wall-face is carved with patterns, the windows are surrounded by scrolled and patterned architraves and the parapet bears busts and is broken by round-headed half-dormers also bearing busts (cf. Tweed Street, Berwick: *see* Perambulation 4, above).

BIDDLESTONE

BIDDLESTONE HALL. The house has been demolished. It was the ancient home of the Selby family, rebuilt in the late C18 and much altered by *Dobson* in 1820. All that remains is the R.C. CHAPEL, built in the early C19 on the substantial remains of a medieval tower, probably of the C14. The vaulted ground floor of the tower was retained. The entrance lobby on the E has a blocked doorway, and a pointed-arched inner doorway with a continuous chamfered surround. There is a continuous offset above the ground floor (except on the w) and, on the N side, medieval masonry continuing almost to eaves level. On the w

side, where the chapel adjoined the house, are two blocked c 16
or c 17 mullioned windows with moulded surrounds. The chapel
is built of ashlar and has Y-tracery windows.

The BIDDLESTONES, 100 metres SE in the wood to the l. of the
track to the chapel. Two stones. One is uncut; the other is the
base of a medieval cross.

ELILAW, 2 m. E. A large and impressive farm group of the mid-
c 19. The house is a standard three bays but faced in ashlar and
set on a mound. The buildings are not formally arranged because
of their position on a hillside, but they are all of a piece and typical
of a long line of large farms that mark the break between the
Cheviots and the valleys around.

CLENNELL HALL, 2 m. W. The s (garden) side still gives an
impression of the original house. Recessed to the r. is a late tower.
It was not mentioned in the 1415 list of castles, fortalices and
towers in the county, but is recorded in 1541. Attached to the l.
is a house of 1567 with scattered fenestration, largely renewed,
and an off-centre doorway with a multi-moulded surround. This
addition shows no sign of being defensible: an unusually early
example of an ordinary house so close to the Border.

Inside, the tower is vaulted at ground level and has a large c 17
bolection-moulded fireplace on the first floor. The c 16 house has
a fireplace with a moulded four-centred arch, and also a charming
hunting scene in plaster, probably from elsewhere.

Everything else, including the single-storey corridor in front of
the tower, the pavilion to the r. and the large Tudor-style additions
to the rear were done in 1897 for Anthony Wilkinson.

Conspicuous HILLFORT on the sw spur of Clennell Hill, high above
the River Alwin; two ramparts and a rocky interior.

BILTON

WATERMILL. Only a gutted two-storey mill building, of light-
coloured sandstone rubble with well-dressed openings, remains,
with a cart-shed alongside. In 1786 this was a flint mill owned by
James King of St Anthony's Pottery on Tyneside, and it was still
shown as a flint mill on a map of 1827, but it probably became a
corn mill shortly afterwards.

BINGFIELD

2 m. NW of Great Whittington

ST MARY. Some medieval masonry; the rest early c 18 and of 1875.
The round-headed s doorway is c 18, and so is the bellcote, with
rusticated sides and ball finial. c 19 kingpost roof with angle struts
and V-struts; some of the timbers are old and reused. – Large c 18
baluster FONT.

BIRNEY HALL *see* DISSINGTON HALL

BIRTLEY

ST GILES. Norman, *see* the completely plain chancel arch on chamfered imposts. The masonry of the nave and the chancel N wall is Norman also; especially fine the squared stone of the W end. Blocked C 16 doorway in N wall of the nave. All the rest appears to be of 1884, including the W porch and fancy SW turret with spirelet. – STAINED GLASS window by *Powell*. – INSCRIBED STONE. On the chancel N wall, with a cross and the letters ORPE, dated *c*. 700. The cross is of the type with cross-bars at the end of the arms, as in the Lindisfarne Gospels. – MONUMENTS. Several medieval cross slabs built into the W porch. Medieval STOUP also built into the porch.

In the former vicarage garden, a ruinous TOWER, probably late C 16 or early C 17, facing the steep slope down to the valley. The walls stand up 2.5 or 3 metres (8 or 10 ft) high. One slit window remains with widely splayed reveals. The SW corner is rounded.

CARRYCOATS HALL, 4 m. NE. A three-bay Tudor-style façade of the 1830s, but behind this an older house with a broad C 18 staircase and much older, possibly C 16 masonry to the rear.

TONE HALL, 2 m. NE. Originally a larger than average bastle. It has walls *c*. 1.3 metre (4 ft) thick and a blocked ground-floor doorway on the E gable end. Converted *c*. 1800 into a five-bay house with sash windows in raised stone surrounds. A rear span was added at the same time.

BITCHFIELD *see* WEST BITCHFIELD TOWER

BLACK CARTS *see* CHESTERS

BLACKHEDDON
2 m. N of Stamfordham

BLACKHEDDON FARMHOUSE. 1613 and one of the earliest unfortified houses in the county, showing the standard Northumbrian pattern of a two-cell, three-bay house with a central doorway already established. The doorway has a finely moulded Tudor-arched surround with lintel inscribed IHS/JS 1613 MD. The mullioned windows have been altered to sashes, but the double-chamfered surrounds and the hoodmoulds remain.

BLACKHEDDON HALL. 1824. Ashlar. Two storeys and three bays. Plain and classical, a standard early C 19 form.

BLAGDON

BLAGDON HALL. The seat of the Ridley family. The present house seems to have been begun *c*. 1735, incorporating a little of its C17 predecessor. An old engraving of the E front shows it as two-storeyed, with heavy pilasters and a balustraded parapet. A second phase of work seems to have been completed by 1752 (the date on some surviving rainwater heads): a second floor was added and the S front built. *Garrett* may have been the designer. In 1778–91 *James Wyatt* made various alterations, making the early C18 E front conformable with the S. The rather plain N wing, partly by *John Dobson*, is an addition of *c*. 1820. *Bonomi* worked on the house in 1826 and 1830, but his additions have largely been erased by later changes, principally those made in a restoration of 1948–9 by *Robert Lutyens* following severe fire damage in 1944. The E front, seven bays wide, still shows traces of its early C18 giant pilasters. The central doorway is by Robert Lutyens. The S front has the same number of bays but is of wider proportions, and is distinguished by a three-bay pediment. The architecture is very restrained, its chief excellence being the beautifully mild colour of the stone. The first-floor windows are all pedimented, with coats of arms and garlands. To the l. is a one-storey three-bay attachment of *c*. 1820. Inside, the mid-C18 is chiefly represented by the staircase with Venetian window and plaster decoration on the walls, sparingly disposed (the ceiling is renewed). The imperial stair, rather surprisingly, has only plain stick balusters. The plasterwork may have been done by the Italian team of Wallington. The staircase proceeds from a columnar screen and reaches another at its upper landing: the lower screen is Roman Doric, the upper Ionic. Mid-C18 also some rooms on the first floor. Otherwise the principal rooms are mostly of Wyatt's time, again remarkably reticent in style. The finest is the former dining room. The saloon in the centre of the S front was originally two-storeyed.

STABLES. By *Wyatt*, 1791. A quadrangle with a tall arched entrance below a lantern. In front of the entrance, in the centre of a *rond-point* by *Lutyens*, a *Coade* stone urn on a pedestal.

GARDENS. Partly remodelled by *Sir Edwin Lutyens*, the work being completed in 1938. The principal features are a paved terrace on the S front, extending W through a section with radial brick paving to a pair of obelisks and beyond a circular pond enclosed by three segments of walling each flanked by bronze urns, and a canal, or what Lutyens would have called a 'sky mirror', set at right angles to the house, 177 metres (580 ft) long, and ending in a circular basin with a big statue of Milo by *Lough* at the centre.

The grounds N of the Hall have much of interest as well. 200 metres NW of the house the Snitter Burn was dammed in 1783 to create a lake, now somewhat reduced in size. The stream then flows W through the Cascade Dene, spanned by three BRIDGES. The WHITE BRIDGE is a single-span cast-iron footbridge of somewhat unusual design. A pair of slightly arched cast-iron beams support cast-iron balustrades to form, in effect, a pair of trusses; timber decking is carried by the cast-iron beams. Beneath, the span-ends are tied with a pair of wrought-iron bars which in turn carry short vertical struts up to the base of the beams, now like a lenticular truss. The bridge is itself supported on dressed stone abutments which have corner piers carrying marble busts of the Ridley family by *Lough*. Through the w abutment is a carriage arch, with triple keystones inscribed 1859 MWR on one side, but similar keystones on the other side are incorporated into the abutment wall and are inscribed MWR AD 1784; perhaps the iron bridge replaced an earlier stone bridge. The STONE BRIDGE has three main full-centred arches on thick, recessed piers, pentagonal voussoirs and a plain parapet; rustic masonry except for stringcourses, voussoirs and soffit. Smaller-span carriage arches at both sides with urns in recesses. Inscribed John Donkin, Mason and MWR 1860. The IRON BRIDGE of 1881 with three wrought-iron spans supported on paired piers of plain concrete which apparently encase cast-iron columns rising above the concrete just below the bottom girders; openwork cast-iron balustrade. The engineer for this bridge was *J. Cresswell* of Newcastle; contractor *J. A. Somerset* of the St Nicholas Ironworks, Newcastle.

E of the S end of the Stone Bridge is a round ICEHOUSE built into the valley side, and just beyond it the SCULPTURE GARDEN: five more classical figures, probably also by *Lough*. Further away from the house, on the N bank of the lake, are a rustic late C18 BOATHOUSE, barrel-vaulted and semi-subterranean, a GOTHIC RUIN (reputedly built of medieval material from the hospital near Hartford Bridge), a SUMMERHOUSE and a circular TEMPLE from Heaton Hall, Newcastle, re-erected without its former dome. It was built in 1783 by *William Newton*. Beyond, in the wood, the remains of a medieval CROSS, said to be from Shotton; a base with leaf ornament at the corners carries a broken octagonal shaft with roll-moulded angles.

GATE LODGES. Both on the former A1. SOUTH LODGE, ¾ m. SE of the Hall, 1786 by *Wyatt*. A pair of octagonal lodges with domed niches and festoons on their parapets, linked by a Roman Doric screen. The main gatepiers are topped by big carved bulls (supporter animals of the Ridleys), painted white. NORTH LODGE, 550 metres NE of the Hall, is of 1887 by *Lish*, in a rather fussy eclectic style. Just inside the gates on the N is the CALE CROSS, another re-erected monument, formerly a conduit head, which stood in Newcastle at the foot of The Side. It was designed by *David Stephenson* and presented to the town by one of the Ridleys in 1783. Open three-bay Roman Doric structure carrying urn finials and a lion couchant.

MILKHOPE, ¾ m. s. Farmhouse dated 1806. Extensive planned farm buildings dated 1865, specifically as a cattle farm. Shelter sheds with full-height spine walls and arcades of segmental arches. Converted to workshops in 1985–6 by *Wiseman*: one of the better examples of reuse of old farm buildings, keeping much of the character of the group.

BLANCHLAND

BLANCHLAND ABBEY was founded for Premonstratensian canons
in 1165. After a troubled history because of the Scottish wars, it
was dissolved in 1539 and the conventual buildings became a
house. In the mid-C18 the estate came into the hands of the
Crewe Trustees, who created the delightful village we see today,
a village which despite its appearance is a result of the meta-
morphosis rather than the full-scale rebuilding of the monastic
buildings.

ST MARY THE VIRGIN. The Crewe Trustees found the monastic
church in ruins, with a little post-Dissolution chapel built against
the w side of its tower (where its roof weathering may still be
seen). Using what walls still stood, they built an L-plan church
incorporating the monastic chancel, crossing and N transept, at
the end of which stands the tower. So today we have a chancel of
c. 1200–10 with two lancets in each side wall, the mid-C13 transept
with Y-tracery windows on the w, and the substantial C13 tower
with its C14 belfry stage, opening from the transept by a tall triple-
chamfered arch. As well as the C18 repairs, the transept aisle was
rebuilt in 1854 and the E end in 1881. The transept arcade is of
two bays with a circular pier and double-chamfered arches with
broaches; the blocked openings above are not a medieval clerestory but the windows of an C18 schoolroom on an upper floor
(removed in the C19). The transept arch has triple-shafted jambs,
the central shaft with a fillet. In the chancel are much-restored
triple sedilia, with to the w the quirked jambs of a door to a former
sacristy; there was never a S transept. Late C19 are the carved
and panelled chancel CEILING, sanctuary PANELLING,
REREDOS and SCREEN. – STAINED GLASS. Some small late
medieval panels, including two with figures of Premonstratensian
canons. – COFFIN LIDS. Six on the floor of the transept, two with
abbots' croziers and two with foresters' emblems.

Outside in the churchyard, the wall bounding the garden of the
Lord Crewe Arms is in fact the S wall of the long and narrow (36
by 10 metres; 118 by 34 ft) monastic nave. It stands highest at its
w end, where it joins the inn: here is a blocked lancet and a
strangely sited double piscina; its SW corner buttress can be seen
from inside the Lord Crewe. From the inn garden, where the
ground level is much lower, the remains of a blocked doorway
can be seen at each end of the wall, and one corbel for the cloister
roof survives. Also in the churchyard is a good C13 CROSS.

The SQUARE, the centre of the village, seems to represent the L-
shaped outer court angled around the main abbey buildings at
its NE corner. Around it would stand barns, storehouses and
workshops, afforded the protection of some sort of perimeter wall.
Slag found under the houses on the w shows that lead or silver
smelting was carried out there at some time. Into the Square
through the segmental-arched passage of the embattled C15
GATEHOUSE (now incorporating the village post office), medieval
fabric is apparent in the three-storey house adjoining on the w
and also in the adjacent terrace on the w side of the Square.
Opposite this, the LORD CREWE ARMS, which is in fact the w
range of the main monastic buildings, a picturesque amalgam of

genuine medieval and C 18 Gothick. At its N end is another big embattled tower, probably C 15 and perhaps the Abbot's Lodge, incorporating the E wall of a narrower C 13 range; further S, at the rear, the segmental-moulded arch of the monks' lavatory survives, but the upper part of the range has been largely rebuilt at various C 18 dates. Inside, the vaulted basement of the tower is intact, and its original low-pitched roof structure with heavy cambered tie-beams. Further S are two big fireplaces, perhaps representing the monastic kitchen. Round the corner is the monastic S range, presumably the refectory, heavily disguised as a row of cottages. The hollow-chamfered jambs of the original large first-floor windows remain visible. The houses on the S of the Square are C 18 and C 19, with some older masonry thought to survive from the abbey mill at the rear. There was probably another gatehouse at the SE corner. On the E side, GOWLAND'S COTTAGE is an altered C 15 building with a good beamed ceiling inside, the S extension of the E cloister range. All around the Square are built-in fragments of medieval carved stone, and in the centre the 1897 PANT commemorating Queen Victoria's Diamond Jubilee.

The best views of Blanchland are from the S, as one drops down into the village across the sloping C 18 two-arch bridge. N of the church, outside the monastic enclosure, less formally arranged terraces of C 18 and early C 19 houses step up the hillside. Below is the former SCHOOL of c. 1860, thought to be by *S. S. Teulon*, who was responsible for the planned village of Hunstanworth just across the county boundary in Durham. Free C 13 style. ABBEY COTTAGE to the NE has a 'wrestler' roof (cf. White Heather Cottage at Beltingham).

SHILDON, ½ m. N up the drovers' way by the Shildon Burn. Here important LEADMINES were worked from medieval times up to the C 19. Relics include the shell of an ENGINE HOUSE of the Cornish type (locally known as 'Shildon Castle'), with a tall stack alongside. A Boulton & Watt engine was housed here; after its removal the engine house was converted into flats. Nearby is a little tramway bridge over the Burn with a segmental arch on impressive megalithic jambs. SHILDON HOUSE and SHILDON COTTAGE are the only survivors of an extensive settlement: thick walls in Shildon House and the ruins adjacent to the cottage suggest a C 17 or earlier date.

BAYBRIDGE. *See* p. 160.

BLENKINSOPP
2 m. W of Haltwhistle

BLENKINSOPP CASTLE. Licensed to crenellate in 1340 and mentioned as a *castrum* in 1415. The castle seems to have consisted of a central tower or keep c. 15 metres (50 ft) square, which was tightly enclosed by a tall curtain wall only 3.6–4.5 metres (12–15 ft) outside it. By 1800 a poor-house had been built inside; by c. 1832 a castellated mine agent's house, probably by *Dobson*, had been added; and by 1870, as old photographs show, a tall chimney or ventilation shaft for the local colliery, combining Gothic and classical detail, had risen from the centre of the castle. Then in 1877–80 it was rebuilt as a country house in a Tudor Gothic style by *William Glover*; this was gutted by fire in 1954 and its main block is now a sad ruin. The E wall of the original tower survives, with a blocked arch that may have been the main entrance, and some of the curtain at the NW corner, incorporated in the present house. The S wall of the 1832 agent's house has a reset C 16 window with a cable-moulded surround.

BLENKINSOPP HALL. The building is mentioned as recent in 1812; this no doubt refers to the five-bay two-storeyed S front, with windows in plain raised surrounds. The embattled parapet and the porch on the E front are additions of 1877. A tower and other additions made by *Dobson* in 1835 have mostly been demolished. – STABLE BLOCK to the NW; embattled front range dated 1903, rear range dated 1833 in pediment.

RAILWAY BRIDGE. Over the main drive to Blenkinsopp Hall is a small but attractive accommodation bridge, ashlar-faced and with low, crenellated, octagonal towers rising from each parapet end. False arch work beneath level deck and good curving wing walls; the bridge still carries the Newcastle and Carlisle Railway, which here opened in 1838. Just beyond the bridge the EAST LODGE of *c.* 1840, with a pyramidal roof carried out over a verandah on slender stone posts.

BLYTH

Blyth is very much a development of the later C 19 and early C 20. A map of 1813 shows a brewery, salt pans, a dockyard and two shipbuilding yards set along the S side of the mouth of the River Blyth; inland there was only Northumberland Street and Bath Terrace. Growth came with the railways and the coalmines. The railway has now gone, and so have most of the mines. So, sadly, have most of Blyth's C 18 buildings, especially from the suburb of Cowpen. Despite the protection afforded by statutory listing, much has been demolished in the last thirty years. In the town centre a scatter of worthwhile buildings still survive.

ST CUTHBERT. Plessey Road. 1884–93 by *W. S. Hicks*, Neo-Dec, with a big crossing tower, short transepts and chancel, and a broad unaisled nave with a flat-roofed W narthex entered by a timber-framed W porch. Shilbottle (q.v.) is a slightly smaller version of the same design. Inside, the crossing has alternating pink and buff dressings, and there are smaller arches obliquely placed between nave and transepts.

ST MARY, Wanley Street. 1864 by *Austin & Johnson*, as a chapel of ease to St Mary, Horton. Chancel and W end nave extended, and N aisle added in 1897–1902 by *W. S. Hicks*, after the church became parochial. C 13 and C 14 styles: the chancel has a SW turret with a timber belfry and spire. – STAINED GLASS. E window (Christ in Majesty), 1911 by *Atkinson Bros*. N aisle window 1950 by *L. C. Evetts*.

OUR LADY AND ST WILFRID (R.C.), Waterloo Road. 1861 by *A.*

M. Dunn. Quite imposing rock-faced church in a C14 style: aisleless nave with SE bell turret and spirelet, S transept and polygonal apse. A covered walk or cloister links the transept with buildings to the E which formerly housed a small community of Benedictine monks. – STAINED GLASS. Adoration of the Lamb, in the W windows, an impressive composition. Maker apparently unknown.

UNITED REFORMED CHURCH (formerly Presbyterian), Waterloo Road. 1874–6 by *Thomas Oliver Junior*. Red brick with ashlar dressings. Tall NW tower with spire.

For public buildings, *see* Perambulation, below.

PERAMBULATION

We start on WATERLOO STREET between the R.C. and United Reformed churches (*see* above) and walk E towards the town centre. S of, and parallel to, Waterloo Street are BONDICARR TERRACE, MARINE TERRACE and MIDDLETON STREET, three streets which provided the best housing Blyth had to offer in the 1870s and 1880s. Some quirky designs: TWEED HOUSE (now the Social Services Office), 1889, of white brick with red sandstone dressings, is typical. Waterloo Road ends in the wide and rather bleak MARKET PLACE. Behind St Mary's Church at the NW corner (*see* above) is the former NATIONAL SCHOOL of 1858 by *A. M. Dunn*; the part nearest to the church, with seg-mental-pointed window heads and a hipped roof, was the head-master's house. Beyond the Market Place, continue E along BRIDGE STREET past, on the r., the LIBRARY (former Mech-anics Institute), 1882, red brick with stone dressings and a clock tower. Then on the l. is LLOYDS BANK, 1898, ashlar-fronted and free Baroque in style. Where the road swings to the r., the BOATHOUSE TAVERN, on the l., probably the oldest building in Blyth. Open-pedimented gable above openings in architraves with pulvinated friezes and triangular or segmental pediments. This late C17 building was part of a big brewery complex in the C19. A little further on, on the same side, the big HARBOUR COMMISSIONERS' OFFICES of 1913 by *Cackett & Burns Dick*. Built on a curving corner site; ashlar ground floor with channelled rustication, brick above. The entrance is flanked by oval windows draped with garlands, all within a Roman Doric blind arcade. Inside, a circular entrance lobby, a stair with ship's wheel motifs in its wrought-iron balustrade, a panelled boardroom with an ornate plaster ceiling and various panels of Dutch glazed tiles taken from the S.S. *Walmer Castle*, broken up at Blyth in 1932. On the other side of the road, the towering POLICE STATION, 1896 by *John Cresswell*, and probably the best building in Blyth. Red brick with ashlar dressings and lots of carved detail. The style is an Italianate Gothic. The main entrance is flanked by black marble piers carrying a carved lintel with three-dimensional chained mastiffs. Steep hipped roofs with terracotta ridges and finials, and above the entrance a belfry and spirelet. Further on, past St Cuthbert's Church on the r., the line of Bridge Street is continued by BATH TERRACE. After the sadly decayed early C18

OLD VICARAGE, Nos. 5–10 are a brick terrace of *c.* 1790. No. 11, slightly later, is the former bath-house and has a prostyle porch. In the backland at the rear is a pleasant surprise, the HIGH LIGHT of *c.* 1789, a circular stone tower with little Gothick quatrefoil and cross loops. Stone newel stair inside. The brick top is later.

HARBOUR works began *c.* 1689, but the main developments were made after 1855, firstly by *James Abernethy* of London, then by *Thomas Meik* of Sunderland (from 1862) and *J. Watt Sandeman* (from 1882). In 1961 Blyth shipped more coal than any other port in Europe.

COWPEN, 1 m. w, until recently had a number of quite large C 18 houses. Now all that survives is the SIDNEY ARMS with its first-floor windows in keyed architraves extending down to enclose panelled aprons, and the KING'S ARMS, notable only for an extraordinary oval doorhead and fanlight. COWPEN CEMETERY has big wrought-iron gates and a pair of Dec chapels linked by a porch with a spire, all of *c.* 1875.

BLYTH LINKS. Remains of a 1914–18 coastal defence FORT and, further N, a DEL (defence electric light) station of the same date with two light turrets and, a little inland, a generator house which now serves as a public lavatory.

HORTON. *See* p. 344.

BOCKENFIELD

1½ m. s of Thirston

1090

House of *c.* 1660 probably by *Robert Trollope* for the Heron family, incorporating earlier walling visible in the gable ends. A relatively small four-bay building. The windows are (or were) mullioned and transomed, and surrounded by a bold cable moulding as at Swarland, except for the ground-floor far right, in a surround which on close inspection turns out to be a reset C 17 fireplace! The angle bays of the five-bay house are emphasized by rusticated pilasters with odd stunted capitals and pineapples on top – all this below the eaves and not touching them, a remarkably unstructural treatment of structural elements. The doorway is flanked by columns with spiral fluting. Segmental hood above.

BOLAM

2 m. N of Belsay

0080

ST ANDREW. Late Saxon w tower. Tall and unbuttressed. A break in the masonry at mid-point may indicate two separate builds. The bell openings are of two lights. They have shafts with bulbous bases and big corbelled-out stones to attain the thickness of the wall above. Above the bell openings on each side, there is one small window, three of them being triangle-headed. The original ground-floor windows are only visible fragmentarily from outside but more can be seen inside. The present windows are a replacement of *c.* 1762. Renewed parapet. The quoins of the nave, and its W wall, are Saxon also. The unmoulded tower arch is too broad to go with the date of the tower and is probably C 12. The colonnettes with low capitals exhibiting unmistakably Norman foliage may well have been carved *in situ* slightly later. The Norman style is indeed what sets the tone of the fine varied interior. The chancel arch has responds of three strong shafts, cushion capitals (carved on the N side with faces at the corners), two roll mouldings in the arch and an outer billet moulding. To the E the arch is simply single-stepped. In the chancel are the responds of the former sanctuary arch, removed when the chancel was lengthened in the C 13. They are round, with cushion capitals, and above them, reset in the wall, the former voussoirs with saltire crosses. Arcade of three bays between nave and S aisle, also round-arched but clearly later, of *c.* 1180–1200. It has quatrefoil keeled piers with simply and broadly moulded capitals. Bolam is the only parish church in the county to have such piers. The arches are single-stepped. The arch between the S chapel and the chancel is still round but double-chamfered and slightly later again. In the S chapel a broad, pointed, double-chamfered arch resting on C 14 corbels, and in the E end of the chapel there are indeed other C 14 forms; the big ogee arch of a large, upright, deep niche to the l. of the altar, and a vesica above the Norman window. All of these point to a widening of aisle and chapel at this time. But the C 13 has so far hardly been mentioned, and this is the period to which the S door and the E part of the chancel belong. The doorway may follow immediately on the aisle, because it still has a round arch. On the other hand such a demonstrative use of dogtooth ornament is no doubt C 13. One order of colonnettes and two orders of dogtooth in the arch, presumably under the influence of Hexham. They are both carried right down to the ground, though in the case of the outer band this is done so incompetently that the arched and the upright parts do not join up. The outermost order of the arch is decorated with the so-called nutmeg motif, which is on the whole characteristic of *c.* 1200. The chancel windows, in so far as they are not new, are lancets or two-light lancets with Y-tracery. Sedilia with single-chamfered arches and octagonal shafts.

Later elements include a two-light N window of *c.* 1600 with segmental heads to the lights, a small rectangular window in the chancel almost like a low-side window, and the Gothick windows of *c.* 1762 in the S aisle. – FONT. Plain, medieval; octagonal. – GLASS. Clear glass, but with beautiful leaded patterns, typical of so many Northumbrian churches and installed by *F. R. Wilson* here as in so many other places *c.* 1880. – MONUMENTS. Several CROSS SLABS. Fragment of a hogback built into the S porch. – Effigy of a knight, probably Sir Robert de Reymes, † mid-C 14; cross-legged, though much of the legs is now missing. – John Horsley † 1770. In the chancel. A standing monument with ver-miculated rusticated base and swan-neck pediment supporting a coat of arms.

VICARAGE. Mid-C 18. A quiet three-bay, ashlar house in a beautiful setting beside the church.

BOLAM HALL. Built for Robert Horsley, who died in 1809. Two

five-bay ashlar wings at right angles, each with a central pedimented doorway. The E wing has a Venetian window above the
door and tripartite windows on the ground floor. Elsewhere, sash
windows in architrave surrounds.

The GROUNDS, including a large and beautiful lake, were laid
out in 1816–18 by *Dobson* for the Hon. J. W. Beresford. Hodgson
says that he undertook the work 'to give employment to the poor
in the scarce, disastrous winters of 1816 and 1817'. The lake and
its immediate surroundings now form a country park.

GALLOWHILL, 1 m. SE. 1882 by *Septimus Oswald* for a Mr Perkins.
Large red-brick house (now a school), vaguely early C 18 in style,
but with a four-storey entrance tower and a group of elaborate
conservatories to the right. The stable block, though much altered,
is in a late C 19 Romantic style with a high pyramid roof over the
entrance tower.

POIND AND HIS MAN. Bronze Age barrow and an attendant standing stone, broad and weathered, prominently sited on the crest of
the ridge SW of Bolam West Houses. The barrow contained a
burial cist; a second stone is now at Wallington (q.v.). Mentioned
as a landmark in the Middle March, 1552. The Devil's Causeway,
the Roman road to Berwick, is clearly visible as a low mound just
to the NW.

SLATE HILL. On the N edge of Bolam Lake Country Park, a
multivallate Iron Age hillfort, its interior almost obliterated by
quarrying.

SHORTFLATT TOWER. *See* p. 569.

BOLTON   <small>1010</small>

BOLTON CHAPEL. A chapel of ease to Edlingham. The chancel
arch is C 12 and very simple, being stepped towards the nave only,
and carried on an impost band too worn to show any detail. The
chancel masonry may be medieval, but all the rest is C 19; the
nave and N transept early C 19, the porch and vestry *c.* 1868. All
these parts are neo-Norman and quite lavishly done, see the triple-
arched screen to the transept, and the carved FONT. There is also
a smaller and simpler font dated 1732. – MONUMENTS. C 18 and
C 19 wall tablets, including one with a draped urn to the Forster
family, 1790–1809, by *R. Blore*, and another to Lewis-de-Crespigny Buckle † 1864 (*see* also Edlingham).

BOLTON HALL. The plain classical S block is early C 19 and may
be by *John Dobson*. It has a five-bay front with sill bands and eaves
cornice, and a central *trompe-l'œil* doorway quite unrelated to the
internal plan. The lower NE range is late C 17 (doorway dated
1689 at rear). It was refenestrated and a rear stair wing added in
the mid-C18. The stair wing also served an earlier three-storey
structure, perhaps a medieval tower or a stronghouse, which
the C 19 block replaced. Late C 18 GARDEN WALL to the SW,
embattled and with Gothick loops.

JENNY'S LANTERN, 1¼ m. NE. Iron Age hillfort consisting of what
appears to be a wide and massive inner wall, heavily robbed, with
an outer dump rampart (two for extra strength, with inner ditches,

on the N and W). Immediately E, along the S crest of the hill, is a straggling settlement of Romano-British type; stone-walled homesteads containing circular houses, and other contemporary houses only partly enclosed; their irregular fields are on the slopes to the S and E. N of the hillfort are ruins of an C18 eyecatcher on a prominent hilltop. It took the form of tall screen wall with the coping stepping down on short returns, enclosing a shepherd's cottage. Its appearance is reminiscent of Crawley Tower; Jenny was the shepherd's wife who showed a lantern to guide her husband back across the marshy moortops from the inn at Eglingham.

SHAWDON HALL. *See* p. 567.

BOTHAL

2080

ST ANDREW. A C13 and C14 church with a complex building history. Externally there is a strong contrast between a chancel with a high-pitched roof and nave and aisles with parapets and roofs so flat that these parts seem roofless. The church of *c.* 1200 (the nave walls may be older) had a four-bay N aisle and a SE chapel. The N arcade has triple-shafted responds with stiffleaf foliage and double-chamfered arches. The E respond of the S arcade is a corbel with nail-head decoration. Later in the C13 came the chancel with its lancet windows (some renewed), sedilia (with trefoiled heads on shafts with fillets) and round-arched piscina with nail-head ornament on the projecting bowl. At the SW corner beside the low-side window is a recess exposing the lintel of an earlier squint carved with stiffleaf foliage. In the C14 the S chapel was extended W into a full aisle by cutting two new arches through the nave S wall, the piers being chunks of solid wall rudely chamfered into a polygonal shape. The Perp aisle windows and clerestory of small trefoiled ogee lights may be of *c.* 1398, when the Holgate Chantry was founded. The very plain low-pitched roofs may be of the same date, although one truss is said to be dated 1576. The W bellcote may be post-Reformation; it rests on a broad buttress like a chimney breast and has two lower openings (one reusing a C14 cusped head) with one above, under a pyramidal cap. The priest's door N of the chancel may be late as well. It has a monolithic triangular head like the door of a bastle. In 1887 the E end of the chancel was rebuilt with a triplet of lancets replacing a Perp three-light window, and the S porch was added. – Octagonal C14 or C15 FONT. – ALTAR RAILS. Jacobean, with turned balusters. – SCULPTURE. Fragment of a Saxon cross in N wall of chancel. At the W end of the N aisle, many C12 and C13 architectural fragments built up into a screen. – STAINED GLASS. Quite extensive remains of contemporary medieval glass in the heads of the aisle windows. Annunciation in the N aisle, Coronation of the Virgin and Instruments of the Passion in the S aisle, Holgate arms, and various other fragments. – MONUMENTS. Two C14 or C15 CROSS SLABS in the floor of the N aisle; others reused in the fabric. – Alabaster altar tomb with effigies of Ralph Lord Ogle † 1516 and his wife. The effigies are badly worn, but against the sides of the tomb-chest, small, better-preserved standing figures of mourners and angels. Concave-sided little gables and buttresses with pinnacles to separate the statuettes. Not great art or sculpture.

BOTHAL CASTLE. Bothal is built on a spur overlooking the Wansbeck on the S and Brocks Burn on the E. The end of this spur rises into an abrupt hill, an obvious strong-point, crowned by the castle. The hilltop controls the irregular plan of the elongate bailey defended on the N by a big gatehouse tower, probably built soon after 1343, when Robert Bertram obtained licence to crenellate. The 'Yethouse Court' lay in front of the gatehouse, towards the village. Early C 18 drawings show that whilst the gatehouse was always (as at Dunstanburgh) the dominant feature of Bothal, there were also a number of square towers around the bailey and one (the Ogle Tower) at the N W corner of the Yethouse Court. The gatehouse was restored in 1830–1 as a house for the Sample family; the W wing was added c. 1858 and extended in 1909. On the N, the gateway is flanked by polygonal turrets; below the embattled parapet is a display of carved shields, and on two of the merlons stand worn stone figures to frighten or confuse enemies (cf. Alnwick, and Raby and Hylton in County Durham). Projecting from the S W corner of the tower is a taller square turret containing a newel stair which ends in a pretty umbrella vault. The gate passage has a pointed vault on chamfered ribs, with three murder holes, and is flanked by guard rooms with semi-circular vaults on plain square ribs. Apart from single-light loops the only original windows to survive are three at first-floor level, each of two trefoiled lights with a quatrefoil above. The transomed Perp window on the S was brought from Cockle Park Tower (q.v.), as was the drawing room fireplace. The surviving fragments of the curtain, of rubble and perhaps earlier than the gate tower, do not tell us much; the section at the S W corner has angle buttresses and blocked chamfered windows. The W face of the C 19 stable range running N from the N W corner of the 1858 wing incorporates some masonry of the W wall of the Yethouse Court.

The village of Bothal is no more than a single street; on its W, an attractive row of estate cottages remodelled in 1885 with latticed windows and fancy bargeboards. The VILLAGE HALL of 1895 is in the same vein.

BRAINSHAUGH

2000

1½ m. N W of Acklington

Set on a wooded hill above the Coquet, Brainshaugh is not a large house, yet its elevations give surprisingly different impressions. The ashlar-faced W front of 1805 has canted bays flanking a central *trompe-l'œil* doorway (completely unrelated to the internal arrangements, as at Bolton Hall); the five-bay S front is early C 18 with a bolection-moulded doorway and windows in architraves; the E wall is older still, with blocked mullioned windows of the C 16 or C 17.

1010
BRANDON
1½ m. ENE of Ingram

Ruined CHURCH. The remains, hardly rising above the ground, point to a C 13 church on the foundations of a Saxon one; for they consist of a nave, a chancel of the same width, and a longer and narrower sanctuary with a narrow arch to connect it with the chancel. The sanctuary had a S chapel nearly as large as itself.

BRANDON FARM. One of those typical Northumbrian farmsteads which in fact comprises the whole village. The late C 18 farmhouse is a particularly attractive example, with architrave surrounds to windows and pedimented doorway, and a fine hipped Scottish slate roof. Extensive ranges of farm buildings round two court-yards, inscribed RL ALLGOOD/1831. Across the road a long row of single-storey workers' cottages and a forge.

0010
BRANTON
1½ m. E of Ingram

Former PRESBYTERIAN CHURCH. 1781. The façade of the usual arrangement; six bays, the outer bays with doorways and arched windows above, the four other bays with full-height arched windows.

BRANTON WEST SIDE is a farm in the village whose redundant buildings were well converted into workshops and cottages by *Reavell & Cahill* of Alnwick *c.* 1980.

8030
BRANXTON

ST PAUL. Neo-Norman of 1849, built of dark brown rhyolite with sandstone dressings. NW tower with stone pyramid roof. Internally one feature survives from the original Norman church: the chancel arch on responds which are single-stepped to the W and E, have shafts in the angles and a broad semicircular shaft in the middle. The bases have spurs and the capitals are scalloped. The arch, however, is of the C 13, pointed and double-chamfered with broaches. – ALTAR RAILS. Late C 17, with fat balusters.

MEMORIAL DRINKING FOUNTAIN. 1910 by *George Reavell*. Classical style; to the memory of William Askew Robertson.

FLODDEN MEMORIAL; ½ m. SW. Erected in 1910 by the Berwick-shire Naturalists Club. A very plain granite cross.

1090
BRINKBURN PRIORY

The Priory (for Augustinian canons) was founded between 1130 and 1135. No more enchanted spot could have been found. The buildings lie at the bottom of a deeply cut dene almost surrounded by a loop of the Coquet river. The church was in ruins until restored in 1858–9 by *Thomas Austin* at the expense of the Cadogan

family. There was enough left to make the restoration archaeologically almost entirely reliable. The surfaces may no longer be
as attractive as they had been, but architecturally, in the proper
serious sense of the word, nothing has been lost, except the SW
corner of the nave, which could not be rebuilt in its original form
as it had entirely disappeared. The church consists of a six-bay 25
nave with a N aisle only, a crossing with a low tower, transepts
with E aisles and a straight short chancel. Above the chancel,
before the restoration, were the remains of an added upper
chamber, as at Tynemouth; there was also an added chamber
above the nave aisle and a sacristy on the N of the presbytery.
These additions have been abolished for the sake of purity, that
of the period c. 1190–1220. The date of the building of the church
at Brinkburn must in fact be almost identical with that at Hexham.

The style is a fine example of the transition between Norman
and E.E.; round and pointed arches are mixed to such an extent
that the order of building is difficult to determine. The principal
doorways and most of the upper windows are round-headed,
whilst the lower windows and those in the W end are lancets.
Building may have begun at the E end; this has three tiers of
windows, pointed below and round-headed in the gable. The 26
lower tiers have shafted outer jambs. The buttresses between the
windows pass from square to semi-octagonal to keeled section as
they rise. Inside, the N and S walls have blank arcading with
pointed arches, but the upper windows are again round-headed.
The crossing piers and the octagonal piers of the transept aisles
have the plainest moulded capitals. The crossing piers consist of
groups of three shafts, a broad semicircular one flanked by two
slender ones in the re-entrant angles. The tower above barely rises
above the ridges of the adjacent roofs. The transept aisles are
vaulted with single-chamfered ribs, but the tympanum and clerestory above are the same as in the nave, and with the nave and
aisle appear a little later in date. The gable end of the N transept
has a central stair turret, capped by an 1866 timber bellcote which
was not part of the medieval design; neither was the wheel window
in the S transept gable (which had fallen before the restoration).
The nave has rather short octagonal piers with more elaborate
abaci, carrying double-chamfered arches. Above the arcade, the
tympanum openings, set above the piers, each have twin round
arches beneath a superordinate arch of the same form. Above
that, and placed above the arches of the arcade, are the round-
headed clerestory windows. The aisle shows moulded springers
for a vault which never seems to have been completed.

The nave has three doorways. The most sumptuous one led to
the outer world on the N side. It is placed in a projection (as at
Kelso and Holy Island) and has an exuberant display of late
Norman ornament, with beakheads, chevron, zigzag and a billet
hood. Yet right above, in the gable, is the chastest, purely Gothic
arcade of three trefoiled-pointed arches on detached shafts. Also,
down the angles of the projection run bands of dogtooth. On the
S side are the customary E and W processional doors to the
cloister, with a blind arcade of trefoiled arches between and five
tall round-headed windows above. There is another doorway into
the cloister on the W side of the S transept, with a book cupboard

beside it. The W end is probably of *c.* 1220; at the base is a blind arcade of pointed arches beneath a similar but taller arcade incorporating three tall lancets, with three stepped lancets in the gable above.

The general absence of furniture and fittings inside the church accentuates the surprising impression of height and length achieved by a building only 40 metres (130 ft) long. – MONU-MENTS. One good CROSS SLAB with inscription to Prior William † 1484. – Plain pink marble slab to Cadogan Hodgson Cadogan, the restorer, † 1888. – STAINED GLASS. One grisaille window (S of presbytery) by *Austin*, incorporating medieval glass fragments recovered at the restoration. – Other windows by *Clayton & Bell* and *Wailes*. – ORGAN. 1868 by *William Hill*.

MONASTIC BUILDINGS. Not a great deal survives. The S end of the S transept shows a blocked door from the night stair to the dorter. Adjacent to the transept are the ruins of a vaulted passage which may have been either a slype or the chapterhouse vestibule. The more substantial remains of the S range are incorporated within the MANOR HOUSE and only visible internally; these comprise the N wall of the range, with the moulded segmental arch of the C13 lavatory recess beside the frater door, part of the S wall, and a cellar beneath the range with an inserted barrel vault perhaps of the C16. After the Dissolution the range was converted into a house for the Fenwick family (cf. several blocked mullioned windows inserted in the medieval N wall) and remodelled in a simple Gothick style in 1810. The E part of this Gothick house survives; the W part was swallowed up in a major extension of 1830–7 by *John Dobson* in the castellated Neo-Tudor style of Beaufront. The house makes an ideal foil for the Priory Church; it is a pity that most of its interiors have been lost to the ravages of dry rot.

The remainder of the site has never been excavated. The tall riverside wall NW of the Manor House is largely medieval; a pair of gatepiers adjacent to it (near the early C19 Gothick stable block) are formed from the moulded jambs, possibly *in situ*, of a C15 or C16 archway, presumably part of a gatehouse. E of the Manor House is a long length of wall forming one side of the priory main drain, later converted into a millrace. (For the mill, *see* below.) An L-plan TUNNEL NE of the mill is presumably an C18 or early C19 garden feature, the sort of place that sometimes temporarily housed a 'hermit' for the benefit of visitors seeking the romantic.

WATERMILL. A watermill at Brinkburn is first noted in 1535 but the present structure is probably early C19. A compact mill building of squared and coursed rough masonry, with an adjacent cottage of later build and superior construction. Both have mullioned, drip-headed window openings, perhaps in deference to the nearby Priory. Originally a water-powered corn mill, it was apparently modified to allow for electricity generation from the iron water-wheel.

A FORT, presumably of Iron Age date, was economically con-structed on the promontory above the Priory. The strong natural defences were completed on the NE by a rampart and ditch cutting off the neck of land.

BRINKHEUGH, ½m. E, higher up on the other side of the river. A nice five-bay, two-storey house with rusticated quoins, a doorway with a bolection-moulded surround and an open scrolly pediment, windows with raised convex-moulded surrounds and cornices, and a walled front garden. The date is late in the C 17 (worn doorhead inscription dated 16..), and there are some contemporary internal features such as door surrounds and a fine open-well stair. The lower parallel range at the rear, however, is a C 16 or early C 17 bastle house with 1.2-metre (4-ft) thick walls and quite a number of original openings. Both doorways are in the E gable-end (cf. Thropton Peel). The doorways and several windows show the unusual feature of stop-chamfered surrounds.

BRUNTON see WALL

BUDLE
2 m. W of Bamburgh

1030

BUDLE HALL. Built in 1810 for a Mr Grieve Smith; the architect is unknown. The stone is a delicate pink ashlar. The house is square, five by five bays, with a Roman Doric porch and large two-storey bow windows on each side elevation. Inside, among much well-designed early C 19 detail, a spacious staircase hall with a glazed dome and a cantilevered stair with lyre-pattern iron balusters.

BURRADON
3 m. N of Longbenton

2070

BURRADON TOWER. C 16 tower-house in the grounds of the C 19 farmhouse. Tiny (externally only 7.7 by 6.9 metres – 25¼ by 22½ ft). Ruinous but still complete in the tunnel-vaulted ground floor, and on the E as far as the top corbels, with machicolation over the elliptical-headed doorway. *See* Introduction, p. 63.

BYKER see NEWCASTLE UPON TYNE

BYRNESS

7000

ST FRANCIS OF ASSISI. Dated 1796 on the inner doorway. Paid for by the Rev. Dutens, vicar of Elsdon. Of tiny dimensions. Round-headed doorway and windows. The windows were given decorated tracery and the chancel was partly rebuilt in 1884 by *F. R. Wilson*, who also remodelled inside. – STAINED GLASS. A famous S window of 1903 commemorating those who died during the construction of the Catcleugh Reservoir, and surely the only such to illustrate a narrow-gauge steam railway. Beside it a brass plate records the names.

CATCLEUGH RESERVOIR, 1 m. w. 1891–1905 by *T. & C. Hawksley* for the Newcastle and Gateshead Water Company. Earth-faced dam with overflow channel and compensation arch and the usual ancillary buildings, all on a grand Baroque scale. Below the dam, a WOODEN HUT, like a hut in the Klondike, is the last vestige of the shanty town used by the navvies and their families.

BYRNESS VILLAGE. A Forestry Commission village planned by *Dr Thomas Sharp* in the 1950s (cf. Stonehaugh).

THE THREE KINGS, in the forest SW of Cottonhopesburn Foot, 1½ m. S of Byrness. A 'four-poster' stone circle – a type more common in Scotland: a square setting of upright stones (one now fallen), probably marking a central cremation burial of the earlier second millennium B.C.

0060

BYWELL

Bywell is probably the most beautifully placed, picturesque and architecturally rewarding group of buildings in the Tyne Valley. It is set a little above the wide river and possesses, besides the large landscaped grounds of Bywell Hall, two ancient churches next to each other, and a castle. Both churches and the castle deserve close attention for aesthetic and archaeological reasons. Bywell cannot strictly be called a village, since its houses and cottages were swept away by mid-C19 landscaping and its villagers resettled in Stocksfield, conveniently out of sight on the S bank of the river.

7 ST ANDREW possesses a first-rate Saxon W tower, the best in the county. It is tall and unbuttressed, with massive side-alternate quoins, and stringcourses above and below the belfry. Just below the belfry on the S is a high-level doorway with an arched head and projecting imposts and bases linking to a stripwork surround. The bell openings are treated in a similar manner, except that each is of two lights, divided by a mid-wall shaft, and with a pierced circle above and between the lights – a kind of prophetic plate tracery (cf. Ovingham and also Billingham in County Durham). The tower arch into the nave is low and slightly pointed: it has been interfered with, perhaps in the C19. The upper parts of the tower look *c.* 1000, but the base, of more massive browner stone, is thought to be earlier, and may have formed a W porch, as at Corbridge.

The rest of the church – aisleless nave with S porch, transepts, and quite a long chancel with N chapel and vestry – is a little disappointing. It was altered in 1830 and again in 1850 by *Dobson*, and again in 1871 by *William Slater*, when the N transept, chapel, vestry and S porch were all added. There is Saxon masonry in the nave walls, and C13 fabric in the S transept and lower chancel walls (although a blocked opening S of the chancel looks to pre-date the C13 plinth), but all the windows are C19. Inside there are old double-chamfered arches to the chancel and S transept (the latter on corbels with nail-head). – In the chancel a piece of

SAXON CROSS SHAFT set on a carved block which is probably
Roman. – CROSS SLABS. A splendid collection, twenty-five in all.
Many are built into the N exterior wall and are beginning to suffer
from weathering. Notice especially a big C 14 slab with an odd
ten-armed cross and a shield with a rampant lion.

ST PETER. The nave N wall and the W parts of the chancel side
walls are now generally recognized to be parts of a large Saxon
church, perhaps as early as C 8, and quite possibly the building in
which Bishop Egbert of Lindisfarne was consecrated in 802. The
most apparent Saxon features are four windows high in the N
wall of the nave, with their round-arched heads cut into large
rectangular blocks, and upright slabs forming each jamb; there
are also traces of a doorway near the W end of the wall. The Saxon
nave was longer than the present one; its megalithic side-alternate
E quoins are visible, but at the W end it has been truncated. The
original footings can be seen continuing alongside the N wall of
the squat C 14 W tower. In the N wall of the chancel is a blocked
square-headed door with the jamb stones laid in 'Escomb fashion'
(i.e. alternately flat and upright), with still visible above it the
roof-line of the *porticus* into which it opened; this overlapped the
junction of nave and chancel in a rather strange way. The Saxon
church was unusually large: its nave was at least the size of that
at Monkwearmouth. What seem to be early foundations jutting
out beyond the present E end, and outside the SW corner of the
S aisle, may also be pointers to the size of the early building.

The medieval parts of the church are better preserved than at
St Andrew, although here too the C 19 has been over-zealous. In
1849 *Benjamin Ferrey* rebuilt the S aisle and S porch and added
the vestry, and there were further alterations in 1873. The chancel
was remodelled in the early C 13, with lancet windows including
a typical triplet in the E end. The double-chamfered chancel arch
on triple-shafted corbels is said to be an 1849 copy of what was
there before. Of the same date the four-bay S arcade with double-
chamfered arches on tall round piers. The W end of the nave (now
within the C 14 tower) may date to a reconstruction after a 1285
fire. The tower itself is severely plain and may have been intended
to be defensible. Apart from the W door the only openings are
twin lancets to the belfry and an odd blocked high-level door on
the W. The tower top has had a pitched roof (as both Corbridge
and Longhoughton once had): the outline of the original gable
can be seen on the E. Mid-C 14 the nave N chapel, with two- and
four-light windows with reticulated tracery under square heads.
The two-bay arcade is C 19 in its present form. Outside, on the N
of the chapel, are the springers of three arches. These never seem
to have been constructed; it is difficult to envisage what sort of
structure the builders had in mind. There is another puzzle on
the S side of the chancel, where a straight-headed two-light low-
side window (cf. Corbridge) opens into the E end of the S aisle,
which overlaps the chancel. Although the aisle was largely rebuilt
by Ferrey it is on the old foundations: early masonry (possibly
the E wall of a Saxon *porticus*) survives in its E wall. – STAINED
GLASS. Windows in N chapel and chancel possibly by *Wailes*. –
MONUMENTS. Outside the E end of the S aisle a strange slab that
seems to mix pre-Conquest influences with medieval heraldry.

The cross is flanked by shears and an angular pattern that looks like ill-remembered knotwork. Above the cross the bottom half of a rampant lion. Other CROSS SLABS in the porch and elsewhere. – Worn C 15 incised effigy under a trapdoor in the N chapel. – Epitaph of 1820 by *Davies* of Newcastle.

The churchyard is entered between GATEPIERS dated 1706, with bulgy rustication (cf. Capheaton Hall and Halton Tower) and ball finials: they formerly stood on the W of the churchyard near the C 18 HEARSE HOUSE.

VILLAGE CROSS, to the E of St Andrew's Church. C 13 shaft with worn nail-head at the corners, now with C 18 ball finial. It originally stood further SW in what are now the Hall grounds.

OLD VICARAGE, to the N of St Andrew. Symmetrical five-bay front elevation. The central door has a big broken pediment with the arms of the See of Durham and an inscription dated 1698: the windows have surrounds of stepped section, and floating cornices. In the E end some interesting little oval and lozenge-shaped windows. Major extensions to the rear of 1901. Inside, a framed newel stair with splat balusters. The lofty garden wall to the SW, known as the 'Spite Wall', was built to screen the house from the view from the Hall: when Bywell village was cleared, the vicar could not be persuaded to move too.

BYWELL CASTLE. A big rectangular gatehouse tower, built early in the C 15 for Ralph Neville, the second Earl of Westmorland. It is roofless, but the shell remains virtually intact. The gatehouse faced S (i.e. towards the river) and was intended to be part of a large enclosure, which may never have been completed. The front has a central double-chamfered arch, still with its old doors, and two floors above with windows of two trefoil-headed lights. The centre section of the embattled parapet is set forward on machico-lations (there is a similar arrangement at the rear), and there are taller corner turrets with octagonal corbelled-out tops. On the ground floor the gate passage and flanking chambers have plain barrel vaults. The floor above has been divided by a later C 15 cross-wall towards the E end, whilst the top floor seems to have held a single large room. The stair starts off in the thickness of the rear wall on the W of the gate passage, and continues as a newel in the NW corner. Several fireplaces survive, along with garderobes in the SW and NE corners. The gatehouse-cum-tower-house concept has its origins in some Norman castles (Newark, Exeter, Richmond): its later medieval reappearance in Nor-thumberland also gives us the grander Dunstanburgh and on a humbler scale the Willimoteswick gate tower. The only other remains are a length of curtain wall running E from the gatehouse to the vaulted basement of a projecting rectangular tower. These are both incorporated in the C 19 Bywell Castle House.

BYWELL HALL. A grand villa built in 1766 by *James Paine* for William Fenwick. The main S front has three wide bays, each with a pediment, above a slightly projecting rusticated ground floor. The central pediment, with a coat of arms flanked by cornucopia, rests on giant Ionic columns. The ground-floor windows in the side bays are flanked by arched niches. The side pediments are broken at the base, as Paine liked it. A lower four-bay block to the NW, in the same style, is late C 19 pastiche. The interior has been altered and Paine's interesting staircase does not survive. One room preserves an original carved marble fireplace and Palladian compartmented ceiling. Paine is said to have incorporated parts of an older house in his design: some C 17 work, with blocked mullioned windows, survives in a detached stable block behind.

BYWELL HOME FARM (Estate Office), 1 m. N. Farmhouse and buildings with some Gothick touches. The house has a three-bay front with a quatrefoil above the doorway and twin gables disguised and linked by an embattled parapet.

BYWELL BRIDGE, ½ m. NE. 1838 by *George Basevi*. Ashlar, with five segmental arches and a panelled parapet.

STYFORD HALL, 2 m. W. Three-storey five-bay house of *c.* 1800. The slightly projecting pedimented centre has an arched doorway with radial fanlight. Interior and rear wings altered *c.* 1965. To the rear, a pretty little stable block with a cupola-cum-clock tower.

MOTTE, ⅓ m. NW of Styford Hall, on the lip of the steep slopes above the river. A simple but substantial conical mound, up to 6.6 metres (21 ft) high, surrounded by a ditch (except on the S, where the natural slopes do very well instead). The barony of Styford was granted to Walter de Bolbec by Henry I.

STYFORD HIGH BARNS, ¾ m. N of Styford Hall. A planned farm of *c.* 1840, with an engine house whose stack is of rusticated ashlar at the base and yellow engineering brick above, with a stone modillion-corniced top.

NEWTON HALL. *See* p. 519.

CALLALY

oooo

CALLALY CASTLE. One of the most interesting and varied houses in Northumberland. It would deserve a monograph all to itself. The house as one sees it today is essentially classical, of *c.* 1675–1890. It was owned by the Claverings from medieval times until 1877, when it was bought by the Brownes. It became one of the very earliest houses in the country to have its own power station for electricity. In 1987 it was divided into flats by *Ainsworth Spark Associates*. It is a large house on an entirely irregular plan and particularly needs to be considered one range at a time.

The most important is the SOUTH RANGE, which has a centre with two projecting wings. It is evident immediately that though all three elements of the façade are fine in themselves they are all quite different from each other. What cannot be guessed from outside, however, is that the wing to the l., the SW angle of the house, is a medieval tower. Three of its walls still stand and in one corner is the spiral staircase, though the stone steps have been replaced by timber. Its W wall was rebuilt in 1840, but the others, refaced in 1749, are over 2 metres (6½ ft) thick. The problem is to decide how the rest of the façade relates to this tower, and when it was all built. The centre must have been a hall range like those attached to towers elsewhere. Inside it a fireplace with a lintel dated 1619 is preserved, though that is unlikely to be the date when this range was first built, because the wing projecting to the

1   Smoking room
2   Drawing room
3   Morning room
4   Entrance hall
5   Staircase
6   Ballroom
7   Music room or pavilion
8   Museum wing
9   Nursery /
    maid-servants' wing
10 Courtyard
11 Men-servants' wing

Callaly Castle. Plan as it was *c.* 1900

r., that is at the SE angle, puts one in mind of the third element of a standard three-bay medieval house. The wing is dated 1707, but once again its walls are over a metre thick, and preserved in the house are two pieces of painted Elizabethan panelling found behind early C18 panelling in this wing when the morning room was redecorated in 1934. The present appearance of the SOUTH FAÇADE contains much of interest on its own. The centre was remodelled or rebuilt in 1676, no doubt by *Trollope*, the architect of Capheaton. The new façade is of five bays and three storeys. All the windows have thin open pediments, with ornamental carvings of trophies, dolphins etc. The doorway, with Corinthian columns, a moulded surround and a four-centred-arched lintel, is absurdly squeezed between the neighbouring windows (cf. Eshott), and since above it is an inscription surrounded by scrolly strapwork one might assume that this piece was kept from the building of 1619; however, the 'RMC' of the inscription refers to Ralph and Mary Clavering, the owners in 1676, so perhaps this is Trollope mixing his stylistic metaphors. Above is a sumptuous coat of arms and a sundial. The top window pediments were cut off in 1749, when a new cornice was substituted for Trollope's original, whose appearance we do not know. The cornice was made, of course, to tally with the refacing of the SW wing. But this came only after the SE wing had been refaced or rebuilt in 1707 in the plainest Queen Anne style, with no more than an ingeniously detailed lintel of keystones to each window. The remodelling of the SW tower in 1749 was even plainer. The windows, some of which are sham, have moulded surrounds and that is all.

The WEST FRONT also has two projecting wings, one of which is, of course, the tower that forms part of the S range. This façade also has some curious details. There are blank arches of Vanbrughian type which were originally an open two-storey arcade on the N side of the tower; and there is an asymmetrically placed doorway with a heavy Gibbs surround. It is dated 1727. The arcade looks about the same date but it does not join up with the doorway. The N wing of this W front, the former nursery and maid-servants' wing, was remodelled in 1893 (see below). The EAST FRONT is in two sections. The l. part is the E façade of the S range. It is the main entrance to the house and has a three-storey, six-bay, mid-C18 façade with a Venetian doorway and Venetian windows in the fourth bay. The r. half of the E front is part of an extensive remodelling and enlargement of the N and E sides of the house undertaken by Major A. H. Browne. The architect was *James Stevenson* of Berwick; work began in 1890. The nursery and maid-servants' wing was created out of the former stables. A new courtyard and men-servants' wing was added on the N side of the house, but it is the E front which has the most interesting work of this stage of the house's development. It was done in harmony with, indeed in literal imitation of, the Trollope front. It involved the conversion into a ballroom of the former chapel (the Claverings had been Roman Catholic) and the creation of a new museum wing. It makes an impressive façade.

The showpiece of the INTERIOR is the DRAWING ROOM 77 behind the Trollope front, which was completely redecorated in 1757. It is the *chef d'œuvre* of the Italian team which also worked at Wallington, and it is of quite fabulous richness, a riot of exuberant Rococo plasterwork. It is two storeys high, with a coved ceiling and balconies at each end on marble Tuscan columns and with balustrades in Chinese Chippendale style and Gothick centre panels. The staircase behind the drawing room looks 1720–30. Most of the other rooms are of minor interest. The SMOKING ROOM on the ground floor of the tower was redecorated in the French style in 1840. It has the Clavering crest in the ceiling. Of the later C19 work, the only room to note is the PAVILION or MUSIC ROOM deep in the heart of the house. It is an ultra-

Victorian piece with stone walls, a glazed roof on steel ribs and a free-standing iron spiral staircase.

STABLES. 1892 by *Stevenson*. A large quadrangle with glass and elaborate cast-iron canopies around the inside.

LORBOTTLE HALL, 2 m. SW. Probably built for Adam Atkinson, who bought the property in 1797. Five bays, with the centre bay treated as a Venetian doorway and a Venetian window above. The door and window surrounds are completely plain, very severe – typical of many houses of this period in the county.

CASTLE HILL. A dramatically sited Iron Age hillfort on the summit, apparently with later occupation. It consists of a strong, angular bivallate enclosure, with two progressively weaker and lower 'annexes' to the W. Without excavation the interpretation of this puzzling earthwork is speculative, but it is likely that the massive rock-cut ditch, with its upcast banks on the W lip of the summit, represents a later division. The original Iron Age phase may be represented by the much slighter bank of the inner of the two W 'annexes', the line of which is continued around the modified E end. Foundations of two rectangular buildings survive within this well-defended E enclosure and are set on the highest point to give the best outlook over Whittingham Vale. This could be Old Callaly, a castle mentioned in 1415. Despite the difficulty of telling chicken from egg, there is a strong local tradition of two castles, of which the lower one proved the more durable.

0080

CAMBO

HOLY TRINITY. 1842 by *J. & B. Green*. Aisleless four-bay nave and polygonal sanctuary in simple lancet style. Quite a modest church, but made to conform more with the scale of Wallington by the addition of a big sound neo-Perp W tower (and a N vestry) in 1884. Elaborate barrel ceilings. – Eight medieval SEPULCHRAL SLABS from a previous chapel (six in the tower and two in the vestry) include an incised effigy, partly recut in the C 19, showing a man with a sword at his hip, his hands raised and a dog at his feet.

The village is beautifully placed on a ridge to the N of the Wallington grounds and consists mainly of Wallington estate cottages in terraces, possibly laid out by *Daniel Garrett*. Most are of *c.* 1750, remodelled and given first floors by Sir Charles Trevelyan in the 1880s. The POST OFFICE, however, is a bastle house, probably C 16, and unusual in that it appears to have been three-storeyed from the first. Traces of the original first-floor door can be seen above a shopfront dated 1818 on its lintel. The TWO QUEENS at the W end of the southernmost row of cottages was formerly an inn, closed *c.* 1846 when Sir Walter Trevelyan (first president of the United Kingdom Alliance for the Total Suppression of the Liquor Traffic) inherited the estate. Inside, in the old kitchen, is an *in-situ* DOG WHEEL. In the centre of the village is a granite DRINKING FOUNTAIN formed by a vigorous life-size Trevelyan dolphin, part of Sir Charles's remodelling.

CAPHEATON

CAPHEATON HALL. 1668 by *Robert Trollope* of Newcastle for Sir John Swinburne. One of the most interesting houses of its date and character in England, and far too little-known. The character is that of the provincial and endearing Mannerism indulged in between 1630 and 1675 by those who were oblivious to or unimpressed by the academic virtues of Jones, Pratt and Wren. It is the exuberant character of Bolsover, of the Old Ashmolean at Oxford, of Clare College and St John's College Third Court at Cambridge, and of Nottingham Castle – the latter perhaps the building most closely comparable to Capheaton, except that Capheaton is doubly attractive because all its ornamentation was done by the rustic masons of the neighbourhood.

SOUTH FRONT (facing the garden) of five bays, two storeys 66 high, divided by giant pilasters which are flatly rusticated at the bottom, with banded intermittent rustication higher up and with thick, bulgy rock-like rustication at the first-floor level. No real capitals and no connection with the cornice. The doorway has columns carved with vines, bases with figures of a knight and a beggar carved in relief and a fantastic version of the curly open pediment so popular in the county in the later C 17. The windows are tall but divided only by a stone mullion, not the more usual mullion-and-transom crosses. Moreover, they are thickly framed by rounded bands of leaf garlands. In addition there are carved flower vases above the two outer windows and sundials above the others. The dials have a most remarkable revival – dogtooth decoration. The three-bay W side is similar, but on the E side there is a doorway with thick fruit and leaf garlands on the lintel and hanging down by the sides. The new NORTH FRONT added in the late C 18 by *William Newton* is very plain but really quite grand. Seven bays with a three-bay pediment and lower L-plan projecting wings. At the same time Trollope's wooden cornice was replaced by a more elegant one of stone. The INTERIOR was redecorated in the middle of the C 18. Of that time there are a number of restrained stucco ceilings. Newton's later C 18 work includes a number of minor rooms with charming segmental-vaulted ceilings. Of the same time the centrally placed staircase with glass dome and strangely plain handrail, and the library with a good Adamish plaster ceiling.

In the C 17 the house had a formal GARDEN with a walled front garden and long avenues in the French taste, but they were landscaped *c.* 1760 and a large lake was formed. A FOLLY RUIN of a chapel W of the house dates from that time. There is no evidence to support the tradition that *Capability Brown* was responsible for this work. The GATEPIERS of the original front garden were moved when the landscaping took place and now stand at the entrance to the park from the village. They have carved trophies.

VILLAGE. Rebuilt as a model village late in the C 18 with terraces of one-storey two-room sandstone houses facing S onto the village street. They have (or had) small square casement windows. The main rooms have segmental-vaulted ceilings. According to John Hodgson, the roofs were originally segmental also, and made of cement, but were covered, alas, by conventional roofs at an early date. The LODGE looks as if it might be by *Newton*.

DOVECOTE, ¼ m. w. Late C 18. Gothick, with quatrefoils. Brick with stone dressings.

CLOCK MILL, ¾ m. NE. A near complete C 18 water corn mill. Overshot wheel for two pairs of stones on a hurst frame. Good mill race. Probably closed down early in the C 20; it was ruinous before partly restored in the early 1980s.

EAST SHAFTOE HALL, 1½ m. NE. A most complicated house, reroofed and partly re-windowed *c*. 1800, so that from a distance it looks vaguely and irregularly Georgian. However the l. third is a tower, the ground-floor vault remarkably strengthened inside by eight closely set mighty transverse arches. The date is probably C 14, and this would match the pointed-arched doorways with continuous chamfers from the vault into the projecting stair turret on the NW corner, and into the main body of the house on the E. The present S door into the tower is round-headed, with a roll-moulded surround, and looks C 16 or early C 17. Attached to the tower is a hall range. It must have been built, or rebuilt, at the same time as the S door, because its back wall, now inside the house, partly obscures the original entrance to the tower. The front wall of this section is early–mid-C 17, with a chamfered plinth and stringcourses above each storey. The staircase is of the same date and has heavy turned balusters of symmetrical profile. The E third of the house projects slightly. It has a C 17 doorway to one side and C 17 windows. The walls, except around the doorway, are once again very thick, and it was probably a C 16 cross-wing with a C 17 porch in the angle between it and the hall range. Finally, *c*. 1800 the house was widened at the back, made of even height and given a single hipped roof.

SE of the house, against the wall of a farm building, there is a large double late C 13 CROSS SLAB with two foliated crosses and a shield with traces of heraldic decoration. It comes from the church which formerly stood close by. A C 12 round FONT, from the same source presumably, is used as a planter.

Multivallate Iron Age HILLFORT on top of the cliffs of Shaftoe Crags which provide natural protection on the S and W.

NEW DEANHAM. *See* p. 518.

CARHAM

7030

Two parts of C 10 cross shafts found here are now in the Museum of Antiquities in Newcastle. Carham was also the site of a small cell of Augustinian canons established here from Kirkham in Yorkshire *c*. 1131.

ST CUTHBERT. Close to the River Tweed. 1790, by an amateur, *R. Hodgson Huntley* (who was lord of the manor). Aisleless nave with quoins and gothicized windows still round-arched within. Tower and chancel 1870. – FURNISHINGS. Box pews and choir stalls. Late C 18. – MONUMENT. Anthony Compton † 1830. Wall tablet by *Davies* of Newcastle.

CARHAM HALL. Mid–late-C 19, for the Compton family, but on the site of an earlier house of which a few fragments survive in the garden. Extended to the l. in *c.* 1920 for Mrs Burrell. It is a quite large beige and pink sandstone house in a rather formless Tudor style. Inside, the dining room has excellent C 16 panelling brought from elsewhere, including linenfold and medallion heads.

PRESSEN BASTLE, 2 m. SE. A C 16 building among the farm buildings and now used as a workshop. Very similar in form to Akeld Bastle (q.v.) and, like Akeld, more a stronghouse than a bastle. It is *c.* 20 by 8 metres (65 by 26 ft), with a high rounded tunnel vault, much of which has been removed, on the ground floor. As at Akeld, the ground-floor doorway (blocked) is in the middle of a long side; the first-floor doorway was in the W gable.

WEST LEARMOUTH, 2 m. ESE. A substantial planned farm of the mid-C 19. Large classical farmhouse and well-preserved E-plan farm buildings. S of this, a long row of single-storey workers' cottages.

RAILWAY VIADUCTS. Two, immediately N and NE of West Learmouth farm. 1849 for the York, Newcastle and Berwick Railway. One has seven arches, the other five skew arches. Both are of rock-faced stone with brick soffits to the arches – the same pattern as on the Royal Border Bridge at Berwick.

WARK-ON-TWEED. *See* p. 610.

CARRAWBURGH

2½ m. N of Newbrough

The bold rectangular platform of the ROMAN FORT of *Brocolitia* extends S from the road, immediately W of the car-park. The fort was described by Gordon in 1726 as 'by far the most intire, and best preserved, of any upon the whole Wall', with walls up to 3.7 metres (12 ft) high. It has suffered considerably since then and only fragments of masonry are visible: one guard-chamber of the W gate and, further S on the W wall, the footings of an interval tower. Excavations have demonstrated that the fort was one of the last to be added to the revised Hadrianic scheme for the Wall, probably sometime shortly after A.D. 130. The Vallum had already been driven down this hillside and its earthworks had to be levelled to make way for the fort. It was by then considered unnecessary for the fort to project N of Hadrian's Wall (now under the modern road), which therefore formed its N side. Instead of the usual rounded corners the E and W walls of the fort met Hadrian's Wall at right angles.

The Roman service road for the Wall (the 'Military Way') can be clearly seen on the W as it descends through a series of narrow terraces on the hillside: these mark the positions of the long narrow buildings of the dependent civil settlement of the C 3 and C 4, which stood gable-on to the road (cf. Vindolanda and Housesteads). Many of the walls of these buildings have been robbed for their stone, and their positions are marked only by slight trenches. Two prominent banks surviving on the outer lip of the fort's W ditch, towards its S end, seem to be part of some

late Roman defences; that area of the civil settlement must have
been cleared away to make room for them.

In the marshy bottom of the little valley to the W is the TEMPLE
OF MITHRAS, dedicated to an Eastern religion that focused on
the struggle between light and darkness. Twice rebuilt and twice
refurbished between the beginning of the C3 and the first years
of the C4, it is displayed in its final, C4 form, with some features
partly but convincingly reconstructed in concrete. Inside the S
door, a simple narthex or antechapel for the uninitiated was
screened off from the nave. A hearth lay W of the door; against
the E wall is a statuette of an anonymous mother goddess, with a
basket on her knees, who was apparently adopted by the cult's
adherents. In the aisles the congregation sat or knelt on low
platforms; the faces of these were of wattle, and incorporated
the oak roof-posts. At the S ends of these platforms stand the
fragmentary statues of the god's attendants: on the E is Cautes,
with his torch raised, symbolizing the dawn, light and life; on the
W the remains of Cautopates, whose lowered torch would indicate
sunset, darkness and death. The sanctuary, at the N end, contains
replicas of the three ALTARS found there, each dedicated by a
senior officer of the garrison. The W altar shows Mithras as the
Unconquered Sun; his pierced radiate crown or halo allowed a
light to shine through from a lamp placed in the niche at the back.
In the gloomy interior, probably lit by no more than a clerestory,
it must have heightened the mystery for the tremulous initiate.
On the N wall, resting on the shelf in the niche above the altars,
was a relief of Mithras killing the bull at the dawn of Time, thereby
releasing and taming all the forces of Creation for the benefit of
man. The original was smashed in antiquity, perhaps by Chris-
tians at the beginning of the C4, or as the result of a more
general iconoclastic order. Rising water levels flooded the site soon
thereafter. The finds and a reconstruction of the interior of the
mithraeum are in the Museum of Antiquities in Newcastle.

Another shrine, known as COVENTINA'S WELL, was built
round a powerful spring, 170 metres NW of the *mithraeum*; lying
W of the field-wall and enclosed by a wooden fence, the immediate
area is frequently a morass. Coventina was a rather superior water
goddess of uncertain antecedents. The spring dedicated to her
was encased in masonry and surrounded by a rectangular shrine,
perhaps no more than a low wall or parapet, open to the sky.
When excavated in 1876 this sacred wishing-well contained about
sixteen thousand coins, along with twenty-four altars and inscriptions, rings, brooches and more utilitarian ancient rubbish. The
shrine seems to have been carefully dismantled late in the C4.

CARR SHIELD

Carr Shield is a former leadmining village deep in the Pennine fells.
It is to the valley of the West Allen what Allenheads is to that of the
East Allen. The scenery here is wilder, however, with few trees, and
traces of mining are more apparent.

CHRIST CHURCH of 1822 has been demolished, but the

METHODIST CHAPEL survives, dated 1857 and of the usual
three-bay type, with a central porch and rusticated round arches
to the flanking windows. The former SCHOOL, dated 1851, is now
the Carrshield Expedition Centre.

WHITELEY SHIELD, at the N end of the village, has a mid-C18
three-bay farmhouse with a ruined bastle house to the N.

HARTLEYCLEUGH, 1 m. N of Carr Shield, has a well-preserved
bastle house.

The remains of LEADMINING include, at the S end of the village,
the CARRSHIELD MINE OFFICES, c. 1840, with rusticated
quoins and door surrounds, and further S an interesting but
ruinous group around the entrance to the BARNEYCRAIG HORSE
LEVEL: a bridge, the level portal itself and a range of buildings,
including the miners' shop (changing and overnight sleeping
accommodation) and blacksmith's shop.

COALCLEUGH. *See* p. 234.

CARTINGTON

oooo

1½ m. N of Thropton

CARTINGTON CASTLE. A fortified manor house rather than a
castle proper; licence to crenellate was granted only in 1441. The
medieval building is of several C14 and early C15 builds; it seems
to have consisted of a rectangular court with, on the N, a first-
floor hall with its solar in the NE tower. A smaller tower at the SE
corner contained the garderobes; another tower at the SW corner
may have contained the gatehouse. The buildings were altered
and extended in the C16 and C17 (to which date the remains of
the E range belong), then partly demolished after a siege in 1648.
The NE tower and part of the hall range were remodelled afterwards, but had fallen into ruins by the early C19. In 1887 repairs
and some reconstruction work – which complicates an already
complicated picture – were carried out by *C. C. Hodges*. The
courtyard is now entered through a C17 gateway with rusticated
piers on the W. The N side of the courtyard stands up high, but
its moulded doorway and three two-light windows are all Hodges's
reconstruction (admittedly using old materials): only the semi-
octagonal stair turret, at the SW corner of the NE tower, is a
genuine feature. In front of the wall is the base of a C17 external
stair; the doorway it served has been erased by Hodges's restoration. One of the three chambers beneath the hall retains its
segmental barrel vault: the W chamber has a stair turret on the N.
The base of the tower is divided into three vaulted chambers, one
with a well shaft in the corner; the top had bartizans at the E
corners, resting on carved figures. The much smaller SE tower
has a vaulted basement and a SW garderobe turret. The S courtyard wall is largely C17; only low fragments of the SW tower
survive.

CARVORAN *see* GREENHEAD

CASTLE HEATON *see* TWIZEL

CATCLEUGH *see* BYRNESS

CAWFIELDS

This group of Roman sites is reached by turning N at the Milecastle
Inn towards the car-park in the former quarry. Milecastle 42
comes into sight ahead, but before the first bend in the road
the earthworks of a ROMAN FORTLET will be seen on the l.,
immediately E of the Haltwhistle Burn, where Stanegate swings
down to a ford. The site is unusual in having an outwork, on all
sides except the W, breached by causeways to S and E. The
internal buildings, not now visible, were a précis of those to be
found in a fort: barrack, officers' quarters, stores and a tiny
headquarters. Established soon after A.D. 105 as a base on the
Stanegate, the fortlet seems to have been dismantled under
Hadrian, perhaps in *c.* 124 or no later than the building of Great
Chesters fort.

MILECASTLE 42 is similar to Milecastle 37 (Housesteads),
being of a type built by the Second Legion: a short N–S axis, and
with two pairs of responds in each gate. The N wall is at the
original Broad gauge, but on either side the curtain wall was
reduced immediately in thickness. The N gate opened uselessly
onto the Whin Sill cliffs and was walled across. Nothing is known
of any buildings in the steeply sloping rocky interior, which must
have made the opening of the doors tricky.

The surrounding area contains a remarkable series of ROMAN
CAMPS; some were probably short-lived encampments for those
building the Wall, others may have been thrown up by troops on
manoeuvre. Each has a single rampart which appears as a low
mound like an old field-dyke, with an outer ditch and curved
angles; the gates were protected by a traverse mound and its
attendant ditch, placed a short distance in front of the opening.
Here too, bordering the natural trough that runs behind the Wall,
the VALLUM comes westward down the slope from Shield-on-
the-Wall. Few finer views exist of the Vallum than this; here there
is a splendid opportunity to study the great earthwork, and the
crossings cut through the mounds when they were slighted *c.* 142
(at the time of the construction of the Antonine Wall). Later
cleaning out and the removal of these Antonine causeways
produced the extra mound on the S lip of the ditch.

To the E of Milecastle 42 a fine length of Wall has been
consolidated; offsets in the S face are common. It stands to a
height of thirteen courses in the dip known as Thorny Doors, on
the steep E side of which the stonework was laid horizontally,
whereas on the W side the courses followed the contours. Of

TURRET 41a, only low walls were left after demolition in the early
C 3: the recess in the S face was walled up and the broad wing-
walls on either side were reduced. The original internal N face of
the turret is visible in the core material. To the N, a short length
of the Ditch had to be provided in this gap in the crags.

MARE AND FOAL. Two prehistoric standing stones, beside the
Stanegate on a prominent ridge, ¾ m. E. A third stone still stood
in 1769.

Several small field LIMEKILNS lie to the S of Cawfields, as at
Moorfield, with two pointed arches and an oval pot; Hallpeat
Moss, similar; and a larger kiln with four segmental arches to the
NE of Fell End.

CHATTON   0020

HOLY CROSS. 1770, and still C 18 in its masonry. The N aisle was
added in 1846 by *Salvin*. The rest of the windows were gothicized
and a saddleback roof put on the tower in 1897. – REREDOS. 1895
by *Arthur Moore*. – STAINED GLASS. E window and chancel S
window of 1851 by *Wailes*. – MONUMENTS. Several medieval
CROSS SLABS built into the baptistry floor. – WALL TABLET to
Matthew Culley † 1849, by *Davies*, with a draped urn. – J. Wilkin
1804, by *R. Blore*, a small plain wall tablet.

   VICARAGE, with big stepped gables, by *Dobson*, 1845.

The village, part of the Duke of Northumberland's estate, has rows
of mid-C 19 Tudor-style cottages. Next to the Post Office, a small
unspoilt mid-C 19 BLACKSMITH'S FORGE.

BRIDGE, ¼ m. E. Early C 18 with two broad segmental arches and
triangular cutwaters. Doubled in thickness in the mid-C 19, probably by *Dobson* in 1857.

CHATTONPARK, 1 m. E. A large mid-C 19 farmhouse built by the
Duke of Northumberland and bearing his crest in the porch frieze.
Four by four bays, with twelve-pane sashes and projecting eaves
on big stone brackets. BROOMHOUSE, 1 m. SW of Chatton, is
another farm of the Duke's, with a fine range of planned farm
buildings, including a gingang.

CUP-AND-RING-MARKED ROCKS. Puzzling but relatively common
on the Fell Sandstone moors. Examples with a cup and multiple
rings are visible on Weetwood Moor, 250 metres and 1,200 metres
ENE of Coldmartin Lough.

Two prominent CAIRNS, 3 m. ESE, on the ridge W of Chatton
Sandyfords. Excavation of the N one illustrated the complex
history of some of these burial mounds: two successive burials
with Beaker pottery of *c.* 2000 B.C. were covered by a large cairn;
a third similar burial was later inserted before a substantial kerb
of finely dressed stones was constructed. Subsequent intrusions
included one cremation in a large Bronze Age urn, and another
without grave-goods. Sherds of a C 3 Roman flagon could suggest
a further burial then or just an *al fresco* lunch. Of the rash of much
smaller cairns in the area, most seem to consist of stones cleared
off new fields – perhaps as early as 2000 B.C.

FOWBERRY TOWER. *See* p. 286.
HETTON HALL. *See* p. 317.

FOWBERRY TOWER. *See* p. 286.
HETTON HALL. *See* p. 317.

CHEESEBURN
1 m. E of Stamfordham

0070

CHEESEBURN GRANGE. Designed *c.* 1813 by *John Dobson* for
Ralph Riddell. The three-bay entrance side has a tall castellated
centre bay with a castellated porch and a large five-light stair
window above. Attached to the l. of this façade is the chapel,
with a three-light mullioned-and-transomed window with arched
heads to the lights. The garden side has rather curious detail for
this date. It is of five bays, with tripartite windows in Tudor-
arched recesses. This façade was remodelled by Dobson from the
existing C 17 house. Later work by *Joseph A. Hansom, c.* 1860, was
all demolished *c.* 1973.

At the same time as he remodelled the house, *Dobson* also laid
out the GROUNDS in a characteristically early, C 19 Picturesque
manner. In the garden, an arbour, framed by a reused door
surround from the earlier house. It is dated 1694 and has a
bolection-moulded surround, broken semicircular pediment
bearing a shield and beasts' heads on scrolled brackets.

CHESTERS
½ m. W of Chollerford

9070

The Roman fort of *Cilurnum* is set on a terrace above the North
Tyne, in the handsome parkland created by Nathaniel Clayton
after 1796. Built to guard the bridge over the river, the fort was
garrisoned by a cavalry regiment, five hundred strong. In the
original Hadrianic scheme, the Wall and its ditch ran unin-
terrupted up this hillside. However, when the decision was taken
to station the troops on the line of the Wall itself, this short line
of curtain had to be demolished to make way for the fort. The
levelled foundations of Turret 27a have been found beside the NE
corner of the later headquarters building.

The fort was laid out with nearly half its area and three of its
gates projecting N of the Wall. Despite later ploughing the raised
platform of the fort is still prominent, but the depression marking
its external ditches is only intermittent. The main gates conform
to a standard type, with guard-chambers below flanking towers;
the two doors in each of the twin portals closed against an upstanding stone stop. At the NORTH GATE, the W portal was blocked,
probably fairly early on, before the threshold could be worn. The
E portal is displayed at its C 3 level with an aqueduct channel
entering beneath the threshold. Walking anti-clockwise around
the fort, the visitor can see that at the WEST GATE the thresholds
are unworn and that the gates, soon blocked, were eventually
walled up solidly. Note in the S portal the iron collar, set in lead,
which held the door-pivot in place. A small aqueduct emptied

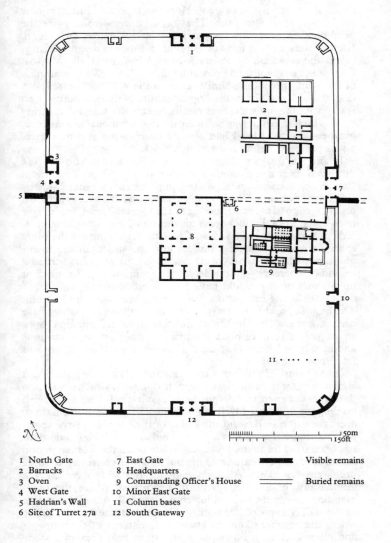

1 North Gate	7 East Gate
2 Barracks	8 Headquarters
3 Oven	9 Commanding Officer's House
4 West Gate	10 Minor East Gate
5 Hadrian's Wall	11 Column bases
6 Site of Turret 27a	12 South Gateway

Visible remains

Buried remains

Chesters, Roman fort. Plan

into a tank (now gone) in the N guard-chamber. Outside the gate-tower (to minimize the fire risk), an oven was inserted into the thickness of the rampart. At this gate, and at the main E gate, Hadrian's Wall is seen joining the S guard-chamber as the Narrow Wall on a Broad foundation. Two oblique walls, one of which cut across this junction, belonged to a much later, post-Roman building. Along the S front, facing onto the site of the civil settlement, the remains of two interval towers are visible, with, between

them, the SOUTH GATEWAY. Here the E portal illustrates how
road levels rose with time. The fort's SE angle-tower, like the
neighbouring interval tower, stands over 1.8 metres (6 ft) high.
(In the interior of the fort at this point an exposed row of columns
marks the verandah of a barrack-block.) Further N, the MINOR
EAST GATE was a single portal for the Military Way, running S
of the Wall; there was a similar gate on the W. The MAIN EAST
GATE is well preserved: the impost-mould of the rearward S arch
is in position, with sockets cut in its top for the wooden centring
upon which the arch was built. Again the thresholds are unworn,
but here the road level had already been raised and new gate-
pivots provided before the gate was blocked.

In the NE quarter of the fort some BARRACK-BLOCKS are
displayed, facing one another across a street with an axial drain.
Each block consisted of separate compartments arranged side by
side under one roof; their W gables lie beyond the excavated area,
on the E edge of the road leading to the N gate. There would have
been room in each block for a maximum of nine compartments,
only five of which are on view. Close to the E rampart the more
spacious officers' quarters project into the street. In the men's
quarters each compartment held a mess-unit of eight; behind a
verandah where they could clean their equipment and cook their
meals, the interior would have been subdivided to give a small
dormitory at the rear, and a living space and store at the front.
The building to the N, of which only one wall is visible, may have
been a stable. That to the S, fronting onto the principal E–W
street, seems to have been subdivided into quite separate units
and may have been one of the C 4 'chalet' type of barrack-blocks
(cf. Housesteads).

In the centre of the fort is the HEADQUARTERS or *principia*. It
is best to enter it through its central N doorway, which opens into
the usual enclosed and arcaded front courtyard. Carved in relief
on the paving near the well is a large *phallus*, a common charm to
avert the evil eye. Beyond the S side of the court is a large cross-
hall; its single N aisle has a door at either end. The E side-door
has been used for carts, presumably late on in the Roman period
as standards deteriorated and the building was converted to more
utilitarian functions. At the W end of the wide nave are the
foundations of a raised platform or *tribunal* where the commanding officer sat to hold his courts-martial. Along the N side
of the wall is a row of five rooms. The central one was the shrine
where the regiment kept its standards, a statue of the emperor
and other objects of official worship. In its rear portion a stone
staircase leads down to a tunnel-vaulted strongroom (for regimental funds), which may have been a C 3 insertion. When first
found, in 1803, the vault retained intact its iron-bound oaken
door. The vaulting juts high into the room above, the floor of
which must have been raised; here, and in the room adjacent,
the pay-clerks were housed. The two rooms W of the shrine
accommodated the regimental records and the clerks who kept
them. The whole building is an excellent example of its type,
which was in large measure common to every Roman fort.

To the E of the headquarters, beyond an elongated workshop
or store, lay the COMMANDING OFFICER'S HOUSE, a com-

plicated building that was so often altered that it is now difficult
to interpret from surface remains alone. A large number of hypocausts have been inserted, the floors supported on pillars made of
tiles or reused stonework. In the NE corner were the Commander's
private baths: cold plunges or tanks made of tile on the N, and a
hot room in the apse on the E.

A   Changing room
B   Sauna
C   Stoke-hole
D   Ante-room
E1, E2 Hot steam rooms
F   Hot bath
G   Boiler
H, I Warm rooms
J   Later cold bath
K   Cool room
L   Earlier cold bath
M   Latrines
N   Lobby
O   Porch

Chesters, Roman bath-house. Plan

The BATH-HOUSE. Close to the riverbank lie the impressive
remains of the garrison's bath-house. A walk through it offers an
opportunity to understand something of this most civilized of
Roman amenities, provided at every permanent fort, in each town
and within all country houses of consequence. So essential a
building received many refurbishments, alterations and improvements but the general plan is clear enough.

   The building is still entered through a small N porch (O on the
plan), an addition which opens into a large changing room (A).
The W wall of this is distinguished by a series of seven arched
niches of unknown purpose. The broad span of this room (9
metres: 30 ft) made a central row of columns a necessity. To the
E lay the latrines (M), their seating missing and the buttressed
riverward wall broken away; however, the stone guttering for the
outfall sewer is still intact, leading towards the river.

A lobby (N) provided three choices: l. to the cold baths, r. to the sauna, or straight on into the Turkish baths. Bathers who opted for a Turkish bath moved through the warm rooms into the hotter ones, where a hot bath and the steamy atmosphere encouraged vigorous perspiration. The alternative was the intense dry heat of the sauna, but the result was the same: the skin, anointed with oil, was scraped clean. Retracing their steps, bathers took a rapid cold bath to close the pores, thus preventing a chill. From the lobby a door leads into the cold suite. Here an early bath (L) went out of use and was walled up; it was replaced by a much smaller one (J). A douche was provided in the cool room (K) by a basin, the base of which survives (with two drains of different dates). A door in the s wall of (K) leads into a small ante-room (I) and then into a much larger warm room (H). Both of these had heated floors, their hypocausts being connected below the door that divided them. The s end of (H) seems to have been extended to provide a furnace there. Doors in the w walls of these rooms led into the hotter part of the Turkish baths. Later these doors were blocked (their thresholds are still visible), and access was only possible through the lobby (N). The hottest room (E2) was next to the boiler at (G); the latter may have had a bath over it, but there was certainly a hot bath in the apse (F), which originally had its own furnace. Although the floor of this bath has disappeared, there are interesting remains of the hot-air flues which heated it from below and the hole which took the outlet pipe from the bath through the wall of the apse. This wall contains a window opening, once glazed, a feature which few Roman buildings in Britain now stand high enough to exhibit; it is widely splayed on the inside to admit the maximum amount of light through the least (heat-losing) window space. A little of the rendering of finely broken tile and lime that acted as a damp-proof coating in the hot and steaming room survives on the wall of the apse. A similar mix would have deeply covered the flags of the floors. Throughout the Baths the ceilings were barrel vaults. Carefully shaped voussoirs (two of which form the steps down from N into E1), some of them cut from specially chosen light-weight tufa, were used as ribs over this hottest room; the spaces between them were bridged with large tiles to form a hollow flue between each rib. Thus both the vault and the walls were fitted with hot-air shafts, effectively combating condensation. The whole of the exterior of the Bath-house, including the vaults, seems to have been rendered.

Notice low down in the E wall of (E1), below the blocked door, carvings of a *phallus*, a bird and a single word, NEILO. It is probable that this room had originally been a sauna offering intense dry heat; this was later moved to D, and finally to B (when D became an ante-room). The doorway between these rooms retains its impressive stone jambs; these must have been the norm everywhere in the Baths to avoid the warping and rotting to which wooden frames would have soon succumbed. Box-tiles incorporated into the walls of B enabled the hot air from the hypocaust (heated from C) to circulate upwards. Portions of the metal ties that held these tiles can still be seen.

Finally, the position and general function of the Bath-house deserve note. It stood on the riverbank, above flood level, sheltered from the prevailing wind and warmed by the sun from early morning until early afternoon. Since heat had to be retained long after the furnaces were raked out, this was a sensible provision in any climate. The establishment was not a luxury. Regular and hygienic bathing must have promoted good health and morale. It was not, however, an idle pastime. If each trooper of the regiment, 500 strong, received a weekly bath, then the building would have been constantly in use, to a well-regulated timetable.

The MUSEUM, c. 1891 by *Norman Shaw*, has openings in Gibbs surrounds and deeply overhanging eaves. It was built to house a notable assembly of Roman inscriptions, sculptures and objects from the central sector of Hadrian's Wall, between the North Tyne and the Irthing. The collection was formed in the C 19, when John Clayton owned many of the sites, having bought them to save them from destruction. The display is little changed and reflects the taste of the Victorian antiquary. The most memorable items include those from the shrine of the water-nymph Coventina at Carrawburgh, altars and sculptures of Mars Thincsus from Housesteads, the statue of Julia Regina from Chesters, and the bronze corn-measure of Domitian from Carvoran, along with milestones, iron weapons and tools.

ROMAN BRIDGE. The remains of the bridge that carried Hadrian's Wall across the North Tyne are visible on each bank of the river. On the w, close to the Bath-house, is the embankment that took the Military Way to bridge level and through a gatehouse-tower on the western abutment. The most impressive remains, however, are on the E bank and are approached from Chollerford by a path alongside the old railway to Bellingham and Riccarton.

A short stretch of the Wall itself (in the Narrow gauge, replacing the original Broad Wall, two courses of which survive) leads down to the broadly splayed E abutment of the bridge. This grand fragment of antiquity still stands 2 metres ($6\frac{1}{2}$ ft) high on its N wing. It is constructed of well-dressed blocks (in alternating courses of headers and stretchers), neatly punched in curving furrows, their upper surfaces bearing lewis-holes (by which they were lifted into position) and the grooves for iron ties set in lead. A large *phallus*, carved low down on the N face, was a defiant insurance against bad luck. The s wing of this abutment was extended s, presumably to counteract scouring eddies; the joint between the two phases of work is clearly visible. The super-structure of this bridge (probably c. A.D. 206) was of stone; its parapet probably incorporated pairs of columns, one of which survives. The Wall ends on the square gatehouse-tower which stood at the head of the approach ramp for the Military Way. A covered water-channel, made of gargantuan slabs, passed through the tower, probably to a mill downstream; this is a secondary feature. When the river is very low the masonry of two of the three piers can be seen.

Portions of a C 2 predecessor, only wide enough for pedestrians, can also be seen. The foundations of one of its eight hexagonal piers are encased in the stonework of the later E abutment, immediately w of the tower; the position of the abutment of this earlier bridge is marked out on the floor of the tower itself.

TURRET 29a is in a fine stretch of Hadrian's Wall at Black Carts,
1¾ m. WNW of Chesters. The Broad wing-walls survive, bonded
into the Narrow Wall; the SE doorway is dressed to receive monolithic jambs.

Immediately W of the lane to Simonburn, on the uphill side
(from which it was easiest to load carts), the Wall has been robbed
away. Further W it is consolidated and in good condition, before
reverting to a picturesque state of decay.

LIMESTONE CORNER is at the summit, giving fine views over
Tynedale to Simonside and to the Cheviots. Unusually, the rigid-
ity of the Hadrianic design was here relaxed; although the ditch
of the Vallum (well-preserved, S of the road) was cut through the
dolerite, the ditch of the Wall was left unfinished. Huge blocks
had already been removed; one remaining bears the marks of the
quarrymen's wedges.

CHESTERS. Looking down on the Roman fort from the W, a substantial house of two-and-a-half storeys built by *John Carr* in 1771
for John Clayton, greatly enlarged in 1891 by *Norman Shaw*. The
old house, with two symmetrical canted bays, forms the centre of
the S front, flanked by Shaw's curved wings. Shaw also added
straight projecting wings on the N side, to form a forecourt, and
made the W front a composition of great splendour, a curve, the
centre of which consists of detached giant Ionic columns behind
which the wall of the house is boldly recessed. The dominant
motif of Shaw's architecture is heavy channelled rustication on
the broad corner pilasters and in the window surrounds. There
are several Venetian windows, and the interior decoration is in the
early C 18 style from which these elements derive. A comparison is
most instructive between Chesters and Shaw's Cragside of twenty
years before. Shaw had been an enthusiastic Tudor romantic. He
now applied the prodigious fertility of his mind to an equally
picturesque, equally romantic interpretation of the English C 18.

CHESTERS STABLES, on the opposite side of the main road
to the house. Ranges around a big rectangular yard, entered under
a pedimented gatehouse which has a cupola, with clock, on the
ridge. A very successful composition in which Shaw's admiration
for Vanbrugh and Seaton Delaval is clear.

8060   CHESTERWOOD
                          ¾ m. NW of Haydon Bridge

Chesterwood seems to have been a defensible hamlet with BASTLE
HOUSES enclosing a small 'green' (cf. Wall). In the late C 19
Tomlinson commented that it was 'chiefly composed of the old-
fashioned buildings known as "Peel-houses"', but only four or
five remain recognizable today. The GOLF HOUSE is the best-
preserved, and seems to have formed part of a central row. External stair on S and byre door on N. On the N of the green, another
shows its blocked upper door, and further W is a pair, reduced in
height, which show several original features. Only one of the S
row remains, near its E end, but this reveals little other than the
distinctive heavy rubble fabric.

LANGLEY BARONY LEADMINES, 1 m. N. Developed in the 1870s, these mines had a short but fairly spectacular life. The most dramatic remains are in the narrow valley floor by the Honeycrook adit of 1871, alongside which are an engine and boiler house with a tall chimney to power a hoist and crushing machinery. Upstream is a small single-arch bridge; downstream, the remains of round buddles used in the ore-dressing operations. On the valley side above are more buddles, reservoirs and conduits, and the remains of more engine houses.

CHESWICK
2 m. NE of Ancroft

0040

LADYTHORNE HOUSE. Formerly dated 1721 on a plaster ceiling. Built for Robert Wilkes. Brick with stone dressings. A lively five-bay S front with segment-headed windows; doorway with ears and a deep segmental cornice; quoins and a parapet. The gables are stepped. The interior has been entirely renewed.

CHESWICK HOUSE. 1859–62 by *F. R. Wilson* for William Cross-man. Very typically High Victorian Gothic, but with numerous round-headed windows. Many of the windows have bizarre but quite strongly personal, heavily detailed tracery, including eight-pointed stars and sexfoil circles. The LODGES and GATES are also by Wilson and reveal the same personality, especially the ironwork of the NE GATEWAY.

EAST HOUSE FARM, *c.* 200 metres E of Cheswick House. Sub-stantial three-bay farmhouse of *c.* 1810–15. Large and impressive FARM BUILDINGS, originally built in 1808 but much extended, roofed over and made suitable for new efficient farming methods in 1879. The S range has a high carriage arch, with a triangular dovecote screen above it, all under a gable. The FARM COTTAGES are also of *c.* 1810–15. An excellent group of single-storey, three-bay cottages stepping down the hill.

CHEW GREEN
8 m. W of Alwinton

7000

The remote site at Chew Green comprises the most remarkable visible group of Roman earthworks in Britain. It will reward the connoisseur of such sites rather more than someone visiting Roman earthworks for the first time, striking though the first impression can hardly fail to be. Though it is accessible by car, this is walking country and a map is essential. Close to the high Border, at the very head of Upper Coquetdale, it can be reached up the winding valley road from Alwinton. When the Army Train-ing Area is open (if in any doubt, seek permission from Range Control at Otterburn) the visitor can take the Roman route from the modern Redesdale Camp at Rochester: up Dere Street, past Featherwood, and over Foulplay Head. From the saddle between Harden Edge and Thirlmoor a fine bird's-eye view can be had of the earthworks, which occupy a shelf between the infant Coquet and Chew Sike on the NE.

The boldest feature is the small fortlet on the summit of the knoll immediately W of Dere Street; it was defended by an inner rampart and triple ditches. Two annexes of similar width extend down the slopes to the SE, parallel with the Roman road. Their context is uncertain, a situation made more complex by the discovery of an earlier fortlet beneath the visible one. Further confusion is introduced by a number of small embanked enclosures (of much later date, but not so different in character) which overlie the Roman defences. A Norman chapel excavated in the centre of the fortlet may well have been contemporary with some of the enclosures. Immediately to the WSW are the prominent ditch and slighter rampart of what seems to have been a fort, almost square on plan, with its NE gate close up against the multiple ditches of the fortlet. Just outside the N corner of the fort is the S rampart of a long and narrow temporary camp, of the usual playing-card shape, extending NW up the hillside; its W side is poorly preserved, but the rampart can be traced on the N, and also on the E, where it is almost parallel with Dere Street. Overlain by all of these separate earthworks is a large square camp, the earliest feature of the site, the rampart of which is best picked up S of the fort, close to the steep natural scarp down to the Coquet. From there it can be followed clockwise (despite being briefly covered by the fort's defences) around its N side, where it is crossed by the S end of the later long and narrow camp.

In order to cross Chew Sike, Dere Street had to turn sharply NE, over the S slopes of Brownhart Law up to the Border. On the W side of the road, just within Roxburgh, are the low sub-rectangular earthworks of a miniature Roman fortlet or watch-tower (staffed from Chew Green), which could have connected the Cheviot watershed with a similar post on Rubers Law between Jedburgh and Hawick.

THIRLMOOR. On the summit (558 metres, 1,830 ft), three massive and conspicuous burial cairns, probably of late Neolithic or Early Bronze Age date. Consisting of surprisingly small stones, they are up to 16 metres (50 ft) in diameter and nearly 2 metres (6$\frac{1}{2}$ ft) high.

CHIBBURN

2090

1 m. NE of Widdrington

CHIBBURN PRECEPTORY. The Preceptory of St John of Jerusalem (Knights Hospitallers) is first mentioned in 1313; in 1338 the community numbered eleven. The only certain relic of the Hospitallers is the ruins of their chapel. The S and E walls stand high, with C 14 detail; the S wall in particular is a real piece of vertical archaeology, displaying evidence of conversion to a two-storeyed range before the end of the medieval period. The most complete part of the ruin, the W range, probably dates to the 1550s, when Sir John Widdrington took over the site for a dower house; this is a complete house and a most interesting building in its own right, with entry via a cross passage behind the principal stack. The upper windows seem to have been of timber, set forward from the wall-face on stone corbels. The C 16 buildings were arranged around a small court, with the chapel on the S. The main entrance seems to have been on the N, although little now survives of the N and E ranges. The whole complex was in much better preservation (the W range inhabited) before the Second World War; after years of neglect and opencast mining all around, which even pared away the moat, it is at last being consolidated (1990).

CHILLINGHAM   0020

ST PETER. Nave, chancel, large S chapel, smaller N chapel and plain bellcote. The bellcote is of 1753; the nave is C 12 in its masonry. The S doorway has one order of colonnettes with block capitals and a roll-moulded arch. The two-light nave windows with depressed heads to the lights are C 16. The chancel has five steps up, to allow for a crypt below. It seems to be late C 12 or C 13 and has one small lancet on the S wall. The S chapel has a blocked C 12 doorway and a tiny blocked C 12 window. It also has two blocked lancets and two two-light C 14 windows with cusped Y-tracery. The nave has a C 16 king-post roof. The chancel arch and chapel arches date from the restoration by *Wyatville* in 1828. The E window was altered in the late 1960s by *John Smith* of *W. B. Edwards & Partners*. It is a large sheet of plain glass framed by a simple grid of steel bars. Some hate it; others welcome the glorious view of the trees beyond. – FONT. 1670, brought from Ancroft. Octagonal shaft and octagonal bowl simply moulded in the Perp tradition. – PULPIT. Simple, Jacobean. – BOX PEWS. 1829. – MONUMENTS. A CROSS SLAB with foliate cross, and parts of four others. – Sir Ralph Grey † 1443 and his wife. A [48] sumptuous monument of considerable artistic importance, because against the tomb-chest there stand fourteen figures of saints in niches separated by figures of angels, and all these figures escaped the iconoclasts of the C 16 and C 17. So here is an example of dated sculpture of *c.* 1450, the date of the Beauchamp Chapel at Warwick, and though the sculptural quality of the Grey tomb is much inferior to the Earl of Warwick's, the stylistic position is the same – drapery folds just breaking, though not so crackly as generally late in the C 15. Rich, thickly encrusted canopy work. Alabaster effigies, and a background or reredos – for the head side of the tomb stands against the wall – with a standing angel and l. and r. two demi-figures of angels holding big helmets. Above that, Jacobean addition with elaborate strapwork cartouche and obelisks.

CHILLINGHAM CASTLE. There was a tower at Chillingham in 1298, when Edward I stayed here, but licence to crenellate was granted to Sir Thomas de Heton in 1344. The castle he built is [67] of the C 14 type, with four roughly square angle towers connected by a curtain wall. The towers are vaulted in the lowest storey. The vaults of the SW and SE towers are plain; that of the NE is ribbed. The NW tower was altered in the C 16. It is not clear when

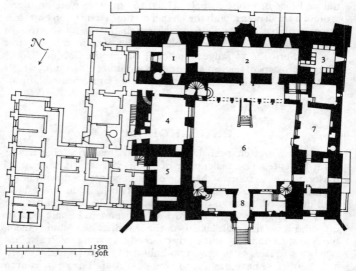

1 SE tower   5 NE tower
2 Great Hall   6 Courtyard
3 SW tower   7 Kitchen
4 Former dining room 8 Long Gallery (on first floor)

Chillingham Castle. Plan

stone ranges were built against the curtain wall between the
towers. It seems unlikely that they were there from the beginning.
For example, the doors with shouldered lintels which lead into
the s towers are now inside the s range, but they appear to have
been external doors originally. The ranges were probably built
early, however, and were provided with tunnel vaults also. The
Great Hall was, and still is, in the s range on the first floor. E of
the hall, in the SE tower, is the former chapel. It has the pointed
rere-arch of a large medieval window, and a small ogee-headed
trefoiled piscina. The N wall and towers, and probably part of the
W range as well, were rebuilt by Ralph Ellerker after a siege in
1536, but the castle remained essentially in its medieval state until
the early C17 when the ENTRANCE WING (N) was remodelled in
a grander way, and to correspond to it a grander entrance to the
Great Hall was also added. The new entrance façade is an addition
just in front of the original N wall. Its principal feature is a three-
storey frontispiece with coupled columns, a motif very popular at
the time and familiar from Oxford colleges, for example, or in
the North from e.g. Stonyhurst (Lancashire). The columns are
Tuscan on all three floors. The archway is reached by a flight of
steps and was therefore not intended for carriages or horses.

The storeys above have two windows each between the coupled columns and an additional column between the windows. There are achievements of arms above the top window and four beasts with shields in front of the parapet.

Inside the COURTYARD, on the front of the hall range a two-storey addition was made. It was rebuilt in the C 18 or early C 19, reusing some of the original detail, so it is impossible to be sure what it looked like. What one sees now is an open arcade (rebuilt) with square piers and segmental arches, for all the world like a farm cartshed. Above this is a closed storey approached by an open stair with coarsely detailed C 17 stone balusters. On top of the upper storey is a terrace with a similar, rather coarsely detailed C 17 balustrade. In front of the arches of the arcade, unrelated to them, and quite clearly reused from an earlier structure, are placed small Ionic columns; above the columns, on corbels, stand six small statues of worthies which closely resemble those which stood on the porch of 1625 at Gibside in County Durham. L. and r. of the doorway on the upper floor are attached Ionic columns identical to those below, and above the doorway the balustrade forms a gable with a seventh statue placed centrally. The whole ensemble is inelegant but interesting. The S FRONT of the hall range was remodelled as a standard seven-bay, two-storey Georgian façade in 1753. In the centre is a canted bay window, with octagonal columns at the angles bearing small figures. At the same time (1753) the grounds were landscaped to the S of the castle and to bring the lawns as close to the house as was liked at that time, the original ground floor of the range was made into a cellar with a tunnel running in front of it, i.e. under the lawn. The only other external alteration of size, if not of note, was the addition in 1872–3 of a large service wing on the E side. This is roofless at the time of writing (1991).

The INTERIOR has also seen vicissitudes. Many of the contents were sold in 1933 and the house remained empty for over fifty years until it was acquired by Sir Humphry Wakefield in the 1980s. During that period of decay much was lost, including plasterwork of the 1750s, a number of rooms remodelled by *John Paterson* for the fourth Earl of Tankerville in 1803, and most of the features introduced in 1828 by *Sir Jeffrey Wyatville* for Charles Grey, the fifth Earl. There have been some survivals. In the Great Hall there are two early Georgian white marble fireplaces brought by Wyatville from Colen Campbell's Wanstead House, Essex, which had been demolished in 1822. In the room above the Hall is a good Jacobean ceiling with patterned ribs and pendants, which had survived in poor condition but was restored in 1988. In the former dining room on the ground floor of the E range is a gallery with a C 17 balustrade and panelling. The overmantel of the fireplace has a relief of Susannah and the Elders. The crest with its strapwork decoration was transferred from another room; the relief is said to have come from one of two fireplaces in the Long Gallery above the N entrance. The other fireplace has a relief of the sacrifice of Isaac, still *in situ*. In the W wing, a large early C 18 kitchen.

The GROUNDS and park are of very considerable extent and interest. Around the house are gardens mainly laid out *c.* 1827–8 by *Wyatville*. There are long avenues of trees and high castellated walls and terracing. Immediately to the w of the house is a parterre surrounded by one of these sets of walls, which incorporates, at its w end, much older masonry, including a round-headed archway. More old masonry, including a round-headed arched gateway, is to be found among trees *c.* 100 metres N of the castle. E and s of the castle is the PARK, famous for its herd of indigenous wild white cattle. It is 2,430 hectares (6,000 acres) in extent and was emparked in the C 13. Its wall is still complete, though it has been rebuilt and repaired many times. The park itself, within the wall and the circle of protecting trees, retains the character of a medieval landscape, apparently uncultivated since that time.

The EAST LODGE, in the village, by *Wyatville*, 1828, is octagonal and castellated.

The WEST LODGE, ½m. SW, with its fantastic Jacobean-style gatepiers, is by *Edward Blore* and dated 1835.

The VILLAGE was largely rebuilt by the Earl of Tankerville in the 1830s. His architect was *Edward Blore*, who designed a number of Tudorish blocks, each of four two-storey houses, quite ingeniously planned though rather dull to look at. Blore's surviving drawings show the houses single-storey. The MANOR HOUSE, formerly the Vicarage, was designed in 1828 by *Wyatville* in the Tudor style. It has a strange irregular plan, almost lozenge-shaped.

HEPBURN BASTLE, I m. SE but still within the park. Not a bastle in the sense in which the word is now applied, but an oblong stronghouse of the C 15, unroofed but well-preserved. First mentioned in 1509. Vaulted ground floor. C 16 one- and two-light windows, also several cross windows. Twin-gabled roof. The spiral staircase in the SE corner has collapsed.

HEPBURN CRAG, I m. SE. Univallate hillfort almost slipping off the edge of the moorland plateau overlooking the Till. In the plantation to the s, a Bronze Age burial cist has been reconstructed beside the carriage drive.

ROS CASTLE, 1½ m. E. Spectacular views of the Cheviots, the Farnes and the coastal castles distract attention from the simple hillfort defences around the summit: a single bank with internal and external quarry ditches and an everted NE entrance. The firing of the beacon here in 1804 began a celebrated false alarm of a French invasion.

8070

CHIPCHASE CASTLE

4 m. NW of Chollerton

43 Sited on a gently sloping plateau high above the North Tyne with beautiful views to the W and S, the castle is a splendid-looking combination of a large-scale mid-C 14 tower with a Jacobean mansion and Georgian additions and alterations. It became the property of the Heron family in 1348, but nothing is known for certain about the date of the tower except that it was in existence by 1415. Comparison, with e.g. Bothal (1343) or Belsay (*c.* 1370), provides the rest. It measures *c.* 16.3 by 11.7 metres (53 by 38 ft) and has a vaulted ground floor and three storeys above. The

ceilings of these are not preserved. The first floor has a big fireplace. The second floor was the hall, which has an even bigger fireplace, a garderobe in the s w corner, a tiny room with a fireplace in the s e corner which may have been used as a withdrawing room, and a small chapel in the n e corner which has two windows with pointed trefoiled heads. A second chamber is in the n w corner. On the third floor was the upper hall with a kitchen, two chambers and a garderobe in the corners. The tower is entered in the s e wall. To the r. of the door, a spiral stair goes up all the way to the roof. The entrance has the rare feature of a wooden portcullis, and above it the guardroom and portcullis chamber are still in their original state. The w face rises sheer and is only broken by two garderobes corbelled out at different heights and in different places, and by a blocked two-light window with trefoiled heads to the lights. The crowning motif is four circular corbelled-out bartizans. The tower is not embattled but has thickly corbelled machicolations.

Did the tower stand alone or as part of a complex, like the towers at Edlingham and Etal? As the house stands now, it is a courtyard house with the tower in the s w corner and the Jacobean mansion forming the s e range. Linking the tower and the Jacobean mansion is the s w range, which is Georgian in its detail but much older in its masonry and in which can be seen a complex pattern of blocked openings and alterations. This range could be the 'manor of stone' which adjoined the 'fair towere' in 1541, but without much more detailed investigation it is impossible to be sure. It is equally difficult to say when it was built. It seems unlikely, however, that the Jacobean house would have been added completely independently at such a distance from the tower, so perhaps one might suggest that this s w range existed at least as early as the c 16.

The Jacobean house is dated 1621 and is easily the best example 65 of its time in the county. It has a three-storey, E-shaped front. The frontispiece consists of a projecting porch with ornamented inaccurate Ionic columns flanking a round arch and canted upper storeys with mullioned and transomed windows. Above the third floor, some fanciful pierced cresting. The windows between the three arms were sashed and georgianized for John Reed the elder between 1734 and 1754, and the bow windows in the outer arms of the e received sashes too. These were replaced by mullions and transoms again in the c 19, probably by *Dobson* in 1819. At the same time (i.e. the mid-c 18) the s w façade was put in order or systemized. In the process even the tower received three tiers of dummy Georgian windows to balance the façade. This whole front now has a middle doorway with Roman Doric columns and a straight entablature and is nine bays wide and embattled. In 1784 the lower ranges at the back were built or rebuilt by *John Dodds* for John Reed the younger.

Inside most of the decoration is of the mid-c 18, i.e. for John Reed the elder, who died in 1754. The alterations comprised the replanning of the Jacobean ground floor into three symmetrical apartments. Above the middle one is the two-storey music room, with a rather coarsely detailed Rococo ceiling. The entablature is finer, with an acanthus frieze and modillion cornice, and there are Palladian doorcases with pulvinated friezes and modillion cornices. In this room, a re-erected, extremely sumptuous Jacobean fireplace with four allegorical figures, a large relief of Father Time with the four Elements, and biblical as well as other small reliefs.

CHAPEL, opposite the Jacobean range. Described as ruinous in the early C18, it was rebuilt for John Reed after 1735. In the N wall, possibly medieval masonry remains. Arched doorway and s windows with heavy frames and keystones. Heavy quoins. The bellcote is Vanbrughian in its heavy details. Inside, the chapel has the finest C18 church furnishings in rural Northumberland: BOX PEWS, READING DESK and CHOIR STALLS all with fluted Ionic pilasters. Two-decker PULPIT with enriched panelling, a tester and a back-board with Corinthian pilasters. – ALTAR RAILS with slender turned balusters.

GATEPIERS, N of the castle. Late C17, with rustication in imitation of shells, and acorn finials.

BOATHOUSE, S of the castle. A ruined Gothick cottage of the late C18.

STEWARD'S HOUSE, ½m. E. Mid-C18, two-and-a-half storeys and five bays. Pedimented stone door surround with pulvinated frieze.

9070

CHOLLERFORD

CHOLLERFORD BRIDGE. 1785 by *Robert Mylne*. Five round arches, with big triangular cutwaters carried up as refuges. At the W end, the GEORGE INN, the old part C18, with a Venetian window in the end of a wing overlooking the river. At the E end, a former RAILWAY STATION on the Border Counties Railway of 1862, now converted to a house.

CHESTERS. *See* p. 218.

WALWICK. *See* p. 608.

9070

CHOLLERTON

ST GILES. Quite sizeable. W tower with quoins, of before 1769, raised by an extra storey, given battlements, crocketed pinnacles and a two-stage wood-shingled spire in 1873 – unarchaeological, maybe, but picturesque. Nave and aisles under one roof; lower chancel. This is all externally of the mid-C18, with two-light cusped ogee windows of 1873. The chancel N wall has three early medieval headstone crosses built in, but the great surprise is the interior and its S arcade of four bays. This is of *c.* 1150 and consists of four Roman monolithic columns, probably from Chesters. Very simple, rather low moulded capitals and double-chamfered pointed arches. The N arcade has C14 octagonal piers, also with double-chamfered arches. – FONTS. One font is a reused and inverted Roman altar, dedicated to Jupiter, found buried in the churchyard in 1827; the other is a plain circular bowl on a C13 foot with four shafts and moulded capitals. Jacobean FONT

COVER with thick double scrolls. – CHANCEL STALLS and ALTAR BACK with domestic-looking Jacobean carving. They may well be reused material. – ORGAN. Reputed to contain work by *Father Schmidt*; given to the church *c.* 1850. – MONUMENTS. In the S porch and elsewhere there are a number of cross slabs, especially an important double slab (cf. East Shaftoe: *see* Capheaton) in the sanctuary floor. – Rare post-Reformation cross slab to Henry Widdrington † 1637, in the S aisle E wall. – GRAVESTONE. SW of the church, a headstone of 1837 to John Saint, owner of the Cocklaw fulling mill, with a relief carving of the mill on the top.

CHURCH STABLE AND HEARSE HOUSE. By the gate. Probably of the early C19, though the little lancets on either side of the arched door may well be genuinely medieval and reused. Hipped stone slate roof.

CHOLLERTON GRANGE, formerly the vicarage. By *Dobson*. Dated on different sections CB/1830 and CB/1847, for two Christopher Birds, father and son, both successively vicars of Chollerton.

RAILWAY BRIDGE, over the A6079. Disused. Designed for the Border Counties Railway by *Robert Nicholson* and/or *John Furness Tone*, his nephew and successor as Engineer to the line. The contractor was *William Hutchinson*. Opened 1858. Two skew arches.

CHOLLERTON FARM. One of the most interesting farms in the county. The FARMHOUSE is an elegant five-bay early C19 ashlar house with a Lakeland slate roof. Three-bay centre, with pedimented, slightly projecting wings. The garden front has a broad two-storey central bow. Large and impressive FARM BUILDINGS with four big ranges round a farmyard. Within the yard a seven-storey, tapering threshing-machine WINDMILL, circular, with steps up to the first-floor doorway, and one large opening on each floor. The sails have gone. Attached to the outside of the W range, and completing a nice object lesson in historical development, is a mid-C19 ENGINE HOUSE with a tall square brick chimney. Mid-C19 also the long ranges of two-storey COTTAGES, STABLES and CARRIAGE HOUSE to the N of the farm buildings. The farm has always been part of the estate of the Swinburnes of Capheaton.

BARRASFORD. *See* p. 159.
CHIPCHASE CASTLE. *See* p. 230.
COCKLAW TOWER. *See* p. 234.
COLWELL. *See* p. 235.
ERRINGTON. *See* p. 272.
GREAT SWINBURNE. *See* p. 290.
SWINBURNE CASTLE. *See* p. 290.
TONE HALL. *See* p. 188.

CHRISTON BANK

1 m. NW of Embleton

In the village beside the level crossing, an unaltered mid-C19 GOODS SHED, presumably by *Benjamin Green*, of the same type as at Acklington (q.v.).

CHRISTON BANK FARM, ¼m. S. Long two-storey house: the five-bay E part probably *c.* 1700, the three-bay W part and rear outshut mid-c 18. Rendered and quite plain, but with contemporary fittings, including some panelling and a closed-string stair. Collared common-rafter roof to the mid-c 18 part.

CHRISTONBANK LIME WORKS, $\frac{1}{2}$ m. SE. Long disused, but an impressive pair of LIMEKILNS remains in the middle of a wood. Early c 19 circular kiln with three round draw arches; later c 19 square kiln with three segmental arches.

CLENNELL *see* BIDDLESTONE

CLENNELL STREET *see* ALWINTON

8040

COALCLEUGH
$1\frac{1}{2}$ m. S of Carr Shield

Formerly an important lead-mining centre at 555 metres (1,821 ft) above sea-level, active at least from the c 17 until *c.* 1890. Most of the buildings of this once populous settlement have now gone, and all of the mine buildings have been demolished since the 1970s. On the W side, a substantial house, perhaps once used by the mine agent, still survives, as do climbing shafts, levels, and a cottage on the E side. An underground hydraulic engine was installed here in 1765 by *William Westgarth*; it was much admired by John Smeaton.

COANWOOD *see* EAST COANWOOD

9070

COCKLAW TOWER
$\frac{3}{4}$ m. SE of Chollerton

Well-preserved shell of a late c 14 or c 15 tower, 15 by 10.6 metres (50 by 35 ft) in size. Large squared masonry, probably reusing Roman material. The barrel-vaulted basement is entered by a central door (protected by a machicolation at parapet level) in the S end, with a newel stair on the E of the entrance lobby. At first-floor level is another doorway, on the E, and two two-light windows. To the S end of the main apartment, a barrel-vaulted mural chamber with fragmentary remains of c 16 wall paintings, and an *oubliette* in the floor. The second floor had only chamfered loop windows: at parapet level there was a taller turret or guardroom at the S end. The first-floor E doorway poses a problem. It was clearly not the main entrance: sockets for timbers show that it communicated via a roofed bridge to an adjacent structure, possibly a chapel.

East Cocklaw Farmhouse and West Cocklaw Farm-
house, 1832. An identical pair, each with two single-storey rear
wings.

Cocklaw Mills, ½m. sw. Big late c 19 limekiln beside the
old railway line. Two pairs of segmental drawing arches; rock-
faced dressings.

COCKLE PARK TOWER   *2090*
1 m. sw of Tritlington

L-plan tower of the early c 16. The N corners have corbelled-out
bartizans, with a machicolation between (*see* Introduction, p. 63).
This end has a barrel-vaulted ground floor and a NE newel stair
with a gabled top. The s part, altered in the c 17, has an added
stair and mullioned-and-transomed windows on the w: the
windows on the s and e were enlarged and vaguely gothicized
c. 1790. The N chamber at first-floor level was the solar; it had an
oriel window on the w side which fell in 1828. About the same
time a two-light window and a fireplace were removed to Bothal
Castle.

COLDSTREAM *see* CORNHILL

COLWELL   *9070*
2½m. NE of Chollerton

Just a single street of nice varied houses and cottages, starting, at
the w end, with the Manor House, a fragment of the early c 17
house belonging to the Swinburnes. It is of two storeys and three
bays, with thick walls. It had two-light windows, but only the
stumps of the mullions remain. Near here, the former library.
Early c 19, single-storey, four bays with sixteen-pane sash
windows. e of this, a cottage with a very steeply pitched roof and
finely squared stonework; c 17 or early c 18. It may well have been
a long-house.

Limekilns, just to the w of the village. Mid-c 19. Three large
triangular corbelled arches.

COQUET ISLAND   *2000*
Off the mouth of the Coquet, 1 m. e of Amble

Apparently a monastic site from at least the c 7, but the present
c 14 or c 15 remains are those of a Benedictine monastic cell of
Tynemouth. The buildings seem to have consisted of a chapel, a
two-storey domestic range to its w, and a tower (mentioned in
the 1415 list of castles, fortalices and towers in the county) to the
s of the w end of the domestic range, to which it may have been

linked by a bridge. An early C 19 lighthouse-keeper's cottage occupies the site of the chapel and incorporates its E end (with the double-chamfered sill and jambs of a large window). A projecting turret at the NW corner of the chapel, which seems to have been solid at ground-floor level with a sacristy above, suggests that the chapel had a gallery at its W end, as the chapels of secular manor houses sometimes did. The domestic range and tower have been incorporated in 1841 Trinity House buildings. The tunnel-vaulted undercroft of the range survives intact, with a blocked newel stair on the S and later cross walls. The relatively small three-storey tower (too small to have been a tower-house in its own right) became a lighthouse in 1841, with the addition of a new top stage; some blocked square-headed chamfered windows survive, and the pointed barrel vault in the basement may be ancient. The castellated and whitewashed 1841 buildings and the medieval remains, which have not been whitewashed, together make up an unusual and evocative group on this bleak island site.

9060

CORBRIDGE

The Anglo-Saxons chose a spur of land on the N bank of the Tyne as their village and monastery site, half a mile E of the ruins of the Roman town. The village grew into an important medieval market town, defended by a ditch on the N. The ditch is no longer visible but the town plan remains and with it many buildings of interest. Of particular note are the number of good buildings sited at the end of streets, which provide stops or backdrops in several attractive townscapes. The only unhappy note is the epidemic of sun lounges and C 20 extensions along the river front, which confronts the traveller entering from the S.

ST ANDREW. The most important surviving Saxon monument in Northumberland, except for Hexham crypt. The lower parts of the W tower are probably of before 786 (the year in which a bishop was consecrated in the monastery of Corbridge) and formed the W porch of an aisleless nave, as at Monkwearmouth. Stubs of wall show that there was an adjacent structure further W (again as at Monkwearmouth), but the doorway that formerly led into it is now blocked; its voussoirs show worn saltire crosses. Above it, a round-headed window. Inside, the original arch from the porch into the nave survives; it seems to be Roman in its entirety, including jambs, voussoirs and also the finely moulded imposts. The Saxon nave was 5.36 metres (17 ft 8 in.) wide and 8.8 metres (29 ft) high to the top of the walls – a typically Northern proportion (cf. Monkwearmouth and Escomb): its original W gable window is now in the E tower wall above the modern roof. The upper parts of the tower seem to be of the C 11, and make it look tall and slender, with none of the enrichments of Bywell and Ovingham. The bell openings are of 1729 and the crenellated parapet above replaces a gabled cap; blocked openings can be seen immediately below on both E and W. Saxon masonry also survives in the side walls of the nave, above the arcades; two early window-heads can be seen on the N. The footings of the side walls of an earlier narrower chancel were found last century. Norman evidence is scantier, limited to the S doorway (inside the early C 20 porch) with one order of colonnettes, scalloped capitals and two orders of zigzag in the arch.

The C 13 remains, however, are again important and impressive; three separate building campaigns have been traced. The E view, which is mainly of C 13 parts, is indeed the best of the church. All the windows are lancets (although the widely spaced stepped E triplet is of 1853). The priest's door on the S side of the chancel, with a pointed trefoiled head, looks like a later insertion, as the straight-headed mullioned 'low-side' window certainly is. The chancel arch rests on short coupled shafts starting from plain corbels. A little later the arch was widened by cutting back the lower jambs. The chancel has an original N chapel of four bays; the nave has aisles on both sides, and transepts. The N transept has a W aisle; the S transept received no aisle as such, but the centre bay of the adjacent nave aisle was widened instead. The nave arcades are of three bays with octagonal piers, moulded capitals and double-chamfered arches with small broaches. The transept arcade and the lower and narrower chancel arcade are of the same type. Finally, also of the C 13, a puzzling structure N of the tower which seems to stand on pre-Conquest foundations. It may at one stage have served as a W bay to the N aisle, but was later converted into a residence for the priest, before he moved to his grander living quarters S of the churchyard.

Trefoiled PISCINAE in chancel and S transept; and below the N transept N windows, a low segmental-arched recess for a MONUMENT. In it, a slab with an inscription referring in all probability to the father of one who was a burgess of Corbridge in 1296. – Recently reset in the S transept floor, a late C 13 slab with a cross and an inscription to Lady Alicia de Tynedale. – Many other cross slabs and slab fragments in the floor and walls. – A 1708 floor stone in the chancel is a medieval altar slab reused. – The fittings and furnishings are otherwise late C 19 and early C 20.

On the S of the churchyard, an embattled LYCHGATE of 1919 and the VICAR'S PELE, a very Northumbrian conception of a vicarage and by far the best-preserved of its type. It is a tower-house, perhaps as late as the mid-C 14, built of Roman stones from Corstopitum; restored and reroofed in 1910. The E entrance to the tunnel-vaulted ground floor still has its old door of oak boards bolted onto an iron grille. A mural stair rises to a lobby, with shelf and sink, and the first-floor room, with fireplace, cupboards and window seats. At second-floor level, one window has a book-rest built into the jamb. Small windows, parapet, and square corbelled-out angle bartizans. The tower now houses a collection of medieval and earlier CARVED STONES; several medieval cross slabs are reused in the fabric, mostly as lintels. – In the churchyard, the memorial slab to John Grey of Dilston † 1868, father of Josephine Butler.

By the tower door, the old MARKET CROSS: Roman capital as base, worn C 13 shaft with dogtooth, and plain C 18 head.

RAILWAY STATION, ½ m. outside the village. Quite unlike the other stations on the Newcastle and Carlisle Railway, for it was built

when a level crossing by the original station of 1835 was replaced
by a bridge *c.* 1848. Towards the line, the station is of two storeys
and seven bays, with hooded drip moulds over lower openings.
Apart from the platform canopy, supported on Tuscan columns
of cast iron, it looks like a medium-size private house.

CORBRIDGE BRIDGE. Stone road bridge of seven unequal segmental spans, giving a total span of 146 metres (160 yards).
Completed in 1674. The s arch was rebuilt in 1829, and the whole
was widened by 0.9 metre (3 ft) in 1881 by corbelling out the
parapets. Huge pointed cutwaters up and down river, stepping
back in three phases to form half-hexagonal retreats in the parapet.
This was the only Tyne bridge to survive the flood of 1771, saved
probably by the wide flood plain to the s.

For other public buildings, *see* Perambulation, below.

PERAMBULATION

In the MARKET PLACE, the remarkable CROSS of 1814. Quatrefoil
shaft with shaft rings and cross on top, all made of cast iron. Cast-
iron cap also to the 1815 PANT. None of the houses in the Market
Place is specially noteworthy, but there is at Corbridge a nice
standard of C19 terraces of low two-storeyed stone houses, of
which examples, some dated, can be seen in the main streets as
well. To the SE of the church, such a terrace bends round by the
Vicar's Pele, and the METHODIST CHAPEL (now used by the
Brethren), of as late a date as 1867, fits in without seeming effort.

From the church and Market Place, three parallel streets run E:
HILL STREET is the northernmost. Here, HERON HOUSE, of
three bays with a good pedimented door, is probably of *c.* 1700.
Closing the E end of the street, the TOWN HALL of 1887 (by *F.
Emily*), a pretty Norman-Shavian stone building with four oriels
and a central tower. The ornament is a feathery acanthus. Further
s, MIDDLE STREET, with the BLACK BULL INN, dated 1755
and 1765, and FRONT STREET, with more typical terraces and
the PANACHE RESTAURANT, an earlier C18 building.

To the E of the end of Middle Street, the very wide MAIN STREET.
Here, at the beginning on the l., the ANGEL INN, ten bays wide,
with a C17 centre (arched door and four-light mullioned-and-
transomed window) and Georgian and later alterations. Further
along a nasty shock – a little C17 house with mullioned windows
and a pretty attic dormer but with the whole ground floor punched
out by an atrocious mid-C20 shopfront. The adjacent three-storey
house shows C16 or C17 masonry in its lower parts. At the end
of old Corbridge, Main Street narrows and the vista is successfully
closed by MONKSHOLME, an early C17 house restored in 1891,
but with genuine attic dormers of the same type as seen in Hexham
and elsewhere.

Across the road to the N is LOW HALL, probably Corbridge's
most interesting house. C13 or early C14 rectangular block with
ground-floor hall, with the storeyed solar at the E end raised into
a tower in the C15, the main block remodelled in the C16 and
again, with larger mullioned windows, *c.* 1675. Restoration and
major extension to rear *c.* 1890. Of the first house, part of the

cross-passage door can be seen in the front wall and a little lancet at the w end, and inside, two doorways from hall to solar undercroft, which is barrel-vaulted E–W, despite its longer axis being N–S. The tower stair starts in the thickness of the wall but in the later upper parts is a conventional corner newel.

On the s of Main Street, pleasant but minor c 19 villas and terraces and two larger c 18 houses, CORBRIDGE HOUSE and the RIVERSIDE HOTEL, which is said to have been built c. 1760 with stone from Dilston Hall. Looking back along the street, the view westwards is also successfully closed, this time by LLOYDS BANK, c. 1890, tall with a hipped mansard roof and some unconventional classical detail. To the s here is BRIDGE BANK, with a good c 18 and c 19 group dropping steeply down to the pantile-roofed FORGE. Beyond is CORBRIDGE BRIDGE (see above).

Away from the town centre, off STAGSHAW ROAD, two noteworthy houses. OLD PRIOR MANOR on the E is the former rectory, held in medieval times by the Prior of Carlisle. The earliest architectural features, which include several fireplaces, are c 17. The head of a plate-tracery window reset in the gable of a barn across the road probably comes from the manorial chapel. Also w of the road, and down in a little valley, ORCHARD VALE, a three-storey five-bay house dated 1731, with a good interior, including a contemporary stair.

Another medieval CHAPEL gives its name to St Helen's Street. What may be the base of its w end is incorporated in the boundary wall w of the Parish Hall, but no features survive. Further E, at the junction with PRINCES STREET, is CROSS HOUSE, an odd semi-detached pair of 1754 with a pedimented centre looking down Princes Street and forming yet another satisfying stop to a streetscape.

The industrial archaeologist will be lured a little further afield, up MILKWELL LANE, to the remains of CORBRIDGE POTTERY (established c. 1840). Two impressive early c 19 'BOTTLE OVENS' are the most prominent feature; there is also a pair of 'Newcastle' horizontal kilns and other bits and pieces. The pottery closed c. 1910, but its name can still be seen on many salt-glazed ceramic troughs, including several associated with the town's wells and pants.

ROMAN TOWN

The centre of what was, in the c 3, a busy garrison town is displayed $\frac{1}{2}$ m. NW. Roman occupation here began after the withdrawal from Scotland N of the Forth–Clyde line, a move which was complete by A.D. 90. A series of three successive forts, mainly built of timber, was constructed to guard the bridge by which Dere Street (the Great North Road of the day) crossed the Tyne. The re-occupation of Scotland and, therefore, the increased importance of Dere Street led to the building of a fourth fort, largely of stone, c. A.D. 140. The dignified retreat from Scotland in the 160s again reduced the value of Corbridge as a military base, and the site began to change into a town – the most northerly in the Empire. This process was complete by the earlier c 3, and it is this phase,

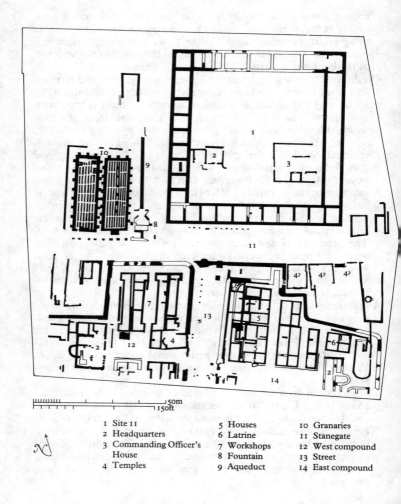

Corbridge, Roman town. Plan

1 Site 11	5 Houses	10 Granaries
2 Headquarters	6 Latrine	11 Stanegate
3 Commanding Officer's House	7 Workshops	12 West compound
4 Temples	8 Fountain	13 Street
	9 Aqueduct	14 East compound

principally, that is on display. Much of the new urban centre (the prosperity of which was still directly linked to the presence of the army) lies under the surrounding fields. Its layout is only occasionally revealed to the airborne camera as the crops wither over the walls of the buried buildings. Most of these were the long and narrow 'strip-houses', set gable-on to the main road, Stanegate, and to the streets opening off it.

The first buildings to be seen are also the most impressive: the two heavily buttressed GRANARIES, their floors of massive slabs resting upon dwarf walls. Vents below the floors maintained a healthy level of air circulation. The w granary displays at its N end the lower vents and floor levels of an earlier phase. In its final form the roof of the E granary was supported by an axial row of columns. Porticoes at the S end of each building provided a sheltered loading bay, until the level of Stanegate rose impossibly high through repeated repairs.

Immediately E, a raised aqueduct supplied an ornate fountain; the water was discharged into a large aeration cistern, flanked by statue-bases, and then into a simpler tank for common use. The sides of the latter have been scalloped almost out of recognition by the sharpening of blades. Note the butterfly clamps holding together the heavy polygonal base of the cistern.

Further E again is a large square courtyard surrounded by small rooms; the purpose of this ('Site II') is uncertain but it may have been intended to be a market with lock-up shops. Its masonry is undistinguished; although set in position the large blocks were still not dressed. The project was destroyed, unfinished, c. 180, although the shops fronting the Stanegate were later occupied. Within the wide open space are exposed fragments of the first stone fort of c. 140: parts of the headquarters and of the commanding officer's house. Outside the SE corner, a more humble and much later (C 4) house encroaches on the Stanegate.

S of the road, at the E end of the site, a simple shop with a well lies next to the fragmentary remains of what may have been temples; their sites were converted to industrial use in the C 4. These buildings, together with those opposite the granaries, were deliberately excluded from the two military compounds, built in the Severan reconstruction of c. 200, which occupy this side of the street. Originally separated by a road running N–S, the compounds were linked in the C 4 by a wall and a gateway on the Stanegate frontage. The zigzag wall of the E compound encloses houses for officers, and perhaps for other ranks, along with fragments of a small administrative block and apsidal buildings that have been interpreted as officers' clubs. The W compound contains double workshops, set back-to-back, and a three-bay administrative block with a rear apse tacked onto the central shrine. From here some steps lead down through stone jambs into a flagged strongroom; surviving corbelling indicates how low the vault was. Living quarters, including a bath and a latrine, were later added to the N end of this block. A simple apsidal building just N of the gate and respected by the compound wall was probably an earlier temple: a colonnade was subsequently added. The marked ripple of the masonry, especially pronounced in the W compound, is due to subsidence over the ditches of one of the earlier forts.

The fine MUSEUM (1975–83, by the *Napper Collerton Partnership*) has many interesting inscriptions, sculptures and smaller objects of everyday life. It is a single-storey stone building with a timber colonnade fronting the central glass section facing the Roman remains. Blue slate roof with a clerestory.

DILSTON. *See* p. 251.
FARNLEY. *See* p. 277.
SANDHOE. *See* p. 558.
STAGSHAW. *See* p. 575.

CORNHILL

St Helen. 1840 by *Ignatius Bonomi*, incorporating in the nave
some of the masonry of the preceding church of 1751. The exterior
is all High Victorian Gothic of 1866, when the chancel was built
(probably by *F. R. Wilson*, who built the adjoining vicarage).
Inside, w gallery on thin Tuscan columns, no doubt of 1840,
though it bears a mid-c 18 carving of the Collingwood arms in a
frame of openwork Rococo mantling. It was formerly at the E end
of the nave. – PULPIT and READING DESK, also 1840. Neo-
Norman with waterleaf columns at the angles.

CORNHILL HOUSE, at the w end of the village. Described by
Mackenzie in 1825 as 'the ancient cross-shaped seat of the Col-
lingwoods'. White-painted, quite irregular and very Scottish in
feel, with its steeply pitched roofs and crowstepped gables. The
detail is all early c 18, but the core of the house, the section
running E–W, is much older, with walls in excess of a metre thick.
Inside, one panelled room; solid early c 18 staircase with heavily
moulded arches leading to the passages. In the attic, an early c 17
fireplace with geometric patterns in the lintel.

COLLINGWOOD ARMS. Early c 19 coaching inn. Seven bays.

COLDSTREAM BRIDGE. A very fine bridge with five segmental
arches each of 18-metre (60-ft) span and smaller segmental land
arches at each end; constructed 1763–6. Designed by *Smeaton* for
the Tweed Bridges Trustees, borrowing the architectural devices –
triple projecting keystones to the main arches, modillions under a
plain cornice at the parapet base, and in each spandrel a blackened
blind-eye decoration surrounded by a masonry ring with projecting keystones on its horizontal and vertical diameters – from
an earlier design by *Robert Reid* of Haddington, who became
resident engineer for the work. Smeaton used these devices on his
later bridges at Perth and Banff in Scotland and at Hexham
in Northumberland. Downstream cauld (weir) added *c.* 1784;
foundations protected with concrete in 1922, strengthened with
concrete relieving arches and widened by cantilevered footpaths
in 1960–1.

MELKINGTON, *c.* $1\frac{1}{2}$ m. NE. Very plain five-bay ashlar house of
c. 1800. Older buildings at the rear.

CORNHILL CASTLE, $\frac{3}{4}$ m. NW. A substantial ditch, crossed by a s
causeway but with no inner rampart, crosses the angle between a
deeply cut burn and the river cliff above the Tweed. There was a
tower here in 1385. It was newly repaired in 1541 and still complete
with barmkin in 1561. No masonry survives.

TWIZEL. See p. 586.

CORSENSIDE

St Cuthbert. In an exposed and solitary position. Nave and
lower chancel. Basically Norman, *see* the chancel arch, which is
unmoulded and rests on the plainest imposts. c 17 priests' door
with a chamfered surround. s door and w bellcote added in 1735.
The nave has domestic-looking mid-c 19 sash windows. The
chancel has one c 18 sash and a Victorian E window with inter-

secting tracery. – FONT. C 18. Octagonal. – ALTAR RAILS. Also
C 18, with turned balusters. – MONUMENTS. Four CROSS SLABS,
two of normal size, two very small. – Outside, against the S wall,
are three C 18 wall monuments to members of the Reed family.
One, of 1735, has two large cherubs seated on a memento mori
and leaning against a cartouche.

CORSENSIDE, beside the church. A relatively early example for
the county of a complete, non-defensible house, already in the
standard two-cell form with central doorway. It is dated 1686
above the door. Three storeys and three bays. Doorway with four-
centred-arched lintel. Formerly two-light mullioned windows
throughout, now replaced by sashes on the first two floors.

THE BRIGG, $\frac{1}{4}$ m. N, and COLDTOWN, $\frac{1}{2}$ m. S. Two farms which
include more or less complete bastle houses. Both are now used
as farm buildings.

COUPLAND CASTLE
1$\frac{3}{4}$ m. S of Milfield

9030

Tower-house of a late date, possibly 1594, the date scratched on the
jamb of a ground-floor doorway. The tower is T-shaped, that is a
plain parallelogram with a short stair projection in the middle of
the E side. A broad square newel stair in the projecting wing goes
up as far as the first floor. Above this point a narrower round
newel stair is corbelled out in the angle between the stair wing
and the main tower. The basement of the tower is tunnel-vaulted.
On the first floor is the former hall, containing a big fireplace with
a four-centred-arched lintel inscribed GW 1619 MW, for George
and Mary Wallis. The tower has a pitched roof and a walkway
behind a plain corbelled-out parapet. It is not clear how long the
tower stood alone. There is a C 16 or C 17 doorway into the kitchen
range to the rear; and at the S end of the house there is a three-
bay C 18 section. Most of the additions to the tower, however,
were rebuilt in 1820–5 in neo-Tudor style. The name of the
architect is not recorded, but he did a competent job both at the
house and at the two LODGES, which are small Tudor-style
buildings of some originality. The house also benefits from being
built of volcanic rock, soft pinks and greys with buff sandstone
dressings. It is one of the few major buildings in the county to be
built of volcanic rock.

In the garden an ICEHOUSE, rather decayed; and a complex,
multi-faceted SUNDIAL of the Scottish type. It must date from
the late C 17 or early C 18.

EWART PARK. See p. 274.

LANTON. See p. 373.

YEAVERING. See p. 637.

CRAGSIDE
                           1 m. E of Rothbury

The dramatic country seat of the first Lord Armstrong, in a highly
romantic situation in the centre of an estate of 5,665 hectares
(14,000 acres), high on the E side of the Debdon Burn valley
amidst extensive woods (all the product of Armstrong's planting).
No other house is visible in any direction. The original Cragside
of 1864 – its architect is unrecorded – was relatively humble;
despite its gables and a pyramid-roofed tower it was a pale shadow
of what was to come when *Norman Shaw* transformed it into the
most dramatic Victorian mansion in the North of England. Shaw
is said to have sketched out his plans in one day, although his
whole scheme required three campaigns of work, 1870–2, 1872–7
and 1883–5. The site is Wagnerian, and so is Shaw's architecture.
It has none yet of the finesse of his Chelsea houses of a few years
later. Its origin is the Tudor style, both in its stone and its black-
and-white versions. The Northumbrian hills are not a black-and-
white region, but that did not worry Shaw. What he was concerned
with was high picturesqueness for his design, and he has without
106   doubt achieved it. The entrance side has stone walls, on the l. at
two different levels crowned by timber-framed gables or storeys,
on the r. carried right up as a tower under which an archway leads
into a courtyard enclosed by rather mechanical post-Shaw wings
(perhaps by Armstrong himself), built in the 1890s. At the r. end,
the stone drawing room wing of 1883–5 projects, built straight
onto the sandstone crag at second-floor level relative to the rest
of the house. Behind it is the billiard room extension of 1895 by
Frederick Waller, and, rising from the bare rock above, a strange
detached chimneystack fed by subterranean flues. The main front,
which looks out across the Debdon Burn, is again a complicated
composition of forward and backward and higher and lower
elements, though the general impression is one of towering height
everywhere. The N side, shaded by trees, is less striking; the
gabled gateway of 1874 was originally more or less detached.

Inside the house there is a disorientating contrast in scale
between the rooms around the entrance hall, where far more of
the pre-Shaw house remains than the exterior suggests, and the
grander apartments towards the extremities of the building. One
of the arches from the stone entrance hall leads through a majolica-
tiled passage, the central artery of the original house, to the library,
which has some exceptionally good *William Morris* glass in the
top lights of the windows, and the dining room, which has a big
inglenook fireplace with much carving. Both rooms are part of
Shaw's 1870–2 campaign. The kitchen, reached via the back
corridor and the butler's pantry, is a large apartment, extended
after 1885; here Armstrong's technical ingenuity is demonstrated
to the full by the hydraulically turned spit and dumb waiter. All
this is at the level of the entrance; the 1870–2 extension has a
lower storey, housing, beneath the library, another unusual item
in the form of a Turkish bath suite. Back in the entrance hall, the
curiously insignificant main staircase leads up to the second-floor
gallery (the timber-framed top floor of the entrance front), with
its arch-braced roof trusses; this was initially constructed in 1872–

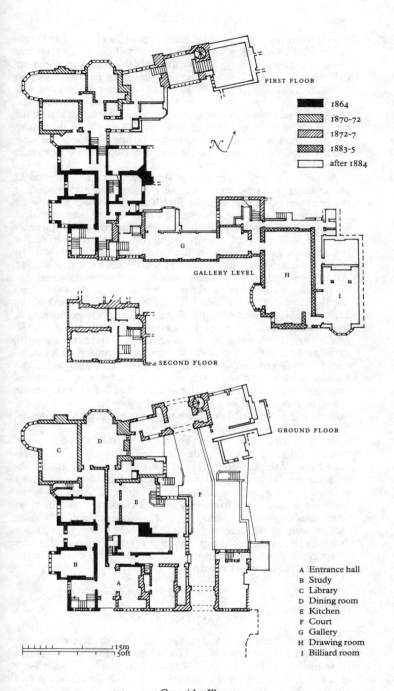

FIRST FLOOR

1864
1870–72
1872–7
1883–5
after 1884

N

GALLERY LEVEL

G

H

I

SECOND FLOOR

GROUND FLOOR

C

D

E

F

B

A

15m
50ft

A Entrance hall
B Study
C Library
D Dining room
E Kitchen
F Court
G Gallery
H Drawing room
I Billiard room

Cragside. Plans

4 as Armstrong's personal museum, giving access to his observatory in the Gilnockie Tower; in the 1883 changes the museum became a gallery, giving access through the tower to the huge drawing room beyond, with its overpowering chimneypiece in Italian marble, designed by *W. R. Lethaby* and carved by *Farmer & Brindley*. The origin of the style – with Mannerist figures, strapwork cartouches and plenty of *putti* – is the decoration of Hardwick and Hatfield at their most spectacular. Throughout the house are contemporary paintings and statues, demonstrating, amongst other things, what was permissible to the Victorian nobleman in the way of erotica.

As well as being an arms magnate, Armstrong was famous as an inventor and innovator, and he was especially interested in water power. Cragside was the first house in the world to be lit by hydroelectric power. Of considerable historic and technical interest, albeit relatively plain architecturally, are the TUMBLE-TON RAM HOUSE of *c.* 1866, below the dam $\frac{1}{4}$ m. NW of the house, which powered the hydraulic equipment in the kitchen and elsewhere; $\frac{3}{4}$ m. NW the DEBDON SAWMILL, where in 1881 Armstrong coupled the turbine to a Siemens horizontal generator to produce the first hydroelectric power source in the world, and the BURNFOOT POWER HOUSE of 1883–7 on the E bank of the Debdon Burn, just N of the B6344. Of more significance in the Cragside landscape are the IRON BRIDGE, manufactured at Armstrong's Elswick Works in the 1870s, arching across the Debdon Burn ravine below the W front of the house, and, $\frac{1}{4}$ m. N, the TUMBLETON STABLES (*c.* 1864, remodelled 1892–3), like Cragside itself built on a site cut into the hillside. These are arranged round a courtyard with pyramid-roofed gateway on the S and towers topped by timber-framed gables at the centre of E and W ranges. The influence, although not, apparently, the actual hand, of Shaw is obvious.

CRAGSIDE PARK HOUSE, $\frac{1}{2}$ m. SW on the W bank of the Burn. A detached part of the Cragside Complex. The house (formerly called the Cottage in the Park) of 1864 is Tudor, of one-and-a-half storeys, and was presumably designed by the anonymous architect of the original Cragside. Evidence of Armstrong the inventor is seen again in the big CONSERVATORY with its rows of rotating ceramic pots, and a hypocaust-style underfloor heating system with a long underground flue (just like that of a C19 lead-smelting mill) running to two chimneys on the hill above. He may also have designed the mechanism of the elaborate CLOCK in the pretty little clock tower nearby.

2070

CRAMLINGTON

The important thing about Cramlington is that it is there at all. Like Killingworth (q.v.) it was a New Township based on an old village, initiated in the 1950s and built without government-funded New Town status. Existing local authorities run both Cramlington and Killingworth, and built them in co-operation with Northumberland County Council (under the County Architect, *Arthur Lawson*). But whereas Killingworth was designed to take overspill from Tyneside, Cramlington was to be a growth point for industrial and residential development, and the County Council, Seaton Sluice UDC and two firms of private housing developers were to be the partners.

Cramlington was officially inaugurated in 1964. There were to be 'no long drab streets', and vehicles were to be segregated from pedestrians. It was expected that 15,000 people would be employed on the industrial estate. The initial plan of 1958 envisaged four stages of development, and a final population of 50,000; the population was 20,000 by c. 1973, with a target of 80,000, and by 1990, with the third stage almost complete, it had reached 30,000. In 1991 a consortium of British Coal and Blagdon Estates announced plans to build 2,700 houses and create 2,000 jobs in the course of the next twenty years in the SW sector.

The last pit in the area closed in 1961, but the knowledgeable traveller can spot the stump where once the colliery waste was piled high in a conical heap. Alexandra Park is an open space on the site of another pit-heap. The huge area of c. 1961–1980 low-rise housing is of the normal type put up by commercial developers, no better and no worse than many others of this time. The SHOPPING CENTRE, CONCORDIA LEISURE CENTRE and LIBRARY, opened in 1972, are by the County Council architect *Arthur Lawson*.

The industries of the 1980s in the 69 hectares (170 acres) of the NW quadrant of the town leave no such landmarks as the old pit-heaps, and are housed in low wide buildings. The most recent are the most interesting, e.g. the BRITISH GAS LINE INSPECTION DEPOT of 1979 by *Ryder & Yates* (as the refurbishment of a factory which they had originally designed for Courtelle), which makes bold use of curved surfaces towards the road and has a very 1930s-style round-fronted gatehouse; the buildings of the depot are less co-ordinated when seen from other points of view.

Caught up within the new town are the original village centre with its parish church and Cramlington Hall, and a scatter of other older buildings of some minor note.

St NICHOLAS. 1868 by *Austin & Johnson*, quite a proud church in a free E. E. style, the design said to have been adapted from one by *Dobson*. Four-bay aisled nave, big W tower and chancel. Plate-tracery windows, with foiled circles as clerestory. – STAINED GLASS. Two windows by *Cottier*, 1868.

St JOHN THE BAPTIST (R.C.), Annitsford, 2 m. S. 1906 by *Parxour*, modelled on Ostend Cathedral, and using Belgian crafts-men. Tall aisled nave with SW porch and pyramid-roofed NW baptistry, and aisled chancel with canted apse and ambulatory. The junction of nave and chancel is emphasized rather oddly by tall octagonal pinnacles rising from aisle and nave walls. Clere-story of foiled circles and a big vesica above two lancets in the W end. The arcades have narrow and steeply pointed arches.

CRAMLINGTON HALL. Mid-C18 Palladian villa: five-bay centre-piece flanked by the ends of lower hip-roofed wings. Modillion cornices all round.

CRAMLINGTON STATION. 1855. Economy buildings (station and goods shed) of brick, to the designs of the *N. E. R. Civil Engineer*.

AGED MINEWORKERS' HOMES, Front Street. 1927. Brick. Three

blocks, totalling ten cottages in all, arranged around a little grassy square behind a front wall with a central gateway.

ARCOT HALL (Golf Club), I m. sw. L-plan house. Late C 18 three-bay block facing w, its centre bow capped by a lead dome (cf. Hartford Hall); this part was built for George Shum-Storey, an Indian adventurer who was present at the siege of Arcot near Madras. Another three-bay block with a Roman Doric porch, facing s, was added in 1805.

EAST HARTFORD, I m. N. Farmhouse with (restored) mullioned windows under straight labels, with contemporary attic dormers and a circular window above the front door. The date is probably in the third quarter of the C 17.

PLESSEY HALL, 2 m. NW. The farm stands on an important medieval site; the present house seems to be C 17 in parts, but is difficult to interpret. PLESSEY MILL, ½ m. E, is C 18, remodelled in the mid-C 19; the adjacent mill house has a similar history. On the hilltop s of the track to the Hall, the remains of a WINDMILL, dated 1749. Circular straight-sided tower with chamfered surrounds to its door and windows, and stonework of near-ashlar quality. Sockets in the outer wall suggest a possible reefing stage, but if so the tower must once have been considerably higher.

2020

CRASTER

ST PETER THE FISHERMAN. 1877. Little mission church with w porch and bellcote.

The village, picturesque but disappointing architecturally, is clustered round the tiny harbour, with Dunstanburgh (q.v.) omnipresent on the horizon. Craster was a fishing haven as early as 1626, but the HARBOUR works date from 1906–10, designed by *J. Watt Sandeman* of Newcastle; the contractors were *McLaren & Proude*, also of Newcastle. The harbour is a simple affair, comprising a mass concrete s pier and a N one of shuttered concrete with rubble fill. Three 27-metre (90-ft) silos supported on a concrete arch were added in 1914 to facilitate the shipment of whinstone chippings; these were demolished *c.* 1936 and only the arch remains. Little fishing is done from here now, but Craster's famous kippers (another North-East of England invention) are still cured in a typical mid-C 19 smoke house which has outer walls of whinstone, pantiled roofs, and a wooden ridge ventilator.

CRASTER TOWER, ½ m. w, well away from the sea. The three-storey embattled tower, mentioned in the 1415 list of castles, fortalices and towers in the county, has a basement vault with entrance lobby and newel stair at the SE corner. The adjacent wing on the E has 1.2-metre (4-ft) thick walls, suggesting a medieval or C 16 date, but it was extended and thoroughly remodelled in the C 19. In 1769 a new house was built on to the s side of the tower. This has a three-storey five-bay s front faced with squared whinstone, with a central pediment. The central doorway is tripartite, with Tuscan pilasters and an open pediment. The second-floor window beneath the main pediment has a detached section of cornice above, just as on the w front of Shawdon Hall. This and other features suggest the hand of *William Newton*. Later in the C 18 there were Gothick alterations, *see* the big tripartite windows to the upper floors of the tower (on the W) and a pretty screen between two ground-floor rooms of the 1769 block. The tower rooms are said to have Gothick interiors as well. There are some impressive embattled GARDEN WALLS of the same later C 18 date, along with the triple-gabled STABLES with quatrefoils in the gables. Also Gothick the embattled GATEWAY, a four-centred arch, which spans not the entrance to the house but the road down to the village.

DUNSTANBURGH CASTLE. *See* p. 257.

DUNSTAN HALL. *See* p. 260.

CRAWLEY TOWER
½ m. E of Powburn

0010

The curious case of a C 14 tower ruin utilized in the C 18 as one of the Shawdon Estate's hilltop eyecatchers (*see* also Shepherd's Law near Shawdon and Jenny's Lantern near Bolton); at the same time a small house was built inside the ruin. The tower was licensed in 1343, but was in decay by 1541. The S and W sides of the tower stand more or less to full height, with the stubs of the other two walls; the odd crenellation and stepping-down of the wall tops is C 18. The S wall preserves two original windows at second- and third-floor levels, each of two lancet lights (the upper with a segmental rear-arch and jamb seats). The base of a similar window is visible on the W. The tower was probably part of a larger building; it is set within a rectangular earthwork, possibly a barmkin, consisting of a broad ditch and an outer bank.

CRESSWELL

2090

On the coast looking N across the wide sweep of Druridge Bay.

ST BARTHOLOMEW. Built, probably in 1836, for the Baker-Cresswells, whose family pew formerly occupied most of the chancel. Neo-Norman, with nave and lower chancel and bellcote. Good grotesque corbel tables. – STAINED GLASS. A considerable amount of glass by *Willement*, 1836–9. The two E windows each have six medallions with scenes in white and yellow in a style remarkably well and intelligently copying that of *c.* 1200.

E of the church, contemporary ESTATE COTTAGES and former SCHOOL, neo-Tudor.

CRESSWELL TOWER. A rectangular three-storey tower of the late C 14 or C 15, now roofless. Barrel-vaulted ground floor with newel stair at the NE corner. Original door at first-floor level on the N. Inside are contemporary fireplaces, mural recesses and garde-robes, but the embattled parapet is of the C 18, when a new house was built onto the N side of the tower. The house was pulled down in the early C 19 except for its pedimented front doorway, which survives as part of a later field-wall.

CRESSWELL HALL. The Hall, a large house of some interest by an architect of considerable interest, *John Shaw*, was pulled down in 1937. It was in the Grecian style and dated from 1821–5. Only a ruinous Roman Doric GALLERY survives, with a curving sixteen-column arcade linking pavilions with latticework parapets, and the STABLES of 1829. These enclose a courtyard, the N range having an imposing tower with garlands hanging down to the l. and r. of the clock faces, a lantern with groups of three square Doric angle pilasters and an Italianate low pyramid roof.

HOME FARM, 1 m. S. Planned farm, probably contemporary with the Hall. The barn has an engine house with an elaborate tower ingeniously combining the functions of chimney and dovecote.

3070

CULLERCOATS
1 m. N of Tynemouth

A pier was built here in 1677, but closed in 1730; the attractive harbour of today owes more to the fishing trade than to the coal trade of the C 17. Even the fishing is not so apparent as it was throughout the C 19 and up to the years just post-1945, when the rows of fishermen's cottages were cleared away and houses with more hygiene but less charm replaced them. In the later C 19 and early C 20 the area became a fashionable dormitory for Newcastle and the streets of desirable residences reflect changing tastes, although none is exceptional enough to be singled out here.

ST GEORGE, Beverley Gardens. 1882–4 by *J. L. Pearson* for the sixth Duke of Northumberland as a memorial to his father. An impressive land- and sea-mark, standing at the edge of the sea, its spire punctuating the sweep of the Long Sands. As Pearson's major churches tend to be, it is noble, honest, earnest, yet a little cold, but externally it gives a fine accent to a drab sea-front. Nave and aisles, transepts, polygonal apse, and a bold tower with tall spire at the E end of the S aisle. Lancet windows and windows with plate tracery. W end with two groups of stepped lancets. The interior has the great Pearson advantage of being stone-vaulted throughout, uniquely so among C 19 churches in Northumberland: sexpartite bays in the chancel and transepts, quadripartite in the crossing and nave. Circular piers; dogtooth decoration to the crossing arches. Very large clerestory windows. High, blind apse arcade. W gallery over a vaulted, arcaded baptistry. Such a church is in a way a C 13 ideal rarely achieved in the C 13, when a less scholarly approach to design and changes of style (owing to the time which building took) tended to interfere with purity and at the same time created life. – On the E pier of the S nave arcade, a plaque commemorating the building of the church. The chancel has a terrazzo and marble floor and a free-standing REREDOS. – Stone COMMUNION RAIL and PULPIT by Pearson. – FONT also original and probably by Pearson: square, on pedestal and four columns, with a Stanhope marble base. – Art Nouveau LIGHT FITTINGS by Pearson in the aisles. – STAINED GLASS by *Kempe* in the apse clerestory.

ROCKET GARAGE, John Street. 1867. Apparatus house for Cullercoats Life Brigade. A modest building, easily overlooked, rep-

resenting a great C19 philanthropic movement. Built for the
second such brigade in the country (for the first, *see* Tynemouth).
Rocket-fired lifelines were used to bring survivors off ships
wrecked on the nearby rocks.

CULLERCOATS WATCH CLUB HOUSE, on the edge of the harbour
in Victoria Crescent. 1877–9 by *F. W. Rich*, for Cullercoats Life
Brigade as a lookout house. Rough sandstone, with rock-faced
quoins and dressings. A stone-mullioned window faces the street
under the high gable of the big plain-tiled roof, which is hipped
at the polygonal, seaward end, with a catslide over a wooden
verandah. A tall clock turret and shingled belfry complete the
composition.

DALLY CASTLE *see* GREYSTEAD

DALTON
2 m. E of Stamfordham

1070

HOLY TRINITY. 1836 by *John Green*. Small, with nave and short
chancel. Lancet windows. The E end has three stepped lancets.
THE OLD SCHOOLHOUSE, opposite the church. 1843. Small, well-
built and pretty in the Tudor style.

DENTON *see* NEWCASTLE UPON TYNE

DENWICK

2010

CHAPEL. 1872. A plain little rectangle with lancet windows, but
forming a picturesque group with the SCHOOL of 1907 and some
big trees.
Denwick is a small village with a row of one- and two-storeyed
C19 Tudor estate cottages, and two PANTS, each dated 1859.
DENWICK HOUSE, set back to the S, is a three-bay estate farmhouse dated 1808, of the type with the front door set in a round-
arched panel; it was enlarged in the later C19. It was built as the
factor's house for the Duke of Northumberland's estate.

DILSTON
1 m. SW of Corbridge

9060

DILSTON CASTLE. L-plan tower-house (cf. Cockle Park) with a
barrel-vaulted basement to the S part and a corbelled-out round
turret in the re-entrant angle. The tower was altered *c.* 1620, when
it was incorporated into a wing of Dilston Hall, the home of the

Radcliffes, later the Earls of Derwentwater. The mullioned-and-transomed windows on the w side are of this date: the large windows with plain stone surrounds on the E are from a second remodelling, of 1711–15. After the execution of the last Earl for his part in the 1715 rebellion, and the death of his son a few years later, the estates passed to the Greenwich Hospital Trustees, who demolished the hall but left the tower as a roofless ruin. The basement has some interesting arched loops with circular gun-ports below their sills. Several fireplaces of c 16 type on the upper floors.

CHAPEL. s of the Castle, a rare example of a post-Reformation recusant chapel of the early c 17, still roofed and furnished. It is a small rectangular building still in the Tudor style (several windows of three pointed lights under straight hoodmoulds). Odd stair turret, to a former w gallery, projecting from the w end, which has a fairly conventional bellcote. The E end is raised above a rib-vaulted undercroft. c 18 interior, with panelled pews and balustraded altar rail. In the external E wall, a ROMAN GRAVE-STONE carved in low relief; under an architrave supported by pilasters, the robed but weathered figure of a woman standing beside a stool.

Attached to the E end of the chapel, a length of wall and a classical GATEWAY, with a keyed segmental arch, dated 1616. This seems to have been the main entrance to the Hall courtyard.

Other relics of the Derwentwaters are the EARL'S BRIDGE, 140 metres NW of the Castle, dated by Jervoise to 1621, a graceful elliptical arch rising from w to E and spanning the Devil's Water, and the (reset) early c 18 GATEPIERS at the entrance to the Hall grounds, with bulgy rustication and ball finials. The present DILSTON HALL is a house of 1835, with considerable later alter-ations.

WATERMILL. Although the mill has been converted into a house, its long head-race, which in part is carried through a rock-cut tunnel, leads back to a well-built masonry dam of horseshoe construction, with ashlar flank walls, dated 1808. The dam and head-race were designed by Messrs *Walton and Forster*, then the Receivers (i.e. agents) for the Greenwich Hospital Northern Estates. After powering the waterwheel at the mill, the tail-race was taken across the Devil's Water on an aqueduct to drive another waterwheel for a threshing machine at Dilston Haugh Farm.

PRIVATE BRIDGE. By the mill head-race is a single, segmental-span stone bridge with a narrow roadway over, rising from w to E and leading into Dilston Park. Jervoise dates it to 1621.

BRICK AND TILE WORKS, ½ m. W. The remains of three brick and tile kilns of red-brick construction but with firebrick linings; prob-ably mid-c 19 and possibly built at the instigation of John Grey of Dilston, Receiver to the Greenwich Hospital Northern Estates from 1833 to 1863, a great believer in agricultural improvement and the father of Josephine Butler (*see* Kirknewton).

DINNINGTON

St Matthew. Dedicated in 1886. Paid for by Captain Henry Bell of Woolsington (£3,000), it replaced a church of 1835, which accounts for the large yews in the churchyard. Well-proportioned, in local stone with a Lakeland slate roof. Steep-gabled s nave porch. The w window is set in a chamfered arch which springs from the big w buttresses below a typically Northumbrian gabled w bellcote. Geometric tracery and diamond-stopped drip-moulds. – Reredos. 1882, Perp with painted panels, given by the women of the new diocese for the chapel at Benwell Towers, the Bishop's Palace (see Outer Newcastle West), and transferred here in 1959.

Parish School (now a community club). Dated 1874 on the door lintel; paid for by Matthew Bell. Rock-faced sandstone. It stands beside the church and shares attractive C19 wrought-iron railings on low stone walls.

New Horton Grange Farm, 1¼ m. to the N. A fine planned farm built in the middle of the C19 for Sir Matthew White Ridley. Kelly's *Directory* for 1858 describes it as the most complete and extensive model farm in Northumberland. There are three groups of buildings. The working farm is planned round a courtyard, with granaries and corn-drier at the N end, hemmels at the sides in front of storage sheds and two detached turnip houses. On the s side a low range of pigsties and hen-houses with a central dovecote which has an 1863 datestone. E of these the farmhouse (now a hotel), dated 1864 on the reset lintel. Unpretentious but satisfying, with good plain masonry, a hipped roof and conjoined ashlar chimneys. Behind it the cart and coach sheds, dated 1858.

To the w of the farm ranges, two rows of two-storey, three-bay sandstone cottages with half-glazed doors, sash windows and nice half-hipped gabled dormers breaking the deep eaves of the Welsh slate roofs.

DISSINGTON HALL

3 m. wsw of Ponteland

1794 by *William Newton* for Edward Collingwood. A perfectly plain house of seven bays by five bays and two-and-a-half storeys. The centre of the s front is a full-height canted bay window. The room behind it on the ground floor is octagonal and has a triglyph and metope frieze with achievements of arms. Plenty of classical detail in other rooms and good fireplaces. Imperial staircase with a screen of Ionic columns on the ground floor, Corinthian on the first floor.

Dissington Old Hall, 1 m. se. A walled garden of the early C17 is all that remains of the original manor house. In the garden, two broken C17 statues.

Birney Hill Windmill, 2 m. se. Tapered stone three-storey tower with a tablet inscribed 'Call at the Guide Well Mill on Berney Hill 1727'. It operated until the turn of the present century, after which the machinery was apparently stripped out and sent to Amsterdam, and the tower was converted into a cottage.

PINE DENE FOLLY WINDMILL, $1\frac{1}{2}$ m. SE. Picturesque folly at
South Dissington, the whimsical creation of a Newcastle solicitor
in the 1920s. Built in wood to resemble a smock mill.

BIRNEY HALL, Dissington March, 2 m. SE. Late C 17 or early C 18
(a reset datestone of 1701 with the initials R & M E possibly
referring to the Errington family). Extended and much restored
in 1907. The original building is three bays and two-and-a-half
storeys with mullioned-and-transomed windows, much renewed.
In front of the house, tall rusticated C 18 GATEPIERS with rusticated friezes and ball finials.

0030   DODDINGTON

ST MARY AND ST MICHAEL. The extremely strange thing about
this C 13 church is that it seems to have consisted originally of
nave and chancel, plus a W chamber the width of the nave. The
original chancel has entirely disappeared and was replaced in 1838
by a small new one in the lancet style by *Ignatius Bonomi*. In
1893 *George Reavell* made the new chancel into a baptistry and
converted the W chamber into a chancel. So today nothing seems
odd. That the W chamber was the original chancel seems most
unlikely in the C 13, when orientation was a matter of course
unless there were irresistible reasons against it. What can it have
been? It has original lancets on the S and W. The arch into it is
double-chamfered with octagonal responds and C 13 moulded
capitals. The N aisle has a low arcade with similar arches and
piers. The S porch, much of the N side and the roof were all
rebuilt in 1893. – REREDOS. By *Hems* of Exeter, 1903. – STAINED
GLASS. In a N lancet there is a most distinctive C 20 window by
Nuttgens, showing a cascade of brightly coloured angels. – In the
churchyard a plain WATCH HOUSE of *c.* 1826.

VICARAGE. A good plain classical house of 1835–6. It is rendered
and painted, with very plain and severe pink ashlar dressings.

DODDINGTON BASTLE, or rather stronghouse, for it is of that
distinct group quite separate from the main group of bastles and
towers (cf. Witton Shields Tower and *see* Introduction, p. 64). It
was built in 1584 for Lord Grey and is T-shaped, with the staircase
in the small projecting wing. The door is on the ground floor and
the house was never vaulted. The ground floor indeed has a large
fireplace and seems to have been the kitchen. The house was three
storeys high. The S wall has collapsed, except for the stair tower,
and so no windows have survived. The N wall stands to *c.* 6 metres
(20 ft), the W end to full height with the remains of a parapet in
the SW corner.

FENTON HOUSE, 2 m. NNW. *c.* 1870 by *Thomas Farrer* for Lord
Lambton. Tudor Gothic style, with a high asymmetrically placed
tower. The spire was added later. The stonework has been
painted. On a side elevation there is an elaborate wrought-iron
outside stair and balcony. Contemporary STABLE BLOCK.

FENTON HILL, 1 m. N of Fenton. Excavation of the hillfort SE of the
farm has illustrated the complex history (dated by radiocarbon) of
many such earthworks. The habitable area increased in each of

five successive phases, except the last: (1) a small and unusually early example of a palisade (partly a single, partly a double line) surrounding a farmstead of C 9 B.C.; (2) a larger settlement within a single palisade; (3) a C 5 timber 'box' rampart of earth from an outer ditch, used to fill the spaces between transverse wooden bracing behind a timber face; (4) a second box rampart replaces the first in the late C 3 B.C.; (5) the multivallate fort still visible was subsequently built with three ramparts of dumped earth enclosing a much smaller area.

DOD LAW. The most prominent of many antiquities here is the Iron Age hillfort on the crest beside the Shepherd's House, over-looking the Till. Two ramparts have continuous 'hairpin' ends flanking the E entrance. Excavation showed that the outer rampart, surmounted by a palisade, was built first; it was followed by a massive stone wall, now much robbed, on the inner line. Some time after the C 1 A.D. this collapsed and the outer rampart was refurbished. Circular stone-founded houses of Romano-British type are visible in the interior. An annexe, more lightly defended, extends to the NW.

Rock outcrops just NE of the hillfort bear some very fine CUP-AND-RING MARKS, including unusual rectangular forms which enclose a number of cups.

THE RINGSES, 1 m. E. Strongly defended multivallate hillfort on the crest of a steep W slope. Its three principal ramparts are not concentric, and several structural phases are probably represented. An entrance passage, formed by two transverse banks, runs through the defences on the SE.

ROUGHTING LINN. A steep-sided riverine promontory, with cliffs and a waterfall to the NW, was converted into a large Iron Age fort by an impressive array of five ramparts across its neck; an inturned entrance lies on the NE. It is, however, for its much earlier CUP-AND-RING MARKS that this site is so famous. The sloping face of a large outcrop of Fell Sandstone, immediately to the E, bears a variety of designs: most of the cups are surrounded by a multiple annular or penannular rings, and many have short grooves leading away from them.

The QUARRY for the famous and much-used Doddington red sand-stone is just to the E of the village.

DOTLAND PARK
2½ m. s of Hexham

9060

Former hunting lodge of the Priors of Hexham. The s front was refenestrated in the C 18 but still shows several blocked medieval openings. The W gable has a cinquefoil-headed light with the arms of Prior Smithson (1491–1524) in the spandrels. The same arms appear in the spandrels of two-light windows in the former rear wall, now within a later outshut. Old roof structure of tie-beam trusses with curved principals and collars.

DOTLAND, ½ m. SW. Still a substantial settlement in 1769, reduced to earthworks that mark a row of tofts and crofts parallel to and s of the road between the two modern farms.

1020

DOXFORD

DOXFORD HALL. 1818 by *John Dobson* for Henry Taylor. A nice plain classical house with a five-bay front and a Greek Doric porch *in antis*. The house was enlarged and remodelled in 1910 by *Robert Mauchlen, see* the gateway at the end of the E wing with a Doric screen and a moulded roundel above, flanked by giant panelled pilasters, and also the charming little external stair in the angle of the N and E wings. Mauchlen was also responsible for the formal garden E of the house, beyond the balustraded terrace; this has a tall sundial in the centre in line with a small pond and a pair of piers holding a wrought-iron gate at the far end. The house also has two attractive GATE LODGES of *c.* 1900, each T-plan with a polygonal front end to the cross-wing and an all-round verandah on cast-iron columns.

DOXFORD FARM, ½ m. SW of the Hall. The farmhouse is a plain three-bay villa of the early C 19, with, inside, some marble fire-places brought from the Hall in 1910. More interesting are the unusually extensive and early planned farm buildings, con-temporary with the farmhouse. The centrepiece of the long N range backing the three yards (now covered in) is a T-plan barn, the projecting middle bay holding a large round arch with stepped voussoirs and an impost band; above is a date panel. The rear part of the barn has an attached watermill as a power source for threshing. N of the main group is a contemporary pyramid-roofed DOVECOTE.

2090

DRURIDGE
1½ m. E of Widdrington

At the centre of a wide sandy bay, which at the time of writing is threatened with being the site of a nuclear power station. Picturesque and little altered group comprising C 18 house and barn with reverse-stepped gables and pantile roofs, and early C 19 ranges with segmental arches. Some reused medieval fragments, doubtless from Chibburn Preceptory (q.v.).

9040

DUDDO

ALL SAINTS, ¾ m. NE. 1879 by *F. R. Wilson.* Dec, though the W bellcote and the buttresses which support it are modelled on St Mary, Holy Island. Pretty lead patterns in the windows and a typical fanciful Wilson hammerbeam roof. The VICARAGE is also by *Wilson.*

The former church of ST JAMES, in the village, became part of the school and is now a private house. It was built in 1832 in an effective neo-Norman by *Ignatius Bonomi.*

DUDDO TOWER. No more than one crag of a wall on a hill with rocks outcropping towards the village street. It had a projecting wing with a corbelled-out turret in the angle (cf. Coupland Castle). Late C 16. A predecessor was destroyed in 1496.

DUDDO HOUSE. A large plain classical farmhouse of 1820–30.
STONE CIRCLE, $\frac{3}{4}$ m. NW. Small but impressive circle of five bulky
   and very weathered stones, up to 2.2 metres (7 ft) high. Victorian
   excavations suggested that two further stones on the NW completed the circuit; cremated bones were apparently found in the
   centre.

DUKESFIELD
2 m. w of Slaley

DUKESFIELD HALL. Tall three-bay C18 house, incorporating
   some C17 fabric in the outbuilding range to the E, which has a
   doorway with a broad moulded surround. To the S, the OLD
   GRANARY, a building of c. 1700 with central moulded doorway
   and chamfered windows.
DUKESFIELD MILL, $\frac{1}{4}$ m. N. In the wooded valley of the Devil's
   Water. The only remnant of a once important LEAD SMELTING
   MILL, demolished c. 1836, is a bridge-like structure with two tall
   pointed arches, carrying the flues from the mill to two adjacent
   chimneys.

DUNSTANBURGH CASTLE
1½ m. N of Craster

The gaunt ruins of Dunstanburgh on their dolerite promontory are
   one of the most moving sights of Northumberland. Finds of Iron
   Age and Roman pottery strongly suggest that the site was first
   defended as an Iron Age fort, later overlain by a Romano-British
   settlement. As well as forming a dramatic landscape, the remains
   of the medieval castle are rewarding architecturally, although
   much less survives than at many other castles in the county. Yet
   what there is is pure and not adulterated as at Alnwick, Bamburgh,
   Ford or Lindisfarne. The castle is much later than at first it looks.
   When the English lost Berwick to the Scots after Bannockburn,
   Thomas Earl of Lancaster, who held the castle, seems to have
   decided to build a fortified port here. In 1314 part of the moat
   was dug and the great gatehouse was under construction. The
   master mason was one *Master Elias*. The licence to crenellate
   followed in 1315. After the execution of Earl Thomas in 1322 the
   castle remained in royal hands. The principal buildings seem to
   have been complete by then. Important alterations were made by
   John of Gaunt as Lieutenant of the Scottish Marches in 1380–4.
   The castle is ideally placed. To the N it did not even need walls,
   so sheer are the dolerite cliffs down to the sea. That is how it
   could occupy a larger area than any other in Northumberland, a
   full 4.5 hectares (11 acres). The W and E sides also are by nature
   well protected, and only to the S does a gentler slope make
   stronger fortifications necessary. Yet it is on that side that the
   main living quarters were placed. It is true that the Inner Ward
   which John of Gaunt constructed in the S corner is amply pro-

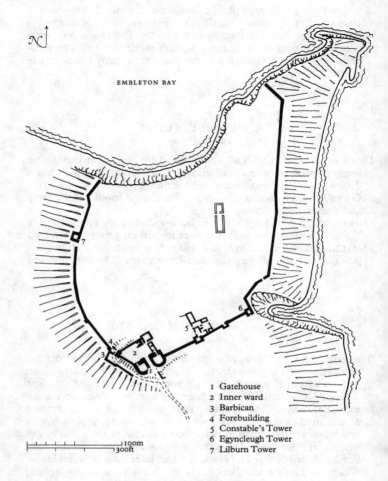

EMBLETON BAY

1 Gatehouse
2 Inner ward
3 Barbican
4 Forebuilding
5 Constable's Tower
6 Egyncleugh Tower
7 Lilburn Tower

100m
300ft

Dunstanburgh Castle. Plan

tected by the gigantic gatehouse which contained the great hall
and principal chambers, yet it remained a fact that the ultimate
defence was the first that would face attackers. This arrangement
was not satisfactory, as John of Gaunt realized, but it is the same
that Edward I's great engineers had used e.g. at Harlech. As at
Harlech – Master Elias certainly looked to Wales for inspiration –
the GATEHOUSE has two flat semicircular towers. There is on the
ground floor one large room in each of them and a small guardroom. An interesting feature of the latter is that the flues of their
fireplaces were carried up to first-floor level and ended in semi-
octagonal caps with holes to let the smoke escape. The gateway
has a tunnel vault with transverse ribs, murder holes and a portcullis slot. The gatehouse was three-storeyed. On the first floor

were rooms of unknown function, with two-light windows, on the second floor lay the hall, with the kitchen at one end (w) and the dais and great chamber at the other. Above the three storeys of the gatehouse the semicircular towers were carried up in two further storeys, still curved at the front but square at the rear. On the inner sides of the once spectacular front elevations of the towers two square stair turrets were continued even higher. One of them stands to full height. There were also newel stairs at the rear corners of the gatehouse; the NE has been restored and shows traces of an umbrella vault, a typical Northumbrian feature (cf. Belsay, Bothal, Warkworth), at its top. At second-floor level the chambers in the towers opened onto the principal apartments by wide segmental arches; one of these survives.

Outside the gatehouse was a barbican, of which only foundations remain. Above these are the foundations of a square FOREBUILDING, which replaced the barbican when John of Gaunt removed the entrance to the castle to the w, converting the former gatehouse into a great tower or donjon. A parallel conversion can be found in Wales, this time at Llansteffan in Carmarthenshire. The entrance of c. 1375–80 was an ingenious piece of fortification, with a mantlet-wall below and parallel to the curtain wall of the castle, and a barbican within which the aggressor had to turn by 90° to reach the new gateway, which opened into the main enclosure just beyond the new Inner Ward; the master mason here was *Henry of Holme*. The INNER WARD is a small trapezoidal enclosure with a projecting square tower at the NE corner protecting an adjacent gateway on the E; it is all much ruined.

The main s curtain runs E from the gatehouse, and stands high. Midway along, beyond a mural garderobe, is the two-storey CONSTABLE'S TOWER with a spiral stair in its NE corner; adjacent was the Constable's House, of which foundations are visible. Further E is a square turret and then, at the SE corner of the castle, the EGYNCLEUGH TOWER. This contained the 'Water Gate' referred to in 1368, and had a drawbridge across the moat with a barbican or turret (shown on a C17 drawing but now vanished) at its outer end. The gate passage has a tunnel vault on heavy square ribs. The two upper floors each have a room with a fireplace and a garderobe. On the w side of the castle the curtain is more fragmentary. The main feature is the LILBURN TOWER, of three storeys with taller angle turrets originally connected by stepped parapets. The SE corner, which contained the stair, has fallen. At first-floor level the E wall contained in its thickness a passage forming part of the curtain wall-walk, into which the two-light E window of the first-floor room opens. Immediately N of the tower is a small postern. The curtain wall on the E is lower and of poor-quality masonry; it contains two posterns and some small mural chambers. Little is known of buildings within the main enclosure. Grassed-over footings near the centre of the E curtain probably represent a large barn mentioned in C15 records. There was also a castle chapel, but its location is now lost.

DUNSTAN HALL
1 m. WNW of Craster

A quite small but very complex house. The lower part of the SW turret, of big whinstone blocks, may pre-date the main block, which seems to be C 14. The E gable of this block has two small lancet windows. There were remodellings in the C 15 (upper part of the E gable and top of the turret) and C 16 or early C 17 (W end of the main block rebuilt and a stair wing added). An early C 18 NW wing, which had fallen into ruins by the early C 20, was rebuilt in 1939, when the house was restored by *H. L. Honeyman* for Mrs Ursula Merz. The four-bay S front of the main block has a chamfered doorway with a worn 1652 (?) date, and a variety of windows, of which the larger ones may be early C 18, with moulded surrounds and cornices; to the l. the turret rears up, its monopitch roof and crowstepped copings the result of an C 18 conversion of the top stage to a dovecote. High on its E wall are what look like the remains of a pendant garderobe. On the W front, the gable end of the main block with a big bolection-moulded first-floor window, with mullioned windows below and above; to the r. is the turret and to the l. Honeyman's wing, which incorporates quoins, dressings and window surrounds from the late C 17 Gloster Hill near Amble. The interior of the house is as varied as the exterior, with an arched vault in the turret (perhaps a later insertion), one good early C 18 panelled room, and more imports from Gloster Hill in three fireplaces and the jointed upper-cruck roof trusses of the 1939 wing. One of the outbuildings is worthy of note: Honeyman's DAIRY (1939) is a charming little square structure with rounded angles, a door in a heavy oak surround and a bell-shaped pantile roof.

DYE HOUSE
3 m. S of Hexham

METHODIST CHAPEL. Dated 1865; still in the Georgian style, with twin round-arched windows in each gable end.

BLACK HALL. C 18 house much altered in the early C 20. BLACK HALL COTTAGE to the N, dated 1725, is an early example of the two-storey three-bay farmhouse type.

EACHWICK HALL
2 m. ESE of Stamfordham

Mainly early C 18, altered to the rear in 1768 and on the W side in the early C 19. The S front is of the early C 18. It is nine bays long. The narrow windows have moulded sills and roll-moulded jambs. The doorway is unusual, with Tuscan pilasters superimposed on taller square cornaced piers with urns on top. On the frieze, an elaborate cartouche bearing a shield. The outer bays are castellated. The W side has a castellated porch with a Gothick window above. Inside, an early C 18 staircase and two panelled rooms with full-height fluted pilasters flanking the fireplaces, and niches with shaped shelves. A third room has similar pilasters, a panelled overmantel and a frieze of triglyphs and metopes.

EARSDON

2 m. w of Whitley Bay

There has been a village here, on the high ground w of the coastal plain, since the Middle Ages. Now on the edge of the Tyneside conurbation, it retains some signs of pre-c 18 origins in its layout along two sides of the E–W street and in one house.

St Alban, Front Street. A dominating church in an elevated position. A chapel was founded here before 1250, but the much-altered medieval building was replaced with the present church of 1836–7 by *John & Benjamin Green*. The lower chancel is said to be of 1889, but this is not apparent. Big w tower with polygonal spirelets between the lower stage and the equally square but recessed upper stage. The bell openings here incidentally are in groups of three stepped lancets. Battlements and pinnacles. Aisleless nave with chamfered buttresses and lancet windows. w gallery on banded quatrefoil columns. Queen-post roof with Gothic struts. – The STAINED GLASS includes some reset pieces given to Earsdon in 1874 by Lord Hastings, who had bought them in 1840 when Willement was restoring Hampton Court Great Hall. Attributed to *Galyon Hone*, Henry VIII's Flemish Master Glazier. *Willement* seems to have repaired and extended the 1531 glass (according to Jill Kerr), but it is not easily assessed through protective glazing and wire mesh. There are the full armorials of Henry VII and Henry VIII: greyhounds, dragons and lions as supporters, each shield of arms with garter, crown and motto; above are the rose and portcullis badges. All in glowing colours. Restored 1958 by *L. C. Evetts*.

Edward Eccles Church Hall, Front Street. 1910–11 by *Wilkinson & Crawley*, the gift of the J. P. whose name it bears. A very satisfying small building in Domestic Revival style. Hammer-dressed sandstone in courses of varying thickness, tall sloping buttresses, octagonal porches, and a roof of graduated Lakeland slate, with tall windows breaking the swept eaves under hipped dormers.

Hartley Disaster Memorial, ne of the church, in the graveyard extension. By *Edward Elliot* of Earsdon, commemorating an infamous disaster which led to improvements in mining practice. An obelisk on a moulded pedestal which is of necessity large, since it has to bear the names of the 204 men and boys who died as a result of the accident in the Hester pit on 16 January 1862.

Front Street still shows signs of age, and not only in the names of Manor House on the N and The Garth on the S. These are of local stone, unsophisticated in treatment; probably c 18 and c 17 respectively, although altered. The Garth has a large flat-Tudor-arched door lintel hidden by a porch. Bleak Hope House, w of The Garth, is also stone but in ashlar and with early c 19 elegance. Two storeys, three bays, with Tuscan porch on the street front and full-height bows in the outer bays on the garden front. To the rear, a stable and carriage shed beside square piers and serpentine walls.

6050

EAST COANWOOD

2½ m. E of Lambley

FRIENDS' MEETING HOUSE. Plain parallelogram, with rusticated quoins and a surround to a doorway dated 1760. Movingly simple interior with stone flagged floor and plain wooden benches.

EAST SHAFTOE HALL *see* CAPHEATON

1000

EDLINGHAM

13 ST JOHN THE BAPTIST. A typically Northumbrian parish church; squat, with a low pyramid-roofed W tower where windows are kept to a bare minimum – not even large bell openings, perhaps a sign of provision against Border raids. The nave may date from just before or just after the Norman Conquest; its SW quoins are inordinately long (they might be reused grave covers). The original W front, now only seen from inside the tower, has a severely simple doorway with massive dressings and a sunk semicircular tympanum; round-headed window above and a circular loop in the gable top. The S door looks C 12; it has a billet hood and a moulded arch on shafts with block capitals, and a smaller C 17 doorway set within it. The very plain but quite broad chancel arch, stepped towards the nave and set on the simplest imposts, is probably of the same date. In the late C 12 the N aisle was added. The low arcade of four bays has round piers with moulded capitals on which vertical bands of nail-head imitate scalloping; there is also nail-head on the bases. The round arches have chamfered inner and square outer orders. The W tower may be *c.* 1300 but is so plain that it is difficult to tell. The three stages are slightly set back. The windows are chamfered square-headed loops, except for a S lancet at the base. Of the C 14 the frame of a window on the S of the nave and a segmental-arched tomb recess. The barrel-vaulted S porch has been claimed as C 12 but looks more likely to be C 17 work; the outer arch has a distinct keystone. The windows of the church have mostly been enlarged to take sashes, but these were replaced (not unsuccessfully) by wooden tracery with C 14 motifs in *Plummer*'s careful restoration of 1902. Only the neo-Norman E window of 1864 is out of character: the window and its contemporary GLASS ('The Sea gave up the Dead which were in it') are a memorial to Lewis-de-Crespigny Buckle, who died at sea on the S. S. *Nemesis* (there is another memorial to him in Bolton Chapel). Across the chancel arch, the base of a stone SCREEN with a central entrance. –

SCULPTURE. In the tomb recess in the nave, part of a pre-Conquest cross shaft with vine scroll, and a C 14 cross slab. A cross slab in the aisle has a primitive slightly cusped cross in bold relief; it may be pre-Conquest. Another slab, now the threshold of the S door, has the unusual emblem of a pair of scissors. – Balustraded ALTAR RAILS of 1726. – Plain octagonal FONT dated 1701. – In the churchyard S of the chancel are the socket stones of two CROSSES; one is a well-cut block of tapering section, and might be pre-Conquest.

G Gatehouse
K Kitchen
H Hall house
S Solar tower

Edlingham Castle. Plan

EDLINGHAM CASTLE. The first edition of this book described Edlingham Castle as 'no more than the ordinary tower-house'. That view has been radically revised since the excavation of the site in 1978–82. That excavation, more than any other, shed light on the development of Northumberland's smaller castles and towers. Before 1978 Edlingham was little more than one ruined tower, admittedly with some surprisingly elaborate detail, and a chaos of grassy mounds. The footings and lower walls now exposed show the complete ground-plan of a small but complex fortified manor or castle, of which the tower was only one part.

The moated enclosure probably dates from the mid-C 13 but the first stone building, an impressive hall house, is thought to have been built *c*. 1295–1300 by Sir William Felton.

This consisted of a block *c*. 24 by 9 metres (80 by 30 ft) externally, with a projecting octagonal turret at each corner (a fragment of the SE turret still stands high). An external stair on the N gave access to the first-floor hall in the centre of the range, which had a central hearth; to the W were service rooms (including a basement kitchen) and to the E the private apartments. In the mid-C 14 these were supplanted by the addition of the tower on the S, a square three-storey structure with diagonal buttresses capped by corbelled-out bartizans, and a projecting stair turret on the N alongside the lobby-cum-bridge giving access from the hall to the lofty first-floor chamber in the tower. This may in fact have had a semi-public function as a kind of subsidiary hall; it has remains of a rib vault springing from corbels with caryatid figures, and a spectacular fireplace with an elaborately joggled lintel. On the N is a recess with a well shaft. The chamber has two levels of windows, the lower with jamb seats. A stone curtain wall and a gatehouse were also built at this time; structural problems seem to have caused the curtain to be rebuilt again at the end of the C 14, enclosing a rather smaller area. Other late medieval alterations include the enlargement of the gatehouse and the building of domestic ranges around the courtyard between hall house and gate.

RAILWAY VIADUCT, NE of the castle ruins, and forming an effective backdrop to them. *c*. 1885.

BIGGES PILLAR, 1½ m. SE. A circular rubble structure, roughly faced, which may be a medieval beacon base.

CORBY'S LETCH BRIDGE, ¾ m. NE of the castle. A stone-built turnpike bridge first constructed *c*. 1755 but now a complex structure through modifications and strengthening. The original was probably a full-centred arch, with later infilling of the arch and added buttresses, presumably to prevent slippage of the abutments and expansion of the haunches. This was followed by a general raising of the upper part of the structure to its present road level. Adopted by the County in 1860.

ABBERWICK. *See* p. 375.

LEMMINGTON HALL. *See* p. 374.

EGLINGHAM

ST MAURICE. Much restored but picturesque; a particularly complicated mix of medieval and post-medieval builds. The aisleless nave and its N chapel are medieval work of uncertain date; Honeyman thought the N wall of the chancel late C 12, but it is now plastered over. The W tower is probably C 13 and has paired lancets to the belfry (as at Ingram), but the present tower arch seems C 19. Thereafter the problems are post-medieval. The church was sacked by the Scots in 1596; this might explain the C 17 rebuilding of the S wall of the chancel (with a four-centred priest's door flanked by windows of three round-arched lights, all with hoodmoulds), the s wall of the nave and probably also the semicircular chancel arch which may incorporate older material. The vestry is dated 1826. Alterations of c. 1837 by *J. Green* included the addition of the broad s transept. The N porch of 1865, a memorial to Archdeacon Coxe, was 'designed under his own eye', as a plaque relates; it is typical of the date. Tower parapet and spire are of 1870; the present E window is early C 20. – FONT. Dated 1663, with octagonal moulded shaft and bowl; simple carved ornament mixed up with a garbled inscription. – MONUMENT. Elaborate and unusually late CROSS SLAB of c. 1530 in the N chapel, with the Ogle arms. – In the churchyard wall to the W of the tower is a reset moulded arch, perhaps a former W door.

OLD VICARAGE, to the s of the churchyard. Large house of c. 1840. Tudor style, with canted bay windows on the s.

The single village street has some pleasant buildings, though none of outstanding interest. The stable range to an older vicarage, alongside the approach to the church, and the POST OFFICE both show C 19 picturesque gothicization of C 18 fabrics, with shouldered arches. Rather earlier Gothick features in MILL HOUSE (a big blind window flanked by quatrefoils in the gable end) and DELPH COTTAGE (a small lodge-like cottage dated 1823). The VILLAGE HALL, with tall arched windows, is an early C 20 conversion of a former mill.

EGLINGHAM HALL. A substantial small country house of some interest. A rainwater head of 1728, admittedly reset, probably dates the main block. This has a seven-bay s front with a recessed three-bay centre. The rusticated quoins, central arched doorway between rusticated pilasters and window architraves with heavy triple keystones betray the influence of Seaton Delaval. Eglingham was built for Robert Ogle; his architect is unknown, although the names of *William Etty* (Vanbrugh's executant architect at Seaton Delaval) and *William Wakefield* have been suggested. The dining room retains a chimneypiece flanked by giant Ionic pilasters; a bedroom above shows a similar arrangement but with giant Doric pilasters. The main stair was remodelled to an imperial form c. 1780, when the Venetian stair window may have been inserted, although its wrought-iron balusters probably date from the 1903 alteration. The W wing incorporates part of an older house; this may be late C 16 or C 17, but shows few datable architectural features apart from a simple fireplace and some C 17–style panelling, both reset. The NE wing, which contains the present entrance, is of 1903 by *Temple Wilson*. To the N is a stable range with a chamfered doorway dated 1704, blocked mullioned windows and three small round windows with cable-moulded surrounds. The arched gateway at the W end is C 18, but the pretty little bellcote on its roof is by Temple Wilson. GATE LODGE. Tudor, dated 1826.

COCKHALL, ½ m. W. Foldyard group of farm buildings, with one gable end gothicized c. 1800 as an eyecatcher.

HAREHOPE HALL, 1½ m. W. Quite a large Tudor-style house of 1846, built as a shooting lodge for the Baker-Cresswell family. Triple-gable s elevation, and on the E a projecting porch with a four-centred arch underneath a canted oriel. Contemporary stable block to the NW.

WEST DITCHBURN, 1½ m. NE. Five-bay house, probably of
1769 (reset datestones in farm buildings), with central doorway in an architrave with pulvinated frieze and cornice, and
windows in plain raised surrounds. A second floor was removed
c. 1965.

OLD SHIPLEY, ⅓ m. E of Shipley Lane. N and E of the cottage and
W of the burn are earthworks of the former village. Mounds mark
the position of three rows of cottages and their garths around a
rectangular green apparently entered from the NW. The present
cottage occupies the W half of the S row. There were eleven
taxpayers in 1296, and still six tenants and four cottagers in 1693;
the site was abandoned in the C 18.

On the moors to the S of Eglingham are a number of late prehistoric
settlements. The most prominent is THE RINGSES, ⅔ m. SW, a
multivallate hillfort with deep defences and a disproportionately
small interior. Later circular stone houses on the NW. A well-
preserved Romano-British rectangular homestead, 400 metres E
of the Ringses, has an E entrance and the stone foundations of
three circular houses at the rear of its modest bivallate enclosure.
Two other homesteads, less regular in plan, lie 200 metres further
E. At the SW end of Hunterheugh Crags, SW of Kimmer Lough,
are two adjacent settlements, one with stone-built round-houses,
the other with radiating enclosure walls. Rock-cut channels are
more modern partly quarried millstones.

₁₀₂₀ # ELLINGHAM

ST MAURICE. 1862, to the designs of the *Rev. J. F. Turner.* Of the
predecessor of this church no more remains than the head of a
lancet in the S transept and a piscina. Crossing-tower with
pyramid roof. Rather bleak large geometrical tracery in the
windows, except the E window, which has three stepped lancets
with black marble shafts inside. – STAINED GLASS. Several interesting windows. The E window looks like C 17 Flemish glass (cf.
Bamburgh Church and Ryton Church, County Durham, two
other churches associated, like St Maurice, with Archdeacon
Thorp). The centre light has a risen Christ and a Christ in majesty
with two sleeping soldiers. The N light has St Luke; S light St
Paul. The windows are very well preserved. The N transept has
excellent glass of 1871 with pictures of the Creation, Hell etc.
The nave S window is especially entertaining; it depicts notable
moments in the history of ecclesiastical building ranging from the
Ark in 2248 B.C. to Ellingham Church itself. – FITTINGS. Good
elaborate brasswork of 1862, including OIL LAMPS on brackets
and a LECTERN with branching candelabra. – MONUMENTS. S
transept: Sir Carnaby Haggerston † 1756, with a garlanded urn in
front of an obelisk. – N transept: Phillis Craster, wife of Edmund
Craster of Preston Tower, † 1813, by *Davies*, with an especially
touching inscription. Winefrid Haggerston † 1815, by *Davies*;
draped urn and obelisk.

OUR LADY OF THE ROSARY (R.C.; the chapel of Ellingham Hall).
c. 1897 by *Dunn, Hansom & Fenwicke.*

ELLINGHAM HALL. Presumably by the same firm and of the same
time as its chapel (*see* above). Big and ordinary in a rather formless
Tudor.

THE OLD VICARAGE, w of the church. Late c 18 and early c 19,
with some Gothick touches. Inside there is an imposing late
c 17 oak staircase brought from Durham in the mid-c 19 by the
incumbent, Archdeacon Thorp. It has a closed string enriched
with festoons and alternately twisted and acanthus-bud balusters.

PRESTON. *See* p. 544.

ELSDON

ST CUTHBERT. On an island site in the middle of the village green.
A church with a complex history; it was once larger than it is. The
buttress in the SW corner is almost certainly the cut-back wall of
an earlier wider aisle, and the two W buttresses are part of the
walls of a demolished tower. The evidence for this is clearer inside,
where there is a blocked tower arch of most odd profile. It may
well be a c 12 arch reset later as a pointed arch. The W responds
of the arcades are also c 12, semicircular, with primitive capitals
and the bases decorated with small knobs. These are the earliest
surviving parts of the church. The two W windows of the aisles
come next. They are early c 13 lancets with shouldered rere-
arches, and therefore they are part of the earlier wider aisles.

The first rebuilding must have occurred in the c 14, when the
arcades, with their octagonal piers, moulded capitals and double-
chamfered arches, were built. The second pier on the S side has
foliage carving in the capital. The arcades are four bays plus the
arch into the transept. The transept piers are square, with unusual
chamfered edges, the stops to the chamfers carved with figures or
tracery. The transept arcades resemble the nave, and this is a
puzzle as there are indications that the transepts were originally
aisleless; in particular there is a c 14 angle buttress embedded in
the N wall of the N transept. The aisles themselves are also
something of a mystery and perhaps the most remarkable thing
about Elsdon. They are very narrow, with thick outer walls (the
windows are c 19) and they have quadrant vaults, an exceedingly
unusual device. The most likely date for such a feature is the c 16
or early c 17 and the most likely reason is defence. The chancel
is c 14. The N wall is blank and the E end a c 19 rebuild, but the
S wall is especially picturesque with a priest's door and three
windows each of different pattern. One has a pointed arch with
reticulated tracery, another, also reticulated, is straight-headed,
while the third, of one light only, has curious blank flowing tracery
in the head. Inside, the plain single-chamfered triple sedilia is also
of the c 14.

The c 18 (*c.* 1720, to be more precise) added the bellcote, the
most conspicuous feature of the church, a heavy square piece with
two tiers of ball finials and a stumpy spirelet. It is splendidly wild
and rustic. The church was restored twice in the c 19, in 1837,
when the S porch was built, and again, by *F. R. Wilson*, in 1877.
He installed the chancel roof and more impressively the clear glass

and leaded glazing of most elaborate patterns. – MONUMENTS.
In the N aisle, two Roman inscriptions: a gabled ROMAN TOMB-
STONE found NE of the fort at High Rochester, erected to a
commanding officer, Rufinus, by his wife Lucilla, daughter of a
senator; also a fragmentary dedication slab from Risingham. –
Several medieval grave slabs, including four in the N transept,
one of them with a defaced figure. – William Brown, 1741. A
painted stone cartouche on a pier of the N arcade.

ELSDON TOWER, to the N of the church, was recorded as a 'vicar's
pele' in 1415 and has always been regarded as a C 14 tower. But
the physical evidence suggests that it was rebuilt in the C 16: the
stonework is large, rough and irregular, not at all what one would
expect in the C 14; moreover the building is of a decidedly Scottish
C 16 type, with a high, solid parapet, slightly corbelled out, and,
behind the parapet, a half-storey cap-house with a steeply pitched
roof. The original entrance, now inside on the N side, is a C 16
form too, round-arched with a roll-moulded surround. It is protected from above by a short stretch of machicolation on four
large corbels. Finally, on the first floor there is a doorway with a
four-centred arch.

At various points on the outer walls there are crests and shields
belonging to families which have been associated with the house –
the Umfravilles (who originally built it), the Percys and the
Howards of Overacre. All of these are likely to be conscious
historicisms of the later C 18. In the NE corner a short mural stair
leads to a very fine ashlar spiral staircase. The ground floor,
vaulted as usual, was prettily stuccoed with thin Gothick ribs by
the Rev. Singleton after 1812. Singleton also added the attached
house, the castellated porch and the lean-to entrance hall which
covers the original doorway. In the hall, another Gothick frieze
of Percy, Lucy and Howard shields. The Gothick decoration in
a room on the first floor and a frieze of hanging arches on the
second floor of the tower are distinctly earlier in character and
were probably done by the Rev. Dutens in the late C 18.

24 ELSDON CASTLE, at the N end of the village, perched high above
the Elsdon Burn. The finest earthwork castle in the county. A
powerful ringwork, with a surrounding ditch, it was carved out of
the tip of a natural spur. The steep descent to the burn made
artificial defences almost superfluous on the W. The bailey, also
bounded by a substantial bank and ditch, lies along the ridge to
the N. Changing needs meant that the castle was not obscured by
later fortifications. It was presumably built by Robert de Umfraville to guard his Liberty of Redesdale, granted early in the C 12.
The castle would have been of timber, but two fragments of a
Roman dedication slab to the god Matunus, found here c. 1715,
could suggest some limited rebuilding in stone by the mid-C 12.
The defences were probably dismantled and abandoned shortly
after 1157, when Henry II regained Northumberland. The passage
across the Border through Upper Coquetdale was thereafter controlled by the new Umfraville stronghold at Harbottle.

The large village green is surrounded by diverse but harmonious
one- and two-storey C 18, C 19 and C 20 houses and cottages,
some of them unusually ambitious, e.g. the former inn, THE
BACCHUS, early C 18 to the r., with a statue of Bacchus on a

barrel over the door; later c 18 to the l., with a Venetian window on the first floor. THE CROWN, another former inn, is dated 1729.

WHITLEES BASTLE, 1 m. ESE. At first sight this looks like a bastle that has lost most of its upper floor. The walls are of huge, rough stones; there is a blocked doorway on the gable end and a small square window with a chamfered surround and a grille of iron bars, but the window is at ground-floor level and there is a smaller blocked window above, implying that this was a ground-floor house with a low first floor.

Other BASTLE REMAINS near Elsdon include fragmentary but unmistakable masonry in the walls of TOWNFOOT at the s end of the village, and more substantial remains standing to c. 1.5 metres (5 ft) among sheepfolds at BOWERSHIELD, 1 m. N.

WINTER'S GIBBET, 2½ m. SE, on the fine summit of the old drove road. The gibbet is a modern replica of the one on which the body of the murderer William Winter was hung in chains in 1791 (within sight of his crime at Raw; *see* Hepple). The medieval cross base known as STENG CROSS lies beside the gibbet.

At Tod Crag, 1¼ m. SE of Winter's Gibbet, a fine prehistoric CUP-AND-RING marked rock on the edge of the forest. A single design (one cup surrounded by two rings) is repeated six times in a broad arc over the level rock surface.

MANSIDE CROSS, on a summit deep in Harwood Forest, 3 m. ESE. A sub-rectangular double-ditched fort, probably of Iron Age date, with a counterscarp bank. Excavation revealed that the low ramparts had been revetted with stone walls, and that the interior contained Romano-British round stone-founded houses. A timber palisade ran parallel with and between the two ditches. Outside the NE corner, the stump and base of the eponymous CROSS.

TOLLHOUSE, ½ m. W. A single-storey stone-built cottage standing at the junction of a drover's route and the turnpike of 1752; much altered and extended.

OTTERCOPS. *See* p. 538.

ELSWICK *see* NEWCASTLE UPON TYNE

ELTRINGHAM

1 m. w of Prudhoe

0060

At CHERRYBURN, Thomas Bewick was born in 1753; the farm is now a museum devoted to his life and work. The farmhouse is later than Bewick's time, but the white-painted farm buildings incorporate the engraver's birthplace.

ELTRINGHAM HOUSE, 200 metres N. From the front, just a neat three-bay ashlar house of c. 1800, with a pedimented doorcase and windows within architrave surrounds. However, the walls are 1.4 metres (4½ ft) thick, and on the w gable end, visible from outside, there are two blocked doorways, one on the ground floor and the other almost directly above it. So the house started life as a bastle, a large one – 14.9 by 7.1 metres (49 by 23 ft) externally – and the closest so far recorded to Newcastle. Blocked windows in the E gable show it to have had three storeys.

ELYHAUGH
1090

1¾ m. SE of Longframlington

ELYHAUGH FARM HOUSE. 1732. Two-storey five-bay house almost identical with the early C 18 front of Acton Hall (q.v.). Bolection-moulded doorway, the mouldings carried up over a semicircular lintel panel with the arms of the Lisle and the date. Above is a cornice on console brackets and above that one of the detached segmental bands that fulfil the function of pediments for the ground-floor openings.

EMBLETON
2020

HOLY TRINITY. That the church has a varied building history is clear externally, but as usual the earlier stages are only visible within. The W tower is quite tall; its early C 14 upper parts are of squared stone, and have two-light belfry openings with transoms and trefoiled heads and, a rarity in the North, a pierced openwork parapet with trefoil-headed panels and small pinnacles. The S porch is also later medieval (perhaps as late as the early C 16), with its four-centred arch beneath a tall niche, and a flat roof. Much of the remainder looks C 19: the aisle W bays (1850 by *John Dobson*), all the aisle and clerestory windows, and the bold chancel of 1867 by *F. R. Wilson*, with its Geometrical tracery, gabled buttresses and steep roof with alternating bands of purple and green slate. The interior is both rewarding and informative. The base of the tower has a pointed barrel vault on three chamfered ribs, but these cut the rere-arches of blocked early Norman windows. The three-bay nave arcades are early C 13, with octagonal piers, moulded capitals and double-chamfered arches. The E responds are corbels with upright stiff-leaf foliage, the leaf-tips hanging down. The arch chamfers have stops which are either broaches or single big dogtooth (cf. Whittingham), whilst the hoodmoulds have big nutmeg decoration, with stops that are heads on the N and disks with crosses on the S; some of these details look either C 19 or recut, however. The E wall of the S aisle shows head corbels and a rebated aumbry, and the E window of the N aisle is flanked by C 14 niches and piscinae; again there seems to have been some C 19 interference. On the N of the N aisle a double-chamfered segmental-pointed arch opens into the small Craster Chapel. Both aisles have plain late medieval roofs. The chancel arch is C 19 on C 13 corbels, but the wall above is old and shows the weathering of the steep C 13 nave roof, and a large blocked window probably coeval with the previous chancel of *c.* 1800. The 1867 chancel internally has bands of pink and yellow stone, and an elaborate collar-beam roof. – MONUMENTS. Several medieval CROSS SLABS in the S porch and another, along with a miscellany of architectural fragments, in the vestry. – Wall tablets of 1696, 1718 and 1810 reset at the W end of the S aisle. – Wall tablets to the Grey family of Fallodon in the N aisle. – STAINED GLASS. Chancel glass by *Kempe*, 1884: quite striking, especially the E window, with Northumbrian saints.

UNITED REFORMED CHURCH (formerly Presbyterian). 1833, with the usual disposition of doorways and windows (cf. Branton and Glanton), which are here pointed and not, as usual, round-arched. The interior was redone *c.* 1920.

OLD VICARAGE, adjacent to the W wall of the churchyard. Often cited as a 'vicar's pele' (cf. Corbridge), but the oddly elongated tower which forms the E wing of the present building may have begun as a more conventional house (or perhaps a cross wing to a larger building) in the early C14 before being remodelled as a tower late in the century. Its basement has two chambers with segmental vaults at r. angles to the axis of the tower. Apart from one or two loops, the oldest windows to survive are the mullioned ones on the E. Corbelled-out embattled parapet, with gabled cap-house in the Scottish tradition. By the C18, if not earlier, the tower was once again reduced to being a wing of a larger house. This was largely rebuilt in 1828 by *John Dobson* in his castellated Tudor style, using local whinstone. Attached to his W wing is a contemporary CONSERVATORY, an elongated octagon in plan, with a swept hipped roof. Dobson's interiors are well-preserved with good cornices and Gothick fireplaces; this is one of his smaller houses but among the most attractive. 90 metres to the N is a C18 DOVECOTE, brick and quite large, with a pantiled pyramid roof.

Embleton village is huddled in the lee of the whinstone bluff which provided much of its building material. The broad Front Street beside the United Reformed Church provides a centre of sorts; here is a PANT of 1911 by *George Reavell*, with an older pump alongside. The journalist W. T. Stead was born in 1849 in the OLD MANSE (early C19) alongside. The MOOT HALL on Station Road may incorporate medieval or C16 masonry, but its visible features are C17 (mullioned windows in the rear wing etc.) and later. SYCAMORE COTTAGES, E of the Creighton Memorial Hall (SE of the parish church), are a pair of 1927 prefabs, with cavity walls of reinforced concrete. They were shown in the North East Coast Exhibition of that year on Newcastle Town Moor. Finally, at the S end of the village and occupying almost all the back garden of No. 4 Sunny Brae is another DOVECOTE: circular, of sandstone rubble, with a convex profile. It can hardly be later than the C17, and might even be medieval.

CHRISTON BANK. *See* p. 233.
FALLODON HALL. *See* p. 275.

ERRINGTON

2 m. E of Chollerton

ERRINGTON FARMHOUSE. Dated 1704 on sundial, but incorporating C 17 parts. Five-plus-one bays. The main part has a central doorway with an open curly pediment, and windows in raised surrounds. Older thick-walled single-storey range at rear.

ESHOTT

ESHOTT HALL. Five-bay two-storey front block perhaps by *Robert Trollope*, *c.* 1660, but much recast *c.* 1850 and in 1881. Curly open pediments to the windows (the central first-floor window is a C 19 insertion). The present porch is of *c.* 1850, of the same period as the sumptuous plasterwork in the drawing room, done in the style of 1750 by the Italian *stuccatori* who worked at Alnwick Castle (and also at Newton-on-the-Moor) at this time. The older central block which lay behind was demolished in the early 1960s, but the 1881 N wing, copying the style of that on the S, was retained as a separate house.

ESHOTT HAUGH, 1 m. W of the Hall. Here the original front door of the Hall has been reused. The bolection-moulded architrave is reset in a farmbuilding, but the flanking Ionic columns, with spiral foliage patterns carrying a moulded cornice with urns, form an unlikely frame for the front door of the C 19 Gothic farmhouse.

ESHOTT CASTLE, ½ m. N. In low-lying ground, the E and S sides of the castle moat with traces of a curtain wall and angle towers. Roger de Mauduit received licence to crenellate it in 1310; it was held by Sir John Heroun in 1415.

ESLINGTON PARK

1½ m. W of Whittingham

A large stone mansion of the C 18, the main parts of 1715–20 for Sir Henry Liddell, Bart. Nine by nine bays and two storeys. Very simple but very dignified. Windows with moulded surrounds, eaves cornice and parapet. The S side has a Tuscan porch with metope frieze. On the E side, angle bays slightly broken forward and quoined, and in the middle an Ionic porch with a pulvinated frieze. In 1797 an addition was made to the W end of the S front. This work was done for Henry George Liddell. It is three bays long, slightly lower and has a parapet pierced like a honeycomb. The entrance hall has at the back a screen of two Corinthian columns. Behind this, the principal staircase, with a fine coved and stuccoed ceiling. The plasterwork is a mid-C 20 facsimile of the damaged original. On the first floor the staircase landing is again provided with a screen of Corinthian columns. A handsome Venetian opening leads on to the corridor. The staircase itself is C 19, with simple square-section balusters. A back staircase has the original balusters, one columnar and one twisted to each tread.

STABLES and OFFICES attached to the W of the house. 1858, for
the first Baron Ravensworth. At about the same time he provided
all the gates, walls, bridges and fences which form the architectural
approaches to the house.

LADY'S BRIDGE, $\frac{1}{4}$ m. E. A small early C 18 hump-backed bridge,
picturesque in its setting; the subject of a famous woodcut by
Thomas Bewick.

ETAL

ST MARY THE VIRGIN. 1858 by *Butterfield* for Lady Fitzclarence,
in memory of her husband, who had died in India in 1854. Built
in the grounds of Etal Manor, just W of the house. Not an
outstanding work of the architect. Nave and chancel under excessively steep roofs, steep bellcote at their junction, and S chapel
under exceedingly steep roof of its own. Pink sandstone with
bands of buff. Windows in the Dec style. Scissor-brace roof in
the chancel, the beams painted with stars and rosettes. The S
chapel is separated from the chancel by a two-bay stone screen
with oversized Dec tracery. In the chapel, the MONUMENT to
Lord Frederick Fitzclarence is a plain slab with a foliated cross
and a sword and may well have been designed by *Butterfield* too.

ETAL MANOR. Quiet, restrained Georgian house built for William
Carr in 1748 and enlarged for him in 1767. Pink sandstone. Seven
by seven bays, two storeys, no pediment and only a plain triangular
pediment to the doorway and another to the centre window on
the side façade. The original house was L-plan. The work of 1767
filled in the angle between the two wings. In 1888 the house was
extended to the rear for James Laing in a style very similar to the
original buildings.

From the Manor to the Castle runs the village street, one of the
prettiest in the county. Some of the cottages are thatched, as so
many were throughout this area of Northumberland until the
beginning of the C 20; others are roofed in big rough stone slates.
Almost all are white painted. They owe their appearance to Lord
Joicey, who rebuilt most of them after he bought the estate in
1907.

ETAL CASTLE. Licence to crenellate granted to Robert Manners
in 1342. The remains are not generous, yet of great interest: SE
gatehouse, NW Great Tower, a smaller SW tower and some curtain
wall. The GREAT TOWER is 14.1 by 9.8 metres (46 by 32 ft) in
size and four storeys high. It seems, however, that it pre-dated
the licence to crenellate and was originally a three-storey hall
house of the C 13 or earlier C 14; its top floor is clearly an addition,
of yellowish as opposed to reddish sandstone. There is a patch
low down on the S side where the original entrance might have
been. The present forebuilding or stair turret on the E is all of the
later yellowish sandstone. The entrance was on the ground floor
and led to a tunnel-vaulted room with seven chamfered transverse
arches. The springing survives. Large segmental-arched fireplaces
on the first and second floors and, on each floor, a two-light
transomed window with cusped heads to the lights. The GATE-

HOUSE was tunnel-vaulted also, with triple-chamfered transverse
arches. Again only the springing remains. Guardrooms l. and r.
also tunnel-vaulted and also with transverse ribs. Straight staircase
in the N wall, again with transverse arches. Dec two-light windows
and fireplace on the first floor. From here a spiral stair led up to
the second floor. It lies in one of the two square projecting towers
flanking the gateway. In the other is the camera. Disturbances to
the stonework on the front of the gatehouse seem to suggest some
sort of timber forework and gallery rather than the stone barbican
which has been postulated. In particular, on the inner faces of the
turrets there are four big drawbar tunnels with corresponding
sockets on the wall opposite. High up on the N turret there is also
a doorway. The curtain wall survives relatively intact on the S side
and there are more fragmentary remains attached to the Great
Tower, but it does not look original; where it comes off the Great
Tower, in an odd place just short of the W end of the S wall, it
looks an addition; and there is no sign of any curtain wall joining
the N side of the gatehouse. Was it added late, only to disappear
completely, or did the castle make do with a stockade instead?
Only the ground floor of the small square SW TOWER survives; it
is plainly tunnel-vaulted. Attached to its W side is the former
PRESBYTERIAN CHAPEL and MANSE. The manse is mid-C 18.
The chapel was rebuilt in 1800. It is of four bays, with tall arched
windows in the centre two bays.

EVISTONES see HORSLEY

9030

EWART PARK
2 m. E of Coupland Castle

An irregular castellated Gothick house of 1787–90. Designed for
himself by *Count Horace St Paul*. The centre of the entrance side
and the most striking feature of the house is a circular tower
inspired by those St Paul saw being built at the nearby Twizel
Castle. W wing added in 1870. The house is empty and partly
derelict at the time of writing. LODGES of 1794.

THIRLINGS, I m. NW. Late C 18 or early C 19, extended and given
its Italianate detail *c.* 1860–70. The main block is of five by three
bays and has a hipped roof with widely projecting eaves and many
stone brackets. It is rendered with ashlar quoins and surrounds.
The later wing is brick and seven bays long.

EWART BRIDGE, over the River Till. 1799. Brick; one broad segmental arch and fifteen low flood arches. The bricks for this bridge
were made in the adjacent KILNS. The Ewart clay was considered
the best in the county. It is a particularly warm red when fired
(*see* Introduction, p. 80).

FALLODON HALL
1¾ m. NW of Embleton

Early C 18 brick house of seven bays, the centre of the W front set
forward with an arched doorway between plain columns carrying
a metope frieze; the windows all have segmental heads with triple
keystones (cf. Acomb House). The house was built *c.* 1730 for
Thomas Wood; after his death in 1755 it passed to the Grey family,
who were prominent in national politics in the C 19 and early
C 20. The bow at the centre of the three-bay S elevation is clearly
a later addition, perhaps of 1796 (rainwater heads). *John Dobson*
worked here in 1815 and may have been responsible for the pink
sandstone E wing. The kitchen wing to the N, refronted in C 18
brick, incorporates something of a previous C 17 house belonging
to the Salkeld family. The main block was completely remodelled
internally, and a second floor removed, by *George Reavell* in 1924,
after a serious fire; he added the present entrance lobby and porch.

The STABLE BLOCK is of pink sandstone, like the E wing, and
may be part of Dobson's work. NE of the house is the WALLED
GARDEN; Samuel Salkeld was a noted horticulturalist in the late
C 17, and some of the masonry of the walls, especially at the N
corner, may be his. This section has a furnace and heating ducts,
and thus may be a very early example of a heated garden wall.
The EAST LODGE is dated 1849. The nearby private railway
station (built to serve the Hall) has been demolished.

FALSTONE

ST PETER. Badly damaged by a fire in 1891. The interior, the porch
and the window tracery all belong to the restoration done then by
Plummer & Burrell. The rest is clearly original, and that means of
1824–5, by *John & Benjamin Green*, who, following a public
subscription, built a church almost entirely modelled on H. H.
Seward's churches at Wark, Greystead etc. – MONUMENTS. In
the churchyard, a number of early C 18 GRAVESTONES with rustic
but very animated carvings on them. One has a little girl holding 73
hands with a skeleton.

UNITED REFORMED CHURCH (formerly Presbyterian). 1807;
restored and the small W tower with its pyramid roof added in
1876. Four bays. The two central round-headed windows are
original, the outer ones of 1876.

FALSTONE FARM, S of the church. The house incorporates a
bastle. The lintel of the ground-floor doorway, now inside the C 18
extension, is dated 1604 and carved with an inscription which,
though hard to decipher, appears to be no more than the first ten
letters of the alphabet, minus the I. The ground floor has a high
round tunnel vault, partly removed at the E end to make way for
a mid-C 18 staircase; evidence at attic level suggests that there was
an original internal stair (cf. Woodhouses Bastle, Holystone).

JUBILEE DRINKING FOUNTAIN. 1897. Cast-iron and quite elaborate.

FALSTONE BRIDGE. 1843 by *Henry Welch*, Engineer. Part of the toll road to Scotland surveyed by *Telford* and paid for by Sir John Swinburne (*see* Kielder). Three broad segmental arches with bold voussoirs.

HAWKHOPE, ½m. NW, and RIDGE END, 1 m. S, are two very well-preserved bastles still in use as houses. Neither is vaulted. Ridge End is particularly interesting, with such features as original doorways with roll-moulded surround. It was given larger windows in the later C 17.

A rectangular earthwork at SMALESMOUTH, 1½m. SSE, has two banks, a medial ditch and perhaps two entrances. Date unknown: plausibly Iron Age. It encloses the slighter remains of a smaller settlement of later Iron Age or Romano-British type.

FARNE ISLANDS

2030

The most easterly outcrop of the Great Whin Sill. There are between fifteen and twenty-eight islands, depending on the state of the tide. The largest is Inner Farne. The view of it from the mainland is dramatic, and the view from it, looking over its dolerite cliffs towards the other islands or towards Bamburgh, is superb. Only three of the islands, Inner Farne, Longstone and Brownsman, are of architectural interest.

INNER FARNE

It is recorded by Bede that St Aidan occasionally retired to Inner Farne for solitude. St Cuthbert built himself a cell on the island and died there in 687. Later hermits followed him, and in 1246 a small Benedictine cell was established from Durham, probably on the same site as Cuthbert's original settlement. The remains are all of the monastic period, and they form an intensely romantic group in this wonderful place.

ST CUTHBERT'S CHURCH is no more than a chapel, without any structural division between the nave and the chancel. It was built *c*. 1370, though the lower part of the N wall has C 12 or C 13 masonry. It was restored by Archdeacon Thorp, who bought the islands in 1861. Ogee-headed doorway, renewed by Thorp. Only one original window (the others are renewed): it has simple decorated tracery. At the W end are the ruins of a small room, possibly a galilee. Apart from the setting, the most interesting thing about the church is that the Archdeacon brought part of the FURNISHINGS of Durham Cathedral here. They were made under Bishop Cosin, probably *c*. 1665, and are examples of his remarkable brand of Gothic Revival. In the STALLS no more than the cherubs' heads are Baroque; the rest is Gothic, with a mixture of round-headed cusped arches and crocketed pinnacles. The SCREEN has balusters and garlands and less of the Gothic. In the chancel there are also two seats with misericords. – MONUMENT. Erected by Thorp to Grace Darling. The inscription by Wordsworth begins 'Pious and pure, modest and yet so brave ...'.

Originally, and most unusually, St Cuthbert's was balanced by another church, St Mary's, across the court to the s, but only its base course remains, now part of the National Trust information centre. It seems to have been contemporary with St Cuthbert's, but whether it acted as a pilgrimage chapel, or whether its existence reflects the tendency of Celtic monasteries to have more than one church is not known. In the court between the two buildings there is a C 15 FONT with concave sides; also a large medieval stone COFFIN and three CROSS SLABS.

PRIOR CASTELL'S TOWER, to the w of the church, was erected (according to Leland) by the prior c. 1500; but it appears to incorporate some earlier work, notably the small lancet windows on the stairs and the trefoiled piscina in the former chapel on the first floor. It is an oblong tower of rough masonry and has no projections. Stair turret on the sw corner. Round-headed doorway on the e side; on the w three Gothick windows. The ground floor has a steeply pointed tunnel vault. Mural stair to the first floor given, in the early C 18, a handrail and splat balusters. On the first floor, apart from the piscina, there is a garderobe and two segmental-arched C 18 fireplaces, one of them incorporating some older stonework. The original room has been divided into two by a screen of mid-C 18 panelling with two cupboards.

A fragment of the GUEST HOUSE of the Benedictine cell, built c. 1360, lies to the l. of the path from the landing place to the church and tower.

LIGHTHOUSE. 1809 by *David Alexander*, for Trinity House, Newcastle. White-painted and extremely pretty.

LONGSTONE

LONGSTONE LIGHTHOUSE. 1826 by *David Alexander*, for Trinity House, Newcastle. Enlarged later in the C 19 by *Joseph Nelson*. The lighthouse is painted red and white and looks splendid on its bare rock. It was the home of the Darling family at the time of the renowned rescue.

BROWNSMAN

BEACON. Erected in the late C 18 after a similar beacon on Staple Island had been destroyed by fire in 1783. It is square and c. 7.5 metres (25 ft) high. Attached to it is a cottage and the stump of a round lighthouse erected in 1810 but later abandoned in favour of the Longstone.

FARNLEY

1 m. SE of Corbridge

FARNLEY FARM. C 18 farmhouse altered in the later C 19. Behind it, a good group of early C 19 planned farm buildings, including a gingang and (until recently) an ingeniously designed pair of pigsties with a dovecote above: access to the dovecote door is by a raised walkway dividing the pigs' exercise yards. Sadly the whole complex has been converted into twee neo-Georgian homes; statutory protection has failed to protect this and other good groups of farm buildings in Tynedale.

FARNLEY GATE HOUSE. 1777. A former toll cottage on the Gateshead to Hexham Turnpike. A small single-storey cottage of rubble masonry but with cut quoins and dressings: slated hipped roof with central stack. The roadside façade has a central door flanked by sash windows, and there is a sashed viewing window in each end, offset towards the roadside.

FARNLEY SCAR TUNNEL. 1834. One of two tunnels on the Newcastle–Carlisle line, and 155 metres (170 yds) long. Although bypassed by a later open cutting, the tunnel alongside remains intact. Of the two portals the W is the more elaborate, with a rusticated arch.

6060   FEATHERSTONE CASTLE

Beautifully situated in large grounds in the wooded valley of the South Tyne, Featherstone is a castle which, even allowing for the fact that much of the fabric is early C 19, does full justice to its situation. A drawing of c. 1770 shows the castle as consisting of ranges around a rectangular courtyard (except at the SE corner, where there was an embattled wall with a gateway facing E), with a single large SW tower. The courtyard plan survives, and with it the old tower and W range. The range incorporates the remains of an early C 13 house, perhaps a ground-floor hall; the principal survival of this is a doorway at the E end of a passage opening into the courtyard, with colonnettes and a deeply moulded arch. At the NW corner of the range is a C 13 stepped buttress of exactly the same distinctive type as those at Haltwhistle Church (q. v.). Two windows, each of two lights with transoms and cusped trefoil heads, may have been reset from the tower. The tower itself seems to be a C 14 addition and is a substantial L-plan structure of four storeys, with rectangular projections at the W corners (the NW containing a newel stair, the upper parts of which survive) and one set diagonally at the NE corner. The two basement chambers have low elliptical barrel vaults, but otherwise the interior is much altered. The embattled parapet is carried on corbels, some carved; the projections at the N corners are carried up as turrets, and the projecting part of the S front has corner bartizans. The buildings around the courtyard were remodelled in the C 17; from this phase survive the W doorway of the passage in the W wing, with its flattened ogee head (cf. Bellister Castle) and several mullioned windows. Then came the Hon. Thomas Wallace, who in the 1820s raised the N end of the W range into a tower, and built new ranges on the other three sides of the courtyard, with towers at the NE and SE corners as well; he also built a new porch onto the W side of the C 14 tower and placed a big semicircular bow at the centre of the new S front. All this is in a castellated style, with embattled parapets and mullioned-and-transomed windows with cusped or arched heads to the lights. Wallace also girdled the castle and its gardens with an outer wall with turrets and gateways, and built a mausoleum-cum-chapel just inside the E wall for his wife, Lady Jane Hope, † 1828. Time has mellowed Wallace's work. The outer walls are ivied and the mausoleum in ruins; the overall effect is as romantic as the C 19 could have desired. The NW gateway, with its four-centred arches, heraldic panel and embattled parapet with a bartizan, is delightful.

FEATHERSTONE BRIDGE, ½ m. N. c. 1775. Ashlar; a single wide segmental arch.

WYDON EALS, ½ m. NW of Featherstone Bridge, on the w bank of the South Tyne. Three-bay farmhouse dated 1759, with rusticated door surround, raised window surrounds and quoins. Good FARM BUILDING group around a yard at the rear.

FELTON

ST MICHAEL. A happy puzzle for the antiquarian and an impressive, if a little incongruous, sight for the layman: C 19 high-pitched chancel roof; the other roofs so low that nave and S aisle look as if they were roofless. The heavy and robust bellcote, with plain square-headed openings (two on E and W, one on N and S) and a pyramid roof of stone, is C 16 or C 17 and coeval with the present nave roof; the broad projection on which it rests, containing a truncated newel stair, is the lower part of a small W tower or bell turret of C 12 or early C 13 date. It is inside the church that the real puzzles begin. Generally speaking, the interior strikes one as low and cut up, owing to the many vicissitudes in the building history of the church. The S arcade especially is baffling in many ways. The solution of its problems may be as follows: the second arch from the W is in fact the c. 1200 S door of an aisleless nave, its inner order cut away. Its outer order is still carried on colonnettes. The tall round-headed rere-arch of the door and a blocked round-headed window faintly visible above it may point to a C 12 origin. This doorway had a rib-vaulted porch attached in the later C 13; the innermost rib remains above the doorway, and the outermost now forms the rere-arch of the present S door into the aisle. The remains of the diagonal buttresses belonging to this porch are clearly visible externally. The W arch of the arcade is double-chamfered, on semicircular responds; presumably this opened into a SW chapel, or perhaps the base of a tower, of the same date as the porch. The chancel is basically early C 13 as well; the double-chamfered chancel arch springs from semicircular responds with moulded capitals, and on the S are three restored lancets. In the C 14 (a chantry was endowed in 1331), aisles were added to the nave, that on the S incorporating parts of the earlier porch and chapel. The C 14 arcades have octagonal piers, moulded capitals and double-chamfered arches; that on the N is all of a piece except for the semicircular E respond, which could be a reused piece or might indicate a C 13 N transept. The five-light E window of the S aisle has Geometrical tracery, with a central circle no longer foiled but of an eight-petalled flower or rose-window pattern: remarkably, all this is cut from a single stone. The present porch, rib-vaulted like its predecessor, is of *c.* 1400. The known post-medieval alterations are best chronicled briefly: N aisle extended *c.* 1845, vestry and w windows 1870, E end rebuilt 1884, N aisle extension partly rebuilt *c.* 1900. – MONUMENTS. In the N aisle, fragment of a C 14 low-relief effigy of a priest. – James Muncaster † 1797, with elegant urn in shallow relief, by *Fisher* of York. – Robert Lisle † 1800, with draped urn, by *T. King* of Bath. – Alexander Davison † 1829, elaborate Gothic canopied niche.

Felton village stands on the N bank of the Coquet, which the old Great North Road crosses by OLD FELTON BRIDGE, probably C 15, with three ribbed arches and triangular cutwaters carried up as pedestrian refuges. Close to the bridge and looking s across the river is No. 6 RIVERSIDE, still of great interest despite a 1960s 'restoration'. It is a long-house, divided by a stone-walled cross passage near the E end. The passage has flat-pointed doorways at each end and internally, opening from the passage into the house proper. The unheated room E of the passage served in the C 18 and C 19 as a distillery for an adjacent public house. The house proper was entered from the passage by a lobby between a big fireplace under a bressumer beam and a small newel stair recessed into the N wall. The date is probably early C 17. Nos. 10–16 RIVERSIDE are an attractive two-storey terrace of *c.* 1800. Of the same date the pretty little bridge at the w end of Riverside, flanked by pilasters with arched niches, and the adjacent PARK LODGE (a former gate lodge to Felton Park) of the same date, with a canted front bay and a pyramid roof. A short distance NW, on the Swarland road, the remains of an interesting mid-C 19 rural GASWORKS (Gasworks Farm); the retort house has round-headed iron-framed windows and an all-iron roof structure.

FELTON MILL. With its Victorian mill house, some mill cottages, a stable block and a small stone house, this forms a splendid complex of buildings on a site possibly dating back to the C 13. It was one of the finest and largest watermills in Northumberland and the last in the county to operate. It was converted to domestic accommodation in the late 1980s.

A wide horseshoe WEIR, rather similar to Smeaton's at the former ironworks at Guyzance (q.v.), is just up-river and supplied water to the head-race, whose masonry embankment projects well beyond the weir itself, terminating in a bank of three steel sluices. A large fish-pass is located at the head-race side of the weir. The head-race is nearly 0.4 km. ($\frac{1}{4}$ mile) long and rock-cut for much of the way. It forms a channel *c.* 3 metres (10 ft) square and leads to the mill, which had three waterwheels. The MILL, of a mellow sandstone and with hipped roofs of blue slates, lies on a sloping site. It is of two distinct periods. The earliest, three-storey part, possibly an C 18 rebuild, lies across the head-race and, though used latterly as a sawmill, it may have been used as a corn mill and a malting floor earlier. Adjoining this wing is the later, four-storey main block, L-shaped, with one bay parallel to the head-race and the other crossing it. The tail-race passed beneath it and was discharged to the river through a rock-cut tunnel. The wing immediately downstream housed a square high (drying) kiln and a low kiln for the manufacture of 'crowdie'.

FELTON PARK. A large house of 1732, probably by *Canston*, remod-

elled in 1799 and mostly pulled down in 1951. The surviving part
is the E (kitchen) wing, consisting of a plain 1799 front block and
an L-plan range of 1732 to the rear, with rusticated quoins and
windows in moulded surrounds. Long and tall C18 GARDEN
WALL to the E; attached to it, a well-preserved GREENHOUSE of
c. 1830 with a curved pent roof and fishscale glazing. W of the
house, and formerly linked to the demolished W wing, is the
CHURCH OF ST MARY (R.C.), 1857 by *Gilbert Blount*. Rock-
faced, with a small SW tower and needle spire; free Dec style with
lots of carved detail. – MONUMENT. Brass to Thomas Riddell of
Felton Park, 'the Founder of this Church', † 1870. Foliate cross
with Virgin and Child in the head, and at the foot Thomas Riddell
holding a model of the church.

ACTON. *See* p. 124.
BOCKENFIELD. *See* p. 195.

FENHAM *see* NEWCASTLE UPON TYNE

FENTON *see* DODDINGTON

FENWICK

1½ m. WNW of Matfen

FENWICK TOWER. Crenellated in 1378. One wall of the tower, *c.* 3
metres (10 ft) thick and *c.* 6 metres (20 ft) high, survives attached
to farm buildings. Beside this, on the rear gable of the farmhouse,
is more medieval masonry, including the springing of the ground-
floor vault. The house has a façade of the early C19 but is in parts
much older. The r. half of the façade has old thick stonework and
window jambs with sections of double-chamfered surround. The
rear wing, adjoining the tower, has similar masonry and a door
with a four-centred arch.

FORD

ST MICHAEL AND ALL ANGELS. The church stands in the
grounds of the castle, near enough to be dominated by it when
one sees the two together. Yet when the church was built, nothing
yet stood of the present castle. St Michael is an early C13 building,
and it has one feature which is archaeologically as interesting as
it is architecturally successful, its bellcote – a sturdy, masculine
structure, direct in the expression of its function with hardly any
embellishments. It stands on a broad heavy central buttress up
the W front like a chimney breast. Above that there is a chamfered
offset, then the first bell stage, with single-chamfered lancets on
all four sides. The sides then slope in sharply, like those of a

pitched roof, to carry the second bell stage, with a lancet opening
to the E–W only. The finishing motif is a pyramid roof of stone.
The church consists of nave and long lower chancel, and N and
S aisles. It was over-restored and much altered by *Dobson* in 1853.
The E bay of the chancel is his and the whole of the N aisle. All
other windows are also renewed, except for the narrow W window
of the nave, N of and close to the bellcote. It has a shouldered
rere-arch. All the other windows are lancets with rere-arches. At
the SW and SE corners of the S aisle are medieval angle buttresses.
The SE buttress has two image niches on top of each other. They
have pointed-trefoiled heads. Inside the church, the S arcade is
original, three wide arches on circular piers with plainly moulded
octagonal capitals (one with nail-head decoration). The W pier
has dogtooth. Double-chamfered arches. The E and W ends of
the arcade rest on corbels with small heads as decoration. –
REREDOS. Elaborately Late Gothic by *W. S. Hicks*, 1892. –
PULPIT by *Hicks* also. – MONUMENTS. Six medieval CROSS
SLABS set into the floor at the W end of the nave. One of them is
carved with a set of bagpipes. – In the churchyard, a heavy
oversized headstone in the pre-archaeological Gothic taste; to
three children of the Black family † 1829–35. – Also in the churchyard the monument to Louisa, Marchioness of Waterford (of
Ford Castle), † 1891, designed partly by *G. F. Watts*. Two kneeling
angels hold a shield with the Waterford arms. In front of this a
recumbent Celtic cross. – A stone simply marked 'George Culley'
marks the grave of one of the most influential farmers of C 18
Britain.

FORD CASTLE. The architectural importance of the castle lies in
the fact that it belongs to the quadrilateral type with four corner
towers and apparently no stone buildings against the high curtain
wall as an integral part of the design. That is, Ford is of the same
type as Chillingham, but the licence to crenellate is earlier than
there. It was given to Sir William Heron in 1338. Two, possibly
three, of the towers survive, of unequal bulk. The biggest is KING
JAMES'S TOWER at the NW corner. It has the usual vaulted
basement strengthened by pointed transverse arches. Very
unusually, though, they are square in section. Including the basement the tower stands five storeys. In the N wall is one small
pointed-trefoiled window of the C 14. There is a mural stair from
the first to the second floor. The SW tower also exists, but is now
isolated. It is called the COW TOWER or the Flag Tower. It has
a recessed upper stage. The battlements and some of the openings
are C 18; the others are C 19. The third tower, that at the NE
corner, is clearly shown on old prints as rectangular, rather like
the tower at Etal Castle, and it may well have been an earlier hall
house which was incorporated into the later castle. It may still
exist in part, buried in later building. Its present visible walls,
those to the N and E, seem to be old masonry, probably reused
with C 18 quoins. The SE tower is gone completely. Of the curtain
wall, a little survives – a stretch to the S of King James's Tower;
and much of the N wall is submerged in the house within the
present N wall. The castle was called 'in decay' by Leland. The
N RANGE was rebuilt as a mansion in the Elizabethan age, and
more precisely before 1589 (*see* Introduction, p. 67). This range

was remodelled to a certain extent in 1694 by Sir Francis Blake, who inserted new windows and built the staircase projection in the angle of the w wing.

Since then the house has passed through two major stages of development. The first was in the second half of the c 18. From 1761 onwards, Sir John Hussey Delaval gothicized the house with an arrangement of pointed-arched windows with intersecting glazing bars. Two names are associated with this work: *George Raffield*, a carpenter, who was certainly employed from 1761, and *James Nesbit* of Kelso, who was involved from 1771 onwards. It is not at all clear who did what, and, to complicate the issue, in 1791–5 more Gothick additions were made by *Alexander Gilkie*, a master builder from Coldstream. He built the walls of a large forecourt with two gateways; probably to the designs of Nesbit. Of this Gothick phase the house retains virtually nothing – no more than a few stretches of frieze with pierced quatrefoils. But the c 18 forecourt is complete and beautiful. The gateway to the E has two circular towers with friezes of little hanging intersected arches, and typical Gothick quatrefoil openings below their battlements. The PORTCULLIS GATE, to the s of the castle, has the fantastic ornament of alternating bands of vermiculated rustication and again quatrefoil openings. The forecourt walls, of course, are castellated, with higher corner towers. ⁸³

The second stage of development occurred in 1861–5 when Louisa, Marchioness of Waterford, having been deprived of her husband while she was still very young (she had met him at the Eglinton Tournament), decided to live at Ford and to make it suitably baronial. Her chosen architect was *David Bryce* of Edinburgh. On the s front, Bryce did little more than replace the Gothick windows with c 17-style cross windows. Indeed this façade now looks very similar to that recorded in Purdy's sketch of the house in 1716. It has a regular E-plan façade, two storeys plus attics and basement. The windows of course are Bryce's, but most of the masonry has not changed since the c 17. On the N side, though, Bryce built a new façade which is quite nobly baronial and irregular, with large mullioned-and-transomed windows, an oriel and a heavy stone balcony with stone steps up to it. The interior of the castle contains little of this period or of any earlier period. Apart from the medieval basement of King James's Tower, there is one c 16 beamed ceiling and one mid-c 19 Gothic room in the rooms above, a number of plain c 16 or c 17 stone fireplaces, and that is all.

Bryce added terracing to the W and N of the castle and presumably he was also responsible for the charming little GAME LARDER to the NE of the castle. It is round, with an overhanging conical roof and little square windows with boxed-out moulded surrounds just below the eaves. In 1907 the castle became the property of Lord Joicey. It is, in 1991, an outdoor centre.

PARSON'S TOWER, NW of the church and SW of the castle. Near enough to the church to be accepted as one of the Northumbrian fortified 'vicar's peles', the type best represented at Corbridge. Of the tower-house at Ford, which is first mentioned in 1541, little remains to date or describe. Only the vaulted ground floor is recognizable, with an entrance lobby and mural stair on the E. It stands to *c*. 4 metres (13 ft).

The VILLAGE. About 1860 Lady Waterford began to build the model village E of the grounds of the castle. It consists of one street, with houses l. and r. The best of them were built as late as *c*. 1914 by Lord Joicey. The original ones are grey and joyless. The street starts at the W end with a pillar of polished Aberdeen granite carrying the figure of an angel. This is a MEMORIAL to the Marquis of Waterford, dated 1859. At the E end of the street is the pretty SMITHY of 1863; single-storey, with a stone horseshoe as a door surround, patterned on a smaller one in County Waterford. In the middle of the street is the WATERFORD HALL, built by the Marchioness in 1860 as the school and now used as a museum and village hall. It is quite an elaborate high Victorian Tudor building with mullioned windows, richly patterned roof and high steep gables bearing roundels with the date and the Waterford crest. Inside, *Lady Waterford* painted a large series of biblical scenes for children, such as the Finding of Moses, David the Shepherd etc. The pictures look at first like frescoes but are in fact watercolour on paper. Lady Waterford started in 1861 and finished in 1882. The models for the figures are mostly village people, but the style chosen has given them a Michelangelesque, Raphaelesque turn. Against the W wall, a large painting of Christ and the Children, opposite Jesus among the Doctors. Ruskin, who was not Lady Waterford's taste ('He is the reverse of the man I like') but whose views she respected, was dissatisfied with the work of this pupil of his. 'I expected', he wrote, 'you would have done something better.'

WATER-POWERED INDUSTRIES. The availability of waterpower to a landowner keen to improve an estate in the second half of the C 18 could be of considerable benefit. The Delaval family, who acquired the Ford estate in 1718, developed a small water-powered complex on the River Till around a group of pre-existing mills. The history of the use of waterpower at Ford is rather complicated. There was at least one water corn mill on the Heatherslaw (W) side of the River Till in the C 13 and possibly two. By the C 14 there was another on the Ford (E) side – the Manor Mill. By the C 17 a walk (fulling) mill had been added, probably on the W side, and in 1767–9 an iron forge (*see* below) was built on the E side, where there was also to be a dye house, saw pit and joiner's shop. Much of this development destroyed or obscured the pre-C 18 structures but provided a small industrial complex suited to an improving estate. It seems not to have been paralleled elsewhere in the county.

HEATHERSLAW WATERMILL. A fine Northumbrian watermill, the only one in the county open to the public at the time of writing. The earliest parts may date from the mid-C 18 but most of the building is C 19. It was not until after 1856 that an extension of the mill covered the previously exposed waterwheels – an idea first mooted in 1806. The mill continued in partial use until 1946. Essentially two bays of three-and-a-half storeys, each having an open float-board wheel with low breasting in the floor of the race, driving three pairs of stones, a pearl barley machine and ancillary equipment. There is an attached three-storey, five-bay granary block, constructed *c.* 1808, which may also have been used for malting, and a detached, two-storey high kiln and one-storey stable block. The high kiln is unusual for Northumberland: it is built into sloping ground so that its drying floor at first-floor level is approached direct from the rear. All this is built of coursed rubble with well-dressed openings, and with hipped, blue-slated roofs, except for the kiln block, which has red pantiles. The foundation of an early HORSESHOE WEIR can sometimes be seen at low water (as can the former ford near the bridge); both this and the later STRAIGHT WEIR lead direct to the wheels of the corn mill on one side and to the former forge (*see* below) on the other.

FORD FORGE. A group of one and two-storey buildings in a good industrial vernacular style, the earliest of them of 1779; in the 1830s and/or 1840s it was greatly extended. It was initially a forge for the production of nails, firedoors, grates and hand tools, made of iron imported from Austria, Russia and Glasgow. At first it was run directly by the estate but it was leased out from 1778 and eventually it became a spade forge. The forge hammers were said in 1897 to be silent, but the assembling of spades continued until the 1920s, after which the buildings were converted into the estate sawmill. The surviving buildings originally served as the iron warehouse, the finishing shop and a dwelling house. The small field just N of the bridge on the E side of the river was the tenterfield for the fulling mill.

ROAD BRIDGE. The C18 bridge consisted of a small land or flood arch on the W side and a main hump-backed segmental span. During upstream widening in 1807, the main arch collapsed; it was rebuilt in 1807–8 with two equal segmental spans. The original W arch was, however, incorporated and has four ribs with mason's marks. It looks C16.

COLLIERY, 1 m. E at Ford Moss. Extensive remains on a site worked at least since the C17. It was redeveloped under the Delavals from 1718, continued by the Waterfords throughout the C19 and closed in 1914. Around the Moss the remains of about thirty colliers' houses can be distinguished, some with gardens. A round-sectioned boiler-house chimney, made mainly of curved bricks, stands by the former engine pit; around the Moss to the N are the walls of a beam engine house, with a probable winding engine house alongside, all possibly mid-C19.

Several good examples of planned and unplanned FARMS surround Ford. ENCAMPMENT FARM, 1½ m. W of the village, has a farmhouse of 1780 with later extensions and farm buildings of the 1780s to the 1860s. HAY FARM, ½ m. N, mainly mid-C19, has a former house of 1780 and a probably earlier dovecote; the present house is of 1910. The well-planned farm buildings are dominated by the chimney of the boiler house, which supplied steam for a threshing machine engine. FORD WESTFIELD, ½ m. SW, is a mid-C19, E-type planned farm, formerly steam-powered. FORD HILL, ½ m. E, is another mid-C19 planned farm, water-powered this time and on a site a few hundred metres S of its predecessor. WEST FLODDEN, 2½ m. SW, is not a planned farm, its buildings being added to piecemeal, giving it a more complex chronology than its neighbours, but none of it earlier than the mid-C18;

a horse-powered thresher with a gingang (horse wheel house) provided post-1786.

BRICK AND TILE WORKS, 1½ m. SW. A kiln and some ancillary buildings survive from the works established in 1768 to provide bricks and pantiles for the development of the estate (*see* Introduction, p. 94).

PALLINSBURN. *See* p. 540.

8060

FOURSTONES

ST AIDAN. 1892. Pretty little wooden building.

FOURSTONES FARM. Early C19 farmhouse and planned farm buildings; a gingang and later engine house, with a tall brick stack, were built alongside. As elsewhere, the gin and engine might have been used in tandem.

FOURSTONES STATION is no more, but the single-storeyed STATIONMASTER'S HOUSE of c. 1835 survives, ashlar-fronted with a central bow. Just W of the station a very large bank of LIMEKILNS, some double-piled. Five can be identified, but there must have been more, with both segmental and round draw arches: post-1835.

PAPER MILL, 1½ m. SE. Established in 1763 and still in production (*see* Introduction, p. 88). The oldest surviving buildings are C19 and include a two-storey stone shed with a gable-end bellcote. Preserved within the complex is the country's oldest Fourdrinier paper-making machine, dated to 1860.

0020

FOWBERRY TOWER
1 m. NW of Chatton

Oblong tower-house of the C15. Rebuilt as a more comfortable house in 1666 for Mr Strother. Only a few details of that house survive, e.g. the eaves cornice, now inside. The N side was rebuilt in 1776 by *Nesbit* of Kelso for Sir Francis Blake. He made the house wider and added lower one-bay wings to the l. and r. The façade is of three bays and two storeys on a vaulted basement. Each bay has a group of three stepped lancets of not-quite-correct form. The basement has tripartite segmental windows under segmental arches. The S side is heavier Gothick, with four-centred arches to the windows. This front was added in 1809 for Matthew Culley; the architect is not known. Delightful interiors in the 1776 part, especially the staircase with a kind of fan-coving, the drawing room with two doorways surmounted by crocketed ogee arches, and the dining room with the usual serving screen at the back, which is here of two arches with a slim quatrefoil shaft in the middle.

GARDEN HOUSE or GAZEBO, ¼ m. W. A two-storey square brick building with a pyramid roof, very plain from the outside but with an elaborate Rococo ceiling inside. It is mid-C18 and decidedly different in character from the work in the house itself.

LODGE and GATEWAY. Inscribed MC 1829 (for Matthew Culley) but probably of the 1770s. Single-storey, three-bay lodge with ogee door and windows, projecting centre bay with castellations over. Inside, a charming rustic Gothick fireplace. The GATEPIERS have hounds' heads on top.

BRIDGE beside the main house. 1825, for Matthew Culley. Segmental arch over the river and a lower segmental accommodation arch over the drive to the house.

GARLEIGH MOOR see HESLEYHURST

GATEHOUSE
1 m. N of Thorneyburn Church

A hamlet with two relatively complete bastles of c. 1600 and fragmentary remains of at least two others.

The NORTH BASTLE is among the finest surviving. It has slightly later stone stairs to the first-floor doorway, and two small original windows, one with a blank segmental arch over. There is no vault; instead huge twisted oak beams support the first floor.

The SOUTH BASTLE has three walls standing to eaves height. The S wall was rebuilt in the C19. The blocked ground-floor doorway in the gable end has a roll-moulded surround.

GATEHOUSE FARM, 100 metres SE, has a boulder plinth very like a bastle plinth. Also, about 30 metres S of the house, parts of two walls of another bastle, incorporating a slit window.

BLACK MIDDENS, 1 m. NW of Gatehouse. Yet another bastle house; now in the care of English Heritage. Roofless but standing to eaves level. A little altered on the ground floor, but all the original openings remain.

NW of Black Middens, in the forest, there are remains of three more bastles, at SHILLA HILL, HIGHFIELD FARM, and CORBIE CASTLE or BOG HEAD. This is the most complete of the three; its vault has fallen but the ground-floor doorway remains, with a quenching hole above (see the Introduction, p. 65).

HIGH GREEN MANOR, 2 m. NE. An incongruous but not unpleasing sight to find up here on these wildest of wild moors – a Victorian country house. It was built c. 1885 for Mr Morrison Bell and extended to the r. in 1894. Quite an ordinary building, such as one might find in any prosperous Victorian suburb, except for the very nicely detailed round corner towers with their tall conical roofs. They turn the house into a chateau. The single-storey GARDEN COTTAGE, $\frac{1}{4}$ m. SW, is an eclectic, deliberately asymmetric design of the 1890s.

GILSLAND

The Poltross Burn, which flows through the middle of the village, is the boundary between Northumberland and Cumbria.

RAILWAY STATION (originally called Rose Hill). 1836. Closed in 1967 and now converted to domestic accommodation, with some unfortunate dormer windows, but unmistakably one of the Newcastle and Carlisle Railway's Tudorish designs, rather similar to Wylam and Greenhead (q.v.). The former stationmaster's house and waiting-room-cum-office have a projecting cross gable corbelled out over the platform, hoodmoulds over the windows etc. Facing across the tracks is the STATION HOTEL (formerly the Rose Hill Hotel), probably mid-C19 but perhaps a little earlier, for this was once a spa town.

WARDREW HOUSE, 1 m. N. Built in 1752 by James Carrick (date and initials in pediment of front door) on the site of an early seat of the Thirlwall family; it had become a hotel by the later C18. Guests included Robert Burns and Sir Walter Scott (who met his future wife here). Formerly of three storeys and five narrow bays, with architraves and rusticated quoins. Remodelled (after having been a ruin) in 1980, as a two-storey house. Front terrace wall with its coping swept up to a central pair of gate piers.

GLANTON

UNITED REFORMED CHURCH (formerly Presbyterian), at the W end of the village. The original building of 1783 is a simple rectangular block with thin corner pilasters linked by an odd horizontal strip across each gable; above the strip at each end are a round window and a cruciform loop. On the S side, two tall arched windows and two shorter windows at each end (the lower ones were doorways). The upper end windows lit the gallery, which formerly extended round three sides of the church; the same pattern is seen again at Branton in 1781 (in a six-bay form) and at Embleton as late as 1833. The N porch and stair projection, in a free Baroque style, are of 1912, by *George Reavell* of Alnwick.

The VILLAGE, set on rising ground overlooking the broad and green Vale of Whittingham, is rewarding enough architecturally to merit a short perambulation. Starting at the E end, on the S of the road is GLANTON HOUSE, described as 'new-built' in 1763–4. The S front is of five quite narrow bays, with rusticated quoins. The central doorway has a lugged architrave, pulvinated frieze and pediment. The roof is still steeply pitched, with interesting trusses of a jointed upper-cruck type. To the S of the house, a handsome circular DOVECOTE, perhaps C17. Then comes WHICKHAM HOUSE, also facing away from the road. This looks a conventional villa of *c.* 1800, but has older fabric, including a doorway dated 1693 in the back wall. On the N side of the road, SOUTH FARM has a good late C18 foldyard, with the usual reverse-stepped gables. The W range has a long arcade of segmental arches on round piers. The barn on the N side has a shaped keystone placed in the course above the door lintel, another typical C18 feature.

Then comes a rather smart terrace of the 1840s, with two old
shop fronts, rather surprising in such a small village, and a good
but plain ashlar three-bay house of 1796, now the WORLD BIRD
RESEARCH CENTRE. In the grounds behind are some early C18
cottages, part of a row built on the N side of the village green
before it was enclosed in the late C18. More C18 houses further W,
including TOWN FARMHOUSE, given a big cornice on moulded
corbels in the early C19, and PROSPECT HOUSE with keyed
supra-lintels like those at South Farm.

GLANTON PIKE, ¾ m. w. A house of *c.* 1780, extended to the rear
by *John Dobson* in 1829. The ashlar five-bay s front has doorway
and window detail akin to Glanton House (*see* above), but the
proportions are broader and the roof low-pitched and hipped; the
actual difference in date may be only twenty years, but it feels
much more. The plainer E front, also of five bays, received a
central porch in the C19. WALLED GARDEN to the E with the
usual heated rear wall; the DOVECOTE amongst the trees to the
sw is a castellated tower, combined with a little shelter shed for
animals. The date is probably late C19.

GOSFORTH *see* NEWCASTLE UPON TYNE

GREAT BAVINGTON
3 m. sw of Kirkwhelpington

The village formerly consisted of two rows of houses (reduced to
earthworks) facing each other across a broad green aligned E–W.
The existing buildings are at the W end of the S row, which
extended to Mires Farm. A parallel N row is represented by the
earthworks of houses, backed by about a dozen crofts. The Poll
Tax listed 37 adults here in 1377. The surface of the main (and
only) street of the present hamlet is the bare bedrock. On one
side, EASTER HOUSE and COTTAGE, an altered C17 house; on
the other, the PRESBYTERIAN CHURCH, built in 1725 but altered
and gothicized in 1869.

BAVINGTON HALL. *See* p. 159.

THOCKRINGTON. *See* p. 583.

GREAT CHESTERS
2 m. N of Haltwhistle

ROMAN FORT. Added to the original scheme for Hadrian's Wall
no earlier than A.D. 128 (*see* Introduction, p. 39). The outline of
the fort is clear, but much of the N side (formed by the Wall) is
overlain by farm buildings. Of the fort wall, only the NW angle
tower and parts of the inner face can be seen; various buildings
are set close inside it on the NW. In the interior is the sunken vault
of the strongroom under the regimental shrine in the headquarters
and, in the sw quadrant, the turf-covered ghost of five 'chalets'

of a C 4 barrack-block (cf. Housesteads). The W gate is of unusual interest in that it is the sole visible and undisturbed example of a common occurrence: the sealing of a gateway. First the S portal of the gate was blocked with masonry for extra defence; then (probably later in C 4) the N portal was walled up also. Usually these blockings have been removed by zealous early excavators (an action akin to some Victorian church restorations).

A narrow winding AQUEDUCT, visible only in places, was cut as an open leat for six miles from the Caw Burn near Swallow Crags to supply the fort.

GREAT CHESTERS FARMHOUSE. Tall early C 18 block with lower C 19 extension. The older part has raised window surrounds and an upper-cruck roof.

GREAT SWINBURNE
2 m. N of Chollerton

9070

SWINBURNE CASTLE. Of the original castle nothing exists, and the C 18 house which replaced it has gone too. However, the buildings which do remain, though fragmentary and in poor repair, are worthy of attention. These include a MANOR HOUSE, built probably in the early C 17, which later became the W wing of the C 18 mansion. It has hoodmoulded windows and a big projecting chimneystack. Attached to it, an early C 18 STABLE and BARN with a large, finely carved coat of arms. E of this, the later C 18 STABLES (seven bays with pedimented centre) and a pretty ORANGERY of the same period, with elongated Tuscan columns and an Adamish frieze. The SW GATEWAY has similar elongated Tuscan columns in pairs with niches between. The high round carriage arch has a pediment over.

R.C. CHAPEL. 1841. Small and simple, with arched windows and a W porch.

TITHE BARN (or so it is called), N of the chapel. C 18 Gothick with quatrefoils, arched windows and cruciform ventilation slits.

STANDING STONE, $\frac{1}{2}$ m. S of the Castle. The most striking in the county, over 3 metres (10 ft) high. Red stone covered with grey lichen; vertical end grooves on top, cup marks on the SE face.

EAST GUNNAR PEAK. See Gunnerton.

GREAT TOSSON
2 m. SW of Rothbury

0000

TOSSON TOWER. C 14. In ruins. It is interesting to see the rubble core where the ashlar stones have been ripped off. All four walls stand to c. 6 metres (20 ft). No features of interest, except the remains of the staircase in the NE corner, a mural chamber on the first floor, and the springing of the ground-floor vault.

LIMEKILN, $\frac{1}{4}$ m. N. 1888 by *George Reavell* of Alnwick. A beautifully constructed kiln in coursed masonry blocks on a polygonal plan but flanked by projecting wing-walls. The single pot has three round-headed drawing arches.

TOSSON BURGH, on the end of a spur overlooking Coquetdale. A conspicuous oval hillfort defended by a single rampart; its contours have been softened by ridge-and-furrow.

CAIRN, within the forest ½ m. s of Great Tosson. It contained two cists (still visible) and an urned cremation.

At NEWTOWN, ½ m. NE, a dwelling house with the remains of a three-storey woollen mill alongside.

GREAT WHITTINGTON 0070

METHODIST CHAPEL. 1835. Small, with a pedimented front.

WINDMILL, ½ m. SE. Before 1828. Slightly tapered tower in coursed masonry with well-quoined openings. Sockets in external wall and elevated door openings indicate the addition of a reefing stage when the mill was heightened. No machinery.

WATERMILL, c. 200 metres SE of the windmill. Probably a late C 18 building on a C 13 site; presumably associated with the windmill (cf. Acomb). The three-storey mill building has been gutted and converted to a farm store. The wheel house on the W gable formerly housed an overshot wheel; mill-cum-farmhouse adjacent.

BINGFIELD. *See* p. 187.

HALLINGTON. *See* p. 297.

HALTON. *See* p. 297.

GREENHEAD 6060

ST CUTHBERT. 1826–8 by *Dobson*. Four-bay aisleless nave with lancets, and narrow W tower with slender octagonal spire. The usual early C 19 preaching box in plan, but more purely E. E. than most of its type; had Dobson been studying Haltwhistle Church? The three-bay chancel with Geometrical tracery was added in 1900 by *Hicks & Charlewood*.

STATION HOUSE. c. 1836. A typical Newcastle and Carlisle Railway station of three bays, with a big corbelled-out half-dormer over the central door (cf. Wylam and Riding Mill).

BRIDGE over the Tipalt Burn. Late C 18. Two segmental arches with flush arch rings and a triangular cutwater; widened to the S c. 1970.

GLENWHELT, on the N side of the Military Road. Six-bay range dated 1757, with rusticated quoins, a doorway with a segmental pediment carried on Corinthian columns, and ground-floor windows under vermiculated friezes and cornices. A parallel rear range is earlier and may incorporate a bastle.

CARVORAN, ½ m. NE. A Roman fort guarding the crossing of the Tipalt; probably pre-dating Hadrian's Wall, it stood at the junction of the Stanegate with the Maiden Way leading S to Whitley Castle (*see* Introduction, pp. 36 and 43). Visible remains (SW of the Roman Army Museum) are unimpressive: a low fort platform, levelled on the E; the only masonry is the NW angle tower.

A large Roman temporary CAMP, 1 m. E of Carvoran, occupies the summit E of Fell End. Stanegate, much disturbed, crosses it from E to W.

LOW OLD SHIELD, 1 m. NW. Bastle house with 1.2-metre (4-ft) thick walls and a blocked roll-moulded byre door set centrally in the W end, remodelled in the late C 17; in the S wall, chamfered windows, formerly mullioned, and a wave-moulded doorway with a flattened triangular head within a square frame.

ALLOA LEE, 2 m. NE. House, probably early C 18, formerly with a cross passage, its doorways (that to the rear segment-headed) now blocked. Substantial upper-cruck roof trusses.

GREYMARE HILL
2 m. NW of Shotley Bridge

ST ANDREW. On a lonely hilltop site, visible for miles around. Rebuilt 1769 and remodelled 1892. Equal-armed cruciform plan, with a porch at the end of the S transept. Pedimented W bellcote and round-headed windows. Intersecting segmental arches, dated 1769, span the crossing. Medieval relics are the heads of two small CROSS SLABS built into the E end and a CROSS BASE in the churchyard.

The HOPPER MAUSOLEUM, in the NE corner of the churchyard, is of a scale which dominates the church and skyline. It is a fantastical domed structure reminiscent in its rustic style of Brittany or Cornwall. Square, with rudely carved statues in niches; some of the niches have shell decoration but pointed heads. Above on each side, an open broken pediment with seated figures. Then the dome, with an undulating outline, and obelisks at the corners. Open lantern with obelisks on top. The mausoleum is usually said to have been built by Humphrey Hopper in memory of his wife, who died in 1752; however, an earlier Humphrey was recorded in 1663, a date more in accord with its style. Also in the churchyard three HEADSTONES, to the Chatt family (1822), Robert Gibson (1820) and Thompson family (1819), recorded as being the earliest pieces of monumental sculpture by *John Graham Lough*.

GREYSTEAD

ST LUKE. 1818 by *H. H. Seward*, for the Commissioners of Greenwich Hospital. A sister church to those at Humshaugh, Wark and Thorneyburn (qq.v.). The same windows, the same pretty internal proportion. The W tower, however, has the distinguishing motif of a group of three lancet bell openings.

GREYSTEAD RECTORY, by the church and contemporary with it. Also by *Seward*. Three bays with tripartite windows.

DALLY CASTLE, 1 m. S, on the Chirdon Burn. The castle seems to be the tower that Sir David Lindsey was building in 1237, causing Hugh Bolbec to complain to Henry III. Occupying the

SE end of a ridge above the Chirdon Burn, the castle is defended
from the NW, the line of easiest approach, by a broad, deep ditch.
A slighter ditch was dug on the SE and possibly on the N also. It
was an oblong hall-house with projecting turrets on three corners.
Nowhere do the walls stand more than 1.5 metre (5 ft) high, but
the castle is nevertheless eminently worthy of attention because
of the quality of the surviving fragments. There is a finely cut
plinth, and more particularly several arrow slits or parts of arrow
slits, extremely finely detailed, with rounded jambs projecting like
stone shutters over the steeply sloping sills and lintels.

SNABDAUGH, 1 m. E of Dally. A bastle house of *c.* 1600 with the
unique survival of a pointed tunnel vault of neatly cut stone at
roof level; at one end of the attic, a window with seats in the
jambs. At first-floor level on the S, remains of a door and two
windows with roll-moulded surrounds. Big external off-set at first-
floor level. There was probably a vault to the basement as well,
but it has been cut away.

FOOTBRIDGE, ¼ m. N of Greystead. A suspension bridge over the
North Tyne in a beautiful and isolated situation. Built to connect
the S bank of the river with the Border Counties Railway, which
opened in 1862.

# GUNNERTON					9070

ST CHRISTOPHER. 1899 by the *Rev. J. C. Hawes*, who was curate
here, later became a Roman Catholic and built several churches
in Australia. He ended his life as a hermit on Cat Island in the
Bahamas. Quite an original, if somewhat mannered, design. Nave
and higher chancel. Rough stone. The nave has three broad,
low, arched windows. The chancel has a four-light window with
segmental heads to the lights, in an ashlar surround. The E end
is blank except for two slit windows. Large oculus window at the
W end. The chancel roof is hipped to the E but gabled to the W,
with a gablet projecting to carry the bell. Unusual interior, with
the walls plastered and the stone arbitrarily exposed only in the
pointed arch to the N chapel and in the jambs and rere-arches to
the E end slit windows. Canted wood-boarded ceilings. – WEST
GALLERY. Low, with panels of excellent openwork naturalistic
Arts-and-Crafts-style carving. – FONT. Old and octagonal on a
C 20 base. Other medieval fragments built into the S wall. –
HARMONIUM. An ultra-Victorian piece.

CLOSE HOUSE. A cottage in the village street. Its origins are not
known, but the date is probably *c.* 1600. Two storeys, with a long
single-storey addition to the l. The whole has walls *c.* 1.2 metres
(4 ft) thick and three doorways with Tudor-arched lintels.

MONEY HILL, ½ m. N. A fine motte (its top mutilated by fruitless
Victorian excavations), with a deep ditch and slight counterscarp
bank, crosses the W half of the neck of a steep-sided promontory;
the E half is closed by a massive bank and ditch. A second outer
bank and ditch is much slighter and may not be contemporary.
The natural triangular bailey required only a minimal peripheral
bank.

A string of SETTLEMENTS, apparently Iron Age and Romano-British in date, occupy the Whin Sill crags between Gunnerton and Colwell. They include an extensive cluster of stone-founded houses within a subdivided rectangular enclosure on East Gunnar Peak, 1 m. w of Swinburne Castle, and the group of well-preserved circular stone houses within the wall that hugs the natural defences of Blue Crags, ½ m. NW of Colwell.

GUYZANCE

2000

Guyzance village is only a single street, flanked by single-storey C 18 cottages remodelled in the mid-C 19 (the former SCHOOL is dated 1852). The number of cottages has been reduced since the C 19, and only one (on the S) keeps its original rear outbuilding with attached pigsties, privies and midden.

GUYZANCE HALL. A rather rambling country house created from the original C 18 Barnhill Farmhouse by means of major extensions of 1894 by *W. H. Knowles* and a central tower of *c.* 1920 which replaced a less ambitious tower by Knowles: all in a free neo-Tudor style. SE of the house are castellated garden walls with an attached octagonal summerhouse and gateway, also probably by Knowles.

GUYZANCE MILL, ½ m. SW. A very neat watermill immediately adjacent to its oblique weir but with a tail-race of considerable length. The mill is an early C 19 three-storey stone structure with additions to provide for a low kiln and a high kiln, the latter bearing the date 1889. A pantiled lean-to covers the wheel house, located at the river-end gable. MILL HOUSE nearby is partly C 17, with a moulded flat-pointed doorway, and a taller C 19 extension.

CHAPEL RUINS, ¾ m. S. On a level haugh almost surrounded by a meander of the Coquet, the picturesque ruins of a chapel which might belong either to the small Premonstratensian nunnery of 'Gysnes' founded *c.* 1147 (and extinct by 1500) or to the 'ecclesia de Gisyng', which seems to have been a separate structure. Most of the N and W walls of the nave stand high; the masonry looks late C 11 or early C 12 in character, but the only feature to survive is the lower part of a narrow W window. On the S are the bases of the E respond and the round pier of a two-bay arcade. The chancel seems to have been rebuilt in the C 14, and both side walls survive in part. On the N is a blocked door with a crude pointed head, and on the S a priest's door with a double-chamfered arch between the remains of a large C 14 window and of what may have been a 'low-side', and a trefoiled piscina with twin bowls. The plan and features suggest a parochial rather than a monastic structure, but footings projecting from under the wall enclosing the C 18 graveyard on the S point to other presumably medieval buildings.

GUYZANCE BRIDGE, SW of the chapel ruins. *c.* 1865. Rock-faced and of three segmental arches.

THE DYE HOUSE, immediately SW of Guyzance Bridge. Formerly Park Mill. Built 1775 as a tin and iron foundry, converted to a woollen mill in 1791, and finally used in 1915–30 for making hydrate of alumina as a white pigment. Long three-storey block, with a brick top floor, now converted into flats. Contemporary with the original mill is the horseshoe-plan DAM designed by *Smeaton*, 365 metres upstream.

HADRIAN'S WALL

Selected portions of the Wall and of its associated structures are described under the following gazetteer entries, listed from E to W:

Wallsend	Carrawburgh
Newcastle (including	Sewingshields
Benwell and Denton)	Housesteads
Heddon-on-the-Wall	Cawfields
Halton	Great Chesters
Wall	Walltown
Chesters	Greenhead

For the Stanegate, *see* Corbridge, Newbrough, Vindolanda and Greenhead. For the outpost forts, *see* Woodburn and Rochester.

For the history of the Wall, *see* the Introduction, pp. 36–42; there is a map on p. 296.

HAGGERSTON

2½ m. SE of Ancroft

oo40

HAGGERSTON CASTLE. The ancient home of the Haggerston family had been rebuilt in 1777 and much altered in 1805. In 1893–7 it was entirely rebuilt by *Norman Shaw* for a new owner, Thomas Leyland. It was an enormous house in Shaw's grandest and heaviest Baroque style, the style of Bryanston and of course, in Northumberland, of Chesters. The house had to be restored by *J. B. Dunn* of Edinburgh following a fire of 1903. In 1933 most of the house was demolished; its contents and its fabric were sold off and are to be found in other houses all over the county (e.g. at Holystone Grange, q.v.). What remains here of the Shaw house is a monumental combined WATER TOWER and belvedere, twelve storeys high and exaggeratedly slender; and the ROTUNDA, the former entrance. It is of one storey but tall, with the windows divided by giant pilasters of banded rustication. The doorway has a tremendous Gibbs surround and pediment, and the windows heavy triple keystones. The interior is faced throughout in rusticated ashlar and the openings are framed by giant attached Tuscan columns connected by segmental arches with coffered soffits. The ceiling is domed. On this evidence the house must have been astonishing.

The STABLE BLOCK is dated 1908. The detail is similar to the house, with boldly rusticated surrounds to the doors and windows. The interior to the courtyard is especially fine. Beside the stables is the ITALIAN GARDEN, a large early C20 walled garden. Wrought-iron Rococo-style gates. Apsidal W wall with statue niches. The interior is divided by stone paths into twelve areas, all slightly different. There are sunken gardens and pergolas. Against the E

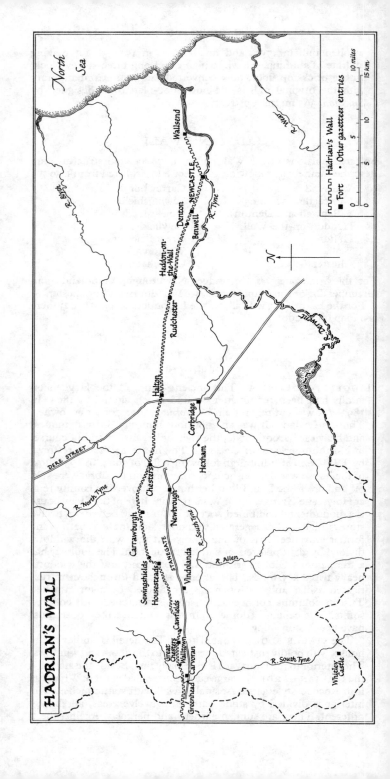

HADRIAN'S WALL

North Sea

R. Blyth

R. Wansbeck

DERE STREET

R. North Tyne

Carrawburgh
Sewingshields
Housesteads
STANEGATE
Chesters
Great
Chesters
Walltown
Cawfields
Greenhead
Carvoran
Vindolanda
Newbrough
R. South Tyne
R. Allen
R. South Tyne
Whitley
Castle

Halton
Corbridge
Hexham
R. Tyne

Rudchester
Heddon-
the-Wall
Denton
Benwell
NEWCASTLE
Wallsend

R. Derwent

N

Hadrian's Wall   · Other gazetteer entries
■ Fort

0   5   10   15 km
0   5   10 miles

wall a Roman Doric gazebo. Against the N wall a single-storey garden house; inside it, two naturalistic plaster ceilings of vines growing through trellises. ICEHOUSE, just E of the stables, a tall grassy hump. Presumably early C 19.

CHAPEL HOUSE, c. 180 metres N of the Castle. Later C 18. Now a private house, but formerly a R.C. chapel and priest's house (the Haggerstons were a Roman Catholic family). Gothick windows.

ANTELOPE HOUSE, in a field by the A1 immediately S of the Castle. A prettily detailed little wooden animal shelter. It is a relic of the private zoo established at Haggerston by Thomas Leyland at the end of the C 19. More shelters, brick this time, are visible to the NE.

WINDMILL, ¼ m. W of the Castle. A small, tapered stone tower, once a windmill but converted in 1828 into a dovecote by lining the inside of the towers with c. 500 brick nesting boxes. Several blocked doors and windows, and some arch stones at the present ground level. Wooden potence extant but decayed. The tower is c. 7.6 metres (25 ft) high, but it stands on an earth mound c. 1.5 metres (5 ft) high in a field of prominent ridge-and-furrow.

BRIDGE MILL, ½ m. NW of the Castle. Mid-C 18 corn mill and miller's house in fine pink sandstone ashlar.

HALLINGTON

9070

4 m. NW of Great Whittington

HALLINGTON HALL. Built in 1768 for Ralph Soulsby, but with late C 18 and early C 19 additions and alterations. It has an attractive three-storey, five-bay entrance front, with pedimented door surround and flanking Venetian windows on the ground floor, sash windows in raised stone surrounds above, and gabled half-dormers on the second floor.

RESERVOIRS, 1 m. W of the village. Two adjacent reservoirs designed for the Newcastle and Gateshead Water Company by *John Frederic La Trobe Bateman*, the E one of 1863, the W of 1880. Beyond them, to the NW, the Little Swinburne and Coltcrag Reservoirs of 1880, for the same company and also by *Bateman*.

HALTON

9060

2 m. S of Great Whittington

CHURCH. Originally Norman, though the nave NW quoins may even be Saxon. The unmoulded chancel arch, on the plainest imposts, is undoubtedly Norman. All the other features are of the C 16 or early C 17, and the church was re-roofed in 1706. The S door is segmental-arched and has a roll-moulded surround. Two-light windows with round heads to lights, and a similar five-light E window. Embattled parapet and a bellcote. The interior is white-painted, simple and moving. The roof has massive timbers with very short king- and queen-posts. – ALTAR TABLE. C 17. The

top rests on heavily rusticated stone arches. – ALTAR RAILS. C 18.
In the churchyard, a weathered ROMAN ALTAR.

HALTON TOWER. A delightful group. What one sees first is a
completely preserved C 14 tower and a late C 17 house attached
to it on the E. The story starts, however, at the rear of the house,
where there are fragments of a late C 13 or early C 14 house. What
remains of this period, apart from masonry, is no more than one
doorway with a shouldered lintel from the cross passage into the
former hall. *c.* 1400, it would seem, the tower was added. It is
built of Roman stones, stands up four storeys high with corbelled-
out bartizans at the corners, and has a vaulted basement. The
details are all of the latest C 14, especially the two-light windows
with cusped four-centred-arched lights, and the doorways within
with four-centred arches. In the late C 15 the house to the rear
was extensively altered. Of this period the finely moulded beams
of the former hall, later the kitchen. The C 17 house was added
by John Douglas in 1696. It is only two storeys high and its
horizontal emphasis contrasts with the sheer height of the tower.
It has five bays, cross windows, and a central doorway with a
big curly open pediment. Inside, a staircase with boldly twisted
balusters.

In front of the house is a WALLED GARDEN and two GATE-
POSTS with urn finials and fat bulgy rustication. Attached to the
S front of the tower, a stretch of medieval wall which, it has been
suggested (most recently by Borne and Dixon), may represent
part of the barmkin of the manor house which preceded the tower.
In the garden wall, a ROMAN TOMBSTONE, depicting a man
reclining at a funeral banquet. Another tombstone is to be found
in the E wall of the tower: it is a relief of the upper part of a woman
in a niche.

The ROMAN FORT of Haltonchesters is crossed by the main road
(B6318: on the line of Hadrian's Wall) and by the N drive of
Halton Tower. Built when the decision was taken, *c.* A.D. 124, to
bring the forts onto the line of the Wall itself. Mainly lying S of
the road, the earthworks present little immediate coherence, but
the general outline is clear. The N third, long in arable use,
projects beyond the Wall. Abandoned during the occupation of
Scotland in the mid-C 2. An unusual W extension was added at
the beginning of the C 3. The fort was garrisoned in the late C 4,
but there may have been earlier periods when it was left to decay.

HALTON LEA GATE

The old village is little more than a hamlet, on the A689 close to
the Cumbrian border. In the village street the only building worth
note is a three-bay Georgian house with rusticated quoins and
doorway.

HALTON LEA, $\frac{1}{2}$ m. N. Farmhouse which seems to have originated
as a large bastle house, with good early C 19 farm buildings,
including a smithy.

HALTWHISTLE   7060

Despite C 19 and C 20 industrial developments, Haltwhistle remains a country market town with its centre quite unspoilt. There is no individual building of wrong scale or manner, if no secular building of great value either. The motorist passing through on the A69 sees the parish church between the old vicarage and a row of substantial late C 19 houses, one with ornate half-timbering; this prospect belies the character of the old town centre further N, which has elements reminiscent of both Lowland Scotland and the West Riding of Yorkshire.

HOLY CROSS. A quite exceptionally complete and well preserved E. E. parish church, typically North Country in proportion and details. It lies back from the S side of the Market Place, with the churchyard open to the Tyne Valley. The long and narrow chancel has four lancets on each side and a stepped triplet in the E end; a two-light mullioned 'low-side' window on the S may be a later medieval insertion. The E lancets are nook-shafted inside (with shaft rings) and have handsome trefoiled rere-arches. The four-bay aisled nave is considerably taller than the chancel, and almost square in plan. The small lancets in the aisle side walls are mostly of 1870, when the church was restored by *R. J. Johnson*; enough survived to show that they follow the original pattern. The taller double lancets in the E end of each aisle are largely original. Both aisles have restored doorways with colonnettes. The buttresses all round the church seem to be original C 13 work, and are rather interesting; almost square in plan, they diminish in size by big chamfered setbacks to a small pyramid-topped top stage. The W end, with its pair of too tall lancets below a big oculus, and bellcote, seems to have been entirely rebuilt in 1870, when a new vestry was added on the N of the N aisle.

The arcades have double-chamfered arches under indented hoodmoulds, on circular piers with moulded bases and irregular octagonal capitals. The chancel arch is also double-chamfered, with a hoodmould on head stops, and springs from filleted responds; above, to l. and r., are semi-octagonal corbels (one with nail-head) for the rood beam. There are three stepped SEDILIA, with trefoiled arches on filleted shafts, and a small PISCINA of the same date and design, much daintier and almost entirely renewed. Another small piscina, rather battered, in the S aisle. The chancel roof was painted, probably to designs by *Kempe*, in 1881; now much faded.

FONT. Circular; the rustic incised designs and the date 1676 may be secondary. – STOUP. Big rudely circular bowl on a slender shaft, at W end of S aisle. – STAINED GLASS. The E lancets have an important composition of 1872 by *Morris & Co.*; the main Crucifixion group was designed by *Burne Jones*, the emblems above by *Philip Webb* and the three lower panels by *Ford Madox Brown*. Four female figures by the same company, to Burne Jones designs, in the N aisle, 1898. – The chancel S and some aisle windows are by *C. E. Kempe*, 1903–4. – MONUMENTS. In the chancel, mutilated effigy of a knight, with Blenkinsopp arms; C 14. Also three C 14 CROSS SLABS, with foliated crosses in uncommonly high relief. Two bear the Thirlwall arms and the third and most elaborate, with the sword, pilgrim's staff and purse as its emblems, the Blenkinsopp arms. Also a ledger stone to John Ridley † 1562, with a long rhyming inscription.

METHODIST CHURCH, Westgate. Mid-C 19. Lancet style, with stepped gable flanked by octagonal pinnacles.

UNITED REFORMED CHURCH (formerly Presbyterian), Westgate. 1899. Rock-faced free Gothic: the tower has a cross-gabled top and a pyramidal spire; timber clerestory.

OLD VICARAGE, at the SE corner of the churchyard. The two-storey canted bays on the S are probably part of alterations by *John Dobson* in 1826, but the core of the building is C 17 or even earlier. Big stepped stack at E end.

RAILWAY STATION. An assemblage of buildings and structures which will interest the industrial archaeologist. The former stationmaster's house, ticket office and waiting room are of 1838 and may be by *Green*, in his usual Tudor style. Cast-iron WATER TANK, with sea-horse motifs on three-arched stone base, dated 1861, designed by *Peter Tate* and built by *F. Wylie & Co.*, and two WATER COLUMNS with ball finials; together these constitute a rare survival. Late C 19 the SIGNAL BOX, timber on brick base, and a cast-iron FOOTBRIDGE. The railway platforms also post-date the original design. S of the station is HALTWHISTLE TYNE BRIDGE (now a footbridge), 1875, designed by *G. G. Page* and built by *Stansfield & Son*. Cast-iron superstructure of three segmental arches with latticed spandrels and a quatrefoil-pierced parapet, on tapering piers of brick below and stone above.

DESCRIPTION. Early in the C 19 Archdeacon Singleton wrote that 'Haltwhistle is full of uncouth but curious old houses which betoken the state of constant insecurity and of dubious defence in which the inhabitants of the Border were so long accustomed to live'. Such bastles and stronghouses that remain today are so much altered and disguised as to be hardly recognizable, although a good example on Castle Hill was demolished as late as 1963. The same rather stern and utilitarian aspect is reflected in the C 18 buildings which survive. The MARKET PLACE is a relatively small square. On the S, screening the churchyard, is a low and irregular row of largely C 18 buildings, including the BLACK BULL INN. At the SW corner is the MIDLAND BANK, Baroque and ashlar-faced, of *c.* 1900, and at the SE corner a taller Italianate Gothic block, also once a bank, of *c.* 1870. On the N a taller row of C 18 buildings, incorporating some older thick walls and rubble plinths from C 16 or C 17 bastles. One lower two-storey building, now a fish-and-chip shop, has an upper-cruck roof. Adjoining this is the RED LION HOTEL, which consists of a rare urban tower with an attached three-storey C 18 wing (again with upper crucks). The tower does not have a vaulted basement; the stair is in the thickness of the W return. The corbelled-out parapet (restored at the front but otherwise original, with several old waterspouts) encloses a gabled cap-house (cf. Embleton Old Vicarage). How does this tower, of traditional medieval form, relate in date and purpose to the sub-medieval defensible houses in the town? One window, lighting the mural stair, has a cable-moulded surround of C 17 type, but this may be an insertion; a second-floor fireplace has a moulded segmental arch on corbels, and may also be C 17.

MAIN STREET runs E from the Market Place. On the S is the
MANOR HOUSE HOTEL, a tall C 18 double-pile house, with,
adjoining it, a two-storey house (now an office) dated 1740 on its
door lintel: this date marks a remodelling of an older bastle, the
E end of which shows a typical byre door (now blocked), with an
irregular surround of big blocks, set centrally. On the opposite
side of the road further E is the former TOWN HALL (now the
Georgie Girl Unisex Hair Salon) of 1861: ashlar, seven bays,
with echoes of Vanbrugh. Rusticated ground floor: the central
segmental-pedimented gablet originally contained a clock. E again
are PLEASANT PLACE HOUSE, a three-bay early C 19 villa, on
the N side and an early C 19 terrace on the S. WESTGATE runs W
from the Market Place: its best building is probably the MECH-
ANIC'S INSTITUTE of 1900, beside the Methodist Church. This
is a three-storey building of rock-faced stone, with a central rusticated arched entrance beneath a carved date panel. Pilasters
divide the front into three bays, except at the second floor, which
is set slightly back and subdivided by additional pilasters corbelled
forward at mid-height.

ALSTON ARCHES VIADUCT, $\frac{1}{4}$ m. SE. Six-arch viaduct of 1852 by
Sir George Barclay-Bruce, carrying the former Alston branch across
the South Tyne (cf. the Burnstones Viaduct at Knarsdale). Rock-
faced stone. Four wide segmental skew arches span the river. The
piers are cut by round arches for an intended pedestrian walkway.

HALTWHISTLE BURN INDUSTRIES. The burn from Cawfields to
the N, running down to its confluence with the Tyne, once witnessed or supported a variety of industries. Cawfields whinstone
quarry at the N end was served by a narrow gauge TUBWAY 1902–
52, which ran alongside the burn to a connexion with the mainline railway in Haltwhistle. This tubway, however, incorporated
earlier sections of line associated with limekilns and a colliery at
the N end of the valley; its alignment and bridges now make a
useful pathway down the valley.

From N to S the walker will meet in sequence a pair of collapsed
LIMEKILNS on the E bank from the first half of the C 19 and a
probably earlier single kiln on the W bank, with three pointed
draw arches, disused by 1856. A COLLIERY SITE associated with
the E bank kilns was certainly active in the mid-C 19, with a
prominent chimney, cylindrical on the outside but with a square-
sectioned flue, stone-built but with a brick top section (perhaps
a later addition); engine beds nearby and a collapsed level. 1 m.
S, past the sites of two woollen mills and the South Tyne Colliery
and Brickworks of 1848, (all active in the mid-C 19 but closed
down before 1921), are the remaining buildings of the later site
of the SOUTH TYNE COLLIERY, *c.* 1871–1930s, a range of two-
storey brick buildings which once housed blacksmith and joiners'
shops, stores and offices; the fire-clay works alongside started in
the 1940s and closed in the 1960s. Further SW, and on the W side
of the burn, is the site of the 1856 'Haltwhistle Gas Light Company
Incorporated', whose chairman by 1886 was also the proprietor
of the colliery. Just beyond, and on the opposite side of the burn,
OAKWELL TERRACE, probably built in 1848 for coal workers,
for it had a tubway spur to the rear for delivering concessionary
coal. S of the main road bridge on the E side of the burn, a group

of buildings comprising a house, a short row of two-storey cottages and a small cart shed, were once a BREWERY, established before 1825. Beyond these, a three-storey house with outbuildings was formerly a WOOLLEN MILL, which seems to have begun operations in 1762. On the opposite bank of the burn, where now stands the depot of a haulage contractor, once stood the short-lived Haltwhistle Ironworks, established in 1856 with a blast furnace, calciners, coke ovens etc. but probably closed in the 1860s.

BELLISTER CASTLE. See p. 166.

BLENKINSOPP. See p. 192.

CAWFIELDS. See p. 216.

GREAT CHESTERS. See p. 289.

PARK VILLAGE. See p. 540.

WALLTOWN. See p. 607.

9000   HARBOTTLE

CASTLE. A motte-and-bailey, first constructed for Henry II by the Umfravilles shortly after 1157. The castle, which crouches on an isolated ridge above the River Coquet, commanded the routes through upper Coquetdale and was the stronghold of the Lords of Redesdale. It had an active history and was taken by Robert the Bruce in 1318. The Umfravilles died out in the C15 and the property passed to the Talbot (Tailbois) family, who in turn exchanged it with Henry VIII for property elsewhere (see Introduction, p. 67). By 1604 the castle was described as 'much decayed'. It is one of the finest medieval earthworks in the county. The motte, surrounded by its own ditch, is at the centre of the s side of the original semicircular bailey, of which only the w half was later fortified in stone. A causeway crossed the bailey ditch from the E, just below the motte, but the motte could only be approached from the w, i.e. from within the bailey. In the C13 the motte received a shell keep with projecting towers, like a smaller version of the keep at Alnwick. At the same time the bailey was divided in two by a curtain wall, parts of which (notably a long, high and dramatic stretch on the E side, ending in a square tower at the NE angle) retain much of their original stonework. At the s end of this wall, protecting the causeway already mentioned, was a gatehouse, with a later barbican on its E side. These have gone, but there are two other substantial fragments of curtain wall on the w side of the bailey. The C13 keep was reconstructed after 1545 as a towerless shell with gun-posts. Several of the small oval gunloops remain, along with two quite substantial chunks of masonry. To the E of the castle, the E half of the original bailey may have been unfortified during these later phases; to the E of that, the slightly sunken causeway which led down to the village can still be identified.

CASTLE HOUSE, at the s end of the village. 1829 by *Dobson*, possibly incorporating an earlier core. Plain, square, two-storey, five-bay villa in beautiful pale buff sandstone ashlar. Slightly later stone porch on the entrance side over the original doorcase, which has attached Tuscan columns. Built for Thomas Clennell.

The STABLES, 100 metres W, a simple L-shaped range, are probably also by *Dobson*; well converted into a house *c.* 1980.

The VILLAGE street is exceptionally pretty, though without any buildings of note. It draws its appeal from the harmonious variety and the even beauty of its stonework, which is a pale biscuit-coloured sandstone cut in large satisfying blocks. The SCHOOL is a National School of 1834 in the Tudor style. The CLENNELL MEMORIAL FOUNTAIN, 1880 by *Macmillan* of Alnwick, is high Victorian Gothic, inappropriate but good fun. Disused PRESBYTERIAN CHAPEL of 1854, with a corbelled-out octagonal bellcote over the gable. An early C 19 ICEHOUSE, which belonged to Castle House, is now in the garden of Windley Cottage.

DRAKE STONE. Huge boulder of Fell Sandstone within Harbottle Crags Nature Reserve. A MILLSTONE QUARRY, immediately W, exploited from the C 16 to the early C 19, is marked by extraction scars and rejected rough-outs; deeply cut sledge tracks descend the hillside.

HAREHAUGH *see* HOLYSTONE

HARNHAM   *0080*
c. 2 m. NW of Belsay

HARNHAM HALL. Not at all a large house, and rather plain, with its pebbledashed façade; but a house rich in history and atmosphere. There was a *'fortalice'* recorded here in the 1415 list of castles, fortalices and towers in the county, and indeed the site is well chosen for defence, with steep rocky slopes on two sides. Among the walls lining these slopes are patches of decidedly medieval masonry which may represent the remains of this fortalice. The present house seems to be of later date. There is a tower at the back, high up the rocky bank and on a daring substructure, but it appears to be C 16 or even C 17. Its walls are no more than 0.6 metre (2 ft) thick, and its windows are all C 16 or C 17. The house in front is probably also C 16, much altered in the C 17 and C 18. It has two doorways. The original doorway to the l. led into a former cross passage. The later, almost central, doorway is late C 17; it still has a four-centred-arched lintel, but it is decorated with small nail-head – a remarkable example of medieval revival. The windows are all C 18 sashes. Inside is an early C 18 staircase, quite finely detailed with turned balusters. The main room, which is low and cottagey, is dominated by a huge segmental-arched fireplace into which an early C 18 fireplace has been inserted, and by a splendid plaster ceiling of *c.* 1670. It shows a dragon in a circle of high-relief oak leaves: quite barbaric.

The dragon represents the crest of the Babington family, who owned the house from *c.* 1660 to 1677. Dame Katherine Babington was a dissenter, the militant daughter of Sir Arthur Hazelrigg. She is said to have plotted with the village blacksmith to have the vicar of Bolam pulled out of his pulpit during church service. As a result she was excommunicated, and when she died in 1670 she was refused burial in consecrated ground; so she was buried in a sepulchral vault hollowed out of the rock in the garden below the house. The TOMB is tunnel-vaulted. There are two inscriptions; one in stone and one in wood which reads:

> In hopes of future bliss contented here I lie
> Though I would have been pleased to live, yet was
> not displeased to die.

On the wall above the tomb, a series of C 18 Janus-headed busts.
The VILLAGE or hamlet is tiny – just a series of byres and three houses descending the ridge on which the hall stands. The farm buildings are all dated and initialled by members of the Leighton family who owned Harnham in the C 18. The dates vary from 1736 to 1799. The houses are also early to mid-C 18, except for SUNDIAL HOUSE at the bottom of the village, which has a blocked bastle-type doorway and two small oddly decorated C 17 windows. The walls, however, are not thick enough for a real bastle, so a late C 17 date seems more likely.
BRADFORD, ¾ m. SW. The present farmhouse is C 19, but amongst the farm buildings the OLD HALL is a rare example in the county of a mid-C 16 house that is neither tower, strong house nor bastle. Much altered externally, the house is two-storeyed and has a ground-floor hall containing a big moulded fireplace with the inscription G.O. [Gabriel Ogle] 1567.

HARTBURN

The church and vicarage lie beautifully on a tongue between two streams with a steep fall down to the N.

ST ANDREW. An intriguing church, with a pre-Conquest core, late C 12 to early C 13 W tower, and a chancel of the same date extended in the later C 13. The tower is broad and in three stages, the setback buttresses being a later addition. It has round-headed as well as lancet windows, two-light pointed bell openings with typical C 13 shafts, and an original corbel table and parapet. Later W window of three lights with Perp panel tracery. Barrel-vaulted ground floor. The blocked round-headed tower arch is an insertion into an earlier W wall, cutting into an arched high-level doorway above. The nave has massive pre-Conquest E quoins, those on the S tooled to represent coursed masonry, with low aisles added in the C 13. The E and W aisle windows are original and of lancet-type outside, with shouldered rere-arches of two different types inside. Those at the E end are especially curious. Near the E end of the S aisle a piscina with trefoiled-pointed arch, the moulding comprising a roll with a fillet. The S doorway has one order of colonnettes, a keeled roll moulding and the uncommon motif of a band of dogtooth all up the sides and round the arch (cf. Bolam). It looks like the work of an over-enthusiastic Hexham mason. The S porch is probably late C 13 but has a good C 18 tilted sundial as a finial. The chancel is also clearly C 13 (except for the parapet and roof-line), long, as was usual in the

North, with a group of three separate stepped lancets at the E end and single lancets to the S. No windows to the N. The E lancets are separated outside by semi-octagonal buttresses (cf. Brinkburn and Hexham) and inside by tall shafts with shaft rings and keeled arches. On the S side one of the lancets is a 'low side' window. The head has two little crockets so as to make it appear cusped. The priest's door has a shouldered lintel.

The interior arcades are of four bays with octagonal piers and moulded capitals. One of the capitals on the N side introduces the curious motif of beads or blobs hanging down over the bell of the capital from the abacus. The chancel arch is taller than the arcade arches and has semi-octagonal responds, enriched originally by accompanying shafts towards the chancel. – SEDILIA with keeled roll in the arch mouldings. PISCINA, trefoiled-pointed; a second piscina or stoup E of the priest's door. – FONT. Circular bowl on pillar with three shafts. – MONUMENTS. Frosterley marble slab on chancel floor with Lombardic inscription to Sir Thomas Errington † 1310. – Lady Bradford † 1830, by *Chantrey*, dated 1834. White marble, reclining figure propped up by a cushion and leaning against the head of an Empire couch. The background of stone is in Perp Gothic. – Tablet to Hodgson, the historian of Northumberland, † 1848, against the back of a sedilia arch. – J. H. H. Atkinson, by *Armstead*, 1873, white marble recumbent effigy, with figures of Christ and two angels in relief behind. – Medieval stone COFFINS. – STAINED GLASS. E window of S aisle by *Kempe*, 1904.

In the CHURCHYARD the best collection in the county of well-preserved C18 HEADSTONES, many carved on both faces. [72] Cherubs, death's heads and various mortality emblems abound. That to Joseph Hepple † 1754, with a death's head on a vermiculated field, is one of the best.

OLD VICARAGE. The heavy rubble and thick walls of the three-storey six-bay main block suggest a C16 date, although most visible features are C18. The lower N wing incorporates a barrel-vaulted ground floor with opposed doorways, perhaps a kitchen passage through the solar undercroft of a C13 or early C14 house (cf. Low Hall at Corbridge). Mid-C18 SE wing, altered in the early C19.

Dr Sharp, vicar of Hartburn in 1749–92, 'improved' his vicarage grounds c. 1760. A lancet-arched FOOTBRIDGE survives on the path down to his GROTTO. This is partly rock-cut, in a cliff above the Hart Burn. There are Gothick arches and a fireplace inside, and a slab-roofed tunnel down to the Burn for discreet bathers.

OLD SCHOOLHOUSE. 1762, also by Dr Sharp. A tower rising in three steps on the bank above the Burn. Castellated, symmetrical with a big heavy ogee arch to the principal window.

TEMPLE THORNTON, 1 m. E. Here is an early C19 dovecote modelled on the parish church tower. The adjacent house, rebuilt in the C19, retains a doorhead dated 1694 with a stepped moulding above a flattened triangular arch, a simpler version of that at Corridge (*see* Middleton).

ANGERTON. *See* p. 147.
MIDDLETON. *See* p. 388.

2080
HARTFORD HALL

Country house of 1807 by *William Stokoe* of Newcastle for William
Burdon; latterly a miners' rehabilitation centre. In a fine position
overlooking the wooded valley of the Blyth. The s front has a
central three-window bow. Old prints show it flanked by symmetrical single-storey blocks. These were swept away in extensive
alterations of *c.* 1875, which left the bow with its lead dome but
added a big porch and *porte cochère* on the N. High Victorian
interior. The stable block to the E was converted at the same time
into a covered exercise yard surrounded by an iron balcony; it is
now a gymnasium. Spectacular heavy and lush wrought-iron
GATE SCREEN by the *Coalbrookdale Co.*, made for and exhibited
at the Vienna Exhibition of 1873; some of the detail, such as the
shaping of the ends of the top rail into human hands grasping the
bar tops, is difficult to take seriously.

HARTFORD BRIDGE. Largely rebuilt in 1904, but the triple-chamfered N arch (only visible from the E, as the bridge has been
widened) is late medieval. HARTFORD BRIDGE HOUSE, looking
across the bridge, is probably of 1836 (date on outbuilding).

HARTLEY *see* SEATON SLUICE

HARTSIDE *see* INGRAM

0020
HAUGH HEAD
1 m. S of Wooler

SURREY HOUSE, on the A697. Formerly a coaching inn called the
George and Dragon. Said to be C 17 in origin. The present building is early–mid-C 18, of three bays and plain, but with its fine
dressed stone, pantiled roofs, and cluster of irregular lean-tos it
makes a picturesque sight. Daniel Defoe stayed here in 1727.

On the hill beside it, a later C 18 Gothick DOVECOTE. It is
octagonal with quatrefoil openings, and must have been built as
a gazebo, as the interior is rib-vaulted and has traces of painted
decoration. The nesting boxes are built into the blocked window
openings.

9070
HAUGHTON

34 HAUGHTON CASTLE. Haughton Castle now appears as an elongated tower-house with embattled parapets and taller turrets at
the corners and corbelled out above the centre of the S side. The
aesthetic delight in this fine, tall, symmetrically grouped front is
matched by the archaeological interest of the building history and
the details. As H. L. Honeyman first pointed out, the castle is the

product of at least two stages of development. In its original c 13 form it was a first-floor hall house on the lines of the recently excavated hall block at Edlingham, which is a building with rather more pretensions to defence than houses like Aydon. It had corner turrets (rectangular rather than polygonal, as at the later Edlingham) projecting from the end walls only, with the exception of that at the s e corner, which does not project at all. Each of the long sides of the block (which measures 14.9 by 32 metres, 49 by 107 feet) had a row of five tall arches in front of it, 'murder holes' in the soffits protecting the wall foot. Above, at the w end of the s wall, was the hall doorway, presumably reached by some form of external stair. This survives, but now only opens in a lobby in the wall thickness: it has a filleted arch with nail-head ornament. To the e of the hall was the solar, and a room above with an oratory (still with its piscina) at its s e corner. This end of the building may have been carried up as a tower from the first. In the late c 14 the building was remodelled and heightened to its present form; the turrets are presumably of this date. The wall-arcades were presumably infilled at this time, to provide additional support for the walls. This interpretation is not proven in detail: Honeyman and others considered the wall-arcades to be a c 14 addition to the original fabric. They are certainly a very unusual feature. Single giant arches used to protect entrances occur at Lumley Castle and the fortified c 13 hall house at Old Hollinside (both in County Durham). The hall block or tower-house did not stand alone – a drawing made in 1538 shows the ruins of a curtain wall and gateway – but it was certainly the principal component of the castle. The interior has been much altered over the last two centuries (*Dobson* was at work here in 1845) but retains twin segmental vaults running the length of the block at basement level and a newel stair in the s w turret ending in a pretty umbrella vault. The n w turret has corbelled-out garderobes on the n. Two rooms have large Jacobean overmantels imported from a house in Sandhill in Newcastle; but most features, including many of the windows, are c 19. The main stair is an insertion of 1886. At second-floor level on the s are three c 14 two-light windows with trefoiled ogee heads and transoms. The oriels on the s and e are a c 19 invention, as is the external stair (1812, with an attractive late c 19 timber-framed superstructure) at the e end. To the w is a lower embattled wing of 1876 by *Salvin*. More embattled walls and a mock gatehouse beyond are mostly of 1816.

CHAPEL. A solitary ruin in the park 150 metres s e of the Castle, partly demolished *c.* 1816, when the village of Haughton was cleared and the park enclosed. All that stands is the e gable, with a ragged hole where a window was, and the base of the s e corner of the nave. Excavation showed it to have been a two-cell building of typically c 12 form. In the ruins lies the head of a c 13 window, of two lancet lights with a pierced quatrefoil in the spandrel. This is said to come from the second-floor oratory in the castle.

HAUGHTON MILL, ¼ m. e of the Castle. The mill itself is partly demolished: the remaining building is the offices and drying shed 117 of a paper mill founded in 1788 (*see* Introduction, p. 88). This has a projecting centrepiece with a rusticated doorway below a large arched opening breaking into the pedimented gable above:

the side parts have large wood-slatted openings to the first-floor drying shed. In 1793 French *assignats* were forged here to lower the value of the currency of the French revolutionary government.

WESTER HALL, ¼ m. E of the Castle. Five-bay house of 1732 (date on reset lintel in garden wall) remodelled as a villa in the early C 19. In the garden to the s an early C 18 summerhouse-cum-dovecote, brick on two sides, with some rustic sculpture over the door and one window.

HAYDON BRIDGE

The small town straddles the South Tyne. The Greenwich Hospital Commissioners, to whom the Derwentwater estates passed in the C 18 (*see* Dilston), were responsible for a number of interesting buildings. The tall C 18 ANCHOR HOTEL on the s bank turns its back to the bridge approach, all except for the rear wing with sash windows and arched doorway with fanlight, which was the former Rent House for the Commissioners. On the hill above, the Commissioners' SHAFTOE TERRACE, a group of almshouses of *c*. 1805; two-storey warden's house flanked by single-storey cottages, and a two-storey house at each end. At the back a tall embattled garden wall.

ST CUTHBERT, on the N bank of the river. 1796; built by the Commissioners. N transept added in 1869 to accommodate children from the Shaftoe Trust School. Chancel enlarged and s elevation gothicized in 1898. The older parts have round-headed windows. Nice W tower, narrower than the nave, with a concave pyramid, i.e. pagoda-like, roof. – MONUMENT. C 14 effigy under a crocketed canopy, damaged, from the Old Church. – STAINED GLASS. *Kempe* glass in chancel.

HAYDON OLD CHURCH, ½ m. N, where the medieval village of Haydon lay. The church had a W tower, nave with s aisle, and chancel with s chapel. The W parts were demolished to provide stone for the new church, the surviving chancel and chapel being restored by *C. C. Hodges* in 1882. The chancel is C 12 and probably quite early in the century, *see* the three round-headed slits in the E end, a similar window on the s and a blocked square-headed N door. The chapel is C 14, with a two-light Dec E window. Inside, the E end has a moulded sill string and shafted jambs to the windows. The two-bay arcade and good king-post roof are C 19. – FONT. A recut Roman altar. – MONUMENTS. Inscribed C 14 CROSS SLAB on the chancel floor and pieces of others reset in blocked N door.

VICARAGE, E of St Cuthbert. A three-bay house of *c*. 1820.

ST JOHN OF BEVERLEY (R.C.), off the E side of Church Street, 1873. Nave, chancel and W bellcote; trefoil-headed lancets and a cusped round window in the W gable.

CEMETERY, E of the village. Some white ceramic crosses of the 1920s bear the stamp of 'The Langley Barony Coal & Fireclay Co., Sanitary Ware Manufacturers'.

TICKET OFFICE AND STATIONMASTER'S HOUSE, now No. 2 Station Cottages. Built *c*. 1835 for the Newcastle and Carlisle

Railway, possibly by the *Greens*; an attractive stone building with a three-bay N portico with flattened Tudor arches.

BRIDGE. A bridge across the South Tyne existed here in 1309, but it, or more likely a successor, was lost in the 1771 flood. A new bridge was opened *c.* 1776 but a 28.5-metre (95-ft) span reputedly collapsed in 1805. In 1816 there was still a temporary bridge across the river, but a six-arch bridge is recorded in 1824 as having been recently repaired and widened. The six arches are of unequal span, built of ashlar masonry with massive pointed cutwaters carried up as half-hexagonal retreats. The N arch was rebuilt *c.* 1969. The new road bridge alongside was built in 1970.

ALTON SIDE, 1 m. E. An extended C16 bastle house, with an unusually elaborate moulded upper door on the N.

ELRINGTON HALL, 1¼ m. SE. Late C17 T-plan house rewindowed in the C19 but retaining its collar-beam truss roofs.

THREEPWOOD HALL, 1 m. S. Once similar to Elrington Hall but remodelled in the late C18; picturesque three-storey five-bay front with sashes in raised and chamfered surrounds. Closed-string open-well stair of *c.* 1690.

LIPWOOD HOUSE, 2 m. W. Ashlar-fronted five-bay house of *c.* 1800, with a Tuscan porch. Four-bay S front with broad central bow. The largely contemporary interior has a Regency staircase with cast-iron balusters. Stable block with projecting pedimented centre.

CHESTERWOOD. *See* p. 224.

HEALEY

0050

ST JOHN. 1860 by *Major C. E. Davis* of Bath. Neo-Norman style. Nave with apsidal sanctuary and S porch. Davis originally planned a stone vault but this was abandoned after two collapses. Some rather bizarre detail, such as the W rose-window, must be seen to be believed: it is circular, but the tracery is only about three eighths of that of a normal rose-window, i.e. a fan-shape of four columns and three arches. It is reset in an otherwise sober W tower added in 1890 by *Montgomery and Carr.* – STAINED GLASS. Attractive Dickinson memorial window of 1912 (the infant Samuel) and three windows by *L. C. Evetts*, 1955–1960 (scenes from the life of St Cuthbert).

VICARAGE, immediately S of the church. 1877 by *Ewan Christian*. Big, in Tudor style. Rock-faced stone.

HEALEY HALL, ¾ m. SW of the church. Old drawings show a tall building with an embattled look-out turret on one gable end, i.e. a stronghouse rather like the demolished Low Hirst 'Tower' near Ashington and the Melkridge bastle house (both demolished in the C20). In 1834 this was replaced by the present Tudor-style house, with a symmetrical twin-gabled entrance front. Part of the C17 N wing of the old house survives in the stable block behind.

HEALEY MILL, ¾ m. W of the Hall. A delightfully located and very fine watermill complex, with three-storey mill, two-storey house and one-and-a-half-storey stable block, all in line. Stone-built, with better-quality stonework reserved for the house; blue slates and some roofing flags. A converted kiln house projects from the mill. All the millwrighting still exists: it is largely C 19. The curved DAM still holds water. The head-race is partly in a rock-cut channel, partly in an iron pipe and finally in an open wooden launder supported on a stone wall. Disused since *c.* 1900 but still cared for.

MINSTERACRES. *See* p. 390.

HEATON *see* NEWCASTLE UPON TYNE

1080   # HEBRON

ST CUTHBERT. A two-cell medieval church remodelled in 1793. The chancel masonry may be C 12, but the only recognizably medieval feature is the double-chamfered C 14 or C 15 chancel arch. Gothick the nave windows and the pretty W bellcote.

1060   # HEDDON-ON-THE-WALL

ST ANDREW. A church of considerable archaeological fascination. First there is evidence of the Saxon church. At the SE corner of the nave there are massive Anglo–Saxon quoins on edge. The W part of the chancel is said to be early Norman, rather than Saxon. It has a very narrow blocked priest's door with a plain tympanum and masonry which matches it in date. Inside there is another tympanum over the door to the vestry. Presumably this early church was apsed and the apse removed to provide the new square sanctuary in the C 12. It is a remarkable piece of architecture but visible from outside only in one tiny round-headed N window. Inside it is rib-vaulted. The ribs rest on odd diagonally squeezed-in thick shafts at the E corners and on triple responds with similar shafts at the sanctuary arch. Of the three thick shafts which stand side by side there, two support the sanctuary arch with its unmoulded soffit and big zigzag towards the W; only the third supports the ribs. The ribs are of two parallel roll mouldings, meeting in one big keystone in the middle. The next phase of development was the building of a N aisle *c.* 1200. It is of three bays, with round piers and capitals but pointed arches with a single narrow chamfer. The last capital and the E respond have leaf decoration, one with a thick crocket-like frieze, the other with waterleaf. A little later in the C 13 the chancel was remodelled and the S aisle added. The chancel has on the S side two pairs of very long thin lancets with a pierced circle above bearing a stone head – a kind of minimum plate tracery. The S aisle has circular piers, like the N aisle, but the arches are normal double-chamfered. The chancel arch also has a double-chamfered arch resting on semi-octagonal responds. The N capital has nail-head. The S door is C 13 too; it has one order of colonnettes with moulded capitals. The S porch appears to be the latest medieval element in the church. It cuts partly across the c 13 doorway and has a steep tunnel vault. The outer doorway has a continuous chamfer. It was probably built in the later c 14 or the c 15. Finally the c 19. The N and S aisles were raised and rewindowed in 1839. The W end and the W bay of the nave were added, which incidentally involved turning the W responds, rather cleverly, into complete piers. The E window was restored c. 1875. – FONT. c 17; small and round, on a round base with a moulded foot. – GLASS. E window by *Kempe*, 1875: a 'Jesse' window. – MONUMENT. The head of a Saxon wheel-head cross on a chancel N window sill.

EAST HEDDON, 1 m. N. Among the farm buildings at the back of the farmhouse there is a much-altered c 16 or early c 17 house, now used as byres and granary. It has various windows of that date and several fireplaces also. The roof and floor timbers are all old. The roof has nine bays, with five different forms of roofing truss.

HEDDON HALL, ½ m. SE. C 18, extended in the early c 19 and extensively remodelled in 1824 for I. M. Bates in Grecian style. Five bays, two storeys, with a higher two-storey tower on the l. Quite a good, if restrained, interior, with coffered ceilings, an extremely Greek fireplace in the hall and an imposing cantilevered stair with hexagonal balusters.

HOUGHTON, a hamlet ½ m. W of Heddon, has a nice group of early c 19 farmhouses and cottages. Several of them dated. The best is the Old School House, of c. 1800; five bays and two storeys with all the openings in raised stone surrounds.

CLOSE HOUSE, ¾ m. SW. 1779 for Calverly and Mary Bewick, but on the site of an earlier house. The architect is unrecorded; it looks as if it might be by *Newton*. A fine restrained five-bay front of two-and-a-half storeys, with a slight three-bay projection and a three-bay pediment. Doorway with broken pediment on Tuscan columns. One room inside with rich imitation dixhuitième stucco work. Could it be by the Duke of Northumberland's Italian team of c. 1850 at Alnwick? Another room has an early c 18 fireplace with a bolection-moulded surround flanked by full-height fluted Ionic pilasters. It has an Adam-style ceiling.

The GARDENS have several features. To the NW of the house, an ORANGERY of five bays with Tuscan columns. W of that, a deep dene crossed by a high late c 18 ashlar BRIDGE. SW of the house there is an ICEHOUSE. The grounds are landscaped with a ha-ha. The cricket pitch at the bottom (the house now belongs to Newcastle University) has a pavilion and score board of 1894 by *Septimus Oswald*.

TIDESTONE, on the bank of the Tyne S of Heddon Hall. A stone c. 1 metre high inscribed with the shield of Newcastle upon Tyne and the date 1783. It marks the tidal limit of the river and the limit of jurisdiction of the Port of Tyne Authority.

WEST HEDDON, 1½ m. NNW. Beside the farmhouse is a cottage in an almost ruinous condition. It has, however, a tiny but sophisticated c 17 façade, most surprising for this area, with hoodmoulds, mullioned windows and a door with a four-centred arch, all in good-quality dressed stone.

RUDCHESTER, 1½ m. WNW. A late Georgian five-bay house with

Gothick windows. But the SE corner, hardly visible at all from outside, is a medieval tower with walls *c*. 1.5 metres (5 ft) thick. From outside the only indication that this part is any older is a small window with a cusped ogee head. Inside, this opens out into a window embrasure with a Caernarvon lintel. In the roof space the parapet and a water spout survive; and on the ground floor a large fireplace with a moulded surround and a lintel carved with shields and two crocketed swags.

RUDCHESTER ROMAN FORT (*Vindobala*). Little more than a rectangular platform is visible, best preserved on the S and W. Its S half is immediately N of the farm buildings, whilst the N half projects beyond Hadrian's Wall, here marked by the B6318. The Wylam–Stamfordham road runs just outside its E wall. A Hadrianic foundation, it was allowed to decay in the late C 3, until reoccupied in the late C 4.

HADRIAN'S WALL. Just E of Heddon-on-the-Wall, on the S side of the Throckley road, a long stretch of the Wall is seen, in its original broad gauge. Towards the W end a much later limekiln has been carefully built into the ruins.

BAYS LEAP FARM, just N of Heddon-on-the-Wall, built on former coal opencast mining land in the 1960s. A simple two-storey farmhouse with large steel-framed sheds alongside – the appropriate style for mixed arable farming in the mid-C 20.

0010

HEDGELEY HALL
1 m. NE of Powburn

The house seems to have begun as a relatively small building of the C 17 or early C 18, extended to the E in the late C 18. Of this period are the big Gothick bow and embattled screen wall at the W end, their style obviously influenced by Adam's work in and around Alnwick. Some other detail, however, is rather odd, such as the roll-moulded angle pilasters and window surrounds, and the crowstepped E gable. This house was enlarged to the N in the C 19, but these extensions were swallowed up in a major remodelling of 1910–14 by *George Reavell* for Colonel Henry Carr-Ellison. The old house became no more than a S range to a new Tudor-style mansion; some internal detail (mostly doors and fireplaces) was brought from Dunston Hill (Gateshead) and Hebburn Hall in County Durham. Also early C 20 the GATEHOUSE and various outbuildings, including the tackroom with a tall stepped gable containing a dovecote.

LOW HEDGELEY, 1 m. NW. The home farm to the Hall. Extensive and interesting complex of farm buildings, which began as a late C 18 foldyard group and was extended at various C 19 dates. The mid-C 19 parts, characterized by gable finials and lots of shouldered arches, are by *F. R. Wilson*. A group of shelter sheds to the NE have timber arcades on padstones, an unusual feature in Northumberland; they are probably late C 18. The covered yards of *c*. 1900 have arcades of cast-iron columns.

HEDGELEY MOOR   *0010*

PERCY'S CROSS, 1 m. SW of Wooperton, E of the A697 just N of
a row of cottages, down a short footpath. Memorial to the 1464
battle, when Sir Ralph Percy fell leading the Lancastrian army.
The head is missing, but the shaft stands to 3 metres (10 ft) and
is carved with a variety of Percy emblems.

HEDLEY ON THE HILL   *0050*

METHODIST CHAPEL. 1837. Now a house.
WOODHEAD, ¾ m. SE. C 17 farmhouse, perhaps originally a bastle.
   Door with flat-pointed head, and remains of mullioned windows.
HOLLINGS, 1 m. SE. Later C 17 farmhouse, refronted and extended
   in the early C 19. Three-bay upper cruck roof.

HEIFERLAW TOWER   *1010*
3 m. N of Alnwick

Built as a lookout tower for Alnwick Abbey; it is too small to have
been residential. The form of the Percy arms, on both S and E
sides, dates it to between 1470 and 1489 (Hugill). The shell is
fairly intact, although the parapet has gone. Three low storeys,
with windows mostly single lights (one cusped on the E). An
inserted C 18 Gothick quatrefoil on the S. The first floor was
carried on big transverse beams, not a vault; the stair must have
been of timber as well.
HECKLEY FENCE, ½ m. SE, has a pyramid-roofed Gothick dovecote
   with more quatrefoils.
HECKLEY HOUSE, 1 m. S. Late C 18 five-bay house with open-
   pedimented doorway and *trompe-l'œil* windows on the l. return.

HENSHAW   *7060*

ALL HALLOWS. 1888–9. Aisleless, in E.E. style.
The hamlet of TOW HOUSE, on the S side of the A69, has a trio of
   interesting buildings. TOWER HOUSE is, despite its name, an
   excellent bastle house, with a massive boulder plinth and quoins.
   Blocked roll-moulded byre doorway set centrally in the W end.
   The basement has heavy ceiling beams and a tight newel stair in
   the SE corner; is this an original feature (cf. the Old Schoolhouse
   at Snitter or Woodhouses Bastle near Holystone)? The roof has
   a heavy truss, with a cambered tie-beam and a collar. Across the
   road to the NW is another rarity, a heather-thatched CRUCK BARN
   with four full cruck trusses (cf. High Meadow near Bardon Mill),
   recently restored by the *Doonan and Haggie Partnership*. Across
   the road N of the barn is a former house, now a BARN, of
   the bastle period but not a bastle as such; it has thick walls, a

bastle-like doorway, timber-mullioned windows in the gable end, and evidence of former crucks (cf. Whitlees, at Elsdon).

EAST TWICE BREWED, $1\frac{1}{2}$m. N, on the Military Road. Three-bay farmhouse dated 1776; doorway in architrave and windows in simple raised surrounds. The farm buildings are probably contemporary.

9000

HEPPLE

CHRIST CHURCH. 1893–4 by *J. Hodgson Fowler*. Very simple solid neo-Perp, with three-light E window and mostly three-light windows. The division between nave and chancel is marked by a well-detailed bell turret. Beautiful views over the Coquet valley. The nicely kept interior gains much from its brightly painted colour scheme. The chancel is more richly furnished, with a SCREEN, painted REREDOS and linenfold panelling. – FONT. Very primitive Norman, from the old church; cylindrical, but with figures standing tightly under arches; only one of them – a bearded man – is still clearly visible. – MONUMENTS. Two CROSS SLABS near the font.

HEPPLE TOWER. C 14. The W side is fairly complete, though without battlements or turrets. A little of the N wall stands also to full height and about half of the S front. The centre of the S front was originally a stair projection; the lower part of it remains. Much of the ground-floor vault survives. Corbels set into it must have supported a wooden loft. The tower is built of very precise squared blocks of buff sandstone.

HEPPLE WHITFIELD, 1 m. S. In a beautiful situation. A small country house built in the late C 19 for Sir J. W.B. Riddell and extended for him by *J. Hodgson Fowler c.* 1897. Tudor style.

Hepple parish has a number of BASTLE HOUSES on the moors W of the village. At CRAIG FARM, 2 m. WSW, is a fairly complete bastle among the farm buildings. The vaulted ground floor is intact, except where a doorway has been opened into the S side; in the SW corner is a very narrow mural stair, which, as it is original, is a very rare feature. The RAW FARM, $2\frac{1}{2}$m. SW of Hepple, has another very complete bastle among its farm buildings. It too is vaulted and it has the unusual feature of a window on the E side carved with a human hand, a rosette and tassels. In 1791 this bastle was the scene of the murder of Margaret Crozier by William Winter, whose body was hung in chains on Winter's Gibbet, Elsdon (q.v.). There are two bastles *c.* $\frac{1}{2}$m. NW of the Raw. HIGH SHAW, on the military ranges, is complete on the ground floor; it is vaulted and has gunloops. IRONHOUSE is ruinous but particularly impressive. The gable-end walls stand to *c.* 6 metres (20 ft); the side walls are not so high, but the masonry is very massive, and round about the bastle there are enclosure walls of equally massive stone work.

WITCHY NEUK, $\frac{3}{4}$m. WSW. A well-preserved D-shaped Iron Age hillfort on the crags W of Hepple Whitfield. A ditch fronts a single rampart, revetted by a stone wall, which was probably preceded by a timber palisade. Excavation revealed timber houses; a frag-

ment of c 3 Rhenish glass suggests continuous or later occupation.
A second palisade linked the fort to a linear earthwork which
extends SSE; their relative chronology is uncertain.

HEPSCOTT

HEPSCOTT HALL. A rather puzzling house, consisting of a three-
storey block with a taller square tower at the rear. The original
windows, where they survive, are mullioned or simply chamfered
single lights. The segmental-pointed arch of the front door looks
c 16 or early c 17, but all else, including the stair in the tower, is
late c 17. The tower looks like a conscious revival of the Northumbrian tower-house tradition, but it is thin-walled and has
never been defensive. A big c 18 hipped roof covering both main
block and tower was removed c. 1965 after a fire. The present flat
roofs on both parts may represent the original form. Early c 18
the rusticated GATE PIERS and the brick DOVECOTE to the NE.

HESLEYHURST
c. 2 m. s of Rothbury

HILLFORT, on Garleigh Moor, N of Lordenshaw. Multivallate Iron
Age defences, with a w entrance, less well-preserved on the SE.
A much smaller central enclosure, approached between flanking
banks from both E and W, may not be strictly contemporary in
origin. The broad space between these two inner and outer entities
is subdivided by radial banks, springing from the central enclosure, which are probably later than the hillfort. A sprawling settlement of round stone houses, probably Romano-British in date,
spills out over the line of the fort's ramparts on the SE.
    To the w and E a remarkable series of CUP-AND-RING-
MARKED ROCKS. The finest is 260 metres wsw of the centre of
the hillfort; partly quarried away, it still bears a wide variety of
symbols: simple cups, and others with single or multiple rings,
larger basins and sinuous grooves. On the E slopes of the hill,
amid a number of small burial cairns, nearly twenty other outcrops
bear many of the simpler symbols; the carved rocks extend ENE
from a point 180 metres SE of the fort to the vicinity of an exposed
burial CIST, 450 metres N of it.
BROCKLEY HALL FARMHOUSE, c. 1½ m. w. Probably originally a
bastle house of the c 16 (it was recorded in 1579); refronted by
Thomas Warton in 1666 and again restored in 1858. The doorway
has a finely moulded surround, with a four-centred arch, the lintel
dated and bearing a shield surrounded by foliage trails.

HESLEYSIDE
2 m. WNW of Bellingham

A courtyard house which has always been the home of the Charltons. Most of what one sees now is C18 work and of considerable interest. Inside the courtyard, however, is a blocked C17 loggia and a date 1631 on a stone over a door. Entry into the courtyard was by an archway through the S range. This range was refronted in 1719; it has nine bays, not quite regularly disposed, with thin giant angle pilasters, heavily segment-headed windows and a parapet. The archway remains but has a door and a window of the later C18 set within it. The r. two bays are an addition of 1796 in identical style by *William Newton*, who at that time was rebuilding the E range with a seven-bay, two-and-a-half-storey façade with three-bay pediment. Doorway with Ionic pilasters; a pedimented window above it. The main entrance is now on the N side and has to the l. a porch of 1796, moved from the E front in the mid-C19. To the r. of this, the courtyard is closed by a three-bay screen with a central rusticated carriage arch, and above it a two-stage clock tower in an Italianate style with an open-arcaded upper stage and a pyramidal roof. This façade and the much plainer W range are largely a rebuilding of 1847 by *Ignatius Bonomi*, who was a friend and distant relative of the Charltons.

Inside, in the centre of the E range, an imperial stair with cast-iron balustrade in a rectangular hall, a screen of Ionic columns at the foot of the stair, a screen of Corinthian columns on the first floor and an Adamish plaster ceiling. The plasterwork was done by *William Burnop*. In 1847 the entrance hall in front of the stairs was made into a dining room and prettily painted with stencilled decoration by *Thomas Worthington*.

HETHPOOL
2 m. SW of Kirknewton

TOWER. Ruins of a tiny tower. Three walls stand to *c.* 6 metres (20 ft), but the details are entirely obscured by rampant vegetation; probably a place of occasional refuge rather than a tower house.

HETHPOOL HOUSE. The house incorporates some masonry, including a dated door surround, of 1687; but essentially it was rebuilt in 1919 by *George Reavell* of Alnwick for Sir Arthur Munro Sutherland, a Tyneside industrialist. The style is a solid Tudor Arts-and-Crafts, rough-cast, with pink ashlar dressings. In 1928 *Robert Mauchlen* made most sensitive additions. At one corner he put a rounded tower with a conical roof and extruded from it a second, lower tower with a conical pent roof. The inspiration is Charles Rennie Mackintosh's Hill House, and the effect is most satisfying.

Mauchlen also designed the adjacent HETHPOOL COTTAGES in 1926. They too are in the Arts-and-Crafts style. Two pairs of semi-detached cottages linked by an archway; again, as at the house, there is a low tower at one end with a conical roof. The roofs are beautiful, with strangely iridescent slate, and the situation is superb.

The valleys of COLLEGE BURN and its tributaries are rich in the remains of early settlement, especially late prehistoric and Roman-period farmsteads scooped into the steep hillsides. Access is controlled by College Valley Estates.

The well-developed series of CULTIVATION TERRACES on the slopes of White Hill, immediately NW of Hethpool, may be prehistoric in origin; ploughing continued sporadically into post-medieval times: the latest phase of ridge-and-furrow crosses the contours.

RING CHESTERS, $1\frac{3}{4}$ m. W, is a multivallate hillfort with fragmentary wall-faces still visible and a staggered SE entrance. The foundations of stone houses (probably Roman in date) overlie the hollows of their Iron Age timber predecessors. Further SW, on the summit of Coldsmouth Hill, are two Bronze Age cairns; each had a central cist containing a cremation.

On the top of GREAT HETHA, $\frac{3}{4}$ m. SW, is an impressively sited hillfort surrounded by two stone walls, entered from the E. Excavation of a settlement 400 metres WNW towards Hetha Burn revealed four phases of occupation before the C3 A.D.: (a) an unenclosed timber house; (b) a rectilinear walled farmstead with two stone houses, later (c) increased to four; final expansion (d) took in five more buildings within an irregular S extension. Another broadly similar settlement lies close to the burn on the WNW.

HETTON HALL

3 m. N of Chatton

A house which incorporates a tower, said to date from 1580. The tower is of three storeys and rendered on the front. A semicircular stair projection rests on a large corbel at first-floor level: the corbel has ovolo mouldings. At the top the projection is corbelled out to receive a square turret, but this has now gone. The parapet has also vanished and has been replaced by a pitched roof, but some of the rounded corbels which once supported it remain on the r. return. In the gable, a small C16 window within a moulded surround. The range to the r. is also old in its masonry but has C19 mullioned windows. The range to the l. is later C18. Inside, only part of the ground-floor vault remains. On the top floor is a fireplace with four-centred-arched lintel.

SOUTH HAZELRIGG, 1 m. SE. A large farm with a house of 1828 built for Carnaby Haggerston, and extensive planned farm buildings presumably of the same time. They comprise a symmetrical E-shaped range and, facing it, a cartshed with twelve segmental arches on the ground floor and a granary over.

HOLBURN MILL, $1\frac{1}{2}$ m. N. An early C19 corn mill, relatively intact though in poor repair. It has a three-storey mill building, still with its wheel and most of the rest of the machinery. Next to it, a detached square corn-drying kiln with battered sides. The original miller's house, rather unusually, occupies just the ground floor of a two-storey cottage, which has granaries above.

HETTON HOUSE

½ m. E of Fowberry

A five-bay early–mid-C 18 house, its windows within architrave surrounds, its door with architrave, pulvinated frieze and cornice. To the rear, the hipped-roofed stair projection has a round-headed stair window with thick glazing bars. The C 18 interior is unusually complete and elaborate. There are several panelled rooms with modillion cornices; note especially the Green Room, which has a fireplace with bolection-moulded surround flanked by full-height Ionic columns and elaborate niches. The handsome staircase has two alternately twisted and fluted balusters to a tread.

HEXHAM

The old centre of Hexham crowns a bluff on the S bank of the Tyne, just below the confluence of North and South Tynes. The bluff is part of a dissected terrace of sands and gravels, isolated between the valleys of the Cockshaw and Halgut Burns (on the W) and that of the Skinners Burn (now culverted) on the E and SE. In terms of both history and architecture the name of Hexham is usually

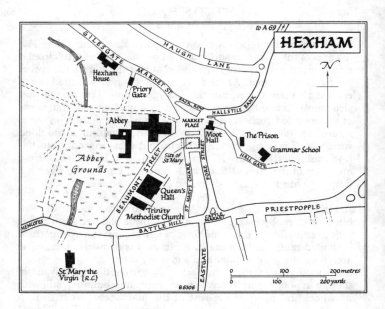

associated with its monastic history and the 'Abbey' (a misnomer:
the present church was that of a medieval priory). The monastic
buildings and precinct are set back from the edge of the terrace; the
'prime site', the spur-like end of the bluff E of the Market Place, is
now occupied by the Moot Hall and Manor Office. These mark the
administrative centre of the medieval Hexhamshire estates of the
Archbishop of York; do they occupy the site of a royal residence
pre-dating the granting of the estate to Wilfrid and his monks?

PRIORY CHURCH

The first church was built by Wilfrid c. 675–80, according to his
  biographer Eddius, in such a way that none other this side of the
  Alps could be compared with it. He describes it as 'supported by
  various columns and many side aisles' and 'surrounded by various
  winding passages with spiral stairs leading up and down'; the
  building was enriched with gold and silver and precious stone. Of
  this church the crypt remains virtually intact (Eddius's *profunditas
  politis lapidibus fundata*), and excavations have revealed what is
  now thought to be a detached apsidal chapel E of the crypt. There
  have been several attempts to reconstruct the plan of Wilfrid's
  church based on the foundations planned when the present nave
  was built (and the footings incorporated in its W and N walls),
  but recent research suggests that these are largely post-Conquest.
  Hexham was the see of a bishop from 681 till 821. By then Danish
  raids had begun, and Hexham was sacked most severely in 876.
  Nothing is known of the fate of the church in the following
  centuries, until it was refounded as the church of a priory of
  Augustinian canons in 1113. They rebuilt it with a nave aisled on
  the N only (all that is visible of this is the base of the W respond
  of the aisle, which looks in its profile rather late C 11 than early
  C 12, cf. Westminster Abbey and the chancel gallery at Gloucester)
  and an apsidal E end which has been excavated in the third bay
  from the W of the present chancel. The nave seems to have been
  rebuilt again in the C 15, but only its lower W and S walls survive.
  With these exceptions the church as we see it today belongs
  essentially to two periods: c. 1180–1250, and c. 1850–1910. The E
  end dates from 1858, the nave from 1907–9, the rest is E.E.
    EXTERIOR. The church exposes to the Market Place a dis-
  appointing Victorian E front of 1858 by *Dobson*, modelled on the
  example of Whitby Abbey. It replaces a far more varied medieval
  E end, and this was never meant to be seen from the Market
  Place. A row of houses backed by the precinct wall marked the
  boundary between the world of the town and the world of the
  priory. The E end consisted of five low C 14 chapels of even height
  and extending across the width of chancel and chancel aisles. The
  chancel E window above was Perp (probably replacing two tiers
  of lancets) until altered in the C 18 and again by Dobson thirty
  years before its eventual demise. The chancel N and S walls have
  lancet windows in the aisles formerly enriched by nook-shafts,
  and broad, flat buttresses between. The clerestory also has one
  lancet for each bay, but placed in the middle of a triple blank
  arcade with narrower l. and r. arches. The arches rest on shafts,

and the edges of the buttresses between each bay are moulded as well. All this is clearly late C 12 to early C 13. The crossing-tower – the church has no W towers and the crossing-tower is not high – also has blank arcading. The bell openings are (correctly) renewed with tracery typical of the ending C 13 – lancets with Y-tracery. The tower is crowned by battlements.

The S transept has an E aisle. Its southernmost bay is on the ground floor given over to the slype – an unusual arrangement (but cf. Oxford Cathedral); the slype normally lies between transept and chapterhouse. The E entrance to the slype has a round arch with a plain roll moulding without capitals – a remarkably early-looking motif – with, above it, the two small barred windows of the treasury. The lower E windows of the transept are lancets with nook-shafts, as in the chancel, but the buttresses between them are now of semi-octagonal shape, a motif also to be found at Brinkburn (cf. also Hartburn, Ovingham, Simonburn). The upper windows in their blank arcade also have semi-octagonal attached shafts. On the S front of the S transept (owing to the adjoining chapterhouse vestibule and dormitory) there are only windows high up – three separate large lancets with double-chamfered surrounds. The gable has turrets l. and r. The W side has the cloister against its lowest stage, at triforium level plain lancet windows with double-chamfered surrounds, and a clerestory as on the E.

The nave was added in 1907–9 by *Temple Moore*. It is in a quiet Dec style, a shrewd choice to avoid uniformity with the original C 13 work. C 15 masonry stands to 2.5–2.7 metres (8–9 ft) on either side of the renewed W door and also on the S (see the cloister); a couple of courses of old walling on the N may be C 12 or C 13. Finally the N transept. Its W side has tall lancets between impressive semi-octagonal buttresses, below a clerestory of the same type as in the S transept. The N front has three excessively long lancets, originally with nook-shafts, alternating with blind arches. The nook-shafts have two sets of rings. Above these are lancets with two-storeyed semi-octagonal shafts. On the E side the aisle windows are set in tripartite arcades with circular shafts, as in the chancel clerestory. The buttresses are again semi-octagonal. The clerestory is the same as that in the S transept. All round the transept is an impressive moulded plinth with nail-head ornament.

What will be remembered about Hexham is that the E parts were clearly built without major, though not without minor, changes of plan; it remains unclear whether the C 12 nave was remodelled to match the E end before its assumed destruction in the Scottish raid of 1296 and later rebuilding; it is not certain that this rebuilding was ever completed. The lapse of a century or so before rebuilding was started is probably explained by the parish already having a church of its own, St Mary, across the Market Place (*see* below).

INTERIOR. In the CHANCEL, E of the crossing, the lower courses of a Saxon apse have been exposed; this may well have been that of a detached chapel immediately E of the main church, which probably had its own sanctuary above Wilfrid's crypt. The two early churches at Jarrow were similarly separate. The Gothic church was begun, it seems *c.* 1180, from the E. As the present E

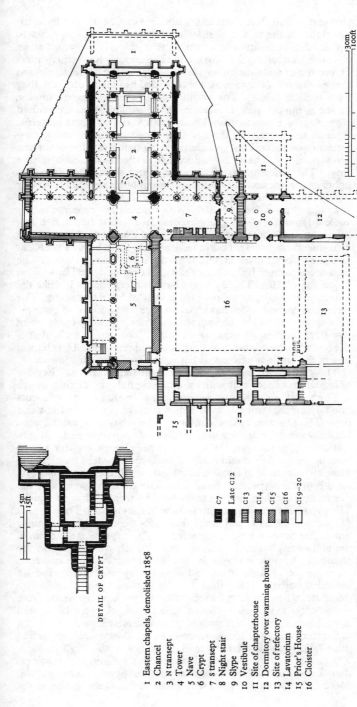

DETAIL OF CRYPT

C7
Late C12
C13
C14
C15
C16
C19–20

1 Eastern chapels, demolished 1858
2 Chancel
3 N transept
4 Tower
5 Nave
6 Crypt
7 S transept
8 Night stair
9 Slype
10 Vestibule
11 Site of chapterhouse
12 Dormitory over warming house
13 Site of refectory
14 Lavatorium
15 Prior's House
16 Cloister

Hexham Priory. Plan

bay and E wall date from 1858, nothing can be said of its composition. Of the N and S sides of the chancel the S appears in certain details a little earlier than the N side. The chancel is six bays long, including the C 19 E bay. The arcades have sturdy piers of four major and four minor shafts, all keeled, and finely moulded arches. On the S the capitals are moulded but plain; on the N they have stiffleaf foliage. The hoodmoulds have nutmeg decoration on the S, but no such decoration on the N. The aisles are vaulted with elegant ribs and have bosses with various foliage patterns. Against the outer wall the vaulting rests on simple, rather Cistercian-looking corbels, trefoiled in section on the S and of varying forms on the N. The aisle windows are shafted and the shafts have rings. The triforium arches are large and subdivided into two lights under one arch for each bay, the subordinate lancets in their outer shanks following the same curve as the main arch. The shafts have moulded capitals. The spandrels are ornamented by sunk quatrefoils of diverse varieties. In the last bay and a half to the W, i.e., near the crossing, some dogtooth decoration is introduced, and this is continued on the N in all bays. That looks as if the triforium was first built on the S and then on the N. The bays are separated by vaulting shafts, resting on dwarf corbels just below the sill-line. These corbels have stiffleaf decoration like the N arcade capitals, again perhaps a sign of later beginning. The clerestory on both sides has tripartite arcading and a wall passage. The arcade is thickly shafted, the shafts being oddly made up of two tiers (instead of using shaft rings). The centre arch, that is the one with the window, has a shouldered rere-arch. The chancel was in the end not vaulted. It has a C 15 roof with nice bosses.

The CROSSING has tall arches on substantial piers. They are of five shafts to each side with moulded capitals and circular abaci.

The SOUTH TRANSEPT is exceptional in that the SLYPE cuts one bay off the ground floor. It is a passage rib-vaulted in three bays. The ribs are single-chamfered. The E bay is separated from the other two by stubby semi-octagonal responds and a triple-chamfered arch. Inside the S transept the canons' NIGHT STAIR goes up in a wide straight flight of well-trodden steps – one of the most monumental of English medieval stairs. It leads to a balcony on top of the slype, and from there one doorway went into the dormitory, another into the treasury. The transept has an E aisle. The piers here are more complex than in the chancel. They consist of four major shafts, and in the diagonals slender tripartite minor ones. The bases are twice chamfered. The capitals are moulded, the arches triple-chamfered, no longer subtly moulded as in the chancel. The aisle is rib-vaulted, without bosses. The vault rests on tripartite vaulting shafts (all with fillets), and these stand on moulded corbels. The triforium is as in the chancel, but has no dogtooth. The clerestory has shafts no longer in two tiers and very stilted arches (without trefoiled rere-arches) above. The W wall is plain where the night stair is placed against it and has only a tall arch holding the lower doorway to the cloister. Higher up are plain lancets flanked by lower blind arches, with a wall passage. The rear arches are sharply pointed and have minimal mouldings; their form might almost suggest post-medieval reconstruction. More elaborate mouldings, with jamb shafts, were started at the s end, and were either not continued or have been erased by subsequent alteration. The clerestory is as on the E side. The s wall has a triforium of two groups of three stepped arches and, above the dormitory roof, one group of three lancets with shafts at the foot and excessive stilting. The timber roof is of the C 15.

The NORTH TRANSEPT is quite different and probably a little 28 later. The whole ground floor here is adorned with blank trefoil arcading, though one discrepancy exists between the body of the transept and its E aisle. The arcading in the transept body, as if unsuccessfully set out, ends at the s end of the w wall and the E end of the N wall with half-arches. A vertical dogtooth strip is applied to give some suggestion of a proper ending. The spandrels of the arcade have sunk quatrefoils. In the E aisle there are broad stiffleaf arrangements instead, some of odd and interesting composition. The aisle arcade has richly moulded arches with foliage-carved hoodmould stops, and the bases (all recut in the C 19) are of the 'waterholding' variety and decorated with curious knobs. The aisle is rib-vaulted with foliage bosses of flat disk-shape. The ribs rest on leaf-corbels against the E wall and not on vaulting shafts. The gallery is identical with that in the chancel, except for some dogtooth in the arches. The clerestory cor-responds to that in the s transept. The w wall has lancets oddly shafted below, but double-chamfered higher up – the moment of the break between the two systems of window surrounds at Hexham. The clerestory is of the familiar pattern. The N wall of the transept shows a break of system: the principal lancets are divided by short clustered piers at the level of the wall passage and higher up by a triple wall shaft which stops short at the upper tier of lights, which have inordinately rich moulded surrounds standing proud of the wall-face, carried on pairs of clustered piers at the level of the upper wall passage. The timber roof is again C 15.

The medieval NAVE has almost gone, but the C 13 arch from the N transept into the N aisle survives. This has a filleted respond, with vertical bands of nail-head. The rere-arch of the C 15 W door survives, along with a mural passage in its s jamb containing a stair (now blocked) which one presumes led to the w range and the prior's lodgings.

The whole of the E. E. architecture at Hexham is charac-teristically North English and finds its nearest parallels in such churches as Darlington (County Durham) and Jedburgh.

CRYPT. Reached by descending a partly original stair in the 9 central aisle of the nave, this is historically the most moving part of the church and perhaps the most moving monument of medieval Northumberland. It was built from Roman stones, many of them carved with ornament or inscriptions. The stair descends to a small vestibule tunnel-vaulted N–S, with, beyond, a round-arched door into the main relic chamber, which has an E–W tunnel vault; there are three small recesses for oil lamps in the relic chamber and one in the vestibule. On the N of the vestibule is a yet smaller chamber with a triangle-vault from which a slab-roofed passage runs E to turn N up steps and then E again to where it is now blocked. One might surmise that pilgrims would have entered down the present stair, viewed the relics through a grille from the vestibule, and left via the N passage. The clergy seem to have had their own access to the relic chamber via a small chamber (with another triangle-vault) in its S wall, from which a third slab-roofed passage led up steps to the E, then S and finally E again. A recent excavation has showed that the southward leg of this passage passed beneath the main S wall of the Wilfridian church, and so either came up outside it or in an adjacent *porticus*. The vault of the relic chamber has still much of its original plaster – as hard as concrete.

FURNISHINGS. Hexham is richer in medieval furnishings than any other church in the county but poor, considering its size and importance, in monuments. The furnishings will here be described topographically, from W to E.

NAVE. *Temple Moore*'s new nave walls incorporated a number of recesses made to house many of the SCULPTURAL FRAGMENTS that came to light during his work. Roman inscriptions and reliefs, probably all from Corbridge, include: a fragment of figured scenes divided by a pilaster; part of a frieze with garlands and birds; a bearded man in profile; a palm tree from the altar of an oriental cult. Free-standing by the NW door is an ALTAR dedicated by the second-in-command of the Sixth Legion to the native god Maponus, equated with Apollo the Harper. There are also pre-Conquest pieces spanning the whole period from Wilfrid to the Norman Conquest. Some fragmentary panels and one complete one with a large rosette might either be Roman work or late C 7, whilst sections of impost or frieze with balusters are almost certainly of Wilfrid's period. There are grave markers of *c.* 800 and *c.* 900, fragments of C 10 cross shafts, a late C 10 hogback and part of an early C 11 cross; mixed in with these are a few medieval fragments, including Norman scalloped capitals. – FONT. Big circular bowl, perhaps of Roman origin, on a C 13 foot with four shafts and dogtooth decoration. Simple Jacobean-looking cover of ogee-shaped ribs. The tall canopy, made by a Belgian refugee in 1916, incorporates some bits of C 15 woodwork. Against the S wall near its E end a fragment of a PULPITUM with C 13 mouldings.

SOUTH TRANSEPT. ROMAN TOMBSTONE of Flavinus, standard-bearer of the crack cavalry regiment known as the *ala Petriana*; *c.* A.D. 80–98. He is portrayed in full-dress uniform gay with plumes, using his dumpy pony to ride down a hirsute barbarian who cowers on his knees but still clutches his sword. The only references to death are the dedication to the Spirits of the Departed and the mouldering Tritons decorating the top of the pillared niche in which Flavinus is set, an allusion to the voyage to the Isles of the Blessed. The stone was found in 1881 forming part of the footings of an earlier wall beneath the floor of the slype. Opposite stands the partially reconstructed ACCA CROSS: Bishop Acca, who died in 740, was said to have had stone crosses 'ornamented with wonderful carving' standing at the head and foot of his grave; that at the head was inscribed, and this may well be it (although most of the inscription is now too worn to be legible). The rear face bears a double-stranded plant scroll forming interlaced oval medallions enclosing leaves and bunches of berries. There is a similar scroll on one narrow side, and a complex spiral

scroll crossed by spoke-like strands on the other. Rosemary Cramp
has shown that most of these motifs can be paralleled in the
mosaics and plated tie-beams of the Dome of the Rock in Jerusalem; she sees the style as one introduced, already mature and
fully developed, into C 8 Northumbria. A smaller section of cross
shaft standing alongside is of the same date, and bears a worn
Crucifixion. – SCREEN. Skeletal remains of a C 15 screen in the
transept aisle. – STAINED GLASS. Barker Memorial Window,
1901 by *Henry Holiday*, very much in the late Pre-Raphaelite taste.
In the SLYPE is a Roman altar, without an inscription.

CROSSING. PULPIT. *c.*1908, but appearing to incorporate
older painted panels. – ROOD SCREEN. The inscription on the
cornice commemorates Prior Smithson (1491–1524). The screen
is of verandah type. The W front has a middle entrance and two
arches on each side filled with most intricate Flamboyant blank
tracery. These rather French-looking Flamboyant motifs were
especially popular in Northern England and Scotland in the early
Tudor period. The dado has a series of paintings of the bishops
of Hexham and Lindisfarne. Ribbed coving on both fronts, supporting an original loft with parapets. On the W front the parapet
has twenty-one little niches. On the E front (altered in 1865) is a
central projecting balcony with two paintings of saints. In the
centre passage l. and r., paintings of the Annunciation and Visi-
tation in the Flemish style.

NORTH TRANSEPT. Between the transept aisle and choir aisle
is a MONUMENT consisting of a richly moulded segmental arch
between corbels formerly carrying statues, with little vaulted canopies above. Under the arch is an incised slab with a foliate cross
from which spring vineleaves covering the whole surface of the
stone; both laying-out and execution are of the highest quality.
The base of the cross emerges from the mouths of two grotesque
heads (cf. a slab at Norton Priory, Cheshire).

CHANCEL. STALLS. Two rows, now without their back canopies; the carving relatively plain. On the elbows and ends carvings, several of pelicans. Misericords with flowers, shields and
grotesques, also not especially sensitive. – FRITH STOOL (also
called Wilfrid's Chair). A stone chair, probably of 675–700, a
precious relic of the first monastery. Tub-shaped, i.e. with solid
arms and back of equal height, ornamented with a plait pattern
on the arms and triangular knots at the back corners. – SEDILIA
of five seats, wooden, C 15, with small figures of angels on the
elbows. – LECTERN probably from the Refectory. Wooden, with
parapet l. and r., the front painted. – Above this, PAINTINGS of
the Passion and the Dance of Death, formerly displayed on the
rood loft. – Above these, the former REREDOS of an altar with
seven large painted figures of bishops; above the canopies are
painted shields, one of Archbishop Neville of York (1464–76). On
the S of the sanctuary, the CHANTRY CHAPEL of Prior Ogle
† 1410, surrounded by wooden screens; fragmentary remains of
brass, and a C 16 triptych said to be a copy by *Pieter Coecke* after
an original by *Quentin Metyz*. On the N of the sanctuary the
CHANTRY CHAPEL of Prior Leschman † 1491. The lower part is
of stone, with a multitude of rustic carvings, a St Christopher and
assorted grotesques, some of them surprisingly inappropriate for

such a purpose. In the ornamental parts even some survival of
interlace. The upper part is much more refined, of timber with
49 fine Flamboyant decoration. Inside is a stone effigy on a tomb-
chest, very stiff and angular, almost as if deliberately stylized. The
cowl of the Prior is drawn over his eyes. Against the wooden E
wall are wall paintings, e.g. of the Instruments of the Passion.

NORTH CHANCEL AISLE. MONUMENTS. Effigies of a C 13
lady, much worn, and a cross-legged knight identified as Sir
Thomas de Devilstone † 1297. In the rather chaotic museum,
two pre-Conquest cross slabs and lots of medieval pieces; also a
window head from the Prior's house, with Prior Leschman's arms.
In a mural recess, fragment of a C 15 priest's effigy.

SOUTH CHANCEL AISLE. MONUMENTS. Effigies of a cross-
legged knight, identified as Sir Gilbert de Umfraville † 1307 and
his lady. Well-preserved C 14 slab with inscription to Matilda,
wife of Philip the Merchant, and a pair of shears.

CRYPT. Used as an arch-head in the N passage is another
Roman altar dedicated to Maponus Apollo; a roof slab at the E
end of the same passage has a fine building inscription of Severus,
Caracella and Geta, dating it to 205–8. An attempt was made to
erase Geta's name, but it remains faintly legible. Another fragment
of the same inscription is now in the N wall of the nave by the NW
door.

THE MONASTIC BUILDINGS AND PRECINCT

The CLOISTER lay S of the nave. The N walk adjoined the nave S
wall; the C 15 W processional door, with continuous mouldings,
and a big recess with a moulded four-centred arch survive, along
with corbels for the roof. On the W side of the S transept is a
continuous wall-arcade incorporating a blocked door into the
transept, the door to the slype, and continuing S to the W end of
the VESTIBULE to the chapterhouse; this has a central doorway
flanked by the empty frames of quite large windows (cf. Black
Friars, Newcastle). Springers of the vaulting prove that the room
had nine square vaults on four central columns, dividing it into
three aisles. The roofless shell was restored in 1955 as a chapel,
and in 1984 the SONG SCHOOL was built above it by *John
Glanfield*; this looks almost Gothick, with a triplet of lancets,
echoing those in the transept gable above, between square turrets
capped by squat pyramid finials.

All that survives of the CHAPTERHOUSE are traces of the wall
bench, blank arcading above and vaulting on the S wall of the
transept E aisle. S of the vestibule are some ruined walls of the
WARMING HOUSE, its S end removed when Beaumont Street
was made; the dormitory above has gone, as have all traces of the
rere dorter and infirmary which one presumes lay E or S of
the range. The S range contained the REFECTORY above an
undercroft; all that survives is a stub of the W end of the N wall,
with one vaulting springer, and higher up the W jamb of the
refectory doorway, with elaborate C 14 mouldings and foliage-
carved capitals to its shafts. More remains of the W range, although
its upper floor was rebuilt *c.* 1790 and altered again (after a fire)

by *Dobson* in 1819. The most important feature is the LAVA-TORIUM of *c*. 1300 with its group of seven gabled blank arches. The middle one is wider and taller than the others. The tracery with pointed trefoils, pointed trefoil lights, and quatrefoils and a cinquefoil in circles confirms the suggested date. The shafts between the arches rest on head corbels and have naturalistic foliage capitals. The ground floor of the range contains two large chambers with ribbed barrel vaults divided by a passage which has a similar vault replacing an earlier groined vault, of which two springers remain. At the N end of the range is a smaller chamber with, in its E wall, a blocked door to the cloister with a plain semicircular tympanum; this looks late C 11 or early C 12 and may be a remnant of a cloister without a W range (cf. Jarrow).

The passage through the range led into a courtyard with the PRIOR'S HOUSE on the N and the priory barn on the W. Most of these buildings were destroyed by the 1819 fire. The Prior's house range was rebuilt; the gateway through it replaces an earlier one. On the N of the range is a C 16 block with mullioned windows having depressed arches to the lights and an embattled parapet above a stringcourse with a leaf ornament of oddly medieval type. A carved panel includes the arms of Sir Reginald Carnaby (granted the buildings after the Dissolution) and the date 1539.

The canons' CEMETERY lay on the S side of the choir; an important group of GRAVE COVERS was unearthed here in 1830. They simply bear the canons' names in incised uncial capitals; three are inside the church but three more have recently been laid down as paving in the cloister, where they lie mossed and decaying; one would have thought they deserved better treatment.

N of the church is FLAG WALK with a pretty gateway to the cemetery (1828) and further N the PRIORY GATE leading out to Gilesgate. This is a remarkable structure of *c*. 1160, from which an upper storey may have been removed. It has at each end a large round arch resting on single-chamfered responds with thick demi-shafts. The interior was vaulted in three bays. Between the N bay and the others was originally a wall pierced by a carriageway arch and a smaller doorway for pedestrians (cf. Easby, Yorkshire).

OTHER CHURCHES AND PUBLIC BUILDINGS

ST MARY'S CHURCH. What remains of the medieval parish church is encased in cottages on the market place. *See* Perambulation, below.

ST MARY THE VIRGIN (R.C.), Hencotes. Gothick of 1830, by *Fr Singleton* (after a design by Bonomi had been rejected). Rectangular nave with pinnacles and odd battlements. The W end has polygonal buttresses copied from the Priory and a stone bas-relief of the Vatican arms in the gable. The E end is very strange, with low chapels projecting from a taller sanctuary with a canted apse, capped by a polygonal bellcote. Aisleless interior with W gallery and large blank traceried arches l. and r. of the sanctuary.

Former BROADGATES INDEPENDENT (later Congregational) CHAPEL. 1790. Rubble preaching box with sharply pointed Gothic windows. Attached school room on the E.

METHODIST CHURCH (now converted into shops), corner of Battle Hill and Beaumont Street. 1909 by *Cackett & Burns Dick*. Entrance at the street corner between thick semicircular bastions. Finely traceried windows; cupola. Of a fanciful style, remarkably free of period precedent.

Former PRIMITIVE METHODIST CHAPEL, St Mary's Chare. Pedimented three-bay front entirely Georgian in feel, but dated 1862.

TRINITY METHODIST CHURCH, Beaumont Street. *c.* 1880. Free C 13 style; here the pinnacles are copied from *Dobson*'s E end of the Priory.

ST ANDREW'S CEMETERY, West Road. Gateway, flanking lodges and a pair of chapels, 1858–9 by *A. M. Dunn*. Lots of ornament; the chapels have quiet and pious faces on the window hoodmould stops, in contrast to the grotesques on the adjacent buttresses. Between the chapels, a reconstruction of Acca's Cross by *C. C. Hodges*, carved by *Robert Beall*.

QUEEN'S HALL, Beaumont Street. 1865–6. Designed by *John Johnstone* as the Town Hall and Corn Exchange. Rather French and exuberant with lots of fancy ironwork on the roof.

OLD GRAMMAR SCHOOL. *See* Perambulation, below.

FELLSIDE MIDDLE SCHOOL (formerly Queen Elizabeth Grammar School), Wanless Lane. 1909–10 by *Oliver, Leeson & Wood*. Main building symmetrical neo-Elizabethan with a Gothic cupola.

QUEEN ELIZABETH HIGH SCHOOL, Allendale Road. The S wing is a private house of the 1860s, greatly enlarged in 1878–9 to form the Hexham Hydro Hotel. Free French Renaissance style, with pavilion roofs and debased dixhuitième and other detail; the main block has a tall mansard-roofed tower as its centrepiece.

PERAMBULATION

A walk through Hexham must start with the MARKET PLACE, overlooked by the Priory on the W and the Moot Hall (*see* below) on the E. In the square are the SHAMBLES, a handsome open building with Tuscan columns on three sides and wooden posts on the S, erected in 1766 by Sir Walter Blackett, and the Temperley Memorial FOUNTAIN of 1901. On the N side, Nos. 27 and 28 is a big four-storey five-bay double-span house with a pedimented doorway and architraves; the rear elevation has three segmental-headed stair windows one above the other and a rainwater head with the date 1749. On the S side, a humbler row of C 18 houses, within which are encased considerable remains of ST MARY'S CHURCH, the parish church of the town in the Middle Ages. By going through an archway into ST MARY'S CHARE one can see part of the N arcade of the church, with an octagonal pier; the arcade was blocked in the later medieval period and a window inserted. This C 13 church was the successor of one built by Wilfrid which was described by Prior Richard in the C 12 as having a tower surrounded on all four sides by *porticus*; fragments and foundations recorded in the late C 19 show that the church of

c. 1200 was a fully aisled seven-bay rectangle, an unusual plan at
that date.

On the E side of the Market Place stands the MOOT HALL, an 53
impressive and menacing building of the later C 14. It housed the
courthouse of the Archbishop of York, who was Lord of the
Liberty and Regality of Hexham. In plan it is allied to castles like
Haughton, Langley and Thirlwall, a rectangular block (here of
three storeys) flanked by taller turrets at the S end; internal
corbelling suggests that there was a pair of smaller turrets at the
N angles. The difference here is that a vaulted passage runs right
through the ground floor at the S end. Each turret is pierced by
a tall arch with a machicolation behind it, in front of a much lower
double-chamfered arch in the wall of the main block. There is a
third arch towards the W end of the passage. N of the passage is
a single barrel-vaulted chamber. The first-floor apartment is now
reached by an external stone stair, probably C 17, on the E. The
doorway and virtually all the features of the first-floor chamber
are restoration of *c.* 1910. The principal apartment is on the second
floor; this too is heavily restored, but retains an original garderobe
set in a buttress-like projection on the E, and an interesting recess
at the N end of the W wall, lit by a narrow loop in its r. jamb; this
seems likely to have been a buffet (cf. Dirleton Castle in East
Lothian) intended for the display of plate or silverware. The
timbers of the low-pitched roof are also old. The SE turret contains
a newel stair and, above the gateway arch, small chambers including a chapel with a restored piscina and a two-light window. The
parapets are set on moulded corbels.

The Moot Hall must have served as a gatehouse to an enclosure on
the E, where there is now HALL GATE, a secluded little square
containing the PRISON (the former MANOR OFFICES), a second
and even more forbidding medieval tower, built in 1330–2. As a
purpose-built gaol for the Archbishop, this is a great rarity. It is
a plain rectangular building with a setback above the first floor
and a corbel-table similar to the one at the Moot Hall, except that
here the parapet has been removed. The renewed entrance on the
W opens into the N of two barrel-vaulted chambers divided by a
cross-wall with a blocked central doorway. Each has a trapdoor
into a similar basement vault below. The first floor has a shallower
segmental vault; the top floor, presumably the gaoler's lodgings,
preserves two fireplaces, along with its original windows, some of
two trefoil-headed lights. The interior was altered when it was
converted into solicitors' offices in the 1860s, and the original
newel stair, on the N of the entrance lobby in a turret projecting
internally only, was partly removed.

Beyond the Prison is a lane leading to the GRAMMAR SCHOOL,
1684, of whitewashed rubble with stone dressings and rusticated
quoins. The schoolroom has two tiers of mullioned windows with
unusually broad lights, the lower with trefoiled semicircular heads;
the doorway is set centrally and has a curly open segmental
pediment. The upper window at the N end, of three narrower
trefoil-headed lights, looks like a C 14 piece reused. The former
headmaster's house forms a NW wing, with the single-storey
caretaker's cottage at the end; the whole is an exceedingly pretty
and eloquent group. N of the Prison is the sprawling PROSPECT

HOUSE (Tynedale District Council Offices), essentially neo-Jacobean, by *Oliver & Leeson, c.* 1888–90. It is of brick, with some odd
stone and brick trim, and incorporates some older building.

Back in the Market Place, HALLSTILE BANK drops away steeply
at the NE corner. On the r. near the top is a C 18 brick building
(part of Prospect House) raised on an older and larger groin-
vaulted basement; the details of this look C 17 or early C 18 rather
than medieval, although a length of walling just beyond, with
reused Roman masonry, might well be part of the enclosure wall
associated with the Moot Hall and Prison. Further on, No. 14 is
a pretty early C 18 brick house with a lugged architrave to its door,
stone wedge lintels and shaped gables; No. 32, near the bottom,
has a doorway with a cornice on consoles and windows in architraves. Beyond is a reset gateway of *c.* 1700 with rusticated jambs
and a segmental pediment, set in the front wall of the HENRY
KING MEMORIAL ALMSHOUSES, Tudor of *c.* 1891.

The main street of old Hexham ran NW from the Market Place. Its
first part is now called MARKET STREET, becoming GILESGATE
beyond the Priory Gatehouse. In Market Street, Nos. 20 and 22
are a picturesque late C 17 house of symmetrical design with two
canted bay windows, two bolection-moulded doorways with curly
open segmental pediments (cf. the old Grammar School), a centre
window above of the same design, and three dormers, still with
low mullioned windows. In Gilesgate facing the Priory Gate,
the MINISTRY OF AGRICULTURE OFFICES (formerly the Post
Office), a three-storeyed five-bay house of *c.* 1730 with segmental-
arched windows in moulded surrounds with keystones. Over the
road, and facing S into its own grounds, is HEXHAM HOUSE.
The house is of the mid-C 18, stone, five bays wide and three
storeys high, with rusticated quoins at the ends and defining the
centre bay, big moulded stringcourses and an added porch on
square pillars; to the r. a lower early C 19 wing. In the grounds to
the SW, a little BRIDGE over the Cowgarth Burn. Along with the
embattled screen wall behind, this looks early C 19 Gothick, but
closer inspection (which may entail getting one's feet wet) reveals
the four chamfered ribs of a C 13 predecessor beneath.

Back on the N side of Gilesgate, the SWIMMING BATHS is an
ingenious conversion of an 1883 wool warehouse by the *Napper
Collerton Partnership,* 1975. At the foot of the hill in HOLY
ISLAND, No. 2 is dated 1657 and still entirely Elizabethan in style,
with mullioned windows, a stringcourse stepped up over the
four-centred doorway, and big gabled dormers. To the l. here is
COCKSHAW, where No. 10, dated 1688, has a moulded doorway
under a window in a bold convex-moulded surround. At the
bottom of Gilesgate one can cross Haugh Lane and follow the old
continuation of Gilesgate (technically Burn Lane; street names
hereabouts are misleading), beside an early C 19 tannery spanning
the Cowgarth Burn, to see the HOUSE OF CORRECTION, a small
building with narrow slit windows; inside, the ground floor is
groin-vaulted, whilst the cells above still have their heavy iron
doors and wall shackles, a chilling reminder of what it was like to
fall foul of the law in the early C 19. Burn Lane ends at the open
TYNE GREEN, flanked by the brick RIDLEY and HEBRON
TERRACES, dated 1864 and 1866 respectively.

Back uphill yet again to the Market Place and s down FORE
STREET, which has divers quoined Georgian stone houses, a
highly Victorian shopfront (originally Messrs Gibson), and,
closing the s view, the MIDLAND BANK, 1896 by *George Dale
Oliver* of Carlisle, a very successful solution to the problem of a
small island site; in plan it is a triangle with an apsidal N end. The
features are in a free C16 Renaissance style with a delightful red
sandstone frieze of putti, foliage, sovereigns, shillings and pennies.
Fore Street ends in a T-junction with what is really the main street
of the town and the through route for traffic; to the E of Fore
Street this is called Priestpopple, to the w Battle Hill. Turning
along PRIESTPOPPLE, first two more banks: LLOYDS BANK,
c. 1896, probably by *J. W. Dyson* of Newcastle, brick on a ground
floor of rusticated grey granite; then BARCLAYS BANK of about
the same date, Baroque with a good Arts-and-Crafts frieze.
Further along, beyond a bleak mid-section with the bus station
on the s and modern shops on the N, No. 19 on the s is a good
early C18 house with quoins and rusticated window surrounds,
rather like Simonburn Rectory. Then a tall former mill dated
1884, of snecked stone (recently renovated) and the COUNTY
HOTEL, which is C17 in origin (one wing has an upper-cruck
roof). Down the hill to the NE, ORCHARD HOUSE and
ORCHARD PLACE, early C19 stone houses with Ionic porches.
Orchard Place is dated 1825 and Orchard House incorporates an
early C18 brick wing with rendering tooled to simulate ashlar; it
has a prettily detailed porch set asymmetrically. At the foot of the
hill, the Tudor-style and well-kept STATION of 1835 (cf. Wylam).
Across the road from Orchard Place and a little further E is the
POOR LAW INSTITUTION, later the hospital and now a nurses'
home. The buildings are of 1839, utilitarian, with classically proportioned windows, but the Jacobean centre with a cupola is dated
1883. On the N side of CORBRIDGE ROAD, just beyond the
hospital, is HALLIWELL DENE, an early C19 Gothick villa with
a triple-arched portico.
Returning to Priestpopple and s up Argyll Terrace, then w along a
narrow back lane parallel to the main road; the long low building
on the s, now fairly mute except for its extraordinary proportions,
is the former ROPERY, a rare survival, built before 1856 and
replacing an open-air ropewalk shown on a map of 1826. Beyond
is the former Broadgates Independent Chapel (*see* above), for a
long time a warehouse.
Back to the Midland Bank and w along BATTLE HILL, which has
some plain C18 houses above later shopfronts but nothing of real
note. At the entrance to ST MARY'S CHARE, the NATIONAL
WESTMINSTER BANK, mid-C19, with a curving ashlar façade.
A detour N up the Chare is worthwhile; narrow and slightly
curved, this is Hexham's best old street. On the E side, No. 20 is
C17 with a moulded doorway and remains of mullioned windows;
on the w, Nos. 17 and 19 are an excellent later C17 pair with
characteristic gabled dormers. No. 17, the former George and
Dragon Inn, has windows under swan-neck pediments with
central rosettes, and fancy shaped gablets to its dormers; inside,
an original stair with fat turned balusters and heavy panelled
newels with ball finials and pendants. All these C17 buildings have

upper-cruck roofs. Just beyond is the former Primitive Methodist Chapel (*see* above).

At the W end of the Battle Hill, at the junction with Beaumont Street, a bronze STATUE of Lieut. Colonel Benson, *c.* 1910, a local Boer War hero, larger than life and striding resolutely forward holding his binoculars. HENCOTES continues w, with a nice variety of minor Georgian buildings. First BURN BRAE HOUSE, brick, with tripartite windows and, in the gable end, two Venetian windows with a lunette above. On the other side of the road, a house, colour-washed over brick, with a pedimented central tripartite doorway now blocked, under a window in a lugged architrave with broad swept feet; later c 19 bows to either side. Further along, TEMPERLEY PLACE, dated 1826. No. 9 West End Terrace (on the r., overlooking the Cockshaw Burn) has a reset c 17 doorway from a house in the Meal Market (between Fore Street and St Mary's Chare) demolished in 1883.

Back to the top of Battle Hill and down BEAUMONT STREET with some of the showier later c 19 buildings of Hexham, including the former Town Hall (*see* Queen's Hall, above). Next door to the Queen's Hall is an essay in free Baroque, now the UNIVERSAL BUILDING SOCIETY. Across the road a late c 17 or early c 18 GATEWAY from the White Hart Inn in Fore Street, reused in 1919 as a war memorial, opening into the grassy expanse of THE SELE, originally within the Priory precinct; here is a BANDSTAND of 1912 with some pretty ornamental ironwork.

On the outskirts of Hexham the following buildings ought to be noted.

HEXHAM BRIDGE, N of the town. Hexham had troubled times with bridges over the Tyne in the c 18. *Smeaton* designed one in 1756 but it was not built; a bridge by *William Gott*, 1 m. upstream, was opened in 1770, only to be destroyed in the 1771 flood. Then *Smeaton* designed another, and this was built and opened in 1781, only to be destroyed by a flood the next year. The present bridge is essentially to Smeaton's design, but it was built on extensive timber piling by *Robert Mylne* and was opened in 1793. There are nine round or segmental arches, with blank roundels each with four keystones in the spandrels (cf. Coldstream Bridge at Cornhill); elegant and vigorously curved roadway. This is not only an uncommonly handsome bridge, but it offers the best general view of the town. Before the Forum Cinema ruined it most ruthlessly, this was one of the best town vistas in England, somewhat Italian in character, with the Priory, the Moot Hall and the Prison all on the skyline.

DUKE'S HOUSE, 1 m. SE. 1873 by *Frank Caws* for Edward Back-house of the Quaker banking family, as a country retreat. Roman-tic Gothic, with conical-roofed towers, steep roofs and a host of tall chimneys. Whilst the S front (before an E extension of *c.* 1920 was built in a slightly watered-down version of the same style) attempted symmetry, the w front utterly abandoned it.

MIDDLE SHIELD HOUSE, off Dipton Mill Road, ½m. S. A good early c 18 five-bay three-storey house, with a bolection-moulded doorway under a broken pediment and windows, apparently unmullioned, in chamfered surrounds under cornices.

LEAZES, 1 m. w. An older house remodelled in 1853 by *John Dobson*. Not one of his better efforts; vaguely Tudor, in whitish brick with sandstone dressings.

SUMMERRODS, 2 m. w, off the Allendale Road. Later C 18 five-bay brick house with pedimented centre doorway and sill bands; at the back an earlier C 18 part, also brick, with wedge lintels. C 19 extensions.

The SPITAL (now a golf club), ¾ m. NW. The site of the medieval St Giles' Hospital. Elegant Palladian house of finely dressed stone. The three-bay front has a rusticated basement. The pedimented centrepiece has two curved stairs leading up to a tripartite doorway with Tuscan columns and a big radial fanlight; the side bays have windows in large blank arches. To the l. a lower two-bay link to the still lower hip-roofed kitchen with a Venetian window beneath a tripartite lunette. At the back the main block has a central three-window bow. The date is said to be after 1802, and the architect is unknown. The stables have a concave front between hip-roofed pavilions with keyed round windows above pairs of segmental arches.

ANICK. *See* p. 147.

DOTLAND PARK. *See* p. 255.

DYE HOUSE. *See* p. 260.

LINNELS. *See* p. 377.

NEWBIGGIN. *See* p. 403.

WEST WHARMLEY. *See* p. 622.

HIGHAM DYKES
2½ m. NW of Ponteland
1070

Late C 17 five-bay brick house with shaped gables. Long narrow windows in roll-moulded wooden surrounds. Pedimented doorcase, probably added in the later C 18. The rear façade is irregular. It incorporates the original projecting stair wing of the front range but is mainly late C 18 or early C 19. Inside, the staircase is probably late C 17, with thick turned balusters and a moulded string. In front of the house a pretty square SUMMERHOUSE of the early C 18, with a pyramid roof.

HIGH CALLERTON
2 m. S of Ponteland
1070

The single street is almost part of Darras Hall and the suburban outskirts of Ponteland, but it is still quite distinct in character, pretty and rural.

CALLERTON HALL. The main part has a slightly irregular seven-bay façade in rock-faced stone, with a massive rock-faced plinth rising to ground-floor sill level. The date is uncertain, but it is probably early C 18 Baroque. Inside, of this period there is a staircase with fat turned balusters, a nice panelled room and plenty of other detail. In 1892 *Norman Shaw* made alterations to the house. He added the two-storey canted bay window on the gable end and made extensive alterations to the service wing and stable block. Inside is a fine fireplace of this period.

CALLERTON HOUSE, opposite the Hall. Dated 1724 but still with cross windows in raised stone surrounds, and above the door an oval panel with the initials I F, i.e. features more suggestive of a late C 17 date. An interesting example of the late survival of these forms in the North.

REBELLION HOUSE. A C 16 bastle house, altered in the early C 17. The walls are over a metre thick and the original first-floor doorway is now a window on the E gable end. To the r. of it is a gunloop. On the ground floor there are a C 17 doorway and a two-light window with hoodmoulds. Inside, on the first floor a huge C 16 fireplace with wooden lintel on rough rounded corbels. On the ground floor, a C 17 fireplace with a finely moulded surround. Two-bay upper-cruck roof with collar beams, saddles and double ridge pieces.

HIGH HAUXLEY

2000

1 m. s of Amble

HAUXLEY HALL. A house of two quite separate parts, now sub-divided. Three bays of the three-storey N front are dated 1724, with the central doorway and the windows of the two lower floors in moulded surrounds; the single-storey W wing contains the kitchen, probably originally detached (a late example of a medieval tradition). The two E bays of the N front match the early C 18 part in style but belong to what was in effect a separate house of *c.* 1790, facing E. This has a symmetrical seven-bay E front with sill bands, and a three-bay S front with two Gothick bows. This later part has one delightful surprise inside, a spectacular entrance hall holding a big spiral stair with wrought-iron twist balusters. The three-bay Tuscan screen at the foot of the stair seems to be a later insertion. Several rooms have good Gothick detail, with carved fireplaces, panelled plasterwork and arcaded cornices.

HAUXLEY FARMHOUSE, W of the Hall. Model farmhouse of 1914. Snecked rubble. Arts-and-Crafts hints in the flat-faced mullioned windows and moulded stringcourse; at the back a pent-roofed verandah on two concrete posts, with a cross window above.

LOW HAUXLEY, $\frac{1}{2}$m. SE. A square of fishermen's cottages, like those at Newton-by-the-Sea, but stripped of its character by late C 20 remodelling.

HIGH ROCHESTER *see* ROCHESTER

HOLE
2 m. ENE of Bellingham

HOLE BASTLE. The usual plain parallelogram of the late C 16 or early C 17, 10.7 by 6.7 metres (35 by 21 ft), with vaulted ground floor and pitched stone-slate roof. The original ground-floor doorway is blocked and inside a later byre; the present doorway at this level is later. Access to the upper floors is by an outer stone stair, probably of the C 18. The first-floor doorway with chamfered surround is flanked by C 18 windows. The original small square windows were moved to the second floor also in the C 18, at the time when a sleeping loft was inserted inside, with an extremely rustic stair leading to it. The ground-floor vault is pierced by a tiny ladder-hole.

Attached to the l. of the bastle, a good group of early C 19 FARM BUILDINGS with a GINGANG to the rear.

A prehistoric BURIAL CIST is visible immediately behind the bastle, inserted into the natural knoll.

HOLY ISLAND

Holy Island from the mainland is not an especially impressive sight. The rock on which the castle is placed is visible but distant, and the rest of the island is flat and uneventful. Yet there is an almost ethereal monotony to the stretching sands and the vast sky, and one cannot help a feeling of awe as one treads the ground where St Aidan arrived from Iona in 635, invited by King Oswald to found a see and monastery. It was organized in the Irish way, but where its buildings were and what they looked like we cannot be sure. They were destroyed by the Danes. After 875 there seems to have been no monastic life on the island, though the earliest remains in the parish church perhaps point to the existence of a church in the years before the site was refounded in 1083 by the Bishop of Durham, William of St Calais (de St Carilef), as a cell of the Benedictine monastery of Durham. Building began at Durham in 1093 and it is clear from the similarity between the architecture of the Priory and of Durham Cathedral that building began on Holy Island at almost the same time.

The PRIORY CHURCH makes a glorious ruin. The stone is dark red 19 and has weathered into the most curious vermiculated surfaces. There is enough standing for the building to be both an object of eminently picturesque interest, against the background of fields and the sea, and an object of intense architectural interest, though it has to be acknowledged at this point that a considerable part of the ruin (notably the w front and parts of the monastic buildings) was effectively rebuilt during restorations in 1855–6 and early in the C 20.

The church was comparatively small, short and compact, only 44 metres (142 ft) long to the original apse (as against the c. 115 metres (375 ft) of the original Durham Cathedral). Building must have begun at the E and have been completed by c. 1140. It comprises a short two-bay chancel with an apse (whose footings are now exposed inside the later E end), short transepts with E apses, a six-bay nave, and a W end with turrets instead of towers. There was also a crossing-tower. As soon as building was completed, the chancel was extended and given the characteristically English straight E end.

The EXTERIOR is divided into bays by flat buttresses. The windows have nook-shafts. The transept apses are given an even stronger articulation: sturdy attached shafts instead of buttresses. In the N transept, a large N window. On the S side, the monastic buildings are attached in the usual way to the S transept. The nave S wall has virtually gone, but much of the rest of the church stands to a considerable height and the outer wall of the N aisle has a stringcourse at sill level, arching round a simple blocked doorway in the third bay from the W, and a second stringcourse higher up arching round the window heads. The W front has a portal projecting in front of the wall (cf. e.g. Kelso). It has three orders of columns with block capitals and zigzag work in the voussoirs of the arch. The geometrical motifs between the columns are lively enough to exclude a date earlier than c. 1135–40. To the l. and r. of the doorway are on each side two blank arches, also with block capitals. The projecting corner turrets are shafted at the angles. Above the door is one very plain window, and above that another with moulded arch and block capitals, and then a later parapet wall with cross slits.

The INTERIOR has many features of great interest.

The E end was lengthened, apparently as early as 1140–50, and then given a straight end, an early case (cf. Romsey and Southwell) of the typically English preference for straight over rounded forms. The windows of this addition were renewed in the C 14, but the tracery of the new windows has not survived, though the arches are complete. Chancel and transepts seem to have been rib-vaulted from the start, though whether a vault was contemplated in the design is hard to decide, for the surviving springers all rest on corbels (in the form of block capitals). There is nothing in the lower courses of the walls to make provision for a vault. The ribs had a central roll and two hollows at the sides (cf. Durham, chancel aisles). Some of the corbels stood on carved human heads. The crossing piers are composed of groups of three shafts. One of the crossing ribs has survived intact with its keystone. It is elaborately chevron-moulded and a most dramatic sight. Then the nave and aisles. The piers are the same as at Durham. As at Durham there is (or was) alternation of compound piers with circular ones, and the circular piers have the carved-in patterns of zigzag, diaper and fluting which are familiar from Durham. The Holy Island piers are not so colossal, but even so they appear very massive, because they stand much nearer each other than at Durham. They have block capitals – there are no scalloped capitals anywhere – and carry arches with a central roll, a hollow and a second roll at each side. The aisle walls are divided by responds

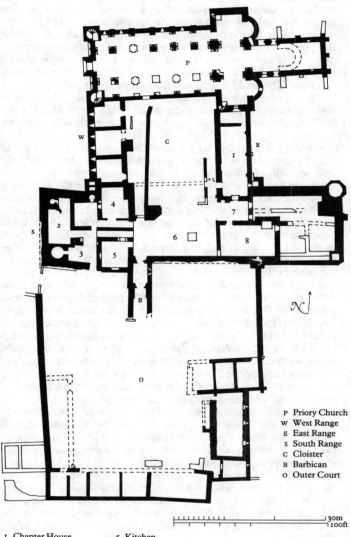

P Priory Church
W West Range
E East Range
S South Range
C Cloister
B Barbican
O Outer Court

30m
100ft

1 Chapter House   5 Kitchen
2 Brew house   6 Refectory
3 Bake house   7 Parlour
4 Larder   8 Warming house

Lindisfarne Priory. Plan

for transverse arches. The responds are of alternating shapes, semicircular and compound. The aisle rib vaults are like those further E. Above the arcade was a gallery, apparently with twin arches for each bay with short stubby columns, and above this the clerestory with a wall passage. The inner w wall emphasized the portal by giving it two orders of columns with block capitals and finely moulded arches. Above this is a narrow wall passage open to the nave in an arcade of five arches on short columns. The middle arch is a little larger than the others, and the detail of the whole arcade is curiously coarser, almost rude and primitive, by comparison to much of the other detail in the building. Above this is the large window seen already from the outside.

The MONASTIC BUILDINGS are all of the C 13 or later. They made use of a grey not a red stone. The cloister walls can be traced only fragmentarily. In the E range was an oblong chapterhouse with vaults on semicircular supports. To its N was the slype, to its s the parlour and the warming house. The fireplace here is preserved, and the fireplace above that, which may have belonged to the Prior's quarters, and also the big chimneystack. E of these buildings and attached to them was probably the infirmary, built in the C 14. The w range is impressively well preserved. It is especially fortunate that the w wall with six small lancet windows can still be visualized, the wall that the Priory showed to the outside world. Behind it there were storerooms and the kitchen with offices, while a C 14 w projection housed brewhouse and bakehouse. The area of the refectory s of the cloister is no longer clearly recognizable. To the s of the whole quadrangle was an outer courtyard of larger size. C 13 gatehouses led into it from the w and from the cloister. In the C 14 the cloister received a barbican, a reminder of the dangers to which the Priory was exposed.

A MUSEUM by the Priory Gate houses a large and impressive collection of Saxon crosses and gravestones from the Island.

St MARY. At first sight the parish church appears as a late C 13 building with a fine long chancel, but its position immediately w of, and more or less in alignment with, the Priory Church should arouse suspicions of much earlier origins. And so there are; outside the church the only clear evidences are the early quoins at the E end of the nave, but inside, the wall above the C 13 chancel arch shows part of the head of a narrower round arch, and high above that a very typically Saxon doorway (cf. Hart in County Durham), with its jambs of large blocks laid in 'Escombe fashion', cut straight through the wall. Saxon work may also survive in the walls above the nave arcades, although these are largely plastered. The question of the date of the Saxon fabric is currently unanswered; could the shell of an early monastic church have survived the Vikings? Or is this a C 10 or early C 11 church which the Norman chroniclers failed to mention? In support of this latter hypothesis it is interesting to note that a large proportion of the pre-Conquest carved stones in the Priory museum date from after the flight of the Cuthbert community. As John Blair has pointed out,* the proportions of the original nave (allowing for the loss of

* 'The Early Churches at Lindisfarne', *Archaeologia Aeliana*, 5th series, XIX, 1991.

half a bay in the C13) would tie in well with early Northumbrian
churches elsewhere, and the pre-C13 chancel arch looks to be an
insertion in a still earlier wall.

To later medieval complexities. The chancel of c. 1200 has
three lancets on the s, one on the N, and three, with stepped
buttresses between, in the E end; there is also a blocked priest's
door and an interesting pair of low-side windows. The N aisle has
windows of two and three grouped lancets, with their spandrels
pierced, i.e. work of c. 1300. The s aisle windows may have been
similar, but they have been replaced by broad early C19 lancets
and only their outlines are visible. The aisle roofs are now flat,
creating an impressively fortified appearance. The w front has a
pyramid-roofed bellcote, recast in the C18, resting on a pair of
massive buttresses linked high up by a pointed arch – an unusual
and very forceful motif. The N arcade, seemingly of c. 1200, is of
four bays; the E three bays have tall and wide semicircular or
elliptical double-chamfered arches on circular piers with moulded
capitals, whilst the w has a much narrower pointed arch. The use
of alternating voussoirs of red and white sandstone is a rarity
in England. The narrower w arch would seem likely to be a
reconstruction resulting from the nave being shortened – or has
there been post-medieval alteration? At any rate, the first aisle
was narrower than at present; its E wall, built in ashlar like the
chancel, survives, and contrasts with the rubble of the widened
aisle of c. 1300. The s aisle poses problems too; its piers are all
octagonal, but the two E arches are lower, and have sunk hollow
chamfers to their inner orders; was the aisle built in two parts?
Sequential replacement of Saxon *porticus* might be invoked. There
are further mysteries in the w wall of the aisle, where an arched
doorway largely below the present ground-level can only have led
into a crypt, and a blocked window at the head of the wall, with
a broad semicircular rere-arch, looks older than anything else in
the aisle; its height is such that the original aisle must have had a
separate gabled roof, or was there a tower here? Other anomalies
are too numerous to catalogue; sufficient to say that this is a
building that would repay a very detailed study. But what looks
like a little N porch (its outer door now blocked) does deserve
mention; it was built in the early C19 as a mortuary for the victims
of shipwreck. The main restoration of the church was done by
F. R. Wilson in 1860. – FONT. C18, with a fat, bulgy, octagonal
baluster stem. – LECTERN. Incorporating some reused C17
woodwork. – GLASS. E window, 1883 by *Mayer* of Munich.

LINDISFARNE CASTLE. A small fort built by the Crown in 1549– 107
50 in a splendid position on a dramatic outcrop of the Whin Sill.
It had batteries for gun emplacements on two levels and was
approached up a shallow ramp on the s side to a portcullis gate.
The fort continued to be used for a garrison until 1819, and it was
used later in the C19 by the coastguards. However, when Edward
Hudson, the owner of *Country Life*, bought the castle in 1902 it
was in a very poor condition. The outside walls were still complete,
but the interior was derelict. He chose his trusted architect, *Sir
Edwin Lutyens*, to convert the castle for him, and no one could
have been more suitable to discover the potential of the site. Much
of what one sees, of course, is old – Lutyens knew when to leave

well alone. He left the approach ramp, for example, but removed its protective parapet to heighten the drama. The walls, too, are largely as they were, though without their battlements; and inside a great deal remains, most notably two fine steeply pointed tunnel vaults in the dining room and the Ship Room; but around this framework Lutyens added and altered at will and with great sensitivity, creating a vision of passages hewn into the rock, of large vaulted chambers, of strong short circular pillars and low arches, and of beamed ceilings – nothing vast like Castle Drogo in Devon, but something equally romantic.

WALLED GARDEN, 500 metres N of the castle. Laid out in 1911 by *Gertrude Jekyll* on a s-facing slope. Very small, with three high walls and a low s wall. Largely stone-paved, with the plants growing through the paving.

LIMEKILNS. Just above the beach, immediately SE of the castle, is a large bank of limekilns, built in the 1860s by a Dundee company which sought to use the island's limestone but had to bring coal from Scotland for its burning. The kiln structure, one of the largest in Northumberland, consists of six lime-burning pots, each with three or four drawing arches, and an internal tunnel giving access to internal drawing arches. To the rear of the kilns is the embankment of the railway which brought the stone to the kilns from quarries on the N side of the island and also carried the coal from, and the burnt lime to, a timber jetty, some fragments of which remain w of the castle. The enterprise had ceased operation by 1896, and the kiln bank, which forms a splendid group with the castle, is now in the care of the National Trust.

The HEUGH, a hill to the s of the harbour and the Priory, received a small fort in the late C 17, designed by *Robert Trollope*. There are a few bits of stonework at the E end which may be part of it but nothing eloquent. The WAR MEMORIAL on the top of the hill is a perfectly plain but elegant cross by *Lutyens*.

The little town is a curious mixture of the pantiled vernacular and the pebbledashed bungalow. The main street is MARYGATE, which has several agreeable houses but nothing special. At the E end, the IRON RAILS was a pub and has a good early C 18 staircase and several panelled rooms. ST OSWALDS, the last house on the way to the castle, is said to be by *Lutyens*, and with the fineness of its vernacular detail it could well be. w of St Oswalds is a walled enclosure known as the BISHOP'S PALACE. There is indeed much old walling, including a chamfered plinth which is clearly medieval, but what it all was does not seem to have been recorded. It looks like a site which deserves examination. In the MARKET PLACE is the VILLAGE CROSS, rebuilt by *John Dobson* in 1828 at the expense of H. C. Selby. Finally, around the harbour and just below the castle there are a number of fishermen's stores made from upturned boats, Northumbrian cobles, cut in two. In the C 19 many such boats were used as dwelling places on the Northumberland coast, and with their little weatherboarded doors, even now they look quaintly habitable. At the w end of the harbour, behind the upturned boats, a group of stone buildings round a cobbled yard was formerly a SMOKE-HOUSE, probably early C 19, from the days of the island's herring fishery.

ST CUTHBERT'S ISLAND, ¼m. SW of the Priory, contained a

monastic cell from the C 7, but the low remains visible on the
island today are from a medieval chapel.

NAVIGATION BEACONS, 1 m. S on Ross Sands (i.e. on the
mainland). Built some time between 1820 and 1840 for Trinity
House by *John Dobson*. Two tall, very slender, tapering pyramids
of sandstone ashlar *c.* 150 metres (500 ft) apart.

HOLYSTONE   9000

Of the nunnery at Holystone, founded by the Benedictines in 1124
and taken over by the Augustinians in the C 13, only a little survives
in situ, in the nave of the church, in the churchyard wall and
probably in Mill Cottage in the village.

ST MARY. The nave was the chancel of a much larger nunnery
church. The S wall and the lower part of the N wall are medieval.
In addition, the E respond of the former S arcade is still attached
to the SW corner of the church outside. All the rest was rebuilt in
modest Norman style by *G. Pickering* in 1848–9. Three medieval
CROSS SLABS were built into the outside of the chancel S wall.

The VILLAGE is tiny but sweet. The SALMON INN is a former
cross-passage house of the C 17 or early C 18. It has a large external
chimney breast. PRIORY FARM, opposite the church, is also
C 17, with thick walls and slightly irregular openings. It has the
distinction of a garden with two square, stone-roofed pavilions at
the corners; probably early C 18. Below the farm, ST MUNGO'S
WELL, an early C 19 pant in the Tudor style. MILL COTTAGE
(The Kennels) has squared medieval masonry and a number of
architectural fragments built into its walls, including a C 14
window head and a medieval CROSS SLAB.

THE LADY'S WELL, $\frac{1}{4}$ m. NW, is a well or water tank, extensively
restored in 1788. It has a low stone kerb all around, a C 19 cross
in the middle, and an C 18 medievalizing statue brought in 1788
from Alnwick Castle to represent St Paulinus, who was
erroneously reputed to have conducted mass conversions here on
Easter Day in A.D. 672. Whatever the origins of the pool, it is a
place of the deepest atmosphere.

HOLYSTONE GRANGE, $1\frac{1}{2}$ m. SE. An early C 19 three-bay house
with canted two-storey bay windows; much extended, quite inap-
propriately but entirely successfully, in the Tudor style in 1897
by *F. W. Rich* for his own use. The SUMMERHOUSE to the W of
the garden is probably his also. The beautiful garden, however,
including the equally beautiful GARDEN HOUSE, was all reconstructed here in 1933 out of material bought when Haggerston
Castle (q.v.) was demolished. It was originally laid out at Haggerston in 1889–93 by *Norman Shaw*. In front of the house a
ROMAN ALTAR.

WOODHOUSES BASTLE, just outside the garden of Holystone
Grange. One of the best, most complete and most dramatically
sited of all the bastles. It stands to full height. The standard
ground-floor doorway in the gable end has a relieving arch over
and a date stone inscribed 1602 WP BP TAM, probably for

William Potte, who is recorded as owning land here. The ground floor is tunnel-vaulted in the usual way, but far less normally there appears to have been no upper door. Instead there is a stone staircase piercing the SE corner of the vault. The first-floor doorway and the windows on the N side were inserted by *F. W. Rich*.

HAREHAUGH, 2m. SE. A small, ruined, mid-C17 house, still entirely in the Tudor tradition. It incorporates one wall of a C16 bastle. (For the fort, *see* below.)

CAMPVILLE FARM partly overlies the triple defences of an Iron Age fort, the S side defended by the slopes above Dovecrag Burn.

FIVE KINGS, 900 metres W of Holystone Grange. An alignment of four standing stones; the fifth was removed to make a gate post.

FIVE BARROWS, $\frac{1}{2}$m. S of Holystone. The most prominent of a large group of cairns. Two excavated in the C19 produced cremations, a cist and Bronze Age pottery.

HAREHAUGH. Iron Age hillfort on the E end of a steep-sided spur above the Coquet, 1m. upstream from Hepple. Multivallate defences protect the vulnerable W approach along the ridge; on the E an extra counterscarp bank was provided; elsewhere two ramparts were sufficient. A scarp cutting across the interior from NW to SE suggests that the heavily defended fort was preceded by a much smaller univallate pear-shaped enclosure that subsequently formed its W half.

3070   HOLYWELL

ST MARY. 1885 by *W. S. Hicks*. A pretty little half-timbered chapel, with a W bellcote cleverly carried on the gablet of the half-hipped W end.

MANOR HOUSE (Strother Farm). The surviving range of Sir Ralph Bates's house, dated 1654, looks like a service or lodgings wing. Ground-floor windows formerly mullioned, with hoodmoulds: smaller chamfered windows above in flat-topped half-dormers. Several original fireplaces inside, including a large one, perhaps for a kitchen, at the W end. Remains of another C17 building on the E side of the walled garden – was this the main house? On the W, to the road, big gateposts with heavy bulging rustication of *c.* 1700.

9040   HORNCLIFFE

HORNCLIFFE HOUSE. Seven-bay red sandstone house built *c.* 1800 for William Alder. Two-and-a-half storeys high, with three-bay pediment. Porch added later. To the r. and l., concave single-storey wings of five arched bays leading to pavilions with one Venetian window in each façade – a handsome Palladian composition. Behind the r. wing, a mid-Victorian conservatory with a terracotta crest of Sir Hubert Jerningham, who lived here in the late 1860s.

LONGRIDGE TOWER, 1¾ m. E. Designed *c.* 1876 by *J. C. & C. A. Buckler* for Sir Hubert Jerningham. Large picturesquely composed neo-Tudor mansion with big *porte cochère*, tall tower with bartizans and plenty of pinnacles.

LOAN END. *See* p. 379.

HORSLEY

1 m. SE of Rochester

HOLY TRINITY. 1844 by *J. & B. Green*. Neo-Norman, with low apse. W tower with pyramidal roof. – Even the FONT is neo-Norman. The other FURNISHINGS are of 1895. – ROMAN ALTAR, in the porch. It comes from Featherwood, 3½ m. N of High Rochester, and is dedicated to Victory and Peace.

REDESDALE ARMS. The part to the l. incorporates the thick rubble walls of a bastle.

OLD EVISTONES, 1 m. W. A deserted hamlet surrounded by its ridge-and-furrow. A tight cluster of at least four ruinous bastles, with other lesser buildings and their garths, huddles around a defensible space which is more a large farmyard than a diminutive green. One bastle, already used as a cow byre in 1827, still has half of its barrel vault standing, the corbelling springing from low walls.

EVISTONES, just E of the old hamlet. A shooting box. Typically Victorian Tudor of 1878.

ROMAN FORT, Blakehope, within the bend of the A68 where it leaves the line of Dere Street 400 metres SW of Elishaw Bridge. Late C 1 and early C 2. A broad rampart (known to be of turf) within a narrow ditch encloses an almost square area. The gap for the N gate is well preserved, and a S annexe embraces the more N buildings of Blakehope farm. A much larger concentric enclosure, superficially Roman in character, appears to be later in date.

HORSLEY-ON-THE-HILL

A house on the N side of the village street is dated 1700 and yet is still of the early C 17 type with mullioned windows under hoodmoulds and a centrally placed doorway with just a straight hoodmould and a slightly pointed head.

WELTON HALL, 2 m. NW. A ruined C 15 tower built of Roman stones from the nearby Wall. The basement is tunnel-vaulted as usual. Entrance into the basement very low and narrow. One pointed-trefoiled window higher up. Attached to this, an L-shaped house which appears to be of 1614 (date above the doorway). The inner sides of the L have mullioned windows with hoodmoulds. The doorway has a pointed head whose sides are straight, with one break, instead of curved. On the S side is the showpiece of the house, a two-storey canted bay with mullioned and transomed windows of three, four and three lights. However, all of this house is much older in its masonry and represents a C 13 or early C 14 house to which the tower was added, as a heightening of an existing NW wing. Evidence for this assertion includes the fact that the lower stages of the tower are clearly coursed-in with the house beside it, and the W gable of the original wing is clearly visible. Also, in the N gable of the attached house is a C 14 window, and there is another small window with a cusped head blocked on the S side. Inside, on the first floor of the hall wing, the segmental rere-arch of a large blocked window is visible and there is a pointed doorway into the tower, which has one continuous chamfer. All of these are C 14 motifs. Outside again, on the W side is a massive external stack which started originally from the first floor on big corbels, suggesting, with the other details, a first-floor hall house. The house deserves a more detailed investigation.

WELTON DESERTED VILLAGE. Earthworks run E–W, on the S side of the road, from the Hall to Slate House. Eight taxpayers were recorded in 1296. Two rows of building foundations can be seen, with crofts and then open fields extending to the S. SLATE HOUSE itself is a small C 17 farmhouse.

NAFFERTON CASTLE, immediately N of the dual carriageway, 1¼ m. W of Horsley, on the W lip of the steep-sided Whittle Dene. A substantial rectangular embanked enclosure, breached on the N and W. In its SE angle there is a single pinnacle of masonry, the remains of a later tower. Philip of Ulecotes was building an unlicensed castle here in 1218, much to the annoyance of the Umfravilles of Prudhoe. It was demolished on the King's orders in 1221. Standing within the rampart, with a deep ditch on the N and S, it was probably built largely of wood. Excavation suggested that work had begun on substantial stone buildings of good quality but the project was never finished. The simple sub-rectangular tower was inserted in the C 15 or C 16.

WHITTLE DENE RESERVOIRS, immediately N of Welton Hall. A group of four reservoirs, the earliest major works of the Whittle Dene Water Company (later absorbed into the Newcastle and Gateshead Water Company). The first three were designed in 1846 and completed by 1848. The engineer was *Robert Nicholson*. In 1848 *John Dobson* designed the very pretty Tudor-style SUPER-INTENDENT'S HOUSE between two of the reservoirs. The octag-onal tower with the large windows provided a meeting room for the directors of the company. In 1850 Dobson added the fourth small reservoir.

2070   HORTON
                   3 m. SW of Blyth

ST MARY. Alone on a hilltop. A preaching box of 1827, retaining a late C 18 or early C 19 N transept which had been added to its medieval predecessor. Gothicized and a S porch added to the W tower in 1903 by *W. S. Hicks*. Inside the porch the 1827 S door has a reset C 12 tympanum with a diaper pattern. – MONUMENT. Built into the S wall outside, the tombstone of Anne Harbottle †1517, an oddly thin slab with name, date and a pair of shears.

LOW HORTON, ½ m. E. Mid-C 18 three-bay house, extended to the

rear in brick *c.* 1800. A detached farm building group to the w is
on the site of HORTON CASTLE (licensed in 1292); only faint
earthworks are now visible.

BEBSIDE HALL, 1 m. N. Mid-C19 house; on the s side of the
road was BEBSIDE OLD HALL. It is not clear whether various
earthworks related to a medieval grange of Tynemouth, or are
garden features associated with the post-dissolution mansion; a
GROTTO, probably mid-C18, is made of big blocks of magnesian
limestone quarried near Sunderland (County Durham). The
house, which contained a tower, was demolished *c.* 1853; some
C18 outbuildings and a pair of massive ball finials from its gatepiers are all that survive.

HOSEDON LINN *see* ALWINTON

HOUSESTEADS
3 m. N of Bardon Mill

The most celebrated ruins of a Roman fort in Britain are exposed
on the line of Hadrian's Wall 500 metres NW of the car-park
beside the C18 Military Road. The site chosen slopes awkwardly
towards the s and SE but had the advantage of providing a clear
view into the shallow valley of the Knag Burn to the E. The
defences on the N are reinforced by the natural strength of the
Whin Sill. In order to make the most of the little level land
available, the long axis of the fort lies parallel to the Wall, which
forms its N side.

The hillside to the s was originally crossed by the Vallum (the
s boundary of the Hadrianic military zone), *c.* 90 metres s of the
fort. As tension eased, the growing civil settlement was no longer
banished to the lower slopes beyond the Vallum, and in the C3
and C4 it was allowed to blossom immediately outside the s and
E gates of the fort. The hillside was probably cultivated fairly early
on, and the terraces that would have been required for this were
reused, remodelled and extended well into post-medieval times.
Arable farming did not cease here until the C18 and so the
prominent series of terraces that the visitor sees on the slopes
below the fort are partly of Roman and partly of more recent
origin.

Every visit has to start at the small MUSEUM (beside the farm),
designed in the 1930s to replicate the plan dimensions (but not
the superstructure) of the buildings in the Roman civil settlement;
it was extended w, less successfully, in 1954.

The fort was an early addition to the original Hadrianic scheme.
The foundations of the Wall and of Turret 36b (21 on the plan)
had already been laid out, on a slightly more s line, when the
decision to build the fort was taken. Entry to the fort is by the s
gate, outside which the neat footings of a few CIVILIAN BUILD-
INGS are exposed; some had their thresholds grooved to take
shuttered fronts, and probably served as taverns or workshops.
Their superstructures were probably timber frames (on two floors)

infilled with wattle and daub; the same was probably true of most of the barracks, workshops and stores within the fort itself. The buildings impinge upon the line of the road leading s from the gate, the E portal of which must already have been blocked before the civil settlement was allowed to encroach into the immediate environs of the fort. A single building of more superior masonry, just to the W, has its corner lopped off, suggesting that another road ran SW from the s gate.

The SOUTH GATE itself is of conventional plan: double portals with a guard-chamber on either side. Its unusual interest lies in its conversion, in the late medieval period, into a BASTLE, a small two-storey fortified farmhouse. This could conceivably have been the home of the Nixons and Armstrongs, who were notorious horse-thieves here in the C 17. The original W door of the guard-chamber was blocked and another one was punched through the s wall into a new sub-rectangular room. This had a W doorway which, like the N one, had the refinement of chamfered jambs. Splayed vents survive in the E, W and S walls and (externally) in the N wall of the former guard-chamber. An external stair on the E later provided access to an upper level, although by that time this may have led only to the head of the corn-drying kiln inserted into the old guard-chamber when the bastle had gone out of use. (A small circular drystone wall, halfway back to the museum, surrounds a C 18 well sunk outside the front door of the con-temporary farmhouse. Another farm was recorded inside the fort in 1725.)

Once inside the Roman s gate, the surviving portion of a long and narrow building (19 on the plan) restricts access to the W; it was found to block the N–S road and is probably of early post-medieval date. Turning E along the s wall of the fort, passing the first of a series of late interval towers, the visitor reaches the communal LATRINES (20). A deep sewer runs around three walls, the base gently graded anti-clockwise to reach an outfall by the fort's SE angle. The cosy wooden seating has gone, but some of the slab floor remains. A graded channel in front of the incum-bent's feet allowed the sponges that were used instead of toilet paper to be rinsed; the flow was arranged clockwise to maximize the scarce water resources available for flushing. An adjacent cistern (a common feature in this fort, where rainwater was precious), outside the SE angle tower, was jointed and sealed with lead and may have a lead lining.

The EAST GATE is on the crest of the slope. Although designed as the fort's main entrance, its s portal was soon blocked; the guard-chamber on this side was converted into a coalshed. The N side, which remained open, has its threshold deeply cut by the passage of carts. It is worth leaving the fort to see the GATEWAY through Hadrian's Wall, close to the point where the Military Way from the E gate crossed the Knag Burn. Such a gate was a rare provision which must have been increasingly necessary as the doors of the milecastles and forts were reduced in width or blocked. Here simple rectangular guard-chambers opened into the gate-passage between the pairs of double doors. The burn flows through a culvert to the W, but this stretch of Wall has been horribly neatly over-restored.

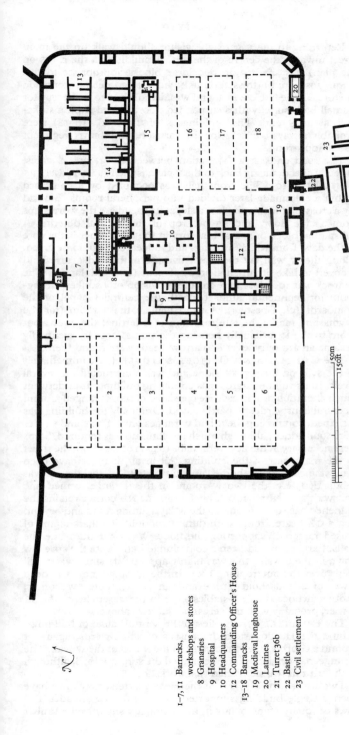

1–7, 11 Barracks,
workshops and stores
8 Granaries
9 Hospital
10 Headquarters
12 Commanding Officer's House
13–18 Barracks
19 Medieval longhouse
20 Latrines
21 Turret 36b
22 Bastle
23 Civil settlement

Housesteads, Roman fort. Plan

Returning to the E gate, the visitor should walk up the main street towards the centre of the fort. A building on the r. (15 on the plan) has smartly dressed large blocks appropriate to this prime position; buttressed on its N side, it had been a workshop or store. In the late C 4 its E end was demolished to make way for a small bath-suite, with a suspended floor, heated from a stoke-hole at its N end. The buildings S of the road (16–18) were probably always barracks for the garrison, an infantry regiment about 800 strong.

The road ends at a T-junction between the N and S gates. Directly ahead, facing back to the E gate, is the HEADQUARTERS BUILDING (10). The front half was occupied by a courtyard within a colonnade later divided into peripheral rooms. Beyond lay a cross-hall with a single E aisle; at its N end are the worn steps from a side door, and an outcrop of the natural dolerite. A substantial block of coarse masonry in the NW corner is the core of the dais, from which briefings and judgements could be given. Along the W wall lay the usual five rooms behind a threshold grooved to take ornamental stone screens (cf. Vindolanda). The bedrock was too close here for the provision of a sunken strong-room for regimental funds beneath the central Chapel of the Standards (cf. Chesters). A short wall in the S room (for the paymaster) marks the late insertion of a latrine; the equivalent room to the N, originally housing the unit's records, eventually became an armoury: over 800 arrow-heads were found there.

The COMMANDING OFFICER'S HOUSE (12), immediately to the S, is on a steep SE slope and was constructed on several levels. In its ruinous state it is a confusing building. It underwent much alteration, but in essence consisted of rooms ranged around a central courtyard, still partly paved. Originally the building was L-shaped, comprising the N and W ranges only. The E and S sides were soon added, although much levelling-up was required. Steps were necessary in the new verandahs to gain access from the street to the main part of the building. All in all, it must have been a most inconvenient home, and ultimately, in the C 4, it was subdivided (e.g. the two W rooms in the N range formed one unit with a W entrance). A kitchen in the NE corner retains the reddened base of an oven. To the W lay a dining room and beyond that a C 4 heated room with dumpy monolithic pillars (some of reused material) supporting the floor. Warm-air flues line the walls. Earlier this had been a cold plunge-bath (note the apse low down in the S wall); this was highly appropriate since water still seeps over the outcropping rock. In the W range, note the deep sewer of a household latrine and, in the extreme SW corner, another hypocaust. The stables were in the basement at the SE corner, probably with the servants' quarters above.

The HOSPITAL (9) also lies in the central range of buildings, behind the Headquarters. It consists of small wards, again set around a courtyard, entered close to the N end of the W wall. The N range may originally have contained the surgical ward, although in the C 4 this was converted to a workshop.

Two GRANARIES (8), N of the Headquarters, may once have been a single building supported by a central colonnade. The rows of square stone pillars in the N granary supported a timber floor (*see* the provision for joists in the S wall), under which splayed vents provided the essential circulation of air. The threshold of the W doorway retains its door-pivots and holes for drop-bolts. The S granary has been much altered, particularly by the insertion of a corn-drying kiln; like the one at the S gate this is probably associated with the C 17 and C 18 farmhouses known to have stood first inside and then outside the fort. (The present farm buildings are of *c.* 1860.)

The NORTH GATE has massive foundations (best seen from the outside), necessary because of the terracing required here in order to make the most of the restricted site. A roadway leading up to the gate has been removed. Hadrian's Wall joins the N wall of the fort just to the W of the NE angle. A tower was originally provided in the normal place within the arc of the corner, but it was soon succeeded by another one, which was positioned to give a view of either side of the Wall down to the Knag Burn.

To the S are two BARRACK-BLOCKS (13, 14) of C 4 type (cf. Chesters and Great Chesters), consisting of individual 'chalets', some with a common rear wall. All the rooms faced N but were distinct enough to be built of different lengths, with party-walls or without.

Returning to the N wall of the fort, a thicker block of masonry marks a staircase to the wall-head. Immediately S of this, within an excavated hollow and partly overlain by later buildings, the footings of the intended Turret 36b are exposed; fragments of the S face of the Broad Wall foundation survive on either side. All this was laid out on the crest of the escarpment before the decision was taken, *c.* 124, to bring the frontier garrison into new forts on the line of the Wall itself. Further W, the rearward third of the fort would have been occupied by barrack-blocks, but apart from some later buildings along the W wall everything in this area remains buried.

The WEST GATE, however, is particularly well-preserved, standing up to 2 metres (6½ ft) high in thirteen courses. Note how, as in the other three gates, the blocks are only roughly dressed, except for their chiselled margins. The effect is sturdy. The masons' marking-out lines can be seen on the forward edges of the piers, and the bolt-holes for the locking-bar survive. The S portal was blocked before the N one, which probably remained open until the C 4. (All this blocking was removed in the C 19.) Outside, double banks cut across the line of the Roman Military Way and are presumably associated with this final phase of retrenchment.

No one should leave Housesteads without taking the short walk W to MILECASTLE 37. The Wall rides along cliffs fluted by vertical pillars of dolerite and the views to the N are magnificently grand, melting into a dark green coniferous horizon. To the S roll the Pennines, high and bare, the summits lined in procession from Cold Fell to Cross Fell, with the green and wooded valleys of the South Tyne and the Allen in the foreground. Even the face of the Wall itself here is no longer so bland: small offsets on the S side probably mark repairs and the end of individual gang-work.

Milecastle 37 is known from an inscription to have been built by the Second Legion and its plan is of their distinctly dumpy 'short-axis' type. Its walls, and especially the N gate, are well preserved. In the N wall, still over 2 metres (6½ ft) high, two bonding courses of thin slabs are visible; it is suggested that a third would bring the Wall to its original height. The N gate is formed of large blocks, but compare the rather rough masonry of its N face with the S face of the SW respond, which is neatly dressed: a snecked joint here was evidently an economical use of the available stone. The S arch was partly reassembled in 1990. Later in the Roman occupation, this gate was reduced, with smaller masonry, to a postern, its threshold considerably above the original level. The S gate was probably also narrowed in this way but (being more accessible to carts) has been severely robbed. Fragments of a small barrack-block for about eight men survive in the E half of the interior. On the W there had once been a wooden store. Just S of the Milecastle the Military Way leads back through all the field-gates to the W gate of the fort: as good a Roman road as is visible anywhere in Britain.

INFORMATION CENTRE, beside the modern road. By *Malcolm Newton*, 1982; inspired by Northumbrian steadings, it blends in well.

PERAMBULATION: HADRIAN'S WALL, FROM HOUSESTEADS TO STEEL RIGG

On Cuddy's Crags, W of Milecastle 37, the walker should look E again for the classic view of Hadrian's Wall, justifiably a photo-graphic cliché. Between Housesteads and Hotbank, offsets in the S face of the Wall are particularly common. The Military Way is also in especially good condition here and around Milecastle 39: a smooth broad green stripe, often with a line of kerbstones (set to retain the road metal) visible on the S side. Milecastle 38, opposite Hotbank Farm, is marked by little more than a robber trench.

Further W, beside the track leading to Hotbank and between the Wall and the Vallum, rubble and boulders mark the site of the Romano-British native SETTLEMENT at Milking Gap. Excavations revealed a sub-rectangular enclosure wall, entered from the E. The subdivided interior focused on a well-built cir-cular central house; an internal French drain and a ring of posts around the inner face of its uncoursed drystone wall may or may not have been contemporary. The site was occupied in or around the C 2.

Returning to the line of the Wall, Crag Lough is spread out at the foot of the cliffs, a beautiful but impregnable defence. Before reaching Milecastle 39, on the E side of a steep dip known for obvious reasons as Sycamore Gap, a consolidated stretch of well-preserved Wall (up to 2.3 metres (7½ ft) high) retains fragments of the hard white mortar rendering that must have made the whole structure so dazzlingly dramatic. Note on the W side of the Gap the tight bend in the curtain successfully achieved on the solid rock. On the summit, a short section of Broad Wall foundation is entirely detached from the later Narrow Wall, for which a line was chosen closer to the lip of the crags. Throughout this area there is evidence that much of the curtain was drastically rebuilt *c.* 200, using the resilient white mortar and replacing the shoddier Hadrianic fabric. In the lee of the Wall, abutting its S face, are the foundations of simple medieval shielings. These could have been permanently occupied long-houses but were probably houses for the shepherds in the higher summer pastures. Partitions suggest a division between a byre or pen and the dwelling.

MILECASTLE 39 occupied the next gap to the W (Castle Nick), 4 overlying the original Broad Wall foundation visible inside its NE corner. The less substantial construction of the S gate suggests that a tower was provided only over the N one. In its late phases the S gate was narrowed to a postern, and probably the N gate also. Two small buildings on the W side, with curving porches, overlay an earlier barrack contemporary with three smaller buildings on the E.

On Peel Crags, the site of TURRET 39a is visible only because of the unusual long basal blocks, chosen to carry the S face of the Wall across the recess when the turret was demolished *c.* 200. Beyond, in the low ground of Peel Gap, three separate phases of the Wall can be seen: Broad foundations and the standard Narrow Wall (cut by separate culverts), together with a further reduction in width, a rebuilding of the early C 3. A TOWER, with a surprisingly limited view to the N, stood watch in the bottom of the Gap. Similar in dimensions to a turret, it was less well built; it was not recessed into the Narrow Wall but as an early addition simply abuts onto it. This tower was an extra provision, inserted into the regular pattern of two turrets in each mile, set between Turrets 39a and 39b. These were rather further apart than normal, leaving some dead ground in Peel Gap poorly guarded. Like the majority of turrets, by the early C 3 the tower had gone out of use.

ROMAN CAMP, 1 m. NW of Housesteads. A simple earthwork high above the S shore of Greenlee Lough. It was constructed over the narrow ridges of earlier fields, still visible to the discerning eye near the SE corner. An IRON AGE HILLFORT 200 metres to the ENE is overlain by the footings of a number of simple rectangular drystone buildings; some are subdivided and most have a doorway roughly central in the S long wall. These are medieval shielings, used by medieval shepherds when their flocks were on these higher pastures in summer.

HOWICK   2010

ST MICHAEL, in the wooded grounds of Howick Hall. A classical chapel of 1746 was remodelled in 1849 by *F. J. Francis.* The chapel was four bays long and had arched windows with frames on pilasters. The pilasters remained, a Romanesque window trim was put in, and the fifth bay, chancel, vestry and Romanesque W front with bellcote were added. The Romanesque work is quite lavishly done, with lots of carving. – MONUMENTS. Charles, second Earl Grey, † 1845. White marble table tomb with inlaid brass cross; designed by *John Francis,* carved by *J. Bedford,* 1850. The monument originally stood in the chancel under an ornate

canopy, only one panel of which remains – wall tablet to Victoria
Sybil Mary Grenfell † 1907, by *Eric Gill*. – In the churchyard s of
the chancel, a group of probably C 13 GRAVE COVERS, plain
tapered slabs with moulded edges; there are similar monuments
in the Cathedral Yard at Durham. Another, further s, has a worn
cross and sword.

HOWICK HALL. Built for Sir Henry Grey in 1782 from designs by
William Newton of Newcastle. Paine and other architects had been
asked to submit designs. The s front is indeed close to Paine's
style: it is nine bays wide, with a slightly projecting three-bay
pedimented centre. The ground floor is rusticated, and the upper
floors of the centrepiece have giant unfluted Ionic attached
columns. At first-floor level the centre window of each part of
the façade is pedimented. On either side are plain straight one-
storeyed wings, leading to five-bay pavilions with three-bay pediments and square lanterns. The drive went to the s front. In 1809
this was changed by *George Wyatt*. The N side became the entrance
side, and a Tuscan one-storey addition was made there to receive
the entrance hall. The wings were converted into quadrants, and
terraces built in front of the s façade. The entrance hall survives,
although reduced a little at the sides, where, inside, big Roman
Doric columns once stood free and now stand close to the wall.
The metope frieze and plaster ceiling are original. The rest of the
house was remodelled, after a serious fire, in 1928 by *Sir Herbert
Baker & Scott*. Theirs is the new N door, with a Cape-Dutch
fanlight. They converted a large central stair hall and made within
it a new inner courtyard set at first-floor level, opening to the N
(i.e. above the entrance hall) by a screen of two giant Tuscan
columns, flanked by circular and shoulder-headed windows,
beneath a carved pediment of some twenty years earlier. Inside,
beneath the inner courtyard, they put, as the new centre of the
house, a roof-lit rotunda with columns as a kind of vestibule, not
at all high, nor large. Most of Baker's fittings and furnishings have
now been removed, and the interior of the house left empty and
bleak. Newton's W pavilion is used as the present house, his E
one as the stable block.

Wyatt designed the GARDEN TERRACES on the s front. His
upper terrace has ashlar balustrades; the middle terrace is a simple
stone wall, incorporating near the W end a doorhead dated 1714,
sole relic of an older house on the site. 180 metres NW of the Hall
is the late C 18 WALLED GARDEN, with a ha-ha wall enclosing a
narrow terrace in front of the s wall.

The original Howick VILLAGE lay near the church and has disappeared. Its C 19 successor, ½ m. E of the Hall, is no more than
a hamlet. The principal feature is the LONG ROW, a terrace of
Tudor-style estate cottages; a central gabled tower bears the Grey
crest and motto, with the date 1841. The back of the tower seems
to incorporate C 18 masonry; perhaps it was once a dovecote.

BATHING HOUSE, superbly sited on the rocky coast E of Howick
village. A C 18 cottage remodelled *c.* 1840 for the Grey family,
with Tudor windows and tall moulded terracotta chimney pots.
The salt wind has eaten deep into the sandstone dressings. Below
the house, a flight of rock-cut steps descends to a small quarried-
out bathing pool.

1. The Cheviots, near Kirknewton

2. The coast, looking south to Dunstanburgh

3. Old Bewick, Iron Age hillforts

4. Hadrian's Wall, Castle Nick,
west of Housesteads, Milecastle 39

5. Chew Green, Roman fortlet (*left*), fort (*right*) and temporary camps

6. Ingram, medieval ploughing around the Iron Age fort, Middledean, and Romano-British settlements, Haystack Hill

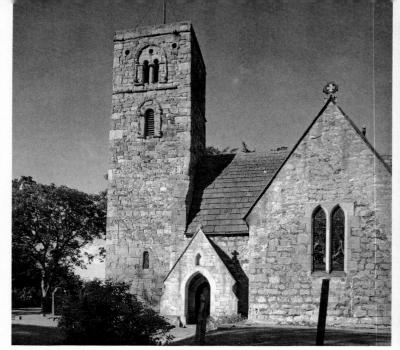

7. Bywell, St Andrew, late Saxon tower

8. Ovingham, St Mary, late Saxon tower,
the rest mostly thirteenth century

9. Hexham Priory,
crypt,
late seventh century

10. Rothbury, All Saints,
cross shaft of *c.* 800,
reused as font shaft

11. Hexham Priory,
Frith Stool,
late seventh century

12. Woodhorn, St Mary,
late Saxon window
above the south arcade

13. Edlingham, St John, eleventh-century nave,
tower probably of *c.* 1300 and seventeenth-century porch

14. Warkworth, St Laurence, north wall of nave, early twelfth century

15. Norham, St Cuthbert, chancel, *c.* 1170, with fourteenth-century east bay

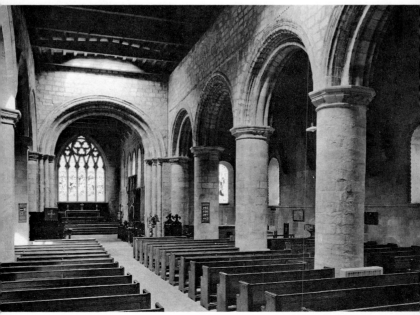

16. Norham, St Cuthbert, south nave arcade and chancel arch of *c.* 1170

17. Newcastle upon Tyne, St Andrew, chancel arch, late twelfth century

18. Kirknewton, St Gregory the Great,
Adoration of the Magi, probably twelfth century

19. Holy Island, Priory Church, *c.* 1100, looking east

20. Seaton Delaval, Our Lady, chancel and sanctuary arches,
early twelfth century

21. Alnwick Castle, begun in the twelfth century,
aerial view

22. Prudhoe Castle, gatehouse from the outer bailey;
early twelfth century, raised in the thirteenth century

23. Bamburgh Castle, begun in the mid-twelfth century, from the south-west

24. Elsdon Castle, ringwork and bailey, early twelfth century

25 and 26. Brinkburn Priory, early thirteenth century,
restored 1858–9 by Thomas Austin

27. Hulne Priory, sedilia, mid-thirteenth century

28. Hexham Priory, north transept, early thirteenth century

29. Ryal, All Saints, cross slabs, medieval

30. Kirknewton, St Gregory the Great,
tunnel-vaulted chancel

31. Tynemouth Priory, east end, *c.* 1190,
with Percy Chantry, fifteenth century

32. Whalton, St Mary Magdalene,
north arcade of chancel, Early English

33. Aydon Castle, solar window of *c.* 1280

34. Haughton Castle, general view,
thirteenth and late fourteenth centuries; west wing 1876 by Salvin

35. Newcastle upon Tyne, the Castle: keep 1168–78, Black Gate 1247;
1618 additions; 1883 restoration by R. J. Johnson

36. Alnwick Abbey, gatehouse, fifteenth century

37. Morpeth, St Mary, chancel, later fourteenth century

38. Seaton Delaval, Our Lady, effigy,
perhaps of Sir Hugh Delaval, early fourteenth century

39. Newcastle upon Tyne, Cathedral of St Nicholas,
interior, fourteenth century

40. Alnwick Castle, barbican, *c.* 1310–1320,
figures on battlements eighteenth century

41. Belsay Castle, tower of *c.* 1370, house 1614, remodelled 1862

42. Langley Castle, late thirteenth or early fourteenth century, remodelled *c.* 1350, restored *c.* 1890 by Cadwallader Bates

43. Chipchase Castle, tower, mid-fourteenth century

44. Newcastle upon Tyne, Cathedral of St Nicholas,
from the Castle: crown, late fifteenth century

45. Alnwick, St Michael, Perpendicular

46. Hexham Priory, rood screen, between 1491 and 1524

47. Newcastle upon Tyne, Black Friars,
east range: chapterhouse late thirteenth century

48. Chillingham, St Peter,
Grey monument, 1443

49. Hexham Priory,
effigy of Prior Leschman, 1491

50. Newcastle upon Tyne, Cathedral of St Nicholas,
font and cover, late fifteenth century

51. Newcastle upon Tyne, Cathedral of St Nicholas,
Maddison monument, c. 1635

52. Warkworth Castle, keep, fifteenth century

53. Hexham, Moot Hall, later fourteenth century

54. Newcastle upon Tyne, Town Wall, looking towards the Heber Tower; late thirteenth century

55. Berwick-upon-Tweed, the bridges

56. Berwick-upon-Tweed, Brass Bastion, 1558–69

57. Berwick-upon-Tweed, Holy Trinity Church, 1650–2

58. Newcastle upon Tyne, Trinity House Chapel, furnishings of *c.* 1635

59. Newcastle upon Tyne, Guildhall, Merchant Venturers' Hall,
overmantel, 1636

60. Newcastle upon Tyne, Guildhall, Town Court, c. 1660
by Robert Trollope

61. Hexham, No. 2 Holy Island, dated 1657

62. Newcastle upon Tyne, John George Joicey Museum
(Holy Jesus Hospital), 1681

63. Newcastle upon Tyne, Sandhill,
seventeenth-century merchants' houses

64. Newcastle upon Tyne, Nos. 28–30 the Close,
late sixteenth- to seventeenth-century plasterwork

65. Chipchase Castle, south-east range, 1621

66. Capheaton Hall, south front, 1668
by Robert Trollope

67. Chillingham Castle, fourteenth century,
remodelled in the early seventeenth century

68. Halton Tower, tower fourteenth century, wing 1696

69. Newcastle upon Tyne, All Saints, 1786–96
by David Stephenson

70. Newcastle upon Tyne, All Saints, interior

To the memory
of HENRY ASKEW, of REDHEUGH, ESQ;
WHO DIED X. MARCH, MDCCXCVI. AGED LXVI.
ALSO OF DOROTHY ASKEW, HIS WIFE;
WHO DIED XVIII. MARCH, MDCCXCII. AGED LII.
THE PROTECTORS OF TWELVE ORPHAN NEPHEWS AND NIECES,
IN GRATITUDE
TO THE BEST OF GUARDIANS,
GEORGE ADAM ASKEW, OF PALLINSBURN-HOUSE, ESQ;
AND ANN ELIZABETH ASKEW, HIS WIFE,
ERECTED THIS MONUMENT.
MDCCCI.

71. Newcastle upon Tyne, Cathedral of St Nicholas,
Askew monument, 1801 by Henry Webber

72. Hartburn, St Andrew,
headstone,
mid-eighteenth century

73. Falstone, St Peter,
headstone,
early eighteenth century

74. Seaton Delaval Hall, south front, 1718–29
by Sir John Vanbrugh

75. Seaton Delaval Hall, north front

76. Wallington Hall, from the south-east, 1688,
remodelled *c.* 1745 by Daniel Garrett

77. Callaly Castle, drawing room, plasterwork 1757

78. Wallington Hall, Clock Tower Gate, 1754 by Daniel Garrett

79. Wallington, bridge over the River Wansbeck, 1755
by James Paine

80. Simonburn, rectory, early eighteenth century

81. Matfen, Corneyside, early eighteenth century

82. Belford Hall, 1754–6 by James Paine

83. Ford Castle, Portcullis Gate, 1791–5

84. Alnwick, Brizlee Tower, 1781, probably by Robert Adam

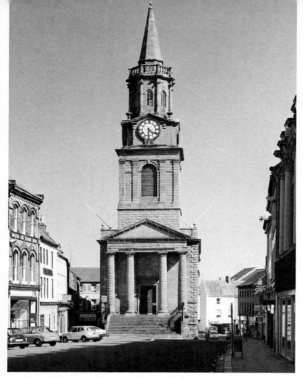

85. Berwick-upon-Tweed, Town Hall, 1754–61
by S. & J. Worrall

86. Berwick-upon-Tweed, Quay Walls, Georgian houses

87. Newcastle upon Tyne, Assembly Rooms, 1774–6
by William Newton

88. Newcastle upon Tyne, Cathedral of St Nicholas,
Thomlinson Library, 1736

89. Woodburn, Low Cleughs, ruined bastle near Low Leam, *c.* 1600

90. Sinderhope, Rowantree Stob, byre doorway of a bastle-derivative house, probably later seventeenth century

91. Vindolanda, Causeway House, dated 1770. Heather thatch

92. Chollerton, St Giles, headstone to John Saint, 1837

93. Belsay Hall, 1807–17 by Sir Charles Monck

94. Belsay Hall, central hall, 1807–17 by Sir Charles Monck

95. Longhirst Hall, 1824 by John Dobson

96. Longhirst Hall, central hall, 1824 by John Dobson

97. Newcastle upon Tyne, Leazes Terrace, 1829–34
by Thomas Oliver

98. Newcastle upon Tyne, Theatre Royal, 1836–7
by John & Benjamin Green

99. Newcastle upon Tyne, St Thomas, 1827–30
by John Dobson

100. Newcastle upon Tyne, Roman Catholic Cathedral of St Mary, 1842–4
by A. W. N. Pugin; spire *c.* 1872 by A. M. Dunn & E. J. Hansom

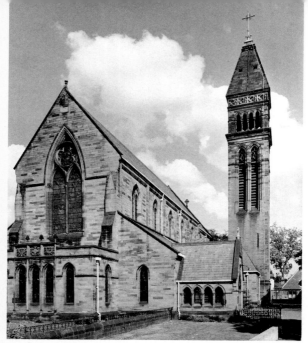

101. Newcastle upon Tyne, Jesmond, St George, 1888–9
by T. R. Spence

102. Newcastle upon Tyne, Jesmond, St George, interior

103. Morpeth, St James, 1843–6 by Benjamin Ferrey

104. Morpeth,
St James,
interior, with
frescoes of 1871
by Clayton & Bell

105. Beaufront Castle, 1836–41 by John Dobson

106. Cragside, largely of 1870–85 by Norman Shaw, entrance front

107. Holy Island, Lindisfarne Castle, 1549–50, remodelled 1902
by Sir Edwin Lutyens; limekilns *c.* 1860

108. Ford, Waterford Hall, painting by Louisa, Lady Waterford

109. Tynemouth, Collingwood Monument, 1847,
statue by James Lough, monument by John Dobson

110. Newcastle upon Tyne, St Nicholas' Square, Queen Victoria, 1903
by Alfred Gilbert

111. Rothbury, Addycombe Cottages, 1873 by Norman Shaw

112. Newcastle upon Tyne, Blackett Street,
Emerson Chambers, *c.* 1903 by Simpson, Lawson & Rayne

113. Loan End, Union Chain Bridge, 1819–20 by Captain Samuel Brown R.N.

114. Newcastle upon Tyne, the bridges

115. Preston, Chathill Station, 1847 by Benjamin Green for the York, Newcastle and Berwick Railway Company

116. Newcastle upon Tyne, Central Station, 1845–50 by John Dobson, *porte cochère* executed 1863 by Thomas Prosser

117. Haughton, paper mill offices and drying shed, *c.* 1788

118. Lemington, glassworks cone, 1797

119. Langley, Stublick Colliery,
early nineteenth-century coalmine buildings

120. Newcastle upon Tyne, Hanover Street warehouses, 1841–4,
Shap granite cart track

121. Dinnington, New Horton Grange Farm.
Mid-nineteenth-century planned farm

122. Newcastle upon Tyne, Northbourne Street, Elswick,
Tyneside flats, late nineteenth century

123. Newton-by-the-Sea, Newton Seahouses, The Square, fishermen's cottages

124. Tynemouth, Life Brigade Watch Club House, 1886–7 by C. T. Gomoszynski

125. Newcastle upon Tyne, Heaton, Wills Factory, 1946–50 by Cecil Hockin

126. Newcastle upon Tyne, Civic Centre, 1960–8 by George Kenyon, City Architect

127. Killingworth, Norgas House, 1963–5
by Ryder, Yates & Partners

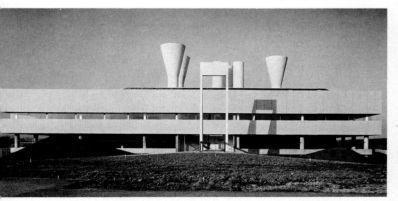

128. Killingworth, British Gas Engineering Research Station, 1965–7
by Ryder, Yates & Partners

129. Newcastle upon Tyne, Byker Wall, 1973–80
by Ralph Erskine Associates

130. Newcastle upon Tyne, Central Station, 1845–50 by John Dobson;
Ticket and Information Office, c. 1982 by British Rail Architects Department

HOWICK GRANGE, ½m. SE of the Hall. Ashlar-faced Regency villa
with twin segmental bows, extended early in the C 20.

HOWTEL

HOWTEL TOWER. Probably of the C 15. The N wall stands to nearly
full height and the W wall a little lower. The ground floor was
vaulted; the springings remain.

BOWMONT HOUSE, ½m. SW. A former Scottish Presbyterian chapel
and manse, now a house and workshop. 1850. The chapel has the
usual tall round-headed windows with intersecting glazing bars.

KILHAM HOUSE, 1½m. SW. A large farmhouse or small country
house. Irregular. Mid-C 19; well extended in 1926.

SHOTTON HOUSE, 4m. SW. 1828, for H. C. Selby. A three-bay
ashlar farmhouse, with a Tuscan doorcase in a rusticated segmental-arched recess. Angle pilasters with odd patterned capitals,
and a plain parapet with a central date panel.

HULNE PRIORY

2 m. NW of Alnwick

Hulne was one of the earliest English foundations – if not the
earliest – of the Carmelites or Whitefriars. It was founded in 1242
by William de Vesci, and is among the best-preserved friaries in
England. Its ruins lie on the end of a spur above the Aln, two
miles up river from Alnwick; the medieval friary remains, late
medieval fortifications and C 18 gothicization (Hulne is in the
Duke of Northumberland's park) give them a memorable three-
fold character.

The entire complex is contained within a C 15 CURTAIN WALL,
essential for any religious house in the Border region. The wall
stands to c. 3.6 metres (12 ft) high all round, and forms an irregular
quadrilateral in plan. Near the centre of the S side is a very plain
square gatehouse tower with a narrow barrel-vaulted passage. On
the E and at the SW corner are C 18 Gothick gateways. The
CHURCH, of which the S and W walls stand in fairly good condition, was a rectangle 36.3 by 5.8 metres (119 by 19 ft) internally.
Nave and chancel were divided, after the usual fashion of the
friars in England, by two cross walls flanking a walking place; the
footings of these were found in excavations of 1888–9 and may
be the earliest example of the feature in the country. In the S wall
of the church are, from E to W, triple stepped sedilia and part of
a shafted piscina niche, then a doorway to the sacristy, and two
two-light windows with unfoiled circles in the spandrels, typical
mid-C 13 work. They gave onto a small courtyard at the N end of
the E range of the cloister. Beyond is a doorway to the walking
place, and three small cusped lights high in the wall so as to clear
the roof of the cloister walk. The W gable has a tall lancet with
a vesica above. The two-storeyed SACRISTY is of considerable
interest; its ground floor has a piscina and a recess with bowl,

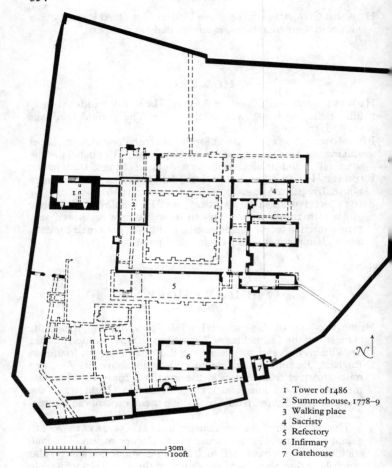

1 Tower of 1486
2 Summerhouse, 1778–9
3 Walking place
4 Sacristy
5 Refectory
6 Infirmary
7 Gatehouse

Hulne Priory. Plan

shelf and flue, interpreted as being used in the preparation of wafers for Holy Communion.

A large yew tree in the centre of the CLOISTER GARTH was recorded in *c.* 1567. What now appears as a N–S walled corridor is in fact the E part of the ground floor of the E range; the surviving S gable shows how the cloister walk itself formed the W part, another typical feature of friary planning. The CHAPTERHOUSE projects to the E, and was reached by a lobby (now part of the 'corridor'; its side walls have gone). It has four trefoiled lancets on the S and the remains of a five-light E window. At the SE corner of the E range, a narrow rectangular building projecting E seems to have contained the WARMING HOUSE (with fireplace) and, at the E end, the REREDORTER (with drain). The S range contained the REFECTORY; only its N wall survives, with openings which are mostly the result of post-Dissolution conversion to domestic use. Little remains on the W side of the cloister, where the site of the N part of the range is occupied by a two-storey Gothick SUMMERHOUSE built in 1778–9 as part of an 'improvement' of the site by *Robert Adam* and *Capability Brown*. To the W of the summerhouse stands a big rectangular TOWER, which forms the dominant feature of the site: an inscribed slab (now reset inside) relates that this was built in 1486 by Sir Henry Percy. It has taller turrets at the W angles and one the full width of the E end, which has an original canted oriel with cinquefoil-headed lights. The tower has a barrel-vaulted basement and mural stair: its two upper floors were thrown into a single tall room in the C18. Tower and summerhouse are linked by a C18 stone BRIDGE, perhaps replacing a medieval one linking the tower to the W range. Both buildings have excellent Gothick interiors with carved fireplaces, crocketed doorcases and plaster decoration. Other domestic buildings of the friary stood against the curtain to the S and W of the cloister, and some fragments survive. The C13 INFIRMARY, now a private house, stands detached immediately NW of the gatehouse. It follows a typical medieval hospital plan, consisting of a hall (three-light W window with intersected tracery) and a smaller chapel to the E (two-light E window with plate tracery). Outside their curtain wall (which has blocked doorways on N and W) the friars must have had their gardens. Beyond was an outer PRECINCT WALL, 2.7 metres (9 ft) high, of which a considerable stretch remains to the NE. – MONUMENTS. In the nave floor, an unusual slab with a tau cross pierced by three nails. A slab built into the nave W wall is from Alnmouth; a third, inside the summerhouse, has a sword and spade as emblems.

STANDING STONE in a wood $\frac{3}{4}$ m. NNW. Probably Bronze Age, but a landmark in a charter of 1283.

HILLFORT, $\frac{3}{4}$ m. NE, beside Chester Cottage. Circular and multivallate, using the end of a natural spur.

HUMSHAUGH   *9070*

ST PETER. 1818 by *H. H. Seward*. Broad aisleless nave with W porch, N organ chamber and small sanctuary. Bellcote-like turrets on both E and W gables of the nave, the latter being the real belfry. E window with intersecting tracery, and side windows with Y tracery. Flat white ceiling, as in the other Seward churches (cf. Greystead etc.). – STAINED GLASS. Window on the S by *Kempe*, 1901.

The picturesque VILLAGE street has a few houses of interest. On the S side is LINDEN HOUSE, which began as a pair of late C16 – early C17 bastle houses, with a C18 DOVECOTE, partly of brick, in the garden to the SE. On the N, TEESDALE HOUSE, dated 1690, and DALE HOUSE, dated 1664, have moulded doorways and mullioned windows; Dale House and the attached cottage are also bastle houses, remodelled in the C17. The EVANS ALMSHOUSE (precisely dated to 'St David's Day 1864') has a PANT of

1854 incorporated in its garden wall. Further E is the larger
HUMSHAUGH HOUSE, a five-bay early C18 brick house with
rusticated quoins, a pedimented doorcase and windows with rusticated lintels. An internal wall over a metre (4 ft) thick suggests
that earlier fabric was incorporated.

₀₀₂₀

ILDERTON

ST MICHAEL. Late C18 church of pink sandstone with a polygonal apse (the E window Victorian). Plain pointed windows (the
thin wooden tracery also Victorian). Round chancel arch with
keystone. Only the embattled W tower in its lower parts is medieval, probably late C13. It has one pointed-trefoiled lancet in the
W wall. Angle buttresses. The tower arch is single-chamfered; it
is so excessively low only because the floor of the nave and part
of the tower have been heightened. – FONT. 1727.
The pillar has an odd corn-cob shape; the bowl has cherubs'
heads. – MONUMENT. C14 CROSS SLAB in the floor of the
tower. – In the churchyard, the plain RODDAM MAUSOLEUM
of 1795.
VICARAGE. 1841 by *John and Benjamin Green* in the Tudor style.
ILDERTON HALL. Dated MTI/1733. Six bays in pink ashlar. The
door is in the fourth bay; the date panel is above the ground-floor
window of the third bay. All the openings have raised stone
surrounds. Inside, a panelled entrance hall and a broad staircase,
probably also of 1733.
MIDDLETON HALL, 3 m. NNW. 1807, for the Commissioners of
Greenwich Hospital, who had acquired the property (part of the
Earl of Derwentwater's estates) after the 1715 Rebellion. Rendered with ashlar dressings and a Scottish slate roof. Just 1:3:1 bays,
but nicely placed on an eminence and with ten steps up to the
Tuscan porch. Rusticated quoins and windows in raised stone
surrounds. The courtyard at the back, formed by the projecting
rear wings, is closed on the fourth side by a high castellated wall
with a round carriage arch.
NORTH MIDDLETON HALL, 2 m. NNW 1830–40. A most unusual
façade. Rendered with an ashlar frame of plinth, frieze and pilaster
strips, all completely plain. But set within this frame are four giant
Tuscan pilasters supporting three blank segmental arches. The
first-floor windows have segmental lintels to fit beneath the arches.
RAILWAY STATION, 1 m. N. 1887. Another fine station on the
Alnwick to Cornhill railway, similar to Akeld (q.v.).
BRANDS HILL, 1 m. W of North Middleton. On the NE and SE
hillsides a complex and extensive late prehistoric and Romano-
British landscape survives: unenclosed stone houses, field boundaries, trackways, enclosed curvilinear and rectilinear settlements,
and much subsequent ridge-and-furrow. A Bronze Age cist is
exposed in a burial mound near the river.
MIDDLETON OLD TOWN, ½ m. W of North Middleton. The earthwork remains of two rows of houses and tofts to the N and S of a
broad green, on the N side of which stands the present cottage.

Thomas Grey of Chillingham had eleven tenants here in 1580; a
few houses by the burn on the E remained *c.* 1800.

THREESTONEBURN, 3¼ m. W of Roddam. Stone circle on the edge
of the forest. Thirteen stones visible; only five standing, up to 1.4
metres (4½ ft) high. Unenclosed settlement of round stone houses
high on TATHEY CRAGS, ½ m. further NW, probably of Bronze
Age date.

INGOE

2½ m. NNE of Matfen

0070

SOUTH HALL. A fine early C18 manor house. Two-and-a-half
storeys and seven narrowly set bays. The windows are in raised
moulded surrounds. There are apparently two doorcases with
Gibbs surrounds, in the second and sixth bays; the one to the r.,
however, surrounds a window and not a door, because although
the façade is symmetrical the plan is not. The hall and staircase
are at one end of the house, with two rooms to the r. On the gable
end, a Venetian stair window with Tuscan columns. The house
has a very complete interior, with several panelled rooms and a
fine open-well stair with carved tread ends and thick turned
balusters. On the first-floor landing, instead of balusters there is
a large openwork Baroque panel.

WARRIOR STONE. A prehistoric standing stone in an impressive
position S of Sandyways Farm. Nearly 2 metres (6½ ft) high and
decorated with cup marks.

INGRAM

0010

An upland parish around the higher reaches of the River Breamish.
Agricultural decline since the C14 has preserved many prehistoric
and Roman settlements from destruction by the plough.

ST MICHAEL. W tower, nave and aisles, transepts and chancel.
The church has changed its appearance dramatically over the past
two hundred years. The original S aisle (which appears to have
been vaulted) was demolished in the early C18, the spire dismantled in 1803, the N aisle demolished in the early C19. Both
arcades were blocked up and became the side walls of the church.
The chancel became unsafe. Restoration began in the 1870s. The
aisles were rebuilt in 1879, the chancel a little earlier. The broad
unbuttressed tower was underpinned with new concrete foundations and systematically rebuilt in as convincing a facsimile as
possible, so that the lower parts still seem early Norman, the
upper parts C13 with paired lancet bell openings (cf. Eglingham).
Despite all these changes the interior has retained to a great extent
the atmosphere of a small medieval church. The ground floor of
the tower has one small round-headed window with deep inner
splays. The C11 tower arch is unmoulded and rests on the simplest
imposts. The W responds of the arcades might belong to the same
date, but rest, oddly enough, on semi-octagonal bases. Unless

these were an attempt, at once given up, at remodelling the C 11 work in the likeness of the C 13 arcades, it is difficult to see how the discrepancy can be explained. The arcades are two bays with octagonal piers, C 13 moulded capitals on the S, possibly C 14 on the N, and double-chamfered arches, those on the S side with fleur-de-lys at the springing of the arches. But, curiously, beyond the arcades are short stretches of solid wall and then the C 14 arches into the transepts. What do they mean? The chancel arch also seems C 14. – FONT, dated March 11th 1662. Octagonal, with elementary geometric patterns and an odd tree of life. – FITTINGS. Altar, pulpit, organ etc. all 1911–12 by *Hicks & Charlewood*. – STAINED GLASS. E window by *Heaton, Butler & Bayne*, 1912. Two nice windows in the S aisle by *Powell*; St Michael and St George, 1915, in one, and in the other, St Oswald, 1934, with a picture of the unaltered Roddam Hall (q.v.) behind the saint's head. – MONUMENT. Lower half of the figure of an ecclesiastic reset in the N wall of the chancel. Two small figures to the l. and r. of his feet. C 14. – Good LYCHGATE of 1928.

VICARAGE. Large and irregular in plan. Begun 1803 and added to throughout the C 19.

INGRAM FARM. By *J. Green*, but nothing special. Probably of 1826, the date on the farm buildings.

LINHOPE LODGE, *c.* 3 m. W. Shooting lodge built in 1905 for W. J. Joicey. It is a large spreading bungalow with long projecting wings and a narrow centre dominated by a fine, sturdy wooden porch.

The hillsides around Ingram, especially Heddon Hill (1 m. NE) and beside the Middledean Burn (1 m. SW), have been extensively ploughed in the past, probably reaching their maximum extent in the early C 14. Prominent CULTIVATION TERRACES (evidence of population pressure and a favourable prehistoric or medieval climate) developed along the contours. Some are cut across by later ridge-and-furrow.

The DESERTED MEDIEVAL VILLAGE of Alnhamsheles, an outlying settlement in Alnham parish, is 500 metres W of Alnhammoor in the upper Breamish. On either side of the Rowhope Burn are the footings of nearly twenty rectangular buildings, both houses and ancillary structures. Some are attached to small enclosures; others stand within them. The settlement was first mentioned in 1265; eleven tenants are recorded in 1314, but by the mid-C 16 the site was abandoned. Excavation of the most SW house indicated that from *c.* 1300 it was a three-bay building, *c.* 12 metres (40 ft) long, its roof probably supported by crucks. Its walls of stone and earth suggest a hipped roof rather than gables. The interior was subdivided: a small W living room and a larger E byre. In the C 16 the building was extended E and its width reduced.

Small promontory FORT defended by double ramparts and a stone wall at the S tip of Knock Hill, ½ m. E of Greensidehill.

BROUGH LAW, 1¼ m. W. A fine bivallate Iron Age hillfort set in a commanding and conspicuous position on the high S lip of the Breamish gorge. The techniques used in its construction (in about the early C 4 B.C.) are most uncharacteristic of Northumberland, for it was built entirely of rubble. The inner wall, which may have been as much as 3 metres (10 ft) high, is particularly unusual: its vertical faces enclose a rubble core and also an internal revetment, one metre inside the outer skin. The slightly narrower outer wall had no integral strengthening; it converges with the inner wall on the N and W where the steepness of the scree slopes (the Glidders) made the second defensive line superfluous. Staggered entrances lie on the E; when excavated, the inner one revealed evidence of a timber gateway. Artefacts and a round stone building in the SW of the interior suggest occupation in the Roman period.

GRIEVE'S ASH. Bivallate Iron Age fort on the hillside shoulder E of Linhope. A staggered E entrance leads into an interior occupied by stone-founded round-houses of Romano-British date. These later buildings straggle E, suggesting a prosperous and expanding settlement. Similar houses stood high above stockyards cut deeply into the slopes 200 metres NE. Small cairns and banks E of the plantation probably mark the associated field systems.

SETTLEMENTS on the S edge of the saddle of Hartside Hill, $\frac{1}{2}$ m. SE of Hartside Farm. A well-preserved group of five sub-circular homesteads of Romano-British type, consisting of stone-founded round-houses that overlooked enclosed and sunken yards (presumably for stock). Medieval and later ridge-and-furrow laps around all sides of them except the NW. On the summit to the E is a univallate Iron Age hillfort within a massive stone wall. Further E, on the lower slopes, is an irregular cluster of enclosed and unenclosed late prehistoric round-houses, from which a series of field-walls radiate.

The DESERTED MEDIEVAL VILLAGE of Hartside survives as earthworks 1 m. NE of Hartside Farm: a cluster of more than a dozen rectangular buildings with garths attached. Some appear to have been simple single-chambered structures, others were evidently subdivided internally; most have sizable boulders as the basal course of their walls. There is a corn-drying kiln at the E end of the settlement. The village fields, fossilized as ridge-and-furrow, stretch away to the S.

HAYSTACK HILL, $1\frac{1}{4}$ m. SW. A well-preserved group of egg-shaped 6 Romano-British settlements survives as an unploughable island in a sea of medieval ridge-and-furrow. The SE example is the most typical: in the rear portion of the enclosure the footings of three round stone houses are clearly seen, facing out onto stockyards which have been deeply scooped into the hillside below them.

MIDDLEDEAN, $1\frac{1}{2}$ m. SW. Bivallate promontory fort with stone-revetted ramparts and a staggered NE entrance. Later occupation traces include some round stone houses (probably Romano-British); a subsequent enclosure occupying the SW corner of the interior has a long rectangular building forming its N side.

WETHER HILL. Finely sited bivallate hillfort on the summit, $1\frac{1}{4}$ m. SSW, defended from the higher ground to the SW by a double cross-ridge dyke. The entrance is on the NW. The thin soils that necessitated internal quarry-scoops to provide the rampart material also ensured the continuing visibility of the overlapping circular foundation trenches of nearly twenty tightly packed timber 'ring-groove' houses (see the Introduction, p. 35).

OLD FAWDON HILL. Conical summit $1\frac{1}{3}$ m. S, encircled by traces of a slight bank marking the course of an Iron Age palisade. There are signs of two further, fainter, palisades circling within the

interior, the steep slopes of which are densely covered with scores
of scoops and platforms for round timber houses.

The SETTLEMENT on Ingram Hill, ½ m. SW, occupies a position
with no natural defences. Visible now only as a circular bank; its
external ditch has been levelled by the medieval cultivation around
it. Excavation revealed that the bank had a stone-revetted forward
face but incorporated the trench and packing for a substantial
fence or palisade. This must have risen high above the bank,
which was constructed in about the C 3 or C 4 B.C. Radiocarbon
dates suggest that this unassuming settlement, consisting of round
timber buildings, was probably contemporary with the sophisticated hillfort on Brough Law, I m. WNW. The social and
architectural implications of this are unexplained. After the deser-
tion of the settlement, and following a period of cultivation within
it, at least seven rectangular buildings were constructed, all but
one of them set around the internal perimeter. Each had bowing
stone walls and a single doorway in one long side. This phase is
undated but seems to represent a simple medieval farm.

BRANDON. *See* p. 200.
BRANTON. *See* p. 200.

JESMOND *see* NEWCASTLE UPON TYNE

₆₀₉₀

KIELDER

Kielder has become, in the mid–late C 20, a landscape of superla-
tives: the Forestry Commission's largest forest, the largest man-
made reservoir in Europe – combinations of scale which are
not necessarily encouraging. At Kielder, however, the effect is
successful. The KIELDER DAM, its downstream face carefully
shaped and planted, merges as well as it could with the surrounding landscape; and the reservoir, its edges planted with
deciduous trees, looks satisfyingly natural. The dam was built
for Northumbrian Water in 1975–81 and opened in 1982; the
designers were *Sir Frederick Gibberd & Partners*, the consulting
engineers *Babtie Shaw & Morton*.

UNITED REFORMED CHURCH (formerly Presbyterian). 1874 by
F. R. Wilson. Small and Norman style. Rock-faced stone. Pretty
patterned roof of different coloured slates.

KIELDER CASTLE. 1775 by *William Newton* for the Duke of Northumberland. It was built as a shooting box and displays the light,
somewhat flimsy style of the Duke's Gothick work at Alnwick.
Unfortunately, as at Alnwick, the fourth Duke, in the mid-C 19,
gave the S front unwanted Tudor solidity; but, projecting from it,
a surprisingly convincing Gothick extension of 1926 again lightens
the mood. More C 18 details survive on the other sides.

KIELDER VIADUCT. Designed for the Border Counties Railway
by *Robert Nicholson* and/or *John Furness Tone*, his nephew and
successor as Engineer to the line. The contractor was *William
Hutchinson*. Opened 1862. A fine long bridge of skew arches with
a castellated parapet and Gothic touches in the spandrels.

BLOODYBUSH PILLAR, 4 m. WSW, on the Border line. A toll-road pillar of 1830 with a long detailed inscription giving the names of the proprietors, the toll rates and the distances to places on the road. The road was constructed by Sir John Swinburne of Capheaton, principally for the haulage of coal from his mine at Lewisburn (now beneath the reservoir). The surveyor was *Telford*, the engineer *James Wilson* of Greena. The line of the road is still used by the Forestry Commission's road W past The Forks and Akenshawburn. Several bridges remain, though the main one, at Akenshawburn, appears to be a mid-C 19 reconstruction.

On the shoreline of Kielder Water, at the tip of the peninsula NE of the Information Centre at TOWER KNOWE, a low wall of boulders enclosed a rectangular homestead. The N half of the site is usually submerged. Excavation revealed that the surviving wall, faced with orthostats, overlay an earlier palisade. In the interior had stood at least two circular timber houses, one of which was twice reconstructed. These were replaced by three circular stone-founded buildings occupied in the Roman period; the timber period is unlikely to have been significantly earlier.

DEVIL'S LAPFUL, ¾ m. SE of the Castle. A Neolithic long cairn deep in the forest. Partly robbed, but measuring 58 by 14 metres (190 by 45 ft) and 2 metres (6½ ft) high at its well-preserved lower (SW) end.

KILLINGWORTH

1 m. N of Longbenton

Killingworth Township lies N and W of the old village, almost detached from it. Though not officially a post-war New Town, it is an independent settlement of 8,518 people (in 1991), planned on New Town lines in the 1960s for a much larger population (20,000). Killingworth was known in the C 18 for the large tract of moor on which Newcastle Races were held and, in the C 19, for the pioneering engineering work of George Stephenson at West Moor Colliery. Collieries, opened in the C 19, dominated the area by the C 20 but suffered the same decline after the Second World War as the rest of the North-East Coalfield. In 1960 the Ministry of Housing and Local Government gave the County Council approval to develop 'an unsightly area of land' (according to the *Killingworth Township Handbook*), and a Comprehensive Development Area was defined under the Town and Country Planning Acts. Longbenton Urban District Council was the housing authority. The co-ordinating architect planner was *R. J. A. Gazzard*. The lynchpin of the layout is an artificial lake crossed by the main access road. To the N of the lake lies a rigid box of public and commercial facilities within a long loop of distributor road, from which the network of houses opens. There is more housing to the NW and an industrial estate W and S of the lake near the railway. Before the linked blocks of concrete deck-housing were demolished in 1989, the distant impression from the N over the coastal plain resembled nothing so much as

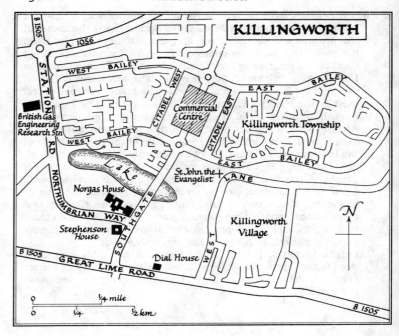

a set for Fritz Lang's *Metropolis*. Houses of a more traditional style
have been built since 1970, and even the supermarket is the usual
1980s rural barn.

ST JOHN THE EVANGELIST, West Lane. The church of the old
village: 1869 by *E. Bassett Keeling*. Nave, s aisle (the N aisle was
never built), chancel with polygonal apse. No tower, no bellcote.
Of iron-streaked sandstone, with bands of red at sill and impost
levels. Plate tracery in the large E and W windows; the others
cusped lancets, paired in the clerestory. On the buttresses, the
crescent emblem of the Dukes of Northumberland. Inside, the N
arcade is blocked to form the N wall. Big stiffleaf capitals to both
arcades, bracketed shafts to the moulded chancel arch and a blind
arch in the chancel N wall. High crocketed hoodmould over the
priest's door. Wagon roof, with stencilled stars in the chancel; its
floor is of tiles and Frosterley marble, with a MEMORIAL BRASS
to the first vicar, J. S. Blair † 1890.

KILLINGWORTH VILLAGE

WEST LANE turns through 90° beside St John's, and becomes a
village street. On the N just after the turn is NORTH FARM-
HOUSE, dated on the lintel 1725 DP (Deborah Potts). It is a
typical modest farmhouse, in coursed squared sandstone on a
plinth, with two storeys, a near-central door and three windows.
Steep pantiled roof, originally thatched; the triangular blocks
which form a strong edge to the return gables would have pre-

vented the thatch lifting in high winds. There are several C 18
houses, and much infill and alteration. Of the C 18 Killingworth
Hall by *Lancelot Coxon* no trace remains (it was demolished in the
1960s), but on the S side of the street, opposite its site, is a pair
of poured reinforced concrete houses of *c.* 1926. One still has its
battlemented parapets. Just beyond the village, ½m. to the E, is
KILLINGWORTH COTTAGE, a pleasant late C 18 house with
ornamental overlight. A little further, on the S side, is a picnic site
at the head of the former waggonway, with a resited winding wheel
as a reminder of the days when coal waggons trundled down, past
Dial Cottage (now Dial House) and on to the Tyne. DIAL
HOUSE (No. 108 Great Lime Road), an unremarkable late C 18
or early C 19 rubble and pantiled cottage with additions, would
be merely a pleasant vernacular survival in a sea of ribbon development if it had not been the home from 1803 to 1815 of George
Stephenson and his son Robert. Together, while Robert was a
schoolboy, they made the sundial over the door, dated 11 August
1816. George was brakesman of the winding engine at West Moor
Pit, and first showed his engineering talent when he improved a
pumping engine at Killingworth High Pit. On 25 July 1814 his
locomotive *Blucher* began working on the adjacent waggonway.

KILLINGWORTH TOWNSHIP

Along NORTHUMBRIAN WAY, the road which curves between the
lake and the industrial estate, some fine buildings for the gas
industry by *Ryder, Yates & Partners*; they are Killingworth's claim
to architectural fame. The best distant view is across the lake from
Southgate. First, at the E end, NORGAS HOUSE of 1963–5, with 127
its back to the S shore of the lake. Clear, uncluttered elevations;
three floors of soft grey glass and bands of vertical enamel panels.
The round piers can be glimpsed through the windows. The flat
roof has gleaming white cylindrical ventilators. In front, a low
round projection of blue brick sweeps up to a point; it contains
air-conditioning plant. A low block set back at the l. houses the
kitchen and dining room, the latter top-lit from a fibreglass roof-
sculpture, representing the Mycenean Minotaur's horns. The
Computer Block extension to the E (1972–5) is a complementary
glass-clad block, subdued and not drawing the eye away from the
main building. Next, STEPHENSON HOUSE of *c.* 1965, on the
opposite side of the road. With three bands of white concrete
cantilevered from hidden piers, and bands of windows deeply
recessed, it echoes, but does not copy, Norgas House. The whole
group takes on a special quality at night when lights and reflections
on glass, concrete and water create new patterns. By day, even
insensitive signs and heavy concrete lamp standards cannot
entirely mar the effect. Further W, the architects' own office of
1964–5 is a clever miniature and an important element in the
group. Two slabs of white float above ground, parting to reveal a
strip of windows and interrupted to allow doors.
Then, further away on STATION ROAD N of the junction with
Northumbrian Way, the BRITISH GAS ENGINEERING
RESEARCH STATION, 1965–7, with a rear extension of the early 128

1970s, also by *Ryder, Yates & Partners*, is just as striking as the other Gas Board buildings. It looks like a moated block with a high-fronted drawbridge; in reality the fall of the land is used to give vehicle access to low-level workshops at one side and to car-parks at the other. The eye is drawn to the 'drawbridge' by the tall narrow trilithon standing at the approach, its slender rear-sloping piers supporting a deep beam. The upper floors of the building are in the slabbed style of Stephenson House, with a recessed window strip. The trilithon is highest of all, its elegance emphasized by the array of tall white cylinders and funnels on the roof. Designed to provide flexible laboratory and workshop space, it is successful and satisfying. The SCHOOL OF ENGINEERING alongside, to the E, of 1977 and by the same architects, is a glass-clad foil to its neighbour.

0080

KIRKHARLE

ST WILFRED. Essentially a Dec church, though the nave was partly rebuilt in 1771–8 and extensively restored in 1884. W porch, nave and lower chancel. The chancel N windows are original, three-light with reticulated tracery. The corresponding windows on the S side are of the restoration, though the openings and especially the labels seem to be at least partly original. The five-light reticulated E window is C 19. The priest's door, on the other hand, is original, with two continuous hollow chamfers. So are the two cusped 'low-side' windows. The W porch and the dignified and heavily moulded bellcote were rebuilt for Sir William Loraine in 1731. – SEDILIA with pointed-trefoiled arches; adjoining trefoiled PISCINA with petalled drain and a fluted stem. Two more tre-foiled piscinae in the nave. – FONT. Perp, from All Saints Church, Newcastle; C 15. Big for this small church. Octagonal, with concave sides and decoration by shields. – An unusually fine and complete set of late C 19 FURNISHINGS in the Dec style. Especially attractive hammerbeam ROOFS. – MONUMENTS. Two medieval CROSS SLABS in the chancel. – In the nave, a simple mid-C 20 memorial to 'Capability' Brown, who was born at Kirkharle.

KIRKHARLE MANOR, the former vicarage. Early C 19. The garden front has three broad bays with a central canted two-storey bay window.

KIRKHARLE FARMHOUSE is the partly rebuilt wing of the mansion of the Loraine family, who were '*Capability*' *Brown*'s first employers. The present house has a three-bay centre and pro-jecting one-bay wings. Hipped roof. Sir William Loraine rebuilt his house in 1718 or shortly after, but it is not clear how much of the present fabric dates from that time. It is equally unclear how much the surrounding landscape owes to the early work of Brown, who was with Sir William from 1732 to 1739. Sir William was certainly a great 'improver', and John Hodgson felt that Brown played a significant part in these improvements. What is more sure is that Brown returned to Kirkharle to work for a second Sir William, the fourth Baronet, who made extensive changes in the 1770s.

LORAINE MEMORIAL STONE, just S of the Manor. 1728. A simple stone tablet, about 1.5 metre (5 ft) high, like a gravestone, recording the murder of Robert Loraine by the Scots in 1483.

LITTLEHARLE TOWER. *See* p. 378.

KIRKHAUGH

6040

A hamlet delightfully sited on the E bank of the South Tyne, amongst trees at the foot of a steep hillside.

HOLY PARACLETE. 1868–9; designed in C 13 style by the vicar, the *Rev. Octavius James*, after he had visited churches in the Black Forest. In the w end there is a genuine C 13 two-light window from the previous church. A simple rectangle with a steeply pitched roof and a corbelled-out turret on each gable, the w carrying a belfry with an absurdly thin needle-spire. Lofty interior accentuated by the absence of fitted seating (the intention from the first). – Plain medieval FONT. – In the churchyard, a Saxon hammerhead CROSS on a C 19 base, without any carved design.

In the area several BASTLE HOUSES and similar C 16 or C 17 buildings. Examples can be seen at UNDERBANK immediately S of the church, WHITLOW, ½ m. SW, WHITE LEA 1½ m. E (remodelled in the later C 17; a ground-floor two-light window has a foliage-carved lintel dated 1682), and the interesting LOW ROW, ½ m. N, which is probably a late C 17 or even C 18 house built when the need for defence was passing, but still with traditional bastle features. The walls are relatively thin but the ground-floor doors are still set centrally in the gable ends. Mullioned windows to all three floors.

KIRKHEATON

0070

ST BARTHOLOMEW. Nave and chancel. Some old masonry in the base courses and the N wall, but otherwise as rebuilt in 1755 for Mrs H. D. Windsor and drastically altered and gothicized in 1866–7 by the curate, the *Rev. T. Harris*. The most notable feature of the church is the fantastic w bellcote. The base has, at each corner, an obelisk capped by volutes; the bell stage has trefoiled heads to the lights and again obelisk finials at each corner. On top there is a stone pyramid with a ball finial. It all looks C 17 but could, one supposes, date from 1755. There are also four grotesque heads at the angles of the nave. They also look C 17 but may be later. The interior is all of 1866–7.

KIRKHEATON MANOR. A C 16 bastle or strong-house refronted in the early or mid-C 17 with hoodmoulded, three-light mullioned windows and a doorway with a hoodmould and a depressed pointed head. To the r. an ashlar-faced, square, taller addition of *c.* 1740. It has large Georgian sashes with a string above the ground-floor windows and triple keystones above the first-floor ones. Inside, the walls of the older part are *c.* 1.5 metres (5 ft) thick, except the front wall, which has been rebuilt and is slightly thinner. There are a number of stone c 17 fireplaces, including one in a bedroom with the lintel supported on big rounded corbels. The Georgian addition has a panelled room on the first floor. The house was partly ruinous in 1925 and restored *c.* 1930. The restoration included slightly heightening the front windows of the old part. The rainwater heads and downpipes were also brought here at this time – from Hornby Castle in Yorkshire, it is said.

WALLED GARDEN with rusticated gatepiers in front of the house.

On the N side of the VILLAGE green, the lower parts of the walls of a BASTLE.

WHITE HOUSE. A five-bay c 18 farmhouse built around the core of a much older house with walls *c.* 1.4 metres ($3\frac{1}{4}$ ft) thick. Large and impressive mid-c 19 LIMEKILNS *c.* 600 metres s of the house.

1070   KIRKLEY
                         3 m. N of Ponteland

KIRKLEY HALL (Northumberland College of Agriculture). The house was largely rebuilt by *Burns Dick* following a fire in 1928. It has a five-bay centre, with one-bay projecting wings and to the rear a large *porte cochère* with square Tuscan columns. The previous house had been built in 1832 by *Ignatius Bonomi*; the house before that was of 1764. All of these dates are represented by reused rainwater heads and reused window lintels with dates and inscriptions to members of the Ogle family whose house this was. – The STABLES of 1764 have an open colonnaded lantern. – SOUTH LODGE is probably of 1832, the first floor added early in the c 20. – To the W of the house, an OBELISK erected in 1788 by Newton Ogle and dedicated to the *vindicata libertas publica*.

BANK HEAD FARM, just E of the Hall. Mid-c 18. Brick. Among the farm buildings, a Gothick DOVECOTE.

BENRIDGE HALL, 1 m. S. The s front, of the late c 18, is in Flemish bond brick, rather a rarity in the county. It has five bays, with a central Venetian doorway set in a blank arch. Behind this, an earlier c 18 range.

9030   KIRKNEWTON

ST GREGORY THE GREAT. Externally a c 19 church in the lancet style, with a nave of 1860 by *Dobson* and a Perp NW tower of the late c 19. On closer examination, however, it can be seen that the s transept is of old masonry, and so are the side walls of the chancel. The s wall of the chancel has a priest's door with a chamfered surround and a flat lintel, and a small square window with a chamfered surround. These suggest that there is more to the church than meets the eye, and indeed inside there are two exciting survivals of a very northern and primitive kind, a chancel and a s transept, both with pointed tunnel vaults starting so low that in the transept there is no vertical wall at all, and in the chancel so little that the small window forms a penetration into the vault. The date of these vaults is rather problematical. On the strength of the double-chamfered chancel arch they are usually assigned to the C 13 or early C 14, but the priest's door and S window are more likely to be C 16. The vaults could be from either date, but it barely matters, since their barbaric qualities match so perfectly our vision of what the Borders were like. Dobson had no feeling for that character; Lutyens or perhaps Oliver Hill would have been equal to it. Dobson simply put up with these barbarities and made a neat and correct building of a good period. – FONTS. One, at the W end, of 1663; octagonal, with simple geometrically decorated patterns. The other, in the S transept, an C 18 marble baluster. – SCULPTURE. Relief of the Adoration of the Magi, the background cut off above the figures. Very rude workmanship; the Virgin, e.g., raises an arm stiff like a pole to greet the Kings. The date is most probably C 12. – STAINED GLASS. E window by *Dunston J. Powell*, 1904. – S aisle, 1915 and 1930, by *Atkinson Bros*. Colourful. – MONUMENTS. Andrew Burrell † 1458, and his wife. Large slab with incised figures. Heads and hands were set in brass. – Rev. T. Orde † 1776, by *I. Jopling*, in the chancel. – Also in the chancel, a lively tombstone of 1732 to the Rev. John Werge. – Josephine Butler † 1906. The great reformer is buried just W of the church.

WEST HILL, ½ m. SW. A univallate hillfort on the summit is defended by a stout stone wall, entered from the E. Traces of circular houses are visible in the NW. An outer rampart, not concentric, is overlain by a sub-rectangular settlement of Romano-British type, containing at least three circular stone buildings.

HETHPOOL. *See* p. 316.

YEAVERING, YEAVERING BELL. *See* p. 637.

KIRKWHELPINGTON
9080

ST BARTHOLOMEW. Sturdy W tower with Perp two-light bell openings, battlements and thin pinnacles, much and irregularly buttressed later. Plain Perp W door. Long aisleless nave and a long C 13 chancel with renewed E end, S lancet and plain priest's door. The nave also has an original-looking lancet on the N side. The S doorway into the nave is C 13 also. It has two orders of filleted shafts and capitals with nail-head decoration. The two roll mouldings of the arch are also filleted. However, the doorway is probably not *in situ*, for excavations have revealed the former existence of aisles and transepts (indeed the base and lower few feet of an octagonal pier can be seen embedded in the S wall). The story is even more confused by the presence of a steeply pointed tower arch to the nave which has two orders of scalloped capitals, the outer order with finely scrolled volutes, and extremely bold zigzag decoration in the arch both towards the E and W. It is too large to have been a W entrance before there was a tower, and so presumably it is evidence that the tower is older in its

masonry than it appears. The infilling of the arch includes many
Norman and c 13 bits placed there in the restoration of 1896. The
chancel arch certainly belongs to the chancel. It has rather low
octagonal responds and a tall steep double-chamfered arch. –
SEDILIA. Double, plain, pointed-trefoiled, with a shaft between
the two seats. – FONT. Plain octagonal and probably c 17, but
resting on the reversed capital of a c 14 or c 15 pier. – PULPIT.
Small, plain, of mahogany, with a tester; 1797. – STAINED GLASS.
Nave s window of 1909, and N window of 1914, by *Heaton, Butler
and Bayne*. – MONUMENTS. Gawen Aynsley † 1750, and his wife
† 1746. Large inscription plate with coat of arms, in a big surround
of Corinthian pilasters and open pediment. – In the chancel floor
there are several c 18 marble tablets with interesting inscriptions
to members of the Aynsley family. – Also in the chancel floor, an
unusual post-Reformation CROSS SLAB; 1632, to Robert Widdrington. – Several medieval cross slabs used as lintels and sills. –
In the churchyard also there are a number of c 18 and early c 19
HEADSTONES with inscriptions which are worthy of notice.

The VICARAGE was the home, in the early c 19, of John Hodgson,
the Northumbrian historian. c 18. Five bays, with lower one-bay
side wings. Stone slate roof. Inside, parts of two thick walls of a
former tower, or more likely bastle, more of which was in existence
in Hodgson's time.

The VILLAGE is quite large, with the church attractively placed on
an island site right in the middle. No houses of special distinction,
but several that are attractive in a quiet, well-built early c 19 way.
The best are CLIFF HOUSE and THE OLD TEMPERANCE,
both to the s of the church. To the N of the church is the OLD
POLICE STATION, now a private house. It is of 1840–50, with
hard ashlar and even harder corners, an uncompromisingly law-
abiding house.

KIRKWHELPINGTON BRIDGE. 1819. Erected at the instigation of
John Hodgson. A single broad segmental arch, and end piers with
pyramidal caps.

Most dominating on the Kirkwhelpington landscape is a large
WIND-POWERED GENERATOR erected *c.* 1984 on the ridge at
Knowesgate, 1 m. N of the village. It seems to be the first of its
type in the county.

At CATCHERSIDE, just N of Knowesgate, is a BASTLE, now a
cottage. It has the usual thickness of walls, but its blocked gable-
end doorway with a round-arched lintel is of a type more typical
further s in the county. Another bastle, at RAY DESMESNE
c. 2 m. NW, stands to *c.* 2 metres (6½ ft).

A SETTLEMENT of Romano-British type with double banks ¾ m.
NW of Catcherside. The interior is masked by ridge-and-furrow
and the E entrance obscured by a later wall.

THE FAWNS, 1 m. NE. Well-preserved medieval earthworks consisting of an enclosure in the shape of a buckled two-centred arch.
A wide enclosing ditch is flanked by two mounds, the inner one
faced with stone. The interior is crossed by dividing walls, and
there are four rectangular building-platforms along the SW side.
An abrupt re-entrant beside the entrance on the NE must have
respected an earlier structure at this point. Sir John Fenwick had
a tower or bastle at The Fawns in 1541.

At the DESERTED MEDIEVAL VILLAGE of West Whelpington, ½ m.
WSW, two dozen houses and their gardens were set around a
village green. Flourishing in the C 12 but deserted c. 1720. Now
quarried away except for its W end. Excavation revealed the
general sequence of building. In the first phase, which ended in
a Scots raid after Bannockburn, there were small long-houses
(with some evidence of integral byres) built of timber on stone
foundations. One house had a cross-passage and some had a door
in the centre of a long side. Roofs (probably of heather, roots or
bracken, perhaps over turf) may already have been supported on
crucks. After some decades of stagnation, four terraces of long-
houses were laid out round the green, perhaps as late as the early
C 15. These were of whinstone boulders bonded with clay to the
full height, up to the eaves. A cross-passage divided byre from
living room; some houses were glazed. c. 1675 the long-houses
were converted into a smaller number of discrete houses and
byres.

A simple univallate Iron Age HILLFORT is set on Great Wanney
Crag, ½ m. NW of Sweethope Lough.

GREAT BAVINGTON. See p. 289.

KNARSDALE   6050

In the Pennine valley of the South Tyne, a landscape more akin to
the more northerly Yorkshire Dales than one's usual impressions of
Northumberland.

ST JUDE. 1833 preaching box, gothicized and the chancel added in
1892. Vestry and porch 1906. – MONUMENTS. Medieval CROSS
SLABS, one with shears, in the N wall of chancel; two others, very
worn, in the graveyard to S. – STAINED GLASS. E window of 1904
by *Kempe*.

KNARSDALE HALL is a C 17 house perched on a steep-sided
mound, probably an older defensive site. Five-bay, extended by
two bays later in the C 17. Two-light mullioned windows with
straight hoodmoulds. Contemporary outbuilding with similar features to the SW.

BURNSTONES VIADUCT. A curious stone-built, double-skew
viaduct on the Alston Branch Railway of 1852. Probably by *Sir
George Barclay-Bruce*. A single elliptical road arch skewed at one
angle, an adjacent blind arch with non-parallel piers, then several
full-centred land and river arches, all skewed at a counter angle
to the road arch; it gives the illusion of one more arch on the W
side than on the E. Curved cutwaters to the river and land piers,
pilasters to the road piers, and a strong, curved stringcourse at
the base of the parapet.

Near the viaduct, two attractive late C 18 houses.

0040
KYLOE

ST NICHOLAS. 1792 by *Geo. Robinson and Thomas Hindmarsh.*
The prominent W tower has the typical 'churchwarden' lancet
windows and battlements. The W window, though, is a pretty
ogee-headed sash. The nave masonry is also of 1792, but the
tracery is geometrical and of 1868. The apsidal chancel and the
porch were added in 1862. All this work was done by *F. R.
Wilson.* – Undecorated late Saxon CROSS in the churchyard, S of
the church. – Fine views to the sea.

EAST KYLOE TOWER. Immediately attached to a farm building.
Probably C 14. The tunnel-vaulted ground floor is relatively complete, and the S wall stands *c.* 3 metres (10 ft) higher. The vault
has corbels to support a floor, and there are two slit windows
with deep inner splays. The newel stair in the SW corner has a
small tunnel-vaulted antechamber at its foot. The original
door is blocked and covered by the farm buildings on the
S side.

BEAL, 2 m. NE. A large farmhouse dated 1674 on a doorway with
an unusually fanciful surround for the county. It has crenellations
up the jambs and along the lintel. The farm buildings are an
impressive planned mid-C 19 group round a farmyard, of the same
type and clearly by the same builder as others in the area (cf. East
House at Cheswick).

BUCKTON, *c.* 2 m. SE. In a field by the farmhouse, a partly ruined
medieval DOVECOTE, of the 'beehive' type like those at Bamburgh
and Embleton.

LOW LYNN, *c.* 1½ m. NW. A ruined house, probably built for John
Gregson, who died in 1774. Mid-C 18, in fine beige ashlar, five
bays wide, with architrave surrounds to all the windows. The
middle window on the first floor has an eared and shouldered
architrave surround. Extended to the l. in the early C 19, using a
delicate pink ashlar.

BERRINGTON HOUSE. *See* Ancroft.

KYLOE HILLS, 1 m. S. On the cliff-edge W of Bogle Houses,
afforestation partly masks a hillfort with two widely spaced ramparts.

6050
LAMBLEY

Below the village the spectacular thirteen-arch VIADUCT of the
former Alston Branch of the Newcastle and Carlisle Railway,
1852; probably by *Sir George Barclay-Bruce.*

ST MARY AND ST PATRICK. 1885 by *William Searle Hicks.* A
very attractive little church; aisleless nave and chancel in
C 13 style. Quadripartite vault to the chancel and an elaborate timber roof to the nave. A second bellcote on the E end
of the nave holds a BELL reputed to come from Lambley
Priory.

LAMBLEY FARM, ½ m. N, stands close to the site of the Priory, a
Benedictine (or possibly Augustinian) nunnery founded before
1190. Sundry architectural fragments have been reused in the
house and farm buildings; others lie in the garden. The house,

remodelled in the late C 18, has thick walls which might be medieval; the adjacent outbuildings on the E have been bastle-type
dwellings.

EAST COANWOOD. *See* p. 262.

LANGLEY   8060

LANGLEY CASTLE. An extremely impressive tower-house, 42
impressive partly owing to *Cadwallader Bates*, who restored the
ruined shell in the 1890s. It says much for the quality of the
original masonry that so much had survived; the castle had apparently been in ruins since it was destroyed in 1405 by Henry IV in
the course of putting down Archbishop Scrope's rebellion. The
castle is first referred to as such in 1365; in its present form it
seems to be the product of a mid-C 14 remodelling of an earlier
first-floor hall house (cf. Haughton Castle). The plan is that of a
letter H, with an undivided central apartment 25 by 7.6 metres
(82 by 25 ft) and four square towers, projecting from the E and W
faces, with the entrance on the E. In the remodelling the main
block was carried up from three to four storeys, and the corner
towers to five. In addition a rectangular forebuilding was built
onto the E front, containing the main door and a newel stair to
the upper floors. The towers each contained separate chambers
entered from the principal apartments; they do not have their own
stairs. The top of the pre-C 14 work is marked by a chamfered
setback and a change in the colour of the ashlar wall-facing to a
lighter biscuity colour. Round-arched windows at second-floor
level on the S and W, the former blocked, survive from the first
phase; quite a number of two- and three-light windows of *c.* 1350
survive, with tracery showing the transition from the Decorated
to the Perpendicular styles. Other windows, notably those on the
ground floor, and the S door are insertions by Bates. The N and
S fronts each have two tall stepped buttresses capped by bartizans;
enough of these survived to justify Bates's restoration. The
embattled parapets of the towers are wholly late C 19. The double-
chamfered E doorway has a portcullis slot, and inside is a roof
boss in the form of a mask, through the mouth of which the
portcullis chain passed. The entrance to the first-floor hall from
the newel stair is a double door, the outer arch set slightly skew,
with moulded arches and foliage-carved capitals. The S part of
the forebuilding contains a ground-floor chamber opening only
to the outside, with above it four small chambers at levels different
from those of the main floors; these have segmental or four-
centred vaults, the only vaults in the castle. The SW tower contains
a unique series of garderobes, arranged above each other in three
groups of four, under pointed arches, and with external vents on
the S and W, through which a stream could be turned. The top
room of the SE tower, with its little two-light window, is said to
have been a chapel, and was restored as such in the early C 20,
but has no old ritual arrangements.

Bates also erected the MEMORIAL CROSS beside the A686 to the
two Jacobite Earls of Derwentwater beheaded in 1716 and 1746

'for loyalty to their lawful sovereign'; a sentiment that could be publicly expressed only 150 years later!

TOLLHOUSE, by the roadside near the Castle on the Alston Roads Turnpike (1824). A one-storey cottage of unusual design but similar to Alston Loaninghead and Langwathby (both in Cumbria but on the same turnpike). It resembles two back-to-back mono-pitch buildings of unequal length but with a common ridge, the shorter facing onto the roadside with the main entrance door and a sash window, but also a sash viewing window in each return to the longer section. Chimneystacks at each end of the longer section and also small additions at each end. Stone-built, with dressed quoins and openings; blue slate roof.

119 STUBLICK COLLIERY. Coal has been worked hereabouts at least since 1700, and hundreds of bell pits pockmark the fell to the s of the smelter chimney. Deeper mining necessitated the driving of a drainage level which discharges into the smelt mill reservoir (Nillston Rigg), but a beam pumping engine was installed, possibly c. 1830, to permit even deeper working. The ashlar-built engine house and boiler house with chimney alongside is now in farm use, as is an adjacent and contemporary engine house which may have been constructed for a winding engine but is described as a saw mill on the first edition of the Ordnance Survey, c. 1856. A dramatic group of industrial buildings, set on an outlier coalfield amongst the high moors, with which there is nothing to compare on the main coalfield.

LEAD INDUSTRY SITES. Langley smelt mill of c. 1770 and the adjacent Blagill Mill of 1704 have largely collapsed or been dismantled, but Langley's horizontal flue leading SE is partially intact and its terminal vertical chimney was restored in 1986. Alongside the flue, small reservoirs, now waterless, suggest that the scraped residues were washed back down the flue for subsequent resmelting. Nearby are former smallholdings and a very large reservoir, still holding water, which supplied power for driving the furnace bellows. Hollowed packhorse routes lead to the mill from the s, while the turnpike of 1778 crosses over the flue near its vertical chimney. This turnpike was remodelled by *Macadam* in the 1820s, and to the SW of the mill an abandoned section of the 1778 turnpike runs to the s of the newer turnpike. A branch of the new turnpike runs from Carts Bog to Haydon Bridge; a cross road links old and new turnpikes via a small river bridge of the 1820s and passes along the W boundary of the smelt mills with another reservoir. Near the small bridge, the Greenwich Hospital Commissioners' school of 1852 and a Primitive Methodist chapel of 1870 stand by a few cottages. Finally, passing along the s edge of the mill site is the disused Allendale Branch Railway of 1867, with its neat STATION and its platform buildings in timber still serving as the local post office. A bridge was built over the railway to carry the horizontal flue, and a retaining wall near the station is provided with tethering rings for packhorses. All these features, from packhorse ways to reservoirs, were a direct result of the lead industry. *See* also Chesterwood.

STAWARD. *See* p. 579.

LANTON
1 m. W of Coupland Castle

The LANTON OBELISK stands on top of a hill, a landmark from afar. It represents no national occasion but a private act of remembrance – or rather two. It was probably erected in 1827 by Alexander Davison of Swarland Park in memory of his brother, John Davison of Lanton. In 1828 Alexander died, and he is commemorated in an inscription dedicated by his son, Sir William Davison of Lanton. There is also an inscription reading 'Alexander Davison 1795'. 1795 is the year in which Alexander bought Swarland Park (q. v.), so the inscription may merely record that event. He was Lord Nelson's chandler, and at Swarland in 1806 he dedicated another obelisk to Nelson's memory.

LEE HALL
3 m. N of Wark-on-Tyne

Early Georgian stone house of five bays and two-and-a-half storeys with quoins, windows in heavy frames, an arched doorway in the middle with heavy keystones, and an arched window above it. Behind this there is earlier work, including a large stone fireplace of the C 17.

LEMINGTON
1 m. E of Newburn

Although some $4\frac{1}{2}$ m. up river from Newcastle's low-arched bridge of 1781 and therefore accessible by river only with keels, Lemington witnessed the establishment of two large industrial concerns in the last decades of the C 18. Here was one of the few available areas of low-lying land adjacent to navigable water, with a co-operative landowner in the Duke of Northumberland and easy access to coal.

HOLY SAVIOUR, Scotswood Road, Sugley. 1836–7 by *Benjamin Green*. E. E. style. Aligned N–S, with lancets flanking the wide chamfered buttress under the W gable bellcote. – STAINED GLASS by *Wailes*, including an E window of the 1840s in Pugin's style. – PARISH HALL of 1838, possibly also by *Benjamin Green*. Stone-mullioned three-light windows with floating cornices.

ST GEORGE (R.C.), Scotswood Road. Church and presbytery of 1868–9 by *A. M. Dunn*, the church paid for by Richard Lamb of West Denton. They burst into view in a rash of polychrome brick, the fronts white in Flemish bond and each with Lombard frieze. The church has shouldered lintels, W lancets with nook-shafts below a cinquefoil, and a S tower with gargoyles. Interior re-ordered.

The GLASSWORKS, between the main valley-bottom road and the old bed of the river (the 'Gut') were begun in 1787 by the newly formed 'Northumberland Glass Company'. The location had to be suitable for river transport, as sand, alkali and suitable clay for the melting pots had to be brought in by sea and river. Initially flat glass was the main product, and soon four large GLASS CONES had been erected, the largest of which survives (although disused). It is *c*. 36.5 metres (120 ft) high and is reputed to have required 1.75 million bricks when it was built in 1797. It is one of the most important industrial monuments in the North East. The works continues to produce specialist commercial glass products which require all of the skills of traditional glassmaking such as marver blowing, block blowing and the hand drawing of capillary tubing.

Immediately E of the glassworks, and also with its own river quay, stood the first integrated IRONWORKS in the North East, established on a 20-acre site in 1797 by the Tyne Iron Company, with coke ovens, calciners, blast furnaces, foundry, wrought-iron plant and rolling mills. There were also 40 workmen's dwellings with gardens attached, a 'most commodious mansion house with large garden and pleasure grounds' and a public house. The works had closed by *c*. 1876 and was largely demolished *c*. 1890. To the N of the road (driven through the abandoned works for an electric tramway in 1913) are the remains of coke ovens and calciners. To the S, a rough road passes an arched ramp, which formerly led to one of the blast furnaces, and a rubble wall showing blocked openings of the houses and pub. At the foot of the track, overlooking the 'Gut', are the former offices. Another prominent ramp incorporates rooms for unidentified purposes.

On a part of this former ironworks site is an early, two-bay POWER STATION, brick-built with round-headed openings and a ridge ventilator. It was built for the Newcastle and District Electric Lighting Company (DISCO) in 1903. Though it ceased generating in 1919, it continued as a substation until 1946. Riverside locations are no longer so important for industry, and much of the ironworks site was never redeveloped.

S of the glass and ironworks sites is the 'Gut', formerly the bed of the Tyne, with fragmentary wooden STAITHS and WAGGONWAY alignments leading back from it. River improvements by the Tyne Improvement Commissioners in the 1880s left this section of the river a backwater (a new channel was cut across a large meander) but it was kept dredged as long as the staiths were in use.

NEWBURN. *See* p. 405.

1010 # LEMMINGTON HALL
1¼ m. NE of Edlingham

A mid-C18 country house altered towards the end of the C18 by *William Newton*. By the late C19 the house had become a roofless ruin. It was restored in 1913 for Sir Stephen Aitchison and is now a convent. The S front is of nine bays. The projecting centre bay has a Venetian doorway under a tripartite window and a pediment. The two bays at each end of the façade are set slightly back; it is not apparent that those at the r. end are in fact the refaced S wall of a C15 tower-house. To the rear the tower-house is more evident, although the traceried windows and embattled parapet are all early C20. The tower is L-plan: the basement barrel vault

and part of the newel stair in the s turret survives. Its first floor is
now a chapel; surviving features at this level are a mural chamber
with an oubliette, and a reset c 16 roll-moulded fireplace now
behind the reredos. The remainder of the house is mostly early
c 20 inside, with older material from both Camelford House, Park
Lane, London (stair balustrades, door surrounds etc.), and the
château at Bar-le-Duc (chapel panelling).

To the NE of the house are various outbuildings with the
same half mid-c18, half early-c 20 character. The long embattled
GARDEN WALL is of the former period, the STABLES of the latter.
The pretty GARDEN COTTAGE is late c 18 and brick; it has a
porch flanked by Venetian windows, with circular windows above.

COLUMN, ¼ m. SE of the Hall. 1786 by *Sir John Soane*, as a memorial
to the parents of James Evelyn (a distant relative of the diarist
John Evelyn). It was originally sited at Felbridge Park in Surrey,
and was brought to Lemmington simply as an ornament in 1928.
It stands on a platform incorporating c 17 and c 18 architectural
fragments, and has a moulded base encircled by a self-swallowing
serpent, an c 18 symbol of eternity found on many headstones.
The tapering column is unfluted, and carries a capital with a
scrolled pattern, supporting a corniced block and a fluted altar.
The shaft carries a variety of inscriptions.

LEMMINGTON BRANCH, 1 m. E. A late c 18 hilltop eyecatcher with
three towers linked by a screen wall, all embattled. Farmhouse and
buildings incorporated at rear.

ABBERWICK MILL, 1½ m. N. Picturesque early c 19 group of mill,
mill house and corn-drying kiln.

ABBERWICK, 1 m. N. Substantial earthworks, especially w of the
farm, of a village that still had seventeen householders in 1665. A
prominent mound may mark the site of a tower first mentioned in
1572. Around about are house-platforms and attached enclosures.

LESBURY   *2010*

ST MARY. The exterior is much restored. Apart from the w tower
(given a Victorian pyramidal roof), all the s side is of 1849,
although the buttresses and lancets s of the chancel and perhaps
also the s door (moulded round arch on shafted jambs) reproduce
what was there before. The E end, however, has a three-light
window of *c*. 1300 cutting an earlier c 13 chamfered stringcourse;
the NE vestry is c 17 or c 18, and the chancel N chapel and nave
N aisle have medieval masonry with a restored c 14 window in
the chapel and strange little blocked square-headed windows
(c 13?) in the aisle. There are so many changes of masonry in the
tower that it defies easy interpretation (it was described as 'like
to fall' in 1604), but the big squared stonework of the lower
stage might be c 12. The interior is extremely puzzling, basically
because much of the detail has been recut. The two-bay arcades
to aisle and chancel chapel, the tower arch and the chancel arch
are all double-chamfered and the arcade piers circular. The nave
responds have heavy imposts, chamfered beneath, carried back
along the chunks of solid wall at each end of the arcade; the

chancel arch springs from a similar chamfered band. One might presume that a Norman church (the tower arch has semicircular responds) was remodelled early in the C 13 with the addition of aisle, chancel and chapel; beyond this it is not safe to go. Of the later medieval period there is only the low-pitched chancel roof (preserved beneath a high-pitched C 19 one), which has cambered tie-beams linked by strange longitudinal members beneath and quite separate from the ridge-piece (cf. Alnwick); the timbers have relief-carved bosses and Percy emblems. – More Percy emblems carved on the C 15 octagonal FONT.

OLD VICARAGE, E of the church. A three-bay villa of c. 1865, still in the early C 19 tradition. 1765 doorhead reset at rear.

LESBURY HOUSE looks S across the river. Five-bay villa of c. 1800, with plinth and sill bands, incorporating an earlier C 18 wing at the back. Major mid-C 19 extensions.

LESBURY BRIDGE. Handsome C 15 bridge over the Aln. Two triple-chamfered arches of 10-metre (34-ft) span, one segmental and the other pointed, with sharply pointed cutwaters between carried up as refuges. Widened on the E in the C 19.

RAILWAY VIADUCT, ½ m. NW. 1848–9 by *Robert Stephenson*. Eighteen segmental arches spanning the Aln valley. Rock-faced, with a big moulded top cornice.

LILBURN

LILBURN TOWER. 1828–9 by *Dobson* for Henry Collingwood. A large and quite splendid house in the Tudor style, with shaped gables. Symmetrical garden front of three broad bays. The entrance side has a large *porte cochère*. The house, though Tudor, follows the same L-shaped plan as so many of Dobson's classical houses. The main rooms are richly decorated. The ballroom has a coffered ceiling with pendants, the library a panelled Tudor-style ceiling and Dec wall panels. In the dining room, a large built-in sideboard by Dobson himself, who designed many of the fittings. There is a Gothic staircase with cast-iron balusters and a very large mullioned-and-transomed stair window (containing glass by *Wailes*). The stair was originally part of a full-height hall, but in 1843 Dobson was recalled by a new owner, John Collingwood, to make alterations. A ceiling was inserted into the hall and the staircase was partitioned off. The *porte cochère* (which had formerly been placed centrally in the entrance front) was moved a little to the l., so that entry could be made into the hall through a draught lobby.

The house is set in a large garden with beautiful views and balustraded terraces, probably also by *Dobson*. In the grounds, several items worth noting. The OBSERVATORY, 100 metres SW of the house, was attributed by *The Builder* to *Moffatt*, a pupil of Dobson who actually lived at Lilburn. 1843. It has a copper dome and an embattled parapet. WEST LODGE and GATEWAY. A single-storey Tudor lodge. Beside it tall gatepiers with large eagles on top, flanked by Gothic screens of five pointed arches. This is also by *Dobson*. DOVECOTE and BYRE, 200 metres N of the house.

Early C19. Three bays; raised castellated centre with a pyramid roof.

WEST LILBURN TOWER, ¼ m. W of Lilburn Tower and still part of its grounds. A ruined C 15 tower. Most of the N wall stands to *c.* 10 metres (34 ft) with much of the ashlar facing and two small square windows within chamfered surrounds. On the inside of the wall the springing of the ground-floor vault, and on the upper floor two arched openings and a mysterious attached shaft between them.

LILBURN CHAPEL, beside the ruined tower. The walls of a ruined early Norman chapel comprising nave and chancel, with a long C 13 S chapel (*see* the one remaining respond). No window shapes survive, but the masonry is eloquent. – In the S chapel, two medieval GRAVE SLABS, one with the inscription 'Alexander'; in the nave another slab.

Just S of the grounds of Lilburn Tower, the Lilburn Burn is crossed by two bridges of contrasting type. LILBURN BRIDGE is early C 19 and of dressed stone with three segmental arches. LILBURN WEST BRIDGE, on the A697, is an early pre-cast ferro-concrete design of 1906 by *Ferro-Concrete Construction*, using the *Hennebique* patent. It is a single span supported on five pre-cast segmental arches and has a pretty cast-iron parapet.

LINDEN HALL
1¼ m. N of Longhorsley

1090

A very plain and beautifully ashlared house of 1812 by *Sir Charles Monck* of Belsay for Charles William Bigge. Now a hotel. It has an oblong central hall in which the staircase goes up along three walls, under an oval roof lantern. To the W an extremely heavy and severe four-column porch with unfluted Greek Doric columns. Stable block and outbuildings converted to domestic accommodation in the 1980s by *Ainsworth Spark*.

LINDISFARNE *see* HOLY ISLAND

LINNELS
1½ m. SE of Hexham

9060

LINNELS BRIDGE. Narrow (2.95-metre (9 ft-10 in.) roadway) segmental-arched bridge of 14.5-metre (47½-ft) span over the ravine of the Devil's Water. Probably of 1698, with the date tablet from a previous bridge of 1581 reset under the arched pediment at centre of parapet.

LINNELS MILL, just up river from the bridge, on the W bank. A very small but important mill, of early compact form and virtually complete. The building is probably C 17, mainly of rubble construction with a flagstone roof. Inside, the machinery of a hurst-frame mill of C 18 type is still extant. The mill closed down late in the C 19, and an early water turbine was inserted between the spokes of the pitchback wheel and drove a dynamo; this, like the race and dam, still survives.

LITTLEHARLE TOWER
½ m. NE of Kirkharle

The GARDEN FRONT reveals a nicely varied house. To the l. and slightly projecting is a three-storey medieval tower with a blocked arched door on the ground floor; the ground floor is still vaulted. Adjoining the tower to the r. is a range which now looks entirely early C 18, apart from the Victorian doorway; it is, however, at least partly medieval and contains a stone newel stair. This range is of two storeys and five bays: the sash windows have largely retained their early C 18 thick glazing bars. To the r. is a section which looks entirely Victorian. It was designed by *Thomas Anderson*, the owner, in 1861–2 and includes a large two-storey canted bay window with cinquefoil windows on the first floor and panels of blank Geometric tracery above. However, this part is also older than it appears, and contains a mid-C 18 staircase and one rather splendid room with a plaster ceiling of *c.* 1745 in the style of the Italians who worked at Wallington, two pedimented doors with pulvinated friezes, and a white marble fireplace with side terms and a broken semicircular pediment framing a bust. On the ENTRANCE SIDE, everything is of 1861–2, including the large Gothic *porte cochère*. Much more of the same period was demolished *c.* 1980.

LITTLEHOUGHTON
1 m. NW of Longhoughton

LITTLEHOUGHTON HALL. The main block has a four-bay front with sill bands and windows in architraves, and a hipped roof. To the rear is a wing dated 1686 (on the fireplace lintel inside), but between the two parts is a still older fragment with thick walls of massive rubble and a blocked square-headed doorway on the E. It is recorded that a tower was demolished here in 1818 (when the front block was built), but the surviving fragment looks C 16 rather than medieval; it might have formed part of a wing added to the tower. Inside is a big roll-moulded fireplace backing onto a cross-passage in the 1686 wing; this has a moulded doorway at each end, with above the E doorway the remains of a cable-moulded surround probably belonging to a sundial (cf. Callaly), and windows which have lost their mullions.

LITTLEMILL
<small>¾ m. E of Rennington</small>

2010

LITTLE MILL FARMHOUSE. L-plan house, with a doorway dated 1714 in the N wing. The main five-bay front, with a badly damaged bolection-moulded door surround and moulded stone frames to the windows, looks a little later.

LITTLEMILL LIMEKILNS, by the level crossing. Probably the largest kiln bank in the county, being some 10 metres (33 ft) high, 16.8 metres (55 ft) wide and 33.5 metres (110 ft) long, with a long earth loading ramp. Within the bank, two rows of four kilns face inwards towards a high internal Gothic arch which took a rail line into the centre of the kiln block. Behind are the quarries and beside is an earlier and smaller kiln with three round-headed draw arches.

LITTLE SWINBURNE
<small>1¼ m. SW of Thockrington</small>

9070

LITTLE SWINBURNE PELE. In ruins. Clearly recognizable, half the arch of the doorway and the lower part of the mural stair. A roof mark on the W side, along with a mound on the same side, suggests that there may have been a hall range. Not mentioned as in existence in 1415, but mentioned in 1541. The date is probably C 15.

LITTLE SWINBURNE FARMHOUSE. Built in 1808 for Sir William Loraine and, with its five bays, rather more substantial than the usual farmhouse, but still completely plain. Attractive cobbled courtyard behind the house, with a high rubble wall and segmental carriage arch.

RESERVOIR. *See* p. 297.

LOAN END
<small>1 m. NE of Horncliffe</small>

9050

UNION CHAIN BRIDGE. 1819–20, to the design of *Captain Samuel Brown R. N.*, who later designed the chain piers at Newhaven and Brighton as well as other bridges. *John Rennie* advised on the abutments and the design of the tower. It was the first suspension bridge in Europe to carry vehicular traffic, for although Telford had completed his design for Menai in 1818, using Brown's suspension chain link patent of 1817, Menai was not completed until 1826. Large iron suspension bridges were first built in America (e.g. James Finlay's chain bridge of 1801 at Jacobs Creek, and White and Hazard's wire rope bridge at Fairmont, Philadelphia, 1816), but the next developments took place in Britain and France. What makes Brown's contribution technically important is his invention of the wrought-iron chain link; its application brought about the beginnings of long-span suspension bridges in Britain. In the Union Bridge the link bars are no more than five centimetres (two inches) in diameter, and so from a distance they are almost invisible against the darker waters of the Tweed. The Scottish support tower is a free-standing structure whose sides have a marked batter (as suggested by Rennie) and a large round-headed vehicle arch. The English side has no tower as such, for the anchorages are here embedded directly into a rock outcrop at 12 metres (40 ft) above the roadway; the cliff face below the anchorages was faced with masonry to match the Scottish tower, and a small toll collector's lodge with a Tuscan porch stood at the foot. This lodge was removed in 1955, but its façade was incorporated into the anchorage wall. The span of the suspension chains is *c.* 146 metres (480 ft) – several times larger than any existing spans of any sort then in western Europe – but the bridge deck span is only *c.* 120 metres (390 ft) to an abutment on the English side which allows the roadway running parallel to the river to turn onto the bridge. The entire bridge cost only £7,700, about one third of the cost of an equivalent masonry bridge, and it took only eleven months to complete. The original suspension hangers were replaced in 1870–1, and in 1902 additional wire suspension ropes and suspension hangers were provided. General refurbishment has continued in the C 20.

2060   LONGBENTON

There is a village street discernible among the 1930s housing estates. The parish church is inexplicably sited a mile to the N, halfway to Killingworth.

ST BARTHOLOMEW, Station Road. The medieval church was rebuilt in 1790 by *William Newton* (as G. W. D. Briggs has shown), so that St Anne's, Newcastle, can no longer be said to be this architect's only church. This is, moreover, in Gothic style, designed after a career devoted almost entirely to the classical. The square W tower, with its wide, pointed belfry openings, pinnacled battlements and short octagonal spire, was drawn by Richardson in 1840 so must be by Newton. The shape of the C 18 church can still be felt in the aisleless nave, but the details are due to various C 19 remodellings: repairs of 1842; rebuilding of the chancel in 1855; alterations in 1873–5 by *R. J. Johnson* and in 1888 by *W. S. Hicks*. – AUMBRY and PISCINA medieval, probably reset, although the masonry of the external face of the N chancel wall is less regular than the rest of the fabric. – FONT. 1857, with octagonal pedestal and bowl, carved in Gothic style on alternate sides. – STAINED GLASS. C 19 E window, resited in the S organ chamber; perhaps the work of *Hardman* in 1856, as may be that in the N chancel.* – Non-pictorial late C 20 glass by *L. C. Evetts*. – MONUMENTS. Two small incised CROSS SLABS reset over the aumbry and piscina. – Well-carved GRAVESTONES reset beside the chancel arch have coats of arms and inscriptions. One to John Fenwick † 1581; the other, apparently altered in the C 18, to John Killingworth and his family † 1587–1720. – In the tower, similar slabs to Edward Hindmarsh † 1708 and Ralph Anderson † 1687. – SUNDIAL, S of porch. 1858, restored.

* Information kindly given by Mr G. Long.

CHURCH HALL. 1980 by *Tony White*, completed by *D. G. Simpson*.* An attractive octagonal addition, low, with bold plain openings and cruciform hipped roof, linked by a corridor to the NW of the nave.

ETHEL WILLIAMS HALL, Front Street. A University of Newcastle upon Tyne hall of residence, comprising two old houses and modern buildings. The w building (the annexe) is the former VICARAGE, once known as North House. It was built *c.* 1734 for C. Hayton; the entrance hall and dining room were added *c.* 1757. Five bays, two storeys and attics, in coursed sandstone. The windows are narrow plain sashes. Some original panelling and doors, one with a lugged pedimented architrave surround. To the E, the present NORTH HOUSE, a late C18 house altered in the C19. Ashlar. Two storeys, five bays, and slightly lower two-bay wings. The main block has a central broken-pedimented Tuscan doorcase, and sill and floor bands. One-storey, three-bay wing at the l., with low-pitched hipped roof. Running N–S along the E side of the site, the MAIN HALL block of 1951 by *W. B. Edwards & Partners* for King's College, Newcastle. Typical of the period's best. Thin bricks, projecting stone-like window frames, pitched slate roofs, and an ashlar porch with stylized classical detail.

BENTON HOUSE CONSERVATIVE CLUB (formerly Benton House), Hoylake Avenue; it backs onto the s side of Front Street. A farmhouse built for T. C. Bigge (1739–94). Good ashlar; two storeys, five bays, with wings. The central door has been made into a window but retains the Tuscan porch with fluted necking. A C20 fire destroyed the interior. The w wing appears to have been classicized when its N front was made into a shop, probably *c.* 1900. Both N and S elevations are pedimented, with keyed oculi. In front among the flowers a ha-ha, sheltering the bowling green.

At FOUR LANE ENDS, the MANOR HOUSE, Front Street, in a prominent position beside the roundabout. Early C18 vernacular converted to late C20 flats. Large sandstone blocks with a coarser stone for dressings; lintels cut to resemble voussoirs over renewed sash windows. The shape of the steeply pitched roof suggests it conceals upper-cruck trusses. Behind, a conical roof proclaims a former gingang. The farmhouse seems to have just escaped the clutches of the METRO STATION to the N, a wide low group of russet brick, smoke glass and brown roof panels. (For the Metro system, *see* Newcastle upon Tyne: Public Buildings.)

KILLINGWORTH. *See* p. 362.

LONGFRAMLINGTON
1000

ST MARY. Nave, chancel and s porch. Nave and chancel are basically of *c.* 1190, although changes in masonry-type suggest that older fabric might be incorporated. The s doorway and chancel arch both have waterleaf capitals (cf. Newminster); both have round arches, the door of three and the chancel arch of two square orders. The jamb shafts of the door are missing, but the

* Information kindly given by Mr G. Long.

chancel arch has three quite detached shafts on each side, with waterholding bases. Also contemporary may be the two round-headed windows on the s of the nave (renewed except for their rere-arches) and the round-headed 'low side' window on the s of the chancel. The w end is a puzzle: two round-headed windows, which look c 19 except for their inner jambs, flank a central broad buttress, dated 1740, which seems to block a w door. The buttress probably goes with the bellcote, which has twin pointed openings and a pretty top with corner finials and a central pyramid-capped turretlet. The chancel was largely rebuilt in 1882 by *John Wardle* of Newcastle. In 1896 the nave was restored and the vestry added (incorporating a c 14 two-light window formerly in the s wall of the chancel) by *Hicks & Charlewood*.

OLD VICARAGE. 1894 by *Boolds & Hardy* of Morpeth. Jacobethan.

In the VILLAGE centre, on the corner of Church and Front Streets, a picturesque curving row of varied late c 18 and early c 19 houses are the back-drop to a 1911 pant. On Rothbury Road is ROOKWOOD HOUSE, dated 1717: two storeys and five bays with rusticated quoins, sill bands, central doorway with lugged architrave and pediment, and windows in architraves. At the N end of the village, to the E of the main road, is EMBLETON HALL (now the Embleton Hall Hotel), incorporating a very similar five-bay house said to be of *c.* 1730. This c 18 part now forms a wing to a Tudor-style mansion of 1893.

LOW TOWN, $\frac{3}{4}$ m. SE. Another two-storey five-bay house, this time dated 1750 and severely plain. Contemporary rear outshut under steep catslide roof.

ELYHAUGH. *See* p. 270.

NEWMOOR HALL. *See* p. 518.

WELDON BRIDGE. *See* p. 620.

LONGHIRST

$2\frac{1}{2}$ m. NE of Morpeth

A good c 19 estate village. Most of the cottages are of the early c 19, remodelled *c.* 1880. One row has a low first floor at the downhill end only, lit by little Yorkshire sashes decreasing in height. On the E the three-bay church hall (formerly READING ROOM) and a house with fancy bargeboards to its dormers.

ST JOHN, a little way s of the village. 1876 by *Sir Arthur Blomfield*. Rock-faced. NW tower with spire, low s aisle with dormers, and rather mechanical geometrical tracery. Chancel screen carved by the *Rev. Proctor* (1885–1916) and his parishoners; good-quality tiled floors and carved bench seating. – LYCHGATE of 1885.

LONGHIRST HALL, amongst trees SE of the village. An especially fine villa of 1824 by *Dobson* for William Lawson, reminiscent of Shaw's Cresswell Hall (begun three years earlier, and now sadly demolished). Simple five-bay, two-storey s front, with the three middle bays projecting as a large bow. Behind this front was originally, it is said, just one large room, now subdivided; beyond this is the *pièce de résistance* of Longhirst, the ashlar-faced central hall, oblong with apsed ends and a circular glass dome over the middle. On the N, open to the hall beyond two columns, the staircase, covered by a coffered segmental vault at r. angles to the hall. The staircase starts in one arm and returns in two. Fine cast-iron balustrade with anthemion ornament. The hall is reached from the W by a large porch with giant Corinthian columns *in antis*.

On the E of the house a CONSERVATORY with Tuscan pillars and glass walls. Further NE a WALLED GARDEN with early C 19 glasshouses, one formerly an aviary.

LONGHORSLEY 1090

OLD CHURCH, in the fields some distance SE of the village and sadly derelict. 1783 nave and lower 1798 chancel, on medieval foundations. Three wide side lancets of typical 'churchwarden' dimensions, and an odd trefoiled chancel arch.

ST HELEN. Built in the mid-C 19 as the village school: the porch was brought from the Old Church in 1982. Adjacent school-master's house of 1751, refronted *c.* 1850, and C 18 schoolroom with bellcote.

ST THOMAS OF CANTERBURY (R.C.). 1841. Nave and chancel with a pair of sacristies making the plan cruciform. Lancet style.

HORSLEY TOWER. Substantial early C 16 tower with a mid-C 17 N wing, restored in 1930. Square-headed windows with hood-moulds, some renewed. Embattled parapet and higher SE stair turret. Barrel-vaulted ground floor and stone newel stair. Original large fireplace on the first floor, early C 18 panelling on the second. The third floor was used as a R.C. chapel in the late C 18 and early C 19.

OLD VICARAGE. Three-bay house described as 'newly built' in 1826. Rear stair wing with the usual arched window, flanked by lower canted projections. A ruined outbuilding to the W of the house has two arched doorways said to be from the medieval church, and a two-light mullioned window.

LINDEN HALL. *See* p. 377.

LONGHOUGHTON 2010

SS. PETER AND PAUL. The walls of the nave and W part of the chancel are probably mid-C 11; then comes the early C 12 W tower, and *c.* 1200 the addition of the S aisle, the lengthening of the chancel and perhaps the remodelling of the upper part of the tower. There is little that is later medieval: the top of the tower was rebuilt *c.* 1840 after a fire (old engravings show it much taller, with a strange gabled top) and the remainder was heavily restored in 1873 by *Streatfield*. The chancel arch belongs to the earliest phase. It is slightly stilted, absolutely plain, and rests on an impost band chamfered beneath; to the S is a big squint. With the chancel arch goes the rubble masonry in the lower part of the nave N wall,

with the jambs of a blocked door. The semicircular tower arch
has quite elaborate mouldings and rests on stepped jambs; the
base of the tower has narrow round-headed loops. The Saxon-
looking belfry openings and embattled parapet are of course c 19,
but old masonry survives on the E and shows some intriguing
former roof-lines. The three-bay arcade has double-chamfered
pointed arches, with moulded caps and bases. The s wall of the
aisle was rebuilt in 1873, but the E end retains a c 14 or c 15 two-
light window with a panelled square head, above which the top
of the original c 13 lancet remains visible. The s porch (round
arch with keystone) must be c 18. The s side of the chancel shows
small rubble masonry of the c 11 original and the squared stone
of the *c.* 1200 extension, but the upper parts of the walls and all
the windows are c 19. – MONUMENTS. In the churchyard, a small
CROSS, almost certainly intended to mark a grave. It consists of
a single slab narrowing to a cross of slightly 'hammerhead' form.
Is it pre-Conquest?

WESTFIELD HOUSE (formerly the vicarage), N of the Church. An
attractive Tudor-style building of 1839.

LONGHOUGHTON HALL FARMHOUSE. The present three-bay
front with simple raised surrounds to door and windows is a mid-
c 18 remodelling of an older structure. A blocked door in the E
end looks a bit like that of a bastle, although the wall-thicknesses
and small blocked windows in the w end are more of a later c 17
type.

LITTLEHOUGHTON. *See* p. 378.

LONGSHAWS *see* STANTON

LORBOTTLE HALL *see* CALLALY

LOW BUSTON
1½ m. NW of Warkworth

LOW BUSTON HALL. L-plan house of *c.* 1800, with a late c 17 wing
(some chamfered windows) at the rear and an E front, all windows,
of 1907. The best feature is the entrance hall with a Gothick stair
window and a Chinese Chippendale-style staircase.

BUTLESDON HOUSE. Almost certainly a bastle house, although
later alterations have obscured the original door positions. Thick
walls and one small N window with sockets for a metal grille.
Formerly dated 1604.

DESERTED MEDIEVAL VILLAGE, on a tongue of land SE of the
hamlet. The hollow of the village street is flanked by remains of
houses, with garden-plots descending to the Tyelaw Burn. In
1296 there were eleven taxpayers, and in 1538 the village could
muster thirty-one men. Emparked *c.* 1800.

BUSTON BARNS, ½ m. E. Four-bay house of *c.* 1700, with wave-moulded door surround and quite large windows in recessed and chamfered frames.

EASTFIELD HALL, ½ m. S. 1858 by the *Rev. H. C. Hingeston-Ralph* for Anthony Strother. Gothic. Largely rebuilt in the mid-C 20 after a fire.

STURTON GRANGE, ½ m. SW. Slightly superior late C 18 three-bay farmhouse, in brick with cut sandstone dressings. Rusticated quoins and small circular gable-end openings to attics.

SOUTHSIDE, ¾ m. SW. C 17 or early C 18 house (blocked mullioned window at rear), remodelled in the later C 18; openings in raised stone surrounds. Extensive complex of FARM BUILDINGS of varied C 18 and early C 19 dates.

LOWICK

0030

ST JOHN. 1794. The architect's name, recorded in an inscription over the doorway, was *Henry Penny Selby Morton*. Gothicized *c.* forty years later; the chancel and vestry were added by *F. R. Wilson* in 1887. Of 1794 the masonry of the tower and nave with thin quoins, but not of course the saddleback roof of the tower.

VICARAGE. 1879, in the early C 18 style. A relatively early example of the style for the area.

ST EDWARD (R. C.), Main Street. 1861 by *Stevenson* of Berwick, who added the brick presbytery in 1864.

PRESBYTERIAN CHURCH OF SCOTLAND, Cheviot View. 1821. Four bays with a hipped roof. Three bays have tall round-headed windows. The r. bay has two sash windows. Restored and refurnished in 1878. Attached to the l., the MINISTER'S HOUSE, a standard three-bay house with sixteen-pane sash windows. Also of 1821.

LOWICK HIGH STEADS, 1 m. S. Mid-C 18. A three-bay farmhouse, in pink sandstone, with ogee-headed windows in raised surrounds, an unusual architectural treatment for the area. The adjoining FARM BUILDINGS are picturesque; the main part is an almost symmetrical range, with six segmental arches and a high square central dovecote tower with quatrefoil openings and a pyramid roof.

WHITE HOUSE, opposite. Dated 1728 and now a standard three-bay farmhouse, with later C 18 sash windows; the blocked mullioned windows, however, are an indication of how late such features were retained in the county.

LIMEKILN, 1 m. N at Old Dryburn. A large and imposing early C 19 kiln with segmental-arched openings. Lowick was the centre of an extensive lime trade.

CASTLE, 1¼ m. E, near Lowick Low Steads. A small ringwork consisting of a very substantial bank and ditch all round the SE arc. These defences cut off the end of a level promontory formed by the angle between the steeply cut slopes down to the narrow haughland of The Low on the W and an unnamed tributary on the N. A slighter bank survives on the W crest of the interior, with traces of the outer ditch below it.

BARMOOR. *See* p. 158.

LOW LEAM *see* WOODBURN

1030

LUCKER

ST HILDA. Late C 18; largely rebuilt in 1874 by *George Reavell*. In the Norman style with an apse.

2080

LYNEMOUTH

ALCAN ALUMINIUM SMELTER. By *Yorke, Rosenberg, Mardall*; contractors *Gleeson Civil Engineering Ltd*. Commenced production in 1972, using electricity from Alcan's own power station (large enough to supply a city with all its electricity needs), fuelled from the nearby Lynemouth Colliery. The clean lines of the vast smelting shop, dominated by eight chimneys 80 metres (263 ft) high, are an excellent example of modern industrial architecture advertising its own product through the extensive use of aluminium in its construction. The 390MW power station, with a 95-metre (312-ft) chimney, is equally utilitarian in design. (*See* the Introduction, p. 103.)

LYNEMOUTH COLLIERY. The PITHEAD BATHS, 2 m. S, by *F. G. Frizzell*, 1938, are now a rare survival. White brick, well grouped. The tower which is a functional necessity of pithead baths has on one side a curved glass projection containing a spiral staircase. Inside, white tiles topped by a single band of red; slatted steel lockers with polished metal mirrors on the doors.

0070

MATFEN

MATFEN HALL. 1828–30 by *Rickman*, but continued by the owner, *Sir Edward Blackett*, who wanted an Elizabethan rather than Rickman's intended Gothic house. The exterior, large and solid, is Elizabethan or Jacobean, that is, with mullioned-and-transomed windows, shaped gables, and a porch-tower with an elaborate canted oriel window above the door. The S front is mainly symmetrical but has a service wing to the W which invalidates the symmetry. Inside, the chief apartment is most emphatically Gothic, a vast hall of Fonthill or Ashridge dimensions, with arcades on both sides, a huge geometric church window to the W, a big Gothic oak staircase with castellated newels running up one long wall, and a hammerbeam roof. In one of the rooms, a white marble fireplace by *Chantrey*, with female figures in the jambs and shells in the frieze. It was made for Buckingham Palace and in the upsets of 1830 not paid for. The former library has an early C 17 fireplace with terms and an overmantel with strapwork and demi-figures. In the W wing there is a reused later C 17 staircase with twisted balusters.

Early C 18 GATEPIERS W of the house. Quite elaborate, with shell niches, oak-leaf friezes and urns with faces and swags.

HOLY TRINITY. Also by *Sir Edward Blackett* for himself. 1841–2; spire 1853–4. In the E. E. style. Quite powerful, with its very high broach spire. There is a certain sculptural quality about parts of the building, e.g. the walls and stairs that lead up to the tower doorway. – Inside, four small C 17 alabaster RELIEFS, very Baroque and of good quality. They are said to be Dutch. – FONT. C 13 style with the bowl on four colonnettes. – LECTERN. A splendid naturalistic wood eagle. Signed 1881 by *Signor Bulletti*, one of the Italian craftsmen who had worked on Alnwick Castle.

The VILLAGE is an estate village, almost all of the mid-C 19 in the Tudor style. The DOWER HOUSE is a simple classical design of 1828 by *Dobson*.

CORNEYSIDE, 1 m. N. The most completely classical Georgian 81 farmhouse in the county. *c.* 1730–40, in fine ashlar. It is of five bays and three storeys, with a slightly projecting pedimented three-bay centre. The door has an architrave surround, pulvinated frieze and a pediment on scrolled brackets. The windows, also in architrave surrounds, have retained their original thick glazing bars.

STOB STONE, opposite STANDING STONE FARMHOUSE. 2.1 metres (7 ft) high and decorated with cup marks. The farmhouse is of *c.* 1700, with later C 18 Gothick alterations.

FENWICK. *See* p. 281.

INGOE. *See* p. 357.

RYAL. *See* p. 556.

MELDON 1080

ST JOHN. Nave and chancel in one. Early C 13, restored by *Dobson* in 1849. The bellcote belongs to the restoration. Lancet windows in the W end and side walls. Priest's door with shouldered arch. The E end has a restored triplet of lancets within an original arch with hoodmould. In the chancel S wall, a PISCINA with a pillar support. C 19 panelled ceiling. *Minton* TILES in the sanctuary. – MONUMENTS. Sir William Fenwick † 1652, reclining on his side, his cheek propped up by his hand. The effigy no doubt belonged to a more composite monument. – Isaac Cookson (of Meldon Park) † 1851. Elaborately neo-Dec recess in the chancel N wall.

In the churchyard close to the S door, the rare survival of a C 13 CROSS SLAB (very worn) along with its HEADSTONE. Close to it an unusual pair of early C 18 HEADSTONES slotted between grooved octagonal stone posts.

MELDON PARK. 1832 by *Dobson* for Isaac Cookson. Large ashlar-faced square villa, with a four-column Ionic porch on the W side, a bay window in the centre of the S side, and a lower wing with a conservatory (cf. Longhirst) to the NE. In the middle of the house, with a tripartite window on the N, an imperial staircase, altered *c.* 1930 by *Lutyens*. Good stable block to the N.

MELDON PARK FARM. Extensive planned farm buildings of 1809, including a WATERMILL, a tall block built out onto the steep valley side, with five storeys at one end as opposed to two at the other; unfortunately it is now a ruin, although the races and weir survive. To the E the DEERKEEPER'S COTTAGE, a pretty little late C 17 two-storey building with mullioned windows and fire-places set in the corners of the rooms.

RIVERGREEN KENNELS, ½ m. E of the village. Early C 19 planned farm, converted in 1889 into the Morpeth Hunt Kennels. Together with the houses flanking the centre block, an attractive roadside group.

MELKRIDGE

7060

MELKRIDGE HALL. Three-bay villa of c. 1830.

NEW HIGH TOWN. An attractive L-plan group of cottages formed out of an early C 19 brewery.

(MELKRIDGE BASTLE. Demolished in 1955. It was a rather superior three-storeyed bastle house, probably of the early C 17. 11.5 by 7.3 metres (38 by 24 ft) externally, with a vertical pair of flat-pointed doorways on the S, two gunloops on the N of the basement (cf. Black Cleugh Bastle, near Unthank Hall), small chamfered windows, and a lookout turret capping the E gable (cf. Monk near Whitfield, Healey Hall, and the demolished Low Hirst 'Tower' near Ashington). The turret was carried on corbels; the gable coping and the surrounds of the small apertures in its walls were ornamented with cable moulding.)

HIGH TOWN HOUSE, ¼ m. N. Farmhouse with a round-arched doorway in a broad rusticated surround dated 1741; windows in plain raised surrounds.

WHITCHESTER, I m. W. Mid-C 18 house, enlarged c. 1870 by the addition of a big canted bay and twin round towers with conical lead roofs.

MICKLEY
1½ m. SW of Prudhoe

0060

ST GEORGE. Originally of 1825, but almost entirely remodelled in 1886 by *W. S. Hicks* in the Dec style. Small but satisfying.

MIDDLETON
2 m. W of Hartburn

0080

The village is no more than a picturesque row formed by the CON-GREGATIONAL CHURCH and MANSE, both of 1877, a couple of earlier cottages and the OX INN, a standard but good-quality three-bay early C 19 house. Over the road to the S, a C 17 or early C 18 FOOTBRIDGE with an irregular pointed arch and low parapets.

CORRIDGE, I m. S. An attractive C 17 house, altered in the C 18. It is a tall three-bay building with a central doorway with its mouldings stepped above the head in West Riding fashion; the original fenestration has been displaced by sashes. To the E a tall garden wall returns to end in a pyramid-roofed dovecote-cum-privy.

SOUTH MIDDLETON, $\frac{3}{4}$ m. SW. The earthworks of a deserted village on the s bank of the Wansbeck, on either side of the road from Bolam to Scots Gap. A line of crofts, extending E–W, had houses at their N ends, overlooking a green which was later encroached upon by ridge-and-furrow. A sporadic row of houses stood on the N side of the green, especially W of the modern road. Twelve taxpayers were listed here in 1296; in 1635 there were still twelve messuages and four cottages.

MILBOURNE
3 m. NW of Ponteland

1070

HOLY SAVIOUR. 1869, probably by *R. J. Johnson*. The gift of Miss Jane Anne Bates of Milbourne Hall. Nave, chancel and SW tower over the porch. The tower has a broach spire. The chancel has geometric windows, the nave cusped lancets. The tower has bell openings with waterleaf capitals. Quite an eclectic building, in fact. Inside, the FITTINGS are all of 1869. – REREDOS. A copy in stone of *The Last Supper*.

MILBOURNE HALL. 1807–9 by *John Paterson* of Edinburgh for Ralph Bates. Built of beautiful stone from the Belsay quarries, a pale golden sandstone flecked with nodules of iron which rust and stain the surface of the stone to the most delicious colours. Externally the house is quite severe, and the canted bay windows and other canted sides would hardly make one expect a plan ingeniously worked out so that nearly every room inside is oval. In conformity with this geometrical game, the STABLE BLOCK is a large octagon. It is joined to the house by a short linking range containing the entrance, a tripartite doorway and a porch with paired Roman Doric columns. The stable entrance, the most ornamental external motif of the house, has a pedimented archway, square lantern with Tuscan pilasters and a cupola.

MILFIELD

9030

PRIMITIVE METHODIST CHAPEL. 1855. Three by three bays with tall round-headed windows.

MAELMIN, $\frac{1}{2}$ m. W. Cropmarks have revealed the site of a vanished C7 PALACE, the successor to Yeavering (q.v.), on the crest of a gravel ridge immediately S of the Till. Within a polygonal double-palisade, 400 metres (1,300 ft) across, the principal cropmarks represent a heavily buttressed grand hall with a smaller annexe at each end. Another hall, on the same axis, lay beyond its E end. Humbler huts with sunken floors clustered to the NW.

COUPLAND CASTLE. *See* p. 243.

MINSTERACRES

0050

2 m. SE of Healey

The former residence of the Silvertop family, now a Passionist monastery, on a hilltop site approached up a long avenue of giant redwood trees. The original L-plan house is of 1758, with rusticated quoins and windows in architraves. The second floor was added in the early C 19 (two 1811 rainwater heads; large additions by *John Dobson* are recorded in 1816). Another wing was added in 1865. Inside the house, the morning room, ballroom (former library) and chapel (former dining room) have High Victorian decoration, including painted ceilings and carved chimneypieces by *Lough*.

ST ELIZABETH OF HUNGARY (R.C.). 1854 by *Joseph Hansom*. Formerly the Silvertops' private chapel, and attached to the house. Free Dec style. In the angle between the nave and the transept-like S vestry is a tower, square below and octagonal above, with an openwork quatrefoil lattice to its belfry, and a stone spire. Quite elaborate interior, including a N gallery below an arcade of paired arches with foiled circles above.

To the NW of the house is the plainer late C 18 STABLE BLOCK, now a retreat centre. At the main entrance on the A68, a SCREEN of *c.* 1860, rusticated ashlar with round-headed pedestrian arches flanking the main gate. The EAST LODGE, halfway up the drive, and paired WEST LODGES are older and in the Gothick style. E of the West Lodges is a farm building group comprising a big Gothick barn and extensions dated 1856.

MITFORD

1080

ST MARY MAGDALENE. The memory of the church will be one of enviable wooded surroundings and a building of C 19 appearance. The building contains, however, much evidence of an interesting but troubled past. Being near the castle, it has shared in its vicissitudes and has been damaged and rebuilt several times. By the mid C 12 it was already a church of noble proportions, with a five-bay aisled nave, at least a S transept, and probably an apsidal sanctuary. This big Romanesque church itself seems to have been the product of at least two building phases: the aisles were probably an addition. What survives is three-and-a-half bays of the S arcade (with thick circular piers, bases with broad angle spurs, square multi-scalloped capitals and moulded arches), one pier of the N arcade with a foliage-carved capital, and the priest's door in the S wall of the chancel. The slightly pointed form of the arch suggests that this may have been reset: it is of two enriched orders, the outer on shafts with scalloped caps. Mitford village was burned by King John in 1216, and the castle was besieged by Alexander of Scotland in 1217: after this the N nave wall was rebuilt without an aisle. Later in the century the present chancel was built, with six lancets on the S, two on the N, and an E triplet. The lancets are shafted inside (two shaft rings each) and have moulded arches, and there are contemporary sedilia with a roll moulding and fillet and a piscina in a moulded square frame. The castle seems to have been destroyed early in the C14, being described as 'wholly burned' in 1327. Once more the church suffered (reddened masonry on the N of the chancel shows where a sacristy or vestry was destroyed by fire). The ruins were patched up, the nave, reduced to three-and-a-half bays, having now lost both aisles: a little later the present transeptal chapels were added, with their square-headed windows of two ogee-arched lights. In 1705 fire yet again gutted the nave, which remained a ruined shell until c. 1840, when it was restored and roofed. A two-light Neo-Norman W window of this date has been reset as a picturesque but incongruous entrance to the vicarage garden from the churchyard. Finally in 1870 *R. J. Johnson* extended the nave half a bay to the W, built the W tower and spire, and added the N organ chamber. – STAINED GLASS. In the S aisle, Mitford window († 1895) by *Kempe*. – MONUMENT. Bertram Reveley † 1622. Recumbent effigy on a tomb-chest with rustic chip-carved lozenge panels and a 'reredos' of even more rustic Jacobean detail, e.g. short broad tapering pilasters. – Pretty oak-framed LYCHGATE, dated 1889.

MITFORD CASTLE is perched on a steep-sided sandstone knoll, with the Wansbeck to the N and various courses of the Park Burn to the W, S and E. On the NW edge of the knoll is a motte, occupied by the later shell keep. Traces of the surrounding ditch are visible on the N; a clue to its depth is the half-buried postern in the wall on the SW. The bailey may at first have covered the whole summit, but only the S half was subsequently enclosed by the curtain wall, leaving a lightly defended barmkin on the NE. A ditch was cut through the SW skirts of the knoll to provide a steep natural counterscarp. A similar arrangement seems to have defended the SE side of the bailey also, but extensive quarrying makes interpretation difficult. The S end of the bailey (probably the site of the main gate) was quarried away before 1810. The original timber defences may have been replaced in stone as early as 1138. The castle was occupied by William the Lion in 1175 and by John in 1216; it was the headquarters of the rebellious Sir Gilbert Middleton in 1317 and of outlaw Scots in 1318, when it was irreparably damaged. Considering this chequered history, there is still a surprising amount of stonework. The tall, probably early C12 wall of the shell keep survives on the W, along with a fragment on the E containing a round-arched gateway which seems to be largely C19 reconstruction. The W wall has one big round arch, which perhaps gave access to a balcony. Inside, and almost touching the shell wall, is the basement of a smaller, early C13 five-sided keep. Footings of a rectangular structure with splayed loops immediately S of this keep may be of an earlier tower or 'blockhouse' which it replaced. The keep basement is divided by an axial wall into two barrel-vaulted chambers, which seem to have been used as cisterns for water storage. Enough survives at first-floor level to show an entrance lobby at the S corner, reached by an external stair. Quite a lot of the bailey curtain, probably of later C12 date, still stands. On the W is a shoulder-arched postern into the motte ditch and, further S, some footings of an adjacent range of buildings. On the N are some remains of a gateway to the barmkin, and on the E a long well-preserved stretch with mural chambers and a garderobe. Within the bailey, just on the brink of the old quarry, is a fragment of a late C 12 CHAPEL. What survives is the lower courses of the E end of the N wall; the E part is thickened, presumably to carry the vault of a sanctuary or short chancel entered by an arch of which the moulded base and jamb shaft of one respond remain. N of the chapel was a graveyard. A rather haphazard excavation terminated by the outbreak of war in 1939 exposed several C 12 graveyard monuments *in situ*, but most of these have been destroyed by vandals. Two small headstones remain, one with an incised cross. Its body stone, a tapering slab bearing an expanded-arm cross with its shaft flanked by a sunk chevron pattern, now lies in the churchyard.

OLD MANOR HOUSE, SW of the church. Mostly in ruins. It consisted of a main block facing E, with rear wings flanking a courtyard. It seems to be largely of C 16 date; the E front was remodelled with a central porch-tower in 1637. This tower is the main surviving feature, with an arched doorway surmounted by an ornate entablature with an armorial panel, strapwork and finials. The two upper storeys have mullioned-and-transomed windows, with stringcourses stepped over them as hoodmoulds. In the sides of the porch are reset C 14 window heads. Of the main block itself the rear wall survives, with a variety of fireplaces. The N wall of the SW range is intact, with small two-light windows. The NW range, remodelled as a house in 1961–2, contained the kitchens.

FOSS BRIDGE, spanning the Wansbeck close to the castle. Mid-C 18, with two segmental arches.

MITFORD BRIDGE, spanning the River Font at the E end of Mitford village. Late C 19. Single segmental arch.

SPITAL HILL. On the hill N of Mitford Bridge, a medieval hospital site. A late C 18 villa remodelled *c.* 1880 with some quite elaborate detail, including a carved armorial pediment above the porch.

MITFORD HALL, $\frac{1}{3}$ m. W, on the N bank of the river. Designed by *John Dobson* in 1823 for Bertram Osbaldeston Mitford, but not built until 1828. Ashlar-faced, two-storeyed villa with projecting eaves and balustrade. The three-bay W front has its centre recessed behind a Greek Doric entrance porch *in antis*. Twin service wings to the N. The central section of the longer NE wing was demolished in 1970, but its tower-like end section is complete, as is an attached conservatory (cf. Longhirst and Meldon Park) with Tuscan pilasters. Typical Dobson STABLE BLOCK to the N, with a cupola on a ridge. GATE LODGE with Tuscan portico, and many-pillared GATE SCREEN.

MITFORD STEADS, $\frac{1}{2}$ m. S. The farmhouse is a typical early C 19 villa. Extensive planned FARM BUILDINGS, with a late C 18 foldyard group, reusing big squared masonry from the castle, extended several times in the C 19. The C 18 barn has at the rear a gingang and the ruins of a watermill; both seem to have turned a common drive shaft to the threshing machine.

HIGHFORD BRIDGE, $\frac{3}{4}$ m. E. Dated 1750. Three segmental arches.

NEWTON UNDERWOOD. *See* p. 521.

NUNRIDING HALL. *See* p. 533.

MONDAY CLEUGH *see* AKELD

MORPETH

Morpeth began beside a crossing of the River Wansbeck. Curiously, though, the major buildings, the castle and the parish church, developed s of the river, while the town itself grew on the N bank. There were three main streets, Bridge Street, Oldgate and Newgate, radiating out from the Market Place. These are still the main streets today, and though the town has grown, its core and coherent heart remain the same. The older buildings and the major modern buildings are of beige sandstone, but the town suffered a fire in the late C 17 and most of the smaller houses were rebuilt in brick. The fashion remained throughout the C 18 and the town is dominated visually by brick in a way which distinguishes it from all the other towns in Northumberland.

ST MARY. Low w tower with a concave-sided lead roof of pagoda type, nave and aisles with low-pitched, almost invisible roofs, higher chancel with a steeply pitched roof. A picturesque sight. There are a few E. E. remains, probably not *in situ*; they comprise two brackets for images or perhaps imposts for arches in the w wall, and three others in the N wall. It is also clear that the aisles are an addition to an earlier aisleless nave. But essentially St Mary is a C 14 church. The w tower has diagonal buttresses and bell openings with cusped Y-tracery. The nave, aisles and side chancel windows are of the same design or reticulated. The reticulated E 37 window of five lights is, outside Newcastle, the most ambitious of its date in the county. It has a hoodmould enriched by head-stops. S of it, in the buttress, two image niches on top of each other. The chancel also has a 'low side' window and a priest's door with its original iron HINGES. They are of 1350–1400, strap hinges, each with six pairs of branches ending in leaves. The s door is original too, and has a DOOR KNOCKER of the same period. Interior with five-bay arcades of octagonal piers and double-chamfered arches. The first two piers on the N are plainer than the others. The s aisle responds are enriched by knobbly leaves. Tall and broad recess in the s aisle, probably built to hold a monument. Double-chamfered tower arch dying into the imposts. The tower is vaulted, a rib vault with subsidiary ribs springing from the centre of each side. Double-chamfered chancel arch with octagonal responds. Several of the aisle windows have shouldered rere-lintels but one, the NE, has a hoodmould with head-stops. All the chancel windows have head-stops also. In the chancel, SEDILIA richer than usual in the county, with crocketed ogee heads and small figures on the buttresses between. Opposite, on the N side of the chancel, an aumbry and the vestry doorway. Both have original DOORS with ironwork similar to the priest's door; *c.* 1350, with branched hinges ending in leaves. The VESTRY poses a problem. It is of two storeys and contemporary with the chancel. The plinth and the stringcourse of both are contiguous. It also has two gargoyles. Its w wall, now inside the church, looks like an external wall and has two windows in it, including a small

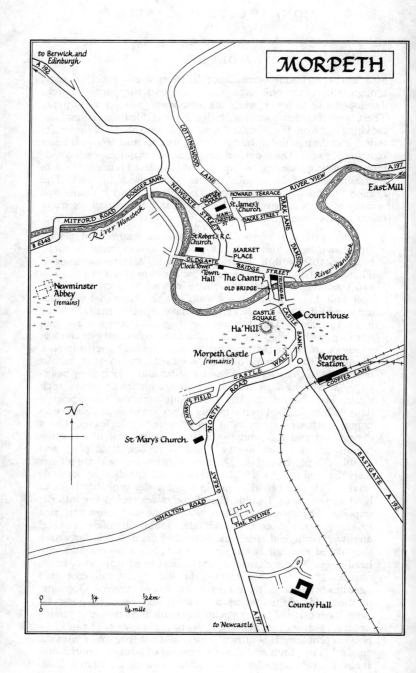

MORPETH

to Berwick and Edinburgh
A 192

A 197

COTTINGWOOD LANE

East Mill

DOGGER BANK

NEWGATE STREET

RIVER VIEW

HOWARD TERRACE

COPPER CHARE

MANCHESTER ST

DACRE STREET

St James's Church

MITFORD ROAD

B 6343

River Wansbeck

St Robert's R.C. Church

DAMSIDE

River Wansbeck

Newminster Abbey (remains)

OLDGATE

Clock Tower

Town Hall

MARKET PLACE

BRIDGE STREET

The Chantry

TELFORD BR.

OLD BRIDGE

DARK LANE

CASTLE SQUARE

Ha'Hill

Court House

CASTLE BANK

Morpeth Castle (remains)

CASTLE WALK

Morpeth Station

COOPIES LANE

ST MARY'S FIELD

NORTH ROAD

N

St Mary's Church

EASTGATE A 192

GREAT NORTH ROAD

WHALTON ROAD

THE KYLINS

County Hall

to Newcastle
A 197

0   ¼   ½ km
0   ¼ mile

quatrefoil window. There is a straight join in the masonry where the N aisle meets the vestry, suggesting that the aisle is an addition and that the vestry stood alone. What was its purpose? Original ROOFS in nave and aisles; in the nave, arched braces forming round arches. The angles between them and the ridge-beam and the purlins filled by plain cusping. Odd, very small recess in the W jamb of the S doorway, provided with a flue. The S porch is the only element of the church added after the C 14. It is probably C 16, with a round-headed doorway.

FONT. C 13. Octagonal, on four attached shafts. – SCREEN and PULPIT. of c. 1900, in C 15 style. – STAINED GLASS. Jesse window at the E end, much renewed by *Wailes*, yet still the most important C 14 glass in the county. All the main lights and all the reticulations in the head are filled with figures. Also Christ and two Saints in the S aisle E window, which is otherwise filled with glass of the 1870s by *Clayton & Bell*. – The chancel glass is by *Wailes*. Mid-C 19. – MONUMENTS. Robert Fenwick † 1693; cartouche in the S aisle erected in 1711. – In the churchyard c. 100 metres NW of the church, the very plain memorial to Emily Davison † 1913. – Rev. Bullen † 1860. A large Gothic pinnacle, c. 150 metres NW of the church. – Also in the churchyard a small WATCH HOUSE with pointed windows, 1830. – LYCHGATE. 1861. Stone, in the E.E. style; in memory of A. R. Fenwick of Netherton.

ST JAMES, Newgate Street. By *Ferrey*, 1843–6, one of his earliest 103 buildings. An ambitious effort in the neo-Norman style. Nave and aisles, crossing with tall crossing-tower open to the inside, taller round NW stair turret, transepts, chancel with aisles and apse. Quite a dramatic interior. The nave has quatrefoil piers with 104 waterleaf capitals and arches with manifold mouldings. The crossing has paired semicircular responds, cushion capitals and arches with two parallel roll mouldings, three rows of bold zigzag and a billet moulding. Two-bay chancel with heavy round piers. One of the arches has a stone screen of intersecting arches. The apse has a frieze of intersecting arches with marble colonnettes. – The FURNISHINGS were almost all designed by *Ferrey* and are contemporary with the church. – FONT. Square on four colonnettes. Elaborately carved. PULPIT, CHOIR STALLS and ALTAR RAILS are all neo-Norman with intersecting arches. – SCREEN. 1887, 'much enriched by a class of wood carvers in 1905', it says on an inscription. – LECTERN. A vigorously carved wooden eagle. – ORGAN. By *Harrison*, 1870. – FRESCOES in the apse and on the screen to the S of the chancel designed by *Clayton & Bell*. There are saints in the intersecting arches, and three large panels above – an Agony in the Garden, Crucifixion and Risen Christ. The paintings were done in 1871 in memory of W. T. Shields, a former curate. – TILES in the chancel; elaborate and varied. – STAINED GLASS by *Wailes*, c. 1850. – MONUMENTS. Brass in the S aisle to the Rev. J. Bolland † 1857. – Brasses to the Rev. F. R. Grey and his wife † 1890 and 1891. The Rev. Grey was the rector of Morpeth and the instigator and chief benefactor of St James.

The church lies a good deal back from the street. The gateway and churchyard wall on Newgate Street is a screen of Norman columns and arches, very ornate, with Frosterley marble columns.

It was built after 1890 as a memorial to the Rev. F. R. Grey.

St Robert (R.C.), Oldgate. 1850, in the E. E. style, with a high octagonal spire over a porch-tower. It might have been designed by *C. Brown*, by whom a drawing dated 1848 exists; or it might be by the incumbent, *Fr Lowe*.

St George United Reformed Church (formerly Presbyterian), Bridge Street. 1860 by *M. Thompson*. Facing the whole length of the street with its perversely stepped-up w tower ending in an octagonal spirelet. The roof to the river side goes very low down over the aisle. The double row of dormer windows dates from 1963, when a ceiling was inserted into the church.

Primitive Methodist Chapel, Howard Street. 1904 by *J. Walton*, in a free Perp. Sensitive additions of 1986 by *Cyril Winskell*.

Gospel Church (formerly Congregational), Dacre Street. 1898. Rock-faced stone; lancet windows.

Former Presbyterian Church, Cottingwood Lane. *See* Perambulation.

Former Wesleyan Chapel, Manchester Street. *See* Perambulation.

The Chantry, Bridge Street. Formerly All Saints Church, a bridge chantry, founded, it is said, by Richard of Morpeth in 1296, though the remains look earlier than that. They comprise, on the N side, one lancet window, the single-chamfered priest's door and the blocked N transept arch. The w end is relatively complete; pointed-arched doorway in a multi-moulded surround, two double-chamfered windows above (with C 19 timber tracery), and a bellcote. The s and E sides were remodelled in 1738. To the E, two gables with heavily arched coupled windows and oval windows above; to the s, five arched windows; all the details severe, in the Vanbrugh taste. Inside the C 18 arcade, three bays with round piers and round arches with architrave surrounds. In the old part, two blocked C 13 doorways, and medieval timbers in the roof. The building suffered some indignities in the later C 19 and C 20, but an excellent restoration in 1980 returned it to an appropriate state.

Morpeth Castle. There have been two castles at Morpeth. The first seems to have been on Ha' Hill, in Carlisle Park, immediately s of the river. The NE end of a narrow ridge appears to have been artificially scarped to form a motte guarding the crossing of the Wansbeck. The defences on the sw are less clear. It is said that there was a castle here in 1095, when it was apparently captured by William Rufus. Scalloped capitals and voussoirs with billet mouldings, found here in 1830, may suggest that a stone keep crowned the motte in the C 12. Apparently destroyed by John in 1216 and not rebuilt.

The existing castle was built *c.* 200 metres s of Ha' Hill on Castle Walk. Its early history is very unclear because of the uncertainty, whenever it is referred to, whether this site or the original one on Ha' Hill is being described. It seems likely, however, that it was begun in the C 13 by the de Merlays. A map of Morpeth, surveyed in 1604, shows quite distinctly a keep in the middle of a bailey with a gatehouse and an outer ward. The keep has disappeared entirely. What remains is the gatehouse, large sections of curtain wall, and in the outer ward a fragment of wall with two buttresses. The curtain wall has been patched and repatched many times, but parts of it appear to be early. The mid-c 14 gatehouse has a four-centred arch and a pointed tunnel vault. L. and r. are vaulted guardrooms. The doorways into them also have four-centred arches. All of this looks c 15, though to the l. of the archway there is a small window with a cusped head which looks earlier. Above are two floors with two-light windows restored in 1857–8 for the Earl of Carlisle; and above that a parapet and corner turrets on close-set triple-step corbels, which though also restored in the mid-c 19 are faithful to what was there before. The first-floor arrangements are unusual – an external doorway at the s end opened into a lobby with a newel stair to the second floor, and a mural passage from which two doorways gave access to the same large chamber, possibly a court room. Pitched roof. Inside the castle there are mildly Tudor–Gothic stables of the mid-c 19.

WAR MEMORIAL, on the bank immediately E of the castle. 1922 by *Franklin Murphy*.

COUNTY HALL, Queen Elizabeth Avenue. 1979–82 by *D. C. Jeffrey*, County Architect. A large informal three-storey building grouped around two gardens. Well-detailed red brick with continuous strips of windows with brown wood frames, this pattern broken periodically by full-height mullioned-and-transomed windows. Shallow hipped copper roofs. A humane and agreeable building, though the approach to the main entrance is poky and insignificant. Inside, in the lobby, impressive rubbed-brick reliefs of Northumbrian history by *John Rothwell*.

TOWN HALL, Market Place. 1714 by *Vanbrugh*, the front renewed and the back replaced after fire damage by *R. J. Johnson* in 1869–70. A fine broadly designed five-bay front, with a pedimented three-bay centre lying back a little behind the corner towers. The towers rise a full extra storey. They have large arched openings, wider to the N and s than to the E and W, which makes the towers oblong instead of square. The whole front, except the top floor of the towers, is banded-rusticated. The ground floor has round-arched openings, originally an open arcade in the centre but now with a wrought-iron grille by Johnson. The windows have segmental heads. Johnson's new building behind is brick and ordinary. Inside, his staircase is quite imposing. It has a bust of the seventh Earl of Carlisle by *Foley*. On the first floor, a large panelled room.

CLOCK TOWER. Belfry in the middle of Oldgate. Such isolated belfries are rare in England (cf. St Albans). Since it is not shown on the 1604 map, this one probably dates from the early c 17, reusing earlier masonry from elsewhere, including the cusped head of a c 14 window. The top floor was added in 1705 and an inscription records repairs of 1760. The round-arched windows, the cornice and the parapet with moulded coping are presumably of this latter date. Small stone figures in c 18 dress stand on the corners.

THE KYLINS (Castle Morpeth Borough Council), Great North Road. A three-bay villa of *c.* 1880. Red brick with stone dressings.

COURT HOUSE. An overpoweringly heavy gateway to the former gaol. Designed by *Dobson* in 1821 and built 1822–8. Castellated Gothic style, inspired, the architect said, by Caernarvon, Conway and Beaumaris. Massive square front block, 22 metres (72 ft) high, with square side towers and an eight-sided apsidal back. Vaulted passageway through the building into the yard behind. Corbelled-out battlements. Inside, an imposing stone Gothic imperial stair leads to the large semicircular courtroom above. This has an eight-sided stone gallery and a rib-vaulted ceiling. It is very similar to Thomas Harrison's court room of 1788 at Lancaster Castle. The gaol itself, which was octagonal and on a highly systematic plan, was demolished in 1891.

OLD BRIDGE. Only the central pier and the abutments are preserved, w of the New Bridge. The present iron footbridge, which incorporates the remains, was built in 1869.

TELFORD BRIDGE (NEW BRIDGE). 1829–31. Hodgson claims that *Thomas Telford* chose the site and supervised the work, while *Dobson* supplied the design. The inscription on the parapet gives the credit to Telford. Three rusticated arches with *cornes-de-vache* voussoirs – a broad splay at the beginning which dies away to nothing at the crown. Triangular cutwaters, topped by tapering panelled pilasters rising to original cast-iron lamp-standards with decorative scrolled ironwork.

LOWFORD BRIDGE, Mitford Road. 1836 by *Dobson*. Plain and simple.

MORPETH STATION, Coopies Lane. 1847 by *Benjamin Green* for the York, Newcastle and Berwick Railway. Tudor-style. The glazed canopies on elaborate cast-iron supports were added *c.* 1890.

Opposite the station, the former terminus of the BLYTH AND TYNE RAILWAY. 1864. Five bays with central porch and round-headed windows. Now an agricultural store.

PERAMBULATION

The centre of Morpeth and the starting-point for this perambulation is the broad triangular MARKET PLACE, which is dominated by roads and road traffic, with the insignificant HOLLON FOUNTAIN of 1885 in the middle. Fortunately the Town Hall and the Clock Tower on the s (*see* above) give the space presence; on the N side there is a relatively pleasing jumble of minor buildings. No. 4 is late c 18 brick; three bays with a pedimented centre bay. No. 2 is plain and ashlar, dated 1815. No. 1, on the corner of Newgate Street, is a good early c 18 brick house with segment-headed windows, the keystones rising to form short pilasters in the parapet.

NEWGATE STREET, which runs N from the Market Place, is the best street in the town, though at the time of writing constant traffic makes it difficult to enjoy what one sees. On the E side the street starts with a series of early c 18 brick houses, one of them with a shaped gable. LLOYDS BANK, on the opposite side of the road, was built in 1904 by *George Reavell* in a sophisticated, very free late c 17 style. Nos. 23 and 29 are two three-bay, mid-c 18

brick houses with sandstone dressings; No. 29 in particular has
quite elaborate details, including shouldered architrave surrounds
to the windows and a pulvinated top frieze and parapet. It has a
contemporary staircase inside. The yard to the rear of this house,
OLD BAKEHOUSE YARD, is one of the best-preserved of the
many yards and courts which give access to the rear of the buildings on the main streets and creates an impression and a model
of what the others might be like; smaller in scale than the main
house, well-preserved and well-used. At the foot of the yard are
the BAKEHOUSE STEPS, the last surviving set of stepping stones
across the River Wansbeck. There used to be seven such sets.
From the steps can be seen PERCY COTTAGE, with an ashlar
façade of c. 1820 and a wooden balcony on curved stone brackets.
Earlier brickwork behind, and inside there is a room with a series
of mural paintings of 1822 by J. Ferguson, in the Romantic style.
Also from the steps a good impression of the quieter side of the
town can be gained – the park on the W side of the river and the
backs of the houses on Newgate Street, with their fine terraced
gardens down to the river. Back on Newgate Street, No. 41 is a
good five-plus-one-bay stone house with a pedimented doorway
and a segmental carriage arch. No. 88 (Dunedin) has horrible
render and altered windows but is basically late C 17 or early C 18,
with a queer ornate doorway which has a segmental pediment on
brackets. No. 90 is mid-C 18, brick, with a pedimented door
surround, a brick stringcourse and a cornice of cogged bricks.
Next door to it, No. 92 is also of brick, but, being an end house,
its gable is visible, revealing the tumbled-in brickwork which is
characteristic of so many mid-C 18 houses in the town. No. 94
was formerly the Girls' Grammar School and before that the home
of Joseph Crawhall, Senior, and birthplace of Joseph Crawhall,
Junior, the engraver. It has two sections; quite a substantial neo-
Tudor section of c. 1840, all in stone, and a brick section of the
mid-C 18, with rusticated quoins and moulded stone keystones to
the flat arches of the windows. On the opposite side of the road,
THE BEESWING, formerly a pub, a nicely detailed building of
c. 1820 built in beautiful ashlar. No. 101 is a real oddity – a two-
bay early C 19 stone house with each bay set in a shallow full-
height recess. Each recess has a convex quadrant moulding, with
an outer roll moulding to the l., and a hollow chamfer to the r.
No. 105 has a doorcase of c. 1760 with attached Ionic columns
and an ogee pediment. The house was altered internally c. 1810
and given a pretty staircase, and Roman Doric arches on the first-
floor landing. This N end of Newgate Street is called BULLER'S
GREEN and has an agreeable cottagey feel to it. No. 19, to judge
by the thick walls with large blocks of random rubble, must be
C 16 or early C 17. Near the N end, BOW VILLA, a solid square
ashlar house of 1824.

Halfway back down Newgate Street and along Copper Chare
past St James's Church into an attractive area of small C 18
cottages and more substantial Edwardian housing. Nothing needs
special mention except, near the corner of COTTINGWOOD
LANE, the former PRESBYTERIAN CHURCH of 1722, restored
and sensitively converted into a house in 1987. It has the characteristic Nonconformist pattern of two large arched windows in

the middle and two smaller arched windows over the doorways in the outer bays. The façade is of brick with stone dressings. John Horsley the historian was minister here.

Back on to Newgate Street and then off again into MAN-CHESTER STREET, which contains the BOYS' BRIGADE HEAD-QUARTERS (formerly a Wesleyan Chapel); 1884, with a Perp façade as part of the street frontage. On to DACRE STREET, where the HOWARD CASTLE COURT comprises two houses linked together by a plain but decent 1980s extension. To the l. is HOWARD CASTLE, a three-bay castellated house of 1860; to the r., the former PRESBYTERIAN MANSE of c. 1830, ashlar with angle pilasters and a pediment over the centre bay. The MASONIC LODGE (No. 13) was built in 1855.

That completes the walk to the N of the Market Place. To the W of it, past the Clock Tower lies OLDGATE, which has, on the N side, COLLINGWOOD HOUSE, quite a large late Georgian brick house of seven bays which belonged to Admiral Collingwood. It used to have a big garden and a summerhouse overlooking the river which Collingwood called his 'quarterdeck'. Summerhouse and garden have been replaced by St Robert's Church (see above), of which the house is now the presbytery. The S side of Oldgate has a number of C 18 brick houses. Nos. 5–7 were the former Queens Head Coaching inn. Five bays with a moulded brick stringcourse and a plain parapet. Original staircase inside. Beyond the Georgian houses, the excellent BONDGATE DEVELOPMENT main-tains the line of the street with arches leading through to houses round courtyards behind. It was done in 1979 by the *Borough Engineers' Department*, with a real sense of what the site demanded. Adjoining it to the E on the riverbank is the equally successful COLLINGWOOD COURT of 1987 by *Jane and David Darbyshire*. Finally No. 35 (MATTESON'S), 1889 by *Boolds & Hardy* of Morpeth, in a very free, almost Arts-and-Crafts Tudor. The house behind the shop is equally freely composed.

BRIDGE STREET, the main shopping street of the town, leads E from the Market Place over the New Bridge and the capricious façade of St George's United Reformed Church (see above), which closes the far end of the street. As with so many shopping streets there is more a sense of what has been lost than of what has survived. However, halfway along is the BLACK BULL, with a nice Adamish doorway and a two-storey bow window projecting pleasantly into the street, and, behind this gentle Regency façade, a bold C 17 staircase with twisted balusters. Above JENNINGS GARAGE can be seen a glimpse of a glory that was; fine Ionic pilasters, cornice and parapet of a mid-C 18 house entirely gutted on the ground floor. No. 57 is early C 18, with a brick stringcourse above each floor. On the S side, Nos. 26–32 have façades of the early C 19, but they are on the site of, and partly incorporate masonry from, the Old Gaol and Governor's House, founded in 1704. This in turn stood on the site of, and probably incorporated masonry from, an earlier building shown on the map of 1604. To the rear, a rainwater head dated 1704 and a rear wing still of early C 18 character. Between Bridge Street and the river stands OLIVER'S MILL. This group of buildings comprises a stone-built, three-storey mill of 1830 and a brick-built mill of 1899.

They make up a good example of the use of waterpower for industrial purposes in a small town. The stone-built mill was almost certainly constructed as a woollen mill, its size, window distribution and floor spaces all indicating textile manufacture. Internally the floor, roof construction and cast-iron columns are fairly typical of the early C 19. The adjoining brick-built mill, added for steam milling, is typical late Victorian industrial architecture, with fine brickwork details to the office block above the waterwheel pit and to the tower at the NE corner; there are also some good window details.

Across the river the road leads on to the Court House and Castle and out of the town. In CASTLE SQUARE, No. 1 was the tollhouse to the New Bridge; early C 19, single-storey and semi-octagonal. Nos. 3–7 (PETHGATE COURT) are early C 18 brick, with stringcourses above each floor and architrave surrounds to the windows. A good early C 18 staircase inside.

Of buildings further out, only two need mention. EAST MILL, $\frac{1}{2}$ m. E on the A197, is a water mill dated 1798 but incorporating earlier masonry. It was extended to include an engine house in the early C 19 and then again as a full power-driven corn mill in 1892. Attached to the side of the 1892 mill is the miller's house, which is also early C 19. GRANGE HOUSE, Mitford Road, is an unusually substantial mid-C 17 farmhouse for the area. Central doorway, five bays with two-light mullioned windows. Inside there are several C 17 fireplaces, old beams throughout and an upper-cruck roof.

LONGHIRST. *See* p. 382.
NEWMINSTER ABBEY. *See* p. 518.

MORWICK
2 m. SW of Warkworth

2000

MORWICK HALL. Georgian house of brick with stone quoins and dressings. The five-bay centre of the S front is of *c.* 1740–50; later C 18 the two-bay W extension and the rear stair wing; early C 19 the central polygonal Gothick bow and the two-bay E extension. C 18 ranges round the stableyard at the rear. In the garden to the E, a MONUMENT to Catharine Maria Grey † 1786. An upright slab between fluted pilasters, with swept top carrying a globular urn, set at the end of a walk lined by tall privet hedges and flanked by a medieval COFFIN and CROSS SLAB imported for picturesque effect; their provenance seems unknown. On the S drive, two sets of late C 18 GATEPIERS, octagonal with acanthus friezes. These were brought here *c.* 1860 from a house in Tynemouth.

CUP-AND-RING MARKS. Just downstream from Morwick Mill, a cliff on the S bears an exceptional variant on the familiar carvings. Their position, on vertical rock faces, is as unusual as their designs, which include multiple spirals and concentric rings.

WATER TOWER, on a hill $\frac{1}{2}$ m. SE of the Hall. 1970 by *W. B. Edwards & Partners*. Concrete, and of a dramatic funnel-like shape.

NAFFERTON CASTLE *see* HORSLEY-ON-THE-HILL

2080

NEDDERTON
1½ m. w of Bedlington

NETHERTON HALL. A tall rather plain house, now subdivided. The oldest part, at the E end, is probably C 17; it was enlarged to the W in the early C 18, heightened and refenestrated later in the same century, and enlarged to the rear in the early C 19.

SCHOOL, on the same side of the main road as the Hall but further E. 1846. Gothic. The projecting entrance bay has a four-centred arch with a pretty oriel above, and the crest of the Earl of Carlisle in the gable.

NETHERTON BLUE HOUSE, ¾ m. NE. Dated 1716. Three-bay front with big pilasters and a little pediment over the narrow centre bay, flanked by slightly lower end bays. The house was restored *c.* 1987 from being a derelict and gutted shell.

1090

NETHERWITTON

ST GILES. Medieval chancel with a C 15 three-light E window, a priest's door dated 1691 and a double-chamfered chancel arch. The nave was rebuilt in the late C 18 as a preaching box, but, with the exception of the virile bellcote crowned by an obelisk, it was remodelled in the later C 19, when the three-bay arcades were inserted. – FONT. C 13 or C 14, with a plain circular bowl. – MONUMENTS. C 14 effigy of a lady. – C 15 cross slab with armorial bearings. C 13 cross slab top, together with C 12 chevron voussoirs, set in the vestry wall.

NETHERWITTON HALL. Undated, but probably *c.* 1685. The house is thought to have been designed by *Robert Trollope* for Sir Nicholas Thornton, in a rather more sober version of the Capheaton tradition. A rectangular block seven by three bays, with top balustrade and quoins. All windows with pediments, but three varieties are used in a complicated order; each type – straight-sided broken, segmental broken and swan-necked – is ranged to form a series of chevrons pointing into the centre of the front (e.g. the swan-necked form occurs on the ground and second floors of the W end bay of the S front, and in the first floor of the second bay, etc.). The window surrounds are moulded on the S side, raised on the E and W, as if ready to receive the wreath decoration of Capheaton. Also recalling Capheaton, the sundials, with frames decorated in a medieval fashion, here with zigzag, at Capheaton with dogtooth. The back of the house is earlier, with two projecting stair turrets: that to the E contains a stone winder stair and might survive from a C 16 'stronghouse' of the Stanton Old Hall type.

Inside the house, several rooms with robust Queen Anne panelling, some of it reset. Late C 17 main stair. The fireplace in the entrance hall is another survival from a late C 16 or early C 17 building. Plasterwork of *c*. 1770 in the former library.

N of the house, a spacious square STABLEYARD, as at Wallington and Capheaton. Some buildings are contemporary with
the house; others, including the central GAME LARDER, could
belong to the date of the S doorway and rainwater heads (1790s).
The GATEPIERS to the grounds, however, with their banded
rustication, are clearly of *c*. 1700 or earlier.

By the burn a MILL building of stone, 1794, eleven bays wide and
three storeys high, with a three-bay pediment. It began as a cotton
mill, but was soon converted to woollens and finally became a
saw mill. Well restored as a number of housing units in 1988,
after lying derelict.

STANTON. *See* p. 578.

WITTON SHIELDS. *See* p. 631.

NEWBIGGIN

3080

ST BARTHOLOMEW. In a remarkably impressive situation, on a
bleak and treeless headland away from the village. There is a
tradition that the church was founded by the Lindisfarne community, and its site is certainly of the type beloved by Celtic
monks. The church, in particular its interior, is archaeologically
fascinating. There is no definite pre-Conquest evidence, but the
long and narrow proportions of the nave (even allowing for a C 19
extension into the chancel) and some features of the strange little
unbuttressed W tower, heavily remodelled in the C 13, hint at early
origins. Reused in the nave walls are a number of stones with
geometric patterns which deserve a close study. Undoubtedly of
the C 12 is a capital, perhaps from a chancel arch, reset as a bracket
at the E end. The nave is of six bays: although both aisles were
destroyed after the Middle Ages, their arcades remain intact. That
on the S stands just inside the line of the S wall. The N one was
reopened when a new aisle was built in 1913. The arcades look
C 13, with their W parts later than the E: where the division comes
is not quite clear. Only the two E piers on each side have distinctly
early C 13 billet ornament and foliage carving; the two W arches
are broader, with clumsy chamfer stops. All the arches are double-
chamfered, and the piers octagonal. The tower has small spheric
triangle windows (cf. Westminster Abbey, *c*. 1250) and two-light
belfry openings with a quatrefoil in the spandrel. The pointed
tower arch looks like an insertion in an earlier wall (there is a
blocked high-level doorway above with an odd corbelled head),
but it was in turn blocked up when a low barrel vault was inserted,
presumably in the C 13, as the window positions seem to relate to
the inserted floor level. The chancel is in part C 13 (reset N lancet),
but the two three-light S windows, one with intersected tracery
and one with three stepped lancets under one arch, look early
C 14, as does the E window of five stepped lights. Also C 14 the
simple spire standing directly on the square tower parapet. The
church did not have a happy post-medieval history; by the early
C 19 both aisles were gone and the chancel was a roofless shell.
The chancel arch too had been removed (perhaps in the C 15 or

early C 16?). The chancel was restored in 1845, with a new chancel arch 3 metres (10 ft) E of the original position; the nave was refaced at the same time and its external walls extended E so as register the new division externally. The two-light windows on the S of the nave are all of this date, although the erosive powers of the salt wind have given them an air of greater antiquity. In 1898 *W. S. Hicks* carried out a second restoration in which the present chancel arch was built, its 1845 predecessor being utilized in the new organ chamber. – MONUMENTS. An important collection of over twenty CROSS SLABS, mostly C 13. The best are in the internal walls of the N aisle: note particularly two at the E end, with crude fleur-de-lys springing from the cross shafts, and with shears and keys alongside – a combination of emblems, common in Northumberland but rare further S, denoting a woman's grave.

NEWBIGGIN HALL
9060

2 m. S of Hexham

Mid-C 18 remodelling (sundial dated 1756) of an older house: a late C 17 plaster ceiling survives in the rear wing. A pair of canted two-storey bays flanking the Tuscan front door were added in the early C 19. To the W is the Italianate STABLE BLOCK of *c.* 1840. Behind, at a lower level, planned FARM BUILDINGS round a yard including a watermill on the W.

NEWBROUGH
8060

A pleasant Tynedale village, its wooded setting a contrast to the omnipresent moors on either side of the valley. It retains its rural integrity, and displays some architectural variety amongst its buildings. There are three quite large houses of *c.* 1800.

ST PETER, on its own, to the W of the village. 1866, simple C 13 style. The site is older, but the only medieval relic is a GRAVE SLAB with an incised sword. – STAINED GLASS. Aisle window of 1899 by *Kempe*. – The church stands on the site of a ROMAN FORTLET beside the Stanegate. Apparently occupied in the C 4, it lies midway between Corbridge and Vindolanda and may have been part of the late C 1 chain of forts along this road.

On the N side of the village street, the rather surprising Italianate TOWN HALL of 1876 and the WOMEN'S INSTITUTE of 1848, enlarged in 1890, and further E the early C 18 RED LION INN. At the W end of the village the segmental-arched NEWBROUGH BRIDGE is dated 1830.

NEWBROUGH PARK turns its back to the S side of the village street. A plainly classical house of *c.* 1790, probably designed by the owner, *Richard Lambert.* The lower E wing incorporates something of an older building.

NEWBROUGH HALL, ⅓ m. N. 1812. An early *Dobson* house, with a five-bay ashlar front and doorway with broad radial fanlight under a round-arched recess. Alterations and internal remodelling by *Deas* in 1902, with some good Arts-and-Crafts wood and plasterwork. In the garden, POWER HOUSE, also by *Deas*, and, as its name implies, originally housing an electricity generator; now a cottage. A pretty little square building with an ogival pyramid roof and a taller semi-octagonal turret. Edwardian LODGE and gatescreen.

Amongst C 19 farm buildings N of the Hall is THORNTON TOWER, a rectangular medieval tower-house, reduced to crags of rubble wall core except for the W face, of massive squared stone, exposed within an adjacent barn.

NEWBROUGH LODGE, ½ m. NW of the village. Three-bay centre of 1796 flanked by two-storeyed porches of 1928. On the lawn, a weathered ROMAN ALTAR now carrying a sundial.

At HIGH STONECROFT, 2 m. NW, is the ruin of a mid-C 19 brick Cornish pumping-engine house of a former lead and witherite mine.

CARRAWBURGH. *See* p. 213.

NEWBURN

1060

Newburn, the first village upstream from Newcastle, was independent and had a far-sighted Urban District Council until it was incorporated into the new District of Newcastle in 1974. Newburn has an ancient past, though this can be seen now only in the parish church of St Michael and All Angels. It was a royal borough at the lowest safe fording point on the Tyne and at the head of the tideway. In 1068 Copsi, the Earl of Northumberland, was murdered in his hall here. Newburn played an important part in the Civil War, when it was of strategic importance in the defence of Newcastle. In the late C 18 the availability of coal and of easy river transport brought glass- and iron-making to Lemington (q. v.), E of the old village, followed in 1822 by steel manufacturing (*see* Introduction, p. 97). Some evidence of these industries remains, but the developing and clearing of the steel works swept away the Manor House. In the C 20 the Urban District Council was noted for its high standard of public building. *William A. Harvey*, one of the consulting architects for Bournville, was U. D. C. architect for the streets built *c.* 1920 E of Union Hall Lane, centred on the 'horseshoe' of WAVERLEY CRESCENT. Many of the houses have been altered, but the layout remains intact.

ST MICHAEL AND ALL ANGELS. A fascinating church, with a bonus for students of railway history; two pioneers, Hedley and Hawthorn, are commemorated and a third, George Stephenson, was married here in 1802. Early Norman W tower, sturdy and with shallow clasping buttresses, small windows and belfry openings of two round-arched lights under a large round arch; some features, such as the megalithic blocks of the jambs of the blocked W door, still look Saxon, although the date may be after 1123, when Henry I bestowed the church on the Chapter of Carlisle. The megalithic quoining glimpsed at the SE angle of the nave may well be genuinely pre-Conquest. The chancel with its (renewed) lancets seems largely C 13, although earlier (C 12?) masonry is incorporated; the transepts are C 14 or C 15, but the aisle walls were rebuilt in 1827; it was probably then that they were extended w to flank the tower. The clerestory of round windows is also C 19. Vestries and porch by *W. S. Hicks*, 1885 and 1896. Inside, the plain square-section tower arch is strangely high and wide – has it been enlarged in the 'gallery era'? Above (and only visible from the belfry) is a blocked high-level doorway, another feature betraying Saxon influence. The arcades are of four narrow bays, the eastern pair spanning the transepts. The N arcade of *c.* 1175 has plain square-section arches on round piers with waterleaf capitals, and the C 13 s arcade pointed double-chamfered arches and alternating round and octagonal piers. The chancel arch seems to go with the s arcade; C 19 openings between the tower and aisles. In the N chancel wall, a segmental-arched tomb recess or Easter sepulchre; above it the rere-arch, also segmental, of a late medieval window, probably that reset in the N wall of the organ chamber; the simple panel tracery of its head, although renewed, is still cut in a single block in the Northumbrian tradition. N transept distinctively refitted in 1941 as a war memorial. – FRESCO above the chancel arch. 1898. – REREDOS. 1896 by *W. S. Hicks*. – ROOD SCREEN and PULPIT. 1885, carved by *Ralph Hedley*. – STAINED GLASS. N aisle by *Ballantine & Gardiner*, Edinburgh, 1904. – s aisle by *W. H. Atkinson*, commemorating the Hedley family and their help in establishing the bishopric of Newcastle in 1882. – N transept window by *L. C. Evetts*. – BRASSES. Michael Spencer † 1889. – Hedley family, including the railway pioneer, William († 1843, buried in the churchyard), with an engraving of his first locomotive, 'now in the Kensington museum'. – MONUMENT. Thomas Longbridge of Walbottle † 1725; in the s chancel wall, with a bust in a broken pediment.

The CHURCHYARD has an interesting collection of memorials, not outstanding artistically but still *in situ*, preserving the atmosphere of a village churchyard. Just s of the chancel, graves belonging to the Hedley family (*see* above). – In the s corner, the family grave of another railway pioneer, Robert Hawthorn, † 1842, marked by an obelisk. – LYCHGATE. 1896 by *W. S. Hicks*, showing how well the late C 19 could pick up the medieval mood. Well-built, with pegged timber-framing and stone-flagged roof. Figure of Christ on the E gable.

ST MARY, Newburn Road, Throckley, uphill from Newburn. 1887 by *W. S. Hicks*. Partly paid for by John Spencer, ironmaster, of Whorlton Hall, as a memorial to his wife † 1882. A sensitive design, using hammerdressed snecked sandstone with iron streaking; roof of graduated stone slates. It is in the spirit of the late C 12, with narrow lancet windows, a s baptistry door with a moulded arch on impost bands, and a high narrow nave, with boarded barrel vault. – STAINED GLASS. Large E window in memory of Spencer. The baptistry has one window of Christ with children, by *Baguley*, and a particularly fine N lancet of 1893 by *Burlison & Grylls* with Christ the Good Shepherd.*

Former COUNCIL OFFICES, Newburn Road. An example of Newburn U.D.C.'s high standard of public building; this is a

---

* According to Neil Moat.

miniature of municipal Baroque by *E. Cratney*, 1910. Brick, with ashlar dressings, including the Ionic doorcase and carved garlands above.

NEWBURN PUMPING STATION, Tyne Riverside Country Park. 1854–5; engineer *Robert Nicholson*, contractor *R. Cail*, for the Whittle Dean Water Company. Part of the mid-C19 response to the problems of waterborne disease after the cholera epidemic of 1853. Rock-faced sandstone, vermiculated dressings and quoins, arched windows. The engine (now removed) pumped water from the gravel beds of the Tyne.

NEWCASTLE AND GATESHEAD WATER COMPANY FILTER BEDS, Hexham Road. Of the next generation of water engineering. On the N side of the beds, a small square valve house of *c.* 1870, with pyramidal roof and wide eaves. On the S side of the main road, a valve house of *c.* 1890, Tudor-style brick, with ashlar dressings.

ROAD BRIDGE. A simple steel lattice-girder bridge with riveted trusses, supported on concrete-filled cylindrical wrought-iron piers braced in pairs. There are four main spans, the river piers being at 31.5 metre (103½ ft) centres; 5.5 metre (18 ft) wide road deck at *c.* 6.4 metres (21 ft) above high water mark. Built in 1893 for the Newburn Bridge Company by *Head Wrightson* of Thornaby on Tees to the designs of *Messrs J. W. Sandeman & J. M. Moncrieff* of Newcastle, to incorporate a 0.56-metre (22-in.) water main on either side of the bridge. Formerly a toll bridge, with its tollhouse at the NE end (long demolished).

PERAMBULATION

This perambulation goes from W to E and then down to the river, starting at the foot of Newburn Road outside the former Council Offices (*see* above). E of this, on CHURCH BANK, is St Michael's Church (*see* above). In HIGH STREET, next to the church, NEWBURN ALMSHOUSES (1870 by *R. J. Johnson*, paid for by Hugh Taylor, bailiff to the Duke of Northumberland), twelve single-storey houses of three bays each, with elliptical-headed doors and windows, shaped gables, hipped dormers, and tall corniced banded chimneys. Next to the E, the plain stone DUKE OF NORTHUMBERLAND'S HOUSE, dated 1822, with the Duke's emblem, a crescent, over the door. To the S, the mid-to-late C18 NEWBURN HOUSE, with its plainer side to the street and a pedimented Tuscan porch on the garden side. Station Road off the S side of High Street leads to WATER ROW and, just to the W of Newburn Bridge, the BOATHOUSE PUBLIC HOUSE, a pleasant stone house of *c.* 1830; the r. quoins are marked with the levels of the floods of 1771, 1815, 1830 and 1856. George Stephenson worked at the nearby Water Row pit, where his father, Robert, was fireman and he was in charge of Robert Hawthorn's new pumping engine from 1798 to 1801.

LEMINGTON. *See* p. 373.

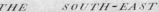

THE SOUTH-EAST PROSPECT

2060

NEWCASTLE UPON TYNE

Two things which the eye can see and the aesthetic sense appreciate distinguish Newcastle from Leeds or Bradford or Sheffield or any other industrial city of the North. One is the river, the other Richard Grainger. The river – and this is perhaps the most exciting visual experience of Newcastle – has steep banks, and so the most violent contrasts of level are met with everywhere in the old centre; bridges high overhead, a hundred steps winding their way down, buildings rising on top of buildings. In what way Grainger's work forms a special distinction needs nowadays hardly be emphasized. He gave the whole centre of the town a dignity and orderliness which even the twentieth century has not succeeded in destroying.

The description of Newcastle in the following pages is divided into Inner and Outer Newcastle. Much of the Inner Newcastle described here lies within the line of the medieval town wall, which remained the boundary on the W and most of the E side up to the

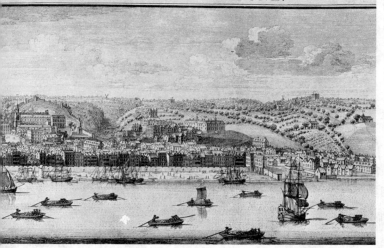

Newcastle upon Tyne. The south-east prospect by Buck, 1745

C 18. The Roman fort of *Pons Aelius*, which lies under the Castle Garth, is known only from excavation: it was built no earlier than the late C 2. The royal castle was built in the same advantageous situation high above the River Tyne in the late C 11, but of this castle there is only a fragment. The typically late Norman keep is late C 12 35 and the major survival of the outer defences, the Black Gate, mid-C 13. The medieval town wall, which was begun in the late C 13, still 54 survives in long stretches on the W side. Within it the town thrived. The earliest known charter was granted *c.* 1175. The town was allowed a mayor by 1216 and granted county status in 1400. The town's prosperity was commercial, based on wool and hides first, on coal digging and exporting later. A coal trade existed in the C 13, and pits were being made instead of open-cast quarrying in the C 15. Workings were on the Town Moor, and at Elswick and Benwell and other outlying places on both sides of the Tyne.

St Nicholas was the chief parish church of Newcastle. There were, 39, 44 and still are, three more churches within the walls: All Saints (rebuilt in the C 18), St Andrew and St John. The town gradually expanded 17 from the high ground round the castle and St Nicholas's Church. Three main streets led to them from gates in the wall – Pilgrim Street, Westgate, and the long street of markets with Newgate at its head. The Lort Burn flowed through the middle, between Pilgrim Street and the Bigg and Flesh Markets, joining the Tyne at Sandhill, and the Pandon Burn ran through the E part of the town, emerging just to the E of Broad Chare, with beyond it the vill of Pandon, absorbed in the town in 1298. At the edges of the town there

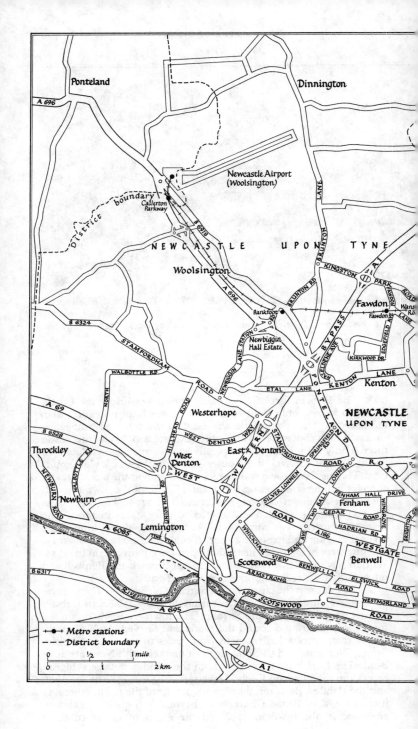

NEWCASTLE
UPON TYNE

Dudley

Burradon

Wide Open

BACKWORTH LANE

A 1056

SANDY LA.

High Gosforth Park

Killingworth

D I S T R I C T

GREAT LIME ROAD B 1505

Palmersville

Tyne Tunnel

Long benton

GOATHLAND AVE

Benton

Regent Centre

HOLLYWOOD AVE

WEST FARM AVE

Four Lane Ends
Longbenton

FRONT STREET A 191

WHITLEY ROAD

Gosforth

CHURCH RD

STATION RD

BENTON PARK ROAD

COACH LANE

South Gosforth

FREEMAN ROAD

Ilford Road

NEWTON

High Heaton

COAST ROAD A 1058

JESMOND DENE RD

JESMOND RD

West Jesmond

NEWCASTLE–TYNEMOUTH ROAD

Wallsend

Jesmond

Heaton

HIGH ST A 193

Wallsend

BIDDLE ST A 187

WARWICK ST

ROTHBURY TERR

Walkergate

Chillingham Road

SHIELDS ROAD

FOSSWAY A 187

Walker

BYKER BR

Byker

WELBECK ROAD

Byker

WALKER ROAD A 186

River Tyne

St Anthony's

N

The Inner City map is on pp. 462–3

were the precincts of at least eight religious houses, including a Benedictine nunnery (St Bartholomew, founded by 1135 and commemorated in the name Nun Street). The friars, the typical religious orders of the towns and the later Middle Ages, had four houses: the Franciscans or Grey Friars (founded by 1237) on Pilgrim Street; the Austin Friars (founded by 1291; a fragment of their church survives within the Holy Jesus Hospital); the Carmelites or White Friars (founded before 1262) in the SW corner of the town (the present Forth Street and Orchard Street); and the Dominicans or Black Friars near the W boundary. Of all these houses only Black Friars, 47 probably built by 1250, survives (in Monk Street). Down beside the river, the area now known as the Quayside developed as a series of lanes or chares downstream from the bridging point at Sandhill (where the Swing Bridge is now). Though this pattern has largely survived, the only medieval buildings that remain in the chares belong to a group in Broad Chare that became Trinity House in the early C 16. Many merchants lived close to the river in the Close, Sandhill and the Quayside area. In the Close and Sandhill a handful of their houses survive, but the wealth and wide connections of some of the merchants can now perhaps best be judged from their benefactions and memorials. Robert Rhodes, who died in 1474, gave money for the building of St Nicholas, of St John and of All Saints; Roger Thornton, who died in 1429 and whose brass, of foreign manufacture, is one of the most ornate in the country, endowed in 1425 the Hospital of St Catherine (the Maison Dieu), one of more than a dozen hospitals in the city. The pattern of the medieval town, with dense settlement by the river, a more spacious layout higher up, and with suburbs outside Sandgate by the river, Newgate, Westgate and Pilgrim Street Gate, is still seen clearly in the late C 16 bird's-eye view of the town in the British Library's Cotton collection and in Speed's plan of 1610.

During the C 17 and C 18, Newcastle became a major coal-exporting port. Impressive timber-framed houses were built during the 63-4 C 16 and C 17 and some survive in the Close and on Sandhill, and 60 in 1655 the Corporation commissioned *Robert Trollope* to rebuild the town court and weigh house there, which he did in a very idiosyncratic mixture of Gothic and classical styles; this, much remodelled, remained the town hall until the mid-C 19. By 1698 Celia Fiennes could say of the town that 'it most resembles London of any place in England, its buildings lofty and large of brick mostly or stone, the streetes very broad and handsome'. Both merchants and markets thrived, and the gardens behind the houses began to fill with smaller houses, workshops, stables, brewhouses and all sorts of ancillary buildings, in the type of yard development preserved at Wilson's Court in the Groat Market and the George Yard in the Bigg Market. So, though James Corbridge's map of 1723 still shows much open space within the medieval town boundary, by the time Charles Hutton's map was published in 1770, there were fewer gardens and more buildings. Successive maps show clearly how first one piece of open ground then another was filled with new brick houses and new squares and streets, such as Hanover Square (begun in 1720 but never completed), Charlotte Square by *William Newton*, begun in 1770, and the contemporary Saville Row off Northumberland Street, just N of the town wall. Newton also designed

the town's first purpose-built Assembly Rooms close to the town's 87
first formal square, Charlotte Square, in the 1770s; they indicate a
growing social and architectural sophistication. The Corporation
also laid out new streets to ease traffic congestion. The T-shaped
insertion of Dean Street and Mosley Street in the 1780s was designed
by David Stephenson to fit between two strands of the web of
medieval streets and to ease the climb from the river. Collingwood
Street, laid out in 1809–10, completed the wide E–W route by linking
Mosley and Westgate Streets, and the Lort Burn dene was partly
filled in to provide a new site for the flesh or meat market behind
Pilgrim Street and Cloth Market.

The great change that began in the late C 18 gathered momentum
c. 1825. Good local architects like William Newton (1735–90), who
also designed St Anne, Newcastle's first classical church, in 1764–
8, and *David Stephenson* (1756–1819), who trained in London and
designed All Saints and the new houses of Mosley and Dean Streets 69
and, with Newton, a new N front for the Guildhall, were followed
by *John Stokoe* (c. 1756–1836), the designer of the Moot Hall (1810–
12), and then by the architects who worked for the visionary entre-
preneur and speculative builder *Richard Grainger* (1797–1861) – *John
Dobson* (1787–1865), *Thomas Oliver* (1791–1857), *George Walker,
John Wardle*, and the *Greens, John* (1787–1852) and *Benjamin (c.
1811–1858)*. The Moot Hall was the city's first and most severe
Greek Revival building; that style predominated until Grainger
introduced a wider repertoire of styles.

Grainger began in 1819–20 with Higham Place (still in brick) but
quickly followed this by schemes in which the use of ashlar marks a
turn to a new scale and metropolitan ambitions (Newcastle, which
between 1750 and 1800 had grown in population from about 20,000
to 28,000, and had reached 35,000 only in 1821, then rose rapidly
to 88,000 in 1851). Eldon Square of 1825–31 and Leazes Terrace of 97
1829–34 are the monuments to this turn, exceedingly well built,
with the ashlar façades that took over completely from brick and
which characterize the C 19 centre of Newcastle. Eldon Square, laid
out on the N side of Blackett Street (which had just been developed
by Grainger along the line of the town wall), was designed by *Oliver*
and *Dobson*. It was (until two-thirds demolished) a spacious square
of the type already built in many large towns, perhaps most significantly in Edinburgh's New Town, only 80 miles to the N. The
suburban Leazes development by Oliver was obviously influenced
by Nash's spectacular work for the Regent, but the grand terrace
goes one better in stone, not stucco. With the Royal Arcade (now
existing only in replica on the ground floor of Swan House, on the
Pilgrim Street roundabout) Grainger entered the centre of the old
town in 1831–2, and followed this up with nothing less than the
planning and building of a completely new commercial centre on
an almost virgin site. The land he purchased had belonged to the
Franciscan friary and to St Bartholomew's Nunnery, which had
become, by 1580, the property of Robert Anderson. Anderson had
demolished the nunnery buildings and on the site of the friary had
built a large house, called 'Newe House' on Speed's town plan of
1610. It passed in 1675 to the Blackett family and was sold in 1782
to a Newcastle builder, George Anderson, who called the house
Anderson Place. Mackenzie said in 1827 that the Corporation had

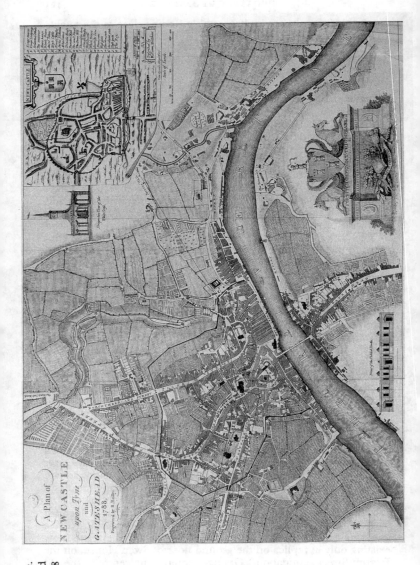

Newcastle upon Tyne.
Map engraved
by Ralph Beilby, 1788

considered buying it then, but had too many other expensive undertakings. The estate extended from Pilgrim Street (E) to the rear of
the properties on Newgate Street (W), and from High Friar Street
and Blackett Street (N) to High Bridge (s). In July 1834 the Common
Council accepted Grainger's proposals, with Grey Street (at first
called Upper Dean Street) planned to run from Blackett Street to
Mosley Street, where it would join Dean Street. This plan involved
demolishing Stephenson's Theatre Royal in Mosley Street (only
opened in 1780) and the new meat market. Grainger's solution was
to undertake to build at his own expense a bigger, better and covered
market on the Nuns' Field within the grounds of Anderson Place,
to be in use before Grey Street was built. By 1839 he had demolished
Anderson Place and built Grainger Market, Grey Street, Grainger
Street and Clayton Street, as well as the shorter streets crossing
them, and had rebuilt part of Pilgrim Street. The result is that
Newcastle can claim to be the only major city in England with a
planned commercial centre of that date, with shops below houses,
workshops and offices. The architecture is classical, competent and
resourceful in the varying of the limited number of elements with
which a classical architect could operate, and convincing in its
appearance of solidity. It escapes from uniformity and boredom by
not being a grid, by exploiting the dramatic possibilities of the steep
slope to the river and by being set within an existing network of
medieval and c 18 streets.

Grainger's streets improved E–W access. Then in the 1840s the
railway arrived, and the Central Station (designed by *Dobson* and
one of the best in England) was built in 1845–50. Neville Street was 116,
laid out to continue the line of Mosley Street and Collingwood 130
Street W to the station and beyond. Grainger's extension to the
town centre was not, however, directly linked with the station until
thirty years later, when Grainger Street was extended S. By then the
Gothic Revival, seen first in the 1820s in Dobson's St Thomas's 99
Church and most notably in *Pugin*'s Roman Catholic St Mary's 100
of 1842–4, was in widespread use for churches and major public
buildings, like the Mining Institute of 1870–4 by *A. M. Dunn*. The
railway cut ruthlessly through the castle between the Black Gate
and the keep, but it drew business and trade to the new streets and
away from the river. *Robert Stephenson*'s High Level Bridge for the
railway (1845–9) brought out the precipitous character of riverside
Newcastle more than ever before, and at the same time provided a
high river crossing for road traffic, flying over the old business
area round Sandhill and bringing traffic directly to Grainger's new
commercial streets in the higher part of the town. However, there
was a slight shift back to the river in 1854, after a disastrous fire in
the Quayside area had destroyed many buildings. In the subsequent
redevelopment the medieval chares, which ran N–S, were replaced
with the rectangular office block of Exchange Buildings and other
new offices for the shipping and insurance firms which still found it
convenient to be near the Quay. The street plan was by *Dobson* for
the Corporation of Newcastle, but Exchange Buildings and other
offices were designed by *William Parnell*. Intense commercial pressure meant that in the later c 19 and early c 20, houses near the new
centre, e.g. in Mosley Street and Blackett Street, were gradually
replaced with offices and shops. It was the familiar pattern in many

English industrial towns, and the Victorian and Edwardian commercial styles are familiar too, with some of the most individual contributions coming from *B. F. Simpson*.

Expansion after 1851 had assumed a new rate: 1851, 88,000; 1871, 128,000; 1891, 186,000; 1911, 267,000. In 1882 Newcastle became a city. The rapid growth based on commercial success, especially in the heavy industries of shipbuilding and engineering, obviously 122 created the need for far more houses, and many streets of Tyneside flats (*see* Introduction, p. 98) were built in the industrial suburbs, once villages, like Walker and Byker, Elswick and Benwell, both E and W of the town. They were built speculatively and rented by the engineering and shipyard workers. To the N, development was somewhat more genteel, slower and restricted on the NW by the Town Moor, still a welcome open space of 375 hectares (927 acres). In the mid-C19 Jesmond had been the retreat of industrialists like Armstrong and Mitchell, but in 1883 Armstrong gave his Jesmond Dene, a wonderfully romantic natural park, to the city, and by 1890 most of Jesmond had been built up with suburban terraces, designed with a restraint that continues on a smaller scale Newton and Grainger's classical tradition. There are none of the Gothic doorcases, shafted windows and turreted roofs then fashionable elsewhere in England; just good bricks and slates and good craftsmanship with, perhaps, some bands of coloured brick, pierced bargeboards and castellated chimney pots.

After the First World War, the city spread as the local authority built estates of well-designed houses in the garden suburb tradition on its edges, for example at Walker, Benwell (the Pendower Estate) and High Heaton. In the decades since 1945, further public housing needs have been met by the inevitable tall blocks of flats, not all unattractive (e.g. those in Jesmond Vale – *see* Vale House – are well designed), but in 1968 a more imaginative solution was found at 129 Byker by *Ralph Erskine*, who showed how a community and designers could work together to rebuild a neighbourhood in a comfortable and practical way; the result is surely one of the most attractive C20 housing developments in Britain.

The Inner Newcastle described here has been as radically transformed in the C20 as it was in the C18 and C19. The main catalyst has been, as it was in the past, the need to accommodate increased traffic. The Tyne Bridge, built in the 1920s, transformed Pilgrim Street into an arterial road, with a group of buildings, including the handsome Carliol House by *Couves* with *Burnet, Tait & Lorne*, on a new and larger scale. Then the building in the 1960s of Central Motorway East truncated Pilgrim Street and smashed some of the mid-C19 suburbs on the E side of the city. Most of the buildings built in association with this road planning and with the contemporary pedestrianization plan for the centre are brutally assertive, to say the least, though some, e.g. the Central Library of 1966–8 by *Sir Basil Spence, Glover & Ferguson*, should not be dismissed. The 1960s also 126 gave Newcastle a very grand Civic Centre, redolent with symbolism. Grainger's commercial centre of the 1830s is remarkably complete, but his Eldon Square has almost entirely fallen prey to the typical introverted shopping centre of the 1970s. Work of the 1980s has concentrated on the rehabilitation of the Quayside, with old buildings restored and some of high quality (the Law Courts and the

Copthorne Hotel) added; elsewhere, many of the city's long-neglected buildings of all periods, e.g. the medieval Black Friars, the C 17 Alderman Fenwick's House and the C 19 Tyne Theatre, have been brought back to life. The mania for façadism has also taken over Grey Street, Nelson Street, Blackett Street and Clayton Street West and threatens to spread. The population of the whole of Newcastle levelled out from its early C 20 peak of 267,000 to 262,000 in 1951, and since then has dropped slightly as industries have closed and population moved to New Towns and development areas. The population of Newcastle, including Gosforth (which was incorporated in 1974), is now just over 190,000. Newcastle was from the end of the C 19 part of a huge Tyneside conurbation, with Wallsend, Tynemouth and, across the river, Gateshead, South Shields and so on. This was recognized in 1974 by the creation of the metropolitan county of Tyne and Wear, and Newcastle lost its function as Northumberland's county town. At the time of writing this county's brief life is threatened with extinction and whether Newcastle will be given back the status she held for 574 years has yet to be revealed.

CATHEDRALS

CATHEDRAL CHURCH OF ST NICHOLAS, St Nicholas Street. Newcastle became a city in 1882; in the same year the diocese of Newcastle was created out of the ancient diocese of Durham, and St Nicholas became the cathedral. It had been until then a parish church, and a parish church in character it has remained, distinguished by its proud spire which, in the words of William Grey, 44 Newcastle's first historian (*Chorographia*, 1649), '. . . lifteth up a head of majesty high above the rest, as a cypresse tree above the low shrubs'.

The church's architecture, with small exceptions, belongs entirely to the C 14 and C 15 – a very rare thing among the churches of Northumberland. The exceptions are of two periods, late C 12 and E.E. Of the former are a part of the outer face of a blocked round-headed window with roll-moulded surround, which has been revealed in the N wall where the N arcade joins the NW crossing-pier, and other fragments detached from the fabric, which seem to have been lost, i.e. fragments of late C 12 vaulting ribs, which were drawn in the C 19; chevron-moulded stones of the same period, which were also drawn; and some waterleaf capitals, which were photographed *c.* 1932 along with fragments of lozenge moulding, said to be 'in a wall at High Fell' (Honeyman). Of the latter period, exposed within the C 14 NW crossing-pier itself, are keeled shafts and a moulded capital on part of a square pier; also keeled, and so E.E., is the surviving part of the E respond of the earlier S arcade. Of uncertain date is the masonry of roughly shaped small blocks into which the taller C 14 arcades were inserted. These survivals allow one to reconstruct in one's mind an earlier church, of unknown length, to which N and S aisles were added in the C 13 (*see* the corbels for the N aisle, and the sawn-off corbels for the S aisle), possibly replacing earlier aisles. Also in the C 13, crossing-piers of square core with four big semicircular keeled shafts were built. There is,

then, no visible evidence to support the suggestion of the C 18
writers Bourne and Brand that the church was founded in the
C 11, nor any documentary evidence. More useful for dating is
the Henry I charter of *c.* 1120, which granted the (unnamed)
church at Newcastle to the cathedral priory of Carlisle; and a
further reference, made in 1194 (in which the dedication of the
church was first given), to a grant of the church's tithes.

As for the later Middle Ages, the C 14 dominates inside, the
C 15 outside, the latter thanks chiefly to the remarkable design of
the W tower and its spire (total height 59 metres, 193½ ft). The
date of completion of the tower is not known, but the ribbed
internal vault bears the arms of Robert Rhodes, M.P., †1474, on
the bosses around the octagonal bell-hatch, which also bears the
motto *Orate pro anima Roberti de Rodes*; his arms are on the
font below, too. The tower rises on a sturdy square base, with
diagonally placed chamfered buttresses. On the N and S sides are
C 19 porches, but the W side has a C 14 doorway below a large
window of five lights with panel tracery, although both doorway
and window – and in fact all the windows in the building, save
for a small internal roundel – have been renewed. On the next
stage are small two-light windows and much solid masonry. The
belfry above has tall, paired openings separated by slender buttresses which continue as pinnacles above the pierced parapet;
the diagonal buttresses reduce to narrow shafts which support
statues in front of big corner pinnacles. From behind these rises
the most surprising part of the structure: an open crown of four
flying buttresses supporting each other and holding aloft a tall
square lantern, itself battlemented and pinnacled, with four miniature flying buttresses balancing a slender octagonal spire, its ribs
crocketed. Crockets also adorn the ogees which flow up the crown
to the lantern and the spirelets on all the pinnacles. What began
with solid lower stages ends as an extraordinarily airy confection
with a flurry of gilded wind-vanes. The design of this structurally
most ingenious crown seems related to that of the pre-Fire St
Mary-le-Bow in London. Although the crown burnt there in 1666
was apparently C 16, its C 14 predecessor was probably similar. In
Britain, such spires seem to have started with St Mary-le-Bow I
c. 1357 or after, followed in the latter part of the C. 15 by St
Nicholas, Newcastle; then by St Giles, Edinburgh, *c.* 1495; King's
College, Aberdeen, *c.* 1500; and St Mary-le-Bow II by 1512. It
has to be said that the crown at St Nicholas was rebuilt in 1608
and again in the C 19 by *Sir George Gilbert Scott*, and it was repaired
at least twice in the C 18. The stability of the tower has frequently
caused anxiety. In 1834 it was found to be leaning 12 inches
(30 cm) to the S. *John Green* and *John Dobson* between them
repaired the foundations, did much tying up with iron bands, and
added N and S porches in 1833–4, but problems remained. Scott
was more successful; he re-underset the tower to 4.3 metres (14 ft)
below the nave floor and put in concrete foundations.

The C 14 work at St Nicholas can be dated with some certainty.
Mayors of 1348, 1350, 1361 etc. are recorded as amongst those
who helped in the building. An indulgence of 1359 was offered to
those who would help in the founding and endowing of new
chapels. Money was left in 1369 for the fabric of one chancel

window. The heraldry of the roof bosses refers to the years 1390 to 1412. It seems likely that nave and transept were complete by *c.* 1350 and that the chancel followed *c.* 1360 etc. The Chapel of St Margaret attached to the S aisle was established in 1394; it is clearly later than the aisle, since inside it crudely breaks into the regular row of tomb recesses along the S wall. The design of the windows does not help much in defining phases more precisely than this. All have been renewed; some are as original, partly Dec with flowing tracery and partly Perp, some are C 19 imitation of the two. *John & Benjamin Green* rebuilt the N aisle in 1834–6, we do not know how correctly, and also St Margaret's Chapel, making it different. *Dobson* rebuilt the N end of the N transept in 1824, and in 1859 the E wall; in both cases he altered the windows, and he removed a high E roundel. Of other windows the following are Dec: N and S transepts, S aisle and clerestory. They are probably not all of the same date and can be sorted out as follows. Cusped intersected, i.e., early C 14, S aisle and N chancel chapel N and E. On the N side the neighbouring window has flowing tracery, so perhaps intersecting was still used as late as 1335 or so. Flowing tracery also in one W window of the W aisle of the N transept. On the other hand, the upper W windows of this transept are of the late Dec type, with three ogee-headed lights under one shallow segmental arch. The same design all along the clerestory and in the S transept's W aisle, although there with a transom, which may be Scott's and certainly is not shown in Horseley's engraving of 1715. In the S transept E wall there are side by side a window with flowing tracery and one that is straight-headed with reticulated tracery. The other windows are Perp.

To complete the exterior it must be added that in 1736, at the expense of Sir Walter Blackett of Wallington, a LIBRARY was 88 built, with a vestry below, to house books left to the church by Dr R. Thomlinson. This is pure Palladian, attributed to *Daniel Garrett* on stylistic grounds (Colvin) and because Garrett worked for Blackett at Wallington. Rusticated ground floor, giant Ionic pilasters above, with alternating window pediments on the first floor.

The INTERIOR impression is of unity of style, mellow and 39 sober, particularly since it was emptied of many of its monuments in the over-enthusiastic restoration of 1783–7 by *David Stephenson* and *William Newton*, done as what Mackenzie described in 1827 as 'a scheme ... for converting it into a kind of cathedral'. The church is not high – the arches spring from a low point on the piers, and the clerestory is small. Also, although the total length is 75 metres (245 ft), it is so cut up that it is never quite felt. The nave has only four bays, the crossing breaks the axial vista, and the chancel with another four bays remains a separate unit. Yet the design is remarkably unified. It is characterized by the use of octagonal piers with chamfered arches dying into them without any capitals, forming a continous sweep of chamfers below hood-moulds along the arcades to the crossing, where even the chancel arch dies into the wall. The clarity thus produced is reinforced by the great width of the aisles, the outer walls well back from the arcades. The crossing-piers are the only element of something like cathedral scale. Moreover they are very uncommon in design:

triple-chamfered with no capitals at all. In the nave, the slightly lower chancel and the N transept, the arches are also triple-chamfered; in the S transept they are double-chamfered. The hoodmoulds rest on head-stops.

Of other features, the graceful little oculus with a wheel of five mouchettes low down in the W wall of the N chancel chapel (St George's) must be mentioned first of all. It is typical of 1330 or 1340 and gives some borrowed light to an oblong CRYPT below part of the N transept. The crypt is vaulted with five heavy, single-chamfered transverse arches, and has a triangular-headed piscina. In the S transept wall there is a round-arched tomb recess. The pointed-arched recesses already referred to, originally eight in an unbroken row along the S aisle wall, are thought to have been tomb recesses inserted in the C 13 for 'founders' tombs', suggesting that the nave aisle walls were not rebuilt in the C 14. The arches at the W end of the aisles do not appear in John Bell's survey of 1831–2, and are part of the extra support for the tower added in the C 19. Finally, the tower opens into the nave with one arch in which the disregard for capitals at St Nicholas is carried to the extreme of a six-fold chamfering. The timber roofs of the church are mostly medieval, with a series of medieval heraldic bosses supplemented by others dating from the C 18 and later, and of sturdy northern character. Only the W tower bay is vaulted, with liernes and a central octagonal bell-hole which has already been mentioned because of its Rhodes inscription. It sits slightly uncomfortably in the tower structure, and the presence of the arms of Jacques on the tower arch jamb, taken with the form of the rere-arch of the W window, has been seen by Honeyman as evidence of the insertion of the vault into a C 14 structure.

MEDIEVAL FURNISHINGS. – FONT made of lower carboniferous limestone, not Frosterley; possibly from Tournai (according to J. Senior). Probably late C 15, for the bowl has eight slightly concave sides bearing the arms of Robert Rhodes on five of them, and on a sixth is a shield in which Rhodes and different arms, said to be those of his wife, are impaled. The same type of font also in other Newcastle and Northumberland churches. – FONT COVER, c. 1500. Wooden, with elaborate Gothic tracery, gables, pinnacles, foliage and crockets. Inside, a tiny rib vault, with an exceedingly pretty boss of the Coronation of the Virgin. The C 17 must have repaired some of the woodwork; *see* the brackets in the first tier of openings. It may well have done more. Again, such elaborate font covers occur also in other Newcastle churches. – CHOIR PEWS reset against the S chancel wall. One row with plain hinged seats fastened down. – LECTERN. Eagle lectern of brass of c. 1500, the same type as more than twenty others in England, e.g. at Southwell (Oman, *Archaeological Journal*, 87, 1930).

OTHER FURNISHINGS. – ORGAN CASE built for a *Renatus Harris* organ in 1676; enlarged 1891. Excellent carving in the classical style, no doubt London work. The trumpeting angel over the centre replaces an earlier figure. The case added in 1710 for additions by Harris now faces into St George's porch in the N transept. – Carved ROYAL ARMS of Charles II on the S transept W wall. – CATHEDRAL FITTINGS, sensitively designed in Gothic

style *c.* 1882 by the cathedral architect, *R. J. Johnson*, include the
REREDOS, executed with great skill by *Robert Beall*, in Uttoxeter
stone; wings with sedilia of sandstone. One band of dark red
Italian limestone across the base (information from J. Senior).
Figures by *J. S. Westmacott*. – PULPIT, also Johnson and Beall,
also Uttoxeter alabaster. – ROOD SCREEN, BISHOP'S THRONE
and CHOIR STALLS also by Johnson, carved in the medieval spirit,
with varied poppyheads, by the local master *Ralph Hedley*, the
canons' stalls with well-carved misericords.

STAINED GLASS. The only medieval glass is a fine C 15 roundel
set in the E window of St Margaret's Chapel (*see* below). The rest
of the glazing is mainly late C19 and C 20. – E window to the
organist Thomas Ions, 1860 by *William Wailes* of Newcastle.
Crucifixion, Last Supper and the Four Evangelists, in mixed
medieval and Renaissance styles. – N CHOIR CHAPEL. E window
1901 by *Clayton & Bell*; N wall, from E, in the Chapel of the
Resurrection, the symbols of the Passion set in clear glass by *L. C.
Evetts*, 1962; the next is a plain window; the third an outstanding
window of 1907 by *Caroline Townshend* (according to Peter
Cormack), showing Northumbrian saints and St Nicholas; the
fourth, 1902 by *Kempe* to W. H. Wilkinson, who developed an
early reinforced concrete in the 1860s; the fifth, 1902 by *H. W.
Bryans*; the sixth, *c.* 1900, unsigned but of high quality and attributed by Neil Moat to *Percy Bacon*. – S CHOIR CHAPEL. E
window in the Chapel of the Ascension, 1962 by *L. C. Evetts*; S
wall, from the E, first window 1861 by *Wailes*, as is the part of the
second remaining after the blocking caused by the 1736 library,
with one light to Spoor † 1856 and in the simple style of the mid-
century, examples of which are becoming rarer. Three further
blocked windows, then the sixth to Rev. James Snape † 1886, and
the seventh, 1861 by *Wailes* (restored 1980), to Joseph Garnett, a
local chemist. – CHOIR. In the clerestory a series by *Kempe, c.*
1900, with the E on the S wall a Sanctus window of great beauty. –
ST GEORGE'S CHAPEL. Four windows of 1934–6 by *A. K.
Nicholson* to the local industrialists Charles Parsons and Andrew
Laing, including pictures of oil wells and the S. S. *Mauretania*. –
N TRANSEPT. Over the crypt door, a 1971 abstract by *S. M. Scott*;
in the clerestory, two by *W. E. Tower* of *Kempe & Co.*; in the
CRYPT, four charming small lights to A. J. C. Ross † 1931, by
Barber (according to Canon Strange), depicting a family scene,
fishing and shipbuilding; and good lead in the medieval roundel
with five mouchettes. – S TRANSEPT. The E wall has two windows
(1870 and 1880) by *Powell Bros.* of Leeds; one on the S wall is by
Powell, and there is a fine *Kempe* W window of *c.* 1900; the
E clerestory has three windows by *Kempe & Co.* showing the
prophets. – NAVE N AISLE. From the E: first window, World
War I Memorial, 1921 by *P. C. Bacon*; second, Indian Mutiny
Memorial, 1851 by *Wailes*; third and fourth, Boer War Memorial,
1903 by *Bryans*. – NAVE S AISLE. From the E: the first two a gift
of 1889, by *E. R. Frampton* (according to Neil Moat); the third in
the aisle, to A. Burchby † 1897, by *Kempe*. Off the aisle, ST
MARGARET'S CHAPEL. E wall, a fine C 15 roundel of the upper
half of a Virgin and Child, the cathedral's only medieval glass; S
wall, an unpleasing late C 19 window by *Mayer & Co.*; W wall, by

Tombleson of *Kempe & Co.*, to Mrs C. G. Bruce † 1896. – S PORCH. 1870 by *Wailes*, with figures of SS. John the Baptist and Evangelist which David Connors identifies as copied from C 15 glass in All Saints, North Street, York. – W WINDOW. Tree of Jesse, 1866 by *Clayton & Bell.*

BRASSES. The THORNTON BRASS, resited after 1959 from All Saints', hangs on the wall of the S chancel chapel, but is to be moved to the rear of the high altar (1992). It is said to be the largest brass in the country, and is certainly one of the finest. Roger † 1429, his wife † 1411. Made before his death, probably N German, with the figures incised, not cut out and set in the stone. Framing the two large principal figures are shafts with seven tiers of saints on buttresses. A remarkable detail is the fact that the outer buttresses have additional figures appearing in profile and only half visible, an early case of a trick of perspective. Seven sons and seven daughters appear below, and there are other narrative figures in the canopies. Also Bishop Wilberforce, first Bishop of Newcastle, † 1907.

MONUMENTS. A selection in topographical order: first the CHANCEL from N to S. N CHANCEL CHAPEL. Set in the choir screen, Bishop Lloyd, 1908 by *Oliver & Leeson*, with recumbent smooth alabaster effigy by *F. W. Pomeroy*; elaborate tomb-chest and canopy; all Gothic. – On the N wall: Major Robert Buggin † 1688, citizen and haberdasher of London; cartouche in richly carved frame with putti and drapery. – Patrick Crowe, 'Armiger', † 1694; white marble on black ground, deeply carved skulls round a cartouche with his arms above. – Danish Church memorial, 1983 by *R. G. Sims*. Steel rods with slate panels; to the Danish seamen who died 1939–45. – Sir Robert Shafto Hawks † 1840; coat of arms and brass plaque on a black stone mount. E wall: James Bell Hostman † 1795; tall flat obelisk in marble. – Major George Anderson † 1831; white high-relief sarcophagus on black ground. – Nicholas Ridley, Esq., Senior Bencher of Gray's Inn, † 1805, a big high relief of a weeping woman leaning on an urn. S wall: John Collingwood Bruce † 1892, signed 1890 by *George Simonds*. Recumbent marble effigy on sarcophagus, his feet resting on an open book, his own *Roman Wall*; the page displayed contains the acknowledgements. – Matthew Ridley, Esq., † 1788, 1787 by *J. Bacon*; the best monument in the cathedral. Large seated figure, in Roman style, against a wide obelisk, very tenderly felt and delicately carved, on a base with a medallion representing the town of Newcastle as a woman crowned with turrets (Mackenzie (1827) explains all the symbols). – Henry Askew † 1796 and his wife † 1792, 1801 by *Henry Webber*, with portrait heads in a roundel on an urn which is surrounded by a big group of allegorical figures. This rare sculptor's best work. – Edward Collingwood of Chirton † 1783; large well-cut inscription on a console supporting an urn, the base of the table with enamel medallions. – Matthew Duane, trustee of the British Museum, † 1785; high wide obelisk in green marble, with white marble inscriptions.

TRANSEPTS. S TRANSEPT: The most appealing of all monuments in the church, the painted and gilded marble of *c.* 1635 to the Maddison family, with six kneeling figures of Henry † 1634,

Elizabeth † 1653 and their parents, and their sixteen children below. Arranged with the couple facing each other across a prayer desk, the parents at the sides and facing front (her father in armour, the mothers half-hidden by Corinthian columns) and the children ranged along the bottom. The lively carving of the figures contrasts with the architectural setting, which is a pair of shell-canopied niches in a projecting frame of deep base, with side columns and central desk on jewelled panels, the entablature elaborately carved with high broken pediment crested with arms, and figures of Faith, Hope and Charity rising over all. The whole projects in a shallow triangular plan because it formerly stood against one of the crossing-piers. It is supported on a richly carved leafy bracket. – Also in the S transept in a recess in the S wall, the only surviving medieval effigy: a C 14 knight in armour, his shield with a faint escutcheon. – Rev. Hugh Moises † 1806 by *Flaxman*, his portrait medallion on the column which supports a severely undecorated urn, and on which a bored Religion rests an elbow. – Thomas Hedley † 1877, whose legacy helped to endow the new bishopric; and a bronze plaque signed *THCo* to David Oliphant † 1900 at Peking.

N TRANSEPT: Joseph Bainbridge † 1823 by *E. H. Baily*, with a portrait head in a roundel below an urn. – William Peareth † 1775, by *Westmacott*, a large well-cut inscription which Mackenzie considered 'chaste and elegant'. ST GEORGE CHAPEL (N transept): several interesting C 17 and C 18 grave slabs in the floor, with well-carved arms. W WALL: William Hall † 1631 and his wife, Jane, † 1613, a good Renaissance piece, with the usual two kneelers and the six children in half-relief below. The entablature has a high broken pediment and figures of Faith, Hope and Charity. – E WALL: Robert Shafto † 1705; undulating cartouche in a deeply carved frame of skulls. – Thomas Surteis † 1629, a rather eroded panel in a wide aedicule, with coat of arms and French motto.

NAVE. N AISLE: Calverley Bewicke † 1815, by *E. H. Baily* from a design supplied by *Theed*, exhibited at the Royal Academy in 1819. The dying man sits on a chair supported by his daughter and faced by a standing allegorical female. The figures are in the round, against a simple Gothic background with a long slender flying angel. – Hannah Mosley † 1784, a big obelisk and a sarcophagus, by *Fisher* of York. There are many other wall memorials which warrant a careful inspection, but the W end has the most significant in historical terms: Admiral Lord Collingwood † 1810, by *Rossi*, showing a bust set on a high pedestal against full drapery. The pedestal has the wave motif – so apt here. Designed by *C. R. Cockerell*. – Sir Matthew White Ridley † 1813, by *Flaxman*. Standing figure in toga against the conventional obelisk. – R. Hopper Williamson † 1835, by *Dunbar*. Seated figure on a comfortably padded chair; well-characterized face. S AISLE: In St Margaret's Chapel, medieval CROSS SLABS, all four unfortunately painted white c. 1960; one the rare type with carving representing openings in the shroud, through which head and feet are revealed. They are exceedingly small, and if one reconstructs the whole figure hidden by the slab, with its cross, sword hammer and pick, one obtains quite preposterous proportions.

HALL, LIBRARY and VESTRY added 1926 by *W. H. Wood* and entered from the S chancel chapel. Restrained Gothic. Stair and upper floor inserted by *R. R. Simms* to form offices *c.* 1980. Railings with Gothic-lettered frieze also of 1926.

CATHEDRAL OF ST MARY (R. C.), Clayton Street West. 1842–4 by *A. W. N. Pugin*; it became the cathedral in 1850. Pugin's design for a spire was not executed; the present spire, 68 metres (222 ft) high, which is so important to the effect of the whole building, was completed in 1872 by *A. M. Dunn & E. J. Hansom*. The baptistry chapel was added in 1902, probably by *Goldie*, and restoration of 1980–8 was carried out by *The Napper Collerton Partnership* (job architect *C. Rainford*). As so often with Pugin churches, the exterior is much finer than the interior. Bold group of three big E windows (ritually E, in fact SE), each under its own gable; Dec tracery. Aisles with three-light windows, W front with three gables and big Dec windows, the S with ballflower decoration running round the tracery. W double door with elaborate hinges in moulded and shafted surround beneath the central window. In niches flanking the window are statues of SS. Bede and Cuthbert. To the ritual SW, the polygonal baptistry chapel, now adapted as entrance porch, and to the E of this the original S porch in the tower, which is crowned by a noble needle spire with spirelets. To the SE, the cathedral library below and the chapter room above were added by *Goldie* in 1851. Adjoining these, the presbytery, by *E. W. Pugin*, was added in 1858 and extended in 1869 by *A. M. Dunn*, in Tudor style, with an interesting variety of window shape, a canted porch and a square stair turret, steep roofs and polygonal chimneys. The whole forms a most successful group, varied, yet not with any levity.

INTERIOR. Arcade of six bays, a narrow chancel bay and a slightly projecting chancel. No clerestory, no specially good proportions or details – all rather uninspired compared with the exterior. Now reordered, and the interior, already lightened by the removal of the rood screen, has been further lightened by the removal of the side choir screens and by cleaning away the grime of the C19. The carved altars, of Caen stone and also by Pugin, were restored in the 1980s to their original stone surface; an account of *c.* 1870 said that they had been 'barbarized' by being painted. They have carving in three quatrefoil panels; reredos also with much carving. Stencilled painting on the roof of the 1980s, new work on new roof structure, picking up the pattern of the mid-C19 floor tiles. The tiled frieze of *c.* 1880 around the nave, below the windowsills, bears the names of local saints. – STAINED GLASS. All the pictorial windows of 1844 were designed by *Pugin* and made by *Wailes*; these included the splendid trio of richly coloured E windows, the central a Tree of Jesse, the Blessed Sacrament Chapel to the N having The Good Shepherd, the Lady Chapel to the S, the Virgin and Child flanked by SS. George and John. Other glass described in an 1848 account is in the two N windows of the N chancel chapel, and the remainder all in the S aisle: E–W, the first to Rev. James Worswick; the second to Rev. J. L. Eyre; the third, the Bede Window, presented to the church by Wailes. Windows described in 1870 added to these the S aisle fourth (St Elizabeth of Hungary) by *Barnet*, *c.* 1862, fifth (St John) and sixth (Baptism of Christ) by *Wailes*, the latter including a view of the church with unfinished tower. In the N aisle, first and second by Wailes (SS. Robert and Thomas the Apostle), the third by *Barnet* ('Go ye and teach'), and the sixth being erected to the late Elizabeth Dunn. – BRASS to James Worswick † 1842 by *Pugin*, made by *Hardman*.

CHURCHES AND MONASTIC REMAINS

ALL SAINTS, Pilgrim Street. 1786–96 by *David Stephenson*. Deconsecrated in 1961 and successfully converted in 1983–4 into offices and an auditorium for Town Teacher (an urban studies educational charity) and the City of Newcastle with the Joint Conservation Team of Tyne and Wear and *M. Pearse*. In the restoration the golden sandstone emerged from nearly 200 years of soot to reveal the very high quality of the carving. This church was the successor to a medieval church with, according to an C18 drawing, a C12 doorway. A boss with the arms of Robert Rhodes proves that the church received a new tower vault in the C15.

Stephenson's is an excellent job, original in its plan and most 69 effective in its exterior. It is set at the edge of the virtual cliff of the river valley, a steep bank with the Quayside chares between it and the Quay. Before the building of the new Tyne Bridge in the 1920s, it held such a dominant position that its spire was the strongest accent on Newcastle's skyline. The spire, which was an afterthought, crowns a tower placed to the S of the church and is detailed throughout with uncommon care and sensitivity. The problem of how to combine a tower with a church front, for which Gibbs at St Martin-in-the-Fields had found so questionable a solution (a solution all the same imitated for nearly a hundred years all over England), is here treated in a far more satisfactory way. The whole tower projects in front of the church and the entrance is marked by a further detached portico in front of the tower. This portico is of four slender Doric columns, Greek in form (i.e. without a base) though Roman in their capitals and their slender proportions, carrying a pediment. A flight of stairs leads up to the portico. The tower then has one storey with one broad tripartite window and a pediment, a second with only a semicircular window, then the clock stage, square with diagonally projecting bases for the coupled Tuscan columns which mark the diagonals of the next, octagonal, stage. The columns are placed exceptionally far from the body of the octagon. Then an intermediate stage and openwork balustrading and a final smaller octagon with single Tuscan columns and the thin obelisk spire. The whole is as much a filigree of transparent forms as any Italian Baroque spire. To the l. and r. of the tower are subsidiary rooms with charmingly designed tripartite windows. Behind these and the circular domed lobby inside the tower, to the N, the church itself curves round, an oval with added shallow apses to the W and E.

Inside, it can be seen that the one difficulty Stephenson had 70 not solved was how to overcome the surprise and confusion which arose from the sudden change of axis on leaving the lobby and expecting to find the altar in front. This is only slightly less surprising now that there is no altar, for the change of axis remains and is all the more painful as there are box-pews and a curved gallery all orientated towards the E apse. So one arrives inconspicuously below one side of the gallery. One would expect at least another entrance of equal weight opposite, on the N (and another tower?) to restore balance. The galleries rest on Tuscan columns. All the woodwork is of solid mahogany. The reredos along the back of the apse, with tall Corinthian columns, is of 1904. In the conversion the SW part was altered to accommodate offices. In the nave (now auditorium) the floor was adapted so that the central pews could be sunk, the woodwork restored, and the ceiling repainted in a lively C 18 style. – BOARDS with painted Our Father, Creed and Commandments, now in the former SE vestry. Moved to the lobby, the medieval FONT and some of the better MONUMENTS. Edward Moses, son of the master of the Grammar School, †1813, a low-relief obelisk with Latin and Greek inscriptions, and a plaque commemorating David Stephenson, architect of the church, †1819: both by *Davies*. – The Thornton Brass has been moved to the Cathedral of St Nicholas (*see* above).

CHRIST CHURCH, Shieldfield Green. 1859–61 by *A. B. Higham*. The stepped frontage formed by the NW porch, W end of the church, SW tower and hall attached to the S was designed to follow the side of the Green but is none the worse for that. In Dec style, with crocketed gables, flower capitals, and gargoyles. The broach spire provides relief from the visual boredom of the surrounding streets. The interior is as decorative, with crocket capitals on quatrefoil piers. – FONT. Medieval but reconstructed. – Curious papier-mâché FIGURE of Christ the King suspended over the chancel; early C 20.

ST ANDREW, Newgate Street, in a churchyard with tall trees, that is, not entirely swallowed up by the town. The sturdy W tower, with NW stair turret and large SW clasping buttress, was surmounted by a gun in the Civil War of the 1640s. The church was probably therefore damaged through being a target in the siege; there were neither baptisms nor sermons for a whole year. In 1788 the third pier of the N aisle was removed and the flanking arches thrown into one. Restoration of 1866 by *T. Oliver*, who restored the N arcade, removed the galleries and renewed the aisle windows. S transept remodelled in 1844 in neo-Norman style by *John Dobson*. Restoration and vestries added in the 1950s and 1960s by *Caröe & Robinson*.

The lower courses of the tower are C 12, but the exterior is too much repaired to be of much use archaeologically. The upper part of the tower, the chancel with S porch, and the N transept are of *c.* 1300; *see* the chancel arch and the stepped lancet lights under one two-centred arch on the N side of the transept and the S side of the chancel (the chancel window is of 1866, supposedly an exact copy of the original). Of the C 14, the N chancel chapel (1380s endowment by Sir Adam de Athol) and the S nave porch, though the outer doorway was remodelled in 1726 in Baroque style. Perp clerestory. Inside, the earliest piece is the late C 12 chancel arch, ambitious, tall and wide, chevron-moulded, of two orders, with keeled responds and one additional shaft to the W which has two shaft-rings. The nave arcades may well be part of the same building operation; four bays, circular piers with very plainly moulded octagonal capitals and single-stepped round arches (the N arcade restoration of 1866 can be quite clearly seen below the arch of 1788). The small blocked clerestory windows on the S side look late C 12. The E parts of the N and S walls of the chancel are of c. 1300, as has already been recognized from the outside. The proof inside is the double piscina. The N chancel chapel, known as the Trinity or Athol Chapel from the image it held and from the C 14 benefactor, has semi-octagonal responds and wide double-chamfered arches. In the tower there are springers and wall-ribs below the beams of the next floor, suggesting that a C 15 vault has been removed. – FONT COVER. C 15; of the same type as the font cover of the Cathedral, but the upper stage has specially large, eight-light 'windows' with Perp panel tracery. – PULPIT and CHOIR STALLS. 1906–7 by *Ralph Hedley*. – ROYAL ARMS of George IV, carved, over the high arch of the W door. – STAINED GLASS. Trinity Chapel, E window (The Ascension), 1900 by *Kempe*; mid-C 19 N window by *Gibson*. – Other windows, 1976 by *L. C. Evetts*, not stained but reglazed with varied vertical and horizontal leading, and Monkwearmouth hand-made glass, in a style developed by Wilson in Northumberland in the C 19; very attractive and allowing a soft clear light into the church. – MONUMENTS. Indent of the brass of Sir Aymer Athol † 1387 and his wife, in their chapel. Of the brass only a fragment survives, now in the Museum of Antiquities store. – H. Griffith † 1837, an inscription tablet by *Dunbar*, with a seated allegorical figure above a profile relief portrait. CHURCHYARD. *See* Perambulation 1, below.

ST ANNE, City Road. 1764–8 by *William Newton*. Built for the Corporation of Newcastle as a chapel of ease to All Saints'. It replaces a medieval chapel. A stately classical church in sandstone ashlar, miniature, however, with a plain and well-designed W tower. Behind the one-storeyed pedimented portico of four Tuscan columns the nave rises to a broader pediment, and behind this the tower itself is placed. Square clock stage, two octagonal stages and spire. The nave is rectangular, of five windows (reduced in size in the C 19) in arched panels, the outer bays set back slightly. The shallow apse is of the same height as the nave and has three windows. Parapets, no balustrade. Simple interior with boarded dado. – REREDOS. 1911 by *Hicks & Charlewood*. Impressive, in classical style, with broken segmental pediment on columns.

ST JOHN THE BAPTIST, Westgate Road. In the exterior the W tower dominates, although it is not high and is partly masked by clasping aisles. Grainger Street was laid out alongside it and caused it to rise starkly from the very pavement, with city traffic flowing alongside its rough and decayed masonry. The tower is of the C 15, with quite elaborate pinnacles, and dated inside by a boss on the vault referring to Robert Rhodes, who gave money for it. His arms and the same inscription, '*Orate pro anima Roberti Rodes*', appear, restored, on the S transept gable. He died in 1474. The only external features of the church which are older than the

c 15 are some N windows, three ogee-headed lights under a
shallow segmental arch (cf. Cathedral) which seem to be late c 14.
The N transept is also c 14, with the distinction of a W aisle, not
unusual in the c 13 here in the North. Of the c 15 the s transept,
without an aisle, and the low clerestory. The chancel was mostly
rebuilt in 1848, and the greater part of the E wall, with its tracery,
was re-erected in the garden of The Lodge, Front Street, Whit-
burn, s of the Tyne (formerly County Durham). The interior has
c 14 nave arcades, modelled on the pattern of St Nicholas, without
capitals, and here double-chamfered on octagonal piers. Shields
as hoodmould stops over the N arcade. But in the N transept the
pier is short and has a moulded capital. High single-chamfered
tower arch, higher than the vault behind it, and hollow-chamfered
N and s arches. There is at least one survival from a much older
church, the head of a Norman window in the chancel, above the
vestry door. Near it, a cross-shaped slit in the wall. A reordering
of 1965–73 by *Dykes Bower* provided CHANCEL SCREEN, and in
front of it COMMUNION RAILS. The delicately turned and widely
spaced balusters do not impose on the ancient fabric. – FONT.
Partly restored. Said to be the gift of Andrew Bates (appointed
lecturer (minister) to the church in 1689), to replace the destroyed
medieval font. Octagonal, of the type of the font in St Nicholas;
the bowl with Bates's arms among the shields on the concave
sides. – FONT COVER. C 17; tall, bristling with canopies and
pinnacles. – PULPIT. Late c 17, with unfluted Corinthian
columns, but still the diamond-studded arches of the Jacobean
style in the panels; the frieze has acanthus leaves, but also pendants. Restored by *Dykes Bower*, with new pedestal and stair. –
STAINED GLASS. Medieval fragments roughly assembled in the
N chancel window contain some pictures. – Lady Chapel N and
one s aisle window by *Wailes*. – N transept. Two E windows of *c.*
1946 (Nativity and Tree of Jesse), signed *G. E. R. Smith*. – Facing
them a good but anonymous window with St Barbara and St
George; a memorial of the Boer War; and one of World Wars I
and II. – s transept E, c 19 window with good heraldic glass.
Atkinson Bros., *c.* 1906. Faith, Hope and Charity by *H. & M.
Barnett*, 1865. – MONUMENTS. s wall of chancel. J. Taylor by
Dunbar, 1835, with frontal bust. – In the s nave wall, beside the
door, a Gothic memorial of 1888 to Richard Grainger † 1861: 'A
citizen of Newcastle ... does not need to be reminded of the
genius ... a stranger is referred to the principal streets in the
centre of this city.'

ST MATTHEW, Summerhill Street. 1877 by *R. J. Johnson*. Tower
by *Hicks & Charlewood*, 1895. Embedded in c 19 terraces; only
the w front is easily visible as a whole, but its big W tower makes
good use of its position at the top of a hill where the street turns
slightly, so that there is a shock awaiting pedestrians approaching
from below as they round the corner. Tall and wide, the tower
dominates this area. It has a five-light window in its second stage,
paired two-light bell openings, and a battlemented parapet with
recessed elaborate pinnacles with wind-vanes. Clasping double
aisles balance this weight. Dec tracery in the tower, Perp elsewhere. Paired two-light clerestory windows between pilasters surmounted by more pinnacles. Inside, the walls are of red sandstone

ashlar, in varied shades; blind traceried frieze below the arch-braced roof with pendants and bosses. Five shafts to the high tower-arch, with delicately carved flower capitals. The nave arcades have quatrefoil piers with moulded capitals except for the easternmost, where the tower-arch capitals reappear. The outer arcades pick up the local medieval style; they have octagonal piers from which double-chamfered arches spring without capitals. Attention is focused on the E end, where the chancel floor is of inlaid marble, there is a sedilia, and a wall of blind tracery is the setting for a magnificent six-light window. – REREDOS. 1896 by *Hicks & Charlewood*, in memory of R. J. Johnson, with niches and canopied statues of Caen stone. – C19 FONT AND COVER, in C14 style, from the demolished St Cuthbert's, Melbourne Street (it was by *A. R. Gibson*, 1871). – CHANCEL RAIL. 1905, of carved stone, with wrought-iron gates. – STAINED GLASS. E window, 1899 by *Kempe*; S aisle, late *Kempe & Co*.

ST PAUL, Havelock Street, Elswick. 1854 by *Benjamin Green*. Small polygonal SW turret. Some plate tracery, but mostly lancets, paired in the aisles, and at the W end two flanking a large buttress. Aisled nave and chancel without division. – STAINED GLASS. W window of N aisle, 1903 by *Wailes & Strang*. – W window by *Morris & Co.*, 1911. – MONUMENT. Marcus Allen † 1843, by *R. G. Davies*; low-relief portrait set in a pillar, against which a weeping female rests.

ST PHILIP, St Philip's Close, High Elswick. 1871 by *Redmayne*, as a national memorial to Charles Thomas Longley, Archbishop of Canterbury and previously Bishop of Durham, † 1868. Paired S transepts, N porch. Lancets. Built of ashlar, except for the N wall, which is of rubble, presumably because a N aisle was intended. – The chancel panelling includes a WAR MEMORIAL to men of the parish who died in the Great War, listing 252 names. – The STAINED GLASS (probably contemporary with the church) in the upper lights of each window and in one S chancel memorial window is of high quality; so is the WROUGHT IRON of the door hinges.

ST THOMAS, Barras Bridge. A 'peculiar', without a parish. The church belongs in its character to the newer parts rather than the old centre of Newcastle, although its origins are ancient. It was built 1827–30 to replace the medieval chapel of St Thomas at the end of Tyne Bridge. The design is by *John Dobson*, chosen from two by Dobson and one by John Green; the style is a personal interpretation of E.E. The church is essentially a Georgian preaching box with Gothic treatment. W tower with very tall coupled bell openings – so tall and so transparent that they give the whole tower an openwork effect. Clasping aisles of the same height as the nave have pierced parapets; the buttresses end in big pinnacles; flying buttresses over the sloping W parapets support the tower. Tall lancet windows, paired in the five-bay nave and triple, with shafts, in the E front. The interior is a large, light space, with slim quatrefoil piers from which plaster vaults with stone ribs spring over nave and aisles. Galleries inserted in 1837 interrupt the flowing lines, but provided the seating which became necessary as the suburbs grew. There is no chancel, only a slight projection to hold the altar (now without its platform), for the Chaplain of

the Chapel at the time of rebuilding was Robert Wastney, a noted
Evangelical. – ORGAN CASE of 1837 inserted in the W gallery
1960. – STAINED GLASS. E window, 1881 by *Baguley*, according
to Neil Moat. – MONUMENTS. Tablet to Robert Wastney † 1836,
by *C. Tate*; standing woman beside altar with profile portrait on
it. White marble.

ST DOMINIC (R.C.), New Bridge Street. 1869–73 by *A. M. Dunn*.
The ritual E is at the S. The W end is partly obscured by a porch
of 1956, but above there is a blind arcade, with damaged statue
(of St Dominic?) in a niche, and in the gable a large wheel
window flanked by symbols of the Evangelists. To the r., the
priory gateway, under a tower which was never completed. E.E.
windows, triple in the large clerestory and higher in the polygonal
E apse. Inside, walls of polychrome brick, mostly yellow, with
ashlar dressings. Round piers with stiffleaf capitals support
moulded arches, with carved heads in the spandrels. Frosterley
marble shafts with clasping bands to the chancel and chancel aisle
arches. The most striking feature is the set of CHOIR STALLS, in
C 14 style, with crocketed canopies. These were designed by *Blore*
in 1827 for Peterborough Cathedral (woodwork by Mr *Ruddle*),
and brought here by a parishioner in the 1890s when Pearson
was restoring the cathedral. – COMMUNION RAIL and FONT of
marble. Worth noting. – PULPIT. 1879, in alabaster, with scenes
from the life of St Dominic. – STAINED GLASS includes the S
aisle window by *Atkinson Bros*.
    The PRIORY attached is by *Dunn & Hansom*, 1887. Brick, with
terracotta dressings in Gothic style.

ST MICHAEL (R.C.), Westmorland Road, Elswick. 1889–91 by
Dunn, Hansom & Dunn. This impressive church (with its presbytery, now demolished) originally dominated steep terraces of
Tyneside flats where Armstrong's engineering workers lived. The
strong composition of the cruciform-plan church with aisled nave,
large clerestory and big octagonal crossing-tower looks (in 1991)
even more imposing now it is surrounded by open space, with
low school buildings to the S. Dec tracery, aisles with gargoyles
and coped parapets, tower with gargoyles, pierced battlements
and pinnacles, the carving as good as the best of the period. The
richness of the exterior continues inside. The five-bay arcades
have alternate round and octagonal piers, the high crossing-arches
are subdivided by shafts to the transepts. Angels for corbels to the
boarded barrel roofs, the chancel ceiling painted, the tower with
tierceron ribs. – High-quality REREDOS. Alabaster with statues
in niches; matching COMMUNION RAIL. – LADY CHAPEL
REREDOS. 1914 by *Giles Gilbert Scott*; richly carved Gothic. –
STAINED GLASS. E window *c.* 1891 by *Westlake*; W and others by
Atkinson of Newcastle.

BRUNSWICK METHODIST CHAPEL, Brunswick Place. 1820–1.
The successor to the Orphan House in Northumberland Street,
which was founded by Wesley. E. Mackenzie wrote in 1827 that
it was 'built after the plan of Waltham Street chapel at Hull,
constructed by Mr [*W.*] *Sherwood*, architect, who liberally sent
all the necessary drawings and specifications.' Brick with ashlar
dressings, a two-storey, five-bay front with arched openings and
three-bay pediment; wide steps up to the panelled double door in

a Tuscan porch with prominent cornice. The r. bay obscured by later building; the returns are of six bays, with a pediment over the last three to Northumberland Court. The interior was described in 1827 as 'one of the most handsome and commodious chapels in the north of England', but is sadly not so now. In 1983 a floor was inserted at gallery level, giving space on the ground floor for various pastoral needs. Inappropriate textured brick partition walls have been erected. The chapel above, at the former gallery level, is all that is needed now for an inner-city congregation. Corinthian pilasters frame the W apse with wide, panelled pulpit. The ceiling retains its delicate stucco.

CHURCH OF THE DIVINE UNITY, Ellison Place. 1939–40 by *Cackett, Burns Dick & Mackellar*. On the site of Dobson's church of St Peter. Light brick, with, along Ellison Place, from W to E, a tall tripartite stone portal screen into a small forecourt; the nave has six tall straight-headed windows, and a square tower with yet taller window. Inside, aisles and clerestory. The beams carrying the clerestory have no intermediate supports at all. Flat ceilings. The detail of the woodwork somewhat modernistic.

ST JAMES UNITED REFORMED CHURCH (formerly Congregational), Northumberland Road. 1882–4 by *T. Lewis Banks*. A big raised central tower dominates this group of cruciform church, Sunday school, church hall and caretaker's house. The style is free C13, the whole in remarkably original condition. Much C19 STAINED GLASS, including some by *Atkinson Bros.* and *G. J. Baguley & Son*.

Former TRINITY PRESBYTERIAN CHURCH, Northumberland Road, now the Trinity Building of Newcastle Polytechnic (*see* Public Buildings, below). 1885 by *Marshall & Dick*. Snecked sandstone, ashlar dressings, graduated Lakeland slate roof with red ridge tiles and finials. A complete group with school and caretaker's house. The church in a free treatment of Perp forms (note especially the ogee gables of the openings). – STAINED GLASS of *c.* 1900 of some quality in the W window by *Atkinson Bros.*; other windows of interest in N aisle and N transept. Timber mullions to the school windows; house half-timbered.

WESTGATE ROAD BAPTIST CHURCH, Westgate Road. 1885–6 by *James Cubitt*. Snecked sandstone and Lakeland slate. An attractive grouping of church and associated buildings. The front facing Westgate Road has paired arches to the doors under paired two-light windows, and to the l. a high NW belfry with nook-shafts and a stone spire. Inside, Gothic panelling at the E end, where the baptistry is of cream marble. The HALL, behind, has tall transomed windows and swept eaves.

Former SYNAGOGUE, Leazes Park Road. 1880 by *John Johnstone*. It forms a strong element in the street frontage but has been converted to a shopping arcade. Damaged by fire in 1990 but to be restored. The style is North Italian, the materials ashlar with pink granite shafts. Doors in the end bays and a Lombard frieze on the gable over the central three. Upper windows paired under round arches with the Star of David carved in the tympana.

BLACK FRIARS, Monk Street. The Dominican friars were established in Newcastle by 1239. In 1250 the Prior was criticized by the

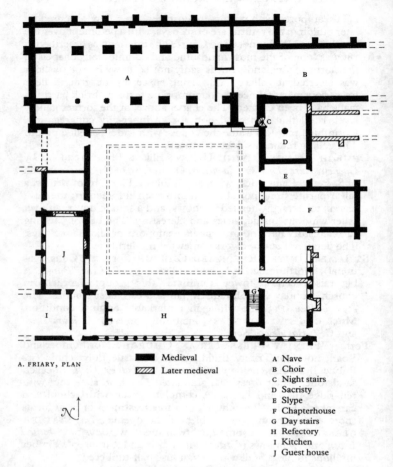

Newcastle upon Tyne, Black Friars

General Chapter of the Order for his architectural extravagance.
What remains of that extravagance and of later building can be
seen in three claustral ranges, the w, s and e. The church, which
occupied the N side of the cloister, was demolished in the c 16
and is known only from excavations. After the Dissolution the
property was sold to the mayor and burgesses of Newcastle, who
in 1552 leased it to nine of the town's craft companies. Thereafter
the general pattern of use was that each company held meetings
in the upper room and used the ground-floor room of their section
as almshouses. Each range was divided into three, which necessitated some insertion of walls. Gradually, after some rebuilding,
the companies let their premises for other uses, and squalor set
in. In the 1930s the many families who by then were living on

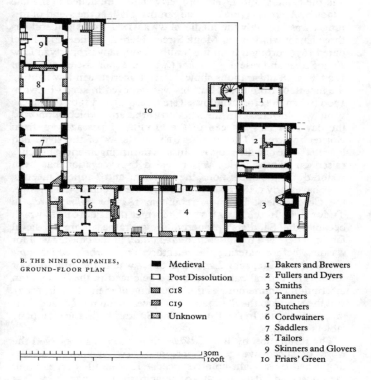

B. THE NINE COMPANIES,
GROUND-FLOOR PLAN

■ Medieval
□ Post Dissolution
▨ C18
▨ C19
▧ Unknown

1 Bakers and Brewers
2 Fullers and Dyers
3 Smiths
4 Tanners
5 Butchers
6 Cordwainers
7 Saddlers
8 Tailors
9 Skinners and Glovers
10 Friars' Green

|⊢⊢⊢⊢⊢⊢⊢⊢⊢⊢⊢⊢⊢⊢⊢⊢⊢⊢⊢⊢⊢⊢⊢⊢⊢⊢⊢⊣ 30m
⊢⊢⊢⊢⊢⊢⊢⊢⊢⊢⊣ 100ft

'Friars' Green' had to leave, as the sanitary authorities used their powers. Restoration, and the preceding excavation, did not begin, alas, until after 1973, when Newcastle's Planning Committee commissioned a report from *Wales, Wales & Rawson* on how to secure the buildings. Restoration by this firm was completed in 1981. In 1991 Black Friars houses craft shops, a restaurant and an educational resource centre, but some rooms still await a use.

A description conveniently starts at the N and makes a clockwise circuit. The church's plan is marked out; it was aisled, and the cloister walk ran along the S nave wall. The choir extended beyond the E wall of the E RANGE. The N end of this range was demolished after the Dissolution, so that it ends now with the W part of the CHAPTERHOUSE, which was occupied after 1552 by the Bakers 47 and Brewers Company. The arched doorway is flanked by two-light windows with cusped tracery, of which the N is original. From the excavations of the church site (and now in the chapterhouse), part of a large blue stone GRAVE COVER, the matrix for a C 15 Flemish brass which was perhaps as fine as the Thornton Brass (*see* St Nicholas's Cathedral). The chapterhouse and the Fullers' and Dyers' property were remodelled in the late 1890s by *Matthew Graham*. The Smiths' Hall, at the S end of this range, was probably the medieval WARMING HOUSE; it still has three lancet windows to Monk Street. Here is a a fine door lintel dated 1679, brought from the Smiths' Company property in Low Friar Street and reset by *Thomas Oliver* in a staircase extension of 1827–8. C 18 illustrations show a large traceried window lighting the first floor from the S, but this was removed in stages between 1709 (when the cross windows were inserted) and 1803 (when the gable was lowered). In the S RANGE, the arch which supported the day stair can be seen in the SLYPE, or passageway, from cloister to street. The REFECTORY to the W of the slype had lancets, some of which survive. Inside, the arrangement of benches raised on plinths which was revealed by excavation has been restored. On the upper floor, the Butchers' and Tanners' meeting halls have early C 18 cross windows. At the W end of the S range, the Cordwainers' Hall was rebuilt in 1843 by *John Wardle* in Tudor style. In the W RANGE, the former GUEST HOUSE, which became the Saddlers' property, shows rather more medieval fabric. There is a trefoil-arched *lavatorium* in the cloister wall for washing before entering the refectory, and corbels which supported the cloister roof. Lancets in the W wall lit the ground-floor room. The central part of the range belonged to the Tailors (an inscription commemorates the rebuilding of their block in 1787), and the N end to the Skinners and Glovers, who remodelled their property in 1712. In the Tanners' and Smiths' halls, the Company tablets remain.

The restoration by *Wales, Wales & Rawson* has preserved the work of successive generations, and new openings are distinguished by straight-pointed arches. This motif is repeated in the houses and flats of 1989–91 imaginatively designed by *Jane Darbyshire Associates* to complement but not copy the medieval fabric; they lie N of the church site. The buildings of the 1990s to the E are less successful in their attempt to compromise between the medieval building and the C 19 warehouses they replace.

THE CASTLE AND TOWN WALL

Owing to the ruthlessness of the Victorian railway company, Newcastle's chief medieval monument, from which the town derives its name, can be appreciated as a castle only with effort. All there is to a significant height is a late C 12 keep, a mid-C 13 gatehouse (the Black Gate), and the S postern with much of the S curtain wall, cut about by the railway lines with their curtain of stone and steel.

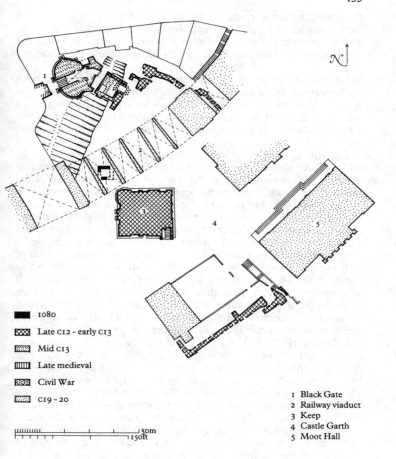

1080
Late C12 - early C13
Mid C13
Late medieval
Civil War
C19 - 20

50m
150ft

1 Black Gate
2 Railway viaduct
3 Keep
4 Castle Garth
5 Moot Hall

Newcastle upon Tyne, the Castle

The ROMAN FORT of *Pons Aelius* lies under the Castle Garth. It
faced N, away from the bridge it guarded and from which it took its
name. The N defences are likely to have been close to the Black
Gate, overlooking the steep slopes down to The Side; the river-cliff
dictated the limit on the S. The fort, known only from excavation,
was built in stone no earlier than the late C2. The W portion of the
central headquarters building, including the regimental shrine in
the middle of the rear range, is outlined in setts immediately W of
the keep (which overlies the E side of the Roman building). Also
marked out is a fragment of the commanding officer's house to the
W and, below the railway arch, part of the W granary with its heavy
buttresses and the sleeper walls supporting the floor.

Symeon of Durham wrote that the New Castle was built by
Robert, William the Conqueror's eldest son, in 1080. It overlooked

the lowest bridging point on the river. One must try to visualize Newcastle as one can visualize Norham or Dunstanburgh. The Black Gate is at the N apex of a roughly triangular shape which has surviving curtain wall on the S. S of this the bank falls steeply to the river.

Of the first Norman castle, there is now only a spread of clay, with the lowest courses of a small rectangular stone building embedded in it at the NW, the base of which can now be seen under the second arch from the W of the railway viaduct. No evidence survives of any structure above this level, nor indeed of the original surface of the clay.

35   Refortification from 1168 to 1178, under Henry II, cost £1,144, and was completed in the reign of John. This included the building of the surviving stone keep in the NW part of the castle, and of the North Gate, of which fragments survive. This gate was inserted into an earth rampart. On the NW side there was a ditch, and some 7 metres (23 ft) back from this there was the small stone building already referred to. Inside the ditch there was probably a ring-bank, upon which the curtain wall seems to have been built after the North Gate had already been constructed. All evidence of this stretch of wall has been removed by later levelling. Other survivals from this period include the S curtain wall, which can still be seen in a stretch of Norman masonry with the Norman (tunnel-vaulted) postern gate. On the N and NE there was a steep bank. Excavations in 1906 revealed the E curtain and the plan of the Moot Hall E of the keep, which stood alongside the roadway from the gate (underneath the old County Hall), and which had circular piers in an aisled nave, and pointed arches in its N wall. The North Gate was superseded when a barbican, with what is now known as the Black Gate (*see* below), was added to the defences by Henry III between 1247 and 1250. It was built into the NW of the former North Gate, with a bridge-pit between the two; alongside the bridge-pit was an ashlar-lined pit, the Heron Pit, with a garderobe in the building above it.

When the Town Wall (*see* below) was built in the late C 13, the castle lay well inside it. The castle ditch became a town dump and the fabric of the buildings was then allowed to decay, though some repairs were made to a curtain wall in the C 14. In the C 17 two storeys were added to the Black Gate, and a bastion was constructed beside the keep, thereby preserving the small early Norman building. From then on more and more was built within the castle area, which became a refuge for those wishing to live outside the jurisdiction of the town authorities; by the C 19, the ancient buildings had fallen into decay. This decline was halted as antiquarian interest increased. In 1809 Newcastle Corporation bought the keep and gave it a roof and battlements, so that when the Moot Hall (*see* Public Buildings, below) was opened the new road to the courts led past a presentable building and not a crumbling ruin. In the mid-C 19, the railway viaduct was built across the site, between the Black Gate and the keep, and it was doubled in width in the 1890s. In 1847 considerable restoration was carried out by *John Dobson*; the Society of Antiquaries of Newcastle then leased the keep from the Corporation. Because of late C 20 excavation and restoration of the land around the keep, the railway now appears more like an overlay than an incursion.

The KEEP is a late example of keep design and in its details typical 35
of the latest phase of the Norman style. It is roughly square, 19
by 17 metres (62 by 56 ft), with slight square projections at three
angles and a bigger, irregularly polygonal one at the fourth (NW).
The battlements are all early C 19 restoration, yet in conjunction
with the broad areas of golden sandstone they determine one's
memory of the Newcastle keep. The keep preserved its forebuilding, an element often not surviving (cf. the White Tower,
London, and Castle Hedingham in Essex). At Newcastle it is
particularly elaborate and ingenious, and it contains a staircase
straight up to the second, not the first, upper floor. This feature
recurs at Dover and at Dover only, a fact of considerable biographical interest, because in the Pipe Rolls for 1174–5 *Mauricius
Caementarius* receives 20 shillings for work on the keep, while in
1181–2 and later *Mauricius Ingeniator* (i.e. engineer) is paid in
connection with the keep at Dover.

Each floor of the keep has one principal room with small rooms
off it set in the thickness of the walls. Stairs, garderobes, a well
room and galleries are also contained within the thickness of the
walls. On the GROUND FLOOR are two distinct sections, originally
unconnected: the chapel and the principal room known as the
'garrison room'. The chapel takes up the narrow space in the
forebuilding below the upper parts of the staircase and was entered
only from the outside until an entrance was broken through from
a barrel-vaulted chamber beside it. This chamber and the larger
room were accessible only from above, by a spiral stair in the SW
corner, although now they are also reached from a comparatively
modern doorway in the S wall. The main room, popularly called
the GARRISON ROOM, is rectangular, with a circular central pier
which has a many-scalloped capital. From this pier eight heavy
single-chamfered ribs radiate to the corners and the middle of the
sides – a conception clearly heralding the chapterhouses of the
C 13. The CHAPEL has a two-bay nave and, at the N end, set at
right angles to it so that the altar was at the E, a one-bay chancel
with a small W recess. The ribs of the oblong nave bays and nearly
square chancel are decorated with chevron moulding in one bay,
chains of beads in the others, and rest on corbels as if not originally
planned. The nave is divided from the chancel by an arch on plain
responds, but the two nave bays are separated from one another
by an arch with a chevron frieze. The short W annexe is the barrel-
vaulted chamber already mentioned.

The FIRST FLOOR consists of the middle part of the outer
staircase, with a doorway with one order of (decayed) colonnettes,
and a hall and smaller chambers in the body of the keep. One
small passage from the SE spiral stair led to the hall and another
to a small barrel-vaulted chamber to W of it. Modern doorways
have been broken through from this chamber to the hall at one
side and the external stair at the other, creating a quite different
pattern of access. The hall is divided into two parts by means
of a circular pier with plain octagonal capital and two single-
chamfered arches. Off its N side, in the thickness of the wall, is
the QUEEN'S CHAMBER. The small room off to the E was for
observing the outer stair. When the external staircase reaches the
SECOND or HALL FLOOR, steps to the l. lead from the landing

to the main entrance. To the N, at the head of the staircase, is a room decorated with restored chevron moulding; it has been suggested that this room was a chapel (cf. a room in a similar position at Dover). The hall door, restored in 1847 by *Dobson*, is unusually ornate, with an order of columns and voussoirs with lozenge and nail-head decoration. The lozenge frieze is placed at r. angles to the wall. To the S a little higher up is a shafted window in a broad shallow buttress projection. The middle buttresses on the N and S sides are narrower, that on the W side, where the C 19 hall fireplace and its flue are, much broader. The hall is not subdivided. To its S, in the thickness of the wall, is a chamber some 6.7 by 2.4 metres (22 by 8 ft), perhaps identifiable as the KING'S CHAMBER. To the NE is a smaller room, the WELL ROOM. At this level a straight stair opens off the SE spiral stair and goes along the E wall, passing through the window opening and so allowing a view down into the Great Hall. It leads to a NE spiral stair. The spirals lead first to a high wall-passage which has openings looking down into the hall from all four sides, and above that to the doors to the roof. The ROOF PLATFORM, and the NW corner turret on it, date from *c.* 1811.

35 The BLACK GATE dates from 1247 onwards. It is a fortification of the new improved C 13 type, allowing flanking fire, and is, as has been said, a barbican gate, set well forward from the main gate behind it. It is roughly oval in shape, i.e. a gateway between two semicircular rib-vaulted guardrooms. The gateway is in three parts, an outer with a portcullis, a middle with a gate, and then a vaulted inner part. In front was a drawbridge; the slots in which the counter-weights swung can be seen below the roadway, sharp-edged sandstone ashlar piers forming three slots 4 metres (13 ft) long by 4 metres deep. There is a 4.3-metre (14-ft) space between them and the opposite abutment. Behind was another turning bridge, possibly of bascule type, since the pit walls are not sub-stantial enough for a tower. This pit is 3.3 metres (11 ft) in length and depth. On top of the two lower floors of the Black Gate a brick house with mullioned-and-transomed windows was erected after 1618, and it is this which makes the building picturesque and lovable. The clearance of old property in 1855 to make a road to the High Level Bridge caused the building to emerge from the huddle of houses which had surrounded it. Strong local opinion prevented not only its demolition but also the erecting of any other building which 'would destroy one of the most picturesque combinations of medieval architecture existing in any English city'. After much campaigning it was restored and a new staircase built to replace the *ad hoc* arrangements of the many families who had lived in it until then. Much original detail survives, notably in the guardrooms with their ribbed vaults; the restoration was carried out with great skill by *R. J. Johnson*. It now houses the library of the Society of Antiquaries of Newcastle.*

Within the CASTLE GARTH, the Moot Hall and the former County Hall (*see* Public Buildings, below).

* The archaeological contents of the Society's museum which was established there in the C 19 have been transferred to the Joint Museum of Antiquities in the Department of Archaeology of the University.

TOWN WALL. Newcastle began to receive its wall in the time of
Henry III. Murage was first granted in 1265. In 1280 the Dominicans obtained permission to make a postern gate through the
wall, and in 1290 the Hospital of St Mary the Virgin in Westgate
obtained a similar privilege. So the wall existed by then at those
W points. Building began on the N, and carried on round E and
W sides of the town simultaneously, not enclosing all buildings
but protecting most of the town. Then at both sides the line
changed. The W part, which had been curving in as if towards the
castle, turned sharply S to the river; at the E, the line was thrown
further out in a great curve, enclosing Pandon, which was granted
to Newcastle in 1298. Much strengthening went on in the time of
Edward III; and c. 1540 Leland could still say that the 'strength
and magnificence' of the walling of Newcastle 'far passith all the
waulls of the cities of England and most of the cities of Europe'.
In spite of widespread destruction in the C 18 and C 19, there is
still more in existence than in any other English town except for
Chester, Chichester, Southampton and York.

The wall was 2.13–3.04 metres (7–10 ft) thick and 6.09–9.14
metres (20–30 ft) high, including the parapet and merlons protecting the wall-walk. There were six principal gates, other less
important gates and posterns, and seventeen towers. The towers
were semicircular projections from the line of the wall, with three
loopholes; between the towers extra shelter was provided by
turrets flush with the external face of the wall and corbelled out
from the wall-walk on the inner face. A lane ran along the inner
side of the wall, and a ditch along the outside. The Dominicans
were given permission to build a wooden bridge over the ditch in
1312.

Of all this structure there can now be seen whole stretches of 54
the W part of the wall, individual features of the E, and part of
the lane, sometimes with and sometimes without its wall. The
best stretch to see and understand the wall of Newcastle is from
the junction of Newgate Street and Percy Street (where the New
Gate stood) to the W and then the S. A stretch of wall appears on
the N side of St Andrew's Churchyard. Then West Walls run in
a SW direction from EVER TOWER, which has survived up to the
deep splays of the arrow slits. MORDEN TOWER has a picturesque upper storey put on c. 1700 by the Company of Plum-
bers, Glaziers and Pewterers. The turret SW of here is the best-
preserved of all the turrets. It shows the passageway and external
stair to the roof platform. The tower to the SW, HEBER TOWER,
is almost intact, still with its pointed barrel vault, but had a large
window inserted by the Company of Armourers, Curriers and
Feltmakers when they restored it in 1770–1. Here the wall turns
SE. DURHAM TOWER is the best-preserved in this stretch, retaining its barrel vault. Next, in Westgate Road, came the West Gate,
which does not exist any longer. It had been greatly strengthened
by Edward III and provided with a big barbican. The wall carried
on to the SE, a line marked still by PINK LANE, where the site
of Gunner Tower can be seen, and diagonally across the site of
the Central Station, and then turned S. Of this part, a section
which stands intact up to the parapet can be seen between FORTH
STREET and HANOVER STREET. From White Friar Tower

(demolished) at the s end of this stretch on high ground it
descended steeply to the Close. This stretch, known as BREAK-
NECK STAIRS, can be seen but is not accessible to the public.
Close Gate has vanished, but the short piece of wall from it to the
river, and the lower courses of the riverside tower and a wall along
the shore, were revealed and recorded in the City of Newcastle's
excavation ahead of redevelopment. This, the Copthorne Hotel
by *Arup Associates* (*see* Perambulation 2a, below), has been
planned so that its piling straddles the medieval structure.

The line of the wall resumes at Sandhill, beside the medieval
bridging point, but there is very little to be seen in this E part and
none at all along the Quay. In Buck's engraving of 1745 (*see* pp.
408–9) the town wall is still there, running E from the Maison
Dieu on the s side of Sandhill, cutting Sandhill off from the river
and continuing along the Quayside as far as Sandgate, the gate
across the road at the E end of the Quayside. From here it turns
northwards, enclosing the vill of Pandon. It can be imagined along
the w side of Milk Market and climbing to the Wall Knoll,
crowned by the WALLKNOLL or SALLYPORT TOWER, which
became the meeting hall of the Ships' Carpenters' Company in
1716. They then built their superb, bold hall above the minor
gateway, in such confident style that comparisons have been
drawn with the work of Vanbrugh. No architect for it has yet been
identified. It is ashlar, with pilasters and big eaves cornice; two
windows in each long side in rusticated keyed round-headed
surrounds, another in the short side to the w. On the E, steps lead
to the hall door, which is set under a round overlight in a rusticated
corniced panel; above the cornice is a carved relief of a ship's
hull – proclaiming the trade of the company. But the most striking
feature is the assemblage of turrets on the corners, cubes with
small round-headed openings (blocked) and with ball finials on
stone pyramid copings.

From this tower the wall dipped westwards, crossing the deep
gulley of the Pandon Burn. A short section of the next part could
still be seen in 1990, revealed by the demolition of C 19 buildings
and in the shadow of the retaining wall of City Road. It climbed
to the Corner Tower, where two turrets joined to guard the right-
angled turn created by the change of line to enclose Pandon.
Excavation in 1978 showed that the s buttress here was just that,
and not a continuation southwards which had been superseded
by the change in the boundary of Newcastle.

From here the line runs N to New Bridge Street, and w again
as far as Newgate Street. The only section remaining in all of
this is another tower – PLUMMER TOWER, remodelled by the
Company of Masons as a meeting hall in 1740. The refinement
which had taken place in the twenty-five years or so since the
Ships' Carpenters built their hall is evident. This is Palladian,
with none of the bold gestures of the other tower, but a fit
showpiece for the expert skills of its builders. On the medieval
tower base, its plan semicircular on the outer face, they built the
two-storey hall in local sandstone, with a gently curved roof. The
flat front to Plummer Street has keyed architrave surrounds to
the door and windows in the rusticated ground floor. Above this
strong base is the sharp contrast, almost *chiaroscuro*, of smooth

stone not finely enough jointed to be called true ashlar, setting off the prominent surround of a grand Venetian window, with full Doric order with plinth and cornices, flanked by pilasters set in from the corners and supporting a deeply modelled eaves cornice. The round head of the window has bold rustication; the sashes still have their original glazing bars.

Beyond this were Carliol Tower, demolished when the C 19 Central Library was built, Pilgrim Street Gate across Pilgrim Street, demolished in 1810 to allow traffic to flow more freely, and a further stretch of wall with towers, all lost under the buildings on the S side of Blackett Street. And so Newgate is reached and the circuit of the walls is complete. Almost all of medieval Newcastle lay S of this line; what lay to the N were the suburbs which are now Percy Street and Northumberland Street.

PUBLIC BUILDINGS

Former COUNTY HALL, N of the Moot Hall. The headquarters of Northumberland County Council until 1974; it remained empty until 1988, and in 1991 is in the process of conversion into an hotel. The nucleus is of 1910 by *J. A. Bain*. This was extended and raised in 1929–34 by *Cackett, Burns Dick & Mackellar*. They extended it to the rear and E, carrying the building down four storeys to reach The Side, making eleven storeys on the E front. Bain's restrained classicism echoes the Moot Hall opposite. The later work picks up Bain's theme but not in any slavish way, and, with shallow pilasters and prominent cornices below the stepped-back top floors, solves the problems of the site's change of levels impressively. The tiled stair wells carry the Northumberland arms. In the former council chamber, a good inlaid hardwood panelled dado, and, originally, fretwork grilles with silhouettes of birds and animals. Outside, the iron railings to The Side are among the best in the city.

CIVIC CENTRE, Barras Bridge. 1960–8 by *George Kenyon*, City 126 Architect. A lavish building which vigorously expresses both civic pride and the council's spiritual, as well as actual, move away from the old centre of the town. It is clad in Portland stone, mostly Whitbed, but with the more heavily pitted Roach Bed on the banqueting hall, and has much specially commissioned decorative detail. It is planned in monastic fashion, with four ranges round a green space and a high round council chamber off to one side like a chapterhouse. The similarity ends with the plan; the N range of offices is ten storeys high, the others only three. A louvered turret sits over the lift shaft at the E end of the highest block. It has thin vertical fins topped by seahorses' heads (supporters of the Newcastle arms) by *J. R. M. McCheyne*, and, high above, the three golden castles of the City's arms. The ceremonial part of the building lies along the W side. The banqueting hall projects N of the council chamber. Hall and chamber are formed from great vertical masses of stone, the hall with long recessed slit windows, the chamber a drum with deep vertical grooves, raised on slender piers arranged to form a *porte cochère* to the ceremonial entrance and Grand Stair Hall. Cast-aluminium

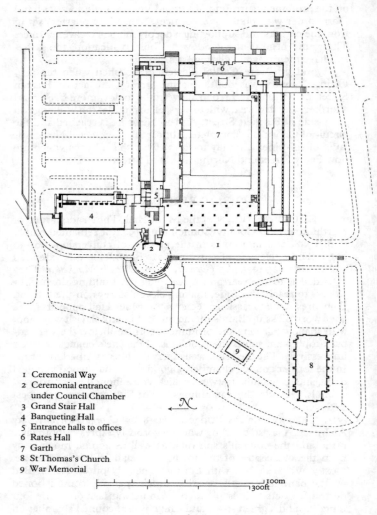

1 Ceremonial Way
2 Ceremonial entrance
   under Council Chamber
3 Grand Stair Hall
4 Banqueting Hall
5 Entrance halls to offices
6 Rates Hall
7 Garth
8 St Thomas's Church
9 War Memorial

Newcastle upon Tyne, Civic Centre

entrance PORTALS and reveals by *Geoffrey Clarke*. GLASS
SCREENS in the Grand Stair Hall engraved by *John Hutton* with
images of local history from the time of the Romans to the C 19.
The w range is also on *pilotis*, with the high windows of committee
rooms above looking out over the Ceremonial Way towards the
trees of St Thomas' Green. Between the *pilotis*, sliding sculptured
metal SCREENS by *Charles E. Sansbury* (who also designed the
FLAMBEAUX along the Ceremonial Way). When open these
screens reveal a view of a long pond with a SCULPTURE of swans

in flight by *David Wynne*, who also created the Tyne River God FOUNTAIN, suspended from the wall facing the approach. The watery theme is continued by a moat, lined with granite setts (once familiar in Newcastle's streets); it curves round the W side of the council chamber.

The three office wings are plainer, although in the high N range Cornish granite and Broughton Moor spandrels soften the great mass of windows. The other elevations facing the central lawns are of warm brick. Windows are in bronze frames. Worth noting inside: the LIFT DOOR motifs in Blocks 1, 2 and 3 by *Sansbury*; cast-aluminium GRILLES, also by Sansbury, and a TAPESTRY by *John Piper* in the banqueting hall; a pendant LIGHT FITTING by *A. B. Read* in the stair hall; MURALS by *Elizabeth Wise* in the marriage suite and by *Victor Pasmore* in the rates hall. Throughout, there are INCISED INSCRIPTIONS by *David Dewey*. Italian marble is lavishly used, with a different colour lining the lift hall of each floor. Outside, the rates hall in the E range has Rosso Levanto marble spandrels on the side facing the green, and the window of the Grand Stair Hall reception area a white Sicilian marble plinth.

GUILDHALL, Sandhill. A complex building. The E end is chiefly a neo-Grecian remodelling of a medieval building, by *Dobson*, 1823–5; the main structure was built in 1655 by *Robert Trollope*, but was given a conventional classical N front in 1794–6 by *Stephenson* and *Newton*, and a classical S front in 1809 by *John and William Stokoe*. King John granted Newcastle Guild Merchant in 1216, and the first reference to a guildhall occurs in 1400. In 1425 Roger Thornton endowed the Hospital of St Catherine, soon to be known as the Maison Dieu, which he had built at the E end of the Guildhall. The town's accounts mention building the 'new house' in 1509. Grey, writing in 1639, said this was the place where the town's revenues were received, that it was above a weigh house and next to the Maison Dieu, and that the Merchant Venturers' court was above the Maison Dieu. This group of buildings can be seen in the bird's-eye view of the town drawn *c.* 1590. In 1655 the Town Council ordered a new town court to be built. *Robert Trollope*, a mason from York, won the contract and the work was finished by 1660. A property to the W of the existing town court was bought so that the new building could run E–W, and the present plan was thus established: the town's court E–W at the W, with the Merchant Venturers' Hall at the E end. Buck's view published in 1745 (*see* pp. 408–9) shows the river front with the Merchants' Court a crenellated tower and the Town Court Trollope's long hall with round turrets at each end. Trollope managed the junction between the old E and the new W with an ingenious stair tower facing Sandhill to link them. It had two flights of stairs set behind loggias, with fat turned balusters and classical arches except for the upper large pointed arch. Above this was an octagonal turret and spire if the illustration in Brand (1789) is to be believed; it shows classical loggia arches on square piers with imposts. Trollope's Town Court was more classical in composition if not in detail, simply five bays and two storeys. The ground-level exchange and weigh house had an open arcade to Sandhill, with classical arches on rusticated square piers, and closed arches towards the river, where the windows were round-headed, apart from the principal pointed first-floor window, with balcony and wheel tracery (incorporating a sundial). Pilasters ended in picturesque spiral finials at the roof parapet. The N front (with a low attic storey) was broken at the second bay to the r. of the stairs by a much taller pointed arch with strange tracery; Gothic survival or revival? This arch can still be seen, without tracery, inside the building, as can two of the finials on the S side: the only reminders of what the exterior was like before it was classicized in 1796 (N front, by *Stephenson* and *Newton*) and 1809 (S front, by the *Stokoes*).

What we see today and now know collectively as the GUILD-HALL is the result of these alterations to the W part and the stair, and of alterations by *Dobson* in 1823–5 to the old Maison Dieu and Merchants' Court at the E end. To take the W PART first: in 1794–6 Stephenson and Newton removed the stair tower and rebuilt the entrance stair, using an unfluted giant Ionic Order with a pediment in a design closely resembling Newton's Assembly Rooms in Westgate Road, but with necking on the attached columns *à la* Adam. W of the stair, they refaced the Town Court, replacing the mullioned windows with sashes, encasing the internal ground-floor pillars in sandstone, and generally smoothing out all the rustication to make a more refined and more fashionable building. They also made a hipped roof out of Trollope's pitched one, and added a smaller hipped roof to the stair forebuilding. In 1807 it was decided that the S front should be similarly 'improved'; this was done in 1809 (according to Mackenzie, who was writing in 1827) by refronting, and making a newsroom by walling off part of the ground floor. This caused the removal of all Trollope's jolly tracery and pilasters, leaving only two finials.

The E END was partly also the town's (they had purchased the Maison Dieu in the C17), and partly the Merchant Venturers' (they had their hall on the first floor). It was all replaced in 1823 with one of *John Dobson's* first buildings in Newcastle. The plan is D-shaped, the style Greek Revival: a very satisfying solution, attractive from all angles and allowing better passage of men and goods from Quay to Sandhill. The FISH MARKET below has unfluted Greek Doric columns with the stumpy proportions dear to the French architects of the 1790s, supporting an entablature with triglyph frieze. On the first floor, sashes in architrave surrounds to offices adjoining the Merchant Venturers' Court; the roof is low-pitched and curved. The Merchant Venturers' Court was reconstructed by Dobson, with windows corresponding to those of the Town Court. The change to smoother masonry on the river front is still clear to see. Later in the C19 the Fish Market arcade was sensitively blocked, and the N front arcade less skilfully filled in.

Inside this classical shell, much of *Trollope's* building survives, especially the first-floor TOWN COURT with its double-hammerbeam roof (the ends altered for the hipped roof of 1796) and a small Tudor-arched window to a barred cell. The court fittings, which include balustrades and arcaded panelled benches and spiky railings to the dock, seem to be mostly mid-C18, with some early C 19 additions. On the N side, a high gallery (at attic-storey level) has rusticated pointed arches of suspiciously sharp detail, which may belong to the gallery Dobson put in in 1845. The rusticated wood balustrade between them is entirely convincing as Trollope's work and may have been reused. The blank wall below divides the court from the MAYOR'S PARLOUR, which is reached from the N side of the Court via a lobby. Here, in the outer wall, can be seen the pointed arch that survives from Trollope's N front (*see* above). Two C 17 doors with good panels and original hinges. That to the r. leads to the small room with the Tudor-arched window (*see* above); that to the l. to the Mayor's Parlour. This has rare (in Newcastle) and interesting decoration, mostly of the C 17: a chimneypiece with Corinthian pilasters and a high broken pediment bearing Newcastle's arms; a typical plaster ceiling with strapwork weaving round motifs of leaves and Tudor roses; and panelling with painting on the main panels said to have come from the Mansion House in the Close. They mostly depict old buildings in Newcastle. The MERCHANT VENTURERS' HALL, on the E side of the Town Court, is on a quite different and astonishing scale. This tall square space was entirely rebuilt in C 17 style by Dobson in 1823. He is said to have copied the original ceiling detail (the usual strapwork) but rather naughtily included a date 1620 – which has been the cause of confusion. The carved wooden chimneypiece he also copied, but incorporated the magnificent original OVERMANTEL dated 1636. It has two large 59 reliefs of the Miraculous Draught and the Judgement of Solomon, and small reliefs of *trionfi* above. The two figures on the sides are contemporary, but a C 20 addition. Also remarkable the eared doorpiece. The panelling is said to incorporate the original frieze. The STAIRCASE has an iron balustrade of late C 19 design, but on the inner wall of the first flight a round-headed niche contains a C 17 STATUE of Charles II in Roman tunic, without toga or mantle, from the gate on the old Tyne Bridge.

MOOT HALL (Crown Court), Castle Garth. Designed by *John Stokoe*, 1810–12, as Northumberland County Court and Prisons, but called the Moot Hall because it replaced the medieval one (*see* Castle, above). It is an early example of the confident use of the Greek Doric order, made even more striking by the high quality of the sandstone ashlar. Eleven bays, two storeys, the portico of four colums with pediment. In 1877 *W. Crozier*, Durham County Architect, blocked the S portico, inserted windows in blank bays, and extended the N steps from the court-yard across the full width, lessening the impact of the portico. This last alteration has been reversed in the recent restoration by the *Napper Collerton Partnership* (job architect *W. R. Foster*, who converted the building to a Crown Court *c.* 1984).

LAW COURTS, Quayside. 1984–90 by the *Napper Collerton Partnership*. Steel-framed and clad in red brick and red Dumfries sandstone, which introduces a new colour into the Quayside. The scale is entirely appropriate to this important site; as it emerges in the view from all approaches the building shows interesting diversity of detail. Large round windows echo the nautical associations of the Quayside at the sides and rear of the building, where they look over chares and warehouses. At the front the colossal

columns support a full-width gallery, curved and projecting, interrupted by a high wide lift tower. Windows in the mansard are
grouped above the glazed gallery, which itself has a rhythm
imposed by round columns. These rise above the colossal granite
order. Inside there are circular courtrooms, light and bright with
light oak panelling, and big uncluttered public spaces with an
excellent view of the river from the gallery.

CENTRAL POLICE STATION, MAGISTRATES' COURTS AND
FIRE STATION, Pilgrim Street and Market Street. 1931 by
Cackett, Burns Dick & Mackellar. Part of the redevelopment of
the approach to the New Tyne Bridge (the police station was the
third on this site since 1840). Portland stone, with recessed giant
columns on the upper floors characteristic of between-the-wars
architecture in the City of London.

CUSTOM HOUSE, Quayside. 1766; refronted in 1833 by *Sidney
Smirke*. A gracious ashlar-faced two-and-a-half-storey building
with arched windows on the ground floor, pedimented windows
on the first floor and the typical heavy doorpiece of the 1830s,
with Tuscan pilasters and big architrave; parapet with pilasters.

POST OFFICE, St Nicholas Street. 1871–4 by *James Williams*. A
splendid composition, with two superimposed giant orders –
Roman Doric for the porch *in antis*, Corinthian above. Between
the Corinthian pilasters, the second-floor windows have alternate
pediments, the central being segmental on Ionic pilasters.

CENTRAL LIBRARY, Princess Square. 1966–8 by *Sir Basil Spence,
Glover & Ferguson*. Five floors, the ground floor hidden from the
main entrance, which is at first-floor level from the raised deck of
Princess Square. This square and the footbridge network which
leads away from it eastwards were the first stage in the building
of what was to have been a solution to the problem of city traffic.
The walkways link major buildings at first-floor level. The library
has five floors running N–S, the lowest really a basement alongside
John Dobson Street and cut off visually from those above, which
are hidden by groups of concrete fins. Behind these fins the
windows are set back behind balconies, allowing light but not
glare to filter through. The building has not worn well; over twenty
years of northern rain have streaked the concrete with patchy
black and reduced the power of the good proportions and strong
lines. In sympathetic light it still looks what it is, a fine example
of the public architecture of its time. The interior has naturally
been rearranged to meet changing needs, losing much original
detail.

LAING ART GALLERY, Higham Place. By *Cackett & Burns Dick*,
the gift of Alexander Laing to the City of Newcastle in 1903–4,
and built as an addition to the Central Library of 1884, which was
demolished in 1968–9 to make way for John Dobson Street.
This street, ironically, now separates the gallery from the Central
Library of 1968 and also effectively from the town centre. Neo-
Baroque style with *art nouveau* elements. The entrance (E), on
Higham Place, is protected by *art nouveau* wrought-iron gates.
To the l., the corner with New Bridge Street is marked by a tower
with a rusticated ground floor, a tall blank second storey, and
a topmost stage with three-light window below a high-relief
frieze and an open octagonal lantern, culminating in a stone

ball-finialled dome. Opulent interior, with real and Frosterley marble.

BLANDFORD HOUSE (Science Museum, Tyne and Wear Museums Service and Archives Service), Blandford Square (formerly West Blandford Street). Built as a Co-operative Wholesale Society warehouse and offices by *Oliver, Leeson & Wood*, 1899. A striking symbol of commercial success. Bright red brick with sandstone and terracotta, and a Lakeland slate roof with copper domes. Fifteen bays long, four storeys high and two further setback storeys. The stylish entrance hall and directors' suite (now the Archives Department) were altered *c.* 1930 in Art Deco style, with marble stairs, a stained glass wheatsheaf in the landing window, walnut panelling, and glass-and-chrome light fittings. The gentlemen's toilets are the most amazing in the city, with blue tiles glowing like lapis-lazuli.

JOHN GEORGE JOICEY MUSEUM, City Road. The site of the Augustinian Friary, retained by Henry VIII for the use of his Council of the North when it was not sitting at York, and referred to as 'the King's Manor'. The Corporation of Newcastle acquired it in the C 17 and in 1681 built the HOLY JESUS HOSPITAL to house a master and thirty-nine poor freemen or poor freemen's widows. It is a building of honest character, one of only two 62 complete C 17 brick buildings to survive in Newcastle (the other is Alderman Fenwick's House in Pilgrim Street; *see* Perambulation 4a, below). Thirty brick arches on square pillars, the arches of moulded brick to give the impression of bulging rustication. The walls above have moulded strings and small horizontal three-light windows, on the first floor with alternated segmental and triangular pediments, on the second with flat brick arches. In the centre of the front, above the inscription with its carved frame, a segmental pediment on grotesque masks, a motif typical of the provincial northern later C 17, as the shaped gables are also. The l. gable was partly renewed when a soup kitchen was added as a parallel rear range in 1886. The original arrangement has been retained in the city's restoration of *c.* 1969, with little rooms opening off long corridors. There is also a fine central staircase. The carved lion finials from the newels are displayed in the C 20 successor to the C 17 building, the Mary Magdalene Hospital sheltered housing built on the W edge of the Town Moor, off Claremont Road.

The TOWER OF THE MANORS to the rear of the E end has often been misnamed Austin Friars' Tower but is probably mostly of the second half of the C 16, incorporating in its S side part of the N wall of the choir of the friary church. Excavation showed that the lower part of the W wall was a surviving fragment of the friary sacristy, but the other external walls could only have been built after the Dissolution. Inside, a fine medieval EFFIGY of a knight, found during excavation. In the S wall a pointed-arched window minus its tracery.

CITY HALL AND BATHS, Northumberland Road. 1928 by *C. Nicholas* and *J. E. Dixon Spain*. A dull neo-Georgian design in which the colonnaded entrance to the City Hall (a concert hall) is balanced by that to the baths.

ASSEMBLY ROOMS, Fenkle Street. 1774–6 by *William Newton*, paid 87 for by public subscription. The ashlar façade strongly resembles Newton's other Newcastle public building – the entrance to the Guildhall – which he designed with David Stephenson. A giant Ionic order supports the pediment over the projecting three-bay centre, all in very high-quality masonry: the sides are brick. The central door was blocked and double side doors under a canopy inserted in alterations of *c.* 1900. On the curved drive, good wrought-iron lampholders, replacements for the originals. Inside (now a club and banqueting hall), carved chimneypieces and doorcases, classical columns (some now masked) and pilasters, and delicate stucco ceiling decoration. The subscribers were very satisfied with this setting for balls and dinners, as well as with the newsroom, where the London papers could be read on the day they were published.

NEWCASTLE PLAYHOUSE AND GULBENKIAN STUDIO THEATRE. *See* University of Newcastle, below.

98 THEATRE ROYAL, Grey Street. 1836–7 by *John & Benjamin Green*. An essential element in the composition of Grey Street. The majestic portico has six Corinthian columns, the outer ones paired on tall heavily moulded plinths. In the pediment are the Royal Arms, carved by *Tate*. Otherwise the design accords with the rest of the street: Corinthian pilasters frame the outer bays, which project like pavilions and have top-floor windows in aedicule surrounds and top balustrades. After a fire in 1901, the entrance and interior were remodelled with his usual bravura by *Frank Matcham*, with stucco by *de Jong*. In a later remodelling (by *Renton Howard Wood Partnership* in 1987) Matcham's balconies and boxes were retained and a second staircase inserted.

TYNE THEATRE, Westgate Road. Built as a theatre and opera house in 1867 by *W. B. Parnell* for Joseph Cowen, but used after 1919 as The Stoll Tyneside's Talkies Theatre, as the painted gable proclaims. The Italianate front is of some interest and suggests an association with grand opera, but more miraculous is the C19 interior, which completely survives: three tiers of balconies and boxes, a shell-shaped ceiling (good acoustically), a high proscenium arch and – said to be the only such in the country – all its contemporary stage machinery. Skilfully restored in 1977–86 by the New Tyne Theatre Trust.

M.E.A. HOUSE, Ellison Place. By *Ryder & Yates*. Completed 1974, the first British building to be purpose-built to house a range of voluntary services. Height limitations (to accord with adjacent early C19 terraces) and the need to provide pedestrian decks and ramps and a road through the site were admirably met by hanging the main floors from four main girders set at roof level, with nine steel yokes slung across them acting as roof trusses. The main block is mirror-glass-clad, with three service towers. A long E ramp leads to the pedestrian deck system, and a wide W curve of brick envelops an auditorium. Structure gives character here. The building's juxtaposition with the C19 houses of Ellison Place is less happy, but on a good day a link is formed by the sharp reflections of the brick houses in the glass wall.

UNIVERSITY OF NEWCASTLE. On a site extending a half a mile W from the Haymarket and Barras Bridge, a miscellany of buildings has appeared since 1888, when the College of Physical

Science left its quarters at the bottom of Westgate Road, behind the Lit. and Phil., and moved into its new building on Lax's Gardens. The college had been founded in 1871 and was incorporated into the University of Durham in 1874. The building of 1888 was the first phase of a roughly four-sided group built by the college, which in 1904 was renamed Armstrong College in memory of Lord Armstrong, the local industrialist who had laid the foundation stone in 1887. The other college of Durham University in Newcastle at this time was the Newcastle School of Medicine and Surgery, founded in 1832 and incorporated into the University in 1870. It too occupied a building behind the Lit. and Phil. in the 1880s, and had to find new premises (the North Eastern Railway Company had bought the sites as part of the plans to double the main line). The College of Medicine moved to a new building on Northumberland Road (*see* Newcastle Polytechnic, below: Sutherland Building) and came to the Haymarket site only in 1937, when it joined with Armstrong College to become King's College in the University of Durham. By 1937 there were many more departments and buildings, and after the Second World War a master plan for the development of the site was drawn up by *W. B. Edwards*, the Professor of Architecture, and *Sir Howard Robertson*. In 1963 King's College became the University of Newcastle. The campus is now so extensive and the buildings so varied that a perambulation seems the most convenient way to describe them.

PERAMBULATION. We approach from the town centre. From the Haymarket, the most striking of all the University buildings is seen to the l., towering over Percy Street. This is the HERSCHEL BUILDING, by *Sir Basil Spence*, completed in 1962 for the Physics Department. The Lakeland slate-clad Curtis Auditorium fans out in a cantilever from its narrow end towards the Haymarket; behind it the end of the eight-storey block is faced in darker slate. The clean lines of the long elevations are set off by the recessed ground floor with dark piers and second floor with gleaming white piers. Set back behind the slits which define the parapet is a penthouse. On the forecourt of granite setts, a tall metal SCULPTURE by *Geoffrey Clarke*, 1962. In complete contrast, in ELDON PLACE, at the extreme E end of the Barras Bridge, a pair of modest brick houses used as offices, a sad fragment of what was once an entire terrace of modest early C 19 town houses. To the l. of them the GULBENKIAN STUDIO THEATRE and the NEWCASTLE PLAYHOUSE (University Theatre) of 1970 by *William Whitfield*, with a green roof of vigorous form strongly streaked by weather.

On the S side of King's Walk (the former College Road) are the PHYSICAL EDUCATION CENTRE, built in 1889 as the Grand Assembly Rooms and with a jolly, overdecorated façade, and the STUDENTS' UNION of 1924, by *Cackett, Burns Dick & Mackellar*, neo-Jacobean in red brick and Portland stone. At the back of the Union, a refectory and debating chamber (the latter straddling King's Road), added in 1960–4 by *William Whitfield*. With their strong shapes in exposed aggregate, granite and bronze mesh, they assert themselves in characteristic late C 20 fashion amongst their historicist neighbours. Enormous bronze lions, from the University's coat of arms, overlook the road from both sides of

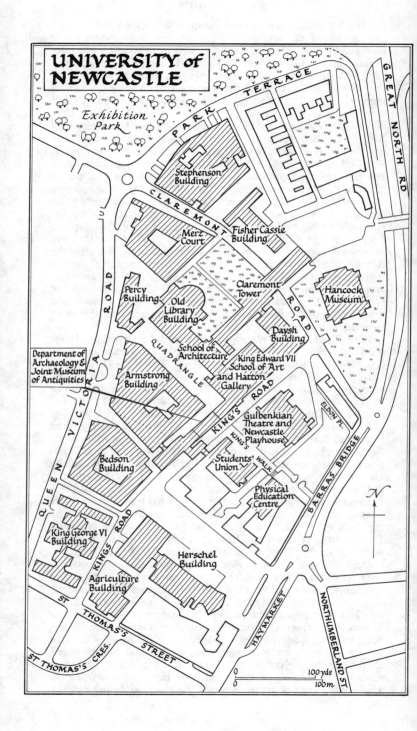

UNIVERSITY of NEWCASTLE

Exhibition Park

PARK TERRACE

GREAT NORTH RD

Stephenson Building

CLAREMONT

Merz Court

Fisher Cassie Building

Percy Building

Claremont Tower

Hancock Museum

Old Library Building

ROAD

Daysh Building

School of Architecture

VICTORIA ROAD

Department of Archaeology & Joint Museum of Antiquities

QUADRANGLE

King Edward VII School of Art and Hatton Gallery

Armstrong Building

KING'S ROAD

ELDON PL.

Gulbenkian Theatre and Newcastle Playhouse

KING'S

Bedson Building

Students' Union

KING'S WALK

BARRAS BRIDGE

Physical Education Centre

QUEEN VICTORIA ROAD

KINGS ROAD

King George VI Building

Herschel Building

HAYMARKET

NORTHUMBERLAND ST

Agriculture Building

ST THOMAS'S STREET

ST THOMAS'S CRES.

N

0   100 yds
0   100m

the debating chamber. Behind the Herschel Building, on the w side of King's Road, are the red-brick blocks of the KING GEORGE VI BUILDING built for the medical school (1938–9 by *P. Clive Newcombe*) and raised in the 1950s. To the N of this is the BEDSON BUILDING (now School of Chemistry) by *W. B. Edwards & Partners*, 1949 and 1959, a simple modern design of four storeys, the top one recessed behind a canopy roof. S of the Herschel Building, and complementing it on a different axis, parallel to King's Road, the eight-storey AGRICULTURE BUILDING of 1964 (also by *W. B. Edwards & Partners*) thrusts a slate-clad auditorium towards the NW and draws the eye up to a spider-like greenhouse on the roof. Back N along King's Road, between the students' debating chamber and the arched gateway (known as The Arches) to the Quadrangle lies the DEPARTMENT OF ARCHAEOLOGY and the JOINT MUSEUM OF ANTIQUITIES,* a simple two-storey building of 1949 designed by *W. B. Edwards & Partners* for the Department of Physical Chemistry. It is entered from the Quadrangle.

Within the QUADRANGLE, the S side is formed by the buttressed ARMSTRONG BUILDING. This was the first range to be built, in 1887–8, by *R. J. Johnson*, who described the style, with large stone-mullioned windows and interesting detail, as 'early Jacobean English'. It is continued on the l. return by the E range of the 1890s with the gate to the courtyard in the JUBILEE TOWER. This exuberant block of 1890–4 was also designed by R. J. Johnson but executed by *F. W. Rich*. The tower (built with money remaining from the 1887 Town Moor Exhibition, which celebrated Queen Victoria's Jubilee) has a vaulted archway below a four-storey oriel, and octagonal corner turrets. Beside it the remarkably cheerful banded chimney of the boiler house (*c.* 1925). The w front to Queen Victoria Road was added in 1904–6 by *W. H. Knowles*, who revised Johnson's original design and incorporated another grand tower. The details owe more to Knowles than to Johnson. Within this N range, many delights, not least the KING'S HALL, with hammerbeam roof and minstrels' gallery, and several memorial plaques, some in the best *art nouveau* metalwork. Also on Queen Victoria Road, S of the Armstrong Building, the SCHOOL OF MINING, a distinguished Tudor building by *A. Dunbar Smith*, 1929.

Now back to THE ARCHES, which is part of the KING EDWARD VII SCHOOL OF ART (now the Fine Art Department), designed in 1911 by *W. H. Knowles*. J. B. Simpson of Bradley Hall (near Ryton, County Durham) gave £10,000 for it, so that wood, metal and craft design could be taught. Tudor-style in red brick, with a statue of Edward VII in a niche set in blind tracery over the paired arches, and large mullioned-and-transomed windows beneath the battlemented and pinnacled parapet. Within the Quadrangle on the NE side a wide flight of steps to the one-storey HATTON GALLERY in front of the teaching block. Both are entered via a doorway with paired Ionic columns carrying an open

* The collection of the Society of Antiquaries of Newcastle was transferred here from the Black Gate (*see* Castle, above). The displays concentrate on the Roman period and Hadrian's Wall but include artefacts from prehistoric and medieval Northumberland.

segmental pediment with the Royal Arms. Next to the School of Art, the former SCHOOL OF AGRICULTURE of 1913 (now part of the School of Architecture), also by *Knowles*, continues the historical theme with more mullions and transoms, and buttressed end bays with oriel windows. Next comes what was designed in 1922 as the SCHOOL OF BACTERIOLOGY (now also part of the School of Architecture) by *Knowles, Oliver & Leeson*. Attached to this, and completing the N range of the Quadrangle, is the OLD LIBRARY BUILDING (no longer a library), 1923–6 by *A. Dunbar Smith*, with diaper-patterned brick, high canted bay windows, and large hipped roof of plain tiles which breaks forward over the end bays – a strong simple building which continues the vernacular revival of the early years of the C 20. To the rear, a plain extension of 1949 supplemented by a full-height apse-like LIBRARY EXTENSION of 1959 by *Easton & Robertson, Cusdin, Preston & Smith*, part of the post-war master plan. It looks towards Claremont Road. The Quadrangle itself was planted in a low and gentle style as a War Memorial in 1947–9 to the design of *J. S. Allen*, Professor of Town and Country Planning. This W end is now closed by the PERCY BUILDING of 1958–9 by *W. B. Edwards & Partners*, which houses the Schools of English and Classics, including the Greek Museum. It was also part of the post-war master plan.

CLAREMONT ROAD lies beyond the rear of the Old Library. All along the S side of this block is post-war development, including additions to the Schools of Art and Architecture, by *Sheppard, Robson & Partners*. MERZ COURT, the DAYSH BUILDING and the CLAREMONT TOWER (all opened in 1968) rear sharp edges of alternate bands of brick and glass high over the lower link to the Art School. All in the same red brick, enlivened by the use of recessed external galleries and occasional breaks in the horizontal rhythm occasioned by the higher windows of taller laboratories. Despite good clean lines, these buildings lack character and, moreover, are spoilt by an unfortunate jumble of huts, notices and barriers round the plain and recessed ground floor. On the N side of Claremont Road, opposite the Old Library, is the STEPHENSON BUILDING, 1952 by *Edwards & Manby*, the first building of the master plan. Classical proportions, four storeys, with recessed central entrance framed by dark columns which contrast with the grey brick. The long curved W front has all the necessary vehicle entrances. Face to face with it is the FISHER CASSIE BUILDING of 1955, in similar style. At the E end of Claremont Road is the oldest building of this N group, the HANCOCK MUSEUM, 1878 by *John Wardle*, built for the Newcastle Natural History Society (now the Natural History Society of Northumbria). It is almost unbelievably Dobsonian for that date, with Dobson's beautiful ashlar, his Doric pilasters and heavy attic, and even the sans-serif capital letters of the pre-Victorian C 19. Facing it, on the E side of the road cutting, is the ROBINSON LIBRARY, completed in 1980–2, by *Faulkner Brown Hendy Watkinson Stonor*. Dark red brick, its proportions reflecting those of Carlton Terrace in Jesmond Road. Long slit windows set diagonally to filter the light.

NEWCASTLE POLYTECHNIC, E and SE of the Civic Centre. To be renamed (1992) the UNIVERSITY OF NORTHUMBRIA AT NEWCASTLE; the Polytechnic was founded in 1969 incorporating the Rutherford College of Technology. To its inherited buildings and others adapted to its needs, some bright new ones have been being added. Of the older buildings, most notable is the SUTHERLAND BUILDING on Northumberland Road and College Street, designed as the UNIVERSITY OF DURHAM MEDICAL SCHOOL in 1887 by *Dunn, Hansom & Dunn*. Late Gothic, of dark red brick and red terracotta with ashlar dressings. Entrance tower like a gatehouse, with barrel vault, stone benches, niches and oriel window. All windows with mullions and transoms; gargoyles below the battlemented parapets of the central and corner towers. Next to it the TRINITY BUILDING, which started life as Trinity Presbyterian Church (*see* Churches, above). The ELLISON BUILDING, the LIBRARY and the LIPMAN BUILDING, built for Rutherford College of Technology in the 1960s by *George Kenyon*, City Architect, were intended to be part of an educational precinct E and S of the Civic Centre, linked by walkways with the central shopping area.

NEWCASTLE COLLEGE: SCHOOL OF ART AND DESIGN, Rye Hill. 1987 by *George Oldham*, City Architect. A 'high-tech' building. Blue and grey tubes and glass, with internal balconies so that the central space is top-lit. Interesting STAINED GLASS in the gable by *Susan Bradbury* in a diagonal pattern of graduated colour.

Former DAME ALLEN'S SCHOOLS, College Street and Northumberland Road. Now the Careers Advice Centre of the City of Newcastle Education Department. 1882 by *R. J. Johnson*. In the Norman Shaw style, both his Chelsea and his Queen's Gate varieties. A charming building, far more than the sum of its parts, with fat Tuscan columns flanking the entrance under an Ipswich oriel, between ogee-hipped towers, thick-framed sash windows, and, in front, fine entrance piers, repeated at the smaller entrance to Northumberland Road, and linked by iron railings.

Former OUSEBURN SCHOOLS, Albion Row. 1893 by *F. W. Rich*. A lively, vigorous design by an architect who often surprises. Planned like a courtyard house, and with keyed arches, alternating block jambs, *œils-de-bœuf* and sashes with glazing bars. The whole C17–18 effect is emphasized by the swan-neck pediment in the central of the three shaped gables of the N range. On the S, three-storey entrance blocks ('BOYS' and 'GIRLS') which have steeply hipped roofs set against tall square towers. These overshadow all else, both literally and metaphorically, having ogee-hipped roofs surmounted by three tiers of eaves, octagonal except for the top, which is a high-pointed concave cone; lower and upper levels have hipped dormers. These roofs would not look out of place on an Eastern temple, and this striking group sited near the river makes a strong contribution to the townscape.

ROYAL GRAMMAR SCHOOL, Eskdale Terrace. 1907 by *Sir Edwin Cooper*. Friendly neo-early-Georgian. Brick with stone dressings. Not high; various ranges connected by colonnaded galleries. Central clock turret.

ROYAL VICTORIA INFIRMARY, Queen Victoria Road. 1900–6 by
W. L. Newcombe & Percy Adams. The most important building is
the Administration Block (although the Nightingale wards are
good examples of the pavilion plan). It is approached by a curved
drive, as if it were a large house. The quality of the architecture
and the internal decoration sustains that illusion as far as is
reasonably possible. The style is Baroque, the materials are bright
red brick, ashlar and soft grey-green slates from Borrowdale. A
porte cochère in the three-bay centre is balanced by pavilions at the
ends of the seventeen bays, and there are pediments over ends
and centre, the central segmental and the end ones carried on
pilasters. The high roof, hipped over the end bays, has attic
windows and a central lantern. Groined inner porch, then in the
hall and gallery inlaid panels, a stucco frieze, and a ceiling with
lavish floral decoration. The CHAPEL has a Greek cross plan with
central dome. Rich mosaics and stained-glass windows. – In the
children's wards, no fewer than 61 charming *Doulton* TILE PIC-
TURES, mostly nursery rhymes, with landscapes in a side room.
Signed by the artists *J. H. McLennan, William Ross* and *Margaret
E. Thompson*, and paid for by the Lady Mayoress and her friends. –
STATUE of Queen Victoria, on a terrace in the centre of the
garden. 1906 by *George Frampton*. The gift of Sir Riley Lord, says
an inscription. Larger than life; a wonderfully slim and graceful
figure, in flowing *art nouveau* style.

HOUSE OF RECOVERY, Bath Lane. Built in 1804 as a fever hospital,
in the restrained classical style then favoured for public buildings.
The local sandstone provides excellent ashlar. Two storeys high,
five bays wide, the central three slightly higher and projecting,
and originally with a pediment. Restored in 1988 for the North of
England Museums Service.

DENE CENTRE, Freeman Road. *See* under Heaton, below.

ARMSTRONG PARK, Jesmond Vale Lane. *See* Heaton.

ELSWICK PARK. *See* under Elswick, below.

EXHIBITION PARK, Claremont Road. A bite taken out of the Town
Moor to provide a site for the Royal Jubilee Exhibition of 1887.
Of the layout of that period all that survives is the BANDSTAND
at the E side, in the shadow of the urban motorway. Octagonal,
with scrolled iron balustrade, thin columns, and a big roof sweeping out from a little dome. The North East Coast Exhibition of
1929, for which the layout and most of the buildings were designed
by *W. & T. R. Milburn* of Sunderland, left rather more behind:
not only the well-known 'Exhibition Ale' but also a promenade
from the Claremont Road entrance to the lake, and, on the far
side of the lake, one of the buildings erected to display exhibits.
Most were meant to be temporary, but this, the Palace of Arts,
was steel-framed and clad in artificial stone for permanence and
the security of the valuable works of art displayed. It is now the
privately owned MILITARY VEHICLE MUSEUM, but was for
many years the Newcastle Museum of Science and Engineering,
a direct successor to the exhibition. It is typical of its time, its
style owing much to the classical, especially as interpreted in
European exhibitions, though its decoration was determined as
much by a scarcity of funds.

HEATON PARK, Heaton Park Road. *See* under Heaton, below.

JESMOND DENE PARK, Jesmond Road. *See* under Jesmond, below.

LEAZES PARK, Barrack Road. Part of the Castle Leazes, laid out as a public park in 1872 when the population of Newcastle was increasing rapidly.

GRAINGER MARKET, Grainger Street, Clayton Street, Nun Street and Nelson Street. The commercial hub of Grainger's scheme for his new commercial centre. To convince the Corporation of the value of his scheme, Grainger had to promise the building of a market to replace an existing one of 1808, which impeded the proposed line of Grey Street. The new building (attributed to *Dobson*) was opened in 1835 and fills a large area between four of the newly planned streets. The internal arrangments are very satisfactory: four long top-lit clerestory alleys from N to S, crossed by four arched passages from E to W. Much of the original detail, including original shopfronts with fish-scale cast-iron grilles above, still survives. At the W side, a very impressive larger hall, the Vegetable Market, with a roof of glass and latticed-steel arches which replaces the timber and glass one (of 95.5 by 17.5 metres, 313 by 57 ft) which burnt down in 1901. The external walls – forty-six bays on the long sides, thirty-four on the short ones – are very plain and articulated, like the rest of Grainger's scheme, with a classical order. In this case, Corinthian pilasters flank the entrance bays and the end pavilions.

Former FISH MARKET. *See* Perambulation 2a, below.

Former NEWCASTLE AND GATESHEAD GAS COMPANY OFFICES, Grainger Street, facing St John's Church. 1884–6 by *John Johnstone*. Exuberant use of French Renaissance style with an arcaded ground floor and a central two-storey oriel on each front. The curved oriels have balustraded parapets in front of elaborate three-stage pilastered gables, and are flanked by shallower projections below smaller pedimented gables. The corner is marked by a corbelled turret rising to a dome, topped by a cupola. All these verticals are balanced by banded rustication on what wall spaces remain, and panelled floor-level blocking courses in each storey's entablature.

CENTRAL STATION, Neville Street. Newcastle is unusual amongst major cities in the United Kingdom in having only one large mainline station, a situation encouraged by Richard Grainger, who as early as 1836, when several railway companies were planning to bring lines into Newcastle, argued for a 'Concentration of Termini'. The station was built between 1845 and 1850 for the York, Newcastle and Berwick Railway Company. The grandeur of *John Dobson*'s original design, in which coupled columns marked the bays and those of the portico supported giant seated figures, was diluted before construction began, probably because of the railway company's financial difficulties. Moreover, the North Eastern Railway Company, formed in 1854, decided to accommodate its offices in the building. The *porte cochère* was not executed until 1863, by *Prosser*. (The extensions of *c.* 1890 were by *W. Bell.*) The station is nevertheless a very fine, broad, single- 116 storeyed composition with its deep central *porte cochère* of seven arches, and angle pavilions at the ends. The windows and the openings of the *porte cochère* are arched. Emphasis by Doric pilasters, coupled at the angles of the pavilions and on the portico, and by heavy attics. Some of the detail is no longer of the purity of Dobson's earlier work. The pavilions have high plinths, attached Roman Doric columns and rusticated, hollow chamfered arches with mask keystones. Diocletian windows in the façade arches light the upper-level offices.

130   Behind the portico, three arches lead to an astonishing train shed, curved to a radius of 243 metres (800 ft) and with its longest platform 407 metres (1,335 ft); roofed in timber and glass on tied, curved, wrought-iron ribs, supported by plain, slender, cast-iron columns 7 metres (23 ft) high. The whole covers an area of c. 3 acres (1.2 hectares). The original roof has three segmental spans of 18.3 metres (60 ft), the central span springing from a slightly higher level than those which parallel it. In detail the main ribs are formed from curved, built-up I beams, fishplated together to give the full span. Except at the junction of the roof with the rear of the station offices, where every rib springs from pilasters set between the arcades, the ribs are supported on longitudinal, two-tier girders (hidden by simple wooden panelling), themselves supported on cast-iron columns located beneath every third rib. Every rib is tied across its ends with a wrought-iron rod, and a vertical wrought-iron hanger links the centre of the tie to the crown of the arch. This was the first train shed roof to be constructed in this way, a design which came to be much copied in modified form elsewhere. In his presidential address to the Northern Architectural Association in 1859 Dobson explained that he had perceived that curved, wrought-iron sections could easily be made by providing a rolling mill with bevelled rollers and that this innovation made his design a commercial possibility (at about the same time Richard Turner produced curved wrought-iron ribs for the Palm House at Kew, but these were fabricated straight and then bent over templates). The train shed was extended s in 1894 with less adventurous but still quite elegant arched roofs. Originally, station offices included stationmaster's room, a waiters' room and bedroom, a bar sitting room, a smoking room, booking facilities, and separate waiting, refreshment and washing rooms according to sex and class. A former REFRESHMENT ROOM has *Burmantoft* faience hidden behind a later disguise. The TICKET AND INFORMATION OFFICE by *British Rail Architects Department*, c. 1982, is unashamedly of the 1980s, with mirror glass and a steel frame that leaves the historic structure untouched.

At the E end of the station were the platforms built to accommodate the North Tyneside Loop of 1904, an electric line which linked Newcastle with its coastal dormitories, Tynemouth and Whitley Bay. The former ticket office linked the main station building with the STATION HOTEL, further E along Neville Street. *Dobson* was responsible for the earliest part of the building (ten bays, with architraves and pediments to the windows); it was extended in 1890. No expense was spared for the public rooms. Much of the *Burmantoft* faience remains, though painted over.

To the w, No. 1 NEVILLE STREET is very grand, in the best European tradition. It must have been built c. 1870, and uses again a combination of ashlar and cast and wrought iron to great effect, with a French-looking roof over the front range, which was at one time the Railway Auditor's Office. The former GOODS STATION building behind it, now housing the railway police etc., incorporates structural ironwork transferred from the former goods station on the other side of Forth Banks.

Integral with the station is the High Level Bridge (*see* below).

The RAILWAY VIADUCTS from the E end of the Central Station follow two great curves, one to the High Level Bridge, the other carrying the main line to Edinburgh. Engineering of great beauty. Particular attention must be paid to the amazingly high stone elliptical arch over the Side, with a second arch on the N side of 1894. The lines are also carried over the N approach to the High Level Bridge, but not at a great height, and so are supported by cast-iron arches with lattice spandrels. That on the S has the makers' plate '*Abbott & Co. Gateshead 1848*'.

OUSEBURN RAIL VIADUCT. 1869. Like its sister viaduct on the Newcastle and North Shields Railway at Willington (*see* Wallsend), this is a closely copied wrought-iron reconstruction of the original laminated timber viaduct constructed by *John Green* in 1837–9. Green pioneered the structural use of laminated timber in this country, both for bridges and roof trusses, using techniques which were later to be emulated by such as Locke, Vignoles and Brunel. The viaduct is 280 metres (918 ft) long, with four stone approach arches, including an accommodation arch over Stepney Road, and five main arches carrying the deck at a height of 33 metres (108 ft) above the stream. The reconstruction retained the original stone approaches and piers (which had been designed with possible reconstruction as a conventional viaduct in mind) and repeats the three arch ribs and openwork spandrel bracing of the original.

METRO SYSTEM. A rapid-transit electric system, based on the old North Tyneside Loop and its South Tyneside counterpart, which serves the built-up areas of the Tyneside conurbation. The Tyneside Metropolitan Railway Act received Royal Assent in 1973. Massive engineering works were involved: tunnelling under Newcastle for lines and stations, strengthening C19 viaducts and 41 kilometres of existing permanent way, building 12.8 kilometres of new track as well as new viaducts and stations. The first section was opened in 1981; an extension to Newcastle Airport (*see* Woolsington) opened in 1991. A report on possible extensions to Washington and Sunderland is expected in 1992.

Three local practices provided station designs, to guidelines from the consultant architects, *Faulkner Brown Hendy Watkinson Stonor*. An overall scheme using white vitreous enamel panels for internal surfaces and high-quality synthetic stone flooring has produced clean, uncluttered interiors. The external materials are chocolate brown and red bricks, ribbed concrete, tubular supports, and plastic-covered steel canopies for the 'bus-stop' suburban stations. The executive architects were: *L. J. Couves & Partners*, who designed the underground stations and those between Jesmond and Gateshead Stadium, and St James to Manors; *Waring & Netts Partnership*, Byker to Chillingham Road, including the Byker realignment, and Tyne Dock to South Shields; and *Ainsworth Spark Associates*, the four interchanges at Four Lane Ends, Regent Centre, Gateshead and Heworth, and

the lines from West Jesmond to Tynemouth and to the Airport.
An admirable achievement, in which warm materials and strong
design discipline are combined with an unusual degree of sensitivity to the character of individual sites.

The BYKER VIADUCT (consultant engineers *Ove Arup*) is especially
notable for its elegance. Parabolic reinforced-concrete trusses
carrying a curved deck across the Ouseburn, not far from the
earlier Ouseburn Rail Viaduct (*see* above).

BYKER BRIDGE, over the Ouseburn. The first road bridge to
link Newcastle with Byker at a high level. Opened in 1878 for
pedestrians, 1879 for road traffic. Built by a private company as
a toll bridge.

OUSEBURN BRIDGE. In the shadow of Byker Bridge and far below
it is an c 18 stone-arched hump-backed bridge. A pleasing urban
survival.

BRIDGES OVER THE TYNE

114 Newcastle developed as a guarded bridging point from Roman times
on. The Roman bridge, perhaps on the site of the present Swing
Bridge, was probably a wooden superstructure on stone piers. The
first complete stone bridge was built by 1175; like the famous London
Bridge, it had towers, houses, shops and workshops built on it,
more on the Bishop of Durham's half than on the Corporation of
Newcastle's. It was severely damaged in the great flood of November
1771, and a new nine-arched stone bridge was built in 1775–81 by
Robert Mylne, designer of the Blackfriars Bridge in London and
several bridges in Northumberland. It had to make way for the
Swing Bridge, which could allow larger and higher-masted vessels
than keels to navigate up river. A ribbed arch of the medieval bridge
remains under the roadway at the N end of the Swing Bridge.

The Newcastle bridges are here described in chronological order,
but those further up river at Scotswood are described from E to W.

HIGH LEVEL BRIDGE. 1845–9 by *Robert Stephenson*, with *T. E.
Harrison*, a superb example of Stephenson's use of materials
appropriate to their function. Its design followed at least nineteen
different proposals by such as Samuel Brown, Robert Stevenson,
John Green, John Dobson and I.K. Brunel, for both high and low
level bridges to augment a low level bridge built to the design of
Robert Mylne in 1781. The final impetus was the need to link the
railway from Darlington to Gateshead with the Newcastle and
Berwick railway, necessarily at high level. In 1845 the decision
was taken to build a combined road and rail bridge giving 120 ft
(36.5 metres) clearance above low water. In its overall length of
1,400 ft (425.6 metres) it approached the scale of Stephenson's
Britannia Tubular Bridge, but here long spans were not essential,
hence the design with six main spans of 125 ft (38 metres), with
smaller land arches. Masonry piers on massive timber piles (first
use of Nasmyth's steam hammer for piling) support the main
spans, each of which consists of four cast-iron ribs of I section
tied with wrought-iron chains; the rail deck above is supported
by cast-iron columns rising from the main ribs, while the road

deck is slung from the ribs by wrought-iron hangers encased in cast-iron box sections to match the columns above. The main ribs were cast by Hawks Crawshay of Gateshead. There have been few changes since the bridge opened, except for additional road suspension rods strengthening the structure to take tramcars in 1922.

TYNE SWING ROAD BRIDGE. 1868–76 by *W. G. Armstrong & Co.*, with the Tyne Improvement Commission. At the time of its opening, the largest such bridge in the world. A necessary development to allow for upriver navigation by sea-going vessels, but it required the removal of Mylne's nine-arched stone bridge of 1781. Armstrongs also constructed the superstructure, but the Commissioners were responsible for the foundations and abutments, a 592-ft (180-metre) temporary bridge aiding the work, which commenced in 1864 with the removal of the Mylne bridge. The wrought-iron superstructure, which is 281 ft (85.6 metres) long and weighs 1,450 tons, is supported centrally on cast-iron rollers and gives two 95-ft (29-metre) river openings. The whole is driven by the original Armstrong hydraulic engines, but in 1959 small electric pumps replaced the steam pumps which once raised the hydraulic accumulators to store the hydraulic energy. The bridge, which swings only rarely now, is controlled from the attractive cupola above the superstructure. All services, water, once gas and now electricity, are brought down the central pier of the High Level Bridge. Since it began life in 1876, nearly half a million ships have passed through.

KING EDWARD VII RAIL BRIDGE. 1902–6 by *Charles A. Harrison* for the North Eastern Railway, with Cleveland Bridge and Engineering Co. as contractors. The original plan was for two lattice girder spans with land approach arches until it was discovered – surprise, surprise – that old coal workings at both ends meant that most of the arches had to be abandoned. Consequently the bridge was built with four massive steel lattice girder spans carrying four rail tracks, each 28 ft (8.5 metres) deep and up to 300 ft (91 metres) long, supported on solid stone piers. It cost just over £500,000 and is very much a workaday design.

NEW TYNE ROAD BRIDGE. 1925–8, designed by *Mott, Hay & Anderson*, with *R. Burns Dick* as architect and Dorman Long of Middlesbrough as contractors. Newcastle's modern-day symbol was first proposed in 1921, to augment existing road and tram provision at high level and to provide a job creation scheme. The corporations of Newcastle and Gateshead, in anticipation of a 65 per cent government grant towards construction, obtained an Act of Parliament in 1924. Work commenced in 1925. Special construction techniques were needed, as the Tyne Improvement Commissioners insisted on full navigational clearance, both height and width, throughout the work and thereafter; they also claimed to be anxious to have the Swing Bridge removed and the High Level Bridge rebuilt with larger spans to make river traffic easier. The demand for full navigational clearance required a single-span bridge with level deck, and the designers came up with a reduced version of the bridge they had already designed for Sydney Harbour – a two-hinged steel arch of 531-ft (161.4-metre) span, with a suspended road deck at 84 ft (25.5 metres) above high water. Massive concrete foundations support abutments for the hinges, and the huge, Cornish-granite-faced pylons above, which are of minimal structural significance, were designed to house warehouses (never used as such) and goods and passenger lifts. The Newcastle approach road is carried on continuous steel girders supported by two pairs of octagonal steel columns, each pair being skewed to accommodate the existing street plan below. Cast-iron balustrades and lanterns by *MacFarlane & Co.* of Glasgow. The largest single-span bridge in Britain at the time of opening.

QUEEN ELIZABETH II METRO BRIDGE. 1976–80 by *W. A. Fairhurst & Partners* with Cementation Construction Ltd and Cleveland Bridge and Engineering Co. as contractors. A rather inelegant (but, at £4.9 million, presumably cheap) through-steel-truss construction with fabricated box chords. Three unequal spans with a total length of 360 metres (1,184 ft).

REDHEUGH ROAD BRIDGE. 1980–3 by *Mott, Hay & Anderson* in association with Tyne and Wear County Council and built by *Nuttall/HBM* to replace a steel truss bridge of 1897–1901. The most striking of the new Tyne bridges and a good example of modern medium-span bridge design. A post-tensioned concrete box construction with four traffic lanes and one footpath over three spans totalling 360 metres (1,184 ft) in length, the main span being 160 metres (526 ft), with a 353-metre (1,161-ft) approach viaduct on the N side. Internal ducts within the box sections carry gas, water, electricity and telephone services, with portholes in the box sections to prevent possible explosions; piers fluted to suggest lightness. Contract value was £15.35 million.

SCOTSWOOD ROAD BRIDGE. 1964–7 by *Mott, Hay & Anderson* and constructed by *Mitchell Construction/Dorman Long* to replace a suspension bridge of 1831 by John & Benjamin Green. A steel arch of 100.5-metre (330-ft) span with suspended box girder deck, the two arch ribs originally tied with wire cables which rapidly corroded and were replaced with tie-bars. A very lively bridge, which has regularly been repaired and modified since it opened; come back, John and Benjamin Green!

SCOTSWOOD RAIL BRIDGE. The present bridge, now disused, is the third on this site. The first, of 1839, by John Blackmore for the Newcastle and Carlisle Railway, a timber truss bridge on the skew with eleven spans each of 60 ft (18.2 metres); it burnt down in 1860 during a board of trade inspection. A temporary bridge which replaced it lasted until 1871, when the present bridge, with wrought-iron hog-back girders each of 127 ft (38.6 metres) on cast-iron cylinder piers, was opened.

BLAYDON ROAD BRIDGE. 1987–90, the most recent bridge over the Tyne; designed by *Bullen & Partners* and built by *Edmund Nuttall Ltd* for the Newcastle western bypass. The bridge is a twin, five-span, prestressed, post-tensioned, concrete box structure 330 metres (1,086 ft) long, the main arch being of 108-metre (355-ft) span; constructed using the balanced cantilever method. Paired elliptical-section piers of reinforced concrete on common cutwaters. Seventeen-span approach viaduct on the S side.

PERAMBULATIONS

1. The medieval market street – from Newgate to the Castle

This perambulation starts from the N end of Newgate Street, the
site of the New Gate in the town wall, and follows the route of
medieval travellers to markets, church and castle, i.e. down Newgate
Street, then Bigg Market, and through the triangle of the market
area formed by Groat Market and Cloth Market, with the church
as the third side. In the Middle Ages these rows of buildings were
interrupted only by narrow lanes leading to the other main streets
of the town. In the last two centuries breaches have been made by
Clayton Street, Grainger Street, Mosley Street and Collingwood
Street.

The New Gate has gone, but in ST ANDREW'S CHURCHYARD,
to the N of the church (for which, *see* above), is a section of the
town wall with the corbels of a turret. Part of it is embedded in a
block of shops and offices which was built facing GALLOWGATE
in 1898–9 by *Oliver & Leeson* in free Baroque style, with a striking
corner turret and, at the rear and overlooking the churchyard, a
big roof with tiers of the cheerful little steeply roofed dormers
associated with the town halls of the Low Countries. On the other,
S side of Gallowgate is the former G.E.C. BUILDING, *c.* 1930
(originally called Magnet House), with the same terracotta motifs
of strong diagonal composition, showing men at work, that were
used inside G.G. Scott's Battersea Power Station to express
power generation. The large office block to the l. is WELLBAR
HOUSE, the first high-rise office block in Newcastle, a speculative
development of 1961 designed by *Williamson, Faulkner Brown &
Partners*. Twelve storeys on a wide two-storey podium; exposed
aggregate concrete panels, black concrete verticals, white mosaic
panels below the long strips of windows. From here one can
glimpse, further up Gallowgate, another high-rise, the SCOT-
TISH & NEWCASTLE BREWERIES offices, by the company architect, *C. P. Wakefield-Brown*, more interesting than most of its kind
because it curves gently. Now back to St Andrew's, where the

NEWCASTLE UPON TYNE
INNER CITY AREA

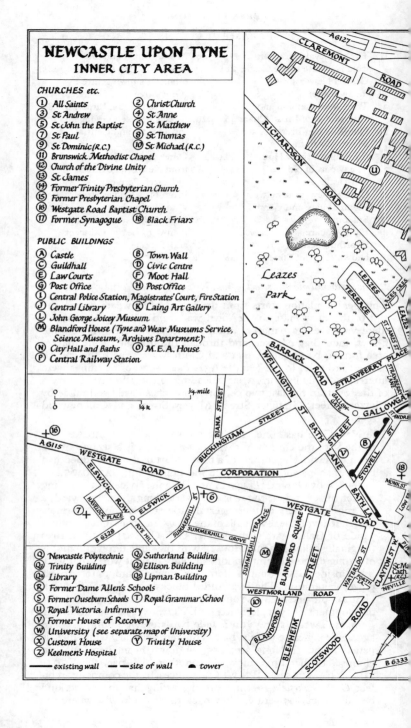

CHURCHES etc.

① All Saints
② Christ Church
③ St Andrew
④ St Anne
⑤ St John the Baptist
⑥ St Matthew
⑦ St Paul
⑧ St Thomas
⑨ St Dominic (R.C.)
⑩ St Michael (R.C.)
⑪ Brunswick Methodist Chapel
⑫ Church of the Divine Unity
⑬ St James
⑭ Former Trinity Presbyterian Church
⑮ Former Presbyterian Chapel
⑯ Westgate Road Baptist Church
⑰ Former Synagogue
⑱ Black Friars

PUBLIC BUILDINGS

Ⓐ Castle
Ⓑ Town Wall
Ⓒ Guildhall
Ⓓ Civic Centre
Ⓔ Law Courts
Ⓕ Moot Hall
Ⓖ Post Office
Ⓗ Post Office
Ⓘ Central Police Station, Magistrates' Court, Fire Station
Ⓙ Central Library
Ⓚ Laing Art Gallery
Ⓛ John George Joicey Museum
Ⓜ Blandford House (Tyne and Wear Museums Service, Science Museum, Archives Department)
Ⓝ City Hall and Baths
Ⓞ M.E.A. House
Ⓟ Central Railway Station

¼ mile
¼ k

Ⓠ Newcastle Polytechnic
Ⓠ₁ Sutherland Building
Ⓠ₂ Trinity Building
Ⓠ₃ Ellison Building
Ⓠ₄ Library
Ⓠ₅ Lipman Building
Ⓡ Former Dame Allen's Schools
Ⓢ Former Ouseburn Schools
Ⓣ Royal Grammar School
Ⓤ Royal Victoria Infirmary
Ⓥ Former House of Recovery
Ⓦ University (see separate map of University)
Ⓧ Custom House
Ⓨ Trinity House
Ⓩ Keelmen's Hospital

—— existing wall – – site of wall ▲ tower

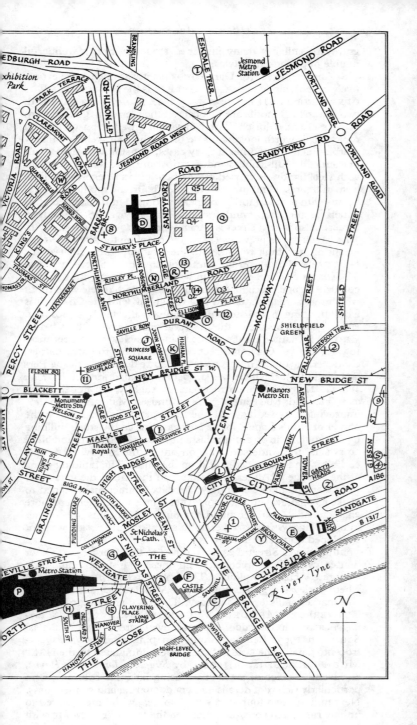

graveyard still has many inscribed stones *in situ*, a wonderful jumble of periods and styles.

s of St Andrew Street (or Darn Crook, as it was once more evocatively called), along NEWGATE STREET is the NEWCASTLE CO-OPERATIVE SOCIETY, 1931–2 by *L. G. Ekins*, a big store with two towers. All motifs are vertical, on the German 1920s pattern of Messel and Olbrich. The l. bays are an addition of 1959 in replica. It is worth looking inside to see the stair wells, originally marble-lined with corner display cases, but still with zigzag rails in front of the full-height window strips, and solid stair balustrades with steel handrails carried on the bent backs of expressive little human figures, climbing with their load. On the top floor several beams with a wave motif, originally also used in the stained glass panels of the shop windows (one bay survives in St Andrew Street). Also in that street is a fragment of a 1902 extension by *E. Shewbrooks* to the previous (1870s) 'Co-op' on the site. The 1959 extension was built to link with the contemporary, eight-storey NEWGATE HOUSE on the corner of Low Friar Street by *Edwin M. Lawson & Partners*. Curtain wall construction, with bands of colour, originally bright green and with a low-relief wave motif which was perhaps intended as a visual link with the Co-op. It is a dull building in dull surroundings much affected by 1960s road engineering. The site of the medieval market cross (the WHITE CROSS) is marked on the traffic island. As Newgate Street turns towards the SE, Clayton Street breaks in with a rounded corner, characteristic of all Grainger's town-centre development (*see* Perambulation 4); this part was probably designed for him by *John Wardle*. Then Newgate Street narrows slightly, but not so much as it once did; Mackenzie, in 1827, praised Major Anderson for improving it by setting back the frontage of his property on the corner of Nun's Lane. No. 22 Newgate Street, the stone building he put up then 'in an antique fashion', has cusped lights and blind cross slits, the Anderson arms on one of the narrow turret-like end bays, and an eroded shield on the other. The building stood at the W edge of Anderson's estate, on the site of the gatehouse to St Bartholomew's Nunnery: were its Gothicisms designed to evoke its medieval predecessor? After Nun's Lane, there are more characteristic Grainger buildings on the l. turning the corner into Grainger Street (*see* Perambulation 4c); the r. side was not developed until later in the C19.

Beyond Grainger Street the sweep down to the river begins. Older houses can still be recognized in these old streets, alongside elaborate Victorian buildings. The first stretch is BIGG MARKET, where barley (bigg) was sold in the Middle Ages and there are still market stalls every Tuesday, Thursday and Saturday. The RUTHERFORD MEMORIAL FOUNTAIN, 1894 by *Charles S. Errington*, stands in the middle; it was moved here from St Nicholas' Square in 1903. Red sandstone and pink granite with Quattrocento detail. The E side of the street is dominated by the HALF MOON CHAMBERS, of 1902–5 by *Simpson, Lawson & Rayne*, an inventive piece of *art nouveau* using fat Ionic columns, with particularly rich roof details and good lettering and stained glass. Next to it are two four-storey C18 houses, with lintels carved to imitate rusticated voussoirs, those on the top floor of No. 10 with the central stone jewelled; the gable of No. 8 has C 18 tumbled-in brickwork. Finally in this block, on the corner with High Bridge, is SUNLIGHT CHAMBERS (Nos. 2–4), built in 1901–2 by *W. & S. Owen* for Lever Bros. Tall and vigorous, with strongly rusticated windows and, above the ground floor, a broad mosaic frieze with images of harvest and industry. (High Bridge, off the E side, is worth a diversion to experience the dip in the road where the medieval bridge once crossed the Lort Burn and led to Pilgrim Street.) After that, Bigg Market appears to split into two, with Cloth Market the l. fork and Groat Market the r. one. In fact the street widens, but the central space of the medieval market triangle has been taken over by the more permanent successors of the market stalls. The timber-framed houses which were there in the C 19 were succeeded by a Town Hall, a distinguished classical building of 1858–63 by *John Johnstone*, which incorporated the Corn Exchange by *John & Benjamin Green*. This has given way in turn to a less distinguished office block of *c.* 1975, which has reduced GROAT MARKET architecturally to a mere service lane and, alas, means that the approach to the Cathedral of St Nicholas passes ugly vehicle entrances. Down PUDDING CHARE, a lane off to the SW, just before the fork, is a surprising C 18 building (Nos. 24 and 26). The two upper storeys are lit entirely by Venetian windows; they have imitation sashes with intersecting glazing bars which sadly lack the subtlety of the originals (removed in 1986). On the first floor the windows are in arched recesses. Below, C 19 shopfronts flank an archway to WILSON'S COURT, a reminder of the warren of yards and courts which once filled this neighbourhood.

On the corner of CLOTH MARKET, No. 54 was designed in 1902 by *J. Oswald & Sons* as the BEEHIVE INN, with a particularly successful corner turret and a ground-floor extravaganza in faience. Next downhill, the grey brick and ashlar Nos. 44–48, 1869 by *R. Fairbairn* for Pumphrey & Carrick Watson, still has its C 19 shopfronts. Fairly sober, but with a fine mansard roof, its central bay high and hipped, with iron crestings, Sobriety ends inside, where, in 1897, *Oliver & Leeson* fitted out coffee rooms in a distinctive version of Arts-and-Crafts style, with panels of Moorish fretwork, slatted seats with parcel racks above copper-covered tables, and a panelled stair well. The Oak Room was redecorated *c.* 1914. Beyond the wide arch between the shops is the OLD GEORGE, the last coaching inn to survive in Newcastle. The inn, on the l. of the yard, is a sequence of buildings, the oldest parts C 17 or earlier, with many alterations of the C 18 and early C 19. Mostly stucco-covered, with some mock timber-framing. Inside, a wide segmental fire-arch and much C 18 structural joinery. Nos. 14 and 16 Cloth Market is an important survival, perhaps medieval in origin, of the merchants' houses that once lined this street. On the ground floor, modern shops now flank the arch to the White Hart Yard, but above, although the original jetty has been cut back and brick-faced, the four-bay, two-storey front leans forward slightly and hints at the interesting interior. Against the rear wall on the first floor, two stone fireplaces with moulded double-curved corbels on chamfered jambs, the chamfers with convex broach-stops; these could be either medieval or late C 16. The big beams (also in the rear wing) and moulded joists, chamfered with well-cut run-offs, are of C 17 type. The main roof is of local type (cf. No. 35 the Close and Trinity House Rigging Loft, in Perambulation 2a and 2b). King-post construction, with mortices for longitudinal bracing to the ridge; sturdy tie-beams rest on curved braces. Further on, down the narrow alley behind No. 10, two houses can be seen if the gate is open. They are no later than the mid-C 18, one with thin box timber-framing and brick nogging, the other of brick with floor-strings. Both have wide-boxed sashes and the door overlights also have the wide glazing bars of the first half of the C 18. Just beyond is BALMBRA'S, rebuilt in 1902 by *A. Stockwell* in a simplified Baroque.

Now we return to the Bigg Market to start our walk down GROAT MARKET. On the r. there are two evidently C 18 buildings (No. 33 (much altered) and Nos. 35–7); *see* their lintels cut to imitate voussoirs. Halfway down the right-hand passage, there is a C 17 rubbed brick arch; and inside Nos. 35–7 there are early C 18 splat balusters in the upper flights of the staircase, and delicate Rococo plasterwork on a wall panel beside the stair and on the long first-floor ceiling, split by an inserted wall. Most of the rest of the block is taken up with THOMSON HOUSE, designed in the 1960s for the Thomson Press by *Cackett, Burns Dick & Mackellar*. Its front of Portland stone and dark grey mosaic is not very sympathetic to its surroundings, but the strong rhythm of well-defined floor levels and clear bay divisions was intended to echo the C 19 Town Hall, which then stood opposite, and, with it, to form a frame for the view of the medieval buildings beyond. Further downhill the medieval street is interrupted by Collingwood Street, which broke into the Groat Market in 1809, and by Mosley Street, which broke through Cloth Market *c.* 1787.

The best view of St Nicholas's Cathedral (*see* Cathedrals, above) is from the bottom of Groat Market, and it is worth pausing here to look at the tower and its steeple. In ST NICHOLAS' SQUARE is the QUEEN VICTORIA MONUMENT by *Alfred Gilbert*, unveiled in 1903, the gift of W. H. Stephenson to commemorate 500 years of the shrievalty of Newcastle. It is a modified version of Gilbert's Queen Victoria Jubilee Monument of 1888, now in Windsor Castle. The figure sits under a domical wrought-iron canopy; the ornamental detail shows all the sculptor's exuberant mannerisms. On the E side of the square, the fine palazzo-style office built *c.* 1850 for the Newcastle Joint Stock Bank. It has been attributed to *Benjamin Green*. Arched openings on the two lower floors, the upper ones with keyed surrounds; pediments over the second-floor windows. The top two floors are more heavily modelled, with giant Ionic columns, architrave window surrounds, panelled pilasters and a balcony on large brackets. The roof is particularly successful, low and hipped on an entablature with modillioned cornice.

Along the w side of the square runs ST NICHOLAS STREET, which was laid out *c.* 1851 to lead to the road deck of the High Level Bridge. REFUGE ASSURANCE HOUSE, on the s corner of Collingwood Street, was built for the BANK OF CHICAGO by *Mauchlen, Weightman & Elphick*, 1971–4. Smooth, unadorned ashlar cladding and full-height oriels acknowledge the cathedral. The Italianate mood of the E side of the square is seen again here in the General Post Office (see Public Buildings, above) and in the Venetian Renaissance buildings N and S of it. The S one, ST NICHOLAS' BUILDINGS, by the local architect *William Parnell*, is contemporary with the laying-out of the street. The same features occur on the corner building N of the Post Office. The main line to Edinburgh is carried over the street on a railway viaduct of two parallel iron arches (see Public Buildings: Central Station). The Castle lies off the E side of the street and must be investigated now (see Castle and Town Walls, above). Part of the medieval ditch is clearly visible in front of the Black Gate, and beyond the Black Gate is the Castle Garth with the keep, the Moot Hall and the former County Hall (for the last two, see Public Buildings). By the side of the High Level Bridge, the BRIDGE HOTEL, an attractive *art nouveau* public house of *c.*1899 by *Cackett, Burns Dick* for J. Fitzgerald. From here we can admire the engineering genius of *Robert Stephenson* at close quarters (see Public Buildings: Bridges over the Tyne). From the footpaths which cross the bridge, we can also appreciate the contrast between the medieval river crossing, among the crowded buildings on the narrow strip of flat land below, and the open approach to the town at a higher level which the bridge achieved.

The next perambulation leads down to those lower levels and to the long extent of Quayside to the E and the Close to the W that we can see from here in one sweep.

2a. Central Newcastle – the riverside: the Close, Sandhill and Quayside W of Broad Chare

Beginning at the Castle (see above), where the first perambulation ended, this circuit (2a–b) investigates what the C19 called 'the lower parts of the town'. Some energy must be saved for the climb back up at the end of 2b. From beside the Moot Hall (see Public Buildings), the CASTLE STAIRS descend. Like so many other stairs in the town, these are of hard-wearing Scottish granite. To the r. of the first landing there is a restored medieval WELL. From this level, the S curtain wall of the Castle can be seen. Beyond the postern arch, and before the next flight of steps, a footpath to the r. leads under the High Level Bridge (see above) and along to the Long Stairs, allowing glimpses of the rear of the properties in the Close. Particularly worth looking at here is the restored rear gable of Nos. 28–30 the Close, which will be examined later. Back at Castle Stairs, only one building survives of the many which used to stand on either side. The mid-C19 fluted cast-iron handrail supports are worth noticing.

The CLOSE starts at the bottom of steps. We turn r. and our route takes us to the W along it. Its width here makes nonsense of its name, but until the C19 tall merchants' houses faced each other across a very narrow passage. Then came the building of the High Level Bridge, followed by street widening, and the demolition of property on the S side. Now, one pier of the bridge stands isolated on a large roundabout and the bridge itself towers over what few houses remain. On the N side, Nos. 28–30 appears to be a plain

C 18 brick building with some C 19 ground-floor alterations. The
interior tells a different story. The ground floor (probably used
for commercial storage over a long period) is plain, with cast-iron
piers which were probably inserted in the early C 19. The single
fireplace, of uncertain date, is at the rear of the E part. Above this
the astonishing truth about the building is revealed: here we have
64   a late C 16–early C 17 merchant's house. What must have been
one long room has close-set plastered beams with Renaissance
decoration, in a style reminiscent of Scottish painted ceilings of
the C 16. The sides have quasi-classical mouldings, the soffits a
variety of repeated motifs, with pairs of herons, thistles, flowers
and arabesque patterns filling the surfaces. Like Nos. 41–44
Sandhill nearby (*see* below), the property belonged in the 1930s
to the Hon. S. R. G. P. Vereker, later seventh Viscount Gort, who
possibly inserted the first-floor Tudor-arched fireplace. *Simpson &
Brown* of Edinburgh are, in 1991, restoring the building for the
Tyne and Wear Building Preservation Trust. They have built a
rear wing, with upper-cruck roof trusses, to replace a C 17 stair
wing imported in the 1930s.

Next door, beyond the narrow gap of the Long Stairs, No. 32 (THE
COOPERAGE), a less sophisticated building, is also of more than
one period, the earliest part perhaps being C 15. The ground floor
is of large stone blocks; it supports a front-gabled timber frame,
with diagonal corner bracing and rendered infill in the two upper
floors, which are jettied at the front. On the r. return to the Long
Stairs, there is brick nogging, and here carpenters' marks of two
periods show that the frame has been altered at least once.
The front roof truss has curved principals tenoned into the tie-beam;
the internal trusses have similar principals, but some are truncated, with a collar at the apex. C 18 engravings show that many
buildings in the Close had access to the river; they were the storage
and business premises of wealthy merchants. No. 35, a group of
buildings (now a restaurant) enclosing a yard, is the only remaining example of this type of property. The street fronts of No. 35
again do not promise very much; they date from the C 19 widening
of the Close. A walk around the l. side towards the river frontage
reveals more – a timber-framed gable, and an apparently C 18
range facing the river, which until the building of a riverside walk
in 1984 stood right on the river's edge. In the yard the E range is
of two builds, in stone and brick; its most interesting feature is
the C 16 roof, with king-posts, set into arched tie-beams and
supporting a ridge which is set square in the side of jowls in the
king-posts and braced lengthwise. This is a local type also found
in Nos. 14 and 16 Cloth Market (*see* Perambulation 1) and in the
Trinity House Rigging Loft (*see* Broad Chare, below). The range
parallel to the river has a similar roof and a timber-framed upper
floor with brick nogging. In the wall facing the yard, an inserted
early C 18 Venetian window with broad glazing bars. The W
range, difficult to date, is all stone, with some early ground-floor
openings, and two stacks of loading bays, one still with a hoist.
The ventilation dormers are entirely of 1989.

From this yard there is a good view of the Victorian warehouses of
Hanover Square which stand on the high ground to the N and
tower over the Close like cliffs. They were built in 1889 and 1893

to designs by *F. W. Rich*. On the s side of the Close, at a point about halfway along, the site of the Mansion House (a grand turreted brick building, erected by the Town in 1691, which burnt down in 1895) is being redeveloped in 1991 with the COPTHORNE HOTEL by *Arup Associates*; all its rooms will look towards the river. The piling of the Copthorne Hotel straddles the line of the TOWN WALL which crossed the Close to the water's edge and was pierced by the Close Gate (a plaque on the n side of the Close marks where the gate stood). The wall had, according to excavation, a tower beside the shore, and possibly continued at least a short way along the river. The wall can still be seen climbing steeply up the hillside (most of which has been cleared and land-scaped as part of the regeneration of the area) in the stretch known as Breakneck Stairs. There are no old buildings by the river along the w part of the Close, and no new buildings have been completed at the time of writing; but, on the n side, dramatic BONDED WAREHOUSES, built in 1841–4 for, and probably by, *Amor Spoor*, cover the hill between here and Hanover Street (*see* Perambulation 3). On this front they have an ashlar plinth, and tall, wide, rusticated stone arched entrances. The brick bond is Flemish, unusual for Newcastle until much later in the c 19. *L. J. Couves & Partners* added the lower curved w extension in 1960 for the Newcastle Warehousing Co. Ltd.

Returning E from here one can conjure a picture of the narrow street, flanked by high houses all the way to the old bridge, that is, where the Swing Bridge is now. The cleared space around the High Level Bridge is, of course, a c 20 phenomenon, but the high, narrow arch of that bridge across the Close probably reproduces something of the old relationship between street and structures. On the r. and facing the river, between the two bridges, is the former FISH MARKET (now offices, NEPTUNE HOUSE), 1880 by *A. M. Fowler*, a distinguished building, Baroque in its details and its rhythm. It is one storey high, seven bays long and three wide, with a long, hipped ridge ventilator in the low-pitched hipped roof. The arched entrances are closed by elaborate wrought-iron gates, with Newcastle's arms in the semicircular grilles; the street side is the plainest, with blank walls below high lunettes; the ends and the river front have pilasters and columns with dramatic entasis and big square intermittent rustication. Above the river entrance, a group of statues with a big Neptune. Beyond, perched on the approach to the Swing Bridge (*see* Public Buildings: Bridges over the Tyne), is a building of *c.* 1870 on the site of the former TOLLHOUSE.

SANDHILL is the roughly triangular area beyond the bridge, between the river and the three routes leading to it – the Close, the Side and the Quayside. The first known reference to the name is of 1310. In 1649 William Grey, in *Chorographia*, wrote that there were many shops and stately houses for merchants in Sandhill. The houses now seen on the n SIDE have their backs against the castle hill. Next to the Castle Stairs is a brick building in the c 18 style built in 1991. The other houses are a handsome mixture of c 17 timber-frame construction and c 18 brick. Nos. 47–52 at the w end, near to Castle Stairs, have altered ground-floor shopfronts and look entirely late c 18 above. The next house, No. 46, belongs

to earlier in that century, as can be seen by the tumbled-in
brickwork of the l. return gable; the c 18-style architrave surrounds are early c 20 additions, and the shopfronts are more
modern still. The next two houses (which have been known for
some time as BESSIE SURTEES' HOUSE, because of Bessie's
elopement from No. 41 with the future Lord Eldon, Chancellor
of England, in 1772), are timber-framed and of the mid-c 17,
though the l. four bays, No. 44, were underbuilt in the early c 18
and given a brick front with sash windows and a high parapet.
The timber frame, with brick nogging and a casement window,
is revealed in the l. return gable. The houses are five storeys high;
as in all these Sandhill houses, the range parallel to the street is
one room deep and extra space is provided in rear wings. The
rear wing here has a roof of upper-cruck construction. Not all in
Nos. 44 and 41 is as it seems. They were acquired in 1931 by the
Hon. S. R. G. P. Vereker, later seventh Viscount Gort, and he
'restored' them with great vigour and with the help of a retired
engineer, *R. F. Wilkinson*, who scoured town and country for
material from old buildings to incorporate. The present ground-
floor front of Bessie Surtees' House, with its fine old door, was
created by him. Nevertheless, it is very likely, on the evidence of
its initials and arms, that the carved chimneypiece on the first
floor of No. 41 belongs there. No. 44 has a fine *in-situ* late c 18
pedimented doorway at the r., opening into a passage to the yard
behind. Here almost all that can be seen is the creation of Lord
Gort, for he rebuilt the property at the rear of the yard out of old
materials; it provides a surprise for anyone who wanders to the
back of the Moot Hall on the hill above and looks down to the
rear of the Sandhill houses. Both houses were acquired by the
City of Newcastle and restored by the *Napper Collerton Partnership*
c. 1982–9. The dramatic contrast presented by the black-and-
white fronts of these timber-framed houses is the most remarkable
feature of this street, and the reason why these houses have been
drawn and photographed so often. Bands of window glass stretch
right across, alternating with bands of white render between floor
and windows. The frame is a simple construction of posts and
bressumers, but the posts have been treated in a classical manner
as very shallow Roman Doric pilasters, contrasting with the sturdy
beam ends of the jetty of each successive floor. Spear-like beading
decorates the pilasters. The whole treatment is apparently without
parallel in England. The ground-floor front of No. 41 has a
different rhythm (the principal posts do not support those of
the first floor), but above first-floor level the pattern is strictly
maintained. All windows are transomed and rest on narrow scroll
corbels; lights have small panes. Nos. 39 and 40, also timber-
framed, is a three-bay house with four storeys and a small gabled
dormer. It has classical pilasters only at the ends of each floor,
but an interruption in the cable moulding along the first floor
shows where there was a projecting bay. There seem to be fewer
altered windows here and, inside, there is more of the panelling
seen already on Sandhill, and, in a room with c 17
panelling, another of the Jacobean-style carved chimneypieces (this overmantel dated 1658, with the initials W C and C R)
such as we saw in Bessie Surtees' House. The next house (Nos.

36 and 38) has a c 17 timber frame hidden by a c 18 brick front
of four storeys and four bays with altered windows. As the street
curves round to the n the timber frame of Nos. 33 and 34, known
as DERWENTWATER CHAMBERS, jetties forward at each floor
from its brick-fronted neighbour. It is also four storeys high, but
five bays wide and, although the proportions are those of the other
contemporary houses, the detail is slightly different; here the sill
brackets rest on corded strings on every floor, and there are no
pseudo-classical pilasters. On the first floor there is a wide Tudor-
arched chimneypiece under a brick relieving arch, and at the rear
a chamfered Tudor-arched stone doorway, with another on the
floor above, as if to a stair wing. At No. 32 another c 17 timber-
frame is concealed by a genteel c 18 brick front with brick strings
and a high parapet like No. 44's. It is of five storeys and only three
bays, with sashes in old, wide boxes and lintels carved to look like
rusticated voussoirs (cf. houses in Bigg Market and Groat Market;
see Perambulation 1).

On the s SIDE, where the Swing Bridge opens into Sandhill, there
stood until 1830 the Bridge Chapel of St Thomas the Martyr,
removed because it obstructed traffic. WATERGATE BUILDING,
which took its place, was designed by *John Dobson*, the architect
of the new St Thomas' at Barras Bridge (*see* Churches). Of ashlar,
this building has the same classical features and proportions as
those in Richard Grainger's development higher up the hill (*see*
Perambulation 4). It was extended E in the same style later in the
century. A ribbed arch of the medieval bridge remains underneath
the roadway (reached from the cellar). The Guildhall (*see* Public
Buildings) is next to the E, on the other side of a narrow lane,
Watergate.

At the E SIDE of Sandhill there is a sudden change of character, due
to much more than architectural fashion. This has always been
so, for the area we now approach is what is properly (though
nowadays, confusingly, not exclusively) called the Quayside. In
the densely occupied block between Sandhill and Broad Chare
many narrow alleys – 'chares' – led from the river front, the
Quayside itself, to the higher ground. They had a succession of
names according to their characteristics or their owners. The w
part of this area was laid waste in 1854 by 'the Gateshead Fire',
when burning debris was flung across the river from a warehouse
explosion. Subsequently these streets were redeveloped in a way
which reflects the intense commercial activity of the c 19, with
shipping and insurance offices predominating, rather than the
intense domestic occupation of the previous centuries, still evident
in the chares at the E part of the Quayside. Most of this front of
Sandhill survived the 1854 fire but succumbed to commercial
pressures after the opening of the Swing Bridge in 1879 and was
rebuilt in the late c 19 in classical style. The N corner, however,
was rebuilt not long after the fire. This is No. 18 (now flats, called
PHOENIX HOUSE), designed for the Royal Insurance Co. in
1869 by that undervalued Newcastle architect *William Parnell*. It
has a well-judged curved corner; Tuscan on the ground floor,
a giant Corinthian order above, a Palladian arcade on the third
floor, and the carved arms of the insurance company over the
door.

To the N is the SIDE, the medieval street to the higher part of the town from the bridge and as impressively steep and demanding today as ever. Dean Street, a late C 18 attempt to provide an easier ascent, which forks off it to the r. higher up, is now the main road (*see* Perambulation 4b). The lower part of the Side is dominated by CALE CROSS HOUSE, an uncompromising glass-clad tower block of 1972–8 by *Hubbard, Ford & Partners*, with a lower block towards the Side (not an aesthetic success) clad in brick and with diagonal boarding hiding the car-park. It is named after the medieval market cross, which stood here and was replaced in the late C 18 by an elegant structure designed by *David Stephenson*, now at Blagdon Hall (q.v.). On the W, an Italianate building of 1867 by *Matthew Thompson* (Nos. 26–31 Sandhill and No. 1 Side) curves round into Sandhill. Groups of windows are set between free Corinthian pilasters and beneath archivolts with keystones; each floor is corniced, the top two with brackets, and roof balustrades link the dormers. Altogether a successful solution to the problems of a site which is visible from many points of view. In the central bay an arched passage leads to a flight of stairs flanked by workshops and warehouses, a densely packed strip of land between Side and Castle. The CROWN POSADA at Nos. 31 and 33 is of 1880 by *W. L. Newcombe*, in a squashed but confident Baroque full of swags and mouldings; the Pre-Raphaelite stained glass, unexpected in a pub, adds to the charm of the well-preserved interior. No. 35, next door, and Nos. 39–41 are plainer, domestic survivors from the C 18 to early C 19, with ground-floor shops. Then the street is astonishingly interrupted by the vigorous iron railings and, behind them, the cobbled court and ten-storey rear elevation of the former County Hall (*see* Public Buildings). Beyond, Nos. 69–75 are plain brick in late C 18 style.

AKENSIDE HILL leads E from the Side, past the back of PRINCES BUILDINGS, another classical office block begun *c.* 1863, after the Gateshead fire. At the top of Akenside Hill is the sad remnant of the lower part of PILGRIM STREET (for the rest, *see* Perambulation 4a). It is now barely recognizable as a street, cut off as it is by the ALL SAINTS OFFICE DEVELOPMENT by *T. P. Bennett & Sons* in conjuction with *Sir Basil Spence*. This was planned in 1969 as a complete redevelopment of the area, with similar blocks intended to spread across the bank as far as Broad Chare, but mercifully it was not completed. The materials (exposed aggregate) and the style (pre-cast boxes with floor levels marked by deep grooves) demonstrate amazing self-confidence. Only ST CUTHBERT'S HOUSE and ST AIDAN'S HOUSE were built, to the W and N of the delicate ALL SAINTS' CHURCH (*see* Churches), which rises triumphantly over its surroundings.

On the return to Sandhill, we pass QUEEN STREET, and a walk along it as far as the steps is worthwhile for the sake of the sudden view of All Saints' framed by Princes Buildings in Akenside Hill (*see* above), and for No. 23 Queen Street, 1871 by *Matthew Thompson*, again classical with Corinthian detail. The courtyard of BLUE ANCHOR QUAY – not a quay at all, but a housing development of 1987 by the *Napper Collerton Partnership*, which fronts onto the Quayside – can be glimpsed here. It keeps to the scale of the Trinity House Almshouses (*see* below). The S side of Queen Street is walled by the N elevation of Exchange Buildings (*see* Quayside, below).

The perambulation resumes its waterside course back on the QUAY-SIDE. The towering New Tyne Bridge of 1925–8 (*see* Bridges over the Tyne, above) dominates this area, not least by the massive size of the circular bearings on which its parabolic arches rest. Inside the bridge pier there is a lift – an easy way for pedestrians to reach higher ground. From the quay at this point there are good views across to St Mary's Church, Gateshead, and both up and down river – up towards the Skinner Burn, down towards the Ouse Burn. Along the mid-C19 nosed granite quay wall are cast-iron bollards of sculptural shape, rubbed smooth by the hawsers of thousands of steamships. The bustle of ship-borne trade has gone, but left behind are the shipping companies' offices, a fine Victorian assortment. From Sandhill to Broad Garth nothing can be earlier than 1854 and the devastation of the fire which followed the Gateshead explosion. First is EXCHANGE BUILDINGS (No. 9) by *William Parnell*, *c.*1861–2, with rusticated ground floor, much classical detail, and emphasis placed on the central entrance bay by the use of tripartite windows. In the stair well, heraldic glass by *Caroline Townshend*, *c.*1908. Then, on the next corner, No. 25 King Street has a narrow but distinguished frontage to the Quayside; 1875 by *R. J. Johnson*, in a mixture of Jacobean and Elizabethan styles, with well-carved mouldings and a hierarchy of orders rising from ground-floor Tuscan, through Ionic to Corinthian, all with pulvinated friezes in the entablatures. Stone mullioned-and-transomed windows and leaded casements lend a domestic air. By contrast, MERCANTILE BUILDINGS (Nos. 15–23 Quayside) is French-style; 1883 by *J. C. Parsons* for Thomas Harper. It has high cyma-moulded aprons below the ground-floor windows, pediments to those above, and an entablature over each floor. The earlier BROAD GARTH HOUSE (Nos. 25–27), 1869 by *John Wardle*, is less imposing. At this point the post-fire block is left behind, and another phase of the street's history is reached. First, the front range of Blue Anchor Quay (already seen in Queen Street), with modern idioms in a frontage of old proportions. The Custom House (*see* Public Buildings) comes next, with an arch at the l. giving access to the development along the chares. To the r., Trinity Chare leads to the rear of Trinity House (*see* below). The plainer C18 to C19 buildings at this end of the Quayside have lost the battle against commercial redevelopment, and the only survivor, with changes, is No. 63. CORONATION BUILDINGS at No. 65 was built *c.* 1902 for Pyman Bell & Co.; Edwardian Baroque, with serpentine balconies. It seems small for the premises of one of the big shipping companies, but it has lost its rear wing. The early C20 BALTIC CHAMBERS next door – the very name says so much about the Quayside – is in an attenuated classical style. The empty corner is being redeveloped in 1991 to designs by *Ryder Nicklin*.

Those of vigorous constitution may now begin the next part of the riverside perambulation from the Law Courts, up Broad Chare and eastwards.

2b. Central Newcastle – the riverside: Quayside E of Broad Chare and streets to the N (including Trinity House)

This part of Perambulation 2 starts at BROAD CHARE, still inside
the medieval town, but very near its eastern wall. Broad Chare is
so named because it was wide enough for a cart, unlike the other
chares. It is even wider today, because it incorporates another
lane, Spicer Chare. The houses between were demolished. The
r. side of Broad Chare is now taken up entirely by the Law Courts
(see Public Buildings). At the corner with the Quayside, a building
by *Ryder Nicklin* with a corner turret is going up in 1991. Most of
the brick buildings on the l. side of Broad Chare are C 19 warehouses converted to other uses, but the pedestrian walking up the
street, perhaps expecting a view of All Saints' spire, will suddenly
come across, on the l., a modest Tudor-style entrance arch of
1841.* Inside the secluded court behind the gate one feels transported to some small Dutch town. This court belongs to the
TRINITY HOUSE OF NEWCASTLE UPON TYNE, a private corporation which had, from 1536, responsibility for lighthouses. In
1505 members of 'The Fellowship of Masters and Mariners of
ships of the town of Newcastle upon Tyne' signed an agreement
to build a chapel, meeting house and almshouses on the site they
had acquired that same 'date and day . . . of old time called Dalton
Place', from 'Rauff Hebburne squyer'. Many changes have been
made to their premises since then, though the mainly C 18 and
C 19 buildings retain some of the earlier work. To the r. of the
entrance arch lies the CHAPEL. Its four-light window was renewed
in 1841 but there is much older masonry, patched and of varying
sizes and golden hues: the small round-headed niches flanking
the window, and the asymmetrical gable peak above are shown
in James Corbridge's map margin picture of 1723. In that illustration, to the l. of the entrance arch, the pretty brick façade
with nine shaped gables belongs to a row of three houses with
warehousing. They were built by Trinity House *c.* 1678 and rebuilt
in 1841 by a 'Mr Oliver, Architect' (either *Andrew* or *Thomas
Oliver*), with *Dobson* advising the House. The same Oliver rebuilt
the gateway. On the r. of the passageway to the main courtyard
are the doorway and windows to the cellar under the chapel
(restored by *Dobson*).

The COURTYARD now reached is the most important of three
yards. On the E side is a graceful flight of steps, wide-curved at
the foot, to the pedimented Tuscan doorcase of the ENTRANCE,
crowned by an open pediment. It was approved by the Board of
Trinity House in 1800; the mason was Mr *Reed*, and Mr *Stokoe*
was paid for work which included 'his trouble respecting the new
entrance'. Next to it is the SECRETARY'S OFFICE, built in 1849.
On the W side, facing the passage, are brick ALMSHOUSES with
a big plaque recording their rebuilding in 1787. There was once
another block of almshouses on the far side of the raised yard,
behind these. The steps up to this yard, which run along the s end
of the C 18 almshouses, abut a much older stone wall, probably
C 16 on the evidence of the flat Tudor-arched doorhead and a

* This gate and that in Trinity Chare are, at the time of writing (1991), open only
during office hours. There have been gates on these sites since at least 1540.

1 Almshouses
2 Almshouses (now demolished)
3 Banqueting Hall
4 Former rigging loft
5 Entrance Hall
6 Chapel
7 Board Room
8 Trinity House Yard
9 High Yard
10 Low Yard

Newcastle upon Tyne, Trinity House. Plan as it was in 1869

small square stone window surround. This superimposing and intermingling of the work of different centuries is part of the charm of Trinity House. On the N side of this courtyard is a three-storey stone building, known in the C 17 and C 18 as the RIGGING LOFT. This is the site and probably the actual building which Trinity House acquired in 1524 from Thomas Hebborne. The stripping of render has revealed small square blocked windows on the top floor. The door and window architraves are recent additions and the sundial of 1721 was probably moved from the Banqueting Hall, but there are two buttresses – a truncated one at the l. end and another between the fourth and fifth bays – and a wide garderobe projection at the E end, with a shouldered lintel to the inner doorway. The ground- and first-floor rere-arches are pointed and chamfered: could these be C 14? The roof, steep now, can be seen from the gables to have been even steeper, and the W gable coping has an eroded fleur-de-lys finial. It has king-post trusses. The BANQUETING HALL of 1721, on the S side of the yard, has original sashes and glazing bars in elliptical-headed windows. The central plaque is particularly good. The parapet shown on Corbridge's map is still there, over a gutter cornice which was carefully matched along the w side of the yard when the almshouses were rebuilt in 1787. A covered gallery links the chapel with the hall at first-floor level, i.e. the principal floor of all these buildings; the ground floor was used for storage.

The ENTRANCE HALL is the w bay of the chapel, separated from it by a Jacobean SCREEN with glazed two-light openings. In the CHAPEL, excellent Jacobean STALLS, a two-decker PULPIT, and a DESK and the READER'S DESK facing one another – a very complete and attractive ensemble, with much lively detail. *Richard Newlove* was paid for carving the cherubs' heads in 1635. The roof was renewed in 1651, with moulded tie-beams, using trees newly cut from Walker wood, and ceiled with deals in 1656. The walls were lined with panels in the early c 20. The VESTRY was the little room to the s, over the arch to Broad Chare. The BANQUETING HALL has its 1721 panelling, stucco ceiling decoration with a central oval compass, and a Jacobean overmantel trimmed down to fit. The central panel of this bears the Royal Arms with 'CR'. All the windows open to the N onto the courtyard, though there are two on the s which were blocked when the school (now barristers' chambers) was rebuilt higher in 1753; they were decorated with paintings in 1768.

A flat-roofed passage runs from the courtyard, under the Hall, to a narrow alleyway between the Hall and the former school. At the start of the alleyway, on the E, the blank brick wall is all that can be seen from outside of the BOARD ROOM (or Election Room, as it was once called); the plaque here records its rebuilding in 1791. The architect was *John Stokoe*. Even inside, the room is not elaborately decorated, though dignified with dado and modillioned ceiling cornice; it is lit partly by a c 20 stained-glass window opening onto a hidden yard and partly by borrowed light through the half-glazed entrance screen, opening from the first-floor passage. This passage was built in 1791 to a plan by Mr *Newton* to lead from the hall to the vestry, now the MASTER'S ROOM. The wall on the s of the alleyway belongs to the SCHOOL, rebuilt in 1753. At the other end, the alley passes under a stair wing linking school and Hall (although, inside, there is now apparently no communication) and opens into Trinity Chare. Skirting the w end of the school, we reach a second, larger COURTYARD, formerly called the Low Yard, which in the c 17 was the Brethren's bowling green; railings separate it from the chare. On the N is the school's façade, strangely sunk below the level of the yard since the building of the ALMSHOUSES on the E side in 1782. These are (in 1991) occupied by the Live Theatre Company, which also occupies the most southerly of the three Broad Chare warehouses, rebuilt by Trinity House in the 1840s. They lie parallel to the almshouses and are linked to them by covered yards. On the s side of this yard is the gable end of a modest ALMSHOUSE block dated 1820, and beside it a little outbuilding contemporary with the 1782 almshouses. All these c 18 and c 19 buildings are of brick.

The perambulation continues from the Broad Chare gate of Trinity House, where we turn l. and then pause at the foot of Dog Bank. Here, at the head of Broad Chare, where Cowgate leads to Manor Chare, a low shrubbery has taken the place of old houses which used to crowd together before they were cleared away in the interests of public health. Among the plants a long flight of stairs leads up to the Corner Tower of the Town Wall (*see* Castle and Town Walls); in 1990 a section of the wall can still be seen in waste ground to the E, but it may be obscured by a new building before long. Now back to the Quayside.* The line of the street between Broad Chare and Milk Market was set further back around 1900; some old buildings were demolished, others altered. The handsome Law Courts (*see* Public Buildings) now dominate this stretch of the riverside. Beyond the Courts, between LOVE LANE and MILK MARKET is a large brick warehouse of *c.* 1830 on a plinth of stone blocks. It was converted in 1991 into flats. A similar warehouse to the w between Love Lane and Cox Chare was sadly destroyed by fire in 1989 and has been replaced with a block of flats which imitates it in style. A third warehouse, in PANDON, was the oldest of the group, built in 1827. This was destroyed by a fire in February 1992. These three were reminders of the former intense concentration of trade and shipping premises near the Quayside, and their scale, rhythm and grouping were important elements in the character of the area. Beyond Milk Market, the CO-OPERATIVE WHOLESALE SOCIETY WARE- HOUSE built in 1899 and 1900 of early reinforced concrete by *T. G. Gueritte* of the firm of *L. G. Mouchel,* with *F. E. L. Harris* of the C. W. S. Architect's Office, using the *Hennebique* method. The Hennebique foundation raft was used because of the great depth of made ground, silt, sand and gravel. A bare concrete structure, eight storeys high including the basement, and with an attic storey of 1910; the three-bay giant order of plain pilasters without frieze stands on a triple-arched corniced podium. The eastern Quayside area between Milk Market and the Ouseburn is the subject of redevelopment proposals at the time of writing.

Sandgate in the Town Wall lay to the s of the corner of Milk Market and from here the wall turned N to the Sallyport Tower (*see* Castle and Town Walls), which is reached from a flight of steps up to Tower Street from the N side of CITY ROAD. To the E of these steps, the KEELMEN'S HOSPITAL, a plain brick quadrangle of 1701, looks down over the area where the keelmen lived in crowded chares until the decline of their trade in the C 19. The s range has a central square clock tower, pilasters in two primitive orders flanking the pedimented plain doorcase and at the angles of the tower, which has a commemorative panel and a sundial. The domed top stage has a single clock face. Dormers with shaped gables have slightly clumsy scroll decoration and central lozenges. The whole building has been much repaired and restored, and it is difficult now to believe that once there were front and back towers, though it is shown like that on C 18 illustrations. Now a Polytechnic students' hostel. With the SALVATION ARMY MEN'S HOSTEL next door, *c.* 1976, *Ryder & Yates* have respected the height of the older neighbour and its relationship to the road by sweeping the building back in an asymmetrical curve of brick and glass.

---

* Just downstream from Broad Chare, the Pandon Burn flowed into the Tyne. The land to the E was the vill of Pandon, which was incorporated into Newcastle in 1298.

We now turn back towards the city centre via MELBOURNE
STREET, past the former NEWCASTLE TRAMWAYS OFFICES,
1901 by *B. F. Simpson*, with an imposing *art nouveau* entrance to
the electricity generating station behind (machinery removed long
ago), past the top of Croft Stairs and the Corner Tower of the
Town Walls (*see* above; we can cross here to look at the wall's
inner face); and on to the former Holy Jesus Hospital (now
restored as the John George Joicey Museum: *see* Public Buildings),
where this perambulation ends.

3. The west part of old Newcastle

This perambulation takes us close to the line of the Town Wall to
see what remains of a fashionable C18 suburb. In the W part of
the town, long stretches of the medieval Town Wall have survived
from St Andrew's Churchyard southwards. The N sections of the
wall were the first to be built, and the request of the Dominican
friars in 1280 to have a postern for access to their land outside it
gives us the date of at least that part of the construction (but
see Castle and Town Wall, above). We start from St Andrew's
Churchyard, where Perambulation 1 began. Leaving the churchyard, we cross St Andrew's Street (Darn Crook) to STOWELL
STREET, laid out in the mid-1820s with a row of houses parallel
to the wall. It was praised by Eneas Mackenzie in 1827 as 'dry
and airy ... judiciously planned ... well adapted for families of a
certain rank, whose convenience is seldom consulted by building
speculators'. A few houses survive at the far S end. The N end
was rebuilt in the late C19 as a C. W. S. WAREHOUSE; *see* the
wheatsheaf symbol with the motto 'Labour and Wait'. The
emerald green pagoda eaves that project over the door in an
exuberant disregard for sober brick indicate that, in the 1990s,
this street is the heart of Newcastle's Chinatown, with numerous
restaurants and shops making good use of all kinds of older
buildings. Along the E side, the lively range of housing by *Jane
Darbyshire Associates* (going up in 1991) is part of the development
of Black Friars (*see* Churches). The area between here and the
Tyne Theatre in Westgate Road is the THEATRE VILLAGE, one
of the Newcastle Initiative Zones, in which private enterprise has
been harnessed by the City Council in an attempt to revitalize
declining neighbourhoods. The lane behind Stowell Street follows
the line of the medieval lane alongside the inner face of the wall.
Here can be seen first, behind the GALLOWGATE BUS STATION
(1930s brick in modernist idiom), Ever Tower, then Morden and
Heber Towers (*see* Castle and Town Walls, above). In Bath Lane
at the S end of Stowell Street is the former House of Recovery
(*see* Public Buildings), which stood in purposeful isolation on the
other side of the ditch which ran around the Town Wall. The
scale of the ditch can be appreciated here, since it has been
excavated and displayed.

MONK STREET leads E from Stowell Street. The C19 warehouses
on one side and the late C20 flats on the other do not prepare
one for the venerable stone of Black Friars beyond (*see* above),
with its S elevation towards the street and an arched passage

leading to the cloister. Opposite, groups of small houses have
been carefully planned by *Barnett Winskell, c.* 1984, to respect
both Black Friars and CHARLOTTE SQUARE, of which they form
part. They fill a gap caused by a serious fire. The square, built in
1770 on part of the former friary precinct, is unique in Newcastle –
an C 18 square in the London style, with three sides of tall brick
houses around a garden. The houses have attractive doorcases,
the usual floor and sill bands and just one or two roof alterations.
William Newton was the architect. He also designed the Assembly
Rooms of 1774–6 (*see* Public Buildings), which lies lower down
the hill in FENKLE STREET. CROSS HOUSE fills the wedge-
shaped site opposite the Assembly Rooms, between Fenkle Street
and Westgate Road. It is an early (1911) *Hennebique* concrete
structure with Portland stone cladding by *Cackett & Burns Dick*.
In front, a fine STATUE by *Tweedy*, 1906, of Joseph Cowen (1831–
1900), newspaper proprietor, social reformer, friend of Italian
freedom, founder of the Tyne Theatre and Opera House (*see*
Public Buildings).

This part of WESTGATE ROAD has, on its S side, two groups of
houses of the first half of the C 18, remarkable despite the inevitable later shopfronts. From the corner with Grainger Street first,
the five-bay No. 53 (in 1723 Lady Clavering's house, according
to Corbridge's map), bright red brick with ashlar dressings. The
sashes are in architrave surrounds linked vertically by stone panels
and aprons, a columnar effect reinforced by the tapered pilasters
at the ends of the three upper floors and by the cornices running
along each floor. The 1960s shopfront is a brutal addition. At
Nos. 55–57, a charming mid-C 18 three-storey house built of
ashlar. Graduated Lakeland slates (favoured as roofing material
for high-quality buildings in Newcastle in the C 18) still cover half
of the roof, which has one of the understated C 18 dormers that
are so much more suitable for C 18 houses than the big gabled
dormers often inserted later.* Only one rusticated pilaster survives
on the ground floor (l.); above, the bays are grouped 2:3:2 by
giant pilasters which are linked by floor bands and support an
entablature. The sashes all have architrave surrounds. Inside, a
grand stair ascends both sides of the hall to a gallery with doors
to a long first-floor room. Much Rococo stucco on the walls and
ceilings; a phoenix on one wall, portrait medallions on the stairs,
and eagles, cornucopias, garlands, putti and clouds. It looks very
much like the work of the York school of *stuccatori*. A big Venetian
window with a Doric surround lights the staircase. The house is
now part of the NEWCASTLE ARTS CENTRE, which occupies a
big restored group of buildings further up the hill. The first and
oldest house (No. 67) was the town house of Sir Matthew White
Ridley in the C 18. Brick, with gauged flat arches and a modillioned
eaves cornice; a segmental-headed dormer (cf. No. 57) is half-
hidden by the roof parapet. No. 69 is a late C 19 building, with
typical iron roof-crestings. Nos. 71–75 have the render typical of
the later part of the C 18, but the gabled rear wing of No. 71 shows

---

* Corbridge's map marks this house as the Assembly Rooms, but his illustration in
the border does not show this front, so it must have been rebuilt in the mid-C 18 (as
the interior, especially, suggests).

tumbled-in brickwork. We should go further up Westgate Road beyond Clayton Street now to see the Tyne Theatre (*see* Public Buildings), before going s via FORTH LANE, which leads through the Westgate Arts Centre from beside No. 67 Westgate Road. The Town Wall and the town boundary used to run along the rear of these Westgate Road properties; *see* the TOWN BOUNDARY STONE, with the town's three castles set above the arch at the rear of the Forth Lane passage. Beyond Pink Lane and the line of the wall, we reach BEWICK STREET, with, on the N side, BEWICK HOUSE of 1884 by *Austin & Johnson* for the Tyne Improvement Commission. In 1911 *W. H. Wood* added three more floors. At the top, under the deep, bracketed cornice, are the arms of the local authorities represented on the Commission. The side of St Mary's R.C. Cathedral (*see* Cathedrals, above) flanks the s side of the road. Facing the w end of the Cathedral from CLAYTON STREET WEST is part of Grainger's redevelopment of the town centre (*see* Perambulation 4c). Nos. 6–24 were probably designed for Grainger by *John Wardle*, but now only the façades remain to screen a large housing development of 1979–82 by *Barnett Curry Smith*. The other face of this scheme (thoroughly of our time and well-proportioned, in brick and dark glass, with long oriel windows) can be seen to the w in WATERLOO STREET. At the w end is a pink and grey granite MEMORIAL FOUNTAIN to Richard Grainger by the *Elswick Court Marble Works Co.*, *Newcastle*, 1892.

Now we go E from the R.C. Cathedral, past the long and grand façade of the Central Station (*see* Public Buildings), to Orchard Street at the side of the Station Hotel. It leads s under the railway lines to FORTH STREET, where a stretch of the Town Wall (*see* Castle and Town Wall, above), is exposed since the demolition of a brewery. In CLAVERING PLACE, the attractive brick CLAVERING HOUSE, *c.* 1784, is a reminder that this was a fashionable development before the railway came in 1849 with viaduct, smoke and noise. Two canted bays, and a pedimented central doorcase with narrow side windows, like a Venetian window. This is echoed above by a window, with a blind arched head and blind side windows. Next door another big house of the 1780s, now part of Messrs Turnbull's premises; their warehouse behind is seen to better advantage from the Close (*see* Perambulation 2a). On the opposite side is the former PRESBYTERIAN CHAPEL built in 1822 by *John Green* for the United Secession Church, with Gothic intersecting glazing bars and Tudor arches. Clavering Place leads to HANOVER SQUARE, a very early planned development, begun in 1720 in the reign of George I (as the name suggests) but never completed. One building has an C18 lower storey with a good Tuscan doorcase and a C19–20 top storey. In HANOVER STREET, off to the s, BONDED WAREHOUSES of 1841–4 by *Amor Spoor* (*see* also Perambulation 2a) form an admirable composition of almost Piranesian grandeur, with the curve and fall of the street accentuating the rhythm of the pediments. Big bond numbers on the walls and the cobbled street surface, with strips of Shap granite to take the weight of cartwheels, are strong reminders of C19 commerce.

From here the Hanover Stairs descend through the warehouses –

an arched brick canyon – to join the Close and the riverside. To the N (our direction) modern steps lead to the Town Wall and Orchard Street, where the ROYAL MAIL SORTING OFFICE has an extension of the 1980s by *Ryder, Nicklin & Yates*. Between these two buildings, a lane leads to SOUTH STREET, where part of the STEPHENSON LOCOMOTIVE WORKS of *c*. 1867 can be recognized by its tall, round-headed windows; No. 20, an early C 19 house, was part of the offices. In the Post Office yard behind, it is possible to see the glazed roof of the boiler shed of *c*. 1848. Back in Forth Street, a big water tank sits high on the top of an Italianate office building, part of the enlargement of the Central Station done by the North Eastern Railway in the 1890s.

4. Central Newcastle between Eldon Square and Central Station

Perambulation 4a–d takes in the planned redevelopment of the medieval town which began at the end of the C 18 and continued until late this century. It is discussed in more detail on pp. 412–17, but in order to understand the present layout of the area it is necessary to know something of the medieval plan. Pilgrim Street is medieval in origin, and led from All Saints' Church N to the Town Wall (*see* Castle and Town Wall), the line of which is followed between Carliol Tower (E) and Newgate (W) by New Bridge Street and Blackett Street. Pilgrim Street Gate stood at the present junction of Pilgrim Street and Blackett Street. To the S, inside the Town Wall and between Pilgrim and Newgate Streets were precincts of two medieval religious houses (Grey Friars and St Bartholomew's Nunnery) which, after the Dissolution of the Monasteries, became the grounds of a house. It was on the site of that house, which in *Richard Grainger*'s time was called Anderson Place, and in the grounds that in 1835–9 Grainger laid out his network of wide streets and sophisticated buildings – a new commercial centre, in the northern part of the medieval town. It created E–W links between the medieval Pilgrim Street and Westgate Street (now Road) and N–S links between Blackett Street and Eldon Square of the 1820s and Mosley Street and Dean Street of the 1780s. By thus connecting the bridge with the upper town by straight, wide roads it transformed Newcastle. The new commercial development was very soon thought of as the centre of the town.

4a. Central Newcastle between Eldon Square and Central Station: Eldon Square and to the NE (Northumberland Street) and SE (Pilgrim Street)

GREY'S MONUMENT is the focus of Grainger's developments, though they were planned before the column was proposed. The monument, designed by *Benjamin Green* in 1838, is a Roman Doric column, *c*. 41 metres (135 ft) high, on a tall pedestal. There is a balcony above the capital and then a square pedestal for the statue of Earl Grey, which is by *Baily*. A long inscription on the pedestal extols Earl Grey as the 'Champion of Civil and Religious Liberty' who had 'safely and triumphantly attained ... the great measure of Parliamentary reform'.
To its W, and on the N side of Blackett Street, lies ELDON SQUARE, one of Grainger's earliest enterprises (1825–31). Here a new atti-

tude of expansion, and more ambitious design and execution, could be seen before all but the E side was demolished in the 1960s for the shopping centre that confusingly bears its name. The first designs for the square were made by *Thomas Oliver*, and then, according to Oliver's own account of 1831, the elevations were drawn up by *John Dobson*, who had surveyed Blackett Street as early as 1815, when it was a muddy lane alongside the Town Wall. The designs, executed in ashlar of the highest quality, staked a claim to formality and monumentality that was new to the town and must at once have doomed the modest houses of Saville Row (*see* below). It must, of course, not be forgotten that at that time nothing yet existed of Grainger Street and Grey Street; that is, most of the centre of Newcastle was still narrow and unplanned. The spaciousness of Eldon Square was a thing quite unheard-of, as was the high-quality ashlar facing (Nash's London work was in stucco). The three ranges of houses were treated with Greek simplicity; the N range had a taller central projection, and the W range was like the surviving E one, which has Doric pilasters defining the five-bay end projections, an entablature with prominent cornice and a lower attic storey above. Steps lead to doors above basements protected by area railings. A Grecian honeysuckle-patterned cast-iron balcony links the pavilions at first-floor level. No more was done to show the superior quality of these houses. Now the N and W sides of the square, and part of the S side of Blackett Street, are dominated by the ELDON SQUARE SHOPPING CENTRE, 1969–75 by *Chapman Taylor & Partners*, in conjunction with the City Planning Officer, *Wilfred Burns*. The height of the new development was kept to that of the surrounding buildings, though a multi-storey hotel (designed by *Arne Jacobsen*) was originally intended for the N side: Grey on his monument fortunately still towers over all. Like most late C20 shopping centres this one is introverted. On Blackett Street and around Eldon Square there is nothing but panelled brick walls, with only a colonnaded balcony on the N side opening out to echo the level of the surviving E side of the square. The W side looks oddly unfinished; it was designed as the podium for Jacobsen's hotel tower, which was to have been clad in bronze anodized aluminium. On the terrace, a bronze SCULPTURE, 'Man and pigeons', by *André Wallace*, 1976, faithfully captures a traditional Tyneside image. The linking bridge high over Blackett Street was in 1988 dressed up with a huge gable of bright blue glass. The NW side, facing Percy Street and Newgate Street, with a bus concourse and service access, is almost blank, because a dual carriageway was planned along here; the shop windows are later insertions. Inside, the wide walks (named to recall medieval Newcastle) are enlivened by varied levels, frequent seats and planters, and occasional points of interest – a cluster of giant pencil-seats, a fountain – and public spaces. The shopping centre is still spreading: in 1988 it was extended to the Newgate Street–Clayton Street corner of Grainger's development, and in 1989 it took a leap over Percy Street to ELDON GARDEN, 1987–9 by *Fitch Bennoy* (job architect *M. Hassnip*), one of the newer generation of shopping malls, lighter and airier, with lavish decorative surfaces. In the grassed centre of Eldon Square, a WAR MEMORIAL of *c.* 1920, a vigorous equestrian bronze St George, on granite and Portland stone base, by *Chas. Hardman.*

To the E in BLACKETT STREET, EMERSON CHAMBERS forms a 112 backdrop to the Grey Monument. This wonderfully inventive Free-Style piece was built *c.* 1903 by *Simpson, Lawson & Rayne* as a restaurant, shops and offices (now offices and a single shop): a glorious confection of canted oriels, strapwork and friezes, balconies and domed turrets, dormers and little roof-lights with high pyramidal roofs, and high corniced chimneys. Fat Ionic columns of granite with bronze decoration and capitals at the former entrance to the restaurant, and fine (restored) *art nouveau* glazing. Of the grand circular staircase to the basement restaurant, only the ceiling survives. Further E, along the N side of Blackett Street, a domed corner in Grainger's manner, and the well-preserved façades of three tall narrow shops (including the jolly No. 30 of 1902 by *Marshall & Tweedy* and Nos. 18 and 22 of 1895 and 1892 by *James Cackett*) are just a skin-deep screen for MONUMENT MALL, a shopping development by *Hugh Martin & Partners*, 1989–92. On the S side, ELDON BUILDINGS (Nos. 29–33) stands at the important junction of Grey and Blackett Streets; 1893 by *Oliver & Leeson.* It turns the corner in a satisfactory manner with a giant Composite order and Venetian windows below a parapet with carved panels. Its neighbour is GEM HOUSE (Nos. 23–27), 1904 by *Newcombe & Newcombe*, with a different order on each floor of the two broad shallow bows, and a serpentine dentilled cornice below a top balustrade and swan-necked pediments. The *art nouveau* shopfront of 1906 for Reid & Sons is similar to Simpson's work at Emerson Chambers. Then come two decent late C19 buildings before the corner with Pilgrim Street is rounded by the showy NORTHERN GOLDSMITHS' building of *c.* 1890 by *James Cackett* with a corner dome on a tall drum. The bracket clock was added in 1932 by *Cackett, Burns Dick & Mackellar*, the female figure above by *Alfred Glover.* The original fittings and showcases by *Sopwith* are a pleasure to see.

NORTHUMBERLAND STREET runs N from the crossroads. In the C18 it was a suburb of the medieval town with three-storey brick houses. At the time of writing it is mostly lined with C20 commercial architecture of the most depressing kind. Some enjoyment can be gained further up on the E side from the little early C19 house-turned-shop, with jolly pargetting added in 1953 to commemorate the Coronation of Queen Elizabeth II. On the W side, the three-bay building with statues of local heroes in niches was built for Boots & Co. *c.* 1900; it looks like one of *Morley Horder*'s typical productions for the company. Off the E side of the street, further up, is SAVILLE ROW, or what survives of this C18 development, built *c.* 1770, and called a 'retired and elegant street' in the early years of the C19. Only one side remains, and that has been sadly altered, but we can still get an impression of the neat brick architecture of the late C18 from the upper floors of decent brickwork and the remaining lintels with carved keystones. RIDLEY PLACE beyond is slightly later and only slightly less altered; and opposite Ridley Place the proportions of the C18 may be discerned behind some of the garish C20 fronts on the W side of the street.

We turn back now to PILGRIM STREET. At its junction with
Blackett Street stood the Pilgrim Street Gate (demolished in
1802). This medieval street has been transformed, first in the
1920s, when the New Tyne Bridge was built to bring Great North
Road traffic over the river, and again in the 1960s, when the
Central Motorway East abruptly truncated it. The street is now
dominated by large C20 buildings, and the view from the top is
filled by an offensive brutalist tower raised over the road on a
street-level podium. This is COMMERCIAL UNION HOUSE,
designed by *Howell Brooks Tucker & Partners* and completed in
1971. Brutal blocks like this and the Norwich Union in Westgate
Road (*see* below) galvanized support for the conservation of the
city centre in the late 1960s and 1970s. Next to it, on the corner
of Market Street, one of the best inter-war buildings in Northumberland, CARLIOL HOUSE of 1924–8 by *Burnet, Tait &
Lorne*, with the Newcastle firm *L. J. Couves & Partners*, for the
pioneering North Eastern Electric Supply Company. It is a magnificent Portland-stone-clad building of classical proportions and
with the barest of classical decorative motifs. The long front to
Market Street is broken by an entrance flanked by massive
columns of dark limestone, the rounded corner to Northumberland Street marked by a low dome. On the opposite
corner of Market Street, the Central Police Station and Magistrates' Court of 1931 (*see* Public Buildings), which, with Carliol
House, belongs to the transformation brought about by the building of the New Tyne Bridge. On the W side of Pilgrim Street
stood the Franciscan friary. This became part of the Anderson
Place estate developed by Grainger in the 1830s, so that side of
Pilgrim Street, between High Friar Lane (where Grainger was
born) and High Bridge, is the E edge of Grainger's scheme and
can be identified by the distinctive classical style (*see* Grey Street
etc., below). (High Bridge was truly a bridge once, as can be
guessed from the gradient; it crossed the Lort Burn.) The line of
the medieval Pilgrim Street as it drops towards the river has been
almost obliterated by the 'improvements' which accompanied the
building of the New Tyne Bridge and the Central Motorway East.
All the more remarkable, therefore, is the survival of some older
houses, reminders that this was once where wealthy merchants
lived. The MARKET LANE PUBLIC HOUSE (W side) shows by
pilasters and proportions that it is an early C18 house, with a
contemporary building of unknown function at the rear of its
yard. A little further down, the late C17 No. 96 was one of the
stateliest houses; it is shown on James Corbridge's map of 1723 as
'ALDERMAN FENWICK'S HOUSE'. Its similarity to Schomberg
House of 1698 in London's Pall Mall is noticeable; in each, the
single outer bays project squarely from the three central bays and
stand on rusticated stone piers, but this house is of more severe
aspect, with heavily moulded brick cornices on each floor, and a
parapet. The 1723 map shows a cupola and balustrade behind
the pitched roof, from which the Fenwicks would have had an
excellent view of town and river. The stair, in a rear wing, still
continues up to the roof, where the steep pitch over the main
building is interrupted by a passage through the centre. The
staircase, one of only two *in-situ* C17 staircases in Newcastle (for

the other, *see* Public Buildings: John George Joicey Museum), is open-well, with a wide grip handrail on fat turned balusters. In the full-width first-floor room, fine bolection-moulded panelling of *c.* 1700, and a ceiling with strapwork stucco and little pendants. Restoration of No. 96 and of the adjacent late C 18 No. 100 was begun in 1982 by *Simpson & Brown* for Buttress (the Tyne and Wear Preservation Trust) and continues at the time of writing. Edwardian commerce is represented by Nos. 112–118, an office block of *c.* 1902 by *C. E. Oliver* for the Consett Iron Company. On the E side, the BANK OF ENGLAND, 1968–71 by *Fitzroy, Robinson & Partners*, is clad in roach bed Portland stone in big vertical slabs which step back as they ascend the curve of the street: a vigorous building which respects the scale of its neighbours. Soaring overhead where the Central Motorway East cuts off the S end of Pilgrim Street is SWAN HOUSE, designed (like all the pedestrian traffic routes round and beside it) by *Sir Robert Matthew* in the early 1960s. Within lies a sorry reproduction of the interior of Grainger's ROYAL ARCADE of 1831–2 by *Dobson*. It was a noble composition with giant Corinthian order over a Doric ground floor, the shops and offices lit by a series of glass domes.

4b. Central Newcastle between Eldon Square and Central Station: Mosley Street and Dean Street

MOSLEY STREET, which opens into the W side of Pilgrim Street, belongs to the late C 18 improvements in which this street and Dean Street were cut through the medieval town to make it easier to move from the river to the higher ground. It dips down to a hollow, where the Lort Burn, now culverted deep below the traffic, once ran between the plots of Pilgrim Street and Cloth Market. The plan, and probably the buildings, of the 1780s were the work of *David Stephenson*. Little remains of his buildings in this street, but a hint of the original scale is provided by Nos. 3–5 on the N side, a single house which seems only to have been refronted *c.* 1900 but not rebuilt. On the corner of Pilgrim Street, two large office buildings: the N one is a block of offices and shops of 1899 designed with considerable style by *Benjamin Simpson*; the S one is of 1908, by *Newcombe & Newcombe* for the Alliance Assurance Co., with its rounded corner and classical forms in the common but attractive combination of sandstone ashlar walls and granite plinth. We are now approaching the heart of the business community of late C 19 Newcastle. Next on the S side, with a second-floor oriel window, is a tall, narrow, ashlar and bright red brick building of 1906 by *W. H. Knowles*, who had his office here; it makes lively use of the orders. On the same side, at the corner with Dean Street, another but larger red sandstone and bright red brick building in free early Renaissance style, with mullioned-and-transomed windows, recognizable as a design by *Alfred Waterhouse*, 1891, for the Prudential Assurance Company. In the granite plinth are magnificent iron window grilles. On the N side, only the façade remains of the building (Nos. 17–19) in which Swan carried out early experiments with incandescent electric light bulbs; it was designed by his nephew, *Alfred Swan*, for Mawson and Swan. Next to it, offices of 1906 by *Fred T. Walker*

for the Edinburgh Life Assurance Company, with a suitably solid
red granite ground floor and ashlar above, with classical motifs
topped by a sort of Egyptian temple. It runs through to Grey
Street, where the same materials are easily recognized in a single
tall bay. On the corner, wrapped round by this building, is the
last piece of Grainger's work in Grey Street (*see* below); it is best
seen from Dean Street which turns off to the s (*see* below). On
the sw corner with Dean Street stands one of *Gibson*'s elegant
designs for the National Provincial Bank (now NATIONAL
WESTMINSTER BANK), 1870–2; High Italian Renaissance with
upper windows in aedicules and a rusticated ground floor. Big
and useful inscriptions on the friezes. Next, at Nos. 28–30, an
interesting façade (of 1894 by *Armstrong & Knowles*, with a shop
of 1902 by *Watson & Curry*) which meets the challenge of a tall
narrow frontage by breaking the verticals with banded pilasters,
enclosing the first and second floors in a giant Ionic order, and
framing the arched top-floor windows with squat, mannered Ionic
pilasters: big corniced chimneys are important in the balance of
the composition. Remarkably, two houses of the 1780s (Nos. 32–
40) survive on this side, although they are now offices and have
a c 20 ground floor and dormer. On the N side, the Baroque No.
27, completed in 1890 by *W. L. Newcombe* for the North British
and Mercantile Assurance Co., and SCOTTISH PROVIDENT
HOUSE (No. 31), which stands at the corner of Cloth Market. It
was built by *S. D. Robbins* in 1906, the first framed structure of
American type in Newcastle, so it is claimed. The exterior is
severely classical, in Portland stone, with grey granite for the
Tuscan porch on the corner and for the pedimented doorcase,
and good wrought-iron gates and window guards. Back E now to
Dean Street.
When DEAN STREET was built over the Lort Burn by *David Stephenson*, contemporaneously with Mosley Street, there was for the
first time a wide approach to the higher part of the town from the
area round the bridge. In 1849 the railway companies flung an
enormous stone arch across Dean Street; then in the 1890s
another was added to widen the track (*see* Public Buildings:
Central Station). So the wide curve of the c 18 street now makes
a fine composition with the c 19 arches. There is still a row of
brick houses of 1789 or so down the E side. Some even have their
original Lakeland slate roofs, and several retain the little dormers
of the period. The *art nouveau* shopfront of No. 50 is a remodelling
done in 1902 by *Benjamin Simpson*. These modest houses are,
alas, interrupted by an unseemly car-park and office block of 1989
with gaping entrances and a peculiar roof-line; the steelwork is
hidden behind brick and stone which apes the c 18 but fails to
match its quality. Another c 18 house intervenes before Nos. 12–
14, a warehouse and offices by *Oliver, Leeson & Wood*, 1901. This
too has a steel frame but it is used as the slim basis for an
interesting design, with borrowed Jacobean motifs for details and
for the tiled panels in blue and ochre between the floors. At
the top of the w side of the street, the exuberant CATHEDRAL
BUILDINGS (also of 1901 by *Oliver, Leeson & Wood*) has giant
Jacobean columns, big corbels supporting five-storey oriel
windows, and a tetrastyle porch. These architects did the remain-

der of the block, beyond the steps to the Cathedral, most of it
MILBURN HOUSE, 1902–5, which occupies a steeply sloping
triangular site between here and the Side, with entrances on many
levels, and a rich range of decoration inside. The internal spaces –
light wells, stair wells and corridors, glazed screens and panelled
walls – are handled in masterly fashion. The Side belongs to the
walk along the riverside (Perambulation 2a), so we return uphill
now to the foot of Grey Street.

*4c. Central Newcastle between Eldon Square and Central Station:
Grainger's town centre (Grey Street and Grainger Street to Clayton
Street)*

Now we have reached that part of the city centre laid out by Grainger
between 1834 and 1839 with three grand new streets, Grey Street,
Grainger Street and Clayton Street, the streets cutting across
them, and his new covered market. GREY STREET is no doubt
the best of Grainger's city streets, and one of the best streets in
England. It curves gently as it rises, and both of these difficulties
have been turned into assets. As early as 1838, before the street
was completely finished, an observer* remarked 'The proportion
and correspondence of every part in the whole, and the admirably
grand effect produced by the perspective view from Mosley Street,
are calculated to impress the beholder with indelible surprise.'
Despite the impression given in *A Memoir of John Dobson* (1885)
by his daughter Margaret, *Dobson* was not the principal architect.
C 19 evidence suggests that he designed the E side between Mosley
and Shakespeare Streets and that *John & Benjamin Green* designed
the whole block between Market and Shakespeare Streets which
includes the Theatre Royal. *John Wardle & George Walker*, who
began their partnership in Grainger's office, designed the remainder, and also all the other streets in the scheme, with the exception
of the interior, and perhaps the exterior, of Grainger Market,
which was by *Dobson*.

We can see that the ranges of Grey Street are not completely
symmetrical from a drawing-board point of view, but on both
sides they are so well balanced that the alternation of plain and
adorned sections comes off perfectly. End and intermediate pavilions, of three storeys with attics behind balustraded parapets,
are enriched with the Corinthian order, either as attached columns
or as pilasters, standing on rusticated ground floors. These points
of emphasis are linked by lower plainer blocks which have plain
entablatures and prominent cornices below the attics; the central
section on each side is, however, given more importance by an
attached giant colonnade. The low unadorned plinths on which
the buildings stand form a series of shallow steps which carry the
large elevations gently round the curve of the street, as gracefully
as a Georgian staircase ascends a stair well. Grey Street has
suffered numerous changes, many of them arrogant and insensitive, though in 1991 the Grey Street Initiative is attempting to
revive its fortunes. Some of the buildings have been restored (and
in a few of them original details survive inside on the upper floors).

* M. A. Richardson, *Descriptive Companion through Newcastle upon Tyne and Gateshead*
(1838).

Others have been demolished except for their façades, which gives some of the buildings the character of late C 20 office blocks, with their plinths destroyed and uncomfortable clashes between façades and the floor levels behind. Shop windows are in as many styles as there have been fashions since the mid-C 19; some are aggressively out of keeping, others quite appropriate, with slender mullions and modest decoration. There are no original shop-fronts: a typical three-bay property originally had a central door to the shop and a door recessed at one side giving access to the house above. Cast-iron columns within the shop windows (still visible in some places) supported the upper floors and permitted generous use of glass. The side streets, both here and off Grainger Street, are designed as return elevations of the blocks facing the main street, and share their character.

First, looking at *Dobson*'s range on the E SIDE, we notice that it is articulated into clearly defined blocks, with heavy and somewhat unorthodox classical detail. For example, the Corinthian pilasters that frame the projecting outer bays of the pavilions have pilasters half-hidden behind them. These outer bays have pedimented first-floor windows. Between them on the first floor, tripartite windows with balustraded balconies below them, and above them big cornices on scrolled brackets which emphasize the stepped rhythm of the blocks up the hill. The overall rhythm has been interrupted by later alterations and additions, particularly in the initial stretch from the corner of Mosley Street, which made a quiet transition to the C 18 houses in Dean Street and, before they were replaced, those in Mosley Street. This corner, Nos. 2–8, with its neat low-pitched curved roof, was the last piece of Grey Street to be built, completed in 1842 with the aid of a grant from the Corporation. *Dobson* seems to have designed it (his signature appears on one of the three surviving alternative designs); it has more Italianate details than the link blocks. Here the cornices on brackets originally had balustraded balconies. Next comes a much-mutilated block comprising the narrow bay of No. 10 (the office entrance of 1908 for No. 31 Mosley Street); the late C 19, fussily modelled terracotta face of Nos. 12–16; and two mid-C 19 bays. Nos. 18–26 is a Dobson pavilion made more elaborate *c.* 1890 by *Newcombe*. The next six-bay linking section and five-bay pavilion are almost unspoilt, but the design of the central section of Dobson's design (Nos. 42–50) was drastically altered in 1910, and again in 1969, by *L. J. Couves & Partners* for the Midland Bank. They restored the attached Corinthian colonnade *in antis* (half the columns had been removed in 1910) but hung the façade on a steel frame, so the stepped progression up the hill is interrupted by a ground floor expressive of the new structure rather than classical logic. The composition is completed by another stretch (Nos. 52–78) of pavilion-link-pavilion. Between High Bridge and Shakespeare Street, a detached block (Nos. 80–96) with corner pavilions has much simpler and rather less correct detail, with unusual simplified acanthus capitals. This block's restraint prepares us for the giant Corinthian portico of *John & Benjamin Green*'s Theatre Royal of 1836–7 (*see* Public Buildings), which boldly juts forward at the highest point in the arc of the street in a way that combines the monumental classical tradition with the English

Picturesque. The composition echoes that of the rest of the E side.

We return now to the bottom of Grey Street to look at the W SIDE as far as High Bridge. This is probably by *John Wardle*. It has fewer, narrower pavilions than the E side, but strikingly rich and monumental Corinthian columns and longer, plainer links. In the links a variety of texture is provided by the use, in alternate sections, of architrave surrounds to windows and of plain reveals. The first corner is a much grander quadrant than its E counterpart, with a narrow curved bay clasped between the giant pilasters of the straight sides. Behind the curved glass of the windows can be seen the cast-iron columns which support the front beam behind the shop fascia. The Baroque corner doorway is an alteration of *c.* 1900. Then comes a simpler twelve-bay link range and, with a Giant Corinthian order above, the wide elliptical-arched entrance to a lane. The main sequence is a full fifty-seven bays. It extends to High Bridge and has flanking pavilions and a boldly modelled ten-bay centrepiece (Nos. 33–41), built for the Bank of England and the Northumberland and District Banking Co. in the manner of a grand palazzo. It is subtly different from Dobson's centrepiece almost opposite. Again there is a giant Corinthian order *in antis*, but the wall behind is more heavily textured, with pediments over the first-floor windows, and the attic completely hidden by a balustrade. The next ten bays (Nos. 43–51) are merely a façade screening offices of 1990. (Just round the corner in HIGH BRIDGE, the bright red brick and yellow sandstone WARD'S BUILDINGS, 1902 by *Cackett & Burns Dick*.) Beyond High Bridge, opposite the theatre, the twenty-seven bays of Nos. 55–85 are a quieter variation on the original theme, corresponding with the more subdued block opposite. In the centre, designed as the front of the Turk's Head Hotel, four bays of giant Ionic columns *in antis*, flanked by narrow pilastered bays. The end pavilions also have giant pilasters rather than columns. All are being altered in 1991. The range has been made lopsided by the two-storey mansard added to the N part in the early years of the C 20 by *Cackett & Burns Dick*. It was altered again in 1982 by *Gordon E. Andrews*, who made the ground floor blank and inserted an atrium.

Beyond Market Street we look again at the E SIDE, at LLOYD'S BANK, 'considered one of the most chaste and neatly decorated buildings in the town' in 1851; the architect is unknown. This palazzo fulfils an important role at the top of the curve and as a neighbour to the Theatre Royal. The Northumberland and District Bank originally occupied the centre, with private houses (perhaps for bank officials) in the corner bays. The theme of the rest of the street is taken up in this façade; the centre has attached Corinthian columns *in antis*, the outer bays pilasters. First-floor windows are pedimented. Below the attic an elaborate entablature with a dentilled and modillioned cornice. The rusticated ground floor has round-headed openings between Tuscan pilasters. Inside, nothing original; the interior has been rebuilt with a dramatic atrium, 1987. (Round the corner in HOOD STREET, the NORTHERN COUNTIES CLUB, the former Union Hotel of 1839, has a Greek Doric porch.) Nos. 104–108, the large Edwardian shop, was a redevelopment by *W. H. Knowles & T. R. Milburn* in 1904 for Messrs Mawson, Swan & Morgan. This is a Mannerist variation on the rest of the street, with a giant Corinthian order and ornate windows. Those on the second floor have large elaborately shaped pediments taken from Rossi's *Studio d'Architettura Civile di Roma* (1702). The W SIDE is completed by the EXCHANGE BUILDINGS, a grand triangular composition between Market Street, Grey Street and Grainger Street, probably designed by *Wardle*, and built by Grainger *c.* 1837 as the Central Exchange and News Rooms. The three corners are rounded with ribbed domes on emphatic columned drums. Nash's London schemes seem to have been the inspiration for the composition (West Strand Improvements of the 1830s) and for the finials of bronze feathers on each dome (Sussex Place of 1822). The CENTRAL ARCADE, with its glorious profusion of yellow and brown faience, was cut through the block in 1906 by *J. Oswald & Sons*; paving by *Rust's Vitreous Mosaics* of Battersea. We now go from the Monument (*see* above), the hinge of Grainger's great scheme, down Grainger Street.

GRAINGER STREET is straight, in contrast to Grey Street's curve. It leads to the station but is Grainger's only as far as Newgate Street and Bigg Market. First on the W is smoky glass screening a corner of the Eldon Square Shopping Centre (*see* above), which continues behind the façade of a block typical of the W part of Grainger's scheme. The blocks down Grainger Street are organized in the same way as those down Grey Street, with pavilions punctuating long plainer stretches, but here the decoration is kept to a minimum and the effect relies upon well-judged proportions and details; the horizontal lines of windows between bands and cornices look especially crisp in such high-quality ashlar. On the E side, the Exchange Buildings (*see* Grey Street, above). The S corner of Market Street is an obtuse angle, turned by a gentle curve with a giant Ionic order on the upper floors. The same order marks the centre and the end pavilions of the return façade to MARKET STREET, the approach from Grey Street to *Dobson*'s Grainger Market on the W (*see* Public Buildings), which fills the block between Nelson Street and Nun Street with its elegantly articulated classical façades of superb ashlar. Nelson Street and the streets further W are worth a detour. NELSON STREET has an interesting variety of C19 façades that now screen the Eldon Square Shopping Centre: they originally belonged to the GAIETY THEATRE, dated 1838, with tall round-headed panels containing two storeys of arched windows; an attractive warehouse of *c.* 1899 by *Marshall & Tweedy*; the plain five-bay DISPENSARY of 1838 (later the Fruit Exchange); and the CORDWAINERS HALL, dated 1838, with nice Egyptian lettering. The final rounded corner effects the transition back to the shopping centre's glass wall in Clayton Street. The vista down Nelson Street is closed by the great double-bowed front of the LORD COLLINGWOOD pub in CLAYTON STREET, matched by the similar DUKE OF NORTHUMBERLAND further S, which looks down Nun Street. This symmetrical pair is the foil for the Grainger Market opposite. We return down Nelson Street to Grainger Street. The Ionic order continues on the E side but now as pilasters, the dominant motif

as far as Bigg Market. The w side between Nun and Newgate
Streets is plainer, the only accent being the projection of the three-
bay end pavilions.

*4d. Central Newcastle between Eldon Square and Central Station:
streets between Grainger's town centre and Central Station*

We now leave Grainger's development. The last stretch of Grainger
Street, beyond Newgate Street and Bigg Market, was originally
the muddy St John's Lane, which ran from the church in Westgate
Street to Newgate Street and was improved in 1869 to lead to the
railway station, which had opened nineteen years earlier. Since
the first part of Grainger Street had been built in the 1830s,
architectural fashions had changed. In this later section classical
simplicity was abandoned and the Gothic and Renaissance styles,
with an abundance of carved decoration, were fervently embraced.
On the E side, after Bigg Market, are the Italianate VICTORIA
BUILDINGS (Nos. 42–50), by *Matthew Thompson* for (Sir) Walter
Scott, 1874; the Jacobean Nos. 34–40 of 1874; and John Johnstone's No. 30 for the Newcastle and Gateshead Gas Company,
1884–6 (*see* Public Buildings). Worth noting on the w side, the
richly Gothic CHAUCER BUILDINGS (Nos. 53–61), incorporating a Freemasons' Hall, probably by *Gibson Kyle*, *c.* 1869; and,
on the corner with Westgate Road, a bank (now the TRUSTEE
SAVINGS BANK) built in 1862–3 by *J. E. Watson*, in classical style
with engaged Ionic columns supporting pediments with a carved
tympanum on each front. Before we reach the railway station,
which lies ahead and distracts both eye and mind, we see, on the
E side, St John's Church (*see* Churches) and, on the w, the eclectic
COUNTY HOTEL, of two builds: the N one, on Grainger Street
and Westgate Road, of 1874 by *John Johnstone*, the s, fronting
Neville Street and with three bays to Grainger Street, of 1897 by
M. H. Graham.

In WESTGATE ROAD,* next to the Church of St John, is the UNION
CLUB, a splendid French château of 1877 by *Manning*, sadly
neglected at the time of writing. Its neighbours, the unspeakably
ugly and intrusive WESTGATE HOUSE and NORWICH UNION
HOUSE of 1965–71 by *Cartwright Woolatt & Partners*, provide a
painful contrast; ironically the latter was designed, according to
a contemporary account, 'to fit into the stone character of this
part of the City'. On an island between Westgate Road and Neville
Street stands the STEPHENSON MONUMENT by *J. G. Lough*,
1862, a bronze statue on a big plinth with, at the corners of the
pedestal, four seated bronze figures representing the fields of
engineering in which George Stephenson triumphed. It was
shown further w on Dobson's watercolour proposal for the
station, but looks very effective here. The full-blooded Victorian
Gothic building facing the Station Hotel (*see* Public Buildings:
Central Station) across Orchard Street belongs to an institute
important in the history of Tyneside but not well known beyond
it. The NEVILLE HALL, 1869–72, is the offices and library of the
North of England Institute of Mining and Mechanical Engineers

---

* For Westgate Road w of Grainger Street, *see* Perambulation 3.

(known as 'The Mining Institute'). It was designed by *A. M. Dunn* for the Coal Owners' Association on behalf of the Institute, and built of Prudham sandstone banded with red, with griffins adorning the pilasters which flank each gabled dormer. (The griffins have been removed, two of them up the hill to No. 271 Westgate Road.) The amphitheatre inside is a 1902 alteration of some splendour by *Cackett & Burns Dick*. The institute's associated WOOD MEMORIAL HALL LIBRARY is Romanesque, with an arched and glazed roof, and contains a seated marble statue of Nicholas Wood by *Wyon*. Next to it is the home of Newcastle's LITERARY AND PHILOSOPHICAL SOCIETY, which was founded in 1793. This Neo-Grecian building is of 1822–5 by *John Green*; three bays, two-and-a-half storeys, entrance with Greek Doric columns *in antis*, the first one-and-a-half storeys with giant pilasters, then a Doric frieze and pediment. Alterations and extensions, not visible from the street, were made in 1888–9 by *A. R. Gibson*, who copied Green's internal details. The glass-domed roof was done by *F. W. Rich* after a fire in 1893. Inside, among many interesting sculptures, a statue of James Losh by *Lough*. The cheerfully Baroque BOLBEC HALL, next door, was designed by *Rich* in 1907–9 for the Lit. and Phil. to let speculatively.

COLLINGWOOD STREET starts opposite and is full of interest. It was made in 1809–10, and named after the local hero who was Lord Nelson's Admiral. In the course of the C19 most of its original three-storey brick houses with ground-floor shops were redeveloped, and now none is left. On the N corner, the former BARCLAYS BANK, with COLLINGWOOD BUILDINGS (Nos. 28–62), was begun in 1899 by *Oliver & Leeson* as a hotel, but completed in 1903 by *Cackett & Burns Dick* for Barclays. Italianate, with a giant Corinthian order, Diocletian windows (to the E part), and a magnificent marble-lined ground-floor banking hall, still with the mahogany fittings made to the architects' designs by *Waring & Gillow* and stucco ceiling decoration by *Laidler*. At the corner with Groat Market, the NORTHERN ASSURANCE BUILDINGS (No. 2) of 1878 and later by *Austin, Johnson & Hicks*, with vermiculate plinth and serpentine balconies. The S corner facing the Lit. and Phil. is filled by the SUN INSURANCE BUILDING of 1902–4 by *Oliver, Leeson & Wood* in French Renaissance style, with much fine detail, including Atlantes at the main entrance, a roof balustrade of linked letters S, and a large sunburst in the pediment to Westgate Road. The ashlar is golden, the copper roof now a beautiful green. Further E, Nos. 9–17 was also designed as a bank, by *R. J. Johnson* for Hodgkin, Barnet, Pease, Spence & Co. in 1891 (converted in 1990 into offices with mezzanine). Its long Italian Renaissance façade has a polished red granite plinth and portal, Gibbs jambs and alternating pediments to the first-floor windows (that is an Anglo-Palladian touch), top frieze with garlands, and a balustrade. Near the E end, No. 7 is the sole reminder of the scale of the original street, although with a C19 front; then comes the restrained No. 5 of 1898 by *J. W. Taylor* for J. C. Eno before the compromising Refuge Assurance House on the corner of St Nicholas Street (*see* Perambulation 1, p. 466). A splendid view of the spire of the Cathedral of St Nicholas makes a cheering end to this perambulation. The next one starts to the NE of Grainger's town centre in New Bridge Street.

5. Outer central Newcastle from New Bridge Street to Leazes Terrace

Perambulation 5a–b takes us through some of Newcastle's early-to-mid-C19 suburbs, much cut about on the E side by the Central Motorway and the roads created c.1970 to lead to it, but well-preserved on the NW.

5a. Outer central Newcastle from New Bridge Street W to Haymarket

NEW BRIDGE STREET, which follows the line of the Town Wall from Pilgrim Street to the site of Carliol Tower and continues E, was laid out at the same time as the new bridge was built over Pandon Dean, in 1812, when the Pandon Burn still ran down a green valley. Villas began to be built along the road in the 1820s. Today the street only starts being architecturally interesting when John Dobson Street is reached. Here on the S is *Dobson*'s Tudor-style LYING-IN HOSPITAL of 1826, a beautiful little building in pale ashlar, with Perp tracery in the oriel over the Tudor-arched doorway, flanked by cusped windows below and cusped canopies above. In 1991 it awaits a new use; until 1987 it was the BBC's North East headquarters. Extra studio space was added in 1932 by *Wells Coates*, with complete disregard for the original building. This addition has itself been much altered, and, in 1991, seems likely to be removed. Facing the hospital is *Dobson*'s own house (now part of TIFFANY'S CLUB) with a pleasant honeysuckle frieze and, inside, some stucco decoration by *Ralph Dodds*. It is spoilt, alas, by nasty alterations. Continuing E along New Bridge Street, we encounter the brave new world of the Central Motorway East which cut mercilessly through here in the late 1960s. The pedestrian walkways over it provide good viewpoints. To the E, beyond the filled-in dean, RIDLEY VILLAS are just recognizable as smart semi-detached houses of the 1820s, and N of them rises the spire of Christ Church, Shieldfield Green (*see* Churches). Behind the former Lying-in Hospital in CROFT STREET, part of the Town Wall, with Plummer Tower, can be seen (*see* Castle and Town Wall). Off the N side of New Bridge Street, HIGHAM PLACE is a welcome oasis among the late C20 hotels and offices. On its E side, three terraced houses (brick-built in English bond, with stone dressings and sash windows, some of which still have original glazing bars) are all that remain of the row built for William Batson in 1819–20 by *Richard Grainger*, right at the start of his distinguished career. Facing them, the remarkable entrance and strong corner tower of the Laing Art Gallery (*see* Public Buildings), built as an extension to the previous Central Library, which was demolished in 1968–9 to allow the construction of John Dobson Street.

JOHN DOBSON STREET, designed by *Bradshaw* (City Engineer) and opened in 1970, leads to the Civic Centre. It is flanked by a late C18 terrace (the remains of the W part of NORTH STREET, threatened with demolition at the time of writing) and C20 buildings of no distinction. On a deck above the new street sits BEWICK

COURT, 1969–71 by *T. K. Powell & Partners*. The wind-swept
piazza in front of this dull block of flats leads to the back of the
Central Library, and from there walkways extend E to M. E.A.
HOUSE (*see* Public Buildings) in Ellison Place, where the Church
of the Divine Unity (*see* Churches) stands on the S side, and there
are some brick houses of the 1840s on the N, next to Newcastle
Polytechnic's Ellison Building (*see* Public Buildings).

NORTHUMBERLAND ROAD crosses John Dobson Street. On its N
side, the City Hall and Baths, the former Dame Allen's Schools
(now the Careers Centre), and St James United Reform Church
(*see* above). On the S side is the former RIDING SCHOOL of the
Northumberland Yeomanry, 1849, perhaps by *Dobson*, in brick
with stone-dressed tall-arched recesses under a pediment. Inside,
bare brick walls and exposed roof-trusses. It is being restored in
1991 by *David Lesley Design* for Newcastle Polytechnic. E of it,
BURT HALL, 1895 by *John W. Dyson*, for the Northumberland
Miners' Association. Brick and terracotta, with good ashlar dressings, a Lakeland slate roof, and on the gable a statue of a miner
by *Canavan*, modelled on the figure in R. Hedley's painting *Going
Home*: altogether a fine tribute to Thomas Burt, M. P. Facing it
across College Street, Newcastle Polytechnic's Sutherland Building and, next door, Trinity Building, the former Trinity Presbyterian Church (*see* Public Buildings, above). Back N up John
Dobson Street to the Civic Centre (*see* above).

Here ST MARY'S PLACE is reached. St Thomas's Church (*see*
Churches) stands among tall trees, and facing it is an ashlar-
fronted terrace in Tudor style, built to designs by *Dobson* in 1830
to complement his church. In the grounds of the church, two
WAR MEMORIALS. Beside the W end, a memorial to the ROYAL
TANK REGIMENT, *c.* 1920, by *J. Reid* in Portland stone and
granite, with curved Barras benches flanking a statue of St George. To
the N, facing Barras Bridge, a powerful sculptured group by *Sir W.
Goscombe John*, *c.* 1923, to the NORTHUMBERLAND FUSILIERS.
Marching soldiers with their families alongside, bronze figures
against a high block of grey Shap granite with an angel above.

5b. Outer central Newcastle from Haymarket NW *and then* W *to Leazes
Crescent and Terrace*

HAYMARKET, the wide space just SW of St Mary's Place and Barras
Bridge, with Percy Street running along one side, is not very old
as a market place: the market was established as late as 1828. Here
the SOUTH AFRICAN WAR MEMORIAL dominates the skyline.
A heroic-sized winged Victory stands on a tall tapered octagonal
column and a figure with unfurled flag clasps the column's base;
very dramatic, the effect heightened by the octagonal steps and
the big low-relief panels and garlands. It is signed and dated *T.
Eyre Macklin*, 1907; the founders were the *Montacutelli Bros*.
Beside it is the dark glass drum housing the entrance to the Metro
Station (*see* Public Buildings) and, behind PERCY STREET, we
get a first glimpse of the University – the Herschel Building by
Sir Basil Spence (*see* Public Buildings), with the crisply rectangular
slab rising above the upswept projecting auditorium. Also now
part of the University, the former NEWCASTLE BREWERY

OFFICES, 1896–1900 by *Joseph Oswald*, in red sandstone and bright red brick with a grey granite plinth. Much Jacobean carved ornament, first-floor oriels conveniently providing second-floor balconies, and a corbelled corner turret with copper fishscale dome. There is an *art nouveau* wrought-iron grille in the big doorway and, inside, much faience, strapwork stucco, and a marble staircase.

BARRAS BRIDGE to the NE was indeed a bridge once; the stone arch is still beneath the road. It is flanked by the extensive buildings of the University of Newcastle (W) and by the ceremonial face of the Civic Centre (*see* Public Buildings). The bridge (shown amongst tall trees in Thomas Richardson's painting in the Laing Art Gallery) connected the town to the GREAT NORTH ROAD, the main route to Edinburgh before the Tyne Tunnel diverted it many miles to the E. On the E side, just beyond Barras Bridge, a short terrace (Nos. 14–20) of the early 1830s, probably by *Dobson*. Most of the pretty cast-iron balcony with Greek honeysuckle motif has survived; it is of the pattern also found in Eldon Square (*see* Perambulation 4a). At the junction with JESMOND ROAD, which forks to the NE, is the Robinson Library of the University (*see* Public Buildings). The first block on the W side is CARLTON TERRACE of *c.* 1838, probably also by *Dobson*, a balanced composition with tripartite windows and Tuscan pilasters in the end pavilions. On the E side we see the more usual type of mid-C 19 terrace development, with standard houses repeated as many times as necessary. Brick – by then fashionable once again – is used for the front, and homely sandstone rubble for the rear of the earliest phase, built *c.* 1840. As we turn back to Barras Bridge, we can catch a good view of the Hancock Museum (*see* Public Buildings: University) standing beyond the chasm of the motorway. In front of the Hancock, the ARMSTRONG MEMORIAL, 1905–6 by *Hamo Thornycroft*, with an imposing bronze figure of the great industrialist, flanked by low reliefs showing some of his factories' products (guns being lowered into a ship; the Newcastle Swing Bridge).

University buildings stretch all along CLAREMONT ROAD, with the Royal Victoria Infirmary (*see* Public Buildings) beyond off the W side. A path parallel with Claremont Road outside the railings along the N side of the hospital leads to a small early C 19 development. There are tall terrace houses in CLAREMONT PLACE (Nos. 25–26), and, beyond it, later pale red brick ones of *c.* 1850 in FRAMLINGTON PLACE. Nos. 18–21 look as if they come from a London suburb, with pediments over each pair. The cap-less WINDMILL further up Claremont Road overlooks the Town Moor and forms a handsome distant accent. This octagonal timber-framed tower mill of 1782 by *Smeaton* was the first windmill to have five sails (sails removed in 1924, fantail in 1933). We return E to QUEEN VICTORIA ROAD, the axial approach to Exhibition Park opened in 1887 (*see* Public Buildings). Beyond the Royal Victoria Infirmary, in ST THOMAS'S STREET, TERRACE, CRESCENT and SQUARE, is a group of modest brick houses built *c.* 1840–58, and rehabilitated in exemplary fashion in the 1980s for North Housing. The terraces in St Thomas's Street are typical and have the doorways with sturdy Doric pilasters and heavy architraves that are characteristic of the first half of the C 19 in Newcastle and its neighbours, e.g. North Shields. At the rear of No. 3 St Thomas's Crescent is the brick stable (marked by a plaque) which was used as a studio by William Bell Scott, whom Rossetti visited in 1853. From here it will be seen that brick was used only for the house fronts, the rear being rubbly sandstone.

But the very best of Newcastle's early C 19 housing, Leazes Crescent and Leazes Terrace, lies further to the W round the S end of Leazes Park, created from Castle Leazes in 1870. They were designed by *Thomas Oliver* for Richard Grainger and were begun while Eldon Square (*see* Perambulation 4a) was still being built. LEAZES CRESCENT of 1829–30 is first on the l., facing Leazes Park. These charming terraced cottages have stuccoed fronts and nothing higher than two storeys. The rinceau frieze in the end bays of each block (not always surviving) and the pretty Egyptian-lettered street-name panels ought to be noticed, and also what remains of the original cast-iron railings. These little houses are the delightful preliminary to the masterpiece that looks down on 97 them. LEAZES TERRACE is also by Oliver, 1829–34. Like Eldon Square – or rather Eldon Square as it once was – it is composed in the accepted Palladian fashion of, e.g., John Nash's Regents Park terraces, which were completed not long before this terrace was begun. Like them it has accents on the angles and the centre. It is a long hollow block of four ranges, projecting boldly into the Leazes; inside the block were back-yards, now cleared for car-parking. The size beats even Nash: eighty-six bays to the E, twenty-one to the S. The architecture is of three storeys, with Corinthian pilasters to accentuate angles and centres. No more is done than that. The precise ashlar work and proportions of the clean-cut windows do the rest. Grainger, with this and with Eldon Square, set a new standard characterized by the use of ashlar, worked with great precision, and, in contrast to Nash's and the Regent's taste in London, an almost complete abstention from ornament. The terrace has been restored after a long period of neglect, and the honey-coloured stone is as dazzling as when it was new. The W range is, alas, overshadowed by the concrete stand (1970–3 by *Williamson, Faulkner Brown & Partners*), of ST JAMES' PARK (Newcastle United's football ground), an interesting structure but a brutal neighbour.

LEAZES PARK ROAD, which leads back to Percy Street, was probably designed by *David Stephenson c.* 1811 as Albion Place, the continuation of Albion Street. There is one early C 19 terrace of three-storey houses with some original sashes, and, then, in the S block, the Leazes Arcade, built as a synagogue (*see* Churches, above), and some altered early C 19 houses.

OUTER NEWCASTLE EAST

BYKER (including ST LAWRENCE)

Of the old village of Byker there are no visible remains, but it was centred on what is now Avondale Road. The 1960s Water Company offices occupy the site of Byker Hall. In 1549 the boundary of

Newcastle was extended E along the riverbank to include a strip of the Manor of Byker, so as to provide space for ballast quays. In 1835 the remainder became part of Newcastle. In the early C 19, access to Byker from Newcastle was restricted to steep lanes from the Ouseburn, crossed by small bridges, one of which survives in the shadow of the Victorian Byker Bridge. In 1839 the railway was carried across the dene by the Ouseburn Viaduct, and in 1878 a major road bridge (Byker Bridge) was built. Collieries, the turnpike road to North Shields (Shields Road), the Tynemouth and North Shields railway, the potteries, the engineering works at Heaton and the shipyards at St Peter's in succession rapidly accelerated the development which changed Byker from village to suburb. In St Lawrence, the area E of the Ouseburn and near the Tyne, one of those potteries (the famous Malings, now a furniture storage depot) can still be seen. By 1900 farmland was completely covered by regimented rows of Tyneside flats, some of which remain to the E of Byker Village.

The highly successful redevelopment of much of Byker in the 129 second half of the C 20 was one of the milestones in the development of community architecture. *Ralph Erskine*, his project leader *Vernon Gracie*, and their colleagues were both architects and planning consultants for the scheme. They ensured from the beginning (1969) that their plans would take into account the opinions of the local community. Alongside concern for the 3,000 inhabitants who needed rehousing went care for the landscape. Varied shapes and textures, materials and colours, flow along the contours of the hillside and rise steeply to the peak of a single wedge-shaped block (TOM COLLINS HOUSE, an old people's home) at the W and the escarpment of a wall of flats along the N. This undulating BYKER WALL is blank to the N, save for tiny lights to minor rooms, in order to make a barrier against traffic noise from the Byker bypass, which was finally opened in 1990. From the homes in the wall that face the sun, there are panoramic views of the river valley. On this S side are cheerful timber balconies and window-boxes. In contrast the hill below is filled with small houses laid out in short terraces and threaded with gently rising steps and well-planted pathways to create an atmosphere far removed from that of the severe rows of cobbled streets, flagged pavements and brick terraces of Tyneside flats which filled this site before. Those older streets had their own remarkable character, but as a solution to the problems of a steep site and the need to shape a new setting for an old community, the Byker redevelopment (1969–71) is highly satisfactory and set new standards for local authority housing.

ST MICHAEL WITH ST LAWRENCE, Avondale Road. 1862–3 by
    W. L. Moffatt, with a gabled N aisle and vestry of 1936 using
    materials from the demolition of *Dobson*'s church of St Peter in
    Ellison Place, Newcastle. Dec style, with broach spire. Enclosed
    within the new community, sensibly preserved when all around
    has been rebuilt, its Gothic sturdiness maintains a link with the
    past.
ST SILAS, Clifford Street. 1886 by *R. J. Johnson*. Snecked sand-
    stone, with mostly square-headed windows, the eaves of the
    gabled N aisle the same height as those of the terrace of Tyneside
    flats which formerly continued the street frontage. A pleasing

composition, with polygonal NW turret (now without its
bellchamber) between nave and aisle; the little apsidal projection
N of it is the baptistry. Alterations of 1899: two W doors; Gothic
REREDOS, in Caen stone; a new E window; and STAINED GLASS
in the baptistry window and the E window by *Atkinson Bros*.

NEWCASTLE AND GATESHEAD WATER COMPANY OFFICES
AND DEPOT, Allendale Road. 1967–70 by *W. B. Edwards &
Partners*. Bold and uncompromising.

MALING FORD B POTTERY, off Walker Road, St Lawrence. Now
a furniture repository. When built in 1878 on a fourteen-acre site,
with an investment of £100,000, this was the largest single pottery
in Britain, producing 1½ million articles a month (mainly jam
pots). Pottery manufacture ceased in 1963 and many buildings
were demolished. Good ranges of three and four storeys remain,
brick-built with stone dressings; they are the only pottery buildings
now left on Tyneside.

BYKER BRIDGE, BYKER (METRO) VIADUCT and OUSEBURN
VIADUCT. *See* Public Buildings, above.

WALKER

The old settlement and the church were near the river. The banks
must have been heavily wooded, for in the C 17 Trinity House sent
men to Walker to cut rafters for their chapel. Later there were
coalmines here with associated industries, and in the middle of the
C 19 the shoreline was considerably changed by river improvements.
Shipbuilding became the major industry, and by 1939 there were
shipbuilding and repairing yards all along the bank here and downstream at Wallsend. Housing estates rapidly filled the fields to sup-
plement the colliery cottages and Tyneside flats. Some of the most
interesting housing is the small development of 'model cottages'
(WALKERVILLE) N of Shields Road in HOLME AVENUE,
BRIARWOOD CRESCENT and ROSEWOOD CRESCENT, some
designed by *E. Cratney*, others by *K. B. Spurgin* and *White & Stephenson*, for the Walker Model Housing Exhibition of 1908; and
the post-1919 WALKER ESTATE designed by *F. L. Thompson, R.
Dann & S. P. Taylor*. Late C 20 redevelopment of the riverside with
light industry and speculative housing has left hardly any trace of
the old heavy industries.

CHRIST CHURCH, Church Street. 1848 by *A. B. Higham*; chancel
lengthened later. Nicely placed in a churchyard with old trees.
Tower and spire at the E end of the S aisle. Late C 13 forms, cross
gables to the aisle bays. Vestry added 1882. – STAINED GLASS
(according to Neil Moat): E window, *Clayton & Bell*, 1901–3, paid
for by Charles Mitchell; W, by *Kempe*. In the S aisle, first window
by *Wailes*, the next two and one in the N aisle by *Bennet*.

LIGHTFOOT SPORTS STADIUM, Wharrier Street. 1963–5 by *Williamson, Faulkner Brown & Partners*. A successful use of new
materials to achieve a large span. A polyester resin dome rests on
laminated timber ribs, reaching to 14 metres (45 ft) above the
ground, with a diameter of 60 metres (197 ft). Refurbished 1990.

OUTER NEWCASTLE NORTH

The C 19 suburbs of Jesmond and Heaton lie respectively W and E of the Ouseburn, as did the two medieval settlements. It is good fortune for such a large town as Newcastle to have a dene, with its burn and densely wooded banks, so close to its centre. The first Lord Armstrong gave the dene to the city in 1880 and 1883; it forms a string of public parks, Heaton Park, Armstrong Park and Jesmond Dene. Gosforth abuts Jesmond on its N edge. Before 1974 it was not part of Newcastle, and in 1991 it still has a distinct identity.

GOSFORTH

The modern suburb is only partly within the city boundary, though it is described as a whole here. It was formerly Gosforth Urban District and Castle Ward Rural District, but in 1974 these were both included in the new District of Newcastle upon Tyne, and the former Urban District became part of the City of Newcastle. Gosforth is, however, still quite distinct from Newcastle. It is separated from the rest of the city by the Town Moor and reached from it by the Great North Road, which crosses the moor. It is around that road that C 19 and C 20 Gosforth has grown, spreading out from South Gosforth, which lies, with its medieval church site, to the E. There is little evidence, before quarries and coalmines brought workers to the area, for anything other than the early churches, the one in South Gosforth on high ground overlooking the Ouseburn, the other now buried in a C 20 housing estate in what is called North Gosforth. Once past the Town Moor the traveller encounters the High Street, flanked by prosperous C 19 and C 20 houses, then the commercial centre, solid and unpretentious, and beyond lies a sprawl of red brick houses, halted only by the open space of golf courses, rugby fields and Gosforth Park, much of which is (in 1991) succumbing to housing. But do not be deceived by the Great North Road; the gentle delights of Gosforth lie away from it.

ALL SAINTS, West Avenue. 1855–7 by *R. J. Johnson*; W tower added in 1896 as a memorial to Lyulf Cochrane. The tower is square and prominent, and the church altogether a good, competent example of the large late Victorian ecclesiastical building in a prosperous suburb. High buttresses; straight-headed Perp aisle and clerestory windows, large seven-light E and tall four-light W windows; gargoyles, Tudor-flowered corbel tables, and battlements. Very tall octagonal piers to the five-bay nave and two-bay chancel, and a very tall chancel arch. – FURNISHINGS. Much wood-carving by *Ralph Hedley*, including a lacy chancel screen, choir stalls with poppyheads, and the reredos designed by *Johnson*. – FONT and cover, a fine example of 1906 by *Crawford Hick*, dedicated to William Cochrane, a benefactor of the church. – STAINED GLASS. An interesting set of windows. – N aisle, one with Northumbrian saints by *Bayne* (to F. W. Bindley, Rector, † 1892); another to W. S. Hicks, 1904 by *Bryans*. – The striking E window of 1887 is by *Heaton, Butler and Bayne*.

ST NICHOLAS, Church Road. 1799 by *John Dodds*, classical but on a medieval site. To Dodds's simple plan of W tower, nave, and

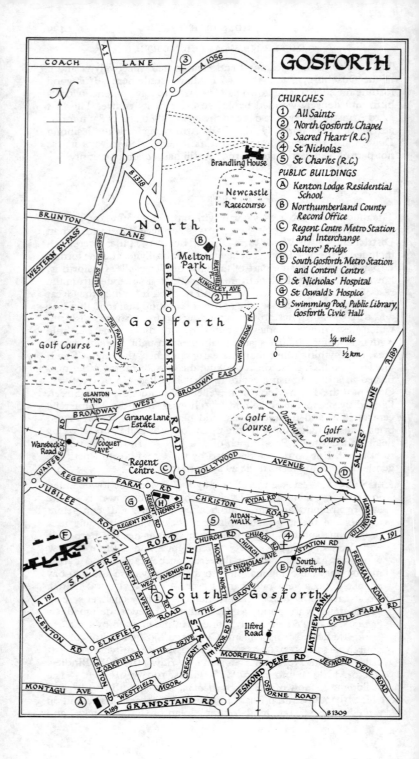

GOSFORTH

CHURCHES
① All Saints
② North Gosforth Chapel
③ Sacred Heart (R.C.)
④ St Nicholas
⑤ St Charles (R.C.)

PUBLIC BUILDINGS
Ⓐ Kenton Lodge Residential School
Ⓑ Northumberland County Record Office
Ⓒ Regent Centre Metro Station and Interchange
Ⓓ Salters' Bridge
Ⓔ South Gosforth Metro Station and Control Centre
Ⓕ St Nicholas' Hospital
Ⓖ St Oswald's Hospice
Ⓗ Swimming Pool, Public Library, Gosforth Civic Hall

0 ¼ mile
0 ½ km

B 1309

apsed chancel, with W gallery, *John Dobson* in 1818–20 added galleried N and S aisles and broke a new door through in the S aisle between the two westernmost windows. The S tower porch was added in 1833. Restoration of 1884, and addition of N porch, by *R. J. Johnson*. In 1913 *Hicks & Charlewood* extended the building E, making the nave a bay longer, blocking Dobson's door, building a new, wider chancel, and adding a Lady Chapel and a second N aisle; they also removed the galleries. Clergy vestry of 1959.

Hammer-dressed sandstone blocks and tooled ashlar dressings are (in 1991) in varying shades of sootiness. The stone spire is swept out gracefully at the base to meet the square tower. The tower porches provide the principal entrances, that on the N having two reset fragments of medieval dripmould. Another door has been inserted near the E end of the S aisle. Recessed round-headed windows throughout. The alterations of 1913, including the curved Venetian apse window, are all in keeping with the earlier work. *Dobson*'s aisles have Tuscan colonnades with wide segmental arches. *Hicks & Charlewood* used the same style for the nave extension and the second N arcade; their Ionic columns support the chancel and apse arches. Their apse window has a keyed surround. Plain tower arch. The *œils-de-bœuf* which were provided to light the galleries now give a good light to the nave. – REREDOS and chancel wood-panelled, with the ALTAR in the same restrained classical style, all by Hicks & Charlewood. – STAINED GLASS. E window and W tower window by *Kempe*. – S aisle W window, *c.* 1840 by *Wailes*, designed for the E apse, but resited by him in this position *c.* 1860; strong blue and red in Gothic style, with figures of the Evangelists in a large central medallion, and their symbols in four smaller medallions. – Several memorial windows to young men who died in the Great War, including the N aisle window to G. H. S. T. Bullen † 1917, signed *Swaine Bourne*. – N aisle above vestry door by *L. C. Evetts* (Flight into Egypt), *c.* 1952. – Two more by Evetts in the chancel: N with arms of local families, 1985; and S with symbols of the Eucharist and the Passion. – MONUMENTS. In the N aisle, several plain reset tablets of the 1830s and 1840s, some by *G. Green* and one by *Davies*, both of Newcastle; and one to William Vincent Von Hompesch 'of the ancient house of Nassau', and Count of the Holy Roman Empire, † 1839. – In the S wall, a reset coat of arms of the Blenkinsopp Coulson family, with two crests. – In the CHURCHYARD many headstones still fortunately *in situ*, and the large severely Greek vault of the Brandling family to the NE of the church, probably early C 19. – Beside the NW path a stone inscribed MAIN DIKE will be understood when its companion (*see* Perambulation, below) is reached.

NORTH GOSFORTH CHAPEL, Kingsley Avenue, Melton Park. A ruin within a housing estate of the 1950s, built in the grounds of Gosforth House. The first reference to the chapel was made in 1296. Only a few courses of masonry remain to show that there was a small nave with S door and a chancel with a N door. Medieval and later grave covers are set in the turf.

SACRED HEART (R.C.), Sandy Lane, North Gosforth. Built *c.* 1865, for T.E. Smith of Gosforth House, on a site within the Park;

bought by the R. C. diocese of Hexham and Newcastle in 1912. Unremarkable except for its STAINED GLASS by *Morris & Co.*; E window, 1875 by *Burne-Jones*, and the others of uncertain date in N chancel. – S aisle E by *Burne-Jones*, and S chancel and N aisle E by *William Morris*.

ST CHARLES (R.C.), Church Road. 1864. Not a particularly interesting church, with vaguely Perp windows and oddly incorporated W towers from an E.E.-style church in New Bridge Street, Newcastle (then recently demolished). Nevertheless, not to be missed by students of STAINED GLASS, because there are three extravagantly rich windows by *Harry Clarke*.

NORTHUMBERLAND COUNTY RECORD OFFICE, Heathfield Place, Melton Park. Exceptionally secure because it was a wartime defence bunker (1939–45). Concrete.

GOSFORTH CIVIC HALL, SWIMMING POOL and PUBLIC LIBRARY. *See* Perambulation (Regent Centre).

NEWCASTLE RACECOURSE. *See* Gosforth Park, below.

KENTON LODGE (Residential School), at the junction of Kenton and Grandstand Roads. A careful Queen Anne Revival house of *c.* 1908 by *Newcombe & Newcombe* for Max Holzapfel (i.e. crabapple; hence the central bunches of iron apples on the wrought-iron gates). Good lettering in low relief on the later Newcastle Education Committee panel over the gate.

ST NICHOLAS' HOSPITAL, Jubilee Road. 1869, with additions of *c.* 1900 and later. An assortment of buildings punctuated by two Italianate square towers. The recreation hall of 1900 has large round-headed windows with two sub-arches and a roundel in each, not very different in style from the buildings around, but there is one astonishing feature – a *Doulton*-tiled proscenium arch by *W. J. Neatby* in *art nouveau* style, the only one of its kind in any hospital. Female figures in flowing robes float beside richly coloured trees with sinuous branches and roots, while tall flowers rise from ground carpeted by simple daisies.

ST OSWALD'S HOSPICE, Regent Avenue. 1984 by *J. & D. Darbyshire* (project architect *Jane Darbyshire*); landscape architects *Kendrick Associates Landscape*. Warm stone, low-pitched roofs and an interesting garden with roofed walks give this small group of buildings a reassuringly domestic air. Bedrooms look onto the garden, and the whole group is sheltered from the street by a courtyard-like car-park.

SOUTH GOSFORTH METRO STATION AND CONTROL CENTRE, Station Road. 1980 (for the Metro system, *see* Newcastle Public Buildings, above). It took the place of the 1865 station of the Blyth and Tyne branch of the North Eastern Railway Company. All that survives from 1865 is a sturdy cast-iron footbridge, wisely kept when the station house was demolished. The new station has the usual clean lines, its principal windows a band of smoked glass on the first floor, the flat roof not much higher than the sides of the cutting. The warm russet bricks are also used for walls by the footpaths, and thick metal tubes support the curved corrugated roof of the E platform shelter.

REGENT CENTRE METRO STATION AND BUS AND TRAIN INTERCHANGE, Great North Road. Built *c.* 1980. Exposed aggregate piers and vitreous enamel panels – no-nonsense finishes – for the station and its roof car-park. A *porte cochère* for buses has open-deck roof. (For the Metro System, *see* Newcastle Public Buildings, above; for the Regent Centre, *see* Perambulation, below.)

SALTERS' BRIDGE, Salters' Lane, over the Ouseburn. The medieval fabric consists of one arch, pointed with three broad ribs, the E end of the bridge on the upstream side, and the adjoining cutwater, which rises to a square pedestrian refuge in the parapet. The W arch was renewed and the whole bridge widened with segmental arches at an unknown date.

GOSFORTH PARK, North Gosforth. Gosforth House, now called BRANDLING HOUSE, was designed by *James Paine* and built in 1755–64 for Charles Brandling, coalowner and M.P. It lies in the heart of the Park, backing on to the drive, and facing S over the landscape towards Newcastle, which was far distant when it was built. The interior was burnt by suffragettes in 1914. The exterior has suffered as much from being made the back premises of the grandstand of the racecourse established there in 1881 by the High Gosforth Park Company Ltd.

The NORTH ENTRANCE FRONT is of three storeys and seven bays, the central three bays projecting slightly under a dentilled open pediment. Above Paine's typical rusticated half-basement are Paine's typical windows in architrave surrounds. Those at the centre and ends of the *piano nobile* have Paine's blind balustrades to the aprons, and long slender curves at either side below segmental pediments, the central one on brackets. Over the corresponding window of the attic storey is a floating cornice, carrying the eye to Paine's typical open pediment. Similar discipline controls the plainer wings flanking the yard, which have E and W sides developed as minor façades, also with projecting middle bays and pediments. Of the seven-bay SOUTH FRONT, only the rusticated basement with end niches and the first-floor windows with architrave surrounds are visible: the whole composition can be imagined only with difficulty. It had a slightly projecting three-bay centre stressed by coupled pilasters at the angles and single pilasters between. The principal windows are pedimented, the central first-floor window arched; there was a top three-bay pediment. The GRANDSTAND which obscures so much is itself not without interest. Late C19 quasi-Ionic cast-iron columns support the glass roof.

PARK HOUSE, across the drive to the NE, was the house for the estate steward, and may well be of 1760 by *Paine*. Sandstone, with two-storey, three-bay centre and lower two-bay wings. The main block has a central open pediment, but alterations have destroyed its original symmetry, which had a central door below a round-headed window. Deeply cut voussoirs to other windows, and rusticated quoins.

The ENTRANCE to Gosforth Park and the racecourse from the B 1318 is thoroughly impressive: two large gate piers of 1830, by *Dobson*, incorporate the Brandling arms carved in high relief. The lodge is simple, with a classical doorcase.

KENTON BAR ESTATE. 1964–8 houses, in terraces without any fussy detail, by *Ryder & Yates & Partners* for the City of Newcastle.

PERAMBULATION. Our perambulation begins in Church Road at
South Gosforth Metro Station opposite St Nicholas's Church (for
both of which, *see* above). N of St Nicholas lies a cluster of well-
planned PREFABRICATED HOUSES, provided by the Government under the Housing (Temporary Accommodation) Act 1944
and put up by Gosforth U. D. C. In RYDAL ROAD they are the
'Howard' type of house, designed by *F. Gibberd*: two storeys, now
with brick cladding and porches. In the group of streets named
after Northumbrian saints they are one-storey, with later
pebbledash.* At the E end of AIDAN WALK, a round-topped slab
of sandstone set in the grass verge is the MAIN DIKE STONE,
which commemorates Gosforth Colliery's conquest of the 'main'
or '90 fathom dike', a fault which causes a vast drop in the strata:
it was the blight of mining engineers in SE Northumberland. In
1829 the colliery owners held a celebratory ball a thousand feet
below ground. Guests hewed their own souvenir lumps of coal.
There is another such stone within St Nicholas's churchyard (*see*
above), which also marks the underground line the dike follows.

In ST NICHOLAS' AVENUE, SW of the church, the head office
of PROCTER & GAMBLE (UK), formerly Hedley House, is an
example of the humanized style of its period and an asset to the
surrounding area: 1951–3, by *Sidney Burn*, Staff Architect of Thos.
Hedley & Co., soap manufacturers, with *Anthony Chitty* as consultant architect. The entrance block is the hub of four two-storey
ranges extending in various directions. Light yellow brick; some
roofs flat and some gently pitched; variation is also provided by
an occasional wall of dark blue or russet bricks. Entrance and
windows altered. Set in a landscape by *B. Hackett* where well-
chosen trees punctuate greensward. Inserted rather close to the
street is the WEST BUILDING by *Sir Basil Spence & Partners*
(opened 1964); black ribs articulating Portland stone cladding.
More additions and alterations in progress in 1992. THE GROVE,
leading E from St Nicholas's Church to the High Street, has at
its end two mid-C19 stone terraces on the r., each house of two
bays, with long gardens in front. In the HIGH STREET, part of
the Great North Road, two more stone terraces of larger Victorian
houses. All these are in almost original condition. On the W side
of the street, the former lodge to Coxlodge Hall, now No. 2
THE DRIVE. It has keyed stone surrounds to elliptical-headed
windows, oddly French-looking in the midst of Northern sobriety.
The former STABLES (now offices), further along The Drive,
were built *c.* 1796 for Job Bulman of Coxlodge Hall (demolished
c. 1938). In good local sandstone, gold and brown, this symmetrical block of three times three bays has a clock tower over a
pedimented centre, and keyed oculi. The incongruous Corinthian
porch is surely an addition. Further W, at the junction of Kenton
and Grandstand Roads, lies Kenton Lodge School (*see* above).

At the N end of High Street, BULMAN VILLAGE is recorded
in an inscription in the front gable of the building N of the
Brandling Arms, which was supposedly carved at the behest of
the builder, Cuthbert Burnup. It used to refer to the group of

* There are more post-1945 prefabricated houses off the Great North Road N of the
Regent Centre on the GRANGE LANE ESTATE in Coquet Avenue and Glanton Wynd.

houses built after the 1826 election to create freeholds with votes. All that survives of them is a group of plain stone buildings behind the shops, and this reset stone. Further N up the Great North Road we come to the REGENT CENTRE, an office and leisure complex served by the Metro Interchange (*see* above). The LIBRARY and SWIMMING POOL, by *Waring and Netts*, 1967–8, are brick and concrete, with copper fascias and much glass. High-quality materials are used for the office blocks, all otherwise undistinguished, except for the NORTHERN ROCK HOUSE, 1967–8 by *Richard Turley Associates*, a wide two-storey block below a tall slender tower, with narrow vertical panels of gleaming white tiles and frame-sawn slate counterbalancing the horizontals of the base. SE of this group, GOSFORTH CIVIC HALL, a concert hall of 1974 by *Mauchlen, Weightman and Elphick*, is on a more do-mestic scale, with warm red bricks and a polygonal theme carried through from entrance hall to raised flowerbeds and tiled forecourt, the latter unfortunately disfigured (in 1990) by clumsy bollards.

HEATON

Heaton Park was originally part of the grounds of Heaton Hall, which belonged to the Ridleys of Blagdon; but by 1868 the whole township was owned by Lord Armstrong. By 1898 much of it had been covered with houses, some in terraces conveniently close to the various engineering works which were growing beside the railway, and some villas for the more prosperous families. Develop-ment then spread N into the High Heaton area, where housing estates were built between the wars.

ST GABRIEL, Heaton Road. 1898–1905 by *F. W. Rich*, on land given by Lord Armstrong. The church hall to the E of the tower was added in 1924; Lady Chapel and S transept completed in 1931 by *H. L. Hicks*. A big cruciform church, with aisles, N and S porches, NE tower and porch; the whole makes a good group from Heaton Road. Snecked sandstone with well-carved dressings; graduated Lakeland slate roof. Free use of Gothic styles, with Dec and Perp windows, particularly large in the transept gables and at the E and W ends. The W gable's octagonal corner turrets and the battlemented porches prepare the eye for the important tower, which has three tall stages, the uppermost with paired bell openings below a Gothic-lettered frieze and pierced battlements. The angle buttresses lead up to octagonal corners which look none the worse for the absence of the intended pinnacles. Three-bay arcades with richly carved foliage capitals, and taller enriched arches to the Lady Chapel and to the tower organ loft. Hammer-beam roof. Rood beam. – Large carved triptych REREDOS with niches and statues. – FRESCO on the E wall. The principal effect is of light and spaciousness. – MONUMENTS. Alabaster War Memorial of *c.* 1920, with enamel plaques of archangels. – Brass in N transept to Walter Baston, churchwarden and the contractor who built the church, † 1913.

ST THERESA (R.C.), Heaton Road. 1972 by *David Brown*. An octagonal church with the roof (re-covered with shingles in 1990) pleated into eight radiating pitches with high gables; a *flèche* marks the centre. The altar is to the N, with the pews in six radiating blocks and the seventh of the eight sides occupied by the Blessed Sacrament Chapel. The simple materials are carefully used; the low walls are of warm-toned Flemish stretcher bond brick, the gables filled with glass. Altars, font and communion rail are good simple shapes in granite.

NONCONFORMIST CHAPELS. It is rewarding to walk along HEATON ROAD from S to N. Of the following, none is particularly outstanding, but they make a fine cross-section of C 19 Nonconformist architecture. From S to N: CUTHBERT BAINBRIDGE MEMORIAL CHURCH (Methodist), 1885 by *S. Oswald & Son*, in the lancet style, with SW tower with pyramid roof. The former HEATON CONGREGATIONAL (now Elim Pentecostal), 1880–2 by *Oliver & Leeson*, very plain, with C 13 tracery and a *flèche*. HEATON UNITED REFORMED CHURCH (formerly Presbyterian), 1895–6 by *W. L. Newcombe*, E.E., with polygonal turret just l. of the doorway; aisles with cross-gables, late E.E. tracery. HEATON BAPTIST, 1904, plain, red brick, with lancet windows. HEATON METHODIST, 1902 by *Hope & Maxwell*, Gothic with some perverse details, such as the many ogee labels; a SW polygonal turret and a NW semicircular projection like the base of another turret.

HEATON BRANCH LIBRARY, Heaton Estate. 1968 by *Williamson, Faulkner Brown & Partners*. Very like the library at Jesmond (q.v.) by the same firm: circular plan, with zigzag perimeter so that full-height windows light the bookcases on each recess.

DENE CENTRE, Freeman Road. 1983–5 by *J. Lynn* for the Disabled Income Group. Simple materials are used to great effect, and the site has been skilfully exploited to preserve the setting and the view. A low grassed mound and the gentle slopes of long ramps are the base of a composition, which has the low wide pyramid of the roof as the centre and Jesmond Dene behind as the middle distance. On the horizon the long ridge of Simonside at Rothbury can be seen on a clear day. The two adjacent SCHOOLS (one for handicapped children, the other a church primary school), although older (1970s) and more basic, are similarly and sensitively massed.

HEATON MANOR SCHOOL, Newton Road. Designed as Heaton High School in 1928 by *H. T. Wright*. The C 17 style is used in a free manner for long ranges which originally had arcaded fronts to admit fresh air. The air proved too fresh, and alterations have been made which have not been so well designed.

HENDERSON HALL, Etherstone Avenue. A men's hall of residence of *c.* 1932 by *A. Dunbar Smith* for Armstrong College (now the University of Newcastle). Attractive Queen Anne revival, using warm-coloured brick and tile. Wonderful big roofs with hipped dormers, and ridges and hips – mere constructional details – with sculptural strength of line and form.

ARMSTRONG PARK, Jesmond Vale Lane, is that part of the valley of the Ouseburn lying E of the stream and N of the lane, which was given to the City by Lord Armstrong in the 1880s. On the higher ground is HEATON WINDMILL, disused for at least 130 years and now without cap, sails and machinery. C 18; nearly straight sides.

HEATON PARK, Heaton Park Road. The first part of the valley of
the Ouseburn to be given to Newcastle by Lord Armstrong, in
1879. Part was laid out as a formal park, with balustraded terrace
(restored in the 1980s). Within its boundaries on the s side of
Jesmond Vale Lane, what is known as ADAM OF JESMOND'S
CAMERA (or sometimes, for no clear reason, King John's Palace),
a tower-house built before 1267 and probably empty by the c 17;
repaired in 1897 by *W. H. Knowles*. N and E walls surviving to
first-floor level; NW corner turret; pointed doorway on the N side;
round-headed first-floor window.

PERAMBULATION. An interesting progression of house types and
ecclesiastical styles can be seen by walking from s to N along
HEATON ROAD from Shields Road (which is properly in Byker).
At first the churches (*see* above) are late c 19 and early c 20,
contemporary with the Tyneside flats all around. These are recognizable by their paired doors, one to the downstairs flat, a second
to the upstairs flat. Then comes Heaton Park and the late c 20
St Theresa (R.C.) (*see* above). The terraces here are of larger
houses. Beyond there are late c 19 villas on the E side and 1920s–
30s semi-detached houses on the w. St Gabriel was built to serve
the villas.

Beyond the major E–W traffic route, Stephenson Road, we
come to HIGH HEATON. Here, in NEWTON ROAD, just s
of Heaton Manor School (*see* above), is WYNCOTE COURT,
interesting 1960s houses by *Waring & Netts Partnership*, non-
traditional in style and plan and with their construction clearly
expressed in a rhythm of brick and glass. Off the E side of Newton
Road, the HIGH HEATON ESTATE, one of Newcastle's best
inter-war housing estates. It was designed by *R. G. Roberts*, the
Corporation Architect, and built in the 1930s using vernacular
revival forms and materials in garden-suburb tradition. Some
houses are Queen Anne style, of brick with pedimented doors,
sash windows, and high roofs covered in an interesting variety of
tiles and slates. Others have tile-hung first floors, and bright red
tile roofs; yet others are built of concrete blocks in imitation of
stone and have roof tiles in subtle shades to look like stone slates.
The original doors were simply boarded with small glazed panels,
the sashes had glazing bars and architraves, and the gables bargeboards; although many of these details have been lost, the overall
impression is still of village houses transported to a suburb. The
layout is in concentric crescents, with space provided for garden
allotments behind them. In the centre is a row of shops in a long
'Queen Anne' block which in 1991 retains most of its original
detail. Behind this block is THE SPINNEY, 1963, tower flats by
the *City Architect*. The blank sides are given life by a grid of low
pyramidal projections. At its foot is the Heaton Branch Library
(*see* above). The Heaton Estate houses are being refurbished by
the City of Newcastle in 1991. To the E of the estate lies Henderson Hall (*see* above).

A mile to the E along the COAST ROAD, right on the city
boundary, is the former WILLS FACTORY. Although built in 125
1946–50 it is a fine example of the style of factory architecture
familiar from the 1930s. Designed by the Imperial Tobacco
Company architect, *Cecil Hockin*, using brick and sandstone on a

steel frame; engineer *J. H. Burn*. In 1991 it is being adapted to
other uses.

JESMOND

Jesmond became part of Newcastle in 1835. Then there were water-
driven mills (at least four for flint-grinding) and a forge on the banks
of the Ouseburn; but no industry of any great size developed, and
Jesmond remained no more than a village up to the middle of
the C 19, when it became the residential suburb for Newcastle's
wealthiest inhabitants (pop. 2,100 in 1851, 6,100 in 1881, 21,400 in
1911). For them were built the substantial brick terraces in the
Tyneside classical tradition that give the suburb its character.
Sufficiently isolated from the town to support a full range of shops
and services, and yet close enough for a brisk walk to the centre, it
still prospers (pop. 11,620 in 1990).

HOLY TRINITY, Churchill Gardens. Chancel of 1908 by *Hicks &
Charlewood*; nave, aisles, tall W tower and spire completed 1920–2
by *Hoare & Wheeler* as a war memorial, the gift of the Dalgliesh
and Hoare familes. This striking building is made even more
prominent by its site on the rim of Jesmond Dene. The high
quality of design and craftsmanship is continued in the windows
(with Dec tracery), filled by contemporary STAINED GLASS with
military insignia by *Nicholson Studios*.

JESMOND PARISH CHURCH, Eslington Road. 1857–61 by *John
Dobson*; vestry by *R. J. Johnson*, 1874. Paid for by public subscription to commemorate Richard Clayton, a leading evangelical
minister. Late E.E., with big pinnacled tower, planned to receive
a spire which was never built, and cross-gabled aisles. Six bays
plus two chancel bays; octagonal piers; no clerestory. Much rich
carving, with gargoyles and varied tracery. The interior expresses
the evangelical principles of its founders, and has no separate
chancel (originally the communion table stood on a timber floor,
with rails on three sides) and N and S galleries. The galleries were
given new fronts in 1907, and the W gallery removed so that a
baptistry could be made as a memorial to the Laing family, with
an enamel roundel of great beauty set on the N gallery to record
the fact. – STAINED GLASS. By *Atkinson Bros.*, Newcastle, in S
baptistry and N aisle. E window of N aisle, 1886 by *J. B. Capronnier*,
Brussels. Tall five-light E window, 1956 by *Lawrence Lee*. – *Johnson's* VESTRY is interestingly domestic, with wide stone fireplace
and hammerbeam roof.

ST GEORGE, Osborne Road. 1888–9 by *T. R. Spence*. A very
ambitious church, built and furnished at the expense (£30,000)
of Lord Armstrong's partner, Charles Mitchell, collector of pictures and father of the painter *Charles W. Mitchell*, who contributed to the decoration. Spence had already enlarged Mitchell's
house, Jesmond Towers (now La Sagesse School, *see* below). Here
he followed the precepts of the Arts-and-Crafts movement and
integrated the decoration with the structure; all is expensive and
well-executed, and very progressive in style for its date. Good
local sandstone ashlar, and roof of graduated Lakeland slate. A
strong composition, E.E., with a high clerestory with five large

windows rising from wide aisles with paired lancets, the gable of
the s w porch rising over the eaves at one end, and the campanile –
'tower' is too English a word for it – standing forward at the other,
its pyramidal top in complete harmony with the steeply pitched
main roof. Three E lancets are placed high in the wall; a long two-
light w window rises above a wide gentle baptistry, where over a
row of lancets is a band of low relief carved with natural forms in
the firmly controlled flowing manner found in all the other external decoration. The interior is high and dramatic, an inspiring 102
setting for ritual, and now a unique witness to Spence's importance as a designer of such schemes (e.g. his decoration – now
overpainted – of the former All Saints, Ennismore Gardens,
London). The approach through the s porch prepares one for the
quality beyond, for it has fine wrought-iron GATES made to
Spence's designs by *Alfred Shirley* (who did all the metalwork)
and delicate stained glass. High, simple arcades with round piers
are the foil for the richness to E and w. The w wall is panelled
with tracery in Caen stone above the three baptistry arches, and
has a central canopied niche containing a bronze STATUE of St
George by *Spence*. – The superb STAINED GLASS window above,
by *John W. Brown*, is filled with angels at the Last Judgement. All
the windows were made by *Gateshead Stained Glass Co.*, except
for the two w aisle windows, by *O'Neil Bros.* Brown also designed
the figures in the E window, a rich, glowing Nativity which is
matched in splendour by the surrounding MOSAIC in the chancel,
with figures designed by *C. W. Mitchell*, the benefactor's son, and
executed by *Rust & Co.* Below the mosaic, glazed tile with roundels of the Evangelists by *G. W. Rhead*, set in a surround of natural
and abstract curving, interlacing leafy shapes by *Spence*. The focus
of all this is the richly carved ALTAR AND REREDOS of Pavonazza
marble, by *Emley & Sons* of Newcastle, who also made the matching FONT. Richly carved wood PULPIT by *Ralph Hedley*,
and SCREENS by him and Messrs *Robson & Co.* – ROOFS
stencilled and painted by *C. S. Wardropper* of Gosforth
to designs by *Spence*. – MEMORIALS by *Frampton*, in the
N wall to Charles Mitchell (1898) and in the s wall to Charles
W. Mitchell † 1903. Of bronze, carved stone, and enamel. –
Fine War Memorial (1920) by *Hicks & Charlewood*, brass and
alabaster.

St HILDA, Thornleigh Street. Daughter church of St George's,
Jesmond. 1900–5 by *Hicks & Charlewood*, with attached school, all
inscribed with the date 1900. Good materials – snecked sandstone,
graduated Lakeland slate – and Perp style. Copper-covered
central *flèche*.

JESMOND UNITED REFORMED CHURCH (formerly Presbyterian), Burdon Terrace. 1887–8 by *W. L. Newcombe*. Good materials – sandstone and Lakeland slate – in free Gothic style.
Windows fill the wall above paired doors, which are set between
pink granite shafts with stiffleaf capitals. s w tower. Consistently
well designed and decorated inside, with more pink granite
columns and a king-post roof. Behind the chancel arch the space
is filled by the organ, a familiar Presbyterian arrangement; w
gallery over the vestibule. – STAINED GLASS. By *Kempe & Co.*,
1904, in ritual E and transept windows. By *H. Dearle* of *Morris &*

Co., 1921, in W, over the doors. S clerestory and N and S aisle windows of 1938 and 1933 by *H. Hendrie.* – WAR MEMORIAL, *c.* 1920, in high relief by *Walter Gilbert*, with soldiers, St George, and an angel flanking the Crucifixion.

ALL SAINTS' CEMETERY, Jesmond Road. 1856 by *Benjamin Green.* Gothic. The gateway and chapels demonstrate very nicely the change in taste that twenty years can bring when compared with the Greek Revival Jesmond Cemetery (*see* below). The chapels are set well back from the gabled arched gateway, and the mood is not sombre and powerful but rather cheerful, with nook-shafts and dripmoulds, buttresses and belfries. Elaborate iron gates and railings complete the picture.

JESMOND CEMETERY, Jesmond Road. 1836 by *John Dobson* for the Newcastle General Cemetery Company. A fine composition, in excellent ashlar; Greek classicism, in a suitably sombre vein, but not slavishly so – for the entrance is after all an arch, which belongs to Rome, not Athens. Loudon wrote of it in 1843 that it was 'the most appropriate cemetery lodge' that he knew, 'because it can never be mistaken for an entrance to a public park or to a country residence'. The strong horizontals at the three main levels – entrance, flanking towers and chapels – are balanced by corner pilasters, paired under pediments at each end of the chapels and supporting parapets with iron grilles in the towers. Spear-headed iron gates with acanthus decoration for the principals. The chapels were converted to offices in 1978. – The SOUTH GATEWAY is equally monumental and Greek, with antefixae and acroteria and a severe lodge. – The GRAVEYARD itself, also laid out by Dobson, rewards the curious with many famous names as well as with a sense of the great prosperity of C 19 Newcastle: architects and artists, shopkeepers and writers, engineers and doctors lie in a sort of Tyneside Père Lachaise. In the SW part, John Dobson's own grave († 1865) is commemorated by a dis-appointing marble headstone of 1905; much better is the plain sandstone slab in the centre, inscribed *J. D.* – In contrast, a huge Gothic tower of 1843 to Archibald Reed (NW section), signed by *Dobson.* – By the W side of the principal path, a touching monu-ment with a baby on a couch under a Tudor canopy, to the Keenleyside children † 1841 and 1842, aged one, twelve and ten. The dates are those of a cholera epidemic.

CHAPEL OF ST MARY, Reid Park Road. Ruins, off Jesmond Dene Road and Reid Park Road, on the edge of Jesmond Dene. A fragment of the nave, chancel and sacristy. There is a C 12 chancel arch on fat, semicircular responds; the S capital has coarse volutes, the shafts cushion capitals, and there are some voussoirs with roll and chevron mouldings. In the S wall of the chancel, a C 14 two-light window with cusped tracery. The N chapel (or sacristy) is curiously long and seems to be mid-C 14 work. In its N wall, two cusped ogee-headed lights in a square-headed opening. Piscinae in the chancel S wall and sacristy E wall.

JESMOND BRANCH LIBRARY, St George's Terrace. 1962–3 by *Williamson, Faulkner Brown & Partners* for the City of Newcastle. Like Fenham Branch Library (*see* p. 516), this is typical of the best of its date. A corner site with narrow frontage is used to advantage by setting a circular reading room in a bed of whinstone cobbles and granite setts. The perimeter wall is zigzag in plan, each glass-fronted fin enclosing a bookcase against a lower panel of red granite chips in its longer side. These full-height glass fins lead the eye by stages round the corner.

AKHURST SCHOOL, The Grove, Jesmond. Now an independent school, but built as a private house in 1831 for Matthew Anderson. Strongly reminiscent of *Dobson*'s work of the period, e.g. Jesmond Towers (*see* La Sagesse School, below). Tudor style, in good ashlar, with much original detail inside.

LA SAGESSE HIGH SCHOOL, Bermersyde Drive, occupying JESMOND TOWERS, a large house on the w rim of Jesmond Dene. The first part was built as West Jesmond House in the early C 19, and added to in 1817 and 1823–7 by *Dobson* for Sir Thomas Burdon. It was enlarged by *Thomas Oliver Junior* in 1869 and by *T. R. Spence* in 1884 and 1895 for Charles Mitchell, Lord Armstrong's partner (*see* also St George's Church, above). As might be expected from its slow evolution, it does not have a clear plan. An overall Gothic atmosphere prevails, especially on the front elevation to the s, which is mostly Dobson's. There are traceried windows, blind traceried buttresses with big polygonal pinnacles, pierced parapets and battlemented gables. The additions by Spence respect Dobson's design and show the same high-quality mason work. Internal detail of this period includes much fine carving executed by *Ralph Hedley*. The stone for the 1884 additions, for which *Walter Scott* was the contractor, came from Kenton quarries. The entrance is through a vestibule with a tiled floor incorporating many medieval motifs. To the r. is a stone-arched hall (now partitioned). The main stair of Dobson's building, at the rear opposite the entrance, has gone, but at the r. of the entrance and hall is a Gothic stair probably designed by him, with a cast-metal and timber traceried balustrade. At first-floor level, a triple arch with pendants, and the soffits of the doors off the stair have blind tracery. The stair is lit by an oriel window. Off this stair hall to the E on the ground floor is a room (now the sun parlour) designed as a MORNING or DRAWING ROOM, with an Arts-and-Crafts dado painted with flowing leafy stems bearing many-petalled flowers; similar flowers appear in the lights of the stone tracery of the square bay window at the s end. This window and the dado seem to have been added between 1885 and 1910; Mitchell's son, the artist *Charles W. Mitchell*, may have been involved. It was to provide him with a studio that the central tower was raised between 1869 and 1884. To the l. of the entrance hall, the former BILLIARD ROOM (now library), lit by an oriel window and with a traceried stone arcade. The door surrounds were elaborately carved by *Hedley*, and the richly coloured stained-glass window to the corridor is by *Sowerby* and *Barnet* (according to Neil Moat). It belongs to the 1884 work, and so do the grisaille windows with inset panels of flowers in the top-lit former PICTURE GALLERY (now school hall), which was added to the w end of the house by Spence to display Mitchell's collection. It also has an elaborately carved triple-panelled surround and an ornate stucco frieze and cornice to the panelled ceiling.

The former SOUTH LODGE, now dissociated from Jesmond Towers in Osborne Road, is dated 1880 in the pargetting, which has the initials C M (presumably for Charles Mitchell). Its Arts-and-Crafts style, in red brick and tile, with an attractively steep roof extending over the pargetted eaves of the big front window, is advanced for the area. Was this designed by *Spence*?

JESMOND DENE HOUSE (Residential School), Jesmond Dene Road, sitting within the dene, on slightly higher ground at the N end, 1822 by *Dobson* for T. E. Headlam, but enlarged for Sir Andrew Noble, another of Armstrong's partners, who acquired the house in 1871. The extensions (which almost obliterate Dobson's house) are in two stages: rear wing (1870–1), rooms towards the front (1875), and billiard room (1885) by *Norman Shaw*; and work of the 1890s, with at least a porch of 1897, by *F. W. Rich*. The later work continues the Tudor style of Shaw's earlier work but in a more cheerful vein, with some half-timbering, some render, an oriel window and a corbel table with Arts-and-Crafts carving. Inside there is a Great Hall with gallery, Jacobean-style panelling, a large fireplace, rich use of stone (Frosterley marble fender) and tiles, and a timber roof with moulded beams, cor-belled arch trusses, and bosses. The staircase is not grand, only a small affair tucked in the thickness of the fireplace wall. Tiles by *De Morgan* in the sitting room fireplace.

The STABLES to the W (now police stables) are plainer but not without interest; two ranges of ashlar with a gabled lodge attached, and some original stalls inside.

The RACQUET COURT, further W, was built *c.* 1900 by *F. W. Rich* for real tennis. Rich made a large hall lively by the application of buttresses, tall octagonal corner turrets, a pent entrance at one end and a single-bay two-storey apartment for the professional player at the other. N gallery and large round S windows. In bright red brick (Flemish garden wall bond), and the plain tiles which are almost Rich's trademark.

NAZARETH HOUSE, Sandyford Road. A convent incorporating VILLA REAL, an early design by *Dobson*, 1817, for Captain Dutton, with a Greek porch.

THE MINORIES, Jesmond Road, just E of Nazareth House. A sheltered housing scheme of 1986 by *George Oldham*, City of Newcastle Architect. Pleasantly informal; one- and two-storeyed buildings of soft-coloured brick with wood balconies and pitched roofs, set in attractive gardens.

JESMOND DENE PARK, Jesmond Road. The natural dene of the Ouseburn, improved by the first Lord Armstrong and given by him to the City in 1883. His house has been demolished, but there is still the shell of the nearby BANQUETING HALL, 1860–2 by *Dobson*. Now a roofless ruin, it is a large, rather dull Italianate apartment with many niches that once held statuary by *Lough*. Diners had wonderful views over the dene. – A GATEHOUSE by *R. Norman Shaw*, 1869–70, lies on the E side of Jesmond Dene Road. Pleasingly irregular, in late Tudor style, with stone-mullioned windows and steep roof. In the park a ruin of one of the flint mills mentioned above.

JESMOND RAILWAY STATION (now the 'Carriage' public house and restaurant). This former station on the Blyth and Tyne Railway dates from 1864 and was probably designed by *J. F. Tone*. A good example of a small suburban station in Tudor style, single-storey, in red brick with stone dressings, strong cross gables on the platform side, some mullioned windows, and octagonal chimney stacks.

ARMSTRONG ROAD BRIDGE. A unique structure, designed and constructed in 1876–8 by *W. G. Armstrong & Co.*, with Messrs *W. E. & F. Jackson* as masonry contractors. Eight equal wrought-iron lattice girder spans to give an overall length between abutments of 168 metres (552 ft), supported by seven pairs of square wrought-iron box-section columns, cross-braced with wrought-iron ties and resting on rock-faced sandstone piers; abutments of similar stone construction. What makes it special are the rocker bearings at foot and head of each column, the sliding bearings at the central columns and the fact that each girder is separately supported, all to provide articulation to compensate for any mine subsidence and thermal variation: clearly a wise precaution, for in the 1970s a trial boring between the E columns was unhappily directly on a mine shaft! It provided a high-level crossing of Jesmond Dene between Jesmond and Heaton and at a maximum height of 20 metres (65 ft) above the dene it gave a splendid view of the landscape, which Armstrong transformed into a park before donating it with the bridge to the Corporation of Newcastle. Pedestrianized in 1960, the bridge has become the setting for a successful Sunday arts and crafts market. Threatened with demolition in the 1970s but rescued in the 1980s thanks to a late-discovered underspend by central government in 1982. Columns replaced with steel replicas, cast-iron pilasters replaced in plastic.

VALE HOUSE, Lansdowne Gardens, S of Jesmond Road and over-looking Jesmond Vale. Tower flats of 1967 by *Douglas Wise & Partners* with the *City Architect*. They can be seen to the S from the Armstrong Bridge over Jesmond Dene. Uncluttered white surfaces with the contrast of a black central staircase strip at the centre of the two shorter sides.

OUTER NEWCASTLE WEST

BENWELL

A Roman fort and a medieval village swallowed in C 19 and C 20 housing.

CONDERCUM, the Roman fort, lay on the hilltop astride Hadrian's Wall (here marked by the West Road); its N third was destroyed by the reservoir. Both fort and attendant civil settlement are now built over, except for the TEMPLE OF ANTENOCITICUS (probably a native god), in Broomridge Avenue: an apsidal building, like a small church, with an E side door. Replicas of C 2 altars found there flank the apse; this probably contained the life-size stone statue of Antenociticus, the head and legs of which are in the Museum of Antiquities in Newcastle.

The VALLUM CROSSING, at the foot of Denhill Park, is the sole visible example of a masonry-revetted original causeway across the ditch of the Vallum. The W pier of the gate that closed the causeway is still in position, built of ashlar of exceptional quality.

Opening northwards, it gave access to the military zone and led directly to the s gate of the fort, 60 metres up the hill. The build-up of successive road-surfaces is displayed.

St James, Benwell Lane. 1831–2, designed as a chapel of ease by *John Dobson*; his first use of Norman style. It became the parish church in 1843; nave and aisle were added in 1864, the original chapel becoming the chancel. Organ chamber and vestry 1879–80; spire, choir vestry and porch by *Hicks & Charlewood*, 1895. Most of the additions are in the Norman style. – In the church-yard, the anonymous sandstone slab, within a T-shaped enclos-ure of Gothic cast-iron railings, is the Grainger family burial place, where Richard Grainger † 1861 lies.

St Joseph (R.C.), Armstrong Road. 1929 by *Stienlet & Maxwell*. A successful brick-and-pantiled church of Mediterranean inspi-ration (cf. The Venerable Bede, below), but more straight-forwardly Romanesque.

The Venerable Bede, Benwell Grove. 1936–7 by *W. B. Edwards*. Brick and pantiles in a style which owes more to the Mediterranean than to Bede's northern Europe. A fascinating church, full of rich detail, mostly structural rather than applied. The w front is particularly pleasing: the high wide tower has a hierarchy of windows: widely spaced and small at the lowest level, then a group of three long lights with arched heads, and at the top a tripartite light under a pitched roof. Set back from this are the porches, with arches of long thin bricks framing low-relief carvings of the life of Bede over the wide sandstone surrounds of the two doors.

St John's Cemetery, Elswick Road. 1856 by *Johnstone & Knowles*. Entrance gateway, lodges and chapels with an archway. The lodges plain, but the remainder Gothic, with a profusion of pinnacles. Amazingly, the cast-iron gates and some railings (cf. All Saints' Cemetery, Jesmond) escaped the Second World War salvage campaign.

Pendower Hall Teachers' Centre, West Road. Built (as a house called Pendower) *c.* 1867 for the banker J. W. Pease, one of the Darlington Quaker banking family. The architect is unknown, but the stair window has armorial glass similar to that at Hutton Hall (North Yorkshire), built in 1866 for another Pease by Alfred Waterhouse. Additions of 1885 by *R. J. Johnson* (A. Greg). A fine house, with French Renaissance and English c 17 elements. The full-height semicircular bay on the s, facing over the valley, is especially successful, with curved mullioned-and-transomed windows. The interior has fittings of high quality. One set of Jacobean-style panelling is dated 1885, the year of the Peases' silver wedding. Stained glass in the billiard room has been iden-tified by Neil Moat as by *Cottier* of Regent Street, in his later style.

Former Whickham View Schools (now Community Centre, but in 1991 threatened with demolition), between Muscott Grove and Norland Road, 1936–8 by the City of Newcastle Education Committee's Building Surveyor *F. W. Harvey*. Two low, wide schools, for boys and girls, linked by a central octagonal tower on concrete piers with inlaid granite bands. Such high style continues throughout, generally recalling Dutch architecture of the 1920s, though the ornament is Art Deco. Large sweeping curves of dark brick, set off by white metal windows, in stepped and linked blocks containing a full range of up-to-date facilities (swimming pool and gymnasiums, craft rooms, assembly halls etc.). Original horizontal oak panelling in the entrance halls, and a compass panel in the ceiling above the twin concrete spiral stairs in the tower.

BENWELL WATERWORKS, Axwell Park View. The LODGE, a pleasant Tudor-style cottage, probably of 1857, was built for the Whittle Dean Water Company, for which *Robert Nicholson* was the engineer. He died in 1855 and was succeeded by his nephew, *J. F. Tone*. Near it, the PUMPING ENGINE CHIMNEY of 1904 for the Newcastle and Gateshead Water Company (consulting engineer *Charles Hawksley*; resident engineer *A. L. Forster*). Octagonal, with classical treatment so that the base has rounded moulding and the top has band and cornice.

BENWELL TOWERS, Benwell Lane. Really a country house – by *John Dobson* for Thomas Crawhall – for it stood well outside Newcastle when it was built in 1831, on the site of the Shafto family seat (which incorporated an older tower, hence the name). One of Dobson's Tudor houses, with Tudor-arched openings, many stone mullioned windows and the usual battlements. Inside, a fine staircase, well-proportioned rooms with panelled ceilings and marble chimneypieces. In 1882 the Pease family gave it to the diocese of Newcastle for the Bishop's residence, and *W. S. Hicks* added the chapel. Awaiting a new use in 1991.

PENDOWER ESTATE, S and SW of Pendower Hall Teachers' Centre (*see* above). An early council housing estate laid out from 1919 according to Garden Suburb principles and continued into the 1920s by *Cackett, Dick & Mackellar*.

W of Benwell, down by the river at Scotswood, is the ARMSTRONG WORKS, 1981–2 by *Ryder & Yates & Partners* for Vickers' Defence Systems, on the site of Armstrong's Scotswood engineering works. A sophisticated shed, with tall slit windows balancing the horizontals of water and riverbank. It is ideally suited to its site, stretching along the shore, and set on the floor slabs and other old surfaces of the previous factory, which provided a good hard foundation. The old factory railway lines are retained within the present floor.

DENTON

HADRIAN'S WALL TURRET 7b is on the side of the West Road, just E of the intersection with the western bypass. Deeply recessed into the Wall, this is the sole visible example of the original design for the incorporation of turret and curtain: the broad wing-walls of the turret bonded in with the Broad Wall on either side. Inside is a stone platform to take the foot of a timber stair or ladder which gave access to the upper floors. Unusually, occupation here lasted into the late C4.

DENTON HALL, 800 West Road. On the porch the inscription '16 A E D 22', which refers to Anthony and Dorothy Errington.

1622 is quite believable for the porch, with its shaped gable and ball finials, and for the whole of the E-plan gabled stone house. Doorways have four-centred arches, windows chamfered surrounds and chamfered mullions. The roof is a fine example of a once common type, pantiled, but with stone slates for the lowest courses. The large c 17 rooms were subdivided in the c 18, and further alterations were made *c.* 1900, when a c 17-style chimney-piece was inserted in the ground-floor hall.

ELSWICK

This was a rural area, with pockets of industry near the river, until it was transformed by the setting up of W. G. Armstrong's engineering works in 1848 and the subsequent rapid spread of
122 housing (*see* p. 98).

CHURCHES. *See* Newcastle, Churches, above.

ELSWICK PARK. Originally the grounds of the classical Elswick Lodge by *W. & J. Stokoe*, 1803, which was bought, with its estate, by Richard Grainger in 1839. Only a small park round the site of the house escaped c 19 development. In place of the house stands ELSWICK SWIMMING POOL by the *Napper Collerton Partnership*, a lively community building of *c.* 1984 in dark wood, red brick and copper and with tubular steel latticework to support the roof.

FENHAM

HOLY CROSS, Ovington Grove. 1935–6 by *H. L. Hicks* of *Hicks & Charlewood*, on land given by J. R. Blackett Ord of Whitfield Hall, whose ancestors lived at Fenham Hall. He also paid for the church and refused to yield to criticism of the plans. A straightforward modern building, made from warm-coloured c 19 bricks, with almost no decoration within and without, other than that provided by the materials themselves. The campanile-like NW tower has rows of long belfry openings and no ornament except a large gilded cross finial. Before reroofing, pantiles made a pleasing rippled pattern. The porch of 1965 is not very appropriate. The long high nave, with low round arches over the altar and to the narrow aisles, is well lit from high clerestory windows, and has a reinforced concrete barrel vault.

ST JAMES AND ST BASIL, Fenham Hall Drive. The church belongs to Fenham the suburb rather than to Fenham Hall and the hamlet of the c 18 and c 19 around it. 1927–31 by *E. E. Lofting*, and paid for by Sir James Knott in memory of his sons James and Basil, killed in the First World War. A solid, prosperous building without extravagant show, but with considerable imagination. The excellent tooled sandstone is said (without any evidence) to have come from Dobson's prison of 1830, which stood in Carliol Square and was being demolished at that time. Nave and s aisle of the same height, in free Gothic style, with a Lombard frieze and high corner spirelet to the big square battlemented tower over the memorial chapel at the E end of the aisle on the street corner. Inside, very tall octagonal piers, a corbelled arcaded frieze below the window sills, Moorish screens filling one arch in the N organ chamber and another in an oriel over the S memorial chapel. King-post roof; ribbed vault to the memorial chapel. – STAINED GLASS. A scheme was designed by *George Jack* but apparently not executed. – N and S windows by *Edward Woore*.

VICARAGE and CHURCH HALL also by *Lofting*. – Well laid-out MEMORIAL GARDEN W of the church, with Lutyens-style paving.

ST NICHOLAS' CEMETERY, Wingrove Avenue. 1857 by *A. M. Dunn*. The chapels have been horribly altered, but the W entrance, in a back lane, is worth a detour. Entirely Gothic in spirit, with gabled buttresses supporting the octagonal piers of the vehicle gate, and low-relief carvings of ships – one wrecked, one in full sail – on shields held by large seahorses. These ships must refer to St Nicholas, patron saint of sailors, and the seahorses to the supporters of the Newcastle coat of arms.

FENHAM BRANCH LIBRARY, Fenham Hall Drive. Opened 1938. Architect unknown. A good miniature, of bright red brick with sandstone ashlar details, with metal attractively used for the fish-scale overlight and the bronze letters over the door. Well-preserved interior, rich in bevelled glass and wood panelling, and with wall and radiating bookcases with fluted friezes. Carefully planned, with double doors to the sides of the vestibule and a single one from it to the issue desk.

CONVENT OF THE SACRED HEART SCHOOL, Fenham Hall Drive. 1903–6. Designed by *Leonard Stokes* as a grammar school for the Sacred Heart Society. He added it to Fenham Hall but made no concessions to the older building other than the use of plinth and rusticated quoins. The strong composition is unified by cornices and parapet, and by Stokes's typical big square and towers with stone bands. The bright red brick with ashlar dressings and the Lakeland slate roof have worn well. FENHAM HALL has a S front of 1748 by *Daniel Garrett,* a N front of *c.* 1800–5 by *William Newton,* and a mid-C19 E front. The interior was burnt out early in the C20. The S front is of seven bays and two storeys, ashlar-faced; decorated three-bay pediment with the arms of the Ord family by *Guthrie*. The details were altered for the convent. The E front is in a rather thick free imitation of Parisian *Dixhuitième*, seen through the eyes of someone used to English C18 houses. The N front is brick, with stone dressings; eleven bays wide, the angle bays projecting and distinguished by giant Tuscan columns and a pediment.

NEW DEANHAM
1¼ m. N of Capheaton

NEW DEANHAM FARMHOUSE, 1670 by *William Nicholson* for John Fenwick. Three-storey four-bay house, with a central moulded doorway beneath a sundial which is an exact copy of those at Capheaton. Otherwise rather plain, with cross windows altered to sashes. Stone winder stair in rear wing.

NEWMINSTER ABBEY
1 m. W of Morpeth

Cistercian abbey founded in 1137 or 1138. It was the eldest daughter of Fountains Abbey and became the mother of Pipewell, Roche and Sawley. These names give an idea of what Newminster might have had to offer to architectural history if more of its buildings had survived. As it is, we can get no more than a dim idea of the architectural character of the abbey and hardly any of the church. It had the usual Cistercian plan with a straight-headed chancel and straight-headed chapels N and S of the chancel. At Newminster there were three on either side. One pier between two of them on the S side is still *in situ*, with four massive keeled major shafts and four minor diagonal ones, also keeled. Plenty of fragments lie about, but they are still awaiting more thorough research. The cloister as usual was S of the nave. Considerable parts of it have been re-erected, with colonnettes two deep carrying dainty arches, mostly pointed but also here and there round. The capitals are waterleaf, i.e., probably of *c.* 1180 or so. The doorway to the chapterhouse has also been reconstructed, with four orders of colonnettes carrying waterleaf capitals and a round arch. The chapterhouse was square, with four sturdy circular piers to divide it into nine rib-vaulted compartments. The range W of the cloister had as usual a vaulted undercroft for stores. This had single-chamfered ribs and was divided by a cross wall. In the N transept Perp fragments with window openings and an embattled top have been found. They may have belonged to a stone screen. The floor of what was probably the Abbot's Chapel has the finest C 13 TILES in the county. This is not exposed at the time of writing (1989).

NW of the ruins, ABBEY HOUSE has a massive external chimneystack and masonry of distinctly medieval character.

NEWMINSTER WOOLLEN MILL, ½ m. W. A picturesque group of mill house and buildings of *c.* 1825, with a loom shed added later. The earlier buildings are in hand-made brick with a pantiled roof, although the millrace arch is faced in dressed stone. Closed in 1945; most of the buildings are now in domestic use.

NEWMOOR HALL
1½ m. NE of Longframlington

A house of *c.* 1720 with a striking front of eight bays, closely spaced, with rusticated quoins, a doorway flanked by big fluted pilasters carrying a bulgy frieze, and windows with heavy surrounds of alternately long and short blocks, under lintels with broad stepped keystones. The influence of Vanbrugh and Seaton Delaval springs at once to mind. The rear wall shows earlier massive squared masonry, possibly medieval.

OVERGRASS TOWER. Strangely sited in the valley bottom a few minutes SE of the Hall, buried in trees and encroached upon by nettles. The tunnel-vaulted ground floor of a C 14 or C 15 tower-house, intact except for the SE corner, which contained the entrance and the stair. Adjacent ruins and earthworks deserve a proper investigation, although the above-ground masonry looks post-medieval. Further S, a ruined C 18 MILL.

NEWTON HALL
2½ m. N of Bywell

ST JAMES. 1857; enlarged in 1873. Small cruciform church with W tower, in C 14 style. The original chapel of ease (the present nave) was modelled on the chapel of St Bartholomew's Hospital, Cowley, Oxford. Quite an elaborate church for its size. Rib vaulting in the tower and S transept, and painted panelled chancel ceiling. – STAINED GLASS by *Clayton & Bell*.

MOWDEN HALL SCHOOL (formerly Newton Hall). 1811; altered in 1851 by *Dobson* and again later in the C 19 (with the interior largely renewed after a fire in the 1970s). The original house is a plain five-by-four-bay block. Later C 19 are the pedimented centrepiece of the S front and a big arched portico of almost railway-station dimensions on the E. Late C 19 STABLEYARD to the NW, including a clock tower. The ruins of the C 14 Newton Hall Tower, just beyond the stables, were demolished *c.* 1980 to provide stone for a new house in the village, a distressingly recent instance of a long-standing tradition.

NEWTON-ON-THE-MOOR

A village largely of single-storey C 18 cottages, many of which have lost their character through C 20 renovations.

JUBILEE HALL AND READING ROOM. An attractive group consisting of the hall, of 1887, set gable-end-on to the main street and with a copper-domed timber bellcote, and adjacent to it an early C 18 five-bay house, which has lost its upper floor but retains one good contemporary panelled room inside.

OLD MANOR HOUSE. Turning its back to the S side of the main street. This is another house made conformable, alas, to the character of the village by the removal of its first floor! It has a bolection-moulded doorway under a triglyph frieze between mullion-and-transom cross windows in moulded surrounds with cornices; another similar window in the W end now opens into the adjacent cottage. It looks C 17, but the doorhead has a worn date beginning 171 (cf. Swarland Old Hall). The plainer single-storey E extension has an upper-cruck roof.

NEWTON LOW HALL, ½ m. NW. Late C 18. Plain, with good-quality close-jointed stonework and hipped roofs. The S front has a central round-headed stair window in a larger arched recess.

VILLA FARM, ½ m. SW. Ashlar three-bay villa of c. 1820, reputedly by *John Dobson*. The house seems to have been built with separate accommodation on ground and first-floor levels, with the front door at the top of a flight of steps serving the latter; but it was remodelled in the mid-C 20 on more conventional lines.

NEWTON GREENS, ½ m. W. Bastle house with thick walls, traces of an upper door, and a byre slit vent at the rear; remodelled in 1668 (dated lintel) and given its present Tudor trimmings in 1889. Foldyard group of farm buildings at the rear, with a barn dated 1744.

NEWTON HALL, ½ m. SW. House of 1772, remodelled and extended in 1864 by the owner, *S. F. Widdrington*, to his own designs but with assistance from *F. R. Wilson*. The result is rambling but picturesque, especially the conservatory, which winds its way round the S front from the oddly detached pedimented porch on the E. It is lined with Italian niches and panels and floored by tesserae, and opens into the entrance hall, which has murals of London and Venice (Widdrington was also a painter). Elaborate plaster ceilings in several rooms by *Giovanni Montiroli* and the Italian team brought over by the Duke of Northumberland in the mid-C 19. There are also two fireplaces with radial cast-iron grates (cf. Acton House).

The garden S of the house has balustrading and a delightful little SUMMERHOUSE lined with C 17 panelling from Shilbottle Church (rebuilt 1884). These and various garden ornaments and wrought-iron gates are all late C 19. The WALLED GARDEN, ¼ m. further S, is older (lintel dated 1771) but was prettified in the C 19.

WATERLOO STONES, ¼ m. NE of Newton Hall. Three headstone-like slabs, the central one, commemorating the Battle of Waterloo, flanked by memorials to two French seamen said to have been drowned off the Northumberland coast.

2020   NEWTON-BY-THE-SEA

NEWTON HALL. Late C 18. Built for Joseph Forster. *William Newton* was probably the architect; the five-bay front elevation of the house is almost identical to that of Togston Hall (North Togston), except that it is raised on a low basement. The house is built of pink sandstone ashlar, and has a flight of stone steps with wrought-iron balustrades sweeping up to the front door; the open pediment is capped by a marble statue and flanked by leafy urns. On the E front is a full-height canted bay. Set back to the W of the house, the gable end of a STABLE BLOCK containing a blind Venetian window under a large round arch.

NEWTON HOUSE. C 18, remodelled as a three-bay villa c. 1800, and with a late C 19 porch. Inside are two fireplaces with elaborate plasterwork said to be by Napoleonic prisoners of war.

123 NEWTON SEAHOUSES (or Low Newton). Fishermen's cottages forming three sides of a square facing out to sea, much better-

preserved than the only other example of this type of settlement, at
Low Hauxley (*see* High Hauxley). The cottages are c 18, improved
and given their little gabled dormers in the mid-c 19. The only
two-storey building is the SHIP INN at the NW corner; this has
a strange semicircular stair projection at the back that might
indicate the presence of older fabric. On the hilltop to the N, a
COASTGUARD STATION of the early c 19, a single-storey T-plan
building with a canted bay window looking seaward, enclosed by
a tall wall giving the appearance of a small fort.

NEWTON UNDERWOOD

1080

1½ m. w of Mitford

An c 18 cottage here has a thick ruined wall, with a rough semicircular arch, attached to its E end. In the early c 19 the site was
known as the 'Old Walls' and there were more extensive remains.
The ruins are probably medieval, and seem to represent something larger than a single tower.

NINEBANKS

7050

ST MARK, ½ m. s of the village proper. 1871 by *Haswell*. Small
aisleless church in the E.E. style, with a three-sided apse and a
sw tower, with spire, linked to the s porch.

SCHOOL, alongside the church. 1845.

NINEBANKS TOWER, adjoining the village post office. An early
c 16 tower (defaced heraldry above a second-floor window relates
to Sir Thomas Dacre, ruler of Hexhamshire 1515–26) built onto
the E gable (all that now survives) of an earlier house. A N stair
turret and an oversailing third floor were added to the tower later
in the same century. The tower walls are only 0.6 metre (2 ft)
thick. The windows are chamfered loops, except for one which
has two pointed-arched lights.

The MANOR HOUSE, over the road from the Tower, has a plain
three-bay front with sash windows in alternating-block surrounds.
Dated 1825 on the door lintel.

OUSTON, ½ m. w. The convincing-looking tower is in fact an
addition of 1938 to a late c 18 farmhouse, built with rubble from
the former Ninebanks Mill and dressings from St Peter's Church,
Newcastle.

FURNACE HOUSE, 1 m. sw. In the Mohope valley, the location of
much former leadmining. A ruined bastle house, unusual in
having a dated lintel (1639) to its byre door. It was extended in
the late c 17 and remodelled in the early c 18.

NORHAM

8040

NORHAM CASTLE. Norhamshire formed part not of Northumberland but of the County Palatine of Durham. The castle
was the chief northern stronghold maintained by the bishops of

Durham, not by the kings of England. The site was well-chosen, with the steep bank of the Tweed to the N and W and a deep ravine to the E. Only to the S and the SW was an artificial ditch necessary. The castle consists of a large quadrant-shaped outer ward, a roughly oval inner ward at the northern apex of the quadrant, separated from it by a deep moat, and a keep filling the SE corner of the inner ward and forming part of its curtain wall. The whole site slopes dramatically from E to W. The castle has undergone so many changes in the course of its history that it is beyond the scope of this book to describe them all; the essential facts are as follows.

Of the castle built *c.* 1121 by Bishop Ranulph Flambard, only earthworks survive. It was a motte-and-bailey, the plan of which determined the layout of the later defences in stone. The motte, formed of upcast from its substantial moat, must have been greatly reduced in height when the keep and inner ward were built; its area is unknown, but portions of its lower skirts may survive on the S. The bailey (later the outer ward) was defended by a moat, part of which is occupied by the modern road on the SW. The internal bank survives on the SW between the Sheep Gate and the West Gate. This motte-and-bailey castle was taken and damaged or destroyed by the Scots in 1136 and 1138. In 1157 Henry II recaptured Northumberland, and it must have been then that Bishop Hugh de Puiset, the greatest builder of all the bishops of Durham, began the present castle. His architect-builder was *Richard of Wolviston*. He built the keep and much more. Part of the curtain wall to the SE of the keep, across the moat and on into the outer ward is C 12 work. So are parts of the West Gatehouse into the outer ward and the gatehouse into the inner ward. The KEEP is 25.6 by 18.3 metres (84 by 60 ft) and now *c.* 27 metres (88 ft) high. It was originally three storeys high, and its high-pitched roof-line can still be seen on the E wall. In 1422–5 it was heightened to five storeys and the W wall was largely rebuilt with a new spiral staircase in the middle. The Norman keep was divided by a cross wall. The basement has three tunnel-vaulted chambers, the vaults divided into bays by broad transverse unmoulded arches; the bays are lightly groined. In the S wall, on the first floor, is a Norman fireplace. At the E end is a splendid arched niche. The W, E and S walls stand to full height; the N wall has largely gone. There are many C 12, C 13 and C 15 windows.

The GREAT HALL lay against the N wall of the INNER WARD. The parts of the walls which remain date from the early C 16. The adjoining GREAT CHAMBER is supposed to be contemporary. The KITCHEN and offices were as usual at the screens-passage end of the hall. The oven can still be seen. The outer S wall of the inner ward towards the moat has two attached towers. One comes out from the SW end of the keep, is oblong and of the C 15. It was the GARDEROBE TOWER. The other is further W, with a pointed face. This is part of the C 16 defences, built with port-holes for artillery. The buildings inside the moat are partly connected with the flooding of the moat and the shutting off of water, and partly with washing. At the N end of the moat and across it lay the chapel, a C 15 structure.

In the OUTER WARD the low early C 16 arches to the E of the

outer gatehouse are casemates for small cannon. The GATE-
HOUSE is partly Norman, *see* the tunnel-vaulted part with shallow
pilasters against the walls. In the C 14 it was closed (cf.
Dunstanburgh), but the early C 15 reopened it and provided it
with a barbican. The drawbridge pivoted round its centre. When
its outer half was raised, its inner half went down into a pit which
can still be seen below the modern bridge. The outer wall on the
S side is hard to understand. It has two semicircular turrets of the
C 13 and a polygonal turret of the early C 16. A fourth turret is
covered by a late C 18 Gothick cottage. So much is easy, but the
remains of the thirteen or fourteen arches which are all that survive
of the rest of the wall have never been satisfactorily explained.
The accepted opinion is that they were the foundations for a stone
curtain wall built on an existing earth wall.

ST CUTHBERT. The name at once reminds one of the connection
with Durham. And the sumptuousness of some and the grandeur
of other surviving Norman parts of the church can only thus be
explained. Unfortunately most of the building belongs to 1837–
52. To deal with these C 19 parts first: they include the oblong
W tower of 1837, with its oversized neo-Norman two-light bell
openings; the S aisle and porch of 1846 by *Ignatius Bonomi*; and
the N aisle and transept of 1852 by *D. Gray*. What remains of the
original building is the S arcade and the chancel of *c.* 1170, though
the N arcade of 1852 has a W respond and one pier base which
are also original. The S arcade is truly majestic for a parish 16
church – in the spirit of Norham Castle and Puiset. Hodges points
out that the distance from pier-centre to pier-centre is larger than
at Hexham. It is now of five bays (though a painting done before
the tower was rebuilt shows it to be of seven bays), with mighty
circular piers, small circular capitals with waterleaf (cf. Puiset's
Galilee at Durham), octagonal abaci, and richly and vigorously
moulded arches. Above the arches runs a small zigzag frieze. The
chancel arch has three tall thin orders of colonnettes with crocket
capitals (that is an early Gothic motif) and a more finely moulded
arch. The chancel has five original windows on each side. They
are placed remarkably high up. On the N side they are perfectly
plain, but on the S side, above an equally plain priest's door, they 15
make a display as gorgeous as in Puiset's Hall at Durham Castle.
Each window is shafted (the colonnettes again have waterleaf
capitals) and has an arch of one order of beak-like voussoirs, one
of zigzag at r. angles to the wall, and then an outer band of flat
zigzag. Very flat buttresses between the windows. The eaves rest
on a corbel table. A sixth bay was added to the E in the C 14. Its
window tracery is renewed. – PULPIT and STALL. Brought from
Durham Cathedral by Archdeacon Thorp in 1840. Elaborately
carved late C 17 work in the Cosin style, with combined Gothic
and Renaissance motifs. – ORGAN. A small C 18 organ case stands
in the tower. – ROYAL ARMS of Charles II; carved wood. –
STAINED GLASS. The E window is by *Bryans*. – The vivid mid-
C 19 armorial glass in the chancel S windows is by *Wailes*. – The
later C 19 W window by *Clayton & Bell*. – Excellent MONUMENT
of *c.* 1320 in the chancel S wall. Worn effigy of a knight and above,
flanked by buttresses, a big gable with pierced early Dec tracery,
the motifs few and large. – Opposite, the monument to Dr Gilly

† 1857 by *Lough*, with recumbent effigy on tomb-chest and Norman arch above; rather dull. – In the N aisle, a composite pillar made up of many different Anglian cross fragments. – Jane, Lady Blake, † 1827, in the N aisle; a weeping relief figure resting on a sarcophagus. – In the chancel, wall tablets to William Alder † 1800 and Mary Ord † 1810, both by *J. Jopling*.

OLD VICARAGE, just W of the church. 1810; enlarged 1830. Three bays with shallow two-storey bow windows flanking the doorway. Hipped roof.

VILLAGE CROSS, in the middle of the village green. Medieval base of six high circular steps. The quatrefoil shaft is surely also medieval, but was restored when the oddly elongated conical cap was added in 1870.

MORRIS HALL, $\frac{1}{4}$ m. E on the road to Horncliffe. Mid-C18; five-bay centre, with slightly projecting one-bay gabled wings of the early C19.

NORHAM STATION. The best surviving station on the Berwick and Kelso branch of the York, Newcastle and Berwick Railway company. 1851 by *Benjamin Green*. The station house and offices are of one storey to the platform side but two storeys to the rear, the whole being a rather functional design in squared masonry but with timber infill buildings along the length of the platform. Signal cabin on a brick tower with stone dressings; goods shed with ramped road access, a coal depot and a covered lime depot.

RAILWAY VIADUCT, over the Newbiggin Dene, 1 m. S. Built *c.* 1849, also for the Kelso branch of the York, Newcastle and Berwick Railway. Six tall segmental arches with brick soffits on battered rock-faced piers. Identical in form to the Royal Border Bridge and so probably also by *Robert Stephenson*, who was engineer for this Kelso branch.

LADYKIRK AND NORHAM BRIDGE. A powerful stone bridge of four segmental arches built for the Tweed Bridges Trust in 1885–7 to replace a two-arch timber lattice bridge of 1838 by John Blackmore. The present bridge was designed by *Thomas Coddrington* and *Cuthbert Brereton* and constructed by *Meakon and Dean*. The central cutwater is rounded and carried up to the parapet to form a retreat; the others are short and pointed. Corbelled stringcourses at the parapet base. Between the spandrel walls are inner arches and voids to reduce weight in the haunches. A late example of a large stone bridge.

NORTH SHIELDS

North Shields owes its beginnings to Tynemouth Priory (*see* Tynemouth). In the early C13 fishermen were settled here by Prior Germanus. Indeed, the parish church was at Tynemouth Priory until the C17. Before *c.* 1760 North Shields was a tiny riverside town with hardly any more to it than the present Clive Street and its immediate neighbourhood. Improvements went on throughout the late C18 and early C19. They can be followed in plans of 1787 and 1827 and consisted of the extension of the old town E and W by the planning and building of Dockwray Square and the New Quay,

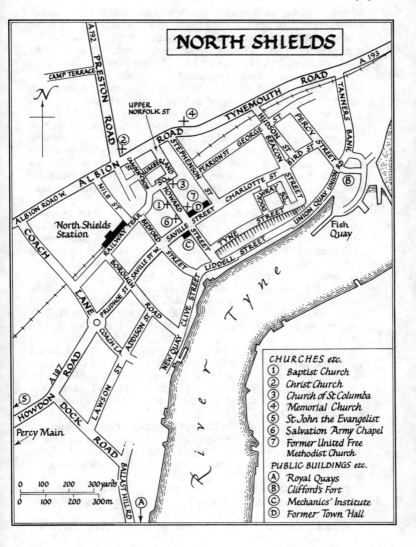

followed early in the C 19 by the development from scratch of a New Town on higher ground behind the old settlement. The C 19 growth of the shipping, shipbuilding and coalmining industries necessitated further expansion, with many new churches, public buildings, houses and shops. Since then, the period which has seen the decline of those industries has also seen radical reshaping of the town centre. Sadly, none of the buildings associated with that redevelopment is worth mentioning here.

CHRIST CHURCH, Preston Road and Albion Road. The first church on this site, of 1654–68 (from 1663 by *Robert Trollope*), was built to replace the decayed church in Tynemouth Priory as the parish church. In 1786–8 a w tower was added and in 1792–3 the rest was rebuilt by *John Dodds*; the chancel was enlarged and the organ chamber added in 1869. Ashlar with rusticated quoins, the tower embattled and the nave with a parapet. Tall round-headed windows; those in the tower have keyed surrounds, as have the blind roundels flanking and above the w door. The three-bay aisled nave has round-headed gallery windows in the end bays, and n and s doors underneath large round windows in the slightly projecting central bays. All the doors have ornamental fanlights. The aisles have Tuscan columns carrying arches as shallow as Soane liked them. The n and s galleries have been removed, but at the w end cast-iron columns support a gallery which now carries the attractive c 19 organ (transferred from the chancel organ chamber, now a vestry). Flat ceiling with classical mouldings in the nave and symbols of the Trinity over the altar. – FONT, in the s aisle. c 18 with a small fluted bowl on a moulded pedestal. – MONUMENTS. Two stone grave covers with coats of arms (E end): to Stephen Dockwray, vicar, † 1681; to members of the Howlett family † 1683 and 1694. – Two monuments by *Dunbar* (John H. Richardson † 1835, with profile medallion; John Hutchinson † 1837, with a standing female figure by an altar). Also tablets by *J. Jopling*, 1822, and *G. Green*, 1837. – N of the church, the former VESTRY, like a house, with a hipped roof on the end facing the church and a plain N gable. To this N gable an entirely sympathetic yet not unoriginal PARISH HALL was added in 1984 by *Rock Townsend*. – In the CHURCHYARD, *c.* 5 metres s of the tower, an interesting chest tomb commemorating Edward Hodgson, Cordwainer, † 1690, one of the founders of the church. Rusticated piers flank panels with low-relief symbols of death; on top, a blank shield with deeply cut helmet, crest and mantling. – GATEPIERS to the s and SE, those at the principal entrance rusticated with ball finials.

ST JOHN THE EVANGELIST, St John's Terrace, Percy Main, 1½ m. SW. 1862 by *Salvin* for the Duke of Northumberland. A simple, dignified church, with aisles to both nave and chancel. Lancets, three stepped at the E, two separated by a massive buttress at the W.

BAPTIST CHURCH, Howard Street. 1846 by *John Dobson*. Ashlar in Romanesque style; door with moulded arch in the centre of the big front gable.

CHURCH OF ST COLUMBA, Northumberland Square. 1853–8 by *John Dobson* for the Anti-Burgher Society, which became Presbyterian. Rather grander than the character of the square – very much in the style of Sanmicheli, i.e. North Italian Cinquecento. Ashlar main block, brick wings with ashlar quoins and dressings.

MEMORIAL CHURCH, Albion Road. 1889–91 by *F. R. N. Haswell* for the Wesleyan Methodists, at the expense of J. Robinson and in memory of his daughter, but now called 'The Cathedral of the Independent North Tyneside Memorial Church'. Sandstone. E.E. with gargoyles on the big tower, which is topped by a much taller octagonal stair turret, a landmark made even more prominent by the demolition of houses to the s. Its ritual w front, with paired doors under a large four-light window, can now be appreciated in full. The interior is a remarkably complete example of the period. Two tiers of cast-iron columns, with stiffleaf capitals under the gallery, ballflower at the top; hammerbeam roof; many original fittings. It makes a good group with the church hall and minister's house.

SALVATION ARMY CHAPEL, Howard Street. 1811 by *John Dobson* for a secessionist church which later became Presbyterian; known as the Scotch Church because the minister had to be a licentiate of the Church of Scotland. Ashlar. Three bays, set well back from the street, with an order of short robust Greek Doric pilasters and a heavy attic; bucrania on the frieze. Somewhat altered but restorable; the SCHOOL of 1841 (attached to the l.) has been mutilated.

Former UNITED FREE METHODIST CHURCH (now Borough Treasurer's department), Howard Street. 1856–7 by *Benjamin Green* in the usual Primitive Methodist pattern of the period, with a big front gable over three full-height arched panels, containing arched doors and windows, tripartite at the first-floor centre. Big blocks support the corniced gable copings.

Former TOWN HALL (now council offices and Magistrates' Court), Howard Street and Saville Street. 1844–5. Designed by *John Dobson* to hold the Town Improvement Commission Offices, Savings Bank, Mechanics' Institute, Museum and Police Station; it became the town hall in 1849. L-shaped and wrapped round the earlier Poor Law Building. Tudor style and of very informal design, not at all demonstratively monumental. Sandstone with ashlar dressings. Battlemented parapet and corniced octagonal chimneys. The former POOR LAW GUARDIANS' HALL which it encloses was built for the Tynemouth Poor Law Union in 1837 by *J. & B. Green* in Jacobethan style, but the lower part of the three-by-three-bay building has been partly rebuilt to match Dobson's Tudor. The central bay in Howard Street is recessed under a corbel table which meets the shaped gables of the outer bays.

Former MECHANICS' INSTITUTE, at the SW corner of Howard Street and Saville Street. 1857–8, designed as the second Mechanics' Institute building by *John Johnstone*, perhaps with alterations by *Dobson*. Plain Italianate, without any flights of fancy. Red brick with stucco trim.

CLIFFORD'S FORT, Union Road. A harbour defence of 1672 designed by *Martin Beckman*, a Swedish engineer, during the Dutch Wars. The gun embrasures were improved in the late C18 when French attack was feared, and the whole was much altered in the late C20, but it is still an important survival. The irregular enclosure makes the best use of natural features. In the C18 there was much reconstruction on the seaward side, when the thick ashlar walls, tapered with fat round string moulding and with many gun embrasures, were built. On the inland stretches of wall (stone below and brick above) there are still some C17 gun slots and musket ports. The building of the fort greatly inconvenienced the Newcastle Trinity House, since it surrounded the Low Lighthouse (*see* Perambulation, below) and made access to it difficult. The force of guns firing damaged the lantern. Obsolete as a battery, the old fort became in 1888 the headquarters of the Tyne

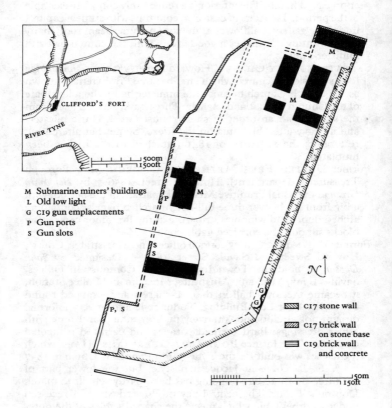

M Submarine miners' buildings
L Old low light
G C19 gun emplacements
P Gun ports
S Gun slots

CLIFFORD'S FORT

RIVER TYNE

500m
150oft

N

C17 stone wall

C17 brick wall
on stone base

C19 brick wall
and concrete

50m
150ft

North Shields, Clifford's Fort. Plan

Division Royal Engineers (Volunteers) Submarine Miners, and
one or two of their purpose-built structures survive (in 1990),
heavily disguised as curing houses (themselves of considerable
historical interest) and storage sheds.

ALBERT EDWARD DOCK, reached from Howdon Road. 1882 by
the engineers *Ure & Messent* for the Tyne Improvement Commission. Originally Coble Dene Dock, but renamed at its opening
by the Prince himself. Now only a reminder of the Tyne's remarkable trading past; planning permission was granted in 1991 for
the ROYAL QUAYS redevelopment with housing, light industry
and a 'water park' (architects *Faulkner Brown Hendy Watkinson
Stonor*). Two fine sets of lock walls and gates, and beside them
the hydraulic accumulator tower which provided the power to
operate the dock machinery. There used to be a clock, wound by
the accumulator, on the four roof panels.

OLD AND NEW LIGHTS. *See* Perambulation, below.

PERAMBULATION

Our perambulation takes us from the riverside to the higher part of
the town and back down to the Fish Quay. CLIVE STREET is
where the original small settlement began. Tall houses used to fill
both sides of the street, with narrow alleys leading to the water
on the s and long flights of steps to the higher ground on the N.
By the middle of this century, only one or two much-altered C 17
brick houses were left; and now that even those have gone, the
historic core of the town has a bland face, with no interesting
buildings, and empty grassy banks flanking the steps. At the E end
of Clive Street is LIDDELL STREET with a now rare early C 19
GRAVING DOCK on the s among 1990s houses. At the w end of
Clive Street is the early C 19 MARKET PLACE or NEW QUAY.
Here, the former NORTHUMBERLAND ARMS belongs to a
scheme designed by *David Stephenson* for the second Duke of
Northumberland, who laid the foundation stone in October 1806.
An 1810 watercolour by John Dobson shows three ranges of
buildings round a square open to the quay, but the only part
completed (in 1817) was the monumental ashlar-faced twenty-
bay N terrace, of which the hotel was the five-bay centre block.
All to the l. of it has been demolished. The terrace has a rusticated
ground floor; the hotel also has a porch and six unfluted giant Ionic
columns supporting the unadorned ramped balustrade, which
originally bore the Duke's arms. To the r. and round the corner
into Borough Road, the SAILORS' HOME, added in 1854–6 by
Benjamin Green for the fourth Duke of Northumberland. At the
w end of the New Quay, a tall BREWERY dated 1871.

The NEW TOWN lies on a higher level reached by Borough Road.
It was developed by John Wright and his sons in the late C 18 and
early C 19, on the former Howard estate. For this part of our
perambulation we pass straight through to ALBION ROAD, on
the N border of the improvements. Here is Christ Church, at the
corner of Preston and Albion Roads (*see* above). Then 300 metres
N along Preston Road a gateway on the w side leads to the early
C 19 CAMP TERRACE. Four houses, each with a broken pediment
over a Tuscan doorcase, and three houses, added not many years
later, which have Greek Doric doorcases. Their gardens are on
the other side of the cobbled street. A little to the w along Albion
Road, Camden Street leads into NORTHUMBERLAND SQUARE,
the focus of the C 19 developments, a square almost too spacious
for the two-storeyed houses on its three sides. The best side is the
N, all of *c.* 1810, in good ashlar and with the original Lakeland
slate roofing on Nos. 13, 16 and 19. Of the thirty-three bays, the
central three and each end pair project slightly, the latter in bows;
each projection has quoins and a coped blocking course. Houses
vary in size, from three to five bays; the doorway to No. 17 encloses
two doors. The doorcases are classical, with open pediments on
columns alternating with engaged-column-and-entablature type.
The whole survives against all odds, to judge from the N side of
the adjacent NORTHUMBERLAND PLACE, built to the w of the
square in 1811 but altered this century in a most insensitive
manner. It could be restored. On the s side of Northumberland
Square, St Columba's Church (*see* above). The w side of the

square is Victorian, the E mostly simple early C 19. The *leitmotif* is doorways with Tuscan pilasters and heavy straight entablature. This motif goes on right through street after street of North Shields as they went up in the first decades of the century, down Camden Street, Stephenson Street, Howard Street and so on. Many streets have their original name-plates.

HOWARD STREET is the most interesting of them, for in addition to the long terraces of small houses, there are a number of churches and public buildings (*see* above), befitting the principal link with the old town. In the block S of Saville Street there are some of the original early C 19 houses, from No. 97 on the corner (altered to make a shop) to No. 100. Then comes the former BANK of 1882, designed by *F. R. N. Haswell* for Hodgkin, Barnett, Pease, Spence & Co. in Italianate style, with giant Corinthian order; and after it another early C 19 house (No. 106). On the other side of the street, overlooking the river, No. 1, built in 1806–7 as the SUBSCRIPTION LIBRARY of the Tynemouth Literary and Philosophical Society, has an ashlar front, with a pediment over the central three of the five bays, a pedimented Tuscan doorcase, and a Venetian window above it. In the pediment, a roundel, which, like the one on the S gable overlooking the river, used to hold a clock-face. On the corner of Saville Street, the former Mechanics' Institute (*see* Public Buildings, above). Little else remains unaltered in the New Town, although there is some architecture of a little more ambition, e.g. in NORFOLK STREET to the E, where the former ALBION ASSEMBLY ROOMS of 1853 by *J. R. Robson* has ten bays and two tall storeys, tall Doric pilasters and arched upper windows. Beyond that the scale of C 19 architecture in North Shields scarcely goes. What little there was of late Victorian and Edwardian commercial exhibitionism has mostly been replaced with late C 20 shops and offices.

Now for the E end of North Shields. Its centre is DOCKWRAY SQUARE, well to the E of the foot of Howard Street. Begun in 1763 by Thomas Dockwray, vicar of Stamfordham, it was the first urban improvement of North Shields, high above the harbour, with fine views to Tynemouth and the sea. The buildings that originally lined it went *c.* 1959 – there has been rebuilding twice since then, lastly with small houses in 1986–7 – but on the S side, in TYNE STREET, the NEW HIGH LIGHT still stands. There are four lights, an Old and a New at High and Low positions, all built for the masters and mariners of Trinity House of Newcastle upon Tyne, who had set up the first pair of lighthouses here in 1539. Navigators aligned the upper and lower lights to find safe passage into the river, the 'new' lights replacing the old after shifting sandbanks had changed the direction of the deepest channel. The New Lights were built in 1808 by *John Stokoe*. The New High Light is a painted ashlar tower which did its job well before the piers were built, and with elegance. The ground floor has a Venetian window and a pediment; the three upper storeys have single windows, the top under a pediment, and a top cornice with iron balustrade in front of the lantern. Attached to the W side is a house of 1860. The OLD HIGH LIGHT of 1727 stands further along Tyne Street, just to the E of the former Dockwray Square. It was used as almshouses for a time after the new light

was built. Painted render and brick, with eroded plaques telling
its story; the lantern has a large ball finial on its ogee-hipped roof.
The lower markers of the alignment are on the flat ground at the
river's edge and the NEW LOW LIGHT is reached down a flight
of steps from Tyne Street to Union Quay. Like its companion
above, it was built in 1808 by *John Stokoe*, and is equally elegant,
but taller. Painted ashlar, and treated like a giant column with
chamfered corners tapering off to the ground floor. Round-headed
windows except on the E face, and curved railings to the lantern
platform. The house attached to the N is dated 1816. Nearby, in
Clifford's Fort (*see* above), the OLD LOW LIGHT. The first
lighthouse here was erected in 1539. This one was built in 1727,
raised in 1775, converted to almshouses in 1830, and in 1988 was
rescued from dereliction by Buttress, the Tyne and Wear Building
Preservation Trust; it is (in 1992) used by the Deep Sea Fisheries
Training Association. The fabric of varied brick bonds, the eroded
plaques and the second-floor sundial express its history. When it
was the front half of the pair of 'old' markers, the end wall facing
the harbour was painted white.

Now a short diversion E to BREWERY BANK, where the LOW
LIGHTS TAVERN at the bottom of the hill is the only old house
remaining from this once densely occupied area. Late C18, with
rendered walls, a plain tile roof and a Tuscan doorcase, a motif
seen abundantly in the higher part of the town. Finally along
Union Road and into TANNERS BANK to see the sturdy coursed
sandstone OLD MALTINGS of *c.* 1800 on the N side, and back
past Clifford's Fort to the UNION or Fish QUAY, notable less for
its buildings than for the fish market held in the sheds each
morning. This is an appropriate place to complete our perambulation of a town which began close by as a riverside fishing
and trading settlement.

NORTH SUNDERLAND   2030

ST PAUL. By *Salvin*, 1834. Quite an early use of the Norman style.
Nave with bellcote, lower chancel and apse. No aisles. The interior
has attractive classical FITTINGS of 1915.

UNITED REFORMED CHURCH (formerly Presbyterian), Main
Street. 1810, with the usual pattern of windows. Small addition
of 1843 to the r.

SHORESTON HALL, 1 m. N. Much altered, but the S side is a four-
bay late C17 façade with a four-centred-arched door. The rest of
the house was extended in an irregular manner in the C19 and
early C20. The GATEPIERS are C18, with banded rustication.
The GARDEN was laid out *c.* 1913 by *Robert Mauchlen*, somewhat
in the Lutyens style, with a particularly attractive GAZEBO incorporated into the high garden wall. The original house was a
property of the Grey family, but the C20 work was done for Sir
Stephen Runciman.

Runciman was also responsible for the group of five COTTAGES
behind the hall, built in 1913 in the Arts-and-Crafts style. The

architect was once again *Robert Mauchlen*. The cottages are linked
by arches and screen walls which incorporate the outhouses. An
informal but entirely successful composition.

SEAHOUSES. *See* p. 559.

SEAHOUSES. *See* p. 559.

NORTH TOGSTON
1½ m. SW of Amble

2000

TOGSTON HALL. An interesting house showing quite a complicated development. The original house seems to have been a
defensible building, perhaps a bastle, with thick walls and small
slit windows; a reset 1546 datestone may belong to it. This was
remodelled in 1685 (central S door, now to a cupboard), with the
addition of a rear stair wing. The upper-cruck roof is probably
contemporary with the remodelling. In the late C 18 the old house
was reduced to serving as rear premises to a handsome new five-
bay front block, of ashlar with sill bands and an open pediment
above the centre bay. The design is very close to that of Newton
Hall (Newton-by-the-Sea), and the architect was probably
William Newton. The interior of the C 18 block is well-preserved,
but the extensive and interesting outbuilding group to the E,
including a bakehouse and brewhouse, has unfortunately been
allowed to fall into ruins.

TOGSTON HOUSE. C 17 and later, but much obscured by render
and pebbledash. Here too there are extensive outbuildings, one
row converted into cottages in the C 19, and a DOVECOTE on the
hilltop to the NE.

NUNNYKIRK
c. 5 m. SSW of Rothbury

0090

NUNNYKIRK HALL. Among the finest of all *Dobson*'s early houses;
1825, for William Orde. Very nobly Greek, with exquisite ashlar
masonry. The stonework of much of the house has banded rustication after the fashion of French Neo-classical architecture.
Dobson may have borrowed it from his friend Ignatius Bonomi,
who was using it at this time on his Burn Hall (County Durham),
begun in 1821. Nunnykirk is a remodelling of an earlier house.
The five-bay centre of the GARDEN FRONT was a Queen Anne
house which Dobson refronted and to which he added lower
projecting wings. The ground floor between the wings has an
Ionic loggia of four columns. Above the loggia the rustication
breaks downwards over the windows to form voussoirs. The top
of the house has a fine honeysuckle frieze. The wings have full-
length tripartite windows, shorter tripartite windows above, and
parapets with scrolls and honeysuckle. The whole effect is most
animated. The wing to the r. continues back to form the
ENTRANCE FRONT, again with banded rustication throughout.
It is of five broad bays, with the outer bays and the centre bay
breaking forward slightly. A loggia of three pairs of Ionic columns

spans the three middle bays and in front of that is a large *porte cochère* with Ionic columns *in antis*.

In the middle of the house, an oblong hall with a coffered dome in the centre and coffered segmental vaults at each end. Excellent plasterwork with scrolls and honeysuckle friezes. The room has a stone balcony with fine metal railings. The staircase, at one end of the hall, is semicircular round a curved screen of Corinthian columns. It has the same balustrade as the balcony and a plaster frieze with Greek figures. There are several other plaster ceilings in the house, especially in the drawing room, which has a sort of close-set trellis with flowers at the intersections. The woodwork is of this same high quality throughout the main rooms. The drawing room has a bizarre white marble fireplace with a high-relief eagle and snake intertwined in the lintel.

A Saxon cross shaft of the C 9 which was formerly in the garden is now in the Museum of Antiquities in Newcastle.

FONTBURN RESERVOIR, 2 m. W. 1901 for the Tynemouth Corporation Water Company. The engineers were *James Mansergh and Sons Ltd*.

COMBHILL, 1 m. W, and SOUTH HEALEY, ¾ m. S. Two farms which incorporate remains of bastle houses. South Healey, in fact, has two – the house itself and one wall of a second one *c.* 100 metres NW.

NUNRIDING HALL

1080

1½ m. NW of Mitford

An odd conjoined pair of substantial five-bay houses, now further subdivided. The W part of the range is a C 17 house built of rubble, with blocked mullioned windows. The taller E part is of squared stone and has a symmetrical front of the mid-C 18. Farm building range at rear with upper crucks.

NUNWICK

8070

A very perfect house of its date, 1748–52. Almost certainly by *Daniel Garrett*, and, if so, perhaps his finest design. L-plan two-and-a-half-storey main block of pecked sandstone ashlar, with five-bay fronts facing S and E. The SOUTH FRONT especially betrays the architect's Palladian sympathies. A band and a sill band emphasize the tall first floor, where the centre window alone has a pediment (the others are corniced). The four-column Roman Doric porch is an addition of *c.* 1829 by *Bonomi*, who may also have been responsible for the broad swept architrave of the centre first-floor window, with ball finials at its feet. Eaves cornice and hipped roof. The EAST FRONT is similar, except that the lower windows have had their sills lowered, probably when Bonomi added the two-storey canted dining room bay at the N end. The INTERIOR is well preserved, with uncommonly fine original fireplaces and Rococo ceilings: Garrett was a pioneer of Rococo decoration, and the plasterer here was *Philip Daniel*. The STAIR opens from the entrance hall beyond a Doric screen, and is lit by a large Venetian window, which looks like a later C 18 insertion, on the W side of the house. Attached to the N end are the servants' quarters and offices, set round a small court. To the S these have a low centre range, capped by a clock by *John Hawthorne* of Newcastle dated 1764, under a cupola, between two-storey end pavilions with arched niches and pediments. On the E the arrangement is similar, except that here the centre range has been heightened in the mid-C 19: the end pavilions have Venetian windows and the centre a tripartite doorway.

In the grounds to the S, the former KENNELS, a 1768 conversion of an older watermill, in the Gothick style with Y-tracery in broad lancet windows (cf. the 1766 alterations at Simonburn Castle, which was made into an eyecatcher with which the main Nunwick drive was aligned). In the garden is a strange SPIRAL COLUMN, said to come from Simonburn Church. It looks like a C 17 or C 18 piece; the square base with vertical roll mouldings at the angles might be medieval or C 17. There was a second drive approaching the house from the SE; this crosses the stream which flows through the park by an attractive little hog-backed BRIDGE of the late C 18 or early C 19, an important feature in what remains very much a planned landscape.

NUNWICK MILL, ¾m. E. Early C 19 three-storey watermill, with two-storey miller's house adjacent; the mill, in commercial operation as late as the 1950s, contains a large overshot wheel. The head-race, fed from a gathering pond filled by an underground stream, was carried in a wooden launder supported on a surviving series of stone columns on its approach to the mill.

OGLE

1½m. SE of Whalton

OGLE CASTLE. An interesting and unusual house, largely of the C 16, an unusual date in Northumberland. There was a quadrangular castle here, licensed in 1341; portions of its double moat survive. A C 17 account speaks of a curtain wall with half-round towers, and a round tower at the E end of the present house was pulled down late in the C 18; but the present building shows little evidence of this. It is of an L-plan, with a main range of squared stone and to the W a taller thick-walled rubble wing usually spoken of as the 'tower'. The evidence of an attic window opening W from the W end of the main range shows that this is in fact the older part. Most of its visible features – straight-headed windows of two and three lights with arched heads and hoodmoulds, big moulded fireplaces and beamed ceilings – are of the earlier C 16, except for two doorways of clearly medieval type, one pointed and one segmental-headed, at the NW corner of the main range. These are difficult to relate to the C 16 building; they would seem to be an *in-situ* remnant of a predecessor. A possible interpretation is that the main range represents the castle's hall block, remodelled when the curtain wall still provided security. The slightly later

wing, perhaps replacing the solar, shows some affinities to later
C 16 'stronghouses' such as Stanton and Tritlington Old Halls.
From this remodelling comes the corbelled-out newel stair in the
angle of main range and wing, directly above the two medieval
doorways. The house has been well restored in the present
century.

VILLAGE EARTHWORKS, well preserved, in the fields N of the
present village street, which runs along the S edge of the former
green. Some of the existing houses stand on the S row of the
old village; behind them extend the earthworks of some original
garths, with the ridge-and-furrow of the open fields beyond. The
modern buildings on the N side of the road are an encroachement
on the medieval green, on the N side of which can be traced the
second row of houses and garths. In 1632 there were sixteen
houses round the green, the castle standing at its E end.

OLD BEWICK   0020

HOLY TRINITY. A small church of nave and chancel only, standing
quite alone among trees ½ m. from the village. The N wall has
stonework which is distinctly Anglo-Saxon in character, but essentially the building is Norman, as is evident from outside in the
C 12 masonry with which the rest of the church is built; in one
unaltered small N window and another, slightly larger, in the
chancel; in the very narrow priest's door; in the outline of the
rounded apse in its lower courses (squared externally in the C 14 –
an interesting comment on the English Gothic builders' belief in
square E ends); and in the S doorway. This has one order of
colonnettes with block capitals, one with remains of carved decoration. Inside, the church is much more impressive and much
more eloquently Norman. The chancel arch is followed by a
Norman apse arch, and that procession of arches is always a
dramatic effect. The chancel arch has semicircular responds on
odd bases something like upturned block capitals, interesting
capitals (the N one carved with big leaves, two beasts' heads and
an abacus with a frieze of saltire crosses, the S one roughly
scalloped, with a similar abacus), an arch with a hollow moulding
and a roll moulding and an outer billet frieze. So clearly somebody
wished to make a display here. The church indeed belonged, from
c. 1110 onwards, to as powerful a body as Tynemouth Priory. The
apse arch is simpler, but the abaci of the imposts again have saltire
crosses. The apse has three windows. Two are at least partly
original, the other C 14. The church was long ruinous and was
restored in 1866–7 by R. Williams. A stone set into the vestry
records an earlier restoration of 1695. – MONUMENTS. Defaced
effigy of a lady under a canopy; C 14. – In the porch several CROSS
SLABS. Another set into the floor at the W end of the nave.

BRIDGE, ¾ m. W. Early C 19 with a single fine broad segmental arch
over the River Till.

Two bivallate horseshoe-shaped HILLFORTS, ½ m. SE, crouch side 3
by side on the lip of the steep slopes above the village, overlooking
the lower Breamish. An outer rampart encloses both forts, but

the relationship between them is a matter of guesswork. Each has an entrance on the SE, although the principal access to the W fort is on the W. Extraction hollows for more recent millstones scar the outcrops within the defences. CUP-AND-RING MARKED ROCKS lie nearby to the E.

BLAWEARIE. An imposing Bronze Age burial cairn, largely reconstructed after excavation, 300 metres WSW of Blawearie. A massive kerb of close-fitting boulders enclosed a rubble core which concealed a central pit and five secondary burial cists. Finds included pottery food vessels, flint knives and a necklace of jet beads. A simple bivallate hillfort, 550 metres SE of Blawearie, makes good use of the steep slopes above the Harehope Burn.

OLD SHIPLEY see EGLINGHAM

9050

ORD

ORD HOUSE, East Ord. The front rooms are of 1789 for William Grieve. Five bays with a three-bay pediment. The rooms to the rear of the house, with the staircase wing and the single-storey square pavilions attached to the rear corners, are early C 18 and were built for the Ord family. These different dates are also reflected inside. The front rooms have restrained Adam-style decoration. The staircase at the back is more robust early C 18, with fat turned balusters and a boldly moulded handrail.

WEST ORD, 2 m. W. A most unusually sophisticated farmhouse for the county. Built 1700–10. A symmetrical rectangular house, with each pair of parallel façades identical. Five by two bays. Angle pilasters, tall narrow windows in raised surrounds, a boldly moulded eaves cornice continuous round the house, and a plain parapet. Inside, three very fine panelled rooms, with fireplaces flanked by full-height Ionic or Corinthian columns. The main room on the first floor has an especially good enriched modillion cornice in wood. At the time the house was built it belonged to Elizabeth Ord, mistress of Sir William Blackett of Wallington Hall.

MIDDLE ORD, 1 m. SW of East Ord. 1788 for J. Grey. Three bays with a pedimented door surround.

MURTON, 2 m. S of East Ord. Large and impressive farm buildings of c. 1880 (cf. East Allerdean, Ancroft). Round-arched carriage entrance under a gable. The yard in the centre roofed over, still with its original king- and queen-post roofs.

CANNY BANK. Earthworks of a sizeable bivallate Iron Age promontory fort where the Canny Burn cuts down through the high river-cliff on the S bank of the Tweed, ½ m. W of the Berwick bypass. The course of the inner ditch and most of the outer rampart are occupied by the broad ridge-and-furrow that covers the interior.

OTTERBURN

ST JOHN THE EVANGELIST. 1858 by *Dobson*. Decorated style, with a large geometrical E window, cusped one-light nave windows and geometrical tracery at the W end. Fussy SW spirelet. – ALTAR FRONTAL. A high-relief copy in wood of *The Last Supper*.

VICARAGE. Late Georgian. Three bays with canted bay windows flanking a pedimented doorway.

OTTERBURN TOWER. A picturesque asymmetrical castellated mansion built *c.* 1830 for a Mr James, but incorporating the masonry of an C18 house which may in turn contain earlier work. There are no vestiges, however, of the medieval tower which stood on or near this site. Extended to the rear and the stable block added in 1904 for Howard Pease by *F. W. Rich*.

OTTERBURN MILL. C18 woollen mill, extended in 1821 and *c.* 1930. Much of the manufacturing process can still be traced. The waterwheels were replaced in the late C19 by a turbine, which still survives; also much early C19 gearing and a fulling hammer. There is a bleach house, a drying house with a perforated iron floor, and a tenter field still with its rows of tenters.

OTTERBURN HALL, $\frac{3}{4}$m. N of the church. Brick with stone dressings. Neo-Elizabethan of 1870 for Lord James Douglas, who received the land as a gift in recompense for the death of his ancestor, the Lord Douglas, at the battle of Otterburn. Much the best part of the house, however, is the E front, altered in 1905 for Sir Charles Morrison Bell; it is still in the same style but shows a great deal more freedom. The interior remodelled after a fire in 1930. To the rear, a large conservatory.

MONKRIDGE HALL, $1\frac{1}{2}$m. SE, on the A696. Built *c.* 1774 for Gabriel Hall. Five narrow bays, with the door and windows in raised moulded surrounds.

OVERACRES, 2m. E. The simple farmhouse is of *c.* 1820 but the sumptuous gatepiers, decorated by shields with knotwork l. and r., are dated 1720, rather later than the style would indicate. The property belonged to the Howards.

PERCY CROSS, $\frac{1}{2}$m. NW. Probably erected in its present form in 1777 but incorporating the medieval cross base. It rests on a plinth of five steps. The shaft is rectangular, *c.* 2.5 metres (8 ft) high and tapering towards the top. It commemorates the battle of Otterburn (1388).

SHITTLEHEUGH BASTLE, $1\frac{1}{2}$m. NW. A ruined C16 bastle, placed dramatically on the skyline. The gable ends stand to full height, the side walls to *c.* 1.8 metres (6 ft). The ground-floor doorway is in the middle of the long side, and there seems to have been a projecting stair turret in front.

REDE, TYNE AND COQUET SPORTS CENTRE, $\frac{1}{2}$m. N of the church. 1987 by *Jowett, Buckley & Curry*. Clad in natural wood with a half-hipped roof like a barn in the Mid-West. An effective treatment.

On FAWDON HILL, $\frac{3}{4}$m. NE, a well-preserved bivallate Iron Age hillfort, entered from the S.

On COLWELL HILL, $1\frac{1}{4}$m. ENE, a fine multivallate hillfort; circular hollows mark the sites of timber houses.

HARE CAIRN. The remains of a mutilated cairn, $1\frac{1}{2}$m. N of Otter-

burn Camp. Robbing in the C 19 revealed three burial cists; two
are still visible.

OTTERCOPS
2¼ m. SSE of Elsdon

OTTERCOPS FARM has a pair of 'semi-detached' bastle houses.
They are of different dates: the E one is recorded in 1604; the W
one is of the early C 17 and partly rebuilt in the C 18. No ground-
floor vaults. Walls *c.* 1.5 metres (5 ft) thick.

OVINGHAM

8 ST MARY. Late Saxon W tower, tall and unbuttressed. The bell
openings exactly as at Bywell (q.v.), two lights with a pierced
circle in the spandrel, all in a thin raised surround rectangular in
section. Saxon windows below the openings. No W doorway, no
original arch from tower to nave, but a high-level doorway, *c.* 12
metres (40 ft) above ground, originally above the ridge of the roof.
The nave SW quoins are Saxon too. The NW quoins are obscured
by a buttress. However, the aesthetic pleasure the church offers
is due to the work of the C 13. Uncommonly fine view from the E
of the long chancel and the long transepts, all with long lancet
windows. The chancel E end in particular has a group of three
stepped, nobly elongated lancets with elegant chamfered buttresses between (for these, cf. Brinkburn and Hexham). The nave
and aisles are C 13 also, though the N aisle was rebuilt in 1857,
and the windows are renewed. The S porch has an inner arch
which is even a little earlier, late C 12 on the strength of its round
arch on two orders of colonnettes, the thin capitals, and the roll
mouldings of the arches.

The interior is of strange proportions. The nave is only two
bays long, the third and fourth bays corresponding to the transept
W aisles and the transepts. There is thus a balance in extension
between nave and transepts, and the long aisleless chancel follows.
In the chancel the minimum of ornament, just a roll moulding
round each of the E lancets. Richer (and probably later) the
SEDILIA, though much restored: trefoiled-pointed arches, shafts
with nail-head and weirdly incorrect capitals and abaci. Some
stiffleaf decoration. The chancel arch is noticeably taller than the
arcade arches of nave and transepts. The arcades have mainly
slender circular piers, and the arches are double-chamfered, with
hoodmoulds on small figured stops. There are, however, a number
of interesting variations. For a start, the crossing piers and E
responds are octagonal; and then, while the capitals are simply
moulded, those on the N side are clearly a little later than those
on the S. The capital of the angle pier between nave and S transept,
furthermore, is carved with pretty foliage in a distinctly C 14 way.
The transept responds are different again. They are also different
from each other, that on the S side being later. Both are short

tripartite shafts on simple corbels. The N respond has nail-head in the capital, the S big dogtooth ornamentation between the filleted shafts. What all this points to, of course, is a building history more complicated than at first appears – a more gradual extension of the Saxon church. – FONT. C 13; circular, on four shafts. – STAINED GLASS. Quite a range of Victorian glass, none of it of especially high quality but much quite satisfactory. *Wailes and Strang* did one window of 1872 in the S transept and two in the chancel S wall. – Between these, one of several by *Baguley* (S transept, NE chancel), early works of the 1850s and much better than most of his. – Nationally known firms are represented first by *Clayton and Bell* (nave NE) of 1882, and more especially a pretty window full of animals in the chancel; and by *Kempe*, 1903–4, in the N aisle, and *Kempe & Co.*, 1910, in the chancel N wall. – SAXON CROSSES. Fragments of two C 10 or C 11 cross shafts, found in 1945 and 1946. One has interlace patterns only, the other also has a saint (?) under an arch and a hunting scene. – MONUMENTS. Fine black marble slab in the chancel, with excellently carved coat of arms and no name at all; it is supposed to be to a member of the Addison family who went mad when he was young and died in 1735. – In the porch a large plain stone slab to Thomas Bewick (1753–1828), who is buried in the churchyard. – Parts of a number of medieval cross slabs against the S wall of the nave outside.

VICARAGE, S of the churchyard. The E end of the house is late C 14 and has a two-light window with cusped heads to the lights; it was built to house three Augustinian canons from Hexham (*see* Introduction, p. 51) and the vicar. The remainder, an L in plan, is of various C 17 dates, extended slightly to the rear in the early C 19, but probably also medieval in its core. The front door is not central. It is round-headed, with moulded imposts and a pendant keystone. The façade has one stringcourse rising over the door and another at first-floor level. There were formerly four-light mullioned windows, but only the chamfered reveals remain. So all of this must be early to mid-C 17. The wing to the rear is dated 1694 and has a big segmental-arched fireplace inside with imitation nail-head. There are several other C 17 fireplaces, one with a little original plasterwork, and, in one room, a plaster frieze of affronted dragons.

S of the house, GATEPIERS with big bulgy rustication. They must date from *c.* 1700. Also GARDEN TERRACES of the same period; set into one of them a datestone recording the level of the Tyne flood of 1815; another, much higher, records the level of the disastrous 1771 flood. The drive entrance to the NE of the house is flanked by sections of massive masonry and may be part of the gatehouse of the medieval cell.

W of the church, a pretty little C 18 FOOTBRIDGE of two segmental arches with a triangular cutwater between.

TYNE BRIDGE. A fragile-looking steel bridge of 1883; eight spans with stone abutments but piers of steel tube pylons grouped in fours and cross-braced. The tubes are fabricated of riveted quadrant-sections marked 'Dorman Long, Middlesbrough'.

0060
OVINGTON

OVINGTON HALL. At the E of an outbuilding, facing the road, there is a pointed window with a trefoiled-cusped and sub-cusped head, evidence of the house that was in existence by *c.* 1350. The house itself looks entirely early C 19, but the rear part is much older in its masonry and has broached-stopped beams in the present kitchen.

9030
PALLINSBURN
3 m. w of Ford

The house has been through a series of astonishing transformations. In the later C 18 it had a three-storey three-bay centre block with a canted centre bay, attached by single-storey linking bays to slightly higher pavilions with Venetian windows. Every angle and junction of this façade was marked by high, thin, octagonal columns with pagoda tops, like minarets on a mosque. By the mid-C 19 the single-storey links had been heightened to three storeys and become the highest elements in the façade. Nothing else had changed. All of this work was done for members of the Askew family. In 1912 the house was acquired by Charles Mitchell. He remodelled the house in Jacobean style and then, *c.* 1933, removed the top storey and gave the house a flat concrete roof. Of the original appearance of the house all that can now be seen on the S front is the original brickwork (some of it in old brick, traditionally said to have come from Flanders), the canted centre bay and the lower half of one of the 'minarets'. The ground-floor window to the l. retains the form, though in Jacobean style, of the original Venetian window. On the N side the two projecting wings have kept their C 19 appearance.

Inside, Mitchell created some beautiful rooms, especially the dining room, with a barrel-vaulted Tudor-style plaster ceiling of intersecting ribs with reliefs of wild animals. Reused Jacobean panelling with Ionic pilasters and a frieze with strapwork. The Oak Room has reused linenfold and panels with medallion heads. The decoration of the hall, with its screen of Tuscan columns with acanthus necking, may be genuine late C 18 *in situ*. Much more similar decoration on other rooms.

Beautiful GARDEN including a long, fine avenue planted in 1912.

KING'S STONE, 1 m. ESE. Prehistoric standing stone, 2.5 metres (8 ft) high. The traditional site of the death of James IV at Flodden.

6060
PARK VILLAGE
2¼ m. SW of Haltwhistle

METHODIST CHAPEL. 1850; extended in the later C 19.
The VILLAGE is a tight cluster of C 18 and early C 19 houses. One opposite the chapel is dated 1752; IVY COTTAGE, further N, is dated 1815, an adjacent house 1836.

PEGSWOOD

The old village street retains one or two quite interesting houses. Extensive late C 19 colliery housing further E.

NORTH FARM. Mid-C 18. Brick with rusticated quoins and cut sandstone dressings. Three-bay house with a projecting centre-piece, a little lower than the remainder, with what might be termed a Venetian door (i.e. an arched door between a pair of windows) beneath a lunette. Behind are planned FARM BUILDINGS, a good later C 19 group. The walls are brick inside and snecked stone outside. Engine house at rear.

EAST FARM. A humbler C 18 brick farmhouse, but with a picturesque foldyard group of FARM BUILDINGS with segmental arches and steep reverse-stepped gables. Early C 19 gingang to the rear on the W.

COOKSWELL HOUSE, at the W end of the village, backing onto the S side of the road. Brick with stone lintels and a slightly chamfered door surround, dated 1768.

RAILWAY VIADUCT, ¾ m. SW, spanning the Wansbeck. Built by engineers *Robert Stephenson* and *T. E. Harrison* for the York, Newcastle and Berwick Railway. Rock-faced stone, with nine segmental arches on tall tapering piers.

LADY CHAPEL, 1 m. S. On the N bank of the Wansbeck in dense woodland, the tumbled footings of a little rectangular C 15 chapel. The only feature now recognizable is the jambs of a W doorway.

PLANETREES *see* WALL

PLENMELLER

On the S bank of the South Tyne looking across to Haltwhistle on the N.

WEST PLENMELLER FARMHOUSE. Bastle house, reconstructed *c.* 1800; the blocked byre entrance door is visible in the E end. Mid-C 18 barn added at the rear, and attractive later C 19 buildings complete the group enclosing the foldyard.

UNTHANK HALL. *See* p. 596.

PONTELAND

ST MARY. Norman W tower of typical sturdy proportions. There are several small original windows and an original W doorway with one order of colonnettes and two orders of zigzag in the arch. It has a tympanum, blank, but still quite a rarity in the county. The tower has at least three stages of masonry: the lower two are Norman; the bell stage with the cusped bell openings and the parapet is C 14. The buttress is, of course, C 19. There are Norman remains inside the church as well. The responds of the tower arch and that on the W side of the S transept arch both look Norman.

Moreover the pier of the s aisle to which this respond belongs is not really a pier at all but part of a solid wall pierced at a later date to make a s aisle. So that tells in favour of a Norman church without a s aisle but with a transept. Then there is the w respond of the N aisle which looks even more elementarily Norman. If that is accepted then the Norman church had a N aisle. Conversion and enlargement began in the c 13, when the fine chancel and the equally fine N transept were built. The transept is still in its original condition. It has a stepped group of three lancets in the N wall and two lancets in the E wall. They are plainly single chamfered outside, and inside have either shouldered rere-lintels (N wall) or pointed-trefoiled rere-arches (E wall). The chancel was altered in the c 14, as will be seen, but it had similar lancets divided by buttresses. Two of the windows on the N side, and all of the buttresses, survive, though the E buttresses survive only in the lower courses. The chancel arch is double-chamfered and rests on large coupled human faces, completely recut. They represent Adam and Eve before and after the Fall. The piscina in the chancel is very low (the floor must have been raised) with a pointed-trefoiled shape and large dogtooth decoration.

About the middle of the c 14 or a little earlier, the chancel E and s windows and one N window were enlarged and given Dec tracery. The s aisle came after that. It is dependent upon Newcastle (St Andrew for the windows, St Nicholas for the arcade), and H. L. Honeyman dated it c. 1390. It is of three bays. Octagonal piers without any capitals and double-chamfered arches dying into them. There is consequently no w or E respond. The bases of the piers are particularly high and finely moulded. The N aisle was rebuilt in 1810, it is said, but if that is so it was done entirely reusing the old masonry. The N arcade was redone by *Wilson*, who did restoration in 1861 and 1880. He made it just like the s arcade. The s aisle windows are Perp. The s transept is largely Norman in its masonry. Its E window with the shallow segmental head, though totally renewed, was probably later c 14. The porch is c 13 or early c 14. It therefore predates the s aisle and must have been moved. It has a pointed tunnel vault with three chamfered transverse ribs. Inside, the timber roofs are by Wilson.

FONT. In the tower vestry, c 13, with octagonal bowl and stem with broaches. – LECTERN. A good late c 19 naturalistic oak eagle. – ORGAN. 1973 by *Johnson* of Cambridge. – STAINED GLASS. Medieval glass in the heads of the s chancel windows, including one small figure of a kneeling ecclesiastic. – The intricate leaded patterns in the clear glass windows were added by *Wilson*. – MONUMENTS. Built into the tower wall inside is a small round-headed c 10 grave marker which has a circle at the intersections of the arms. – Nathaniel Ogle † 1789, good tablet with urn in front of an obelisk; unsigned. – Richard Newton Ogle † 1794; signed by Coade, i.e. of *Coade* stone. Sarcophagus and trophies on top and an interesting inscription. – Chaloner Ogle † 1750 and Charles Ogle † 1858. They share a tablet made at the later date by *M. W. Johnson*. – Anne Byne † 1769. A wall tablet with a moving inscription. – Joseph Mackay † 1896, a good memorial brass.

BLACKBIRD INN, opposite the church. Handsome gabled front

towards the s, with masonry clearly older than its c 16 mullioned windows. The ground floor of this part of the inn is indeed tunnel-vaulted, and belongs to a c 14 or even c 13 fortified house. The original doorway to it is on the w side and now enters into a modern toilet block. It has a chamfered-shouldered arch, rather damaged, and retains its drawbar socket and tunnel. It opens into a lobby with a murder hole above and a mural stair to the n. On the outside of the building there are chamfered setbacks on the e and s sides but none on the w; there are, however, traces of the pitched roof of a range which formerly adjoined the building on this side. There is also an early window placed right at the s end of the wall so that it might have a view unobstructed by the roof. It seems likely, therefore, that the present inn (at least the s part of it) originally formed only a fortified wing of a larger hall house (cf. Shield Hall).

The house was altered and extended in 1597 by Mark Errington, whose initials appear above a first-floor window, above a door inside and on the lintel of the first-floor fireplace. The alterations include a two-storey gabled bay on the e side, blank on the ground floor and oversailing above on two large rounded corbels. Beside this (with a modern doorway between the two), a large projecting chimney breast, old brick above, stone below. The fireplace behind this has a four-centred multi-moulded arch. That on the first floor is similar but has a crenellated moulding on the lintel incorporating the initials M + E for Mark Errington. The details of the c 17 house attached to the n of the old part are now all c 19.

OLD RECTORY to the s of the inn, on the corner of North Road and Main Street. A nice plain early c 18 brick house, heightened later in the century. Five plus two bays. Inside, two early c 18 panelled rooms. The house was the property of Merton College, Oxford, who were the lay rectors of Ponteland.

VICARAGE, Main Street, next door to the Old Rectory. Now a residential home. By *F. R. Wilson*, probably in 1860. In its garden the ruins of a TOWER-HOUSE, originally no doubt a 'vicar's pele'. Said to be c 14, but the existing remains are all c 16. Three storeys. Two windows with chamfered surrounds and one lintel of a doorway which has a drawbar slot. A blocked doorway on the first floor has part of an early medieval CROSS SLAB as a jamb stone.

BELL VILLAS. A group of nine small detached houses on the main road, built in 1826 by Matthew Bell of Woolsington Hall, the prospective Member of Parliament, to provide extra freeholds and so increase the number of his supporters.

ELAND LODGE (No. 16 North Road). Early c 19. Three bays with widely projecting eaves.

ELAND HALL, ½ m. NE. A substantial early c 18 farmhouse. Five plus two bays. Only one room thick, with two projecting stair wings, both of which contain staircases with thick turned balusters. The front was altered in the mid-c 19. *John Dobson* is said to have built a house here in 1816 for William Barclay, but there is no sign of it.

NORTHUMBRIA POLICE HEADQUARTERS, 1 m. NW. 1903 by *Leeson* for the Newcastle Board of Guardians as cottage homes for children. A civilized crescent of semi-detached houses in the Arts-and-Crafts style. The crescent on the N side of the green is a little later and a little less successful.

DARRAS HALL. Large area of middle-class housing to the S of Ponteland. The land was acquired in 1907 by the Northern Allotment Society with the view of establishing a garden city for Newcastle. The land was auctioned off in lots in 1911 and building began within guidelines on layout laid down by the society. The architecture is of no special distinction.

DARRAS HALL RAILWAY STATION, 2½ m. SW. A timber-built station on the Ponteland Branch extension light railway of 1913, which boasted a royal siding. Long closed, the station is now used for community purposes.

TOLLHOUSE, at the SW end of the Pont Bridge. Early C19. Small sandstone building with a pyramidal hipped roof; presumed to be a bridge toll but not for the present bridge.

DISSINGTON HALL. *See* p. 253.

HIGHAM DYKES. *See* p. 333.

HIGH CALLERTON. *See* p. 333.

KIRKLEY. *See* p. 366.

MILBOURNE. *See* p. 389.

See p. 253. *See* p. 333. *See* p. 333. *See* p. 366. *See* p. 389.

POWBURN

0010

PLOUGH INN. Former coaching inn. C18 and C19, of several builds.

FIELD HOUSE, ¼ m. S on the Glanton road. Formerly a Presbyterian manse. Attractive 1830s Tudor house; its style, with gable finials and corbelled eaves, has affinities with the railway architecture of the Greens.

CRAWLEY TOWER. *See* p. 249.

HEDGELEY HALL. *See* p. 312.

CRAWLEY TOWER. *See* p. 249. HEDGELEY HALL. *See* p. 312.

PRESTON

1020

1 m. E of Ellingham

PRESTON TOWER. A miniature edition of the Langley Castle type, i.e. a hall tower of the C14, originally with four corner turrets (cf. also Tarset Castle). What remain are the two S turrets, the wall between them and parts of the side walls. The present rear wall dates from the restoration of 1864 by *Henry Robert Baker-Cresswell*. The tower is three storeys high, and there are vaulted rooms at each level in the turrets. Three of the rooms have C16 or C17 fireplaces with chamfered surrounds. The springing of the main basement vault is also visible. Cresswell was an amateur horologist and the clock in the tower was made by him.

The HOUSE adjacent to the tower is also called Preston Tower. It was built *c.* 1805 for Edmund Craster; the long E wing was added in 1862 and the entrance side altered in 1915. The architect is not known. The garden front is five bays and classical, with a porch of two pairs of Roman Doric columns, a pediment over the centre three bays, and a parapet with panels of bold guilloche moulding. The entrance front is seven bays. It formerly had a three-bay centre of giant attached Ionic columns, but this was replaced in 1915 by the present plainer centre with the large solid porch. Inside, an imperial staircase with plain balusters.

CHATHILL STATION, 1 m. N. 1847 by *Benjamin Green* for the York, 115 Newcastle and Berwick Railway Company. In the Tudor style. Most attractive and satisfyingly complete; even the waiting shed on the up platform is quite intact.

PRESTWICK LODGE 1070
1 m. SE of Ponteland

By *Dobson*, 1815. A small house and an early one by this architect, but already a very characteristic example of his work. It has the usual plan of a square front block with a service wing and conservatory to the rear. It also has the perfection of masonry finish we expect from Dobson. It is of three bays with nice, swept steps up to a recessed porch with Doric *antae*. The rest is all quite plain. Not so inside: the interior is rather grand, in a miniature way. The entrance hall has a screen of two Greek Doric columns and a coffered ceiling with a triglyph frieze. The dining room and sitting room have ornate plaster ceilings with wreaths of vines and ivy. In the study, a severely neo-Greek fireplace.

Incorporated as part of the service wing is a BATH-HOUSE with a sunken walk-in bath, contemporary with the house.

PRUDHOE 0060

PRUDHOE CASTLE. In spite of the industry around, Prudhoe has kept a narrow belt of green, and the grounds of the castle are beautifully laid out and maintained. The castle was first mentioned when unsuccessfully besieged by William the Lion in 1173 and 1174. Set on a strong natural site, it is protected by the river-cliff above the Tyne to the NW and by a steep-sided dene on the E. The ridge has been scarped into an oval mound by digging a ditch round all except the NW. A short length of ditch was also cut to bar the way up the extreme NE tip of the ridge. Excavations within the E half of the existing castle suggest that in the later C 11 timber buildings there were enclosed by a stout palisade. This was later replaced by a ringwork of clay and stones which had an entrance on the SE. Apart from the tower, these defences were dismantled before *c.* 1150, and a stone curtain wall, a NE postern and the present S gatehouse were substituted. A bailey on the SW (the 'Pele Yard') is defended by a bank and a substantial ditch; it may have been part of the original defences, but the date of its construction, no later than the C 13, is uncertain. Its E end is now confused by the later barbican and the mill-pond.

The present castle, built by the Umfravilles and in the hands of the Percys only from the C 14 onwards, is an important example of the type with the keep free-standing in the inner bailey, and an outer bailey with gatehouse. The KEEP stands in parts to quite a height. It was built either just before or just after the 1174 siege. It is small: only 12.6 by 13.5 metres (41 by 44 ft). It has a fore-building with staircase on the E side, a wall-passage at first-floor level in the W face and a large N window at the same height. This has single-chamfered jambs and a shouldered arch. At the NW corner of the INNER BAILEY is a large semicircular tower, open at the back and probably of the C 13. At the SW corner, the lower courses of an identical tower. A late Georgian Gothick house stands between the inner and outer baileys. Mackenzie, writing in 1825, said it was in 'the most execrable modern taste', but to us it seems particularly pretty. The N end, overlooking the river, is apsidal. The S end retains much medieval masonry and two C 15 windows. Internally also there is medieval work, now largely plastered over, so it is evident that the C 19 range replaces a much older one. The archway between the two baileys has a head corbel of the C 12.

The curtain wall of the OUTER BAILEY is well preserved. The HALL which stood against its N wall has been shown by excavation to be of the C 13 or early C 14. In the S curtain wall is a well-preserved garderobe. The GATEHOUSE is one of the most rewarding in the county. The arches are round-headed and single-chamfered on plain responds. They are clearly Norman, and date indeed from the early C 12. The passageway itself is tunnel-vaulted and has a transverse arch resting on a pair of head corbels. These also are unmistakably Norman (cf. the head corbels at Holy Island). The floor above was built in the C 13, with lancet windows belonging to a small but extremely interesting apartment: the CHAPEL. The sanctuary is irregularly corbelled out and has been called the earliest English oriel window. Its three lancets are quite unsystematically arranged. In addition there is a W lancet in a skew position. The guardroom on the second floor was added later in the Middle Ages. The chapel and the guardroom are reached by a picturesque outer staircase. A BARBICAN was added, initially in the mid- or late C 13 but lengthened in 1326. Again it is one of the best in Northumberland, long, with a prominent outer gateway and small doorways in the barbican walls close to the outer gatehouse. The roadway up through the barbican and the gatehouse is steep and dramatic. At the E end of the outer bailey, a square Gothick tower on old foundations.

OUR LADY AND ST JOSEPH (R.C.), Highfield Lane. By *Dunn, Hansom and Dunn*. Built at Prudhoe Hall in 1891 and reconstructed on the present site in 1904. Nave and chancel with N chapel and S transept. The chancel has two-light Geometric windows but the nave and porch have curious tracery, a mixture of Perp and Flamboyant elements. Vigorous gargoyles.

PRUDHOE GRANGE, South Street. A curious case. At first sight the house looks like an ordinary Victorian villa, except that in the S wall it has a quite splendid C 13 doorway which has two orders of colonnettes, and a two-centred arch with roll mouldings. The hoodmould has nail-head decoration. The doorway is said to have come from Ovingham, but as there was a chantry chapel at

Prudhoe it seems very possible that it is *in situ*. It is certainly in the right position for the S doorway of a church, and the rest of the house, despite its C 19 appearance, has walls 1.2 metres (4 ft) thick and a C 16 fireplace on the first floor. There is also a short stretch of nail-head decoration below the E gable.

PRUDHOE HALL, ½ m. SE. Now the administrative block of Prudhoe Hospital, but originally built in 1878 for Matthew Liddle. Rather formless but redeemed by much excellent naturalistic stone-carved detail. Good interior, especially the hall with a Jacobean staircase and elaborate wrought-iron lamp standards. A bathroom and W.C. are also decoratively Victorian.

BRIDGE over the dene immediately E of the castle. Medieval, of two periods, it would seem, since one side has a steeply pointed single-chamfered arch, while the other has a chamfered round arch. The vault is strengthened by three chamfered transverse ribs.

ELTRINGHAM. *See* p. 269.
MICKLEY. *See* p. 388.

REDESMOUTH
2 m. ESE of Bellingham

8080

REDESMOUTH HOUSE. From the front a simple four-bay early C 19 house with an equally simple but older service wing to the r. However, the rear gable has windows with early C 17 cable-moulded surrounds, and both on the side walls and blocked up inside the house there are early C 18 windows with architrave surrounds. Also inside, early C 18 stone fireplaces and two-panel doors. Upper-cruck roof.

REDE BRIDGE, 900 metres N. Early C 19. An attractive stone bridge of two segmental arches and a smaller flood arch at the NW end. Now used only for farm and pedestrian access.

Romano-British SETTLEMENT, ⅓ m. N. A familiar type: sub-rectangular within a wall, a ditch and a counterscarp bank; round stone houses fronted onto sunken yards. There are suggestions of more than one phase and, unusually, of opposed entrances.

RENNINGTON
2010

ALL SAINTS, 1831, with chancel and N aisle added in 1865. The earlier work is of good solid buff stone, in the lancet style. W tower with large twin-lancet bell openings and embattled parapet on corbels. When the additions were made in a C 14 style, cusped trefoils were inserted into the heads of the nave lancets. – FONT. Plain octagonal font from Embleton Church, probably C 14.

OLD VICARAGE, beside the church. Quirky Victorian Gothic, with many shouldered arches and big mason's marks on many of the stones.

LITTLEMILL. *See* p. 379.

0060
RIDING MILL

ST JAMES. 1858 in a free C13 style by *Matthew Thompson*, with rather more grandiose E parts of 1879.

METHODIST CHAPEL (formerly Baptist), Broomhaugh. 1842, still in plain Georgian style.

RIDING MILL STATION. One of the original Newcastle and Carlisle line buildings; 1834–5, in the usual Tudor style. Taller stationmaster's house to the rear. The ROAD BRIDGE nearby, carrying the A695 over the railway, is of the same date, with a segmental skew arch and channelled rustication.

Riding Mill is largely a mid-C20 commuter village, incorporating three older settlements, Broomhaugh on the E side of the March Burn, Riding on the W of the Burn, and, between them, Riding Mill itself. BROOMHAUGH on the E side of the stream retains its original village street running down to a ford over the Tyne. Two houses here incorporate the remains of bastle houses: BROOMHAUGH FARM HOUSE on the E and STABLE END on the W side of the street. The latter has an original harr-hung byre door (now internal) and an extension dated 1699. At RIDING MILL itself, the MILL stands on a site dating back at least to the C14; the three-storey mill has an attached wheel house. Corn milling continued until *c.* 1900, after which it was used for sawmilling until the 1950s. The buildings were converted to a house in 1972, with some iron gears and part of the waterwheel rim retained for façade decoration. Across the road the WELLINGTON INN has its original doorway dated 1660 between windows which have lost their mullions; on the first floor, two good C17 fireplaces. The old hamlet of RIDING is a little further W along the A695. The MANOR HOUSE, which turns its back on the road, is a complex building, partly brick and of late C17, C18 and early C19 dates. To the N the DOWER HOUSE has a partly C17 front range and a good mid-C18 rear wing. Other C18 and early C19 houses nearby. Hidden in the trees on the S of the road, the surprisingly urban HOLLIN HILL TERRACE, 1864. Pinkish brick and quite grand; only half an hour's train ride from Newcastle, the terrace marks the beginnings of the commuter development responsible for the present nature of the village.

OAKLANDS, in the trees on the hill above the parish church. A playfully Gothic house of 1860 by *Thomas Wilson*, which proved to be a smaller-scale prototype of his later Shotley Hall (q.v.).

THE ROMAN BRIDGE, carrying a footpath across the Burn below the E end of the church, on the line of Dere Street. Segmental C17 arch, but with earlier masonry, perhaps medieval, in the abutments.

RIDING WOOD *see* BELLINGHAM

RIDLEY

½ m. E of Beltingham

RIDLEY BRIDGE. 1792 by *Robert Mylne*. Two lofty segmental arches of 20.6 metres (67½ ft) span over the South Tyne.

RIDLEY HALL. Neo-Tudor of 1891 by *Horatio Adamson*, with a big octagonal Carnarfon-Castle-like tower at the SW corner. Impressive stair hall with coffered ceiling. Fireplace from Mottisfont Abbey (Hampshire); C 16, timber. Another fireplace is said to be by *Samuel Watson*. To the W, the lower stable wing survives from a previous house of 1743, showing two arches with rusticated surrounds.

RIDLEY BASTLE. The road winds round a bastle house which, despite C 20 alterations, shows its original gable-end byre door, a basement slit, part of the upper door, and pairs of corbels on each gable for original end stacks. Original floor and roof timbers inside.

RIDSDALE see WOODBURN

RINGSES, THE see DODDINGTON and EGLINGHAM

RISINGHAM see WOODBURN

ROCHESTER

HIGH ROCHESTER. The hamlet stands within the ROMAN FORT of *Bremenium*; this is reached by turning N off the main road at the old school, the porch of which is a jigsaw puzzle of Roman blocks, including many monolithic gutters and two large stone balls from the Roman single-armed catapults provided in the fort *c.* 220. After two successive timber forts in the late C 1, the site was abandoned until the re-advance into Scotland in *c.* 140, when it was rebuilt in stone. Reconstruction followed in the C 3; occupation probably ended *c.* 312.

Much of the outer facing wall of the fort rampart has been robbed away or buried by debris (short stretches are visible on the W), but the defences still present an impressively daunting external scarp. The ditches survive well as earthworks on the SW and around the NE angle. Some of the best masonry can be seen from the approach road, consisting of part of an internal tower between the S gate and SW angle. The front of the tower has been torn away by stone-robbers, leaving the back and the side walls and a blocked doorway clearly visible. More impressive is the recessed W gate, reached from inside the fort through a field-gate which lies to the S of it. The massive masonry of the flanking towers, flush with the face of the fort wall, is clearly seen, as is also the N impost, the moulded cap and the springer of the arch.

Of the other gates, only a few courses of the outer E jamb of the N gate are exposed. The layout of the internal buildings is known in some detail, but nothing is traceable on the surface. The Victorian excavators found that the sunken strongroom in the headquarters building had a stone door which slid on a pair of iron wheels into a special recess.

The large CEMETERY survives 350–750 metres SSE, between Petty Knowes and Lamb Crag. Most prominent is a circular stone tomb beside Dere Street, built to receive an unurned cremation. More modest low barrows are identifiable, about ninety in all, many with a ditch and outer bank: early C 2 to early C 4.

The HAMLET within the fort includes two C 16 BASTLES. The most complete, known simply as The Bastle, stands alone. Both its original doors are blocked but retain roll-moulded surrounds. The second bastle is called Rose Cottage and forms the S end of the row of cottages. It has been much altered, but the walls are very thick and at the back there is massive masonry. In Rochester village, the BIRDHOPECRAIG UNITED REFORMED CHURCH, inscribed Birdhopecraig Scotch Church. 1826; in an entirely domestic style.

A Neolithic LONG CAIRN occupies a fine skyline site on the SE shoulder of Bellshiel Law, 2 m. NNE. Consisting of an elongated pile of heavy rubble, it is 110 metres (360 ft) long by 18 metres (60 ft) wide and nearly 2 metres ($6\frac{1}{2}$ ft) high; its bulbous E end concealed a rock-cut pit.

WOOLAW, $\frac{3}{4}$ m. W. A well-preserved sub-rectangular late Iron Age and Romano-British settlement, divided by a row of four round-houses strung across the axis. Two E entrances led into separate yards. Originally of timber, the visible houses had low stone-capped walls faced with boulders and apparently lined with wattle. All but the centre of the floor was paved; a timber porch was provided.

ROMAN TEMPORARY CAMPS. A series of nine camps strung out along Dere Street between the Roman fort at High Rochester and Chew Green. Each camp was normally rectangular in plan, enclosed by a single low rampart and external ditch which provided sufficient short-term protection. One of the three superimposed camps 400 metres WNW of High Rochester is very well preserved, its gates protected by a short detached length of bank and ditch set a few metres forward. Two larger camps on Foulplay Head, N of Featherwood, have broadly similar defences. Most of the other examples here are harder to appreciate, being partly obscured by later field banks or ploughing.

GOLDEN POTS. The bases of two wayside crosses: Middle and Outer Golden Pots. In the C 18 there were five or more along Dere Street on the Alwinton–Rochester boundary. The place name, perhaps transferred, was mentioned in 1228.

HORSLEY. *See* p. 343.

ROCK

St Philip and St James. A good small mid-c 12 church in spite of regrettable additions. The Norman building of nave and chancel had a corbel table all round (arcaded on the side walls, with grotesque masks at the w end), carried on pilasters at the angles and on the side walls (dividing the nave into four and the chancel into two bays). The nave angles are shafted, with scalloped capitals. The w end has a central raised panel containing a doorway with chevron ornament, jamb shafts with scalloped caps and a tegulated hood springing from a stringcourse with lozenge ornament. Above the corbel table is another similar string, but the gable top with its window and bellcote is of 1855, when the church was restored by *Salvin*. The s wall of the nave shows one small c 12 loop and two pairs of c 19 lancets. There is another c 12 loop on the N of the chancel, but the apse (and little N vestry) are Salvin additions. The broad N aisle to the nave is of 1866 by *F. R. Wilson*; its N wall is the old nave N wall rebuilt stone-for-stone, with its corbel table, one c 12 loop and two c 19 lancets. In the church is a fine Norman chancel arch, quite broad and low, with an inner order moulded with broad rolls on the angles and an outer order (to the nave) with zigzag; there is also a hood with a sort of chip-carved panelled ornament. The jambs have paired attached shafts with fluted and scalloped caps. Above the arch (towards the nave) is another string with a lozenge pattern. A c 19 triple lancet on the s of the chancel has an obviously older segmental rere-arch beneath a roll-moulded hood with strange disk-like stops. – The rere-arch still bears remains of wall painting (a pattern rather than figures). – MONUMENTS. On the chancel floor, a late c 12 CROSS SLAB with sword and axe. – Nearby, a brass plate to John Salkeld † 1629 and a marble wall tablet to Colonel John Salkeld † 1705. – Marble plaque to Charles Bosanquet † 1850, by *J. Edwards* of London; draped oval medallion with bust in profile, against an obelisk, in the c 18 tradition. – ORGAN. Oversized and occupying most of the N aisle; by *Gray & Davison*, 1881.

Rock Village consists of little more than a single row of mid-c 19 Tudor estate cottages. The VILLAGE HALL (originally built as a Sunday School) is set forward from the centre of the row and is dated 1855, with a reset 1623 date panel from the 'Mid Hall' which occupied the site before. Across the road to the E is the c 18 ROCK FARMHOUSE and a tall octagonal later c 19 DOVECOTE.

Rock Hall (Youth Hostel). Highly picturesque and extremely complicated. What can be read of the building history can mostly be seen in the main E elevation. This is three-storeyed, with a three-bay centre and quite broad end bays set slightly forward; the N end bay is partly ruined and has been so since a fire in 1752. Both end bays show the outlines of the gable ends of two-storeyed cross wings of an early medieval house. In each case the ground floor, up to a chamfered setback, is of good-quality squared stone, and the upper part is rubble. No datable architectural features are exposed but one might assume the c 13 or early c 14; the gables are steeply pitched. Then in the later c 14 or c 15 the walls of the s wing were thickened (the external thickening is obvious at the

SE corner) when it was converted into a tower, and given a short wing or turret on the S. The N wing may have become a tower as well; the surviving fragment of its SE corner shows a circular gunloop at second-floor level (in 1549 the house was the head-quarters of a band of Spanish mercenaries under Sir Julian Romero, engaged to fight the Scots). In the C 17, when the Hall was owned by the Salkeld family, it was remodelled again, with the centre block being raised to three storeys and given a rear W wing. Of this date is the central doorway (now blocked), with a moulded arch within a square frame, and the three-light mul-lioned-and-transomed windows. In the early C 18 the entrance position was transferred to the end of the S cross-wing (doorway with lugged bolection-moulded surround). A 1743 drawing in the estate office shows the house with crenellated parapets all round before the fire which destroyed the N wing and the symmetry of the front. The house was patched up, with a pair of corbelled-out castellated turrets at the N angles where the wing had been; but no major changes were made until *John Dobson* was called in *c.* 1820 to add two strange two-storeyed octagon bays to the S front, which sit uneasily on either side of the S wing turret. Another octagon was planned for the NE corner (its outline is sketched in on the estate office drawing), but only its ground floor remains as a screen wall to the yard behind. Perhaps it was never completed, and was left as a picturesque 'ruin' to match the adjacent fragment of the old N wing. Finally, in the mid-C 19 *F. R. Wilson* added a projecting block at the NW corner of the house with distinctive crowstepped gables. The interior of the house is disappointing; much must lie hidden behind plaster and stoothing. Early C 19 groined plaster ceiling in the entrance hall, and fireplaces of the same date with the Bosanquet arms.

Immediately N of the Hall is an outbuilding called the CHAPEL (a chapel is recorded here in 1359). This has a two-centred cham-fered doorway near the W end of its S wall, blocked in the C 17, when a big fireplace was inserted in the W end. Several mullioned windows probably date from this conversion. The building extended further E, and was truncated in the early C 19. Further N are extensive GARDEN WALLS (the Salkelds were noted gar-deners; cf. Fallodon Hall); the long N wall has furnaces concealed in little embattled turrets, which have a mock gatehouse to match them. These parts must be *c.* 1800, although parts of the walls look earlier C 18.

0020

RODDAM

RODDAM HALL. Five-bay early C 18 centre, with short linking sections to lower, one-bay pedimented wings of 1765–83 by *Lancelot Coxon* for Edward Roddam. The centre has quoins, hipped roof, doorway with pediment on attached Tuscan columns, and windows in moulded frames. To the rear the wings project, forming a courtyard. The centre section was reduced in height from two-and-a-half to two storeys *c.* 1979 as part of a major restoration, and the change in proportion has made the house seem somehow gentler, less Northumbrian.

Several outbuildings, including the STABLES, the GAME
LARDER and the GARDEN COTTAGE, have the cross-shaped
arrow slits typical of late C 18 romantic Gothicism. The stables
are partly castellated also, and the garden cottage has a little clock
tower with a lead spire. This work may have been done by *Vincent
Shepherd*, estate architect to the Duke of Northumberland in the
later C 18.

WOOPERTON HOUSE, I m. E. A plain ashlar house of *c.* 1840, with
a three-bay entrance front but a long irregular garden front with
two shallow segmental bows.

HILLFORT, I m. WNW of Ingram, in the lee of the summit of
Ewe Hill, high above the Breamish gorge. A boulder-faced wall
encloses an irregular oval area within which a single stone-founded
circular house is visible. An unusual annexe was added on the
NNE and a second, internal, wall was built parallel to the S side.
Two hornworks flank the everted ESE entrance, deepening its
defences.

CALDER, I m. SW of Roddam Hall. A farm and row of attached
former cottages dated 1788. The odd thing is that the cottages
were single-storey, with the granaries to the farm on the first floor
above them.

THREESTONEBURN. *See* Ilderton.

ROS CASTLE *see* CHILLINGHAM

ROTHBURY   *oooo*

ALL SAINTS. The rebuilding in 1850 by *G. Pickering* of all but the
chancel and E walls of the transepts was a tragedy, involving the
demolition of a pre-Conquest W tower which seems, like the tower
at Jarrow, to have linked two early churches; the foundations of
the W church, extending beneath the present Church Street, could
be traced in the C 18. Pickering's work is early C 14 in style. His
W tower has a taller gabled SW turret. The surviving medieval
parts unfortunately do not take us before the C 13. The chancel
has a shouldered priest's door and six lancets (the western pair
C 19) on the S, and a triplet of E lancets with double-chamfered
surrounds. The E wall of the S transept has three more lancets,
the smaller one near the N end of the wall being the E window of
the S aisle before the transept was added later in the C 13. The
chancel arch has two continuous chamfers. On the N side of the
chancel are two broad round arches on an octagonal pier and on
the E side of the N transept a C 19 arch on C 14 responds; these
opened into the Cartington Chapel, the ruins of which were
removed when the present vestry was built in 1887. Pickering's
nave is of four bays, with normal octagonal piers and double-
chamfered arches. The only hint of what was there before is the
E respond of the N arcade, a C 13 shafted corbel with nail-head
ornament. The transepts each have a two-bay W aisle (cf.
Corbridge, Ovingham etc.). – FONT. The bowl, dated 1664, has
knotwork and simple interlace motifs doubtless inspired by the

10   shaft, which is the base of a splendid Anglo-Saxon CROSS, with
an Ascension on the front, interlace at the rear, a spiral scroll on
one side and a scene of animals and humans struggling in the
coils of reptiles (Hell?) on the other. The Museum of Antiquities
in Newcastle has two more pieces of the cross, including part of
the head with a Crucifixion. Cramp suggests that the Rothbury
Cross is of the first half of the C 9, and the earliest surviving stone
rood in the country. – MONUMENTS. Two small medieval CROSS
SLABS and a C 12 fragment in the porch W wall. On the N wall
of the chancel, painted wall monument to Mary Tomlinson
†1710.

PERAMBULATION. Rothbury is a pleasant little town to wander
through, and still shows signs of its prosperity as a late Victorian
resort, brought about by the arrival of the railway (now gone) and
the influence of Lord Armstrong and Cragside. Coming in from
the S one crosses ROTHBURY BRIDGE, medieval beneath the
C 20 concrete and steel superstructure. The three N arches have
chamfered ribs; the S arch and a 1759 widening to the E show
plain soffits. Bridge Street beyond ends in a T-junction. Turning
r. along Town Foot, a detour up the steep Brewery Lane on the
111   l. brings one to ADDYCOMBE COTTAGES, built in 1873 by
Norman Shaw to house retired staff from Lord Armstrong's estate.
There are two terraces arranged in an L-plan; that facing S (Nos.
1–12) is the grander, with an almost Bavarian feel to the big
timber-framed gables of the end houses. The windows are mullioned-and-transomed, those to the first floors of the intermediate
houses in steeply gabled dormers. Each house has a little dogleg
timber porch with an ogee-headed doorway. The roofs are of red
clay tiles with terracotta finials (notice in particular the curly ones
on the porches); the chimneys have splayed bases straddling the
ridge. At the back one realizes that the cottages are in fact flats;
those on the upper floors have external stone stairs to balconies
or doors in the short rear wings. Even the attached outhouses
have interestingly asymmetric roofs. The cottages were restored
in 1978 by *Spence & Price* of Newcastle. Returning to TOWN
FOOT and continuing E, ROTHBURY MOTORS is notable, being
a virtually unaltered garage dated 1913. It has a broad rock-faced
gable to the road and a basket-arched workshop entrance to the
l. of the central shopfront; the workshop has cast-iron roof trusses
with diagonal strutting. Beyond are ARMSTRONG COTTAGES
(almshouses), 1896, a pleasant vaguely Tudor group but with
nothing of Shaw's flair; the contrast with Addycombe Cottages is
that between the 1870s and early 1880s at Cragside and the rather
pedestrian later additions.

Returning to the end of Bridge Street and turning W, the first
part of HIGH STREET is relatively narrow. Behind the C 19 street
front on the S, and set at r. angles to the road, is SANDFORD
HOUSE, dated 1722. Built of heavy rubble, tall and narrow with
small mullioned windows, in appearance it is still wholly C 17.
Continuing W, High Street suddenly opens out into a green
triangle with the church at the SE corner, and continues as two
roadways divided by a steep bank with old trees. In the centre of
the triangle is ROTHBURY CROSS of 1902 by *C. C. Hodges*, a
good piece of Arts-and-Crafts work with oak and rose scrolls

inhabited by rabbits, squirrels and stags. The s side of the triangle has a varied c 18 and early c 19 terrace bending round the corner into Church Street. The long frontage on the N side of High Street is rather grander but shows the same character, c 18 houses interspersed with more elaborate c 19 buildings in a pleasing variety of styles, e.g. the Italianate CONWAY HOUSE of 1876 and the TURK'S HEAD INN of 1874; there is some attractive detail both in stonework and wrought iron.

THRUM MILL, ½ m. E, dramatically sited in the wooded Coquet valley where the river rushes though a narrow channel in the sandstone. Rectangular c 18 mill with an external undershot waterwheel at one gable end and a low kiln and high kiln placed on either side of the building. The rocky bed of the river was evidently lowered late in the c 18 to facilitate salmon passage; previously the mill had an overshot wheel. The stone columns near the present wheel did not carry a launder but bearings for a layshaft drive to a threshing machine in an adjacent building. The present masonry weir augmented the rock outcrops and took water direct to the wheel; the tail-race is rock-cut.

OLD ROTHBURY, ¾ m. w. Bivallate hillfort, overlooked from the NE but defended by steep slopes on the s. Stone-founded hut-circles overlie the s part of the interior.

WESTHILLS FARM, 1½ m. w. An old cottage with an attached barn and a detached shelter shed with granary over; probably no earlier than the late c 18 but with impressively steep-pitched roofs and reverse-stepped gables. Immediately N of the farm a small circular HILLFORT, defended by a single inner rampart; a wide berm separates this from two concentric outer ramparts.

CRAGSIDE. *See* p. 244.

GREAT TOSSON. *See* p. 290.

HESLEYHURST. *See* p. 315.

NUNNYKIRK. *See* p. 532.

SNITTER. *See* p. 573.

WHITTON. *See* p. 629.

ROTHLEY

Rothley, although it is *c.* 4 m. NE of Wallington Hall, is part of that estate, and several of its most noteworthy elements are connected with the Blacketts, in particular with Sir Walter Calverley Blackett, who was concerned to create a Picturesque landscape on the northern part of his land as well as closer to the Hall.

ROTHLEY CASTLE. Designed for Sir Walter *c.* 1755 by *Daniel Garrett* as an eyecatcher and viewing-point on his new deerpark, Rothley Park. It is a Gothick folly with a central, two-storey, castellated tower and lower end towers linked by screen walls with cruciform slits. The end towers have arched niches which formerly held large statues. The walls were decorated with the griffins' heads now to be seen on the lawn at Wallington.

CODGER FORT, *c.* 1 m. N. A smaller eyecatcher done for Sir Walter *c.* 1769 by *Thomas Wright*. Like Rothley Castle it is in an intensely dramatic situation above a steep craggy hillside. It is Gothick also, a triangular bastion in shape, and built of huge blocks of roughly dressed stone.

ROTHLEY LAKES. The final element of Sir Walter's Picturesque landscape. Two fishing lakes created on either side of the road by *Capability Brown* in the 1760s (Arthur Young called them 'newly made' in 1770). A dam between the two formed of rustic arches seems not to have been built.

HARTINGTON HALL, 1 m. W. Referred to as a bastle in 1542. The present house may include fragments of that house on the W side but is mainly early C17; the roof, the windows and the rear wing were altered in the mid-C19. Three storeys and three bays. Very plain. Thick walls. Inside, several large stone C17 fireplaces and doorways with four-centred-arched lintels.

KIRKHILL, just E of Hartington Hall. Built into the garden wall, a large relatively complete and well-preserved C14 GRAVE SLAB with a foliated cross. Also part of a second slab and several architectural fragments.

LOW FAIRNLEY, 1 m. NW of Hartington. A very complete C16 bastle house. Stone stairs to the first-floor doorway. The inscription 1723:WB:Bt refers to alteration and the building of the outshut by Sir William Blackett. On the ground floor there are two large well-cut corbels to support the fireplace on the floor above.

GUIDEPOST, at the Rothley crossroads. The stone pillar of a turnpike guidepost, possibly the only such survivor in the county. It is slotted near the top to take wooden fingerposts, which had wrought-iron brackets leaded into the pillar. The road N and W was the ALNMOUTH TURNPIKE (Hexham to Alnmouth) of 1752 and has a good series of turnpike milestones of 1851; the E–W road was the MORPETH TO STENG CROSS TURNPIKE, also of 1752; the section of road from the crossroads W to Gallows Hill was shared by the two Trusts but maintained by the Blacketts of Wallington and their successors, the Trevelyans. Its straightness indicates that the land was unenclosed at the time it was built.

ROUGHTING LINN see DODDINGTON

RUDCHESTER see HEDDON-ON-THE-WALL

RUSSELL'S CAIRN see ALWINTON

0070

RYAL
2 m. NNW of Matfen

ALL SAINTS. A chapel of ease. C12, extensively restored and partly rebuilt in 1870. The nave has much medieval masonry, including, at the W end, two large buttresses which may be the remnants of a tower. Inside is a C 13 chamfered chancel arch. The responds, however, are C 12. The N respond has scallops and saltire crosses, the S has scallops and intersecting arches. Built into the W wall inside are nineteen medieval CROSS SLABS, complete or in parts, 29 and several architectural fragments. The effect is quite dramatic. The C 19 work is also in a mixture of Norman and C 13 styles. The S doorway is a large stylized Norman portal with three orders of columns, a corbel table and two tiers of small round-headed windows on each side. The chancel was restored in E.E. style. – FONT. An C 18 marble baluster.

SOUTH FARM. A very substantial mid-Georgian farmhouse, with a stair wing added to the rear in 1771. Pedimented doorway with a pulvinated frieze.

ST JOHN LEE
½ m. s of Acomb

9060

ST JOHN OF BEVERLEY, prettily situated amongst trees on the valleyside opposite Hexham. 1818 by *Dobson*. Simple preaching box and W tower; thoroughly remodelled and chancel added in 1886 by *W. S. Hicks* in his usual free Perp style. The interior, with its spectacular panelled roofs and carved screens, dates entirely from the remodelling. – MONUMENTS. Outside, set upright against the E wall of the nave S of the chancel, a large C 14 Frosterley marble slab with an inscription in Lombardic script and a brass indent. – Also a few medieval fragments under the tower; an uninscribed ROMAN ALTAR, later converted to a sundial; and a boulder decorated with prehistoric CUP-AND-RINGS and scarred by ploughing. – In the churchyard, some good C 18 HEADSTONES.

RECTORY, W of the church. 1886 by *Hicks*. A five-bay house with a central pedimented doorway; a free version of an early C 18 type.

THE RIDING, ¼ m. NE of the church. Three-bay house of *c.* 1800 with a Tuscan porch; big extensions of 1905. To the N, RIDING FARMHOUSE dated 1834, with an attached DAIRY of *c.* 1900, a very pretty building, semi-octagonal with the overhung eaves carried on a timber arcade, and mullioned windows. Planned FARM BUILDINGS dated 1858: the triple-gabled timber super-structure covering the yards, of rather superior quality, is probably contemporary with the dairy.

THE HERMITAGE, ½ m. SE. On the reputed site of the C 7 hermitage of St John of Beverley. A building called the 'Armytage' is recorded in 1496 but the present house is largely of the mid-C 18, in two phases, with some alterations and additions of *c.* 1890. The s front has a projecting three-bay centrepiece with a lugged architrave to the door and a Diocletian window within the open pediment; the flanking two-bay wings have balustraded parapets. To the r. is a late C 19 addition with a canted bay window facing E. The entrance block on the W is also late C 19. Inside, some early and mid-C 18 fireplaces and a good mid-C 18 stair. The drawing room (with the canted bay) has a late C 19 coffered ceiling with carving of the quality seen in the parish church. – STABLE BLOCK, W of the house, *c.* 1760, with central arched gateway and pyramid-roofed end pavilions; in the shrubbery to the s of it two FLOOD-MARK STONES (1771 and 1817) remind one of the dangers of living on the Tyne floodplain. – E of the house in the walled garden, the GRAVESTONE of George Heslop †1665, an early Baptist.

BOATACRES, on the riverbank to the SE, is a mid-C19 ferry-man's cottage of rock-faced stone with a steeply pitched roof, an early example of domestic revival. N of the Hermitage, and now stranded alone on the N side of the A69 dual carriageway, is a mid-C18 WELL HOUSE with an arch on Tuscan columns and a pyramidal top.

9060

ST OSWALD'S
1 m. NE of Wall

ST OSWALD, in a splendidly isolated position commanding wide views to N and W. 1737; remodelled and gothicized in 1887 by *W. S. Hicks.* It commemorates the battle of Heavenfield (634), where King Oswald of Northumbria defeated the pagan Cad-wallon. Of the C18 only the basic rectangle with its rusticated quoins, and a dated sundial. Hicks's work is in a simple Perp style. His are the s porch and the bellcote, oddly placed on the roof ridge one bay from the w end. Inside, a ROMAN ALTAR decorated with a sacrificial cleaver, wine ladle, vine branch and grapes. It has been made to serve as the socket for a cross, perhaps the predecessor of the modern wooden cross beside the Military Road. – In the porch, fragments of a medieval CROSS SHAFT with roll-moulded angles. – Decorated C12 corbel built into the N wall inside.

FALLOWFIELD, 1 m. SW. C17 house, remodelled in the mid-C18; altered again and extended to the rear in 1928. Inside, a big four-centred-arched fireplace with contemporary plaster bosses at the rear (cf. Ovingham Vicarage), and two other C17 fireplaces of the type where the moulded lintel is set forward on corbels. Also a stair with barley-sugar balusters, clustered in groups of four to form the newels. This stair is said to have been brought from the old Dilston Hall, demolished in the mid-C18.

9060

SANDHOE
2 m. NW of Corbridge

A village amongst trees on the N flank of the Tyne Valley. Beside the road, a WELL, with stone seats made from a variety of late C17 architectural fragments, probably from the house that preceded Dobson's Beaufront Castle (q.v.). SANDHOE HIGH HOUSE is an interesting building of C17 and C18 dates, with a big semi-circular bow to the s. What is now HIGH HOUSE WEST was originally its detached kitchen or brewhouse. More reset bits from Beaufront at APPLETREES (a big Ionic doorcase) and BUTLER'S

COTTAGE (an elaborate panel-traceried Gothic fireplace used as a door surround).

SANDHOE HALL, on the hillside below the village. 1850 by *Dobson* for Sir Rowland Errington. The central of the three finely sited mansions which form such a landscape feature on this side of the valley (the others are Beaufront and Stagshaw House, q.v.). Here Dobson uses a rather eclectic mixture of Tudor and Baroque motifs, but the house is not one of his best, although the porch is rather attractive. Irregular plan, incorporating a heavily disguised earlier building at the rear. Big Gothic ENTRANCE SCREEN dated 1870. 165 metres W a brick-lined ICEHOUSE, with not one but two square chambers, each with a tapering ice well in the floor.

BEAUFRONT CASTLE. *See* p. 162.

SCREMERSTON
0040

ST PETER. 1842–3 by *Bonomi & Cory*. Broach spire. Aisleless nave, narrower chancel, coarsely detailed timber roof.

Contemporary Tudor-style VICARAGE by the same architects.

THE SINK PIT (Scremerston Old Mine), $\frac{1}{2}$ m. s, in a wood to the E of the road. A massive beam pumping engine house, surmounted by a cast-iron panelled water tank. Heavy buttresses at the pumping shaft end of the house, and the remains of a horse whim at the rear. A tablet records that it was erected in 1840 by the Commissioners of Greenwich Hospital with John Grey (of Dilston) as Receiver, *Thomas Forster* as engineer and *W. Elliot* of Tweedmouth as builder. What is presumed to be a winding engine house of the same period and probably the same date is aligned at r. angles to the pump house.

SCREMERSTON TOWN FARM and INLANDPASTURE. Two farms just outside the village rebuilt *c.* 1820 for the Commissioners of Greenwich Hospital. Very plain classical style in sandstone ashlar. Originally they had wind-powered threshing machines, later powered by stationary steam engines. Town Farm had sixteen workers' cottages, each with its own cowhouse, pigsty and privy. The Commissioners had acquired land here, as in many other parts of the county, from the estate of the Earl of Derwentwater, who was executed following the Jacobite Rebellion of 1715.

LIMEKILNS, 1 m. E, by the sea. N of Sea House and at the foot of a cliff, a kiln with three drawing arches is built on a limestone shelf at water level. S of Sea House, a larger but similar kiln with a long loading ramp to the kiln head. Ruins of another kiln nearby.

SEAHOUSES
2030

Really a continuation of North Sunderland (*see* above) and originally called North Sunderland Sea Houses. It was developed from a haven for fishing and limeburning activities. The centre of the little town is sadly altered to cope with the tourist trade, but there are areas of character left, notably the harbour and the fishermen's

houses in the delightful CRASTER SQUARE off South Street.
There are also CURING HOUSES, active, derelict and converted,
in SOUTH STREET and UNION STREET.

METHODIST CHAPEL, Main Street. 1925 by *Mauchlen & Weight-man*. Classical style.

HARBOUR. Original harbour works in large blocks of red and grey
sandstone (part of the present inner harbour) by *Robert Cramond*
of North Sunderland, *c.* 1786; later modifications and new piers
by *Sir John Coode* and *J. Watt Sandeman* in 1886–9. These new
works consisted mainly of a N pier *c.* 300 metres (985 ft) long,
constructed of rubble faced with Portland cement concrete and
having a terminal lighthouse *c.* 9 metres (30 ft) high, also of concrete, and an E breakwater, about the same length as the pier,
built of mass concrete.

LIMEKILNS. A bank of four pre-1825 limekilns lines the quayside.
These, together with the fish trade, led Walter White to describe
the place in 1858 as 'A small common-looking town, squalid in
places ... Signs of trade are however manifest.' The lime trade
ceased soon afterwards, but the kiln arches are still in use as
fishermen's stores.

3070   SEATON DELAVAL

OUR LADY. Within the ha-ha wall of the Hall, and originally the
Delavals' manorial chapel. Ignoring the W porch of 1895, it is
externally a little two-cell building with a tall and narrow nave of
almost Anglo-Saxon proportions. Rubble masonry and a round-
headed loop of early appearance on the N of the nave may in fact
point to a date before the early C 12, to which the rest of the fabric
belongs. The other windows are all C 19 lancets, except for that
in the E end, which is a copy of the three-light window with
reticulated tracery of *c.* 1330 of which the head is now set in the
W porch. The bellcote, oddly placed on the E nave gable, is also
C 19. Blocked straight-headed priest's door S of the chancel, with
a roll-moulded surround of C 16 type. The original W door, now
inside the porch, has a tympanum bordered by zigzag. One head
in the middle, the only motif now recognizable, suggests a Tree
of Life design, cf. Croxdale (County Durham). Three shields in
cusped panels above, and more inside in the W wall, no doubt
came from a C 14 tomb-chest. Inside, the Norman chancel arch
remains and an identical arch into a separate sanctuary. They
have short heavy semicircular responds, with big block capitals
and arch mouldings of a soffit roll between hollow chamfers
(exactly like the earliest ribs at Durham, those in the chancel
aisles), inside an outer order with zigzag and a billet hood. Both
chancel and sanctuary have plain barrel vaults springing from a
chamfered string which is a continuation of the imposts of the
arches. The C 14 E end probably replaces an earlier apse. Also
C 14, an interesting PISCINA with a fluted bowl and a shelf. The
nave has a coved plaster ceiling of the C 18. – MONUMENTS. –
Effigy of a cross-legged knight, perhaps Sir Hugh Delaval; early
C 14. – Effigy of a lady, late C 14 or early C 15.

SEATON DELAVAL HALL. By *Sir John Vanbrugh* for Admiral 74–5
George Delaval. A sombre house of smoke-blackened stone facing
a bleak scene, with the roofs of Blyth and the sea in the distance
to the N. The house is orientated N–S, that is, not in any calculated
relation to the sea; for it was built in 1718–29, and the sea was

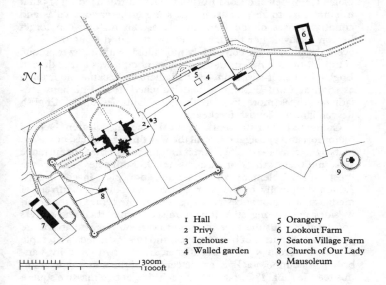

1	Hall	5	Orangery
2	Privy	6	Lookout Farm
3	Icehouse	7	Seaton Village Farm
4	Walled garden	8	Church of Our Lady
		9	Mausoleum

300m
1000ft

Seaton Delaval Hall and grounds

accepted as a picturesque asset only a hundred years later. Vanbrugh was over fifty when he designed the house; the Admiral
was yet older, and both died before the completion of the building
which is the triumph of both. No other Vanbrugh house is so
mature, so compact and so powerful, and the Admiral, we know
from one of Vanbrugh's letters, was 'not disposed to starve the
design at all'.

The arrangement of square symmetrically planned *corps de logis*,
with arcades to the l. and r., breaking forwards at an angle of 90°
and running along the fronts of two service wings to end by the
road in small square pavilions, is Palladian, i.e. the arrangement
customary for villas on the Venetian *terra ferma*. The forecourt or
cour d'honneur is 55 metres (180 ft) deep and 46.5 metres (152½ ft)
wide; the house itself is comparatively small – only about 23 by
23 metres (75 by 75 feet), though with attached towers and turrets.

Now for towers and turrets one would look in vain in Palladio's
serene villas, and Vanbrugh's house, in plan and elevations, utterly
contradicts the overall layout of central block and *corps de logis*. If
they are reminiscent of any Italian designer, only Piranesi's name
would come to mind, and he was born two years after work had
started on Seaton Delaval. What Piranesi had in common with
Vanbrugh is the passion for the cyclopic, and also the theatrical,

and the scorn for homely comforts. Wren, older by one generation, had a much nicer sense of when the grand manner and when a more domestic style was appropriate; Lord Burlington and his protégés, younger by one generation, had a more refined and even manner. So even, indeed, was the strictly Palladian style which Colen Campbell and Lord Burlington had introduced c. 1715 that it is not easy to keep apart in one's mind the various villas and country houses of the Burlingtonians. But no one can forget Seaton Delaval. For though it betrays the hand of its master in every detail, it is yet completely individual, with its own unique composition and mood. In details and mood it was out of date in England when it was built, for Palladianism became the fashion as soon as Lord Burlington had launched it; and perhaps Palladianism was more English than the fantasies of the English descendant of Flemish forebears.

Compared with the work of the Palladians, Seaton Delaval seems forceful and aggressive all the way through; it has, however, in its own terms two quite distinct moods, that of the N or entrance side, and that of the S or garden side. On both sides some of the most unusual elements of the composition play an equal part. Added diagonally to the four corners are polygonal turrets of medieval or Tudor ancestry, and added to the centre of the E and W sides are oblong stair towers raised higher than the turrets and façades. But the tops of these towers do not rise above the pedimented centres of both façades, and this is carried as a temple roof across from N to S. Yet higher are the two typically Vanbrughian chimneystacks over the centres of the E and W eaves of this temple roof. They consist on each side of two massive square shafts connected by a heavy arch. Moreover they are made to look yet more massive by alternating bands of bulgily raised rustication. The same motif is applied to the whole ground floor and first floor of the stair towers, and in addition the house rests on a half-sunk base of yet more thickly bulging rusticated bands. The smooth to Vanbrugh evidently meant the unstressed.

75   Take the NORTH FRONT. A broad open staircase leads to the arched doorway. Above it a semicircular window of considerably greater diameter. The whole of the centre of the front is ashlared with deep and wide joints and flanked by groups of three giant columns of the Tuscan order on each side, arranged angle-wise and carrying a metope frieze which jumps back, and is carried on along the centre above the semicircular window. The part of the façade between the centre and the turrets lies back a little and has windows with heavy keystones. The raised centre with its sculptured pediment has a group of three windows, one arched and two with yet heavier keystones. Even the balusters of the top balustrade are extremely wilful in their details. The upper storeys of the stair towers have smooth ashlaring and Venetian windows.

Now for the wings. The arches of the arcade rest on excessively heavy square piers with bands of rustication, the upper windows have a type of surround which was, during those very years, especially favoured by Gibbs, and the three centre bays project a little and have a pediment. The pavilions by the road again have banded rustication. They are square, with only one large arched window on each side, a parapet and urns. They are lower than the wings, the wings are lower than the house itself, and this reaches up by another storey with its pedimented arches and stair towers. So the skyline is dramatically scaled and broken.

On the SOUTH SIDE all is calmer, although the skyline is no 74 more restful. But instead of the wilfully spaced and closely pressed-in columniation on the N, there is here a comfortable portico of detached, elegantly fluted Ionic columns carrying a balustraded balcony, and the wall behind it to its l. and r. is smooth without any of the farouche rustications of the other sides. A wide staircase leads up to the portico.

Seaton Delaval has had an unlucky history. Its l. wing suffered from a fire in 1752, and a more disastrous fire in 1822 destroyed an added E wing of c. 1770, along with most of the interior of the *corps de logis* itself, which was reroofed but remains little more than a gutted shell. The GREAT HALL is large and stone-faced, of uncomfortably high proportions and provided with heavy blank arcading on the ground floor, arched niches between heavy pillars on the first floor, and a second storey (in the raised centre part) that was originally a separate upper room. The hall was then 9 metres (30 ft) high, as against a width of 7.5 metres (25 ft) and a depth of 13.4 metres (44 ft). On the E is a stone fireplace with male termini caryatids carrying the mantelshelf. The hall is connected with the two stair turrets by vaulted corridors. Similar corridors at first-floor level are linked by a cantilevered stone gallery spanning the S end of the hall. The staircases wind up with unsupported stone steps and wrought-iron balustrades; the stair and gallery balustrades are largely of the 1962 restoration by *Aynsley & Sons* of Newcastle. The S front is occupied by the SALOON, a tripartite apartment, originally with a painted ceiling by *Vercelli*. At the NE corner is one room that escaped the fire, a parlour with bolection-moulded mahogany panelling of 1726. Beneath the whole ground floor is a labyrinth of vaulted cellars and passages.

The centre of the W wing is the KITCHEN, a large room with groin vaults and a shallow curve at its W end. There is a large Venetian window here. The centre of the E wing is the STABLES, divided into three parts by broad segmental transverse arches. The arches are ashlared, and the E wall at the centre again has a shallow apse with a Venetian window. The horses eat their hay out of arched niches.

The GARDEN FEATURES are of considerable interest. The *corps de logis* forms the centre of the N side of a rectangular area c. 365 by 220 metres (1200 by 720 ft) enclosed by a ha-ha wall, raised at the corners into circular bastions. In these stood lead statues: only David and Goliath, probably a C 17 recasting from a lost marble by *Baccio Bandinelli* remains *in situ* at the NW corner. Samson and the Philistine, probably C 17 and a copy of the group by *Giovanni Bologna*, was moved in 1964 from the NE bastion to the C 20 garden W of the house. Diana, formerly on the SE bastion and now in the Orangery, is identical to a statue of c. 1766 by *John Cheere* in the Pantheon at Stourhead (Wiltshire).

E of the house are an attractive early C 18 PRIVY, with a Venetian doorway, and an ICEHOUSE. Beyond, outside the ha-ha wall is a range of farm buildings with an arched C 18 screen wall at the

N end, and then a separate walled garden with on its N side the
ORANGERY, by *William Etty*: five bays with arched openings
between Roman Doric demi-columns; frieze and parapet. The
row of cottages W of the orangery incorporates at its W end a
section of thick walling which may be a remnant of the Delavals'
old castle or tower, which preceded the house. Further away to
the SE, the sad shell of the MAUSOLEUM of 1766, a large square
structure with dome on square drum, designed in the pattern of
the Temple at Castle Howard (Yorkshire). The entrance side has,
as at Castle Howard, a portico. The order is Tuscan. Opposite
the entrance, a broad apse with a Venetian window in the curve.
To the l. and r., two-bay wings with arched windows.

One or two more distant features of the planned C 18 landscape
around the Hall are preserved. In line with the S front but ½ m.
away is an OBELISK, 18.2 metres (60 ft) high. The base of another,
on the N side of the Avenue, 595 metres W of the house, marks
Admiral Delaval's fatal fall from his horse in 1723. Only the end
walls of the gate screen at the far end of the Avenue, 1¼ m. W,
survive.

LOOKOUT FARM. C 17 house remodelled in the mid-C 18. Conventional three-bay front but showing Vanbrughian influence in
the steep stepped and pedimented gables with blind lunettes.

SEATON SLUICE

The small natural harbour, originally known as Hartley Harbour,
was protected by a pier built by Sir Ralph Delaval before 1676,
when, to overcome problems of river silting, which may have been
aggravated by the pier, he arranged for the harbour to be scoured
by low-tide releases of river and high-tide water, dammed behind
a sluice at high tide. The sluice was located near the present road
bridge, and the harbour was thenceforth known as Seaton Sluice.
(Smeaton was sufficiently impressed by its performance to advo-
cate a similar system for Margate.) These original works were
carried out to protect and enhance coal and salt exports, but as
trade built up, the little harbour, which was never easy to enter,
became increasingly inadequate. So a supplementary harbour was
created for Sir John Hussey Delaval between 1761 and 1764 by
driving an easterly rock-cut from the harbour through the headland on its S side, to the sea. It was 9.1 metres (30 ft) wide, 15.8
metres (52 ft) deep and nearly 275 metres (900 ft) long, with lock
gates at either end, probably of the stop-log variety, to provide a
small wet dock. In addition to coal and salt exports (*see* Introduction, p. 90), the Delavals added bottle shipments to the harbour's trade after the establishment of their 'Royal Hartley Bottle
Works' in 1762 on a site now covered by the housing to the SW
of the road bridge; the works became the largest in the country
(*see* Introduction, p. 99). The Hester pit disaster of 1862 (*see*
Earsdon) brought an end to coal shipments, and when the bottle
works closed ten years later, all kinds of shipments ceased and
the harbour works either rotted away or were dismantled. Only
the outlines of the OLD HARBOUR and the impressive CUT now

remain. At the seaward end of the cut a curved retaining wall marks the site of a large capstan, either horse- or manually powered, for raising and lowering the gate there and for winching ships into the cut. Also visible at this point are squared sockets and grooves which held the timber work for the jetty, which reached out into the sea.

The OCTAGON was formerly the harbourmaster's office and looks like an after-dinner idea of Vanbrugh's. It is an embattled octagon with arched windows and an added r. wing with one big Venetian window (converted to a private residence in the 1980s). The KING'S ARMS is another early C 18 building but very plain. On the island formed by the cut is the picturesque little WATCH HOUSE built c. 1876 for the Seaton Sluice Voluntary Life Saving Company. It looks like a miniature church, with a pyramid-roofed tower at one end.

In the Dene of Seaton Burn stood Seaton Lodge, a C 17 house claimed by Sir John Delaval to be 'the finest thatched house in the kingdom'. It was demolished c. 1965. PRIMROSE COTTAGE, a little s of its site, is of the same date, with some mullioned windows. Further up the Dene is STARLIGHT CASTLE, a Gothick gazebo traditionally said to have been built to house one of Sir Francis Delaval's mistresses. It seems to have been a tower with projecting square corner turrets. Only the ground-floor walls of one corner remain, but still make a picturesque object in the landscape.

HARTLEY, $\frac{3}{4}$ m. s. The DELAVAL ARMS is a mid-C 18 building with stepped pedimented gables like those of Lookout Farm at Seaton Delaval. FORT HOUSE to the N incorporates an octagonal tower of c. 1917 which carried the rangefinders for Roberts' Battery, the northern of the Tyne Turrets. The concrete boundary wall has a projecting pill-box at the NW corner, a rare First World War survival.

SEGHILL

HOLY TRINITY. 1849 by *John & Benjamin Green*. Nave, chancel and bellcote, in the lancet style. To the w, the attached church hall of 1981. Inside, still a w gallery on cast-iron columns. – STAINED GLASS. Original patterned glass with coloured borders in the E window and roundel above chancel arch. – E of the church, the VICARAGE by *Dobson*, 1848, in a rather humdrum Tudor style.

SEGHILL HALL, 1 m. w. A villa of c. 1830, with giant pilasters and a distyle-*in-antis* central porch, extended in 1908.

The remains of Seghill Tower incorporated in the Blake Arms Hotel have been demolished; they included a rib-vaulted chamber 13.6 by 5 metres ($44\frac{1}{2}$ by $16\frac{1}{2}$ ft) suggesting that the building was something more than a conventional medieval tower-house.

BURRADON. *See* p. 203.

SEWINGSHIELDS

A perambulation along Hadrian's Wall from Coesike to House-steads.

TURRET 33b is $\frac{3}{4}$ m. E of Sewingshields, close to the point where the Wall and the Vallum diverge from the modern road. (Cars should be parked beside the telephone exchange at the turning to Grindon.) Flanking the turret are Broad wing-walls bonded into the Narrow Wall. In the interior a platform in the SW probably acted as the base for a ladder or stairs to an upper floor. The turret fell out of use by the end of the C 2. Its doorway, on the SE, which had had its threshold raised because of changing internal floor levels, was blocked. Eventually, probably at the beginning of the C 3, the whole structure was demolished and the recess in the S face of the curtain was walled up. The old internal N wall is still visible within the newer core. Outside the NE corner on the N side, in the top surviving course, is a stone roughly inscribed > GRAN, a so-called 'centurial stone' recording building work by the *centuria* (a squad of about eighty men) under the command of Granianus.

To the W the Wall is represented by a mound of rubble, mostly core material robbed of its facing-stones. The low swelling marking the line of the Military Way is readily visible to the S as it splits away from the N mound of the Vallum. The small wood masks the site of Milecastle 34. At this point on the nascent crags, as the Wall begins the long climb W up onto the natural defences of the Whin Sill, its Ditch enjoys a deeply cut finale. Looking S, beyond the modern road into the field E of the telephone exchange, the earthworks of a small ROMAN CAMP are visible, its gates protected by short external traverses. Just to the N, on an island in the bog known as Fozy Moss, is a puzzling earthwork. A raised pear-shaped area, with faint traces of buildings, is defined by a ditch and outer bank broken for an entrance causeway on the E. A deep depression occupies the N end of the enclosure. Quite undated, but plausibly medieval.

Further W, a robber-trench along the line of the Wall attests to the single-minded quarrying of the stone so conveniently available. The next structure exposed, TURRET 34a, is another clear example of the method by which the S face of the Wall was carried across the site of the demolished turret, again *c.* A.D. 200. Both the internal N corners are displayed; the original SE doorway is clear and some internal paving survives. The site was reused in the medieval period, perhaps contemporary with SEWINGSHIELDS CASTLE to the N. This was probably a tower, first mentioned in 1415 but abandoned by 1541; its site is indicated only by the earthworks of the rectangular fish-ponds constructed in its N side.

Sewingshields Farm probably masks Turret 34b, but to the W beyond the wood is a long stretch of consolidated Wall, including MILECASTLE 35. This is rather poorly preserved and has been displayed in confusing complexity. A road entering the S gate was flanked by internal buildings. For once there was no N gate through the Wall: when you are there, the reasons are obvious enough. In the Hadrianic scheme there was a single building in the SE corner, replaced in the early C 3 by another, partly overlying it. At the same time all the W half of the interior was occupied by one long building. In the early C 4 a jumble of crude structures was put up: one, on the W side, had a porch projecting onto the roadway. Abandonment in the mid-C 4 was followed, after a considerable lapse of time, by three successive medieval long-houses, the remains of which have been removed. To the E, a long burial cist of uncertain (but post-Roman) date abuts the S face of the Wall.

Westwards from the Milecastle up to and beyond the summit, short lengths of Wall have been sporadically consolidated, including TURRET 35a. This had stubby wing-walls and was also demolished and walled up in the early C 3. The original NE internal corner is visible. The panoramic views from the summit are exceptionally good, especially over Broomlee Lough, Busy Gap (famous for its late medieval bandits), Housesteads and the line of the Wall along the Whin Sill crags to Winshields and beyond. The underlying geology is readily apparent, with all the outcrops aligned E–W. To the N of the impervious dolerite of the Whin Sill itself, stripes of natural green sward betray the fertile limestone ridges, whereas the jagged crags are of the sandstone from which the Wall was built.

The walker continuing W to Housesteads will pass, on King's Hill, the site of Milecastle 36, of which only traces remain. Like Milecastle 42 (Cawfields) it seems at first to be bureaucratically sited in its metrically correct position irrespective of the impossible slope; in reality it is on an excellent vantage point, exceptionally well placed for its towers to watch over the gaps in the crags to E and W.

SHAWDON HALL
1 m. NW of Bolton

ooio

1779, perhaps by *William Newton*, for William Hargrave. The ashlar S FRONT, two-storeyed and of seven bays, has a three-bay centre-piece with giant pilasters of the form Robert Adam liked, carrying a fluted frieze with paterae and a pediment enclosing a wood carving (1817) of the Pawson coat of arms. A flight of steps leads up to a central Venetian doorway. The five-bay west front has a central open pediment, with a floating cornice over the first-floor window beneath. There is another pediment on a wing set back to the l. Some good internal detail survives. Both upper and lower stair halls have archways with fluted archivolts springing from imposts with paterae; there are also some good fireplaces, including one in black-and-white marble brought from Close House, Wylam. Quite a grand archway (probably part of the alterations of 1858 by *John Dobson*) links the rear wing of the house to a late C 18 stable block. Both GATE LODGES are mid-C 19 and probably by Dobson: that at the South Gate is the more ambitious, and links to an arcaded screen wall.

SHEPHERD'S LAW, 1½m. N. A hilltop ruin (a speciality of the Shawdon Estate), which seems to be of early C 18 date. The surviving part is a screen wall with three-bay round-arched blind arcades flanking a central gateway, between projecting end bays with taller arches. All the arches have alternating long and short voussoirs. Tradition links the structure with a manorial court founded *c.* 1710, but it seems more likely to be another eyecatcher, cf. Crawley Tower and Jenny's Lantern (Bolton). At the time of writing, a small monastic retreat centre is being built on the site; it is intended to retain and restore the C 18 screen.

SHEEPWASH

2080

A hamlet on the N bank of the Wansbeck. The ruins of the medieval Church of the Holy Sepulchre had been removed by the C 18, but the OLD RECTORY survives, a rambling late C 17 and C 18 house. Inside at first-floor level, a spectacular ceiling of the early C 19, with a lattice of faceted timbers covering each roof slope and heavy cornices with Romanesque and Gothic ornament. The discovery in 1988 of a large number of burials across the road from the Rectory and a little to the S suggests that the old church stood nearby. Remains of the N abutment of a medieval BRIDGE survive immediately W of the present road bridge.

SHIELD HALL
1½ m. NW of Slaley

9050

Late C 18 five-bay brick house. Incorporated in the farm buildings to the E, a medieval building which appears to be the cross-wing of a late C 13 or early C 14 house of the Aydon Castle type. Barrel-vaulted ground floor. A mural stair leads up from ground-floor doorway to upper chamber, probably a solar. This has a window in its N gable end with two pointed lights and a pierced lozenge in the spandrel; shouldered rere-arch with window seats. The S end, with a similar window, is C 19 work. The hall presumably lay to the E, for small chamfered windows on both floors of the wing are placed at the extreme N end of the E wall, as if to clear its N wall.

SHILBOTTLE

1000

ST JAMES. 1884 by *W. S. Hicks*. An impressive church in the Dec style, aisleless but cruciform with a strong crossing-tower and taller octagonal stair turret. In its tower and in many details the church is very reminiscent of Hicks's rather larger St Cuthbert at Blyth (q.v.). As at Blyth there are good ceilings, including a panelled vault under the tower. Hicks demolished a small C 12 church but reused its main features: the S door with a moulded segmental arch on shafts with cushion caps, and a billet hood; two round-headed loops in the N exterior of the nave; and the former chancel arch (now serving the organ chamber on the N of the crossing) of two square orders with chamfered hood and imposts. Good-quality fittings and furnishings contemporary with the church, including the FONT, a successful piece of free imitation Norman.

PEEL HOUSE (the former vicarage). House with a medieval tower at the E end, altered and extended in 1863 by *F. R. Wilson*. The tower is quite small; its walls have a pronouced batter up to the top of the first floor; the second floor and embattled parapet with a higher stair turret are entirely Wilson's. The ground floor has a barrel vault and a four-centred doorway; the only old windows are splayed loops in each end of the basement (that to the S enlarged, that to the N now opening inside the 1863 N wing). The three-bay part of the house adjoining the tower looks mid-C 18 (Wilson altered the door position), but its rear wall (now internal), although not especially thick, has the same distinctive batter as the tower walls and so may well be medieval.

Shilbottle VILLAGE is grouped around what is more a series of fields than a village green. There are three PANTS, two simple stone structures, the third more elaborate, with polished granite panels and a domed top. Some of the cottages are early C 18 (the CARRIB NORTHUMBRIA RESTAURANT dated 1701), but there has been much C 20 alteration. Nos. 1–8 LEATHERLAND ROAD, N of the church, are Aged Miners' Cottages of 1927; brick with pebbledash up to a string of shaped tiles at windowsill level. Four pairs of gabled projections, those at the ends with inscribed panels above the windows. Developments of the village at this time were made by the C. W. S., which took coal royalties in the area in 1916.

COLLIERY FARM, ½ m. NW. The farmhouse is one of a small but distinctive group built *c.* 1800 on the Duke of Northumberland's estates. It seems at first sight to belong to the standard two-storey three-bay type, but the central doorway is blind, the entrance being in one gable end below a tall round-arched stair window. All the ground-floor rooms and the stair thus opened off the same lobby or hall. Other members of the group are at Greensfield Moor, 1 m. S of Alnwick, Rennington North Farm and Old Barns at Warkworth.

TOWNFOOT, ½ m. NE. Late C 18 or early C 19 limekiln. Seven-sided, with three round arches.

LONGDYKE, 1 m. NE. The planned farm building group has the oddity of a projecting wing with a granary over an open arcaded ground floor which contained a horse engine.

SHORTFLATT TOWER

1¼ m. SW of Bolam

0080

Licence to crenellate was granted in 1305 to Robert de Reymes, but most of the present house seems much later. There is a small projection on the NE corner of the tower in older masonry with a double plinth which may be a survival of the original house. The present building comprises a tower, probably of late C 15 date, and an attached early C 17 house incorporating earlier masonry. The tower is tunnel-vaulted at ground level. It has a ground-floor doorway with a four-centred head, the lintel carved with a shield. The battlements project slightly on a roll-moulded corbel. Pitched roof behind the battlements. The room in the roof has a medieval fireplace (possibly reused) with a hood supported on corbels. The attached house is of four irregular bays, with C 18 sashes under early C 17 stringcourses which rise above each window. There is an enormous chimneystack between the third and fourth bays.

SHOTLEY

0050

Shotley Bridge, the main settlement, lies on the E side of the Derwent in County Durham. The BRIDGE is of late C 18 date with a single elliptical arch, widened to the N *c.* 1820.

SHOTLEY HALL. 1863 by the owner, *Thomas Wilson*. Quite a spectacular Gothic house, with a wide variety of window types and a pyramid-roofed round tower at one corner. Fine contemporary interior with carved marble fireplaces, elaborately panelled doors and Romanesque arches to the main stair. Painted glass (angel musicians) in the heads of the ground-floor windows.

Similarly fancy STABLE BLOCK to the N. GATE LODGE dated 1856, also by *Wilson*, with a saddlebacked tower. The adjacent gatepiers carry C 18 statues, one of Perseus with the Gorgon's head, brought from the demolished gatehouse at Black Hedley (*see* Snods Edge). Wilson's talents are also evident in THE BARN, an odd cruciform pair of houses across the road from the Hall gates, with his initials and the date 1860 in blue brick on the gable end.

GREYMARE HILL. *See* p. 292.
SNODS EDGE. *See* p. 573.

SHOTTON

2070

1¼ m. SE of Stannington

A hilltop hamlet E of the A1. NORTH SHOTTON FARMHOUSE is a three-storey three-bay house of the later C 18, with stone surrounds to its openings but otherwise quite plain. SOUTH SHOTTON HOUSE is a two-storey house of *c.* 1800. On the hilltop between them, a tall farm CHIMNEY, dated 1860, and with a circular shaft of white engineering brick. The adjacent engine house and barn have been demolished, but the chimney remains as a prominent landmark.

SIMONBURN

8070

ST MUNGO. An attractive church of dark grey stone, consisting of a four-bay aisled nave with W bellcote and N porch, and a long chancel. In essence it is a C 13 building, but despite initial appearances little medieval fabric survives. Externally all that is old are parts of the w end, with its two main buttresses, and a little of the chancel side walls, with the semi-octagonal N buttresses and the retooled 'low-side' window and priest's door on the s. The window (of two pointed lights with a pierced vesica above) and door both have jamb shafts and richly moulded arches. The aisle walls were rebuilt (and a SE transeptal chapel removed) in 1763 by *Robert & William Newton*. The chancel was rebuilt in 1863-4 by *Anthony Salvin*, and the aisles were refenestrated, the w window inserted, the N porch added and the chancel arch rebuilt by *R. J. Johnson* in 1875-7. Inside, the fall of the floor from w to E with the slope of the site gives the unusual sensation of looking downhill to the altar. The nave arcades, of double-chamfered arches on octagonal piers, seem old, but the chancel arch, similar in detail, was heightened in 1877. Two reset rood loft corbels above. In the chancel a reset PISCINA with a moulded trefoiled arch and a shelf, below which twin bowls have been separated by a circular shaft, now removed. – SCULPTURE. In the N porch, part of a Saxon cross shaft with vine scroll, *c.* 875-925, and other fragments including part of an impost or frieze with a baluster pattern, dated *c.* 700-750. – STAINED GLASS. E window and several aisle windows by *Kempe*, 1877, 1878 and 1904. – MONUMENTS. Several medieval CROSS SLABS. At the E end of the s aisle, four defaced figures from the Cuthbert Ridley monument of 1637; three kneeling, and one recumbent child. Sculpture of this date is rare in Northumberland. – Marble wall tablet in chancel to the Rev. Major Allgood † 1696. – In N aisle, wall monument to Robert and Elizabeth Allgood by *Noble*, 1866; standing robed angel holding a cross.

The churchyard has a large number of well-carved C 18 headstones. – LYCHGATE, 1885 by *R. J. Johnson*. C 13 style, cross-gabled, with a groined vault and a memorial tablet to Lancelot Allgood, in the form of a cross slab, set above the entrance.

OLD RECTORY. The style of the front block of 1725 suggests 80 Vanbrughian influence. It is three-storeyed and of five bays with segment-headed openings. Rusticated quoins and surrounds to the openings, and also the panels between, linking them in vertical bands. Hipped roof. The plainer rear wing has a moulded doorway dated 1666; this may be reset.

The small tree-shaded GREEN is enclosed by unassuming late C 18 and early C 19 cottages, one- and two-storied; on the lane entering from the E is STEWARD'S HOUSE, mid-C 18 and of five bays, with a central doorway in an architrave and windows in plain raised surrounds.

SIMONBURN CASTLE, $\frac{3}{4}$m. w on a narrow neck of land between two deeply incised burns (a situation very like Mulgrave Castle in Yorkshire). It was first mentioned in 1415. One wall of the tower was rebuilt in 1766 as a Gothick eyecatcher (*see* Nunwick); this fell in the 1940s, but the medieval barrel-vaulted basement survives in part, with a chamfered doorway on the N. There seems to have been a NW turret, but the remains are much encumbered by fallen debris.

TECKET, $\frac{3}{4}$m. SW. An interesting farmhouse. The walls are thick enough for it to have been a bastle, but the surviving features are of a conventional C 17 house; moulded doorway and formerly mullioned windows, those to the W of the door under a stringcourse. Upper floor rebuilt in the early C 19.

KIRKSHIELD, 1¼ m. SW. Former shooting lodge-cum-eyecatcher dated 1775, built for the Rev. James Scott. The end gables are tall screen walls, that to the S with Gothick windows, capped by squat crocketed pinnacles.

PARK END, 1 m. N. Late C 18 three-bay house with wings of *c.* 1830 which have giant angle pilasters and hipped roofs. LITTLE PARK END is an early C 18 house, still with some blocked mullioned windows, also enlarged in the C 19. At LOW PARK END is a circular C 18 stone DOVECOTE, brick-lined internally, which looks as if it may be a conversion of a C 18 windmill (cf. Plessey near Cramlington).

SINDERHOPE

In mid-Allendale.

PRIMITIVE METHODIST JUBILEE CHAPEL, beside the road. 1860. No longer in use.

TOLLHOUSE, on the Allendale Road turnpike of 1826. Very like the Allendale Bridge End tollhouse, but possibly a little larger.

LEADMINING REMAINS down in the valley at HOLMS LINN, below the waterfall on the Allen. Here are a good waterwheel pit, remains of the head of a shaft which connected with the Blackett Level from Allendale Town, and the miners' 'shop'.

BASTLE HOUSES. Above the road at HAYRAKE, an extended bastle with monolithic triangular doorheads in both parts. At SIN-DERHOPE SHIELD, an almost square bastle or tower extended *c.* 1700 by a three-storeyed block with its first floor lit by large openings under wedge lintels. The opposed doorways to the basement byre still have monolithic round-arched heads in the bastle tradition, and the first floor is of sandstone slabs carried on closely spaced beams; stubs of upper crucks at second-floor level. At ROWANTREE STOB, 1 m. SW, an unusual bastle-derivative house, probably of the later C 17, in ruins, built at the foot of the valley side. The walls are not especially thick, and the first floor could be entered from the hillside without an external stair being required, but the basement byre still has an impressive round-arched doorway.

SLALEY

ST MARY. 1832 by *Milton Carr* (Goodhart-Rendel). Simple two-cell church, with broad lancet windows and wide stilted segmental chancel arch. Alterations in 1907, when the S porch and the diagonal buttresses were added. Blocked windows on the N of the nave, on either side of the two-storied vestry, lit a former gallery.

Slaley consists of a long single street on the crest of a gentle ridge. There are one or two interesting houses in the village. W of the church is SLALEY HOUSE, the former vicarage; late C 18, remodelled as a square villa *c.* 1840. Further E is STANEGARTH, dated 1728; three bays with a moulded central doorway and windows in raised surrounds. Opposite the church is CHURCH VIEW, a C 17 house remodelled in 1769 (dated doorway inside later porch).

QUARRY HOUSE, 1 m. SW. A barn here, in poor condition at the time of writing, is a rare survival of a vernacular type: hip-ended roof, formerly thatched, with unshaped branches as the close-spaced rafters. Probably no earlier than the C 18.

SLALEY HALL, 1½ m. SW. Large Tudor-style castellated mansion of 1911–14.

TODBURN STEEL, 1½ m. NE. The farmhouse consists of a pair of bastle houses. The W bastle was heightened in the early C 19 but retains its blocked byre door in the usual gable-end position: the E bastle has its first-floor door, with a later window set into the blocking.

DUKESFIELD. *See* p. 257.
SHIELD HALL. *See* p. 568.

SNABDAUGH *see* GREYSTEAD

SNITTER
2 m. NW of Rothbury

0000

A pretty village, largely of unexceptional houses. The OLD SCHOOLHOUSE at the N end is in part a bastle house of *c.* 1600. Inside there is the lower part of a finely cut spiral stair, an unusually grand feature for such a building. GLEBE FARMHOUSE, at the S end, is early C 18; three storeys and three bays.

FLOTTERTON HOUSE, 2 m. SW. 1823 by *Dobson* for C. Weallands. Not a large house. Five bays, with a full-height three-bay bow window on the garden side. Angle pilasters. On the entrance side, a recessed porch with two square Tuscan columns *in antis*. The house has a nice cantilevered stair and two rooms with deep friezes of Greek detail, including palmettes and cornucopia.

WARTON FARMHOUSE, 1½ m. SW. C 17; refronted in the early C 18. Reroofed and extended to the rear *c.* 1885. The front is of five bays, with segmental-arched door and windows in raised surrounds with impost blocks and keystones.

SNODS EDGE
1½ m. W of Shotley

0050

ST JOHN, 1836, with mid-C 19 organ chamber and 1903 chancel. Nave in plain lancet style, polygonal chancel apse with external canopied niches at the E end above a MONUMENT to the Walton-Wilson family of Shotley Hall.

BLACK HEDLEY, ¾m. SW. Mid-C 18 five-bay house with a good
doorway and round-arched windows in the gable end. C 18 garden
walls and farm buildings. The DOCTOR'S COTTAGE is a picturesque combination of a house and a lectern DOVECOTE. The
carvings of a fox and an otter on the parapet are reputed to be the
work of *Lough*, who was born in 1798 at GREENHEAD, ¼m. W,
where a castellated gatehouse to Black Hedley was largely demolished in 1964 (but *see* Shotley, above).

SOUTH CHARLTON

ST JAMES. 1862 by *James Deason* of London for the Duke of
Northumberland. Small but good-quality church in E.E. style.
VICARAGE (now Grovewood House, an old people's home). Of the
same date, and also by *Deason*, but Tudor.
THE OLD SCHOOLHOUSE. A bastle house, uncommon so far E.
Remodelled *c*. 1840. Thick walls and the remains of both doors;
that to the byre in the E end with a relieving arch above; the upper
door as usual on the S.
CHARLTON HALL, 1½m. NE. Small late C 18 country house, in the
style favoured by *William Newton*. Main block of five by four bays;
the Venetian doorway and tripartite window over are reminiscent
of Lemmington Hall (q.v.). Modillion eaves cornice and hipped
roof. Well-preserved contemporary interior.
NORTH CHARLTON, 1½m. N. Medieval wayside cross. Stepped
base and headless shaft.

SOUTH MIDDLETON *see* MIDDLETON

SPARTYLEA

In a picturesque stretch of Allendale now largely healed of its C 19
mining scars.

ST PETER'S CHURCH. A disused preaching box of 1825, gothicized
in 1893, standing close to the early C 19 CORN MILL FARM-
HOUSE with its adjacent old mill, and a little rubble BRIDGE over
the Allen; together they form a charming group.
LEADMINING REMAINS. At SIPTON, 1 m. N, the main road crosses
the Sipton Burn by an unusual early C 19 BRIDGE with an arch-
within-an-arch. Further up the Burn, another impressive BRIDGE
dated 1878 carries the LONG DRAG, a well-graded mine road
from Allendale over the moors to Whitley Chapel and Hexham.
In the field S of Sipton Terrace, a small gabled stone structure
was the C 19 POWDER HOUSE for the leadmines.
BASTLE HOUSES. In the Swinhope valley, 2 m. SW, at HOPE HEAD
is the best-preserved bastle in the area, with a C 19 house built on
one end. The top floor with its upper-cruck truss may be a late
C 17 addition. Also late C 17 is HIGH SWINHOPE SHIELD, a

post-bastle dwelling with heavy rubble masonry and mullioned windows.

SPITTAL *see* BERWICK-UPON-TWEED

STAGSHAW

1½ m. N of Corbridge

ST AIDAN. 1885. Designed by *W. S. Hicks* for John Straker of Stagshaw House as a private chapel. Aisleless nave and chancel, with octagonal SW bell turret and spire. Hicks's characteristic Perp style and typically good quality. Much good stone and wood carving inside and out. – STAINED GLASS. 1898 by *Kempe*.

STAGSHAW HOUSE. Three-storey mid-C19 house with canted bays on the S, extended and altered in 1920 by *Hicks & Charlewood*. Little conical-roofed GAME LARDER, probably early C19, to the N. Italianate mid-C19 STABLES to the NW, and GATE LODGE on the A68. ICEHOUSE 45 metres SE of St Aidan's Chapel.

HOLLY HALL BARN, ¼ m. W of the church. Barn conversion of *c.* 1985 by *Ralph Crowe*. Simple and effective, in contrast to the much less happy domestic conversions of old farm buildings elsewhere in the area.

STAMFORDHAM

ST MARY. Possibly Saxon quoins at the SW corner of the nave, a blocked Saxon or early Norman arch in the W wall of the tower, and a round rere-arch to the tower ground-floor lancet. Otherwise the church is C13, much restored, in fact partly taken down and rebuilt by *Benjamin Ferrey* in 1848. The broad sturdy W tower has small lancets on the lower two floors and on the S a two-light bell opening with roll-moulded arches and a central column with waterleaf capital. The parapet appears to be original. The exterior detail of the nave is all of 1848 and so is much of the detail of the chancel, though the lancet windows and the masonry of the S wall are more clearly reused C13 material. Inside, the tower-arch is low, unmoulded and slightly ogival. The responds are curiously carried on and broken round to continue as a hoodmould. Two aisles with four-bay arcades of recut but original double-chamfered arches. The octagonal piers are replacements. The capitals of the two W piers have stiffleaf decoration of a decidedly early character – too early indeed for the nave and perhaps too freely renewed by Ferrey. The E responds and the double-chamfered chancel arch have short tripartite filleted shafts standing on plain corbels. The chancel is long and fine, with roll mouldings around the N and S lancets and a multi-moulded surround to the tall stepped three E lancets. The priest's door has a shouldered lintel and there is a large trefoiled piscina in an elaborately moulded surround on the S wall, and a smaller recess of the same form in the N wall. – REREDOS in the S aisle, a very coarsely carved

Crucifixion with two saints l. and r. in a frame of Dec tracery, C 14. – STAINED GLASS. *Kempe* glass of 1886 in the E window and of 1904 in the chancel N window. – Chancel S window, *Clayton & Bell.* – MONUMENTS. C 13 effigy of a priest in a very low segmental recess in the chancel N wall; the arch is decorated with dogtooth and the effigy is probably the earliest in the county. – Also in the chancel, mutilated effigies of a knight with crossed legs, *c.* 1300, and of another of *c.* 1400. – In the porch, two panels from a C 15 tomb-chest with angels holding shields, probably belonging to the effigy of *c.* 1400; and three CROSS SLABS. – In the N aisle, a large tomb-chest to John Swinburne of Blackheddon †1623. With thick fruit and scroll panels. Its back wall has arms, a broad frame, and scrolls, the carving very lush but very rustic. – Members of the Dixon family, 1721. Brightly painted coat of arms in a moulded frame. – In the S aisle, a painted cartouche of 1776 to Wm Akenside and Sam, his son. – Against the nave S wall, outside, a GRAVESTONE to Joseph Fothergill, gardener, has a roundel bearing a beautifully carved basket of flowers. Late C 18.

VICARAGE. The rear of the house, i.e. towards the church, has a C 17 section to the l. in thick masonry, with a large external chimneystack. To the r. is a section added by *Dobson* in 1847. It is ashlar, with a Tuscan door surround and twelve- and nine-pane sash windows. The front of the house is also in two sections. To the r., a four-bay section with a doorway in the l. bay. It is pedimented with a pulvinated frieze, dated 1764 and inscribed AEDES HAESCE LABENTE REFECIT THO DOCK-WRAY. The pediment bears a shield and Rococo decoration. To the l., an early C 18 section with a steeply pitched roof and windows with triple keystones. Inside, the drawing room is probably also of 1764. It has panelling with enriched mouldings and a restrained Rococo fireplace.

VILLAGE. A remarkably long GREEN with rows of houses on both sides, the N row lying higher than the S. In the middle of it is the BUTTER CROSS of 1735; erected, according to an inscription, by Sir John Swinburne of Capheaton. It is square, with one round arch on each side and pillars with banded rustication. Pyramid roof with a little square turret on top also with a pyramid roof. Nearby, on the green also, is the VILLAGE LOCK-UP. Early C 19, small and rectangular, with a studded door and tiny ventilation slits for windows. The row of houses on the N SIDE makes a fine sight. Nos. 1 and 2, at the E end, are early C 18, stone with sash windows and steep roofs. Then comes the mid-C 19 PRES-BYTERIAN CHURCH, three bays and part of the terrace. It has a round-headed doorway and round-headed windows with Y-tracery. No. 3 was the manse. It is dated 1715 and is of five bays with door and windows in moulded surrounds. The row of brick council houses next to this is said to have replaced early C 18 brick houses in the 1950s. The high point of the N side, literally and architecturally, is No. 22, CROSS HOUSE, late C 18, brick, three storeys and three bays, with a pedimented doorway and single-storey bow windows. The S SIDE starts at the E end with THE CROFT, dated 1711. Brick, with stone dressings and a doorway with a rusticated surround. No. 13, in the centre of the row, has rainwater heads of 1744. The core of the building is older, though, late C 17 or early C 18. The house was formerly three storeys instead of the present two, and the original ground-floor windows and porch are partly visible in a cellar beneath the roadway. Inside, a staircase with splat balusters. The rest of the row W of here is all attractive, with mainly C 18 stone houses except for WID-DRINGTON HOUSE, whose front range has walls *c*. 1.3 metres (4½ ft) thick. It was probably a bastle of the C 16 or early C 17. The original first-floor doorway, blocked up within the house, was in the original W gable end. Massive beams on the ground floor and C 17 roof timbers.

HAWKWELL, a sweet hamlet immediately S of the river, is really part of Stamfordham. HAWKWELL HOUSE has a three-bay façade rendered and refenestrated in the early C 19, but the doorway with the two-light mullioned overlight is inscribed PRE 1679 and round the corner is a bay with a four-light mullioned window on each floor. Inside, two late C 17 panelled rooms. They are quite grand. The study also has a fireplace with a bolection-moulded surround, but the dining room has an earlier C 17 stone fireplace. The main stair is a replacement of *c*. 1930, but the back stair has original splat balusters. In front of the house there is a walled garden with tall rusticated gatepiers.

MAINSBANK, ½ m. NW. An early C 18 five-bay farmhouse with the narrow windows characteristic of the county at that time.

BLACKHEDDON. *See* p. 188.

CHEESEBURN. *See* p. 218.

DALTON. *See* p. 251.

EACHWICK HALL. *See* p. 260.

STANNINGTON

ST MARY THE VIRGIN. 1871 by *R. J. Johnson*. Quite an imposing church in the Dec style. The tall W tower, with twin square-headed belfry openings, is perhaps modelled on Bedale in North Yorkshire. It replaced an interesting medieval church of which the N arcade, much renewed, survives. Round piers, with double-chamfered pointed arches. Both arcades have C 13 waterleaf capitals to the responds. – STAINED GLASS. Medieval heraldic glass in the organ chamber window, presented to the church in 1772 by the second Baronet Ridley. – E window by *Clayton & Bell* – Rather fine chancel N and S windows by *Bacon Bros*. – W window by *Kempe*, 1885. – MONUMENTS. In the floor under the tower, an assortment of medieval CROSS SLABS, including two with quite remarkable crosses, reminiscent of the great collection of Celtic monks' graveslabs at Clonmacnoise in Ireland. Are they C 12 or C 13 copies of C 7 or C 8 originals? – First Viscount Ridley 1904; recumbent bronze effigy by *Sir W. Reynolds Stephens* on a cruciform marble base by *Detmar Blow*. – Outside the S wall, a massive stone COFFIN, the upper parts of its sides tooled as if they were to form the visible part of a monument. – CHURCH-YARD CROSS. Celtic, *c*. 1890. Good timber-framed LYCHGATE of 1893.

VICARAGE, E of the church. Five-bay house, said to be of 1745, with keyed lintels. Later rear wing, and linked porch-and-bay-windows of 1910. In the garden behind, ARCHITECTURAL FRAGMENTS from the old church.

Until 1987 Stannington VILLAGE was bisected by the A1: it is now bypassed to the E. On the main road in the village are two pretty little BUS SHELTERS by *Laurence Whistler*, presented to the village to mark the coronation of George VI in 1937. They are wooden, with swept slate roofs, and arched iron-framed casement windows in one end. In the E part of the village, one or two attractive mid-C19 houses and cottages and, N of the Ridley Arms, a HEARSE HOUSE dated 1871.

SWAN HOUSE, $\frac{1}{4}$ m. S of the village. Superior-quality three-bay farmhouse, with rusticated quoins and architraves.

VALE HOUSE, $\frac{3}{4}$ m. S. Late C18 three-bay house with tripartite sashes in the end bays and an eaves cornice. All the openings have raised panels above, giving the impression of wedge lintels.

CATRAW, $\frac{3}{4}$ m. W. The farmhouse, dated 1930, is by *Sir Edwin Lutyens*. Big hipped roof to the N, otherwise quite plain. The older house to the NE, demolished c. 1970, was probably a bastle house. Some lower walls remain.

BELLASIS. *See* p. 164.

SHOTTON. *See* p. 570.

1090

STANTON

STANTON OLD HALL. A three-storey 'stronghouse', probably dating to the later C16; oblong, with a projecting stair wing or turret on the E. Some medieval fabric is incorporated: the outline of a lower gable can be seen on the N end, and on the E is a corbelled fireplace in what is now an external wall-face. The earlier house may have consisted of a tower (containing the fireplace), with an attached two-storey wing heightened to form the present main block. This in turn received a new S front c. 1700, with rusticated quoins and cross windows with swan-necked pediments. Inside, a stone winder stair in the turret, several C16 and C17 fireplaces, and unusual roof trusses, each with one convex and one concave curved principal.

ROMAN FORTLET, on the cliff-top above the River Font, $\frac{1}{3}$ m. S, near Longshaws. A square fortlet with inturned E and W gates, defended by two ramparts and ditches. The inner ditch is flanked on each side by a level berm, and beyond the outer ditch another substantial bank survives in places. Probably dating from very early in the Roman occupation, perhaps the late A.D. 80s. A slighter enclosure, which may be contemporary, lies in the trees 20 metres WSW.

STAWARD

STAWARD PELE is an enigmatic ruin in a stunning, impregnable position on a precipitous spine of rock between the Allen on the W and the Harsondale Cleugh on the E. The approach from the SE is guarded by a ditch cutting across the neck of the promontory; a fragment of an internal bank survives on the E. About 100 metres further on the width between the cliff-tops narrows to only 2.7 metres (9 ft). After 50 metres more the NE corner of a gatehouse (?) stands on a slight rise. The rough masonry incorporates many Roman stones (including, formerly, the altar to Jupiter now at Staward Manor: *see* below), reused from an unknown site. The 'pele' itself, first mentioned in 1327, stood on the tip of the promontory; the lower parts of three walls survive, of beautiful squared stone with no features other than a triple-stepped plinth. What is their date? A broad ditch outside the NW wall has an external upcast bank.

STAWARD MANOR, formerly Low Staward, has its origin in a pair of bastle houses extended and altered in the late C18 and *c.* 1840. The W bastle is still recognizable, with a blocked upper door dated 1668 between two three-light mullioned windows with open scrolled pediments. Both date and detail are late for the bastle period proper; they probably relate to a first remodelling. On the lawn is the ROMAN ALTAR from Staward Pele (*see* above), with a weathered inscription and a relief carving of a bull's head.

HIGH STAWARD has a fine farmhouse and planned farm building group of the early C19. Two-storey three-bay ashlar house with a hipped roof. Main farm building group with barn and gingang to rear, a detached pigsty with poultry loft and dovecote, and detached smithy. 300 metres W is HIGH SHAW, a good example of the previous generation of Northumberland farmhouses; early C18 with a hood bressumer to its fireplace and three upper-cruck roof trusses.

STOCKSFIELD

ST JOHN THE DIVINE. 1927. Small and Gothic, in the tradition of fifty years earlier.

BAPTIST CHURCH. 1906 by *Dixon & Sons*. Snecked stone, low and cruciform.

Stocksfield is a rather scattered Tyne Valley village, now largely a commuter settlement. The station on the Newcastle to Carlisle line retains its STATIONMASTER'S HOUSE, somewhat altered, with a cluster of other mid-C19 buildings nearby. On the S side of the A695, and turning its back on the road, is an older house (now an outbuilding) with a stone slate roof and a moulded doorway dated 1724. On the road running N towards Bywell Bridge are three good Tudor Gothic buildings, BEAUMONT HOUSE (a former school), STOCKSFIELD HOUSE (the headmaster's house) and WENTWORTH HOUSE AND COTTAGE. Dated 1851, 1852 and 1853 respectively, these were built by W. B. Beaumont of Bywell Hall to displace the last remnants of Bywell village to the s side of the river. Two estate cottages in the same style nearby on the N side of the A695.

To the s of that part of the village known as BRANCH END, the extensive well-wooded Painshawfield Estate on the E side of the Stocksfield Burn valley. Here on Bat House Road, there are two houses of interest: BAT COTTAGE, the original Bat House farmhouse, mid-c18, with Yorkshire sash windows; and CRANFORD, built in 1903 for the Steel family and enlarged in 1907 and 1913. Pebbledashed brick with some timber framing. Some good-quality Arts-and-Crafts detailing. At the rear a GAS GENERATOR HOUSE which produced acetylene and looks like a little tile-hung lighthouse. The tower held a water tank which fed a generator holding calcium carbide beneath, on the same principle as the old carbide lamp.

STOCKSFIELD HALL, on an isolated valley-floor hillock SE of Bywell Bridge. Early c18 three-bay house and early c19 planned FARM BUILDINGS with an apsidal gingang at the rear of the N range.

OLD RIDLEY, ¾ m. s of Stocksfield Station. Late c17 or early c18 house, much altered in the c19. In the garden, a c18 DOVECOTE, square, with a pyramid roof and wooden cap. Late c18 farm buildings to the N, with one odd corniced-and-pedimented gable end.

RIDLEY MILL. Little remains other than the overshot wheel of c. 4.8-metre (16-ft) diameter, sited at the gable end of a two-storey building.

BROOMLEY, 1 m. SW. The oldest house in this hamlet is WEST FARMHOUSE, with a three-bay mid-c18 front but incorporating older fabric. In the W end, a stone with a vigorous relief-carved dolphin, a puzzling piece but perhaps c18.

WHEELBIRKS, 2 m. S. Restrained Gothic farmhouse of 1868, extended when the small estate was transformed in the first decade of the c20 by David Richardson, a Quaker. He built six estate cottages, and adorned both them and the bridges, roadside walls and seats in the woods with carved texts and aphorisms (*see* Wheelbirks Bridge on the B6309). His most surprising innovation was a SANATORIUM, left unfinished on his death in 1913. Apparently intended for TB sufferers from his own leather works at Elswick, it is a cruciform construction of steel-reinforced concrete (with floors of hollow concrete blocks), white engineering brick and predominantly glass, standing as if on stilts in a hollow and reached by bridges from higher ground on three sides. Across the fields to the s the remains of a c16 BLAST FURNACE on the W bank of the Stocksfield Burn.

7070

STONEHAUGH
4 m. w of Wark-on-Tyne

A Forestry Commission village designed in 1951 by *Dr Thomas Sharp*. Simple terraces of two-storey houses, rather incongruous in this remote setting. Boldly and imaginatively painted and landscaped in 1986–7 by the Commission's *Design Branch*.

STYFORD *see* BYWELL

SWARLAND   *1000*

SWARLAND PARK. At Swarland one historic landscape is superimposed upon another. The earlier is that which surrounded
Swarland Park (or Swarland New Hall), built in 1765 and pulled
down in 1947. Alexander Davison, the early C 19 owner, who
made much of his friendship with Nelson (cf. Felton, Nelson
Monument), planted out trees in his park to represent the position
of the fleets in the Battle of the Nile. The only buildings to remain
from this C 19 phase are: two GATE LODGES, one early C 19,
octagonal and much altered, the other late C 19; SWARLAND
HALL COTTAGE, which was built in the late C 19 as a generator
house (Swarland Park followed Cragside as one of the first houses
in the country to have electric light); some of the buildings of the
HOME FARM and two ANIMAL SHELTERS in the S corners of
the Park, which look a little like escaped gingangs.
The SWARLAND SETTLEMENT, which overlay the parkland, was
laid out in 1934–9 by Commander Clare Vyner and the Fountains
Abbey Settlers Society, to house unemployed craftsmen from
Tyneside. Seventy-seven houses were built, along with several
community buildings in the village centre: *Miss M. P. Reavell* was
the architect. There are four different house types: flat-roofed
bungalows (e.g. Nos. 2 and 4 NELSON DRIVE); larger bungalows
with pitched roofs (e.g. No. 10 THE AVENUE, No. 40 PARK
ROAD); two-bay houses with attics and gabled dormers (e.g. Nos.
24 and 28 PARK ROAD); and the three 'Dutch houses' with
mansard roofs in KENMORE ROAD. All are of brick, generally
rendered and colour-washed; roofs were originally of red clay tiles
or wooden shingles.
SWARLAND OLD HALL. A highly picturesque and rather puzzling
house. Front of four narrow bays; the moulded doorway has a
rustic triglyph frieze incorporating two fat angel faces, and the
former cross windows have cable-moulded surrounds below semicircular pediments which are not really connected with them,
those on the first floor with carved keystones. The house has been
linked with Capheaton and *Trollope*, but the doorhead bears a
worn date in the 1730s (cf. the Old Manor House at Newton-on-
the-Moor). The rear part of the house is certainly older, with
some thick walls, but few datable features; it might be late C 16
or C 17. The E gable end was nicely gothicized towards the end
of the C 18, with three lancet arches and battlements.

SWINBURNE CASTLE *see* GREAT SWINBURNE

7080

TARSET

TARSET CASTLE. Impressive earthwork castle defended by a deep ditch cut across a steep-sided promontory above the Tarset Burn. Destroyed on the SW by the railway cutting of 1860. Inside, on the E side of the enclosure, the almost incomprehensible fragments of a long narrow building with rectangular angle turrets. One short stretch of well-cut double-chamfered plinth. The castle was occupied by the Scots until 1244, licensed by John Comyn in 1267, then burnt in 1525 by the Scots in league with the men of Tynedale.

The farmhouse called THE REENES, NW of Bellingham, incorporates a number of architectural fragments said to have come from the castle, especially a late C15 or early C16 two-light window with cusped heads to the lights.

REDMIRE BRIDGE, over the Tarset Burn, ¼ m. W. Early C19. Two segmental arches with keeled cutwaters.

RAILWAY BRIDGE, behind Tarset Hall. 1860. Two skew arches.

On the road W from Tarset to Falstone along the N bank of the river, fragmentary remains of bastles: CAMP COTTAGE (a few lumps of walls); DONKLEYWOOD (parts of two walls).

THORNEYBURN. *See* p. 584.

TATHEY CRAGS *see* ILDERTON

THIRLMOOR *see* CHEW GREEN

6060

THIRLWALL CASTLE
½ m. N of Greenhead

The dramatic ruins of a small castle, at the top of the steep W bank of the Tipalt Burn. It was a stronghold of the hall-house type (cf. Haughton; Dally, near Greystead; Langley). In plan it consisted of a rectangular three-storey block 14.3 by 5.8 metres (47 by 19 ft) internally, with square turrets at the N corners and a larger projecting tower at the S end of the E side carried up to four storeys. The entrance was near the N end of the E side. There was a mural stair in the N wall between the first and second floors; the hall may have been on second-floor level, with the solar at its S end. The floors were timber, carried on setbacks of the internal wall-faces and corbels, except for the strange pyramidal vaults in the tiny chambers in the NW turret. The walls are 2.7 metres (9 ft) thick, pierced by remarkably few windows; all those that survive are small single lights, square-headed except for trefoiled loops lighting the head of the mural stair and on the S side of the top floor of the SE tower. Thirlwall must have been a gloomy and prison-like fortress with few concessions to either architectural detail or comfort. Although its plan has affinities with those of the hall houses of the C 13, the emphasis on defensibility suggests a date in the first half of the C 14, after the troubles with the Scots had begun in earnest.

THIRSTON

1000

Looking across the Coquet to Felton is a long row of C 18 and early C 19 houses, including the NORTHUMBERLAND ARMS, c. 1820, with two full-height segmental bows.

PETH FOOT, across the road and a little further s, was remodelled in the C 19 but retains a doorway dated 1617 (beneath an inscribed panel with a long and garbled quotation from Proverbs) and two immensely thick (2.5 metres, 8 ft) walls which may survive from a still earlier tower guarding the approach to the bridge.

THIRSTON HOUSE, on the hill above the river, is said to be an early work of *Dobson*; four bays wide with a Tuscan porch. Remodelled inside in 1902.

HEMELSPETH, beside the old A1 s of the village. An early C 19 two-bay cottage (now a farm outbuilding) in front of a pleasant small-scale farm building group of c. 1800, with an added early C 19 gingang on the E.

BOCKENFIELD. *See* p. 195.

THOCKRINGTON
1½ m. sw of Great Bavington

9070

ST AIDAN. High up and solitary, except for one farm with its old trees. Nave and lower chancel. The church is really Norman, although that appears externally only by one tiny window on the N and one on the s side. Internally there is the unmoulded chancel arch on the plainest imposts and an identical arch against the E wall. There must have been a Norman apse here. It was replaced by a straight E end in the C 13; *see* the one E lancet with a rere-arch. The most interesting thing about the Norman church, however, is that the chancel is tunnel-vaulted with the window arches penetrating it. Externally the most prominent features are the heavy diagonal buttresses of the chancel and the yet heavier buttress with many offsets in the middle of the w front to support the curious big, slightly projecting square bellcote with its stone roof. All this may be as late as the C 17. The nave is largely a mid-C 19 rebuild. – FONT. Plain, big, circular. Probably C 13, with a C 17 FONT COVER. – MONUMENT. Decayed effigy of a lady. – Lord Beveridge († 1963) is buried in the graveyard.

The present hamlet is surrounded by the slight and scattered EARTHWORKS of the former village. Footings of rectangular buildings and their garths are visible, especially on the crag N of the church and N of the existing cottages. In 1296 there were eighteen taxpayers; eleven houses were listed in the Hearth Tax of 1666. Major depopulation took place in the early c 19.

LITTLE SWINBURNE *See* p. 379.

THORNEYBURN
1 m. N of Tarset

ST AIDAN. 1818 by *H. H. Seward* for the Commissioners of Greenwich Hospital and very similar to his churches at Humshaugh, Wark and Greystead. Small, embattled w tower, windows with the same Y-tracery as at the other churches. Nice proportions inside, flat ceiling, no division between nave and chancel.

The church, like all the others, forms a group with the RECTORY, STABLE, CHURCHYARD WALLS etc., all by Seward; a curiously urbane group in the midst of these wild moors.

REDHEUGH, ½ m. N. A farmhouse with thick walls inside, suggesting that it started life as a bastle. Over a side window, a reused c 16 doorhead with a roll-moulded surround and an apparently meaningless inscription of jumbled letters and numbers. The house was refronted in 1732 by William Charlton. Opposite the house, an early c 18 DOVECOTE with a pyramid roof.

GATEHOUSE. *See* p. 287.

THREE KINGS *see* BYRNESS

THREESTONEBURN *see* ILDERTON

THROPTON

ALL SAINTS (R.C.). Late c 18 or early c 19; remodelled and the w end rebuilt in 1842. Broad lancets with Y-tracery. The remarkable feature inside is the separation of the apsidal sanctuary from the nave by a pendant screen of three arches – a kind of pelmet effect. The church began as a chapel attached to Thropton Old Hall, which was replaced in 1811 by the present PRESBYTERY (*see* Introduction, p. 72).

UNITED REFORMED CHURCH (formerly Presbyterian). 1863 by *F. R. Wilson*. Rock-faced, in the rather mechanical Gothic of the period, but with some interesting detail, e.g. the rather perverse NW porch-cum-turret.

Thropton village has a few buildings of interest. The hogbacked THROPTON BRIDGE of 1810 spans the Wreigh Burn at the E end of the single street. A short distance W, on the N side of the road, is SELBY HOUSE, dated 1728 (on a rear door), with a moulded doorway and raised stone window surrounds. On the s of the road, just beyond the United Reformed Church, is the

THREE WHEAT HEADS INN, of various C 18 dates with some Gothick windows and quatrefoil loops. Further W is THE PEEL, a well-preserved bastle house. The byre door in the E end has a heavy block surround with rounded arrises, and a rough relieving arch above. The first-floor door (unusually for a bastle) is in the same end-wall, above and to the right. The basement has a quite tall barrel vault with an original ladder hole at one corner. An original first-floor window, with sockets for an iron grille, survives on the N. The second or attic floor is an addition, although still perhaps in the bastle period; it preserves a chamfered loop on the S. The larger windows are mostly of 1863. Sympathetic late C 20 E extension.

WREIGHBURN HOUSE, ¼ m. SE. A picturesque and rambling complex of C 18 and C 19 builds, thought to be on or near a medieval hospital site. In the garden on the N, an incised CROSS set on a C 20 plinth; it may be a C 12 grave slab.

CARTINGTON. *See* p. 215.

TILLMOUTH *see* TWIZEL

TITLINGTON HALL
¾ m. NE of Shawdon Hall

1010

Five-bay two-storey house, with the projecting centre bay carrying three antefixae instead of a pediment. An inscription on a NW corner quoin states that the house was rebuilt in 1824 for W. M. Pawson (a lower quoin has the date 1745, probably that of the preceding house). At the far end of the entrance hall is a handsome curved stair behind a two-bay screen with fluted columns. A fireplace and other internal features are said to have been brought from Lemmington Hall (q.v.). The stable range to the NE is C 18, remodelled in the early C 19.

TOSSON *see* GREAT TOSSON

TOWER KNOWE *see* KIELDER

TOW HOUSE *see* HENSHAW

TRITLINGTON

2090

TRITLINGTON HALL. Early C 19 five-bay house, ashlar-fronted but brick at rear. Brick also the rear wing and a stable range dated 1854.

TRITLINGTON OLD HALL. Splendid early C 18 gatepiers, with finials carved as baskets of fruit and flowers. The house, which looks humble in comparison, is a rather complicated building which seems to be an C 18 reworking of a medieval tower (its newel stair partly survives in a rear turret) and a wing dated 1595.

TRITLINGTON LODGE, in the village, is a mid-C 19 *cottage orné*.

COCKLE PARK TOWER. *See* p. 235.

2020

TUGHALL
2 m. SW of Beadnell

TUGHALL HALL. Early C 19 front, extended and remodelled *c*. 1927 by *Robert Mauchlen*. But, as is evident at the back, it was added to an older house, late C 17 or early C 18 with a much more steeply pitched roof. Inside this section, a staircase of the same period, with fat turned balusters and closed string.

TUGHALL CHAPEL. Sad fragments of this early Norman chapel surrounded by a sub-rectangular burial ground. A map of *c*. 1620 shows a broad village street extending SW along the present farm road, with houses on either side. Declining in C 17, the village was almost abandoned by early C 19.

TWEEDMOUTH *see* BERWICK-UPON-TWEED

8040

TWIZEL
3 m. NE of Cornhill

TWIZEL BRIDGE is said to date from the C 15. A narrow bridge, flung across the river at a spectacular height, with a span of 27 metres (90 ft); the largest single-span stone arch in Britain until the Causey Arch (County Durham) of 1727. The arch is reinforced by five very narrowly placed single-chamfered ribs, and the roadway arches too. The whole makes a beautiful shape and has the advantage of a beautiful setting, with the bending River Till forming a deep pool just by its side and the wooded glen rising steeply on its NW.

On the ridge of that glen, with views along the high plain into Scotland and on to distant hills, stands TWIZEL CASTLE, the ruins of a large Gothick house begun *c*. 1770 by *Sir Francis Blake*, for himself, around the remains of a medieval house on the site. Building continued for over fifty years, but the house was never quite completed. Sir Francis was assisted by *Nesbit* of Kelso. The house is rectangular, with four round corner towers. Now it is only two storeys high, but originally it had five storeys. It was also stone- or brick-vaulted throughout, though only the vaults on the ground floor and the springing of a groin vault on the first floor survive. The ground floor along the S front has three rooms with tunnel vaults and a large room behind the central bow window with a groin vault and two flanking tunnel vaults. The corner towers were vaulted also, though in the two N towers only the springing remains. The N wall has collapsed and revealed an internal wall which formed part of the medieval house. It is almost 2 metres (6½ ft) thick and has blocked C 17 and earlier openings.

TILLMOUTH PARK HOTEL, ¼ m. S. Neo-Elizabethan; 1882 by *Charles Barry Jun*. Most of the decoration of the house is ultra-Victorian, but there are many fireplaces of *c*. 1810 from an earlier house (also called Tillmouth Park) which had been built by Sir Francis Blake (*see* Twizel Castle) and demolished by his son to build the present house.

The GARDENS of the earlier house survive, however. The features all date from *c.* 1810 and include much castellated walling, archways, niches, lodges, a bridge and a tunnel. Sir Francis also started a new bridge across the River Till, but this was never completed and only one arch stands. It is known as BLAKE'S FOLLY.

ST CUTHBERT'S CHAPEL, *c.* 1 m. W of Tillmouth Park, in a beautiful situation near the mouth of the Till. A ruinous plain parallelogram, with pointed windows and W door. Built by Sir Francis Blake in the early C 18 or early C 19. Some reused medieval stone in the walls.

DOWER HOUSE, opposite the entrance to Tillmouth Park. A farmhouse converted in 1976 by *Felix Kelly* for Sir Francis Blake, descendant of the original Sir Francis. A light and delicate Gothick pastiche.

RAILWAY VIADUCT, over the Till. 1849, for the Newcastle and Berwick Railway. Six brick segmental arches on very high battered stone piers.

CASTLE HEATON, 1 m. SE of Tillmouth Park. The castle of the Greys has largely disappeared, but among the farm buildings is a late medieval building in form very similar to Akeld and Pressen bastles. It is *c.* 20 metres (68 ft) long, with a high round tunnel-vaulted ground floor.

WATERMILL, by the Till, on the opposite bank to the hotel. This fine and beautifully sited mill underwent selective demolition in the 1980s. It was a double-wheeled mill with attached high kiln. The mill dam appears to have been formerly a horseshoe type, perhaps breached and thereafter made oblique. The detached mill house still survives.

TYNEMOUTH
3060

Tynemouth was the parent of the modern North Shields, as has been made clear in that entry, but the settlement here was never much more than one street leading to the great Castle and Priory. Even on Wood's map of 1827 there are only a few houses beyond that street (Front Street). By 1863, when the first Ordnance Survey map was published, the railway had arrived, bringing with it the middle classes who bought houses in new terraces built S of Front Street, which had itself already been partly redeveloped with new houses. Later in the C 19 shops were fitted into the older houses, or occasionally purpose-built with some care. C 20 development was less happy until a Civic Trust scheme of the 1950s raised standards, but, despite the spread of houses during the last hundred years, the dominant elements of the town are still headland and harbour at the mouth of the Tyne.

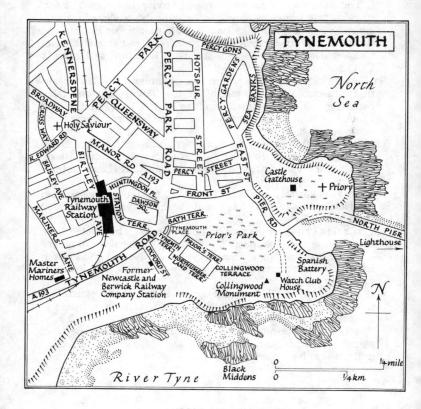

TYNEMOUTH PRIORY AND CASTLE

This magnesian limestone promontory, with high cliffs on three
sides, guarded the approach to the river and afforded a site which
could be defended by the erection of a fairly narrow barrier. Circular
timber buildings revealed by excavations immediately N of the
church suggested that the headland was the site of an Iron Age
promontory fort with Roman native secondary occupation. Three
adjacent rectangular timber buildings, were pre-Conquest. Two of
these had construction trenches dug for close-set posts and the
third used sill beams. A fourth building, poorly preserved, had a
semicircular end wall. There was a monastery here at the time of
Bede, possibly founded as early as the mid-C7, but the buildings
excavated could just as well have been secular as monastic.

St Oswin is supposed to have been murdered and buried here in
651. More certain is that the Priory existed by 800, when it was
sacked by the Danes. This, and its destruction in 875, is mentioned
by Matthew Paris. A long silence follows, broken by the stories of a
chaplain of Earl Tostig finding shelter in the 'ecclesiola' in C11 and
of the discovery in 1065 of what were believed to be St Oswin's
bones. In the reign of William I, Tynemouth, with its ruined church,

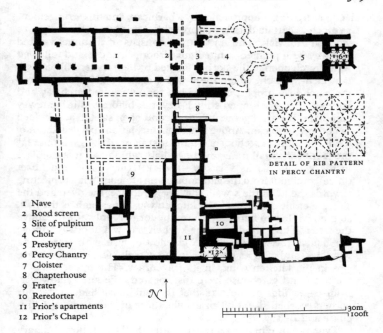

DETAIL OF RIB PATTERN
IN PERCY CHANTRY

1 Nave
2 Rood screen
3 Site of pulpitum
4 Choir
5 Presbytery
6 Percy Chantry
7 Cloister
8 Chapterhouse
9 Frater
10 Reredorter
11 Prior's apartments
12 Prior's Chapel

Tynemouth Priory. Plan

was granted first to monks from Evesham, and then became dependent on Jarrow, and therefore also dependent on the Benedictines of Durham, under a charter of Earl Waltheof confirmed by Bishop Alberic. At this stage, *c.* 1083, the church was restored, only to be transferred in 1090 to the care of the Benedictines of St Albans by Earl Robert Mowbray, who had quarrelled with the Bishop of Durham. The connexion with St Albans remained for centuries. The Priory was dissolved in 1539.

Right through the Middle Ages the Priory was as much a fortress as a monastery. The site is similar to Bamburgh and Dunstanburgh. The cliff, which on the N and E falls almost perpendicularly to the sea, made the Priory buildings on their plateau impregnable. The fall to the S is steep too, though less rocky, and only on the W was it necessary to defend the monastery seriously. Of the defences of the earlier Middle Ages nothing has survived. But in 1296 licence to crenellate was granted, probably soon followed by the renewal of the curtain wall and its towers. In the C14, Edward III considered the fortress to be one of the strongest in the Marches. But the main defensive work of Tynemouth, the gatehouse, is later still, and followed a double attack – by nature and the Scots – which crumbled cliffs and burnt buildings. It dates from the time of Prior John de Whethamstede, uncle of the more famous abbot of St Albans. He ruled from 1393 to 1419. The work was completed by the early C15 with the help of money from Richard II and John of Gaunt.

The GATEHOUSE is approached by a barbican, and this arrangement as much as certain details was probably copied from the early C 14 work at Alnwick. The BARBICAN consists of a tunnel-vaulted archway with pointed-vaulted guardrooms l. and r. and followed by a stretch open to the sky but flanked by high walls. This crosses the filled-in ditch, where there was a drawbridge. Then follows the gatehouse proper, again with a tunnel-vaulted archway and with another small stretch beyond, before a third gateway completes the arrangement. The second open stretch acts indeed as another barbican. Above it are machicolations corbelled out of the E wall of the gatehouse. On the first floor of the gatehouse lay the HALL, with tall transomed two-light windows and a fireplace in the E wall. To its s is the KITCHEN (now shop and ticket office), built out from the gatehouse as an attached wing projecting towards the E. In the s wall, the large fireplace, the oven and the sink are easily discerned. The kitchen was not as high as the hall, so that, while two floors lay above the former, only one lay above the latter. The E window of the kitchen is now a doorway. Above the hall is the SOLAR of the gatehouse, also with transomed windows, and with its fireplace in the W wall. The main staircase was in the kitchen wing, in its NE corner. The upper parts of barbican and gatehouse have disappeared. We know, however, from engravings of the C 18 that the gatehouse had, at its four corners, corbelled-out bartizans like those of the towers at Chipchase and Belsay.

Tynemouth remained a fortress after the Dissolution. Military buildings were erected at divers times and have obscured the medieval evidence a great deal. In addition landslides have carried off on the s side the ground on which the outer wall stood. But while for the archaeologist who wishes to study medieval fortifications Tynemouth is thus disappointing, for the architectural historian the splendid ruin of the Priory Church is of the highest value.

PRIORY CHURCH. No Saxon church has come to light. But the NORMAN CHURCH of 1090, which was sufficiently complete by 1110 to receive the relics of St Oswin in a new shrine, is relatively well known to us. Little of it stands to any great height, and the imaginative mind has to do a great deal to reconstruct its appearance. Although it belonged to St Albans, its architectural design did not depend on that abbey either in plan or in elevation – a fact worth remembering. The plan of Norman Tynemouth, as laid out on the ground after excavations had determined it, had a chancel of a size to have two bays, and five divisions in the apse, with an ambulatory which had three radiating chapels. The aisled nave was seven bays long, and there were N and S transepts with an E chapel each. The plan is similar to that introduced into England at Battle Abbey and St Augustine, Canterbury, and then used frequently. At Tynemouth the nave is unusually short.

As for the elevation, we cannot say anything of this chancel. Of the crossing piers, two stand almost complete, though badly worn, and there is part of a third. They had groups of three strong shafts to each side and block, single- or double-scallop capitals. They probably carried a square lantern-tower. Evidence on nave and aisles comes particularly from the E bay of the N aisle, where a typical round pier, not very high, supports a plain round arch. It has survived because it was walled off after the Suppression to enclose the nave as a parish church. Above that is the E jamb of the gallery arcade. On the S side plenty of square Norman masonry is at once recognized in the outer wall, and there is in addition a round-headed doorway to the cloister. Shallow buttresses survive on both N and S walls.

But whereas the evidence on the C 11 and early C 12 is as scanty as this description has shown, of the EARLY ENGLISH ADDITIONS, begun c. 1190, enough stands to allow for a very strong aesthetic impact. The E wall of the rebuilt CHOIR AND PRESBYTERY belongs to the best E.E. compositions we possess and has the additional advantage of a superb position, whether one sees the blue sky made a deeper blue by the frame of the lancet windows, or whether gusts of wind drive the rain through the unglazed openings. From outside, the E wall is very sheer, and must have been even more striking before the addition of the Percy Chantry. No decoration at the foot, a group of three very tall stepped lancets with the plainest chamfered jambs and arches, separated and flanked by buttresses, a second row of windows, small lancets l. and r., a higher vesica-shaped window in the middle, and then above this one more lancet. This alone has the decorative enrichment of stepped blank arcading l. and r., inside the gable, the lines of which are at once evident. In the C 14 or C 15, however, above all this another upper chamber or hall was built on top of the vault of the presbytery and the flat roof of the choir; no record has been found which names its function. It had large windows, two of which survive in part in the S wall. The addition of this chamber must have ruined thoroughly the calculated proportions of the E elevation.

Inside there is much more enrichment. Blank arcading ran above the whole length of a wall bench. The group of three E lancets above the arcade is perhaps over-richly shafted, with two ringed shafts in the jambs of each window, and tripartite shafting between, so that there are groups of seven shafts. In addition there is dogtooth ornament in the arches. Above is a stringcourse, and more dogtooth in the vault. The presbytery was aisleless, of four bays and vaulted. Each bay had an oblong quadripartite vault, but the E bay was given an additional two ribs springing from the E wall. The springers survive. Now to examine the S wall, for on the N only the bench survives. Its composition was quite different from that of the E wall – another example of the remarkable lack among English early C 13 designers of any desire to see two walls together as one unit. The designer of Tynemouth was obviously a man of high architectural power; but then, not even at Salisbury Cathedral are walls conceived together. Above the blind arcading the S wall has ringed double shafts framing lancets lower than those in the E wall, with the stringcourse above their heads reaching the springing point of the E windows. The vault ribs spring from this level, and frame a second row of windows with dogtooth up the jambs between paired shafts. Each of these levels has a wall-gallery. The wall above that belonged to the later upper chamber.

In the arcade at the foot of the E wall the space for the reredos can still be seen, with the door to the Percy Chantry broken through it. To l. and r. are two square aumbries. In the S wall-arcade is a deep arched tomb recess (another faces it in the N wall), then an aumbry, and then a pointed-trefoil piscina followed by a pair of arches of similar shape with a shaft between, which have been interpreted as sedilia or as the site of an important shrine. The fourth bay, the transition between presbytery and choir, is narrower. The solid wall there has blank arcading instead of the windows of the other bays, the upper arches paired under a round head. W of it, a newel staircase leads to the wall-passages between the windows of the presbytery, and formerly both gave access on the W to the triforium and clerestory of the choir and climbed in a turret to the upper chamber.

Of the transepts – one pair at the W end of the new presbytery in addition to the Norman main transept further W – less significant detail can be seen, except for the handsome arch from the main S transept into the choir aisle. This is enriched by three orders of shafts. The E transepts were also vaulted, *see* one remaining springer, but the choir proper had only aisle vaults and no high vaults, according to C 18 illustrations, which show it without springers. The arcade piers were of four main shafts with fillets, and four subsidiary keeled shafts on the diagonals. A PULPITUM ran across the E end of the main crossing. The W wall of the main transept was closed by a second stone wall, the ROOD SCREEN, which had doorways l. and r. and blank arcading in the middle. The E face has dogtooth decoration. It marked the E end of the parochial space. The nave remained in its Norman state, except that the aisles were vaulted in the same way as the three bays W of the Norman nave which the early C 13 added. Here, regardless of the Norman design, octagonal piers were used. The E.E. W front has a middle portal of five orders decorated with dogtooth. Above this was a large C 14 window, and also in the C 14 a tower was placed in front of the S part of the façade. It was a kind of barbican to the porch from which the monastic quarters were reached.

The CLAUSTRAL RANGES to the S of the nave are represented by laying out the plan in the grass where no upstanding walls remain. There is fabric from the Norman period to the end of the Middle Ages, with post-Suppression alterations. At the N end of the W range Norman work remains; in the W wall of that range a small section of masonry survives, halfway along its length, with a moulded plinth and the base of a shaft which could have supported vaulting. In the E range was the vaulted C 13 CHAPTERHOUSE, against the S wall of the S transept; the base of its moulded W doorway and the blank arcading of its N wall can be seen. Next to it on the S was the day stair, and beyond was probably the warming house, where there are later tiled floor and fireplace; the dorter would be above. The frater probably lay as usual in the S range; only a large S buttress remains clearly visible, which may relate to the position of the pulpit inside the room for readings during meals. The buttress was in a small enclosed courtyard, to the W of which were the kitchens, and to the S and SE the PRIOR'S APARTMENTS. As the site slopes considerably on the S side, the ground level of the southernmost rooms is 9 metres (30 ft) below that of the nave, and walls stand up higher. The two big blocked mid-C 14 S windows belonged to the Prior's Hall, which was rib-vaulted. To its E was the Prior's Chapel, of two vaulted bays. More survives of this than of any other of the monastic buildings. It dates from the early C 13 and has lancet windows; inside there are interesting architectural fragments. The REREDORTER E of the Prior's Hall has walling of three periods, Norman as well as early and later C 13. To the SE of it the stone-lined drains are worth examining. There were many more buildings E of this, including probably the infirmary, and many more in what might be called the outer bailey, between church and gatehouse. Most of the monastic buildings belonged to the C 13.

But there is one more part of the Priory which has so far been left undescribed, because it is of considerably later date: the PERCY CHANTRY, a small vaulted C 15 chapel at the E end of the church, which was restored by *Dobson* in 1852. A Lady Chapel had been added N of the Presbytery in the C 14, projecting one bay further to the E. The Percy Chantry projects as far, but is much lower. The vault indeed lies heavy on the low walls with their N and S benches and small two-light windows, and their circular window in the E, and it seems all the heavier because it is studded with big figured bosses. A list of what they represent can be found in the English Heritage guidebook to the Priory. The seated figure of Christ is in the middle. The sculptural quality of the bosses is indifferent. The design of the rib vault, on the other hand, is very ingenious and with its interlacing of different patterns deserves study. The chapel is of three bays, each having a rib vault with diagonal ribs and longitudinal as well as transverse ridge ribs. Superimposed on this design is a second which is based as a unit on the half size of a bay. Each of these square halves has exactly the same design as the whole bay, its own diagonal ribs and its own longitudinal and transverse ridge ribs. The resulting shapes and curvatures of the cells are confusingly varied. – STAINED GLASS. In the E bay of the N wall (the other two windows have blind tracery), the gift and work of *W. Wailes*, 1854. – In the S wall, the W window commemorates W. Gibson, historian of Tynemouth, † 1871.

The GRAVEYARD has a special appeal because of its romantic setting. There are some fine early C 19 examples of the Greek Revival style, but the most important stone is much earlier and is resited; it is the MONK'S STONE, a C 9 interlace cross shaft. At the E end of the promontory are early C 20 gun emplacements. Also deserving attention is the strongly sculptural COASTGUARD STATION of *c.* 1968.

CHURCHES AND PUBLIC BUILDINGS

HOLY SAVIOUR, Cross Way. 1839–41 by *John & Benjamin Green* for the Duke of Northumberland; chancel 1884; C 20 W porch. The embraced embattled W tower has been truncated, but this is still an attractive sandstone church with Perp tracery in lancet-shaped windows. No aisles, but transepts make the plan inter-

esting. The interior, with a hammerbeam roof and stencilled frieze
to the nave, shows the quality of the patronage. – C 19 and C 20
STAINED GLASS by several firms and all of high quality: *Powell
Bros.* of Leeds in nave S and N transept; *T. F. Curtis* of *Ward &
Hughes*, London, in nave N and chancel S; *H. A. Payne* in chancel
S; *Wailes (& Strang)* in nave N; *L. C. Evetts* in S transept. There
is more good glass in the E windows of the transepts.

Former CONGREGATIONAL CHURCH, Front Street. *See* Perambulation, below.

RAILWAY STATION, Station Terrace. 1882 by *William Bell* for the
North Eastern Railway Company. Twenty-one symmetrical bays
to the front, of bright red brick with stone mullions and drip-
moulds, all well-carved. But the ironwork of the interior canopies
and footbridge is gloriously exuberant, and, in 1991, is being
carefully conserved for the Friends of Tynemouth Station by
Barnett Winskell, who are also accommodating the needs of the
Metro system. On the platform wall, a tile map of the N.E.R.
network.

NEWCASTLE AND BERWICK RAILWAY COMPANY STATION.
See Perambulation.

PERAMBULATION

The centre of the town is the QUEEN VICTORIA MONUMENT
signed by *Alfred Turner*, 1902. Bronze on a Portland stone base.
It shows the Queen in old age, seated, and is a noteworthy study
of character. On the green to the W are MEMORIALS to the dead
of the FIRST WORLD WAR and beyond of the SOUTH AFRICAN
WAR (1899–1902), each typical of their time, the former tall and
simple in granite, the latter in red sandstone with buttresses and
cornice. From the centre, the old street of the settlement, Front
Street, runs E to the sea, Manor Road (with Holy Saviour's
Church, *see* above) goes NW, and HUNTINGDON PLACE lies to
the W, with, along most of it, a post-1827 brick and ashlar terrace
of three-storey houses with basements. No. 9 (MARSDEN
HOUSE), however, is early C 18, of three storeys and a basement,
and five bays. The sashes were renewed in the early C 19, possibly
at the same time as the incised render was applied. Pantiled roof.
Tuscan doorcase within a C 19 porch. The pediment (dated 1760)
on the porch was removed from the S elevation, that is the front,
before the surrounding land was developed (*see* Northumberland
Terrace and Dawson Square in Tynemouth Road, below). Huntingdon Place curves S to the railway station (*see* above) and
Station Terrace, which continues to Tynemouth Road. Just to
the W off the S side of Tynemouth Road, TYNEMOUTH PLACE,
another terrace built *c.* 1830, leads to the fine mid-C 19 NOR-
THUMBERLAND, COLLINGWOOD and PRIOR TERRACES, still
in the Georgian tradition and outward-facing from a large hollow
block to catch views over the harbour.

In TYNEMOUTH ROAD Nos. 1–3 are of *c.* 1790, ashlar with bands
and open-pedimented Tuscan doorcases. Just beyond in
OXFORD STREET, the former NEWCASTLE AND BERWICK
RAILWAY COMPANY STATION, 1846–7 by *John & Benjamin*

Green, is Tudor-style in ashlar, with an arched porch and coats of arms to give shelter and dignity. The station was restored in 1986–7 but the early (*c.* 1847) hotel and refreshment rooms beside the platform were replaced by sheltered housing, rather gimmicky, in polychrome brick with oriel windows in panels (architects *Browne, Smith, Baker & Partners*). About 300 metres further w along Tynemouth Road, KNOTT'S FLATS, by *Tasker & Child*, in collaboration with *Charles Holden*, were erected by Sir James Knott to replace the Duke of Northumberland's Percy Square of 1758, and opened in 1939. They are a remarkably large example of the style which the London County Council used for its flats *c.* 1930, light brick, with horizontal balconies and loggias and recessed hipped roofs; entirely c 20 in character and rather over-powering in their position above the harbour. N of them, on the other side of the road, the MASTER MARINERS' HOMES built as almshouses in 1837 by *J. & B. Green* for the Tyne Mariners' Benevolent Institution. The land was given by the Duke of Nor-thumberland, whose statue by *C. Tate* (finished by *R. G. Davies* after Tate's death in 1841) adorns the garden in front. They are also Tudor in style, E-plan and built of ashlar. Each cottage is three bays wide, the outer ones in gabled wings. Central clock tower with plaque. Casement windows and conjoined octagonal chimneys. Altogether an attractive sight. The short walk back along Tynemouth Road to Queen Victoria's statue passes, on the r., NEWCASTLE TERRACE and DAWSON SQUARE, both built in the mid-c 19 in the grounds of No. 9 Huntingdon Place (*see* above).

Part of FRONT STREET was demolished when Percy Park Road was created to lead from here to the seafront. E of this road there are a few pleasant houses, e.g. No. 14 (HOLLY HOUSE), basically late c 18, with ramped brick walls in front; it is the only house in the E part of the street to retain its front garden. On the s side, the former CONGREGATIONAL CHURCH, 1868 by *Thomas Oliver*, marks the corner with an imposing tower. E from here the houses worth noting, plain but pleasant and mostly c 18, begin with Nos. 57–59 (all one group; Harriet Martineau lodged in No. 57 in the 1840s), followed by Nos. 56–52, and Nos. 47–45. At this end of the street the CLOCK TOWER of 1861 by *Oliver & Lamb*, in polychrome brick and eroded pink sandstone. Before entering the Priory, a r. turn s down PIER ROAD takes us to the COL-LINGWOOD MONUMENT of 1847, by *Dobson*, with a statue by *Lough*. Surprisingly large, so that the sight of the local hero would greet mariners entering the river. The large base has slit windows and a door. On his high pedestal, the colossal figure of the Admiral (7 metres, 23 ft) is draped in a cloak. Four guns from his ship, the *Royal Sovereign*, were set flanking the steps in 1848. The view must be admired from here. The PIERS and LIGHTHOUSES, begun in 1854 and finished in 1895, were partially rebuilt in 1909 after storm damage, for the Tyne Improvement Commissioners. Even while the piers were being built the notorious Black Midden rocks, just below this spot, were claiming victims. Their plight brought into being the first Life Brigade in the country, and the Tynemouth Brigade's WATCH CLUB HOUSE of 1886–7, by *C. T. Gomoszynski*, the Borough Engineer, stands E of the monument, with the weatherboarded BRIGADE COTTAGE, still with a sliding storm shutter to one window. Immediately E of the Collingwood Monument, a broad ditch (with a bulge in its E side marking the site of a bastion) is almost all that remains visible of the SPANISH BATTERY, the Castle's mid-C 16 outworks, constructed to command the river mouth. Deep C 20 gun emplacements can be seen further E, with concrete arcs. We then reach the Priory and Castle (*see* above), and from there can finally stroll N to admire the grand crescent of PERCY GARDENS, mostly of *c.* 1860, with substantial three-storey terrace houses in a nice variety of styles, a private road and entrance lodge, and wonderful views of Priory and sea.

CULLERCOATS. *See* p. 250.

ULGHAM

2090

ST JOHN THE BAPTIST. Chancel of 1842, the remainder 1863. Neo-Norman. Built into the internal E wall of the N aisle, a piece of genuine Norman SCULPTURE, the shape of the stones of which forms the heads of small Norman windows. Carved on it, in a style entirely that of children's art, a standing woman in a long straight skirt with long triangularly hanging sleeves, two birds on her r. (above the window head) and to the r. again a man on horseback. The horse is of the type of the White Horse of Uffington. In the outer W wall of the church another undecorated stone of the same type. – MONUMENT. Fragments of a C 17 monument, long used in the churchyard wall.

MANOR HOUSE, immediately S of the church. The much-renovated exterior conceals an interesting house of unknown date. The thick ground-floor walls, of rubble-and-clay construction, are reported to be built on heavy timber sills, and predate the six-bay upper-cruck truss roof (trusses with cambered collars) and the added rear wing containing a dogleg stair of *c.* 1680, with turned balusters and panelled newels.

In the centre of the village a much-worn medieval CROSS. ULGHAM HALL is an early C 18 remodelling of an older building; open well stair of *c.* 1720.

ULGHAM GRANGE, ½ m. E, on the site of a medieval grange of Newminster. Mid-C 18 brick house, enlarged in the early C 19. Some tumbled-in gables and segmental-headed windows.

UNTHANK HALL
1 m. E of Plenmeller

7060

A medieval seat of the Ridleys (cf. Willimoteswick). The house was remodelled in 1815 in a plain classical style and again in 1865 in a free neo-Tudor, each time by *John Dobson*. Altered again *c.* 1900; reduced in size in 1965. The only pre-C 19 evidence now is a 1.2-metre (4-ft) thick wall in the house and some reset C 16 features in the former kitchen wing to the SE, detached since the

1965 demolitions. The rich mid-Victorian internal details were mostly brought from a house at Pallion (Sunderland) c. 1900.

SHANKFOOT, 1½ m. E. A late C 17 farmhouse with a moulded door surround and contemporary fireplaces with corbelled-out Tudor-arched lintels.

BLACK CLEUGH, remotely situated on the moors 2 m. SE. An interesting ruined bastle house with a circular gunloop in the surviving gable end, and a byre door in the side rather than the end wall. Remains of other buildings nearby.

VINDOLANDA

1 m. NW of Bardon Mill

7060

A Roman fort and civilian settlement on the Stanegate, the road from Corbridge to Carlisle, the course of which is followed for a mile by visitors approaching from the W. The site is on the level crest of a short promontory above the Chineley Burn; beyond, to the E, rises Barcombe Hill crowned by a Roman signal station (*see* below).

The first fort, built of timber in the A.D. 80s, lies under the later civil settlement; it was greatly enlarged c. A.D. 95 to extend under the major part of the fort now visible. It was not until 122–4 that the first stone fort was constructed, contemporary with Hadrian's Wall. It apparently had a military annexe on the W, the forerunner of the civil settlement. In c. 223–5 the fort was almost entirely rebuilt; only portions of the earlier E and W walls were retained. A civil settlement was laid out but this was largely abandoned by the end of the C 3 (*see* Introduction, p. 41). Occupation within or near the fort continued after 400, perhaps into the C 6. For the most part it is the second stone fort and its civil settlement which are consolidated for display.

The CIVIL SETTLEMENT lies outside the W gate of the fort; though only partly revealed, it consists mainly of long narrow 'strip-houses' set gable-on to the main street. These seem to have been mainly domestic in character although a few workshops have been identified along the side street that runs close to the fort-wall. Approaching from the W, the first substantial building the visitor sees is on the S side of the main street. This was apparently a *mansio*, an inn for official travellers; Hadrianic in origin, it was laid out as a series of rooms opening off an elongated courtyard. Entering the courtyard from the street and moving clockwise, the rooms were: three guest apartments (with another three opposite); a latrine; furnace room, and the two hypocausted baths it served, one bath having an E apse. Vertical flues here carried the warm air from beneath the floor up the walls. Along the S side of the courtyard, furthest from the street, were what seems to have been the entrance lobby and a changing-room for this bath-suite. In the W range the largest room has an oven-base in one corner and may thus have been a kitchen.

On the N side of the road lie two strip-houses divided by a narrow alley that leads towards the main bath-house of the fort. The W house had an unusual apsidal end on the N. Excavation revealed that in their original form these houses were a single unit with a markedly oblique N wall: in an unusually sophisticated arrangement, six rooms flanked a central corridor which later became the alley.

The BATH-HOUSE of the fort is well preserved and stands on the N edge of the civil settlement that grew up around it. The W wall is over 2 metres (6½ ft) high. The long room on the E side is the changing-room; from there, bathers passed rapidly through a cool lobby, on the S side of which was a cold plunge-bath floored with the pink waterproof plaster *opus signinum*; on the N was a more welcoming hypocausted sauna. To the W of the lobby lay a warm room, also with a hypocaust, leading into the Turkish bath; the prominent W apse of the latter contained the hot plunge. Walls and floors were lined with *opus signinum*, some of which survives. The whole exterior was apparently also plastered. The two N rooms were for the furnaces; that on the W must have allowed inspection of the water level in the iron boiler. On the extreme NE of the building are the remains of a deep latrine, which was economically flushed by all the waste water from the baths.

The FORT. The W gate, the first reached by the visitor, was a single archway; the stop for its wooden doors is still visible. The gateway's flanking towers, markedly rectangular, are unusual in that they project forward of the fort wall. A clockwise walk round the outer face of these walls reveals a repertoire of Roman stone-dressing: oblique, cross and diamond-broaching, even filled tri-angles. At the NW angle, beside a small internal tower or platform, is an arched latrine-drain with a tall monolithic division. Next to the N gate (similar in design to the W one), the arcs of six circular buildings of *c.* 205 can be seen. Once they stood inside the N part of the earlier fort, when it was only partly occupied; they are overlain by the wall of its successor of *c.* 225. They may have housed a civilian workforce under military control. By the NE angle is a well-preserved latrine, its twin water supplies flowing into sewers around three sides; these were flushed through the fort-wall along a divided outfall. The E wall survives to nearly 2.5 metres (8 ft) but of the simple E gate, which had no guard-chambers, only a short return remains. (The S gate was similar in design.) The date of the broad diverging foundations of an earlier fort-wall, further S, is uncertain.

The HEADQUARTERS BUILDING is the only substantial structure visible in the interior. Largely dating to A.D. 223–5, with some later modifications, it faces N and lies on top of its Hadrianic predecessor, which faced S. Traces of this earlier building are seen here and there, its presence also betrayed by the waves of masonry where some of the later walls break their backs over earlier foundations. Sadly the extraordinary building technique, unique in Roman Britain, which was used in parts of the Hadrianic structure is not visible: concrete blocks set on a sill of soft sandstone panels divided by harder piers.

The building on display had a front verandah and a central entrance; this led into a small courtyard surrounded on three sides by four rooms, asymmetrically arranged. Beyond the courtyard lies the remains of the cross-hall, at the W end of which there is a fine tribunal, a platform from which briefings or judgements were delivered. Its front was renewed with a shallow slot for a decorative stone dado, unfortunately robbed away. Out of the cross-hall, along its s side, opens the usual row of five rooms, the administrative and emotional centre for the garrison. The central room was the regimental shrine; it had an antechapel and a raised floor, below which a trench (said to be for strong-boxes) extends around the back and side walls. The two flanking rooms, for the pay-officers and clerks, have broad grooves at the front to take a decorated stone screen. One slab of this is still in position, another retains the holes in its top for an iron grille, appropriately reminiscent of a counter in an Edwardian bank. Later alterations meant that the room in the sw corner lost its little heated extension, but it was then given its own hypocaust. Living quarters were carved out of the se suite, and a long narrow latrine was added at the rear. These changes are also very apparent elsewhere; the whole verandah and two of the rooms around the courtyard were converted into stores (for foodstuffs) with ventilation under the floors. Beside one of them a well was sunk to the bedrock. In the antechapel of the shrine there was a huge open hearth, completely out of harmony with the room's original purpose and eloquent of the drastic changes introduced within the fort by its last garrisons of soldier-farmers and their families.

RECONSTRUCTIONS. To the sw of the fort a didactic reconstruction of two representative segments of Hadrian's Wall was built in 1971–4. The section built in stone is to the original Broad Wall gauge and incorporates a turret. In the length of Turf Wall (a structure soon replaced, and found only in Cumbria), the turf has been laid to give an almost vertical exterior face and a more gentle internal revetment. This all had to be renewed in 1984. The timber gateway is based on those found in milecastles on the Turf Wall. The ground-plans, and the general profile of the Turf Wall, are accurate enough, but all other details are conjectural; the height of the Wall and of the towers, the design of their roofs, the existence of a parapet-walk and of the crenellations are all unknown. The conjectures may be quite right; they may be quite wrong.

MAUSOLEUM. Immediately N of the reconstructions is an original small square mausoleum. An outer wall enclosed a central block of coursed rubble containing the setting of upright slabs that protected the cremated remains.

MUSEUM. Housed in Chesterholm, the 'cottage in the Abbotsford style', of 1831, E of the fort beside the burn.

ROMAN MILESTONE, still in its original position where Stanegate crosses a ford NE of Codley Gate farmhouse. A plain cylinder, 1.8 metres (6 ft) high, it was never inscribed; its message must have been painted on. The stump of a second milestone stands beside the access road (Stanegate) 1 m. to the w.

BARCOMBE HILL, ¾ m. ENE. A small univallate Iron Age hillfort on the crest high above Stanegate, within sight of Vindolanda. A much smaller enclosure within the w corner of the hillfort originally consisted of a turf rampart within a single ditch; this was a Roman signal station or watch-tower, probably of the late C 1. The whole site is much disturbed along its N edge by later quarrying.

91 CAUSEWAY HOUSE, ½m. W on the Stanegate. A precious survival
of a heather-thatched house, dated 1770. Restored and rethatched
by *Stewart Tod and Partners* in 1989. The openings have plain
raised surrounds, the upper windows being square and tucked
close beneath the eaves. The gables have reverse-stepped copings
and are, as one would expect, very steeply pitched. The roof
trusses are of a simple collar-beam type, not upper crucks, as one
might have expected. At the E end is a lower outbuilding with a
similar roof.

WALKER *see* NEWCASTLE UPON TYNE

9060   WALL

ST GEORGE. 1895 by *Hicks & Charlewood*, not on an old site.
Orientated N–S. Snecked stone. Perp style. An aisleless six-bay
rectangle which is a near copy of St Cuthbert's Church at Beltingham. The usual good-quality fittings and furnishings.
METHODIST CHAPEL, on the S side of the green. 1868; extended
in the late C19.
Wall is one of the most attractive of Tynedale villages, and its plan
is of considerable interest. The layout today is of a large square
GREEN, in which the church and some houses form an island,
with the main Hexham-to-Chollerton road (A6079) forming in
effect a 'back lane' on the W. There is considerable evidence,
however, that the green was once larger: its original NW corner
can be seen in a house which juts out awkwardly from the W side
of the main road, its position aligning with the N side of the green.
Several of the older houses seem to have been BASTLE HOUSES
of the 'terraced' type, i.e. with both byre and upper doors in the
long front wall; other near-contemporary houses adjoined one or
both ends. So Wall in the late C16 and early C17 seems to
have been a defensible village, enclosing a large green into which
animals could be driven at night or when the threat of a raid was
not strong enough to have them secured in the bastle byres. The
N side of the green is the best place to see remains of bastles:
GREENHEAD HOUSE at the W end shows remains of both original doors, with a reset 1631 lintel, perhaps dating a remodelling.
Further E is a much-altered bastle showing little more than its
distinctive masonry, and then ST OSWALD'S COTTAGES with
blocked slit windows in each gable end and a post-bastle moulded
doorway dated 1642. On the E side of the green, only traces of
bastle-type fabric. On the W side of the original village (i.e. the W
side of the main road), a pair of cottages N of the Hadrian
Hotel has a blocked upper door. The S side is less clear. TOWN
FARMHOUSE, which now turns its back on the green, is a late
C17 remodelling of an older building. Several interesting features
survive from the remodelling, including an upper-cruck roof.
Island development within the green had begun before the end
of the bastle era, as witness STABLE COTTAGE, with a good
triangular-headed upper door. There are some minor but pleasant

later buildings as well, e.g. the C18 MILESTONE COTTAGE and early C19 PENRHYN (the former Temperance Hotel), both on the W side of the main road. On the green, a HYDRANT AND TROUGH dated 1858. To the S of the green the attractive VICARAGE, probably contemporary with the church.

WALL MILL, ½m. S. Late C18 corn mill. A three-storey building built into the steep riverbank: wooden-spoked undershot wheel and other machinery, mostly of wood.

PLANETREES. Halfway down Brunton Bank, W of Planetrees Farm (cars must be parked with care), a short stretch of Hadrian's Wall includes on its S face a dramatic point of reduction from the Broad Wall (10 Roman ft: 2.9 metres) on the E to a very thin Narrow Wall (only 6 Roman ft: 1.7 metres) on the W. This Narrow Wall continued down hill to Brunton turret (see below). The Broad Wall foundations, with a culvert, had already been laid, and these are also visible.

BRUNTON. Hadrian's Wall Turret 26b, reached by a signposted path from the Hexham–Chollerton road S of the crossroads at the foot of Brunton Bank, is one of the best-preserved turrets, standing well over 2 metres (6½ft) high. The threshold is dressed to receive monolithic door-jambs. Broad Wall on the W side, but not on the E, where the turret's stumpy Broad 'wing wall' joins awkwardly to the stretch of very thin Narrow Wall extending E to Planetrees. The core of the wall, now reinforced in mortar, was set by the Romans in puddled clay which still retained its resiliency when uncovered in 1950.

ST OSWALD'S. See p. 558.

WALLINGTON

0080

The present Wallington Hall, a square of 120 by 120 ft (36.5 by 36.5 metres), was built by Sir William Blackett in 1688 on the site of an earlier house of the Fenwicks, out of the proceeds of coal- and leadmining, shipping, and Whig convictions. It was a courtyard house, and its courtyard was larger than it is now. That is all we can say of it with certainty, although it may be safely assumed that Sir William favoured a more classical or more metropolitan style than that of Capheaton and Netherwitton. From engravings we know how classical the added wings of Anderson Place, Sir William's Newcastle house, were – very much in the same style as the Mansion House in Newcastle, which was erected in 1691. At Wallington, none of the details we now see date from Sir William's time, although the form of the E front – a compressed E-plan – may. The house was altered by his great-nephew, Sir Walter Calverley Blackett, from 1727 onwards, chiefly c. 1745. It is now known that *Daniel Garrett* was his architect. It was altered further a century later for the Trevelyans, with advice from *Ruskin*.

The house is of honey-coloured sandstone, two storeys high and nine bays wide, with hipped roof, three-bay pediment and quoins. The E doorway has two Tuscan columns and a pediment, the S doorway an open pediment, and the S windows have moulded frames. Otherwise there is no enrichment. Behind, to the N, lies

1 Wallington Hall
2 Clock Tower Gate
3 The Arches
4 Portico House
5 Owl House
6 Garden House
7 Walled garden
8 Privies
9 Icehouse (disused)

500m
1500ft

Wallington Hall and grounds

a large turfed stable-yard with low ranges of offices, cottages etc. –
just as at Capheaton, Nunwick and others, but at Wallington it
leads to a fine showpiece forming the N entrance or CLOCK
TOWER GATE, a three-bay building with a central archway
between large coupled Tuscan columns and crowned by a big
lantern with a cupola on an open rotunda of columns. It is of 1754
and by Garrett; it was originally intended to be a chapel, and to
have Venetian windows.

Inside the house, Sir Walter reduced the size of the courtyard (roofed
in the C 19; see below) by adding vaulted corridors on the E and
w and a fine, large staircase on the S which starts N of the central
saloon in one flight, turns round by 90° into two and again by 90°
to reach the upper landing. The principal rooms were redecorated
too, more sumptuously and – what is more – in a more fashionable,
courtly and elegant style than the county had known before. A
gang of Italian *stuccatori* was established at Cambo in 1740–2
under *Pietro Francini* and they did their work, while some of
the best English marble carvers (among them *Cheere*) did the

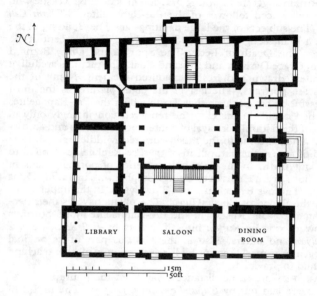

Wallington Hall. Ground-floor plan

fireplaces, and the woodwork was in the hands of craftsmen of equal standing. The showpiece is the SALOON in the middle of the S front, made higher than the other rooms by resting the ceiling on a big coving. The plasterwork has the French ribbon ornament of Bérain, and thin acanthus trails, and heads and sphinxes. The walls also are given elaborate panels, framing, l. and r. of the fireplace, oval recesses for porcelain. In the space above the mantelshelf is a relief of Apollo and Midas. The fireplace has to the l. and r. caryatids in profile coming out of big scrolled termini, and in the middle a relief of *putti* and grapes. The full-length portrait of Sir William C. Blackett by *Reynolds* was painted for the place where it hangs. To the E is the DINING ROOM, with its E end screened by Corinthian columns and a similar, though more restrained, stucco ceiling, and to the l. is the LIBRARY with a stucco ceiling also in the same style framing an oval relief with *putti*. The Ionic columns are a late C 18 alteration. N of the library, facing W, where the present study is, was the staircase of 1688, a spacious apartment with steps leading up three walls round an open well. The staircase walls also have plaster decoration, but the ceiling with its deep coffering is said to be C 19 work. Even some upper rooms are equally rich, notably the Tapestry Room.

In 1855, on the advice of *Ruskin*, a friend of the house, which had by then become Trevelyan property, the courtyard was roofed in and given Italian arcades on square pillars and an arched gallery. The walls on the N and S, where the arcades were blind, the pillars, the spandrels, and the upper spandrels were all painted. The architecture was commissioned from *Dobson*; for the paintings Ruskin suggested a young drawing master at Newcastle who was a convinced follower of the Pre-Raphaelites, *William Bell Scott*. The subjects of the large paintings are The Building of the Roman Wall, King Egfrid and St Cuthbert, The Descent of the Danes, The Death of Bede, The Spur in the Dish, Bernard Gilpin, Grace Darling, and Iron and Coal. The pictures are full of accurately drawn and freshly coloured incident. Many of the heads are portraits. The last of the eight pictures is the most successful by far, because that Truth which the Pre-Raphaelites preached could, in the C 19, be rendered convincingly only in terms of the faithful portrayal of contemporary events and accessories. When it came to the much-admired Middle Ages and the world of poetry the naturalism of the Pre-Raphaelites tended to drive out truth. In the spandrels, a series of portrait heads in medallions, from Hadrian to George Stephenson, including Duns Scotus, Thomas Bewick and two Trevelyans. In the upper spandrels, the Ballad of Chevy Chase. The pillars have as their decoration a typically Ruskinian and Pre-Raphaelite motif, portraits of flowers, one by *Ruskin* himself, others by *Bell Scott, Pauline Trevelyan* and others. Also in the Hall, as part of its original setting, a large marble statue by *Woolner*, a young mother teaching her child to pray.

The GARDENS are some distance away from the house to the E. They were laid out by *Capability Brown c.* 1766. The mid-C 18 PORTICO HOUSE made in the centre of a long high late C 17 brick wall may be by *Garrett*. It is a summer-house with a Roman Doric screen with a coved ceiling inside as at Capheaton (q.v.). To the S, Brown created a big lake, with further E a walled garden; the flower gardens within are, in their present form, the work of *Lady Trevelyan* in 1938. C 17 lead figures, Dutch, on the terrace wall; in the wall behind is the OWL HOUSE, a mid-C 18 quoined and pedimented brick gazebo. In the woods to the N, two C 18 PRIVY HOUSES, brick with ashlar dressings and round-arched doors. On the N horizon, an eyecatcher, THE ARCHES, originally built in 1735 as a three-bay gate-screen to the Hall courtyard, but found to be too narrow for coaches and replaced by the Clock Tower Gate; round arches on piers with bulgy rustication, and projecting pedimented centre. E of the walled garden, the nobly simple three-bay GARDEN HOUSE; ashlar, dated 1766 and perhaps by *Brown*. S of the Hall a BRIDGE over the Wansbeck; 1755 by *James Paine*. Segmental arch flanked by smaller round arches, rusticated voussoirs, steeply rising balustraded parapet. Also, in the East Wood a STANDING STONE, 2.3 metres ($7\frac{1}{2}$ ft) high, beside the China Pond. It probably came from the barrow known as 'The Poind and his Man' near Bolam West Houses. On the lawn E of the Hall, four grotesque DRAGONS' HEADS from Bishops Gate, London (the story is that they were brought N as ballast in one of the Blacketts' coal boats); in the West Wood, an ICEHOUSE.

79

WALLSEND

The name refers to the E end of Hadrian's Wall, where there was a fort; but what can be seen in the late C 20 is largely the result of two centuries of coalmining and shipbuilding. The Rising Sun pit has now gone, the shipyards need fewer men, but new industries and housing estates have spread across the fields where the miners used to walk to the colliery. The population in 1801 was 3,100; by 1871 it was 10,458, by 1911, 41,461. Thereafter it rose only slowly (in 1961 it was nearly 50,000) and thirty years later it had dropped back to 44,599. It is not easy to see where Newcastle ends and Wallsend begins. Perseverance is rewarded by the discovery of a medieval chapel and a village green on the high ground of opposite sides of Wallsend Burn, well to the E of the industrial town.

CHURCHES AND PUBLIC BUILDINGS

ST LUKE, Station Road. 1885–7 by *Oliver & Leeson;* W vestries 1895; tower, chancel and Lady Chapel by *Oliver, Leeson & Wood*, 1906. A big serious E.E. church built of sandstone in the very heart of C 19 Wallsend. Tower at the E end of the N aisle. E end with five tall stepped lancets. – STAINED GLASS. Much that is only average, but the E window is a First World War memorial by *Wilhelmina Geddes*, 1922, of quite exceptionally high quality. Crucifixion, with the Deposition in small figures below the figure of the Crucifixus.

ST PETER, Church Bank. 1809, paid for by a tontine (in which the last survivor of several subscribers gains the prize) and by the Dean and Chapter of Durham. It lies on the opposite side of Wallsend Burn from the medieval Holy Cross Chapel (*see* below), which it replaced, and nearer the Tyne. Enlarged and gothicized in Perp style by *W. S. Hicks*, 1892. Except for the shape of the nave (without aisles), there is nothing late Georgian left. Good hammerbeam roof by Hicks, with large angels. – FONT. Medieval, from Holy Cross; completely plain octagonal bowl. – STAINED GLASS. N: central window by *Wilhelmina Geddes*, c. 1912; another signed by *Ethel Rhine Strang*, c. 1921. – S chancel chapel second window by *Michael Healey*. – E window by *Bacon Bros*. – GRAVE-YARD. Near the porch, the STOCKS of 1816, to punish sabbath-breakers. They have three holes.

HOLY CROSS CHURCH, Valley Gardens. The remains of the small C 12 parish church and its C 17 porch. Consolidated as a ruin in 1909 by *W. H. Knowles*.

ROMAN FORT, Buddle Street. The positions of the fort wall, gates and towers (known from excavation) are outlined effectively in concrete; the barrack blocks N of the road are marked by grass. Fragmentary footings of the E gate survive; those of the S gate are modern masonry, as is the stump of Hadrian's Wall which runs down from the SE angle to its ultimate end, in the river. The lowest courses of the central headquarters building are exposed; a colonnaded court, entered from the N, a cross-hall and offices beyond, with a central sunken strongroom. A cistern lies outside the SE corner. This was one of the forts added to the original scheme for the frontier in the Hadrianic modification that brought the forts up onto the line of the Wall itself. As an adjunct to this, the Wall was extended (in a narrow gauge) E from the bridgehead at Newcastle as far as this point in order to cover the N banks of the Tyne.

Former TOWN HALL (now North Tyneside District Offices), High Street East. 1907–8 by *E. F. W. Liddle & P. L. Brown*, a vigorous composition expressive of the town's prosperity. Baroque, in the spirit of John Belcher's winning design of 1897 for Colchester Town Hall. Bright red brick with ashlar plinth and dressings. Eleven bays and a r. corner turret, a tripartite window with a balustraded balcony over the central door, attached Ionic order on the first floor, the borough arms, and a copper roof on the turret. – The FIRE STATION behind, in Lawson Street, and the PUBLIC BATHS, which complete the block, were all part of the same scheme.

BUDDLE ARTS CENTRE, Buddle Street. This was the Buddle School, called after a notable mining engineer of the early C 19. 1876 by *J. Johnstone* in sandstone, with Scottish crowstepped gables; three rear wings. Contemporary former headmaster's and caretaker's houses complete the group.

SIR G. B. HUNTER MEMORIAL HOSPITAL, The Green. Built as Wallsend Hall in the early C 19. Brick with sandstone sill bands, and a Westmorland slate roof. Three storeys and seven bays, with pedimented Tuscan porch.

BURN CLOSES BRIDGE, St Peter's Road. 1912 for Wm T. Weir, built of what was then called ferro-concrete; the method of construction was patented by *Hennebique*. The engineer *L. G. Mouchel* was Hennebique's agent, with a Newcastle office. Five trestles carry a slightly arched roadway over the deep dene of Wallsend Burn.

WILLINGTON VIADUCT, further SE over the same stream. 1837–9 by *John & Benjamin Green* for the Newcastle and North Shields Railway Company. The seven large arches, with spans from 35 to 39 metres (115 to 128 ft), were originally of laminated wood resting on stone piers. In 1869 the wood was replaced with wrought iron in a similar latticed pattern. The latest alteration has been the strengthening necessary for the Metro trains. An ACCOMMODATION ARCH at the E end allows Ropery Lane through the embankment; it is a skew arch, of fine ashlar.

PERAMBULATION

THE GREEN, E of Station Road, is worth a stroll, for there are still a few houses of the C 18–19. The former Wallsend Hall (now a hospital, *see* above) and LILY COTTAGE lie to the N; JASMINE HOUSE and CROSS HOUSE at the E end were a school and the schoolmaster's house, given to Wallsend in 1748 but altered since. At the E end, Crow Bank was the paved way for funerals to descend the dene. It may be followed to the Wallsend Burn and from there a path leads to Holy Cross Church (*see* above). From the church, another path along the valley-top S of Valley Gardens leads under Burn Closes Bridge and past the post-1918 WAR MEMORIAL – a striking object on the skyline with a bronze angel of victory on a high granite obelisk (perhaps by *R. A. Ray*; cf. the memorial in Burdon Road, Sunderland, formerly County Durham) – to Ropery Lane. (A ropery used to lie along the valley.) The Willington Viaduct (*see* above) can be seen from here, and a short walk along the lane leads to the beautiful skew accommodation arch through the E embankment. Now N again to Church Bank and W to St Peter's Church (*see* above), then along HIGH STREET EAST to see an attractive Edwardian group of Town Hall and pub between Coach Road and Lawson Street. The COACH AND HORSES is of *c.* 1907, by *Watson*, the company architect of the brewers W. B. Reed. Its bright red brick with ashlar dressings respects but does not imitate the adjoining Town Hall (*see* above). Just SW along VINE STREET there are typical Tyneside flats (*see* p. 98), with separate front doors for each flat. Vine Street takes us to Station Road and St Luke's Church (*see* above). On the N side of FRANK STREET, set in the arcade of the Hunter Memorial Hall, is another First World War WAR MEMORIAL, to the staff and men of the Swan Hunter and Wigham Richardson Ltd shipyard; it has particularly appealing industrial scenes in low relief, signed by *R. Hedley*, who also did the bronze statues. Some distance to the S, the Roman Fort (*see* above) makes a green oasis traversed by BUDDLE STREET. Here also is the cast-iron shipyard CLOCK which, when on its original site at the N side of the street, encouraged the workforce to be good timekeepers. From here there are good views of the river, with industrial parks and landscaped open spaces on each shore instead of the clamour of shipbuilding.*

WALLTOWN
2½ m. NW of Haltwhistle

6060

Those walking W from the Roman fort at Great Chesters see Hadrian's Wall in poor condition at first; the Ditch is a shadow of its usual self and for some reason seems never to have been finished. A ROMAN MILESTONE, moved from the Military Way, has been reused as the W post of a gate at the NW end of the wood on Cockmount Hill. Its inscription must have been painted on. Only a robber trench marks the site of Milecastle 44 (and also that of 45, to the W). Just E of Alloa Lea (*see* Greenhead), the N face of the Wall is up to nine courses high, but the S face survives incognito, no more than three courses high, as the base of a scruffy field-wall. Further W the facing stones have been robbed, leaving a long mound of core material. Close to Walltown, the Ditch reappears to defend each gap in the crags. TURRET 44b is well preserved; set in a sharp angle on the cliffs overlooking Walltown Nick, both its N and W sides are recessed into the Wall itself. A fragment of a monolithic arch, preserved in the interior, is broad enough to have come from an original doorway.

Immediately beyond Walltown Nick, only a mound of core material marks the line of the curtain; however, to the W of the

* The offices of Messrs SWAN HUNTER by *Richard Sheppard*, 1943 and *c.* 1948–52 (described at length in the first edition), survive but have been spoilt by later alterations.

smaller of the two former quarries is one of the prettiest and best-preserved stretches of the whole Wall. As it wriggles between the clifftop of the Whin Sill and the outcrops behind, the Wall stands up to 2 metres ($6\frac{1}{2}$ ft) high in twelve courses. Some culverts are visible at its base. TURRET 45a is on the summit of Walltown Crags. Butt-joints on either side suggest that it was built early in the Hadrianic sequence, before the adjoining lengths of Wall; conventionally explained away as a signal-post in service during the construction of the Wall. Unusually, some dressed Whin blocks are used in its fabric. To the w the curtain was mercilessly cut away by the former Walltown quarry, its savagery now muted by landscaping.

WALWICK
1 m. w of Chollerford

9070

As its name suggests, a hamlet on the line of Hadrian's Wall. There are two houses of some size: WALWICK HALL, a large irregular house which is largely C18 (one pyramid-roofed canted bay, as at Chesters), incorporating some older fabric, and LITTLE WALWICK, its main part a three-storey five-bay early C18 block with quite plain detail.

LINCOLN HILL, $\frac{1}{2}$ m. NE. The influence of Carr's Chesters is seen again in a three-bay house dated 1799, with broad canted bays and a big eaves cornice. Other parts earlier C18. Away to the E, a walled garden with a pyramid-roofed DOVECOTE.

WALWICK GRANGE
1$\frac{1}{2}$ m. s of Chollerford

9070

An early C18 house, splendidly sited above the North Tyne. Three-storey five-bay river front, with a tall arched stair window at the centre; windows in stone surrounds with keystones. Wing to the rear altered and entrance porch added in the early C19. Good C18 stair with moulded balusters. There is said to be a medieval tower incorporated, but if anything of it survives it is well disguised.

WARDEN
9060

Handsomely situated among the trees near the confluence of the North and South Tynes; traditionally the site of an oratory of St John of Beverley founded c. 700.

ST MICHAEL. Unaisled cruciform church. The w tower is one of the Tynedale pre-Conquest group. It is tall and unbuttressed and has large irregular quoins and small round-headed windows, deeply splayed internally; the belfry stage is probably of 1765. The arch towards the nave is low and narrow; the moulded imposts may be reused Roman blocks, but the rubble arch is probably a post-medieval reconstruction. The transepts belong to the C 13. They are remarkably long and have lancet and coupled lancet windows, single-chamfered outside and with hoodmoulds continued as a stringcourse. Broad clasping buttresses at the transept angles. The transept arches are C 19 on older jambs; piscina in S transept and aumbry in N. Nave and S porch (with good sundial) 1765, rewindowed in the C 19; chancel rebuilt 1889. – Several MONUMENTS. – A coped and tegulated gravestone in the chancel. – C 13 CROSS SLAB in sanctuary floor. – Various pre- and post-Conquest slabs and fragments in the porch, including a grave slab split from a large Roman altar: a full-length figure with outstretched arms, much worn, is cut in relief; flanked by interlace panels and interlinked loops. Early C 11. – STAINED GLASS. Much *Kempe* glass, 1889 and 1891.

In the churchyard, S of the tower, a crudely cut hammerhead CROSS, perhaps as early as the C 7. LYCHGATE of 1903, with a richly carved timber superstructure.

An earthwork CASTLE (a partial ringwork) lies 150 metres W of the church: the tip of a promontory made defensible by a ditch and bank on the NW. The steep natural slopes on the S and E have been artificially scarped to give, from below, an imposing motte-like appearance.

LOW WARDEN HOUSE. Late C 17, altered in the C 18. Three-bay three-storey front with hipped dormers.

HIGH WARDEN, ½ m. NW. A finely sited early C 19 house, with additions of 1834 by *Dobson*. Enlarged again later in the C 19, but recently reduced in size.

WAREN MILL
2 m. W of Bamburgh

1030

WATER MILL. An ancient site, and the last water mill in the region to be involved in the grain trade. A tablet attached to an external wall outlines its history from its first mention in 1187 to the addition of a malting block in 1924 (*see* Introduction, p. 86). Originally water-powered; the millrace still passes through the mill, but it was an early user of steam power (1819) and probably dependent on coal brought in by sea. Its site on the tidal limit of Budle Bay was considered advantageous for shipping purposes when the mill was offered for sale in 1858. The main mill block is of four-and-a-half storeys and is masonry-built; the three-storey malting block forms a massive extension to the W. The stone-built mill house faces E; the whole makes up a fine set of buildings. Closed as a mill *c.* 1980.

WARK-ON-TWEED

CASTLE. This, one of the most important of all the castles of the Border, is in a poor state; yet in the C 16 it was described as 'a jewel of noysaunce' against the Scots and 'The stay and key of all this country'. The site is on the crest of a narrow ridge that runs roughly parallel with the Tweed, at a point where the river's S bank is a high cliff commanding a former ford. Here Walter Espec built a motte-and-bailey in the early C 12; his earth-and-timber castle was probably rebuilt gradually in stone from the late C 12 onwards, although its overall plan was probably little changed. Besieged with great frequency by the Scots, a castle in such a strategic position was too important to be left wholly in private hands; for nearly five centuries the Crown commandeered it as and when required, or contributed to its garrisons or upkeep.

The most prominent feature is the MOUND (containing the ruins of the keep) on the site of the motte at the W end of the village; a W ditch, still visible, defended it from attack along the ridge. To the E, in line, lay an inner and an outer ward. Part of the inner one survives, still partly surrounded by the remains of a substantial wall, as a level area immediately E of the motte, but the outer ward is occupied by the modern village. The river-cliff provided impregnable defences on the N; the S side is marked by the irregular S row of cottages built on a very distinct steep-sided spine: probably the natural ridge adapted to be the bailey-bank itself. The gatehouse into the outer ward must have been close to the E end of this row.

Shortly before Flodden the castle was captured and partly destroyed by James IV. After a massive rebuilding programme in 1517–19, the keep on the motte stood four storeys high and had been adapted for artillery: 'The said dongeon [i.e. the keep] is made of foure howses hight, and in every Stage, there is fyve grete murdour holes, shot with grete voultes of Stone, except one stage which is with Tymbre. So that grete bumbardes may be shot out at icheon of them. And there is a well made with trap dores thorow the middest of every hows for the heasing up of ordinaunce.' From the top the watchman could see Norham Castle and 'all the boundes of Berwyk'. The surviving mound, containing the ruins of the keep, still rises over 13 metres (43 ft) above the ditch to the W, and towers even higher over the N and S flanks. Nevertheless, the foundations of this donjon were found to be only two feet (0.6 metre) deep and much at risk from mining. In 1543–7 the keep was encircled by 'the Ring', a wall 1.8 metres (6 ft) thick and over 7 metres (23 ft) high. Twelve embrasures were provided for artillery, which were set on a rear platform more than 7 metres broad. Although all the facing-stones have been robbed away, it is the rubble core of the Ring that now forms the sheer W face of the 'motte'. The artillery platform is visible as a terrace at the wall-head, well below the top of the mound.

An Elizabethan description records a 'stonehouse' in the outer ward and, in the inner one, a bakehouse, a kitchen and a house for the constable. By this time the keep was decayed and ruinous; despite further repairs the castle continued to deteriorate and in 1633 the royal artillery was finally withdrawn.

WARK-ON-TYNE

St Michael. 1818 by *H. H. Seward,* a pupil of Soane. Built at the expense of the Commissioners of Greenwich Hospital, whose house architect Seward was. Wark had been part of Simonburn parish, which had belonged to Greenwich since the break-up of the Derwentwater estates after the 1715 Rebellion. They built Wark (and Greystead, Humshaugh and Thorneyburn, qq.v.) to provide livings for navy chaplains. Thin embattled w tower, broad aisleless nave, narrower and lower chancel. E window of inter-sected tracery, the other windows with Y-tracery, all in very broadly chamfered surrounds. Redecorated 1883–4 and 1920. – STAINED GLASS. 1900 by *Kempe,* next to the pulpit.

RECTORY. Also designed by *Seward* at the same time. Three bays with tripartite windows.

Wark was the capital of the regality of Tynedale, and formerly had a motte-and-bailey castle at the s end of the village. There is still something of a small-town feel about the village. It has a square green with rows of neat C 18 and C 19 stone cottages and, to the s, a TOWN HALL, formerly the Mechanics Institute, of 1873. About a hundred metres up the Stonehaugh road is the PINFOLD or stray animal pound of the mid-C 19, a rather mysterious yard with high wall and a doorway with the crescent moon of the Duke of Northumberland.

The road from Wark along the Warks Burn passes several bastles. MORTLEY and HORNEYSTEAD are both ruinous, only the ground floors standing, but both have fine doorways under bold relieving arches. LOW STEAD, *c.* 3 m. NW, near Hetherington, is more complete and was converted into a house in the C 18. Attached, a smaller building with walls of the same thickness; might it have been a granny bastle?

SHITLINGTON CROSS, 1 m. N of Low Stead. The base and octag-onal shaft of a medieval cross.

A 'four-poster' STONE CIRCLE at the w end of Ravensheugh Crags, 2¼ m. SW. The ESE stone bears cup marks; the central cremation burial, of the earlier second millennium B.C., has been robbed.

LEE HALL. *See* p. 373.

WARKWORTH

Warkworth must be approached from the N. With its bridge, its bridge-tower, then Bridge Street at an angle joining the main street up a hill to the towering, sharply cut block of the keep, it is one of the most exciting sequences of views one can have in England. The church does not form part of it. Walking back from the Castle, down the street with its fine quiet terraced C 18 and C 19 houses on the l. and r., one reaches the Market Cross, and there the road forks, to the r. Bridge Street and to the l. Dial Place, leading to the church. The whole village is enclosed by a loop of the Coquet, and its layout is entirely medieval, each house on the main strip having its own long strip of land running to the 'back lane' (called The Butts on the E, The Stanners on the W) on the riverbank.

ST LAURENCE. Warkworth Church is unique in Northumberland
in being a large fairly complete Norman church. The Norman
building originally consisted of an unusually long and narrow
nave – 27.5 by 7.5 metres (90½ by 25 ft) – and a chancel. The w
tower and s aisle are both later. Externally the fine Norman N
wall of the nave has broad flat buttresses, a blocked door and five
completely plain windows. A stringcourse runs at sill level, and
another at the level of the springing of the arches, banding round
them as hoodmoulds. Inside, the windows have nook-shafts. The
doorway is set in a sunk gable-headed panel within a broad
pilaster-like projection; it has one order of colonnettes and the
arch two slight chamfers. Another shallow projection at the E end
of the wall housed a newel stair to a mural passage above the
chancel arch, which gave access to a former chamber above the
chancel vault. In addition the Norman W wall survives, but that
can only be seen inside. It had three tall windows, also with nook-
shafts. A doorway was broken in when the tower was built. The
chancel is even more remarkable. Externally it has some small
Norman windows and an extremely narrow s door, but internally
there is a display of richness directly derived from the example of
Durham Cathedral. There are few vaulted chancels of the C 12 in
English parish churches; Warkworth possesses one of them. The
vaulting is reinforced by ribs, again on the pattern of Durham,
and the ribs have zigzag decoration. This appears for the first time
at Durham in the nave vaults, i.e. *c*. 1130, so the Warkworth
chancel is unlikely to be earlier. The vault consists of two bays.
They rest on short shafts with scalloped capitals, and these stand
on the stringcourse which runs along at sill level. The windows
are nook-shafted; those at the E end date from the restoration of
1860 (nave by *Dobson*, chancel *Ewan Christian*). The chancel arch
has rectangular responds with one central demishaft and two in
the angles. The capitals are single- and double-scalloped, the arch
decorated with an outer band of ornament of a curious fan-like
triangular motif and another of beads. The W tower is an addition
of *c*. 1200, sturdy and not in need of buttresses. It has narrow
lancets which are only just pointed. The belfry, with openings of
paired, quite broad pointed lights, and the plain broach spire of
moderate height, are regarded as additions of the C 14. The N
vestry is probably C 13, with its small lancets and the curious three
small W openings cut out of one stone. Finally the s aisle. It
represents the C 15. The arcade of five bays has quatrefoil piers
with slender shafts in the diagonals. The capitals are circular and
moulded, and the arches moulded with remarkable finesse. The
aisle windows are large, with four-centred arches: the un-
imaginative panel tracery, of five lights at the E end, of three
otherwise, is all C 19 (besides renewing these windows Dobson
destroyed a C 15 clerestory). The s porch has a rib vault with
ridge-ribs, and an upper chamber reached by a stair turret on the
E. – COMMUNION RAIL. Fine wrought-iron work of *c*. 1710 with
crest and monogram of Matthew White of Blagdon. – STAINED
GLASS. Medieval fragments in head of s aisle E window. – MONU-
MENTS. Two headstone crosses and a round-topped grave
marker, all probably C 11, in chancel. – In s aisle, well-preserved
EFFIGY of cross-legged knight, *c*. 1330; expressive face and

sharply cut detail. It rests on a c 17 table tomb. – Various late c 18 and early c 19 wall tablets, many by *Davies* of Newcastle.

UNITED REFORMED CHURCH (formerly Presbyterian), The Butts. 1828. Plain ashlar front with Tuscan doorway and oculus in pediment; extended to rear *c.* 1860.

WARKWORTH STATION, 1 m. w on a minor road towards Shilbottle. One of *Green*'s handsome Tudor stations for the Newcastle and Berwick Railway Company (cf. Acklington), now sensitively converted into two houses. A long flight of stone stairs sweeps up to a portico with three pointed arches, still with their old glazing. The single-storey s wing ends in a room with a canted bay window; this is said to have been the Duke's private waiting room.

BRIDGE. C 14: in 1379 John Cook of Newcastle left 20 marks towards its building. It has two ribbed segmental arches of 18.2-metre (60-ft) span, with a sharply pointed cutwater between, carried up as a pedestrian refuge; the road is narrow (3.3 metres, 11 ft). At the s end is the BRIDGE TOWER, making this one of England's few fortified bridges. It is a plain rectangular structure with a rough four-centred barrel vault and a parallel guard-chamber. The first floor is much ruined.

The VILLAGE. The medieval bridge (see above), now bypassed by a new road bridge, is the obvious starting point for a walk round Warkworth. Immediately beyond, in Bridge Street, is BRIDGE END HOUSE, the best house in Warkworth. It is of five bays, with quoins and a good pedimented doorway. The lower two floors have an original eaves cornice below a lower second floor added later in the c 18. In front an excellent, although sadly decayed, wrought-iron gate and railings. Further on on the same side is the WARKWORTH HOUSE HOTEL, a three-storey five-bay house with a pedimented centrepiece, dated 1822. John Forster, who built the house, brought the fine staircase with its patterned wrought-iron balustrade from the Brandenburgh House, Queen Caroline's residence in London. Most of the houses on Castle Street are of the c 18 and c 19. c 17 remains survive in the first group of houses (Nos. 1–4) on the w at the top of the hill, and the thick walls of a much-altered house on BREWERY BANK (a lane running down to the river on the w) may be c 16. Of the early c 18, the seven-bay HERMITAGE INN, brick behind its render, with segment-headed windows, and two houses (Nos. 25 and 37) both dated 1727, all on the E side. The best early c 19 house is No. 5, on the w: it was built in 1818, and is of two storeys and four bays, with a pretty patterned fanlight and a balustraded parapet. At the top of the hill, CASTLE TERRACE runs E, in the shadow of the keep, to the SUN HOTEL, a big house of 1825 with an open-pedimented doorway and patterned fanlight, and tripartite sashes; c 18 wing at rear. Looking down the hill, in the Y-fork of Bridge Street and Dial Place is the MARKET CROSS of *c.* 1830 on an older stepped base. It is octagonal, with traceried panels and a domed top. Behind it, the CO-OPERATIVE SOCIETY, a good piece of inter-war building well fitted to its acute corner site. On the w side of Dial Place, Nos. 6 and 7 (formerly Durham House), a tall semi-detached pair of *c.* 1820, with patterned overlights to the central pair of doors. Further on, opposite the w end of the church, the OLD VIC-

ARAGE, of the same date, has a patterned fanlight. Fanlights and overlights of this type seem to have been something of a trademark of early C 19 Warkworth builders; the design is usually expressed in lead, applied to a single pane of glass. From the churchyard, a footpath runs E to Bridge Street, passing a late C 19 red-brick terrace built into the former TITHE BARN; the outline of its W gable is visible, with slit vents, but gives no clue as to its date. Beyond are the tall C 18 garden walls of Bridge End House; that on the S overlies the site of the chapel of a monastic cell of Durham mentioned in the C 13. Foundations were seen in the C 19, but nothing is visible today. Back at the Bridge again, one can walk E along THE BUTTS to the SCHOOLHOUSE, a plain three-bay building with a worn inscription dated 1736 and chamfered door and window surrounds. It served as the Borough School until *c.* 1890. THE OLD SCHOOL alongside, formerly the National School, is of 1824, extended in 1852, in typical C 19 Tudor style. Further on, COQUET HOUSE is a plain early C 18 house, said to have been built for the Duke of Northumberland's fisherman, but remodelled *c.* 1822 by John Forster of Warkworth House, who here installed another of the stairs he had brought from the Brandenburgh House; this one is of stone, with an anthemion-pattern wrought-iron handrail.

WARKWORTH CASTLE. In 1139 Henry, son of David I, King of Scotland, was made Earl of Northumberland. It has been suggested that he first built, or at least converted from wood to stone, the castle of Warkworth in order to have a fortress capable of vying with the royal castles of Bamburgh and Newcastle. Of his time no more survives than masonry in the E and W curtains. In 1158 Warkworth was granted by Henry II to Roger, son of Richard. His son Robert, who succeeded in 1178 and died in 1214, must have been responsible for the gatehouse, the Carrickfergus and West Postern Towers, and also for the Great Hall, with its E aisle. The Grey Mare's Tail Tower dates from later in the C 13, the Chapel from early in the C 14. In 1332 the castle was given to Henry, second Lord Percy of Alnwick, and it has remained in the Percy family ever since. Its great building period came after the Scottish invasion of 1383–4. The builder was probably the first Earl, who died in 1408; details of the planning and architectural detailing of the keep have been compared with Gilling and Bolton Castles in North Yorkshire,* and a date in the 1390s seems likely. Of this period are the keep or donjon, the remodelled hall, the kitchen, and the laying out and beginning of the collegiate church within the walls of the castle.

In its original form the castle was defended by a deep ditch (conceivably an Iron Age legacy) cutting off the end of the promontory within the bend of the Coquet. Beyond lay an embanked bailey, which was reduced in area when the timber palisades were replaced in stone. Thus the bailey bank is well preserved only on the abandoned E side. The keep stands on the motte of the first castle at the N tip of the promontory. On the N, within the meander, lies the whole village. The present castle faces S, with

---

* M. J. B. Hislop, 'The Date of the Warkworth Donjon', *Archaeologia Aeliana*, 5th series, XX, 1991, pp. 79–92.

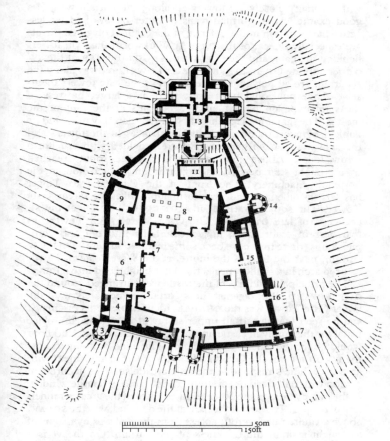

1 Great Gate Tower	7 Lion Tower	13 Keep
2 Chapel	8 Collegiate Church	14 Grey Mare's Tower
3 Carrickfergus Tower	9 Kitchen	15 Stables
4 Solar (above)	10 West Postern Tower	16 East Postern
5 Porch	11 Brew House	17 Amble or Montagu
6 Great Hall	12 Postern	Tower

Warkworth Castle. Plan

the Great Gate Tower at the centre of its S curtain. Behind is the almost square outer ward, with beyond the triangular inner ward narrowing to the keep placed on the Norman motte at the highest point of the site.

The GREAT GATE TOWER represents the improved technique of military architecture that had been developed in the West in consequence of the Crusades, characterized by far greater care for the curtain wall and its strengthening. The Tower of London, with its many closely set towers all along the curtain wall, is a good example; the Norman walls of outer baileys had far less active participation in the defence of the castle. Polygonal turrets are especially typical of the C 13. At Warkworth the twin towers flanking the gate, and the CARRICKFERGUS TOWER at the SW corner and the GREY MARE'S TAIL TOWER midway along the E curtain are all polygonal. The angles of the gate towers themselves have polygonal buttresses; there is a larger buttress of the same type on both E and W curtains at the foot of the motte. The gate passage has a pointed barrel vault, and is flanked by guardrooms; both the front faces of the towers and the side walls of the gate passage are provided with cruciform arrow loops. Above the passage is a large room, reached by a straight stair beyond each guardroom, which housed the portcullis machinery. The front of the Carrickfergus Tower has largely fallen; it had cruciform loops like the Great Gate Tower. The square AMBLE or MONTAGU TOWER at the SE corner is of late C 15 date. The Grey Mare's Tail Tower has two tiers of embrasures, linked externally into tall and complex loops (there may have been some restoration here). On the W curtain, near the foot of the motte, is the West Postern, a two-centred arch in a shallow projection later heightened into a tower.

The principal buildings of the castle were arranged around the OUTER WARD. Built against the S curtain immediately W of the Great Gate Tower was the CHAPEL, identifiable by its piscina. It can be seen that it had an upper storey at its W end, the place usual for the family in castle and palace chapels; the ground floor would be for the tenantry or garrison. The main building against the W curtain was the GREAT HALL, a spacious apartment with an E aisle. The S respond of the aisle arcade survives, a corbel of c. 1200 with nail-head decoration. The N jamb of a large window to the outer ward, on the other hand, is proof of the great remodelling of c. 1400. To the S of the hall, at the dais end, was the SOLAR, above a vaulted undercroft; access from the hall was by means of a straight stair in the thickness of the curtain. On the W is a square-headed window with a lunette over, carved with foliage, within a round arch; the window probably opened onto a timber balcony (there may have been a similar feature at Mitford) overlooking the Coquet. N of the hall are low walls marking the buttery and pantry, with, behind them, the large kitchen with an oven. More prominent than any of these rooms today are the two C 15 TOWER-PORCHES connected with them. The S tower contained a lobby giving access to the S end of the hall, the solar, and (via a short passage) the chapel: it has a tunnel-vaulted ground floor, a rib-vaulted first floor and a broached spire at the top. It contains a spiral stair finishing in a pretty umbrella vault. The N (Lion) tower was built as the main porch to the hall and also to the collegiate church, via a passage on the N; its ground floor has a star vault, or rather a vault of two diagonal and two ridge-ribs, with a Percy lion on the boss. After the abandonment of the college scheme the porch was heightened into a tower and a N stair turret added; the front of the tower, above the main door, has a large figure of the Percy lion carried on two fan corbels and flanked by thin buttresses which rest on angel figures. Opposite the hall, on the E side of the outer ward was a range of stables, now much ruined.

The foundations of the COLLEGIATE CHURCH divide the outer from the inner ward – a functional division rather than a line of defence, and one which may not have existed at all before *c.* 1400. It seems to have been the intention of the first Earl to found a college of secular priests; the outer ward can be visualized in terms of a college quad with gateway, hall, sets of rooms and chapel, with the inner ward no more than a backyard behind the church, as one finds behind some college chapels in Oxford. However, the church was never completed, and little more may have been constructed than what survives today: one can recognize in the turf an aisled nave of four bays (quatrefoil piers), a crossing (piers with groups of three shafts to each of the four diagonals), transepts and a two-bay aisled chancel. There are complete vaults under the N transept and chancel, and a vaulted passage beneath the E end linking outer and inner wards. The inner ward is small and seems to have contained little more than a brewhouse built into the S slope of the motte.

Now for the KEEP. It is placed on the earlier Norman motte. 52 Here is one of the rare cases where the military engineer happened to be a great architect. The design of castles and bastions often has little to do with the art of building. But the Warkworth keep is a work of architecture in the sense that both its mass and its inner spaces are beautiful as well as useful. It was the Edwardian engineers of the late C 13 who for the first time had raised castle building in Great Britain to an art capable of aesthetic effects as intense as those of churches. Harlech and Beaumaris in their crystalline shapes are as much art as the Westminster chapter-house. The C 14 then, thanks to the internal peace on the island, saw a great increase in comfort within the castle – at the expense of formality. (Let nobody argue that informal architecture can also be architecture. Of course it can, but one has little reason to assume that the designer of a fortified manor house arranged rooms, ranges of rooms and towers for aesthetic effect.) The formal symmetrical plan was revived a hundred years later in such castles as Bodiam, where ranges of buildings are disposed around a square courtyard with symmetrical angle towers. Lumley in Durham follows the same type of plan but with less aesthetic self-discipline. Warkworth is the apogee of formal design, and it proves the genius of its designer in that it is at the same time a residence of considerable comfort. Dr Simpson has suggested that, although it appears essentially a keep, that is a solid stone block, its attitude to the planning of rooms ought to be derived from the regular courtyard houses. It has indeed a small light well or 'lantern' in the middle; this in addition housed a cistern collecting rainwater which flushed the garderobe shafts via drainage channels seen in the basement chambers.

The Warkworth keep is a square with bevelled corners and polygonal turrets attached to the middle of the four sides, or, if you like, a Greek cross with bevelled corners superimposed on a square with bevelled edges. The basic shape is not the product of the C 15, for a close inspection of the fabric shows that it is a remodelling of an earlier, probably C 13, keep: traces of this only

survive at basement level, for at the level of the principal apartments all remains of the older structure seem to have been erased.
The evidence for the older keep is seen in the sides of the postern
at the N end of the W wall of the main square, where a C 15
refacing of an earlier wall can be seen, in the two-centred chamfered doorways of the basement chambers, in the contrast between
the rubble masonry of some internal walls and the ashlar of others,
and in the fact that some vaults are cut awkwardly round earlier
openings; at the foot of the mural stair near the NW corner the
springing of an earlier, slightly lower vault can be traced. It is
difficult to disentangle all this and draw out the plan of the earlier
keep, whether it was a square or whether the four projections were
part of the design from the first (or whether there were two pre-
C 15 phases). H. L. Honeyman pointed out that the overall plan
of the Warkworth keep (without the bevelled corners) is similar
to that at Trim in Ireland of c. 1200. But to return to the present
keep: it now rises to three storeys, and seen up the village street
it seems even higher. On that side there is a large panel displaying
the Percy lion, and higher up all round the keep are shields held
by angels. Above and behind the unembattled parapet rises a high
and slim turret with a semi-octagonal stair projection on the N.
It is a shape of great clarity and force. And whereas inside the
earlier keeps, even those with as much space as the White Tower
in London and Colchester (or Norham and Bamburgh), there are
on each floor no more than two or possibly three rooms and some
cells in the thickness of the walls, Warkworth has a complete
system of rooms arranged so as to make sense. On the ground
floor are guardrooms and cellars – all tunnel-vaulted – and four
staircases. The entrance is by a restored doorway on the W side
of the S projection, into a lobby with a pitfall beneath, and then
the largest of the basement chambers, from which a quite spacious
straight stair returns S over the entrance lobby to the ante-chamber
to the HALL. This is 12.2 by 7.6 metres (40 by 25 ft) in size, and
in the disposition of its features is modelled on the halls of less
congested houses. It runs through two floors with the minstrels'
gallery opening in two large depressed arches at the E end of it.
At the W end are the three doors to BUTTERY and PANTRY and
the main KITCHEN which lies in the NW corner and also goes up
through two floors. The dais was at the E end of the Hall. Here,
facing S, is the largest window in the keep, of two lights and so
high that it has two transoms. An adjacent window to the W was
converted into a fireplace in the C 16. Opposite this is a window
to the light well. A doorway on the N links the hall to the CHAPEL.
This is situated in the E projection, the bevelled corners making
a perfect polygonal apse. It has tall two-light windows; on either
side of the central one are brackets for images. As in the outer
ward chapel, the W part was two-storeyed, the E part as high as
the Hall. PISCINA and SEDILIA are well preserved, and again, as
if there were no problems of arrangement in so confined and
formalized a space, the chaplain had his SACRISTY just N of the
chancel, where it would be in a church. N of the chapel, but also
accessible by a passage from the Hall behind the light well, is
another living room, perhaps the solar or principal chamber, with
an inner chamber in the N projection. Both these rooms have

chambers above. Second-floor chambers above the buttery and pantry, and in the s projection above the ante-chamber, were restored and roofed by *Anthony Salvin* in 1853–8, when much of the s elevation was refaced.

From this description it will be patent how ingeniously all the comfort which a rich and powerful man might expect in his house at the end of the c14 was provided within a keep. Yet the accommodation the architect had designed can never have been regarded as more than subsidiary. For, as we have seen, apart from the hall in the keep there was a much larger hall in the outer ward, and the chapel there was also more spacious than that in the keep. However, Percy knew from experience how often and how long stays within an unassailable stronghold might have to be.

BIRLING MANOR, on the A1068 ¼ m. N. Mid-c18 house, of two near-contemporary builds (extension dated 1752). Ashlar four-bay front, with lintels tooled to represent voussoirs.

COQUET LODGE, ¾ m. w on the s bank of the river. An extremely picturesque group. Tudor-style house of *c.* 1840, beside a mid-c18 miller's house (the mill has gone) now divided into cottages. This has three storeys, with the top windows tucked beneath the eaves; the cottages and mid-c19 ranges with cartsheds and kennels enclose a triangular yard.

SHORTRIDGE HALL, 1 m. N. Now an old people's home. 1898 by *W. L. Newcombe* of Newcastle for Mr R. Deuchar. Roman Doric, with a big central stair hall.

WARKWORTH HERMITAGE
½ m. w of Warkworth

2000

One of the best-preserved and most elaborate cave-hermitages in the British Isles, in a wooded cliff on the N bank of the Coquet, and now only accessible by ferry. An extremely curious chapel and sacristy were cut out of the sandstone rock in *c.* 1330–40, with an adjacent domestic block built up against the cliff-face in the c15. The domestic parts had an entrance lobby from which one could turn l. into the hall, with a solar above, or r. into the kitchen. The walls of the hall and solar stand quite high but the kitchen is reduced to footings. A stair now rises from the site of the kitchen to the doorway of the chapel cut in the cliff above: there was obviously some sort of gallery here, as to the E, halfway up the rock-face, a flight of steps commences and winds up through a tunnel cut right through a spur of the cliff, to the hermit's garden on the slopes above. The roughly arched chapel door leads via a small porch or lobby to an inner doorway with a worn crucifix above. The chapel itself is 6.2 by 2.3 metres (20½ by 7½ ft) and is 'vaulted' in two bays, the groined vaulting resting on semi-octagonal wall shafts with moulded caps and bases. At the E end is an altar shelf with a cusped recess above; the detail of the shaft caps seems unfinished at the W end. The chapel is lit by a two-light window on the s, with worn relief carvings on its inner sill which may represent the Nativity. Behind the chapel is a parallel but narrower sacristy with a plain arched roof. This opens to the chapel by a doorway beneath a shield with the Emblems of the Passion, and also by both a cusped squint (so placed that the chaplain could see the altar from his bed in a recess near the w end of the sacristy) and a four-light traceried window. All the architectural detail, the vault, the altar and the window tracery, is cut *in situ* from the native rock. At the w end of the sacristy another door on the s opened into a third chamber immediately w of the chapel, with which it communicated by four strange little slits. The outer rock walls on the s and w of this apartment, and that at the w end of the sacristy, have either fallen away or been removed. There was presumably access from here to the solar in the c 15 domestic block.

Low Buston. *See* p. 384.

Morwick. *See* p. 401.

Low Buston. *See* p. 384.

Morwick. *See* p. 401.

0020
WEETWOOD
2 m. e of Wooler

Weetwood Hall. Externally late c 18, with a three-bay centre and Venetian windows in the slightly projecting wings, but on the rear elevation there are two large buttresses and, inside, the walls of a tower. – Dovecote in the garden; square with a pyramid roof.

Weetwood Bridge. Narrow hump-backed bridge, very picturesque in its setting. Probably c 16; rebuilt in the c 18. Elegant single arch flanked by shallow pilasters, each with a niche. On the N side the parapets end in circular piers with conical finials.

1090
WELDON BRIDGE
1½ m. s of Longframlington

A fine c 18 bridge of asymmetric composition, designed very much with flood conditions in mind, as newly built bridges here had been swept away in 1744 and 1752; this was their replacement. Three segmental arches with stepped keystones, the N one flanked by smaller flood and mill-race arches, and a keyed circular opening in the spandrel between the s two. Some features are reminiscent of Coldstream Bridge by Reid and Smeaton, but there is no documented architect here. N of the bridge, the Angler's Arms, a five-bay c 18 brick house with a projecting castellated early c 19 wing.

Weldon Mill. The last complete watermill to be built in the county, being totally reconstructed after a serious fire in 1891. Milling continued until 1964, and the building was converted into domestic accommodation in the early 1980s. The waterwheel was in a lean-to at the gable end of the four-storey building; an adjoining building housed a low kiln. The whole is constructed of an attractive honey-coloured sandstone.

WELTON HALL *see* HORSLEY-ON-THE-HILL

WEST BITCHFIELD TOWER

¾ m. s of Belsay

0070

A c 14 tower with an attached c 17 house, as at Halton or nearby Belsay. The tower in fact shows some similarities to Belsay. It clearly had at least one bartizan of the same type as at Belsay, though only the corbel remains on the SE corner. It also has a doorway inside the present hall in the same position and of the same mouldings as the entrance to the tower at Belsay, that is a pointed arch with a continuous chamfered surround. The tower is much smaller than Belsay, however – just *c.* 9.5 by 7 metres (31 by 23 ft) – and simpler in its plan, with a vaulted ground floor, two rooms above and a mural stair. What is particularly impressive about West Bitchfield is that the tower is fully inhabited. It was ruinous and was restored in *c.* 1935 by *Caröe* and *Lord Gort,* with taste as well as enthusiasm (the lavatory is in the garderobe niche and the plumbing goes down the old chute). The tower windows, apart from several slit windows and one c 16 window with a moulded surround, are all also of the 1930s, but equally sensitively done.

The attached house has a date, 1622, inside. It was a hall range, with a kitchen at the opposite end to the tower. Both hall and kitchen have huge external chimneystacks on the rear wall and the kitchen (now the dining room) has an equally huge fireplace with a segmental lintel. The large hall fireplace has a bolection-moulded surround, symptomatic of the next stage of development at the house. It was refronted in the last quarter of the c 17 and given a six-bay façade. The doorway has a bolection-moulded surround, a pulvinated oak-leaf frieze and a scrolled pediment. There are cross windows, with roll-moulded sills and cornices on the ground floor. The crosses themselves, however, are renewals of the 1930s; at the same time the top cornice and the parapet were added and the sundial dated 1711 was brought from Belsay and placed above the door. Also in 1935, Caröe added a wing on the E side in similar style.

In front of the house a late c 17 WALLED GARDEN with ornamental gatepiers on the s side, and two doors with bolection-moulded surrounds on the E and W sides.

WEST CHEVINGTON

2 m. NW of Widdrington

2090

WEST CHEVINGTON FARMHOUSE. An oddity in Northumberland. Brick centre of *c.* 1700, with later c 18 wings producing an H-plan. Double band at first-floor level, flat-arched windows and tumbled-in gables.

BULLOCK'S HALL, ¾ m. NE. The site of a medieval CHAPEL N of the road is marked by a prominent mound and a pile of dressed stones, with a few c 14 or c 15 architectural fragments.

WEST EALINGHAM
2 m. S of Bellingham

About 275 metres E and 275 metres W of the present farm are two
ruined bastles of the usual type. Both stand at least in part to
eaves height and both have their ground-floor doorways.

WEST SLEEKBURN
2½ m. NE of Bedlington

ST PETER. 1845 by *Joseph Clarke*. Stone. Transitional style, with
apse; the nave aisles were never built and the arcades remain
bricked up.

WEST WHARMLEY
3½ m. W of Hexham

This farm, well sited on a little hill, seems to have been a defensible
complex of C 16 or early C 17 buildings after the fashion of Wooley
(*see* Allendale). The present farmhouse is a slightly superior ashlar-
fronted building of *c.* 1835, but a long L-plan wing to the E has
thick rubble walls, blocked bastle-type doorways and small slit
windows.

WEST WHELPINGTON *see* KIRKWHELPINGTON

WHALTON

ST MARY MAGDALENE. The W tower is probably C 11. Its openings have been altered, except on the W of the belfry, where
there is a single round-headed light, with a segmental-topped one
directly below. The tall round tower arch is of Saxon rather
than Norman proportions, with chamfers which look like a later
modification. The C 12 W respond of the N aisle, a half-drum with
a scalloped cap, shows that there was at least a N aisle by the
early C 12, but the building took on its present form after a
comprehensive early C 13 remodelling. From this survive the W
lancets of the aisles (the S with a trefoiled rere-arch, the N
shouldered), and the blocked lancets set unusually low in the S
aisle wall. Inside, the double-chamfered three-bay arcades are of
the same date, with broach stops, on slender octagonal piers with
simple moulded capitals. So is the double-chamfered chancel arch
on responds with nail-head; the hoodmould towards the nave
ends in a dragonhead stop above the line of the (removed) rood
beam. The chancel has a two-bay N arcade to the Ogle Chapel.
This has round double-chamfered arches on a central pier with
big vertical dogtooth ornament between filleted angle shafts with

carved masks at the top. At the E end of the arcade is a large corbel with the Ogle arms. There is more nail-head on the responds of the arch from the chapel to the N aisle. The S wall of the chancel is complicated, with a piscina, traces of sedilia, and several blocked openings. There is C 14 reticulated tracery in the chancel E and S aisle E windows. Apart from the W window, a rare survival from the late C 18 (a sash in an arch with imposts and hoodmould), most of the other fenestration has been renewed: the chancel windows date to an 1890 restoration by *Hicks & Charlewood*. The S porch is of 1908. – FONT. Octagonal; probably C 15. – CLOCK. Late C 18 clock mechanism, and single-handed clock face on the E side of the tower. – STAINED GLASS. E window of 1877 by *Kempe*. – MONUMENTS. In the S aisle a tomb recess with a four-centred arch holds a C 13 CROSS SLAB. – Early armorial floor slabs (1564, 1566 and 1613) in the Ogle Chapel. – Also in the Ogle Chapel, wall monuments to John Ogle † 1831, with a kneeling female figure, and to Sara Ogle † 1846, both by *E. H. Baily*.

MANOR HOUSE. An interesting conversion job of *Sir Edwin Lutyens*, 1908–9, for Mrs Eustace Smith. He linked up two older houses, Old Whalton Manor (late C 17 or early C 18, already linked to three cottages by *Lorimer* in the late C 19) and Whalton Mansion, dated 1729. His connecting block has a tripartite gateway with an elliptical central arch, set back behind a fancifully paved approach. The three windows above have aprons and odd projecting blocks of stone between them. To the rear the gateway is flanked by quadrant-shaped rock-faced projections with semi-conical roofs that give a distinctly medieval and military feel, overlooking a concentrically paved yard. Inside, the entrance passage is aisled and groin-vaulted: from it opens a stone-walled hall with Gibbs surrounds to its doorways and a moulded fire-place. From this a stone winder stair with a ribbed barrel vault leads up to the first floor, where the former dining room (now a bedroom) is circular, with a high domed ceiling: it is said to have been a model for the Viceroy's throne room at New Delhi. The W part of the house, the old Whalton Mansion, is now a separate dwelling (WEST MANOR HOUSE) again. It is a little-altered five-bay house and has a moulded doorway with a shaped top, and windows with triple keystones. Contemporary stair inside. Behind the house Lutyens laid out a garden with a pergola, various terrace walls and two SUMMERHOUSES, one chaste and classical and the other a jolly, almost nautical little structure, hexagonal with a round window and a tall pyramidal roof. On the S side of the road, opposite the E end of the house, is a section of wall with a reset medieval ogee-arched doorway, tracery fragments and three CROSS-SLABS, probably from the parish church.

The uncommonly pretty VILLAGE street is long and almost broad enough to be termed a green. It has a number of good buildings. W of the Manor House (at the E end of the street) is the early C 18 MANOR COTTAGE and then LAUNDRY COTTAGE, early C 20 and probably by *Lutyens*, with gabled dormers and an almost Cotswold look. Beyond an early C 19 terrace is WHALTON HOUSE, mid-C 18 with a late C 19 extension, ashlar-fronted with rusticated quoins and architraves. Towards the W end of the village, more C 18 houses.

On the s side of the village, to the E of the lane running down past the church, is the OLD RECTORY. The w wing is C 14 or C 15, and was probably a tower; it has a basement of twin vaulted chambers with a mural stair. The thick walls of the kitchen wing suggest that the tower formed the solar end of a hall-and-cross-wings house, or that the house had attained this form by the C 16. The centre part was rebuilt early in the C 18 with a five-bay s front. The C 19 added bay windows and extended the kitchen wing to the N. At the SW corner of the garden a pier with an iron pivot on top, and a stepped approach rather like a mounting block on the opposite side of the lane, are the remains of the vicar's private swing-footbridge, probably mid-C 19. When the bridge was in position, spanning the deeply sunk lane, one knew that the vicar was in church and that the service had started. Further w, the SEVEN STARS, a late C 18 three-bay former inn, and SOUTH SIDE, a row of single-storey cottages ending in a two-storey house dated 1715, with, inside, remains of the original firehood bressumer and a salt box recess.

WHALTON MILL, $\frac{3}{4}$m. s. Picturesque but ruinous group of C 18 buildings; the house was remodelled c. 1840.

KIPLAW, $\frac{3}{4}$m. w. Five-bay farmhouse, dated 1752 on the lintel of the central chamfered doorway, with a C 19 wing.

OGLE. See p. 534.

7050   WHITFIELD

The village lies amongst trees in the pleasantly wooded valley of the West Allen.

ST JOHN, on the Plenmeller road. Built in 1790 by *Newton* to replace a medieval building. Three bays of the nave and a w tower were demolished in 1859 to provide stone for the new Holy Trinity Church (*see* below). The surviving one-bay nave and chancel were rewindowed late in the C 19. Plain late C 18 unmoulded chancel arch. – MONUMENTS. Part of an elaborate late C 12 coped GRAVE COVER with acanthus leaves and an inscription on the ridge. – Wall tablet to W. H. Ord † 1838, by *Gaffin*, with mourning *putti*.

HOLY TRINITY, in the valley bottom. 1859–60 by *A. B. Higham*. An ambitious church in the E.E. style, with lancet windows, aisles, transepts and a crossing-tower with spire. Contemporary fittings, including some nice STAINED GLASS by *Powell & Sons*; there is also some *Kempe* glass of 1901.

WHITFIELD HALL. 1785 by *William Newton*, incorporating earlier fabric; remodelled and a storey added in 1856. Five-bay s front with a central tripartite ground-floor window reset in a porch of 1969. Remains of the medieval Whitfield Tower are said to be incorporated in the rear wing, but nothing recognizable survives. – COACH-HOUSE AND STABLES. Dated 1786. – In the garden, bronze STATUES of Caprice and Thorsulus, 1891 and 1892 by *Frampton* (*see* Introduction, p. 109), and Apenthe, 1893, by *Luichen*.

TOLLHOUSE, $\frac{1}{2}$m. s of the Hall. On the Hexham-to-Alston Turnpike (1778), but absorbed into the Alston Roads Turnpike of

1824. One-and-a-half storeys; the gable facing the road has a bay window. In the mildly Tudor style of many of the local estate buildings.

MONK, $\frac{1}{4}$ m. SE. In the farm buildings, a long range of bastle-type buildings. The oldest part, at the S end, is an almost square building with a blocked two-centred arch (now internal) which hints at medieval origins ('la Menke' is mentioned in 1547). It may have been carried up an extra storey, as may the N end section, which now has a corbelled-out dovecote capping its gable end which looks as if it might be an adaptation of a lookout turret (cf. Melkridge) or a large stack. The possible arrangement of the centre part of the range being flanked by two 'towers' suggests a degree of elaboration not normally associated with Northumberland farmsteads of the period; there is a tradition that the farm belonged to Hexham Priory. A short distance SW is a CRUCK BARN; the three trusses spring from corbels 1.5 metres (5 ft) above the floor. The barn seems to have been reconstructed in the late C 18 or C 19.

WESTSIDE, $\frac{1}{2}$ m. E. A stronghouse of c. 1610 now forms an outbuilding. Both ground- and first-floor doors, with flat-pointed heads in square frames, are on the S; the upper floor has chamfered windows, including one of two lights. Its details show that it was a house of higher status than the usual bastles common hereabouts.

CUPOLA BRIDGE, 2 m. N on the A686. A fine bridge of three segmental arches, on the turnpike (Act of 1778); curved cutwaters. The name probably relates to the lead smelting mill that stood nearby.

WHITLEY BAY   3070

The manors of Whitley and Monkseaton were granted by Henry I to Richard, Abbot of St Albans, and to the monks of Tynemouth. The Urban District of Monkseaton and Whitley was formed in 1873 and became a municipal borough in 1954. By the end of the C 19 the railways had made it possible for people to work in Newcastle and live in Whitley Bay, and also for those who lived in Newcastle to come to the sands for the day without much expense. The C 20 also brought holidaymakers from Scottish towns and cities, so Whitley Bay became both a popular holiday resort and a dormitory for Newcastle.

ST PAUL, Park View. 1864 by *Salvin*, at the expense of the Duke of Northumberland. Not a church of much architectural merit. E.E., in snecked sandstone. Three-stage tower with a mask corbel table under a stumpy octagonal spire. – STAINED GLASS. W window to William †1883, son of W. B. Wilkinson of Newcastle, who in 1854 patented a successful reinforced concrete. – N aisle first window by *Wailes & Strang*. – Third window, better than the rest of the building, dated 1901, by *Camm & Co.* of Smethwick. – LYCHGATE. 1894 by *W. S. Hicks*.

ST EDWARD (R.C.), Park Parade. 1928 by *E. J. Kay*. Brick Romanesque with a squat crossing-tower.

RAILWAY STATION, Station Road. 1910 by *William Bell* for the North Eastern Railway Company. Free Baroque, in cheerful brick, ashlar and faience. Fat Ionic pilasters in the arcaded ticket office, and cast-iron Ionic columns in the seven-bay train shed. Stone garlands abound on the prominent clock tower, which lends some distinction to an undistinguished neighbourhood.

RAILWAY STATION, Earsdon Road, West Monkseaton. 1936. International style, with curved shops flanking the entrance. White walls, metal windowframes, flat roof.

THE SPANISH CITY, Promenade. A theatre and amusement arcade of 1908–10 for Whitley Pleasure Gardens Ltd by *Cackett & Burns Dick*, with *L. G. Mouchel* as engineers for the construction in *Hennebique* patent ferro-concrete. It is the symbol of the resort, and a landmark in the otherwise unremarkable string of buildings along the sea-front. The high and stately dome (possibly one of the earliest in Britain to be built of ferro-concrete) rises behind a three-bay entrance flanked by towers topped by lively bronze figures. The four-bay wings contain the usual seaside shops.

BEACON HOUSE, Western Way, behind The Links, *c.* 1 m. N of the Spanish City. By *Ryder & Yates*; completed in 1962. Eleven storeys high, with a central tier of recessed stair balconies over the entrance. Four blocks were intended.

ST MARY'S ISLAND, at the N end of the bay, is worth visiting for the experience of walking across at low tide to reach a group of simple stone cottages of *c.* 1800 with pantiled roofs and gabled dormers. The 38-metre-high (125-ft) LIGHTHOUSE of 1897–8 (now a natural history information centre) rises behind them.

EARSDON. *See* p. 261.

6040

WHITLEY CASTLE
2 m. NW of Alston (Cumbria)

A Roman fort of unusual design on the Maiden Way from Kirkby Thore near Appleby to Carvoran on the Stanegate. The normal playing-card shape was distorted into a lozenge to make the best use of the restricted summit of a natural knoll that projects from the E slopes of Great Heaplaw: an excellent vantage point commanding the road and the valley. The defences are exceptionally deep: along the NW side there are five ramparts, and on the SW (where the approach is almost level) the defences bulge outwards to accommodate three additional but much shorter ramparts. A mere three or four was thought sufficient on the NE and SE. The innermost line, representing the fort-wall, is dignified by the provision of an external berm. These defences are unlikely to be of a single period, for the three outer lines stop abruptly close to the NE corner, evidently respecting the site of the fort's external bath-house, excavated *c.* 1810.

The layout of the interior of the fort is not readily apparent and little is known of the site's history. It was occupied *c.* 130 (and possibly earlier) but may have been briefly abandoned in the mid-c 2. Thereafter occupation may have continued into the mid-c 4.

WHITLEY CHAPEL
4 m. s of Hexham

Little more than a hamlet, but nevertheless the largest settlement to
be found within the civil parish of Hexhamshire. It stands on a spur
between the valleys of the Devil's Water and the Rowley Burn.

St Helen. 1742. Five-bay rectangle. Round-arched doorway with
    imposts and keystone, and windows of twin basket-arched lights.
    Later c 19 are the w vestry and n windows. The e window,
    however, is of three pointed lights within a single arch, and looks
    a c 13 piece reset from a previous building.
Methodist Chapel, White Hall. Dated 1871, with the usual
    gable-end porch flanked by round-arched windows.
Holme House, ½ m. sw. An outbuilding n of the house is a well-
    preserved bastle house with both byre and first-floor doorways,
    square-headed and chamfered, in the long s wall.
Steel, 1 m. e. c 16 and later range, now farm buildings, tra-
    ditionally associated with Hexham Priory. Two arched doorways
    and several blocked mullioned windows. A building which
    deserves further attention.
Low Ardley, 1½ m. nw. The farmhouse incorporates an almost
    square structure of heavy rubble with megalithic quoins, with
    walls up to 1.8 metres (6 ft) thick. Was it a bastle or a vernacular
    version of a small tower-house?
White Hall Farmhouse, 2 m. s. Bastle house, remodelled in
    1755 (date on door lintel), still with mullioned windows. ¼ m. se
    is Stone House, now derelict, with mullioned windows and an
    upper-cruck roof.
Hesleywell, 3 m. s. Another bastle house, now a farm building.
    Byre door with gabled monolithic head in the long s wall and
    some slit windows. Unusually sophisticated roof structure, with
    arched collars and notched multi-pegged joints.
boundary stones. Along the parish boundaries on the high
    moorlands are many good-quality c 18 stones with flat or arched
    tops and the incised initials of various landowners and estates.

WHITTINGHAM

St Bartholomew. It throws a significant light on the Victorian
    mentality that Whittingham in 1840 decided to pull down the
    existing Anglo-Saxon tower and rebuild it bigger and better in
    Gothic. In fact, to do Whittingham justice, it was not the village
    but the new vicar, the Rev. Goodenough, who was responsible
    and in the event the job was not completed, so that the lower
    parts remain unmistakably Saxon. They are still linked to the w
    wall of the Saxon nave. The quoins (also those at the e end of the
    nave) are the best in the county. They are long-and-short work,
    a style not found elsewhere in Northumberland and not normally

associated with the North. Adjoining the Saxon work on the s side is c 13 walling with a small trefoil-headed window. The lower courses of the aisle walls are also medieval, and one window with intersecting tracery in the N aisle is partly original. Another, similar, in the N transept now opens into the vestry. The chancel was rebuilt c. 1725 and then extended and gothicized in 1871 by *F. R. Wilson*. The s porch is old, probably c 14, with a pointed tunnel vault strengthened by two chamfered transverse ribs.

The architect responsible for the vandalism to the tower and the virtual rebuilding of the aisles was *John Green*. He left his mark inside also by replacing the existing N arcade. It had been Norman, with round piers, it was now made imitation c 13 – perhaps an even less comprehensible act than what was done to the tower. The s arcade and transept are indeed original late c 13. The arcade is of three bays, with octagonal piers and double-chamfered arches with broaches. The E pier starts with big dog-tooth instead, but the motif was given up after only two had been carved. The responds are also original. The arches have hoodmoulds starting on disks with rosettes. To return to the beginning, though, the tower arch is once again unmistakably Saxon. It is similar to Corbridge and has unmoulded imposts. At the w end of the N arcade is a short stretch of solid wall with a blocked c 11 arch. The chancel arch is by Wilson but the filleted, semicircular responds are c 13 and original. – FURNISHINGS. All of 1906 by *Hicks & Charlewood*. – STAINED GLASS. E window of 1880, vigorous, with figures of saints and symbols of the Evangelists. Sadly unsigned. – MONUMENT. In the N transept by *Craigs* to Reginald Goodenough, killed at Sebastopol (1854). Military emblems above the inscription. – In the churchyard, a plain medieval CROSS HEAD, reset in a cross base.

ST MARY (R.C.), 1 m. N. Reticent neo-Norman of 1877–81 by *Dunn and Hansom*. By the s door an elaborate, richly carved Celtic-style cross of 1881 to Edward Clavering of Callaly, the benefactor of the church.

WHITTINGHAM TOWER, by the village green. Probably c 14 in origin. The lowest courses of stonework are of this period. Above that, stonework which may be c 16 or c 17. The round-headed s doorway with a continuous chamfer looks early c 17. Old masonry continues to the second-floor sill level on three sides and to the first floor on the fourth side. The tower became ruinous and was restored in 1845 by Lady Ravensworth. Her additions can be clearly seen and, just in case we should miss it, she told us all about it in an inscription above her new door.

By the munificence and Piety of
LADY RAVENSWORTH
This ancient Tower which was formerly
Used by the village as a place of refuge
In time of rapine and insecurity
Was repaired and otherwise embellished
For the use and benefit of the deserving Poor
A.D. 1845

The ground floor is tunnel-vaulted.

RAVENSWORTH FOUNTAIN, at the foot of the pretty village green. Designed in 1905 by *George Reavell*. Octagonal basin, with a statue of the third Earl of Ravensworth and his dog set rather incongruously but agreeably in the middle.

The CASTLE INN and CASTLE FARM form the entrance to the village from the S. The inn is three storeys, *c.* 1830. The farmhouse attached to its r. is lower; five bays, early C 18, with a stone door surround and raised stone surrounds to the windows. The back of the building is older. For the OLD BUTCHERS SHOP, *see* p. 81.

WHITTINGHAM STATION, 1½ m. E, just off the A697. Disused. 1887 by *Bell* of York for the Alnwick–Cornhill branch of the North-Eastern Railway. An island station, the only one on this line, with nice cast-iron supports to the canopies.

ESLINGTON PARK. *See* p. 272.

WHITTON
½ m. s of Rothbury

WHITTON TOWER. A C 14 tower-house with an attached Tudor-style house of the mid-C 19. The tower was a 'vicar's pele', the home of the vicars of Rothbury. It is remarkable for having vaults on two of its four storeys. The lowest is a real basement, dug into the bank that the house stands on and only half the width of the house. It is entered by a doorway with a shouldered lintel. The ground floor has a pointed tunnel vault divided into two rooms by a later wall. The entrance has a wall-passage whose outer and inner doorways have two-centred arches and continuous chamfers. A third doorway with a shouldered lintel leads from this passage to the base of the stone spiral stair. Similar doorways lead from the stairs on each floor. The battlements and turrets have been renewed.

SHARP'S FOLLY. In the 1720s the Vicar of Rothbury, Archdeacon Thomas Sharp, not satisfied with his genuine tower, built a folly tower close to his gardens, on a hill with a vista to the s. His tower is round and has below its battlements a classical cornice. Doorway and windows are also classically arched. The Gothic Revival had not yet properly arrived. The idea of an embattled tower at such an early date may be connected with Vanbrugh's visits to the county. The Archdeacon is said to have built his tower partly to alleviate local unemployment and partly to satisfy his taste for astronomy and astrology.

WHITTON GRANGE. 1921 by *Robert Mauchlen* for Sir Angus Watson. The best building of its date in the county. The front is in a quite conventional but very perfect late C 17 style. The rear is a much freer and irregular composition, with an apsidal stair projection. The GARDENS are also by *Mauchlen*, very much in the Gertrude Jekyll style. They incorporate the base of a medieval tower, the walls in places standing to *c.* 2.7 metres (9 ft). The lower courses of the basement vault are visible. To the rear of this, built into a wall of 1921, there is a C 14 piscina with trefoiled head and petalled drain. It may be the one recorded at Whitton Tower in the c 19 and since lost.

WHITTONSTALL

ST PHILIP AND ST JAMES. 1830 by *Jonathan Marshall* (Goodhart-Rendel) with straight-headed mullioned windows under hood-moulds, and a small embattled w tower. More ambitious chancel of 1893 in snecked stone. Inside, fragment of a c 13 respond. – MONUMENT. c 13 slab with no cross, only a centrally placed sword, a type commoner towards the Border.

OLD VICARAGE. About the same date as the church. Three-bay house with projecting gabled centrepiece with stair window strangely placed above the front door.

WIDDRINGTON

HOLY TRINITY. Late c 12 N arcade of two bays, with short, thick circular pier, plainest moulded capital and double-chamfered arches. s arcade mid-c 14 with octagonal piers and double-chamfered pointed arches. The chancel arch, nave arcade, arch from chapel to chancel and arch between chapel and aisle all oddly spring from the same pier. The c 14 chancel has a renewed E window with flowing tracery and s windows which are smallish, of two ogee-headed lights under a straight head. The s aisle windows are identical. The N aisle (long demolished) was rebuilt in the late c 19. The s doorway should be, according to its forms, earlier than the s windows. It looks like reused c 13 material. In the chancel, SEDILIA made simply by taking down the sill of a window to seat level. Next to it a big pointed-trefoiled PISCINA. But at the E corner of the sedilia a small pillar piscina as well which seems to be original. Opposite are two recesses, one perhaps for a tomb and the other an Easter Sepulchre. – MONUMENT. c 13 CROSS SLAB as inner lintel to vestry door.

UNITED REFORMED CHURCH. 1893. Lancet style, with low eaves. The porch is carried up as a square tower capped by an octagonal belfry and shingled spire.

WIDDRINGTON CASTLE. The 'Tower of Widdrington', built *c.* 1341 and later part of a great house, stood immediately E of the church. Old drawings show two towers (one looking very like Belsay), with a hall block between. Earthworks and a few exposed footings further E in the same field seem to relate to a Gothick structure, more folly than house, which replaced it in the mid-c 18 and had a relatively short life.

CHIBBURN. *See* p. 226.

DRURIDGE. *See* p. 256.

WEST CHEVINGTON. *See* p. 621.

WILLIMOTESWICK

1 m. w of Beltingham

A fortified manor of the Ridleys. The buildings seem to have been arranged around a rectangular yard with the house on the s. The house occupies the site of what seems to have been a double-ended hall with narrow towers at each end of the cross wings, a variant on the Langley Castle plan. The E wing and its towers survive, the remainder having been rebuilt *c.* 1900 in Tudor style, reusing c 16 moulded doorways at each end of the screens passage. The GATEHOUSE to the NE is more or less intact, with its tunnel-vaulted carriageway, mullioned windows and corbelled-out parapet. Both house and gatehouse look late c 15 or early c 16, although the plan of the former suggests that earlier fabric may be incorporated; more c 16 features in the E range, and old walling at the rear of the farm buildings on the N.

At PARTRIDGE NEST, ½ m. NE, the late c 18 farmhouse was altered and extended in the early c 19, reusing many features (moulded door and window surrounds, and good-quality c 16 moulded beams inside) presumably from Willimoteswick.

WILLINGTON *see* WALLSEND

WITTON SHIELDS

1½ m. E of Netherwitton

WITTON SHIELDS TOWER is a stronghouse, dated 1608, quite similar to nearby Stanton Old Hall (and cf. Doddington). The entrance is into the base of a gabled stair wing or turret projecting from the centre of the s wall. At first sight the two-storey house appears remarkably complete, but it was in fact shorn of a top floor (which had contained an early Roman Catholic chapel) *c.* 1914, the old roof trusses being reset at a lower level. The rear outshut is of 1680. The garden wall to the SW incorporates the remains of an earlier (c 16?) house.

WOODBURN

There are two settlements, West Woodburn on the A68 and East Woodburn 1 m. to the E.

ALL SAINTS, East Woodburn. 1906 by *Hicks & Charlewood*. An excellent small church with equally excellent woodwork of 1923 by *Hedley & Co.*

There are two BASTLE HOUSES at or near East Woodburn. One, just a fragment incorporated in the farm buildings at TOWN FOOT farm, has a Roman altar from Risingham (*see* below) built into the fabric. It has an inscription to the native god Cocidius and a hunting scene. HAREWALLS, 1 m. E, is relatively complete and still used as a house.

Between East and West Woodburn, CHERRY TREE COTTAGE is another bastle still in use as a house.

89 LOW LEAM, 1 m. W of West Woodburn, has two BASTLES. One, LOW CLEUGHS, on the hillside 600 metres N of the farm, is in ruins but is just a little above average in the quality of its masonry and details. It is of *c.* 1600 and is also unusual in having the upper doorway directly over the lower in the middle of one of the long sides (cf. Westside, near Whitfield, and Shittleheugh, near Otterburn). The other bastle is embedded in the farm buildings at Low Leam. The original lower doorway on the N gable end has a massive lintel with a relieving arch over. Not vaulted, but the very low ceiling of the ground floor has close-set original oak beams.

RISINGHAM ROMAN FORT, 600 metres SW of West Woodburn. An outpost of Hadrian's Wall, built to guard Dere Street at the crossing of the River Rede. The raised platform of the fort, playing-card-shaped, is quite clear as an earthwork (surrounded by ridge and furrow), but masonry is visible only for a short stretch round the outer face of the NE angle. Part of the N side has been eroded by the river. The fort originally faced S but was later reorientated to face W, towards Dere Street. The causeway to the gap in the defences marking the W gate can be seen. The fort was apparently not occupied until the C 2 and may have been abandoned within a few decades. From the beginning of the C 3, however, occupation was continuous until the site was finally given up, probably in the early C 4. In a fort this size there can hardly have been room for its C 3 garrison, which included a unit of scouts and also Swiss pikemen; many troops must have been out-stationed, patrolling far into the Borders. The interior of the fort is almost entirely occupied by the turf-covered footings of later buildings, the last of which was occupied into the early C 19.

ROBIN OF RISINGHAM, at Parkhead Farm, 1 m. SE. Only the lower portion of this Roman sculpture survives, cut in relief on a detached rock-face. The upper part was cut up for gateposts in 1819 to rid the farmer of trespassing visitors. Below a panel for an inscription stood the hunting god Silvanus dressed as an archer, in a belted tunic, with a cloak slung over his shoulder, a quiver on his back and his bow raised; in the other hand he held a purse or a rabbit.

RIDSDALE IRONWORKS, 2 m. SE. Established in 1836, closed down *c.* 1848. It had three blast furnaces with a double-beam blowing engine. The site was substantially dismantled *c.* 1865, but the blowing engine house remains, resembling, in this windswept spot, nothing less than a Border stronghold. Immediately to the N are two buildings which were probably tapping floors, while to the S are the earthworks of coke ovens, calciners and tramways. The entire site is a scheduled ancient monument.

WOODHORN

ST MARY (now Woodhorn Church Museum). Woodhorn may be the 'Wudecestre' (Woodchester) granted by Ceolwulf to the Lindisfarne Community in 739. Externally the church is not promising; except for some masonry in the tower, everything is from an 1842–3 restoration by *B. & J. Green* of Newcastle. Some features, such as the tower W window and the chancel fenestration, including the three E lancets, seem to be a copy of what was there before. The upper parts of the tower are the Greens', and of a rather atrocious neo-Norman with an absurdly top-heavy arcaded parapet. The only hint of the interesting interior is the nave SW quoin of big irregular blocks. Inside, the church is much more worthwhile. Pre-Conquest work, probably of the early C 11, is evident in the nave walls, with the W arch of each arcade cutting into an early single-splayed window. That on the S has an extraordinary incised pattern of concentric circles on its external lintel; is this intentional decoration or (as some have suggested) just an elaborate keying for plaster? The base of the tower may be C 11 too, although the single-stepped round arch is too simple to be used as evidence. The two W bays of each arcade are C 12: the N arcade early in the century, with a squat circular pier carrying a many-scalloped capital and plain square arches, the S arcade a little later with nail-head ornament on the pier bases (the capitals are recut) and stepped arches. Each arcade has a taller C 13 eastern arch opening to a former transept. That on the N has filleted roll mouldings, and a triple-shafted E respond with stiffleaf foliage and a mask; the S arch is double-chamfered. The chancel arch is also C 13 and double-chamfered, on twin-shafted corbels. The chancel itself was wholly rebuilt by the Greens on C 13 foundations; excavations have disclosed the footings of an earlier apse, presumably C 11, beneath its floor. – SCULPTURE. In the chancel the head and two shaft fragments of a C 11 cross show affinities with contemporary sculpture at Durham. – Two medieval BELLS now displayed in chancel. – MONUMENTS. Several C 12–14 CROSS SLABS (some built into the porch and W wall of nave). Some have been recently brought from the Society of Antiquaries' collection at Newcastle, and one inscribed slab from the Kirkhill Chapel site at Hepple near Rothbury. – C 13 effigy of a lady, attributed to Agnes de Valence. Above her head is a canopy with, on its top, a carving of the Virgin seated, worshipped by two kneeling figures. Also the very unusual and charming motif of four handmaids, two holding her feet, two her veil. – Elizabeth Addison † 1807, nice tablet with weeping female figure leaning over an urn; unsigned. – Tablets of 1828 and 1830 by *Davies*.

VICARAGE (now an old people's home), W of the church. Quite a large house, of several C 18 and early C 19 dates.

WINDMILL. *c.* 1880; probably the last windmill to be built in Northumberland. It seems to have ceased operation *c.* 1900. Tapered tower in ashlar masonry, cleaned and externally restored in the 1970s. The outer wall has curve-profiled corbels and high-level sockets which indicate a former reefing stage. The mill cap disappeared early this century, but the sail-stocks and windshaft remained until *c.* 1970, when they were lowered to the ground

and broken up. Otherwise the mill is fairly intact, apart from
rotted floors.

WOODHORN COLLIERY. *See* Ashington.

WOODHOUSES BASTLE *see* HOLYSTONE

WOOLAW *see* ROCHESTER

WOOLER

The best thing perhaps about Wooler is its position on a hill, with
the grey and red roofs, the church rising above them, the little river
below and the hills to the w. However, the town is agreeable in
itself, quite tightly clustered with rows of c 18 and c 19 houses, plain
but unspoilt. Among them no major buildings, but several worthy
of attention.

ST MARY. Wide aisleless nave of 1765 with a dated sundial and a
   moulded cornice. w tower heightened and the w vestries added
   1834. Most of the details were gothicized by *F. R. Wilson* in 1873.
   The chancel is an addition of 1912–13. – STAINED GLASS. An
   attractive w window of 1903 by *Percy Bacon & Bros.* – MONU-
   MENTS. Wall tablets by *Jopling* of Gateshead (1824) and *Davies*
   of Newcastle (1836).

ST NINIAN (R.C.). 1856 by *Goldie*, whose work is commemorated
   in a s aisle window. In the late Geometrical style, not without
   personality. The tower rises over the sw porch and carries a
   saddleback roof. – STAINED GLASS. E window by *Wailes*, 1856.

UNITED REFORMED CHURCH, Cheviot Street. Originally an
   English Presbyterian Church of 1784 of which only the walls
   and the general shape remain. Gothicized and refurnished by
   Stevenson of Berwick in the 1870s and remodelled again by *George
   Reavell* in 1904. The style is Perp, but the detail, particularly of
   the tower and the rainwater heads, is *art nouveau* and of some
   character. The STAINED GLASS is also in a restrained *art nouveau*
   style throughout.

MASONIC HALL, High Street. Formerly the Methodist chapel,
   built in 1818, with the porch added a little later. Typical of the
   date. Tall round-headed windows with intersecting glazing bars.

POLICE STATION, Church Street. 1850, enlarged in 1887. Tudor,
   with a heavy studded door and diamond-paned casement
   windows.

CASTLE. A steeply flanked narrow promontory, once commanding
   the Wooler Water, rises abruptly from the E side of Church Street.
   Eminently defensible but with no sure sign of earthworks, it is
   crowned by a 1920s neo-Celtic War Memorial (a ringed cross)
   and by some massive chunks of rough and tumbled mortared
   rubble. These fragments are all that survive of a tower built *c.*
   1500; although its position was described in 1541 as 'a mervelous

convenyent place for the defence of the countrye thereaboute', it was by then already in decay. (A castle at Wooler was described as a 'waste motte' in 1254, but this could equally well have been Green Castle (*see* below).)

PERAMBULATION. Standing in the MARKET PLACE facing the church, most of the best buildings are close at hand. All of them, it should be stressed, are minor. To the r., on the corner of GLENDALE ROAD, is the BANK OF SCOTLAND, 1904 by *F. W. Rich*. HIGH STREET starts with the RED LION INN, a C19 scored stucco façade with a castellated bay window, and the BLACK BULL opposite, another large pub, remodelled in 1910 by *George Reavell* in the Arts-and-Crafts style. Beyond these are several good C19 shopfronts, especially Messrs PRINGLE & CO., which has thin decorative *art nouveau* glazing bars and lettering. BARCLAYS BANK is a late C19 classical building, quite freely composed. The street ends with LORETO, set back behind its garden walls next to the Catholic church. Built in the late C18 as the town house of Count Horace St Paul of Ewart Park (q.v.). Quite a large three-bay ashlar house, with a pedimented centre bay.

GREEN CASTLE, ¾ m. W. A simple ringwork castle consisting of a massive oval bank, with the remains of an outer ditch and a counterscarp bank; the steep slopes down to the burn on the E and S provided economical natural defences.

FOWBERRY TOWER. *See* p. 286.

HAUGH HEAD. *See* p. 306.

WEETWOOD. *See* p. 620.

WOOLEY *see* ALLENDALE TOWN

WOOLSINGTON

1070

Still separated from Newcastle by fields, and hiding some of its houses behind the hedges of Woolsington Park, Woolsington is now inevitably dominated by Newcastle Airport, which lies to the N of the mid-C20 ribbon development. At the time of writing, there are proposals for redeveloping most of Woolsington with a leisure park and housing.

WOOLSINGTON HALL. The four GATEPIERS on the Ponteland Road at the entrance to South Drive are early C19, round with low domed tops on cornices and fluted bands. This was once the main drive to the house, which is now reached from a lane further N. Its design combines local solidity with the beginnings of the Baroque style, and because some of his stylistic devices appear here it has been suggested that *Robert Trollope* may have been involved. There is, however, no documentary evidence to support this. The centre of the S front is in the Capheaton style, but with mullioned-and-transomed three-light windows. They and the central door are framed by excessively thick mouldings, but bead not cable. Mullions and transoms are timber on the ground floor, ovolo-moulded stone on the floor above. All the windows have a kind of depressed shell motif instead of pediments. Giant angle pilasters, with ball finials, and a parapet frame the composition. The date of all this must be late c 17. The flanking lower wings with vases on their parapets are of 1794. All this side is rendered. The rear has a Venetian stair window with broad (and so probably early-to-mid-c 18) glazing bars, and two cross windows of which one is blind. To the E an early c 19 wing. The ORANGERY has a rainwater head dated 1797, urn finials and the usual round arches.

BULLOCK STEADS. A cheering sight with its glowing red brick by the side of the busy Ponteland Road. It is essentially an c 18 farm group, exhibiting many characteristics of the local vernacular. Tumbled-in brickwork in the gable of the former farmhouse, and a pantiled roof with sandstone flags at the eaves. The present farmhouse has a c 19 brick front and a Welsh slate roof. The (converted) two-storey shelter shed at the back of the yard has seven elliptical arches and a loft above.

NEWCASTLE AIRPORT (Ponteland parish) began in the 1930s with a hut or two. The present TERMINAL BUILDING of 1964–7 is an impressive white-tiled block of pure lines by *Yorke, Rosenberg, Mardall*.

METRO STATION. 1991. A major station, 'the gateway to Tyneside', by *Couves Ltd*, on the basis of designs made by *Ainsworth Spark Associates*. Glass-covered link between airport and station. A split pyramid houses the concourse area. (For the Metro system, *see* Newcastle upon Tyne: Public Buildings.)

1060   WYLAM

ST OSWIN. 1886 by *R. J. Johnson* in memory of William Hedley. Perp, aisleless, with a big s tower, the ground floor of which forms the s transept. The s porch is of timber, very delicate and pretty, deliberately un-Northumbrian, one feels. All the furnishings are contemporary, also Perp in detail, and very attractive. – The former VICARAGE was done by Johnson at the same time.

WYLAM HALL. The core of the house is medieval and includes a tunnel-vaulted ground floor of 18.9 by 5.8 metres (62 by 19 ft) internally. This has a pretty early c 19 Gothick plaster rib vault and is pierced by a curving stair with cast-iron Gothick balusters. Outside, one irregular early c 18 façade has a doorway with a bolection-moulded surround and an open curly pediment. Windows in architrave surrounds. Other façades include work of the 1880s but are mainly irregular c 18 and early c 19. Much was demolished in the 1950s. William Hedley is said to have used the drive to the hall for his experiments in making steam engines run uphill without the aid of rack and pinion.

WYLAM STATION, on the Newcastle and Carlisle Railway. Opened in 1835; one of the earliest stations in the world still in passenger use. Tudor style. Single-storey station to the l., with the two-storey stationmaster's house attached on the r. The platform was an afterthought.

GEORGE STEPHENSON'S COTTAGE, *c.* ½ m. E. The birthplace and family home of the great engineer is a small, typical Northumbrian c 18 house with horizontal sash windows and a central boarded door. Steeply pitched pantile roof, edged in stone slates. At the time of Stephenson's birth the cottage faced directly onto the Wylam horsedrawn waggonway of *c.* 1748, later relaid as the Scotswood, Newburn and Wylam Railway of 1876.

The ROAD BRIDGE by the station has an interesting history. It started life in 1836 apparently as a combined road and railway bridge to connect the Wylam collieries and the proposed ironworks with the newly opened Newcastle and Carlisle Railway on the s bank of the Tyne. Designed either by *John Blackmore* of the railway company or *Benjamin Thompson* of the ironworks, the bridge initially had a timber deck supported on stone piers. It was built by subscriptions, and a toll collector's hut stood at the SE corner of the bridge. Colliery waggons seem not to have used the bridge after *c.* 1890, and between 1893 and 1897 the wooden superstructure was replaced in steel by the Wylam Toll Bridge Company, which also built a new tollhouse at the N end (it still stands). The bridge was acquired by the county in 1936. The superstructure was replaced again in 1946 by *Dorman Long*, and in 1960.

WEST WYLAM RAILWAY BRIDGE, $\frac{1}{2}$ m. W. Disused. 1876 by *William George Laws*. A single-span wrought-iron arch railway bridge with a suspended rail deck. Built for the former Scotswood, Newburn and Wylam Railway at a cost of £16,000. Laws was consulting engineer to the railway company and later became city engineer to Newcastle upon Tyne. The arch is formed of three parallel parabolic wrought-iron lattice ribs stiffened with cross bracing; the abutments were founded on cement and built of masonry. Ironwork by *Hawks, Crawshay & Co.* of Gateshead, masonry and foundations by *W. E. Jackson & Co.* The bridge experienced the usual Tyne flood problems during construction as well as fire to the timbers due to the dropping of hot rivets. It was the first bridge of this type for a railway; the only precedent seems to have been George Leather's road bridge of 1833 over the River Aire at Leeds, where the arch ribs were of cast iron. An obvious descendant of them both is Newcastle's Tyne Bridge.

PUMPING STATION, 1 m. W. A river-water extraction station of the Newcastle and Gateshead Water Company, with a Cornish pumping engine house of 1874, built to house a third-hand engine from Cornwall. Original boiler house and octagonal chimney also survive as well as additional steam engine houses of 1885 and 1894 and buildings of 1918 and 1950 for electric pump sets.

YEAVERING

9030

A monument beside the road, 1 m. E of Kirknewton, marks the site of *Ad Gefrin*, the c 7 rural palace of King Edwin of Northumbria recorded by Bede. Discovered from the air as cropmarks in 1949, its complex structural history has been revealed by excavation.

An arable landscape of the late prehistoric and Roman periods was succeeded by a large stockaded enclosure (perhaps a market centre), and by some simple rectangular cottages, the roofs of which were supported by timber uprights set in individual post-holes. In the mid-c 6 the first halls, with inclined external buttresses, were built, using a distinctive construction technique. The walls were solid, load-bearing structures made up of heavy squared vertical timbers which were close-set (probably with tongues and grooves) in foundation-trenches. Only the lower end of alternate posts rested on the bed of the trench; there were no sill-beams. When St Paulinus stayed here as a guest of Edwin in 627, Yeavering was at its peak. As an indication of quality, at least one of the halls had its wooden walls faced internally with a fine white plaster.

Shortly afterwards the township was destroyed, probably in the eclipse of Northumbria by Penda and Cadwallon in 632–3. It was soon rebuilt, perhaps when Oswald returned from exile, in a lighter architectural style that utilized planks as walling. The buildings were again burnt c. 651–5, but occupation on a reduced scale continued, after a last reconstruction, until c. 685. These latest walls were in a cheaper form of timber cladding held together with clinch nails. By this time, however, Yeavering had been superseded by the new palace of Maelmin, near Milfield (q.v.).

During each major phase in the history of the palace there was one great hall. In the time of Edwin it was 27 metres (90 ft) long internally and had a room partitioned off at the E end. Although varying in detail, it seems that the major halls normally had four doorways, one in each wall, and one or more internal partitions. Some had a narrower annexe at each end, probably private bed-rooms. Lesser halls, almost all of which were domestic in character, were also built in each phase. The exceptions were one used as a weaving-shed, another which was a sunken-floored kitchen, and a Christian church pre-dating the destruction of 651.

One quite extraordinary building seems to have been central to the life of Yeavering from the mid-c 6. This was a 'theatre', constructed as a narrow segment of a circle, with concentric rows of raked seating focused on a small dais. Under Edwin its capacity was doubled to take over 300 people; it may have served as a royal assembly, and no doubt Paulinus preached in it. Its probable social and ceremonial function, potentially serving a wide area, may have been linked to the large stockaded enclosure (or market centre, if such it was) which was not finally abandoned until the 630s.

YEAVERING BELL. The largest and most memorable hillfort in the county, in essence an Iron Age town, embraces the twin summits of Yeavering Bell at a height of 360 metres (1,182 ft). Commanding Glendale at its foot, the views from the Bell extend up the Bowmont into Scotland and E across the lowlands of the Till to the Kyloe Hills and the coast.

The summits are enclosed by a massive wall, composed wholly of rubble, draped around the shoulders of the hill; this perimeter, 950 metres (1,040 yards) long, enclosed an area of 5.5 hectares (13½ acres). Although now spread in a band up to 8 metres (26 ft) wide, this wall seems to have been c. 3 metres (10 ft) broad at the base, tapering in a double batter. A short section, 40 metres E of the N gate, which was tentatively reconstructed after small-scale excavations in the 1950s stands 2 metres (6½ ft) high externally, one metre internally. Elsewhere only brief sections of wall-face survive: the inner face E of the gateway at the midpoint of the S side and S of the W summit, and at the W end externally. A Victorian excavation of the S gateway suggested that there was a 'guard-house' in the thickness of the wall on the W side. Similar bifurcations of the rubble can be seen at the N and E gates. No gate is apparent on the W, but the former existence of one may be indicated by the scruffy and discontinuous arc of an additional outer wall round the W end of the fort. A comparable outwork protects the E gate.

The interior is densely pockmarked by scores of circular hollows and platforms, representing the sites of contemporary timber buildings. These are up to 13 metres (42 ft) across, although the average diameter is c. 8 metres (26 ft). Over 130 have been identified; many more must be concealed by the gentle slopes in the saddle where no levelling up would have been required. In some cases a 'ring-groove' is still visible, marking the trench for a wall of closely set timber uprights; a few other platforms seem to be overlain by simple stone buildings founded on rubble walls. The poor artefacts recovered in the excavations showed that occupation continued from the Iron Age certainly as late as the C 4 A.D.

Around the E summit a narrow sub-circular or polygonal ditch has been dug, cutting through the building-platforms, the upcast thrown outwards to form a slight bank. Access was gained over a narrow causeway on the E. Excavation revealed that the ditch was 1.5 metres (5 ft) wide and deep, tapering to 0.6 metres (2 ft) at the bottom. Its date and function are unknown, although it has been tempting to link it (with no supporting evidence) to the C 7 palace in the valley (*see* above).

BATTLE STONE, 600 metres W of Yeavering. Prehistoric standing stone, 3.1 metres (10 ft) high. Locally associated with a victory over the Scots in 1415. It fell in 1890 and was re-erected in 1924.

GLOSSARY

Particular types of an architectural element are often defined under the name of the element itself; e.g. for 'dog-leg stair' see STAIR. Literal meanings, where specially relevant, are indicated by the abbreviation *lit*.

For further reference (especially for style terms) the following are a selection of books that can be consulted: *A Dictionary of Architecture* (N. Pevsner, J. Fleming, H. Honour, 1975); *The Illustrated Glossary of Architecture* (J. Harris and J. Lever, 1966); *Recording a Church: An Illustrated Glossary* (T. Cocke, D. Findlay, R. Halsey, E. Williamson, Council of British Archaeology, 1982); *Encyclopedia of Modern Architecture* (edited by Wolfgang Pehnt, 1963); *The Classical Language of Architecture* (J. Summerson, 1964); *The Dictionary of Ornament* (M. Stafford and D. Ware, 1974); *Illustrated Handbook of Vernacular Architecture* (R. W. Brunskill, 1976); *English Brickwork* (A. Clifton Taylor and R. W. Brunskill, 1977); *A Pattern of English Building* (A. Clifton Taylor, 1972).

ABACUS (*lit*. tablet): flat slab forming the top of a capital; *see* Orders (fig. 19).

ABUTMENT: the meeting of an arch or vault with its solid lateral support, or the support itself.

ACANTHUS: formalized leaf ornament with thick veins and frilled edge, e.g. on a Corinthian capital.

ACCUMULATOR TOWER: *see* Hydraulic Power.

ACHIEVEMENT OF ARMS: in heraldry, a complete display of armorial bearings.

ACROTERION (*lit*. peak): plinth for a statue or ornament placed at the apex or ends of a pediment; also, loosely and more usually, both the plinths and what stands on them.

ADDORSED: description of two figures placed symmetrically back to back.

AEDICULE (*lit*. little building): architectural surround, consisting usually of two columns or pilasters supporting a pediment, framing a niche or opening. *See also* Tabernacle.

AFFRONTED: description of two figures placed symmetrically face to face.

AGGER (*lit*. rampart): Latin term for the built-up foundations of Roman roads; also sometimes applied to the ramparts of hillforts or other earthworks.

AGGREGATE: small stones added to a binding material, e.g. in concrete. In modern architecture used alone to describe concrete with an aggregate of stone chippings, e.g. granite, quartz, etc.

AISLE (*lit*. wing): subsidiary space alongside the nave, choir, or transept of a church, or the main body of some other building, separated from it by columns, piers, or posts.

ALTAR: elevated slab consecrated for the celebration of the Eucharist; cf. Communion Table.

ALTARPIECE: *see* Retable.

AMBULATORY (*lit*. walkway): aisle around the sanctuary, sometimes surrounding an apse and therefore semicircular or polygonal in plan.

AMORINI: *see* Putto.

ANGLE ROLL: roll moulding in the angle between two planes, e.g. between the orders of an arch.

ANNULET (*lit*. ring): shaft-ring (*see* Shaft).

ANSE DE PANIER (*lit*. basket handle): basket arch (*see* Arch).

ANTAE: flat pilasters with capitals different from the order they accompany, placed at the ends of the short projecting walls of a portico or of a colonnade which is then called *In Antis*.

ANTEFIXAE: ornaments projecting at regular intervals above a classical cornice, originally to conceal the ends of roof tiles.

ANTEPENDIUM: *see* Frontal.

ANTHEMION (*lit*. honeysuckle): classical ornament like a honeysuckle flower (*see* fig. 1).

A   P   A   P   A

Fig. 1. Anthemion and Palmette Frieze

APRON: raised panel below a window or at the base of a wall monument or tablet, sometimes shaped and decorated.

A.P.S.D.: Architectural Publications Society Dictionary.

APSE: semicircular (i.e. apsidal) extension of an apartment: *see also* Exedra. A term first used of the magistrate's end of a Roman basilica, and thence especially of the vaulted semicircular or polygonal end of a chancel or a chapel.

ARABESQUE: type of painted or carved surface decoration consisting of flowing lines and intertwined foliage scrolls etc., generally based on geometrical patterns. Cf. Grotesque.

ARCADE: (1) series of arches supported by piers or columns. *Blind Arcade* or *Arcading*: the same applied to the surface of a wall. *Wall Arcade*: in medieval churches, a blind arcade forming a dado below windows. (2) a covered shopping street.

ARCH: for the various forms *see* fig. 2. The term *Basket Arch* refers to a basket handle and is sometimes applied to a three-centred or depressed arch as well as to the type with a flat middle. A *Transverse Arch* runs across the main axis of an interior space. The term is used especially for the arches between the compartments of tunnel- or groin-vaulting. *Diaphragm Arch:* transverse arch with solid spandrels spanning an otherwise wooden-roofed interior. *Chancel Arch:* W opening from the chancel into the nave. *Nodding Arch:* an ogee arch curving forward from the plane of the wall. *Relieving* (or *Discharging*) *Arch:* incorporated in a wall, to carry some of its weight, some way above an opening. *Skew Arch*: spanning responds not diametrically opposed to one another. *Strainer Arch:* inserted across an opening to resist any inward pressure of the side members. *See also* Jack Arch; Triumphal Arch.

ARCHITRAVE: (1) formalized lintel, the lowest member of the classical entablature (*see* Orders, fig. 19); (2) moulded frame of a door or window (often borrowing the profile of an architrave in the strict sense). Also *Lugged Architrave*, where the top is prolonged into lugs (*lit*. ears) at the sides; *Shouldered*, where the frame rises vertically at the top angles and returns horizontally at the sides forming shoulders (*see* fig. 3).

ARCHIVOLT: architrave moulding when it follows the line of an arch.

ARCUATED: dependent structurally on the use of arches or the arch principle; cf. Trabeated.

ARRIS (*lit*. stop): sharp edge where two surfaces meet at an angle.

ASHLAR: masonry of large blocks wrought to even faces and square edges.

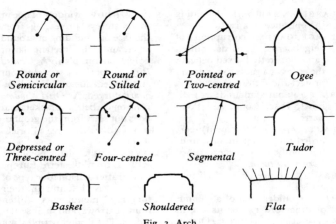

Round or Semicircular

Round or Stilted

Pointed or Two-centred

Ogee

Depressed or Three-centred

Four-centred

Segmental

Tudor

Basket

Shouldered

Flat

Fig. 2. Arch

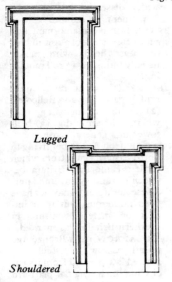

Lugged

Shouldered

Fig. 3. Architrave

ASTRAGAL (*lit.* knuckle): moulding of semicircular section often with bead-and-reel enrichment (q.v.).

ASTYLAR: term used for an elevation that has no columns or similar vertical features.

ATLANTES (*lit.* Atlas figures, from the god Atlas carrying the globe): male counterparts of caryatids (q.v.), often in a more demonstrative attitude of support.

ATRIUM: inner court of a Roman house; also open court in front of a church.

ATTACHED COLUMN: *see* Engaged Column.

ATTIC: (I) small top storey, especially within a sloping roof; (2) in classical architecture, a storey above the main entablature of the façade, as in a triumphal arch (q.v.).

AUMBRY: recess or cupboard to hold sacred vessels for the Mass.

BAILEY: area around the motte or keep (qq.v.) of a castle, defended by a wall and ditch.

BALANCE BEAM: *see* Canals.

BALDACCHINO: free-standing canopy, properly of or representing fabric, over an altar supported by columns. Cf. Ciborium.

BALLFLOWER: globular flower of three petals enclosing a small ball. Typical of the Decorated style.

BALUSTER (*lit.* pomegranate): a pillar or pedestal of bellied form. *Balusters:* vertical supports of this or any other form, for a handrail or coping, the whole being called a *Balustrade. Blind Balustrade:* the same applied to the surface of a wall.

BARBICAN: outwork defending the entrance to a castle.

BARGEBOARDS: corruption of vergeboards. Boards, often carved or fretted, fixed beneath the eaves of a gable to cover and protect the rafters.

BARROW: burial mound; see Bell, Bowl, Disc, Long, and Pond Barrow.

BARTIZAN (*lit.* battlement): corbelled turret, square or round, frequently at a corner, hence *Corner Bartizan.*

BASCULE: hinged part of a lifting bridge.

BASE: moulded foot of a column or other order. For its use in classical architecture *see* Orders (fig. 19).

BASEMENT: lowest, subordinate storey of a building, and hence the lowest part of an elevation, below the main floor.

BASILICA (*lit.* royal building): a Roman public hall; hence an aisled building with a clerestory, most often a church.

BASTION: one of a series of semicircular or polygonal projections from the main wall of a fortress or city, placed at intervals in such a manner as to enable the garrison to cover the intervening stretches of the wall.

BATTER: intentional inward inclination of a wall face.

BATTLEMENT: fortified parapet, indented or crenellated so that archers could shoot through the indentations (crenels or embrasures) between the projecting solid portions (merlons). Also used decoratively.

BAY LEAF: classical ornament of formalized overlapping bay leaves; *see* fig. 4.

Fig. 4. Bay Leaf

BAYS: divisions of an elevation or interior space as defined by any regular vertical features such as arches, columns, windows, etc.

BAY-WINDOW: window of one or more storeys projecting from the face of a building at ground level, and either rectangular or polygonal on plan. A *Canted Bay-window* has a straight front and angled sides. A *Bow Window* is curved. An *Oriel Window* rests on corbels or brackets and does not start from the ground.

BEAD-AND-REEL: *see* Enrichments.

BEAKER FOLK: late Neolithic settlers from western Europe named after a distinctive type of pottery vessel found in their funerary monuments (often round barrows) and their settlements. The Beaker period saw a wider dissemination of metal implements in Britain.

BEAKHEAD: Norman ornamental motif consisting of a row of bird or beast heads with beaks, usually biting into a roll moulding.

BELFRY: (1) bell-turret set on a roof or gable (*see also* Bellcote); (2) chamber or stage in a tower where bells are hung; (3) belltower in a general sense.

BELGAE: Iron Age tribes living in north-eastern Gaul, from which settlers came into Britain between 100 and 55 B.C. and later. These immigrants may not have been numerous, but their impact on material culture in southern Britain was marked.

BELL BARROW: early Bronze Age round barrow in which the mound is separated from its encircling ditch by a flat platform or berm (q.v.).

BELL CAPITAL: *see* fig. 8.

BELLCOTE: belfry as (1) above, usually in the form of a small gabled or roofed housing for the bell(s).

BERM: level area separating ditch from bank on a hill-fort or barrow.

BILLET (*lit.* log or block) FRIEZE: Norman ornament

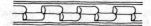

Fig. 5. Billet Frieze

English

Flemish

Fig. 6. Bond

consisting of small half-cylindrical or rectangular blocks placed at regular intervals (*see* fig. 5).

BIVALLATE: (of a hill-fort) defended by two concentric banks and ditches.

BLIND: *see* Arcade, Balustrade, Portico.

BLOCK CAPITAL: *see* fig. 8.

BLOCKED: term applied to columns etc. that are interrupted by regular projecting blocks, e.g. the sides of a Gibbs surround (*see* fig. 13).

BLOCKING COURSE: plain course of stones, or equivalent, on top of a cornice and crowning the wall.

BOLECTION MOULDING: curved moulding covering the joint between two different planes and overlapping the higher as well as the lower one, used especially in the late C17 and early C18.

BOND: in brickwork, the pattern of long sides (stretchers) and short ends (headers) produced on the face of a wall by laying bricks in a particular way. For the two most common bonds *see* fig. 6.

BOSS: knob or projection usually placed at the intersection of ribs in a vault.

BOW WINDOW: *see* Bay-window.

BOWL BARROW: round barrow surrounded by a quarry ditch. Introduced in late Neolithic times, the form continued until the Saxon period.

BOWSTRING BRIDGE: with arch ribs rising above the roadway, which is suspended from them.

BOX FRAME: (1) timber-framed construction in which vertical and horizontal wall members support the roof. (2) in modern architecture, a box-like form of concrete construction where the loads are taken on cross

walls, suitable only for buildings consisting of repetitive small cells. Also called *Cross-wall Construction*.

BOX PEW: *see* Pew.

BRACE: subsidiary timber set diagonally to strengthen a timber frame. It can be curved or straight. *See also* Roofs (3) and figs. 24–8.

BRACKET: small supporting piece of stone, etc., to carry a projecting horizontal member. *See also* Console.

BRATTISHING: ornamental cresting on a wall, usually formed of leaves or Tudor flowers or miniature battlements.

BRESSUMER (*lit.* breast-beam): big horizontal beam, usually set forward from the lower part of a building, supporting the wall above.

BROACH: *see* Spire.

BRONZE AGE: in Britain, the period from *c.* 2000 to 600 B.C.

BUCRANIUM: ox skull used decoratively in classical friezes.

BULLSEYE WINDOW: small oval window, set horizontally, cf. Oculus. Also called *Œil de Bœuf*.

BUTTRESS: vertical member projecting from a wall to stabilize it or to resist the lateral thrust of an arch, roof, or vault. For different types used at the corners of a building, especially a tower, *see* fig. 7. A *Flying Buttress* transmits the thrust to a heavy abutment by means of an arch or half-arch.

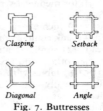

Clasping   *Setback*

Diagonal   *Angle*

Fig. 7. Buttresses

CABLE MOULDING: originally a Norman moulding, imitating the twisted strands of a rope. Also called *Rope Moulding*.

CAIRN: a mound of stones usually covering a burial.

CALEFACTORY: room in a monastery where a fire burned for the comfort of the monks. Also called *Warming Room*.

CAMBER: slight rise or upward curve in place of a horizontal line or plane.

CAMES: *see* Quarries.

CAMPANILE: free-standing bell-tower.

CANALS: *Pound Lock*: chamber with gates at each end allowing boats to float from one level to another. *Flash Lock*: removable weir or similar device through which boats pass on a flush of water. Predecessor of the pound lock. *Tidal Gates*: single pair of lock gates allowing vessels to pass when the tide makes a level. *Balance Beam*: beam projecting horizontally for opening and closing lock gates. *Roving Bridge*: carrying a canal towing path from one bank to the other.

CANOPY: projection or hood usually over an altar, pulpit, niche, statue, etc.

CANTED: tilted, generally on a vertical axis to produce an obtuse angle on plan, e.g. of a canted bay-window.

CANTILEVER: horizontal projection (e.g. step, canopy) supported by a downward force behind the fulcrum.

CAPITAL: head or crowning feature of a column or pilaster; for classical types *see* Orders (fig. 19); for medieval types *see* fig. 8.

CARREL: (1) niche in a cloister where a monk could sit to work or read; (2) similar feature in open-plan offices and libraries.

CARTOUCHE: tablet with ornate frame, usually of elliptical shape and bearing a coat of arms or inscription.

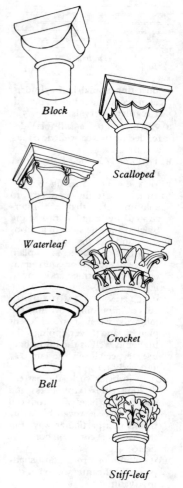

Block

Scalloped

Waterleaf

Crocket

Bell

Stiff-leaf

Fig. 8. Capitals

CARYATIDS (*lit.* daughters of the village of Caryae): female figures supporting an entablature, counterparts of Atlantes (q.v.).

CASEMATE: in military architecture, a vaulted chamber, with embrasures for defence, built into the thickness of the wall of a castle or fortress or projecting from it.

CASEMENT: (1) window hinged at the side; (2) in Gothic architecture, a concave moulding framing a window.

CAST IRON: hard and brittle, cast in a mould to the required shape. *Wrought Iron* is ductile, strong in tension, forged into decorative patterns or forged and rolled into e.g. bars, joists, boiler plates. *Mild Steel* is a modern equivalent, similar but stronger.

CASTELLATED: battlemented.

CAVETTO: concave moulding of quarter-round section.

CELURE OR CEILURE: enriched area of a roof above the rood or the altar.

CENOTAPH (*lit.* empty tomb): funerary monument which is not a burying place.

CENTERING: wooden support for the building of an arch or vault, removed after completion.

CHAMBERED TOMB: Neolithic burial mound with a stone-built chamber and entrance passage covered by an earthen barrow or stone cairn.

CHAMFER (*lit.* corner-break): surface formed by cutting off a square edge, usually at an angle of forty-five degrees. When the plane is concave it is termed a *Hollow Chamfer*. *Double-Chamfer*: applied to each of two recessed arches.

CHANCEL (*lit.* enclosure): E arm or that part of the E end of a church set apart for the use of the officiating clergy, except in cathedrals or monastic churches; cf. Choir.

CHANTRY CHAPEL: chapel, often attached to or inside a church, endowed for the celebration of masses principally for the soul of the founder.

CHEVET (*lit.* head): French term for the E end of a church (chancel and ambulatory with radiating chapels).

CHEVRON: V-shaped motif used in series to decorate a moulding: also (especially when on a single plane) called *Zigzag*.

CHOIR: the part of a church where services are sung. In monastic churches this can occupy the crossing and/or the easternmost bays of the nave.

Also used to describe, more loosely, the E arm of a cruciform church.

CIBORIUM: (1) a fixed canopy of stone or wood over an altar, usually vaulted and supported on four columns, cf. Baldacchino. (2) canopied shrine for the reserved sacrament.

CINQUEFOIL: *see* Foil.

CIST: stone-lined or slab-built grave. If below ground, covered with a protective barrow. It first appears in late Neolithic times and was also used in the Early Christian period in West Britain.

CLADDING: external covering or skin applied to a structure, especially framed buildings (q.v.), for aesthetic or protective purposes.

CLAPPER BRIDGE: bridge made of large slabs of stone, some making rough piers, with longer ones laid on top to make the roadway.

CLASP: *see* Industrialized Building.

CLASSIC: term for the moment of highest achievement of a style.

CLASSICAL: term for Greek and Roman architecture and any subsequent styles derived from it.

CLERESTORY: uppermost storey of the nave walls of a church, pierced by windows. Also applied to high-level windows in domestic architecture.

CLUSTER BLOCK: multi-storey building in which individual blocks of flats cluster round a central service core.

COADE STONE: a ceramic artificial stone made in Lambeth from 1769 to *c.* 1840 by Eleanor Coade († 1821) and her associates.

COB: walling material of clay mixed with straw.

COFFER DAM: a temporary structure to keep out water from an excavation in a river, dock, etc.

COFFERING: arrangement of sunken panels (coffers), square or polygonal, decorating a ceiling, vault, or arch.

COGGING: a decorative course of bricks laid diagonally as an alternative to dentilation (q.v.). Also called *Dogtooth Brickwork*.

COLLAR: *see* Roofs (3) and figs. 25–8.

COLLEGIATE CHURCH: church endowed for the support of a college of priests.

COLONNADE: range of columns supporting an entablature; cf. Arcade.

COLONNETTE: in medieval architecture, a small column or shaft.

COLOSSAL ORDER: *see* Order.

COLUMN: in classical architecture, an upright structural member of round section with a shaft, a capital, and usually a base. *See* Orders (fig. 19).

COLUMN FIGURE: in medieval architecture, carved figure attached to a column or shaft flanking a doorway.

COMMUNION TABLE: unconsecrated table used in Protestant churches in place of an altar (q.v.) for the celebration of Holy Communion.

COMPOSITE: *see* Orders.

COMPOUND PIER: grouped shafts (q.v.), or a solid core surrounded by attached or detached shafts.

CONSOLE: ornamented bracket of compound curved outline (*see* fig. 9).

Fig. 9. Consoles

COPING (*lit.* capping): protective capping course of masonry or brickwork on top of a wall.

CORBEL: projecting block of stone or timber supporting something above. *Corbel Course:* continuous course of projecting stones or bricks

fulfilling the same function. *Corbel Table:* series of corbels to carry a parapet or a wall-plate; for the latter *see* Roofs (3) and figs. 24–7. *Corbelling:* brick or masonry courses built out beyond one another like a series of corbels to support a chimneystack, window, etc.

CORINTHIAN: *see* Orders (fig. 19).

CORNICE: (1) moulded ledge, projecting along the top of a building or feature, especially as the highest member of the classical entablature (*see* Orders, fig. 19); (2) decorative moulding in the angle between wall and ceiling.

CORPS-DE-LOGIS: French term for the main building(s) as distinct from the wings or pavilions.

COTTAGE ORNÉ: an artfully rustic building usually of asymmetrical plan. A product of the late C 18/early C 19 Picturesque.

COUNTERSCARP BANK: small bank on the downhill or outer side of a hill-fort ditch.

COUR D'HONNEUR: entrance court before a house in the French manner, usually with wings enclosing the sides and a screen wall or low range of buildings across the front.

COURSE: continuous layer of stones etc. in a wall.

COVE: a concave moulding on a large scale, e.g. to mask the eaves of a roof or in a *Coved Ceiling*, which has a pronounced cove joining the walls to a flat central panel smaller than the area of the whole ceiling.

CRADLE ROOF: *see* Wagon Roof.

CREDENCE: in a church or chapel, a shelf within or beside a piscina, or for the sacramental elements and vessels.

CRENELLATION: *see* Battlement.

CREST, CRESTING: ornamental finish along the top of a screen, etc.

CRINKLE-CRANKLE WALL: wall undulating in a series of serpentine curves.

CROCKETS (*lit.* hooks), CROCK-ETING: in Gothic architecture, leafy knobs on the edges of any sloping feature. *Crocket Capital: see* Capital (fig. 8).

CROMLECH: word of Celtic origin still occasionally used of single free-standing stones ascribed to the Neolithic or Bronze Age.

CROSSING: in a church, central space at the junction of the nave, chancel, and transepts. *Crossing Tower:* tower above a crossing.

CROSS-WINDOWS: windows with one mullion and one transom (qq.v.).

CROWSTEPS: squared stones set like steps e.g. on a gable or gateway; *see* Gable (fig. 12).

CRUCKS (*lit.* crooked): pairs of inclined timbers, usually curved, which are set at bay-length intervals in a building and support the timbers of the roof (q.v.). The individual cruck is known as a blade. *Base:* blades which rise from ground level to a tie- or collar-beam upon which the roof truss is carried; in timber buildings they support the walls. *Full:* blades rising from ground level to the apex of a building; they serve as the main members of a roof truss and in timber buildings they support the walls. *Jointed:* blades formed from more than one timber; the lower member normally rises from ground level and acts as a wall-post; it is usually elbowed at wall-plate level and jointed just above. *Middle:* blades rising from half-way up the walls to a tie- or collar-beam upon which the roof truss is supported. *Raised:* blades rising from half-way up the walls to the apex. *Upper:* blades supported on a tie-beam and rising to the apex.

CRYPT: underground or half-underground room usually below the E end of a church. *Ring Crypt:* early medieval semicircular or polygonal corridor crypt surrounding the apse of a church, often associated with chambers for relics.

CUPOLA (*lit.* dome): especially a small dome on a circular or polygonal base crowning a larger dome, roof, or turret.

CURTAIN WALL: (1) connecting wall between the towers of a castle; (2) in modern building, a non-load-bearing external wall composed of repeating modular elements applied to a steel-framed structure.

CURVILINEAR: *see* Tracery.

CUSP: projecting point defining the foils in Gothic tracery, also used as a decorative edging to the soffits of the Gothic arches of tomb recesses, sedilia, etc. When used decoratively within tracery patterns called *Sub-cusps.*

CYCLOPEAN MASONRY: built with large irregular polygonal stones, but smooth and finely jointed.

CYMA RECTA and CYMA RE-VERSA: *see* Ogee.

DADO: the finishing of the lower part of an interior wall (sometimes used to support an applied order, i.e. a formalized continuous pedestal). *Dado Rail:* the moulding along the top of the dado.

DAGGER: *see* Tracery.

DAIS: raised platform at one end of a room.

DEC (DECORATED): historical division of English Gothic architecture covering the period from *c.* 1290 to *c.* 1350. The name is derived from the type of window tracery used during the period (*see also* Tracery).

DEMI-COLUMNS: engaged columns (q.v.) only half of whose circumference projects from the wall. Also called *Half-Columns.*

DENTIL: small square block used in series in classical cornices, rarely in Doric. In brickwork *dentilation* is produced by the projection of alternating headers or blocks along cornices or string courses.

DIAPER (*lit.* figured cloth): repetitive surface decoration of lozenges or squares either flat or in relief. Achieved in brickwork with bricks of two colours.

DIOCLETIAN WINDOW: semi-circular window with two mullions, so-called because of its use in the Baths of Diocletian in Rome. Also called a *Thermae Window*.

DISC BARROW: Bronze Age round barrow with an inconspicuous central mound surrounded by a bank and ditch.

DISTYLE: having two columns.

DOGTOOTH: typical E.E. decoration of a moulding, consisting of a series of small pyramids formed by four leaves meeting at a point (*see* fig. 10). *See also* Cogging.

Fig. 10. Dogtooth

DOME: vault of even curvature erected on a circular base. The section can be segmental (e.g. saucer dome), semicircular, pointed, or bulbous (onion dome).

DONJON: *see* Keep.

DORIC: *see* Orders (fig. 19).

DORMER WINDOW: window projecting from the slope of a roof, having a roof of its own and lighting a room within it. *Dormer Head:* gable above this window, often formed as a pediment.

DORTER: dormitory; sleeping quarters of a monastery.

DOUBLE CHAMFER: *see* Chamfer.

DOUBLE PILE: *see* Pile.

DRAGON BEAM: *see* Jetty.

DRESSINGS: the stone or brick-work used about an angle, opening, or other feature worked to a finished face.

DRIPSTONE: moulded stone projecting from a wall to protect the lower parts from water; *see also* Hoodmould.

DRUM: (1) circular or polygonal stage supporting a dome or cupola; (2) one of the stones forming the shaft of a column.

DRYSTONE: stone construction without mortar.

DUTCH GABLE: *see* Gable (fig. 12).

EASTER SEPULCHRE: recess, usually in the N wall of a chancel, with a tomb-chest thought to have been for an effigy of Christ for Easter celebrations.

EAVES: overhanging edge of a roof; hence *Eaves Cornice* in this position.

ECHINUS (*lit.* sea-urchin): ovolo moulding (q.v.) below the abacus of a Greek Doric capital; *see* Orders (fig. 19).

EDGE RAIL: *see* Railways.

E.E. (EARLY ENGLISH): historical division of English Gothic architecture covering the period *c.* 1190–1250.

EGG-AND-DART: *see* Enrichments.

ELEVATION: (1) any side of a building: (2) in a drawing, the same or any part of it, accurately represented in two dimensions.

EMBATTLED: furnished with battlements.

EMBRASURE (*lit.* splay): small splayed opening in the wall or battlement of a fortified building.

ENCAUSTIC TILES: glazed and decorated earthenware tiles used mainly for paving.

EN DELIT (*lit.* in error): term used in Gothic architecture to describe stone shafts whose grain runs vertically instead of horizontally, against normal building practice.

ENGAGED COLUMN: one that is partly merged into a wall or pier. Also called *Attached Column*.

ENGINEERING BRICKS: dense bricks of uniform size, high crushing strength, and low porosity. Originally used mostly for railway viaducts etc.

ENRICHMENTS: in classical architecture, the carved decoration of certain mouldings, e.g. the ovolo (q.v.) with *Egg-and-Dart*, the cyma reversa (q.v.) with *Waterleaf*, the astragal (q.v.) with *Bead-and-Reel*; see fig. 11.

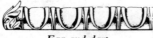

Egg-and-dart

Waterleaf

Bead-and-reel

Fig. 11. Enrichments

ENTABLATURE: in classical architecture, collective name for the three horizontal members (architrave, frieze, and cornice) carried by a wall or a column; see Orders (fig. 19).

ENTASIS: very slight convex deviation from a straight line; used on classical columns and sometimes on spires to prevent an optical illusion of concavity.

ENTRESOL: mezzanine storey within or above the ground storey.

EPITAPH (*lit.* on a tomb): inscription in that position.

ESCUTCHEON: shield for armorial bearings.

EXEDRA: apsidal end of an apartment; see Apse.

EXTRADOS: outer curved face of an arch or vault.

EXTRUDED CORNER: right-angled (or circular) projection from the inner angle of a building with advancing wings, usually in C16 or C17 plans.

EYECATCHER: decorative building (often a sham ruin) usually on an eminence to terminate a vista in a park or garden layout.

FASCIA: plain horizontal band, e.g. in an architrave (q.v.) or on a shopfront.

FENESTRATION: the arrangement of windows in a building.

FERETORY: place behind the high altar where the chief shrine of a church is kept.

FESTOON: ornament, usually in relief, in the form of a garland of flowers and/or fruit, suspended from both ends; *see also* Swag.

FIBREGLASS (or glass-reinforced polyester (GRP)): synthetic resin reinforced with glass fibre, formed in moulds, often simulating the appearance of traditional materials. GRC glass-reinforced concrete) is also formed in moulds and used for components (cladding etc.) in industrialized building.

FIELDED: *see* Raised and Fielded.

FILLET: in medieval architecture, a narrow flat band running down a shaft or along a roll moulding. In classical architecture it separates larger curved mouldings in cornices or bases.

FINIAL: decorative topmost feature, e.g. above a gable, spire, or cupola.

FLAMBOYANT: properly the latest phase of French Gothic architecture where the window tracery takes on undulating lines, based on the use of flowing curves.

FLASH LOCK: *see* Canals.

FLÈCHE (*lit.* arrow): slender spire on the centre of a roof. Also called *Spirelet*.

FLEUR-DE-LYS: in heraldry, a formalized lily, as in the royal arms of France.

FLEURON: decorative carved flower or leaf, often rectilinear.

FLOWING: *see* Tracery (Curvilinear).

FLUSHWORK: flint used decoratively in conjunction with dressed stone so as to form patterns: tracery, initials, etc.

FLUTING: series of concave grooves, their common edges sharp (arris) or blunt (fillet).

FOIL (*lit.* leaf): lobe formed by the cusping of a circular or other shape in tracery. *Trefoil* (three), *quatrefoil* (four), *cinque-foil* (five), and *multifoil* express the number of lobes in a shape. *See also* Tracery.

FOLIATE: decorated, especially carved, with leaves.

FORMWORK: commonly called shuttering; the temporary frame of braced timber or metal into which wet concrete is poured. The texture of the framework material depends on the imprint required.

FRAMED BUILDING: where the structure is carried by the framework – e.g. of steel, reinforced concrete, timber – instead of by load-bearing walls.

FRATER: *see* Refectory.

FREESTONE: stone that is cut, or can be cut, in all directions, usually fine-grained sandstone or limestone.

FRESCO: *al fresco:* painting executed on wet plaster. *Fresco secco:* painting executed on dry plaster, more common in Britain.

FRIEZE: (1) the middle member of the classical entablature, sometimes ornamented; *see* Orders (fig. 19). *Pulvinated Frieze* (*lit.* cushioned): frieze of bold convex profile. (2) horizontal band of ornament.

FRONTAL: covering for the front of an altar. When solid called *Antependium.*

FRONTISPIECE: in C16 and C17 buildings the central feature of doorway and windows above it linked in one composition.

GABLE: (1) area of wall, often triangular, at the end of a double-pitch roof; *Dutch Gable,* characteristic of *c.* 1580–1680; *Shaped Gable,* characteristic of *c.* 1620–80 (*see* fig. 12). *Gablet:* small gable. *See also* Roofs.

GADROONING: ribbed ornament, e.g. on the lid or base of an urn, flowing into a lobed edge.

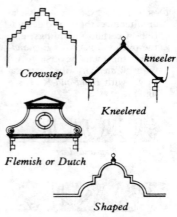

Fig. 12. Gables

GALILEE: chapel or vestibule usually at the w end of a church enclosing the main portal(s).

GALLERY: balcony or passage, but with certain special meanings, e.g. (1) upper storey above the aisle of a church, looking through arches to the nave; also called tribune and often erroneously triforium (q.v.); (2) balcony or mezzanine, often with seats, overlooking the main interior space of a building; (3) external walkway, often projecting from a wall.

GALLERY GRAVE: chambered tomb (q.v.) in which there is little or no differentiation between the entrance passage and the actual burial chamber(s).

GALLETING: decorative use of small stones in a mortar course.

GARDEROBE (*lit.* wardrobe): medieval privy.

GARGOYLE: water spout projecting from the parapet of a wall or tower, often carved into human or animal shape.

GAUGED BRICKWORK: soft brick sawn roughly, then rubbed to a smooth, precise (gauged) surface with a stone or another brick. Mostly used for door or window openings. Also called *Rubbed Brickwork.*

GAZEBO (jocular Latin, 'I shall gaze'): lookout tower or raised summer house usually in a park or garden.

GEOMETRIC: historical division of English Gothic architecture covering the period c. 1250–90. *See also* Tracery. For another meaning, *see* Stair.

GIANT ORDER: *see* Order.

GIBBS SURROUND: C18 treatment of a door or window surround, seen particularly in the work of James Gibbs (1682–1754) (*see* fig. 13).

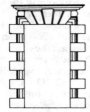

Fig. 13. Gibbs Surround

GIRDER: a large beam. *Box Girder*: of hollow-box section. *Bowed Girder*: with its top rising in a curve. *Plate Girder*: of I-section, made from iron or steel plates. *Lattice Girder*: with braced framework.

GLAZING BARS: wooden or sometimes metal bars separating and supporting window panes.

GOTHIC: the period of medieval architecture characterized by the use of the pointed arch. For its subdivisions *see* E.E., Geometric, Dec, Perp, Flamboyant.

GRANGE (monastic): farm owned and run by members of a religious order.

GRC and GRP: *see* Fibreglass.

GRISAILLE: monochrome painting on walls or glass.

GROIN: sharp edge at the meeting of two cells of a cross-vault; *see* Vault (fig. 35).

GROTESQUE (*lit.* grotto-esque): classical wall decoration in paint or stucco adopted from Roman examples, particularly by Raphael. Its foliage scrolls, unlike arabesque, incorporate ornaments and human figures.

GROTTO: artificial cavern usually decorated with rock- or shellwork, especially popular in the late C17 and C18.

GUILLOCHE: running classical ornament of interlaced bands forming a plait (*see* fig. 14).

Fig. 14. Guilloche

GUNLOOP: opening for a firearm.

GUTTAE: *see* Orders (fig. 19).

HAGIOSCOPE: *see* Squint.

HALF-TIMBERING: archaic term for timber-framing (q.v.). Sometimes used for non-structural decorative timberwork, e.g. in gables etc. of the late C19.

HALL CHURCH: medieval or Gothic Revival church whose nave and aisles are of equal height or approximately so.

HAMMERBEAM: *see* Roofs (fig. 28).

HEADER: *see* Bond.

HENGE: ritual earthwork with a surrounding bank and ditch, the bank being on the outer side.

HERM (*lit.* the god Hermes): male head or bust on a pedestal.

HERRINGBONE WORK: masonry or brickwork in zigzag courses.

HEXASTYLE: *see* Portico.

HILL-FORT: later Bronze Age and Iron Age earthwork enclosed by a ditch and bank system; in the later part of the period the defences multiplied in size and complexity. Varying from about an acre to over fifty acres in area, they are usually built with careful regard to natural elevations or promontories and range in character from powerful strongholds to protected farmsteads.

HIPPED ROOF: *see* Roofs (1) (fig. 23).

HOODMOULD: projecting moulding shown above an arch or lintel to throw off water. When the moulding is horizontal it is often called a *Label*. *See also* Label Stop.

HUSK GARLAND: festoon of nut-shells diminishing towards the ends.

HYDRAULIC POWER: use of water under high pressure to work machinery. *Accumulator Tower:* to house a hydraulic accumulator which accommodates fluctuations in the flow through hydraulic mains.

HYPOCAUST (*lit.* under-burning): Roman underfloor heating system. The floor is supported on pillars and the space thus formed is connected to a flue.

ICONOGRAPHY: interpretation of the subject matter of works of the visual arts.

IMPOST (*lit.* imposition): horizontal moulding at the springing of an arch.

IMPOST BLOCK: block with splayed sides between abacus and capital.

IN ANTIS: *see* Antae.

INDENT: shape chiselled out of a stone to match and receive a brass.

INDUSTRIALIZED BUILDING (system building): the use of a system of manufactured units assembled on site. One of the most popular is the CLASP (Consortium Local Authorities Special Programme) system of light steel framing suitable for schools etc.

INGLENOOK (*lit.* fire-corner): recess for a hearth with provision for seating.

INTARSIA: *see* Marquetry.

INTERCOLUMNIATION: interval between columns.

INTERLACE: decoration in relief simulating woven or entwined stems or bands.

INTRADOS: *see* Soffit.

IONIC: *see* Orders (fig. 19).

IRON AGE: in Britain, the period from *c.* 600 B.C. to the coming

of the Romans. The term is also used for those un-Romanized native communities which survived until the Saxon incursions especially beyond the Roman frontiers.

JACK ARCH: shallow segmental vault springing from beams, used for fireproof floors, bridge decks etc.

JAMB (*lit.* leg): one of the vertical sides of an opening.

JETTY: in a timber-framed building, the projection of an upper storey beyond the storey below, made by the beams and joists of the lower storey oversailing the external wall. On their outer ends is placed the sill of the walling for the storey above. Buildings can be jettied on several sides, in which case a *Dragon Beam* is set diagonally at the corner to carry the joists to either side.

JOGGLE: mason's term for joining two stones to prevent them slipping or sliding by means of a notch in one and a corresponding projection in the other.

KEEL MOULDING: moulding whose outline is in section like that of the keel of a ship (fig. 15).

Fig. 15. Keel Moulding

KEEP: principal tower of a castle. Also called *Donjon*.

KENTISH CUSP: *see* Tracery.

KEY PATTERN: *see* fig. 16.

KEYSTONE: central stone in an arch or vault.

Fig. 16. Key Pattern

KINGPOST: *see* Roofs (3) and fig. 24.

KNEELER: horizontal projecting stone at the base of each side of a gable on which the inclined coping stones rest. *See* Gable (fig. 12).

LABEL: *see* Hoodmould.

LACED WINDOWS: windows pulled together visually by strips of brickwork, usually of a different colour, which continue vertically the lines of the vertical parts of the window surround. Typical of *c.* 1720.

LACING COURSE: one or more bricks serving as horizontal reinforcement to flint, cobble, etc., walls.

LADY CHAPEL: chapel dedicated to the Virgin Mary (Our Lady).

LANCET WINDOW: slender single-light pointed-arched window.

LANTERN: (1) circular or polygonal turret with windows all round crowning a roof or a dome. (2) windowed stage of a crossing tower lighting the interior of a church.

LANTERN CROSS: churchyard cross with lantern-shaped top usually with sculptured representations on the sides of the top.

LAVATORIUM: in a monastery, a washing place adjacent to the refectory.

LEAN-TO: *see* Roofs (1).

LESENE (*lit.* a mean thing): pilaster without base or capital. Also called *Pilaster Strip*.

LIERNE: *see* Vault (fig. 36).

LIFT: in a gasholder, one of the telescopic sections.

LIGHT: compartment of a window defined by the mullions.

LINENFOLD: Tudor panelling where each panel is ornamented with a conventional representation of a piece of linen laid in vertical folds.

LINTEL: horizontal beam or stone bridging an opening.

LOGGIA: gallery open along one side of a building, usually arcaded or colonnaded. It may be a separate structure, usually in a garden.

LONG BARROW: unchambered Neolithic communal burial mound, often wedge-shaped in plan, with the burial and occasional other structures massed at the broader end, from which the mound itself tapers in height; quarry ditches flank the mound.

LONG-AND-SHORT WORK: quoins consisting of stones placed with the long side alternately upright and horizontal, especially in Saxon building.

LOUVRE: (1) opening, often with lantern over, in the roof of a building to let the smoke from a central hearth escape; (2) one of a series of overlapping boards or panes of glass placed in an opening to allow ventilation but keep the rain out.

LOWER PALAEOLITHIC: *see* Palaeolithic.

LOWSIDE WINDOW: window set lower than the others in a chancel side wall, usually towards its W end.

LOZENGE: diamond shape.

LUCARNE (*lit.* dormer): small gabled opening in a roof or spire.

LUGGED: *see* Architrave.

LUNETTE (*lit.* half or crescent moon): (1) semicircular window; (2) semicircular or crescent-shaped area of wall.

LYCHGATE (*lit.* corpse-gate): roofed wooden gateway at the entrance to a churchyard for the reception of a coffin.

LYNCHET: long terraced strip of soil accumulating on the downward side of prehistoric and medieval fields due to soil creep from continuous ploughing along the contours.

MACHICOLATIONS (*lit.* mashing devices): in medieval military architecture, a series of openings under a projecting parapet between the corbels that support it, through which missiles can be dropped.

MAJOLICA: ornamented glazed earthenware.

MANOMETER or STANDPIPE TOWER: containing a column of water to regulate pressure in water mains.

MANSARD: *see* Roofs (1) (fig. 23).

MARQUETRY: inlay in various woods. Also called *Intarsia*.

MATHEMATICAL TILES: facing tiles with one face moulded to look like a header or stretcher, most often hung on laths applied to timber-framed walls to make them appear brick-built.

MAUSOLEUM: monumental building or chamber usually intended for the burial of members of one family.

MEGALITHIC (*lit.* of large stones): archaeological term referring to the use of such stones, singly or together.

MEGALITHIC TOMB: massive stone-built Neolithic burial chamber covered by an earth or stone mound.

MERLON: *see* Battlement.

MESOLITHIC: 'Middle Stone' Age; the post-glacial period of hunting and fishing communities dating in Britain from *c.* 8000 B.C. to the arrival of the Neolithic (q.v.) communities, with whom they must have considerably overlapped in many areas.

METOPES: spaces between the triglyphs in a Doric frieze; *see* Orders (fig. 19).

MEZZANINE: (1) low storey between two higher ones; (2) low upper storey within the height of a high one, not extending over its whole area. *See also* Entresol.

MILD STEEL: *see* Cast Iron.

MISERERE: *see* Misericord.

MISERICORD (*lit.* mercy): shelf placed on the underside of a hinged choir stall seat which,

when turned up, supported the occupant during long periods of standing. Also called *Miserere*.

MODILLIONS: small consoles (q.v.) at regular intervals along the underside of the cornice of the Corinthian or Composite orders.

MODULE: in industrialized building (q.v.), a predetermined standard size for co-ordinating the dimensions of components of a building with the spaces into which they have to fit.

MOTTE: steep mound forming the main feature of C11 and C12 castles.

MOTTE-AND-BAILEY: post-Roman and Norman defence system consisting of an earthen mound (motte) topped with a wooden tower within a bailey, with enclosure ditch and palisade, and with the rare addition of an internal bank.

MOUCHETTE: *see* Tracery (fig. 33).

MOULDING: ornament of continuous section; *see* e.g. Cavetto, Ogee, Ovolo, Roll.

MULLION: vertical member between the lights in a window opening.

MULTI-STOREY: modern term denoting five or more storeys. *See* Cluster, Slab, and Point Blocks.

MULTIVALLATE: (of a hill-fort) defended by three or more concentric banks and ditches.

MUNTIN: vertical part in the framing of a door, screen, panelling, etc., butting into or stopped by the horizontal rails.

NAILHEAD MOULDING: E.E. ornamental motif consisting of small pyramids regularly repeated (*see* fig. 17).

NARTHEX: enclosed vestibule or

Fig. 17. Nailhead Moulding

covered porch at the main entrance to a church.

NAVE: the body of a church w of the crossing or chancel which may be flanked by aisles (q.v.).

NECESSARIUM: *see* Reredorter.

NEOLITHIC: term applied to the New Stone Age, dating in Britain from the appearance of the first settled farming communities from the continent *c.* 4000–3500 B.C. until the beginning of the Bronze Age. *See also* Mesolithic.

NEWEL: central post in a circular or winding staircase; also the principal post where a flight of stairs meets a landing. *See* Stair (fig. 30).

NICHE (*lit.* shell): vertical recess in a wall, sometimes for a statue.

NIGHT STAIR: stair by which monks entered the transept of their church from their dormitory to celebrate night services.

NOGGING: *see* Timber-framing.

NOOK-SHAFT: shaft set in the angle of a pier or respond or wall, or the angle of the jamb of a window or doorway.

NORMAN: *see* Romanesque.

NOSING: projection of the tread of a step. A *Bottle Nosing* is half-round in section.

NUTMEG MOULDING: consisting of a chain of tiny triangles placed obliquely.

OBELISK: tapering pillar of square section at the top and ending pyramidally.

OCULUS: circular opening or window in a wall or vault; cf. Bullseye Window.

ŒIL DE BŒUF: *see* Bullseye Window.

OGEE: double curve, bending first one way and then the other. Applied to mouldings, also called *Cyma Recta*. A reverse ogee moulding with a double curve also called *Cyma Reversa* (*see* fig. 18). *Ogee* or *Ogival Arch: see* fig. 2.

ORATORY: (1) small private

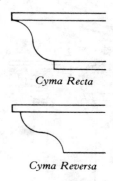

Cyma Recta

Cyma Reversa

Fig. 18. Ogee Mouldings

chapel in a church or a house; (2) church of the Oratorian Order.

ORDER: (1) upright structural member formally related to others, e.g. in classical architecture a column, pilaster, or anta; (2) especially in medieval architecture, one of a series of recessed arches and jambs forming a splayed opening. *Giant* or *Colossal Order:* classical order whose height is that of two or more storeys of a building.

ORDERS: in classical architecture, the differently formalized versions of the basic post-and-lintel (column and entablature) structure, each having its own rules for design and proportion. For examples of the main types *see* fig. 19. In the *Composite*, the capital combines Ionic volutes with Corinthian foliage. *Superimposed Orders:* term for the use of Orders on successive levels, usually in the upward sequence of Tuscan, Doric, Ionic, Corinthian.

ORIEL: *see* Bay-window.

OVERDOOR: *see* Sopraporta.

OVERHANG: *see* Jetty.

OVERSAILING COURSES: *see* Corbel (Corbelling).

OVERTHROW: decorative fixed arch between two gatepiers or above a wrought-iron gate.

OVOLO MOULDING: wide convex moulding.

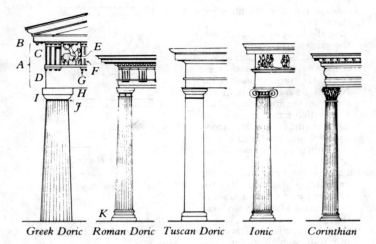

Greek Doric   Roman Doric   Tuscan Doric   Ionic   Corinthian

Fig. 19. Orders: A Entablature; B Cornice; C Frieze; D Architrave; E Metope;
F Triglyph; G Guttae; H Abacus; I Capital; J Echinus; K Base

PALAEOLITHIC: 'Old Stone' Age; the first period of human culture, commencing in the Ice Age and immediately prior to the Mesolithic; the Lower Palaeolithic is the older phase, the Upper Palaeolithic the later.

PALIMPSEST (*lit.* erased work): re-use of a surface. (1) of a brass: where a metal plate has been re-used by turning over and engraving on the back; (2) of a wall painting: where one overlaps and partly obscures an earlier one.

PALLADIAN: architecture following the examples and principles of Andrea Palladio (1508–80).

PALMETTE: classical ornament like a symmetrical palm shoot; for illustration *see* fig. 1.

PANELLING: wooden lining to interior walls, made up of vertical members (muntins q.v.) and horizontals (rails) framing panels (*see* linenfold; raised and fielded). Also called *Wainscot.*

PANTILE: roof tile of curved S-shaped section.

PARAPET: wall for protection at any sudden drop, e.g. on a bridge or at the wall-head of a castle; in the latter case it protects the *Parapet Walk* or wall walk. Also used to conceal a roof.

PARCLOSE: *see* Screen.

PARGETTING (*lit.* plastering): in timber-framed buildings, plasterwork with patterns and ornaments either moulded in relief or incised on it.

PARLOUR: in a monastery, room where monks were permitted to talk to visitors.

PARTERRE: level space in a garden laid out with low, formal beds of plants.

PATERA (*lit.* plate): round or oval ornament in shallow relief, especially in classical architecture.

PAVILION: (1) ornamental building for occasional use in a garden, park, sports ground, etc.; (2) projecting subdivision of some larger building, often at an angle or terminating wings.

PEBBLEDASHING: *see* Rendering.

PEDESTAL: in classical architecture, a tall block carrying an order, statue, vase, etc.

PEDIMENT: in classical architecture, a formalized gable derived from that of a temple, also used over doors, windows, etc. For variations of type *see* fig. 20.

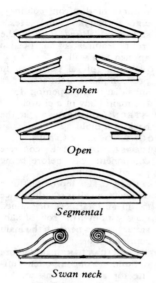

Broken

Open

Segmental

Swan neck

Fig. 20. Pediments

PEEL (*lit.* palisade): stone tower, e.g. near the Scottish–English border.

PENDANT: decorative feature hanging from a vault or ceiling, usually ending in a boss.

PENDENTIVE: spandrel formed as part of a hemisphere between arches meeting at an angle, supporting a drum or dome (*see* fig. 21).

PENTHOUSE: subsidiary structure with a lean-to roof; in modern architecture, a separately roofed structure on top of a multi-storey block.

Fig. 21. Pendentive

PERISTYLE: in classical architecture, a range of columns all round a building, e.g. a temple, or an interior space, e.g. a courtyard.

PERP (PERPENDICULAR): historical division of English Gothic architecture covering the period from *c.* 1335–50 to *c.* 1530. The name is derived from the upright tracery panels then used (*see* Tracery).

PERRON: see Stair.

PEW: loosely, seating for the laity outside the chancel. Strictly an enclosed seat. *Box Pew*: with equal high sides, entered by a door.

PIANO NOBILE: principal floor, usually with a ground floor or basement underneath and a lesser storey overhead.

PIAZZA: open space surrounded by buildings; in the C17 and C18 used erroneously to mean an arcaded ground floor, especially adjoining or around an open space.

PIER: large masonry or brick support, usually for an arch. *See also* Compound Pier.

PIETRA DURA: ornamental or pictorial inlay by means of thin slabs of stone.

PILASTER: flat representation of a classical column in shallow relief against a wall. *Pilastrade*: series of pilasters, equivalent to a colonnade. *Pilaster Strip: see* Lesene.

PILE: row of rooms. The important use of the term is in *Double Pile*, describing a house that is two rows thick.

PILLAR: free-standing upright member of any section, not conforming to one of the Orders.

PILLAR PISCINA: free-standing piscina on a pillar.

PILOTIS: French term used in modern architecture for pillars or stilts that carry a building to first-floor level leaving the ground floor open.

PINNACLE: tapering finial, e.g. on a buttress or the corner of a tower, sometimes decorated with crockets.

PISCINA: basin for washing the communion or mass vessels, provided with a drain; generally set in or against the wall to the S of an altar.

PLAISANCE: summer house, pleasure house near a mansion.

PLATE RAIL: see Railways.

PLATEWAY: see Railways.

PLINTH: projecting courses at the foot of a wall or column, generally chamfered or moulded at the top.

PODIUM: continuous raised platform supporting a building. In modern architecture often a large block of two or three storeys beneath a multi-storey block covering a smaller area.

POINT BLOCK: high block of housing in which the flats fan out from a central core of lifts, staircases, etc.

POINTING: exposed mortar jointing of masonry or brickwork. The finished form is of various types, e.g. *Flush Pointing, Recessed Pointing*.

POND BARROW: rare Bronze Age barrow type consisting of a circular depression, usually paved, and containing a number of cremation burials.

POPPYHEAD: carved ornament of leaves and flowers, generally in the form of a fleur-de-lys, as a finial for the end of a bench or stall.

PORCH: covered projecting entrance to a building.

PORTAL FRAME: single-storey frame comprising two uprights rigidly connected to a beam or pair of rafters, particularly to support a roof.

PORTCULLIS: gate constructed to rise and fall in vertical grooves at the entry to a castle.

PORTICO: a porch, open on one side at least, and enclosed by a row of columns which also support the roof and frequently a pediment. When the front of it is on the same plane as the front of the building it is described as a *Portico in Antis* (Antae q.v.). Porticoes are described by the number of the front columns, e.g. Tetrastyle (four), Hexastyle (six). *Blind Portico:* the front features of a portico applied to a wall.

PORTICUS (plural porticūs): in pre-Conquest architecture, a subsidiary cell opening from the main body of a church.

POSTERN: small gateway at the back of a building.

POUND LOCK: see Canals.

PRECAST CONCRETE: concrete components cast before being placed in position.

PREDELLA: (1) step or platform on which an altar stands; hence (2) in an altarpiece or stained glass window, the row of subsidiary scenes beneath the main representation.

PREFABRICATION: manufacture of buildings or components offsite for assembly on-site. *See also* Industrialized Building.

PRESBYTERY: (1) part of a church lying E of the choir where the main altar is placed; (2) a priest's residence.

PRESTRESSED CONCRETE: see Reinforced Concrete.

PRINCIPAL: see Roofs (3) and figs. 24, 27.

PRIORY: religious house whose head is a prior or prioress, not an abbot or abbess.

PROSTYLE: with a free-standing row of columns in front.

PULPIT: raised and enclosed platform used for the preaching of sermons. *Three-decker pulpit*: with reading desk below and clerk's desk below the reading desk. *Two-decker pulpit*: as above, but without the clerk's stall.

PULPITUM: stone screen in a major church provided to shut off the choir from the nave and also as a backing for the return choir stalls.

PULVINATED: see Frieze.

PURLIN: see Roofs (3) and figs. 24–7.

PUTHOLES or PUTLOCK HOLES: in the wall to receive putlocks, the horizontal timbers on which scaffolding boards rest. They are often not filled in after construction is complete.

PUTTO: small naked boy (plural: putti. Also called *Amorini*.)

QUADRANGLE: rectangular inner courtyard in a large building.

QUARRIES (*lit.* squares): (1) square (or diamond-shaped) panes of glass supported by lead strips which are called *Cames*; (2) square floor-slabs or tiles.

QUATREFOIL: *see* Foil.

QUEENPOSTS: *see* Roofs (3) and fig. 26.

QUIRK: sharp groove to one side of a convex moulding, e.g. beside a roll moulding, which is then said to be quirked.

QUOINS: dressed stones at the angles of a building. They may be alternately long and short, especially when rusticated.

RADIATING CHAPELS: chapels projecting radially from an ambulatory or an apse; *see* Chevet.

RAFTER: *see* Roofs (3) and figs. 24–8.

RAGGLE: groove cut in masonry, especially to receive the edge of glass or roof-covering.

RAIL: *see* Muntin.

RAILWAYS: *Edge Rail:* rail on which flanged wheels can run, as in modern railways. *Plate Rail:* L-section rail for plain unflanged wheels, guidance being provided by the upstanding flange on the rail. *Plateway:* early railway using plate rails. *Sleeper Block:* stone block to support rail in lieu of timber sleeper.

RAISED AND FIELDED: of a wooden panel with a raised square or rectangular central area (field) surrounded by a narrow moulding.

RAKE: slope or pitch.

RAMPART: wall of stone or earth surrounding a hill-fort, castle, fortress, or fortified town.

Rampart Walk: path along the inner face of a rampart.

REBATE: rectangular section cut out of a masonry edge to receive a shutter, door, window, etc.

REBUS: a heraldic pun, e.g. a fiery cock as a badge for Cockburn.

REEDING: series of convex mouldings, the reverse of fluting.

REFECTORY: dining hall of a monastery or similar establishment. Also called *Frater*.

REINFORCED CONCRETE: concrete reinforced with steel rods to take the tensile force. A later development is *Prestressed Concrete*, which incorporates artificially-tensioned steel tendons.

RENDERING: the process of covering outside walls with a uniform surface or skin for protection from the weather. *Stucco*, originally a fine lime plaster worked to a smooth surface, is the finest rendered external finish, characteristic of many late C18 and C19 classical buildings. It is usually painted. *Cement Rendering* is a cheaper and more recent substitute for stucco, usually with a grainy texture and often left unpainted. In more simple buildings the wall surface may be roughly *Lime-plastered* (and then whitewashed), or covered with plaster mixed with a coarse aggregate such as gravel. This latter is known as *Roughcast*. A variant, fashionable in the early C20, is *Pebbledashing:* here the stones of the aggregate are kept separate and are thrown at the wet plastered wall to create a textured effect.

REPOUSSÉ: decoration of metalwork by relief designs, formed by beating the metal from the back.

REREDORTER (*lit.* behind the dormitory): medieval euphemism for latrines in a monastery. Also called *Necessarium*.

REREDOS: painted and/or sculptured screen behind and above an altar.

RESPOND: half-pier or half-column bonded into a wall and carrying one end of an arch. It usually terminates an arcade.

RETABLE: a picture or piece of carving standing at the back of an altar, usually attached to it. Also called an *Altarpiece*.

RETROCHOIR: in a major church, the space between the high altar and an E chapel, like a square ambulatory.

REVEAL: the inward plane of a jamb, between the edge of an external wall and the frame of a door or window that is set in it.

RIB-VAULT: *see* Vault.

RINCEAU (*lit.* little branch) or ANTIQUE FOLIAGE: classical ornament, usually on a frieze, of leafy scrolls branching alternately to left and right (*see* fig. 22).

Fig. 22. Rinceau

RISER: vertical face of a step.

ROCK-FACED: term used to describe masonry which is cleft to produce a natural rugged appearance.

ROCOCO (*lit.* rocky): latest phase of the Baroque style, current in most Continental countries between *c.* 1720 and *c.* 1760, and showing itself in Britain mainly in playful, scrolled decoration, especially plasterwork.

ROLL MOULDING: moulding of part-circular section used in medieval architecture.

ROMANESQUE: that style in architecture (in England often called Norman) which was current in the C11 and C12 and preceded the Gothic style. (Some scholars extend the use of the term Romanesque back to the C10 or C9.) *See also* Saxo-Norman.

ROMANO-BRITISH: general term applied to the period and cultural features of Britain affected by the Roman occupation of the C1–5 A.D.

ROOD: cross or crucifix flanked by the Virgin and St John, usually over the entry into the chancel, on a beam (*Rood Beam*) or painted. The *Rood Screen* beneath it may have a *Rood Loft* along the top, reached by a *Rood Stair*.

ROOFS: (1) *Shape:* for the external shapes and terms used to describe them *see* fig. 23. *Helm:* roof with four inclined faces joined at the top, with a gable at the foot of each. *Hipped* (fig. 23): roof with sloped instead of vertical ends. *Lean-to:* roof with one slope only, built against a vertical wall: term also applied to the part of the building such a roof covers. *Mansard* (fig. 23): roof with a double slope, the lower one larger and steeper than the upper. *Saddleback:* the name given to a normal pitched roof when used over a tower. *See also* Wagon Roof.

(2) *Construction:* Roofs are generally called after the principal structural component, e.g. *crown-post, hammerbeam, king-post*, etc. See below under *Elements* and figs. 24–8.

A *single-framed* roof is constructed with no main trusses. The rafters may be fixed to a wall-plate or ridge, or longitudinal timbers may be absent altogether. A *common rafter* roof is one in which pairs of rafters are not connected by a collar-beam. A *coupled rafter* roof is one in which the rafters are connected by collar-beams.

A *double-framed* roof is constructed with longitudinal members such as purlins. Generally there are principals or principal rafters supporting the longitudinal members and dividing the length of the roof into bays.

(3) *Elements: Ashlar piece.* A short vertical timber connecting an inner wall-plate or timber pad to a rafter above.

Braces. Subsidiary timbers set diagonally to strengthen the frame. *Arched braces:* a pair of

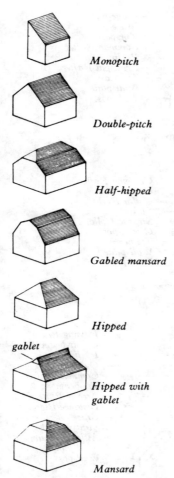

Monopitch

Double-pitch

Half-hipped

Gabled mansard

Hipped

gablet

Hipped with gablet

Mansard

Fig. 23. Roofs: external forms

curved braces forming an arch, usually connecting the wall or post below with the tie- or collar-beam above. *Passing braces:* straight braces of considerable length, passing across other members of the truss. *Scissor braces:* a pair of braces which cross diagonally between pairs of rafters or principals. *Wind-braces:* short, usually curved braces connecting side purlins with principals. They are sometimes decorated with cusping.

Collar-beam. A horizontal transverse timber connecting a pair of rafters or principals at a height between the apex and the wall-plate.

Crown-post. A vertical timber standing centrally on a tie-beam and supporting a collar purlin. Longitudinal braces usually rise from the crown-post to the collar purlin. When the truss is open lateral braces generally rise to the collar-beam, and when the truss is closed they go down to the tie-beam.

Hammerbeams. Horizontal brackets projecting at wall-plate level on opposite sides of the wall like a tie-beam with the centre cut away. The inner ends carry vertical timbers called hammerposts and braces to a collar-beam.

Hammerpost. A vertical timber set on the inner end of a hammer-beam to support a purlin; it is braced to a collar-beam above.

Kingpost. A vertical timber standing centrally on a tie- or collar-beam and rising to the apex of the roof where it supports a ridge.

Principals. The pair of inclined lateral timbers of a truss which carry common rafters. Usually they support side purlins and their position corresponds to the main bay division of the space below.

Purlin. A horizontal longitudinal timber. *Collar purlin:* a single central timber which carries collar-beams and is itself supported by crown-posts. *Side purlins:* pairs of timbers occurring some way up the slope of the roof. They carry the common rafters and are supported in a number of ways: *butt purlins* are tenoned into either side of the principals; *clasped purlins* rest on queenposts or are carried in the angles between the principals and the collar; *laid-on purlins* lie on the backs of the principals; *trenched purlins* are trenched into the backs of the principals.

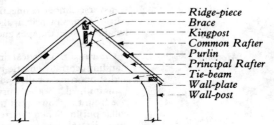

Fig. 24. Kingpost Roof

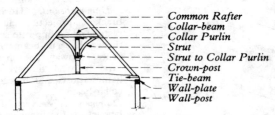

Fig. 25. Crown-post Roof

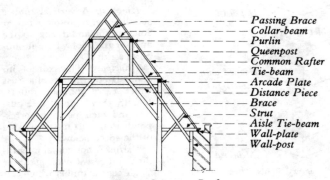

Fig. 26. Queenpost Roof

Queenposts. A pair of vertical, or near-vertical, timbers placed symmetrically on a tie-beam and supporting side purlins.

Rafters. Inclined lateral timbers sloping from wall-top to apex and supporting the roof covering. *Common rafters:* rafters of equal scantling found along the length of a roof or sometimes interrupted by main trusses containing principal rafters. *Principal rafters:* rafters

which act as principals but also serve as common rafters.

Ridge, ridge-piece. A horizontal, longitudinal timber at the apex of a roof supporting the ends of the rafters.

Sprocket. A short timber placed on the back and at the foot of a rafter to form projecting eaves.

Strut. A vertical or oblique timber which runs between two members of a roof truss but

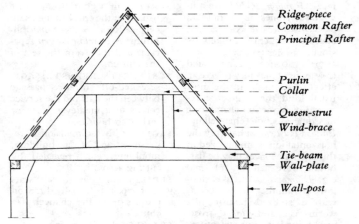

Fig. 27. Queen-strut Roof

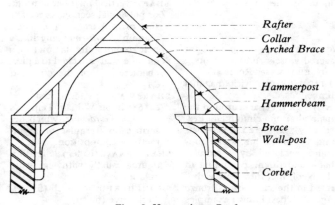

Fig. 28. Hammerbeam Roof

does not directly support longitudinal timbers.

Tie-beam. The main horizontal, transverse timber which carries the feet of the principals at wall-plate level.

Truss. A rigid framework of timbers which is placed laterally across the building to carry the longitudinal roof timbers which support the common rafters.

Wall-plate. A timber laid longitudinally on the top of a wall to receive the ends of the rafters. In a timber-framed building the

posts and studs of the wall below are tenoned into it.

ROPE MOULDING: *see* Cable Moulding.

ROSE WINDOW: circular window with tracery radiating from the centre; cf. Wheel Window.

ROTUNDA: building circular in plan.

ROUGHCAST: *see* Rendering.

ROVING BRIDGE: *see* Canals.

RUBBLE: masonry whose stones are wholly or partly in a rough state. *Coursed Rubble:* of coursed stones with rough faces. *Random Rubble:* of un-coursed stones in a random pattern. *Snecked Rubble* has courses frequently broken by smaller stones (snecks).

RUSTICATION: exaggerated treatment of masonry to give an effect of strength. In the most usual kind the joints are re-cessed by V-section chamfering or square-section channelling. *Banded Rustication* has only the horizontal joints emphasized in this way. The faces may be flat, but there are many other forms, e.g. *Diamond-faced*, like shal-low pyramids, *Vermiculated*, with a stylized texture like worm-casts, and *Glacial* (frost-work) like icicles or stalactites. *Rusticated Columns* may have their joints and drums treated in any of these ways.

SACRISTY: room in a church for sacred vessels and vestments.

SADDLEBACK: *see* Roofs (1).

SALTIRE CROSS: with diagonal limbs.

SANCTUARY: (1) area around the main altar of a church (*see* Pre-sbytery); (2) sacred site consist-ing of wood or stone up-rights enclosed by a circular bank and ditch. Beginning in the Neolithic, they were elabo-rated in the succeeding Bronze Age. The best known examples are Stonehenge and Avebury.

SARCOPHAGUS (*lit.* flesh-consuming): coffin of stone or other durable material.

SAUCER DOME: *see* Dome.

SAXO-NORMAN: transitional Romanesque style combining Anglo-Saxon and Norman fea-tures, current *c.* 1060–1100.

SCAGLIOLA: composition imitat-ing marble.

SCALLOPED CAPITAL: *see* fig. 8.

SCARP: artificial cutting away of the ground to form a steep slope.

SCOTIA: a hollow moulding, especially between tori (q.v.) on a column base.

SCREEN: in a church, structure usually at the entry to the chan-cel; *see* Rood (Screen) *and* Pul-pitum. A *Parclose Screen* sepa-rates a chapel from the rest of the church.

SCREENS or SCREENS PASSAGE: screened-off entrance passage between the hall and the service rooms of a medieval, C16, or early C17 house.

SECTION: two-dimensional re-presentation of a building, moulding, etc., revealed by cutting across it.

SEDILIA (singular *sedile*): seats for the priests (usually three) on the S side of the chancel of a church.

SET-OFF: *see* Weathering.

SGRAFFITO: scratched pattern, often in plaster.

SHAFT: vertical member of round or polygonal section, especially the main part of a classical column. *Shaft-ring:* ring like a belt round a circular pier or a circular shaft attached to a pier, characteristic of the C12 and C13.

SHARAWAGGI: a term, first used *c.* 1685 in Sir William Temple's *Essay on Gardening*, which de-scribes an irregular or asym-metrical composition.

SHEILA-NA-GIG: female fertility figure, usually with legs wide open.

SHOULDERED: *see* Arch (fig. 2), Architrave (fig. 3).

SHUTTERED CONCRETE: *see* Formwork.

SILL: (1) horizontal member at the bottom of a window- or door-frame; (2) the horizontal member at the base of a timber-framed wall into which the posts and studs (q.v.) are tenoned.

SLAB BLOCK: rectangular multi-storey block of housing or offices.

SLATE-HANGING: covering of overlapping slates on a wall, which is then said to be *slate-hung. Tile-hanging* is similar.

SLEEPER BLOCK: *see* Railways.

SLYPE: covered way or passage,

especially in a cathedral or monastic church, leading E from the cloisters between transept and chapter house.

SNECKED: *see* Rubble.

SOFFIT: (*lit*. ceiling): underside of an arch (also called *Intrados*), lintel, etc. *Soffit Roll:* roll moulding on a soffit.

SOLAR (*lit*. sun-room): upper living room or withdrawing room of a medieval house, accessible from the high table end of the hall.

SOPRAPORTA (*lit*. over door): painting or relief above the door of a room, usual in the C17 and C18.

SOUNDING-BOARD: horizontal board or canopy over a pulpit; also called *Tester*.

SOUTERRAIN: underground stone-lined passage and chamber.

S.P.A.B.: Society for the Protection of Ancient Buildings.

SPANDRELS: roughly triangular spaces between an arch and its containing rectangle, or between adjacent arches. In modern architecture the non-structural panels under the windows in a framed building.

SPERE: a fixed structure which serves as a screen at the lower end of an open medieval hall between the hall proper and the screens passage. It has a wide central opening, often with a movable screen, between posts and short screen walls. The top member is often the tie-beam of the roof truss above; screen and truss are then called a *Speretruss*.

SPIRE: tall pyramidal or conical feature built on a tower or turret. *Broach Spire:* starting from a square base, then carried into an octagonal section by means of triangular faces. The *Splayed-foot Spire* is a variation of the broach form, found principally in the south-eastern counties, in which the four cardinal faces are splayed out near their base, to cover the corners, while oblique (or intermediate) faces taper away to a point. *Needle Spire:* thin spire rising from the centre of a tower roof, well inside the parapet: when of timber and lead often called a *Spike*.

SPIRELET: *see* Flèche.

SPLAY: chamfer, usually of a reveal.

SPRING or SPRINGING: level at which an arch or vault rises from its supports. *Springers:* the first stones of an arch or vaulting-rib above the spring.

SQUINCH: arch or series of arches thrown across an angle between two walls to support a superstructure of polygonal or round plan over a rectangular space, e.g. a dome, a spire (*see* fig. 29).

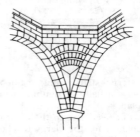

Fig. 29. Squinch

SQUINT: an aperture in a wall or through a pier usually to allow a view of an altar of a church otherwise obscured. Also called *Hagioscope*.

STAIRS: *see* fig. 30. A *Dog-leg Stair* has parallel flights rising alternately in opposite directions, without an open well. *Newel Stair:* ascending round a central supporting newel (q.v.), called a *Spiral Stair* or *Vice* when in a circular shaft. *Well Stair:* term applied to any stair contained in an open well, but generally to one that climbs up three sides of a well with corner landings, e.g. the *timber-framed newel stair*, common from the C17 on. *Flying Stair:* cantilevered from the wall of a stairwell, without newels. *Geometric Stair:* flying stair whose inner edge describes a curve. *Perron (lit.* of stone):

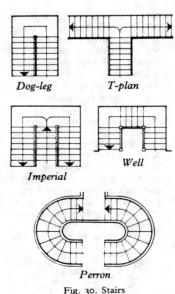

Dog-leg   *T-plan*

Imperial   *Well*

Perron

Fig. 30. Stairs

external stair leading to a doorway, usually of double-curved plan.

STALL: fixed seat in the choir or chancel for the clergy or choir (cf. Pew). Usually with arm rests. Often framed together like a bench.

STANCHION: upright structural member, of iron or steel or reinforced concrete.

STANDPIPE TOWER: see Manometer.

STEAM ENGINES: *Atmospheric*: the earliest type, worked by the vacuum created when low pressure steam was condensed in the cylinder, as developed by Thomas Newcomen. *Beam Engine:* with a large pivoted beam moved in an oscillating fashion by the piston. It may drive a fly wheel or be *Non-rotative*. Different types are the *Watt* and *Cornish* engines (single-cylinder), the *Compound* (two cylinder) or *Triple Expansion* (three cylinders). The cylinders may be mounted in various ways.

STEEPLE: tower together with a spire, lantern or belfry.

STIFF-LEAF: type of E.E. foliage decoration. *Stiff-leaf Capital: see* fig. 8.

STOP: plain or decorated blocks terminating mouldings or chamfers in stone or wood, or at the end of labels, hoodmoulds, or string courses.

STOUP: vessel for the reception of holy water, usually placed near a door.

STRAINER: *see* Arch.

STRAPWORK: late C16 and C17 decoration, resembling straplike interlaced bands of leather.

STRING COURSE: horizontal stone course or moulding projecting from the surface of a wall.

STRINGS: two sloping members which carry the ends of the treads and risers of a staircase. Closed strings enclose the treads and risers; in the later open string staircase the steps project above the strings.

STUCCO (*lit.* plaster): *see* Rendering.

STUDS: subsidiary vertical timbers of a timber-framed wall or partition.

STYLOBATE: solid platform on which a colonnade stands.

SUSPENSION BRIDGE: bridge suspended from cables or chains draped from towers. *Stay-suspension* or *Stayed-cantilever Bridge:* supported by diagonal stays from towers or pylons.

SWAG (*lit.* bundle): ornament suspended like a festoon (q.v.), but usually representing cloth.

SYSTEM BUILDING: *see* Industrialized Building.

TABERNACLE (*lit.* tent): (1) canopied structure, especially on a small scale, to contain the reserved sacrament or a relic; (2) architectural frame, e.g. of a statue on a wall or free-standing, with flanking orders. In classical architecture also called an *Aedicule*.

TABLE TOMB: a memorial slab raised on free-standing legs.

TABLET FLOWER: medieval ornament of a four-leaved flower with a raised or sunk centre.

TAS-DE-CHARGE: the lower courses of a vault or arch laid horizontally.

TERMINAL FIGURE: pedestal or pilaster which tapers towards the bottom, usually with the upper part of a human figure growing out of it. Also called *Term*.

TERRACOTTA: moulded and fired clay ornament or cladding, usually unglazed.

TESSELLATED PAVEMENT: mosaic flooring, particularly Roman, consisting of small *Tesserae*, i.e. cubes of glass, stone, or brick.

TESTER (*lit.* head): flat canopy over a tomb and especially over a pulpit, where it is also called a *Sounding-board*.

TESTER TOMB: C16 or C17 type with effigies on a tomb-chest beneath a tester, either free-standing (tester with four or more columns), or attached to a wall (half tester) with columns on one side only.

TETRASTYLE: *see* Portico.

THERMAE WINDOW (*lit.* of a Roman bath); *see* Diocletian Window.

THREE-DECKER PULPIT: *see* Pulpit.

TIDAL DOORS: *see* Canals.

TIE-BEAM: *see* Roofs (3) and figs. 24–7.

TIERCERON: *see* Vault (fig. 36).

TILE-HANGING: *see* Slate-hanging.

TIMBER-FRAMING: method of construction where walls are built of interlocking vertical and horizontal timbers. The spaces are filled with non-structural walling of wattle and daub, lath and plaster, brickwork (known as nogging), etc. Sometimes the timber is covered over by plaster, boarding laid horizontally (weather-boarding q.v.), or tiles.

TOMB-CHEST: chest-shaped stone coffin. *See also* Table Tomb, Tester Tomb.

TORUS: large convex moulding usually used on a column base.

TOUCH: soft black marble quarried near Tournai.

TOURELLE: turret corbelled out from the wall.

TOWER HOUSE: compact medieval fortified house with the main hall raised above the ground and at least one more storey above it. The type survives in odd examples into the C16 and C17.

TRABEATED: depends structurally on the use of the post and lintel; cf. Arcuated.

TRACERY: intersecting ribwork in the upper part of a window, or used decoratively in blank arches, on vaults, etc. (1) *Plate tracery: see* fig. 31(*a*). Early form of tracery where decoratively shaped openings are cut through the solid stone infilling in a window head. (2) *Bar tracery:* a form introduced into England *c.* 1250. Intersecting ribwork made up of slender shafts, continuing the lines of the mullions of windows up to a decorative mesh in the head of the win-

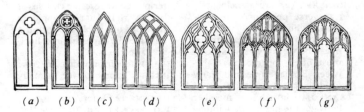

(*a*)   (*b*)   (*c*)   (*d*)   (*e*)   (*f*)   (*g*)

Fig. 31. Tracery

dow. The types of bar tracery are: *Geometrical tracery: see* fig. 31(*b*). Tracery characteristic of *c.* 1250–1310 consisting chiefly of circles or foiled circles. *Y-tracery: see* fig. 31(*c*). Tracery consisting of a mullion which branches into two forming a Y shape; typical of *c.* 1300. *Intersecting tracery: see* fig. 31(*d*). Tracery in which each mullion of a window branches out into two curved bars in such a way that every one of them is drawn with the same radius from a different centre. The result is that every light of the window is a lancet and every two, three, four, etc., lights together form a pointed arch. This also is typical of *c.* 1300. *Reticulated tracery: see* fig. 31(*e*). Tracery typical of the early C 14 consisting entirely of circles drawn at top and bottom into ogee shapes so that a net-like appearance results. *Panel tracery: see* fig. 31 (*f*) and (*g*). Perp tracery, which is formed of upright straight-sided panels above lights of a window. *Dagger:* Dec tracery motif; *see* fig. 32. *Kentish* or *Split Cusp:* cusp split into a fork. *Mouchette:* curved version of the dagger form, especially popular in the early C 14; *see* fig. 33.

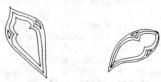

Fig. 32. Dagger   Fig. 33. Mouchette

TRANSEPT (*lit.* cross-enclosure): transverse portion of a cross-shaped church.

TRANSITIONAL: transitional phase between two styles, used most often for the phase between Romanesque and Early English (*c.* 1175–*c.* 1200).

TRANSOM: horizontal member between the lights in a window opening.

TREAD: horizontal part of the step of a staircase. The *Tread End* may be carved.

TREFOIL: *see* Foil.

TRIBUNE: *see* Gallery (1).

TRIFORIUM (*lit.* three openings): middle storey of a church treated as an arcaded wall passage or blind arcade, its height corresponding to that of the aisle roof.

TRIGLYPHS (*lit.* three-grooved tablets): stylized beam-ends in the Doric frieze, with metopes between; *see* Orders (fig. 19).

TRIUMPHAL ARCH: type of Imperial Roman monument whose elevation supplied a motif for many later classical compositions (*see* fig. 34).

Fig. 34. Triumphal Arch

TROPHY: sculptured group of arms or armour as a memorial of victory.

TRUMEAU: central stone mullion supporting the tympanum of a wide doorway. *Trumeau Figure:* carved figure attached to a trumeau (cf. Column Figure).

TRUSS: braced framework, spanning between supports. *See also* Roofs.

TUDOR FLOWER: late Gothic ornament of a flower with square flat petals or foliage.

TUMBLING or TUMBLING-IN: term used to describe courses of brickwork laid at right angles to the slope of a gable and forming triangles by tapering into horizontal courses.

TUMULUS (*lit.* mound): barrow.

TURRET: small tower, usually attached to a building.

TUSCAN: *see* Orders (fig. 19).

TWO-DECKER PULPIT: *see* Pulpit.

TYMPANUM (*lit.* drum): as of a drum-skin, the surface between a lintel and the arch above it or within a pediment.

UNDERCROFT: vaulted room, sometimes underground, below the main upper room.

UNIVALLATE: (of a hill-fort) defended by a single bank and ditch.

UPPER PALAEOLITHIC: *see* Palaeolithic.

VAULT: ceiling of stone formed like arches (sometimes imitated in timber or plaster); *see* fig. 35. *Tunnel-* or *Barrel-Vault:* the simplest kind of vault, in effect a continuous semicircular arch. *Groin-Vaults* (which are usually called *Cross-Vaults* in classical architecture) have four curving

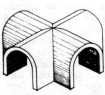

Cross- or Groin-Vault   *Tunnel- or Barrel-Vault*   *Pointed Barrel-Vault*

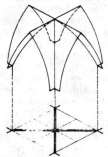
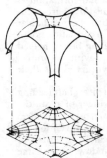

Quadripartite Rib-Vault   *Fan-Vault*

Fig. 35. Vaults

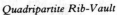
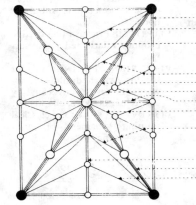

Transverse Rib
Tiercerons
Transverse Ridge Rib

Liernes
Diagonal Rib
Liernes
Longitudinal Ridge Rib
Liernes

Liernes

Transverse Ridge Rib
Diagonal Rib
Tiercerons

Fig. 36. Vaulting Ribs

triangular surfaces produced by the intersection of two tunnel-vaults at right angles. The curved lines at the intersections are called groins. In *Quadripartite Rib-Vaults* the four sections are divided by their arches or ribs springing from the corners of the bay. *Sexpartite Rib-Vaults*, most often used over paired bays, have an extra pair of ribs which spring from between the bays and meet the other four ribs at the crown of the vault. The main types of rib are shown in fig. 36: *transverse ribs, wall ribs, diagonal ribs*, and *ridge ribs. Tiercerons* are extra, decorative ribs springing from the corners of a bay. *Liernes* are decorative ribs in the crown of a vault which are not linked to any of the springing points. In a *Stellar Vault* the liernes are arranged in a star formation as in fig. 36. *Fan-Vaults* are peculiar to English Perpendicular architecture in consisting not of ribs and infilling but of halved concave cones with decorative blind tracery carved on their surfaces.

VAULTING-SHAFT: shaft leading up to the springer of a vault.

VENETIAN WINDOW: a form derived from an invention by Serlio, also called a Serlian or Palladian window. The same motif is used for other openings (*see* fig. 37).

VERANDA(H): shelter or gallery against a building, its roof supported by thin vertical members.

Fig. 37. Venetian Window

VERMICULATION: *see* Rustication.

VERNACULAR ARCHITECTURE: design by one without any training in design, guided by a series of conventions built up in a locality (Brunskill).

VESICA: oval with pointed head and foot, usually of a window or tracery.

VESTIBULE: anteroom or entrance hall.

VICE: *see* Stair.

VILLA: originally (1) a Romano-British farm or country house. The term is one of convenience and covers a wide spectrum of sites, ranging from humble farmsteads to sumptuous mansions associated with large estates. Various architectural traditions, including both classical and vernacular, are evident in villas, but all display some pretension towards fundamental Roman standards. (2) the C16 Venetian type with office wings, derived from Roman models and made grander by Palladio's varied application of a central portico. It became an important type in C18 Britain, often with the special meaning of (3) a country house which is not a principal residence. Gwilt (1842) defined the villa as 'a country house for the residence of opulent persons'. But devaluation had already begun, and the term also implied, as now, (4) a more or less pretentious suburban house.

VITRIFIED: bricks or tiles fired to produce a darkened glassy surface.

VITRUVIAN OPENING: door or window which diminishes towards the top, as advocated by Vitruvius, book IV, chapter VI.

VITRUVIAN SCROLL: classical running ornament of curly waves (*see* fig. 38).

Fig. 38. Vitruvian Scroll

VOLUTES: spiral scrolls on the front and back of a Greek Ionic capital, also on the sides of a Roman one. *Angle Volute:* pair of volutes turned outwards to meet at the corner of a capital. Volutes were also used individually as decoration in C17 and C18 architecture.

VOUSSOIRS: wedge-shaped stones forming an arch.

WAGON ROOF: roof in which closely set rafters with arched braces give the appearance of the inside of a canvas tilt over a wagon. Wagon roofs can be panelled or plastered (ceiled) or left uncovered. Also called *Cradle Roof.*

WAINSCOT: *see* Panelling.

WALL MONUMENT: substantial monument attached to the wall and often standing on the floor. *Wall Tablets* are smaller in scale with the inscription as the major element.

WALL-PLATE: *see* Roofs (3) and figs. 24–7.

WARMING ROOM: *see* Calefactory.

WATERHOLDING BASE: type of early Gothic base in which the upper and lower mouldings are separated by a hollow so deep as to be capable of retaining water.

WATERLEAF CAPITAL: *see* fig. 8.

WATER WHEELS: described by the way the water is fed on to the wheel. *Overshot:* over the top. *Pitchback:* on to the top but falling backwards. *Breastshot:* mid-height, falling and passing beneath. An *undershot* wheel is turned by the momentum of the water passing beneath. In a *Water Turbine* water is fed under pressure through a vaned wheel within a casing.

WEALDEN HOUSE: medieval timber-framed house of distinctive form. It has a central open hall flanked by bays of two storeys. The end bays are jettied to the front, but a single roof covers the whole building, thus producing an exceptionally wide overhang to the eaves in front of the hall.

WEATHERBOARDING: overlapping horizontal boards, covering a timber-framed wall, most common after the mid C18.

WEATHERING: inclined, projecting surface to keep water away from wall and joints below. Also called *Set-off.*

WEEPERS: small figures placed in niches along the sides of some medieval tombs. Also called *Mourners.*

WHEEL WINDOW: circular window with radiating shafts like the spokes of a wheel. *See also* Rose Window.

WROUGHT IRON: *see* Cast Iron.

INDEX OF PLATES

INDEX OF ARTISTS

INDEX OF PATRONS AND RESIDENTS

Indexed here are the names/titles of families and individuals (not of bodies or commercial firms) recorded in this volume as having owned property and/or commissioned architectural work. It includes monuments to members of such families, but not those to other individuals.

INDEX OF PLACES

Principal references are in **bold** type; demolished buildings are shown in *italic*. For Newcastle, see the Index of Streets and Buildings in Newcastle upon Tyne (below).

INDEX OF STREETS AND BUILDINGS
IN NEWCASTLE UPON TYNE

Principal references are in **bold** type;
demolished buildings are shown in *italic*.

THE BUILDINGS OF ENGLAND

COMPLETE LIST OF TITLES
1992

Bedfordshire and the County of Huntingdon and Peterborough *1st ed. 1968 Nikolaus Pevsner*

Berkshire *1st ed. 1966 Nikolaus Pevsner*

Buckinghamshire *1st ed. 1960 Nikolaus Pevsner, revision in progress*

Cambridgeshire *1st ed. 1954, 2nd ed. 1970, Nikolaus Pevsner*

Cheshire *1st ed. 1971 Nikolaus Pevsner and Edward Hubbard*

Cornwall *1st ed. 1951 Nikolaus Pevsner, 2nd ed. 1970 revised Enid Radcliffe*

Cumberland and Westmorland *1st ed. 1967 Nikolaus Pevsner*

Derbyshire *1st ed. 1953 Nikolaus Pevsner, 2nd ed. 1978 revised Elizabeth Williamson*

Devon *1st ed. in vols. 1952 Nikolaus Pevsner, 2nd ed. 1989 Bridget Cherry and Nikolaus Pevsner*

Dorset *1st ed. 1972 John Newman and Nikolaus Pevsner*

Durham, County *1st ed. 1953 Nikolaus Pevsner, 2nd ed. 1983 revised Elizabeth Williamson*

Essex *1st ed. 1954 Nikolaus Pevsner, 2nd ed. 1965 revised Enid Radcliffe*

Gloucestershire: The Cotswolds *1st ed. 1970, 2nd ed. 1979, David Verey*

Gloucestershire: The Vale and the Forest of Dean *1st ed. 1970, 2nd ed. 1976 reprinted with corrections 1980, David Verey*

Hampshire and the Isle of Wight *1st ed. 1967 Nikolaus Pevsner and David Lloyd, revision in progress*

Herefordshire *1st ed. 1963 Nikolaus Pevsner*

Hertfordshire *1st ed. 1953 Nikolaus Pevsner, 2nd ed. 1977 revised Bridget Cherry*

Kent, North East and East *1st ed. 1969, 3rd ed. 1983, John Newman*

Kent, West, and the Weald *1st ed. 1969, 2nd ed. 1976 reprinted with corrections 1980, John Newman*

Lancashire, North *1st ed. 1969 Nikolaus Pevsner*

Lancashire, South *1st ed. 1969 Nikolaus Pevsner*

Leicestershire and Rutland *1st ed. 1960 Nikolaus Pevsner, 2nd ed. 1984 revised Elizabeth Williamson*

Lincolnshire *1st ed. 1964 Nikolaus Pevsner and John Harris, 2nd ed. 1989 revised Nicholas Antram*

London 1: The Cities of London and Westminster *1st ed. 1957 Nikolaus Pevsner, 3rd ed. 1973 revised Bridget Cherry*

London 2: Except the Cities of London and Westminster *1st ed. 1952 Nikolaus Pevsner, being revised, expanded, and reissued under the following three titles*

London 2: South *1st ed. 1983 Bridget Cherry and Nikolaus Pevsner*

London 3: North West *1st ed. 1991, Bridget Cherry and Nikolaus Pevsner*

London 4: North and North East *1st ed. in progress, Bridget Cherry and Nikolaus Pevsner*

Middlesex *1st ed. 1951 Nikolaus Pevsner, revision in progress for incorporation into the above two titles*

Norfolk, North East, and Norwich *1st ed. 1962 Nikolaus Pevsner, revision in progress*

Norfolk, North West and South *1st ed. 1962 Nikolaus Pevsner, revision in progress*

Northamptonshire *1st ed. 1961 Nikolaus Pevsner, 2nd ed. 1973 revised Bridget Cherry*

Northumberland *1st ed. 1957 Nikolaus Pevsner with Ian A. Richmond, 2nd ed. 1992 revised John Grundy, Grace McCombie, Peter Ryder and Humphrey Welfare*

Nottinghamshire *1st ed. 1951 Nikolaus Pevsner, 2nd ed. 1979 revised Elizabeth Williamson*

Oxfordshire *1st ed. 1974 Jennifer Sherwood and Nikolaus Pevsner*

Shropshire *1st ed. 1958 Nikolaus Pevsner*

Somerset, North, and Bristol *1st ed. 1958 Nikolaus Pevsner*

Somerset, South and West *1st ed. 1958 Nikolaus Pevsner*

Staffordshire *1st ed. 1974 Nikolaus Pevsner*

Suffolk *1st ed. 1961 Nikolaus Pevsner, 2nd ed. 1974 revised Enid Radcliffe*

Surrey *1st ed. 1962 Ian Nairn and Nikolaus Pevsner, 2nd ed. 1971 revised Bridget Cherry*

Sussex *1st ed. 1965 Ian Nairn and Nikolaus Pevsner*

Warwickshire *1st ed. 1966 Nikolaus Pevsner and Alexandra Wedgwood*

Wiltshire *1st ed. 1963 Nikolaus Pevsner, 2nd ed. 1975 revised Bridget Cherry*

Worcestershire *1st ed. 1968 Nikolaus Pevsner*

Yorkshire: The North Riding *1st ed. 1966 Nikolaus Pevsner*

Yorkshire: The West Riding *1st ed. 1959 Nikolaus Pevsner, 2nd ed. 1967 revised Enid Radcliffe, revision in progress*

Yorkshire: York and the East Riding *1st ed. 1972 Nikolaus Pevsner with John Hutchinson, revision in progress*